CORPORATIONS
AND OTHER BUSINESS ENTITIES

SEVENTH EDITION

STEVEN L. EMANUEL

Founder & Editor-in-Chief, *Emanuel® Law Outlines* and
Emanuel Bar Review
Harvard Law School, J.D. 1976
Member, NY, CT, MD and VA bars

The *Emanuel® Law Outlines* Series

Wolters Kluwer
Law & Business

Published by Wolters Kluwer Law & Business in New York.

Wolters Kluwer Law & Business serves customers worldwide with CCH, Aspen Publishers, and Kluwer Law International products. (www.wolterskluwerlb.com)

To contact Customer Service, e-mail customer.service@wolterskluwer.com, call 1-800-234-1660, fax 1-800-901-9075, or mail correspondence to:

Wolters Kluwer Law & Business
Attn: Order Department
PO Box 990
Frederick, MD 21705

Printed in the United States of America.

1 2 3 4 5 6 7 8 9 0

ISBN 978-1-4548-2482-4

Library of Congress Cataloging-in-Publication Data

Emanuel, Steven.
Corporations : and other business entities / Steven L. Emanuel, Founder & Editor-in-Chief, Emanuel Law Outlines and Emanuel Bar Review; Harvard Law School, J.D. 1976, Member, NY, CT, MD and VA Bars. — Seventh Edition.
pages cm. — (The Emanuel® law outlines series)
ISBN 978-1-4548-2482-4
1. Corporation law—United States—Outlines, syllabi, etc. I. Title.
KF1414.85.E434 2013
346.73'06—dc23

2013018240

This book is intended as a general review of a legal subject. It is not intended as a source of advice for the solution of legal matters or problems. For advice on legal matters, the reader should consult an attorney.

Dedication

For Samuel Herman,
no longer the littlest Emanuel

Abbreviations Used in Text

CASEBOOKS

A,K&S — Allen, Kraakman & Subramanian, *Law of Business Organization* (4th Ed. 2012)

B,W&P (6th) — Bauman, Weiss & Palmiter, *Corporations — Law and Policy* (6th Ed. 2007)

C&E — Cary & Eisenberg, *Cases and Materials on Corporations* (7th Ed., Unabridged, 1995)

Hamilton (8th) — Hamilton & Macey, *Cases and Materials on Corporations, including Partnerships and Limited Liability Companies* (8th Ed. 2003)

Hamilton (10th) — Hamilton & Macey, *Cases and Materials on Corporations, including Partnerships and Limited Liability Companies* (10th Ed. 2007)

Hamilton (11th) -- Hamilton, Macey & Moll, *Cases and Materials on Corporations, including Partnerships and Limited Liability Companies* (11th Ed. 2010)

K,R&B (8th) — Klein, Ramseyer & Bainbridge, *Business Associations* (8th Ed. 2012)

O&T (6th) — O'Kelley & Thompson, *Corporations and Other Business Associations* (6th Ed. 2010)

S,S,B&W — Solomon, Schwartz, Bauman & Weiss, *Corporations — Law and Policy* (3rd Ed. 1994)

HORNBOOKS

Clark — Robert Clark, *Corporate Law* (1986)

Gevurtz — Franklin A. Gevurtz, *Corporation Law* (2000)

H&A — Henn & Alexander, *Law of Corporations* (3d Ed. 1983, w/1986 supp.)

OTHER MATERIALS

ALI Prin. Corp. Gov. — American Law Institute, *Principles of Corporate Governance* (1994)

Brode — George Brode, Jr., *Tax Planning for Corporate Acquisitions* (1988)

Del. GCL — Delaware General Corporations Law

F,B&H — Ferrara, Brown & Hall, *Takeovers — Attack and Survival* (1987)

K&C — Klein & Coffee, *Business Organization and Finance* (4th Ed. 1990)

Loss — Louis Loss, *Fundamentals of Securities Regulation* (2d Ed. 1988)

Nutshell — Robert Hamilton, *The Law of Corporations in a Nutshell* (3d Ed. 1991)

NY BCL — New York Business Corporation Law

Ratner — David Ratner, *Securities Regulation in a Nutshell* (3d Ed. 1988)

MBCA — Model Business Corporations Act (1999)

'33 Act — Securities Act of 1933, 15 U.S.C. §§ 77a *et seq.*

'34 Act — Securities Exchange Act of 1934, §§ 78a *et seq.*

SUMMARY OF CONTENTS

TABLE OF CONTENTS

Chapter 1

INTRODUCTION

Chapter 2

THE CORPORATE FORM

Chapter 3

THE CORPORATE STRUCTURE

Chapter 4

SHAREHOLDERS' INFORMATIONAL RIGHTS AND THE PROXY SYSTEM

Chapter 5

CLOSE CORPORATIONS

Chapter 6

THE DUTY OF CARE AND THE BUSINESS JUDGMENT RULE

Chapter 7

THE DUTY OF LOYALTY

Chapter 8

INSIDER TRADING (AND RELATED TOPICS)

Chapter 9

SHAREHOLDERS' SUITS, ESPECIALLY DERIVATIVE SUITS

Chapter 10

STRUCTURAL CHANGES, INCLUDING MERGERS AND ACQUISITIONS

Chapter 11

DIVIDENDS AND SHARE REPURCHASES

Chapter 12

ISSUANCE OF SECURITIES

Preface

Thank you for buying this book.

Here are some of its special features:

- **"Casebook Correlation Chart"** — This chart, located just after this Preface, correlates each section of our Outline with the pages covering the same topic in the four leading Corporations casebooks.
- **"Capsule Summary"** — This is an 85-page summary of the key concepts of the law of Corporations, specially designed for use in the last week or so before your final exam.
- **"Quiz Yourself"** — Within or at the end of nearly every chapter we give you short-answer questions so that you can exercise your analytical muscles. There are over 100 of these questions. Most are from the *Law in a Flash* Corporations title, which is available from your bookstore or by visiting **www.aspenlaw.com**. Within the answers to these short-answer questions, we often cross-reference to the relevant substantive discussion in the main text of the outline. So for instance, in the answer to Quiz Yourself Question 1, the notation [6] means that you can find the main discussion of the principle(s) discussed in that answer on p. 6 of the outline.
- **"Exam Tips"** — These tips, at the end of nearly every chapter, alert you to the issues that repeatedly pop up on real-life Corporations exams and the fact patterns commonly used to test those issues. We created these Tips by looking at literally hundreds of multiple-choice and essay questions asked by law professors and bar examiners. You'd be surprised at how predictable the issues and fact patterns chosen by professors really are!

While this book concentrates on Corporations, we give some coverage to Partnerships as well as to two newer forms of business organization, LLCs and LLPs.

I intend for you to use this book both throughout the semester and for exam preparation. Here are some suggestions about how to use it:[1]

1. During the semester, use the book in preparing each night for the next day's class. To do this, first read your casebook. Then, use the *Casebook Correlation Chart* to get an idea of what part of the outline to read. Reading the outline will give you a sense of how the particular cases you've just read in your casebook fit into the overall structure of the subject. You may want to use a yellow highlighter to mark key portions of the *Emanuel*.

2. If you make your own outline for the course, use the *Emanuel* to give you a structure, and to supply black letter principles. You may want to rely especially on the *Capsule Summary* for this purpose. You are hereby authorized to copy small portions of the *Emanuel* into your own outline, provided that your outline will be used only by you or your study group, and provided that you are the owner of the *Emanuel*.

---

1. The suggestions below relate only to this book. I don't talk about taking or reviewing class notes, using hornbooks or other study aids, joining a study group, or anything else. This doesn't mean I don't think these other steps are important — it's just that in this Preface I've chosen to focus on how I think you can use this outline.

3. When you first start studying for exams, read the *Capsule Summary* to get an overview. This will probably take you all or part of two days.

4. Either during exam study or earlier in the semester, do some or all of the *Quiz Yourself* short-answer questions, supplied at the end of most sub-chapters. You can find these quickly by looking for *Quiz Yourself* entries in the Table of Contents. When you do these questions: (1) record your short "answer" on the small blank line provided after the question, but also: (2) try to write out a "mini essay" on a separate piece of paper. Remember that the only way to get good at writing essays is to write essays.

5. A couple of days before the exam, review the *Exam Tips* that appear at the end of nearly every chapter. You may want to combine this step with step (4), so that you use the *Tips* to help you spot the issues in the short-answer questions.

6. Some time during the week or so before the exam, do some or all of the full-scale essay exams at the back of the book. Write out a full essay answer under exam-like conditions (e.g., closed-book if your exam will be closed book). If you can, exchange papers with a classmate and critique each other's answer.

7. The night before the exam: (1) do some *Quiz Yourself* questions, just to get your writing juices flowing; and (2) re-read the various *Exam Tips* sections (you should be able to do this in 1-2 hours).

My deepest thanks go to Barbara Lasoff of Wolters Kluwer, who has been my editor and counselor on all *Emanuel Law Outlines* and *CrunchTime* publications for many years.

Good luck in your Corporations or Business Organizations course. If you'd like any other Wolters Kluwer publication, you can find it at your bookstore or at **www.aspenlaw.com**. If you'd like to contact me, you can email me at **semanuel@westnet.com**.

Steve Emanuel
Larchmont NY
May 2013

CASEBOOK CORRELATION CHART

(**Note:** general sections of the outline are omitted from this chart. **NC** = not directly covered by this casebook.)

Emanuel's Corporations Outline *(by chapter and section heading)*	Klein, Ramseyer & Bainbridge **Business Associations** (8th Ed. 2012)	O'Kelley & Thompson, **Corporations and Other Bus. Assoc.** (6th Ed. 2010)	Allen, Kraakman & Subramanian **Law of Business Organization** (4th. Ed. 2012)	Hamilton & Macey **Corporations, incl. Prtnrshps & LLCs** (11th Ed. 2010)
Ch. 2 — THE CORPORATE FORM				
I. Where and How To Incorporate	NC	159-170	89-114	156-172
II. *Ultra Vires* and Corporate Powers	251-267	686-688	NC	172-182
III. Pre-Incorporation Transactions by Promoters	169-176	659-662	NC	182-205
IV. Defective Incorporation and Its Consequences	NC	NC	NC	NC
V. Piercing the Corporate Veil	176-198	608-657	134-152	206-260
VI. Insider Claims in Bankruptcy (Including Equitable Subordination)	NC	624	127-134	266
Ch. 3 — THE CORPORATE STRUCTURE				
I. General Allocation of Power: Shareholders, Directors and Officers	NC	153-159	102-104	376-406, 515-532
II. Board of Directors	NC	166-169, 176-195, 246-250	104-111, 156-160	410-427, 475-477
III. Officers	NC	185-86, 669-686	111-114	477-483
IV. Formalities for Shareholder Action	516	170-175	160-161	392-406
Ch. 4 — SHAREHOLDERS' INFORMATIONAL RIGHTS, AND THE PROXY SYSTEM				
I. Shareholder Inspection of Books and Records	562-568	251-263	166-168	1083-1105
II. Reporting Requirements For Publicly-Held Companies	NC	196-207	NC	306-309
III. The Proxy Rules Generally	516-517	216-217, 220-222	161-165, 191-195	406-410, 427-432, 567-604
IV. Implied Private Actions Under the Proxy Rules	NC	NC	206-213	605-621
V. Communications by Shareholders	542-562	224-233	195-206	621-637
VI. Proxy Contests	517-575	217, 692-695	594-601	999-1003
VII. Improved Public Disclosure by the Corporation	NC	155, 373, 1153-1163	NC	549-567

CASEBOOK CORRELATION CHART (continued)

Emanuel's Corporations Outline ***(by chapter and section heading)***	Klein, Ramseyer & Bainbridge **Business Associations** (8th Ed. 2012)	O'Kelley & Thompson, **Corporations and Other Bus. Assoc.** (6th Ed. 2010)	Allen, Kraakman & Subramanian **Law of Business Organization** (4th. Ed. 2012)	Hamilton & Macey **Corporations, incl. Prtnrshps & LLCs** (11th Ed. 2010)
Ch. 5 — CLOSE CORPORATIONS				
II. Shareholder Voting Agreements: Voting Trusts and Classified Stock	582-589, 599-612	467-472	NC	418-427, 432-445
III. Agreements Restricting the Board's Discretion	589-594	450-467	NC	NC
IV. Super-Majority Voting and Quorum Requirements	NC	NC	NC	NC
V. Share Transfer Restrictions	NC	531	100-102	445-450, 453
VI. Resolution of Disputes, Including Dissolution	642-674	488-516	316-328	454-475
Ch. 6 — THE DUTY OF CARE AND THE BUSINESS JUDGMENT RULE				
II. The Standard of Care	308-316, 326-331	323-324, 328-350	217-221, 236-265	638-741
III. The Business Judgment Rule	316-319, 334	265-268, 325-327, 350-357	231-236, 406-410, 532-545	647-669, 695-719
IV. Modern Statutory Modifications to the Rules of Director Liability	NC		221-227	NC
Ch. 7 — THE DUTY OF LOYALTY				
I. Fiduciary Status of Directors, Officers and Controlling Shareholders	334-339	265-268, 277	270-276	NC
II. Self-Dealing Transactions	339-345	300-320	276-281	742-790
III. Executive Compensation	311	322-323	329-366	765-768
IV. The Corporate Opportunity Doctrine and Related Problems	345-355	277-300	313-316	790-804
V. The Sale of Control	688-691	801-807	419-443	483-503
VI. Other Duties of Controlling Shareholders	355-365	NC	316-328	NC
Ch. 8 — INSIDER TRADING				
II. State Common-Law Approaches	462-466	1123-1125	607-618	NC
III. Sec. Rule 10b-5 and Insider Trading	466-478	1125-1144	621-653, 662-684	805-864
IV. Rule 10b5 — Who Is an "Insider", "Tippee", or "Misappropriator"?	478-493	1144-1153	653-662	879-917
V. Rule 10b5 — Misrepresentations or Omissions Not Involving Insider Trading	NC	NC	630-637	938-947
VI. Short-Swing Trading Profits and § 16(b)	494-502	NC	618-621	925-931

CASEBOOK CORRELATION CHART (continued)

Emanuel's Corporations Outline *(by chapter and section heading)*	Klein, Ramseyer & Bainbridge **Business Associations** (8th Ed. 2012)	O'Kelley & Thompson, **Corporations and Other Bus. Assoc.** (6th Ed. 2010)	Allen, Kraakman & Subramanian **Law of Business Organization** (4th. Ed. 2012)	Hamilton & Macey **Corporations, incl. Prtnrshps & LLCs** (11th Ed. 2010)
Ch. 9 — SHAREHOLDERS' SUITS, ESPECIALLY DERIVATIVE SUITS				
II. Distinguishing Derivative from Direct Suits	201-209	407	367-370	NC
III. Requirements for Maintaining a Derivative Suit	NC	NC	377-379	729-741
IV. Demand on the Board; Early Termination Based on Board or Committee Recommendation	210-250	398-422	379-406	695-729, 733-737
V. Security-for-Expenses Statutes	206	NC	376	591-592
VI. Settlement of Derivative Suits	209-210	NC	410-414	NC
VII. Plaintiff's Attorney's Fees	209-210	NC	370-377	598-600
VIII. Who Gets to Recover	210	NC	NC	NC
IX. Indemnification and D&O Insurance	209, 503-515	438-446	221-227, 410-414	976-996
Ch. 10 — STRUCTURAL CHANGES, INCLUDING MERGERS AND ACQUISITIONS				
I. Corporate Combinations — Generally	695-697	689-705, 708-711	453-455, 462-471	NC
II. Corporate Combinations — Protecting Shareholders	697-705	705-706, 711-801	480-491	787-789
III. Recapitalizations — Hurting the Preferred Shareholders	NC	NC	NC	331-337
IV. Freezeouts	706-728	720-786	491-510	1008-1009
V. Tender Offers — Generally	749-805	827-837	445-449, 511-515	1003-1009
VI. Tender Offers — The Williams Act, and Other Federal Regulation	835-846	1077-1104	443-445, 449-452	1077-1082
VII. State Anti-Takeover Statutes	835-848	933-938, 1104-1122	587-594	1014-1030
VIII. Hostile Takeovers — Defensive Maneuvers, and the Judicial Response	751-805	838-933	515-532, 540-587, 601-606	1030-1068

CASEBOOK CORRELATION CHART (continued)

Emanuel's Corporations Outline *(by chapter and section heading)*	Klein, Ramseyer & Bainbridge **Business Associations** (8th Ed. 2012)	O'Kelley & Thompson, **Corporations and Other Bus. Assoc.** (6th Ed. 2010)	Allen, Kraakman & Subramanian **Law of Business Organization** (4th. Ed. 2012)	Hamilton & Macey **Corporations, incl. Prtnrshps & LLCs** (11th Ed. 2010)
Ch. 11 — DIVIDENDS AND SHARE REPURCHASES				
I. Dividends — Protection of Creditors	NC	597-599	121-127	345-349, 366-375
II. Dividends — Protection of Shareholders; Judicial Review of Dividend Policy	308-311	NC	NC	337-345
III. Stock Repurchases	NC	599-603	NC	349-366
Ch. 12 — ISSUANCE OF SECURITIES				
I. State-Law Rules on Share Issuance	NC	NC	NC	268-294, 322-337
II. Public Offerings — Introduction	NC	NC	NC	303-306
III. Public Offerings — Mechanics	NC	NC	NC	306-309
IV. Public Offerings — Exemptions	NC	NC	NC	310-318
V. Public Offerings — Civil Liabilities	NC	NC	NC	NC
VI. Public Offerings — State Regulation	NC	NC	NC	NC

CAPSULE SUMMARY

This Capsule Summary is intended for review at the end of the semester. Reading it is not a substitute for mastering the material in the main outline. Numbers in brackets refer to the pages in the main outline where the topic is discussed.

CHAPTER 1

INTRODUCTION

I. CHOOSING BETWEEN CORPORATE AND PARTNERSHIP FORM

A. Partnership vs. corporation: Choosing a form of organization usually comes down to choosing between a ***partnership*** and a ***corporation***. [2]

B. Nature of partnerships: There are two kinds of partnerships: "general" partnerships and "limited" partnerships. [3]

1. General partnership: A "***general*** partnership" is any association of two or more people who carry on a business as co-owners. A general partnership can come into existence by operation of law, with no formal papers signed or filed. Any partnership is a "general" one unless the special requirements for limited partnerships (see below) are complied with. [3]

2. Limited partnerships: A ***"limited"*** partnership can only be created where: (1) there is a ***written agreement*** among the partners; and (2) a formal document is ***filed*** with state officials. [3]

a. Two types of partners: Limited partners have two types of partners: (1) one or more ***"general"*** partners, who are ***each liable*** for all the debts of the partnership; and (2) one or more ***"limited"*** partners, who are ***not liable*** for the debts of the partnership beyond the amount they have contributed.

C. Limited liability: Corporations and partnerships differ sharply with respect to ***limited*** liability. [4]

1. Corporation: In the case of a corporation, a shareholder's liability is normally ***limited to the amount he has invested.*** [4]

2. Partnership: The liability of partners in a partnership depends on whether the partnership is "general" or "limited." [4]

a. General: In a ***general*** partnership, ***all partners are individually liable for the obligations of the partnership***.

b. Limited: In a limited partnership, the general partners are personally liable but the limited partners are liable ***only up to the amount of their capital contribution.*** (But a limited partner will lose this limit on his liability if he ***actively participates*** in the management of the partnership.)

c. **Limited Liability Partnership (LLP):** Most states now allow a third type of partnership, the ***"limited liability partnership"*** or ***"LLP."*** In an LLP, each partner may participate fully in the business' affairs without thereby becoming liable for the entity's debts. [5]

D. Management:

1. **Corporation:** Corporations follow the principle of ***centralized*** management. The shareholders participate only by electing the board of directors. The board of directors supervises the corporation's affairs, with day-to-day control resting with the "officers" (i.e., high-level executives appointed by the board). [6]

2. **Partnership:** In partnerships, management is usually ***not*** centralized. In a general partnership, all partners have an equal voice (unless they otherwise agree). In a limited partnership, all general partners have an equal voice unless they otherwise agree, but the limited partners may not participate in management. [6]

E. Continuity of existence: A corporation has "perpetual existence." In contrast, a general partnership is ***dissolved*** by the ***death*** (or, usually, even the ***withdrawal***) of a general partner. A limited partnership is dissolved by the withdrawal or death of a general partner, but not a limited partner. [6]

CAPSULE SUMMARY

F. Transferability: Ownership interests in a corporation are readily transferable (the shareholder just sells stock). A partnership interest, by contrast, is not readily transferable (all partners must consent to the admission of a new partner). [7]

G. Federal income tax:

1. **Corporations:** The corporation is ***taxed as a separate entity.*** It files its own tax return showing its profits and losses, and pays its own taxes independently of the tax position of the stockholders. This may lead to "double taxation" of dividends (a corporate-level tax on corporate profits, followed by a shareholder-level tax on the dividend). [8]

2. **Partnership:** Partnerships, by contrast, are ***not separately taxable entities***. The partnership files an information return, but the actual tax is paid by ***each individual***. Therefore, double taxation is avoided. Also, a partner can use losses from the partnership to shelter from tax certain income from other sources. [9]

3. **Subchapter S corporation:** If the owner/stockholders of a corporation would like to be taxed approximately as if they were partners in a partnership, they can often do this by having their corporation elect to be treated as a Subchapter S corporation. An "S" corporation does not get taxed at the corporate level, unlike a regular corporation; instead, each shareholder pays a tax on his portion of the corporation's profits. [10]

H. Summary:

1. **Corporation superior:** The corporate form is superior: (1) where the owners want to limit their liability; (2) where free transferability of interests is important; (3) where centralized management is important (e.g., a large number of owners); and (4) where continuity of existence in the face of withdrawal or death of an owner is important. [10]

2. **Partnership superior:** But the partnership form will be superior where: (1) simplicity and inexpensiveness of creating and operating the enterprise are important; or (2) the tax advantages are significant, such as avoiding double taxation and/or sheltering other income. [11]

II. THE LIMITED LIABILITY COMPANY (LLC)

A. Limited Liability Companies generally: The fastest-growing form of organization since the 1990s has been the ***limited liability company***, or ***LLC***. All states have enacted special statutes recognizing and regulating LLC's. The LLC is neither a corporation nor a partnership, though it has aspects of each. Many people think that LLCs incorporate the best features of both corporations and partnerships. [11]

1. **Advantages vs. standard partnership as to liability:** The biggest advantage of the LLC compared with either a general or limited partnership is that in the LLC, a "member" (analogous to a partner) is liable ***only for the amount of his or her capital contribution***, even if the member actively participates in the business.

2. **Taxed as partnership:** The LLC's biggest advantage compared with a standard "C" corporation is that the LLC's members can elect whether to have the entity treated as a partnership or as a corporation. If they elect partnership treatment, the entity becomes a ***"pass-through" entity,*** and thus ***avoids the double-taxation of dividends*** that shareholders of a standard corporation suffer from.

3. **Operating agreement:** Owners of the LLC (called ***"members"***) must agree among themselves how the business will operate (e.g., what kind of a vote is necessary to sell the LLC's assets, or whether the entity will be managed by its members or by a separate set of managers). The members do this by an ***"operating agreement"*** to which they are all party. Usually the operating agreement is in writing. [12]

   a. **LLC is bound:** Most decisions hold that the LLC is itself ***bound*** by the operating agreement, even if only the members, and not the LLC itself, signed the agreement. This means that if one member sues the LLC, the operating agreement will control on matters with which it deals (e.g., the forum in which suits by or against the LLC may be brought).

   b. **Obligation of good faith:** An LLC's operating agreement is a contract, and all contracts contain an ***implied covenant of good faith and fair dealing***. Disgruntled LLC members have frequently argued that another member's conduct, even though expressly allowed by the terms of the operating agreement, ***constitutes a breach*** of this implied covenant. But these arguments generally ***fail*** — where a member exercises a right that is expressly given to her by the operating agreement, courts almost ***never*** hold that that exercise constitutes a breach of the covenant of good faith and fair dealing.

   Example: Inventor, an individual, and Investor, a venture capital company, form an LLC funded mainly by Investor. The operating agreement says that all important decisions, including the raising of further capital, require the consent of both members. The LCC runs out of cash, and can't operate. Investor refuses to consent to the raising of more funds by other investors, and instead sues for dissolution based on the statutory ground of deadlock. Inventor claims that Investor's refusal to allow fundraising violated Investor's implied obligation of good faith and fair dealing.

   Held, for Investor. The operating agreement expressly granted Investor the right to block any financing of which it disapproved. The implied covenant of good faith and fair dealing is a "gap filler," and cannot be invoked where the contract itself expressly covers the subject at issue. "The mere exercise of one's contractual rights, without more, cannot constitute ... a breach ... of the implied covenant of good faith and fair dealing[.]" [*Fisk Ventures, LLC v. Segal*] [13]

4. **Piercing of veil:** Just as a *corporation's* ***"veil"*** may sometimes be ***"pierced"*** (see *infra*, p. C-6), some decisions hold that the veil of the LLC may sometimes be pierced, so as to make the members liable for the LLC's debts. [14]

CHAPTER 2

THE CORPORATE FORM

I. WHERE AND HOW TO INCORPORATE

A. Delaware vs. headquarter state: The incorporators must choose between incorporating in their headquarter state, or incorporating somewhere else (probably Delaware). [19]

1. **Closely held:** For a ***closely held*** corporation, incorporation should usually take place in the state where the corporation's ***principal place of business*** is located. [20]

2. **Publicly held:** But for a ***publicly held*** corporation, incorporation in Delaware is usually very attractive (because of Delaware's well-defined, predictable, body of law, and its slight pro-management bias.) [20]

B. Mechanics of incorporating:

1. **Articles of incorporation:** To form a corporation, the incorporators file a document with the Secretary of State. This document is usually called the ***"articles of incorporation"*** or the "charter." [21]

   a. **Amending:** The articles can be amended at any time after filing. However, any class of stockholders who would be adversely affected by the amendment must ***approve*** the amendment by majority vote. See, e.g., MBCA § 10.04.

2. **Bylaws:** After the corporation has been formed, it adopts ***bylaws***. The corporation's bylaws are rules governing the corporation's internal affairs (e.g., date, time and place for annual meeting; number of directors; listing of officers; what constitutes quorum for directors' meetings, etc.). Bylaws are usually not filed with the Secretary of State, and may usually be amended by either the board or the shareholders. [22]

CAPSULE SUMMARY

II. ULTRA VIRES AND CORPORATE POWERS

A. *Ultra vires:*

1. **Classic doctrine:** Traditionally, acts beyond the corporation's articles of incorporation were held to be ***"ultra vires,"*** and were unenforceable against the corporation or by it. (But there were numerous exceptions.) [24]

2. **Modern abolition:** Modern corporate statutes have generally ***eliminated*** the *ultra vires* doctrine. See, e.g, MBCA § 3.04(a). [24]

B. Corporate powers today: Most modern corporations are formed with articles that allow the corporation to take ***any lawful action***. [24]

1. **Charitable contribution:** Even if the articles of incorporation are silent on the subject, corporations are generally held to have an implied power to make ***reasonable charitable contributions***. See, e.g., MBCA § 3.02(13). [24]

2. **Other:** Similarly, corporations can generally give bonuses, stock options, or other ***fringe benefits*** to their employees (even retired employees). See, e.g., MBCA § 3.02(12). [25]

III. PRE-INCORPORATION TRANSACTIONS BY PROMOTERS

A. **Liability of promoter:** A ***"promoter"*** is one who takes initiative in founding and organizing a corporation. A promoter may occasionally be ***liable*** for debts he contracts on behalf of the to-be formed corporation. [28]

1. **Promoter aware, other party not:** If the promoter enters into a contract in the corporation's name, and the promoter ***knows*** that the corporation has not yet been formed (but the other party does ***not*** know this), the promoter will be ***liable*** under the contract. See MBCA § 2.04. [28]

   a. **Adoption:** But if the corporation is later formed and ***"adopts"*** the contract, then the promoter may escape liability.

2. **Contract says corporation not formed:** If the contract entered into by the promoter on behalf of the corporation ***recites*** that the corporation has not yet been formed, the liability of the promoter depends on what the court finds to be the parties' ***intent***. [28]

   a. **Never formed, or immediately defaults:** If the corporation is ***never formed***, or is formed but then immediately ***defaults***, the promoter will probably be ***liable***.

   b. **Formed and then adopts:** But if the corporation is formed, and then shows its ***intent to take over*** the contract (i.e., ***"adopts"*** the contract), then the court may find that both parties intended that the promoter be released from liability (a ***"novation"***).

B. **Liability of corporation:** If the corporation did not exist at the time the promoter signed a contract on its behalf, the corporation will not become liable unless it ***"adopts"*** the contract. Adoption may be ***implied***. (*Example*: The corporation receives benefits under the contract, without objecting to them. The corporation will be deemed to have implicitly adopted the contract, making it liable and perhaps making the promoter no longer liable.) [29]

C. **Promoter's fiduciary obligation:** During the pre-incorporation period, the promoter has a ***fiduciary obligation*** to the to-be-formed corporation. He therefore may not pursue his own profit at the corporation's ultimate expense. (*Example*: The promoter may not sell the corporation property at a grossly inflated price.) [30]

IV. DEFECTIVE INCORPORATION

A. **Common-law "de facto" doctrine:** At common law, if a person made a "colorable" attempt to incorporate (e.g., he submitted articles to the Secretary of State, which were rejected), a "de facto" corporation would be found to have been formed. This would be enough to shelter the would-be incorporator from the personal liability that would otherwise result. This is the ***"de facto corporation"*** doctrine. [32]

1. **Modern view:** But today, most states have ***abolished*** the de facto doctrine, and expressly impose personal liability on anyone who purports to do business as a corporation while knowing that incorporation has not occurred. See MBCA § 2.04.

B. **Corporation by estoppel:** The common law also applies the "corporation by ***estoppel***" doctrine, whereby a creditor who deals with the business as a corporation, and who agrees to look to the "corporation's" assets rather than the "shareholders'|" assets will be estopped from denying the corporation's existence. [32]

1. **May survive:** The "corporation by estoppel" doctrine probably survives in some states, as a judge-made doctrine.

V. PIERCING THE CORPORATE VEIL

A. **Generally:** In a few very extreme cases, courts may ***"pierce the corporate veil,"*** and hold some or all of the shareholders ***personally liable*** for the corporation's debts. [34]

B. **Individual shareholders:** If the corporation's shares are held by ***individuals***, here are some factors that courts look to in deciding whether to pierce the corporate veil: [35]

1. **Tort vs. contract ("voluntary creditor"):** Courts are more likely to pierce the veil in a ***tort*** case (where the creditor is ***"involuntary"***) than in a ***contract*** case (where the creditor is "voluntary"). [35]

2. **Fraud:** Veil piercing is more likely where there has been a grievous ***fraud*** or ***wrongdoing*** by the shareholders (e.g., the sole shareholder siphons out all profits, leaving the corporation without enough money to pay its claims). [36]

3. **Inadequate capitalization:** Most important, veil piercing is most likely if the corporation has been ***inadequately capitalized***. But most courts do not make inadequate capitalization ***alone*** enough for veil piercing. [37]

   a. **Zero capital:** When the shareholder invests ***no money whatsoever*** in the corporation, courts are especially likely to pierce the veil, and may require less of a showing on the other factors than if the capitalization was inadequate but non-zero.

   b. **Siphoning:** Capitalization may be inadequate either because there is not enough ***initial*** capital, or because the corporation's profits are systematically ***siphoned out*** as earned. But if capitalization is adequate, and the corporation then has unexpected liabilities, the shareholders' failure to put in ***additional*** capital will generally ***not*** be inadequate capitalization.

4. **Failure of formalities:** Lastly, the court is more likely to pierce the veil if the shareholders have ***failed to follow corporate formalities*** in running the business. (*Example*: Shares are never formally issued, directors' meetings are not held, shareholders co-mingle personal and company funds.) [39]

5. **Summary:** In nearly all cases at least ***two*** of the above four factors must be present for the court to pierce the veil; the most common combination is probably inadequate capitalization plus failure to follow corporate formalities.

C. **Parent/subsidiary:** If shares are held by a ***parent corporation***, the court may pierce the veil and make the parent corporation liable for the ***debts of the subsidiary***. [40]

1. **No liability generally:** Again, the ***general*** rule is that the corporate parent shareholder is ***not liable*** for the debts of the subsidiary (just as individual shareholders are not liable for the corporation's debts). [40]

   a. **"Dominance" over subsidiary not enough:** The fact that the parent may in some sense ***"dominate" the affairs*** of the subsidiary will ***not*** by itself be enough to give rise to veil-piercing. Thus the fact that the parent ***drains excess cash*** from the subsidiary, ***demands a***

veto power over significant decisions by the subsidiary, or otherwise exercises some degree of ***control*** over the subsidiary's ***operations***, will not suffice for piercing. So long as the degree of control by parent over subsidiary is within the bounds usually found in corporate America, creditors will probably not be able to attack the parent's assets. [41]

2. **Factors:** But as in the individual-shareholder case, certain acts by the parent may cause veil piercing to take place. Such factors include:

[1] the parent and subsidiary fail to follow ***separate corporate formalities*** for the two corporations (e.g., both have the same board, and do not hold separate directors' meetings);

[2] the parent and subsidiary are operating pieces of the ***same business***, and the subsidiary is undercapitalized;

[3] the public is ***misled*** about which entity is operating which business;

[4] assets are ***intermingled*** between parent and subsidiary; or

[5] the subsidiary is operated in an ***unfair manner*** (e.g., forced to sell at cost to parent). [41]

a. **"Single economic entity" theory:** As the Delaware courts summarize the idea, only if the two companies operate as a ***"single economic entity"*** will the veil generally be pierced, assuming that there is no fraud on creditors. [41]

VI. INSIDER CLAIMS IN BANKRUPTCY (INCLUDING EQUITABLE SUBORDINATION)

A. **Disallowance in bankruptcy:** A bankruptcy court may ***disallow*** an insider's claim entirely if fairness requires. (*Example*: The insider claims that his entire capital contribution is a "loan," but the court finds that some or all should be treated as non-repayable "equity" in the bankruptcy proceeding.) [44]

B. **Equitable subordination:** Alternatively, the bankruptcy court may recognize the insider's claims against the corporation, but will make these claims come ***after*** payment of all other creditors. Many of the same factors used for piercing the corporate veil (e.g., inadequate capitalization) will lead to this ***"equitable subordination"*** in bankruptcy. [45]

CHAPTER 3

THE CORPORATE STRUCTURE

I. GENERAL ALLOCATION OF POWERS

A. **Traditional scheme:** A "traditional" scheme for allocating power in the corporation (reflected in most statutes) is as follows: [50]

1. **Shareholders:** The shareholders act principally by: (1) electing and removing ***directors***; and (2) approving or disapproving ***fundamental*** or non-ordinary ***changes*** (e.g., mergers). [50]

2. **Directors:** The directors ***"manage"*** the corporation's business. That is, they formulate policy, and they ***appoint officers*** to carry out that policy. [50]

3. **Officers:** The corporation's officers administer the ***day-to-day affairs*** of the corporation, under the supervision of the board. [50]

4. **Modification:** This traditional allocation of powers usually may be ***modified*** by the corporation where appropriate. This is often done in the case of closely held corporations. [50]

B. **Powers of shareholders:** The main powers of the ***shareholders*** are as follows:

1. **Directors:** They have the power to ***elect*** and ***remove directors***. [51]

a. **Election:** Shareholders normally elect the directors at the ***annual meeting*** of shareholders. In other words, directors normally serve a one-year term. See Model Business Corporations Act (MBCA) § 8.05(b).

b. **Vacancies:** Shareholders usually have the right to elect directors to ***fill vacancies*** on the board, but the board of directors also usually has this power.

c. **Removal:** At common law, shareholders had little power to ***remove*** a director during his term of office. But today, most statutes allow the shareholders to remove directors ***even without cause***. See MBCA § 8.08(a).

2. **Articles and bylaws:** The shareholders can amend the ***articles*** of incorporation or the ***bylaws***. [51]

a. **Some states limit:** However, some states significantly ***limit the content of bylaws***, and thus limit the ability of stockholders to change how the corporation functions. For instance, in Delaware a bylaw may not specify what ***substantive*** business decisions are to be made by the board, and may mandate only the ***procedures*** by which the board is to make those decisions. [*CA, Inc. v. AFSCME Employees Pension Plan*] [54]

i. **Limit of board's exercise of fiduciary responsibilities:** Thus suppose a Delaware corporation's shareholders vote to approve a bylaw amendment to the company's charter that purports to significantly ***limit the board's discretion*** over substantive matters, in a way that deprives the board of its ability to ***exercise its fiduciary responsibilities*** to all shareholders. The court is likely to hold the bylaw invalid. [54]

Example: Suppose shareholders of a Delaware publicly-traded company vote to approve a bylaw amendment (opposed by management and the board) that says that if any all-cash takeover offer should occur at more than a 30% premium over the previous market price of the shares, the board must approve the takeover. A court would likely hold that the bylaw as amended usurps the board's right and duty to exercise its fiduciary responsibilities to all shareholders (which includes deciding whether a takeover offer is a good one). If so, the court would strike the amendment as a violation of state law.

3. **Fundamental changes:** The shareholders get to approve or disapprove of ***fundamental changes*** not in the ordinary course of business (e.g., mergers, sales of substantially all of the company's assets, or dissolution). [51]

C. **Power of directors:** The ***directors*** "manage" the affairs of the corporation. [52]

1. **Shareholders can't give orders:** Thus shareholders usually ***cannot order the board of directors to take any particular action***. [52]

2. **Supervisory role:** The board does not operate the corporation day to day. Instead, it ***appoints officers***, and ***supervises*** the manner in which the officers conduct the day-to-day affairs. [52]

D. **Power of officers:** The corporation's ***officers*** are appointed by the board, and can be removed by the board. The officers carry out the day-to-day affairs. [53]

II. BOARD OF DIRECTORS

A. **Election:** As noted, members of the board of directors are always elected by the shareholders. [55]

1. **Straight vs. cumulative:** The vote for directors may either be ***"straight"*** or ***"cumulative."*** (In most states, cumulative voting is allowed only if the articles of incorporation explicitly elect to have it.) [55]

a. **Cumulative:** In cumulative voting, a shareholder may ***aggregate his votes*** in favor of fewer candidates than there are slots available. (*Example:* H owns 100 shares. There are 3 board slots. H may cast all of his 300 votes for 1 candidate.) This makes it more likely that a minority shareholder will be able to obtain at least one seat on the board.

i. **Removal of directors:** If cumulative voting is authorized, a director usually may not be ***removed*** if the number of votes that would have been sufficient to elect him under cumulative voting is voted against his removal.

B. **Number of directors:** The number of directors is usually fixed in either the articles of incorporation or in the bylaws. Most statutes require at least three directors. Most statutes also allow the articles or bylaws to set a variable (minimum and maximum) size for the board, rather than a fixed size. (If variable size is chosen, then the board gets to decide how many directors within the range there should be.) [59]

C. **Filling vacancies:** Most statutes allow ***vacancies*** on the board to be filled ***either*** by the shareholders or by the board. [60]

1. **Term:** Statutes vary as to the term of a replacement director: some let him serve the full unexpired term of his predecessor, others make him stand for reelection at the next annual meeting. (This only matters if the predecessor's term was for more than one year). [60]

2. **Classes of stock:** The articles of incorporation may give each separate ***class of stock*** the power to elect one or more directors. [60]

3. **Holdover director:** A director holds office not only for the term for which he is elected, but ***until his successor is elected and qualified***. A director serving beyond the end of his term is called a ***"holdover"*** director. [61]

D. **Removal of directors:** Most modern statutes provide that directors may be removed by a majority vote of ***shareholders***, either ***with or without cause***. Modern statutes also generally say that a ***court*** may order a director removed, but only for ***cause***. [61]

1. **No removal by board:** But in most states a director may ***not*** be removed by his ***fellow directors***, even for cause. [63]

E. **Directors' meetings:**

1. **Regular vs. special:** There are two types of board meetings: ***regular*** and ***special***. A regular board meeting is one which occurs at a regular interval (e.g., monthly). All other meetings are "special." The frequency for regular meetings is usually specified in the bylaws. [63]

2. **Notice:** No notice is necessary for a regular meeting. But prior notice (e.g., two days notice under the MBCA) is required for a special meeting. [63]

3. **Quorum:** The board may only act if a ***quorum*** is present. Usually, the quorum is a ***majority*** of the total directors in office. (*Example*: If there are nine directors, at least five must be present for there to be a meeting.) [63]

   a. **Lower number:** Some states allow the articles or bylaws to set a percentage for a quorum that is ***less than a majority***.

   b. **Super majority:** Conversely, most statutes permit the articles or bylaws to make the quorum ***more*** than a majority (useful as a control device in closely-held corporations). See MBCA 8.24(a).

   c. **Present at vote:** The quorum must be present ***at the time the vote is taken*** in order for the vote to constitute the act of the board. Thus even if a quorum is present at the start of the meeting, a director may leave and thereby remove the quorum.

CAPSULE SUMMARY

F. **Act of board:** The board may normally take action only by a ***vote of a majority*** of the directors ***present*** at the meeting. [65]

1. **Higher number:** In most states, the articles of incorporation may set a ***higher percentage*** than a majority for all or certain board actions. [65]

2. **Requirement for meeting:** The board may normally take action ***only at a meeting***, not by individual action of the directors. (*Example*: A contract cannot be executed by the board merely by having a majority of the directors, acting at separate times and places, sign the contract document.) But there are some exceptions: [65]

   a. **Unanimous written consent:** Nearly all states allow directors to act without a meeting if they give their ***unanimous written consent*** to the proposed corporate action. See MBCA § 8.21(a).

   b. **Telephone meetings:** Many states now permit the directors to act by means of a ***telephone conference call***.

   c. **Ratification:** Also, if the board learns of an action taken by an officer, and the board does not object, the board may be deemed to have ***"ratified"*** this action, or the board may be ***"estopped"*** from dishonoring it. In either case, the result is as if the board had formally approved the action in advance.

3. **Objection by director:** A director may ***disassociate*** herself from board action by filing a written dissent, or by making an oral dissent that is entered in the minutes of the meeting. This will shield the director from any possible liability for the corporate action. [66]

G. **Committees:** The full board may appoint various ***committees***. Generally, a committee may ***take any action*** which could be taken by the full board. (But there are exceptions. For instance, under the MBCA, committees may not fill board vacancies, amend the articles of incorporation or the bylaws, propose actions for shareholder approval, or authorize share repurchases. MBCA § 8.25(e).) [66]

III. OFFICERS

A. **Meaning of "officer":** The term ***"officer"*** describes only the more important executives of the corporation, typically those ***appointed directly by the board of directors.*** Most states leave it up to the board or the bylaws to determine what officers there shall be. [72]

B. **Right to hire and fire:** Officers can be both ***hired*** and ***fired*** by the board. Firing can be with or ***without cause*** (and can occur even if there is an employment contract, though the officer can then sue the corporation for breach). [73]

C. **Authority to act for corporation:** The officer is an ***agent*** of the corporation, and his authority is therefore analyzed under agency principles. An officer does not have the ***automatic right*** to bind the corporation. Instead, one of four doctrines must usually be used to find that the officer could bind the corporation on particular facts: [73]

1. **Express actual authority:** Express actual authority can be given to an officer either by the corporation's ***bylaws***, or by a ***resolution*** adopted by the board. (*Example*: A board resolution authorizes the Vice President to negotiate and sign a contract to dispose of a surplus plant.) [73]

2. **Implied actual authority:** "Implied actual authority" is authority that is ***"inherent in the office."*** Usually, it is authority that is inherent in the ***particular post*** occupied by the officer. [74]

   a. **President:** The ***president*** is generally held to have implied actual authority, merely by virtue of his office, to engage in ***ordinary*** business transactions, such as hiring and firing non-officer-level employees and entering into ordinary-course contracts. But he does ***not*** usually have implied actual authority to bind the corporation to ***non-ordinary-course*** contracts such as contracts for the sale of real estate or for the sale of all of the corporation's assets.

   b. **Secretary:** The ***secretary*** has implied actual authority to ***certify the records of the corporation***, including ***resolutions*** of the board of directors. Therefore, a secretary's certificate that a given resolution was duly adopted by the board is ***binding*** on the corporation in favor of a third party who relies on the certificate.

   c. **Removal:** The board may always explicitly ***remove*** implied actual authority that would otherwise exist (e.g., by notifying President that he may not hire anyone.)

3. **Apparent authority:** An officer has ***"apparent authority"*** if the corporation gives observers the ***appearance*** that the agent is authorized to act as he is acting. There are two requirements: (1) the corporation, by acts ***other than those of the officer***, must ***indicate to the world*** that the officer has the authority to do the act in question; and (2) the plaintiff must be ***aware*** of those corporate indications and rely on them. [75]

   a. **President:** In the case of a president, apparent authority will often flow merely from the fact that the corporation has given him that title — he will then have apparent authority to enter into ordinary course arrangements. (*Example*: If Corp. gives X the title "President," this will signal to the world that X has authority to purchase office supplies. Therefore, if X does purchase office supplies from P, who knows that X has the title "President," X will bind Corp. even if the board of directors has explicitly resolved that X does *not* have authority to purchase such supplies.)

4. **Ratification:** Under the doctrine of ***"ratification,"*** if a person with actual authority to enter into the transaction learns of a transaction by an officer, and either expressly affirms it or fails to disavow it, the corporation may be bound. Usually, P will have to show that the corporation either received benefits under the contract, or that P himself relied to his detriment on the existence of the contract. [77]

IV. SHAREHOLDER ACTION

A. **Meetings:** Nearly all states require a corporation to hold an ***annual meeting of shareholders***. See MBCA § 7.02(a). [80]

1. **Special meeting:** Corporations may also hold a ***"special"*** shareholders' meeting. A special meeting is any meeting other than the regularly-scheduled annual meeting. [80]

a. **Who may call:** The board may call a special meeting. Also, anyone authorized by the bylaws to call a meeting (e.g., the president, under many bylaws) may do so. Finally, some statutes allow the holders of a certain percentage of the shares to call a special meeting. (*Example*: MBCA § 7.02(a)(2) allows the holders of 10% of shares to call a special meeting. But in Delaware, shareholders may not call a special meeting.)

B. **Quorum:** For a vote of a shareholders' meeting to be effective, there must be a ***quorum*** present. Usually, this must be a ***majority of the outstanding shares.*** However, the percentage required for a quorum may be ***reduced*** if provided in the articles or bylaws. [81]

1. **Minimum:** Some states don't allow the percentage for a quorum to be reduced below a certain number (e.g., the number cannot be reduced below one-third in Delaware). But the MBCA sets no floor. [81]

2. **Higher percentage:** Conversely, nearly all states allow the articles or bylaws to set a ***higher percentage*** as the quorum. [81]

C. **Vote required:** Once a quorum is present, the traditional rule is that the shareholders will be deemed to have approved of the proposed action only if a majority of the ***shares actually present*** vote in ***favor*** of the proposed action. [81]

1. **Traditional rule:** In other words, under this approach, an abstention is the equivalent of a vote against. [81]

a. **MBCA:** But the MBCA, in § 7.25(c), changes this by treating abstentions like votes that are not cast.

2. **Breaking quorum:** Once a quorum is present, the quorum is deemed to exist for the rest of the meeting, even if shareholders ***leave***. [82]

3. **Written consent:** Nearly all states allow shareholders to act by ***unanimous written consent*** without a meeting. [82]

a. **Non-unanimous written consent:** A minority of states allow shareholder action in the form of ***non-unanimous*** written consent. (*Example*: Delaware § 228(a) allows shareholder action by the written consent of the same number of votes as would be needed to approve the action at a meeting.)

4. **Meeting in cyberspace:** Some states now allow shareholder meetings to occur on the ***Internet***. See, e.g., Del. GCL § 211(a)(2) (allowing a meeting to occur electronically, so long as shareholders can hear the proceedings and vote by computer.) [82]

CHAPTER 4

SHAREHOLDERS' INFORMATIONAL RIGHTS AND THE PROXY SYSTEM

I. SHAREHOLDER INSPECTION OF BOOKS AND RECORDS

A. Generally: State law generally gives shareholders the right to inspect the corporation's books and records. [89]

1. **Common law:** In most states, shareholders have a common-law right of inspection if they show a "proper purpose" for doing so. [90]

2. **Statute:** Also, many states have enacted statutes codifying the shareholder's right of inspection. [90]

B. Who may inspect: Usually "beneficial owners," as well as holders of record, may inspect. [91]

1. **Size or length of holding:** Some statutes restrict the right of inspection to shareholders who either have held their shares for a certain time, or hold more than a certain percentage of total shares. [91] (*Example*: New York BCL § 624 gives the statutory right of inspection only to one who: (1) has held for at least six months; or (2) holds at least 5% of a class of shares.)

C. What records may be examined: Under most statutes, the holder has a right to inspect not merely specified records, but the corporate records ***in general***. [92]

1. **More limited statutes:** But other statutes are more limited. (*Example*: The MBCA does not give holders an automatic right to inspect sensitive materials like the minutes of board meetings, the accounting records, or the shareholder list. For these, he must make a demand "in good faith and for proper purpose," he must "describe with reasonable particularity" his purpose and the records he wants to inspect, and the records must be "directly connected with his purpose." See MBCA § 16.02(b).) [92]

D. Proper purpose: The shareholder generally may inspect records only if he does so for a ***"proper purpose."*** [92]

1. **Evaluation of investment:** A shareholder's desire to ***evaluate*** his ***investment*** will usually be "proper." (*Example*: A holder will usually be allowed to examine accounting records to determine whether the stock's market price fairly reflects its true value.) [93]

2. **Unrelated personal goal:** Pursuit of unrelated ***personal goals*** will generally ***not*** be a proper purpose. (*Example*: A holder may not inspect if his purpose is to get access to trade secrets which he can sell to a competitor or use himself.) [93]

3. **Deal with other shareholders:** If the holder wants to get access to the shareholder's list to contact his ***fellow shareholders*** to take group action concerning the corporation, this will usually be proper. (*Example*: A holder will usually be given access to shareholder lists to solicit proxies in connection with an attempt to elect a rival slate of directors.) [93]

4. **Social/political goals:** If the holder is pursuing only ***social or political goals*** that are not closely related to the corporation's business, this purpose will usually be improper. (*Example*: P wants to stop D Corp from making munitions for the Vietnam War because he thinks the war is immoral; P's purpose is not "proper," so he cannot have D's shareholder list or its records of weapons manufacture.) [93]

5. **Multiple purposes of which one is proper:** Suppose a shareholder has ***multiple purposes*** for requesting the inspection, of which one (or more) is appropriate and the other(s) not. Here, at least in Delaware inspection must be ***allowed*** — so long as there is ***at least one proper purpose***, the presence of an ***improper*** purpose is ***irrelevant***. [94]

   a. **Court will look to the "real" purpose:** Of course, the court will not blindly accept the shareholder's stated reason(s) for the inspection, and will instead normally try to ascertain the ***"real"*** reasons that are motivating her. If the court concludes that all of the real reasons are ***illegitimate***, the fact that the holder has asserted a different reason that would be legitimate will be irrelevant. [94]

E. **Financial reports:** In most states, the corporation is ***not*** required to send an ***annual report*** or other annual financial information to the shareholder. (But federal law requires publicly held corporations to send a report, and some states require this for all corporations.) [95]

F. **Director's right of inspection:** A ***director*** in most states has a very ***broad***, virtually automatic, right of inspection. (But most states deny him the right of inspection if he is acting with "manifestly improper motives.") [95]

II. REPORTING REQUIREMENTS FOR PUBLICLY HELD COMPANIES

A. **What companies are "publicly held":** Certain reporting requirements are imposed on "publicly held" companies. Basically, these are companies which either: (1) have stock that is traded on a national securities exchange; or (2) have assets of more than $10 million *and* a class of stock held of record by 500 or more people. These companies must make continuous disclosures to the SEC under § 12 of the Securities Exchange Act of 1934 (the "'34 Act"), and must comply with the proxy rules described below. [97]

B. **Proxy rules generally:** Any company covered by § 12 of the '34 Act (companies listed in the prior paragraph) fall within the SEC's ***proxy solicitation*** rules. If a company is covered, any proxy solicitation by either management or non-management (subject to some exemptions) must comply with detailed SEC rules. Basically, this means that whenever management or a third party wants to persuade a shareholder to ***vote*** in a certain way (whether the persuasion is written or oral, and whether it is by advertisement or one-on-one communication), the solicitation must comply with the SEC proxy rules. [97]

C. **Disclosure and filing requirements:**

1. **Filing:** Any proxy solicitation documents that will be sent to shareholders must first be ***filed with the SEC***. [100]

2. **Proxy statement:** Every proxy solicitation must be accompanied or preceded by a written ***"proxy statement."*** This must disclose items like conflicts of interest, the compensation given to the five highest-paid officers, and details of any major change being voted upon. [100]

3. **Annual report:** The proxy rules require than an ***annual report*** be sent to every shareholder. [100]

4. **Anti-fraud:** Any ***false*** or ***misleading*** statements or omissions in a proxy statement are banned by SEC rules. [101]

D. Requirements for proxy: The proxy itself is a ***card*** which the shareholder signs, and on which he indicates how he wants to vote. SEC rules govern the format of this card. [102]

1. **Function:** Most commonly, the proxy will be the method by which the shareholder indicates to management that he is voting for management's slate of ***directors***. The proxy card will also be the shareholder's way of indicating how he votes on some major non-election issue, such as whether the company should merge with another corporation. The proxy is the method of casting shareholder votes in all situations except where the shareholder attends the shareholder's meeting. [102]

2. **Broad discretion:** The proxy form may not confer unduly broad discretion on the recipient. (*Example*: The card must list exactly what nominees management is proposing for election to the board; it may not confer on management the right to vote for unnamed candidates that management desires.) [102]

3. **Must be voted:** The recipient of the proxy (e.g., management or a group of insurgents waging a proxy contest) ***must*** vote the proxy as the shareholder has indicated, even if the shareholder has voted the opposite of the way the person who solicited the proxy would like. [102]

E. Revocation of proxies: Generally, a proxy is ***revocable*** by the shareholder, even if the proxy itself recites that it is irrevocable.

1. **Coupled with an interest:** However, if a proxy states that it is irrevocable ***and*** the proxy is ***"coupled with an interest"*** then it is ***irrevocable***. A proxy is "coupled with an interest" when the recipient of the proxy has a property interest in the shares, or at least some other direct economic interest in how the vote is cast. (*Example*: A shareholder pledges his shares in return for a loan from Bank. The pledge is an interest, so the proxy will be irrevocable while the loan is outstanding.) [102]

CAPSULE SUMMARY

III. IMPLIED PRIVATE ACTIONS UNDER THE PROXY RULES

A. Generally: The Supreme Court has recognized an ***"implied private right of action"*** on behalf of individuals who have been injured by a violation of proxy rules. [*J.I. Case Co. v. Borak*] There are three requirements which the plaintiff must satisfy: [103]

1. **Materiality:** First, P must show that there was a ***material*** misstatement or omission in the proxy materials. In the case of an omission, the omitted fact is material if it would have "assumed actual significance in the deliberations of a reasonable shareholder." [105]

2. **Causation:** Second, P must show a ***causal link*** between the misleading proxy materials and some damage to shareholders. However, P does not have to show that the falsehood or omission directly "caused" the damage to shareholders; he only has to show that the proxy solicitation itself (not the error or omission) was an essential part of the transaction. [107] (*Example*: If holders have to approve a merger, any material defect in the proxy materials will be deemed to have "caused" damage to the holders, since the entire proxy solicitation process was an essential part of carrying out the merger transaction.)

   a. **Minority class whose votes are not needed:** If P is a member of a ***minority class*** whose votes were ***not necessary*** for the proposed transaction to go through, P may not recover no matter how material or how intentional the deception in the proxy statement was. [*Virginia Bankshares, Inc. v. Sandberg*].

Example: FABI, a bank holding company, owns 80% of the shares of Bank. FABI wants to get rid of the 20% minority shareholders in Bank, so it proposes to buy out the minority holders at a price of $42. The minority holders are sent a proxy solitication stating that the $42 price is "high" and "fair." Most of the minority holders approve the transaction. P, a minority holder who opposes the transaction, sues on the grounds that the proxy materials falsely stated that the price was "high" and "fair."

Held, P has no claim here, even if the proxy materials were false. Because FABI could have voted its own shares in favor of the buyout, approval by the minority holders was not legally necessary. Therefore, no misstatements in the proxy materials sent to the minority holders could have "caused" the merger, or contributed to any damage suffered by P or the other minority holders. *Virginia Bankshares*, *supra*.

3. **Standard of fault:** Third, P must show that D was ***at fault*** in some way. If the defendant is an "insider" (e.g., the corporation itself, its officers and its employee/directors), P only has to show that D was ***negligent***. Some courts have also found ***outside directors*** and other outsiders liable for errors or omissions under the proxy rules, where the outsider was negligent. [110]

4. **Remedies:** If P makes these three showings, he can get several possible types of relief: (1) he may be able to get an ***injunction*** against a proposed transaction (where the proxy solicitation was for the purpose of getting shareholder approval of the transaction, such as a merger); (2) he may very occasionally have an already-completed transaction ***set aside***; and (3) he may obtain ***damages*** for himself and other holders, if he can prove actual monetary injury (e.g., he shows that due to lies in the proxy statement, shareholders approved the sale of the company at an unfairly low price). [110]

IV. COMMUNICATIONS BY SHAREHOLDERS

A. **Two methods:** A ***shareholder*** may solicit her fellow shareholders to obtain their proxies in favor of her own proposed slate of directors or her own proposal. Depending on the circumstances, there are two methods for her to do so, in one of which the shareholder bears the expense and in the other of which the corporation bears the expense. [111]

B. **Shareholder bears expense:** Under SEC Rule 14a-7, a shareholder who is willing to ***bear the expense*** of communicating with his fellow shareholders (e.g., printing and postage) has the right to do so. Management must either mail the shareholder's materials to the other stockholders, or give the soliciting shareholder a shareholder list so that he can do the mailing directly. [112]

1. **Few restrictions:** There are very few restrictions on when and how this method is used. For instance, there is no length limit on the materials the shareholder may mail, and management has no right to censor or object to the contents. [112]

C. **Corporation bears expense:** Alternatively, a shareholder may sometimes get a "shareholder proposal" submitted to fellow shareholders entirely at the ***corporation's expense***. Under SEC Rule 14a-8, shareholder proposals may sometimes be required to be included in management's own proxy materials. (*Example*: An activist shareholder may be able to get management's proxy materials to include the activist's proposal that the company cease doing business with China.) [113]

1. **Exclusions:** Many kinds of proposals are ***excluded*** from 14a-8, so management can refuse to include them. Some of the important exclusions are: [113]

a. **Improper subject under state law:** A proposal may be excluded if "under the law of the [state where the corporation is incorporated, the proposal is] not a proper subject for action by security holders." This usually means that the proposal must be phrased as a ***recommendation*** by the shareholders that management consider doing something, rather than as an ***order*** by shareholders that the corporation do something (since under state law shareholders usually cannot order the corporation to do anything). [114]

b. **Not significantly related to corporation's business:** A proposal may be excluded if it is ***not significantly related to the company's business*** (i.e., if it counts for less than 5% of the corporation's total assets and less than 5% of its earnings and gross sales, and is "not otherwise significantly related to the [corporation's] business"). (*Example*: A proposal calls for Corp's widget division to be divested because it has a poor return on equity; if the widget division accounts for less than 5% of Corp's assets, earnings and sales, the proposal may be excluded.) [116]

   i. **Ethical/social issues:** But ***ethical*** or ***social*** issues may usually ***not*** be excluded for failure to meet these 5% tests, if the issues are otherwise related to the corporation's business. (*Example*: The corporation's alleged force feeding of geese to produce pate de fois gras may not be excluded, even though it accounts for less than 5% of earnings, assets and sales.)

c. **Routine matters:** A proposal may be excluded if it relates to the ***"conduct of the ordinary business operations"*** of the company. (*Example:* A proposal that the company charge 10% less for one of its many products would relate to ordinary business operations, and thus be excludible.) [117]

   i. **Compensation issues:** Proposals concerning ***senior executive compensation*** are ***not*** matters relating to the "ordinary business operations" of the company, and may therefore not be excluded. (*Example:* A proposal suggesting that the board cancel any "golden parachute" contracts it has given to senior executives — i.e., contracts that give the executive a large payment if the company is taken over — must be included in the proxy materials.)

d. **Election of directors:** A proposal may be excluded if it's about a particular ***election*** to the company's ***board of directors***. More specifically, the proposal may be excluded if it "(iv) Seeks to ***include a specific individual in the company's proxy materials for election*** to the board of directors; or (v) Otherwise could affect the ***outcome of the upcoming election of directors.***" Rule 14a-8(i)(8). In other words, a holder who wants to propose his own slate of directors, or to oppose management's slate, must pay for the dissemination of his own materials, and may not require the corporation to disseminate for him. [117]

   i. **Proposal to change election rules:** What if a shareholder wants to use the free include-shareholders'-materials mechanism not to try to get a *particular* slate of directors elected or defeated, but instead to ***change the company's bylaws*** so as to ***change the procedures*** for how board elections *generally* work? As the result of a 2011 change, the shareholder ***may*** use the free mechanism for this change-the-procedures purpose. [118]

      Example: Holder is a minority (and dissident) shareholder in Corp, a public company. Holder submits a proposal to Corp. that would (1) let any shareholder own-

C A P S U L E S U M M A R Y

ing more than 1% of the company's shares propose a slate of up to 4 directors as nominees to Corp's Board of Directors; and (2) require such a proposed slate to be included in management's proxy materials at no cost to the proposing shareholder.

Under present (post-2011) Rule 14a-8(i)(8), nothing makes this proposed change to the bylaws excludable by Corp. Therefore, Corp will ***have to include the proposal*** in its next set of proxy materials. Then, if a majority of the shareholders votes in favor of the proposal, Corp's bylaws will be amended so that the default "no shareholder nominations may be included in management's proxy materials" rule of 14a-8(i)(8) is reversed as to Corp. [119]

V. PROXY CONTESTS

A. Definition: A "proxy contest" is a competition between management and a group of outside ***"insurgents"*** to obtain shareholder votes on a proposal. Most proxy contests involve the election of directors, but there can be proxy contests over some non-election proposal as well. (*Example*: A proxy contest over whether the corporation should adopt a proposed "poison pill" takeover defense.) [120]

B. Regulation: Proxy contests are tightly regulated by the SEC. [121]

1. **List access:** The SEC rules do not give the insurgent group access to the shareholder's list. (However, they may have this under state law, as described above.) But as noted, the SEC rules do allow the insurgents to force management to choose between mailing the insurgents' materials or giving the insurgents the list so that the insurgents can do this themselves. (Management will usually mail instead of giving up the list.) [121]

2. **Disclosure required:** Both sides must comply with all disclosure regulations. Thus they must make sure that any "solicitation" (including oral solicitation) is preceded by a written proxy statement, and in the case of an election they must file special information about any "participant" in the solicitation. [122]

C. Costs:

1. **Management's expenses:** The corporation may usually pay for any reasonable expense incurred by management in waging its side of the proxy contest. [122]

2. **Insurgents:** If the insurgents are successful at getting control, they will usually be allowed to have the corporation reimburse them for their expenses (provided that the shareholders approve). If the insurgents are unsuccessful at getting control, they must bear their own expenses. [123]

VI. IMPROVED PUBLIC DISCLOSURE BY THE CORPORATION

A. Improvements to disclosure: As the result of turn-of-the-century corporate scandals, the federal government has made two major attempts to improve the disclosure obligations of public companies: ***Regulation FD*** and the ***Sarbanes-Oxley Act***.

B. Regulation FD: Regulation FD, enacted by the SEC, stops a company from making ***"selective disclosure."*** Selective disclosure occurs when the company gives certain professional investors (e.g., security analysts for big Wall Street firms) information that the public isn't given til later. Now, under FD: [124]

- ❑ If a public company ***intends*** to release material nonpublic information to certain professional investors (e.g., analysts), the company must ***disclose*** the information ***simultaneously to the public***.

- ❑ And, if the public company realizes that it has ***unintentionally*** disclosed material nonpublic information to such a professional investor, it must cure the problem by then ***"promptly"*** disclosing that information to the public.

C. Sarbanes-Oxley Act: The ***Sarbanes-Oxley Act,*** passed by Congress in 2002, increases the responsibilities of people in charge of running the finances of public companies. Here are some of the major responsibilities that Sarbanes-Oxley imposes: [125-126]

1. **CEO/CFO certification:** Most importantly, the company's ***CEO*** and ***CFO*** must each ***certify the accuracy*** of each quarterly and annual filing with the SEC.

2. **Rules about Audit Committee:** Each member of a company's ***Audit Committee*** must be ***"independent"*** of the company (e.g., not an employee, consultant, etc.)

3. **Auditor independence:** The company's ***outside auditors*** (the CPAs that perform the annual audit) must also be much more ***independent*** than previously. The auditors may no longer do other — potentially more lucrative — tasks for the company, such as bookkeeping, designing the computer system that does financial record-keeping for the company, etc.

CAPSULE SUMMARY

CHAPTER 5

CLOSE CORPORATIONS

I. INTRODUCTION

A. What is close corporation: A "close corporation" is one with the following traits: (1) a ***small number*** of stockholders; (2) the lack of any ***ready market*** for the corporation's stock; and (3) substantial participation by the ***majority stockholder(s)*** in the management, direction and operations of the corporation. [134]

B. Significance of close corporation status: Close corporations present special problems relating to control. The various devices examined here are mainly ways of insuring that a minority stockholder will not be taken advantage of by the majority holder(s). [134]

II. SHAREHOLDER VOTING AGREEMENTS, VOTING TRUSTS AND CLASSIFIED STOCK

A. Voting agreements: A ***"shareholder voting agreement"*** is an agreement in which two or more shareholders agree to ***vote together*** as a unit on certain or all matters. Some voting agreements expressly provide how votes will be cast. Other agreements merely commit the parties to vote together (without specifying how the vote is to go, so that the parties must reach future agreement). [137]

1. **Generally valid:** Shareholder agreements are generally ***valid*** today. [137]

2. **Enforcement:** There are two ways that a voting agreement may be ***enforced:*** [138]

a. **Proxy:** First, the agreement may require each signatory to give to a third person an ***irrevocable proxy*** to vote the signer's shares in accordance with the agreement. Usually this irrevocable proxy arrangement will be enforced today.

b. **Specific performance:** Second, most courts today will grant ***specific performance*** of the terms of the voting agreement. See, e.g., MBCA § 7.31(b).

B. **Voting trust:** In a ***voting trust***, the shareholders who are part of the arrangement ***convey legal title*** to their shares to one or more ***voting trustees***, under the terms of a voting trust agreement. The shareholders become "beneficial owners" — they receive a "voting trust certificate" representing their beneficial interest, and get dividends and sale proceeds. But they no longer have voting power. [139]

1. **Validity; requirements:** Most states enforce voting trusts, if they conform with statutory requirements. Usually, these requirements include the following: [140]

a. **Maximum term:** There is almost always a ***maximum term*** for the voting trust (usually ten years).

b. **Disclosure:** Usually the trust's terms must be ***publicly disclosed*** (at least to the shareholders who are not part of the agreement).

c. **Writing:** The trust must generally be ***in writing***, and must be implemented by a ***formal transfer*** of the shares on the transfer records of the corporation.

2. **Strict compliance:** These requirements must be ***strictly adhered to***. If not, the court is likely to hold the entire agreement unenforceable. [140]

C. **Classified stock and weighted voting:** Shareholders may reallocate their voting power (and give minority holders a bigger voice) by using ***classified stock***. The corporation sets up two or more classes of stock, and gives each class different voting rights or financial rights. [141]

1. **General valid:** The use of different classes and weighting of voting is generally valid.

CAPSULE SUMMARY

III. AGREEMENTS RESTRICTING THE BOARD'S DISCRETION

A. **Problem generally:** If the shareholders agree to restrict their discretion ***as directors***, there is a risk that the agreement will violate the principle that the business shall be managed by the board of directors. If a court finds that the board's discretion has been unduly fettered, it may refuse to enforce the agreement. [141]

B. **Present law:** However, this danger is not very great today. Most courts will probably uphold even a shareholder agreement that substantially curtails the board's discretion, so long as the agreement: (1) does not ***injure*** any ***minority*** shareholder; (2) does not injure ***creditors*** or the public; and (3) does not violate any express statutory provision. [142]

IV. SUPER-MAJORITY VOTING AND QUORUM REQUIREMENTS

A. **Modern view:** Most statutes allow the shareholders to agree that a ***"super-majority"*** will be required for a vote or a quorum. In general, such super-majority quorum and voting requirements are upheld, even if they require unanimity. (*Example*: Under the MBCA, the articles of incorporation may be amended to require some percentage greater than 50%, even unanimity, both for a quorum for a shareholders' meeting and for shareholder approval of proposed corporate action.

Also, either the articles or the bylaws may impose a super-majority quorum or voting requirement for directors' meetings and directors' action.) [145]

1. **Changing a requirement:** If the charter is drafted to impose a super-majority voting or quorum requirement, some statutes allow the super-majority provision to be ***removed*** or ***changed*** only by the same super-majority percentage. (*Example*: Once the charter is amended to require two-thirds shareholder vote for any merger proposal, a two-thirds shareholder would be required to remove the super-majority provision.) In other states, the shareholders must expressly agree to this kind of "anti-amendment" scheme. [145]

V. SHARE TRANSFER RESTRICTIONS

A. **Why used:** The shareholders of a close corporation will often agree to ***limit the transferability*** of shares in the corporation. This lets shareholders veto the admission of new "colleagues" and helps preserve the existing balance of control. [146]

B. **Enforcement:** Today, share transfer restrictions will generally be ***enforced***, so long as they are ***reasonable***. [146]

   1. **How imposed:** Share restrictions may be imposed either by a formal agreement among the shareholders or, in some instances, by an amendment to the articles of incorporation or the bylaws. [147]

C. **Various techniques:** Here are the five principal techniques for restricting share transfers: [111]

   1. **First refusal:** Under a ***right of first refusal***, a shareholder may not sell his shares to an outsider without first offering the corporation or the other shareholders (or both) a right to buy those shares at the same price and terms as those at which the outsider is proposing to buy. (Usually the corporation gets the first chance, and if it refuses, the other shareholders get the right to buy proportionally to their holdings.) [147]

   2. **First option:** The ***"first option"*** is similar to the right of first refusal, except that the price is determined by the agreement creating the option. [147]

   3. **Consent:** Stock transfers may be made subject to the ***consent*** of the board of directors or the other shareholders. [147]

   4. **Stock buy-back:** A ***buy-back right*** is given to the corporation to enable it to buy back a holder's shares on the happening of certain events, whether the holder wants to sell or not. (*Example*: The corporation might be given the right to buy back shares of a holder/employee upon that person's retirement or termination of employment.) The corporation is ***not obligated*** to exercise a buy-back right. [147]

   5. **Buy-sell agreement:** A buy-sell agreement is similar to a buy-back right, except that the corporation is ***obligated*** to go through with the purchase upon the happening of the specified event. (*Example*: The corporation agrees in advance that it will repurchase the shares at a fixed price upon the death of a shareholder/employee.) [148]

D. **Notice and consent:** Not everybody is necessarily bound by a share transfer restriction: [148]

   1. **Signor:** Obviously if the shareholder signs an agreement, he will be bound.

   2. **Subsequent purchaser without notice:** A person who purchases shares ***without actual knowledge*** of pre-existing restrictions will generally ***not be bound*** by the restrictions. However, if the restriction is ***conspicuously noted*** on the share certificates, he will be bound.

3. **Non-consenting minority holder:** Courts are split as to whether a person who is ***already a shareholder*** at the time the restrictions are imposed (and who does not consent) is bound. MBCA § 6.27(a) provides that a person who is already a holder at the time restrictions are imposed (e.g., by an amendment to the articles of incorporation or bylaws) will ***not be bound*** if he does not sign any agreement to that effect, and does not vote in favor of the restriction.

E. **Valuation:** Most transfer restrictions require some ***valuation*** to be placed on the stock at some point. There are four common techniques: [149]

1. **Book value:** The value may be based upon the ***"book value."*** This is basically the corporation's assets minus its liabilities. (Sometimes adjustments will be made to the corporation's historical balance-sheet figures to arrive at the book value used for valuation.) [149]

2. **"Capitalized earnings" method:** If the ***"capitalized earnings"*** method is used, the parties use a formula that attempts to estimate the future earnings of the business, and they then discount these earnings to present value. [150]

3. **"Mutual agreement" method:** If the ***"mutual agreement"*** method is used, the parties agree upon an initial fixed valuation and also agree that from time to time they will mutually agree upon an adjusted number to reflect changes in market value. [151]

4. **Appraisal:** Last, if the ***"appraisal"*** method is used, the parties agree in advance on a procedure by which a neutral third-party appraiser will be selected; the appraiser then determines the value. [151]

F. **Funding of buy-sell:** There are two main ways to ***fund*** a buy-sell agreement: [151]

1. **Life insurance:** ***Life insurance*** can be purchased on each shareholder, in an amount sufficient to cover the estimated purchase price for that holder's shares. [151]

2. **Installment payments:** Alternatively, the parties can agree that the shares will be purchased by the ***installment method***. Usually, there will be a down payment, followed by quarterly or annual payments, usually paid out of the earnings of the business. (Often, life insurance is used to fund the down payment.) [151]

G. **Requirement of "reasonableness":** Transfer restrictions will only be upheld if they are ***"reasonable."*** [152]

1. **Outright prohibition and consent requirements:** Courts are especially likely to strike down an ***outright prohibition*** on the transfer of shares to third parties. Similarly, a provision that shares may not be sold to outsiders without the ***consent*** of the other shareholders is likely to be found unreasonable, if the others are permitted to withhold their consent ***arbitrarily***. [152]

2. **Options, first refusals and buy-sell agreements:** The other types of restrictions — first option, right of first refusal, buy-backs and buy-sell agreements — are more likely to be found "reasonable." In general, if the mechanism chosen by the parties is reasonable ***at the time the method was agreed upon***, it will probably be found reasonable (and upheld) even though it turns out to produce a price that is much higher or lower than the market price at the time of sale. [152]

VI. RESOLUTION OF DISPUTES, INCLUDING DISSOLUTION

A. **Dissension and deadlock:** The courts often have to deal with "dissension" and "deadlock" among the stockholders. "Dissension" refers to squabbles or disagreements among them. "Deadlock" refers to a situation where the corporation is paralyzed and prevented from acting (e.g., two factions each control the same number of directors, and the two factions cannot agree). [152]

B. Dissolution: The major judicial remedy for dissension and deadlock is a court order that the corporation be ***involuntarily dissolved***. Dissolution means that the corporation ceases to exist as a legal entity; the assets are sold off, the debts are paid, and any surplus is distributed to the shareholders. [154]

1. **No general right:** ***No state gives a shareholder an automatic right to a judicially-ordered dissolution.*** Instead, each state has a statute setting forth ***specific grounds*** (strictly construed) on which dissolution may be granted. [154]

2. **MBCA:** Thus under MBCA § 14.30(2), a shareholder must show one of these four things to get dissolution: (1) that the ***directors*** are ***deadlocked***; (2) that those in control have acted in a manner that is "***illegal***, ***oppressive***, or ***fraudulent***"; (3) that the ***shareholders*** are ***deadlocked*** and have failed to elect new directors for at least two consecutive annual meetings; or (4) that the corporation's assets are being "***misapplied*** or ***wasted***." [154]

3. **Judge's discretion:** Most states hold that even if the statutory criteria are met, the judge still has ***discretion*** to refuse to award dissolution (e.g., when it would be unfair to one or more shareholders). [155]

4. **Remedy for oppression:** Most states allow dissolution to be granted as a remedy for ***"oppression"*** of a minority stockholder. (*Examples*: (1) Majority holder sells property to the corporation at inflated prices. (2) Majority holder tries to squeeze P out by refusing to pay him either a salary or dividends.) [155]

5. **Buy-out in lieu of dissolution:** Under many statutes, the party opposing dissolution has the right to ***buy-out*** the shares of the party seeking dissolution at a judicially-supervised fair price. [157]

6. **Dissolution of an LLC:** Most states allow for judicial dissolution of ***LLCs***, just as for corporations.

   a. **Delaware:** For instance, the Delaware LLC Act says that on application by any member of the LLC, the court may "decree dissolution of [the LLC] whenever it is ***not reasonably practicable*** to ***carry on the business*** in conformity with [the LLC agreement]." §18-802. [157]

      i. **Factors to be considered in Delaware:** The Delaware statute does not specify what factors the court should consider in determining whether it is "reasonably practicable" to carry on the business in accordance with the operating agreement. But the cases show that there are ***three circumstances*** that, when present, are likely to persuade the Delaware courts to approve dissolution:

         [1] "[T]he members' vote is ***deadlocked at the Board level***";

         [2] "[T]he ***operating agreement*** gives ***no means of navigating*** around the deadlock"; and

         [3] "[D]ue to the ***financial condition of the company***, there is effectively ***no business to operate.***"

      [*Fisk Ventures, LLC v. Segal*] The three factors ***need not all be present*** for the court to approve dissolution. [*Fisk*] [159]

Example: Recall the facts of *Fisk Ventures*, *supra*, p. C-3: Inventor, an individual, and Investor, a venture capital company, form an LLC funded mainly by Investor. The operating agreement says that all important decisions require the consent of both members. The LCC runs out of cash, and can't operate. Investor refuses to consent to the raising of more funds by other investors, and instead sues for dissolution based on the statutory ground of deadlock.

Held, for Investor; dissolution granted. The "consent of both" clause creates a board-level deadlock as to the raising of additional capital, and the operating agreement gives no means of navigating around the deadlock. Since the company can't operate without new capital, there is effectively no business to operate. The fact that new capital might be raised if Investor would surrender its veto right over capital-raising decisions is irrelevant: Investor expressly negotiated all of the rights it held under the operating agreement, and was therefore within its rights to exercise its negotiated leverage even if the effect was to benefit solely itself. The court will not "redraft the [operating agreement]." [*Fisk Ventures, LLC v. Segal*] [159]

C. Alternatives to dissolution: There are a number of alternatives to dissolution, including: (1) arbitration; (2) court appointment of a provisional director (to break a deadlock); (3) court appointment of a custodian (who will run the business); (4) appointment of a receiver (who will liquidate the business); and (5) a judicially-supervised buy-out in lieu of dissolution. [160]

1. **Fiduciary obligation of majority to minority:** A few states (especially Massachusetts) have formulated a theory of ***fiduciary obligation***, under which a majority stockholder in a close corporation has a fiduciary obligation to ***behave in good faith to a minority shareholder***. [161]

   Example: P is a minority stockholder who has inherited her shares from her husband, an employee of Corporation. Corporation has previously bought back shares from its majority stockholder at a high price, but refuses to buy P's shares back at anything like the same price. *Held*, the controlling stockholder owed P a fiduciary duty, and was therefore required to cause Corporation to repurchase shares from P in the same portion, and at the same price, as it had purchased from the majority holder. [*Donahue v. Rodd Electrotype*]

   a. **Where applied:** The few courts that have recognized this "fiduciary obligation of majority to minority" tend to find it violated only where the majority holder causes the corporation to take action that has ***no legitimate business purpose***. (*Example*: Majority holders fire P, end his salary, drop him from the board, and refuse to pay dividends; *held*, these actions had no legitimate business purpose, and were used merely to deprive P of a reasonable return on his investment, so the majority holders violated their fiduciary obligations. *Wilkes v. Springside Nursing Home, Inc.*)

2. **Award of damages:** If the court does find that the majority has violated a fiduciary obligation to the minority, it can award ***damages***. [161]

CHAPTER 6

THE DUTY OF CARE AND THE BUSINESS JUDGMENT RULE

I. INTRODUCTION

A. Duty generally: The law imposes on a director or officer a ***duty of care*** with respect to the corporation's business. The director or officer must behave with that level of care which a ***reasonable person*** in ***similar circumstances*** would use. [169]

1. **Damages vs. injunction:** If a director or officer violates this duty of care, and the corporation consequently loses money, the director/officer will be ***personally liable*** to pay ***money damages*** to the corporation. Separately, if the board of directors has approved a transaction without using due care (and the transaction has not yet been consummated), the court may grant an ***injunction*** against the transaction. [170]

2. **Rare:** It is ***very rare*** for directors and officers to be found liable for breach of the duty of due care. (When this happens, it's usually because there is some taint of ***self-dealing***, but not enough to cause the court to find a formal violation of the duty of loyalty.) [170]

3. **Directors and officers:** The same duty of care is imposed on both ***officers*** and ***directors***. However, what is "reasonable" conduct will often be different for an officer than for an outside director (since the officer normally has a better understanding of the corporation's affairs). [171]

II. THE STANDARD OF CARE

A. Basic standard: The basic standard is that the director or officer must behave as a reasonably prudent person would behave in similar circumstances. [171]

1. **No "accommodation" directors:** There is no such thing as an "accommodation" or "dummy" director. If a person sits on a board, he automatically (and non-waivably) bears the burden of acting with due care. [171]

2. **Egregious cases:** However, liability for breach of the duty of due care is generally imposed only when the director or officer behaves ***"recklessly"*** or with ***"gross negligence."*** (*Example*: D, a director, fails to attend board meetings, fails to read financial reports, fails to obtain the advice of a lawyer or accountant even though he is on notice that the corporation is being mismanaged — taken together, these acts amount to recklessness, and thus justify holding D liable for losses suffered by the corporation that could have been prevented by a director who exercised reasonable care. [*Francis v. United Jersey Bank*]) [171]

B. Objective standard: The standard of care is an ***objective*** one: the director is held to the conduct that would be exercised by a "reasonable person" in the director's position. So a director who is less smart, or less knowledgeable about business than an "ordinary" reasonable director nonetheless must meet this higher objective standard. [173]

1. **Special skills:** On the other hand, if the director has ***special skills*** that go beyond what an ordinary director would have, he must ***use*** those skills. Thus a trained accountant, lawyer, banker, real estate professional, etc., if he learns of facts that would make a person in that pro-

fession suspicious, must follow through and investigate even though these facts would not make a non-professional suspicious. [173]

C. Reliance on experts and committees: Directors are generally ***entitled to rely*** on ***experts***, on reports prepared by insiders, and on action taken by a ***committee*** of the board. But all such reliance is allowed only if it is "reasonable" under the circumstances. (*Example*: A director may rely on the financial statements prepared by the corporation's accountants; therefore, unless the director is on notice that the accountants are failing to uncover wrongdoing, the director will not be liable for, say, embezzlement that is not reflected in the financial statements.) [173]

D. Passive negligence: A director will not be liable merely for failing to ***detect wrongdoing*** by officers or employees.

1. **Director on notice:** However, if the director is on ***notice*** of facts suggesting wrongdoing, he cannot close his eyes to these facts.

2. **Monitoring mechanisms:** Also, in large corporations, it may constitute a violation of due care for the directors not to put into place ***monitoring mechanisms*** (e.g., stringent internal accounting controls, and/or an audit committee) to detect wrongdoing. [175]

3. **Delaware law:** In Delaware, most corporations have exercised their statutory right to include a charter provision that directors ***will not be personally liable for lack of due care***. But such an ***"exculpatory" provision*** can't block liability for breach of the duty of loyalty, or for lack of "good faith." [178] So in Delaware, if the corporation has such an exculpatory clause, ***directors will have liability for poor oversight only if:***

   [1] the directors "utterly ***failed to implement any reporting or information system*** or controls"; *or*

   [2] having implemented such a system or controls, the directors "***consciously failed to monitor or oversee [the system's] operations,*** thus disabling themselves from being informed of risks or problems requiring their attention."

   [*Stone v. Ritter*] [177]

   a. **Knowledge of shortcoming required:** To put it another way, directors who are protected by an exculpatory provision are still liable for lack of "good faith," but failure to supervise won't constitute lack of good faith unless the plaintiff shows that the directors ***"knew that they were not discharging their fiduciary obligations.***" [*Stone*, *supra*.] [177]

      i. **Gross negligence not enough:** So what might be called ***"oblivious gross negligence" won't be enough*** for director-liability in Delaware where there's an exculpatory clause in the certificate of incorporation.

   b. **The "offer to buy the company" scenario:** Where directors protected by an exculpatory clause are accused of bad faith for allegedly ***mishandling an offer to acquire the company,*** the "gross negligence is not enough" principle is manifested in a special test. Only if the directors are shown to have "***utterly failed to attempt to obtain the best sale price"*** will they be liable for bad faith in the takeover context. [*Lyondell Chemical Co. v. Ryan*] [180]

   Example: The directors of Target receive a $48/share buyout offer from Bidder at a substantial premium to the existing share price. Bidder says that this is his final offer, and must be accepted within one week or it will be off the table. During that week, the directors meet several time to consider the offer, solicit and follow the advice of their financial and legal advisors (which is to take the offer), briefly and unsuccessfully attempt to negotiate a higher offer, and approve the agreement. After the board accepts the offer and shareholders approve it, some investors bring a class action, alleging that the board showed bad faith in not doing more to get a higher price.

Held, summary judgment granted against the Ps. In the acquisition context, the directors will be liable for breach of the duty of loyalty only if they are shown to have "***utterly failed to attempt*** to obtain the best sale price." Here, the multiple board meetings, the soliciting and following of the advisors' advice to take the deal, and the brief attempt to get a higher price were more than enough to show that the directors did not fail to even attempt to obtain the best price. *Lyondell Chemical Co. v. Ryan*, *supra*. [180]

E. Causation: In many states, even if a director or officer has violated the duty of due care he is only liable for damages that are the ***proximate result*** of his conduct. (For instance, if the loss would have happened anyway, even had the directors all behaved with due care, there will be no liability in these courts.) However, other states, including Delaware, allow plaintiff to recover without a showing of causation against a director who violated his duty of care. [182]

1. **Joint and several:** If a board member violates his duty of due care, at least some courts hold him ***jointly and severally liable*** with all other directors who have violated that duty, so long as the board ***collectively*** was a proximate cause of the loss. (In other words, a director cannot say, "Even if I had been diligent, the other directors would still have ignored me and the loss would have happened anyway.") [182]

CAPSULE SUMMARY

III. THE BUSINESS JUDGMENT RULE

A. Function of rule: The "business judgment rule" saves many actions from being held to be violations of the duty of due care. [182]

1. **Relation to duty of due care:** Here is how the duty of due care and the business judgment rule fit together: (1) the duty of due care imposes a fairly stern set of ***procedural*** requirements for directors' actions; (2) once these procedural requirements are satisfied, the business judgment rule then supplies a much easier-to-satisfy standard with respect to the ***substance*** of the business decision. [183]

B. Requirements: The business judgment rule basically provides that a ***substantively-unwise decision*** by a director or officer will ***not by itself constitute a lack of due care***. However, there are three requirements (two of them procedural) which a decision by a director or officer must meet before it will be upheld by application of the business judgment rule: [184]

1. **No self-dealing:** First, the director or officer will not qualify for the protection of the business judgment rule if he has an ***"interest"*** in the transaction. In other words, any ***self-dealing*** by the director or officer will deprive him of the rule's protection. (*Example*: X, an officer of Corp, has Corp buy supplies at inflated prices from another company of which X is secretly a major shareholder. X's decision to have Corp buy the supplies in this manner will not be protected by the business judgment rule, because the transaction in question amounted to self-dealing by X.) [184]

2. **Informed decision:** Second, the decision must have been an ***"informed"*** one. That is, the director or officer must have gathered at least a ***reasonable amount of information*** about the decision before he makes it. [185]

a. **Gross negligence standard:** Probably the ***"gross negligence"*** standard applies to the issue of whether the decision was an informed one. In other words, even if the director or officer is somewhat (but not grossly) negligent in failing to gather all reasonably available information, he will not lose the benefit of the rule. But if he was grossly negligent, he will lose the protection.

Example: The Ds, directors of a publicly held corporation, approve a sale of the company without making any real attempt to learn the "intrinsic value" of the company, without having any written documentation about the proposed deal, without learning that no true bargaining took place with the buyer, and while spending only two hours on the decision even though there was no real emergency or time pressure. *Held*, the process used by the directors was so sloppy that their decision was not an "informed" one, so they do not have the protection of the business judgment rule and are in fact liable for the breach of the duty of due care. [*Smith v. Van Gorkom*]

3. **"Rational" belief:** Finally, the director or officer must have ***"rationally believed"*** that his business judgment was in the corporation's best interest. Note that this belief does not have to be substantively "reasonable," but it must be at least "rational" (i.e., not totally crazy). Note also that what must be rational is not the underlying *decision*, merely the *belief* that the decision is in the corporation's best interests. [188]

a. **No review of substance of underlying decision:** Because of this emphasis on the rationality of the "belief," not the rationality of the underlying decision, the court will generally focus on the directors' decision-making ***process***, and will rarely consider the ***merits of the underlying decision.*** [188] Or, as the idea is often put, the court will not use ***"20/20 hindsight"*** when it evaluates the board's decision — only if a transaction is "egregious on its face" will the court review the substance of the underlying decision. [188]

C. **Exceptions:** Even where these three requirements for the business judgment rule are satisfied, there are one or two situations where the court may find the rule inapplicable: [189]

1. **Illegal:** If the act taken or approved by the director or officer is a ***violation of a criminal statute***, the defendant will lose the benefit of the business judgment rule. (*Example*: The Ds, directors of a major corporation, approve the corporation's making of illegal political contributions. *Held*, the directors will not be protected by the business judgment rule, because the transaction in question violated a criminal statute. [*Miller v. American Telephone & Tele. Co.*]) [189]

2. **Pursuit of "social" goals:** Some courts may hold the business judgment rule inapplicable if the director is pursuing his own ***social*** or ***political*** goals (unrelated to the corporation's welfare). But other courts do not agree. [189]

IV. RECENT STATUTORY CHANGES TO DIRECTOR LIABILITY

A. **Some approaches:** Some states have tried to restrict the liability of directors for breaches of the duty of due care. Here are some approaches: [190]

1. **Amendment:** Some states allow the shareholders to ***amend the articles of incorporation*** to eliminate or reduce directors' personal liability for violations of the duty of due care (e.g., Delaware § 102(b)(7)); [190]

2. **Looser standard:** Some states have made the standard of care ***looser***, so that only more outrageous conduct will be covered; [190]

3. **Limit on money damages:** Some states limit the ***money damages*** that may be recovered against the officer or director; and [190]

4. **Indemnification:** Most states now allow the corporation to ***indemnify*** directors and officers for liability for breach of the duty of due care. [191]

CHAPTER 7

THE DUTY OF LOYALTY

I. SELF-DEALING TRANSACTIONS

A. **Definition:** A ***"self-dealing transaction"*** is one in which three conditions are met: (1) a Key Player (officer, director or controlling shareholder) and the corporation are on ***opposite sides*** of a transaction; (2) the Key Player has helped ***influence*** the corporation's decision to enter the transaction; and (3) the Key Player's personal financial interests are at least potentially ***in conflict*** with the financial interests of the corporation. (*Example*: A director/shareholder of Corp induces Corp to buy Blackacre from him at an inflated price.) [198]

B. **Modern rule on self-dealing transactions:** Courts will frequently intervene to strike down (or award damages for) a self-dealing transaction. [200]

1. **General statement:** In most states, the approach to self-dealing transactions is as follows: [200]

   a. **Fair:** If the transaction is found to be ***fair*** to the corporation, the court will ***uphold*** it. This is true regardless of whether the transaction was ever approved by disinterested directors or ratified by the shareholders.

   b. **Waste/fraud:** If the transaction is so unfair that it amounts to ***"waste"*** or ***"fraud"*** against the corporation, the court will usually void it at the request of a stockholder. This is true even though the transaction was approved by a majority of disinterested directors or ratified by the shareholders.

      i. **Standard for "waste":** The typical definition of "waste" is a very ***restricted*** one. Thus in Delaware, a transaction will not be invalidated as constituting waste unless it is "an exchange that is ***so one sided that no business person of ordinary, sound judgment could conclude that the corporation has received adequate consideration."*** Cf. *Brehm v. Eisner*. For instance, in the case of executive compensation, "If ... there is ***any substantial consideration received*** by the corporation, and if there is a ***good faith judgment*** [by the board] that in the circumstances the ***transaction is worth while***, there should be no finding of waste, even if the fact finder would conclude ex post that the transaction was ***unreasonably risky***." *Brehm, supra.*

   c. **Middle ground:** If the transaction does not fall into either of the two above categories — it's not clearly fair, but it's not so unfair as to amount to waste or fraud — the presence or absence of ***director approval*** and/or ***shareholder ratification*** will make the difference. If a majority of disinterested and knowledgeable directors have approved the transaction (or if the transaction has been ratified by the shareholders) the court will probably approve the transaction. If neither disinterested-director approval nor shareholder ratification has occurred, the court will probably invalidate the transaction.

2. **Three paths:** Thus there are three different ways that a proponent of a self-dealing transaction can probably avoid invalidation:

[1] by showing approval by ***a majority of disinterested directors***, after full disclosure;

[2] by showing ***ratification by shareholders***, after full disclosure; and

[3] by showing that the transaction was ***fair when made***.

We consider each of these "branches" below. [204]

C. **Disclosure plus board approval:** A transaction may not be avoided by the corporation if it was ***authorized*** by a ***majority of the disinterested directors***, after ***full disclosure*** of the nature of the conflict and the transaction. [205]

1. **What must be disclosed:** Two kinds of information must be disclosed to the board before it approves the transaction: (1) the material facts about the ***conflict***; and (2) the material facts about the ***transaction***. (*Example*: If D, a director of XYZ Corp, wants to sell XYZ an office building he owns, he must disclose not only the fact that he owns the office building, but also any material facts about the deal, such as whether the price is a fair one in light of current market conditions.) [205]

a. **When disclosure must be made:** Courts are split about *when* this disclosure must be made. Some courts require it to be made ***before*** the transaction. Others allow it to be ***"ratified"*** after the fact (e.g., by a resolution in which the board says that it has no objection to the transaction).

2. **Who is "disinterested" director:** The approval must be by a majority of the ***"disinterested"*** directors. A director will be "interested" if either: (1) he or an ***immediate member of his family*** has a financial interest in the transaction; or (2) he or a family member has a ***relationship*** with the other party to the transaction that would reasonably be expected to ***affect his judgment*** about the transaction. (*Example*: Prexy is president, director and controlling shareholder of XYZ. He wants to sell Blackacre, which he owns, to XYZ. Sidekick, who is an employee and director of XYZ, knows that he owes his job to Prexy. Sidekick will probably not be a "disinterested" director because his relationship with Prexy would be expected to affect his judgment about the transaction; therefore, Sidekick's vote to approve the transaction will not be counted.) [206]

3. **Quorum:** A ***quorum*** for the vote by the disinterested directors merely has to consist of a majority of the disinterested directors, not a majority of the total directors. (Thus if there is a nine-member board, but only three disinterested directors, two of them will constitute a quorum, and both will have to vote in favor of the transaction to authorize it.) [206]

4. **Immunization of unfairness:** The fact that a majority of the disinterested directors (acting after full disclosure) have approved or ratified the transaction does not necessarily immunize it from attack, if the unfairness is ***very great***. But the existence of such approval/ratification ***shifts the burden of proof*** to the person attacking the transaction, and the transaction will only be struck down if the unfairness is so great as to constitute ***fraud*** or ***waste***. [207]

D. **Disclosure plus shareholder ratification:** A self-dealing transaction will be validated if it is fully disclosed to the ***shareholders***, and then ***ratified*** by a ***majority*** of them. [208]

1. **Disinterested shareholders:** The courts are ***split*** about whether the ratification must be by a majority of ***disinterested*** shareholders, or merely by a majority of *all* shareholders (including, perhaps, the one who is doing the self-dealing). [208]

   a. **MBCA:** Under MBCA § 8.63, a majority of the ***disinterested*** shareholders must approve the transaction.

E. **Fairness as key criterion:** Finally, a self-dealing transaction can be validated by a showing that it is, under all the circumstances, ***fair*** to the corporation. Such "overall fairness" will suffice even if the transaction was neither approved by the disinterested directors nor ratified by the shareholders. Fairness is generally determined by the facts as they were known ***at the time of the transaction***. [208]

   1. **No prior disclosure:** In most courts, a fair transaction will be upheld ***even though it was never disclosed by the Key Player to his fellow executives, directors or shareholders.*** [208]

F. **Indirect conflicts:** A self-dealing transaction will be found not only where the Key Player is directly a party to the transaction, but also where he is ***indirectly*** a party, i.e., he owns an equity position in the other party to the transaction. The test is whether the Key Player's equity participation in the other party is big enough to expect his ***judgment*** to be ***affected***. See MBCA § 8.60(1)(i), (ii). (*Example*: Prexy, in addition to being president, director and controlling shareholder of XYZ Corp, owns 20% of ABC Corp. A major transaction between ABC and XYZ will probably be a self-dealing transaction if Prexy influences the XYZ side of it, because Prexy's own 20% stake in ABC is probably large enough to affect his judgment about whether the transaction is good for XYZ.) [209]

   1. **Interlocking directors:** If the Key Player is merely a ***director*** (not a shareholder) of the other party to the transaction, this will usually ***not*** make the transaction a self-dealing one unless the transaction is a non-ordinary-course one requiring board approval. See MBCA § 8.60(1)(ii). [210]

G. **Remedies for violation:** If there has been a violation of the rule against self-dealing, there are two possible remedies:

   1. **Rescission:** Normally, the court will ***rescind*** the transaction, where this is possible. (*Example*: Prexy sells Blackacre to XYZ Corp, of which he is president and director. If the transaction is unfair, and was not ratified by directors or shareholders, the court will rescind it, giving title back to Prexy and the purchase price back to XYZ.) [210]

   2. **Damages:** If because of passage of time or complexity of the transaction it cannot be rescinded, the court will award ***restitutionary damages***. That is, the Key Player will have to ***pay back*** to the corporation any benefit he received beyond what was fair. [210]

CAPSULE SUMMARY

II. EXECUTIVE COMPENSATION

A. **Business judgment rule:** If an officer or director influences a corporation's decision about his own compensation, this is technically a self-dealing transaction. However, courts are reluctant to strike down decisions about executive compensation. Such decisions receive the protection of the business judgment rule: the director's decision will be sustained so long as it is rational, informed, and made in good faith. [216]

B. **Consideration:** In the case of ***deferred*** compensation plans, courts sometimes insist that the plan be set up in such a way that an executive will receive the deferred compensation only if he

remains with the company. Thus a grant of stock options to all executives (regardless of whether they stay with the company) might be struck down as lacking in ***consideration***. [216]

C. Excessive compensation: Even if a compensation scheme has been approved by a majority of the disinterested directors, or ratified by the shareholders, the court may still overturn it if the level of compensation is ***"excessive"*** or ***"unreasonable."*** That is, the compensation levels must be reasonably related to the ***value*** of the services performed by the executive. [216]

1. **Few cases:** But courts very rarely strike down a compensation plan as excessive. One exception may be where a plan makes use of a ***formula*** which is not amended even though conditions change. (*Example*: If XYZ enacts a formula paying its president 10% of pre-tax profits, and the corporation's profits increase so much that the president is earning $25 million a year, the court might strike the plan as excessive.) [217]

III. THE CORPORATE OPPORTUNITY DOCTRINE AND RELATED PROBLEMS

CAPSULE SUMMARY

A. Competition with corporation: A director or senior executive ***may not compete*** with the corporation, where this competition is likely to ***harm*** the corporation. (*Example*: Corp operates department stores in a particular city. A, B, and C, senior executives of Corp, secretly purchase a controlling interest in another department store in the same city. This is competition which is likely to harm Corp, so A, B, and C are violating their duty of loyalty to Corp.) [219]

1. **Approval or ratification:** Conduct that would otherwise be prohibited as disloyal competition may be validated by being ***approved*** by disinterested directors, or by being ***ratified*** by the shareholders. The Key Player must first make ***full disclosure*** about the conflict and the competition that he proposes to engage in. [219]

2. **Preparation to compete:** Usually, courts will find that a Key Player has violated his duty of loyalty even if he just ***prepares to compete*** (rather than actually competing) while still in the corporation's employ. The court often will order the insider to ***return all salary*** he earned during the period of preparation. [220]

3. **Competition after end of employment:** But if the executive first ***leaves*** the corporation, and only then begins preparations or actual competition, this does ***not*** constitute a violation of the duty of loyalty. (However, the insider may not use the corporation's ***trade secrets.*** Also, the insider will be barred from competing if he has signed a valid ***non-competition agreement***.) [220]

B. Use of corporate assets: A Key Player may not ***use corporate assets*** if this use either: (1) ***harms*** the corporation; or (2) gives the Key Player a ***financial benefit***. "Corporate assets" include not only tangible goods, but also intangibles like information. (*Example*: D, the president of XYZ, lives rent-free in a house owned by XYZ; this is a violation of the duty of loyalty to XYZ and to its other shareholders.) [220]

1. **Approval or payment:** Use of the corporate assets will not be a violation of the duty of loyalty if: (1) it is approved by disinterested directors (after full disclosure); (2) it is ratified by shareholders (after full disclosure); or (3) the Key Player pays the ***fair value*** for any benefit he has received. [220]

C. The "corporate opportunity" doctrine: A director or senior executive may not usurp for himself a business opportunity that is found to "belong" to the corporation. Such an opportunity is said to be a ***"corporate opportunity."*** [221]

1. **Effect: :** If the Key Player is found to have taken a "corporate opportunity," the taking is ***per se wrongful*** to the corporation, and the corporation may recover ***damages*** equal to the loss it has suffered or even the ***profits*** it would have made had it been given the chance to pursue the opportunity. [221]

2. **The Delaware multi-factor test:** Delaware law is especially influential in this area. Under Delaware law, a business opportunity presented to a corporate officer or director will count as a "corporate opportunity" if it meets the following requirements:

   - ❑ the corporation is "***financially able to exploit***" the opportunity;
   - ❑ the opportunity is "within the corporation's ***line of business"***;
   - ❑ the corporation has an ***"interest or a reasonable expectancy"*** in the opportunity; and
   - ❑ if the director or officer were to embrace the opportunity, he would thereby be placed in a ***conflict*** with his duties to the corporation.

   [*Beam v. Stewart*] [221]

   i. **Either "line of business" or "interest or expectancy":** The language quoted above sounds as though the opportunity must satisfy *both* the "line of business" and "interest or expectancy" standards. But in practice, the Delaware courts seem to hold that the opportunity must merely satisfy *either* the "line of business" or "interest or expectancy" test, not both.

3. **Other factors:** Regardless of which test is used, here are some factors that courts find important in determining whether an opportunity was a "corporate" one: [222]

   a. whether the opportunity was offered to the insider as an ***individual*** or as a ***corporate manager***;

   b. whether the insider learned of the opportunity while ***acting in his role*** as the corporation's agent;

   c. whether the insider used ***corporate resources*** to take advantage of the opportunity;

   d. whether the opportunity was ***essential*** to the corporation's well being;

   e. whether the corporation is ***closely*** or ***publicly held*** (the case for finding a corporate opportunity is stronger in the case of a publicly held corporation);

   f. whether the person taking the opportunity is an outside director or a ***full-time executive*** (more likely to be a corporate opportunity in the case of a full-time executive); and

4. **Who is bound:** Generally, courts seem to apply the corporate opportunity doctrine only to ***directors***, ***full-time employees***, and ***controlling shareholders***. Thus a shareholder who has only a ***non-controlling interest*** (and who is not a director or employee) will generally ***not*** be subjected to the doctrine. [224]

5. **Rejection by corporation:** If the insider offers the corporation the chance to pursue the opportunity, and the corporation ***rejects*** the opportunity by a majority vote of disinterested directors or disinterested shareholders, the insider may pursue the opportunity himself. The insider must make ***full disclosure*** about what he proposes to do. (Some but not all courts allow ratification ***after the fact***.) [225]

6. **Corporation's inability to take advantage:** Courts are split about whether it is a defense that a corporation would have been ***unable*** (for financial or other reasons) to take advantage of the opportunity. As noted above, in Delaware if the corporation could not have financially exploited the opportunity it won't be deemed to be a corporate opportunity. [225]

7. **No need for pre-approval by corporation:** At least in Delaware, the Key Player does not need to ***disclose*** the opportunity to the board of the corporation ***in advance***, so as to give the board the chance to argue that this is indeed a corporate opportunity that the corporation wishes to pursue. The Key Player is always free to disclose the opportunity and try to get the corporation to say that it's not interested (which would give the Key Player a sort of "safe harbor"), but the Key Player is ***not required*** to make advance disclosure. [*Broz v. Cellular Info. Systems, Inc.*] [223]

8. **Remedies:** The usual remedy for the taking of a corporate opportunity is for the court to order the imposition of a ***constructive trust*** — the property is treated as if it belonged to the corporation that owned the opportunity. Also, the Key Player may be ordered to account for ***all profits*** earned from the opportunity. [229]

CAPSULE SUMMARY

IV. THE SALE OF CONTROL

A. **Generally:** In some (but not most) situations, the court will prevent a "controlling shareholder" from selling that controlling interest at a ***premium price***. [232]

1. **"Control block" defined:** A person owns a "controlling interest" if he has the power to use the assets of the corporation however he chooses. . A majority owner will always have a controlling interest. But the converse is not true: a less-than-majority interest will often be controlling (e.g., a 20-40% interest where the remaining ownership is highly dispersed and no other shareholder is as large). [233]

2. **Generally allowed:** The general rule is that the controlling shareholder ***may sell his control block for a premium, and may keep the premium for himself***. [234]

   a. **Exceptions:** However, there are a number of exceptions (discussed below) to this general rule, including: (1) the "looting" exception; (2) the "sale of vote" exception; and (3) the "diversion of collective opportunity" exception.

B. **The "looting" exception:** The controlling shareholder may not sell his control block if he knows or suspects that the buyer intends to ***"loot"*** the corporation by unlawfully diverting its assets. [235]

Example: ABC is an investment company with $6 per share of assets, but with nearly offsetting liabilities and a net asset value of six cents per share. Buyer offers to buy Seller's control block for $2 per share, a sum many times greater than market value. Because Seller knows or suspects that the only reason Buyer is willing to pay such a huge premium is because he intends to illegally transfer the liquid assets to himself, Seller may not sell his control block to Buyer at a premium price. If he does so, he will be liable to ABC and its other shareholders for damages.

1. **Mental state:** Clearly if the controlling shareholder either ***knows*** or ***strongly suspects*** that the buyer will loot, he may not sell to him. Also, if Seller ***recklessly disregards*** the possibility of looting, the same rule applies. Most, but probably not all, courts would also impose liabil-

ity where the seller merely ***"negligently"*** disregards the likelihood that the buyer will loot. [235]

2. **Excessive price:** In many courts, ***excessive price alone*** will ***not*** be enough to necessarily put the seller on notice that the buyer intends to loot. But an excessive price combined with other factors (e.g., the liquid and readily saleable nature of the company's assets) will be deemed to put the seller on notice. [235]

C. **The "sale of vote" exception:** The controlling shareholder may not sell for a premium where the sale amounts to a ***"sale of his vote."*** [236]

1. **Majority stake:** If the controlling shareholder owns a ***majority*** interest, the "sale of vote" exception will ***not*** apply. Thus even if the controlling shareholder specifically agrees that he will ensure that a majority of the board resigns so that the buyer is able to immediately elect his own majority of the board, this will not be deemed to be a sale of vote (since the buyer would eventually get control of the board anyway merely by owning the majority stake). [236]

2. **Small stake:** If the seller has a very ***small*** stake (e.g., less than 20%) in the corporation, and promises to use his influence over the directors to induce them to resign so that the buyer can elect disproportionately many directors, then the "sale of vote" exception is likely to be applied. [236]

3. **"Working control":** Where the seller has "working control," and promises to deliver the resignations of a majority of directors so that the buyer can receive that working control, courts are split about whether this constitutes a sale of vote. [236]

4. **Separate payment:** Also, if the contract of sale explicitly provides for a ***separate payment*** for the delivery of directors' resignations and election of the buyer's nominees to the board, this will be a sale of vote. [237]

D. **Diversion of collective opportunity:**

1. **Business opportunity:** A court may find that the corporation had a business opportunity, and that the controlling shareholder has constructed the sale of his control block in such a way as to ***deprive the corporation of this business opportunity.*** If so, the seller will not be allowed to keep the control premium. [237]

   Example: ABC Corp, due to scarce wartime conditions, is able to get interest-free loans from its customers. President sells his control block to a consortium of those customers, who then cancel the no-interest loan arrangements and who sell themselves much of ABC's production, although at standard prices. The president may be found to have diverted a business opportunity belonging to ABC, in which case he will not be allowed to keep the portion of the price he received for his shares that is above the fair market value of those shares. See *Perlman v. Feldmann.*

2. **Seller switches type of deal:** If Buyer proposes to buy the entire company, but Seller instead ***switches*** the nature of the deal by talking Buyer into buying just Seller's control block (at a premium), a court may take away Seller's right to keep the premium, on the grounds that all shareholders deserve the right to participate. [239]

E. **Remedies:** If one of these exceptions applies (so that the seller is not entitled to keep the control premium) there are two remedies which the court may impose: [239]

1. **Recovery by corporation:** Sometimes, the court will allow the ***corporation*** to recover. (But this has the drawback that the purchaser who paid the control premium gets a windfall.) [240]

2. **Pro rata recovery:** Alternately, the court may award a ***pro rata*** recovery, under which the seller repays to the ***minority shareholders*** their pro rata part of the control premium (thus avoiding a windfall to the buyer). [240]

V. OTHER DUTIES OF CONTROLLING SHAREHOLDERS

A. **Possible general fiduciary duty:** Almost no courts have held that a controlling shareholder owes any kind of ***general fiduciary duty*** to the minority shareholders. (A few courts have recognized such a fiduciary duty limited to the case of a ***close*** corporation. See, e.g., *Donahue v. Rodd Electrotype*, discussed at the end of the chapter, "Close Corporations," *supra*, p. C-24) [242]

B. **Duty of complete disclosure:** When a controlling shareholder or group deals with the non-controlling shareholders, some courts say the controller owes the non-controllers a ***duty of complete disclosure*** with respect to the transaction, as a matter of state common law. [243]

> **Example:** Controlling shareholders in ABC give notice of the proposed redemption of a minority block, without telling the minority holders that due to secret developments the minority holders would benefit by exercising certain conversion rights. A court might well hold that this failure to give complete disclosure violated the majority's common-law obligation to the minority. [243]

C. **Parent/subsidiary relations:** When the controlling shareholder is another corporation (the ***parent/subsidiary*** context), essentially the same rules apply. [243]

1. **Dividends:** When the parent corporation controls the parent's ***dividend*** policy, this is in theory self-dealing. But so long as dividends are paid pro rata to all shareholders (including the parent), courts will rarely overturn the subsidiary's dividend policy even though this was dictated by the needs of the parent. [243]

2. **Other types of self-dealing:** Other types of self-dealing transactions between parent and subsidiary will be struck down if they are ***unfair*** to the minority shareholders of the subsidiary, and were entered into on the subsidiary's side by a board ***dominated by directors appointed by the parent***. (*Example*: Subsidiary and Parent agree to a price and terms under which Subsidiary will sell to Parent the oil it produces. If Subsidiary's board is dominated by directors appointed by Parent, Parent will have to bear the burden of proving that the transaction is fair to Subsidiary and to the minority holders of Subsidiary.) [244]

3. **Corporate opportunities:** If the parent takes for itself an opportunity that should belong to the subsidiary, the court will apply the ***"corporate opportunity"*** doctrine, and void the transaction. [245]

4. **Disinterested directors:** The parent can avoid liability both for self-dealing transactions and for the taking of corporate opportunities by having the truly ***disinterested directors*** of the subsidiary form a ***special committee*** which negotiates at arm's length with the parent on behalf of the subsidiary. [245]

CHAPTER 8

INSIDER TRADING (AND RELATED TOPICS)

I. INTRODUCTION TO INSIDER TRADING

A. Generally: The term "insider trading" has no precise definition, but basically refers to the buying or selling of stock in a publicly traded company based on material, non-public information about that company. [251]

1. **Not all illegal:** Not all insider trading (as defined above) is illegal. In general, only insider trading that occurs as a result of someone's ***willful breach*** of a ***fiduciary duty*** will be illegal (at least under the federal securities laws, which are the main source of insider trading law). [251]

2. **Illustrations:** Either ***buying on undisclosed good news***, or ***selling on undisclosed bad news***, can be insider trading (and will often be illegal). [252]

   a. **Buying before disclosure of good news:** Thus if an insider at Oil Corp buys stock at a time when he knows, and the market doesn't, that Oil Corp has just struck a huge gusher, this is illegal insider trading.

   b. **Sale before disclosure of bad news:** Similarly, if an insider at Oil Corp sells his stock at a time when he knows (and the market does not) that Oil Corp is just about to report an unexpected large loss, this too is illegal insider trading.

3. **Harms:** The possible harms from insider trading include: (1) harm to the ***reputation*** of the corporation whose stock is being insider-traded; (2) harm to ***market efficiency***, because insiders will delay disclosing their information and prices will be "wrong"; (3) harm to the ***capital markets***, because investors will stay away from what they think is a "rigged" market; and (4) harm to ***company efficiency***, because managers may be induced to run their companies in an inefficient manner (but one that produces large insider trading profits). [254]

4. **Bodies of law:** There are three bodies of law which may be violated by a particular act of insider trading: [257]

   a. **State common law:** A few states impose ***common-law*** restrictions on insider trading.

   b. **10b-5:** The federal ***SEC Rule 10b-5*** prohibits any "fraudulent or manipulative device" in connection with the purchase or sale of security; this has been interpreted to bar most types of insider trading.

   c. **Short-swing profits:** Section 16(b) of the federal Securities Exchange Act makes insiders liable to repay to the corporation all profits they make from "***short swing*** trading profits" (whether based on insider information or not).

   Note: Of these three bodies of law, SEC Rule 10b-5 is by far and away the most important limit on insider trading.

II. STATE COMMON-LAW APPROACHES

A. Suit by shareholder: A shareholder can in theory bring a state common-law action against an insider trader for "***deceit.***" [258]

1. **Face-to-face:** If the insider buys from the outsider in a ***face-to-face*** transaction, the rule is that the insider has ***no duty to disclose*** material facts (e.g., good news) known to him. So usually, even in this face-to-face situation, the plaintiff outsider will not be able to recover in deceit even though he would not have sold at the price he did had he known the undisclosed good news. But there are some exceptions: [259]

   a. **Fraud:** If the insider knowingly ***lies*** or tells a ***half truth***, he will be liable under ordinary deceit principles.

   b. **Special facts:** Many states recognize a ***"special facts"*** exception to the general rule that silence cannot constitute deceit. (*Example*: If the insider ***seeks out*** the other party, or makes elaborate attempts to ***conceal*** his own identity, the "special facts" doctrine may be employed.)

   c. **Minority rule:** A minority of states impose a more general rule that in face-to-face transactions, the insider has an affirmative obligation to disclose material facts known to him.

2. **Garden variety impersonal insider trading:** If the insider trading takes place in an ***impersonal*** rather than a face-to-face way (i.e., it occurs by means of ***open-market purchases*** on the stock market), virtually no states allow the outsider to recover on common-law principles. [260]

C A P S U L E S U M M A R Y

B. **Suit by corporation:** A very few states have allowed the ***corporation*** to recover against an insider who buys or sells based on undisclosed material information. [260]

1. ***Diamond* case:** The best known example is *Diamond v. Oreamuno*, where the corporation was permitted to recover against the insiders who sold before disclosing bad news; recovery was allowed even though there was no direct tangible harm to the corporation. [261]

2. **ALI:** The ALI follows the approach of *Diamond*, by making it an actionable breach of loyalty for the insider to use "material non-public information concerning the corporation" to either cause harm to the corporation, or to secure a pecuniary benefit not available to other shareholders. [261]

III. SEC RULE 10b-5 AND INSIDER TRADING

A. **Summary:** The principal proscription against insider trading is SEC's ***Rule 10b-5***, enacted pursuant to the Securities Exchange Act of 1934. [262]

1. **Text:** SEC Rule 10b-5 makes it unlawful: (1) to "employ any device, scheme, or artifice to ***defraud***"; (2) to make any "untrue statement of a material fact or to ***omit to state*** a material fact. . . ."; or (3) to engage in any "act, practice, or course of business which operates or would operate as a ***fraud or deceit*** upon any person." All three of these types of conduct are forbidden only if they occur "in connection with the purchase or sale of any security." [262]

2. **Disclose-or-abstain:** The insider does not have an affirmative obligation to ***disclose*** the material, non-public information. Rather, he must ***choose*** between disclosure and abstaining from trading. [264]

3. **Misrepresentation:** If an insider makes an affirmative ***misrepresentation*** (as opposed to merely omitting to disclose information), he can be liable under 10b-5 even if he does not buy or sell the stock. [262]

4. **Nature of violation:** Violation of 10b-5 is a ***crime***. Also, the SEC can get an ***injunction*** against the conduct. Finally, a private party who has been injured will, if he meets certain procedural requirements, have a ***private right of action*** for damages against the insider trader. [264]

5. **Private companies:** Rule 10b-5 applies to fraud in the purchase or sale of securities in ***privately-held*** companies, not just publicly held ones. [265]

B. **Requirements for private right of action:** An outsider injured by insider trading has a right of action for damages under Rule 10b-5, if he can meet certain procedural requirements: [267]

1. **Purchaser or seller:** P must have been a ***purchaser*** or ***seller*** of the company's stock during the time of non-disclosure. [267]

2. **Traded on material, non-public info:** D must have misstated or omitted a ***material*** fact. [268]

3. **Special relationship:** If the claim is based on insider trading, D must be shown to have had a ***special relationship*** with the issuer, based on some kind of ***fiduciary duty*** to the issuer. [268]

4. **Scienter:** D must be shown to have acted with ***scienter***, i.e., he must be shown to have had an intent to deceive, manipulate or defraud. [268]

5. **Reliance and causation:** P must show that he relied on D's misstatement or omission, and that that misstatement or omission was the proximate cause of his loss. (In cases of silent insider trading rather than misrepresentation, these requirements usually don't have much effect.) [268]

6. **Jurisdiction:** There is a federal jurisdictional requirement: D must be shown to have done the fraud or manipulation "by the use of any means or instrumentality of ***interstate commerce*** or of the ***mails***, or of any ***facility of any national securities exchange***." In the case of any ***publicly-traded security***, this requirement will readily be ***met***. But where the fraud consists of deceit in a ***face-to-face sale of shares***, especially shares in a ***private company***, then the jurisdictional requisites may well be ***lacking***. [268]

Note: The first five of these requirements are discussed below.

C. **P as purchaser or seller:** P in a private 10b-5 action must have been either a ***purchaser*** or ***seller*** of stock in the company to which the misrepresentation or insider trading relates. [*Blue Chip Stamps v. Manor Drug Stores*] [269]

1. **Non-sellers:** Thus one who already owned shares in the issuer and who ***decides not to sell*** because the corporation or its insiders makes an unduly optimistic representation, or fails to disclose negative material, may not sue. [270]

2. **Options:** Some courts hold that this "purchaser or seller" requirement also means that a plaintiff who buys or sells ***options*** on a company's stock has no standing to sue an insider who trades on the company's stock. [270]

D. **"Material" non-public fact:** D must be shown to have made a ***misstatement*** or ***omission*** of a ***"material"*** fact. [272]

1. **"Material":** A fact is "material" if there is a "substantial likelihood that a reasonable shareholder would consider it important" in deciding whether to buy, hold, or sell the stock. [272]

a. **Mergers:** The fact that the company is engaged in "merger" discussions is ***not*** necessarily "material." This is a fact-based question that depends on how far along the negotiations are, whether a specific price is on the table, whether the investment bankers have been brought in, etc.

b. **Fact need not be outcome-determinative:** To be "material," a fact does ***not*** have to be one that, if known to the investor, would have ***changed the investor's decision***. The "total mix" test means that "a material fact is one that would ***affect*** a reasonable investor's ***deliberations*** without necessarily changing her ultimate investment decision." [*Folger Adam Co. v. PMI Industries, Inc.*]

2. **Non-public:** If the claim is that D traded silently rather than made a misrepresentation, the omission must be of a ***non-public*** fact. But "non-public" is interpreted broadly: even if a fact has been disclosed, say, to a few reporters, it is still non-public (and trading is not allowed) until the investors as a ***whole*** have learned of it. [273]

E. **Defendant as insider, knowing tippee or misappropriator:** In the case of silent insider trading, D will not be liable unless he was either an ***insider***, a ***"tippee,"*** or a ***"misappropriator."*** In other words, mere trading while in possession of material non-public information is ***not by itself enough*** to make D civilly liable under 10b-5. [273]

Example: D is sitting in a taxi, and finds handwritten notes left by the prior occupant. The notes indicate that ABC Corp. is about to launch a tender offer for XYZ Corp. D buys XYZ stock. D won't be liable under 10b-5, because he was not an insider of XYZ, nor a "tippee" of one who was an insider of XYZ, nor a "misappropriator" who "stole" the information from anyone.

1. **Insiders:** An ***"insider"*** is one who obtains information by virtue of his ***employment*** with the company whose stock he trades in. One can be an insider even if one is a ***low-level employee*** (e.g., a secretary). Also, people who do work on a contract basis for the issuing company (e.g., professionals like accountants and lawyers) can be a "constructive" insider. See *infra*, p. C-43. [275]

2. **Knowing tippee:** A person will be a ***"tippee,"*** and will be liable for insider trading, if he ***knows that the source of his tip has violated a fiduciary obligation to the issuer.*** Conversely, if the tippee does not know this (or if the insider has not breached any fiduciary obligation), the tippee is not liable. [276]

Example: X, a former employee of ABC Corp, tells D that XYZ is engaging in massive financial fraud. X is not acting for any pecuniary benefit, but instead just wants to expose the fraud. D tells his clients to sell their ABC stock. *Held*, D did not violate 10b-5, because X was not violating any fiduciary duty, so D was not a knowing "tippee." [*Dirks v. SEC*]

3. **Misappropriator:** A ***"misappropriator"*** is one who takes information from anyone — especially from a person who is ***not the issuer*** — in violation of an express or implied ***obligation of confidentiality***.

Example: Lawfirm represents Behemoth, a big company that is secretly planning a takeover of Smallco. D, a partner at Lawfirm, learns from Behemoth about these plans, and buys Smallco stock. *Held*, D has violated 10b-5, because he misappropriated the information from Behemoth, in violation of an implied promise of confidentiality. This is true even though neither D nor Lawfirm was an insider of Smallco, the issuer. *U.S. v. O'Hagan.* [291]

F. Scienter: A defendant is liable under 10b-5 only if he acted with ***scienter***, i.e., with intent to ***deceive***, manipulate or defraud. Probably this is met if D makes a misstatement ***recklessly***. (In silent insider trading cases, the scienter requirement means that the defendant must have known that the information to which he had access was material and non-public.) [277]

G. Trading "while in possession" of info, vs. trading "on the basis of" info: Is it enough for liability that D was merely ***"in possession"*** of the inside information at the time of the trade, even if the government cannot prove that D in some sense ***"used"*** the information in making his decision to trade? The answer is essentially ***"yes,"*** as a result of the SEC's adoption of an important rule, ***Rule 10b-5-1.*** [271-272]

1. "Awareness" test: 10b-5 (the basic anti-fraud rule) prohibits trading "on the basis of" material nonpublic information. But 10b-5-1 now defines "on the basis of" to *mean* ***"was aware of"*** the information" at the time of the purchase or sale. In other words (except for a "safe harbor" which we'll discuss below), the government or private plaintiff merely has to show that D was ***"aware"*** of the inside information at the time he traded, *not* that the inside information in any sense ***caused or even affected*** D's decision to trade. (So D can't defend by saying, "Sure I sold the stock at a time when I knew that bad news was coming, but my *real* reason for selling was something else.")

a. Safe harbor for preplanned trading: But Rule 10b-5-1 also gives the insider an important ***"safe harbor"***: if before becoming aware of the inside information, the insider adopts a ***"written plan for trading securities"*** that ***locks the insider into making particular types of purchases or sales at particular times*** or under particular circumstances, sales that are made according to this preplanned trading arrangement won't be deemed to be "on the basis of" the inside information, even if the insider knows the information at the time the trade actually occurs. [271]

Example: Prexy, the head of XYZ Corp., owns $100 million of XYZ stock, and would like to gradually diminish the proportion that XYZ stock constitutes of his net worth. In late 2004, therefore, Prexy adopts an irrevocable written contract with Broker, under which Prexy instructs Broker to sell $5 million of Prexy's XYZ stock during the first week of each calendar quarter for the next three years. On June 25, 2005, Prexy learns that XYZ will soon need to announce poor quarterly earnings, which will likely lead to a decline in the stock. On July 2, before the poor earnings are reported, Broker sells $5 million of stock for Prexy.

Even though the sale took place at a time when Prexy was in possession of material nonpublic information, Prexy has not committed insider trading, because he has successfully used the preplanned-trading-arrangement safe harbor of Rule 10b-5-1. The idea is that because in late 2004 Prexy irrevocably made the decision to sell shares in the first week of July, 2005 — a decision that would bind him no matter what happened to the market price or status of XYZ — he won't be deemed to have sold "on the basis of" information that he didn't acquire until after making that irrevocable decision.

H. Causation; reliance:

1. Misrepresentation: If the case involves affirmative misrepresentation (not just silent insider trading), P will be given the benefit of a ***presumption*** that P ***relied*** on the misrepresentation and that it ***caused*** P's injury. In other words, because of the fact that the stock market is usually "efficient," D's misstatement will be presumed to have ***affected the price*** at which the plaintiff bought or sold. (*Example*: D, an insider at XYZ, falsely says, "Profits will be up this quarter." P buys for $20 per share. Profits go down, and the stock drops to $10. The misstatement will be presumed to have affected the market price, and P will be presumed to have relied on the fairness of that price.) But this presumption may be ***rebutted***. [279]

2. **Silent insider trading:** If the case involves silent insider trading, the requirements of reliance and causation are not very important (and probably are ignored by the courts) so you can safely ignore them. [281]

I. **"Contemporaneous trader's" right to sue:** In 1988, Congress specifically allowed any insider-trader to be sued civilly by any ***"contemporaneous trader"*** who traded in the ***other direction***. The plaintiff can recover his own losses up to the amount of gain achieved, or loss avoided, by the defendant. P does not have to prove that the insider trading "caused" P's loss. (The statutory provision creating this right of action doesn't define "insider trading"; that's left to the courts, as it has always been.) [283]

Example: D, Senior Vice President of XYZ Corp., learns from his job that XYZ will soon be acquired by ABC Corp. at a price of $40 per share. D buys 1000 shares of XYZ on March 1 at a price of $20 per share. On March 2, P sells 2000 shares of XYZ at $20 each. The merger is announced on March 3, and the price goes to $40 immediately. D sells at $40, and thus makes a $20,000 profit. P may sue D civilly, and may recover $20,000. That is, P gets the lesser of: (1) P's lost profits (which are probably $40,000, since that's the profit he would have made on his shares if the market had been aware of the inside information at the time P made his sale); and (2) D's gains ($20,000).

1. **Information not from issuer:** This express private right of action applies even though the inside information does not derive from the issuer, but rather, from some third party. However, under court rulings that still apply — like *Dirks*, *supra*, p. C-40 — the trade is not "insider trading" unless the trader knew that the information was obtained by the trader or his tipper in violation of some ***fiduciary responsibility***. [284]

Example: On the facts of the above example, P could recover even if D learned the information while working at ABC, the acquirer, rather than while working at XYZ, the issuer. But if D had learned the information by overhearing a conversation on a park bench — or in any other way not involving a breach of fiduciary responsibility by D or D's source — then this would not be "insider trading" at all, and P could not recover under the express private right of action now given to "contemporaneous traders" injured by insider trading.

J. **Damages:** If P meets all of these requirements for a private 10b-5 action, there are various ways that the ***measure of damages*** might be calculated. [284]

1. **Misrepresentation:** If D has made a ***misrepresentation***, P generally receives damages that would be needed to put him in the position he would have been in had his trade been delayed until after the misrepresentation was corrected. [284]

2. **Silent trading; P is "contemporaneous trader":** If D is a silent insider-trader, and P is a ***"contemporaneous trader,"*** P may recover the lesser of: (1) P's own losses (probably measured by how much gain P would have made, or how much loss he would have avoided, had the inside information been disclosed before P traded); and (2) D's gains made, or losses avoided, from the transaction. See the example to Par. (H) above. [285]

3. **P is acquirer who has to pay more:** If P is an ***acquirer*** who as the result of D's insider trading or tipping in the target's stock is forced to ***pay more*** to acquire the target, P's liability is probably ***not limited*** to the gains made by D. [285]

   Example: Suitor is planning to acquire Target. Target's stock is now $20 per share, and Suitor plans to offer the public $30. Dennis, a managing director at InvestCo., Suitor's investment banker, buys 1000 shares in Target at $20, and tells his friends so they can buy too. As a result of this trading and tipping, the price of Target jumps immediately to $30. Suitor finally has to pay $40, rather than $30, to buy all Target's 1 million shares. Probably Suitor can recover $10 million — the amount it had to pay extra — from Dennis, even though Dennis only made $20,000. *Cf. Litton Industries v. Lehman Bros.*

4. **SEC civil penalties:** Also, the ***SEC*** may recover ***civil penalties*** against an insider trader. The SEC may recover a civil penalty of up to ***three times*** the profit gained or loss avoided by the insider trader. See '34 Act, § 21A(a)(3) and 21A(b). [286]

   a. **"Controlling person's" liability:** Furthermore, as the result of changes made by Congress in 1988 to the Securities Exchange Act, a person or organization who ***"controls"*** an insider trader, and carelessly fails to take steps to prevent foreseeable insider trading, may be liable for the same three-fold SEC civil penalties as the insider. (*Example:* D insider-trades based on information he learned while working as an associate in the mergers and acquisitions department of Law Firm. Law Firm can be liable for three-fold civil penalties if the SEC shows that Law Firm recklessly disregarded the risk that D might insider trade and failed to take reasonable steps to limit this risk of such trading.)

IV. WHO IS AN "INSIDER" OR "TIPPEE"?

A. **Recap:** Remember that only a person who is either an "insider" or a "tippee" is covered by 10b-5. [286]

   1. **Who is "insider":** A person is an "insider" only if he has some sort of ***fiduciary relationship*** with the issuer that requires him to keep the non-public information confidential. [286]

   2. **Who is "tippee":** A person is a ***"tippee"*** only if: (1) he receives information given to him in ***breach*** of the insider's fiduciary responsibility; (2) he ***knows*** that (or, perhaps, ***should know*** that) the breach has occurred; and (3) the insider/tipper has received some ***benefit*** from the breach (or intended to make a pecuniary gift to the tippee). [286]

B. **Acquired by chance:** Thus if an outsider acquires information ***totally by chance***, without anyone violating any fiduciary obligation of confidentiality, the outsider may trade with impunity. (*Example*: The outsider randomly overhears inside information in a restaurant without any fiduciary violation by the speaker or by the outsider.) [288]

C. **Acquired by diligence:** Similarly, if an outsider acquires non-public information through his ***own diligence***, he may trade upon it. (*Example*: A security analyst ferrets out non-public information by interviewing former employees and others who when they speak to the analyst are not receiving or intending to confer any pecuniary benefit.) [288]

D. **Intent to make a gift:** If an insider gives an outsider information with the ***intent to make a gift*** of ***pecuniary value*** to the outsider, the outsider will be a "tippee," and both ***insider and outsider*** will be liable. (*Example: A* gives an inside stock tip to his mistress, *B*, with the intent that *B* be able to make some money by buying the stock. Even though *A* doesn't expect or get any profit himself, *A* and *B* are both liable under 10b-5.) [288]

E. Disclosure between family members: If the tipper learns information from a ***close relative***, this relationship is ***not*** by itself enough to give the tipper a fiduciary responsibility. This is true even if the relative or the relative's family control the issuer, the information "belongs" to the issuer, and the tipper knows all this. [288]

Example: The Waldbaum family, which controls publicly-held Waldbaum Corp., agrees to sell Waldbaum Corp. to another company, for a price higher than the current market price. Ira Waldbaum, President of Waldbaum, tells his sister; she tells her daughter, Susan. Susan tells her husband, Keith, and then tells him to keep the information secret. Keith tells D, his stockbroker, who secretly buys Waldbaum stock for himself. D is charged with the crime of violating 10b-5.

Held, D is not guilty of violating 10b-5. The mere family relationship between Susan and Keith was not enough to make Keith a "fiduciary" regarding the merger information; this is true even though Keith knew the information came from the issuer (Waldbaum Corp.) and knew that the information derived from Susan's family's control of the issuer. (But if Keith had promised confidentiality to Susan as a condition of hearing the news, then he would have been a fiduciary.) Because Keith was not a fiduciary, his tippee, D, has no 10b-5 liability. (But D *is* guilty of violating SEC Rule 14e-3, which prohibits trading on non-public information about a tender offer.) [*U.S. v. Chestman*]

F. Confidential information from other than issuer (the "misappropriation" problem): Where an outsider receives confidential information that is ***not from the issuer***, the situation is trickier. [289]

1. **Criminal liability under other provisions:** Often, trading by the outsider in this situation will constitute ***mail*** or ***wire fraud***. This will be the case if the outsider has "misappropriated" the information from, say, his employer, even if the employer is not the issuer and didn't get the information from the issuer. [290]

   Example: D is a reporter for a financial newspaper. He learns that company XYZ will be the subject of a favorable news story in the newspaper. He buys XYZ stock. A court would hold that even though D's information did not come from the issuer (XYZ) he has "misappropriated" it from his employer, so he will be criminally liable under federal wire and/or mail fraud statutes.

2. **10b-5:** Now, let's consider whether ***10b-5*** is violated when a person trades based on confidential information whose source is other than the company whose stock is being traded. The Supreme Court finally answered this question in the 1997 case set forth in the following example: the defendant ***is liable under 10b-5*** if he has ***misappropriated*** the information, by ***breaching a fiduciary relationship with the source of the information.*** [291]

   Example: Grand Met is planning a secret tender offer for Pillsbury. Grand Met hires the law firm of Dorsey & Whitney to represent it. D is a partner in Dorsey & Whitney, and learns what Grand Met is planning. (D doesn't actually do any work on the matter — he just learns about it from others in the firm.) While the plan is still secret, D goes out and makes open-market purchases of thousands of Pillsbury shares and call options. When Grand Met announces its tender offer, Pillsbury shares skyrocket, and D pockets a $4.3

million profit. The U.S. government brings criminal charges against D for violating Rule 10b-5. A jury convicts D.

Held (in a 6-3 decision by the Supreme Court), against D: 10b-5 liability may be based on the ***misappropriation of confidential data from a person other than the issuer.*** "Investors likely would ***hesitate to venture their capital*** in a market where trading based on misappropriated nonpublic information is unchecked by law. . . . It makes scant sense to hold a lawyer like [D] a [10b-5] violator if he works for a law firm representing the target of a tender offer, but not if he works for a law firm representing the bidder." [*U.S. v. O'Hagan*]

a. **Significance:** *O'Hagan* clearly broadens the population of people who can be liable for violating 10b-5. A person who "misappropriates" confidential information ***from anyone*** can be liable for trading on that information. [291]

- ❑ Thus one who learns of the information as the result of a fiduciary relationship with a company ***planning a tender offer*** for X Corp. can be liable for trading in X Corp. stock. (That's what happened in *O'Hagan* itself.)
- ❑ Similarly, one who learns secret information about X Corp. as the result of working inside a ***publisher or broadcaster*** that's about to publish a story on X Corp. would presumably also be covered, as long as the publisher's or broadcaster's rules of employee conduct made it clear that the information belonged to the employer.
- ❑ Even a person who learns the information as the result of ***securities research*** done at a ***money-management company*** would be liable, if the information belonged to the money-management company.

G. **One's own trading plans:** It is ***not*** a violation of 10b-5 for one who is about to launch ***his own tender offer*** to buy shares on the open market without disclosing his plans.

Example: Raider secretly buys 4% of Target Corp stock on the New York Stock Exchange, without announcing that he plans to institute a tender offer. He then institutes a tender offer at a much higher price. Raider has not violated 10b-5 by his open-market purchases, even though he was concealing the material fact that he would soon be taking an action which would raise the price. [293]

V. RULE 10b-5: MISREPRESENTATIONS OR OMISSIONS NOT INVOLVING INSIDER TRADING

A. **Breach of fiduciary duty:** The fact that an insider has breached his ***state-law fiduciary duties*** may occasionally (but rarely) constitute a violation of 10b-5. [298]

1. **Lie to directors:** For instance, if an insider lies to the board of directors and thereby induces them to ***sell him stock*** on favorable terms, this would be a 10b-5 violation. (*Example*: The chief scientist of XYZ Corp falsely tells the board of directors that there have been no new developments, when there has in fact been a major scientific breakthrough that will improve the company's prospects. The board then issues stock options to the scientist. The scientist will be held to have violated 10b-5, because he violated his state-law duty of disclosure to his corporate employer.) [298]

2. **Breach of duty without misrepresentation:** But if an insider violates his fiduciary duties to the corporation or its shareholders ***without making a misrepresentation***, this will ***not*** constitute a 10b-5 violation. In other words, there is no doctrine of "constructive fraud" to trigger a 10b-5 violation. (*Example*: The controlling shareholder of XYZ Corp carries out a short-form merger on terms that are substantively unfair to the minority stockholders. Even though this violates a controlling shareholder's fiduciary obligations to the minority shareholder, there will be no 10b-5 violation because there has been no fraud or deception. See *Santa Fe Industries v. Green*.) [299]

B. Misrepresentation without trading: If a corporation or one of its insiders makes a ***misrepresentation***, it/he will be liable ***even though it/he does not trade in the company's stock.*** (*Example*: D, the president of XYZ, falsely tells the public, "Our profits will be up this quarter." D can be liable under 10b-5 even though he has never bought any XYZ stock.) [300]

1. **Scienter:** However, remember that D will not be liable for misrepresentation in a 10b-5 suit unless he acted with ***scienter***, i.e., he knew his statement was false or recklessly disregarded the chance that it might be false. That is, D will not be liable for mere ***negligent*** misstatement. [300]

2. **Merger discussions:** If a company is a company is engaged in ***merger*** discussions, and its insiders knowingly and falsely deny that the discussions are taking place, this may make them liable under 10b-5. (Therefore, they should say, "No comment," instead of falsely denying.) [300]

3. **Fraud by one not associated with issuer:** Even a person ***not associated with the issuer*** can commit fraud by knowingly or recklessly ***making a false statement*** about the issuer or the issuer's stock. [328]

C. Omission by non-trader: Where the company or an insider simply ***fails to disclose*** material inside information that it possesses, it/he will ***not*** be liable as long as it/he does not buy or sell company stock. (*Example*: D Corp signs a huge contract which improves its prospects enormously. It keeps the deal quiet for 10 days. So long as neither the company nor its insiders buys or sells any D Corp stock during this period, no violation of 10b-5 has occurred.) [302]

1. **Exceptions:** But there are two exceptions to this general rule that there is no duty to disclose: [302]

   a. **Leaks:** If rumors are the result of ***leaks*** by the company or its agents, the company probably has an obligation under 10b-5 to correct the misapprehension.

   b. **Involvement:** If the company heavily ***involves itself*** with outsiders' statements about the company, it may thereby assume a duty to correct errors in those outsider's statements. (*Example*: X, a securities analyst, submits his estimates of ABC Corp's next quarterly earnings to ABC's investor relations director, W. W knows that these estimates are wrong but says nothing. X releases the estimates to the public. ABC and/or W may have violated 10b-5.)

VI. SHORT-SWING TRADING PROFITS AND § 16(b)

A. Generally: Section 16(b) of the Securities Exchange Act of 1934 contains a "bright line" rule by which all ***"short-swing"*** trading profits received by insiders must be returned to the company. [305]

1. **Gist:** The gist of § 16(b) is that if a statutorily-defined insider buys stock in his company and then ***resells within six months,*** or sells and then ***re-purchases within six months***, any profits he makes must be ***returned to the corporate treasury.*** This rule applies even if the person in fact had no material non-public information. [305]

2. **Who is covered:** Section 16(b) applies to any ***"officer," "director,"*** or ***beneficial owner of more than 10%*** of any class of the company's stock. [306]

3. **Public companies:** Section 16(b) applies only to the insiders of companies which have a class of stock registered with the SEC under § 12 of the '34 Act. Thus a company's insiders are covered only if the company either: (1) is listed on a national securities exchange; or (2) has assets greater than $5 million and a class of stock held of record by 500 or more people. [306]

4. **Who may sue:** Suit may be brought by the corporation or by ***any shareholder.*** But any recovery goes into the corporate treasury. (The incentive is to the plaintiff's lawyer, who gets attorney's fees out of the recovery.) [253]

   a. **P must continue to be stockholder:** P must not only be a stockholder in the corporation at the time she files suit under 16(b), but she must also ***continue*** to be a stockholder as the suit progresses. However, if P is forced to exchange her shares for shares in a different corporation as the result of the target corporation's ***merger***, P may continue her suit as long as she keeps the shares in the surviving corporation. [*Gollust v. Mendell*]

5. **Public filings:** To aid enforcement, any officer, director, or 10%-owner must file with the SEC (under 16(a)) a statement showing any change in his ownership of the company's stock. This must be filed within 10 days after any calendar month in which the level of ownership changes. [306]

B. **Who is insider:**

1. **"Officer":** Two groups of people may be ***"officers"*** for § 16(b) purposes: (1) anyone who holds the title of "President," "Vice President," "Secretary," "Treasurer" (or "Principal Financial Officer"), or "Comptroller" (or "Principal Accounting Officer"); (2) anyone (regardless of title) who performs ***functions*** that correspond to the functions typically performed by these named persons in other corporations. [307]

2. **"Beneficial owner":** A person is a beneficial owner covered by § 16(b) if he is "directly or indirectly" the beneficial owner of more than 10% of ***any class*** of the company's stock (he need not own 10% of the overall equity). [307]

   a. **Attribution:** Stock listed in A's name may be ***attributed*** to B. A person will generally be regarded as the beneficial owner of securities held in the name of his or her ***spouse*** and their ***minor children*** (but usually not ***grown children***). Thus a sale by Husband might be matched against a purchase by Wife; similarly, a sale and purchase by Wife might be attributed to Husband if Husband is a director or officer.

3. **Deputization as director:** A corporation may be treated as a "director" of another corporation if the former appoints one of its employees to serve on the latter's board. (*Example*: ABC Corp owns a significant minority interest in XYZ Corp. ABC appoints E, its employee, to serve on the board of XYZ. ABC will be deemed to have "deputized" E to serve as director, so ABC will be treated as a constructive director of XYZ, and any short-swing trading profits reaped by ABC in XYZ stock will have to be returned to XYZ.) [308]

C. **When insider status required:**

1. **Director or officer at only one end of the swing:** If D is a director or officer at the time of ***either*** his sale or his purchase of stock, § 16(b) applies to him even though he does not have the status at the other end of the trade. [308]

2. **10% owner:** But the same rule does not apply to a 10% owner. A person is caught by the "10% owner" prong only if he has the more-than-10% status at ***both*** ends of the swing. [308]

   a. **Purchase that puts one over:** The ***purchase*** that puts a person ***over 10%*** does not count for § 16(b) purposes. (*Example*: D has owned 5% of XYZ for a long time. On January 1, he buys another 10%. On February 1, he sells 4%. There are no short-swing profits that must be returned to the company.)

   b. **Sale that puts one below 10%:** In the case of a ***sale*** that puts a person ***below 10%*** ownership, probably we measure the insider status ***before*** the sale. (*Example*: D already owns 15% of XYZ. He then buys another 10% on January 1. On February 1, he sells 16%. On March 1, he sells the remaining 9%. Probably D has short-swing liability for 16% sale, but not for the second 9%, since we probably measure his insider status as of the moment just before the sale.)

C A P S U L E S U M M A R Y

D. **What is a "sale," in the case of a merger:** If the corporation merges into another company (and thus disappears), the insiders will not necessarily be deemed to have made a "sale." D will escape short-swing liability for a merger or other unorthodox transaction if he shows that: (1) the transaction was essentially ***involuntary***; *and* (2) the transaction was of a type such that D almost certainly did ***not have access*** to inside information. [309]

   Example: Raider launches a hostile tender offer for Target. On Feb. 1, Raider buys 15% of Target pursuant to the tender offer. Target then arranges a defensive merger into White Knight, whereby each share of Target will be exchanged for one share of White Knight. The merger closes on May 1, at which time Raider (like all other Target shareholder) receives White Knight shares in exchange for his Target stock. On June 1, Raider sells his White Knight stock on the open market for a total greater than he originally paid for the Target stock. Raider does not have any § 16(b) problem, because the overall transaction was essentially involuntary, and was of a type in which Raider almost certainly did not have access to inside information about White Knight's affairs.

E. **"Profit" computed:** If there is a covered purchase/sale or sale/purchase, the courts will compute the profit in a way that produces the ***maximum possible number***. In other words, the court takes the shares having the lowest purchase price and matches them against the shares having the highest sale price, ignoring any losses. [309]

CHAPTER 9

SHAREHOLDERS' SUITS

I. INTRODUCTION

A. **What is a derivative suit:** When a person who owes the corporation a fiduciary duty breaches the duty, the main remedy is the ***shareholder's derivative suit***. In a derivative suit, an individual shareholder (typically an outsider) brings suit ***in the name of the corporation***, against the individual wrongdoer. [318]

1. **Against insider:** A derivative suit may in theory be brought against some outside third party who has wronged the corporation, but is usually brought against an ***insider***, such as a director, officer or major shareholder. [318]

B. **Distinguish derivative from direct suit:** Not all suits by shareholders are derivative; in some situations, a shareholder (or class of shareholders) may sue the corporation, or insiders, ***directly***. [319]

1. **Illustration of derivative suits:** Most cases brought against insiders for breach of the fiduciary duties of ***care*** or ***loyalty*** are ***derivative***. Examples include: (1) suits against board members for failing to use due care; (2) suits against an officer for ***self-dealing***; (3) suits to recover ***excessive compensation*** paid to an officer; and (4) suits to reacquire a ***corporate opportunity*** usurped by an officer. [320]

2. **Illustration of direct actions:** Here are some of the types of suits generally held to be ***direct***: (1) an action to enforce the holder's ***voting rights***; (2) an action to compel the ***payment of dividends***; (3) an action to prevent management from improperly ***entrenching*** itself (e.g., to enjoin the enactment of a "poison pill" as an anti-takeover device); (4) a suit to prevent ***oppression*** of minority shareholders; and (5) a suit to compel ***inspection*** of the company's books and records. [320]

3. **Delaware law on the distinction:** Delaware has a simple ***two-part test*** for distinguishing between direct and derivative actions. In Delaware, the distinction turns solely on the two following questions:

   [1] who ***suffered the alleged harm*** (the corporation, or the suing stockholders individually)? and

   [2] who would ***receive the benefit*** of any recovery or other remedy (the corporation, or the stockholders individually)?

   a. **Summary:** So if the shareholders have suffered the harm (in a way that doesn't derive from harm to the corporation), and they would get the benefit of any recovery, the action is "direct." [320]

   b. **No need for "special injury":** Delaware now ***rejects*** its former "special injury" test, by which an action was derivative, not direct, unless the plaintiff shareholder(s) had an injury that was qualitatively different from that suffered by other shareholders. Now, as long as the injury is suffered by the shareholders alone — and does not derive from an injury to the corporation — the fact that *all* shareholders have been injured in the same way ***doesn't prevent*** the injury from being a direct one. [*Tooley v. Donaldson, Lufkin & Jenrette Inc.*] [320-321]

C. **Consequence of distinction:** Usually, the plaintiff will want his action to proceed as a ***direct*** rather than derivative suit. If the suit is direct, P gets the following benefits: (1) the procedural requirements are much simpler (e.g., he doesn't have to have owned stock at the time the wrong occurred); (2) he does not have to make a demand on the board of directors, or face having the action terminated early because the corporation does not want to pursue it; and (3) he can probably keep all or part of the recovery. [321]

CAPSULE SUMMARY

II. REQUIREMENTS FOR A DERIVATIVE SUIT

A. Summary: There are three main requirements that P must generally meet for a derivative suit: (1) he must have been a shareholder at the time the acts complained of occurred (the ***"contemporaneous ownership"*** rule); (2) he must ***still*** be a shareholder at the time of the suit; and (3) he must make a ***demand*** (unless excused) upon the board, requesting that the board attempt to obtain redress for the corporation. [322]

B. "Contemporaneous ownership": P must have owned his shares ***at the time of the transaction*** of which he complains. This is the ***"contemporaneous ownership"*** rule. [322]

1. **"Continuing wrong" exception:** An important exception is for "continuing wrongs" — P can sue to challenge a wrong that began before he bought his shares, but that continued after the purchase. [323]

2. **Who is a "shareholder":** P must have been a "shareholder" at the time of the wrong. It will be sufficient if he was a preferred shareholder, or held a convertible bond (convertible into the company's equity). Also, it will be enough that P is a "beneficial" owner even if he is not the owner of record. But a ***bond holder*** or other ordinary creditor may ***not*** bring a derivative suit. [322]

C. Continuing ownership: P must ***continue*** to own the shares not only until the time of suit, but until the moment of judgment. (But if P has lost his shareholder status because the corporation has engaged in a merger in which P was compelled to give up his shares, some courts excuse the continuing ownership requirement.) [323]

D. Demand on board: P must make a ***written demand*** on the board of directors before commencing the derivative suit. The demand asks the board to bring a suit or take other corrective action. Only if the board refuses to act may P then commence suit. (But often the demand is "excused," as is discussed below.) [324]

E. Demand on shareholders: Many states require P to also make a demand on the ***shareholders*** before instituting the derivative suit. But many other states do not impose this requirement, and even those states that do impose it often excuse it where it would be impractical. [324]

III. DEMAND ON BOARD; EARLY TERMINATION BASED ON BOARD OR COMMITTEE RECOMMENDATION

A. Demand excused: Demand on the board is ***excused*** where it would be ***"futile."*** In general, demand will be deemed to be futile (and thus excused) if the board is accused of having ***participated*** in the wrongdoing. [326]

1. **Delaware view:** In Delaware, demand will not be excused unless P carries the burden of showing a ***reasonable doubt*** about whether the board either: (1) was ***disinterested*** and ***independent***; or (2) was entitled to the protections of the ***business judgment*** rule (i.e., acted rationally after reasonable investigation and without self-dealing). [326]

   a. **Difficult to get:** But Delaware makes it very difficult for P to make either of these showings. For instance, he must plead facts showing either (1) or (2) with ***great specificity***. Also, it is usually not sufficient that P is charging the board with a violation of the duty of ***due care*** for approving the transaction; usually, a breach of the duty of ***loyalty*** by the board must be alleged with specificity.

2. **New York:** New York follows roughly the same rules as Delaware about when demand will be excused. In New York, demand will be excused if (and only if) the complaint alleges "with particularity" ***any*** of the following:

   [1] "that a ***majority of the board*** is ***interested*** in the challenged transaction." (A director can be "interested" either because she has a direct self-interest in the transaction, or because, although she has no direct self-interest in the transaction, she has lost her independence by being "controlled" by a self-interested director.)

   [2] that the board "***did not fully inform themselves*** about the challenged transaction to the extent reasonably appropriate under the circumstances." In other words, a director who merely "passively ***rubber-stamp[s]*** the decisions of the active managers" does ***not*** thereby exempt herself from liability.

   [3] that "the challenged transaction was so ***egregious on its face*** that it ***could not have been the product of sound business judgment*** of the directors."

   [*Marx v Akers*] [327]

B. **Demand required and refused:** If demand is required, and the board rejects the demand, the result depends in part on who the defendant is. [328]

   1. **Unaffiliated third party:** If the suit is against a ***third party*** who is not a corporate insider, P will almost never be permitted to continue his suit after the board has rejected it. [328]

   2. **Suit against insider:** Where (as is usually the case) the suit is against a corporate ***insider***, P has a better chance of having the board's refusal to pursue the suit be overridden by a court. But P will still have to show either that: (1) the board somehow ***participated*** in the alleged wrong; or (2) the directors who voted to reject the suit were ***dominated or controlled*** by the primary wrongdoer. (These requirements are similar to those needed to establish that demand is "excused," but it is usually somewhat easier to get the court to rule that the demand would be futile and therefore should be excused than to get the court to overturn the board's rejection of a required demand.) [328]

C. **Independent committee:** Today, the corporation usually responds to P's demand by appointing an ***independent committee*** of directors to study whether the suit should be pursued. Usually, the committee will conclude that the suit should ***not*** be pursued. Often, but not always, the court will give this committee recommendation the ***protection of the business judgment rule***, and will therefore ***terminate the action before trial***. [329]

   1. **New York view:** In New York, it is difficult for P to overcome the independent committee's recommendation that the suit be terminated. The court will reject the recommendation if P shows that the committee members were not in fact independent, or that they did not use reasonable procedures. But if the court is satisfied with the committee's independence and procedures, the court will ***not review the substantive merits*** of the committee's recommendation that the suit be dismissed. [330]

   2. **Delaware:** It is somewhat easier to get the court to disregard the committee's termination recommendation in ***Delaware***. Delaware courts take two steps: (1) First, the court asks whether the committee acted independently, in good faith, and with reasonable procedures. If the answer to any of these questions is "no," the court will allow the suit to proceed. (2) Even if the answer to all of these questions is "yes," the court may (but need not) apply its ***own***

independent business judgment about whether the suit should be permitted to proceed. (This second step will only be applied in "demand excused" cases.) [330]

a. Tough standard for independence in Delaware: Concern about whether the members of independent committees are really psychologically independent has led the Delaware courts to impose a ***heavy burden*** on the committee to demonstrate its members' independence. In Delaware, the committee "has the burden of establishing its own independence by a yardstick that must be 'like Caesar's wife' — ***'above reproach.'"*** *Beam ex rel. Martha Stewart Living Omnimedia, Inc. v. Stewart.* [332]

i. Social ties considered: Furthermore, the Delaware courts now ***consider social ties*** — not just direct financial ties — in deciding whether the committee members have carried their burden of showing that they are really independent of the persons whose conduct they are investigating. [*In Re Oracle Corp. Derivative Litigation*] [332]

Example: A derivative suit is brought against the several insiders of Oracle Corp., charging them with insider trading. Oracle appoints a Special Litigation Committee, consisting solely of two directors that Oracle says are independent. The SLC investigates, and finds that the suit is meritless and should be discontinued. But the plaintiff point out that both SLC members have jobs at Stanford (as professors), which two of the defendants attended. The SLC members and the defendants have other social ties as well (e.g., one SLC member supervised one defendant as a graduate student decades previously). Oracle asserts that (1) unless the SLC members were under the "domination and control" of a defendant or of the corporation, the members are automatically independent; and (2) because the SLC members were independent under this test, the SLC's conclusion that the action was meritless and should be discontinued must be followed by the court.

Held, for the plaintiffs. The court rejects the defendants' "domination and control" test, and will consider social ties between the SLC members and the defendants in deciding whether the SLC members are independent of the defendants. Here, those social ties were so extensive that the SLC members were not independent, so the SLC's dismissal recommendation won't be accorded any deference by the court, and the suit will go forward. [*In Re Oracle Corp., supra.*]

3. More liberal view: A few courts are even more willing than the Delaware courts to ignore the committee's recommendation of termination. Such courts believe that even a committee of ostensibly "independent" directors will for structural reasons rarely recommend a suit against insiders, so that the committee should be viewed as biased. In a few states, the solution is a ***court-appointed committee*** of non-directors, whose recommendation the court will accept. [331]

4. MBCA: Under the MBCA, the court must dismiss the action if the committee of independent directors votes to discontinue the action "in ***good faith*** after conducting a ***reasonable inquiry*** upon which [the committee's] conclusions are based." MBCA § 7.44(a). So the court under the MBCA will almost never review the substantive merits of the suit if the independent directors vote to discontinue. [335]

IV. SECURITY-FOR-EXPENSES STATUTES

A. Generally: About 14 states have so-called ***"security-for-expenses"*** statutes, by which P must post a ***bond*** to guarantee repayment of the corporation's expenses in the event that P's claim turns out to be without merit. [336]

B. Not substantial impediment: But such statutes do not usually serve as much of an impediment to the bringing of suits, mostly because the corporation often doesn't take advantage of them for various tactical reasons. [336]

V. SETTLEMENT OF DERIVATIVE SUITS

A. Judicial approval: Most states require that any ***settlement*** of a derivative suit be ***approved by the court***. The court must be convinced that the settlement is in the best interests of the corporation and its shareholders. [337]

1. **Factors:** When the court decides whether to approve the settlement, the most important factor is usually the relation between the size of the net financial benefit to the corporation under the settlement and the probable net benefit if the case were tried. [338]

B. Notice: In the federal courts and in many states, shareholders must be given ***notice*** of any proposed settlement of a derivative action, as well as the opportunity to ***intervene*** in the action to oppose the settlement.

C. Corporate recovery: All payments made in connection with the derivative action must be ***received by the corporation***, not by the plaintiff. [339]

VI. PLAINTIFF'S ATTORNEY'S FEES

A. "Common fund" theory: Courts usually award the plaintiff's attorneys a reasonable ***fee*** for bringing a successful derivative action. Under the ***"common fund"*** theory, the fee is paid out of the amount recovered on behalf of the corporation. [340]

B. Calculation of fee: There are two main approaches to calculating the amount of the fee:

1. **"Lodestar" method:** Under the ***"lodestar"*** method, the key component is the ***reasonable value of the time*** expended by the plaintiff's attorney. This is computed by taking the actual number of hours expended, and multiplying by a reasonable hourly fee. Often, the award is then adjusted upward to reflect the fact that there was a substantial contingency aspect to the case. [340]

2. **"Salvage value" approach:** The other approach is the ***"salvage value"*** approach. Here, the court calculates fees by awarding a percentage of the total recovery (usually in the range of 20-30%). [340]

3. **Combination method:** Some courts combine the two techniques: they begin with the lodestar computation, but set a particular percentage of the recovery as a ***ceiling*** on the fee. [340]

VII. WHO GETS TO RECOVER

A. Pro rata recovery: Usually, the corporation will make the recovery. But occasionally this will be unjust, so the court may order that some or all of the recovery be distributed to ***individual***

shareholders on a ***pro rata basis*** (i.e., proportionally to their shareholdings). Here are two situations where this might be done: [341]

1. **Wrongdoers in control:** Where the alleged wrongdoers remain in substantial ***control*** of the corporation (so that if a recovery were paid to the corporation, it might be diverted once again by the same wrongdoers). [341]

2. **Aiding and abetting:** Where most of the shares are in the hands of people who in some sense ***aided and abetted*** the wrongdoing. [341]

VIII. INDEMNIFICATION AND D&O INSURANCE

A. **Indemnification:** All states have statutes dealing with when the corporation may (and/or must) ***indemnify*** a director or officer against losses he incurs by virtue of his corporate duties. [342]

1. **Mandatory:** Under most statutes, in two situations the corporation is ***required*** to indemnify an officer or director: (1) when the director/officer is completely ***successful*** in defending himself against the charges; and (2) when the corporation has previously bound itself by charter, law or ***contract*** to indemnify. [342]

2. **Permissive:** Nearly all states, in addition to this mandatory indemnification, allow for ***"permissive"*** indemnification. In other words, in a large range of circumstances the corporation ***may***, but need not, indemnify the director or officer. [344]

   a. **Third party suits:** In suits brought by a ***third party*** (in other words, suits not brought by the corporation or by a shareholder suing derivatively), the corporation is permitted to indemnify the director or officer if the latter: (1) acted in ***good faith***; (2) was pursuing what he reasonably believed to be the ***best interests of the corporation***; and (3) had no reason to believe that his conduct was ***unlawful***. See MBCA § 8.51(a). (*Example*: D, a director of XYZ, acts grossly negligently, but not dishonestly, when he approves a particular corporate transaction. XYZ may, but need not, indemnify D for his expenses in defending a suit brought by an unaffiliated third person against D, and for any judgment or settlement D may pay.)

   b. **Derivative suit:** If the suit is brought by or on behalf of the corporation (e.g., a ***derivative*** suit), the indemnification rules are ***stricter***. The corporation may ***not*** indemnify the director or officer for a ***judgment*** on behalf of the corporation, or for a ***settlement*** payment. But indemnification for litigation ***expenses*** (including attorney's fees) is allowed, if D is not found liable on the underlying claim by a court.

   c. **Fines and penalties:** D may be indemnified for a ***fine*** or ***penalty*** he has to pay, unless: (1) he knew or had reason to believe that his conduct was ***unlawful***; or (2) the deterrent function of the statute would be frustrated by indemnification.

3. **Who decides:** Typically, the decision on whether D should be indemnified is made by ***independent members*** of the board of directors. Also, this decision is sometimes made by independent legal counsel. [347]

4. **Advancing of expenses:** Most states allow the corporation to ***advance*** to the director or officer money for counsel fees and other expenses as the action proceeds. The director or officer must generally promise to ***repay*** the advances if he is ultimately found not entitled to indemnification (but usually need not make a showing of financial ability to make the repayment). [347]

5. **Court-ordered:** Most states allow D to ***petition the court*** for indemnification, even under circumstances where the corporation is not permitted, or not willing, to make the payment voluntarily. [348]

B. **Insurance:** Nearly all large companies today carry directors' and officers' (D&O) ***liability insurance***. Most states explicitly allow the corporation to purchase such insurance. Furthermore, D&O insurance may cover certain director's or officer's expenses even where those expenses ***could not be indemnified***. [348]

1. **Typical policy:** The typical policy ***excludes*** many types of claims (e.g., a claim that the director or officer acted dishonestly, received illegal compensation, engaged in self-dealing, etc.). [348]

2. **Practical effect:** Insurance will often cover an expense that could not be indemnified by the corporation. For instance, money paid to the corporation as a judgment or settlement in a ***derivative*** action can usually be reimbursed to the director or officer under the D&O policy. [349]

CHAPTER 10

STRUCTURAL CHANGES, INCLUDING MERGERS AND ACQUISITIONS

I. CORPORATE COMBINATIONS GENERALLY

Note: For the entire following discussion, the business that is being acquired is referred to as "Little Corp" and the acquirer is "Big Corp."

A. **Merger-type deals:** A "merger-type" transaction is one in which the shareholders of Little Corp will end up mainly with ***stock in Big Corp*** as their payment for surrendering control of Little Corp and its assets. There are four main structures for a merger-type deal: [360]

1. **Statutory:** First is the traditional ***"statutory merger."*** By following procedures set out in the state corporation statute, one corporation can merge into another, with the former (the ***"disappearing"*** corporation) ceasing to have any legal identity, and the latter (the ***"surviving"*** corporation) continuing in existence. [360]

a. **Consequence:** After the merger, Big Corp owns all of Little Corp's assets, and is ***responsible for all of Little Corp's liabilities.*** All contracts that Little Corp had with third parties now become contracts between the third party and Big Corp. The shareholders of Little Corp now (at least in the usual case) own stock in Big Corp. (Alternatively, under many statutory merger provisions, Little Corp holders may receive some or all of their payment in the form of ***cash*** or Big Corp debt, rather than Big Corp stock.)

2. **Stock-for-stock exchange ("stock swap"):** The second method is the ***"stock-for-stock exchange"*** or ***"stock swap."*** Here, Big Corp makes a separate deal with each Little Corp holder, giving the holder Big Corp stock in return for his Little Corp stock. [361]

a. **Plan of exchange:** Under the standard stock swap, a Little Corp holder need not participate, in which case he continues to own a stake in Little Corp. However, some states allow Little Corp to enact (by approval of directors and a majority of shareholders) a ***"plan of exchange,"*** under which all Little Corp shareholders are ***required*** to exchange their shares for Big Corp shares. When this happens, the net result is like a statutory merger.

3. **Stock-for-assets exchange:** The third form is the ***"stock-for-assets" exchange***. In step one, Big Corp gives stock to Little Corp, and Little Corp transfers substantially all of its assets to Big Corp. In step two (which usually but not necessarily follows), Little Corp dissolves, and distributes the Big Corp stock to its own shareholders. After the second step, the net result is virtually the same as with a statutory merger. [363] (However, approval by Big Corp shareholders might not be necessary, as it probably would for a statutory merger.)

4. **Triangular or subsidiary mergers:** Finally, we have the ***"triangular"*** or ***"subsidiary"*** merger. [364]

   a. **Forward triangular merger:** In the "conventional" or ***"forward"*** triangular merger, the acquirer creates a subsidiary for the purpose of the transaction. Usually, this subsidiary has no assets except shares of stock in the parent. ***The target is then merged into the acquirer's subsidiary.*** (*Example*: Big Corp creates a subsidiary called Big-Sub. Big transfers 1,000 of its own shares to Big-Sub, in return for all the shares of Big-Sub. Little Corp now merges into Big-Sub. Little Corp shareholders receive the shares in Big Corp.)

      i. **Rationale:** This is very similar to the stock-for-stock exchange, except that all minority interests in Little Corp is automatically eliminated. (Also, the deal ***does not have to be approved by Big Corp's shareholders,*** unlike a direct merger of Little Corp into Big Corp.)

   b. **Reverse merger:** The other type of triangular merger is the ***"reverse"*** triangular merger. This is the same as the forward triangular merger, except that the acquirer's subsidiary ***merges into the target***, rather than having the target merge into the subsidiary. (*Example*: Same facts as above example, except Big-Sub merges into Little Corp, so that Little Corp is now a surviving corporation that is itself a subsidiary of Big Corp.)

      i. **Advantages:** This reverse triangular form is better than a stock-for-stock swap because it automatically eliminates all Little Corp shareholders, which the stock-for-stock swap does not. It is better than a simple merger of Little Corp into Big Corp because: (1) Big Corp does not assume all of Little Corp's liabilities; and (2) Big Corp's shareholders do not have to approve. It is better than the forward triangular merger because Little Corp survives as an entity, thus possibly preserving contract rights and tax advantages better than if Little Corp were to disappear.

B. **Sale-type transactions:** A ***"sale-type"*** transaction is one in which the Little Corp shareholders receive cash or bonds, rather than Big Corp stock, in return for their interest in Little Corp. There are two main sale-type structures: [369]

1. **Asset-sale-and-liquidation:** First, there is the "***asset-sale-and-liquidation.***" Here, Little Corp's board approves a sale of all or substantially all of Little Corp's assets to Big Corp, and the proposed sale is approved by a majority of Little Corp's shareholders. Little Corp conveys its assets to Big Corp, and Little Corp receives cash (or perhaps Big Corp debt) from Big Corp. Usually, Little Corp will then dissolve, and pay the cash or debt to its shareholders in proportion to their shareholdings, in a ***liquidating distribution***. [370]

2. **Stock sale:** Second is the ***"stock sale."*** Here, no corporate level transaction takes place on the Little Corp side. Instead, Big Corp buys stock from each Little Corp shareholder, for cash or debt. (After Big Corp controls all or a majority of Little Corp's stock, it may but need not

cause Little Corp to be: (1) dissolved, with its assets distributed to the various stockholders or (2) merged into Big Corp, with the remaining Little holders receiving Big Corp stock, cash or debt.) [370]

a. **Tender offer:** One common form of stock sale is the ***tender offer***, in which Big Corp publicly announces that it will buy all or a majority of shares offered to it by Little Corp shareholders. (Alternatively, Big Corp might ***privately negotiate*** purchases from some or all of Little Corp's shareholders.)

3. **Differences:** Here are the big differences between the asset-sale and the stock-sale techniques: [371]

a. **Corporate action by target:** The asset sale requires ***corporate action*** by Little Corp, and the stock sale does not. Thus Little Corp's ***board must approve*** an asset sale but need not approve a stock sale.

b. **Shareholder vote:** Similarly, the asset sale will have to be formally approved by a majority vote of Little Corp's ***shareholders***, whereas the stock sale will not be subjected to a shareholder vote (each Little Corp shareholder simply decides whether to tender his stock).

c. **Elimination of minority stockholders:** In an asset-sale deal, Big Corp is guaranteed to get Little Corp's business without any remaining interest on the part of Little Corp shareholders. In the stock sale, Big Corp may be left with some Little Corp holders holding a ***minority interest*** in Little Corp (though if the state allows for a "plan of exchange," this minority may be eliminated).

d. **Liabilities:** In an asset sale, Big Corp has a good chance of escaping Little Corp's ***liabilities*** (subject, however, to the law of fraudulent transfers, the bulk sales provisions of the UCC, and the possible use of the "de facto merger" doctrine). In a stock sale, Big Corp will effectively take Little Corp's liabilities along with its assets, whether it wants to or not.

e. **Tax treatment:** There are important tax differences between the two forms. In general, the tax treatment of an asset sale is much less favorable for the seller than is a stock sale. See below.

C. **Approvals for sale-type deals:**

1. **Asset sale:** In the case of an ***asset sale***, here is how the approvals work: [376]

a. **Target side:** On the Little Corp side: (1) Little's board of directors must approve; and (2) (in most states) Little's shareholders must approve by a ***majority*** of all votes that ***could be*** cast, not just a majority of the votes actually cast. (But the MBCA requires just a majority of the shares actually voting, assuming a quorum is present.) [376]

i. **The "substantially all assets" test:** Not every sale of assets triggers this obligation. Under most statutes, the shareholder approval is required only if all or ***"substantially all"*** of Little's assets are being sold. (Under the MBCA, approval is required if Little would be left "without a significant continuing business activity.") [375]

b. **Acquirer side:** On the Big Corp side of the asset-sale transaction: (1) the Big Corp board must approve; but (2) the Big Corp ***shareholders*** need ***not*** approve.

2. **Stock sale:** In the case of a ***stock sale***, each Little Corp stockholder would decide whether to sell his stock to Big Corp, and no approval by Little's board (or any formal vote of Little's stockholders) is necessary for some or all of Little's stockholders to do this. [376]

   a. **Back-end merger:** On the other hand, once Big got control of Little by having acquired most of Little's shares, it might want to conduct a ***back-end merger*** of Little into Big (or into a subsidiary of Bid), and this would normally require a vote by Little's board and shareholders. But each of these votes would probably be a formality, due to Big's majority ownership and board control of Little.

D. **Approval for merger-type deals:** Here is how approvals work for ***merger-type*** deals:

1. **Statutory merger:** In a traditional ***statutory*** merger: [378]

   a. **Board approval:** The boards of directors of both Big (the survivor) and Little (the disappearing corporation) must approve.

   b. **Holders of target:** The shareholders of Little Corp must approve by majority vote of the shares permitted to vote (except in a short-form merger, as discussed below).

   c. **Holders of survivor:** The shareholders of Big Corp also must approve by majority vote (except in the case of a "whale/minnow" merger, see below).

   d. **Classes:** Under many statutes, if there are ***different classes*** of stock on either the Big Corp or Little Corp side, each class must ***separately approve*** the merger.

   e. **Small-scale ("whale/minnow") mergers:** If a corporation is being merged into a ***much larger*** corporation, the shareholders of the surviving corporation usually ***need not approve***. Under Delaware law and under the MBCA, any merger that does not increase the outstanding shares of the surviving corporation by ***more than 20%*** need not be approved by the survivor's shareholders. (But this assumes that there are enough ***authorized but unissued*** shares to fund the merger; if the number of authorized shares must be increased, this will usually require a shareholder vote to amend the articles of incorporation.)

   f. **Short-form mergers:** Under most statutes, including Delaware and the MBCA, if one corporation owns ***90% or more*** of the stock of another, the latter may be merged into the former ***without approval*** by the shareholders of ***either*** corporation. (*Example*: Big Corp owns 92% of Little Corp shares. Under the Delaware or MBCA short-form merger statute, Little Corp may be merged into Big Corp, and the 8% minority shareholders of Little Corp given stock in Big Corp, or cash, without any shareholder approval by either the Big or Little shareholders. But Little Corp shareholders will have appraisal rights, described below.)

2. **Hybrids:** Here is how approvals work for "hybrid" transactions, i.e., those that are ***"merger-type"*** but not pure statutory mergers: [381]

   a. **Stock-for-stock exchange:** In a ***stock-for-stock exchange***, the proposal: (1) must be approved by the Big Corp board but ***not*** by its shareholders; and (2) need not be formally approved by either Little Corp's board or its shareholders (though in a sense each shareholder "votes" by deciding whether to tender his shares).

   b. **Stock-for-assets deal:** In the case of a stock-for-assets deal: (1) on the Big Corp side, board approval is necessary but shareholder approval is not (as long as there are enough authorized but unissued shares to fund the transaction); and (2) on the Little Corp side, this is like any other asset sale, so Little's board must approve the transaction, and a majority of shareholders must then approve it.

c. **Triangular mergers:**

i. **Forward merger:** In a ***forward*** triangular (or "subsidiary") merger: (1) Big-Sub's board and shareholders must approve (but this is a formality, since Big Corp will cast both of these votes, and Big Corp's board (but not its shareholders) must also approve; and (2) on the Little Corp side, both the board and shareholders will have to approve the merger, just as with any other merger.

ii. **Reverse merger:** In the case of a ***reverse*** triangular merger, essentially the same board and shareholder approvals are needed as for the forward merger.

E. **Taxation:** Merger-type transactions are ***taxed*** quite differently from sale-type transactions. [383]

1. **Reorganizations:** What we have called ***"merger-type"*** transactions are called ***"reorganizations"*** by the tax law. In general, in a reorganization the target's shareholders ***pay no tax*** at the time of the merger. (*Example*: Little Corp is merged into Big Corp, with each Little Corp shareholder receiving one Big Corp share for each Little Corp share. The Little Corp shareholders will not pay any tax until they eventually sell their Big Corp shares, at which time they will pay tax on the difference between what they receive for the Big Corp shares and what they originally paid for the Little Corp shares.) There are three different types of tax-free reorganizations: [384]

a. **"Type A" reorganization:** A "type A" reorganization is one carried out according to state ***statutory merger*** provisions. The principal requirement is that the Little Corp shareholders have a ***"continuity of interest,"*** i.e., that most of the compensation they receive be in the form of Big Corp stock.

b. **"Type B" reorganization:** A "type B" reorganization is a ***stock-for-stock exchange.*** To qualify as a type B deal, Big Corp must end up with ***at least 80%*** of the voting power in Little Corp, and must not give Little Corp shareholders anything other than its own stock (e.g., it may not give any cash).

c. **"Type C" reorganization:** A "type C" reorganization is basically a stock-for-assets exchange. Big Corp must acquire ***substantially all*** of Little Corp's assets, in return for Big Corp stock. (But Big Corp may make part of the payment in ***cash*** or bonds, so long as ***at least 80% of the acquisition price*** is in the form of Big Corp stock.)

2. **Sale-type transactions:** If the transaction is a ***sale-type*** one (i.e., it is not a "reorganization"), here is how it is taxed: [387]

a. **Asset sale:** In an ***asset sale***, the target pays a corporate-level tax; then, if it dissolves and pays out the cash received in the sale to its own shareholders as a liquidating distribution, the target share holders each must pay a tax on the distribution. (*Example*: Big Corp buys all of Little Corp's assets for $1 million cash. Little Corp will pay a tax on the amount by which this $1 million exceeds the original cost of Little Corp's assets. If the remainder is paid out in the form of a liquidating distribution to Little Corp shareholders, each shareholder will pay a tax based on the difference between what he receives and what he originally paid for his Little Corp shares.)

b. **Sale of stock:** In a ***stock*** sale, there is only ***one level*** of taxation, at the shareholder level. (*Example*: Some or all Little Corp shareholders sell their stock to Big Corp. Each shareholder pays a tax on the difference between what he receives per share and what he originally paid per share.) This tax is less, typically, than the combined two levels of tax in the case of an asset sale.

i. **Buyer dislikes:** But the tax consequences on the *buyer's* side are less attractive than in the asset-sale situation. Thus ***the buyer will always want an asset sale and the seller will always want a stock sale***.

F. **Federal securities law:** Here are the federal ***securities-law*** implications of the various types of combinations: [389]

1. **Sale-type transactions:** [389]

a. **Asset sales:** If Big Corp is acquiring Little Corp's assets for cash, and Little Corp is publicly held, the only federal securities laws that are relevant are the ***proxy*** rules. Little Corp will have to send its holders a proxy statement describing the proposed transaction, so that the holders may intelligently decide whether to approve.

b. **Stock sale:** If there will be a sale of stock by each Little Corp shareholder to Big Corp, Big Corp will usually proceed by a tender offer. If so, it will have to send special tender offer documents to each Little Corp shareholder.

2. **Merger-type deals:** [389]

a. **Stock-for-stock exchange:** If the deal will be a ***stock-for-stock exchange***, for securities-law purposes this is the equivalent of public issue of stock by the acquirer. Thus if Big Corp will be acquiring each Little Corp share in exchange for a share of Big Corp, Big will have to file a ***registration statement*** and supply each Little Corp shareholder with a prospectus. Also, the tender offer requirements will generally have to be complied with.

b. **Statutory merger; stock-for-assets deal:** If the deal will be a ***statutory merger*** or a ***stock-for-assets exchange***: (1) Little Corp will have to send each shareholder a proxy statement to get the shareholder's approval; and (2) Big Corp must file a registration statement and supply a prospectus, as if it were issuing new stock to Little Corp's shareholders.

II. CORPORATE COMBINATIONS — PROTECTING SHAREHOLDERS

A. **Appraisal rights:** ***Appraisal rights*** give a dissatisfied shareholder in certain circumstances a way to be "cashed out" of his investment at a price ***determined by a court*** to be fair. [394]

1. **Mergers:** In nearly every state, a shareholder of either company involved in a ***merger*** has appraisal rights if he had the right to ***vote*** on the merger. (*Example*: Little Corp merges into Big Corp. Any shareholder of either Big Corp or Little Corp who had the right to vote on the merger will in most states have appraisal rights.) [394]

a. **Whale-minnow:** In the ***"whale-minnow"*** situation — that is, a merger in which a corporation is merged into a much larger one, so that the increase in outstanding shares of the larger company is small — the surviving corporation's shareholders do ***not*** get appraisal rights (since they would not get to vote).

b. **Short-form merger:** But shareholders of the ***subsidiary*** in a ***short-form merger*** get appraisal rights even though they would not get to vote on the merger.

2. **Asset sales:** In most states shareholders of a corporation that is ***selling substantially all of its assets*** also get appraisal rights. [397]

   a. **Sale for cash, followed by quick dissolution:** But if the selling corporation liquidates soon after the sale, and ***distributes the cash*** to the shareholders, usually there are no appraisal rights. See, e.g., MBCA § 13.02(a)(3) (no appraisal rights where liquidation and distribution of cash proceeds occurs within one year after the sale).

   b. **Delaware:** Delaware does ***not*** give appraisal rights to the stockholders of a corporation that sells its assets.

3. **Publicly-traded exception:** Many states deny the appraisal remedy to shareholders of a company whose stock is ***publicly traded***. So does the MBCA, in most situations. [398]

4. **Triangular mergers:** [399]

   a. **Forward:** In the case of a ***forward*** triangular merger: (1) on the acquirer's side, Big Corp's shareholders will not get appraisal rights; and (2) on the target's side, Little Corp's shareholders generally ***will*** get appraisal rights. [399]

   b. **Reverse:** In the case of a ***reverse*** triangular merger: (1) Big Corp shareholders do not get appraisal rights; and (2) Little Corp holders will get appraisal rights if Big-Sub is statutorily merging into Little Corp, but not if Little Corp is issuing its own stock in return for Big-Sub's stock in Big Corp.

5. **Procedures:** Here are the usual procedures for appraisal:

   a. **Notice:** At the time the merger or sale transaction is announced, the corporation must notify the shareholder that he has appraisal rights.

   b. **Notice of payment demand by holder:** The holder must then give ***notice*** to the corporation, ***before the shareholder vote***, that he demands payment of the fair value of his shares. Also, the holder must ***not vote*** his shares in favor of the transaction.

   c. **Deposit of shares:** Early in the process (in some states, before the vote is even held), the holder must ***deposit his shares*** with the company.

   d. **Payment:** Then, the company's obligations vary from state to state. In some states, the corporation does not have to pay anything until the court finally determines what is due. But under the MBCA, the corporation must at least pay the amount that *it* concedes is the fair value of the shares (with the rest due only after a court decision as to fair value).

6. **Valuation:** The court then determines the ***"fair value"*** of the dissenter's shares, and the corporation must pay this value. [401]

   a. **Don't consider the transaction itself:** Fair value must be determined ***without reference*** to the transaction that triggers the appraisal rights. (*Example*: Little Corp is worth $10 per share in the absence of any takeover attempt. Big Corp, recognizing possible synergies with its own business, acquires Little Corp for $15 per share. For appraisal purposes, the fair value of Little Corp stock will be $10, not the higher $15 price that reflects the benefits of the acquisition.)

   b. **No "minority" or "nonmarketability" discount:** Most courts do not reduce the value of P's shares to reflect that P held a minority or non-controlling interest. Instead, the court usually takes the value of the whole company, and then divides by the number of shares (so P, even though she is a minority holder, gets the same per-share price as the insiders would have gotten.) See, e.g., *In Re Valuation of Common Stock of McLoon Oil Co.*

c. **"Delaware block" method:** Most courts use the "Delaware block" valuation method. Under this, the court considers three factors: (1) the ***market price*** just prior to the transaction; (2) the ***net asset value*** of the company; and (3) the ***earnings valuation*** of the company. These three factors can be weighted however the court chooses.

i. **Abandoned in Delaware:** Delaware itself no longer requires use of the Delaware block approach. Delaware courts will now accept additional evidence of valuation, such as valuation studies prepared by the corporation, and expert testimony about what "takeover premium" would be paid.

7. **Exclusivity:** Appraisal rights are the ***exclusive*** remedy available to an unhappy shareholder in some, but not all, circumstances. [404]

a. **Illegality:** If the transaction is ***illegal***, or ***procedural requirements*** have not been observed, the shareholder can generally get the transaction ***enjoined***, instead of having to be content with his appraisal rights.

b. **Deception:** Similarly, if the company ***deceives*** its shareholders and thereby procures their approval of the transaction, a shareholder can attack the transaction instead of having to use his appraisal rights.

c. **Unfair:** On the other hand, if the shareholder is merely contending that the proposed transaction is a ***bad deal*** for the shareholders, or is in a sense ***"unfair,"*** appraisal normally *is* the exclusive remedy (and the shareholder cannot get an injunction). But if unfairness is due to ***self-dealing*** by corporate insiders, the court may grant an injunction.

B. **"De facto merger" doctrine:** Under the ***"de facto merger"*** doctrine, the court treats a transaction which is not literally a merger, but which is the functional equivalent of a merger, as if it were one. The most common result of the doctrine is that selling stockholders get ***appraisal rights***. Also, selling stockholders may get the right to vote on a transaction, and the seller's creditors may get a claim against the buyer. [405]

1. **Only occasionally accepted:** Only a few courts have accepted the de facto merger theory, and they have done so only in specialized circumstances. They are most likely to do so when the target has transferred all of its assets and then dissolves, and when the target's shareholders receive most of their consideration as shares in the acquirer rather than cash and/or bonds. [406]

Example: Glen Alden Corp. agrees to acquire all of the assets of List Corp. (a much larger company). Glen Alden plans to pay for these assets by issuing a large amount of its own stock to List (so that List will end up owning over three-quarters of Glen Alden). Glen Alden will assume all of List's liabilities, and will change its name to List Alden Corp. List will then be dissolved, and its assets (stock representing a majority interest in List Alden) will be distributed to the original List shareholders. (The purpose of this bizarre structure is to deny the shareholders of Glen Alden appraisal rights, which they would have if Glen Alden was selling all of its assets to List, but will not have if Glen Alden "bought" List.)

Held, this transaction was a de facto merger, so Glen Alden's shareholders have appraisal rights. See *Farris v. Glen Alden Corp.*

2. **Usually rejected:** Most courts, including most notably Delaware, ***reject*** the de facto doctrine. [407]

3. **Successor liability:** But even courts that normally reject the de facto merger doctrine may apply it (or something like it) to deal with problems of ***"successor liability."*** (*Example:* Big Corp acquires the assets of Little Corp, and carries on Little Corp's business. Normally, Little Corp's liabilities will not pass to Big Corp unless Big Corp has explicitly assumed them in the purchase contract. But a tort claimant who is injured by a product manufactured by Little Corp before the sale might be permitted to recover against Big Corp, on the theory that Big Corp should be treated as if Little Corp had merged into it.) [408]

C. **Judicial review of substantive fairness:** Courts will sometimes review the ***substantive fairness*** of a proposed acquisition or merger. This is much more likely when there is a strong self-dealing aspect to the transaction. [408]

1. **Arm's length combination:** If the buyer and the seller do ***not have a close pre-existing relationship*** at the time they negotiate the deal, courts will rarely overturn the transaction as being substantively unfair. For instance, under Delaware law a person who attacks the transaction for substantive fairness must: (1) bear the ***burden of proof*** on the fairness issue; and (2) show that the price was so ***grossly inadequate*** as to amount to ***"constructive fraud."*** P will rarely be able to satisfy this double-barreled test. [408]

2. **Self-dealing:** But if the transaction involves ***self-dealing*** (i.e., one or more insiders influence both sides of the transaction), the court will give much stricter scrutiny. For instance, in Delaware, the proponents of the transaction must demonstrate its ***"entire fairness."*** [410]

   a. **Two-step acquisition:** This test is applied in ***two-step acquisitions***.

   Example: Big Corp attempts to acquire Little Corp by means of a two-step hostile tender offer. Big Corp first buys 51% of Little Corp stock for $35 per share. As the second step, it then seeks to merge Little Corp into Big Corp, with the remaining Little Corp shareholders receiving $25 per share. (In the original tender offer, it announces that it plans to take the second step if the first step succeeds.) An unhappy Little Corp shareholder might (but probably would not) succeed in getting a court to enjoin this second-step "back end merger" on the grounds that it is substantively unfair. (The court would probably scrutinize the transaction fairly closely, but uphold it on the grounds that all shareholders were treated equally and knew what they were getting into.)

   b. **Parent-subsidiary:** Similarly, the court will take a close look for possible self-dealing where the transaction is a ***parent-subsidiary merger***.

   Example: ABC Corp owns 80% of XYZ Corp (with the rest owned by a variety of small public shareholders). Most XYZ directors have been appointed by ABC. ABC proposes to have XYZ merge into it, with each XYZ share being exchanged for one share of ABC. Nearly all of the public XYZ minority holders oppose the merger, but ABC's 80% ownership allows the merger to be approved by a majority of all XYZ holders. A court would be likely to closely scrutinize this merger, because ABC's dominance of XYZ (and its ability to persuade the XYZ board to approve the transaction) amounted to self-dealing. Therefore, ABC will bear the burden of demonstrating that the merger terms are "entirely fair" to the minority holders of XYZ, and the court will enjoin the transaction if this showing is not made. (ABC could guard against this problem by having XYZ negotiate its side of the merger by the use of only "independent" directors, i.e., those not dominated by ABC.)

III. RECAPITALIZATIONS — HURTING THE PREFERRED SHAREHOLDERS

A. Problem: A board of directors dominated by common shareholders (as is usually the case) may try to help the common shareholders at the expense of the ***preferred*** shareholders. Typically, the common shareholders try to cancel an arrearage in preferred dividends, so that the common holders can receive a dividend. [415]

B. Two methods: There are two basic recapitalization methods by which the common shareholders can attempt to eliminate the accrued preferred dividends: [415]

1. **Amending articles:** First, they can cause the articles of incorporation to be ***amended*** to eliminate the accrued dividends as a corporate obligation. (But in most states, the preferred shareholders will have to agree ***as a separate class*** that this amendment should take place. See MBCA § 10.04(a)(8).) [416]

2. **Merger:** Second, the corporation can be ***merged*** into another corporation, with the survivor's articles not providing for payment of any accrued preferred dividends. (Again, in most states the preferred get to vote on the merger as a separate class. But under Delaware law, the preferred would not have this right.) [417]

C. Courts don't interfere: Courts are generally very ***reluctant*** to interfere with such anti-preferred recapitalizations, even where the plans seems to be objectively unfair to the preferred holders. But in addition to possible veto rights, the preferred holders will also generally get ***appraisal rights***. [417]

IV. FREEZEOUTS

A. Meaning of "freezeout": A "freezeout" is a transaction in which those in control of a corporation ***eliminate the equity ownership*** of the non-controlling shareholders. [419]

1. **Distinguished from "squeezeout":** Generally, "freezeout" describes those techniques whereby the controlling shareholders ***legally compel*** the non-controlling holders to give up their common stock ownership. The related term "squeezeout" describes methods that do not legally compel the outsiders to give up their shares, but in a practical sense coerce them into doing so. Squeezeouts are especially common in the close-corporation context, and are discussed briefly below. [419]

2. **Three contexts:** There are three common ***contexts*** in which a freezeout is likely to occur: (1) as the second step of a ***two-step acquisition*** transaction (Big Corp buys, say, 51% of Little Corp stock, and then eliminates the remaining 49% holders through some sort of merger); (2) where two ***long-term affiliates merge*** (the controlling parent eliminates the publicly-held minority interest in the subsidiary); and (3) where the company ***"goes private"*** (the insiders cause the corporation or its underlying business to no longer to be registered with the SEC, listed on a stock exchange and/or actively traded over the counter). [419]

3. **General rule:** In evaluating a freezeout, the court will usually: (1) try to verify that the transaction is basically ***fair***; and (2) scrutinize the transaction especially closely in view of the fact that the minority holders are being cashed out (as opposed to being given stock in a different entity, such as the acquirer). [420]

B. Techniques for carrying out a freezeout:

1. **Cash-out merger:** The leading freezeout technique today is the simple ***"cash-out" merger***. The insider causes the corporation to merge into a well-funded shell, and the minority holders are paid cash in exchange for their shares, in an amount determined by the insiders. [420]

   Example: Shark owns 70% of Public Corp. He wants to freeze out the minority holders. He creates Private Corp, of which he is the sole shareholder, and funds it with $1 million. He now causes both Public Corp and Private Corp to agree to a plan of merger under which each of Public's 1,000,000 shares will be exchanged in the merger for $1 in cash. The 30% minority holders in Public are completely eliminated by the $300,000 cash payments, and Shark receives $700,000 with which to pay down the bank debt that funded Private Corp in the first place. Such a "cash out" merger is allowed by most modern merger statutes, including MBCA § 11.01(b)(3).)

2. **Short-form merger:** A freezeout may also be done via the ***short-form*** merger statute. If ABC Corp owns 90% or more of XYZ Corp, then in most states at ABC's request, XYZ can be merged into ABC with all XYZ holders paid off in cash (rather than ABC stock). [421]

3. **Reverse stock split:** Finally, a freezeout may be carried out by means of a ***reverse stock split***. Using, say, a 600:1 reverse stock split, nearly all outsiders may end up with a fractional share. Then, the corporation can compel the owners of the fractional shares to exchange their shares for cash. [422]

CAPSULE SUMMARY

C. Federal law on freezeouts:

1. **10b-5:** A minority shareholder may be able to attack a freezeout on the grounds that it violates SEC Rule 10b-5. If there has been ***full disclosure***, then P is unlikely to convince the court that 10b-5 has been violated, no matter how "unfair" the freezeout may seem to the court. But if the insiders have concealed or ***misrepresented*** material facts about the transaction, then a court may find a 10b-5 violation. [423]

2. **SEC Rule 13e-3:** Also, SEC Rule 13e-3 requires extensive disclosure by the insiders in the case of any ***going-private*** transaction. If the insiders do not comply with 13e-3, they may be liable for damages or an injunction. [424]

D. State law: A successful attack on a freezeout transaction is more likely to derive from ***state*** rather than federal law. Since a freezeout transaction will usually involve self-dealing by the insiders, state courts will ***closely scrutinize*** the ***fairness*** of the transaction. [424]

1. **General test:** In most states, the freezeout must meet at least the first, and possibly the second, of the following tests: (1) the transaction must be ***basically fair***, taken in its entirety, to the outsider/minority shareholders; and (2) the transaction must be undertaken for some ***valid business purpose***. [424]

2. **Basic fairness:** For the transaction to be "basically fair," most courts require: (1) a fair ***price***; (2) fair ***procedures*** by which the board decided to approve the transaction; and (3) adequate ***disclosure*** to the outside shareholders about the transaction. [424]

   Example: Signal owns slightly more than half of UOP Corp., with the balance owned by the public. Four key directors of UOP are also directors of Signal (and owe Signal their primary loyalty). Two of these directors prepare a feasibility study, which concludes that $24 is a fair price for Signal to pay for the balance of UOP. Signal then offers $21 per UOP share. There is no negotiation between UOP and Signal on this price, and the non-

Signal-affiliated UOP directors are never told about the $24 feasibility study. The deal goes through.

Held, this acquisition did not meet the test of basic fairness to UOP's minority shareholders. The price was not fair (since Signal's own directors admitted that $24 was a fair price); the procedures were not fair (since there were no real negotiations between the two companies); and the disclosure was not fair (e.g., the public was never told about the feasibility study showing $24 as a fair price). See *Weinberger v. UOP, Inc.*

a. **Independent committee:** A parent-subsidiary merger is much more likely to be found fair if the public minority stockholders of the subsidiary are represented by a ***special committee of independent directors*** who are not affiliated with the parent (e.g., if UOP had been represented by non-Signal-affiliated directors in a true bargaining session with Signal, the transaction in *Weinberger* might have been upheld).

3. **"Business purpose" test:** Apart from the requirement that the transaction be basically fair, some but not all courts will strike down the freezeout unless it serves a ***"valid business purpose."*** In other words, in some courts the insiders, even if they pay a fair price, cannot put through a transaction whose sole purpose is to eliminate the minority (public) stockholders. [427]

   a. **Going private:** This business purpose test is especially likely to be flunked when the transaction is a ***going-private*** one (as opposed to a two-step acquisition or a merger of long-term affiliates).

   b. **Delaware abandons:** Delaware has abandoned the business purpose requirement, so in Delaware only the test of "basic fairness" has to be met.

4. **Closely-held corporations:** If the freezeout takes place in the context of a ***close corporation***, most courts will probably scrutinize it more closely than in the public-corporation context. This is especially true of ***"squeezeouts."*** (*Example*: Shark, who owns 70% of Close Corp, tries to coerce Pitiful, his long-time assistant, to sell his 30% stake. Shark fires Pitiful, cuts off his salary, and refuses to pay dividends, then offers to buy Pitiful's stake for a fraction of its true value. A court is likely to strike this transaction on the grounds that it is unfair, since it leaves Pitiful with no way to make a reasonable return on his investment.) [428]

V. TENDER OFFERS, ESPECIALLY HOSTILE TAKEOVERS

A. **Definition of tender offer:** A tender offer is an offer to stockholders of a publicly-held corporation to ***exchange their shares*** for cash or securities at a price higher than the previous market price. [429]

   1. **Used in hostile takeovers:** A cash tender offer is the most common way of carrying out a ***"hostile takeover."*** A hostile takeover is the acquisition of a publicly held company (the ***"target"***) by a buyer (the ***"bidder"***) over the ***opposition of the target's management***.

   2. **Williams Act:** Tender offers are principally regulated by the ***Williams Act***, part of the federal Securities Exchange Act of 1934. [437]

B. **Disclosure by 5% owner:** Any person who ***"directly or indirectly"*** acquires ***more than 5%*** of ***any class*** of stock in a publicly held corporation must disclose that fact on a statement filed with the SEC (a "Schedule 13D" statement). [438]

1. **Information disclosed:** The investor must disclose a variety of information on his 13D, including the source of the funds used to make the purchase, and the investor's ***purpose*** in buying the shares (including whether he intends to ***seek control***). [438]

2. **"Beneficial owner":** A 13D must be filed by a "beneficial owner" of the 5% stake, even if he is not the record owner. [438]

3. **When due:** The filing must be made ***within 10 days*** following the acquisition. (Thus an investor has 10 days beyond when he crosses the 5% threshold, in which he can make further purchases without informing the world.) [438]

4. **Additional acquisitions:** Someone who is already a 5%-or-more owner must refile his 13D anytime he acquires ***additional*** stock (though not for small additions which, over a 12-month period, amount to less than 2% of the company's total stock). [439]

5. **Groups:** A ***"group"*** must file a 13D. Thus if A and B each buy 4% of XYZ acting in concert, they must file a 13D together as a "group" even though each acting alone would not be required to file. (A group can be formed even in the absence of a written agreement.) [439]

6. **No tender offer intended:** The requirement of filing a Schedule 13D applies ***no matter what the purchaser's intent is***. Thus even if an investor has no intent to seek control or make a tender offer, he must still file. [439]

C. **Rules on tender offers:** Here are the main rules imposed by the Williams Act upon tender offers: [440]

1. **Disclosure:** Any tender offeror (at least one who, if his tender offer were successful, would own 5% or more of a company's stock) must make extensive ***disclosures***. He must disclose his identity, funding, and purpose. Also, if the bidder proposes to pay part of the purchase price in the form of securities (e.g., preferred or common stock in the bidder, junk bonds, etc.) the bidder's financial condition must be disclosed. [440]

2. **Withdrawal rights:** Any shareholder who tenders to a bidder has the right to ***withdraw*** his stock from the tender offer ***at any time while the offer remains open***. If the tender offer is extended for any reason, the withdrawal rights are similarly extended until the new offer-expiration date. [441]

3. **"Pro rata" rule:** If a bidder offers to buy only a ***portion*** of the outstanding shares of the target, and the holders tender more than the number than the bidder has offered to buy, the bidder must buy ***in the same proportion from each shareholder***. This is the so-called ***"pro rata"*** rule. [441]

4. **"Best price" rule:** If the bidder ***increases*** his price before the offer has expired, he must pay this increased price to ***each*** stockholder whose shares are tendered and bought up. In other words, he may not give the increased price only to those who tender after the price increase. This is the ***"best price"*** rule. [441]

5. **20-day minimum:** A tender offer ***must be kept open for at least 20 business days***. Also, if the bidder changes the price or number of shares he is seeking, he must hold the offer open for ***another 10 days*** after the announcement of the change. [442]

D. **Hart-Scott-Rodino Act:** The Hart-Scott-Rodino Antitrust Improvements Act (H-S-R) requires a bidder to give notice to the government of certain proposed deals, and imposes a waiting period before the deal can be consummated. H-S-R applies only where one party has sales or assets of more than $100 million and the other has sales or assets of more than $10 million. [442]

E. Definition of "tender offer": There is no official definition of "tender offer." [444]

1. **Eight factors:** Courts and the SEC often take into account eight possible factors which make it more likely that a tender offer is being conducted: (1) ***active and widespread solicitation*** of the target's public shareholders; (2) a solicitation for a ***substantial percentage*** of the target's stock; (3) an offer to purchase at a ***premium*** over the prevailing price; (4) ***firm*** rather than negotiable terms; (5) an offer ***contingent*** on receipt of a ***fixed minimum number*** of shares; (6) a ***limited time period*** for which the offer applies; (7) the ***pressuring*** of offerees to sell their stock; and (8) a ***public announcement*** by the buyer that he will be acquiring the stock. [444]

2. **Vast quantities not sufficient:** Mere purchases of large quantities of stock, without at least some of these eight factors, do ***not*** constitute a tender offer. [445]

3. **Privately-negotiated purchases:** A ***privately-negotiated purchase***, even of large amounts of stock, usually will ***not*** constitute a tender offer. This is true even if the acquirer conducts simultaneous negotiations with a number of large stockholders, and buys from each at an above market price. [445]

4. **Open-market purchases:** Usually there will not be a tender offer where the acquirer makes ***open-market purchases*** (e.g., purchases made on the New York Stock Exchange), even if a large percentage of the target's stock is bought. [445]

F. Private actions under § 14(e): Section 14(e) of the '34 Act (part of the Williams Act) makes it unlawful to make an "untrue statement of a material fact," to "omit to state" any material fact, or to engage in any "fraudulent, deceptive, or manipulative act," in connection with a tender offer. [446]

1. **Substantive unfairness:** This section does ***not*** prohibit conduct by a bidder that is ***substantively unfair***, but that does not involve misrepresentation or nondisclosure. (*Example*: Bidder withdraws an attractive and over-subscribed tender offer, and replaces it with a much less attractive one. *Held*, even though this may be substantively unfair conduct, it is not deceptive, and therefore does not violate § 14(e) of the Williams Act. See *Schreiber v. Burlington Northern.*) [446]

2. **Standing:** Several types of people can bring a suit for a violation of § 14(e), including: (1) the target (which can seek an injunction against deceptive conduct by the bidder); (2) a ***bidder*** (which can get an injunction against the target's management or against another bidder, but which ***cannot*** get ***damages*** against anyone); (3) a ***non-tendering shareholder*** (who can get either damages or an injunction); and (4) a person who ***buys*** or ***sells*** shares in reliance on information disclosed or not disclosed in tender offer documents. [447]

3. **Materiality:** Plaintiff must show that the misrepresentation or omission was ***"material."*** That is, he must show that the omitted or misstated fact would have assumed actual significance in a reasonable shareholder's deliberations about whether to tender. [447]

4. **Scienter:** Plaintiff probably must show ***scienter*** (i.e., an ***intent*** to deceive, manipulate or defraud) on the part of the defendant in a private § 14(e) action. [446]

5. **Reliance:** D must normally show that he ***relied*** on D's misrepresentation (e.g., that he read D's tender offer materials). But there is no reliance requirement if P is complaining about the ***omission*** of a material fact. [446]

6. **Remedies:** A private party may generally get either an ***injunction*** against consummation of the tender offer or ***damages***. [447]

G. **State regulation of hostile takeovers:** Many states have statutes which attempt to discourage hostile takeovers and protect incumbent management. [447]

1. **Modern statutes:** Most modern anti-takeover statutes operate not by preventing the bidder from buying the shares, but instead depriving him of the ***benefit*** of his share acquisition, by: (1) preventing the bidder from ***voting the shares*** he has bought unless certain conditions are satisfied; (2) preventing the bidder from conducting a ***back-end merger*** of the target into the bidder's shell, or vice versa; or (3) requiring the bidder to pay a specified ***"fair price"*** in any back-end merger. [448]

2. **Delaware Act:** The most important modern statute is the ***Delaware*** anti-takeover statute, Del. GCL § 203. Section 203 prohibits any "business combination" (including any ***back-end merger***) between the corporation and an "interested stockholder" for ***three years*** after the stockholder buys his shares. Anyone who buys more than 15% of a company's stock is covered. The net effect of the Delaware statute is that anyone who buys less than 85% of a Delaware corporation cannot for three years conduct a back-end merger between the shell he uses to carry out the acquisition and the target, and therefore: (1) cannot use the target's assets as security for a loan to finance the share acquisition; and (2) cannot use the target's earnings and cash flow to pay off the acquisition debt. [449]

H. **Defensive maneuvers:** Here are some of the defensive maneuvers that a target's incumbent management may use to defeat a hostile bidder. [450]

1. **Pre-offer techniques:** Techniques that can be used before a concrete takeover attempt emerges are usually called ***"shark repellants."*** These generally must be approved by a majority of the target's ***shareholders***. Here are some of the more common ones: [450]

a. **Super-majority provision:** The target may amend its articles of incorporation to require that ***more than a simple majority*** of the target's shareholders approve any merger or major sale of assets. (Alternatively, the target can provide that such a merger or asset sale be approved by a majority of the ***disinterested*** shareholders.) There are called ***"super-majority"*** provisions.

b. **Staggered board:** A target might put in place a ***staggered*** board of directors (i.e., only a minority of the board stands for election in a given year, so that a hostile bidder cannot gain control immediately even if he owns a majority of the shares).

c. **Anti-greenmail amendment:** The target might amend its charter to prohibit the paying of ***"greenmail"***, so as to discourage any hostile bidder bent on receiving greenmail.

d. **New class of stock:** The target might create a ***second class*** of common stock, and require that any merger or asset sale be approved by each class; then, the new class can be placed with persons friendly to management (e.g., the founding family, or an Employee Stock Ownership Plan).

e. **Poison pill:** ***"Poison pill"*** plans try to make bad things happen to the bidder if it obtains control of the target, thereby making the target less attractive to the bidder.

i. **"Call" plans:** A ***"call"*** plan gives stockholders the right to buy cheap stock in certain circumstances. Most contain a "flipover" provision which is triggered when an outsiders buys, say, 20% of the target's stock. When the flipover is triggered, the holder of the right (the stockholder) has an option to ***acquire shares of the bidder*** at a cheap price.

ii. **"Put" plans:** Other poison pills are ***"put"*** plans. If a bidder buys some but not all of the target's shares, the put gives each target shareholder the right to sell back his remaining shares in the target at a pre-determined ***"fair"*** price.

iii. **No approval required:** Shareholder approval is ***not*** generally required for a poison pill plan. Also, such plans may sometimes be implemented ***after*** a hostile bid has emerged.

2. **Post-offer techniques:** Here are some techniques that can be used ***after*** a hostile bid has surfaced: [454]

a. **Defensive lawsuits:** The target's management can institute ***defensive lawsuits*** (e.g., a state suit alleging breach of state-law fiduciary principles, or a federal court suit based on the federal securities laws). Usually, lawsuits just buy time.

b. **White knight defense:** The target may find itself a ***"white knight,"*** who will acquire the target instead of letting the hostile bidder do so. Often, the white knight is given a ***"lockup,"*** that is, some special inducement to enter the bidding process, such as a ***"crown jewel" option*** (i.e., an option to buy one of the target's best businesses at a below-market price).

c. **Defensive acquisition:** The target might make itself less attractive by arranging a ***defensive acquisition*** (e.g., one that causes the target to take on a lot of debt).

d. **Corporate restructuring:** The target may ***restructure*** itself in a way that raises short-term stockholder value. (*Example*: Target borrows heavily from banks and then pays holders a large one-time dividend, possibly followed by large asset sales to pay down the debt.)

e. **Greenmail:** The target may pay ***"greenmail"*** to the bidder (i.e., it buys the bidder's stake back at an above-market price, usually in return for a "standstill" agreement under which the bidder agrees not to attempt to re-acquire the target for some specified number of years).

f. **Sale to friendly party:** The target may sell a less-than-controlling block to a ***friendly party***, i.e., one who can be trusted not to tender to the hostile bidder. Thus the target might sell new shares to its employees' pension plan, to an ESOP (employee stock ownership plan), or to a "white squire." In Delaware, if a friendly party owns 16%, the Delaware anti-takeover statute, GCL § 203, will be triggered, thus preventing a bidder from arranging a back-end merger or asset sale for three years.

g. **Share repurchase:** The target might ***repurchase*** a significant portion of its shares from the public, if insiders hold a substantial but not controlling stake (thus raising the insiders' stake).

I. **Federal securities law response:** A bidder who wants to ***overturn*** the target's defensive measures probably will ***not*** be able to do so using the federal securities laws. If the bidder can show the target's management has actually deceived the target's shareholders, it may be able to get an injunction under § 14(e) of the '34 Act. But if incoming management has merely behaved in a way that is arguably "unfair" to the target's shareholders (by depriving them of the opportunity to tender into the bidder's high offer), there will generally be no federal securities-law violation. [456]

J. State response: The bidder has a much better chance of showing that the target's defensive maneuvers violate ***state law***. [456]

1. **Summary of Delaware law:** Most case law concerning what defensive maneuvers a target may employ comes from Delaware. [457]

   a. **Business judgment rule:** In Delaware, the target and its management will get the protection of the ***business judgment rule*** (and thus their defensive measures will be upheld) under the following circumstances (summarized in *Unocal Corp. v. Mesa Petroleum Co.*): [457]

      i. **Reasonable grounds:** First, the board and management must show that they had ***reasonable grounds*** for believing that there was a ***danger to the corporation's welfare*** from the takeover attempt. In other words, the insiders may not use anti-takeover measures ***merely to entrench themselves in power*** — they must reasonably believe that they are protecting the stockholders' interests, not their own interests. (Some dangers that will justify anti-takeover measures are: (1) a reasonable belief that the bidder would ***change the business practices*** of the corporation in a way that would be harmful to the company's ongoing business and existence; (2) a reasonable fear that the particular takeover attempt is ***unfair and coercive***, such as a two-tier front-loaded offer; and (3) a reasonable fear that the offer will leave the target with unreasonably high levels of debt.)

      ii. **Proportional response:** Second, the directors and management must show that the defensive measures they actually used were "reasonable in relation to the threat posed." This is the ***"proportionality"*** requirement.

         (1) **Can't be "preclusive" or "coerecive":** To meet the proportionality requirement, a defensive measure must ***not*** be either ***"preclusive"*** or ***"coercive."*** A "preclusive" action is one that has the effect of foreclosing virtually ***all*** takeovers (e.g., a poison pill plan whose terms would dissuade any bidder, or the granting of a "crown jewels option" to a white knight on way-below-market terms). A "coercive" measure is one which "crams down" on the target's shareholders a management-sponsored alternative (e.g., a lower competing bid by management, if management has enough votes to veto the hostile bid and makes it clear that it will use this power to block the hostile bid).

      iii. **Reasonable investigation:** Third, the target's board must act upon ***reasonable investigation*** when it responds to the takeover measure.

   b. **Independent directors:** Court approval of the anti-takeover devices is much more likely if the board that approved the measure has a majority composed of ***"independent"*** directors (i.e., those who are not full-time employees and who are not closely affiliated with management). [458]

   c. **Consequences if requirements not met:** If one or more of the three requirements summarized in (a) above are not met, the court will refuse to give the takeover device the protection of the business rule. But it will not automatically strike the measure; instead, it will treat it like any other type of self-dealing, and will put management to the burden of showing that the transaction is "entirely fair" to the target's shareholders. [461]

K. Decision to sell the company (the "Level Playing Field" rule): Once the target's management decides that it is ***willing*** to sell the company, then the courts give ***"enhanced scrutiny"*** to the steps that the target's board and managers take. Most importantly, management and the board must make every effort to obtain the ***highest price*** for the shareholders. Thus the target's insiders must create a ***level playing field***: all ***would-be bidders must be treated equally***. [461]

Example: Target is sought by Raider and White Knight. Target's board favors White Knight. Target's board gives White Knight a "crown jewels option" to buy two key Target subsidiaries for a much-below-market price.

Held, Target's board violated its obligation to get the best price, and it was not entitled to favor one bidder over another, such as by the use of a lockup to prematurely end the auction. [*Revlon, Inc. v. MacAndrews & Forbes Holdings, Inc.*]

1. Detailed consequences: Here is a more detailed list of what the *Revlon* "Level Playing Field Rule" requires:

[1] Once management decides to ***offer the company for sale***, or decides that a sale is ***inevitable***, it may ***no longer use defensive measures***, and must instead make every effort to achieve the ***best price*** for the stockholders;

[2] Getting the best price for stockholders means ***treating all bidders equally***, not preferring one bidder over another;

[3] The use of ***lock-ups*** and the divulging of ***confidential financial information*** to one bidder rather than another are the kinds of actions that probably constitute inappropriate favoritism;

[4] In choosing among offers, the board's sole duty is to the ***common stockholders*** (i.e., to get the highest price), and the board may not attempt to get extra protection for ***employees***, ***creditors***, ***management*** or the ***board itself*** at the expense of shareholders. [463]

2. When obligation begins: If ***no formal offer*** to buy the company has ***so far occurred,*** the *Revlon* Level Playing Field rule is ***not triggered***, even if the board has specific reason to believe that a particular party may well ***soon make an offer.*** Only when the board actually receives an offer ***and starts negotiating with the bidder*** need it take concrete steps to obtain the best price. [*Lyondell Chemical Co. v. Ryan*] [464]

a. Board can "wait and see": Therefore, even though the board may reasonably believe that an offer will ***soon*** be forthcoming, the board is ***free to "wait and see"*** whether the offer occurs, and need not take any concrete steps in ***anticipation***. So before any concrete offer has been made, the board doesn't need to take steps like ascertaining what other potential bidders might exist, gauging the company's value to an acquirer, or plotting how to get the best price. [*Lyondell, supra*]

3. Management interested: If the target's ***management*** is one of the competing bidders, the target's board must be especially careful not to favor management (e.g., it must not give management better access to information). Normally, the target's ***independent directors*** should form a special committee to conduct negotiations on the target's behalf. [464]

L. Sale of control: Just as the Level Playing Field Rule triggers ***enhanced scrutiny*** of board decisions to sell the entire company (as explained in Paragraph (K) above), so there is enhanced scrutiny given to transactions in which the board ***"sells control"*** of the company to a single individual or group.

> **Example:** Target's shares are widely dispersed, with no controlling shareholder. Acquirer, although it's a public company, has a controlling shareholder, Boss, who owns 30% of its shares. Target negotiates a merger agreement with Acquirer, under which each holder of Target will get a share of the combined Target-plus-Acquirer company. Because Target's board is proposing to sell "control" of Target to a single individual (Boss), the court will carefully scrutinize the deal, and make extra sure that all other possible buyers or merger partners are treated equally. [466]

1. **Friendly merger into non-controlled public company:** It is only where the target is merging into a friendly ***"controlled"*** acquirer that enhanced scrutiny will be triggered -- if the target is merged into a friendly acquirer that's ***already held by the public at large*** with no single controlling shareholder or group, there will be ***no enhanced scrutiny***. [*Arnold v. Soc. for Savings Bancorp, Inc.*]

M. Board may "just say no": If the target's board has ***not*** previously decided to put the company up for sale or dramatically restructure it, then the board basically has a right to ***reject unwanted takeover offers***, even all-cash, high-priced offers that the board has reason to think most shareholders would welcome. In other words, the board may ***"just say no,"*** at least in Delaware.

1. **Illustrations:** Thus the target's board may, as a general rule, refuse to ***redeem*** a previously-enacted ***poison pill***, refuse to ***recommend a merger*** or put the proposed merger to a ***shareholder vote***, or otherwise ***refuse to cooperate***. [*Paramount Communic. v. Time*] [469]

N. Particular anti-takeover devices: Here is how the courts respond to some of the particular anti-takeover devices: [472]

1. **Greenmail:** Most courts seem to ***allow greenmail***. (*Example*: If the target's board is worried that a particular bidder will damage the corporation's existence or its business policies, it may buy the bidder's shares back at a premium.) [472]

2. **Exclusionary repurchase:** If the target ***repurchases*** some of its shares at a price higher than the bidder is offering, it ***may*** refuse to buy back any of the bidder's shares as part of the arrangement (at least in Delaware). [*Unocal v. Mesa Petroleum*] [472]

3. **Poison pill plans:** Most ***poison pill*** plans have been ***upheld***. Only where the poison pill plan has the effect of foreclosing virtually all hostile takeovers is it likely to be struck down. [*Moran v. Household International, Inc.*] [474]

4. **Lock-ups:** ***Lock-ups*** are the type of anti-takeover device that is most likely to be ***invalidated***. This is especially true of ***crown jewel*** options. Lock-ups, including crown jewel options, are not *per se* illegal; for instance, they can be used to produce an auction where none would otherwise exist. But if a crown jewel option or other lock-up is used to end an auction prematurely rather than to create one, it may well be struck down. [475]

   a. **Conditions making approval a "mathematical certainty":** A bidder will sometimes demand some sort of lock-up as a condition of entering a bid that binds that bidder — the bidder will often refuse to run the risk of being a ***"stalking horse"*** for some later, higher bidder who will end up taking the company. In Delaware, at least some combinations of ***deal-protection measures*** given to satisfy the first bidder's "I won't be a stalking horse" demand (and thus to lock up the deal for that bidder) will be found to ***violate*** the Level Playing Field rule. If the deal-protection measures constitute, in the court's opinion, ***an "absolute lock up"*** that makes approval of the merger a ***mathematical certainty,*** the combination will be ***invalid***, even if the bidder is the only or highest bidder in the picture, and will walk away if not given the lock up. [476]

Example: NCS is on the verge of bankruptcy. Finally, Genesis offers to buy it in a stock-for-stock merger. But Genesis makes it clear that it won't risk being a stalking horse bidder whose bid might be used to extract a better bid from someone else. Genesis demands, and NCS gives, a package of protections, including a voting agreement in which NCS stockholders controlling more than half the stock irrevocably bind themselves to vote for the merger, and a "force the vote" clause in which NCS' board promises to submit the merger to a shareholder vote even if the board no longer believes the merger is a good deal. NCS insists that there be no "fiduciary out" clause by which the board can refuse to submit the merger for shareholder approval if the board later concludes that its fiduciary obligation to stockholders is to try to avoid the merger. Hours after the NCS-Genesis merger agreement is signed, Omnicare makes a better merger proposal. NCS' board wants to take the better proposal, but the prior NCS-Genesis merger agreement, with its lock up concessions, make that deal's completion a virtual certainty. Therefore, Omnicare sues for an injunction to block the NCS-Genesis deal.

Held, for Omnicare. A target's board can't give a bidder "coercive" or "preclusive" lock up provisions. Where the concessions to the first bidder make it "mathematically impossible" for the target's shareholders to vote down the first merger in favor of a better one, the concessions amount to an "absolute lock up," and will be invalidated. [*Omnicare, Inc. v. NCS Healthcare, Inc.*] [478]

i. **Narrow interpretation:** But *Omnicare*, *supra*, will apparently be narrowly construed in Delaware. For instance, the target's board and controlling shareholders *can* agree that they won't vote for any competing transaction for a substantial period of time, if they also give the target's minority holders the right to kill the first merger by voting it down. In other words, as long as the target's concessions ***still leave a mathematical chance*** that the outside shareholders can disapprove the first deal, the concessions won't be deemed "coercive" or "preclusive." [478]

5. **Stock option:** An option to the acquirer to ***buy stock in the target*** will likely be struck down if it is for so many shares, or for so low a price, or on such burdensome terms, that its mere existence has a materially ***chilling effect on whether other bidders will emerge***.[478]

6. **Termination fee:** A fee payable to the acquirer if the merger should be terminated by the target may be upheld or struck down, depending on the amount and other circumstances. [494]

CHAPTER 11

DIVIDENDS AND SHARE REPURCHASES

I. DIVIDENDS — PROTECTION OF CREDITORS

A. Terminology:

1. **Dividend:** A ***"dividend"*** is a cash payment made by a corporation to its common shareholders pro rata. It is usually paid out of the current earnings of the corporation, and thus represents a partial distribution of profits. [505]

2. **Stated capital:** ***"Stated capital"*** is the stockholder's ***permanent investment*** in the corporation. [507]

   a. **Par stock:** If the stock has ***"par value,"*** stated capital is equal to the number of shares outstanding times the par value of each share.

   b. **No-par:** If the stock is ***"no-par"*** stock (now permitted in most states), stated capital is an arbitrary amount that the board assigns to the stated capital account. (This amount is never more than the shareholders paid for their stock when they originally bought it, but is otherwise whatever the directors decide it should be when the stock is issued.)

3. **"Earned surplus":** ***"Earned surplus"*** is equal to the ***profits*** earned by the corporation during its existence, less any dividends it ever paid out. ("Retained earnings" is a more modern synonym.) [507]

4. **"Capital surplus":** ***"Capital surplus"*** is everything in the corporation's "capital" account other than "stated capital." "Paid in" surplus, "revaluation" surplus, and "reduction" surplus are the main types of capital surplus. [508]

B. Dividends generally:

1. **Authorized by board:** The decision to pay a dividend must always be made by the ***board of directors***. [505]

2. **Two tests:** All states place certain ***legal limits*** (mostly financial ones) on the board's right to pay dividends, and directors who disregard these limits may be liable. In most states, a dividend may be paid only if ***both*** of the following general kinds of requirements are satisfied: (1) payment of the dividend will not impair the corporation's ***stated capital***; and (2) payment will not render the corporation ***insolvent***. [505]

C. Capital tests:

1. **"Earned surplus" statutes:** In most states, there are ***"earned surplus"*** restrictions: dividends may be paid ***only out of the profits which the corporation has accumulated*** since its inception. [509]

2. **"Impairment of capital" statutes:** A substantial minority of states merely prohibit dividends that would ***"impair the capital"*** of the corporation. These states are less strict than the "earned surplus" states: they allow the payment of dividends from ***either*** earned surplus or ***unearned surplus***. [509]

   a. **Paid-in surplus:** Thus an "impairment of capital" statute allows a corporation with no earned surplus to pay its entire ***"paid-in surplus"*** out again as dividends. "Paid-in surplus" is the difference between what the shareholders paid for their shares when they were originally issued, and the "stated capital" represented by those shares.

   b. **Revaluation surplus:** Many "impairment of capital" states also allow the board to create, and then pay out, "revaluation" surplus. This is the surplus produced by "writing up" the corporation's assets to their current market value (rather than using the historical prices normally reflected on a balance sheet).

c. **Reduction surplus:** Finally, a "impairment of capital" statute usually allows the ***"reduction surplus"*** to be paid out. "Reduction surplus" is caused by reducing the corporation's stated capital (which in the case of stock having a par value requires a shareholder-approved amendment to the articles of incorporation).

3. **Nimble dividends:** Some states allow payment of "***nimble*** dividends." These are dividends paid out of the ***current earnings*** of the corporation, even though the corporation otherwise would not be entitled to pay the dividends (because it has no earned surplus in an earned-surplus state, or because payment would impair its stated capital in an impairment-of-capital state). [511]

   a. **Delaware:** Delaware GCL § 170(a) allows payment of nimble dividends: even if there is no earned surplus (normally required for a dividend in Delaware), the dividend may be paid out of the corporation's net profits for the current or preceding fiscal year.

D. **Insolvency test:** Even if a dividend payment would not violate the applicable capital test (earned-surplus or impairment-of-capital, depending on the state), in nearly all states payment of a dividend is prohibited if it would ***leave the corporation insolvent***. [512]

1. **UFCA:** In half the states, this ban is imposed by the Uniform Fraudulent Conveyance Act (UFCA), which has the effect of prohibiting dividends by an insolvent corporation. [512]

2. **"Equity" meaning:** In most states, a corporation is insolvent if it is ***unable to pay its debts as they become due*** (the ***"equity"*** meaning of "insolvent"). A minority of states define a corporation as insolvent if the ***market value*** of its assets is less than its liabilities (the ***"bankruptcy"*** meaning). [512]

E. **MBCA:** The MBCA imposes ***only*** an insolvency test, not a capital-related test. Under MBCA § 6.40(c), no dividend may be paid if it would leave the corporation insolvent under ***either*** the "equity" or the "bankruptcy" definition of insolvent. [513]

1. **Popular:** The MCBA's approach to dividends has been ***popular***: about 37 states have adopted it either wholly or with minor variations. [514]

F. **Liability of directors:** If the directors approve a dividend at a time when the statute prohibits it, they may be ***personally liable***: [514]

1. **Bad faith:** If the directors ***know*** that the dividend is forbidden at the time they pay it, they are personally liable in nearly all states. [515]

2. **Negligence:** If they act in good faith but are ***negligent*** in failing to notice that the dividend is forbidden, they are liable in some but probably not most states. [515]

3. **Creditor suit:** Usually, the suit to recover an improperly-paid dividend must be brought by the corporation (perhaps by means of a shareholder derivative suit, or by a trustee for the corporation once it declares bankruptcy). But some states allow suit to be brought by a ***creditor*** against the director(s) who approve an improper dividend. [515]

4. **MBCA:** Under the MBCA, the corporation may hold liable any director who negligently approves an improper dividend. [515]

G. **Liability of shareholders:** A ***shareholder*** who receives an improper dividend may also be liable. [515]

1. **Common law:** At common law, the shareholder will be liable and required to return the improper dividend if ***either***: (1) the corporation was insolvent at the time of, or as the result of

the payment of, the dividend; or (2) the shareholder ***knew***, at the time he received the dividend, that it was ***improper***. But if the corporation is solvent and the shareholder takes the dividend without notice that it violates the statute, the shareholder does ***not*** have to return it at common law. [515]

2. **Statute:** Some corporation statutes make the shareholder liable to return the improper dividend, even if he would not be liable at common law. Apart from the basic corporation statute, the statute dealing with fraudulent conveyances (e.g., the Uniform Fraudulent Conveyance Act) may permit a creditor or bankruptcy trustee to recover against a shareholder. [516]

II. DIVIDENDS — PROTECTION OF SHAREHOLDERS; JUDICIAL REVIEW OF DIVIDEND POLICY

A. **Generally:** A disgruntled shareholder will sometimes try to persuade the court to order the corporation to pay a ***higher*** dividend than it is already paying. [516]

1. **General rule:** This is left to case law by most states. Usually, P will only get the court to order a higher dividend if he shows that: (1) the low-dividend policy is ***not justified by any reasonable business objective***; and (2) the policy results from ***improper motives*** that harm the corporation or some of its shareholders. [517]

2. **Plaintiff rarely succeeds:** Plaintiffs very rarely succeed in making these showings. Therefore, courts rarely order a corporation to change its dividend policies for the benefit of some group of shareholders. [517]

3. **Closely-held:** Courts are more likely to order an increase in dividend payments when the corporation is ***closely held*** rather than publicly held. Some courts now hold that minority stockholders who are not employed by the corporation are entitled to a ***return on their investment*** in the form of a dividend, even in the face of an otherwise valid corporate objective (e.g., expanding the business). Courts sometimes say that the insiders have a ***fiduciary duty*** to grant a reasonable dividend to the outside minority investors. [518]

III. STOCK REPURCHASES

A. **Repurchases generally:** A ***"stock repurchase"*** occurs when a corporation ***buys back*** its own stock from stockholders. This may happen by open market repurchases, by a "self-tender" (i.e., a tender offer by a public company offering to buy some number of shares pro rata from all shareholders), or by face-to-face selective purchases. [518]

B. **Protection of shareholders:** One shareholder may object to the corporation's repurchase of another shareholder's shares (e.g., on the grounds that the corporation has paid too high a price, or has refused to give all shareholders an equal opportunity to have their shares repurchased). [521]

1. **General rule:** Generally the court will not overturn a corporation's repurchase arrangements at the urging of a shareholder, so long as the board of directors: (1) behaves with reasonable care (i.e., makes reasonable inquiries into the corporation's financial health and the value of its shares before authorizing the repurchase); and (2) does not violate the duty of loyalty (e.g., the directors are not buying from themselves at an above-market price). [521]

2. **Self-dealing by insiders:** The court will look extra closely at a repurchase that appears to ***benefit the insiders*** unduly. (*Example*: Ian, 40% owner of XYZ, induces the board to have

XYZ repurchase his holdings for 50% more than the current stock market price. The court will look upon this as self-dealing, and will strike down the transaction unless Ian bears the burden of proving that the transaction is "entirely fair" to the corporation and its remaining shareholders.) [522]

C. Protection of creditors; financial limits: In general, share repurchases are subject to the same ***financial limits*** for the protection of creditors as are ***dividends***. [522]

CHAPTER 12

ISSUANCE OF SECURITIES

I. STATE-LAW RULES ON SHARE ISSUANCE

A. Par value: If shares have a ***par value***, the corporation ***may not sell the shares for less than this par value***. This rule protects both the corporation's creditors, and also other shareholders. [530]

1. **"Watered stock" liability:** If shares are issued for less than their par value, ***creditors*** will sometimes be allowed to recover against the stockholder who received the cheap stock (usually called ***"watered stock"***). [531]

   a. **"Misrepresentation" theory:** Most courts apply the ***"misrepresentation"*** theory, under which only a creditor who has ***relied*** on the corporation's false assertion that the shares were issued for at least par value, may recover. Under this theory, one who becomes a creditor ***before*** the wrongful issuance, and one who becomes a creditor after the wrongful issuance but with ***knowledge of it***, may not recover since he has not "relied."

2. **Kind of consideration:** In most states, shares may be paid for not only in cash, but also by the contribution of ***property***, or by the performance of ***past services***. States vary as to whether shares may be purchased and returned for ***promises*** to perform services or donate property (e.g., Delaware does not allow payment in the form of a promise to perform future services). [532]

   a. **MBCA:** But the MBCA is more liberal: any kind of consideration is valid, so long as the board acts in good faith and with reasonable care. Thus promissory notes and promises to perform future services are both valid consideration under the MBCA.

3. **Valuation:** If the board of directors sells stock to a stockholder in return for past or future services or property, the board's good faith computation of the value that should be attributed to those services or property will usually ***not be overturned*** by a court. See, e.g., Delaware § 152 ("in the absence of actual fraud in the transaction, the judgment of the directors as to the value of such consideration shall be conclusive"). [533]

4. **Use of no-par or low-par stock:** Observe that all of these problems of "watered stock" are less likely to arise today, because of the extensive use of no-par or low-par stock. [533]

B. Preemptive rights: A ***"preemptive right"*** is a right sometimes given to a corporation's existing shareholders permitting them to ***maintain their percentage of ownership*** in the corporation, by enabling them to buy a portion of any newly-issued shares. (*Example:* Inventor holds 49% of stock in Mousetrap Corp. If preemptive rights exist, then before Mousetrap's 51% holder can induce the board to issue new shares to himself or to the public, Inventor must first be given the right to buy as many new shares as will be needed to maintain Inventor's 49% ownership, on the same terms as offered to the 51% holder or to the public.) [534]

1. **Statutes:** Today, every state governs preemptive rights by statute. All modern statutes allow the corporation to ***dispense*** entirely with preemptive rights if it chooses. This choice by the corporation is embodied in the articles of incorporation. [535]

   a. **Opt-in provisions:** Under most statutes, the preemptive rights scheme is an ***"opt-in"*** scheme. In other words, the corporation does not have preemptive rights unless it expressly elects, in the articles of incorporation, to have such rights. The MBCA follows this "opt-in" pattern; see § 6.30(a).

   b. **Opt-out:** A minority of states give the corporation an ***"opt-out"*** election — the corporation has preemptive rights unless it expressly specifies, in the articles of incorporation, that it does not want such rights.

2. **Exceptions:** Even where preemptive rights would otherwise apply, there are some important ***exceptions*** under most statutes: [535]

   a. **Initially-authorized shares:** Preemptive rights usually do not apply to shares that are part of the amount that is ***initially authorized*** at the time the corporation is first formed. (However, initially-authorized-but-unissued shares *do* become covered by the preemptive scheme if a certain time period — e.g., six months under the MBCA — elapses following the date of incorporation.)

   b. **Treasury shares:** Under most statutes, ***treasury shares*** (that is, shares that were once outstanding, but that have been repurchased by the corporation) are not covered. (But the MBCA does not exclude treasury shares.)

   c. **Property or services:** Shares that are issued in exchange for ***property*** or ***services*** are generally not covered. Similarly, shares issued to allow the exercise of employee ***stock options*** are usually not covered.

3. **"Fiduciary duty" concerning dilution:** Even in situations where there are no preemptive rights (either because they have been waived by the corporation, or because the case falls into an exception where preemptive rights do not apply), courts may protect minority stockholders against dilution by a ***"fiduciary obligation"*** theory. According to some courts, a majority stockholder has a fiduciary duty not to cause the issuance of new shares where the purpose is to ***enhance his own control at the expense of the minority***. [536]

   a. **Unfair price:** The court is most likely to impose this fiduciary duty where the new shares are issued at a ***bargain price*** to those who are already in control.

   b. **Bona fide business purpose required:** Even if the price is fair, the court will frequently strike down the sale of new stock by the corporation to its controlling shareholders if there is ***no valid business purpose*** behind the sale. For instance, if the court becomes convinced that the controlling shareholder has caused the sale to take place solely for the purpose of ***enhancing his own control***, the court is likely to strike the transaction even though the price was fair.

   c. **Preemptive rights as a defense:** If preemptive rights *do* apply, but the plaintiff ***declines to participate*** (perhaps because he doesn't have the money), courts are split about whether P may attack the sale of new shares to other existing shareholders on the grounds that the price is unfairly low. Some courts treat the fact that P declined to exercise his preemptive rights as a ***complete defense*** (so the court will not inquire into whether the shares were sold at an unfairly low price). Other courts hold that the existence of preemptive rights is ***not*** a defense, and that the board must bear the burden of showing that the price of the sale to insiders was at least within the range of fairness.

II. PUBLIC OFFERINGS — INTRODUCTION

A. Generally: Public offerings of securities are extensively regulated by the Securities Act of 1933 (the "'33 Act"). [540]

1. **Section 5:** The key provision of the '33 Act is § 5. Section 5 makes it unlawful (subject to exemptions) to ***sell any security*** by the use of the mails or other facilities of interstate commerce, ***unless a registration statement is in effect for that security***. This "registration statement" must contain a large amount of information about the security being offered, and about the company that is offering it (the "issuer"). Additionally, § 5 prohibits the sale of any security unless there is delivered to the buyer, before or at the same time as the security, a ***"prospectus"*** which contains the most important parts of the registration statement. [540]

2. **Disclosure:** The entire scheme for regulating public offerings works by compelling ***extensive disclosure***. The SEC does ***not*** review the ***substantive merits*** of the offering, and cannot bar an offering merely because it is too risky, overpriced, or valueless. [540]

B. "Security": The '33 Act applies to sales of "securities." "Security" is defined very broadly. It includes not only ordinary "stocks," but "bonds," "investment contracts," and many other devices. [541]

1. **Stock in closely held business:** Even where the owners of a closely held business sell ***all*** of the stock in the company to a single buyer who will operate the business himself, this is still the sale of a "security," so it must comply with the public-offering requirements (unless an exemption applies). [541]

2. **Debt instruments:** ***Debt instruments*** will often be "securities." For instance, a widely-traded ***bond*** will typically be a security. But a single "note" issued by a small business to a bank will typically not be a security. In general, the more a debt instrument looks like an "investment," and the more widely traded it is, the more likely the court will be to find it a "security." [*Reves v. Ernst & Young*] [541]

III. PUBLIC OFFERINGS — MECHANICS

A. Filing process: Here is how the process of going public works:

1. **Filing of registration statement:** The process begins when a registration statement is ***filed*** with the SEC. [542]

2. **20-day waiting period:** The issuer must now wait for the registration statement to become ***"effective."*** This normally happens ***20 days*** after it is filed. [542]

3. **Price amendment:** The registration statement is usually filed ***without a price***. Then, the statement is ***amended*** to include the price term just before the end of the 20-day waiting period. [543]

B. Rules during the three periods:

1. **Pre-filing:** During the ***pre-filing*** period (before the registration statement has been filed with the SEC), no one (including underwriters or issuers) may sell or even ***offer to sell*** the stock. (This means that press releases touting the issue, and oral offers, are forbidden, with narrow exceptions.) [543]

2. **Waiting period:** During the ***"waiting period"*** (after filing but before the effective date), most offers to sell and offers to buy are allowed, but sales and binding ***contracts*** to sell are not allowed. [544]

   a. **Red herring:** The underwriters may (and typically do) distribute during the waiting period a ***"red herring,"*** i.e., a ***preliminary prospectus*** which is identical to the final prospectus except that it typically omits the price.

   b. **No binding offers to buy:** During the waiting period, no offer to buy or "acceptance" will be deemed binding. Thus even if Customer says, "Yes, I'll buy 1,000 shares," he is not bound and can renege after the effective date.

3. **Post-effective period:** Once the registration statement becomes effective, underwriters and dealers may make offers to sell, and actual sales, to anyone. However, the final ***prospectus*** (complete with the final price) must be sent to any purchaser ***before or at the same time*** he receives the securities. [545]

IV. PUBLIC OFFERINGS — EXEMPTIONS

A. **Generally:** There are two key ***exemptions*** to the general rule that securities can only be issued if a registration statement is in force: [546]

1. **Sales by other than issuer, underwriter or dealer:** First, § 4(1) of the '33 Act gives an exemption for "transactions by any person other than an issuer, underwriter, or dealer." Because of an exemption for most sales by dealers, registration will generally be required only where the transaction is being carried out by a person who is an ***"issuer"*** or ***"underwriter."*** (But these terms are defined in a broad and complex way.) [546]

2. **Non-public offerings:** Second, under § 4(2), there is an exemption for "transactions by an issuer ***not involving any public offering***." So if an issuer can show that its sale was "non-public" rather than "public," it need not comply with the registration requirements. [546]

B. **Private offerings:** There are two different bodies of law by which an issuer may have its offering treated as ***"private"*** rather than "public": [547]

1. **Statutory exemption:** First, the issuer may show that the broad ***statutory*** language of § 4(2) (exempting transactions "not involving any public offering") applies. [547]

   a. **Sales to institutions:** For instance, a sale by a corporation of a large block of stock or bonds to one or a few large and sophisticated ***institutions*** (e.g., insurance companies or pension funds) will be a private offering based on this statutory exemption.

   b. **Sales to key employees:** Similarly, stock sales to key employees will usually qualify under this statutory exemption.

   c. **General test:** In general, an offering will not be "private" unless: (1) there are not very many offerees (though there is no fixed limit); and (2) the offerees have a significant level of ***sophistication*** and a significant degree of ***knowledge*** about the company's affairs. (*Example*: XYZ Corp offers shares to 10 secretarial-level employees at the company, without giving them any special disclosure. Since the secretaries' knowledge of the company's financial affairs is probably limited, this is a "public" rather than "private" offering, even though the number of offerees is small. Therefore, a registration statement must be used.)

2. **SEC Rule 506:** Separately, SEC has enacted ***Rule 506***. If Rule 506's conditions are met, the offering will be deemed "private" regardless of whether it would be private under the cases decided under the general § 4(2) statutory exemption. [549]

   a. **Gist:** The gist of Rule 506 is that an issuer may sell an unlimited amount of securities to: (1) any number of ***"accredited"*** investors; and (2) up to ***35 non-accredited*** investors. (An "accredited" investor is essentially one who is worth more than $1 million net of his personal residence, or has an income of more than $200,000 per year.)

   b. **Sophisticated:** Although an "accredited" investor can be very unsophisticated without ruining the Rule 506 exemption, a non-accredited investor must be ***sophisticated.*** (More precisely, the issuer must ***"reasonably believe"*** that the non-accredited investor, either alone or with his "purchaser representative," has such ***knowledge and experience*** in financial and business matters that he is capable of evaluating the merits of the investment.)

   c. **No advertising:** The issuer may not make any general ***solicitation*** or ***advertising***, for a Rule 506 offer. (But an issuer that is willing to sell ***only to accredited investors*** may now conduct general solicitations and advertising, as the result of a 2012 change.) [550]

   d. **Disclosure:** If the offering is solely to accredited investors, there are no disclosure requirements. But if even one investor is non-accredited, then *all* purchasers (accredited or not) must receive specific disclosures about the issuer and the offering.

C. **Small offerings:** Two other SEC rules give an exemption for offerings that are ***"small"*** (as opposed to "private"): [550]

1. **Rule 504:** Rule ***504*** allows an issuer to sell up to a total of ***$1 million*** of securities. (All sales in any 12-month period are added together.) [551]

   a. **Unlimited number:** There is no limit on the ***number*** of investors in a purchase.

   b. **Disclosure:** No particular disclosure is required.

   c. **Advertising:** Generally, the offering may not be publicly advertised or accomplished by widespread solicitation.

2. **Rule 505:** Under Rule ***505***, the issuer can sell up to ***$5 million*** of securities in any 12-month period. [551]

   a. **Number:** The number of investors is limited to 35 non-accredited and any number of accredited investors (like Rule 506).

   b. **Disclosure:** The same ***disclosure*** to all investors as would be required under 506 is required under 505, if there is even a single non-accredited investor.

   c. **Type of investor:** But 505 (in contrast to 506) imposes no requirements concerning the ***type of investor***: the investor need not be either accredited or sophisticated.

D. **Sales by non-issuer:** [552]

1. **Sales by or for controlling persons:** If a ***controlling stockholder*** sells a large number of shares by soliciting a large number of potential buyers, this may be held to be a "public offer-

ing." If so, the shareholder will have to register the shares, or else he (as well as his broker) will face liability for the crime of distributing unregistered stock. The key concept is ***"distribution"***: if a broker sells for a controlling shareholder in what is found to be a "distribution," a registration statement is required. (The larger the number of shares sold, and the larger the number of potential buyers contacted, the more likely a "distribution" is to be found.) [554]

a. Rule 144: But SEC Rule ***144*** provides a safe harbor: if the terms of the rule are complied with, sales by or for a controlling shareholder will not need to be registered. The key requirements for 144, in the case of a sale by a controlling shareholder, are:

i. Limit on amount of sales: The sales must be made ***gradually:*** In any three-month period, the controlling shareholder may not sell more than the greater of: (1) 1% of the total shares outstanding; or (2) the average weekly trading volume for the prior four weeks.

ii. Holding period: The controlling shareholder must normally have held the securities ***for at least two years*** before reselling them. (But this does not apply if he bought the shares in a public offering.)

iii. Disclosure: The issuing company must be a ***"public"*** company (one which files periodic reports with the SEC), or must make equivalent information about itself publicly available. So Rule 144 is not usually usable by the controlling shareholder of a private company.

iv. Ordinary brokerage transactions: The stock must be sold in ordinary brokerage transactions. The controlling shareholder's broker may not ***solicit*** orders to buy the stock.

v. Notice: A ***notice*** of each sale must be filed with the SEC at the time the order to sell is placed with the broker.

2. Non-controlling shareholder: ***Non-controlling*** persons may also sometimes have to register their shares before selling them. A person who has previously bought stock from the issuer in a private transaction, and who now wishes to resell that stock, could be liable for making an unregistered public offering if a court finds that he ***bought with an intent to resell*** rather than for investment. [556]

a. Rule 144: But Rule 144 may help in this situation, too.

i. Held less than three years: If the non-controlling shareholder has held his restricted stock for ***less than three years***, then he may only use Rule 144 if all the requirements listed above for controlling-shareholder sales are met.

ii. Held for more than three years: But if a non-controlling shareholder has held his restricted stock for ***more than three years***, most limitations are removed: a non-controlling shareholder who buys stock in a private offering and then holds that stock for three years may sell ***to whomever he wishes***, and whatever amounts he wishes, by whatever type of transaction he wishes, without reference to whether the company files SEC reports, and without any need to file any notice with the SEC. (But, of course, the resale must not itself constitute a brand new public offering.)

E. Other exemptions: There are two other significant exemptions: [557]

1. **Intrastate offerings:** Section 3(a)(11) of the '33 Act exempts "***intrastate*** offerings." However, this exception is very hard to qualify for, and is rarely used except in isolated areas that are very far from any state border. [557]

2. **Regulation A:** Regulation A is a set of SEC Rules that gives an exemption for certain issues of up to $5 million. Its main use is for offerings made under employee stock option or stock purchase plans. [557]

V. PUBLIC OFFERINGS — CIVIL LIABILITIES

A. **Generally:** There are four liability provisions under the '33 Act, at least three of which impose civil liability in favor of an injured investor. [558]

B. **Section 11:** Section 11 imposes liability for any material errors or omissions ***in a registration statement***. [558]

1. **Who may sue:** A Section 11 suit may be brought by ***anyone*** who buys the stock covered by the registration statement (even if he did not buy at the initial public offering). [558]

2. **Reliance:** P does not have to show that he ***relied*** on the registration statement. (However, D can raise the affirmative defense of showing that P knew of the untruth or omission at the time he purchased it.) [559]

3. **Who may be sued:** A wide range of people may be sued under § 11, including: (1) everyone who signed the registration statement (which always includes at least the issuer and the principal officers); (2) everyone who is a ***director*** at the time the registration statement was filed; (3) every ***expert*** who consented to being named as having prepared part of the registration statement; and (4) every ***underwriter***. [559]

4. **Standard of conduct:** The issuer's liability is ***absolute***; even if the misstatement or omission was inadvertent and in fact non-negligent, the issuer is strictly liable. But all other defendants may raise the ***"due diligence"*** defense. [559]

   a. **Expertised portions:** With respect to any part of the registration statement prepared by an ***expert***: (1) the expert can establish the due diligence defense only by affirmatively showing that he conducted a ***reasonable investigation*** that left him with reasonable ground to believe, and the actual belief, that the part he prepared was accurate; but (2) all other persons (the ***non-experts***) merely have to prove the negative proposition that they "had ***no reasonable ground to believe and did not believe***" that there was any material misstatement or omission. (Thus an ordinary director can entrust to the issuer's accounting firm the preparation of the audited financial statements, as long as he is not on notice of inaccuracies.)

   b. **Non-expertised portions:** With respect to parts of the registration not prepared by experts, D must show that: (1) he made a ***reasonable investigation***; and (2) after that investigation, he was left with reasonable ground to believe, and did in fact believe, that there was no material misstatement or omission. (Inside directors will usually find this harder to show than will outside directors.)

C. **Section 12(1):** Section ***12(1)*** imposes liability on anyone who sells a security that ***should have been registered but was not***. Liability here is imposed even for an honest and in fact non-negligent mistake. However, a buyer may only sue his immediate seller, not someone further back in the chain of distribution. [561]

D. Section 12(2): Section ***12(2)*** imposes liability for untrue statements of material fact and for omission of material fact. Unlike § 11, it is ***not limited to misstatements made in the registration statement***. (For instance, misstatements made ***orally***, or in a writing other than the registration statement, are covered.) Not only the seller but anyone who is a "substantial factor" in making the sale (e.g., a ***broker*** or public relations consultant for the seller) may be sued. A ***negligence*** standard is used. [561]

E. Section 17(a): Section 17(a) imposes a general ***anti-fraud*** provision. Unlike the three sections discussed above, most courts have held that 17(a) does not support a private right of action by investors (merely a right on the part of the government to prevent or punish violations). [561]

VI. PUBLIC OFFERINGS — STATE REGULATION

A. State "Blue Sky" laws generally: Every state regulates some aspects of securities transactions through regulations collectively known as ***"blue sky"*** laws. [562]

1. **'96 Act changes rules:** However, Congress took away a large portion of the states' Blue Sky Powers, in the ***National Securities Improvement Act of 1996.*** State regulation of securities ***issuance*** is now largely ***preempted*** by federal regulation.

CHAPTER 1

INTRODUCTION

I. WHAT IS A CORPORATION

A. Formed by filing with Secretary of State: In every state, one or more people may form a corporation by simply filing a document with the Secretary of State or some similar state official. (The mechanics of this process are described in detail *infra*, p. 21.)

B. Artificial entity: What is this "corporation" that has been so formed? Its key aspect is that it is an ***independent entity***, separate from the identity of its owners (who are, of course, "shareholders"). Even though the corporate entity is artificial, it is treated the ***same as a person*** for many purposes. For instance, it can enter into contracts, own property, and sue or be sued.

C. Key advantages: Why do we need to have corporations at all? Some of the reasons will become clear when we discuss, shortly below, how one should choose between the partnership form and the corporate form in setting up a new business venture. For now, here are the two key advantages that a corporation has over an individual (who if he is operating a business is said to be running a "sole proprietorship") or over a group of individuals (who when they run a business together are said to be operating a "partnership"):

1. **Limited liability:** First and foremost, the corporate form allows for ***limited liability***. Each shareholder is normally liable only for the amounts that he contributes to the corporation; if the corporation runs up large debts, the shareholders are usually not responsible. In contrast, a person operating a sole proprietorship, or a group of individuals operating a partnership, will normally be personally liable for the debts of the enterprise.

2. **Free transferability:** Second, ownership interests in the corporation are ***freely transferable***. Ownership interests in the corporation are represented by shares, and shares can be readily sold. Selling partial stakes in a sole proprietorship or partnership is somewhat more complicated.

II. SOURCES OF CORPORATION LAW

A. Created by a particular state: A corporation is always created ***under the laws of a particular state.*** The corporation is then said to be incorporated "in" that state. (There are virtually no "federal" corporations, only corporations created under the laws of a particular state.) The significance of the choice of the state of incorporation is discussed extensively beginning *infra*, p. 19. For now, you should merely understand that the law of the state of incorporation controls nearly all matters of "corporate governance"; thus the powers of stockholders and of the board of directors, the requirements for corporate acquisitions and mergers, the circumstances under which dividends may be paid, indeed virtually all legal principles described in this book (except for certain matters governed by the federal securities laws concerning publicly-held corporations) are determined by the law of the state of incorporation.

B. Delaware: The state of ***Delaware*** occupies a disproportionately major role in corporate law. Both for historical reasons and as a matter of the state's own business strategy, a large number of corporations headquartered elsewhere are incorporated in Delaware. (For instance, over half of all the corporations listed on the New York Stock Exchange are incorporated in Delaware. See Hamilton (8th), p. 238.) Delaware has a very finely-developed corporation statute and accompanying body of case law. Therefore, we will be paying far more attention to Delaware corporate law than to the law of any other state.

C. Other key states: A few other states have unusual importance in corporate law, not so much because their jurisprudence is so well-developed but simply because these states are the domicile for large numbers of corporations. New York and California are the principal states, apart from Delaware, that we will be focusing on.

D. MBCA: An important source of guidance about corporation law, especially for students, comes from the ***Model Business Corporations Act*** (MBCA). This is a model act prepared by a committee of the American Bar Association. The MBCA has heavily influenced the corporation statutes of more than half the states. Nutshell, pp. 7-8.

1. **Revisions:** The present overall version of the MCBA was drafted in 1984. Major revisions of the portions dealing with mergers and acquisitions, and with appraisal rights, were published in 1999.

E. ALI project: The newest major source of guidance on corporate law is the American Law Institute's *Principles of Corporate Governance*. The ALI text is comparable to the Restatements prepared by the ALI in other subjects; the *Principles* form a sort of "Restatement of Corporations." The *Principles* were completed in 1994.

III. CHOOSING BETWEEN CORPORATE AND PARTNERSHIP FORM

A. Choice between partnership and corporation: A lay person who is setting up a business often assumes that the only sensible form of organization for the business is a corporation. However, this is not necessarily true. Often, it will make more sense to set the business up as a ***partnership***. In this Section III, we examine some of the factors that should be considered in choosing between the corporate and partnership forms.

1. **Non-corporate non-partnership forms:** Before we examine the partnership-vs-corporation decision, let us briefly touch upon two forms of organization that are neither corporations nor partnerships: (1) the ***sole proprietorship***; and (2) the ***limited liability company (LLC)***.

   a. **Sole proprietorship:** If there will only be one "owner" of the business, it may be feasible to set the business up as a ***"sole proprietorship."*** In a sole proprietorship, the owner of the business carries on the business ***as an individual***. This means that he is directly liable for all the debts of the proprietorship, and he reports the gains and losses from the proprietorship directly on his own personal income tax return. In many respects, a sole proprietorship is a "one person partnership" — that is, many of the attributes of partnerships apply to a sole proprietorship. Because of this close resemblance, we will not talk any further about sole proprietorships, and will focus on choosing between the corporate and partnership forms.

b. **Limited liability company (LLC):** Since the 1990s, every state has recognized a fourth form of organization, the ***"limited liability company,"*** or ***"LLC."*** The two most important attributes of the LLC are that: (1) all those with an economic interest in the business ("members," analogous to partners in a partnership) can ***limit their liability*** to the ***amount invested*** (not so easily done with partnerships); and (2) the entity can elect to be ***taxed either as a corporation or as a partnership***, whichever the members prefer. Also, LLCs offer tremendous flexibility in management, financing, and other operational aspects. LLCs are discussed further *infra*, p. 11.

B. **Nature of partnership:** In order to assess the pros and cons of partnerships versus corporations, we must first understand a little bit about the nature of partnerships.

1. **General partnership:** The simple term "partnership" normally refers to a so-called ***"general partnership."*** All partnerships are "general" unless the particular statutory requirements for a limited partnership (see *infra*) are complied with. In all states, general partnerships are governed by statutes patterned on the ***Uniform Partnership Act*** (UPA). The most recent version of the UPA was promulgated in 1997.

a. **How created:** The UPA defines a partnership as "an association of two or more persons to carry on as co-owners a business for profit." § 6(1). In contrast to a corporation, a general partnership can come into existence by ***operation of law***, without the need to file any formal papers with any state official. Thus if Jones and Smith, without signing any agreement between them and without filing any documents with the state, begin to jointly operate a corner candy store, they will have a general partnership. The most important single fact about general partnerships is that ***each*** partner is liable (vis-a-vis the outside world) for all the ***debts*** of the partnership. (See *infra*, p. 4.)

i. **Creation by "estoppel":** Two people who don't actually intend to be in partnership with each other can even be found to have created a partnership ***"by estoppel,"*** if they ***represent*** to the ***outside world*** that they are in partnership together. Thus §16 of the UPA says that "a person. . .[who] represents himself, or consents to another representing him to any one, as a partner in an existing partnership … is liable to any such person to whom such representation has been made, who has, on the faith of such representation, ***given credit*** to the actual or apparent partnership."

2. **Limited partnership:** All states also allow the formation of something called a ***"limited"*** partnership. In all states, limited partnerships are governed by either the Uniform Limited Partnership Act (ULPA) or the newer 1976 Revised Uniform Limited Partnership Act (RULPA).

a. **Formation:** Unlike general partnerships (but like corporations), limited partnerships may only be created by filing a formal document with a state official. Also, there must be a ***written agreement*** among the partners. RULPA § 201.

b. **Nature:** Limited partnerships have two kinds of partner: (1) one or more "general" partners, who are each liable for ***all*** the debts of the partnership; and (2) one or more ***"limited"*** partners, who are ***not*** liable for the debts of the partnership beyond the amount that they have contributed to the partnership.

i. **Corporate general partner:** To allow liability to be limited even further, the general partner(s) may be a ***corporation***, and in fact a corporation with few assets. This means that a limited partnership, if carefully constructed, can be put into place without any individual being exposed to the unlimited personal liability that is characteristic of general partnerships.

ii. **Limited partners cannot participate in management:** Why would anyone ever choose to be a general partner in a limited partnership, rather than being a limited partner? The reason is that a limited partner ***may not participate actively in the management of the partnership***; if he does participate, he will lose his limited liability. (But the problem is not as bad as it sounds. The individuals who will be running the partnership probably can create a corporation of which they are the sole stockholders, and can make the corporation be the general partner; the fact that the individuals are running the corporate general partner usually does not cause these individuals to be regarded as "de facto" general partners who have sacrificed their limited liability.

c. **LLP:** Most states now also allow something called a ***"limited liability partnership,"*** or ***LLP***. LLPs are discussed *infra*, p. 5.

C. **List of factors:** In deciding whether to organize a new venture as a corporation or as a partnership, there are six major factors which need to be considered: (1) limited liability; (2) management; (3) continuity of operations; (4) transferability; (5) complexity and expense of forming and operating the enterprise; and (6) federal income tax considerations. We consider each of these factors in turn.

D. **Limited liability:** It is with respect to ***limited liability*** that the difference between corporations and partnerships is clearest.

1. **Corporation:** In the case of a corporation, as noted, the shareholders' liability is normally ***limited*** to the amount they have invested. If the corporation runs up large debts after the shareholders have made their initial capital contribution, the shareholders are normally not responsible for those debts.

a. **Lenders often require guarantee:** However, this advantage is not quite as significant as it may at first seem to be. The problem is that ***banks*** and ***other lenders*** understand the normal rule of limited shareholder liability just as well as business people do. Therefore, if the corporation is just starting and/or has limited assets, lenders usually simply will not lend money to the corporation without ***personal guarantees*** by some or all shareholders. Therefore, the advantage of limited liability boils down mostly to avoiding liability for (1) debts to ordinary "trade creditors", i.e., suppliers of goods and services to the corporation; and (2) suits by tort claimants (e.g., a person hit by a truck driven by a corporate employee while on corporate business). (But even these two classes of possible creditors may very occasionally be able to recover against the shareholders by "piercing the corporate veil"; see *infra* p. 34.)

2. **Partnership:** The liability of partners, as you might expect, varies depending on whether the partnership is a general or limited one.

a. **General partnership:** In a ***general*** partnership, ***all partners are individually liable for the obligations of the partnership.***

i. **Joint ability to bind partnership:** This joint liability applies even where one partner does not participate in the act that causes the partnership to become liable. For instance, remember Smith and Jones, who are operating the local candy store as a general partnership. Assume that Smith and Jones have signed a partnership agreement that explicitly provides that neither will incur any obligations on behalf of the partnership without the consent of the other. Now, assume that Smith orders a new $50,000 freezer without telling Jones. If the partnership does not pay the bill, the supplier of the freezer will be able to sue Jones as well as Smith — the Smith-Jones partnership agreement does not save Jones from liability vis-a-vis the world (though he will have a claim over against Smith for breach of the agreement).

ii. **Limited Liability Partnership (LLP):** But the modern (1997) version of the UPA gives partners in what would otherwise be a traditional general partnership a chance to avoid the standard individual liability for partnership debts. The partners can elect to be a ***"limited liability partnership,"*** or ***"LLP."*** UPA § 1001. Once the partnership files such a statement of election, ***no partner will be liable for the partnership's obligations*** just by virtue of being a partner. § 306(c). (The partnership must indicate that it has LLP status by appending some variant of the word "LLP" after its name [§ 1002], so that members of the public who do business with the partnership will know that individual partners won't be liable for partnership obligations.)

(1) **Most states now allow:** Most states have now passed statutes, modelled on the UPA provisions, recognizing the LLP.

(2) **Professional service corporations:** The biggest users of LLP status are ***professional service firms***, like ***law firms*** and ***accounting*** firms. The biggest practical benefit of the LLP status to such a service firm is that the individual partners will not be liable for acts of ***malpractice*** committed by other partners.

(3) **Partner can actively participate in management:** The LLP status also has a major advantage over a traditional limited partnership, since a limited partner will lose her freedom from liability by participating in management, but a partner in an LLP will not.

b. **Limited partnership:** In a ***limited*** partnership, as noted, the general partners are personally liable but the limited partners are liable only to the amount of their capital contributions. But remember that the limited partners will lose this limit on their liability if they participate actively in the management of the partnership. (But as noted above, the *LLP*, or "limited liability partnership," does not have this problem – in an LLP, as distinguished from a limited partnership, a partner may participate in management to her heart's content without thereby becoming liable for partnership obligations.)

3. **Summary:** So with respect to limited liability, the corporation is distinctly superior to the general partnership. Also, if individuals want to be able to actively participate in man-

agement without losing their limited liability, the corporation is much superior to the limited partnership (but not superior to the LLP).

E. Management: Corporations and partnerships differ with respect to how the enterprise will be ***managed*** and controlled.

1. Corporation: Corporations follow the principle of ***centralized*** management. The shareholders participate only by electing the board of directors. The board of directors then appoints "officers" (i.e., high-level executives). The corporation is managed under the supervision of the board, with day-to-day control resting with the officers. So if the investors desire to entrust management to non-shareholders, or to some but not all shareholders — which will frequently be the case in a larger corporation — the centralized management structure of the corporation is helpful.

2. Partnership: In partnerships, the "standard" mode of management is ***not*** a centralized one.

a. General partnership: In a ***general*** partnership, ***all*** partners have an equal voice in managing the enterprise, unless they otherwise agree. But it is important to realize that the partners may indeed "otherwise agree." For instance, they may decide that the decision-making powers will be limited to one or a few of them rather than all.

i. Right to deal with the rest of the world: But remember that such internal agreements concerning decision-making authority are ***not binding*** on outsiders who are unaware of these agreements. (Remember our example of Smith, Jones and the freezer, *supra*, p. 5.) Thus even if the 26 general partners in ABC Partnership agree that only partner A will have the right to commit the firm, ***any*** partner may nonetheless bind the partnership in a deal with an outsider, if the outsider is not aware of this agreement. See S,S,B&W, p. 164.

b. Limited partnership: Management in a limited partnership is the same as in a general partnership, except that the limited partners may not actively participate in management without losing their limited liability. In other words, each general partner may bind the partnership vis-a-vis the rest of the world.

3. Summary: So if the management of the entity needs to be entrusted to non-owners or to fewer than all of the owners, and it is important to make sure that only certain people can make deals with the rest of the world on behalf of the enterprise, the corporate form is clearly superior.

F. Continuity of existence: Partnership and corporations differ as to their ability to ***continue in existence*** when ownership changes.

1. Corporation: A corporation has ***"perpetual existence."*** In other words, the fact that ownership (i.e., shares) changes hands, whether by sale, inheritance, gift, etc., does not in any way affect the corporation's continuing existence.

2. Partnership: The rules for a partnership are quite different.

a. General: A ***general*** partnership is ***dissolved by the death*** of any general partner. In fact, even the ***withdrawal*** of a general partner will dissolve the partnership unless the partnership agreement otherwise provides. See UPA §§ 31-32.

i. **Provisions for:** But this is not as big a problem as it sounds. First, the partnership agreement may provide that the withdrawal of a partner will not cause the partnership to dissolve. Furthermore, even the mandatory dissolution on account of a partner's death can be made surprisingly painless — the partnership agreement can (and usually does) provide that the dead partner's interest will be "bought out," and that the remaining partners will then carry on the business with a new partnership. S,S,B&W, p. 165.

b. **Limited:** A ***limited*** partnership is not dissolved by the withdrawal or death of a limited partner. *Id.*

3. **Summary:** If it is important to the owners that the business continue with a minimum of fuss even if one owner withdraws or dies, then the corporate form is somewhat superior. But it may be the case (especially in smaller businesses dependent on the skills of a few owners/managers) that an owner/manager will want the bargaining power that comes from an ability to unilaterally dissolve the partnership. In any event, through careful drafting of the partnership or shareholders' agreement, a corporation can be made to look like a partnership, or a partnership like a corporation, with respect to continuity of existence. See the discussion of shareholders' agreements, p. 133.

G. **Transferability of interest:** The two forms of organization differ with respect to how readily ***transferable*** an ownership interest is.

1. **Corporation:** Ownership interests in a ***corporation*** are very readily transferable. Ownership is, of course, embodied in shares of stock. Unless the shareholders otherwise agree (see the discussion of shareholders' agreements *infra*, p. 146), any shareholder may at any time sell or give his shares to anyone else without consent by the other shareholders. This transferability is especially important where: (1) the business wants to attract "venture capital," i.e., equity investments in a young or start-up business; or (2) the business is large and is owned by many different people.

2. **Partnership:** By contrast, a partnership interest is not really transferable to the same extent. Ordinarily, ***all*** partners must consent to the admission of a new partner. See UPA § 18(g). A partner may "assign" his partnership interest, but this does not make the transferee a partner; instead, the transferee merely obtains limited economic rights.

a. **Pros and cons:** Of course, this limited transferability is not necessarily a disadvantage. It will often be very comforting for each partner to know that no new partner may be thrust upon him without his consent. (Since each general partner can bind the entire partnership, this veto power over new partners is absolutely essential. S,S,B&W, p. 166.)

b. **Limited partners:** ***Limited*** partners, similarly, may in a sense transfer their interests, but the transferee does not really become a limited partner — he merely has certain economic rights. The transferability features of limited partnership interests are strong enough that there actually exist "public limited partnerships" whose limited partnership shares are traded on major stock exchanges. One buys and sells "limited partnership interests" in such partnerships much as one would buy or sell stock in a corporation.

3. **Summary:** If free transferability is important, the corporate form is clearly superior to the partnership form. If it is important to the owners that there ***not*** be free transferability, the partnership form may be somewhat preferable (thought the same results can usually be obtained by a corporation through a carefully-drafted shareholders agreement).

H. Complexity of formation and operation: Especially where the business will at the beginning be small and thinly capitalized, the degree of ***complexity*** and ***expense*** involved in forming and operating the business will be important, and will vary as between corporation and partnership.

1. **Corporation:** It is not all that cheap or simple to incorporate. The would-be shareholders must file a moderately complex document with the Secretary of State, and more importantly, must then comply with a small blizzard of regulatory requirements applicable to corporations. There is likely to be a minimum annual tax (often called a "franchise fee") imposed on the corporation even if it is unprofitable.

2. **Partnership:** By contrast, a partnership (at least a general partnership) can be created and maintained with somewhat less expense and fuss. As noted, no formal documents need to be filed with the state to create a partnership, and indeed, a partnership can come into existence by operation of law (merely by virtue of the joint operation of a business) even though the partners have not explicitly agreed that they will operate a partnership. There tend to be somewhat fewer regulatory requirements, and some states do not impose a fee on the partnership for the mere privilege of existing. (But remember that both a limited partnership and an LLP are like a corporation in that they *do* have to be formally filed with the state.)

3. **Summary:** So if the enterprise will be a very modest one carried on by just a couple of people, ease and inexpensiveness of creating the enterprise and operating it argue in favor of the partnership rather than corporate form.

I. Federal income tax: The ***federal income tax*** consequences of operating as a corporation rather than as a partnership are enormous. We can only touch very superficially on the differences.

1. **Corporation:** The corporation is taxed as a ***separate entity***. In other words, if the corporation has profits or losses, it files its own tax return, and pays its own taxes independently of the tax position of the stockholders.

   a. **"Double taxation":** One consequence of the corporation's status as a separate taxpayer is that there will often be so-called ***"double taxation."*** The corporation pays a corporate income tax on its profits. If the after-corporate-tax profits are then distributed to the shareholders as ***dividends***, the individual shareholders pay a separate, second, tax on these dividends.

   Example: Suppose that ABC Corp. earns one million dollars after paying all expenses (including salaries). Simplifying in terms of tax rates, ABC will pay a corporate-level tax (at 2002 rates) of 34%, or $340,000. If the remaining $660,000 is paid out to the stockholders as dividends, these stockholders will pay individual income taxes. Assuming that each shareholder has taxable income of, say, $150,000 before these dividends and is married filing jointly, the individual federal marginal tax rate on the total $660,000 dividends will be 30% (or additional taxes of $198,000). So the pre-tax profit will go though a combined tax mill equaling about 54% before ending up in the hands of shareholders. (But if the shareholders are corporations, the dividends they receive will be taxed at a much lower rate, on account of special treatment given to "inter-company dividends.")

i. **Deduction of salaries:** But for closely-held corporations, the double taxation problem is usually not as bad as it seems. If the corporation can pay out most of its pre-tax profits in the form of high ***salaries*** to the owner/managers, the problem just about goes away. The reason is that ***salaries are deductible at the corporate level***; therefore, most of the profits will only be taxed at the individual level (when received by the shareholders as salary), not at the corporate level (since the corporate profit after deducting salaries will be little or nothing).

ii. **Reinvested profits:** Also, keep in mind that the double taxation problem only arises when the corporate profits are actually ***paid out***. If the corporation holds onto the profits to reinvest them in the business, then there is *only* the corporate-level taxation. (There is a possibility that these accumulations might be taxed under a separate provision of the Internal Revenue Code intended to discourage unreasonably large accumulations, but this is usually not a problem.)

b. **Subchapter S:** The usual principles of corporate taxation can be avoided if the corporation qualifies for status as a "Subchapter S corporation," and elects to be treated that way. See *infra,* p. 10.

c. **Fringe benefits:** Many ***fringe benefits*** given to owner/managers of corporations receive very favorable taxation. For instance, pension and profit-sharing plans, and stock options, are more available to corporations than to partnerships.

2. **Partnership:** Partnerships, unlike corporations, are ***not separately-taxable entities***. Instead, the partnership is viewed as an aggregation of individuals for tax purposes. True, the partnership files a tax return; but this tax return is merely an ***informational*** return, which shows how much the partnership earned and how those earnings are distributed among the partners. The actual tax is ***paid by each individual***, and is therefore a function of his own tax bracket and the other earnings or losses he has.

a. **Avoids double taxation:** This means that the partnership avoids the "double taxation" problem that can occur in corporations. On our example from p. 8, if ABC operated as a partnership rather than a corporation, the total tax on the $1 million of pre-tax profits would probably be about $300,000, all of which would be reported on the partners' individual tax returns.

b. **Ability to allocate:** Another tax advantage of partnerships is that the partners may ***allocate*** the gains and losses from the partnership to individual partners pretty much as the partners decide.

c. **Shelter:** Partnerships offer significant opportunities for ***sheltering*** gains from other activities (though these opportunities were much reduced by the Tax Reform Act of 1986). So long as a partner is ***actively involved*** in management of the partnership, he may offset his share of losses incurred by the partnership against gains from other activities. Thus if Smith and Jones operate their candy store while each holds down a salaried job somewhere else, and the store loses money, each can subtract his share of the losses from his salaried income and pay individual taxes only on the difference. S,S,B&W, p. 173.

3. **Subchapter S:** If the owner/stockholders of a corporation would like to be taxed approximately as if they were partners in a partnership, they will often be able to do so by having their corporation elect to be treated as a ***Subchapter S*** corporation.

   a. **Tax treatment:** A Subchapter S corporation does not get taxed at the corporate level, unlike a regular (or "Subchapter C") corporation. In a loose sense, stockholders in an S corporation are treated as if they were partners. For instance, if A and B each owned 50% of ABC Corp, an S Corp., and the corporation had pre-tax profits of $100,000, ABC would not pay any tax, and A and B would each report $50,000 of taxable income.

   b. **Shelter:** Like a partnership and unlike a C corporation, an S corporation may furnish the opportunity to ***shelter*** income from other sources. Thus if ABC Corp has a loss of $100,000 instead of a gain, A and B as equal shareholders may each use his $50,000 loss to offset $50,000 from, say, a salary earned at a different job. (However, these losses are limited to each investor's "basis" in his ABC stock, i.e., his investment in the corporation.)

   c. **Requirements:** Not all corporations are eligible for taxation as S corporations. The main requirements are that: (1) there must be no more than 75 shareholders; (2) all shareholders must be individuals, estates or qualified trusts; and (3) there may be only one class of stock outstanding.

4. **LLC:** Similarly, if the members of an ***LLC*** (see *infra*, p. 11) would like to be treated as partners in a partnership, they may so elect.

5. **Summary:** In summary, the investors will probably prefer to be taxed as partners rather than as C corporation stockholders if the business has (after payment of salaries) either losses or large profits. If the partnership form is used, the losses can be offset against other income (at least if the partners are actively involved in running the business) and the profits will be taxed at a lower rate than if they were corporate profits. Conversely, the corporate form is probably better if, after payment of salaries, the corporation makes a modest profit (say between $15,000 and $75,000). The corporate form is also attractive if fringe benefits like pension and profit sharing plans are an important part of the total economic benefit that will be received by the owners. Lastly, many of the benefits of partnership taxation can be achieved by operating as an S corporation or as an LLC.

J. **Overall summary of corporations vs. partnerships:** Summing up our various factors, we can say the following about the corporation-vs-partnership choice:

   1. **Corporations superior:** The corporate form is usually superior: (1) where the owners find it important to limit their liability; (2) where free transferability of interests is important; (3) where centralized management is important, as where there is a large number of owners who cannot all be active in the business; and (4) where continuity of existence, in the face of withdrawal or death of an owner, is significant.

a. **Large number of owners:** These factors taken together mean that if there will be a large number of owners (say more than several hundred), the corporate form is dramatically superior to the general partnership form. (A ***limited*** partnership may be an adequate alternative in this situation.)

2. **Partnerships superior:** Conversely, the partnership form will be superior where: (1) simplicity and inexpensiveness of creation and operation are very important (as where the enterprise is very small and not very profitable); and (2) where there are either losses or large profits, making the fact that the partnership is taxed only at the level of the individual partners significant. (But remember that these tax advantages will often be largely attainable in the corporate form, by operating as an S corporation.)

IV. THE LIMITED LIABILITY COMPANY (LLC)

A. **Limited Liability Companies generally:** The fastest growing form of organization since the 1990s has been the ***limited liability company***, or ***LLC***. All 50 states have enacted special statutes recognizing and regulating LLCs. The LLC is neither a corporation nor a partnership, though it has aspects of each. In the opinion of many business lawyers and business operators, LLCs incorporate the best features of both corporations and partnerships.

1. **Advantages:** Here are the principal ***advantages*** of an LLC over both a corporation and a partnership:

a. **Limited liability:** Recall that in a standard (general) partnership, ***each partner*** is ***personally liable*** for the debts of the partnership. (*Supra*, p. 5.) Even in a limited partnership, there must be a general partner who has full personal liability for partnership debts. (Furthermore, in a limited partnership, a person who wants to be a limited partner and thus have the protection of limited liability may not be active in the business's operations.)

The LLC suffers from none of these undesirable liability-related problems: ***no "member"*** (analogous to a partner in a partnership or a stockholder in a corporation) ***can be liable for anything other than the amount of his investment in the LLC, regardless of how involved that member is in the daily operations of the business.*** So for liability-limiting purposes, an LLC is every bit as good as a corporation.

b. **Taxed as partnership:** Yet the LLC members can elect to have the entity treated, for ***federal tax purposes***, as a ***partnership***. Therefore, unlike the standard "C" corporation (*supra*, p. 8), the LLC can operate as a ***"pass-through" entity and avoid double taxation.***

i. **Flexibility in allocations:** Furthermore, being taxed like a partnership offers great flexibility in the ***allocation of gains and losses***, flexibility that is not present in the one type of corporate structure that is a pass-through, the "S" corporation. For instance, an LLC's two members could agree that *A* (an individual in a high tax bracket) would receive 99% of all operating losses, and that *B* (a low-tax-bracket person) would receive 99% of all operating profits. They could additionally agree that gains on sale of the business would be split, say, 70% to *A* and 30% to *B*, regardless of what percentage of startup capital each provided. This kind of customized allocation cannot readily be done in an S corporation, where the allocations are essentially dictated by each parties' percentage of stock ownership.

c. **Flexibility in operations:** Lastly, the LLC provides nearly total flexibility in how ***operations are to be conducted***. For instance, whereas a corporate Board of Directors may generally take action only by a formal meeting (see *infra*, p. 65), an LLC's members may provide that action may be taken without a formal meeting by a vote of a majority of the "managers" (i.e., the people designated to run the company's business operations.) Similarly, the restrictions that exist by statute on a corporation's right to dispose of its financial resources — see, e.g., the restrictions on dividends discussed *infra*, p. 508 — have no counterpart under the LLC statutes. See Hamilton (7th), p. 190.

2. **Disadvantages:** LLCs, however, do have some ***disadvantages***. Here are a few:

   a. **Complexity in formation:** LLCs are more ***complex to form*** — an LLC requires an ***"operating agreement"*** to specify how it will work (*infra*, pp. 12-14), and the very flexibility that the LLC form allows makes drafting an effective operating agreement more challenging than, say, drafting the more-routine certificate of incorporation and bylaws for a typical corporation. *Id.* at 193.

   b. **Veil-piercing:** It may turn out that it is easier to ***"pierce the veil"*** of an LLC (see *infra*, p. 14) than that of a corporation (see *infra*, p. 34).

   c. **State taxes:** In some states, state income or franchise taxes are applicable to LLCs just as they are to corporations, but are not applicable to partnerships. In these states, this is therefore an advantage to the partnership form. *Id.* at 194.

3. **ULLCA:** Just as there are Uniform Acts governing other types of business entities (e.g., the Uniform Partnership Act, *supra*, p. 3), so there is now a ***Uniform Limited Liability Company Act (ULLCA)***, created in 1994 and revised in 2006. However, the act has not been very widely adopted: as of the end of 2010, only ten states had enacted either the original or the revised ULLCA. Hamilton (11th), p. 1183.

B. **Operating agreement:** Recall that one of the advantages of LLCs is their extreme flexibility. That flexibility derives from fact that state statutes allowing the formation of LLCs contain far fewer absolute rules about how the entity must conduct its affairs than is the case with, say, corporations. Instead, owners of the LLC (called ***"members"***) must agree among themselves how the business will operate (e.g., what kind of a vote is necessary to sell the LLC's assets or change its principal business?). They typically do so by means of an ***"operating agreement,"*** which is a contract among the members.

1. **May be oral:** The better practice is clearly to have the operating agreement be in writing. But many state statutes allow for an ***oral*** operating agreement. See, e.g., ULLCA § 103 ("All members of a limited liability company may enter into an operating agreement, which ***need not be in writing***, to regulate the affairs of the company and the conduct of its business, and to govern relations among the members, managers, and company.")

2. **Company is itself bound:** The parties to an operating agreement are normally the members, and the company itself is not necessarily a member. Therefore, the question sometimes arises, if the LLC itself has not signed the operating agreement, is the LLC

nonetheless ***bound*** by the terms of that agreement? In the principal case on the issue, set forth in the next example, the Delaware Supreme Court has answered ***"yes."***

Example: Two corporations, Elf and Malek, Inc., and an individual, Jaffari (owner of Malek, Inc.) set up an LLC, Malek LLC, and become its members. The three members sign an operating agreement (the "Agreement") for Malek LLC, but Malek LLC does not itself sign the Agreement. The Agreement contains a clause saying that all disputes must be subjected to arbitration, and that if a dispute is not arbitrable it must be tried in the California courts. The members then have a dispute about how the company is being run, with Elf alleging that Jaffari has withdrawn LLC funds for his personal use and otherwise improperly behaved. Elf brings a "derivative action" (see *infra*, p. 318) against Jaffari and Malek LLC in Delaware. Jaffari asserts that the Agreement's arbitration and forum-selection clauses bar this Delaware litigation. Elf counters that because Malek LLC is not a party to the Agreement, the arbitration and forum-selection clauses are not applicable to Elf's suit against Malek LLC.

Held (by the Delaware Supreme Court), for Jaffari. Even though Malek LLC did not sign the Agreement, all of the LLC's members did, and they are the "real parties in interest" (the LLC is "simply their joint business vehicle.") Therefore, the fact that all members have signed the Agreement is enough to make the arbitration and forum-selection clauses in the Agreement enforceable. Furthermore, "the policy of the [Delaware LLC] Act is to give the maximal effect to the principles of freedom of contract and to the enforceability of LLC agreements[.]" This policy dictates enforcing the parties' decision to change the usual rules under which controversies involving Delaware business entities can be litigated in the Delaware courts. *Elf Atochem North America, Inc. v. Jaffari and Malek LLC*, 727 A.2d 286 (Del. 1999).

3. **Adherence to rights can't be breach of implied covenant of good faith:** An LLC's operating agreement is of course a contract, and you'll remember from first-year Contracts that all contracts contain an ***implied covenant of good faith and fair dealing***. Disgruntled LLC members have frequently argued that another member's conduct, even though expressly allowed by the terms of the operating agreement, ***constitutes a breach*** of this implied covenant. But these arguments have ***not fared well*** in the courts — where a member exercises a right that is expressly given to her by the operating agreement, courts almost ***never*** hold that that exercise constitutes a breach of the covenant of good faith and fair dealing.

   a. **Illustration (*Fisk Ventures v. Segal*):** A Delaware Chancery case, ***Fisk Ventures, LLC v. Segal***, 2008 WL 1961156 (Del. Ch. 2008), illustrates this principle.

      i. **Structure:** In *Fisk Ventures*, P (Segal) was a biochemist who formed Genitrix, LLC ("the LLC"), a biomedical company. The LLC had several classes of membership interests. Segal as founder controlled the Class A interest. D (Fisk Ventures), a venture capital company, together with its head, was the principal investor, and in return received control of the Class B interest. The operating agreement was drafted in such a way that ***no significant action*** could be taken except by ***agreement between the Class A and Class B members.***

ii. **Fisk's rights:** In return for Fisk's capital, Fisk and the other Class B members received numerous specially-negotiated protections. For instance, the B members received a "Put Right," which allowed them at any time to force the company to re-purchase any or all of the Class B interests at an appraised value; a key feature of the Put Right was that the Class B interests would have a ***liquidation preference*** superior to any claim by anyone who later invested in the company.

iii. **Company runs short of cash:** The LLC ran short of cash. Segal wanted to bring in new investors, but they would invest only if Fisk would surrender or suspend the Put Right (since the new prospects didn't want to put in fresh money if they would be subordinate to the Class B members). Fisk refused to do this, so the outside investors could not be brought in. Fisk and Segal had various other disagreements, which led to a ***deadlock*** in which the company no longer had any funds, offices, or operations. Fisk sued to dissolve the company, and Segal asserted various counterclaims.

iv. **Segal's counterclaims:** Segal's key counterclaim was that when Fisk blocked the various financing opportunities proposed by Segal, Fisk breached the operating agreement's ***implied covenant*** of good faith and fair dealing. Delaware courts had held that this covenant "requires a party in a contractual relationship to refrain from ***arbitrary and unreasonable conduct*** which has the effects of ***preventing the other party to the contract from receiving the fruits of the bargain***." Segal claimed that when Fisk blocked the outside investors, this action had blocked Segal from his bargained-for opportunity to try to continue the company's operations.

v. **Court rejects:** But the court held against Segal; it decided at the pre-trial motions stage that Segal had not even stated facts showing that he might be entitled to relief. The operating agreement ***expressly granted Fisk the right to block*** any financing of which it disapproved — that right to block was built into the structure that required the Class A and Class B interests to cooperate on any significant company action. The implied covenant of good faith and fair dealing, the court held, is a "gap filler," which can be used only where it is clear from the contract that the parties ***would have agreed to the particular term in question had they thought to negotiate the matter.*** The covenant "cannot be invoked where the contract itself ***expressly covers the subject*** at issue." And every blocking step used by Fisk was expressly authorized in the operating agreement. "The ***mere exercise of one's contractual rights,*** without more, ***cannot constitute*** ... a breach ... of the implied covenant of good faith and fair dealing[.]"

Note: For discussion of another phase of this case, in which the court granted Fisk's request for a judicial dissolution, on the grounds that it was no longer "reasonably practicable" to operate the business, see *infra*, p. 159.

C. **Piercing the veil of an LLC:** The LLC is, as we've just seen, in theory a limited liability device, under which members are not liable for the debts of the LLC no matter how involved they are in the daily operations of the business. The same is theoretically true of corporations. Yet, as we'll see later (*infra*, p. 34), in the case of a *corporation's* liabilities, courts sometimes

"pierce the corporate veil" and hold some or all of the shareholders ***personally liable*** for the corporation's obligations. May a court similarly ***pierce the veil of an LLC in a suitable case***, so as to hold one or more members personally liable for the LLC's obligations? LLCs are sufficiently new that there is not much of a consensus about the proper answer, but it seems clear that in at least some (maybe most) states, the answer is sometimes ***"yes."***

1. **Some statutes apply similar rules:** Some state LLC ***statutes*** contain express provisions requiring that whatever the jurisdiction's rules are about when a corporate veil may be pierced, similar rules should apply to the piercing of LLCs. Cf. B,W&P (5th), pp. 360-61. So in such a jurisdiction, clearly an LLC's veil may sometimes be pierced.

2. **Where statute is silent:** Where the state statute governing LLCs is ***silent*** about veil-piercing, most courts have held that, as a matter of common law, ***rules similar to those governing veil-piercing in corporations*** should apply. *Id.*

   a. **Criticism:** But there is at least one factor often used in corporate veil-piercing cases — ***failure to follow organizational formalities*** — that perhaps ought ***not*** to be interpreted the same way in an LLC-piercing case. Thus one court considering the matter endorsed the general idea that courts have equitable power to pierce the veil of an LLC, but then cautioned that "the various factors which would justify piercing an LLC veil ***would not be identical*** to the corporate situation for the obvious reason that ***many of the organizational formalities applicable to corporations do not apply to LLCs.*** The LLC's operation is intended to be much more flexible than a corporation's." *Kaycee Land and Livestock v. Flahive*, 46 P.3d 323 (Wyo. 2002).

      Example: For instance, when the stockholders of a corporation fail to formally issue shares, or to hold shareholders' meetings or directors' meetings, this is a factor that sharply raises the risk of a veil-piercing (see *infra*, p. 39); on the other hand, members of an LLC are *not required* to issue member certificates or to hold regular meetings, so their failure to do so would *not* support veil-piercing.

Quiz Yourself on ***INTRODUCTION*** *(CHOOSING A FORM OF ORGANIZATION)*

1. Scrooge and Marley own a catering business, the Roast of Christmas Present, Inc. They each own 50% of the shares. Marley dies in a freak accident when one of the corporation's employees, Bob Cratchit, drops a haunch of venison on him. Since Marley was a 50% owner of the corporation, does the corporation terminate along with him? ______________

2. Curly owns part of the Nyuck-Nyuck Wise Guys, a major league baseball team. Curly becomes disgusted with the whole business of baseball when the team makes a $50-million, five-year deal with a free agent, Mr. Potatohead. Without telling the other owners, Curly purports to transfer his interest in the team to Shemp. (Curly is one of several hundred owners.) On the issue of whether Curly's interest is in fact transferable, does it matter whether the team is a partnership or a corporation? ______________

3. After their "excellent adventure," Bill and Ted decide to open up a travel agency, Bill & Ted's Excellent Adventures. They decide the business should be operated as a corporation, so they draw up articles of incorporation and put them in the company safe-deposit box. They purport to carry on the business as a

corporation, putting an "Inc." after the business name and keeping the company records and finances separate from their own. Is the travel agency a corporation? ________________

4. Tarzan and Jane each is a 50% owner of the Me Tarzan, You Jane Charm School, Inc., a standard "C" corporation. Last year, the charm school earned a $10,000 profit, which was spent on new etiquette videos. Do Tarzan and Jane each owe tax personally on their respective (50%) shares of the company's profit? ________________

5. Abe and Barbara want to establish a business entity that will operate a business based on an idea that the two of them have developed. They want to choose a form of business entity that will help them achieve several different objectives: (1) allow each of them to be active in the daily affairs of the business; (2) insulate each of them from liability for claims against the business by third parties to the maximum feasible extent; (3) allow them to put all of the business's operating profits into their own pocket, without paying more than one level of federal income tax; (4) entitle Abe to 40% and Barbara to 60% of the business's profits until the first $800,000 of lifetime profits has been distributed, and thereafter entitling the two to split the profits equally; and (5) give each of them a veto over all major business decisions concerning the business. What is the best form of business entity for them to use, and why?

Answers

1. No. Corporate existence is perpetual, and doesn't depend in any way on the continuity of its shareholders. Therefore, the death, withdrawal, or bankruptcy of any shareholder (even a majority or controlling one) doesn't terminate the corporation. [6]

COMPARE: A *partnership* dissolves when any partner dies, withdraws, or files for bankruptcy, unless the partnership agreement provides otherwise. Uniform Partnership Act § 31(1)(a). This means that, when any one of these occurs, the only authority left in the partners, as to the partnership business, is to wind up and liquidate the business. [6]

2. Yes: if it's a partnership, Shemp isn't an owner, and, if it's a corporation, he probably is. The rule on transferability of ownership for a corporation is that shares are freely transferable unless they are subject to a written restriction on transfer. [7] (Note that shares in a "close corporation" (see p. 146) usually have restrictions on transfer and are therefore similar to a partnership in that respect; that's why we specified that there are several hundred owners, so that this wouldn't be considered a close corporation)

For a partnership, unless the partnership contract provides otherwise, a partnership interest is only transferable with the remaining partners' approval; without it, the transferee cannot become a full partner (e.g., he can't vote). [7] (Keep in mind, however, that if the partnership agreement is silent on the subject a partner can assign his *economic interest* in the partnership, such that the assignee gets the partner's profits from the partnership. But the assignee won't have any other involvement with the partnership, such as the power to vote.)

3. No, it's a partnership. The principal difference in formation between a partnership and a corporation is filing. Creating a corporation requires that articles of incorporation be filed with the Secretary of State for the state in which the corporation is to be incorporated. A partnership doesn't even require a written document, unless it's a "limited partnership" (in which only the general partners can be liable for the partnership's debts). Since the travel agency's articles of incorporation weren't filed with the state, Bill and Ted have a partnership. (That's because a partnership is merely "an association of two or more persons to carry on as co-owners a business for profit" (UPA §6(1)); thus a partnership will come into existence by operation of law, as soon as the two or more owners conduct business without a corporation's having been validly formed.)

SIGNIFICANCE: The most important ramification of partnership v. corporation status is that Bill and Ted, as partners in a general partnership, are ***jointly and separately liable*** for the partnership's debts and obligations; if the agency fails, their personal assets could be reached by a partnership creditor. [5] (Here, conceivably the two might get the protection of the "de facto corporation" doctrine, though modern statutes like the MBCA don't recognize this doctrine. [32]) In a corporation, unless the holders have signed explicit guarantees or there are grounds for "piercing the corporate veil," shareholders are only liable for corporate debts and obligations to the extent of their investment in the corporation. [4]

4. **No.** One of the benefits of conducting business as a standard C corporation is that the corporation is a ***separate taxable entity***, such that unless the corporation's income is distributed to shareholders via a dividend, shareholders don't pay tax on corporate income (and, conversely, can't deduct corporate losses). [8]

   EXCEPTION: Small corporations may elect to be treated more-or-less like a partnership for purposes of income and losses, such that income and losses are attributed to the shareholders and must be reported on their personal tax returns regardless of whether income is distributed. This kind of corporation is called a "Subchapter S corporation." [10] (Note that the same result — pass-through taxation as in a partnership — can be created by using a limited liability company (LLC), a newer form of organization that is neither a corporation nor a partnership. [11])

5. **The limited liability company, or LLC.** The LLC outperforms the general partnership and the limited partnership in terms of simultaneously achieving objectives (1) and (2); all partners are personally liable for the debts of a general partnership (thus failing (2)), and in a limited partnership, limited partners are protected against liability, but only if they are passive partners who do not participate in the daily affairs of the business (thus failing (1)). The LLC outperforms an ordinary corporation (a/k/a a "C Corporation"), because the latter will often result in two levels of taxation (corporate-level and individual-level) if the earnings of the business go beyond what can reasonably be paid out as salaries (thus failing (3)). It's true that an "S Corporation" (which is a "pass-through" entity that is essentially taxed only at the individual level) could fulfill objective (3), as well as (1) and (2). But achieving objectives (4) and (5) simultaneously is quite clumsy with an S corporation (or any form of corporation). That's so because the distribution of profits generally has to be done in proportion to each shareholder's holdings of stock, yet it's cumbersome (though doable, through a "shareholders' agreement") to give persons who own unequal amounts of stock equal veto power over all major decisions. The LLC, since it involves the drafting of an operating agreement that can be highly customized with respect to profit-splitting and decision-making, can accomplish all of these five objectives easily. [11-12]

CHAPTER 2

THE CORPORATE FORM

ChapterScope

This Chapter covers a number of introductory topics about the corporate form. The most important concepts in this Chapter are:

- **Articles of incorporation:** To form a corporation, you file ***"articles of incorporation"*** (also known as a ***"charter"***) with the Secretary of State of the state of incorporation. The articles must include the name of the corporation, a "purposes" clause, and the number of shares the corporation is authorized to issue. The articles can usually be amended only by majority vote of shareholders, followed by a new filing with the Secretary of State.

- **Bylaws:** ***"Bylaws"*** are rules governing the ***internal affairs*** of the corporation. Bylaws are usually not filed with the Secretary of State, and are ***more easily amended*** than the articles of incorporation.

- ***Ultra vires*** **doctrine:** The doctrine of ***"ultra vires"*** says that corporate actions that are ***beyond the corporation's authorized powers*** are ***void***. The doctrine is of much less significance today than formerly.

- **Promoter liability:** A person who arranges for formation of a corporation is called a ***"promoter."*** Under some circumstances, the promoter can be liable for ***pre-incorporation contracts*** that he makes on behalf of the corporation.
  - Generally, whether the promoter is liable for a pre-incorporation contract made in the corporation's name depends on ***the intent of the two parties*** (the promoter, and the other party who expects to deal with the corporation once it's formed.)

- **Shareholder liability:** A key purpose of incorporating is to ***prevent shareholders from being held personally liable.*** However, sometimes things go wrong, and the shareholders are held liable anyway.
  - **Piercing the veil:** Most importantly, sometimes a court may ***"pierce the corporate veil"*** to hold shareholders liable, if the corporation can't or doesn't honor claims against it. This is most likely to happen if the corporation is ***inadequately capitalized***, or if shareholders don't ***follow corporate formalities***.

I. WHERE AND HOW TO INCORPORATE

A. Where to incorporate: The individuals who want to form a corporation have several important initial decisions to make. One of these is ***where*** to incorporate. Usually this decision comes down to choosing between: (1) the state where the corporation will have its ***principal place of business***; and (2) ***Delaware***, which has made a major industry out of serving as the state of incorporation for companies whose principal place of business is elsewhere.

1. **"Internal affairs" rule:** What difference does it make where you incorporate? The main significance is that under the "internal affairs" rule, it is the law of the ***state of incorporation*** that controls issues of ***internal corporate governance***. K&C, p. 142. For example, the rules about circumstances under which a corporation may declare a ***dividend*** (see *infra*, p. 505), and the rules about what percentage of stockholders must approve a merger or sale of all the corporation's assets (see *infra*, p. 376) are set by the state of incorporation.

2. **"Permissive" states:** Some states give the corporation's organizers and shareholders nearly unlimited scope to establish whatever corporate governance rules they wish. Such jurisdictions are usually referred to as ***"permissive"*** ones. For instance, a permissive state might regulate the percentage of shareholder vote required to approve a merger by saying: (1) where the articles of incorporation are silent, a two-thirds majority is needed; but (2) by majority vote, the shareholders may amend the articles to provide any approval threshold they wish. A ***"non-permissive"*** state, by contrast, might provide that a two-thirds shareholder vote is needed regardless of what the articles of incorporation say.

   a. **Delaware as permissive state:** ***Delaware*** is usually considered to be a ***permissive*** state. K&C, p. 143.

3. **Closely-held corporation:** The organizers of a ***closely-held corporation*** should normally choose to incorporate in the state in which they have their ***principal place of business***, rather than in, say, Delaware.

   a. **Rationale:** Even if this "home" state is not so permissive, it usually gives special flexibility to closely-held corporations. C&E, p. 125.

   b. **Costs of using foreign domicile:** Conversely, the closely-held corporation is likely to incur major extra costs if it incorporates "out of state": (1) The corporation will face two sets of taxes (a corporation must generally pay at least minimum taxes to the state of incorporation even if all business is done elsewhere, and of course the state where most business is done will also impose corporate and other taxes); (2) The corporation will have to qualify as a ***foreign corporation*** in its "home-office state," and is likely to be subject to significant regulation there anyway; and (3) The corporation will be subject to suit in the state of incorporation; that state may be far away, and separate local counsel will be required. Nutshell, p. 30.

4. **Publicly-held corporation:** But for a ***publicly-held*** corporation, the cost-benefit analysis often cuts the other way — in favor of incorporating in a place other than the principal place of business, usually Delaware.

   a. **Costs:** On the cost side, the extra taxes payable to Delaware for the privilege of being incorporated there are small relative to the corporation's assets.

   b. **Benefits:** On the benefit side, the managers of the publicly-held corporation (who generally make the decision where to incorporate or whether to push for a change in the state of incorporation) may get two important types of benefits from incorporating out-of-state, especially in Delaware:

      (1) the ability to accomplish specific transactions (e.g., acquisitions, asset sales) ***without a shareholder vote***, or with a lesser percentage of shareholders needed for approval; and

(2) a well-developed ***body of law*** governing corporations.

Advantage (2) is especially important to the management of publicly-held companies because it enables them to ***predict*** with much greater certainty how a particular issue of corporate law would be resolved by the courts than would be the case in a state with sparser corporate statutes and case law. Thus Delaware has an extremely broad, and rapidly updated, body of case law and statutes governing such topics as takeovers, so the managers of a company incorporated there are likely to know with much greater certainty how a litigated issue will turn out than they would in the state of their principal place of business.

B. Mechanics of incorporating: The mechanics of creating a corporation vary from state to state. Here are some of the general aspects:

1. **Articles of incorporation:** In every state, those wishing to form a corporation must file a document with the state official, usually the Secretary of State. This document is usually called the ***"articles of incorporation,"*** or the ***"charter."*** (We'll be using the term "articles of incorporation" throughout this book.) Nutshell, p. 31. A filing fee must be paid with the document.

2. **Review by state official:** The articles are then reviewed by the state officials (usually by a clerk in the Secretary of State's office). If the official determines that the document is in satisfactory form, the official files the document, and the corporation is treated as having been formed. The date of incorporation is usually made retroactive to the ***date of filing***. See, e.g., MBCA § 1.23(a). The state usually shows that it has accepted the corporation merely by issuing a receipt for the filing fee (though some states still issue a more formal "charter" or "certificate of incorporation"). Nutshell, pp. 31-32.

3. **Incorporators:** Since no corporation exists at the time the articles of incorporation are prepared and filed, this document cannot be signed by the corporation's "shareholders." Therefore, the articles can be signed by *any* individual or individuals, who are known as ***"incorporators."*** Most states today require only a single incorporator, who need not reside in the state of incorporation and need not expect to have any connection with the corporation once it comes into existence. In modern legal practice, most incorporating papers are prepared by "corporate service companies" (e.g., CT Corporation Services), and the incorporator is an employee of the service company. Usually the incorporators perform no practical function once they have signed the incorporation papers.

4. **Contents of articles of incorporation:** The articles of incorporation must contain certain minimum information. In most states, these contents include:

   a. **Name:** The corporation's ***name***. The Secretary of State will check the records to see whether this name is still available.

   b. **Purposes:** A ***"purposes"*** clause. Traditionally, such a clause set forth fairly narrowly the purposes for which the corporation was being formed (e.g., "to operate and maintain a railroad"). Today, the purposes clause is almost always as ***broad as possible***, e.g., "for general business purposes" or "to engage in any lawful business." In fact, the MBCA eliminates the requirement of a purposes clause entirely (§2.02), and provides that every corporation "has the purpose of engaging in any lawful business unless a more limited purpose is set forth in the articles of incorporation." (§3.01(a)).

c. **Capitalization:** The ***number of shares*** the corporation is authorized to issue. See MBCA, § 2.02(a)(2). (Even if the corporation does not plan to actually issue that many shares, it lists the number that it is authorized to issue. In fact, this number should usually be ***substantially more*** than the corporation plans to issue in the near future, so that if more shares need to be issued the articles of corporation will not need to be amended by shareholder vote. K&C, p. 125.)

5. **Registered office and agent:** All states require corporations incorporated in the state to maintain a ***registered office*** and a ***registered agent*** at that office. Nutshell, p. 44. Even if the corporation has its principal place of business in the state, the registered office may be different from this principal place of business — for instance, it can be an office belonging to, say, the corporation's attorney. The main purpose of the registered office and agent is that anyone who wants to sue the corporation can make ***service of process*** on the corporation by serving the agent at the registered office. Also, tax notices and other official communications are sent to the registered office. *Id.*

6. **Initial board of directors:** A corporation's board of directors is normally elected by the shareholders. But before the corporation has been formed, there are no shareholders who *can* elect directors. Conversely, without a board of directors there can be no issuance of shares and therefore no shareholders. Therefore, without some special rule giving a mechanism for setting up an initial board of directors, this Catch 22 would prevent anything from getting done. States fix this problem by allowing either or both of the following as solutions:

   [1] the ***incorporators*** may have the power to ***elect*** initial directors; or

   [2] the state may allow initial directors to be ***named in the certificate of incorporation***. C&E, p. 137.

   If option [2] is used, the initial directors can resign at a meeting of shareholders held immediately after incorporation — the initial directors can therefore be persons who will not own shares in, or have anything to do with, the corporation; in this way, the articles of incorporation can conceal the names of the people who will be the actual ongoing directors.

7. **Bylaws:** Once the corporation has been formed by the filing of the articles of incorporation, it should adopt ***bylaws***. A corporation's bylaws are rules governing the corporation's ***internal affairs***.

   a. **Contents:** Here are some of the things that may be specified in the bylaws: (1) Date, time and place for the annual meeting of shareholders; (2) number of directors of the corporation; (3) whether or not cumulative voting for directors (see *infra*, p. 56) will be allowed; (4) a listing of the officers of the corporation (e.g., that there shall be a president, a vice-president, a secretary and a treasurer), together with a description of the duties of each; (5) what shall constitute a quorum for the meeting of directors, etc.

   b. **Not filed:** Bylaws are usually ***not filed*** with the Secretary of State and are not matters of public record. Nutshell, p. 48.

c. **Amendment:** The bylaws may be easily ***amended***; they usually provide that they may be amended either by the board of directors or by the shareholders. (The articles of incorporation, by contrast, are not in all respects amendable by the board of directors alone. For instance, under the MBCA the number of authorized shares must generally be changed by shareholder approval if the corporation has more than one class of shares; MBCA §§ 10.03(b); 10.05(4).)

d. **Conflict:** If the articles of incorporation conflict with the bylaws, the articles control. Nutshell, p. 48.

8. **Organizational meeting:** A number of initial items are resolved at an ***organizational meeting***. For instance, initial ***shares*** are usually ***issued***; officers are elected; the bylaws are approved; a resolution authorizing the opening of bank accounts is usually passed, etc. If the initial directors are mentioned in the certificate of incorporation, then the organizational meeting is usually a meeting of these initial directors, who may issue shares, elect their successors, and then resign. If initial directors are not named in the certificate of incorporation, then the incorporators hold the organizational meeting and issue stock (so that the newly-established shareholders can elect the permanent directors). Nutshell, pp. 49-51.

C. **Amending the articles:** Once the articles of incorporation are in place and the corporation has been formed, the articles can be ***amended*** at any time.

1. **Limits:** Under most modern corporation statutes, there are only two significant limitations to this right of amendment:

a. **Must be allowable as original articles:** First, the articles of incorporation, as amended, must be ones which ***could be adopted*** if the amended articles were being filed as a new (rather than revised) set. In other words, a provision cannot be placed into the charter, or eliminated from the charter, if that placement or elimination would not be allowed for a new charter being filed at the same time as the amendment is taking place. See MBCA § 10.01(a).

b. **Voting rights:** Second, under most statutes any class of stockholders who would be ***adversely affected*** by the amendment must ***approve*** the amendment by majority vote. See, e.g., MBCA § 10.04. For instance, suppose that a particular charter amendment would eliminate the accrued dividends owed to preferred stockholders (a change which would help the common shareholders at the preferred shareholders' expense). Under MBCA § 10.04(a)(3), the amendment would not go through unless it was approved by a majority of the preferred shareholders (even if the preferred stock is otherwise non-voting). This issue is discussed more extensively *infra*, p. 415.

2. **Judicial review of fairness:** Very occasionally, a court may enjoin a proposed amendment on the grounds that it is simply ***unfair*** to some shareholders. Much more often, however, courts decline to review the fairness of charter amendments, relying instead on the fact that: (1) the affected group, under most statutes, gets to vote separately about whether to approve the transaction (as described just above); and (2) an unhappy shareholder whose rights are adversely affected will usually get ***appraisal rights*** (discussed *infra*, p. 394), which permit him to sell his shares back to the corporation at a judicially-determined fair price. See, e.g., MBCA § 13.02(a)(4).

II. *ULTRA VIRES* AND CORPORATE POWERS

A. *Ultra vires* doctrine: The doctrine of ***"ultra vires"*** was once extremely important, but is of little practical significance today.

B. Classical *ultra vires* doctrine: Early statutes governing corporations usually narrowly restricted the activities in which a corporation could engage. If a corporation purported to act beyond the scope of what it was authorized by statute to do (or beyond the scope of its perhaps even more limited certificate of incorporation), the problem arose, What, if anything, was the legal significance of these corporate actions? Such impermissible transactions were labeled "*ultra vires*" (latin for "beyond the power"), and some cases held that ***the corporate action was totally void.***

1. **Use to invalidate contracts:** Most importantly, *ultra vires* contracts were often said to be ***unenforceable*** either ***against*** the corporation or ***by*** the corporation.

C. Modern abolition: Modern American corporate statutes have largely ***eliminated*** the *ultra vires* doctrine. Two distinct developments have made this occur:

1. **Broad powers clauses:** First of all, as noted (see *supra*, p. 21), under most statutes unless the articles of incorporation expressly limit the corporation's powers, it will be deemed to have the power to engage in ***any lawful business activity***. Therefore, the probability that the corporation will try to do something beyond the scope of its charter is much reduced.

2. **Formal abolition of doctrine:** Second, almost all states have explicitly ***abolished*** the doctrine as to lawsuits by or against a ***third party*** who has done business with the corporation. See, e.g., MBCA § 3.04(a): "[T]he validity of corporate action may not be challenged on the ground that the corporation lacks or lacked power to act."

   a. **Exceptions:** Modern statutes generally ***do*** allow the corporation's power to act to be challenged in a few specific types of suits: (1) a suit brought by a ***shareholder*** to enjoin the corporate act (if an injunction would be "equitable"); (2) a suit by the corporation against a ***director or officer***; or (3) a suit brought by the ***state*** to enjoin the act. See MBCA § 3.04(b) and (c). But the *ultra vires* doctrine in its classical function — as a defense asserted by the corporation in a suit brought by one who contracted with it, or as a defense by the third party if suit on the contract was brought by the corporation — is now abolished in virtually all jurisdictions. Nutshell, p. 54.

D. Corporate powers today: The statutory abolition of most applications of *ultra vires* doctrine leaves a few holes, as noted. Most significantly, a shareholder may still sue to enjoin the corporation from acting beyond its powers. If (1) the corporation has a charter that expressly limits its powers, or (2) the charter is silent on those powers and the state has not yet revised its statute to give all lawful powers where the charter is silent, the shareholder may even today be able to obtain an injunction on an *ultra vires* theory.

1. **Charitable donations:** Most shareholder-injunction cases have involved ***charitable donations*** which the corporation has attempted to make. In general, the shareholder who tries to block a corporate charitable donation will lose unless the donation is ***manifestly unreasonable***.

a. **Implied power:** Thus corporations have been held to have the ***implied power*** to make ***reasonable charitable contributions***.

b. **Statutory provisions:** Nearly all states have now enacted statutory provisions explicitly allowing charitable contributions. For instance, MBCA § 3.02(13) allows every corporation (unless its articles of incorporation provide otherwise) to "make donations for the public welfare or for charitable, scientific, or educational purposes. . . ." See also 8 Del. C. § 122(9).

i. **Reasonableness limitation:** However, courts usually read statutory language like this as authorizing only charitable donations that are ***reasonable*** in size and type. As one commentator has put it, donations must be "reasonable in amount in the light of the corporation's financial condition, bear some reasonable relation to the corporation's interest, and not be so 'remote and fanciful' as to excite the opposition of shareholders whose property is being used." Prof. Garrett, quoted in C&E, p. 229. See, e.g., *Kahn v. Sullivan*, 594 A.2d 48 (Del. 1991) (charitable donation to construct and fund an art museum was within the "range of reasonableness" required for a donation to be valid.)

Example: Suppose the president of a business which does all of its activity in Iowa contributes 20% percent of one year's profits to the Metropolitan Opera, and there is evidence that this contribution was made not because there was any real corporate interest in the opera, but rather because the president's wife was a member of the Metropolitan Opera's board. A court might well hold that shareholders were entitled to enjoin the contribution as being unreasonable.

2. **Pensions, bonuses and other fringe benefits:** A related issue arises when the corporation grants an employee or retired former employee a ***bonus***, a stock option, or some other kind of fringe benefit.

a. **Still employed:** Where the recipient still works for the corporation, there is a theoretical benefit to the corporation (the employee will work harder because he has been given the incentive). Therefore, the arrangement will usually not be attackable by shareholders unless it is clearly excessive or based upon self-dealing (see *infra*, p. 216).

b. **Retired:** But if the fringe benefit is given to a ***retired*** employee, the direct-incentive justification no longer applies. Nonetheless, courts will generally stretch to approve the arrangement if it is not excessive or a product of self-dealing. The court may, for instance, reason that the ***rest of the labor force*** will become happier and thus more productive when they see how the retiree has been treated. See Nutshell, pp. 57-58.

c. **MBCA:** MBCA § 3.02(12) explicitly gives corporations the right to institute pension plans, share option plans, and other incentives for its current or former directors and employees.

Quiz Yourself on
THE CORPORATE FORM *(ULTRA VIRES AND CORPORATE POWERS)*

6. Gilligan's Island Tours, Inc. (GITI), runs one-day cruises. Its purpose, as stated in its articles of incorpo-

ration, is "the operation of one-day cruises to nearby islands." Realizing that a desert island to which it sails would make a great resort, the chairman of the board of GITI, Skipper, signs a land sale contract on the corporation's behalf to purchase the island from Mary Ann, its record owner. Before closing, Mary Ann changes her mind. GITI brings suit. Mary Ann has examined GITI's charter, and has noticed the cruises-only purposes clause.

(a) At common law, what defense could Mary Ann make, based on the purposes clause? ________________

(b) Under a modern statute (the MBCA, for instance), would the defense you mentioned in (a) work? ________________

(c) Suppose that Ginger, a major shareholder of GITI, intervened in the suit and sought an injunction against the transaction. Suppose further that GITI's charter expressly said that the corporation "shall not be permitted to own or acquire real estate." Under the MBCA, can the court grant the injunction? ________________

7. Scrooge McDuck is the majority shareholder of the Huey Dewey Louie Real Estate Development Corp. The company makes a $19,000,000 profit one year. McDuck donates $500,000 of it to a nonprofit charity he controls, the McDuck Foundation for the Preservation of Wetlands. Assume that a fairly typical statute (e.g., the MBCA) applies. If a minority shareholder challenges the donation as improper, what result? ________________

Answers

6. (a) The doctrine of *"ultra vires."* At common law, transactions prohibited by the corporation's articles of incorporation were said to be "*ultra vires*" ("beyond the power"), and were often treated as being unenforceable either by or against the corporation. [24] So here, at common law Mary Ann might well wriggle off the hook because of the purposes clause.

(b) No, even though the articles of incorporation limit the corporation's purpose to running cruises. First, under MBCA § 3.02, unless the articles of incorporation provide otherwise, every corporation has "the same powers as an individual to do all things necessary or convenient to carry out its business and affairs . . ." Under sub-section (4) of 3.02, the powers automatically (unless the certificate of incorporation says otherwise) include the right to "purchase . . . real or personal property . . ." The mere fact that the only listed purpose here is the operation of cruises would not be enough to trigger the "otherwise provided in the certification of incorporation" provision, and thus not enough to make the proposed acquisition here beyond the corporate powers.

Second, even if the articles of incorporation expressly said that the corporation's purposes were *only* the operation of cruises, or expressly said that the corporation was not permitted to buy real estate (thus triggering the "articles of incorporation provide otherwise" clause in § 3.02), the ultra vires doctrine *still* wouldn't work here. That's because, according to § 3.04(a), "Except as provided in subsection (b), the validity of corporate action may not be challenged on the ground that the corporation lacks or lacked power to act." [24] Assertion of *ultra vires* by a third party whom the corporation sues for enforcement of a contract is not one of the exceptions listed in (b). (Nor, by the way, would assertion of the defense *by* the corporation, if the third party sued it for enforcement of the contract, be such an exception.)

(c) Yes, if (and only if) the court found that an injunction would be "equitable." Since the articles of incorporation expressly prohibit acquisition of real estate, the general "power to do all things necessary" provision of MBCA § 3.02 (see answer (b) above) doesn't apply. § 3.04(b) says that "[a] corporation's power to act may be challenged: (1) in a proceeding by a shareholder against the corporation to enjoin the act." § 3.04(c) says that "In a shareholder's proceeding under subsection (b)(1) to enjoin an unauthorized corporate act, the court may enjoin or set aside the act, if equitable and if all affected persons are parties to the proceeding . . .." Since GITI and Mary Ann (the two affected persons) are parties, the court has power to enjoin if to do so would be "equitable" (which it might well be, here, especially if Ginger showed, for instance, that she distrusted all real estate investments and relied on the charter prohibition in deciding to invest in GITI in the first place).

7. **The gift is valid, as long as it's in the corporation's interests (and not purely for McDuck's own personal benefit).** The scope of a corporation's powers is determined by its articles and state statutes. Statutes typically allow reasonable corporate charitable gifts. Thus MBCA § 3.02(13) allows corporations to make "donations for the public welfare or for charitable, scientific, or educational purposes." If the amount of the gift were excessive measured by the corporation's financial status, the court might strike it down. But with a $19,000,000 profit, $500,000 (2.5%) is probably reasonable. Note that the fact that McDuck controls the charity in question is relevant to whether the donation was "reasonable," but this fact probably wouldn't change the result. (However, if the charity were a sham, or McDuck was making the gift for purely personal reasons having nothing to do with the corporation's business interests, then the court might strike it down as "unreasonable." [25])

III. PRE-INCORPORATION TRANSACTIONS BY PROMOTERS

A. **Who is a "promoter":** A ***promoter*** is a person who takes initiative in ***founding and organizing*** a business or enterprise. See SEC Rule 405. A promoter may act alone or with co-promoters. A promoter's activities typically include the following:

- ❑ arranging for the ***necessary capital***;
- ❑ acquiring any needed ***assets*** or ***personnel*** (e.g., signing a contract with a person who will manage the business; buying or renting real estate for the plant or office, etc.); and
- ❑ arranging for the actual ***incorporation*** of the business.

When used in its corporation-law sense, the term "promoter" does not have any of the negative connotations that surround the popular use of the term.

1. **Transactions by:** We're concerned in this section with transactions that the promoter undertakes on behalf of the business ***before incorporation***. We're concerned with three questions:

   (1) Under what circumstances does the promoter become ***personally liable*** for transactions he undertakes on behalf of the corporation?

   (2) Under what circumstances does the ***corporation***, once it is formed, become liable based on the promoter's pre-incorporation transactions? and

   (3) What, if any, are the promoter's ***fiduciary obligations*** to the not-yet-formed corporation?

B. Liability of promoter: If the corporation has already been formed, and a promoter makes the contract in the corporation's name, there is normally no issue as to the promoter's liability — the corporation is liable, and the promoter is not. But if the promoter purports to make a contract on behalf of a not-yet-formed corporation, the situation is much fuzzier. Depending on the circumstances, the promoter may or may not be personally liable if the corporation is never formed, or if it is formed but does not perform the contract. We will consider a number of distinct situations:

1. **Corporation not named:** First, suppose the promoter makes the contract in ***his own name***, without referring to the not-yet-formed corporation. Even if the promoter has the ***intent*** to assign the contract to the corporation, the promoter is ***personally liable***. Nutshell, p. 66. In fact, the promoter's personal liability here is so clear that it is rarely litigated.

2. **Contract in corporation's name:** Now, assume that the contract purports to be ***in the corporation's name***, and that the contract does not on its face disclose the fact that the corporation has not been formed as of the contract date. Let us further assume that the other party to the contract ***does not know*** that the corporation does not yet exist.

   a. **Promoter knows:** If in this situation the promoter ***knows*** that the corporation has not yet been formed, he will almost certainly be held ***personally liable*** if the corporation is ***never formed***, or if it is formed but ***does not take over*** and fulfill the contract. This result is usually reached on some kind of agency principle: for instance, the court may assert that "a person who purports to act as agent for a nonexistent principal thereby automatically becomes a principal." Nutshell, p. 65. Other decisions base this result on a ***tort*** theory: the promoter, by concealing the fact that the corporation has not yet been formed, is liable for ***misrepresentation***.

      i. **MBCA:** The MBCA follows this near-universal practice of holding the promoter liable where he knows (and the other party does not) that the corporation is not in existence on the day of signing. MBCA § 2.04 provides that "[a]ll persons purporting to act as or on behalf of a corporation, knowing there was no incorporation under this Act, are ***jointly and severally liable*** for ***all liabilities created*** while so acting."

   b. **Later formation of corporation and adoption of contract:** Suppose that after the contract has been made in the name of the not-yet-existing corporation, the corporation is ***formed***. If the corporation now takes action that may be construed as ***"adopting"*** the contract, the promoter has a somewhat better chance of escaping personal liability.

3. **Promoter unaware that corporation hasn't been formed:** Now suppose that the promoter ***honestly believes*** that the corporation has been formed, but due to some ***technical defect*** of which he is unaware, the corporation doesn't really exist at the time he signs a contract on its behalf. Here, courts are somewhat more sympathetic to the promoter, as you might suspect — they sometimes find a way to relieve him of personal liability, at least if the defect is eventually cured. This class of cases is discussed under the heading "defective incorporation and its consequences," *infra*, p. 31.

4. **Contract states that corporation is to be formed:** Finally, let us consider the last and probably most difficult of the promoter-liability situations: The contract ***recites*** that the

corporation in whose name it is executed has not yet been formed. For instance, the contract may recite that one of those parties is "ABC, Inc., a Delaware corporation to be formed." (Or, alternatively, the other party knows that the corporation has not yet been formed but accepts a contract executed in the corporation's name.) Obviously courts are more sympathetic to the promoter in this situation than where the other party does not know of the corporation's non-existence — here there is no need to worry about misrepresentation by the promoter. Therefore, this class of cases comes down to a question of ***interpreting the parties' intent***.

a. **Corporation never formed:** If the corporation is ***never formed***, the promoter is quite ***likely*** to be held ***personally liable***. The court may reason that the parties obviously intended for ***someone*** to be liable, and that in the absence of a corporation's ever being formed the liable party could only be the promoter. Or, the court may reason that the promoter has made an implied promise to cause the corporation to be formed, and has breached this promise.

b. **Corporation formed, but no adoption:** Now, assume that the corporation is in fact ***formed*** after the signing of the contract. If the corporation never takes any acts to ***adopt*** the contract or to begin performance, the situation is really no different from that in which the corporation is never formed, so the promoter will probably be personally ***liable***.

c. **Adoption by corporation:** If the corporation is eventually formed and then ***manifests its intent to take over the contract***, the promoter has a somewhat better chance of escaping liability. Here, too, the question is one of the intent of the parties. The parties may have meant any of several different things when they made the agreement on behalf of the corporation to be formed, including: (1) that the other party is making a revocable or irrevocable ***offer*** to the non-existing corporation, which results in a contract if the corporation is formed while the offer is still open; (2) that the promoter will be bound but his liability will ***terminate*** if the corporation is formed and assents to be bound; or (3) that the promoter will be ***bound***, and the subsequent formation and assent of the corporation will not discharge the promoter.

   i. **Tendency to bind promoter:** The decision in any case is likely to turn on the facts, since it is the ***parties' intention*** that is being measured. However, in general, courts ***do not release*** the promoter where all that has happened is that the corporation has been formed and has shown its assent, but has not performed. (In other words, they tend to view the case as falling within choice (3) above rather than (1) or (2).)

   ii. **Urging by other side to use corporate name:** If the other party ***urges*** the promoter to contract in the name of the corporation-to-be-formed, the court is more likely to find that the other party intended to look only to the credit of the corporation once it was formed and assented.

C. **Liability of corporation for promoter contract:** Now, let us examine the other side of the coin: Suppose the corporation that did not exist at the time the promoter signed the contract on its behalf *does* come into existence. In that case, under what circumstances does the ***corporation*** become liable under the contract?

1. **No adoption, no liability:** First, even though the contract may have been made in the corporation's name, the corporation does ***not*** become ***automatically*** liable merely by coming into existence. If the corporation does not take any action to manifest its ***assent*** to the contract, it is simply ***not bound***. Nutshell, p. 70.

2. **Adoption by corporation:** If, on the other hand, the corporation after its formation ***does*** manifest its assent to be bound by the contract previously signed in its name, this intent will be ***enforced***: the corporation will be liable just as if it had itself originally executed the contract. In this situation, the corporation is usually said to have ***"adopted"*** the agreement (though it is sometimes said to have ***"ratified"*** the agreement).

   a. **What constitutes adoption:** The adoption by the corporation may be either ***express*** or ***implied***.

   b. **Express:** ***Express*** adoptions present few problems. Thus if the corporation passes a resolution, "Resolved that a certain contract made on the corporation's behalf by Promoter with Landlord for the lease of premises is hereby ratified and adopted by the corporation as if it had entered into such contract initially," the corporation will obviously be bound. (Whether this adoption will relieve the promoter of liability is a different question; this will depend on whether the parties, including the other party to the original transaction, intended a novation. See *supra*, p. 28.)

   c. **Implied:** An adoption may also be ***implied*** from the corporation's acts, and even from its failure to act. Thus if the corporation ***receives benefits*** under the contract without objection, this will probably be held to be an implied adoption. This might be the case, for instance, if the promoter purports to hire an employee in the corporation's name under a contract, and the corporation permits the employee to begin work.

   d. **Effective date:** When adoption occurs, it is usually held ***not to be retroactive*** to the date of the original contract, but merely to run from the date of the corporation's assent.

D. **Promoter's fiduciary obligation to corporation and shareholders:** The promoter may, once the corporation is formed, have dealings with it. Most courts appear to hold that during the pre-incorporation period the promoter has a ***fiduciary obligation*** to the to-be-formed corporation, and therefore may not pursue his own profit at the corporation's ultimate expense.

Quiz Yourself on
THE CORPORATE FORM *(PRE-INCORPORATION TRANSACTIONS BY PROMOTERS)*

8. Marie Antoinette, a promoter for the as-yet-unformed Let 'Em Eat Cake Baked Goods Company, signs a requirements contract on the company's behalf (and in the company's name) with the Wilted Flour Company, covering all the company's flour needs for the next three years.

(a) Suppose that after Let 'Em is formed, and before it takes any action with reference to the contract, its board sends Wilted a letter saying, "We don't want the flour, so don't send it." Can Wilted recover against Let 'Em for breach of contract? _______________

(b) Suppose the letter in (a) was never sent. What action by Let 'Em, if any, would cause Let 'Em to be bound by the contract? _______________

9. Oliver Wendell Douglas, a promoter for the yet-to-be-formed Hooterville Produce Company, contracts to buy a 160-acre farm on Hooterville Produce's behalf from Mr. Haney. Douglas signs the land sale contract in Hooterville's name, without making it clear to Haney that Hooterville (as Douglas knows) doesn't exist yet. The closing is set for August 1st. Hooterville Produce is formed one month before that. The board, consisting of Hank Kimball, Fred Ziffel, and Sam Drucker, passes a resolution ratifying the land sale contract. Shortly thereafter, Hooterville Produce becomes insolvent, and the closing never takes place.

(a) Can Haney hold Douglas personally liable on the land sale contract? ________________

(b) Suppose that before the contract was signed, Haney knew that Hooterville Produce didn't yet exist, and said to Douglas, "Why don't you sign the contract in the corporation's name anyway." Can Haney hold Douglas personally liable? ________________

Answers

8. (a) No. Even though a contract is made in a not-yet-formed corporation's name and for its behalf, the corporation doesn't become liable merely by coming into existence. [30]

(b) Let 'Em's express or implied adoption or ratification of the contract. Let 'Em would be bound if it *expressly* adopted or ratified the contract, say by passing a resolution by the Board of Directors to that effect. Alternatively, Let 'Em would be bound if it *impliedly* adopted or ratified the contract. This might happen if it received the goods and used them (or even kept them very long) rather than returning them. Or, it might happen if the company learned of the contract before the goods were shipped, and didn't notify Wilted not to perform. [30]

9. (a) Yes, in all probability. When a promoter contracts on a corporation's behalf before the corporation is formed and does not let on that the corporation doesn't exist yet, the promoter is personally liable on the contract. [28] If the corporation is later formed and ratifies the agreement, the promoter would be discharged if the other party manifests a willingness to look only to the corporation (not to the promoter) for performance. (Such a substitution is called a "novation.") Here, there's no sign that Haney agreed (even implicitly) to look only to the company for performance. So Douglas remains liable. [29]

(b) Probably not. If the other party knows the corporation doesn't yet exist, and urges that the contract be signed in the corporation's name anyway, this is strong circumstantial evidence that the other party is expecting to look to the assets of the to-be-formed corporation, not to the assets of the promoter. So unless there's some evidence that this isn't what Haney contemplated (and there's no such evidence here in our facts), the court won't hold Douglas liable. [29]

IV. DEFECTIVE INCORPORATION AND ITS CONSEQUENCES

A. The problem generally: The "promoter's liability" cases discussed above are generally ones in which a contract is made at a time when no one has even attempted to form a corporation. Related problems arise when the promoter has ***attempted*** to incorporate, but because of some ***technical defect*** the incorporation has not yet successfully occurred. The issue becomes whether the promoter and/or his passive investors are personally liable.

1. **How defects can occur:** This "defective incorporation" can occur for a number of reasons. For instance, the promoter may send what he believes to be satisfactory articles of incorporation to the Secretary of State, but the Secretary rejects them because they have a missing or incorrect item in them. Or, perhaps the promoter relies on a lawyer to file, and the promoter is unaware that the lawyer has not done the filing. Are the promoter and/or his passive investors liable for debts incurred in the corporation's name before the incorporation actually occurs?

B. **Common law's "de facto" doctrine:** At common law, the ***"de facto corporation"*** doctrine was frequently used to shield the "shareholders" from liability. Under this doctrine, so long as a "colorable" attempt to incorporate was made (e.g., articles of incorporation were drafted and submitted to the state, but rejected), the court would frequently hold that the entity was a "de facto" corporation. That is, the entity was not a true corporation insofar as the state itself was concerned, but it could take advantage of quasi-corporation status vis-a-vis its creditors. Therefore, the "shareholders" were ***not personally liable*** to the creditors of the would-be corporation.

C. **Modern view:** Today, the de facto doctrine is much less frequently used, because of statutory reforms. Far fewer technicalities are typically required to form a corporation than was previously the case, so that a good faith attempt to incorporate is much more likely to be successful today than formerly. In return, most states have statutes that ***expressly impose personal liability*** as the penalty for purporting to do business as a corporation that is not in fact incorporated.

1. **MBCA abolishes de facto doctrine:** Thus, most states have provisions similar to MBCA § 2.04: "All persons purporting to act as or on behalf of a corporation, ***knowing there was no incorporation*** under this act, are ***jointly and severally liable*** for all liabilities created while so acting." Provisions like this one are usually interpreted as having ***abolished*** the de facto doctrine.

   a. **Knowledge of defect:** But MBCA § 2.04 ***relieves from personal liability*** those who act as a corporation ***without knowledge*** that there has in fact been no incorporation. See Official Comment to § 2.04.

2. **Passive investors:** Just as courts have tried to protect those who mistakenly but honestly believe that incorporation has taken place, so they try to protect ***passive investors*** from personal liability, even investors who put up money for the commencement of operations without an honest belief that incorporation has taken place.

   a. **Active investors:** But an ***active*** investor — one who participates in the business' daily operations — ***won't*** get this protection. If an active investor acts on behalf of the corporation while knowing it hasn't yet been formed, he'll be personally liable.

D. **Corporations by estoppel:** The common law has traditionally recognized a second method of avoiding personal liability in defective incorporation cases, apart from the de facto doctrine: the doctrine of "corporation by ***estoppel***."

1. **Creditor dealt with business as a corporation:** The main requirement for the doctrine has been that the creditor must ***deal with the business as a corporation***, and agree to look to the "corporation's" assets rather than the assets of the individual shareholders. Once the

creditor has done this, he is said to be "estopped" from denying the corporation's existence.

2. **Innocent noncompliance:** Most courts that have applied the doctrine also seem to require that the shareholder who is asserting the defense must not have ***known*** that the incorporation was defective. Thus the doctrine is most often used where the shareholder in good faith ***relies on some third party*** (e.g., a promoter or a lawyer) to handle the incorporation, and based on assurances from this third person, falsely but honestly believes that a corporation has been formed.

3. **Easier to get than de facto doctrine:** Most courts have held that even where the defect in the incorporation process is too serious to allow use of the de facto doctrine, the estoppel doctrine can still be applied if the creditor deals with the business as a corporation and the defendant shareholder/promoter has behaved in good faith.

4. **Tort claimants:** Because of the requirement that the estoppel doctrine applies only where the plaintiff has dealt with the business as a corporation and agreed solely to look to the corporation's credit, the doctrine is essentially limited to ***contract*** cases, and is virtually never applied against ***tort plaintiffs***. Obviously, a person who is injured by the act of a business or its employee (e.g., one who is hit by a taxi cab company's cab) has not agreed to deal with the business as a corporation — therefore, it's not fair to "estop" the victim from arguing that since no actual incorporation had taken place by the time of the accident, the individuals running the business should be personally liable. C&E, p. 160-61.

5. **Effect of Model Act:** The MBCA does not explicitly either allow or prohibit the classical corporation-by-estoppel doctrine. But (as noted, *supra*, p. 32), § 2.04 of the act exempts from personal liability those who act as a corporation without knowledge that there has been no incorporation. Since most courts that have applied the classical corporation-by-estoppel doctrine have required such innocence on the part of the defendant anyway, § 2.04 leads to the same result of non-liability without using the estoppel doctrine. Nutshell, p. 79.

Quiz Yourself on
THE CORPORATE FORM *(DEFECTIVE INCORPORATION AND ITS CONSEQUENCES)*

10. Benjamin Disraeli intends to form a corporation, Sceptered Isle Tableware, to manufacture salt and pepper shakers in the shape of British kings and queens. Disraeli fills out the articles of incorporation, and has his lawyer file them with the Secretary of State for the state of Thames on October 1. On October 10, Disraeli, signing as "Sceptered Isle Corp by Ben Disraeli, President," enters into a lease on some manufacturing space owned by Victoria Regina. On December 1, Sceptered Isle runs out of money, and defaults on the lease. On December 15, Disraeli gets a letter from the Secretary of State saying that the articles of incorporation are not valid because they were not signed by the incorporator(s) (a fact that Disraeli didn't realize until he got the letter). Disraeli signs the articles and sends them back promptly, whereupon the Secretary of State accepts them for filing on Jan. 2. Victoria Regina, discovering that Sceptered Isle has no assets, sues Disraeli personally. Ignore any issue of whether the corporation was adequately capitalized.

(a) Under the common law, what doctrine(s) should Disraeli assert as a defense? Will the defense(s) work? ________________

(b) Under the MBCA, will Disraeli be liable under the lease? ________________

11. Snow White wants to incorporate her business as The Poison Apple Produce Company. There are eight shareholders: Snow White, Dopey, Grumpy, Sleepy, Doc, Bashful, Sneezy, and Happy. Each owns an equal number of shares in the company. Bashful and Happy are passive investors, with no involvement in the company except the cash they invested; the rest are actively involved in management. The company becomes insolvent, primarily due to Dopey's mismanagement, which, perhaps, is predictable with a name like that. Evil Stepmother Trucking Company has an outstanding invoice for $20,000 due from Poison Apple. There was a defect in formation that all the Poison Apple shareholders knew about and ignored. Can Evil Stepmother go after all of them personally? Answer both under common law and under the modern approach. ________________

Answers

10. (a) Disraeli should assert the doctrines of "de facto incorporation" and "corporation-by-estoppel." He'll probably succeed with at least one of these. Under the de facto incorporation doctrine, since Disraeli made a "colorable" attempt to incorporate before signing the lease (he tried his best, and did not know of the problem), the common-law court would probably hold that Sceptered Isle was a de facto corporation, thus shielding Disraeli. [32] Under the common-law corporation-by-estoppel doctrine, so long as Victoria Regina thought it was dealing with a corporation (as the form of Disraeli's signature here suggests), and Disraeli was ignorant of the lack of incorporation, Victoria will be estopped from denying that a corporation existed. [32] So here, too, Disraeli would win.

(b) Disraeli won't be liable under the MBCA, either. The MBCA is usually interpreted as having abolished the de facto incorporation doctrine; it's not clear whether it also abolishes the corporation-by-estoppel doctrine. [32, 33] But MBCA § 2.04 implicitly insulates from liability anyone who acts on behalf of a corporation *without knowing* about the defect in incorporation, so Disraeli qualifies. [32]

11. Not all of them — she can go after everyone except Happy and Bashful, under both the common-law and modern approaches. When a defectively-formed corporation becomes insolvent, creditors try to go after shareholders directly, citing the defect in formation. In a situation where shareholders knew about the defect and carried on as a corporation anyway, the common-law defenses of de facto incorporation and corporation by estoppel aren't available. That's the case here; all the shareholders knew about the defect. Under the modern statutory view, as stated in MBCA § 2.04, personal liability is incurred by anyone purporting to act as a corporation knowing of a defect in formation. However, under both the common-law and modern (including MBCA) approaches, the only shareholders who are liable personally for unpaid corporate debts are those who were active in the corporation's management. That excludes Happy and Bashful from liability, since they were merely passive investors.

V. PIERCING THE CORPORATE VEIL

A. Problem generally: One of the key attributes of the corporate form, is of course, ***limited liability***: A properly-formed corporation will normally shield the stockholders from being personally liable for the corporation's debts, so their losses will be limited to their investment (*supra*, p. 4). However this shield is not complete: In a few very extreme cases, courts sometimes ***"pierce the corporate veil,"*** and hold some or all of the shareholders ***personally liable*** for the corporation's debts.

B. Individual shareholders: First, let us consider a situation in which the corporation's shares are held by ***individuals***. (Later, we'll consider the parent-subsidiary situation and the brother-sister-corporations situation.)

1. Factors considered: Courts vary dramatically in their willingness to pierce the veil, though even in courts that are relatively willing to do so, this is a ***very extreme remedy***. There are no hard and fast rules to predict when the corporate veil will be pierced. However, there are a number of factors that seem to be important components of courts' decisions to pierce:

- ❑ whether the case involves ***tort*** or ***contract*** (with the court being more willing to pierce in tort cases);
- ❑ whether the defendant stockholders have engaged in ***fraud*** or wrongdoing (e.g., knowingly siphoning out all the profits of the corporation);
- ❑ whether the corporation was ***adequately capitalized***; and
- ❑ whether ***corporate formalities*** (e.g., the issuance of stock certificates, the keeping of minutes of corporate meetings, etc.) were followed.

We'll be considering each of these factors in turn.

a. Closely-held companies: First, however, you should understand the context in which nearly all veil-piercing suits arise: When the corporate veil is pierced to the detriment of individual shareholders, it is almost always in cases where the corporation is dominated by ***one*** or a ***small number*** of shareholders.

b. Rule of thumb: As a rule of thumb, courts generally require that at least ***two*** (any two) of the above factors be present before the veil is pierced. The most common combination is probably ***inadequate capitalization*** plus failure to follow ***corporate formalities***.

2. Tort claims vs. contract claims (and the "voluntary creditor" doctrine): Courts often distinguish between ***tort*** and ***contract*** claims for veil-piercing purposes — they're much more likely to pierce the veil in a tort case. To see why, let's consider two scenarios in which veil-piercing is sought by the plaintiff. Scenario 1 involves a plaintiff whose claim is based upon contract, and Scenario 2 involves a plaintiff whose claim is based on tort:

Scenario 1: Priscilla is in the business of selling mini-computers to small businesses. She sells a $30,000 computer system on credit to Delivery Corp., a local package delivery service. Dennis, the sole shareholder of Delivery Corp., shows Priscilla Delivery Corp.'s balance sheet, which correctly shows a net worth of $30,000. Shortly after delivery of the system, the local market for package delivery becomes much more competitive. Delivery Corp.'s net worth drops sharply, Dennis is unwilling to add additional capital, and the business fails without having paid the balance due to

Priscilla. Priscilla sues Dennis, seeking to have the corporate veil pierced so that Dennis will be personally liable for Delivery Corp.'s debts.

Scenario 2: Peter, who lives in the city in which Delivery Corp. does business, is hit by a Delivery Corp. van while walking on the street. He, too, brings suit against Dennis, seeking to pierce the corporate veil and have Dennis held personally liable for Delivery Corp.'s debts. (Assume that Delivery Corp. is liable for the van driver's torts under the doctrine of respondeat superior.)

a. **Voluntary vs. involuntary creditor:** In Scenario 1, Priscilla is a ***"voluntary creditor."*** That is, she voluntarily agreed to look to the credit of Delivery Corp. alone. Regardless of whether she actually investigated Delivery Corp.'s credit, she had the ***opportunity*** to do so. She also had the opportunity to ***bargain for a personal guarantee*** by Dennis, and did not do so. Therefore, a court is very ***unlikely*** to pierce the corporate veil for her benefit, even though the corporation turns out to have been undercapitalized for its actual (and perhaps even for its reasonably foreseeable) needs. In Scenario 2, by contrast, Peter is in quite a different position. He obviously didn't voluntarily elect to become a creditor of Delivery Corp. He didn't have a chance to investigate Delivery Corp.'s credit before becoming its creditor. A much stronger case for piercing the corporate veil for Peter's benefit can therefore be made than can be made for piercing the veil for Priscilla's benefit.

b. **Not dispositive:** However, the distinction between tort and contract creditors, or even the distinction between voluntary and involuntary creditors, is ***not dispositive***. First, even an involuntary creditor is very unlikely to be able to pierce the corporate veil in the absence of at least one of the other factors discussed below (e.g., inadequate capitalization). And a contract or other voluntary creditor will sometimes be able to get the veil pierced, especially if a corporation's finances have been administered in a way verging on fraud. Nonetheless the court is substantially more likely to pierce the veil on behalf of a tort or other involuntary creditor than on behalf of one who has voluntarily elected to look solely to the corporation's credit.

3. **Fraud or wrongdoing:** The second factor that courts look to in deciding whether to pierce the corporate veil is whether there has been a grievous ***fraud*** or ***wrongdoing*** by the corporation's shareholder(s). Usually, this refers to some means by which those controlling the corporation have ***siphoned out*** its assets, leaving too little in the corporation to satisfy the creditors. For instance, if the sole shareholder of a corporation draws a salary that changes from month to month, but is always just enough to leave the corporation with practically no assets, this "wrongdoing" makes it more likely that the veil will be pierced. Usually the fraud or wrongdoing amounts to leaving the corporation with inadequate capital, a factor that is discussed below.

a. **Misrepresentation:** Keep in mind that apart from situations where the veil is pierced to hold a shareholder or investor liable, the shareholder/investor may, by his acts, incur ***direct personal liability***. For instance, suppose Shareholder, who owns all the stock of Corporation, knowingly and falsely tells Creditor that Corporation has one million dollars in its bank account. If Creditor lends to Corporation in reasonable reliance upon this statement, Shareholder will be directly liable for the tort of misrepresentation, regardless of whether the corporate veil is pierced.

4. **Inadequate capital:** Probably the single most important factor in most courts' decision whether to pierce is the fact that the corporation has been ***inadequately capitalized***. Inadequate capitalization is especially likely to be a key factor where the claimant is an "involuntary creditor" who cannot be said to have willingly accepted the risk of inadequate capitalization. (See *supra*, p. 35.) But even a contractual claimant might be able to have the veil pierced for his benefit, if he could show the corporation did not have reasonable capital for its foreseeable business needs, and the creditor had no opportunity to ascertain this fact.

   a. **Significance of inadequate capital:** Courts are split as to whether grossly inadequate initial capitalization, by itself, will suffice to pierce the corporate veil.

      i. **Minority rule:** Some courts, but almost certainly a ***minority***, appear to hold that an involuntary creditor may pierce the corporate veil if there has been grossly inadequate capitalization, even in the absence of the other two factors that are commonly considered (fraud/wrongdoing, *supra*, and failure to follow formalities, *infra*).

      ii. **Majority view:** The ***vast majority*** of courts hold that although grossly inadequate capitalization is a factor in determining whether to pierce the veil, it is ***not dispositive***. That is, most courts require that there be either some ***affirmative fraud or wrongdoing*** by the shareholder, or a gross failure to follow the ***formalities*** of corporate existence, before the veil will be pierced. This seems to be true even where the plaintiff seeking veil-piercing is clearly an involuntary claimant who never willingly relied on the corporation's credit worthiness. See, e.g., Clark, p. 81 (referring to the "near absence of cases basing veil-piercing solely on inadequate initial capitalization"). The best-known case representing this majority view is ***Walkovszky v. Carlton***, 233 N.E.2d 6 (N.Y. 1966), set forth in the following example.

      Example: D, an individual, owns stock in ten corporations, each of which owns two taxi cabs. Each cab is insured for the statutorily-required minimum amount of $10,000. Each of the ten corporations has no assets other than its two cabs. The pattern of an individual forming multiple corporations, each owning one or two cabs, is common throughout the taxi cab industry, and is followed for the direct purpose of limiting the liabilities that can arise from any single accident involving a cab. P, who is severely injured by a cab owned by one of D's ten corporations, sues to hold D personally liable. (P also sues each of the other nine corporations owned by D.)

      Held, The pleading is insufficient to state a claim against D individually. "The corporate form may not be disregarded merely because the assets of the corporation, together with the mandatory insurance coverage of the vehicle which struck [P], are insufficient to assure him the recovery sought." It may well be sound public policy to require that corporations take out more than $10,000 of insurance, but this policy should be established by an act of the legislature, not by a court's piercing the corporate veil. (If P can show that D really conducted the business in his individual capacity, or that he siphoned off the corporation's assets in fraud of creditors, he may be able to hold D personally liable; but the pleadings do not allege either of these theories with sufficient particularity.) *Walkovszky v. Carlton*, *supra*.

A dissent argued that "a participating shareholder of a corporation vested with a public interest, organized with capital insufficient to meet liabilities which are certain to arise in the ordinary course of the corporation's business, may be held personally responsible for such liabilities." The dissent conceded that if a corporation was not profitable enough to afford more than the statutorily-required minimum insurance coverage, the veil should not be pierced; but if the corporation did earn such profits, and these were paid out to the shareholder solely for the purpose of insulating the corporation from effective ability to pay tort claims, the veil should be pierced.

iii. **Zero capital:** When the shareholder ***invests no money whatsoever*** in the corporation, courts are especially likely to pierce the veil (more so than if the investment is inadequate but non-zero).

iv. **Insurance as rebutting inference of undercapitalization:** Where the plaintiff is a tort claimant, courts will consider whether the corporation procured ***insurance*** against the type of risk that came to pass — if the corporation procured adequate insurance, this will make a finding of undercapitalization less likely. And this is true even if the insurer later goes bankrupt.

b. **Siphoning of profits:** When courts treat inadequate capitalization as a factor, they are normally referring to inadequate ***initial*** capitalization. That is, they consider it highly relevant that the defendant has set up a corporation without giving it the capital that will almost certainly be needed. A different form of inadequate capitalization occurs when the corporation is set up with adequate initial capital, but the defendant shareholder then ***drains out*** all of the profits and/or capital while the company operates, whether in the form of salaries, dividends, loans to himself, or whatever. Here, too, the court is likely to conclude that this form of inadequate capitalization is a factor strongly militating in favor of piercing the corporate veil. Also, this siphoning of profits will frequently be a form of "fraud or wrongdoing" (the second factor, mentioned *supra*, p. 36).

i. **Fraud on creditors:** In fact, the taking of excess salaries, excess dividends, or other transfers to the shareholder that leave the corporation unable to pay its debts, will frequently be attackable under various state or federal laws allowing the setting aside of ***transfers in fraud of creditors***. See, e.g., The Uniform Fraudulent Conveyance Act, adopted in most states; see especially § 5 of the UFCA ("Every conveyance made without fair consideration when the person making it is engaged . . . in a business or transaction for which the property remaining in his hands after the conveyance is an ***unreasonably small capital***, is fraudulent as to creditors . . . without regard to his actual intent").

ii. **Piercing veil:** But courts frequently prefer to use the veil-piercing doctrine rather than the law of fraudulent conveyances because the latter is extremely technical and requires detailed analysis of each transaction; veil-piercing, by contrast, is a much more flexible equitable doctrine, allowing the court to pursue what it sees as the requirements of justice. See Clark, p. 91.

c. **Failure to add new capital:** Now, let's consider a third form of inadequate capitalization: The corporation at the time it is set up has adequate capitalization for its reasonably foreseeable business needs; however, due to poor economic conditions, unintentional mismanagement, or other facts not evident at the time of incorporation, the business' ***capital diminishes*** to where it is no longer adequate for the then-existing operations. A plaintiff seeking veil-piercing might argue that a stockholder's ***failure to replenish the capital*** is a reason to pierce the veil, just as inadequate initial capitalization would be. However, ***few if any*** courts would accept this argument. "[T]here is no affirmative duty on [shareholders'] part to supply an additional investment to a dying corporation. Such a duty would be in fundamental contradiction to the policy of permitting limited liability." Clark, p. 90.

d. **Business grows:** Finally, suppose that the initial capitalization is adequate, but the business ***grows*** to the point where capital that was once adequate is no longer adequate to meet the new likely responsibilities. A strong argument can be made that this should be considered "inadequate capitalization" of the sort that should make veil-piercing more likely.

5. **Failure to follow corporate formalities:** The last factor that makes it more likely that the court will pierce the corporate veil is that the shareholder has ***failed to follow corporate formalities*** in the running of the business.

a. **Illustrations:** Here are some of the ways in which such failure to follow formalities might occur:

- ***shares*** are ***never formally issued***, or consideration for them is never received by the corporation;
- ***shareholders' meetings*** and ***directors' meetings*** are ***not held***;
- shareholders do not sharply ***distinguish*** between ***corporate property*** and ***personal property*** (e.g., the sole shareholder spends funds from the corporate bank account for his personal use, and/or spends funds in his personal account for corporate use without proper accounting); and
- proper ***corporate financial records*** are ***not maintained***.

See generally Nutshell, p. 89.

b. **Injury to creditor:** When this failure to follow formalities actually ***injures*** creditors, it is easy to see why the failure should increase the court's willingness to pierce the corporate veil. For instance, if the failure to follow formalities consists of the shareholder's taking of cash from the corporation's bank account to pay his personal debts, thus making this money unavailable to corporate creditors, fairness (as well as the law of fraudulent conveyances) dictates that he be required to make good the loss.

i. **Misleading to creditor:** Sometimes, of course, the failure to follow corporate formalities may have injured the creditor by ***misleading him***. For instance, if

Shareholder puts his personal name on the business' door instead of the corporate name, and pays some of its bills with a personal check, Creditor may have been misled into believing he was dealing with Shareholder personally instead of the corporation, even though Shareholder has executed the contract with Creditor in the corporate name. As in the situation where commingling of funds drains the corporation of cash to pay its debts, it is easy to see why this failure to follow corporate formalities should be "punished" by being used as a factor leading to piercing the veil.

ii. **No injury:** But in most of the reported cases where the court pierces the veil based upon a failure to follow corporate formalities, the failure did ***not*** injure the creditors. For instance, if the failure is the shareholder's failure to conduct shareholders' and directors' meetings or issue shares, the tort or contract claimant will almost never be directly injured. Therefore, it is somewhat illogical to point to this conduct as a rationale for piercing the veil.

(1) **Possible explanation:** A possible explanation is that "the shareholder should not be permitted first to ignore the rules of corporate behavior and then later to claim the advantage of the corporate shield." Nutshell, p. 90. However, a complete imposition of personal liability seems like an exceptionally brutal and unfair remedy for a disregard of corporate formalities — especially by an overburdened small business owner — that injures no one.

(2) **Alternative explanation:** A second explanation is that although such failure to follow formalities usually does not ***directly*** show that creditors have been injured, this failure "at least *suggest[s]* that fraudulent transfers may have taken place" (Clark p. 85), and the court is spared the need to apply highly-technical fraudulent transfer law.

6. **Summary:** In summary, in nearly all cases in which a shareholder has been made liable for corporate debts under the doctrine of piercing the corporate veil, at least ***two*** of the above four factors have been present. Probably the most common combination is one in which the corporation is ***inadequately capitalized*** and the stockholders ***fail to follow the formalities of corporate existence***.

C. **Parent/subsidiary structure:** Just as the individual shareholders of a corporation may be held liable for the debts of the corporation, so there are situations in which a ***parent corporation*** may be held liable for the debts of its ***subsidiary***.

1. **Greater tendency to pierce:** In fact, the courts probably have a ***greater*** tendency to pierce the corporate veil in the parent/subsidiary context than in the individual shareholder situation — in the former situation, a large business enterprise is being required to pay the debts, whereas in the latter, an individual's non-business assets are being taken, probably a more sobering thought to most courts. Nutshell, p. 91.

2. **General rule of non-liability:** In any event, it is certainly ***not*** the case that a parent is automatically responsible for the obligations of its subsidiary. The veil will not be pierced, and the parent will not be liable for the debts of the subsidiary, so long as: (1) proper corporate formalities are observed, (2) the public is not confused about whether it is dealing

with the parent or the subsidiary, (3) the subsidiary is operated in a fair manner with some hope of making a profit, and (4) there is no other manifest unfairness.

a. **Illustration:** Thus the parent/subsidiary demarcation will ***not*** be pierced merely because there is a ***close relationship*** between the two entities. For example, the fact that the ***directors*** are mostly or even entirely the same between the two corporations, the ***officers*** are the same, they have common accountants and lawyers, and they file a consolidated tax return, are not by themselves enough to cause a piercing of the corporate veil. See Nutshell, p. 93.

b. **"Domination of affairs" not enough:** The fact that the parent may in some sense ***"dominate" the affairs*** of the subsidiary will, similarly, ***not*** by itself be enough to give rise to veil-piercing. Thus the fact that the parent ***drains excess cash*** from the subsidiary, ***demands a veto power*** over significant decisions by the subsidiary, or otherwise exercises some degree of ***control*** over the subsidiary's ***operations***, will not suffice for piercing. So long as the degree of control by parent over subsidiary is within the bounds usually found in corporate America, creditors will probably not be able to attack the parent's assets. Only if the two companies operate as a ***"single economic entity"*** will the veil generally be pierced, assuming that there is no fraud on creditors.

3. **Factors leading to veil-piercing:** Conversely, there are a number of factors that ***will*** make it likely that the court will pierce the veil and hold the parent liable for the debts of its subsidiary:

a. **Intertwined operations:** Piercing is likely if the business affairs of the two corporations are ***intertwined***, and ***separate corporate formalities*** are not followed. For instance, if both corporations have ***exactly the same board of directors***, ***separate directors' meetings*** of the two corporations are not held, and separate ***sets of minutes*** are not maintained, the court is more likely to pierce the veil. As the idea is sometimes put (in Delaware, for instance), there will be piercing if the two companies operated as a ***"single economic entity."***

b. **Unified business and subsidiary undercapitalized:** Veil-piercing is more likely if subsidiary and parent are operating ***portions of a single business***, and the subsidiary is ***undercapitalized***. For instance, suppose that Parent buys and maintains a fleet of taxi cabs, and purports to lease the cabs to Subsidiary, whose employees do the driving. If Subsidiary is insufficiently capitalized to meet probable tort claims, a court might well hold that the two companies are really operating a single business, and that the veil should therefore be pierced to allow Subsidiary's creditors to attack Parent's assets. (This is one situation in which the presence of a parent/subsidiary context rather than an individual shareholder context might make a difference — thus in *Walkovszky*, *supra*, p. 37, had there been a parent corporation that owned the cabs, the parent might have been held liable.)

c. **Misleading to public:** Veil piercing is more likely if the parent and subsidiary do not make it ***clear to the public*** which entity is handling each particular aspect of the business. For instance, if Subsidiary is listed as being a "division" or "branch office" of Parent, Parent is likely to be held liable for Subsidiary's debts on the theory that creditors who dealt with Subsidiary were misled into believing that they were dealing with Parent through its unincorporated division.

d. **Intermingling of assets:** Similarly, veil-piercing is more likely if Parent and Subsidiary ***intermingle assets***. For instance, if Subsidiary receives the capital it needs merely by an undocumented transfer of funds from Parent's bank account, veil-piercing is more likely. Instead, Parent should cause Subsidiary to sign a formal note, and should then treat the transaction as a formal interest-bearing loan. See Nutshell, p. 93.

e. **Unfair manner of operation:** Perhaps most important of all, veil-piercing is more likely if the court concludes that the subsidiary was operated in an ***"unfair manner."*** Usually this refers to operation of the subsidiary in a way that is for the ***advantage of the parent*** rather than advantage of the subsidiary. Thus if Subsidiary is forced to ***sell at cost*** to Parent, so that Subsidiary can never make a profit, the court is likely to pierce the veil.

See generally Nutshell, pp. 91-93.

4. **Direct liability by parent for exercising control of subsidiary:** So far, in our discussion of parent-subsidiary veil piercing we have been assuming that the parent's liability, if any, is *vicarious*: that is, the plaintiffs first prove that the subsidiary is liable, and then establish that because the preconditions to piercing are met, the parent should be automatically, and vicariously, held liable for the subsidiary's obligations. But there is another, closely-related, path by which the parent may be found liable. That is the path of "***direct***" liability: the parent is found to have been ***so deeply involved*** in conducting the ***particular activity*** that has given rise to the claim that the court finds that the parent is itself responsible, typically under tort principles, and without reference to the doctrine of veil-piercing. For instance, it may be the case that an ***officer of the parent has specifically directed that the subsidiary take a particular action*** that turns out to be tortious — if so, the parent can be found liable not on a veil-piercing derivative-liability analysis but rather on a "direct liability" theory (under which the parent is itself the, or a, tortfeasor). The leading case applying such a direct-liability approach is set forth in the following example.

Example: A federal environmental protection statute imposes "Superfund" cleanup liability upon any "person" who "operates" a facility from which hazardous wastes are disposed. CPC wholly owns Ott Chemical, which in turn owns and operates a Michigan factory that pollutes. After Ott goes out of business, the federal government sues CPC, claiming that CPC "operated" the plant at the time of the pollution even though the plant was owned by a subsidiary.

Held (by the Supreme Court), the case can go to trial against CPC. A parent corporation is not liable for the acts of its subsidiaries merely because the parent controls the subsidiary by such means as electing its directors, appointing some of the parent's executives to executive positions at the subsidiary, etc. So CPC's mere ownership and control of Ott would not make it liable under the Superfund statute. However, such derivative liability (which does not exist here) must be distinguished from "direct" liability: if the parent directly participates in the wrong complained of, the parent may have its own direct, i.e., non-vicarious, liability. So, here, CPC may have taken actions of its own which constituted direct "operation" of the Michigan plant. To show such direct operation, it will not be enough for the federal government to show merely that

CPC controlled the entire subsidiary, Ott. Instead, the government will have to show that CPC directly controlled the relevant operation of the *polluting factory itself.* So if the government merely shows that CPC's actions regarding the factory were those which a parent company would customarily take regarding a subsidiary (e.g., monitoring the subsidiary's performance, deciding on its capital budget, etc.), this will not be enough to show that CPC "operated" the factory. But if, for instance, the government can show that a person who was acting solely as the agent or employee of CPC (rather than as an agent of both CPC and Ott) played a significant role in the decisions surrounding the pollution, this might be enough to establish that CPC should be deemed to have operated the factory. (Case remanded to the trial court for further proceedings on whether CPC in fact operated the plant.) *U.S. v. Bestfoods*, 524 U.S. 51 (1998).

D. Distinction between active and passive investors: The court is far more likely to pierce the corporate veil to the detriment of an ***active*** investor than to the detriment of a ***passive*** one.

Example: Active and Passive each own fifty percent of Corporation. Active runs the company from day to day, controls its bank accounts, and draws the only executive salary. Passive's involvement is limited to supplying initial capital. Active commingles his personal funds with those of the Corporation, fails to see to it that board meetings are held, and misleads creditors into thinking that he is a sole proprietor. In a suit by one of Corporation's creditors against Active, the court is likely to pierce the veil. But it is far less likely to pierce the veil to hold Passive liable (even though, strictly speaking, the corporate form should either be honored or disregarded without regard to which shareholder is the defendant). See Nutshell, p. 101.

Quiz Yourself on
THE CORPORATE FORM *(PIERCING THE CORPORATE VEIL)*

12. The Three Little Pigs are each one-third owners of the Huff 'N Puff Construction Company, Inc. Huff N' Puff has a board of directors (at least on paper), but none of the Pigs are on it. The board never meets or signs any documents. The Pigs don't set regular salaries for themselves; instead, any time any of them needs money for living expenses, he takes it from the safe, without keeping a record of how much he took. Cumulatively over the last two years, the Pigs have taken out $100,000 more for "living expenses" than the company earned. The real estate market suffers a sharp downturn, and Huff N' Puff is unable to pay one of its largest suppliers, Big Bad Wolf Masonry Supplies. Big Bad Wolf seeks payment from the Pigs personally. What result? ________________

13. The Attila the Hun Wrecking Company has a wholly-owned subsidiary, Attila's Army-Navy Surplus Stores, Inc. Army-Navy is run as a separate corporation, with its own board of directors (most of whom are also directors of Wrecking Co.) Army-Navy observes all corporate formalities, such as the holding of board meetings, the keeping of minutes, segregation of funds from those of Wrecking Co., etc. Wrecking Company, through its domination of Army-Navy's board, causes Army-Navy to sell Wrecking Co. product at Army-Navy's cost; these sales from Army-Navy to Wrecking Co. account for 90% of Army-Navy's total sales. Because Army-Navy does not have sufficient operating profits, it can't pay a creditor, the Bambi Freeze-Dried Venison Co. Bambi then seeks payment from the Wrecking Company directly. Can Bambi recover from Wrecking Company? ________________

Answers

12. **Wolf will be allowed to seek payment from the pigs personally.** As a general rule, corporate creditors cannot seek payment directly from the shareholders of a corporation; the shareholders are protected by the corporate "veil." However, when shareholders don't deserve such protection, creditors may "pierce" the corporate veil and seek payment from the shareholders personally. Mere undercapitalization, without more, won't usually be grounds for piercing the veil. But undercapitalization combined with failure to follow corporate formalities *will* be. [35] Here, the Pigs have committed both sins: (1) they have left the corporation undercapitalized, i.e., unable to pay its bills; and (2) they have ignored corporate formalities — the holding of board meetings, the keeping of records of withdrawals, etc. Since the Pigs have ignored the corporate form when such ignorance was to their benefit, a court will disregard that form now that it's to the Pigs' detriment. As a result, the Pigs will be liable personally for Huff 'N Puff's debt to Wolf.

13. **Yes.** In a parent-and-subsidiary context, running the subsidiary for the parent's benefit rather than for the subsidiary's own benefit is likely to be grounds for piercing the corporate veil, especially where this has the effect of stripping all profits from the subsidiary. [42] This makes perfect theoretical sense in that, if the parent is unwilling to view the subsidiary as a separate corporation for profit purposes, it ought not to be able to take advantage of the subsidiary's corporate "veil" so as to avoid the subsidiary's liabilities. Therefore, Wrecking Company will be liable for Army-Navy's obligations.

VI. INSIDER CLAIMS IN BANKRUPTCY (INCLUDING EQUITABLE SUBORDINATION)

A. Generally: When a corporation becomes ***bankrupt,*** its shareholders and officers will often be among the corporation's creditors. The same principles that lead a court to disregard the corporate form to hold the shareholder liable in the veil-piercing context may lead the bankruptcy court to: (1) disallow an insider's claim entirely; or (2) make that claim subordinate to the claims of non-insiders, under the doctrine of "equitable subordination".

B. Disallowance of claim: The bankruptcy court may decide to ***disallow*** the insider's claim ***entirely***.

1. **Payment for services:** If the insider's claim is for ***services*** he has rendered to the corporation or other intangible benefits, the court may reach this result by finding that the claim has not been "proved." For instance, if the sole shareholder/president causes the corporation to agree to pay him a very excessive salary considering the type of work he is performing, the court is likely to disallow his claim for the unpaid portion of this excessive salary.

2. **Transforming loan into capital:** Similarly, if the stockholders have contributed funds to the company, but have denominated all or nearly all of their contribution as "loans" rather than as "capital," the court may treat some or all of this as capital (in which case the stockholders will forfeit this equity in the bankruptcy). The court will generally do this only where the stated capital is very clearly inadequate for the corporation's expected business.

C. Equitable subordination: The doctrine of ***"equitable subordination"*** is a slightly less drastic means of placing the insiders' interest below those of arms-length creditors. Under this doctrine, if it is equitable to do so the bankruptcy court will recognize the insiders' claims against the corporation, but will require that these claims be satisfied ***only after all other creditors*** (and perhaps preferred shareholders) have been ***fully satisfied***. As a practical matter, the use of equitable subordination in a bankruptcy proceeding will usually mean that the insiders receive nothing, since the assets of the bankrupt corporation are rarely sufficient even to satisfy the outside creditors.

1. **Grounds:** There is no cut-and-dry test for determining when equitable subordination should be applied. Since the doctrine derives from equity, the court will apply it whenever it is "equitable" or "fair" to do so. As a practical matter, many of the same factors that would induce a court to pierce the corporate veil may also induce the bankruptcy court to use equitable subordination. Thus ***inadequate capitalization***, ***failure to follow corporate formalities*** and ***fraud or wrongdoing*** by the insider, may all lead to use of this doctrine.

2. ***"Deep Rock"*** **doctrine:** The doctrine of equitable subordination is often referred to as the ***"Deep Rock" doctrine***, named after a subsidiary in a case applying equitable distribution to bar the parent's claim against the subsidiary.

3. **Less wrongdoing required:** Generally, less of a departure from ordinary corporate practice is required for a bankruptcy court to apply the equitable subordination doctrine than for an ordinary court to pierce the corporate veil and favor a creditor. Since the insider is merely required to wait his turn to receive payment on his claim, rather than suffering the much more drastic remedy of having to reach into non-business assets to satisfy business creditors' claims, this lower threshold for the doctrine seems appropriate.

Quiz Yourself on

THE CORPORATE FORM *(INSIDER CLAIMS IN BANKRUPTCY & EQUITABLE SUBORDINATION)*

14. Larry, Curly, and Moe have for several years conducted their house-painting business as a partnership. During that time, they have each kept $50,000 in cash invested as capital in the partnership. They then decide that it would be better to operate as a corporation. Consequently, they incorporate as O-A Wizeguy House Painting Corp. They liquidate the partnership, and each contributes $10,000 to the corporation's stock. At the same time, each lends the corporation $40,000. Shortly thereafter, the corporation becomes insolvent. At that point, it has $200,000 in unpaid debts, of which $120,000 is due to Larry, Curly and Moe ($40,000 each), and the balance of $80,000 is owed to Shemp, a supplier who has no affiliation with the three owners. There is $40,000 in cash available for distribution.

(a) If you represent Shemp, what doctrine will you assert as the basis for getting as much of the cash for your client as you can? ________________

(b) How is the court most likely to divide the cash? ________________

Answer

14. (a) The doctrine of "equitable subordination." Under this doctrine, a bankruptcy court can "subordinate" the claims of insiders, i.e., not pay the insiders anything until all outsiders have been paid in full.

(b) Shemp will likely get 50 cents on the dollar, because there is $40,000 available to pay the $80,000 debt to him. The issue here is whether equitable subordination should apply. If it does, the court will give the entire $40,000 to the outsider, Shemp, and leave the three insiders with nothing. One of the grounds for equitable subordination is inadequate capitalization. The capitalization here was clearly inadequate in light of the fact that the partnership, which undertook the same activities as the corporation, was capitalized for $150,000, and the corporation was only capitalized for $30,000. So the court probably will apply equitable subordination. As a result, the "loans" from Larry, Curly, and Moe would be treated as invested capital, being subordinated to the $80,000 in claims from Shemp, the outsider. Since there's only $40,000 to distribute, Larry, Curly, and Moe would get nothing.

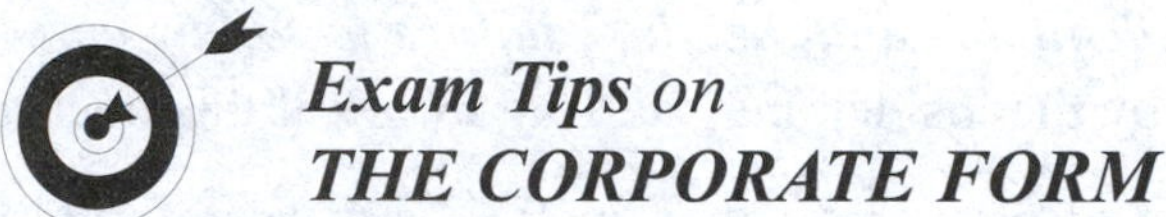

Exam Tips on ***THE CORPORATE FORM***

Here are the main things to watch for in connection with the corporate form:

- If your fact pattern indicates that the corporation is doing something which ***violates a statute*** or a provision of the corp's ***charter***, consider whether the corporate action is unenforceable because of the ***ultra vires*** doctrine.

  - Be especially alert for the ultra vires issue when the pattern involves a ***contract*** between the corp. and a third party, and one of the parties is trying to ***wriggle out*** of the contract on the grounds that the charter doesn't allow the contract. In this situation, discuss the fact that at common law, this might have furnished a defense to whichever party (the corp. or the third party) didn't want to comply, but that under modern statutes ultra vires usually ***won't be a defense*** in this situation.

  - But where a ***shareholder sues to block the transaction***, indicate that ultra vires may still be grounds for an injunction under many modern statutes.

    Example: Corp's charter limits debt to $75,000. The board (which includes all but one shareholder) unanimously decides to borrow $100,000. S, the absent shareholder, sues to block the loan. The court might well issue an injunction on grounds of ultra vires. (But if all shareholders agreed to the loan, and it was the bank that was trying to wriggle out of the contract on ultra vires grounds, then a court would probably *decline* to apply ultra vires.)

- When your fact pattern involves a ***pre-incorporation contract***, here are the issues to watch out for:

  - Is the ***promoter*** (the founder/organizer) liable?

    - The most common exam situation is that the other party to the contract ***knows*** that the corporation hasn't been formed yet, but the promoter *assures him* that it will be. If the corporation is ***never formed***, the promoter will generally be found ***personally liable***.

Example: A, a promoter, induces X to make a contract with "Z Corp., a corporation to be formed." (A tells X that he, A, will be one of the stockholders of Z Corp. when it's formed). Z Corp. is never formed. X sues A. X will probably win, because A has induced X to believe that the corp. will be formed, so A should bear responsibility if it never is.

- ☞ Another frequently-tested situation is that the promoter tells the other party the corp. will be formed, and the corp. ***is formed***, but it defaults. Here, too, the promoter will usually be ***held liable*** (though it's always a question of what the promoter and the other party originally intended).

☞ Is the ***corporation*** liable?

- ☞ Here, remember that the general rule is that the corp. will generally ***not*** be liable under the pre-incorporation agreement, unless the corp. ***expressly or impliedly adopts*** the agreement. (*Example:* If the corp. ***receives benefits*** under the agreement, this is likely to be found to be an implied adoption of the agreement.)

☛ Professors often test the situation in which investors ***attempt*** to form a corp., but ***no corp. is actually formed*** due to some ***procedural defect*** (e.g., failure to pay filing fees). Here, the issue becomes, are the investors liable?

☞ Refer to the possibility that the ***"de facto corporation"*** doctrine will apply, in which case the individual defendants won't be liable. But you should conclude that the doctrine probably ***won't apply***, because most states (and the MBCA) have abolished it. Best odds for the doctrine's applying: where the defendants are purely passive investors, who didn't conduct the business's operations but merely supplied $.

☞ Also, discuss the possibility that the ***"corporation by estoppel"*** doctrine may apply. This has a better chance of working than the "de facto corp." doctrine: if P (the creditor) ***thought the business was a corp.***, and indicated his willingness to ***deal with it as a corp.***, the court may estop him from pursuing the individual would-be "shareholders."

☛ Professors also often give you the issue of whether the ***"corporate veil"*** should be ***"pierced."*** Look for this issue wherever the corporation ends up ***insolvent*** and can't perform its obligations — always consider the possibility that the creditor can sue the individual shareholders (even if the facts don't indicate that the creditor is in fact suing the shareholders).

☞ In veil-piercing questions, keep in mind that the most important factor is whether the corp. was ***inadequately capitalized*** — if it was, P is much more likely to achieve piercing.

☞ But also, keep in mind that in addition to inadequate capital, piercing usually requires ***some other factor***, of which the most common are:

- ☞ ***misrepresentation*** (e.g., "My corp. has all the capital it will need to perform the contract with you"); and

- ☞ failure to ***follow corporate formalities*** (e.g., no board of directors is elected, or shareholder loans are taken from the corp. without repayment or without promissory notes).

- ☞ In the case of a ***parent-subsidiary relationship***, the subsidiary's veil will probably be pierced (so the parent is held liable) if it can be said that the parent and subsidiary operated as a ***"single economic entity."*** But the mere fact that the parent ***"dominated"*** the subsidiary (e.g., by appointing directors, or exercising veto power over major decisions) ***won't*** be enough.

☞ If the case involves an ***LLC*** (as opposed to a corporation), consider whether the veil can nonetheless be pierced. But failure to follow ***formalities*** probably ***won't*** be a reason for piercing (since LLCs have virtually no formalities that they're required to follow). On the other hand, ***inadequate capitalization*** may well be a reason for piercing the LLC's veil.

CHAPTER 3

THE CORPORATE STRUCTURE

ChapterScope

This Chapter discusses the powers of directors, officers, and shareholders, respectively. The main concepts are:

- **Straight vs. cumulative voting:** In all elections for directors, the number of votes a shareholder gets equals the number of shares she holds, multiplied by the number of directors standing for election. But there are two distinct methods by which these shares can be voted, "straight" and "cumulative."
  - **Straight voting:** In ***"straight"*** voting, ***no share*** may be ***voted more than once*** for any given candidate.
  - **Cumulative voting:** In ***"cumulative"*** voting, by contrast, a voter may vote a single share ***multiple times for a single candidate*** (once for each director seat that's open). This increases the ***power of minority shareholders***, since a shareholder may cumulate (i.e., lump together) all his votes so as to be sure to elect a single director.
- **Quorum:** At both a shareholders' meeting and a board of directors' meeting, no action may be taken without a ***"quorum."***
  - **Board meeting:** At a ***board*** meeting, a quorum is usually a majority of the ***directors in office.***
  - **Shareholders' meeting:** At a ***shareholders'*** meeting, a quorum is usually a ***majority of the outstanding shares.***
- **Shareholders' powers:** Shareholders are the owners of stock in the corporation. They have two main sets of powers:
  - **Vote for directors:** First (and most important) they ***elect the members of the board of directors.***
  - **Approval of fundamental changes:** Second, they ***approve or disapprove major changes to the corporation.*** For instance, the corporation cannot sell substantially all of its assets, or merge into another corporation, unless the shareholders so vote.
- **Directors:** The board of directors ***manages the corporation,*** at the ***policy*** level.
  - **Appointment of officers:** A key aspect of directors' powers is that the board votes to ***appoint the "officers" of the corporation***, who are its day-to-day managers. For example, the board elects the president.
  - **Setting of policy:** The board also ***sets major policy.*** For instance, any non-trivial acquisition of another company's stock or assets would have to be approved by the board.
  - **Requirements for board action:** A key focus with respect to directors is, What are the requirements for valid ***action*** by the board? (For instance, there must be a quorum present at a directors' meeting; the board must normally act by majority vote of those present,

etc.)

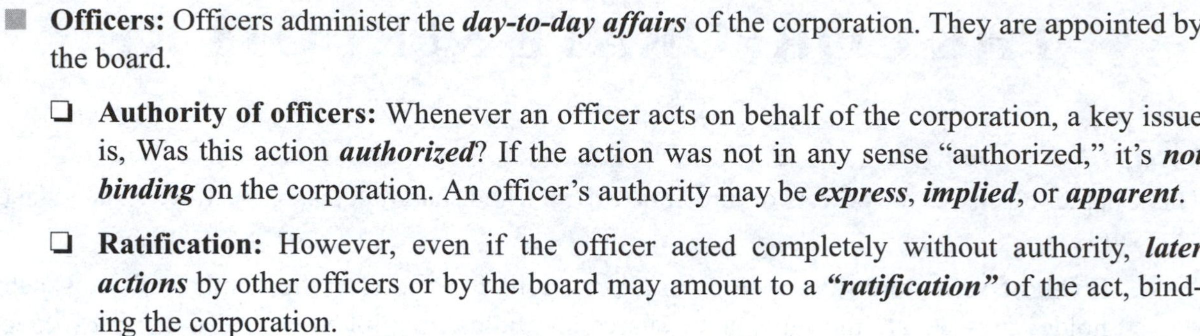

- **Officers:** Officers administer the ***day-to-day affairs*** of the corporation. They are appointed by the board.
  - ❑ **Authority of officers:** Whenever an officer acts on behalf of the corporation, a key issue is, Was this action ***authorized***? If the action was not in any sense "authorized," it's ***not binding*** on the corporation. An officer's authority may be ***express***, ***implied***, or ***apparent***.
  - ❑ **Ratification:** However, even if the officer acted completely without authority, ***later actions*** by other officers or by the board may amount to a ***"ratification"*** of the act, binding the corporation.

I. GENERAL ALLOCATION OF POWER: SHAREHOLDERS, DIRECTORS AND OFFICERS

A. The traditional statutory scheme: Traditionally, powers have been allocated among the shareholders, the directors and the officers of a corporation in a particular way. Even today, most statutes assume that this allocation of powers will be followed. Therefore, we refer to it as the ***"statutory scheme."*** However, most modern statutes allow the corporation, if it observes certain formalities, to ***modify*** this scheme.

1. **The statutory scheme:** The statutory scheme may be summarized as follows:

   a. **Shareholders:** The ***shareholders*** act principally through two mechanisms: (1) ***electing and removing directors***, and (2) approving or disapproving ***fundamental or non-ordinary changes*** (e.g., mergers).

   b. **Directors:** The ***directors*** "***manage***" the corporation's business. That is, they formulate policy, and appoint officers to carry out that policy.

   c. **Officers:** The corporation's ***officers*** administer ***the day-to-day affairs*** of the corporation, under the supervision of the board.

2. **Inappropriate structure for very large or very small corporations:** For very large or very small corporations, this statutory scheme does not reflect reality. For instance, a small closely-held corporation generally does not have its affairs managed by the board of directors — the shareholders usually exercise control directly (they may happen also to be directors, but they usually do not act as a body of directors, and the controlling shareholders often disregard any non-shareholder directors). At the other end of the spectrum, a very large publicly-held company is really run by its officers, and the board of directors frequently serves as little more than a "rubber stamp" to approve decisions made by officers.

3. **Modification of statutory scheme:** Modern statutes generally give the corporation the power to modify this traditional statutory scheme where appropriate. This is especially true for closely-held corporations, as is discussed *infra*, p. 134. (For instance, some statutes allow closely-held corporations to reduce the board to one or two members; see *infra*, p. 59.) But unless a particular modification of the statutory scheme is explicitly authorized by statute, the corporation and its lawyer disregard the statutory scheme ***at their peril***.

Much of this chapter is devoted to an explanation of the statutory scheme in detail, together with a description of the consequences if the traditional scheme is not actually followed by the corporation.

4. **Focus of this section:** The rest of this section I is an overview of the division of powers as among the shareholders, directors and officers. Following that, sections II, III and IV examine the mechanisms by which the board, the officers and the shareholders, respectively, exercise their powers.

B. **Powers of shareholders:** Under the statutory scheme, the shareholders do ***not directly manage*** the corporation, even though they own it. Instead, they can influence the conduct of the business through a number of ***indirect*** methods.

1. **Four methods:** There are four main methods by which the shareholders can influence the corporation's affairs:

   a. **Elect and remove directors:** They have the power to ***elect*** and ***remove directors***;

   b. **Articles of incorporation and bylaws:** They can approve or disapprove of changes to the ***articles of incorporation*** or ***bylaws*** and thereby influence the allocation of power as among themselves, the directors, and the officers. See *supra*, p. 23. (For instance, the powers and duties of executive officers are usually spelled out in the bylaws, so these powers and duties could be cut back or re-allocated based partly on shareholder-approved bylaw changes.)

   c. **Fundamental changes:** They have the right to approve or disapprove of ***fundamental changes*** not in the ordinary course of business, such as a ***merger***, a sale of substantially all of the corporation's assets, or dissolution.

   d. **Void or voidable transactions:** Finally, some transactions by officers or board of directors are ***void*** or ***voidable*** unless ratified by a vote of shareholders. For instance, many transactions between the corporation and a director or officer are voidable on grounds of self-dealing unless the shareholders ratify the transaction by voting to approve it. See *infra* p. 200.

   See generally Nutshell, pp. 155-56.

2. **Election and removal of directors:** Because the shareholders' power to ***elect and remove directors*** is so important, we give it special attention here (as well as on p. 55):

   a. **Election:** Directors are normally elected at ***each annual meeting*** of shareholders. That is, directors normally serve a ***one-year term*** (though of course they can be, and often are, re-elected). See MBCA § 8.05(b).

      i. **Staggered terms:** The one common exception to annual terms is that in most states, if the articles of incorporation so provide, the directors may have ***staggered terms***. That is, the directors may be initially divided into, say, three "classes," with one class having a three-year term, another a two-year term and the last a one-year term. This classification device, which is often used today to make it more difficult for a "raider" to replace the board, is discussed further *infra*, p. 451.

   b. **Vacancies:** Shareholders are generally given the power to elect directors to fill ***vacancies*** on the board, but the board of directors also usually has this power. Therefore, the filling of vacancies is discussed in the treatment of the board of directors, *infra*, p. 60.

c. **Removal of directors:** At common law, shareholders had little power to ***remove*** a director during his term of office. But modern statutes have dramatically expanded this shareholder power. The topic of shareholder-removal of directors is discussed more fully *infra*, p. 61, as part of our more general discussion of the ways in which directors may be removed.

3. **No power to bind corporation:** The shareholders do ***not*** have the power to ***conduct business*** directly on behalf of the corporation. (They must operate through their control of the board.) This means that shareholders cannot ***bind the corporation*** by their own direct actions. And this is true even of actions taken by a majority of shareholders, purportedly in the corporation's name — unless the action is somehow ratified by the board or by an officer with power to bind the corporation to the kind of transaction in question (see *infra*, p. 73), the action by the shareholders has ***no effect***.

   Example: Sam is a majority shareholder of Corp., but does not sit on the board and is not an officer. He goes to Copy Machine Co. and signs a contract (made out in Corp's name) to purchase a copy machine. The board learns of this before the machine is delivered, and sends a letter to Copy Machine saying, "We're not bound to take this copier, and we don't want it." Copy Machine can't hold Corp. to the contract, because Sam is merely a shareholder (albeit a majority one), not an officer, and shareholders *qua* shareholders can't bind a corporation.

C. **The power of directors:** Traditionally, state corporation statutes have provided that the board of directors shall ***"manage"*** the affairs of the corporation. These statutes generally view the board not as agents of the stockholders, but as an ***independent institution*** with responsibility for supervising the corporation's affairs. C&E, p. 287.

1. **Shareholders can't give orders:** Thus traditionally (and probably even under recently-revised statutes), the shareholders ***cannot order the board of directors to take any particular action***. It is the board, not the shareholders, who formulate policy; shareholder control is limited to removing directors (see *supra*) or approving or disapproving certain major actions contemplated by the board (e.g., mergers).

2. **Supervisory role:** Although older statutes still say that the board of directors shall "manage" the corporation, the reality is that day-to-day management is carried out by the corporation's ***officers***, under the ***supervision of the board of directors***. Some modern statutes now recognize this fact. For instance, the MBCA says that "All corporate powers shall be exercised ***by or under the authority of*** the board of directors of the corporation, and the business and affairs of the corporation shall be ***managed by or under the direction***, and subject to the ***oversight***, of its board of directors. . . ." §8.01(b). (The role of officers is described *infra*, p. 72.)

   a. **Sets policy:** Thus today, the board's main function is to ***set the policies*** of the corporation, and to authorize the making of important contracts. Nutshell, pp. 161-62. It is also the board which declares dividends; this responsibility is given to it specifically by statute. See *infra*, p. 505. Beyond this, it is usually up to the board to initiate fundamental changes in the corporation (e.g., mergers or large asset sales), though these must then be submitted to the shareholders for approval.

D. Power of officers: According to the statutory scheme, the corporation's ***officers*** serve under and at the will of the board of directors and carry out the ***day-to-day operations*** of the corporation. In practice, of course, the officers frequently have much greater power than this implies, especially in large publicly-held corporations. But the important thing to remember is that, as far as most corporate statutes contemplate, the officers are essentially ***"agents"*** of the board of directors. (This "agency" view has major implications for the power of an officer to bind the corporation as his "principal"; see *infra*, p. 73.)

E. Sharing of responsibility: From the above discussion, it might sound as though shareholders have very little ability to influence the corporation's affairs, apart from election and removal of directors. However, there are a number of additional ways in which shareholders at least get to ***share*** some of the power over corporate operations:

1. **Shareholder resolutions:** As noted, shareholders cannot require the directors or officers to take any particular action during the corporation's day-to-day operations. However, shareholders can seek to ***influence*** the board by exercising their right to adopt ***shareholder resolutions*** that ***recommend*** particular actions to the board (even though the board can't be required to follow the resolution's recommendations).

2. **Self-interested transactions:** Also, transactions in which the board or officers are ***personally interested*** are almost always put to a shareholder vote. Thus ***incentive compensation*** plans that cover officers, and arrangements whereby the corporation indemnifies directors or officers against liability (see *infra*, p. 341), are almost always put to a shareholder vote.

   a. **Effect of ratification:** If such a transaction in which directors or officers are personally interested is ratified by the shareholders, this generally does not completely immunize the planned transaction against attack. But individual shareholders who vote for it can't attack the transaction later on; also, approval may make it harder for opposing shareholders to attack the transaction on grounds of general unfairness, by shifting the burden of proof to them from management. (But a court will still set aside a transaction involving officers or directors that is fraudulent or "manifestly unfair." See *infra*, p. 200.) See Nutshell, p. 165.

3. **Fundamental changes:** Lastly, shareholders are always given the power to approve or disapprove of certain ***fundamental changes*** in the corporation. For instance, in most states the following kinds of changes are ineffective without shareholder approval:

   [1] ***mergers***;

   [2] ***sales*** of all or substantially all of the corporation's ***assets***;

   [3] ***amendments*** of the articles of incorporation;

   [4] statutory ***share exchanges*** (see *infra*, p. 310), in which all shareholders are required to exchange their shares for those in another corporation; and

[5] ***dissolution*** of the corporation.

But observe that in most states the power to effect these changes does not reside exclusively in the shareholders: Only if the board of directors first decides to put the matter to a shareholder vote does the vote occur. This is sometimes referred to as the board of directors' ***"gatekeeping"*** function. See, e.g., MBCA § 11.04(b) (shareholders only get to vote if the board submits the proposed merger or share exchange to them.)

a. Amendment of bylaws: In recent years, another significant avenue by which shareholders may assert power has begun to emerge: the ability to ***amend*** the corporation's ***bylaws***. Recall (*supra*, p. 23) that most states allow the bylaws to be amended either by the board or the shareholders. Under the law of some states, practically any topic may be covered by a bylaw as long as the bylaw does not conflict with the certificate of incorporation. Although bylaws typically deal with non-controversial ***procedural*** matters (e.g., the date of the shareholders meeting, or how board elections are to be conducted), there is often nothing in state law to prevent bylaws from dealing with weightier matters on which the board and shareholders may disagree. Consequently, the shareholders may be able to change the corporation's policies in major ways over the objection of the board, by voting a bylaw change.

Example: In *Int'l Brotherhood of Teamsters v. Fleming Cos.*, 975 P.2d 907 (Ok. 1999), the court affirmed the right of shareholders of an Oklahoma corporation to pass a bylaw cancelling an ***anti-takeover device*** that the board had enacted.

i. State-law limits on bylaws: But some states do significantly limit the content of bylaws. For instance, in Delaware, "a proper function of bylaws is ***not*** to mandate how the board should decide ***specific substantive business decisions***, but rather, to define the ***process and procedures*** by which those decisions are made." *CA, Inc. v. AFSCME Employees Pension Plan*, 953 A.2d 227 (Del. 2008). So a bylaw amendment to the charter of a Delaware corporation would be unlawful if the amendment purported to significantly ***limit the board's discretion*** over substantive matters, especially in a way that deprived the board of its ability to ***exercise its fiduciary responsibilities*** to all shareholders. See *CA, Inc.* (discussed in detail *infra*, p. 115) for a fact pattern in which such an illegal limitation in a bylaw occurred.

Quiz Yourself on
THE CORPORATE STRUCTURE *(GENERAL ALLOCATION OF POWER)*

15. Alfred Pennyworth is a 51% owner of Metropolis Crimefighters, Inc. Metropolis has two officers who serve as its directors and employees, Batman and Robin. Alfred is not a director or officer of the corporation. Alfred is out shopping one day when he sees a nice, sedate station wagon, the Travel Queen Family Truckster, which he thinks would make a far more sensible company car than the Batmobile. He signs a lease for the Travel Queen on behalf of Metropolis. When Batman and Robin see the Travel Queen, Robin exclaims, "Holy Corporations, Batman! Is Metropolis Crimefighters bound by this lease?" Well — is it? ______________

Answer

15. No. The issue here is the extent to which an *owner* of a corporation (i.e., a shareholder) may conduct corporate business. Here, that's all Alfred is; he's neither a director nor an officer. The rule is that shareholders have no authority to conduct corporate business; the board of directors has such authority, which it may delegate to officers or subordinates. Thus, a shareholder who is not an officer or director cannot enter into a contract on the corporation's behalf, unless the board has explicitly given him authority to do so. And that's true even where the shareholder owns a majority of the shares (and could therefore replace a majority of the board with a compliant one that would do what he wants.) [52]

II. THE BOARD OF DIRECTORS

A. Generally: We cover now the mechanics of the board of directors, including (1) how the board is ***elected***; (2) how it holds its ***meetings***; (3) what ***formalities*** it must observe in order to take action; and (4) how it may make use of ***committees***.

B. Election of board members: As noted, members of the board of directors are always ***elected by the shareholders*** (with the possible exception of the filling of vacancies; see *infra*, p. 60). Normally, a director's term is one year, and the entire board stands for re-election at the annual meeting of shareholders.

1. Pre-conditions for a valid vote: Before we get into the intricacies of board elections, understand that the stockholder vote to elect directors must satisfy the same basic ***procedural requirements*** as a stockholder vote to take any other action (e.g., to approve the sale of the company.) This means that:

a. Notice: Proper ***notice*** of the time and place of the meeting must be given to all shareholders. See, e.g., MBCA § 7.05(a).

b. Quorum: A ***quorum*** must be present. That is, ***more than 50% of the shares eligible to vote*** must be "present," either in person or via a valid proxy. See, e.g., MBCA § 7.25(a). (For a discussion of proxies, see p. 97.)

2. Straight vs. cumulative voting: The vote for directors may either be ***"straight"*** or ***"cumulative,"*** depending on the state's corporation statute and the articles of incorporation.

3. Definition of "straight" voting: In ***straight*** voting, each share may be voted for as many candidates as there are slots on the board, but no share may be voted more than once for any given candidate. Directors are elected by a ***plurality*** (not necessarily majority) of the votes cast. See MBCA § 7.28(a). Each share has one vote.

Example: In a closely-held corporation, A and B are the sole shareholders. A holds 72 shares and B holds 28. The board has three directors. A's candidates are A1, A2 and A3; B's candidates are B1, B2 and B3. If there is straight voting, A cannot cast more than 72 votes for any single candidate, and (most importantly), B cannot cast more than 28 votes for any candidate. Therefore, A's three candidates will receive 72 votes each, B's three candidates will receive 28 votes each, and *A's candidates will get all the seats on the board.*

4. Cumulative voting: The result in the above example looks pretty unfair to B. Although he has almost one-third of the votes, he has no representation on the board. In fact, even if he had 49 votes to A's 51, he still would not get a board seat under straight voting, since each of A's candidates would receive 51 votes and each of B's would get 49. To remedy this inadequate representation of minority shareholders, the device of ***cumulative*** voting was invented. As the name implies, cumulative voting entitles a shareholder to ***cumulate*** or ***aggregate*** his votes in favor of ***fewer candidates*** than there are slots available, including in the extreme case aggregating all of his votes for just one candidate. The consequences are that ***a minority shareholder is far more likely to be able to obtain at least one seat on the board***.

Example: Assume the same facts as the above example: A has 72 votes, B has 28 votes and there are three directors to be elected. This time, however, cumulative voting is permitted. B can therefore take his entire "package" of 84 votes (28 shares x three seats) and put it all on his single favorite candidate, whom we'll call B1. B1 therefore has 84 votes. Now, no matter how A divides up his 216 votes (72 shares x 3 seats), he cannot come up with three candidates all of whom beat B1. For instance, if he casts 85 votes for A1 and 85 votes for A2 (the minimum necessary for A1 and A2 to beat B1), he has used up 170 votes, and has only 46 votes left to put on A3. Therefore, even though B has only 28% of the shares and 28% of the total votes castable in the election, he is assured of at least one seat on a three-seat board by the device of cumulative voting.

a. Formula: Here is a simple formula that shows the minimum number of shares needed to elect ***one director*** under cumulative voting:

$$\frac{S}{D+1} + 1$$

where S = the total number of shares voting and D = the number of directors to be elected.

Using this formula on our above example, there were 100 shares being voted, and three directors to be elected. Therefore, we have:

$$\frac{100}{4} + 1$$

so that even had B had as few as 26 shares (with A having the remaining 74), B would have been able to elect one director on a three-seat board.

i. Multiple directors: An analogous formula tells the number of shares needed to elect n directors:

$$\frac{nS}{D+1} + 1$$

To illustrate the use of this formula, suppose there are three shareholders A, B and

C, and a total of 100 shares to be allocated. The board of directors will have five seats. A wants to know how many shares he will need if he is to deny seats to B and C (assuming that they act together to pool their votes). A will therefore need to elect all five directors, so the formula gives us (500/6) + 1, or 83 1/3 + 1, or 84 1/3. Actually, we can round the resulting number down to the nearest whole share. Therefore, A needs at least 84 of the 100 shares in order to deny B and C a seat on a five-seat board. See generally Nutshell, pp. 184-88.

b. Mandatory or permissive cumulative voting: As of 2002, all states at least ***permitted*** cumulative voting if the corporation desires it, and some states ***required*** it. Hamilton (8th), p. 551. There are three ways in which cumulative voting is handled in statutes:

i. Mandatory: Seven states make cumulative voting ***mandatory*** by a statutory or state constitutional provision. *Id.* In these states, even an amendment to the corporation's articles of incorporation specifically banning cumulative voting will be ineffective.

ii. "Opt in" election: Thirty states permit cumulative voting, but only if the articles of incorporation specifically elect to have it (an ***"opt in"*** election). *Id.* The MBCA follows this path; see § 7.28(b).

iii. "Opt out" election: Finally, thirteen states provide that cumulative voting is allowed unless the articles of incorporation explicitly exclude it (an ***"opt out"*** election). Hamilton (8th), p. 551.

c. Trickiness: When cumulative voting is allowed, voting strategy can be quite tricky. Most dramatically, it can be catastrophic to A to use straight voting when, unbeknownst to him, B is using cumulative voting.

Example: A owns 60 shares, B owns 40 shares and the board consists of five directors to be elected. Suppose A is unaware that cumulative voting is allowed and that B will be using it. A therefore casts 60 votes for each of his five candidates, A1, A2, A3, A4 and A5. B, knowing or suspecting that A is doing this, allocates his votes as follows: B1-68, B2-67 and B3-65 (with nothing for a fourth or fifth candidate). By this strategy, B ends up ***controlling the board*** with three directors even though he has only 40% of the shares!

Note: However, B's strategy in the above example could easily backfire if A learns or guesses what is going on. For instance, A can cast 75 votes for each of A1, A2, A3, and A4 (with nothing for A5). If A does so, B's strategy will have backfired — A will have four of the five seats, one more than he would have gotten had B followed the "conservative" cumulative strategy of splitting his votes among only two candidates (the maximum number that he could be sure of electing regardless of A's strategy).

i. Ties: It is poor strategy for a shareholder to create a ***tie*** among his own candidates. The reason is that if there is a tie for the last place on the board, this will result in a ***separate election*** for the last seat, at which cumulative voting will not apply. This may result in the minority shareholder's losing a seat he could otherwise have gotten. See Nutshell, p. 187.

ii. Advance notice: A few states require shareholders to give ***advance notice*** before they use cumulative voting. California, Hawaii, Minnesota, North Carolina and Ohio are among such states. See H&A, p. 496, n. 19. Similarly, MBCA § 7.28(d) provides that either: (1) the notice to shareholders of the annual meeting must state "conspicuously" that cumulative voting is authorized, or (2) the shareholder must give 48-hour notice to the corporation that he intends to vote cumulatively (in which case the other shareholders may cumulate without any further notice). This helps eliminate the unfair results that can occur if one shareholder votes cumulatively while the other does not, as in the example *supra*, p. 57.

iii. May change vote until announcement: Unfair surprise is also reduced by the fact that a shareholders' vote is ***not final*** until it is ***announced*** by the chairperson at the meeting. Thus even if in the above example A and B have both cast and submitted their written votes, if A suddenly realizes that B is cumulating, he can resubmit his own votes on a cumulative basis. H&A, p. 496.

d. Reduction in board size: Observe that one way to ***reduce the impact*** of cumulative voting is ***to reduce the size*** of the board.

Example: Suppose that A has 80 shares and B has 20 shares. If there are five seats on the board, cumulative voting assures B of getting a seat. (By the formula on p. 56, even as few as 17 of the 100 shares would guarantee B a seat on a five-person board.) But if the board is reduced to three seats, B will lose his guaranteed seats. Now, by the same formula, B needs at least (100/4) + 1, or 26, of the 100 shares in order to guarantee himself a seat.

e. Staggered terms: A second, similar way of reducing the effect of cumulative voting, is the use of ***staggered terms*** for the board of directors. That is, the board may be divided into, say, three "classes" of directors, one class elected for a one-year term, another for a two-year term, and the last for a three-year term. Once the initial election of each class has taken place, re-election of each class is for the same term (probably for three years).

Example: A has 79 shares and B has 21. The board has nine seats. If all directors are elected for one-year terms at each annual meeting, B is guaranteed at least two of the nine seats by cumulative voting — by the formula on p. 56,

$$\frac{200}{9+1} + 1 = 21$$

Now, assume that the board is divided into three "classes," each consisting of three directors; class A will stand for re-election in year one, class B in year two, and class C in year three. Each annual election now involves only three directors and B will go from having a guaranteed two seats to having *zero* guaranteed seats (since by the formula on p. 56, a shareholder needs at least 26 of 100 votes to be sure to fill one of three available seats in an election).

i. Upheld by court: The effect of staggered terms on cumulative voting is so severe that in those states where cumulative voting is required by statute or constitution (see *supra*, p. 57), minority shareholders have tried to convince courts that the adoption of staggered terms amounts to an automatic violation of cumulative voting. In one or two states, this argument has succeeded, but in most it has not. See H&A, p. 496, n. 21.

f. **Merits of cumulative voting:** The merits of cumulative voting depend largely on how widely dispersed ownership is. In a closely-held corporation, cumulative voting serves the very useful purpose of insuring that the holders of a minority, but significant, stake in the corporation are not "frozen out" from the board. But in a publicly-held corporation whose ownership is widely dispersed, cumulative voting can be more of a nuisance than a value, since it greatly complicates the mechanism of voting by proxy, yet will rarely affect the outcome. See Nutshell, p. 187. Management usually opposes cumulative voting, both on this ground and on the ground that it produces an ***adversarial board***. See K&C, p. 124-25.

g. **Removal of cumulatively-elected directors:** Recall that in most states today, shareholders have the right to ***remove*** a director without cause at any time during his term. See *supra*, p. 56 (as well as *infra*, p. 62). How does this right, where it exists, interact with cumulative voting? If an election to remove without cause were done by a straight "yes or no" vote at which the majority of votes cast determined the result, the right of cumulative voting would be ***completely nullified***: the holder of fifty-one percent of the shares could allow the minority to use its cumulative votes to elect, say, four seats on a nine-member board, but then could immediately prevail in a majority-vote election to remove those four without cause. Consequently, most states have a special provision to prevent this; see *infra*, p. 63.

C. **Number of directors:** Traditionally, most statutes require that there be at least three directors. But today, many states allow a board to consist of less than three so long as it is equal to the number of shareholders — thus a one-shareholder corporation can have one director and a two-shareholder corporation can have two directors. (California and New York are among these states. See H&A, p. 551, n. 1.)

1. **Minimums abolished:** A substantial (and growing) minority of states, in fact, now allow a corporation to have a one- or two-member board ***even if there are more than two shareholders.*** This is now true of Delaware (§141(b)) and the MBCA (§8.03(a)). See H&A, p. 552, n. 2.

   a. **Rationale:** There seems little reason to require that there be more than one or two board members merely because there are, say, three shareholders. For instance, suppose that A owns all the stock of a corporation, and is the sole director. If he makes a gift of a few shares to each of his children, all of a sudden he would have to expand his board to three, a move that has no business justification. Nutshell, p. 217.

2. **Stated in articles or bylaws:** The number of directors is usually fixed either in the ***articles of incorporation*** or in the ***bylaws***. Most statutes leave it up to the corporation whether this should be done in the articles or the bylaws; see e.g., MBCA § 8.03(a). Observe that if the number is specified in the articles, it may only be changed by shareholder vote; but if it is set in the bylaws, it may usually be changed by the board itself, under the board's general power to amend bylaws (see *supra*, p. 23).

a. **Restrictions on scope of change:** However, corporation statutes sometimes prevent the board from making very large changes in its size without shareholder approval, even if the bylaws allow the board to change the number of directors. For instance, MBCA § 8.03(b) provides that even if the board has power to change the number of directors, it may increase or decrease the board only by ***thirty percent*** or less without shareholder approval.

3. **Variable board size:** Most statutes allow the articles of incorporation or bylaws to set a ***minimum*** and ***maximum*** size for the board, rather than a fixed size. When this approach is followed, either the shareholders or the board may adjust the size within the range, but only the shareholders may change the range itself. MBCA § 8.03(b) follows this pattern.

   a. **Rationale:** Observe that the MBCA's handling of changes in the number of directors leaves some scope for the board to make modest changes, but requires shareholder approval for large changes. This is true whether the corporation uses a fixed or variable number of directors. Thus under the MBCA scheme the board may usually decide whether to fill one or a small number of vacancies without seeking shareholder approval but may not dramatically expand the power of incumbent directors (by refusing to fill a large number of vacancies) without going back to the shareholders. See MBCA § 8.03(b); see also Nutshell, p. 219.

D. **Filling of vacancies:** Most statutes allow ***vacancies*** on the board to be filled ***either*** by the shareholders or by the board, unless the articles of incorporation provide otherwise. See e.g., MBCA § 8.10(a).

1. **Term:** Some statutes let the replacement director serve the ***full unexpired term*** of his predecessor. Others require her to ***stand for re-election*** at the ***next annual meeting***. The two rules differ only where the board is staggered (see *supra*, p. 58); under the former rule, if A resigns with two and one-half years left on his three-year term, his successor gets to serve the full two and one-half years, whereas under the latter rule the successor must stand for re-election in six months.

   a. **MBCA:** MBCA § 8.05(d) requires that the replacement stand for re-election at the next annual meeting.

2. **Increase in number on board:** Some statutes distinguish between vacancies created by resignation (an "old" vacancy) and those created because the size of the board is increased (a "new" vacancy). States making this distinction usually allow the board to fill old vacancies but not new vacancies. Nutshell, p. 222. But many states have abolished this distinction; see e.g., MBCA § 8.10(a), explicitly giving the board the right to fill vacancies "resulting from an increase in the number of directors."

3. **Election by classes of stock:** In many corporations, especially closely-held ones, a key control device is that each separate ***class of stock*** is entitled to elect a certain number of directors. For instance, if a closely-held corporation has A and B classes of stock, the B shareholders might be given the right to elect four of nine board members, even though they had only 25% of the total voting power of the corporation. If a class has the right to elect a specified number of directors, then ***only that class*** may vote to fill a ***vacancy*** arising from the resignation of one of the directors elected by the class (assuming that it is the shareholders, rather than the board, that fill vacancies). See MBCA § 8.10(b).

4. **Dated resignations:** A director may normally submit a ***dated resignation***, that is, a resignation that is to take effect at some future time. The key advantage of such a prospective resignation is that the resigning director may ***participate in the election*** of his successor (always assuming, of course, that the board is authorized, as is usually the case, to fill vacancies). See MBCA § 8.10(c). This is particularly important where, without the vote of the soon-to-resign director, the board would be deadlocked between competing factions. See Nutshell, p. 224.

5. **Quorum problems:** Any board action normally requires a ***quorum*** (see p. 63), and that's true of votes by the board to elect new directors to fill board vacancies. Well, what happens if so many directors resign (without first voting for their successors), or otherwise leave the board, that a quorum of the board is no longer possible? Most states have a special rule saying that in this situation, the vacancy can be filled by majority vote of the remaining directors, ***even though no quorum is present.*** See the further discussion of this problem *infra*, p. 64.

6. **Holdover directors:** Virtually all states provide that a director holds office not only for the term for which he is elected, but ***until his successor is elected and qualified***. A director serving beyond the end of his term is called a ***holdover*** director. See, e.g., MBCA § 8.05(e) ("[D]espite the expiration of a director's term, the director continues to serve until the director's successor is elected and qualifies or there is a decrease in the number of directors.")

   a. **Rationale:** Without the holdover device, a corporation could become completely deadlocked. For instance, if there were two factions with equal voting power, one faction could refuse to attend an annual meeting or to vote for directors, and the absence of a quorum at the shareholders meeting would prevent any election from taking place; holdover directors would then be the only directors. Of course, the holdover provision means that in this kind of deadlock situation, the original directors would remain in office forever; the remedy might well be involuntary dissolution of the corporation (see *infra*, p. 154). See also Nutshell, p. 225.

E. **Removal of directors:** When may a director be ***removed***? Most statutes allow this to be done by either a ***shareholder vote*** or by ***court order***.

1. **Shareholder vote:** Most modern statutes provide that directors may be removed by a majority vote of ***shareholders***, either ***with or without cause***.

   a. **MBCA:** Thus MBCA § 8.08(a) says that "The shareholders may remove one or more directors ***with or without cause*** unless the articles of incorporation provide that directors may be removed only for cause."

   b. **Minority rule:** Even the ***minority*** of jurisdictions whose statutes do not allow shareholders to remove directors without cause in all circumstances allow it if this right is ***reserved in the articles of incorporation.***

   c. **Protection of groups:** However, removal-of-director provisions are generally drafted so as to ***prevent the majority from undermining*** the effect of cumulative voting and other ***minority-protection devices***.

i. **Cumulative voting:** For instance, if a corporation has ***cumulative voting***, the statute will normally provide that a director cannot be removed if the number of votes cast against his removal would have been enough to elect him. See MBCA § 8.08(c), to this effect.

Example: X Corp. is a closely-held corporation. A, B and C each have 30 shares, and D has 10 shares. X has cumulative voting, and a 5-member board. (Therefore, each shareholder voting for directors has five votes times the number of shares he holds. By the formula on p. 56, anyone who receives 100/6 + 1, or 17 2/3, votes will be elected.) D casts all his 50 votes for himself, so he is elected to the board even though no one else casts any votes for him. A, B and C later decide that they wish to remove D.

Under MBCA § 8.08(c), if D casts his 50 votes against his own removal, D can't be removed, even though A, B, and C collectively cast all 450 (90 x 5) of their votes to remove him. This is so because § 8.08(c) says that "If cumulative voting is authorized, a director may not be removed if the number of votes sufficient to elect him under cumulative voting is voted against his removal," and more than 17 2/3 votes have been cast against D's removal.

d. **Majority of those voting:** To remove a director, it's not necessary that a majority of all shares outstanding be voted against the director, only that a majority of those votes ***actually cast*** be against the director. (This is an application of the more general rule, discussed *infra*, p. 81, that when an action requires shareholder approval, only a majority of shares actually voted, not a majority of shares outstanding, need be voted in favor.)

e. **Meeting required:** Also, keep in mind that a shareholder vote to remove a director requires the ***same formalities*** (e.g., a shareholders ***meeting***) as any other shareholder action. (See *infra*, p. 79, for more about the formalities for shareholder action.) In fact, some statutes say that there must be a special meeting of shareholders, at which the removal of the director is one of the ***stated purposes*** of the meeting. See, e.g., MBCA § 8.08(d), to this effect.

f. **Significance of removal power:** There are at least two situations in which the shareholders' power to remove directors ***without cause*** has a sharp practical significance.

i. **Control shifts:** First, when through a friendly or unfriendly takeover, ***control*** of the corporation ***shifts*** (see *infra*, p. 360), this right of removal allows the new controlling owner to replace directors with "friendly" directors of his own choosing.

ii. **Closely-held corporation:** Secondly, in a ***closely-held*** corporation, the controlling shareholder(s) will frequently want to make sure that directors he elects remain "***friendly***" to him; the unrestricted right of removal helps ensure this. See Nutshell, p. 160.

2. **Court order:** Modern statutes also generally say that a ***court*** may ***order*** a director removed, but only ***for cause***.

a. **MBCA:** For example, MBCA § 8.09 says that the court may order a director removed as the result of a proceeding commenced either by the corporation or by a shareholder's derivative suit, if the court finds both that: (1) the director "engaged in ***fraudulent conduct*** with respect to the corporation or its shareholders, ***grossly abused the position of director,*** or ***intentionally inflicted harm*** on the corporation," *and* (2) "removal would be in the ***best interest*** of the corporation."

b. Why used: Since the shareholders may remove the director without cause, why would a judicial proceeding ever be necessary? There are two situations in which judicial action is the only or better method of removing a director:

[1] First, the director may be a shareholder and may possess ***such voting power*** that he can block removal by shareholder vote. (For instance, if the director was elected by cumulative voting — see *infra*, p. 56 — and votes he controls were sufficient by themselves to elect him under the cumulative scheme, he will be able to block his removal by casting the same number of votes.) Here, the board's ability to start a lawsuit to remove the director would be crucial.

[2] Second, recall that the director can only be removed if a ***special shareholders' meeting*** occurs. If the corporation is ***publicly-held,*** and the director refuses to resign when requested to do so, this special meeting will involve considerable ***delay and expense.*** See Official Comment to MBCA § 8.09.

3. No removal of director by board action: States generally do ***not*** allow the ***board itself*** to remove a director, ***even for cause.***

F. Procedures for a directors' meeting: We now examine the procedural requirements for the holding of a directors' meeting, including (1) frequency of meeting; (2) notice; and (3) quorum.

1. Regular vs. special meetings: There are two types of board meetings: regular and special. A ***regular*** board meeting is one which occurs at a regular interval (e.g., monthly, quarterly or annually). All other meetings are ***"special."*** The frequency for regular meetings is generally specified in the ***bylaws***.

2. Notice: The main distinction between regular and special meetings is that a special meeting must normally be preceded by ***notice*** to the board members, whereas this is not necessary for a regular meeting. Thus MBCA § 8.22(b) provides that a special meeting must be preceded by "at least two days' notice of the date, time, and place," unless the articles or bylaws provide for a longer or shorter notice period.

a. Waiver: In any event, a director may ***waive*** the required notice in writing. Also, if a director ***attends*** the meeting without objecting to the lack of notice, he will generally be held to have thereby waived notice. See, e.g., MBCA § 8.23(b) (attendance constitutes waiver unless the director not only objects upon his arrival but also refrains from voting in favor of, or assenting to, the proposed action at the meeting.)

b. Purpose need not be specified: The notice of a special directors' meeting need ***not specify*** the business to be transacted at the meeting, and any business may in fact be transacted. This is quite different from the rule governing notices of ***shareholders'*** meetings (see *infra*, p. 80). "As a result there is little practical difference between regular and special meetings of directors." Nutshell, p. 220.

3. Quorum: The board of directors may act only if a ***quorum*** is present.

a. **Percentage required:** If the board has a fixed size, a quorum is a ***majority of that fixed number***. This is true even though there are ***vacancies*** on the board at the moment.

Example: The articles of incorporation of C corporation provide that it shall have a nine-member board. At the time of a particular directors' meeting, there are two vacancies. A quorum consists of five, not four, board members, since there must be a majority of the total number of seats, not the number of sitting directors.

b. **Variable board:** But if the articles set up a ***variable-size*** board (see *supra*, p. 60), a quorum is generally set as a majority of the directors ***in office*** at the start of the meeting. See, e.g., MBCA § 8.24(a)(2).

c. **Lesser number:** Some states, but probably still a minority, now allow the articles of incorporation or bylaws to specify a percentage that is ***less than a majority*** as the quorum. For instance, both Delaware (§141(b)) and the MBCA (§8.24(b)) allow the articles of incorporation or bylaws to establish any percentage that is ***one-third*** or greater as the quorum.

d. **Super-majority as quorum:** Conversely, statutes often permit the articles or bylaws to establish a quorum of ***more than a majority***. See, e.g., MBCA § 8.24(a). Such a provision could be used as a control device in a closely-held corporation. For instance, the bylaws could be amended to provide that all three directors must be present for a quorum; this way, a minority shareholder who controls one seat could actively block corporate action by refusing to attend directors' meetings.

e. **Quorum must be present at time of vote:** The quorum must be present ***at the time a vote is taken*** in order for the vote to constitute the act of the board. Thus even if a quorum is present at the start of a meeting, directors may, by leaving, remove the quorum and thereby prevent further board action. (A different rule applies to ***shareholders'*** meetings, at which all that counts is that a quorum be present at the start of the meeting. See *infra*, p. 82.)

f. **Quorum for filling vacancies:** We said just above that the board of directors may not take action unless a quorum is present. There is one exception to this rule: In most states, the board may ***fill a vacancy*** even though less than a quorum of directors is present. Carefully-drafted statutes make it clear that this right exists only where the number of directors ***in office*** is less than a quorum; other statutes leave open the possibility that a vacancy may be filled if less than a quorum is present at the meeting, even though more than a quorum is in office.

Example: Corporation has a board whose fixed size is six directors. A quorum would therefore be four. There are two vacancies at the moment. Under the MBCA, three directors at a "meeting" may not fill the vacancy — the number of directors in office is not less than a quorum, even though the number of directors at the "meeting" is. See MBCA § 8.10(a)(3) and Official Comment thereto. But some older statutes might be interpreted to allow the three members to fill the vacancies; see Nutshell, p. 221. Observe that under the MBCA approach, on these facts a single board member could prevent the board from ever taking action; by staying away, he could prevent there ever being a quorum to fill the vacancies; therefore the vacancies could never be filled, so there could never be a quorum for purposes other than election of directors. (Eventually, however, the *shareholders* could fill the vacancies.)

G. What constitutes act of board: Normally, the board may take action only by ***vote of a majority of the directors present*** at the meeting. See, e.g., MBCA § 8.24(c).

1. **Higher number:** However, many modern statutes allow the articles of incorporation to specify a ***higher percentage*** than a majority for all or certain board actions. For instance, MBCA § 8.24(c) allows a higher number to be required by ***either*** the articles of incorporation or the bylaws.

H. Formalities for board action: Normally, the board of directors may take action ***only at a meeting***, not by individual action of the directors. Directors, unlike shareholders, ***may not vote by proxy***. Clark, pp. 109-110.

1. **Rationale:** Why should there be a rule that the directors must act during a duly-convened meeting rather than as separate individuals? The traditional rationale for this requirement is that "the decision-making process is likely to function better when the directors consult with and react to one another. A ***group discussion of problems*** is thought to be needed, not just a series of yea or nay responses." Clark, p. 110.

2. **Exceptions to requirement of board meeting:** Under modern statutes there are a few ***exceptions*** to the general rule that directors may act only by duly-convened meeting.

   a. **Unanimous written consent:** First, nearly all states now provide that directors may act without a meeting if they give their ***unanimous written consent*** to the proposed corporate action. See, e.g., MBCA § 8.21(a), allowing this unanimous written consent procedure unless the articles of incorporation or bylaws prohibit it. Observe that because the written consents must be unanimous, a ***single director*** who opposes the action can, in effect, require that a meeting be held to discuss the action. Also, note that under this MBCA provision, the consent does not become effective until the ***last director*** has signed the consent; therefore, the consent method ***cannot*** be used as a means of ***ratifying*** a purported corporate action that has taken place before all directors have signed. However, the doctrines of ratification and estoppel discussed *infra*, p. 77, will, if they apply at all, have a retroactive effect in this situation.

   b. **Telephone meetings:** Many states now permit the directors to act by means of a ***telephone conference call***. For instance, MBCA § 8.20(b) authorizes the conducting of a meeting by use of "any means of communication by which all directors participating may ***simultaneously hear each other*** during the meeting." This is not really an exception to the requirement of the meeting, but rather a re-definition of what constitutes a "meeting" — the main purpose of a meeting, that board members be able to simultaneously discuss the proposed matter, is of course carried out when the meeting occurs telephonically.

   c. **Ratification:** In a sense, the related doctrine of ***ratification***, discussed *infra*, p. 77, may serve as a substitute for a formal vote of the board at a duly-convened meeting. That is, if a corporate officer takes an action without board authorization (e.g., signs a contract), and the board later learns about it but does nothing to undo the action, the corporation will likely be held to have ratified the action, preventing the corporation from claiming that the action took place without board approval.

I. Objection by director: A director may sometimes wish to ***disassociate*** herself from action taken by the board, because she feels that the action is unwise, illegal, or a breach of fiduciary duty. It may be quite important for the director to register her dissent, because if she does not do so, she may be personally liable for the board's action even though she remained silent or orally voiced reservations. (See *infra*, p. 171.) Therefore, the director in this situation should either submit a formal ***written*** dissent or abstention, or should make sure that her oral dissent or abstention is ***entered in the minutes*** of the meeting. See MBCA § 8.24(d)(2) and (3).

J. Composition of the board: Board members of a publicly-held corporation can be thought of as falling into three categories: (1) ***insiders*** (executives or employees of the corporation); (2) ***"quasi-insiders,"*** i.e., people who have some other significant relationship with the corporation or its chief executive (e.g., the corporation's lawyer or investment banker); and (3) true ***"outsiders,"*** i.e., those who do not fall into either of the two previous classes. K&C, p. 126.

1. Traditional structure: Traditionally, corporate boards were usually dominated by insiders and quasi-insiders. This structure was often criticized on the grounds that it led to a board that merely "rubber stamped" management's decisions, rather than acting as a truly independent force.

2. Modern trend: Today, especially among the large publicly held corporations, the trend is to have a ***majority of true outsiders*** on the board. For instance, a majority of the boards of most New York Stock Exchange-listed companies is today composed of true outside directors. K&C, p. 126. The ALI's *Principles of Corporate Governance* recommend that even small publicly-held corporations should have at least three directors who are "free of any significant relationship with the corporation's senior executives" (i.e., class (3) above). See §3A.01(b).

K. Committees: Boards increasingly tend to appoint ***committees*** of their members to carry out certain board functions. A committee typically consists of three or more board members, and is given authority to take certain specified action on behalf of the board. The two most common kinds of committees are the ***audit*** and the ***compensation committees***. ***Executive*** and ***nominating*** committees are also frequently appointed.

1. Rationale: There are two main rationales for this increasing use of committees: (1) boards, especially those of large publicly-held corporations, are frequently so large as to be unwieldy, and meet too seldom to stay on top of the corporation's affairs; and (2) some kinds of board actions (e.g., compensation of senior executives) are best handled outside the presence of senior management, and therefore are best handled by a committee composed solely of independent directors.

2. Model Act: The MBCA demonstrates the modern trend of facilitating the use of committees. § 8.25(a) allows the appointment of committees by the board unless the articles of incorporation or the bylaws specifically prohibit them. With a few exceptions, "each committee may exercise the authority of the board of directors. . . ." § 8.25(d).

a. Majority of board: However, a majority of the ***entire sitting board*** must approve the creation of a committee and the appointment of members to it. § 8.25(b). That is, it is not enough that a committee is approved by a majority of the directors present at a meeting containing a quorum (the standard for other types of board action; see *supra*, p. 65). This requirement of an absolute majority reflects the serious authority which can be and often is entrusted to committees.

b. Off-limits actions: Under the MBCA, committees are not allowed to take certain very important types of actions. Some of these off-limits actions include: (1) filling vacancies on the board; (2) amending the articles of incorporation or the bylaws; (3) approving or proposing to shareholders actions that require shareholder approval; and (4) authorizing the issuance or re-purchase of shares. § 8.25(e). The basic idea behind these limits is to "prohibit delegation of important actions that cannot be overruled or overturned by the board of directors." Nutshell, p. 231.

c. Allowed actions: But even with these limitations, committees can take some very important actions in the name of the board, without separate board approval. For instance, a committee may authorize the corporation to take on ***long-term debt*** or to make a large ***capital investment***; it may set the price at which shares shall be issued (so long as the whole board has approved the issuance); it may ***appoint or remove senior management***, and fix the salary of these executives. See Official Comment to § 8.25.

3. Audit committee: Probably the most commonly-encountered committee is the ***audit*** committee. For example, the New York Stock Exchange now requires every listed company to have an audit committee composed entirely of independent directors, and probably most non-NYSE middle-sized and large corporations have also appointed such a committee. See K&C, p. 122. The audit committee typically meets regularly with the corporation's outside ***auditors*** to review the corporation's financial statements and the audit process. *Id.*

a. Rationale: The corporation's outside auditors are usually hired (and fired) by senior management. Therefore, without an audit committee, there is a real chance that management will try to conceal its shortcomings by pressuring the auditors to paint an unduly rosy picture of the corporation's performance. Since audit committee meetings take place outside of the presence of management, the independent directors on the committee can ask the kind of embarrassing questions ("Are earnings being properly stated?" "Are there any contingent liabilities which management hasn't told us about?") that directors would probably not ask at a full board meeting. *Id.*

4. Nominating committee: A ***nominating*** committee nominates candidates to run for ***vacancies*** on the board of directors. Without a nominating committee composed largely of outsiders, the chief executive will tend to nominate either insiders, quasi-insiders, or "outsiders" who are in fact his close friends and whom he expects to be loyal to him. Therefore, if the board is to be more than a rubber stamp for management decisions, it must get a truly independent cadre of outside directors; the nominating committee furnishes a way to do this. For this reason, a nominating committee should have at least a majority of outside directors. Probably only a minority of publicly-held corporations have formed nominating committees, but the number is growing rapidly. K&C, p. 123. (Regardless of whether it is the CEO or a nominating committee that nominates candidates, these "official" candidates almost always win the election; only in the rare case of a successful "proxy fight" — see *infra*, p. 120 — does someone not nominated by management or the existing board get elected.)

5. **Compensation committee:** Most publicly-held corporations now have a ***compensation*** committee composed principally of outside directors. Such a committee sets the salaries and other compensation of the chief executive and other senior management. Again, the theory (though not necessarily the practice) is that a committee composed of outsiders will be less dominated by the CEO and will thus be more objective (and stingier) than the full board would be.

6. **Executive committee:** Many companies have an ***executive*** committee, which essentially performs the functions of the board between meetings of the full board. Such a committee is especially common where the full board meets only a few times a year. *Id.* Unlike the three types of committees discussed above, the executive committee is usually composed of insider or quasi-insider members, since they must be available on short notice and be familiar with the daily affairs of the corporation.

Quiz Yourself on
***THE CORPORATE STRUCTURE** (THE BOARD OF DIRECTORS)*

16. Brady Strippers, Inc., a furniture refinishing company, has two shareholders, Mike Brady and Carol Brady, and three directors, who are elected annually. Mike owns 60 shares of Brady Strippers stock, with Carol owning the other 40 shares. All shares can vote. Mike wants to elect Greg, Peter, and Bobby as directors; Carol wants to elect Marcia, Jan, and Cindy.

(a) You represent Carol. What advice should you give her about what she should do to maximize the number of directors she can elect (and is there any special procedural advice you have for her about how to implement your substantive advice)? ________________

(b) If Carol follows your advice in part (a), how many directors is she likely to end up with? ________________

(c) If Carol doesn't follow your advice, what's likely to happen? ________________

17. The Heavenly Choir Musical Instrument Company has a board of directors whose number is fixed in the charter at 5. Three of these members are Richie Valens, Janis Joplin and the Big Bopper. The three are killed in a plane crash, leaving just two members (less than a majority of board seats, and thus less than a quorum.) Can the two remaining directors fill the vacancies anyway? ________________

18. The Acme Electrical Company — "Let us fix your shorts" — has bylaws providing for regular, quarterly board of directors meetings, which are to take place at the company headquarters on the first Wednesday of each calendar quarter, unless a different time or place is set by prior board resolution. A quorum is three of the five directors. One of the directors is Wile E. Coyote. At the most recent quarterly meeting Coyote was not present, but the other four directors were. At that meeting, the board (by unanimous vote of all present) approved an acquisition. As soon as he found out about the acquisition (2 days after the meeting approving it), Coyote challenged it, stating (accurately) that he did not receive constructive or actual notice of the time and place set for the meeting.

(a) Does the lack of notice to Coyote make the board's action invalid? ________________

(b) What difference, if any, would it make if the meeting had been a special rather than regular quarterly meeting? ________________

19. Spencer Christian is a member of the board of Pitcairn Travel Agency, Inc. Captain Bligh, another director (and majority stockholder), calls a special meeting of the board of directors to discuss changing the location of the annual meeting from an island in the South Pacific to a town in the Midwest, since this would be far more convenient for the company's directors and shareholders. Christian doesn't receive notice of the meeting; however, he happens to be at company headquarters when the meeting starts. He sits in and offers his opinion — he's hotly against the move. A majority of the directors present vote for it, however. Christian then challenges the change, claiming that the meeting was invalid because he didn't receive clear and timely notice of it. What result? (Assume that there are no quorum issues.) ________________

20. Jack is president of the Fee Fi Fo Produce Company. Undertaking a new crop line is considered major enough to require approval of the board of directors. Nonetheless, Jack is at the Cow Tavern one day when Butcher, another patron, proposes to sell him some "magic beans," which Butcher claims will produce giant beanstalks. Fee Fi Fo doesn't plant beans currently. Jack says, "I can't buy the company unless my board of directors approves." Several members of the five-person board are out-of-town. So Jack telephones each board member, one at a time, and asks them to approve the transaction. Four say "yes," but the fifth, Giant, says "no." Is Jack authorized to enter the purchase contract? ________________

21. Same facts as the previous question. Now, however, assume that all five directors say "yes."

(a) What procedural step can Jack take to implement the action without a formal board meeting at which a quorum is present? ________________

(b) Would your answer to part (a) work if Giant persisted in saying "no" to the proposed acquisition, while the other four directors said "yes"? ________________

22. Benedict Arnold is a member of the Libber Tea Company board of directors. He has two years left on his board term. The company does not have cumulative voting. George III, Libber Tea's majority shareholder, sells his interest to George Washington. At the next annual shareholders' meeting, Washington says (to everyone's surprise), "I now move to remove Arnold from the board of directors." Washington does not give any reason in support of his desire to remove Arnold. The motion is duly seconded. All shareholders but Washington vote against the motion (i.e., vote to keep Arnold), but since Washington owns a majority of the shares the motion passes. The jurisdiction has enacted the MBCA. Libber's articles of incorporation are silent on the issue of removal of directors.

(a) Putting aside any issues of notice, was Arnold validly removed from the board? ________________

(b) Now, focusing solely on the issue of notice, was Arnold's removal handled properly? ________________

(c) Would your answer to part (a) be different in a jurisdiction that follows the traditional common-law approach to removal of directors? ________________

23. Melmac Phlegm Industries, Inc., has a board of directors with five members. The corporation's charter authorizes cumulative voting. Alf is elected to the board. He's not an especially impressive board member (he makes off-the-wall comments and rarely says anything intelligent), but he doesn't do or say anything that would be cause for removal in the jurisdiction. Two major stockholders duly call a special stockholders meeting for the stated purpose of removing Alf from the board. By a vote of 1,000 to 800, the shareholders vote to remove Alf, even though his term has one year left to run. Has Alf been validly removed from the board? ________________

Answers

16. (a) You should tell her to use cumulative voting. Of course, depending on the state and on what the company's charter says, Carol may not be able to bring this about on her own. (For instance, MBCA § 7.28(b) allows cumulative voting only if the charter explicitly includes it; if Brady Strippers' charter doesn't, then without Mike's agreement Carol can't get the charter amended and thus can't use cumulative voting.)

You should also tell Carol to give *advance notice* to Mike that she'll be voting cumulatively, if you're in a jurisdiction that requires such advance notice. See, e.g., MBCA § 7.28(d), so requiring.

(b) She'll elect one director. Under cumulative voting, there's no limit on how many shares a shareholder can use for any one candidate. The number of shares needed to elect *n* directors is determined by the formula

$$\frac{nS}{D+1} + 1$$

where *S* is the total number of shares voting and *D* is the number of directors to be elected. So to elect one director, Carol would need 26 shares ((100 total shares ÷ 4) + 1). Since she's got 40 shares (120 votes), she'll be able to do this. She'll want to cast at 61 of her votes for her favorite candidate, let's say Marcia. That way, even if Mike spreads his votes evenly (which is how he comes closest to being able to elect all three of his candidates), he'll have only 60 votes for each, so Marcia will finish first, and one of his 3 will then lose to the other 2 in a run-off election. (If he splits his votes any other way, Marcia will finish third, and will take the third seat.)

(c) She won't elect any directors. With straight voting, a shareholder cannot cast, for any single candidate, more votes than the voter owns shares. Thus, in straight voting, although Carol gets 120 total votes, she can't cast more than 40 of them for any single candidate. Mike is, similarly, limited to 60 votes for any candidate. Therefore, the voting will be: Greg, Peter and Bobby, 60 each, Marcia, Jan and Cindy, 40 each, and Greg, Peter and Bobby will be elected.

17. In most states, yes — even though they don't constitute a quorum. Normally, a board election to fill a board vacancy is like any other board action — it must occur at a meeting at which a quorum is present. But to deal with the situation presented in this question, most states recognize an exception: when the number of directors remaining in office is less than a quorum, each vacancy can be filled by a majority vote of the remaining directors. [64] So in such a state, any candidate who got the vote of both of the remaining directors (i.e., a "majority" of the 2 remaining directors) would be elected. See, e.g., MBCA § 8.10(a)(3).

18. (a) No — The business transacted at the meeting was valid. As a general rule, the board of directors may only take action at a properly convened meeting. The two prerequisites of a properly convened meeting are quorum and notice. The issue here is notice. The general rule is that "regular" meetings — i.e., those whose time and place are fixed by the bylaws or prior resolution — don't require notice of time and place. [63] See, e.g., MBCA § 8.22(a) ("Unless the articles of incorporation or bylaws provide otherwise, regular meetings of the board of directors may be held without notice of the date, time, place or purpose of the meeting.") On these facts, the quarterly meetings are provided for in the bylaws. As a result, business at the meeting was valid, even though Wile E. didn't receive particular notice of it.

(b) The meeting would probably be invalid. Most states *do* require that notice of time and place be given to each director for a "special" meeting, i.e., one which is not a "regular" (e.g., quarterly) one. See, e.g., MBCA § 8.22(b) (at least 2 days advance notice of time and place required for a special board meeting.) [63]

19. The meeting was valid, because Christian waived the notice requirement. As the prior answer says, for "special" meetings — i.e., those whose time is not fixed by the bylaws or prior resolution — all directors must receive clear and timely notice of the meetings (which includes the date, time, and place of the meeting). Here, Christian didn't receive notice, so if he hadn't attended a court would allow him to challenge the board action.

However, Christian waived the requirement by showing up at the meeting and not making a prompt objection to the lack of notice. See, e.g., MBCA § 8.23(b) ("A director's attendance at or participation in a meeting waives any required notice to him of the meeting unless the director at the beginning of the meeting (or promptly upon his arrival) objects to holding the meeting or transacting business at the meeting and does not thereafter vote for or assent to action taken at the meeting.") [63] Therefore, the vote was valid.

20. No. Board action may generally occur only at a duly-noticed board meeting, at which a quorum is present. Most states now treat a director as being "present" if he's part of a telephone conference call. But this "exception" to the requirement of a quorum applies only if enough board members to constitute a quorum are all *simultaneously* on the phone, because the purpose is for them to all be able to discuss the matter at once and receive input from each other. The seriatim phone calls here did not satisfy this requirement. Therefore, no quorum was present, and consequently board action has not occurred. Since the facts say that undertaking a new crop line requires board approval, Jack can't proceed. (If Jack goes ahead anyway and plants the seeds, then the doctrine of "ratification" may apply. [77])

21. (a) Have them sign a unanimous consent to the purchase. Nearly all states now provide that directors may act without a meeting if they give their unanimous written consent to the proposed corporate action. See, e.g., MBCA § 8.21(a). So all should sign copies of a resolution saying that the board approves the purchase.

(b) No. For the "written consent" exception to work, the written consent must be ***unanimous***. Thus Giant, by refusing to sign, can force Jack to call a formal board meeting at which a quorum is present. That way, Giant will get to make his arguments in person to the other directors — he may get outvoted, but he's guaranteed a chance to speak against the action.

22. (a) Yes. Under the MBCA, as in most states today, shareholders can (by ordinary majority vote) remove a director from office at any time, without cause. See MBCA, § 8.08(a). (This rule does not apply if the articles of incorporation say that directors may be removed only for cause, but the facts tell us that Libber's charter is silent on this point.) Thus the holders' action here sufficed to remove Arnold even though no cause (like fraud, or gross abuse of discretion) was shown. [61]

Observe that this very scenario — change of control — is the scenario in which the ability to remove a director without cause is of greatest importance. Without such an ability, Washington would have to wait until the expiration of Arnold's term, two years from now, before he would have full control of the board. And, in fact, if a majority of the board were friendly with George III and had the same two years to run, then Washington wouldn't be able to exercise any control over the company for two years even though he was the majority owner! So the power of removal-without-cause by vote of a majority of shareholders is very important to merger-and-acquisition law.

(b) No. Under MBCA, § 8.08(d), "A director may be removed by the shareholders only at a meeting called for the purpose of removing him and the meeting notice must state that the purpose, or one of the purposes, of the meeting is removal of the director." Since the facts suggest (by the reference to "everyone's surprise") that the notice of meeting did not mention that Arnold's removal would be a purpose of the meeting, the vote was improper. [62] (But Washington could fix the problem at any time, at least under the MBCA. As a more-than-10% owner, he could call a special meeting of shareholders at any time under MBCA § 7.02(a)(2), and state that the purpose was to vote on whether Arnold should be removed. [80] Then, he could cast his votes in favor of the motion and remove Arnold.)

(c) Yes. At common law, directors were only removable for cause; that is, for conduct harmful to the corporation, like fraud, incompetence, or disloyalty. Thus under the traditional rule, Arnold could successfully challenge his removal.

23. No. The fact that cumulative voting is authorized by the corporation makes all the difference. In virtually all jurisdictions, if the corporation has authorized cumulative voting, a director cannot be removed without cause if there are cast against his removal enough votes to have elected him under cumulative voting. (If this were not the rule, the majority could always remove minority-chosen directors, defeating the whole purpose of cumulative voting.) [62] See, e.g., MBCA § 8.08(c). Here, there were 1800 shares voting, and the board has 5 seats. Therefore, by the formula for the number of shares which one must control in order to elect one director (further explained in the answer to question 15):

$$\frac{S}{D+1} + 1 ,$$

Alf could have been elected so long as at least the following number of shares voted for him:

$$\frac{1800}{6} + 1 = 301$$

Since the 800 shares voted against Alf's removal were more than 301, Alf got enough support to have elected him to the board, so he won't be deemed to have been removed. (If the corporation had not authorized cumulative voting, then the analysis would be like that in the prior question, and Alf would be deemed removed by simple majority of those voting.)

III. OFFICERS

A. Meaning of "officer": The term ***"officer"*** is usually used to describe only the more important executives in the corporation. Clark, p. 114. Typically, the term is used to describe those executives who are ***appointed directly by the board of directors***. *Id.*

1. Names of posts: Most older statutes specify the particular officerships that a corporation must have. For instance, many statutes require that there be a president, one or more vice-presidents, a treasurer, and a secretary.

a. Model Act and Delaware: But the modern trend is ***not*** to require specific named positions. For instance, both the MBCA and Delaware leave it up to the bylaws or to the board to determine what officers there shall be. See MBCA, § 8.40(a); Del. GCL § 142(a).

2. **Multiple posts for one person:** Whether or not the statute requires certain named officers, nearly all statutes allow one person to hold ***multiple officerships simultaneously***. In a closely-held corporation, for instance, the president will also commonly be the treasurer.

   a. **Exception for secretary:** The one exception is that the ***president*** and ***secretary*** are usually ***not*** permitted to be the ***same*** person. The reason is that the secretary's principal function is to certify that a person signing a document as chief executive officer is in fact that person; it would make little sense to allow *A* in his role as secretary to certify that he, *A*, is in fact the president/CEO — "an imposter would happily certify these facts." K&C, p. 124.

B. **Right to hire and remove:** The board of directors has not only the power to appoint officers, but also the power to ***remove them***, with or without cause. This is true even though the officer has an employment contract that is still in force — the board has authority to fire the officer, but he in turn has the right to sue the corporation for damages (but not the right to specific performance, i.e., the right to be reinstated).

C. **Authority to act for corporation:** Recall that, under the traditional view, the corporation is managed by the board of directors, not by the officers (*supra*, p. 50). Therefore, even when an officer ***purports to act on behalf of the corporation*** and to bind the corporation, his action ***may not be legally sufficient to bind the corporation***. Since the officer is an ***agent*** of his principal (the corporation), the officer's authority to bind his principal is usually analyzed by use of traditional ***agency principles***.

1. **Not automatically binding:** The most important concept to keep in mind is that an officer (even the president) ***will not automatically have authority*** to bind the corporation to a transaction merely by virtue of his office. Only if one of the doctrines described below applies will the corporation be bound by the act of its officer.

   Example: Brown, the treasurer of ABC Corp., promises Gray that ABC will guarantee a debt owed by Black to Gray. The mere fact that Brown is ABC Corp.'s treasurer does not give him authority to bind ABC. Therefore, unless Gray can show that Brown had express authority, implied actual authority, or apparent authority to bind ABC, or that the board subsequently ratified the guarantee (the four doctrines described below), Brown's action will not cause the corporation to be bound to honor the guarantee, even if Brown honestly believes that he had authority to bind the corporation, and even if Gray honestly believed Brown's statement that he, Brown, had authority.

2. **Four doctrines:** There are four doctrines commonly used to hold that the officer has bound the corporation: (1) ***express*** actual authority; (2) ***implied actual*** authority; (3) ***apparent*** authority; and (4) ***ratification***. We will consider each of these in turn.

3. **Express actual authority:** ***Express actual authority*** is the easiest concept to understand. Usually, this comes into existence by an explicit grant of authority to the officer to act on behalf of the corporation. This explicit grant generally comes from either the corporation's ***bylaws***, or in the form of a ***resolution*** adopted by the board of directors.

   Example: The board adopts a resolution authorizing the Vice President to negotiate and sign a contract to dispose of one of the corporation's surplus plants. This board resolution constitutes a grant of express authority to the Vice President. Therefore, when he signs the contract on the corporation's behalf, the corporation will be bound, even if it is not usually the case (either generally or in this particular corporation) that vice presidents may sign contracts to sell plants.

4. **Implied actual authority:** The doctrine of "***implied*** actual authority" is a much fuzzier one. It is often described as "authority which is ***inherent in the office.***" Clark, p. 115. There are two common ways in which implied actual authority can come into existence:

   a. **Inherent in post:** First, authority may be ***inherent*** in the particular ***post*** occupied by the officer, measured by the ***common understandings of business people***.

      Example: It is today commonly assumed that the president of a corporation has actual authority to sign at least non-extraordinary contracts (e.g., contracts for the corporation to receive supplies that it needs in the ordinary course of its business). Therefore, if President signs such a supply contract on behalf of Corporation, the court would probably hold that President had implied actual authority to bind Corporation to this contract, even though the board of directors never specifically authorized him to sign either this particular contract or any similar contract — authority to sign such contracts is simply found to be inherent in the presidency of a corporation.

   b. **Particular action of board:** Second, the board, by its own ***conduct or inaction***, may have ***implicitly*** granted the actual authority to the officer in question. Thus even if vice presidents in the business world are generally not permitted to sign contracts disposing of surplus plants, the fact that ABC's Corp's board has allowed Vice President to do so in the past without objection, or the fact that the board has known that Vice President was about to sign the particular contract in question, would be enough to clothe Vice President with implied actual authority to sign the present contract on behalf of ABC.

   c. **Particular posts:** There has been a lot of litigation about the inherent power of various corporate posts, especially the presidency.

      i. **Presidency:** Traditionally, the ***president*** had little if any authority to bind the corporation merely by virtue of his office. However, this narrow view conflicted with what most non-lawyers thought the president could do. Therefore, the modern trend is to treat the president as having, by mere virtue of his position, at least the authority to bind the corporation in ***ordinary business transactions***. H&A, p. 596.

         (1) **Illustration:** Thus most courts today would probably hold that the president has implied authority, by virtue of his office, to ***hire and fire*** non-officer-level employees; and the authority to enter into ***ordinary-course contracts*** (e.g., contracts to supply the business' ordinary raw materials requirements, or to sell part of the corporation's output).

         (2) **Beyond the scope:** But other kinds of actions would, even under the more expansive modern rule, probably be found to be ***"extraordinary"*** and thus ***not authorized*** by the president's office alone: ***lifetime employment contracts***; contracts to sell, lease or mortgage ***real estate***; contracts to sell all of the corporation's ***assets***; contracts to issue and distribute ***new stock***; and agreements to ***settle*** important litigation.

         See generally Clark, p. 116; Nutshell, p. 238.

ii. **Chairman of the board:** There is no generally accepted rule about the inherent authority of the ***chairman of the board***. The scope of this post varies dramatically from corporation to corporation — in some companies this post is held by the chief executive officer (with the president being the chief operating officer, or number two executive); in other cases the chairman is largely an honorary figure, who is not the C.E.O. In general, it is not safe to assume that the chairman has ***any*** inherent authority by virtue solely of his position. C&E, p. 302-03.

iii. **Vice president; treasurer:** A ***vice president*** or a ***treasurer*** probably has little if any authority by virtue of his or her position. However, if a vice president has the appearance of standing close to the top of the corporate hierarchy, (e.g., an Executive Vice President), he may under the modern, looser, approach to authority be held to have some limited authority in ordinary-course matters. *Id.*

iv. **Secretary:** The ***secretary*** has one key element of inherent authority in virtually every jurisdiction: He has inherent authority to ***certify the records of the corporation***, including ***resolutions*** of the board of directors. Therefore, a secretary's certificate that a given resolution was duly adopted by the board is ***binding*** on the corporation in favor of a ***third party who relies on the certificate***. C&E, p. 303-04. (But the secretary has no other inherent authority to bind the corporation.)

5. **Apparent authority:** A third way in which the officer may bind the corporation is by the doctrine of ***apparent authority***. Under this doctrine, when the actions of a ***principal*** (the ***corporation***) give the ***appearance to reasonable persons*** that the agent is authorized to act as he is acting, the principal is held responsible for creating the impression that the agent had actual authority to act; therefore, the principal may not avoid the transaction. K&C, p. 123.

a. **Requirements:** Thus for the third party to successfully invoke the apparent authority doctrine, he will have to show that: (1) the ***corporation***, by acts ***other than those of the officer***, ***indicated to the world*** that the officer had authority to do the act in question; *and* (2) the plaintiff was ***aware*** of those corporate indications and relied on them. K&C, pp. 123-24.

b. **Mere position as source of apparent authority:** Sometimes, the plaintiff will be able to point to specific, affirmative conduct by the corporation that indicates to the world that the officer has the authority in question. For instance, if the board of directors is aware that Vice President has routinely been signing large contracts to buy raw materials, and the board does not object, a supplier who can show this past pattern of acquiescence (and who can show he was aware of it at the time of his own contract) would probably succeed in arguing that Vice President had apparent authority. But often, the mere ***post*** held by the officer, when coupled with ***industry practice***, will be enough to create apparent authority. This is most likely to happen where the action is by the company's president, and the action is of a sort that presidents are usually permitted to take.

Example: The board of directors of Corporation appoints Smith as president. Because the chairman's son has long held the post of vice president for Office Supplies, Smith is handed a board resolution expressly denying that Smith has any authority whatsoever to purchase office supplies for Corporation. Nonetheless, Smith, introducing himself to Supplier as president of Corporation, orders office supplies. Supplier does not know of the special limitation on Smith's authority.

Assume (as is probably the case) that by custom, a person holding the title of president will in most corporations have actual authority to order office supplies. If so, Supplier will probably be able to bind Corporation to the contract Smith signed with him, on an apparent authority theory. The board of directors, by clothing Smith with the title of "president," has indicated to the world that Smith has the authority usually found in that post. If the board wishes to deny Smith that authority, it must bear the burden of ***communicating to the world*** (including to Supplier) that Smith does not have this customary presidential authority. Observe that on these facts, Corporation is bound under the apparent authority doctrine even though it is absolutely clear that Smith did not have any kind of actual authority (not even implied actual authority) because of the resolution. See Clark, p. 117.

c. **Representation by agent:** For the apparent authority doctrine to apply, it is ***not*** sufficient that the ***agent himself*** represents to the third party that he has authority to enter into the transaction. The indications of authority must come from ***someone else*** in a position of power at the corporation. Thus if Vice President tells Supplier "I have full authority to contract for the purchase of office supplies," this representation does not create apparent authority, since Supplier should know that Vice President may simply be lying or mistaken about the degree of his authority. (If, on the other hand, the board of directors had appointed him with the title Vice President of Supplies and given him a business card with that title, a person who saw and relied on the card would probably succeed in establishing apparent authority.)

d. **The president and "ordinary-course" transactions:** As we saw in the example involving Smith and the supplies, *supra*, the mere fact that an officer has been given a common title (e.g., president) will itself be enough to give him apparent authority to do certain transactions. In the case of an officer bearing the title of president, the usual modern rule is that the president has apparent authority "to take actions in the ***ordinary course*** of business, but ***not extraordinary*** actions." C&E, p. 300-01. But where is the line between "extraordinary" and "ordinary"? "A useful generalization is that decisions that would make a ***significant change*** in the ***structure*** of the business enterprise, or the structure of ***control*** over the enterprise, are extraordinary corporate actions and therefore normally outside the president's apparent authority." C&E, p. 301-02.

   i. **Illustrations:** Thus the ***issuance or re-purchase*** of ***shares*** by the corporation, the taking on of significant ***debt***, the making of significant ***capital investments***, the ***sale*** of one of the corporation's ***significant businesses***, or its entry into an important ***new line of business***, would all be "extraordinary" (and thus not within the president's apparent authority) in most circumstances. *Id.*

   ii. **Comparison with implied actual authority:** Observe that a similar "extraordinary vs. ordinary" test is also used to determine whether the president has ***implied actual*** authority to take a particular action. (See *supra*, p. 74.) But even though a given act by a president will often indicate that he has both implied actual authority (by virtue of his position) and apparent authority, the two doctrines are not the same. Implied actual authority can always be negated by an express board resolution to the contrary (as in the Smith office-supplies example *supra*, p. 75); but the board cannot negate apparent authority unless it communicates this fact to the third person who is relying.

e. **Question of fact:** In the final analysis, it will often be a ***question of fact*** for the jury whether, taking into account all the circumstances, the officer had apparent authority to do the act in question. That is, there are many situations that are so close to the blurry line between "extraordinary" and "ordinary course" transactions that it cannot be said as a matter of law that the transaction falls into the one class or the other.

6. **Ratification:** Suppose that at the time an officer acts on behalf of the corporation, he has neither actual nor apparent authority. The corporation may nonetheless be bound by its ***subsequent*** actions, under the doctrine of ***"ratification."*** Under this doctrine, if a person with actual authority to enter into the transaction ***learns*** of the transaction and either expressly ***affirms*** it or even ***fails to disavow it***, the court may find that the corporation is bound.

a. **Retention of benefits or reliance by third party:** In most of the cases where the ratification doctrine is applied, either or both of two special factors is present: (1) the corporation has ***received benefits*** under the contract, which it has not returned; or (2) the third party has ***relied to his detriment*** on the existence of the contract. Nutshell, p. 240. However, strictly speaking the mere after-the-fact approval or acquiescence of the board ought to suffice, even without either of these two special factors.

b. **Full knowledge by board:** Of course, the plaintiff who is claiming ratification must show that the ratifier had ***full knowledge*** of the contract. For instance, if the board knows that the president has signed a contract to acquire a company from X, but does not know that the president is receiving a kickback from X or does not know that the contract calls for the corporation to pay a very excessive price, a court would probably not find that the board's mere failure to object constituted ratification.

7. **A "bullet-proof" means of confirming authority:** The above discussion demonstrates that authority is a tricky concept — a third party will often find it hard to be certain that the corporation officer he is dealing with really has authority to bind the corporation to the proposed transaction. However, there is one "bullet-proof" way in which a third party can be certain that the corporation will be bound: He should "require the person purporting to act for the corporation to deliver, prior to the closing of the transaction, a ***certified copy*** of a ***resolution*** of the board of directors authorizing the transaction in question or directing the named officer to enter into the transaction on behalf of the corporation. The certificate should be ***executed*** by the ***secretary*** or an assistant secretary of the corporation, the corporate seal should be affixed, and the certificate should recite the date of the meeting (or a statement that the resolution was approved by unanimous written consent) and quote the resolution itself." Nutshell, p. 237.

a. **Rationale:** The reason that such a certificate is binding on the corporation is that, in all states, the corporation is ***estopped*** to deny the correctness of its secretary's certification that a particular resolution was adopted by the board.

Quiz Yourself on ***THE CORPORATE STRUCTURE*** *(OFFICERS)*

24. Frontier Foods, Inc., appoints Betty Crockett treasurer of the corporation, with the express authority to handle corporate funds, and no express authority to do anything else. However, whenever the other officers and employees have their hands full, Betty steps in and helps out by purchasing inventory on the corporation's behalf. She's purchased hardtack for Frontier Foods from the Tuffas Leather Company several times before, and Frontier has always paid the invoices. Betty now makes out a new purchase order for fifty cases of hardtack, and Tuffas manufactures her order. Before it's delivered, some board members find out that they can get a much better deal on hardtack from a competitor. They try to cancel Betty's hardtack purchase order, claiming that it was unauthorized. Is the purchase order a valid corporate obligation? Cite the doctrines you use in arriving at your answer. ________________

25. Dr. Seuss is the corporate secretary for the Sam I Am Company. The company's office manager usually handles the arrangements for the annual meeting of shareholders, and has the express authority to make all necessary contracts regarding the arrangements for the meeting; however, this year the office manager, Bartholomew, has an oobleck virus and can't set up the meeting. Dr. Seuss steps into the void. He looks through the yellow pages and hires the Cat N. Hat Caterers to provide two hundred servings of green eggs and ham.

(a) Assume that the meeting takes place as scheduled. At the meeting, the directors, officers, and shareholders all eat the green eggs and ham. When Cat N. Hat sends its bill, Sam I Am refuses to pay, claiming that Dr. Seuss, as corporate secretary, had no power to bind the corporation. What result? (Cite any relevant doctrines.) ________________

(b) Assume for this part only that before the meeting, Cat N. Hat sent a document marked "Confirmation," in which he said, "This confirms that we will supply 200 svgs, green eggs & ham, to your annual meeting on 6/14/13." The confirmation is marked, "Attn: President," and the President in fact sees it. He does nothing for two weeks, during which time Cat N. Hat makes substantial preparations (e.g., he makes a special purchase of green eggs.) Three days before the meeting, the President sends a letter to Cat: "The catering order was submitted to you by Dr. Seuss, acting without proper authority. Consider it rescinded." Can Cat hold Sam I Am to the contract (as opposed to merely recovering in quantum meruit for services already performed)? ________________

Answers

24. Yes, on either an "implied actual authority" or "apparent authority" theory. The issue here is whether Betty had authority to bind the corporation. Officers can bind the corporation only if they act within the scope of their corporate authority (unless the corporation subsequently ratifies the officer's action, something that's not relevant to this problem.) There are four types of authority commonly recognized: (1) express actual authority; (2) implied actual authority; (3) apparent authority; and (4) ratification. Here, Betty probably had both "implied actual authority" and "apparent authority."

An officer has "implied actual authority" whenever either: (1) authority is inherent in the particular post occupied by the officer, measured by common business understandings about what people holding that post customarily do; or (2) the corporation, by its own conduct or inaction, has implicitly granted the actual authority to the officer in question. [74] The situation here falls into case (2), because when the corporation on prior occasions allowed Betty to place purchase orders and uncomplainingly paid the bill, the corporation was implicitly giving her actual authority to place such orders. So even if Tuffas hadn't been aware that it was Betty who had placed the prior orders, Frontier would still be bound because it gave Betty implied actual authority.

An officer has "apparent authority" when the corporation indicates to a third person that the officer has authority to act on its behalf, and the third person believes in good faith that such authority exists (whether or not it actually does). [75] So Betty had apparent authority to place the order for hardtack, since Tuffas knew that Betty had placed prior orders with it that the corporation had honored. Therefore, even if Frontier now wishes to change its mind about Betty's authority (or had, unbeknownst to Tuffas, changed its mind before the latest order), Frontier is stuck under the apparent-authority doctrine, because the only issue is what Tuffas reasonably *believed* about Betty's authority, and Tuffas clearly had grounds to believe that Betty's purchase was authorized. (Remember, by the way, that for apparent-authority to apply, the corporation itself, not just the agent, must convey to the third person that the agent has authority. So if there had been no prior orders, and Betty had merely told Tuffas, "I have authority to buy," this would not suffice for apparent authority. It's the corporation's acquiescence in the prior orders by Betty that makes the difference here.)

25. **(a) Sam I Am is liable, on grounds of ratification.** The issue here is a corporate officer's ability to bind the corporation. As a general rule, corporate secretaries by virtue of their post alone have no authority to bind a corporation, certainly not to a purchase order. (In other words, Seuss had no express authority or implied actual authority at the moment he acted, nor did he have apparent authority.) However, even though an act is unauthorized at the moment it occurs, it can become authorized after the fact, if the requirements for "ratification" are met. Ratification occurs when the corporation either expressly adopts the unauthorized act (e.g., by passing an explicit resolution adopting the act) or implicitly indicates, by conduct or inaction, that it approves of the action. [77] The most common way in which a corporation implicitly indicates its approval after the fact is by retaining the benefits from the transaction. Here, by allowing its employees to attend the event and eat the green eggs and ham, Sam I Am implicitly ratified the contract. Therefore, the company is liable.

    (b) Yes; the company is nonetheless bound. Again, the doctrine of ratification applies. A company can ratify an otherwise-unauthorized act not just by retaining the benefits, but even by remaining silent after learning of the proposed transaction. [77] Such "silent ratification" is especially likely to be found where the other party relies to his detriment on the proposed transaction, while the corporation is remaining silent. So when the President (who by his post clearly had authority to enter into the transaction in the first place or to ratify it later), remained silent for two weeks during which time Cat was relying (purchasing special eggs, etc.), this would constitute ratification even before the affair occurred.

IV. FORMALITIES FOR SHAREHOLDER ACTION

A. Generally: We examine now some of the mechanics by which ***shareholders exercise their right to vote*** on certain aspects of the corporation's affairs. In particular, we examine: (1) the giving of notice of a shareholders' meeting; (2) the quorum for such a meeting; and (3) the method of voting at such a meeting.

B. Annual vs. special meeting: Nearly all states require a corporation to hold an ***annual meeting*** of shareholders. See, e.g., MBCA § 7.01(a). Corporations may also hold a ***"special"*** shareholders' meeting; a special meeting is any meeting other than the regularly-scheduled annual meeting. See MBCA § 7.02(a).

1. **No penalty for failure to hold annual meeting:** If the corporation fails to hold an annual meeting, this failure does ***not*** make the corporation's subsequent actions invalid. See MBCA § 7.01(c). However, if the annual meeting is not held when scheduled, a shareholder will probably be able to get a court to ***order*** that one be held. See e.g., MBCA § 7.03(a)(1) (meeting will be ordered by court on application of any shareholder if meeting has not been held six months after the end of the corporation's fiscal year or fifteen months after its last annual meeting, whichever comes first.)

2. **Purpose of annual meeting:** The purpose of an annual meeting always includes at least the ***election of directors***. (See *supra*, p. 51.) However, the annual meeting may also consider any other relevant issue. According to most statutes, any other issue may be considered even if the issue was not specifically referred to in the ***notice*** given to shareholders. See e.g., MBCA § 7.05(b) (notice of annual meeting "need not include a description of the purpose or purposes for which the meeting is called.")

3. **Purpose of special meeting:** A ***special*** meeting is normally called to consider one or a small number of very important matters that cannot wait until the next annual meeting. Unlike the notice of an annual meeting, the notice of the special meeting must ***state the particular issues*** to be raised at the meeting, and no other issues may be considered. See MBCA § 7.05(c) and § 7.02(d).

4. **Who may call a special meeting:** Statutes vary as to ***who may call*** a special meeting. Such a meeting may always be called by the board of directors. Also, any person or group who is authorized by the ***bylaws*** to call a meeting (e.g., the president, under many bylaws) may do so.

   a. **Called by shareholders:** Also, some (but by no means all) states allow the holders of a certain ***percentage*** of the ***shares*** to call a special meeting. The MBCA goes especially far in this respect: Under § 7.02(a)(2) the holders of a mere ***ten percent*** of the shares may cause a special meeting to be held. By contrast, Delaware does ***not*** allow even a larger percentage of shareholders to call a special meeting; only the board or persons authorized in the bylaws may do so; see Del. GCL § 211(d).

      i. **Raider:** Observe that the MBCA approach gives a ***raider*** (i.e., a person attempting a hostile takeover) important powers: If he gains control of a majority of the shares shortly after an annual meeting, he may call a special meeting, ***remove a majority of the existing directors without cause***, and elect his own slate. Under the Delaware approach, by contrast, he probably has to wait until the next annual meeting to gain a majority of the board. (But in Delaware, the raider could probably accomplish the same result by use of Delaware's unusual provision allowing action to be taken by a non-unanimous majority of shareholders based on their written consent; see *infra*, p. 82.)

C. Quorum: Statutes generally require that a ***quorum*** be present at the shareholders' meeting equal to a ***majority of the outstanding shares***. However, the percentage required for a quorum may be ***reduced*** as provided in the articles of incorporation or bylaws.

1. **Minimum:** However, many statutes set a minimum percentage below which not even the articles or bylaws may set the quorum. Many of these require that at least ***one-third*** of the shares be present as the minimum allowable quorum. See, e.g., Del. GCL § 216, setting this one-third figure. But the MBCA makes the articles' or bylaws' minimum quorum provision effective ***no matter how low it is***. See MBCA § 7.25(a).

2. **Higher numbers:** Conversely, nearly all states allow the articles or bylaws to set a ***higher*** percentage as the quorum. This is frequently used as a control device in closely-held corporations; for instance, the articles might require ***all*** shares in a close corporation to be present, as a way of letting the minority shareholder veto action of which he disapproves. Nutshell, p. 177.

D. Vote required for approval: Once a quorum is present, the traditional rule is that the shareholders will be deemed to have approved of the proposed action only if a majority of the ***shares actually present*** vote in ***favor*** of the proposed action.

1. **Explanation:** Observe that this rule contains two important sub-rules: (1) only a majority of the shares ***present***, not a majority of the total shares eligible to vote, must support the proposal being voted on; and (2) a majority of the shares present must ***affirmatively vote in favor*** of the proposal; that is, an ***abstention*** is the equivalent of a vote against.

   a. **MBCA changes rule:** The MBCA ***changes*** the traditional rule with respect to (2), by making abstentions the same as votes that are not cast. § 7.25(c) provides that action on a matter "is approved if the votes cast . . . favoring the action exceed the votes cast opposing the action. . . ."

   Example: Corporation has 1000 shares outstanding. 600 shares are represented at the meeting (a quorum is, of course, 501, assuming that the articles and bylaws do not set a different number). The vote on an action is 280 in favor, 225 opposed and 95 abstaining. Under the traditional approach, the proposal fails, since it needed 301 votes (a majority of the shares present). But under the MBCA, the action is approved 280-225. See Official Comment to § 7.25(c); see also Nutshell, p. 178.

   b. **Election of directors:** The rules for elections of ***directors*** are different from the rules for all other action by shareholders. These director-election rules are discussed in detail *supra*, p. 55. Most importantly, a minority of shareholders will frequently be able to elect one or more members of the board of directors, because of the use of cumulative voting. (Cumulative voting does not apply to shareholder approval of matters other than the election of directors.)

   c. **Super-majority for fundamental changes:** Also, the standard rule that a majority is enough to constitute approval does ***not*** apply to certain issues that are of ***"fundamental"*** importance. Most states now allow the articles or bylaws to set a ***higher percentage*** as the minimum percentage needed to approve any given transaction, and many corporations have instituted such higher requirements for fundamental transactions like mergers. Indeed, a "super-majority" voting requirement before the corporation can be acquired by another corporation is a common anti-takeover device today. See *infra*, p. 451.

2. **Breaking of quorum:** Recall that a quorum of directors is required ***throughout*** the directors' meeting. (*supra*, p. 64.) A comparable rule does ***not*** apply to shareholders' meetings. Once a quorum is present at the beginning of the meeting, the quorum is deemed to exist for the rest of the meeting, even if so many shareholders ***leave the meeting*** that the total number present would be less than the number needed for the quorum. See e.g., MBCA § 7.25(b) ("[O]nce a share is represented for any purpose at a meeting, it is deemed present for quorum purposes for the remainder of the meeting and for any adjournment of that meeting unless a new record date is or must be set for that adjourned meeting.") Thus if a minority block knows that its presence is required for a quorum, and fears that a proposal it opposes will be passed, it should not attend the meeting at all rather than attending and leaving before the vote on the issue. Nutshell, pp. 178-79.

3. **Written consent:** Just as directors may act by unanimous written consent (see *supra*, p. 65), so nearly all states allow ***shareholders*** to act by ***unanimous written consent*** without a meeting. Such a provision is especially useful in closely-held corporations, where the few shareholders are in agreement, and the holders do not want to waste time on a formal meeting. Nutshell, p. 179.

   a. **Written consent by less-than-majority:** Furthermore, about a dozen states now allow shareholder approval in the form of written consent by the number of votes needed to approve the action, even if this is ***non-unanimous***. See, e.g., Delaware GCL § 228(a). Thus in Delaware for ordinary corporate action requiring approval by a majority of the shares, if the holders of a majority sign a written consent to the action, the action will be binding without a meeting, and the minority shareholders will not have the right to dissent publicly at a meeting. (This trend contrasts with the practice as to directors' meetings, where virtually all states require that the directors must either meet or consent unanimously (*supra*, p. 65).)

      i. **Use in takeovers:** Observe that allowing shareholder action to be taken by written majority consent may help a ***raider***: Once the raider acquires a majority of the target's shares, he can carry out shareholder approval of any action needing a mere majority without having to convince the board to hold a special meeting of shareholders. See Nutshell, p. 179.

4. **Meeting in cyberspace:** Traditionally, shareholders have had to be ***physically present*** at the shareholders' meeting in order to count towards a quorum, and to vote. (Unanimous written consent, *supra*, has been the one exception to this rule.) But recently, some jurisdictions have allowed for shareholders meetings to take place ***electronically***, such as via the Internet. For instance, in Delaware the board may authorize shareholders to participate in a meeting "by means of ***remote communication***" and to vote by that same means. Del. G. C. L. § 211(a)(2). What Delaware has in mind is a ***"meeting by website,"*** in which shareholders log in, prove that they are authorized, "hear" the proceedings, and vote, all in a web browser. Cf. Hamilton (8th), p. 559, n. 10. The meeting can be in a particular physical location, with shareholders having the choice of attending physically or logging in;

alternatively, the statute authorizes the meeting to take place "***solely*** by means of remote communication," in which case there would be no physical location at all. § 211(a)(2)(B).

Quiz Yourself on
THE CORPORATE STRUCTURE (FORMALITIES FOR SHAREHOLDER ACTION)

26. Ferdinand de Gama is the chairman of the board of the Cheap & Good Boat Company. Cheap & Good's articles of incorporation have a purposes clause, limiting the company's boat production to pleasure boats no longer than twenty feet. De Gama believes that there is much money to be made in larger, ocean-going vessels. He gets the board to call for a special meeting of the shareholders, to discuss amending the purposes clause in the articles to encompass larger vessels. That's the agenda that's included in the notice to shareholders announcing the special meeting. The corporate president, Marco Polo, convenes the meeting. After the shareholders vote in favor of the amendment, de Gama figures that, since everyone's all together anyway, it would be an ideal place to discuss a merger with the Chinese Junk Company, which specializes in ocean-going vessels. The combined company would be known as the Cheap Junk Company. Discussion takes place, and the shareholders then present approve the merger. Has the merger received proper shareholder approval? ________________

27. Popeye tires of life at sea and decides to open a chain of massage parlors, "Sweet Pea Parlors, Inc." There are 100 shares outstanding. Popeye owns 51 shares, Olive Oyl 30 and Bluto 19. Each shareholder is elected to the 3-person board of directors. At a time when each of the three stockholder/board-members has 2 1/2 years to go on his board term, Popeye sells his shares to Sea Hag. (Assume that there are no share-transfer restrictions preventing this.) The corporation's charter is silent on the issue of cumulative voting. Sea Hag wants to join the board of directors immediately (and in fact would prefer to replace all directors with ones beholden to her.) Because of bad lawyering by Sea Hag's lawyer, the share-purchase agreement did not require Popeye to resign from the board, and he refuses to do so now. The state has enacted the MBCA. What procedural step would you advise Sea Hag to take right away (and how will things work out if she takes that step)? ________________

28. Same basic facts as the prior question. Now, assume that, at a duly-noticed shareholders meeting, Olive Oil and Bluto show up, but Sea Hag doesn't. (Nor does Sea Hag give anyone else her proxy). At the meeting, Olive Oil introduces a motion to change the company's accountant. (Assume that this is a proper subject for shareholder action. Also, assume that the charter and bylaws are silent about all issues relevant to this question.)

(a) Assume that both Olive Oil and Bluto vote their shares in favor of the motion. Is the corporation now authorized to change accountants? ________________

(b) Assume that Olive Oil votes her shares for the motion, and Bluto votes his shares against it. Putting aside any issue of procedural irregularity with respect to the holding of the meeting, has the motion passed? ________________

Answers

26. No, because the merger was not mentioned as one of the purposes of the meeting. Shareholders are entitled to notice of both annual and special shareholders' meetings. If the meeting is "special" (i.e., a meeting other than the annual meeting), as is the case here, virtually all states say that the notice must include a statement of the meeting's purpose. [80] See, e.g., MBCA § 7.05(c) ("Notice of a special meeting must include a description of the purpose or purposes for which the meeting is called.") What this statement does is limit the scope of what may be discussed at the meeting, since no unstated business can be transacted at the meeting. Since the notice didn't mention the merger, it can't be discussed.

(No statement of purposes is required in the notice for the *annual* meeting, by contrast. But even as to an annual meeting, if a merger will be discussed, shareholders must be told in advance that this will happen, and must be given the details of the plan. See, e.g., MBCA § 11.04(d). So even if de Gama was making his merger proposal at the annual meeting as opposed to at the special meeting, the merger couldn't be approved without this proposal's having been mentioned in the notice-of-meeting.)

27. You should advise her to call an immediate special meeting of shareholders, at which Sea Hag will move to remove all directors without cause. Most states now allow the holders of a certain percentage of shares to call a special shareholders' meeting at any time. The MBCA allows any holder or holders of more than 10% to do this (see § 7.02(a)(2)). Then, the shareholders can, under the MBCA (as under the law of most states today), remove any director by majority vote, even without cause. So, because the corporation doesn't have cumulative voting, at the meeting Sea Hag can cast all her votes (51% of the total votes cast) to remove all three directors. She can then elect herself to one of the vacancies by majority vote. Then, she can (either as the sole member of the board or as majority shareholder) elect two new directors to fill the vacancies. Thus she gets complete board control without waiting for the prior directors' terms to expire. (If the corporation had had cumulative voting, Sea Hag would only have been able to remove two directors and control the election of their replacements — by the formula on p. 56, she would have had just exactly the 51 shares (153 votes) needed to elect two of three directors, and not enough to elect all three.)

28. (a) No, because there was no quorum for the meeting. Unless the charter or bylaws provide otherwise (which the facts say they don't), a shareholder meeting requires a quorum of at least a bare majority of the outstanding shares entitled to vote on the measures at issue. Since only 49 of 100 shares were present, shareholder action could not validly take place.

(b). Yes, since we're told to ignore the quorum problem. The real issue in this sub-question is whether the fact that less than a majority (i.e., only 49%) of the total shares outstanding voted for the measure prevents the measure from passing. The answer is "no" — all that's required is that a majority of those shares *actually voting* vote for the measure. (States differ in how they treat abstentions, but that's not an issue here.) Since 30 out of the 49 votes actually cast voted for the measure, it passed.

Exam Tips on *THE CORPORATE STRUCTURE*

Here are the main things to watch for in connection with the corporate structure:

- Whenever your fact pattern describes an attempt to ***remove a director***, here's what you should keep in mind:
  - The ***shareholders***, by majority vote, can always remove a director for ***cause*** (e.g., fraud, gross incompetence, or a breach of the duty of loyalty).

☞ Also, most modern statutes (including the MBCA) let a ***majority of the shareholders*** remove a director ***even without cause***, unless the corp's charter provides differently.

☞ ***Directors***, even by majority vote, ***cannot*** remove a fellow director even for cause, unless the charter or bylaws specifically say they can.

☞ The ***court*** may (under most modern statutes) remove a director for ***cause*** (e.g., fraudulent or dishonest conduct, or gross abuse of power).

☛ If your fact pattern involves the ***removal of an officer*** (e.g., the president), here's what you should remember:

☞ The ***board*** has the power to remove an officer, ***with or without cause***. That's true even if the officer has an employment contract — the board has power to remove the officer anyway (and the officer's only recourse is a suit for damages, not a suit to enjoin the dismissal or to compel reinstatement).

☞ ***Shareholders***, even by majority vote, do ***not*** have the power to remove an officer.

☛ ***Election of directors*** is often tested.

☞ The most common issue about election of directors involves ***filling board vacancies***. Here, the usual rule (and the MBCA approach) is that the vacancy can be filled ***either by shareholder vote*** or ***board vote***.

☞ Don't overlook the possibility that a corp. may have ***cumulative voting***. In cumulative voting, a shareholder may ***aggregate his votes*** in favor of fewer candidates than there are slots available.

Example: A, B and C each own 100 of G Corp's 300 shares outstanding, and are its 3 directors under annual terms. C dies, and D inherits her shares. The bylaws say that a 90% majority is required for election of new directors. You have to say whether, at the next holders' meeting, D can elect herself as a director, against the wishes of A and B. If G Corp. has cumulative voting, D can do so — she can cast all 300 of her votes in favor of herself, and thus come up with a "100% vote" (i.e., 1 vote for each share outstanding) for herself, even if A and B don't vote for her.

☛ You'll sometimes be asked about when shareholders can ***compel the calling of a special shareholders' meeting***. In general, the board is ***not obligated*** to call such a meeting (even if a majority of holders requests it) unless the particular action sought to be accomplished must be approved by shareholders.

Example: P, majority holder of X Corp., wants to remove Pres., the corp's president. P calls for a special meeting of shareholders to consider his motion to fire Pres. The board refuses. P can't compel the board to hold the special meeting, because shareholders don't have the power to fire officers, and therefore don't have the right to call a special meeting to consider the firing of officers.

☛ Issues involving the ***corporate structure*** are often hidden in fact patterns that tell you about the provisions of the corp's ***charter*** and ***bylaws***. ***Be certain to read these charter and bylaws terms carefully***, because they're likely to be implicated in events that you're told about later in the question.

- ☞ If the facts indicate that the board has taken an action which ***conflicts*** with the corp's ***charter***, remember that the charter can ***only be altered by the shareholders***, not the board — so the board's action is probably illegal.

  Example: X Corp's charter says that the board consists of 5 members, who will be elected annually. The board unilaterally votes to expand its size to 9, and to stagger terms. This action will be illegal, because only a majority of shareholders, not a board majority, may vary the charter.

☛ Whenever you have to decide the validity of a particular board action, check for failure to comply with ***notice***, ***quorum*** and ***meeting*** requirements. In particular:

- ☞ A special meeting of the board must normally be preceded by ***notice*** to the board members. The notice must specify the subject(s) (and no unlisted subject may be discussed).
  - ☞ However, the notice requirement will be deemed ***waived*** as to any director who ***attends the meeting*** and does not object at the start of the meeting to the lack of notice.
- ☞ The board may act only if a ***quorum*** is present.
  - ☞ If the board has a ***fixed size***, a quorum is a majority of ***that size*** (even if there are now vacancies).
  - ☞ If the board has a ***variable size***, a quorum is a majority of the directors ***in office*** at the start of the meeting.
  - ☞ Most states let a corporation's charter or bylaws establish a ***supermajority*** requirement for a quorum. (*Example:* Corp's bylaws say that a quorum will consist of 5 out of its 7 directors. This provision will be given effect, so a meeting at which only 4 of 7 are present will be of no effect.)
- ☞ Normally, the board may take action ***only at a meeting***. Directors must be ***present to vote*** (i.e., they ***may not vote by proxy***). (*Example:* Paul, one of Corp's directors, can't come to the board meeting, so he gives his proxy to Steve, and has Steve vote for him at the meeting. Paul won't be deemed present, and his vote won't count.)
  - ☞ Look out for the possibility of a ***telephone meeting***: in most states (and under the MBCA), if the director is present for a conference call in which a quorum participates, the director is deemed to be in attendance at the meeting, and his vote counts.
  - ☞ The board may take action only upon a vote of a ***majority*** of the directors ***present at the meeting***. (So the action doesn't have to be supported by a majority of directors in *office*, only a majority of those *present*, assuming that a quorum is present.)
  - ☞ If the facts indicate that the meeting/quorum/majority-vote requirements ***weren't met***, consider the possibility that the board action is valid anyway, because the directors subsequently ***ratified*** it by affirming it or failing to disavow it.

    Example: No quorum is present when the board purports to approve a contract with a third party. A year later, at a regular meeting, attended by a quorum, a majority of those present vote to approve the transaction. This is a ratification, so the contract is binding as if it had been properly approved the first time. (Same result if the board ***tacitly*** ratifies, as by ***accepting benefits*** under the contract.)

☛ Whenever the fact pattern states that an officer acted on behalf of the corp., consider whether the officer had ***authority*** to bind the corp. under any of these 4 doctrines: (1) ***express actual authority***; (2) ***implied actual authority***; (3) ***apparent authority***; and (4) ***ratification***.

☞ Look for indications as to whether the officer was ***expressly*** authorized to make the contract. An explicit grant of authority usually comes from either the corp's bylaws, or from a resolution adopted by the board. (Usually this form of authority is so easy that you won't find it in your facts.)

☞ If the officer had a ***title*** within the corp. that would typically include the power to make the deal in question, then the officer had ***"implied actual authority"*** (i.e., authority that's "inherent in the office.") (*Example:* Pete, who is actually the Pres. of Corp., signs a deal to buy office furniture "Corp, by Pete, its President." Pete has implied actual authority, because the president of a corporation would typically have authority to make a deal for furniture.)

☞ Look for situations in which ***extraordinary*** action is taken by the corp.'s president, without board approval. Such action is probably ***invalid***, since it doesn't fall within any form of authority.

Example: X Corp. is a 10-employee business with $1 million in annual revenues. Pres., the president of X Corp., signs an agreement to pay a $100,000-per-year lifetime pension to a retiring vice-president. The board isn't told of the agreement, and thus doesn't authorize it. The contract is probably not enforceable against X Corp., because it was an extraordinary contract, that did not fall within any theory of authority. (For instance, the authority isn't "implied actual," because such a deal is too large and unusual to come within the usual powers of the president of a corp. this size.)

CHAPTER 4

SHAREHOLDERS' INFORMATIONAL RIGHTS AND THE PROXY SYSTEM

ChapterScope

This Chapter focuses on how shareholders can get information about the corporation's affairs, and how (at least for publicly-held corporations) the system of "proxy voting" lets shareholders vote on the corporation's affairs without having to physically attend shareholders' meetings. Key concepts are:

- **Inspection of books and records:** Shareholders are normally allowed by state law to ***inspect*** the corporation's books and records, if they are doing so for a "proper purpose."
- **Securities Exchange Act of 1934:** The " ***'34 Act***" is a federal statute that applies to companies traded on a national securities exchange, and to companies traded "over the counter" if the company is above a certain size. The '34 Act requires the company to ***"register"*** its stock, and to continuously ***supply the public with information*** about the company.
- **Proxy rules:** A ***"proxy"*** is a document in which the shareholder ***appoints someone*** (typically management) to ***cast his vote*** for one or more specified actions. For instance, in every public corporation, management annually solicits from each holder that holder's proxy for voting for the board of directors. (This is the means by which a shareholder can vote without physically attending the annual meeting.) The solicitation of proxies is subject to strict SEC rules; these rules include requirements about what ***information must be disclosed*** by the party who's soliciting the proxy. (This information is contained in a ***"proxy statement."***)
    - **Shareholders' proposal:** Under certain circumstances, a minority shareholder may require management to include in management's proxy statement the minority holder's ***proposal for shareholder action***.
    - **Private right of action:** If a proxy statement does not meet the SEC's requirements (e.g., it contains false or misleading information), a shareholder may bring a ***private action*** for money damages, against the party who issued the statement (e.g., the management of the company).
    - **Proxy contest:** A ***"proxy contest"*** is a competition between management and another faction — usually a group of outside insurgents — to obtain shareholder votes. Typically, a proxy contest is for election of ***competing slates*** to the ***board***, and thus is really a competition for ***control*** of the corporation. The SEC has elaborate rules governing proxy contests, which have the effect of somewhat equalizing the outsiders' chances.

I. SHAREHOLDER INSPECTION OF BOOKS AND RECORDS

A. Right of inspection generally: For a shareholder to be able to decide intelligently whether to sell her shares, hold onto them, bring a shareholders' derivative action (see *infra*, p. 317), or otherwise take action on her investment, she needs information. In the case of a publicly-held corporation, the federal securities laws require that much of the needed information be sent automatically to the shareholder; this is discussed below, p. 100, in our treatment of proxy solicitation. But apart from the federal securities regulatory system, ***state law*** generally provides shareholders with a useful alternative method of getting information about the corporation's affairs: This is the right to ***inspect the corporation's books and records***.

1. **Common law vs. statutory right:** This right of inspection can be based upon the common law, a statute, or both.

2. **Common law:** In most states, shareholders have a ***common-law*** right to inspect the corporation's books and records, if they show a ***"proper purpose"*** for doing so. If the corporation does not make the books and records available voluntarily, a shareholder may obtain a ***court order*** compelling the corporation to grant this right of inspection. Clark, p. 97. (What constitutes a "proper purpose" is discussed further *infra*, p. 92.)

   a. **Usually necessary:** The corporation will usually ***not*** voluntarily grant the right of inspection. A corporation's management almost always regards a shareholder request for inspection as a hostile act, and will therefore usually force the shareholder to litigate in order to take advantage of his inspection right. Nutshell, p. 376.

3. **Statutes:** Many states have enacted ***statutes*** codifying this shareholder right of inspection.

   a. **Penalties for non-compliance:** A key feature of most of these statutes is that they buttress the shareholders' common-law inspection right by establishing ***penalties*** if the corporation without cause refuses to allow the inspection. Thus the standard management response to assertion of the common-law inspection right — making a shareholder litigate to exercise his right — is a more dangerous option for management under most statutes.

   b. **Proper purpose:** Because the right of inspection can be used by a hostile shareholder to harass management or to steal corporate secrets, most statutes continue the common-law requirement that the shareholder have a ***"proper purpose"*** for the inspection. Nutshell, p. 377. See *infra*, p. 92.

   c. **Copies:** Virtually all states give the inspecting shareholder the right to obtain ***copies*** of the inspected documents, usually at the shareholder's expense. See, e.g., MBCA § 16.03(b) and (d).

   d. **Right to bring attorney:** Also, the inspecting shareholder generally has the right to have his ***attorney*** or agent do the inspection. See MBCA § 16.03(a).

4. **Model Act:** The MBCA is a good example of a modern statute giving shareholders a fairly broad right of inspection.

   a. **Automatic right:** For some types of corporate records, the shareholder has an ***absolute right of inspection***. Under MBCA § 16.02(a), the shareholder is automatically entitled to inspect and copy the following records: (1) the articles of incorporation; (2) the bylaws; (3) board resolutions creating or governing the rights of each class of stock; (4) minutes of shareholders' meetings for the last three years; (5) all written communications to shareholders within the last three years (including financial statements, which under § 16.20(a) are required to be given to shareholders); (6) the names and addresses of current officers and directors; and (7) the most recent annual report.

b. Other records: This list of records subject to the "automatic" inspection right is limited to "easy" situations, i.e., to information that is rarely considered highly secret by management. Clark, p. 97. A different MBCA section gives shareholders a ***qualified*** right to inspect more sensitive materials. Under § 16.02(b), any shareholder has a qualified right to examine: (1) the ***minutes*** of ***board meetings***; (2) the ***accounting records*** of the corporation; and (3) the corporation's ***list of shareholders***.

i. Proper purpose: Because these three items are more sensitive, and the corporation could be damaged or harassed by their wrongful use, these documents may only be inspected if the shareholder satisfies three requirements: (1) his demand must be made "in ***good faith*** and for a ***proper purpose***"; (2) he "describes with ***reasonable particularity***" his purpose and the records he wants to inspect; and (3) the records are "***directly connected*** with his purpose." Probably these requirements are, collectively, a little more strict than the common law's general "proper purpose" requirement. Clark, p. 98.

c. Penalties: The MBCA follows the recent statutory trend of ***penalizing*** the corporation if it without good cause requires the shareholder to litigate to exercise his inspection right. § 16.04(c) provides that if the shareholder goes to court to get an order compelling inspection, the court must require the corporation to pay the costs (including ***attorney's fees***) that the shareholder incurred in getting the court order. (However, the corporation can avoid this penalty by proving that it refused the inspection "in good faith because it had a reasonable basis for doubt" about the shareholder's right to inspect the records in question.)

5. Litigant's right: Shareholder inspection right statutes virtually never displace a ***litigant's*** right to inspect the corporation's records just as he could inspect the records of any other adversary if those records were relevant to the litigation. Thus MBCA § 16.02(e)(1) makes it clear that the general shareholder inspection right "does not affect . . . the right of a shareholder to inspect records . . . if the shareholder is in litigation with the corporation, to the same extent as any other litigant."

B. Who may inspect: At common law, not only shareholders who are of record but also ***beneficial owners*** of shares have the right of inspection. (Thus one for whom shares are held in trust, or one whose shares are held in "street name" or by a nominee — see *infra*, p. 101 — may inspect.) Statutes vary as to whether they apply to beneficial owners. The MBCA has been amended to include beneficial owners as "shareholders" for inspection purposes. See MBCA § 16.02(f).

1. Size or length-of-holding requirements: Some statutes restrict the right of inspection to shareholders who have either held their shares for a certain ***time***, or hold more than a certain ***percentage*** of the total shares. These requirements are in theory a means of protecting the corporation against harassment and damage from persons who buy a small number of shares for the sole purpose of conducting an immediate inspection.

a. New York: For instance, New York's BCL § 624 generally gives anyone who has held his shares for at least ***six months***, or who holds at least ***five percent*** of any class of shares, the right to examine certain documents (the shareholder list, the minutes of shareholders' meetings, and the current financial statements) without any showing of need or proper purpose.

b. **Criticism:** This kind of discrimination in favor of older or larger shareholders seems arbitrary. It clearly discriminates against small shareholders, and there is no reason to believe that small shareholders are more likely to be motivated by an improper purpose than are large shareholders. For this reason, the MBCA has dropped a prior requirement that was similar to the New York six months/five percent requirement. See Official Comment to § 16.04.

C. **What records may be examined:** Under most statutes, the shareholder has a right to inspect not merely specified records, but the corporation's ***records in general***. Nutshell, p. 379. Under these broadly-worded statutes, the basic idea is that the shareholder can review any documents that have a ***reasonable bearing upon his investment***. Thus a broadly-written statute might allow the shareholder to inspect contracts, correspondence, accounting records, and anything else that bears reasonably upon the corporation's business or finances.

1. **Accounting records:** Other statutes are more narrowly drawn to restrict the shareholder from seeing especially sensitive documents. For example, some statutes do not allow the shareholder to inspect the underlying ***accounting records***, and limit him to the company's financial statements. Thus as noted above (p. 90), the MBCA does not include accounting records within the list of records that the shareholder has an "automatic" right to inspect.

2. **List of shareholders:** Similarly, some statutes deny the shareholder the right to examine the list of shareholders for fear that this list is especially susceptible to misuse. Thus the MBCA makes this list off-limits unless the shareholder makes a showing of good faith, proper purpose, reasonable particularity and direct connection. See § 16.02(b)(3).

a. **Solicitation of proxies:** The most common reason for which a shareholder will want the list of shareholders is to ***solicit proxies*** from them. If the corporation is publicly held, federal law (*infra*, p. 121) gives the shareholder the right to require the company to either mail the shareholder's proxy solicitation materials itself or to furnish the shareholder list to the shareholder so that the latter may solicit directly. If the company is not publicly held, most states grant the shareholder access to the list so long as the solicitation is reasonably related to the corporation's business. See *infra*, pp. 92-93 (including the *Pillsbury* case).

D. **What is a proper purpose:** As we mentioned above, in nearly all states the shareholder will be allowed to inspect corporate records only if he does so for a ***"proper purpose"***. In most states, a "proper purpose" is a prerequisite for any kind of inspection at all; under the MBCA, it is a prerequisite for the inspection of the interesting and sensitive types of corporate documents (minutes of directors' meetings, accounting records and the shareholder list; see § 16.02(b)).

1. **Definition:** There is no universally accepted definition of "proper purpose." The MBCA does not define the term at all. Delaware's definition is reasonably typical: A proper purpose means "a purpose ***reasonably related to such person's interest as a stockholder***." Del. GCL § 220(b).

2. **Four categories:** Shareholders' purposes for inspecting can be placed into four categories which we shall consider in turn: (1) the desire to ***evaluate one's investment***; (2) the pursuit of ***personal goals*** unrelated to ownership of stock in the corporation; (3) the desire to ***deal with other shareholders*** in the corporation as ***investors***; and (4) the desire to pursue ***social or political goals***. As a general rule, (1) and (3) will almost always be found "proper," and (2) and (4) will usually be found improper. See Clark, pp. 100-03.

   a. **Evaluation of investment:** A shareholder's desire to ***evaluate*** his ***investment*** is the easiest situation. Thus the shareholder might want to inspect (1) to determine whether there has been mismanagement (if there are some initial grounds for reasonable suspicion of this); (2) to determine whether the stock's market price currently reflects its intrinsic value; (3) to determine why dividends are not being paid; or (4) to investigate any other aspect of the corporation's financial condition. All of these inquiries will generally be found to be for ***proper purposes***. Clark, pp. 100-01.

   b. **Pursuit of unrelated personal goals:** Conversely, if the shareholder is pursuing a ***personal goal*** that is unrelated to his status of investor in the corporation, his purpose will be deemed ***not*** proper, and he will not be permitted to inspect. Thus if he wants to get access to ***trade secrets*** which he can sell to a competitor or use himself, or if he wishes to get hold of the shareholder list so that he can sell it to a mailing list rental company for junk mail solicitation, his purpose will not be found proper. Clark, p. 102. Of course, it is only the rare (and dumb) shareholder who will concede that these are his real purposes, so it is generally management that must convince the court that these are the real purposes, a burden that management usually cannot carry.

   c. **Deal with shareholders as investors:** The third category consists of cases where the shareholder wishes to ***contact*** his fellow shareholders to persuade them to take some sort of action regarding the corporation. For instance, she may want to ***solicit proxies*** from them (perhaps to elect an anti-management board of directors), or to initiate a ***tender offer*** for their shares. In this situation, courts generally conclude that the shareholder's desire to have a shareholder list constitutes a ***proper purpose*** since the purpose is closely related to the business and financial affairs of the corporation.

      i. **Hostility to management:** The fact that the shareholder who seeks inspection is ***hostile to management*** does not by itself make his purpose improper. Indeed, this is the very situation in which courts are quickest to affirm the right of inspection. So long as the shareholder shows that he is motivated by the desire to maximize the value of his investment, he will be found to have the right of inspection.

      ii. **Suit against corporation:** Similarly, if the shareholder wants to contact other holders in order to solicit them to join in ***litigation against or concerning the corporation***, this will not necessarily be an improper purpose.

      iii. **List of "non-objecting beneficial owners":** Some states' shareholder-list statutes have even been interpreted to allow access to lists of people who are ***"beneficial owners"*** (see *infra*, p. 122) rather than "shareholders of record."

   d. **Pursuit of social and/or political goals:** Where it is clear that the shareholder is pursuing only ***social or political goals*** that are relatively ***unrelated to the corporation's business,*** most courts will find that the shareholder's purpose is ***improper*** and will therefore deny inspection rights. Thus most courts would agree with the result in the leading case set forth in the following example.

Example: P owns one share of D (Honeywell Corp.) in his own name; he is also the beneficial owner of several hundred additional shares in D. P demands the right to inspect D's shareholder list and all records relating to weapons and munitions manufacture. He admits that his purpose is to bring pressure on D to stop producing munitions for use in the Vietnam war.

Held, for D. A stockholder has the right to inspect shareholder lists and other corporate records only if he has a "proper purpose germane to his economic interest as a shareholder." "Proper purpose" means "concern with investment return." Here, it is clear that P has made no attempt to determine whether holdings in D Corp. would make a good investment; he is not interested in the enhancement of the value of his shares, but merely in persuading the company to adopt his social and political concerns. True, P desires to contact other shareholders and attempt to gain the election to the board of one or more directors who would share his views; but although this might be a proper purpose if tied to the corporation's underlying business, here it is merely an aspect of P's desire to impose his political/social views on the corporation. *State ex rel. Pillsbury v. Honeywell, Inc.*, 191 N.W.2d 406 (Minn. 1971).

Note: Observe that P might have prevailed in *Pillsbury* had he been a little more careful and a little less forthright. He could have done some reasonable investigation into the economic prospects for Honeywell, and then asserted that he believed that its economic prospects over the long run would be adversely affected by the poor public relations stemming from its munitions manufacturing. Probably even the Minnesota court would have accepted this as a proper purpose.

3. **Multiple purposes of which one is proper:** Suppose a shareholder has ***multiple purposes*** for requesting the inspection, of which one (or more) is appropriate and the other(s) not. Here, the Delaware courts have held that inspection must be ***allowed*** — so long as there is ***at least one proper purpose***, the presence of an ***improper*** purpose is ***irrelevant***.

   a. **Court will look to the "real" purpose:** Of course, the court will not blindly accept the shareholder's stated reason(s) for the inspection, and will instead normally try to ascertain the ***"real"*** reasons that are motivating her. If the court concludes that all of the real reasons are illegitimate, the fact that the holder has asserted a different reason that would be legitimate will be irrelevant.

4. **Tie-in between purchase date and the act supplying "reasonable purpose":** Suppose the stockholder wants to investigate possible corporate wrongdoing that ***predates*** the moment when the stockholder bought the stock; should this nullify the stockholder's right of inspection? The Delaware Supreme Court has answered ***"no."*** In *Saito v. McKesson HBOC, Inc.*, 806 A.2d 113 (Del. 2002), the court said, "The date on which a stockholder first acquired the corporation's stock does not control the scope of records available under [the Delaware inspection statute]. If activities that occurred before the purchase date are 'reasonably related' to the stockholder's interest as a stockholder, then the stockholder should be given access to records necessary to an understanding of those activities."

E. Financial reports for shareholders: Suppose the shareholder does not make a formal request to inspect the corporate records. Is there any financial information (e.g., an annual report) that he is entitled to receive ***automatically***, without request? Perhaps surprisingly, in most states the answer is ***"no"*** — the corporation is not even required to send an annual report or annual financial statement to the shareholder. Nutshell, p. 384.

1. **Annual financial statement:** Some jurisdictions, however, require at least an annual financial statement to be sent to each shareholder. See e.g., Cal. § 1501(a) (annual financial statement required unless there are less than 100 stockholders and the requirement is waived in the bylaws). See also MBCA § 16.20, requiring an annual financial statement to be sent to every shareholder, together with the accountant's or management's discussion of the method by which these statements were prepared.

2. **Public corporations:** A ***publicly held*** corporation is required by the federal securities laws to supply an annual report to all shareholders. The source of this requirement is described *infra*, p. 100.

F. Director's right of inspection: A shareholder's right to inspect corporate records should be compared with the right of a ***director*** to inspect those records.

1. **Scope of director's right:** A director in most states has a much broader, more automatic, right of inspection than does a shareholder. Since the director is interested in management of the corporation and owes a fiduciary duty to the shareholders, most states grant him very broad inspection powers. In fact, some states hold that the director has an ***absolute*** right of inspection, and that his motives are irrelevant.

2. **Misuse:** Most states, however, would deny the right of inspection if it is clear that the director is acting with ***"manifestly improper motives."*** Nutshell, p. 375. For instance, if a director were shown to have an ***interest in a competitor***, and it were demonstrated that the director wanted to inspect the books and records so that he could aid the competitor at the corporation's expense, most courts would probably deny the right of inspection. But such cases are very rare, and the burden of establishing improper purpose is clearly on the corporation.

II. REPORTING REQUIREMENTS FOR PUBLICLY HELD COMPANIES

A. Overview: For a privately held company, the shareholders' inspection rights described above are the principal way in which the corporation's shareholders can get financial information about the company. For a shareholder with a modest economic investment in a particular corporation, this is often not a very useful right, especially where the corporation requires the shareholder to litigate to exercise his inspection right. But once a corporation becomes ***"publicly held,"*** the shareholder's access to information about it improves dramatically: Under the federal securities laws, the corporation is required to file a great deal of financial information with the Securities and Exchange Commission (SEC), which then becomes available as a public record; also, under SEC rules the public corporation is required to send certain types of financial information to the shareholder automatically. This section II gives a brief overview of the federal securities regulation scheme; sections III-VI then examine in detail the so-called "proxy rules" that are a portion of the federal securities regulation scheme.

1. **Two types of public filings:** To begin with, there are two main statutes that impose filing requirements on publicly held corporations: (1) the Securities Act of 1933 (the " '33 Act"); and (2) the Securities Exchange Act of 1934 (the " '34 Act").

   a. **The '33 Act:** The '33 Act principally regulates the ***initial offering of securities*** to the public. Under this act, before a corporation may issue shares to the public, it must file a ***"registration statement"*** with the SEC. Part of this registration statement is a "prospectus," which is distributed to any prospective or actual purchaser of shares. Once a corporation issues its shares (and assuming that it does not make any additional issues), the '33 Act largely becomes irrelevant. Therefore, we consider its provisions in a later chapter that deals with the initial issuance of securities. See *infra*, p. 539.

2. **The '34 Act:** In this chapter, our principal concern is with the '34 Act. That Act requires ***registration*** of the shares of certain companies, and also requires the ***continuous updating*** of information about companies whose shares are so registered. There are two main ways in which a company's shares may become required to be registered under the '34 Act:

   a. **Listed stocks:** First of all, if the company's stock is ***traded on a national securities exchange***, it is automatically required to be registered with the SEC. '34 Act, § 12(a). This means that not only companies whose stock is traded on the New York Stock Exchange and American Stock Exchange, but also companies traded on the various "regional" exchanges (e.g., Philadelphia, Pacific, Boston, etc.), must be registered, ***no matter how small the company*** or the issue of stock.

   b. **Over-the-counter companies of more than a certain size:** Secondly, even companies whose shares are traded ***over the counter*** (i.e., not on any formal stock exchange) must be registered with the SEC if the company is above a certain size. At present, a non-exchange-listed company must generally register with the SEC if it meets ***both*** of the following requirements: (1) the company has assets in ***excess of ten million dollars***; *and* (2) the company has a class of stock held of record by ***500 or more persons***. See '34 Act, § 12(g)(1) and SEC Rule 12g-1 thereunder. It is this "500 shareholder/ten million dollars in assets" provision that requires thousands of over-the-counter stocks to be subject to the SEC reporting requirements. This includes many of the stocks on the NASDAQ Automatic Quotations System, which in many ways functions like a stock exchange but is not considered an exchange for purposes of the '34 Act.

      i. **Single class of more than 500 holders:** The registration required under the '34 Act is not actually registration of the company, but is rather registration of a particular ***class of stock***. In the case of stock not listed on any exchange, it is the class of stock that must have more than 500 record holders before registration will be required.

         Example: ABC Corp. has 300 record holders of its common stock and 300 record holders of its preferred stock. Neither of these classes will have to be registered with the SEC under the '34 Act (unless one of the classes is traded on a national stock exchange), since neither of the classes, by itself, has more than 500 record owners.

ii. Termination: Once a class of shares has to be registered under the '34 Act, even a reduction of assets or reduction of record holders below the number that would have been required for initial registration will not automatically be enough to remove the registration requirements. The company must keep on registering the class unless the number of shareholders in the class drops below ***300***; see '34 Act, § 12(g)(4). This means that even a publicly-held corporation with billions of dollars of assets can terminate its SEC reporting requirements (and thereby ***"go private"***) if it can reduce the number of record holders of its stock to fewer than 300.

c. Definition of "publicly held": There is no official federal meaning to the concept of a ***"publicly held"*** company. The phrase "publicly held" is an informal one, and usually refers to companies that are subject to the '34 Act disclosure requirements that we've just summarized (i.e., companies that are either exchange-listed or have 500 shareholders plus ten million in assets.)

B. What must be disclosed: Once a company has a class of shares that is required to be registered under § 12 of the '34 Act (the companies described in paragraphs A(2)(a) and (b) above), it must then make ***continuous disclosures*** to the SEC. Among the many kinds of filings that are required are: (1) an ***annual report*** each year on SEC form 10-K; (2) a ***quarterly financial report*** every three months on SEC form 10-Q; and (3) a report of ***major business developments*** (e.g., changes in control, acquisition or disposition of significant assets, resignations of directors, etc.), to be reported within fifteen days of their occurrence on SEC form 8-K.

III. THE PROXY RULES GENERALLY

A. Overview: Few shareholders have the time or inclination to physically attend the shareholders' meeting and vote their shares in person, whether for the election of directors, approval of a merger, or for some other action requiring a shareholder vote. However, recall that shareholder action cannot be taken unless a quorum (usually one-half of the total shares) is represented at the meeting (see *supra*, p. 81). How can a majority of the shares be represented if few of the shareholders are present? The answer is, by use of the ***proxy***. The proxy is a document whereby the shareholder ***appoints someone*** (usually management) to ***cast his vote*** for one or more specified actions.

Example: Consider the most typical case, that of a proxy for voting that is to take place at the upcoming ***annual meeting of shareholders***. X, a shareholder in Corporation, can cast his vote for, say, management's proposed slate of directors, even though X cannot attend. X sends management a signed proxy card (pre-printed by management) on which X authorizes management to cast X's vote in favor of management's slate of directors. Of course, this will only happen if management first sends X this pre-printed form of proxy and requests that X sign and return it to management; if management does this, it is said to be "soliciting" a proxy from X.

1. **How SEC regulation fits in:** Except in rare cases where management directly controls a majority of the voting shares, the corporation could not function without proxy solicitation. For instance, a slate of directors could never be elected, because a majority of the shares would never be present and voting at the annual meeting. It is the all-pervasive proxy system that gives the SEC a broad opportunity to regulate: (1) the mechanics of the proxy system; (2) the information that must be furnished to a shareholder when his proxy is solicited; and (3) even more broadly, the information that must be ***furnished to each shareholder annually***, whether or not his proxy is solicited. The SEC's proxy regulations also furnish a shareholder with the means of submitting a proposal to his fellow shareholders, and dictate special requirements for conducting "proxy contests." The focus of this proxy regulatory system is on making sure that investors have ***adequate information*** before they exercise their right to vote by filling out a proxy card. Clark, p. 366.

2. **Who is covered:** The SEC's authority to regulate the proxy process comes from § 14 of the Securities Exchange Act (the '34 Act). Section 14(a) makes it "unlawful for any person, by the use of the mails or by any means or instrumentality of interstate commerce or of any facility of a national securities exchange . . . in contravention of such rules and regulations as the [SEC] may prescribe . . . to ***solicit*** or to permit the use of his name to solicit ***any proxy*** or consent or authorization in respect of any security . . . registered pursuant to section 12 of this title. . . ."

   a. **Registration pursuant to section 12:** Thus a proxy solicitation is covered by the SEC rules if the proxy is solicited concerning stock registered under § 12 of the '34 Act. As we saw above, *supra*, p. 96), stock must be registered under section 12 if it is the case that ***either***: (1) the stock is traded on a national securities exchange; or (2) the company has at least ten million dollars of assets and the class of stock in question is held by at least 500 record owners. In other words, if the issuer (the company whose shares are being considered) has to file 10-K's and other regular reports with the SEC, it ***must also obey the SEC's proxy solicitation rules***.

3. **What transactions are covered:** As we just saw from looking at the language of § 14 of the '34 Act, the SEC's right to regulate the proxy system is extremely broad: It extends to any solicitation, by any person, of any "proxy or consent or authorization in respect of any security" that is registered with the SEC. The SEC has in turn promulgated rules that regulate most (but not all) of the transactions that the SEC could, under § 14, regulate. SEC rule 14(a)-2 grants certain ***exemptions*** for solicitations that would otherwise be covered. After taking into account these exemptions, here is what is covered by the SEC rules:

   a. **Solicitation by management:** If the solicitation is by ***management***, the solicitation of ***even one person*** falls within the SEC rules.

   b. **Solicitation by non-management:** But if the solicitation is by ***non-management*** (e.g., it is by an ***insurgent faction*** trying to get its own slate of directors elected to the board), the solicitation is not covered so long as the number of persons solicited is ***ten or fewer***.

      i. **Solicitation of eleven or more:** But if non-management solicits eleven or more people, the solicitation falls within the SEC rules even if none of the people solicited actually grants a proxy to the solicitor. C&E, p. 331.

4. **What is a "proxy":** The SEC's definition of "proxy" is extremely ***broad***. Under rule 14a-1(e), the term includes "every proxy, consent or authorization. . . ." For example, the proxy need not be a piece of paper; a shareholder's ***oral consent*** to a request will be enough. Clark, p. 368.

5. **Meaning of "solicitation":** Similarly, ***"solicitation"*** is very broadly defined. Here are some of the requests that are deemed "solicitations" by SEC rule 14a-1(k):

   a. **Oral requests:** An ***oral request*** for a proxy, even if no proxy card is sent to the person being solicited;

   b. **Request not to execute:** A request (written or oral) ***not*** to execute, or to revoke, a proxy ***solicited by someone else***;

   c. **Advertisement:** The "furnishing of a form of proxy or ***other communication*** to security holders under circumstances reasonably calculated to result in the procurement, withholding, or revocation of a proxy." Rule 14a-1(k)(1)(iii). Under this definition a ***newspaper advertisement*** urging shareholders to give or deny one side a proxy would be a "solicitation." (But if the newspaper advertisement merely describes how holders may get copies of the proxy statement, it is not deemed to be a "solicitation". Nutshell, p. 284.)

6. **Communications among shareholders (*Studebaker*):** The very broad definitions of "proxy" and "solicitations" are illustrated by *Studebaker Corp. v. Gittlin*, 360 F.2d 692 (2d Cir. 1966), where the court held that informal contacts by one stockholder with less than fifty other stockholders amounted to a proxy solicitation.

   a. **Facts:** D, a dissident stockholder in Studebaker, wanted to convince shareholders to vote for his proposed directors slate at the upcoming annual meeting. The company refused to give him access to its shareholder list, which he needed for this purpose. He then sued to obtain the right to inspect the shareholder list. Under local (New York) law, D could only gain this inspection right if he held or represented more than five percent of the corporation's shares. (See *supra*, p. 91.) He therefore obtained written authorizations from ***forty-two other shareholders*** who collectively held more than five percent of Studebaker's shares, authorizing him to inspect the shareholder list.

   b. **Holding:** The court held that D's act of ***requesting these other shareholders to authorize him to inspect*** the shareholder list ***was itself a proxy solicitation***. Therefore, D violated SEC rules by making that solicitation without complying with all of the formal requirements for a proxy solicitation (e.g., the filing of proxy materials with the SEC).

      i. **SEC exemption:** But the SEC has effectively ***reversed*** the result in *Studebaker* and similar situations. In 1992, the Commission enacted Rule 14a-2(b)(1), which gives an exemption from the proxy rules for someone who conducts a solicitation of stockholders but "who ***does not ... seek ... the power to act as proxy*** for a security holder" (subject to some limitations, such as that the person doing the soliciting not be affiliated with the issuer, not be a current board candidate, etc.). So in the *Studebaker*-type situation in which one non-controlling shareholder contacts others to discuss how they should all vote in an upcoming corporate matter, 14a-

2(b)(1) is likely to give the contacting holder an exemption from the proxy rules. See A,K&S, p. 193.

B. Four topics: Our remaining discussion of the proxy rules is divided into five main areas: (1) What ***information*** must be disclosed and filed as part of a proxy solicitation (discussed immediately below)? (2) When may a proxy be ***revoked***? (3) What ***private rights of action*** exist for violation of the proxy rules? (4) When must a ***shareholder proposal*** be included by management in the proxy materials? and (5) What special rules apply during a proxy ***contest***?

C. Disclosure and filing requirements: Once a company with stock that is registered under § 12 decides to solicit proxies, it must comply with extensive ***filing*** and ***disclosure*** requirements. (Dissident shareholders who want to solicit proxies must also satisfy some of these requirements; these are discussed in the treatment of proxy contests, *infra*, p. 120.)

1. **Filing with SEC:** Any documents that will be sent to shareholders as part of the solicitation process must first be ***filed with the SEC*** before they are sent to stockholders. Not only the "proxy statement" (defined below), but all other solicitation materials — such as letters, press releases, speeches and even instructions for oral solicitations — must be pre-filed in this manner. (If the solicitation relates only to election of directors or a few other routine matters, and is uncontested, pre-filing is not necessary. See Rule 14a-6(a).)

   a. **Limited review:** The SEC does not conduct a major review of these pre-filed materials. However, if in its cursory review it concludes that information is missing or inaccurate (perhaps because it conflicts with other information on file at the SEC), it will order revisions to be made. Nutshell, p. 284.

2. **Proxy statement:** Every proxy solicitation must be accompanied or preceded by a written ***"proxy statement"***. Rule 14a-3(a). The proxy statement must disclose, among other things: (1) ***conflicts of interest***; (2) details of any ***compensation plan*** to be voted on; (3) the ***compensation paid to the five most highly-paid officers***; and (4) details of any ***major corporate change*** being voted upon. See Clark, p. 369.

3. **Annual report:** Perhaps even more importantly, the proxy rules effectively require that an ***annual report*** be sent to every shareholder. If the solicitation is by management and relates to an annual meeting at which directors will be elected, the proxy statement must be preceded or accompanied by an annual report that includes, among other items, audited balance sheets and audited profit and loss statements. Rule 14a-3(b).

   a. **Significance:** Since under state law directors must generally be elected at the annual meeting, and since a majority of all shares must be present at the annual meeting for there to be a quorum, management generally has little choice but to solicit proxies for the annual meeting. Therefore, as a practical matter management ***must send an annual report to every stockholder.***

      i. **Management-controlled companies:** In fact, the proxy-solicitation rules apply in practice ***even where management itself controls a majority of the stock***, so that it doesn't need any outsiders to grant proxies or show up at the annual meeting. SEC Rule 14c-3 says that even if management is not soliciting proxies, the ***same annual report*** (with all of the same required disclosures) must still be given to shareholders before the annual meeting, as if proxies were being solicited. So minority holders in management-controlled public companies get essentially the same information (and that same information is filed with the SEC) as in the usual situation in which outsiders hold a majority.

4. **Anti-fraud rule:** In addition to the above provisions that require specific documents to be sent to shareholders whose proxy is being solicited, the SEC has a more general ***"anti-fraud"*** rule concerning proxy solicitations. Rule 14a-9(a) prohibits the use of proxy solicitation materials that contain "any statement which, at the time and in the light of the circumstances under which it is made, is ***false or misleading*** with respect to ***any material fact***, or which ***omits*** to state any material fact necessary in order to make the statements therein not false or misleading. . . ." If this anti-fraud rule is violated, a shareholder has the implied right to bring a ***private action*** for an injunction or damages; private actions for proxy violations are discussed *infra*, p. 103.

D. Getting the materials to shareholders (the "street name" and "nominee" problems): If management is to solicit proxies from its shareholders, it must know who they are. This poses far more of a problem than you might think, because of the practice of holding shares in "street name" or "nominee name" (terms defined below).

1. **"Record owner" vs. "beneficial owner":** First, consider that a given share of stock may have both a ***"record"*** owner and a ***"beneficial"*** owner. The record owner is the one who is shown on the ***corporation's own books*** as being the owner of that stock. The beneficial owner, by contrast, is the person who has the real, effective economic ownership of the share. For instance, suppose that Minor is a beneficiary under a trust set up by his grandparents, and the trustee for the trust is Mega Bank. If the trust holds shares of stock in X Corp., X Corp.'s transfer records will probably show that Mega Bank is the record owner of the stock. Minor is the beneficial owner of these shares (it is he who takes the actual economic gains or losses), but X Corp's transfer records will not show Minor's name at all.

2. **Street names and nominees:** Today, about 70% of all shares in publicly-held corporations have a record owner who is not the beneficial owner. Apart from the ordinary trustee/beneficiary situation (illustrated above by our Minor/Mega Bank hypothetical), there are several kinds of procedures that lead to the beneficial owner's not being shown as the record owner on the issuing corporation's transfer books:

   a. **"Street names" at brokerage firms:** First, when an individual buys stock through a broker, the shares will often end up being registered in ***"street name,"*** i.e., the name of the brokerage firm. For example, the individual's shares will be registered in street name if: (1) the individual does not want to bother taking physical possession of the shares, so he decides to leave them with the broker for convenience; or (2) the shares are bought on margin, so that the broker must hold them as collateral.

   b. **Nominees:** Second, large institutional investors (e.g., mutual funds and pension funds) generally hold their shares in the names of ***"nominees,"*** usually a partnership of employees formed for just that purpose. Nutshell, p. 277. The issuing corporation knows only that a certain number of shares are owned by, say, Baker & Co., and does not necessarily know for which institutional investor Baker & Co. is the nominee.

c. **Use of depositories:** The development in the last few decades of the system of ***depositories*** makes things even more complicated. Brokerage firms and other large institutions generally do not keep possession of the shares themselves. Instead, over 70% of all outstanding shares are held by four depositories, which are in effect central clearing corporations. By the use of these depositories, many offsetting trades can be netted out, and only the net change of position noted on the depositories' books.

i. **Depository Trust Co.:** By far the largest of these four depositories is the Depository Trust Co. (DTC), which is a subsidiary of the New York Stock Exchange. All shares held by DTC are shown on the issuer's books as being held by the nominee "Cede and Co." Thus Cede and Co. is the record owner of probably a majority of all publicly-held shares in America!

E. **Requirements for proxy:** The SEC's rules also regulate the form of the proxy itself.

1. **Contents of card:** The proxy is generally a ***card*** which the shareholder signs, and on which he indicates the side he favors. For example, if the proxy form in question is management's form for soliciting a vote for management's slate of board candidates, the card will typically contain a box to indicate that the holder votes for management's slate as a whole, a box to indicate that the holder is withholding authority to vote for management's slate, and an opportunity to withhold support for any particular member(s) of management's slate.

2. **Undated or post-dated proxy forms:** If in a proxy contest (see *infra*, p. 120) a holder gives a proxy to each of two competing sides, the ***last-dated*** proxy controls. Therefore, the SEC's proxy rules ***prohibit undated or post-dated proxy forms***. See Rule 14a-10.

3. **Ban on broad discretion:** The proxy form may not confer unduly broad ***discretion*** on the recipient. For example, management could not send a proxy form concerning the election of directors, that authorizes management to vote for "whomever it believes to be the best qualified person" Instead, the proxy form must list the names of management's nominees. See Rule 14a-4(d).

4. **Must vote for:** The recipient of the proxy ***must*** vote the proxy as the shareholder has indicated. Thus if management sends Holder a card, and the card has boxes both "for" and "against" a proposal backed by management (as Rule 14a-4 requires it to do), management cannot simply disregard those proxies marked "against" that are returned to it — it must vote them as indicated. Rule 14a-4(e).

F. **Revocation of proxies:** When may a proxy be ***revoked*** by the shareholder who gave it?

1. **Generally revocable:** Generally, a proxy is ***revocable*** by the shareholder. This is true ***even if the proxy itself recites that it is irrevocable.*** (In that sense, a proxy is like an ordinary offer at common law — the offer is revocable even if it says it isn't, unless some other special feature, like consideration, is present.)

2. **Proxy "coupled with an interest":** However, all states recognize one major ***exception*** to this general rule of revocability: a proxy is ***irrevocable*** if it meets two requirements: (1) it ***states*** that it's irrevocable; *and* (2) it is ***"coupled with an interest."*** See, e.g., MBCA § 7.22(d); Del. GCL § 212(e).

a. **Meaning of "coupled with an interest":** The idea behind the ***"coupled with an interest"*** concept is that the recipient of the proxy (the person who will be authorized to cast the vote on behalf of the proxy-giving shareholder) must have some ***property interest*** in the shares, or at least some other ***direct economic interest in how the vote is cast.*** MBCA § 7.22(d) gives a catalog of people who will be deemed to hold a suitable "interest." Here are some:

- ❑ a ***pledgee*** (e.g., Holder pledges his shares in return for a loan from Bank, and gives Bank, the pledgee, his proxy);
- ❑ a person who has ***purchased or agreed to purchase the shares***;
- ❑ a ***creditor of the corporation*** (e.g., Creditor says he won't give credit to Corp. unless Prexy, the controlling shareholder, gives Creditor a proxy that's irrevocable while the debt is outstanding);
- ❑ a ***party to a voting agreement*** (e.g., A, B, and C are the shareholders in closely-held Corp; they sign a voting agreement to vote their shares together (see p. 137), which impliedly gives the two shareholders in the majority on any ballot an irrevocable proxy to vote the shares of the third).

b. **Termination of interest:** If the proxy is irrevocable because it's coupled with an interest, the ***irrevocability*** (and the proxy itself) ***lasts only as long as the interest.*** So if, for instance, a borrower who gives the proxy as security for his loan pays off the loan, the proxy will then terminate (even if the proxy document says otherwise).

IV. IMPLIED PRIVATE ACTIONS UNDER THE PROXY RULES

A. **Implied right of action generally:** Nothing in the '34 act or the SEC's rules expressly gives a ***private investor*** the right to sue if the proxy rules are violated. But the Supreme Court has recognized an ***"implied private right of action"*** on behalf of individuals who have been injured by a violation of proxy rules.

1. **Summary of law:** We will consider this private right of action in detail below. For now, the right to sue may be summarized as follows:

a. **Materiality:** The shareholder/plaintiff must show that there was a ***material*** misstatement or omission in the proxy materials. But it is not necessary that the misstated or omitted fact would ***probably*** have caused a reasonable shareholder to change his vote; all that is required is that the fact would have been regarded as ***important***, or would have "assumed actual significance," in the decision-making of a reasonable shareholder. (*TSC Industries, infra*, p. 105.)

b. **Causation:** The plaintiff/shareholder does not have to show that he ***relied*** on the falsehoods or omissions in the proxy statement. Instead, the court will ***presume*** that injury was caused, so long as the falsehood or omission was material (see above) and the proxy materials were an essential link in the accomplishment of the transaction. (*Mills v. Electric Auto-Lite Co., infra*, p. 107.) Thus if proxy solicitation is necessary to gain shareholder approval of a merger, any material falsehoods will be presumed to have "caused" injury to the shareholders since the proxy solicitation process was a necessary part of bringing about the merger.

c. **Standard of fault:** The Supreme Court has never ruled on whether ***scienter*** (i.e., an intent to deceive) must be shown on the part of the defendants. Some lower courts have held that mere negligence is sufficient.

d. **Remedies:** If the plaintiff successfully establishes a cause of action, he may be entitled to damages, to an injunction (i.e., an order blocking the proposed transaction for approval of which the company sought proxies), or in a very extreme case, even an undoing of a consummated transaction.

2. **Implied right of action (the *Borak case*):** The recognition of an implied private right of action on behalf of shareholders for proxy violations occurred in ***J.I. Case Co. v. Borak***, 377 U.S. 426 (1964).

a. **Facts:** P, a minority shareholder in Case Corporation, sued to enjoin a proposed merger between Case and American Tractor Corp. (ATC). P claimed that Case's managers had engaged in illegal self-dealing, that the merger was unfair to shareholders, and (most significantly for our purposes) that the proxy materials were false and misleading in that they did not disclose the true facts about the merger and its value to shareholders. The district court held that even if P established that there had been proxy violations, the court could not grant damages. By the time the case got to the Supreme Court, the merger had been consummated.

b. **Supreme Court finds implied right of private action:** The Supreme Court held that private stockholders have an ***implied right*** to bring a federal court action for violation of the proxy solicitation rules. The Court found that Congress, in passing § 14(a) of the '34 Act (which gives the SEC the right to set proxy solicitation rules), intended to "prevent management or others from obtaining authorization for corporate action by means of deceptive or inadequate disclosure in proxy solicitation." This regulatory scheme was intended to be for the protection of investors, so it was not unreasonable to give investors the right to sue for violations.

i. **Deterrent effect:** Furthermore, the Court held, "[p]rivate enforcement of the proxy rules provides a necessary supplement to [SEC] action. As in antitrust treble damage litigation, the possibility of civil damages or injunctive relief serves as a most effective weapon in the enforcement of the proxy requirements." The Court noted that the SEC has to examine over 2,000 proxy statements a year, and the Commission's own investigatory and enforcement mechanisms are not by themselves adequate to prevent violations.

c. **Remedies:** The Court also stated that if P proved a violation of the proxy rules, the federal district court had the power to grant "all necessary remedial relief." This relief was not limited (as the district court had held) to the granting of an injunction against a not-yet-consummated merger. Thus the Court hinted, but did not find, that damages or even an ***undoing of the already-done merger*** might be appropriate remedies for a violation.

3. **Present state of implied private actions:** During the last few decades, the Supreme Court has become much less eager than in *Borak* to find that a particular statutory provision was implicitly intended by Congress to create a private right of action. Nonetheless, the Court has not overruled or cut back *Borak*, so it continues to be the case that a shareholder who can show that a material violation of the proxy rules has caused injury to him may ***recover damages*** or obtain other relief.

B. Materiality: It is not the case that every falsehood or omission in a proxy statement, no matter how trivial, gives rise to a private right of action on the part of each shareholder. A key requirement is that the falsehood or omission be shown to have been ***material***.

1. **Definition of "material":** The Supreme Court has defined "material" in a way that gives this requirement some real bite. "[A]n omitted fact is material if there is a ***substantial likelihood*** that a ***reasonable shareholder*** would ***consider it important*** in deciding how to vote." ***TSC Industries, Inc. v. Northway, Inc.***, 426 U.S. 438 (1976). By this standard, the plaintiff must show a "substantial likelihood that, under all the circumstances, the omitted fact would have assumed ***actual significance*** in the deliberations of the reasonable shareholder." *Id.* To put it still another way, "there must be a substantial likelihood that the disclosure of the omitted fact would have been viewed by the reasonable investor as having ***significantly altered the 'total mix' of information*** made available." *Id.*

2. **Middle ground:** Thus the Supreme Court in *TSC* steered a middle ground between hard-to-satisfy and easy-to-satisfy standards for demonstrating that the falsehood or omission was material:

   a. **Not easy standard:** It rejected the lower court's standard that material facts include "a fact which a reasonable shareholder ***might*** consider important." The Supreme Court believed that this "might" standard was "too suggestive of mere possibility, however unlikely."

   b. **Rejects most difficult standard:** But at the same time, the Supreme Court declined to hold that the plaintiff must show a probability that disclosure of the omitted fact ***"would"*** have caused a reasonable investor to change his vote. Even if the court concludes that few if any investors would have voted differently had the omitted fact been present, the court will find the omission "material" so long as a reasonable shareholder would have ***considered the information important*** in making his decision on how to vote.

3. **Objective standard:** Observe that the Court's standard for materiality is totally ***objective***: Even if the actual plaintiff was a very skittish or cynical person — who in fact voted to approve a merger but would have changed his vote based upon even a tiny bit of additional information showing the merger was less favorable than it appeared — this will be irrelevant; the test is always what a hypothetical ***"reasonable investor"*** would be likely to do.

4. **Statement of reasons for board action:** Suppose proxy materials contain a ***statement of the reasons*** for which the board is recommending that the corporation or the shareholders take a certain action. If plaintiff shows that this statement of reasons is itself false or misleading, has she made out the requisite "material" falsehood or omission? The answer seems to be two-fold:

[1] A false statement ***can be "material"*** even though it is couched as a statement of reasons rather than as a statement of facts.

[2] *However*, because the proxy rules are violated only by a statement that is "false or misleading with respect to ***any material fact***," it is not enough for P to show that the speaker ***wasn't really acting for the stated reasons*** or didn't believe them. Instead, P must show that the statement of reasons also "expressly or impliedly ***asserted something false or misleading*** about [the statement's] subject matter." "Proof of ***mere disbelief*** or belief undisclosed should not suffice for liability under § 14(a). . . ." ***Virginia Bankshares, Inc. v. Sandberg***, 501 U.S. 1083 (1991) (another aspect of which is discussed *infra*, p. 108).

a. Statement of reasons can be material: Thus in *Virginia Bankshares*, *supra*, the proxy solicitation materials issued in connection with a merger stated that the board was recommending that the public minority shareholders of the corporation approve the merger, because it would give the minority holders the opportunity to achieve a "high" and "fair" price for their stock. P claimed that the directors did not really believe that the price was high, and were instead proposing the merger (into a wholly owned subsidiary of the majority shareholder) so that the board members could keep their board seats. The directors argued that a statement of the ***reasons*** why the board was recommending the transaction could never be a statement "with respect to . . . material facts."

i. Court disagrees: But the Supreme Court ***disagreed*** with the directors' position, holding that the reasons why the board was recommending the transaction could often be (and in this case clearly *were*) the sort of information on which a shareholder might well rely in deciding how to cast her vote; therefore, the statements, although they were about reasons rather than directly about "facts," could give rise to liability.

ii. Must be express or implied misstatement of fact: However, the Supreme Court then attached a big ***caveat*** to its holding. A mere showing that the directors were not acting for the stated reason (and were acting for some other, undisclosed reason), was ***not by itself sufficient***. For instance, the fact that the directors were really motivated by a desire to save their seats, not by any belief that the price was high or fair for shareholders, would ***not*** be enough to confer liability. The Court noted that under the proxy statute, liability can only be premised on a statement "with respect to . . . material ***fact[s]***." The Court then concluded, "we . . . hold ***disbelief or undisclosed motivation***, standing alone, ***insufficient*** to satisfy the ***element of fact*** that must be established under § 14(a)." Instead, P must show "proof by . . . objective evidence . . . that the statement also ***expressly or impliedly*** asserted ***something false or misleading*** about its ***subject matter***."

(1) Satisfied: In *Virginia Bankshares*, this additional element was satisfied: P showed that the price offered was ***in fact not*** "high" or "fair," since there was solid objective evidence that the fair value of the shares was $60, in contrast to the $42 proposed in the merger. Since the statement of reasons (that the price was "fair" or "high") was not only a misleading statement of psychological fact (i.e., misleading on the subject of what was really motivating the directors), but was also an implicit ***misstatement of fact*** (the price was really not "high" or "fair"), P was able to proceed. (But if the price proposed had been fair, but the directors had merely failed to explain that their real motivation was to keep their board seats, P would *not* have been able to go forward.)

(2) P loses anyway: Despite P's victory on whether the proxy misstatements were "material," P ended up losing anyway: he was a member of a class — minority shareholders — whose consent was not legally needed for the merger, so the misstatements were found to not have "caused" any harm; see *infra*, p. 109.

5. Disclosure of management wrongdoing: In *TSC Industries* and *Virginia Bankshares*, as in many private actions brought under the proxy rules, the issue for which stockholders' proxies were sought was whether to approve a merger. In this setting, it is relatively easy to apply the "materiality" rule; the issue is whether the omitted fact would have been considered important by a reasonable shareholder in deciding to vote to approve the merger. But another class of proxy suits involves misstatements or omissions made in connection with the ***annual election of directors***, and the plaintiff's claim is that ***self-dealing*** (or other ***wrongdoing***) by officers and/or directors was not disclosed. Here, it is harder to know how to apply the "materiality" test.

a. Self-dealing: If the proxy materials fail to report accurately that officers and directors have engaged in ***self-dealing***, courts seem relatively willing to find the omission material.

b. Simple mismanagement: But if the false statement or omission relates merely to ***"simple mismanagement"*** as opposed to "self-dealing," courts are more reluctant to find that it is "material."

C. Causation: Once the plaintiff has proved that the falsehood or omission was "material," he has another major obstacle to overcome: He must show a ***causal link*** between the misleading proxy materials and some damage to shareholders.

1. *Mills* case: But here, the Supreme Court has ***eased*** the plaintiff's burden substantially. In ***Mills v. Electric Auto-Lite Co.***, 396 U.S. 375 (1970), the Court held that the shareholder does not have to prove that the falsehood or omission itself "caused" the damage to shareholders. Instead, "a shareholder has made a sufficient showing of causal relationship between the violation and the injury for which he seeks redress, if, as here, he proves that the ***proxy solicitation itself, rather than the particular defect in the solicitation materials***, was an ***essential link*** in the accomplishment of the transaction." How this dramatically eases the plaintiff's burden of proving causation is illustrated by the facts of *Mills* itself.

a. Facts: In *Mills*, Plaintiffs were shareholders of Electric Auto-Lite Co. ("Auto-Lite"). Mergenthaler Linotype Co. already owned over fifty percent of the stock of Auto-Lite, was in control of Auto-Lite's day-to-day affairs, and had named all eleven of Auto-Lite's directors. Auto-Lite shareholders were sent proxy materials asking for their approval of a merger of Auto-Lite into Mergenthaler. The materials stated that the board of Auto-Lite had approved the merger, but did not disclose that these directors were all Mergenthaler nominees (so that they would, arguably, approve a transaction desired by Mergenthaler even if it wasn't in the best interest of Auto-Lite's non-Mergenthaler shareholders). Even though Mergenthaler owned a majority of Auto-Lite stock, state merger rules required approval of Auto-Lite's minority shareholders.

b. **Holding:** Mergenthaler argued that the Ps should have to show that this omission "caused" injury to them, i.e., to show that had the omitted information been supplied, enough minority shareholders would have changed their votes that the merger would not have gone through. But the Supreme Court rejected this approach to causation, reasoning that such an approach would involve the "impracticalities of determining how many votes were affected. . . ." Instead, the Ps merely had to show that the merger ***could not have been carried out without the submission of proxy materials to the minority shareholders***; once this was shown (and the materiality of the falsehoods also shown), the requisite causal link would be deemed established.

c. **Remedies:** The Supreme Court's conclusion that the Ps in *Mills* had established a violation of the proxy rules did not automatically entitle them to relief. By the time the case got to the Supreme Court, the merger had already gone through (the Ps had been unwilling or unable to post a bond to obtain a temporary restraining order against the merger). Therefore, the only possible remedies were money damages or an undoing of the merger. The Court remanded for further proceedings on the damage issue. The trial court awarded damages to the Ps, but the Seventh Circuit reversed this award, because it concluded that the merger terms were fair to the Ps, so that they should receive nothing. The damages aspect of the *Mills* case is discussed further *infra*, p. 110.

2. **Reliance and standing:** Suppose P himself ***refused*** to give management his proxy. When P sues for violation of the proxy rules, the defendant corporation is likely to argue that P has no standing because he was not injured — he was not deceived into giving his consent (since he didn't consent at all). Nearly all courts reject this argument, and ***allow even a plaintiff who did not grant a proxy to sue***. This seems clearly the better reasoning: Even if P did not give a proxy, he may still have been injured by the fact that ***other shareholders*** were ***duped*** into giving a proxy, and into approving the proposed merger or election.

3. **Majority shareholder could approve transaction by himself:** A similar issue is presented when a corporation has a ***majority shareholder*** who controls so much stock that he could effect the proposed action (e.g., election of the board or approval of a merger) ***by himself***, without any minority votes at all. If the majority shareholder was not deceived (e.g., because he was the source of the misrepresentation and the proxy statement, or at least knew the true facts), may the minority shareholders still sue? The Supreme Court has answered ***"no"*** to this question — if the plaintiff is a member of a minority class whose votes were ***not necessary*** for the proposed transaction to go through, the plaintiff ***may not recover*** no matter how material or how intentional the deception in the proxy statement was, because the deception did not "cause" the transaction to go through. ***Virginia Bankshares, Inc. v. Sandberg***, 501 U.S. 1083 (1991).

a. **Facts:** In *Virginia Bankshares*, First American Bankshares, Inc. (FABI), a bank holding company, owned 85% of the shares of First American Bank of Virginia (Bank). FABI wanted to get rid of the 15% public shareholders in Bank. Therefore, the boards of FABI and Bank entered into a merger agreement, whereby Bank would be merged into a wholly owned subsidiary of FABI. FABI (not Bank) hired an investment banking firm to give an opinion on the appropriate price for the minority shares; the investment banker recommended a price of $42. Bank's board agreed to the merger at that $42 price. Bank's minority shareholders were sent a proxy solicitation, in which Bank's directors urged that the merger be approved. In the solicitation, the directors stated that they had approved the merger plan because it would give the minority shareholders the opportunity to achieve a "high" value, and a "fair price," for their stock.

- **i. Not necessary:** The entire proxy solicitation was not necessary under state or federal law — Bank could have used a much less extensive "statement of information" to shareholders. But Bank decided to use a proxy solicitation for reasons that are unclear, but that probably included a desire to maintain the goodwill of the minority shareholders by convincing them that they were receiving a fair price. (Under Virginia law, the 85% of Bank's shares held by FABI would, if voted in favor of the merger, have been enough to cause the merger to go through, even if the 15% held by the public had been entirely voted against the merger.)
- **ii. Minority approves:** Most minority shareholders gave the requested proxies, which were in effect approvals of the transaction. P was a minority shareholder who did not give the requested approval. The merger went through, and P brought a private damage action for violation of the proxy rules; she asserted that her shares were worth at least $60, not the $42 which she and the other minority holders received. A jury found on behalf of P at trial on all issues.

b. Court rejects liability: But the Supreme Court, by a 5-4 vote, ***overturned the verdict***. The Court held that ***no private recovery for proxy misstatements was available*** to "a member of a class of minority shareholders whose ***votes are not required by law*** or corporate bylaw to authorize the transaction giving rise to the claim."

- **i. Board's reasons irrelevant:** It did not make any difference that the proxy solicitation was motivated by the corporation's desire to avoid bad shareholder or public relations. Nor did it matter that the corporation or its board may, by seeking disinterested-shareholder ratification, have been trying to "immunize" the transaction against later conflict-of-interest attack. (One of Bank's directors was also a director of FABI, and Bank's board approval of the transaction might therefore have been attacked by Bank's minority shareholders on the grounds of director conflict-of-interest, an attack which ratification by disinterested shareholders foreclosed. See generally *infra*, p. 208.)
- **ii. Rationale:** Allowing members of a minority shareholder class to recover for misstatements when their vote of approval was not even necessary would give rise to "speculative claims and procedural intractability" — the litigation would get lost in a welter of speculation about why and how badly the board wanted the legally-unnecessary minority-shareholder approval, an issue on which "reliable evidence would seldom exist." Congress could not have intended such a result, the majority held.

c. **Dissent:** The four dissenting Justices would have allowed recovery as long as the solicitation of proxies was an ***"essential link"*** in the transaction (here, the freeze-out merger). Since Bank's board decided that minority shareholder approval should be sought, this was by itself enough to make the solicitation an essential link, the dissenters said.

D. **Standard of fault:** The plaintiff contemplating a private action for proxy violations has a number of possible defendants to sue: the corporation itself, its officers, its directors, and its outside professionals who helped to prepare the materials (e.g., the corporation's lawyers and accountants). In a given situation, some of these individuals will have been much more closely involved with the preparation of materials than others, and are thus much more likely to have actually known of the falsehoods, or at least to have been in a position where they should have known of them. Therefore, the question arises, What is the ***standard of fault*** which must be shown before a given defendant will be held liable in a private suit for proxy violation? Perhaps surprisingly, this is an issue on which the Supreme Court has never spoken.

1. **"Scienter" not required for insiders:** At least where the defendant is an "insider" (e.g., the corporation itself, its officers and its inside directors), nearly all courts seem to hold that ***mere negligence*** on the part of the defendant is ***sufficient***. That is, ***"scienter"*** (knowledge that the statement is false, or reckless disregard of whether the statement is true or false) is ***not*** required.

2. **Outside directors and other outsiders:** Some courts have also found ***outside directors*** and other outsiders liable based on a mere showing of negligence. If such decisions become common, the outside directors of large publicly held corporations (each of which prepares voluminous proxy materials annually) will face a huge burden: Every director will have to read every word of every proxy statement or related material, in order to avoid being held negligent if there is a misstatement. See S,S,B&W, p. 889.

E. **Remedies:** Suppose that the plaintiff does overcome the hurdles of proving a falsehood or omission in proxy materials, materiality, and causation; what ***remedies*** is he then entitled to? The Supreme Court in *Mills*, *supra*, p. 107, discussed the possibilities (though it did not state what form of relief would be appropriate in that case). Depending on the situation, the three major possibilities are as follows:

1. **Injunction:** First, if the proxy solicitation was for approval of a proposed ***transaction***, the court may grant an ***injunction*** preventing the transaction from going forward. For instance, in *Mills* itself, the trial court might have granted plaintiffs an injunction against the consummation of the proposed merger of Auto-Lite into Mergenthaler, until revised proxy materials (including full disclosure) were submitted to shareholders and they re-approved the merger. (But by the time the Supreme Court heard the *Mills* case, decided in favor of plaintiff and remanded to the trial court, this injunction remedy was no longer available, since the merger had been already carried out.)

2. **Setting aside of transaction:** Second, the court may ***set aside*** a transaction that has ***already been carried out***. For instance, it might even order a merger to be undone. However, it will only do this if it concludes, from all the circumstances, that doing this would be fair and in the best interests of all shareholders. It is not surprising that the district court in *Mills*, on remand, declined to do this, since unscrambling a seven-year-old transaction

would have been prohibitively expensive and not necessarily advantageous to the shareholders. Indeed, it is probably only in a quite rare case (and one in which the transaction has only recently been completed) that the court will order the transaction to be undone.

3. **Damages:** Finally, the court may order that ***damages*** be paid to the plaintiff and other shareholders. However, plaintiff bears the burden of proving that actual ***monetary injury*** occurred before he can recover money damages.

   a. **Merger:** In the case of a proposed ***merger***, the plaintiff would, to recover money damages, have to show that the merger reduced the actual or potential earnings or value of his investment. For instance, P in *Mills* might have been able to show that at the time of the proxy solicitation the market valued each share of Auto-Lite at $10, but that shareholders received shares in Mergenthaler following the merger worth only $8. (In fact, the 7th Circuit reversed a monetary award for the Ps in *Mills*, after concluding that the original merger price was fair.)

   b. **Damages for action by board:** It will be even harder for plaintiff to recover money damages where his claim is that proxy materials submitted in connection with the ***election*** of the ***board of directors*** were false. For instance, P might claim that one or more board members had engaged in self-dealing, and that this self dealing was improperly omitted from the proxy materials for the election at which the board member(s) was a candidate. The plaintiff could in theory argue that if the improperly-elected board then took actions which lowered the value of his shares, the false proxy materials (and consequent election) "caused" the injury, since had the board not been elected it would not have taken these actions. But courts generally reject damage claims such as this, on the theory that there is no ***"proximate*** causation" — the link between the falsehood in the proxy materials and the board's conduct is insufficiently close. See C&E, p. 360-61.

   c. **Attorneys' fees:** If the plaintiff establishes that there was a proxy violation but is unable to establish monetary damages, he may still be entitled to ***attorneys' fees***. For instance, the attorneys in *Mills* were awarded fees for their work up to the Supreme Court decision.

V. COMMUNICATIONS BY SHAREHOLDERS

A. **Two methods:** So far, we have spoken only about the means by which the company (i.e., ***management***) may communicate with shareholders to solicit their proxies. But the SEC's proxy rules also furnish two elaborate procedures whereby a ***shareholder*** may communicate with her fellow shareholders, to solicit their proxies in favor of her own proposal or against a proposal of management.

   1. **Shareholder bears cost:** First, if the shareholder is willing to ***bear the costs*** of printing and postage, SEC Rule 14a-7 requires the company to either mail the shareholder's solicitation or give the shareholder a stockholder list so that the shareholder can do the mailing.

   2. **Company bears cost:** Second, in a narrower set of circumstances, Rule 14a-8 requires ***management*** to include a shareholder's proposal in management's own proxy materials, at the corporation's expense.

B. Shareholder bears expense (Rule 14a-7): If the shareholder wishes to communicate with his fellow shareholders and is willing to ***bear the expense*** of doing so (mainly printing and postage), Rule 14a-7 gives him a broadly-applicable ability to do so. This has been called the ***"mail their stuff or give them a list"*** rule. Clark, p. 370. This phrase is quite descriptive of what the rule does: If the rule applies, management must either mail the shareholder's materials to the other stockholders or give the soliciting shareholder a list of shareholders so that he can do the mailing directly.

> **Example 1:** Management of X Corp. announces that it will be soliciting proxies for approval of a merger into Y Corp. Shareholder, who opposes the merger and wants to persuade his fellow shareholders to deny management their proxies on this issue, may use Rule 14a-7 to help him do this. He may force management to choose between either: (1) mailing to all shareholders the opposing proxy materials that he has had pre-printed; or (2) giving him the shareholder list, so that he can mail these materials himself.

> **Example 2:** Management will soon be mailing its materials to solicit proxies to elect the board of directors at the next annual meeting. Shareholder wants to solicit proxies for his own anti-management slate of directors (i.e., he wants to wage a "proxy contest"). Again, Shareholder may use Rule 14a-7 to force management to either mail Shareholder's proxy materials, or to furnish him with a list of shareholders so that he may do the mailing himself.

1. **Requirements for rule:** To gain the assistance of Rule 14a-7, the soliciting shareholder must meet only a few simple requirements: (1) his proxy materials must relate to a meeting in which the company will be making its own solicitation (so that a dissident shareholder can't use this rule to require his communications to be mailed when no meeting has been called); (2) the stockholder must be ***entitled to vote*** on the matter; and (3) the shareholder must ***defray the expenses*** that the corporation will incur in mailing the materials (mainly postage and printing costs).

2. **No length limits or censorship:** If the shareholder meets these requirements, his materials are not subject to any ***length*** limit. (This is in contrast to Rule 14a-8's provision for including shareholders' proposals in *management's* solicitation, under which the entire text is limited to five hundred words.) Also, under 14a-7 management has basically no grounds for ***censorship*** or objection (whereas it has many arguments for exclusion under 14a-8's scheme).

3. **Choice by management:** As noted, management has a choice: It can furnish the list of shareholders to the soliciting shareholder, or it can itself do the mailing on behalf of the shareholder. Management is generally reluctant to surrender its shareholder list (the list might be used for other purposes, such as a later hostile takeover attempt), so it almost always elects to do the mailing itself.

4. **Timing:** To prevent management from unfairly ***delaying*** the mailing, the rule requires that materials be mailed "with ***reasonable promptness.***" However, in the usual case where the mailing relates to an annual meeting, management may put itself on an equal footing with the soliciting shareholder by delaying the mailing until the ***earlier of***: (1) a day corresponding to the first date on which management's proxy materials were mailed in connec-

tion with the ***last*** annual meeting; or (2) the first day on which management makes its solicitation this year.

a. **Rationale:** Date (1) above prevents management from delaying both its own and the shareholder's mailings until so close before the meeting that the shareholder has no opportunity to formulate a reply or drum up support. Thus if management mailed its 2008 materials 60 days before the 2008 annual meeting, it must mail the shareholder's 2009 materials at least 60 days before the 2009 meeting, even if management's own materials won't be going out until a later time. See Clark, p. 371.

C. **Corporation bears expense (Rule 14a-8):** A shareholder who prepares his own proxy materials and uses Rule 14a-7 will bear very substantial expenses. Therefore, that section tends to be used only where the soliciting shareholder has a very large financial stake in the corporation and the matter is of direct and large economic importance (as in the two examples given on p. 112, *supra*). By contrast, Rule 14a-8's ***"shareholder proposal"*** rule costs the proposing shareholder almost nothing, and is therefore today mainly used by persons with small stockholdings who seek to influence the corporation's policies concerning matters of great ***social*** or ***political*** interest. Doing business with South Africa, developing anti-personnel bombs for use in Vietnam, practicing alleged cruelty to animals — these are illustrative of the kinds of policies that shareholders have attacked in the last few decades by use of the 14a-8 shareholder proposal rule.

1. **Included in management's proxy materials:** What makes Rule 14a-8 so attractive to activist groups is that where it applies, the shareholder's proposal must be included in ***management's own proxy materials***. The submitting shareholder bears essentially no expense — he does not have to print up materials, or pay the postage for mailing them. The only real cost is the cost of sending a letter to management submitting the proposal.

2. **Eligibility:** For a shareholder-initiated proposal to be covered by Rule 14a-8, the shareholder must: (1) own either at least 1% or $2,000 in market value of securities in the company; and (2) have held the shares for ***at least one year*** prior to the submission. 14a-8(b)(1). Therefore, it is not possible for, say, an activist group to buy a couple of shares just before submitting its proposal.

3. **Initiated by shareholder:** The shareholder's proposal ***does not have to have anything to do*** with any matter that management plans to raise at the meeting. For instance, if management plans to do nothing more at the annual meeting than to elect directors, a shareholder may nonetheless use Rule 14a-8 to put to a vote his proposal concerning, say, the corporation's doing of business in China.

4. **Length of proposal:** A shareholder may submit only ***one*** proposal for inclusion in management's proxy materials. The proposal and its supporting statement may not together exceed ***five hundred words***.

5. **Exclusions:** To limit shareholders' proposals to ones that are reasonably relevant to the voting and meeting process, Rule 14a-8(i) lists thirteen ***exclusions***, under which management may refuse to include the proposal. We will summarily list each of the thirteen, and then give special attention to the several that are most frequently applicable.

   a. **Relating to proposal itself:** Eight of the exclusions relate to the proposal itself:

i. **(i)(1):** The proposal is ***not a proper subject*** for action by stockholders under ***state law***;

ii. **(i)(2):** The proposal would result in a violation of ***state, federal or foreign*** law;

iii. **(i)(5):** The proposal is ***not significantly related*** to the company's business;

iv. **(i)(6):** The proposal is ***beyond the company's power to implement***;

v. **(i)(7):** The proposal relates to the company's ***"ordinary business operations"***;

vi. **(i)(8):** The proposal relates to a ***nomination or election*** of a candidate to the ***board*** of directors, or to a ***procedure*** for such nomination;

vii. **(i)(10):** The proposal is ***moot*** because the company has already substantially ***implemented*** it; and

viii. **(i)(13):** The proposal relates to specific amounts of ***dividends***.

b. **Abuse of process:** The other five reasons for exclusion are an attempt to prevent ***abuse*** of the shareholder proposal ***process***:

i. **(i)(3):** The proposal or supporting statement violates the ***proxy rules*** (including 14a-9's ban on "false or misleading" statements in proxy materials);

ii. **(i)(4):** The proposal relates to a ***personal claim or grievance***, or is designed to further a personal interest not shared with other stockholders;

iii. **(i)(9):** The proposal is ***counter*** to a proposal to be submitted by the company (so that, say, a holder's statement of opposition to a merger plan being advocated by management could be excluded);

iv. **(i)(11):** The proposal ***duplicates*** a proposal of another shareholder for inclusion in the same proxy materials; and

v. **(i)(12):** The proposal deals with ***substantially the same subject matter*** as a ***prior*** shareholder proposal made at a recent prior meeting, unless the earlier proposal received a sufficiently large vote (e.g., at least 3% if submitted only once during the prior five years, at least 6% at the second of two prior submissions during the five prior years, etc.).

c. **Improper under state law:** Subsection (i)(1) allows management to exclude the proposal if "under the laws of the registrant's domicile, [the proposal is] ***not a proper subject for action by security holders***." Since most state corporation statutes entrust the running of the corporation to the board of directors (*supra*, p. 50), and give authority to the shareholders only as to certain specified matters (generally, the election of directors and fundamental structural changes), this exclusion rules out a large portion of possible proposals.

i. **Proposals that an order be given:** Thus a shareholder proposal to the effect that management be ***ordered*** or compelled to do something will always be excludable under (i)(1) if the thing proposed is something that shareholders do not have the right to vote on under the law of the state where the corporation is incorporated. For instance, if, as in most states, shareholders may not propose a merger, but may merely approve a merger proposed by management, a proposal "that the corporation accept the merger offer recently made by XYZ Corp." would be excludable.

ii. Interference with board's power to exercise fiduciary duties: Similarly, if the shareholder proposal orders the board to behave in a way that would ***violate substantive state law***, that proposal, too, will be excludable. That's because 14a-8(i)(2) lets management exclude the proposal "if the proposal would, if implemented, ***cause the company to violate any state ... law*** to which it is subject." For instance, since most states do not allow the board of directors to ***abdicate their fiduciary responsibilities***, a proposed bylaw that would have the effect of stripping the board of its power to do what it thinks best for all stockholders in a particular case can be excluded, because the bylaw would, if enacted, violate the "no abdication by the board" rule.

Example: AFSCME (a union-affiliated pension plan and investor) attempts to force CA, Inc., a Delaware-chartered public company, to include in its proxy materials AFSCME's proposed bylaw amendment, which if enacted would require the company to reimburse in all cases the reasonable expenses of any shareholder who runs and funds a successful proxy contest (see *infra*, p. 120) to elect one or more non-management-sponsored directors. CA asks the SEC to rule that the proposal is excludable because it would violate Delaware law. The SEC in turn asks the Delaware Supreme Court to say whether the bylaw, if enacted, would violate Delaware law.

Held (by the Delaware Supreme Court), for management. Enactment of this bylaw ***would not be proper*** under Delaware law. "It is well-established Delaware law that a proper function of bylaws is ***not*** to mandate how the board should decide ***specific substantive business decisions***, but rather, to define the ***process and procedures*** by which those decisions are made." If AFSCME's proposed bylaw were enacted, that bylaw might require CA's board to reimburse a shareholder group when such reimbursement would be a ***violation of the board's fiduciary duties*** to all stockholders. For instance, such a violation would occur "if a shareholder group affiliated with a ***competitor*** of the company were to cause the election of a minority slate of candidates committing to using their director positions to obtain, and then communicate, valuable proprietary strategic or product information to the competitor." ***CA, Inc. v. AFSCME Employees Pension Plan***, 953 A.2d 227 (Del. 2008).

iii. Recommendations: However, most states permit shareholders to make ***non-binding recommendations*** or ***requests***. Therefore, (i)(1) and (i)(2) do not exclude proposals that are framed as requests, i.e., so-called ***"precatory"*** proposals.

Example: Under the laws of nearly every state, shareholders would not be permitted to vote on whether the corporation should do business in Country X. Therefore, a shareholder proposal reading, "Resolved, that the Corporation cease doing business in Country X" would be excludable under (i)(1). Similarly, a proposed bylaw amendment ("Resolved, that the Corporation's bylaws be amended to prohibit the Corporation from doing business in Country X") would likely be excludable under (i)(2), at least under Delaware law, since it takes away the board's power to make substantive business decisions, in likely violation of state law restricting bylaws to procedural issues (as in *CA, Inc.*, *supra*).

But a proposal phrased as a ***request*** would not be excluded. Thus the proposal might be phrased as "Resolved, that the shareholders of Corporation request the board of directors to consider whether the Corporation should cease doing business in Country X." See Clark, p. 373.

d. Not significantly related to corporation's business: (i)(5) excludes proposals that are ***not significantly related to the company's business***. The actual text of (i)(5) gives a partly mathematical definition: The proposal is excludable if it "relates to operations which account for less than 5% of the company's total assets at the end of its most recent fiscal year, and for less than 5% of its net earnings and gross sales for its most recent fiscal year, and is not otherwise significantly related to the company's business."

i. Explanation: The 5% tests seem to be the exclusive tests for those proposals which relate solely to economic issues. Thus if the proposal calls for the corporation's Widget division to be divested because it has a poor return on equity or because the cash could be better invested elsewhere, the proposal is automatically excluded under (i)(5) if the Widget division accounts for less than 5% of the company's assets, earnings, and sales.

ii. Ethical issues: But if the reason advanced for the proposal relates to ***non-economic*** issues, apparently failure to meet the 5% test is ***not conclusive***; this is the meaning of the phrase "and is not otherwise significantly related to the [company's] business. . . ." Thus if the proposal is significant because of the ***social*** or ***ethical*** issues that it raises, and these issues are ***related to the corporation's business***, the proposal will not be excludable automatically merely because it doesn't satisfy the 5% tests.

Example: D Corp. has annual revenues of $141 million, with $6 million in annual profits and $78 million in assets. P, a shareholder, submits a proposal urging the board of directors to consider whether the method used by French farmers to force feed geese for the production of pate de foie gras (a product imported by D) causes the geese undue pain and suffering, and if so, whether further importation of the product should be suspended until more humane methods become available. D's sales of pate are $79,000 annually, it has only $34,000 in assets relating to pate, and it loses money on its sales. Thus none of the 5% tests comes close to being satisfied. However, P argues that because of the large ethical and social issues raised by the force feeding of geese to produce pate, his proposal is "otherwise significantly related" to D's business even though it does not satisfy the 5% tests.

Held, for P. The meaning of "otherwise significantly related" is not limited to economic significance. Since P's proposal raises substantial ethical and social issues, and these issues are tied to significant business activity by D (even though that activity relates to less than 5% of sales, assets and profits), D must include P's proposal in its proxy materials. *Lovenheim v. Iroquois Brands Ltd.*, 618 F.Supp. 554 (D.D.C. 1985).

e. **Relates to routine matters:** (i)(7) allows the shareholder proposal to be excluded if it relates to conduct of the ***"ordinary business operations"*** of the company. In other words, if the matter in question, is ***"too routine,"*** it may be excluded on that basis. In a sense, this is the opposite of the ground for exclusion considered just previously ("not . . . significantly related to the [company's] business"). This exception covers some of the same ground as the (i)(1) exception for matters that are not a proper subject for shareholder action under state law — in nearly all states, details of day-to-day operations are to be decided solely by the board and management, not by shareholders. For instance, a proposal recommending that the corporation curtail its research and development spending, or one recommending that the corporation launch more (or fewer) new products, would be excludable.

   i. **Major social, ethical or economic issue:** If the proposal raises a major social, ethical, political or economic issue, the "ordinary business operations" exclusion does not apply, even though the matter might otherwise seem to fall within the corporation's routine business. See *infra*, p. 119.

   ii. **Executive compensation:** The SEC holds that proposals concerning ***senior executive compensation*** are ***not*** matters relating to the "ordinary business operations" of the company, and that shareholder proposals on this topic ***may not be excluded under (i)(7).*** Thus a shareholder proposal that the corporation not make ***"golden parachute"*** payments (payments contingent on a merger or acquisition), a proposal that the board set up a Compensation Committee consisting of independent directors to establish executive compensation, and presumably any other proposal whose thrust is to complain that the corporation is ***paying its senior executives too much money***, are all includible. See, e.g., Feb. 13, 1992 Statement of SEC Chairman Richard Breedon.

f. **Election of directors:** (i)(8) allows exclusion of proposals relating to the ***election of specific individuals*** to the company's board of directors. For instance, (i)(8)(iv) lets the company exclude a proposal that "[s]eeks to ***include a specific individual*** in the company's proxy materials for ***election to the board of directors***[.]"

   i. **Main significance:** The main significance of this exclusion is that a proposal seeking to elect a ***particular slate*** of directors favored by the proposer, or opposing management's slate of directors, ***may not be done through the free "include shareholder's proposal in management's materials" method*** of Rule 14a-8. Instead, a person wishing to solicit proxies for his own slate of board nominees, or to oppose management's slate, must conduct a regular ***"proxy contest,"*** in which he ***bears the cost of mailing his own materials*** under Rule 14a-7 (and complies with the special disclosure rules of Schedule 14B, discussed *infra*, p. 122).

      (1) **SEC adds a new rule to allow shareholder access:** Beginning in the early 2000s, the SEC wanted to at least partially reverse the above ban, so that minority shareholders could sometimes use the company's proxy materials to nominate their own competing slate of directors. Then, in 2010, as part of the Dodd-Frank financial-industry reform statute, Congress gave the SEC explicit authority to do this (though the Commission probably already had that authority). The SEC promptly responded by enacting a new proxy Rule, 14a-11. The

new rule allowed anyone who had owned for the past three years (and still owned) ***more than 3% of a company's shares*** to nominate a slate for up to 25% of the company's board, and to require that the nominating materials be ***included in the company's own proxy materials.***

(2) Big companies oppose: But most public companies hated the idea that every 3% dissident holder would now have an easy and cheap way to nominate a slate of directors to challenge management's nominees. As the president of the Business Roundtable (a group of large public companies) put it shortly after the SEC enacted the new Rule 14a-11, "This is an unprecedented preemption of state corporate law — the bedrock of corporate governance — that will ***turn the boards*** of more than 15,000 publicly-traded companies ***into political bodies and threaten their ability to function.***" Quoted at O&T (6th), p. 251.

(3) Court rejects this rule: The Business Roundtable and the U.S. Chamber of Commerce then sued to overturn the new Rule 14a-11. The U.S. Court of Appeals for the District of Columbia held for the plaintiffs, and ***struck down*** the new Rule 14a-11 as having been improperly adopted. The court found that the SEC had "acted ***arbitrarily and capriciously*** [by] fail[ing] ... adequately to assess the economic effects of [the] new rule." ***Business Roundtable v. S.E.C.***, 647 F.3d 1144 (D.C. Cir. 2011).

(4) SEC gives up: Since that loss, the SEC has ***abandoned*** its efforts to give shareholders this right of proxy access for nominations of rival slates. So it remains the case as of this writing (April, 2013) that in the ordinary situation, no shareholder may require a company to put the shareholder's proposed board nominations into the company's own proxy materials.

ii. Proposal to change election rules: What if a shareholder wants to use the free include-shareholders'-materials mechanism not to try to get a *particular* slate of directors elected or defeated, but instead to ***change the company's bylaws*** so as to ***change the procedures*** for how board elections *generally* work? As the result of an important 2011 change to 14a-(i)(8) by the SEC, the answer is that the shareholder ***may*** use the free mechanism for this change-the-procedures purpose.

(1) Right to propose bylaw amendment: In 2011, shortly after the SEC lost the *Business Roundtable* case, *supra*, the Commission changed Rule 14a-8's language. The effect of the change is to remove anything in 14a-8 that might have been interpreted to prevent shareholders from proposing such a general change to a company's bylaws on how elections are to be run. This modification gives dissident stockholders a chance, one corporation at a time, to reverse the result of *Business Roundtable* (and thereby eventually to force management to include nominations of rival slates in management's proxy materials).

Example: Holder is a minority (and dissident) shareholder in Corp, a public company. Holder submits the following proposal to Corp, and demands that it be included within management's proxy materials for the next annual meeting: "Resolved, that Corp's bylaws be changed so that (1) any shareholder owning more than 1% of the company's shares shall be entitled to propose a slate of up to 4 directors as nominees to Corp's Board of Directors; and (2) such a proposed slate shall be included in management's proxy materials at no cost to the proposing shareholder."

Under present (post-2011) Rule 14a-8(i)(8), nothing makes this proposed change to the bylaws excludable by Corp. Therefore, Corp will ***have to include the proposal*** in its next set of proxy materials. Then, if a majority of the shareholders votes in favor of the proposal, Corp's bylaws will be amended so that the general "no shareholder nominations may be included in management's proxy materials" rule of 14a-8(i) is reversed as to Corp. Thereafter, any holder with 1% of Corp's stock will have the ability, at minimal cost, to force Corp's management to include that holder's rival slate of up to 4 directors as part of management's proxy materials. Cf. K,R&B (8th), p. 553.

(2) **Delaware now allows:** By the way, the statutory law of Delaware has been changed to specifically ***allow*** such an effort by shareholders to change the company's bylaws to make shareholder slates includable in management's proxy materials. § 112 of the Delaware GCL, enacted in 2009, says that a Delaware company's bylaws "may provide that if the corporation solicits proxies with respect to an election of directors, it may be ***required ... to include in its proxy solicitation materials*** ... one or more ***individuals nominated by a stockholder.***" Since Delaware state law has always generally allowed stockholders to amend the corporation's bylaws as long as the amendment does not interfere with the board's own responsibilities to manage the business,[1] § 112 means that a shareholder proposal to amend the bylaws so as to shift the company to this type of "voluntary proxy access regime" for director elections is now also proper. A,K&S (4th), p. 201.

6. **Social/political/ethical problems:** Now let's consider shareholder proposals that take a position on major ***ethical/social/political*** issues that have some tangible link to the corporation's affairs — can management exclude these? Even with all of the grounds for exclusion, the courts and the SEC have tended to ***require the inclusion*** of such proposals, as long as they take the form of a recommendation to the board, rather than an order. For instance, the SEC has required the following proposals to be included:

- ❑ a proposal recommending that Motorola cease business activities in South Africa, even though the company did only a minor volume of business in that country;
- ❑ a proposal recommending that Citicorp disclose political contributions made by its executives;
- ❑ a proposal recommending that Eastman Kodak report to shareholders on contracts to develop weapons for the "Star Wars" program; and
- ❑ a proposal recommending that Phillip Morris get out of the tobacco business.

See S,S,B&W, p. 630.

---

1. For an explanation of this limitation, see *CA, Inc. v. AFSCME Employees Pension Plan, supra,* p. 115.

VI. PROXY CONTESTS

A. What a proxy contest is: A ***"proxy contest"*** is, in the broadest sense, any competition between two competing factions (generally management and outside ***"insurgents"***) to obtain shareholder votes on a proposal. The contest is much like a political campaign: Each side typically takes out newspaper advertising, does direct mailing (of proxy materials), makes personal phone calls to important "voters" (i.e., large stockholders), and does anything else in its legal power to gain more votes than the other side.

1. Election of directors: Most proxy contests involve the ***election of directors***, and are thus direct contests for control.

> **Example:** Bumbling Corp. has a solid basic business, but is generally regarded by Wall Street as poorly and sleepily run, so its profits are less than they could be under a more aggressive management. Tycoon, who has made a huge fortune in the real estate business, decides that he could run Bumbling better than its current management. A few months prior to the scheduled annual shareholders' meeting, Tycoon nominates an insurgent slate of directors (including himself and his close associates) for each seat on the board. Management counters with its own slate, consisting mostly of existing board members running for re-election.
>
> This is a "proxy contest." Each side will now submit its own proxy materials to every shareholder; these materials will contain facts about that side's nominees and arguments why the shareholders should vote for that side. Both sides would also typically take out newspaper advertising disparaging the other's slate, and do massive telephone electioneering of large (usually institutional) stockholders.
>
> If management wins (i.e., its candidates get more votes than Tycoon's) the pro-management slate is re-elected, and perhaps business goes on much as before. If Tycoon's slate wins, the newly-constituted board will probably dismiss the old management, appoint new executives backed by Tycoon (perhaps making Tycoon himself CEO), and may well then sell the corporation's assets or otherwise dramatically restructure.

2. Non-director fights: About one-third of proxy fights do not involve the election of directors. Instead, they are contests over some ***proposal*** by management or by a shareholder-insurgent. Usually, the proposal relates to a corporate takeover or restructuring. For instance, management may be proposing anti-takeover defenses (e.g., a "poison pill," see *infra*, p. 452), which the insurgents are opposing because they want to conduct or at least benefit from a takeover. Conversely, an insurgent may have proposed that the board be asked to remove anti-takeover devices or to seek a buyer for the company's assets.

B. Why contests are waged: In most contests today, the insurgent faction hopes to end up in ***operating control*** of the target, whether by owning a majority of the shares or by merely obtaining a majority of the board seats. In theory, a proxy contest will usually be cheaper than a hostile takeover bid (see *infra*, p. 429), since the insurgents do not have to buy any shares. However, the outsider group is much less likely to win or achieve a profitable compromise in a proxy contest than in a takeover bid.

1. "Wall Street Rule": One reason why proxy contests usually fail is that traditionally, shareholders usually vote in favor of management. A shareholder who thinks management is doing a poor job usually ***sells his shares***, so by a natural process the shareholders on hand at the time of a proxy contest do not include very many who are dissatisfied with management. This tendency to vote-by-selling is known as the "Wall Street Rule."

2. **No benefits for loser:** Furthermore, the unsuccessful insurgent group in a proxy contest is generally left with no benefit at all from its expense, whereas the unsuccessful tender offeror usually has built up a sizable minority stake in the company which it can then sell back to the company or to a "white knight" acquirer. (See *infra*, p. 454.) S,S,B&W, p. 1177.

3. **Consequence:** For these reasons, the number of proxy contests has been flat or decreasing in recent years, whereas the number of tender offers has been increasing.

C. **Regulation of proxy contests:** Proxy contests are unlike a political election campaign in one major respect: Whereas in the political campaign each side may say pretty much whatever it wants, the proxy contest is subject to the same stringent SEC proxy solicitation rules as any other solicitation, with some extra regulations to boot.

1. **Three advantages for management:** At the start of a proxy contest, management has three key advantages: (1) as already mentioned, stockholders usually tend to vote for management; (2) management can use ***corporate funds*** to pay for its side of the contest (see *infra*, p. 123); and (3) management knows who the shareholders are (and how much each owns), whereas the insurgents will usually have to litigate to get access to the list, if they can get it at all. (This access is discussed below.) S,S,B&W, p. 1174.

2. **Insurgents' right to get information from management:** The SEC proxy rules very slightly redress this imbalance by requiring management to give the insurgents limited assistance in communicating with shareholders. SEC Rule 14a-7 requires management to tell the insurgents how many stockholders of record there are, how many beneficial owners there are (if management plans to solicit the beneficial owners through brokers and bankers) and how much it will cost to mail the insurgents' proxy materials to all holders.

3. **Access to list:** It is vital for the insurgents to obtain access to the ***list*** of shareholders. Only through direct access to this list can the insurgents engage in the follow-up electioneering that is usually indispensable (e.g., telephone calls and personal meetings with large holders). Yet the SEC rules do not in fact grant the insurgent this right; however, they may have the right under ***state law***.

a. **Proxy rules:** Recall that under SEC Rule 14a-7 (discussed extensively *supra*, p. 112), any shareholder who wants to solicit his fellow shareholders may require the corporation (i.e., management) to ***choose*** between furnishing the list of shareholders or mailing the shareholder's materials to all holders. Because of the tactical importance of direct list access, management usually chooses to mail the insurgents' materials rather than to give the insurgents access to the list. As far as the federal proxy rules go, management has the perfect right to do this, and nothing else in the rules gives the insurgents any right to inspect the shareholders list.

b. **State law:** However, recall that nearly all ***states*** give shareholders some right of inspection of corporate books and records. This right of inspection may include the right to inspect the shareholders list. Whether and when this inspection is available varies sharply from state to state. For instance, MBCA § 16.02 allows inspection of the shareholder list, but only if the inspecting shareholder makes his demand "in good faith and for a proper purpose," having described "with reasonable particularity his purpose" for inspection, and shows that the records are "directly connected" with this purpose. (A court would probably hold that the desire to wage a proxy fight is a proper purpose, to which inspection of the shareholders list is directly connected.) Similarly, Delaware GCL § 220(b) gives any shareholder the right to inspect the list so long as he has a "purpose reasonably related to [his] interest as a stockholder"; here, too, the desire to wage a proxy fight should be sufficient.

i. **Litigation required:** But even where the insurgents seem to have a state-law right to inspect, this right is of course not self-executing, and management will usually require the insurgents to ***litigate*** the issue. This gives management a valuable time advantage (since in the meantime it can be personally contacting large holders to present its own position).

ii. **Non-objecting beneficial owners:** Some state shareholder-list-access statutes have even been interpreted to allow a shareholder the right to inspect a list of the corporation's ***"non-objecting beneficial owners"*** ("NOBO list"). Recall (see *supra*, p. 101) that the beneficial owner is a person who has the real, effective economic ownership of a share that is held on the corporation's own books in "street name." Thus in *Sadler v. NCR Corp.*, 928 F.2d 48 (2d Cir. 1991), the Second Circuit held that New York law gives any shareholder of a non-New York corporation doing substantial business in New York the right to a NOBO list; in fact, if a NOBO list is required to put both sides in a proxy contest on equal footing, the corporation may be required to ***compile*** the list if it does not already have one.

D. Disclosure required: Both sides in a proxy contest must comply with the usual disclosure and anti-fraud rules of the '34 Act. Thus the insurgents must, like management, make sure that any "solicitation" (including oral solicitation) is ***preceded by a written proxy statement*** (Rule 14a-3(a)). Similarly, both insurgents and management must respect Rule 14a-9's prohibition on any ***"false or misleading" statement*** in the proxy statement or in any other communication (e.g., newspaper advertisements, telephone calls, etc.).

1. **Additional disclosure for election:** Furthermore, in the usual proxy contest involving the election of directors, the insurgent must file special information about each ***"participant"*** in the solicitation (with "participant" defined to include anyone who contributes more than $500 to the contest). For each participant connected with the insurgents' side, there must be filed a Schedule 14B disclosing the person's business background, his interest in the corporation's stock, his financial contribution to the proxy fight, and other information that would assist a shareholder in deciding whether the insurgents' slate is more worthy than management's. This information must be filed with the SEC five days ***before*** the group starts its solicitation, thus giving management an early warning that a contest is about to begin.

E. Costs: Proxy contests are costly — today, it is not unusual for each side's costs to be in the millions of dollars. Therefore, each side would like to have the corporation reimburse it for these expenses. The ability to have the corporation reimburse proxy contest expenses is governed by state law. Most states seem to apply the following rules:

1. **Management's expenses:** All courts agree that the corporation may pay for the basic "bare bones" compliance by ***management*** with federal proxy regulations. Thus the costs of drafting and printing the proxy materials, and of mailing them to shareholders, may clearly be paid by the corporation, since otherwise management would have to choose between not complying with the federal proxy rules or not obtaining a quorum for the shareholders' meeting. Nutshell, p. 294.

   a. **Other solicitation costs:** Of course, the "bare bones" costs just described are only a part (often a very small part) of the total costs on management's side of a proxy contest. Much more significant are the expenses of massive newspaper advertising, retention of proxy-solicitation specialist firms, telephone and private meetings with large holders in many cities, etc.

   b. **Corporation may pay:** Most courts hold that so long as the contest involves a conflict over ***"policy,"*** and is not merely a "personal power contest," the corporation may ***pay for management's reasonable expenses*** in "educating" the stockholders as to the correctness of management's view. Thus in most if not all states, these advertising and other "campaign" costs — even if they only disseminate information that is already in the proxy materials — may be paid for by the corporation. See, e.g., *Rosenfeld v. Fairchild Engine and Airplane Corp.*, 128 N.E.2d 291 (N.Y. 1955).

   c. **Always characterizable as "policy":** The requirement that the contest involve "policy" rather than "personal power" has very little bite: Almost any proxy contest can be (and is) characterized as one involving "policy" or "economic issues," rather than as one involving management's desire to stay in control or the insurgents' desire to seize control. Nutshell, p. 295.

2. **Expenses of successful insurgents:** Suppose the insurgents ***succeed*** and end up controlling a majority of the board of directors. The newly-appointed board will then often approve the corporation's reimbursement of the insurgents' proxy-contest expenses. Here, the courts seem to have generally ***allowed*** such reimbursements, if two requirements are satisfied: (1) the contest involved ***"policy"*** rather than being a pure power struggle (the same requirement as for management's expenses, *supra*, p. 123); and (2) the ***stockholders approve*** the reimbursement. See *Rosenfeld v. Fairchild, supra*, to this effect.

   a. **Payment for both sides:** If the successful insurgents get their expenses covered, the usual result is that ***both sides*** will end up having the corporation cover their expenses. This is because the former management, before leaving office, will have the corporation pay *its* expenses. Nutshell, p. 295.

   b. **Criticism:** Even if shareholders approve the reimbursement of the insurgents' expenses, this is not necessarily a fair or reasonable result. Often, the insurgents will hold a substantial minority of the stock. Therefore, they can get approval from a majority of overall shareholders by convincing a minority of the non-affiliated holders to vote with them. The other shareholders then end up having the corporation paying (out of their investment, in a sense) for both sides of a proxy contest that may well not have benefited these minority holders at all.

3. **Unsuccessful insurgents:** If the insurgents are ***unsuccessful***, they have virtually ***no chance*** of getting the corporation to reimburse them for their expenses. After all, they

have waged an unsuccessful war against management, so management is hardly likely to reward them.

VII. IMPROVED PUBLIC DISCLOSURE BY THE CORPORATION

A. Greater disclosure, generally: At the start of the 21st century, major financial scandals erupted at Enron, WorldCom, Adelphia Communications and other major public companies. Senior executives at these companies seemed to have been "cooking the books" for years. When the book-cooking could no longer be concealed, in many cases the company turned out to be completely worthless (e.g., Enron and Adelphia), and in all cases stockholders suffered major losses. The SEC and Congress responded with several initiatives to improve the quality of financial disclosure by public corporations.

We look briefly here at two of these major attempts to improve the disclosure obligations of public companies: ***Regulation FD*** and the ***Sarbanes-Oxley Act***.

B. Regulation FD: The SEC became convinced that professional investors (e.g., securities analysts) had an unfair advantage over amateur investors, because public companies frequently ***disclosed sensitive information to the professionals before disclosing to the public.*** This gave the professionals a chance to react to the changed information (e.g., by buying up shares in companies with good news or selling shares in companies with bad news) before the amateur public could respond. Therefore, in 2000 the SEC attempted to "level the playing field" by enacting ***Regulation FD*** (which stands for ***"Fair Disclosure"***).

1. Function of Reg. FD: Reg. FD changes the rules about selective disclosure in two ways, one dealing with intentional disclosures, and the other with unintentional ones:

- ❑ If a public company ***intends*** to release material nonpublic information to securities analysts or certain other types of outside professional investors, the company must disclose the information ***simultaneously to the public***.

- ❑ And, if the public company realizes that it has ***unintentionally*** disclosed material nonpublic information to such a professional investor, it must cure the problem by then ***"promptly"*** disclosing that information to the public.

Cf. Hamilton (8th), p. 796.

Example 1: Fred, the header of investor relations for XYZ Corp., has just learned that XYZ's sales and profits for the recently-completed quarter were better than Wall Street expects. Fred would like to be able to tell this news to his buddy, Ralph, a securities analyst who follows XYZ for Big Brokerage Co., at 10 AM, and not alert the public until noon. Under Reg. FD, Fred cannot do this — he must inform Ralph and the public simultaneously. Typically, the public would be informed by a press release or an SEC filing.

Example 2: Same basic facts as above example. This time, however, Fred makes an offhand remark to Ralph in a telephone call, "It looks like it was an unusually good quarter." He then realizes that he's given Ralph material inside information. Fred must see to it that the company "promptly" (essentially, as soon as possible) makes the same information public.

C. Sarbanes-Oxley Act: The most important fallout from the turn-of-the-century corporate scandals has been the passage of the ***Sarbanes-Oxley Act*** by Congress in 2002. Sarbanes-Oxley dramatically increases the responsibilities of people in charge of running the finances of public companies, including the CEO, the CFO (Chief Financial Officer), directors who serve on the company's audit committee, inside and outside legal counsel to the company, and the company's outside auditor. Here are some of the major responsibilities that Sarbanes-Oxley imposes:

1. **CEO/CFO certification:** Most importantly, the company's ***CEO*** and ***CFO*** must each ***certify the accuracy*** of each quarterly and annual filing with the SEC. More precisely, the CEO and CFO must certify:

   ❑ that each quarterly and annual report "does not contain any ***untrue statement*** of a material fact or omit to state a material fact necessary in order to make the statements made ... not misleading";

   ❑ that the financial statements in the report "***fairly present*** in all material respects the ***financial condition and results of operations*** of the issuer[.]"

   ❑ that the signing officer has designed ***"internal controls"*** to ensure that information about the company is made known to the signing officer; the officer must also re-evaluate the effectiveness of those controls each quarter;

   ❑ that the signing officer has disclosed to the company's outside auditors, and to the audit committee of the board, any ***deficiencies in the internal controls***, and any ***fraud*** involving management.

   See §§ 302(a)(2), (3), (4) and (5) of the Sarbanes-Oxley Act. Cf. Hamilton (8th), pp. 717-18.

   Adding to the stakes for the certifying CEO and CFO, the Act imposes ***criminal penalties*** of up to 10 years imprisonment for a "knowing" violation and up to 20 years for a "willful" violation. See § 906 of the Act.

2. **Rules about Audit Committee:** Each company's Audit Committee is much more tightly regulated now, under Sarbanes-Oxley. Each member of the committee must be ***"independent."*** This requirement of "independence" means that (a) no employees of the company or its subsidiaries may be a member; and (b) members may not accept any "consulting, advisory, or other compensatory fees" from the company, other than fees for belonging to the board or to the committee (so that an audit committee member may not, say, serve as a consultant or lawyer to the company).

3. **Whistle-blower rules:** Corporate ***whistle-blowers*** — employees who report, say, the company's financial misconduct to government authorities — get special protection. It is now a crime punishable by up to 10 years in prison for anyone to knowingly retaliate against a person for supplying truthful information about a federal crime to a law-enforcement officer. (Violations of Sarbanes-Oxley are themselves, of course, federal crimes.) Retaliation is defined to include interference with "the lawful ***employment*** or livelihood" of a person. § 1107 of the Act. So ***firing a whistle-blower in retaliation*** is now a ***felony***.

Example: Suppose that CFO learns that Clerk, a low-level accounting clerk, has just told the SEC about an ongoing financial fraud at the company. CFO fires Clerk so that Clerk will be cut off from further information, and in order to be able to be able to say, "Well, Clerk is just a disgruntled employee who was fired for incompetence." CFO has committed a felony under § 1107, and can go to prison for up to 10 years.

4. **Auditor independence:** The company's ***outside auditors*** (the CPAs that perform the annual audit) must also be much more ***independent*** than previously. The auditors must contract with the audit committee of the board, not with management of the company. And the auditors may no longer do other — potentially more lucrative — tasks for the company, such as bookkeeping, designing the computer system that does financial record-keeping for the company, etc. See § 201 of the Act.

Quiz Yourself on
SHAREHOLDERS' INFO. RIGHTS AND THE PROXY SYSTEM *(ENTIRE CHAPTER)*

29. Hannibal Lechter Foods, Inc., a privately-held company, makes a popular meal extender for cannibals, "Manburger Helper" (". . . when you need a helping hand."). Robinson Crusoe, a 1% shareholder, believes that the directors are cooking the books; however, they refuse to allow him to see the corporation's books to find out if he's right. Under the prevailing approach, does Crusoe have a right to examine the corporation's accounting records for this purpose? ________________

30. The Botch Ewlism Food Company has assets of $15 million. It has 350 shareholders of preferred stock and 350 shareholders of common stock. Botch Ewlism's shares are traded over-the-counter.

(a) Does Botch have to file annual and/or quarterly financial reports with the SEC? ________________

(b) Is Botch subject to the SEC's proxy-solicitation rules? ________________

31. Nyuck-Nyuck Corp. is a huge public company, with its shares traded on the NYSE. The management of Nyuck-Nyuck, consisting of Larry, Curly, and Moe, owns a majority of the stock. Therefore, management doesn't need proxies from anyone else in order to arrange a quorum at the annual meeting, or to cause any properly-noticed shareholder action to be approved at that meeting. Consequently, management would like to be able to skip the cumbersome step of sending anything to outside shareholders before the annual meeting. Is there anything that, according to federal proxy rules, management must send to shareholders before the meeting despite the absence of a proxy solicitation (and if so, what)? ________________

32. Sarah Connor owns shares in the Terminator Wrecking Company. Terminator's annual meeting takes place on June 1st, and has a record date of April 15th. On May 1st, Sarah takes out a loan with the Cyborg Bank, pledging as collateral her Terminator shares. Cyborg insists on being granted a proxy as a condition for the loan. Sarah grants the proxy. The proxy says, on its face, that it's irrevocable. Sarah pays off the loan full on May 20th. Sarah shows up at the Terminator annual meeting, intending to vote her shares. Cyborg Bank sends a representative as well, claiming it has an irrevocable proxy and is entitled to vote the shares. Who gets to vote the shares? ________________

33. Clampett Oil Company's stock is traded on the NYSE. Clampett's board of directors wants to merge Clampett with the Drysdale Corporation. Clampett's board has to get shareholder approval for the merger, so it sends out proxy materials soliciting proxy appointments to vote on the merger. The proxy solicitation contains the board's recommendation that the merger be approved. However, the proxy materials don't mention that, because Drysdale owns 54% of Clampett, all of Clampett's directors were named by Drysdale. (Clampett's charter does not allow cumulative voting). The merger is approved by Clampett's shareholders. Ellie May Clampett, a minority shareholder of Clampett Oil, files suit for an injunction against the transaction, on the grounds that the proxy materials omitted a material issue of fact (Drysdale's domination of Clampett's board).

(a) For this part, assume that according to Clampett's charter, the merger needed to be approved by a two-thirds majority of Clampett's shareholders. Will Ellie May get the injunction she seeks? ________________

(b) For this part, assume that only a simple majority needed to approve the merger. Assume also that Ellie May wasn't initially aware of the omission about board domination, voted to approve the transaction, and then found out (after the merger went through) about the domination. She now sues in federal court for monetary damages. (Assume that state law does not allow appraisal rights in this situation, whether or not the holder votes in favor of the transaction.) Will Ellie May get damages? ________________

34. Pongo has owned 10% of the voting stock of the Cruella De Vil Clothing Company for several years. Cruella De Vil stock is traded on the NYSE. Pongo hears that management intends to expand its line of furs to include dalmatian pelts, and he's furious. Pongo wants to submit a proposal under the shareholder proposal rule, 14a-8, to be included in management's proxy materials for the upcoming annual meeting. Pongo's proposal asks management to consider not manufacturing clothing made from furs, which currently account for 10% of the company's product line. Management isn't submitting a proposal on the same subject for the annual meeting. Must management include Pongo's proposal in its proxy materials? ________________

35. Caesar is the CEO of Imperial Rome Corp., a public company. The company's annual meeting of shareholders will be coming up in a couple of months. Management (meaning Caesar) is going to propose in its proxy materials that all incumbent members of the board be re-elected. Cleopatra, a dissident shareholder who has owned 4% of the company's shares for several years and who is not presently on the board, wishes to run for a board seat. She has prepared a brief statement that lists what she believes to be her credentials to be elected to the board, and the steps she would favor if she were elected. Instead of waging an independent "proxy contest" to be elected to the board, Cleopatra has submitted her statement to management, and has requested that the statement (together with a form of proxy enabling shareholders to vote for her by proxy) be included with management's own proxy materials in the mailing that will go to all shareholders. Caesar would like to find a grounds for rejecting Cleopatra's request. You are counsel to the company. What ground, if any, can you cite to Caesar that would justify Caesar in refusing Cleopatra's request?

36. WorldCon, a public company, issues a quarterly report to the SEC reporting that the company made $100 million that quarter. The quarterly report is accompanied by all required certifications about the accuracy of the report, signed by, among others, Bernie Fibbers, CEO and controlling shareholder of the company. Bernie knows that the $100 million of profit was obtained by improperly treating $200 million of expenses as if they had been capital expenditures (thus changing what would have been an $80 million loss into the reported $100 million profit). You are a federal prosecutor, and you have learned the above facts.

(a) What, if any, juicy federal securities-law charge can you bring against Bernie to put him away for a long time? ________________

(b) What will you have to prove to win a conviction on that charge? ______________

Answers

29. Yes. Most states let a shareholder examine the corporation's books and records, provided that this is not being done for an "improper" purpose (e.g., stealing the corporation's secrets so as to compete with it). [90] Confirming or refuting one's suspicions that the books are being cooked certainly qualifies as a proper purpose, so Crusoe should be able to get a court order compelling the company to allow the inspection.

Note that under MBCA § 16.02(c), Crusoe would be allowed to inspect the accounting records, but only if: (1) he made his demand "in good faith and for a proper purpose" (satisfied here); (2) he described with "reasonable particularity" why he wanted to do the inspection (e.g., "I think the books are being cooked," which he could honestly say here); and (3) the records are "directly connected" with his purpose (satisfied here). So Crusoe would get the inspection under § 16.02(c) (and in fact the corporation would probably have to pay his legal fees in getting the court order, under § 16.04(c)). [91]

30. (a) No. § 12 of the Securities Exchange Act ('34 Act), and SEC Rule 12g-1 enacted under it, describe the companies subject to federal proxy rules. A company qualifies if ***either***: (1) Its securities are traded on a regulated securities exchange (e.g., NYSE); ***or*** (2) The company fits *both* of the following requirements: (a) It has assets greater than $10,000,000, and (b) It has 500 or more shareholders of a class of equity securities (e.g., common stock). [96]

The key to this question is that if a corporation isn't traded on a national exchange (as Botch Ewlism isn't), it must have a *class* of stock held by 500 or more people, not 500 or more shareholders all together. That's the problem here: Botch Ewlism has 700 shareholders, but it doesn't have 500 or more holders of any one class. Thus, it's not subject to the SEC's reporting requirements.

(b) No. A company is bound by the SEC's proxy solicitation rules if, and only if, it's required to file financial reports under the '34 Act. So the negative answer to part (a) compels a negative answer to this part as well. [98]

31. Yes — management must send each shareholder material "substantially equivalent" to the material that it would have had to send if it were soliciting proxies. [100] This means that management has to send an *annual report* containing the corporation's financial reports, plus information about the compensation and stockholdings of management and board members, transactions between management and the corporation, and any matter on which there will be a shareholder vote. This information must also be filed with the SEC. So shareholders get as much information about a management-controlled public company as they do about one that is not management controlled. (But remember, the solicitation and filing requirements don't get triggered if the company is not traded on a stock exchange and doesn't have at least 500 holders of some one class of stock — see the previous question.)

32. Sarah. The normal rule is that a proxy is revocable unless it's ***coupled with an "interest."*** This is true even if the proxy says that it's irrevocable. [102] One of the ways in which a proxy can be coupled with an interest is if the stock is pledged as collateral for a loan. [103] That was the case here, so Cyborg is correct in the sense that the proxy it received *was* irrevocable. However, if the condition that made the proxy irrevocable is *lifted* — in the case of a collateralized loan, the loan is paid off — then the proxy is automatically revoked. As a result, Sarah's entitled to vote her own shares. See MBCA § 7.22 (d, f).

33. (a) Yes, probably. Rule 14a-9 of the '34 Act requires that proxy materials be free of misstatements or omissions of "material" fact. Here, the fact that Clampett Oil's directors were all Drysdale's nominees would be likely to influence the Clampett directors' recommendation that the merger be approved. A fact is "material" (so that the proxy materials can't omit or misstate it) if "there is a substantial likelihood that a reasonable shareholder would consider it important in deciding how to vote" (i.e., if the fact would "significantly alter the 'total mix' of available information"). *TSC Industries*. [105] The omission here certainly seems to qualify: a Clampett shareholder would probably give the Clampett board's recommendation much less weight if she knew that the board was controlled by the acquirer than if she didn't know this. So omission of the fact of board domination renders the proxy materials misleading. A federal court has discretion to issue an injunction against the transaction if adequate proxy materials haven't been sent, and there's a good chance the court in this situation would exercise that discretion. [110]

(b) No, probably. The Supreme Court has held that no private recovery for proxy misstatements is available to "a member of a class of minority shareholders whose votes are ***not required*** by law or corporate bylaw to authorize the transaction giving rise to the claim." *Virginia Bankshares.* [108] Here, since Drysdale controlled a majority of the common stock, and only a simple majority had to approve the transaction, the merger would have gone through even if Ellie May and all other shareholders apart from Drysdale had voted against it. Therefore, the omission didn't cause things to turn out differently, and Ellie May hasn't really been damaged. (If Ellie May had been duped into surrendering her state-law *appraisal* rights — as would be the case in a state that grants such rights to those dissenting from a merger, but denies appraisal where the holder votes in favor of the transaction — then Ellie May might still have a federal monetary claim, on the theory that the omission deprived her of her appraisal rights. That's why the facts tell you that Ellie's appraisal rights weren't affected by her vote in favor of the transaction.)

34. Yes. Rule 14a-8 of the '34 Act allows shareholders to include proposals in management's proxy solicitation materials. [113] There are significant restrictions on this right; for instance, the shareholder must have owned 1% or $2,000 (market value) of the corporation's voting stock for at least a year, and any shareholder can only submit one proposal for any one meeting. In addition, there are many grounds on which management may omit a proposal. (For instance, the shareholder proposal can't be counter to a management proposal on the same subject; it can't relate to electing or removing directors; it can't be insignificant, personal, or relate to ordinary business; and it can't have been voted down in the recent past.) [113]

The exclusion that comes closest to fitting these facts is that the proposal must not relate to the "conduct of the ordinary business operations" of the company. But the composition of 10% of the company's product line would probably be held not to relate to the company's "ordinary business operations," especially in light of the extreme public controversy associated with fur products. (Courts have generally held that where the issue is an ethical, social or political one, it doesn't fall within the "ordinary business operations" ban. [117]) So a court would probably order Cruella to include the proposal.

35. That the proposal may be excluded under SEC Rule 14a-8(i)(8)(iv). That Rule lets the company exclude any proposal that "[s]eeks to ***include a specific individual*** in the company's proxy materials for ***election to the board of directors***[.]" This exclusion means that a proposal seeking to elect one or more ***particular*** director(s) favored by the proposer ***may not be done through the free "include shareholder's proposal in management's materials" method*** of Rule 14a-8. [117] So Caesar can reject Cleopatra's request, thus forcing Cleopatra to prepare her own proxy statement under Rule 14a-7 and to pay the costs of mailing it to shareholders.

36. (a) Violations of §§ 302(a)(2) and (a)(3) of the Sarbanes-Oxley Act, triggering a violation of § 906 of

the Act. § 302(a)(2) of Sarbanes-Oxley requires the reporting company's "principal executive officer" (Bernie) to certify that "based on the officer's knowledge, the [quarterly] report does not contain any untrue statement of a material fact[.]" And § 302(a)(3) requires Bernie to certify that "the financial statements ... fairly present in all material respects the financial condition and results of operations of the issuer ... for the periods presented in the report." § 906(a) authorizes an up-to-10-year prison term for certifying any statement covered by §§ 302(a)(2) and (3) while knowing that the report being certified doesn't meet the requirements of those sections. (The penalty is up to 20 years for a "willful" violation, whatever that means.)

(b) You'll have to prove (a) that the report was false; and (b) that Bernie knew that the report was false when he certified it. You *won't* have to prove that Bernie ordered anyone else in the company to cook the books, or that he otherwise actively participated in the fraud — it's enough simply that he *knew* of the falsehood(s) when he certified that the report was accurate.

Exam Tips on *SHAREHOLDERS' INFORMATIONAL RIGHTS AND THE PROXY SYSTEM*

There are three basic fact patterns that are most likely to be tested in connection with this chapter:

(1) A s/h's request to ***inspect corporate records*** has been denied;

(2) Management has refused to ***include a s/h's proposal*** in its proxy materials; and

(3) A s/h is attempting to ***revoke a proxy.***

☛ In fact patterns where a s/h has asked to ***inspect corp. records***, the most testable issue is whether the s/h has stated a proper purpose for the inspection.

- ☞ Remember that a purpose is proper (so that the corp. must allow the inspection) so long as it is ***reasonably related to the requester's interest as a stockholder***, and not likely to ***damage*** the corp.
  - ☞ Anything that relates to evaluating the investor's ***return on his investment*** is likely to be found proper. (Example: P, a s/h in D Corp., wants to inspect D's records to see how much profit D is making, and how much could be distributed as dividends. This is a proper purpose.)
  - ☞ If the s/h wants a lists of other s/h's so he can ***solicit proxies*** to unseat incumbent management, this is generally a ***proper*** purpose.
  - ☞ On the other hand, a purpose is improper where the s/h requests the info in order to pursue ***personal goals*** unrelated to ownership of stock in the corp. (*Example:* P is a s/h of D Corp., but also is the controlling s/h of a competitor of D, X Corp. P wants to review D's detailed product-by-product revenues and costs. If the court believes that P will use this info. to have X Corp. compete more effectively with

D, the court will find the purpose improper.)

☛ Whenever a fact pattern involves a ***shareholder proposal***, consider whether any of the exclusions set forth in SEC Rule 14a-8(i) apply (in which case management may refuse to include the proposal in its proxy materials).

☞ Remember that a proposal doesn't have to be included if it concerns a matter that is ***"not a proper subject for action by security holders."*** Thus make sure that that the s/h isn't proposing to ***order management to do something***, if holders don't have the right to make such an order under state law. (Since s/h's don't normally have the right to order the company to do anything, a lot of proposals are excludible under this ground.)

Example: X Corp. is a nuclear-based utility. An anti-nuke s/h group asks for inclusion of a proposal "ordering the corporation to cease building or operating new nuclear power plants." Because under the law of virtually all states s/h's can't tell the corp. how to conduct its operations, this proposal advocates a step that is "not a proper subject for action by shareholders," and is thus non-includible.

☞ But if the proposal is couched as a ***recommendation*** to management or the board, rather than an order, it's ***not*** excludible on this ground. (*Example:* In the above example, if the s/h proposal seeks s/h approval of a *recommendation* to the board that it commission no new nuclear plants, it's probably includible.)

☞ If the proposal relates solely to the corporation's ***"ordinary business operations,"*** it's ***excludible*** as too routine. (But if the proposal involves a ***controversial*** problem or issue, it won't fall within the "ordinary business operations" exclusion even if it also relates to the company's routine business operations.)

☞ If the proposal relates to the ***election of one or more specific directors***, it's ***excludible*** (so that the s/h group that wants to electioneer has to pay for its own proxy materials). (*Example:* A s/h group opposes management's slate of directors for the upcoming election. The group's statement of reasons for its opposition is excludible, because it relates to the election of particular directors.)

☞ If the proposal relates to ***general economic, political, racial, social*** or other similar causes, it will nonetheless be ***includible*** if it has some ***tangible link*** to the corp's affairs.

Example: An anti-nuke group tenders a "no new nuclear power plants" recommendation to a power company that currently uses nuke plants. The proposal will be *includible* even though it relates to a general social/political cause, because it relates to the company's business. But if a general proposal opposing "all uses of nuclear energy" is tendered to a company that neither uses nor proposes to use nuclear energy in any way, it's probably *excludible* as "not significantly related to the company's business."

☛ If the fact pattern relates to a ***proxy***, you're most likely to be tested on whether the s/h may ***revoke*** the proxy.

☞ Here, remember that the rule is that even if the proxy purports to be irrevocable, it's ***revocable unless*** it's ***"coupled with an interest."*** (Only if the recipient is a person who has a legal interest in the stock, or in the corporation, does the proxy meet the "coupled with an interest" requirement. So if the recipient has a ***contract to buy the stock***, or has lent money with the stock as ***pledge***, the proxy can be irrevocable. But an ordinary proxy given, say, to management, is ***revocable even if it says it's irrevocable***.)

CHAPTER 5

CLOSE CORPORATIONS

ChapterScope

This chapter examines some of the special problems of "close corporations," i.e., non-public corporations owned by a small number of shareholders. Most of the chapter discusses various planning devices the shareholders can use to allocate control. We also discuss methods for resolving disputes about how the corporation is to be run. Key concepts:

- **Definition:** A close corporation is a corporation that has the following characteristics:
  - A ***small number*** of shareholders (usually fewer than 20, and often only 1 or two);
  - The lack of any real ***resale market*** for the corporation's stock;
  - (Usually but not always) a controlling shareholder who ***actively participates*** in the day-to-day ***management*** of the business.
- **Allocation-of-control devices:** Shareholders in close corporations typically use one or more of the following devices to ensure that the minority shareholder(s) will not be ***outvoted*** or ***taken advantage of*** by the majority holder(s):
  - **Shareholder voting agreements:** Under a shareholder voting agreement, some or all shareholders agree to ***vote together*** as a unit on specified matters.
  - **Voting trusts:** Under a voting trust, shareholders relinquish their voting power to a ***"voting trustee,"*** often one who agrees to cast the votes in a prescribed way (e.g., so as to elect certain stockholders to the board). The shareholders retain their economic interest in the business.
  - **Classified stock:** A corporation can set up ***multiple "classes" of stock***, each of which gets different voting rights or financial rights. A common pattern is for a particular group of minority holders to get its own class of stock, which is guaranteed the right to elect one or more directors.
  - **Super-majority voting and quorum requirements:** These devices provide that certain types of corporate action (e.g., payment of dividends, setting of salaries, sale of the business) can only occur if an especially ***high percentage*** of shares or board votes (e.g., 80%) are cast in favor of the measure, and/or an especially high percentage of shares or board members make up the quorum for the measure. The purpose is to give minority holders ***blocking power***.
  - **Share-transfer restrictions:** The corporation often limits each holder's ability to ***re-sell*** her shares (e.g., by requiring that the shares first be offered to the corporation or to the other holders, before they can be sold to a non-holder).
- **Dissolution:** If the holders are deadlocked, one way to undo the deadlock is for the court to order the corporation ***"dissolved."*** Its assets are then sold, its debts paid, and the surplus distributed to the holders.

I. INTRODUCTION

A. **What is a close corporation:** There is no single universally-accepted definition of a "close corporation."

1. **Massachusetts definition:** A definition adopted by Massachusetts, however, encapsulates the concept well. Under this definition, given in *Donahue v. Rodd Electrotype Co.*, 328 N.E.2d 505 (1975), a close corporation is a corporation meeting these three requirements:

   a. **Number of stockholders:** A ***small number*** of stockholders;

   b. **Lack of market:** The lack of any ***ready market*** for the corporation's stock; and

   c. **Stockholder participation:** Substantial participation by the ***majority stockholder*** in the ***management***, direction and operations of the corporation.

2. **Contrast with partnership:** It is sometimes said that a close corporation should be treated almost like a ***partnership***. Indeed, some of the control devices and judicial doctrines we discuss in this chapter have the effect of making close corporations more like partnerships than they would otherwise be. For instance, just as no person can become a member of a partnership without the consent of all partners, shareholder agreements in close corporations often accomplish almost the same result by restricting transfer of the corporation's shares without consent of the other stockholders. Similarly, partners stand in a fiduciary relationship to each other; some courts now impose a corresponding fiduciary responsibility upon stockholders in a close corporation. (See *infra*, p. 162.)

3. **Close corporation statutes:** A typical state corporation statute is geared to the needs of the large, publicly held, corporation. Because a close corporation's needs are usually quite different, a number of states have adopted special ***"close corporation statutes."*** Typically, these statutes are not mandatory — a qualifying corporation must ***elect*** to be covered by the statute. Once covered, a corporation is then permitted (but not required) to enter into certain types of arrangements among shareholders that might not be valid for a regular corporation.

   Example: In many states, under the general corporation statute shareholders are not allowed to make agreements that have the result of tightly restricting the authority of the board of directors. For instance, a shareholder agreement in which both parties agree that X is to be elected president and is to have full control over the policies and operation of the business, might well be held invalid on the grounds that it "sterilizes the board of directors." (See *infra*, p. 141.) But in Delaware, a corporation that has fewer than thirty shareholders, and that has never made a public offering, may elect to be treated as a special statutory "close corporation"; if it does so, this type of shareholder agreement restricting the authority of the board of directors is explicitly validated. See Del. GCL, §§ 341-356, especially § 350.

   a. **Various approaches:** California and Delaware each has a separate set of provisions applicable only to statutory close corporations. Additionally, other states have special provisions, scattered through their statutes, that apply only to close corporations. (For instance, New York, in BCL § 620(c), allows what would normally be the powers of the board to be given to an individual, but only if the corporation is not publicly held.)

b. Model Act: Similarly, the MBCA is now accompanied by a special "Model Statutory Close Corporation Supplement" ("MSCCS"), which applies only to corporations that elect to come under it, and which validates certain inter-shareholder arrangements that might otherwise not be valid under the MBCA. The MSCCS applies to any corporation having ***50 or fewer shareholders*** that ***elects*** this treatment. The corporation makes the election by putting a provision to that effect in its articles of incorporation.

i. Mandatory provision: The MSCCS, unlike the Delaware, California and New York approaches to statutory close corporations, does not merely validate certain kinds of arrangements; it also imposes some ***mandatory*** provisions on corporations which elect to be covered by it. For example, whereas the shares of an ordinary corporation are not subject to any share transfer restrictions unless the shareholders so agree (see *supra*, p. 7), shares of a corporation electing to be covered by the MSCCS may not be transferred unless the corporation is given a ***right of first refusal*** to buy the shares, and declines. See MSCCS, §§ 11-13.

c. Not generally used: Only a tiny fraction of corporations eligible for special close corporation status elect to receive this treatment. One reason is that the kinds of arrangements that used to be frequently struck down by courts are now often valid even for corporations not electing this special close corporation statutory treatment. S,S,B&W, p. 444.

B. Planning devices: A shareholder in a large, publicly held corporation will usually not need the protection of any special contractual arrangement with fellow shareholders or management. The shareholder in a close corporation, by contrast — especially a ***minority shareholder*** in such a corporation — probably will not fare as well economically without a "negotiated arrangement" regarding such matters as who will be on the board of directors, who will be the managers, what salaries and dividends will be paid, how shares may be transferred, etc.

1. Reasons: To see why this is so, let us contrast the public shareholder with the shareholder in a close corporation.

a. Public shareholder: The public shareholder expects to realize economic gains from his shares by either or both of two means: the receipt of dividends and/or the ability to sell his shares for a capital gain. The boards and managers of public corporations know this, and will ordinarily attempt to operate the corporation so as to furnish either dividends, share appreciation or both. (If they do not, bad things may happen to them, such as a hostile takeover attempt.)

b. Close corporation: For a shareholder in a close corporation, by contrast, the economic rewards typically come in very different forms from those received by the public shareholder:

i. Dividends: Such small-company shareholders rarely receive much reward from dividends. For one thing, dividends are taxed twice (at the corporate level and then at the shareholder level), so those running the corporation (generally shareholder-managers) will usually try to find other means of funneling money out of the corporation.

ii. Salaries: For instance, the controlling shareholder(s) of a close corporation is usually involved in ***management***, and therefore often wants to pay out some or all of the corporation's operating profits in the form of ***high salaries*** or bonuses to the managers (including him/themselves). Consequently, a ***minority*** shareholder in a close corporation will be deprived of the fruits of the business' success unless he, too, is ***employed*** by the corporation so that he can receive salary/bonuses. But since the company's officers and managers are controlled by the board of directors, and the board normally operates by majority vote, the majority shareholder(s) has power to deny employment and salary to the minority.

iii. Market for shares: Similarly, the minority shareholder cannot usually hope to ***sell*** his shares at a capital gain to a third party who is not affiliated with the corporation — such a buyer would have the same difficulties (e.g., lack of dividends and no guarantee of employment) as the selling shareholder would have. Therefore, as a practical matter the only possible buyers for the minority shares are likely to be the corporation itself or the other shareholders, especially the controlling shareholders. This lack of competition among buyers, in turn, is likely to induce the corporation or the controlling shareholders to make a "low ball" offer for the shares, or no offer at all.

iv. Keeping out strangers: Finally, since most shareholders in a close corporation are active in the management of the business, each shareholder is likely to want to be sure that another shareholder will not sell or give his shares to an "outsider" who would then seek to become active in management, in a way that would lead to discord. For instance, if *A* and *B* are shareholders, *A* may worry that upon *B*'s death, *B*'s shares will go to *B*'s widow, with whom *A* has no working relationship and who may disrupt the corporation's smooth functioning if she demands to become involved in management.

2. Special contractual arrangements: Therefore, the shareholder of a close corporation, especially a minority shareholder, will normally want to make special ***contractual arrangements*** to preserve her chance to benefit economically from the corporation. Her objectives are likely to include:

- ❑ making sure that she receives ***employment*** with the corporation, including the chance to receive salaries and/or bonuses that reflect her pro rata share of the company's operating profits;
- ❑ arranging a mechanism whereby upon ***death***, ***retirement*** or other important event her shares can be ***sold back to the corporation*** or to the other shareholders for a fair price;
- ❑ being sure that the ***other*** shareholders will not sell or bequeath ***their*** shares to an outsider who may interfere with the functioning of the business; and
- ❑ being sure that, even though she possesses only a minority vote, she can ***participate in important business decisions***, and perhaps can ***veto*** major changes of policy (e.g., the decision to sell all of the corporation's assets, or to go into an entirely new line of business).

The planning devices we will be looking at in this chapter furnish ways for a shareholder, especially a minority holder, to achieve each of these objectives.

II. SHAREHOLDER VOTING AGREEMENTS, VOTING TRUSTS AND CLASSIFIED STOCK

A. Arrangements at the shareholder level generally: We first examine a trio of arrangements that take place at the ***shareholder*** (rather than director) level: (1) shareholder voting agreements; (2) voting trusts; and (3) classified stock. All of these are methods whereby a minority shareholder can reduce or eliminate the chance that a majority will outvote him and take actions that he would like to prevent.

B. Voting agreements: A ***"shareholder voting agreement"*** or ***"pooling agreement"*** is an agreement in which two or more shareholders agree to ***vote together*** as a unit on certain or all matters.

1. Specific agreement vs. "agreement to agree": Some voting agreements attempt to resolve in the agreement itself exactly how the votes will be cast. Other agreements merely commit the parties to vote together, without specifying which way the vote is to go; it is then up to the parties to reach agreement in the future.

Example 1: A and B, the only two shareholders of XYZ Corp., sign a shareholder voting agreement in which A and B each agree to vote for each other as directors for so long as the agreement lasts.

Example 2: A owns 60% of XYZ Corp. and B owns 40%. They sign a shareholders' agreement in which each promises that as to any matter on which a vote of shareholders is required (e.g., a sale of substantially all the company's assets, a merger, a major acquisition, etc.) they will confer with each other and vote together as a unit. This agreement does not specify ***how*** they will vote on such matters, since the issues are not even known at the time of the agreement. However, such an agreement assures B that he will not be "outvoted" (and will have an effective veto power) as to major decisions that require a shareholder vote.

2. Generally valid: Such shareholder agreements are today generally ***valid***. This is true of both the "specific" and the "agreement-to-agree" types. See, e.g., MBCA § 7.31(a) ("Two or more shareholders may provide for the manner in which they will vote their shares by signing an agreement for that purpose.")

a. No restrictions on directors' authority: However, the shareholders can be confident that a court will uphold their voting agreement only if the agreement does not try to deal with matters that are appropriately left to the discretion of the ***board of directors***. A shareholder agreement that does restrict the authority of the board of directors (e.g., an agreement in which the two shareholders of a corporation agree that one of them will serve permanently as President) may be found invalid as an illegal modification of the principle that a corporation's business shall be managed by or under the direction of the board of directors. This very important subject of agreements that limit the board's discretion is discussed extensively *infra*, p. 141.

3. **Time limits:** Generally, voting agreements may remain in force for an ***indefinitely long period*** of time. However, a few states limit such agreements to a specified period (e.g., ten years), as most states do for voting trusts (discussed below). Nutshell, p. 194-95.

4. **Enforcement:** The most interesting legal question concerning voting agreements is how they can be ***enforced***. The problem is that such agreements are not self-enforcing. For instance, if *A* and *B* agreed to vote to elect each other as directors, and *B* reneges and instead votes for *C*, what can *A* do? Without some judicial relief, *A* will simply not be elected, and will be left with a claim for breach of contract. There are two solutions to this problem:

   a. **Proxies:** First, the agreement may expressly provide that each signatory is deemed to give to a third person (let's call him X) an ***irrevocable proxy*** to vote the signer's shares in accordance with the agreement. The proxy holder will then vote the shares as provided in the agreement, and no judicial intervention is necessary.

   Example: A and B, the sole shareholders of XYZ Corp., agree that each will vote to elect the other to the board. The agreement also provides that A and B each give X an irrevocable proxy to vote the shares in accordance with this agreement. When it comes time for the election of directors, X, not A and B, will cast the vote for directors, so neither A nor B will be able to thwart the agreement.

      i. **Must be coupled with an interest:** A proxy is a form of agency — the shareholder is the principal, and the one to whom he gives the proxy is his agent. Under general agency principles, even a proxy that purports to be "irrevocable" may be revoked by the shareholder at any time until the vote is cast. This would make the use of supposedly irrevocable proxies in a shareholder agreement valueless. However, courts have long recognized that a proxy that is given in return for ***consideration*** — usually called a proxy ***"coupled with an interest"*** — may be truly irrevocable. (See *supra*, p. 102). Most courts today hold that where a shareholder has purchased stock in a close corporation in reliance on the existence of a shareholder agreement and the creation of proxies, a sufficient "interest" exists to make the proxies truly irrevocable. Also, some states have simply statutorily eliminated the requirement of an interest for the proxy to be irrevocable. See S,S,B&W, pp. 453-54. However, in some states there is still a risk that the "irrevocable" proxy referred to in a shareholder agreement will be found to be in fact revocable, and thus useless as an enforcement device.

   b. **Specific performance:** The other method of enforcing a shareholder voting agreement is by court-ordered ***specific performance***. That is, the court orders the breaching shareholder to cast his vote as prescribed in the shareholders' agreement. The difficulty is that courts are sometimes ***reluctant*** to order a stockholder to vote a certain way, and instead conclude that this is a matter to be resolved between the shareholders themselves.

   Example: Mrs. Ringling, Mrs. Haley, and Mr. North are the three shareholders of Corporation (which operates the Ringling Brothers-Barnum & Bailey Circus). Mrs. Ringling and Mrs. Haley sign a voting agreement, in which each agrees to consult and confer with the other and to vote their shares together on any issue put to a stockholder vote. They also agree that if they can't agree on how the shares should be voted, their lawyer, Mr. Loos, shall act as arbitrator. At a subsequent shareholders meeting to elect directors, Mrs. Haley and Mrs. Ringling disagree, and the arbitrator is called in. Mrs. Ringling agrees to vote her shares in accordance with the arbitrator's decision, but Mrs. Haley refuses to do so. The chairman rules that the arbitrator may cast Mrs. Haley's vote (i.e., that Mrs. Haley should be deemed to vote as the agreement provides). For reasons that are unclear, Mrs. Ringling (not Mrs. Haley) sues to overturn the election. The court of equity holds that the agreement is valid, and orders a new election at which the agreement is to be followed (with the arbitrator casting the votes if Mrs. Ringling and Mrs. Haley cannot agree).

Held (on appeal), the agreement is valid. (This is not a disguised voting trust and therefore need not be held illegal for failure to meet the statutory formalities for such trusts.) However, the lower court was wrong in holding that the agreement created an implied irrevocable proxy (which would allow the arbitrator to cast the votes of a non-complying shareholder). Instead, Mrs. Ringling's remedy for Mrs. Haley's failure to follow the agreement should be that Mrs. Haley's votes will ***not be counted***. In other words, the court denies specific performance of the agreement (since specific performance would mean allowing the arbitrator to cast Mrs. Haley's vote as he deems fit). *Ringling Bros.-Barnum & Bailey Combined Shows v. Ringling*, 53 A.2d 441 (Del. 1947).

Note: Observe that although Mrs. Ringling was the nominal victor in the suit (the agreement was held valid, and her adversary was found in breach), this was a Pyrrhic victory — what Mrs. Ringling wanted was to have Mrs. Haley vote the same way as she did, so that they would outvote Mr. North. Instead, by refusing specific performance, and ordering that Mrs. Haley's vote not be counted, the court allowed Mr. North to achieve a stalemate with Mrs. Ringling, the very result Mrs. Ringling tried to avoid by making the agreement in the first place.

i. **Statutory and judicial relief:** Today, many if not most courts would ***give*** Mrs. Ringling the specific performance she desired. A number of states have enacted statutes that make the voting agreements specifically enforceable. MBCA § 7.31(b), for instance, provides that "a voting agreement created under this section is ***specifically enforceable***." Also, as noted above, if the agreement expressly grants a proxy to the other party or grants a third person the right to cast votes in accordance with the agreement (a provision which the agreement in *Ringling* did not specifically contain), most courts today would probably recognize that proxy as valid.

C. **Voting trusts:** A second device by which shareholders can agree to limit their voting discretion is by use of a ***"voting trust."***

1. **Mechanics:** To create a voting trust, the shareholders who are part of the arrangement ***convey legal title*** to their shares to one or more ***voting trustees***, under the terms of a voting trust agreement. S,S,B&W, p. 452. The shareholders become "beneficial owners" or "equitable owners" of the shares. Usually they receive a "voting trust certificate" representing their equitable interest. They are entitled to receive dividends and their share of

proceeds of any sale of corporate assets. But they ***no longer have voting power*** — votes are cast by the trustees in accordance with the instructions in the voting agreement.

Example: Eager and Willing are entrepreneurs who want financial backing for their new venture, Corporation. Vulture, a venture capitalist, agrees to supply the financing in return for a one-third interest, but only if he can be certain of controlling the board of directors (and thus certain of being able to discharge Eager and Willing from their posts as officers if they don't run the business effectively). Eager and Willing therefore sign (perhaps reluctantly) a voting trust agreement that appoints Vulture as voting trustee; Eager and Willing convey legal title to their shares to Vulture, and receive a voting trust certificate in return. Vulture now has complete shareholder voting authority (and can thus elect and remove all directors), but Eager and Willing will still receive, collectively, two-thirds of any dividends and two-thirds of any net proceeds if the corporation is sold.

2. **Generally valid:** Originally, courts were reluctant to enforce voting trust agreements. But today, nearly all states have statutes ***authorizing*** voting trust arrangements. S,S,B&W, p. 453. However, these statutes usually ***regulate*** voting trusts. Most statutes impose these requirements:

   a. **Maximum term:** First, the statutes generally set a ***maximum term*** for the voting trust. Generally, the maximum term for such a trust is ***ten years***. Clark, p. 777. See, e.g., MBCA § 7.30(b) (ten year limit, but at any time some or all parties may sign an extension agreement, which may continue the trust as to them for up to ten years from the signing of the extension).

   b. **Disclosure:** Secondly, most statutes require ***public disclosure*** of the trust's terms, so that the existence and terms of the trust will not be hidden from other shareholders. For instance, MBCA § 7.30(a) requires that the trust, together with the list of all shareholders participating in it, must be delivered to the corporation's offices, where it can be inspected by other shareholders.

   c. **Writing:** Lastly, nearly all states require that the trust be ***in writing***, and that the trust be implemented by a formal transfer of the shares on the transfer records of the corporation. See, e.g., MBCA § 7.30(a).

3. **Powers of trustees:** The voting trustees are subject to the ***fiduciary obligations*** of trustees. In general, they may exercise only those powers that are specifically spelled out in the trust, and unless the trust expressly permits they may not vote in a way that ***damages*** the beneficial owners that they represent. H&A, p. 532-33. For instance, suppose the corporation needs funds, and its stockholders agree to create a voting trust in which third persons are made trustees in return for advancing funds to the corporation; unless the trust expressly authorizes otherwise, the trustees cannot act to the detriment of the beneficial owners they represent (e.g., the trustees cannot vote to issue new stock to themselves, or vote to favor creditors over stockholders). See *Brown v. McLanahan*, 148 F.2d 703 (4th Cir. 1945).

4. **Effect of failure to comply:** Precise compliance with all the terms of the statute is very important. In most states, an arrangement that is found by the court to be a voting trust will be held to be ***entirely invalid*** if it fails to meet all the statutory requirements. Nutshell, p.

200. For instance, if the state sets a maximum length of ten years for the trust, and the trust agreement does not state a maximum length, many states would treat the entire arrangement as unenforceable. *Id.*

a. **MBCA loosens rule:** But MBCA § 7.30(b) ***relaxes*** this rule: If the trust does not specify a term, or specifies a term longer than ten years, the trust will be enforceable, but only for ten years.

D. Classified stock and weighted voting: Another way in which the shareholders can re-allocate their voting power, and ensure minority stockholders a bigger voice than they would otherwise have, is by the use of ***classified stock***. The corporation sets up ***two or more classes*** of stock, and then gives the classes ***differing voting powers*** or financial rights. By this means, a minority stockholder may be given voting rights equal to those of the majority even though he does not have equal financial rights. Similarly, two equal shareholders may give a third person (even one who has no real ownership interest) a vote to break a tie between them.

1. **Generally valid:** This use of different classes and weighting of votes is generally ***valid***. Even states that have traditionally been suspicious of attempts to re-allocate voting power by use of voting agreements and voting trusts nearly always uphold the use of classified stock for this purpose.

2. **Representation for minority:** Observe that the use of different classes furnishes an easy way to insure that the minority gets a ***disproportionate*** (perhaps even equal) number of directors.

Example: A owns 90% and B owns 10% of Corporation. There are to be three members of the board. A and B agree that B should always be able to elect one director, even though he holds only 10% of the shares. Cumulative voting (*supra*, p. 41) would not suffice to guarantee B this director, since A can cast more votes for each of three nominees than B can for a single one. The problem can be resolved by creating two classes of stock: Class A (to be owned entirely by A) and Class B (to be owned entirely by B). The certificate of incorporation would be amended to state that one of the three seats on the board is to be elected by a majority vote of the class B shares. So long as B continues to control all of the class B shares, he will be assured of always being able to elect a director.

III. AGREEMENTS RESTRICTING THE BOARD'S DISCRETION

A. How problem arises: So far, we have looked only at shareholder agreements where the participants limit their discretion ***as shareholders*** (e.g., they agree to vote for a certain slate of directors). As we have seen, these shareholder agreements are nearly always valid. A quite different and more severe problem is posed when shareholders agree to restrict their discretion ***as directors***. Such an agreement may be found to violate the principle that the ***business shall be managed by the board of directors***; a number of cases, mostly older ones, hold that agreements that ***substantially fetter the discretion*** of the board of directors are ***unenforceable***.

1. **Rationale:** The courts holding that director-fettering agreements are invalid seem generally to be worried that such agreements will be unfair to ***minority stockholders*** who have not signed the agreement, and possibly to the public (including creditors). The courts rea-

son that the board of directors has a fiduciary obligation to the corporation, all of its shareholders and its creditors; an agreement that results in the board of directors' not being able to use its own best business judgment might result in unfair and unnecessary injury to a minority shareholder who did not agree to the restrictions on the board, or to a creditor.

Example: Suppose that A, B and C each own one-third of the stock of Corporation. A and B sign a secret agreement in which they agree: (1) to vote for each other for the next 20 years as directors; and (2) to cast their votes as directors for 20 years in such a way as to elect A chairman and B president, regardless of whether each does a competent job in that post. Assuming that the state of incorporation requires that a corporation's affairs shall be managed by or under the board of directors, the court will probably refuse to enforce the agreement if it is attacked by C, who can show that A or B's conduct as chairman or president is adversely affecting the value of his investment in Corporation.

2. **Statutory reform:** A number of states have enacted special statutory provisions treating as enforceable shareholder agreements that vest management decisions in the shareholders rather than in the board. But in the absence of such a statutory provision, most courts will still probably refuse to enforce an agreement that fetters the board, at least where the agreement is attacked by a minority shareholder who did not consent to it, and who can show that his interests are adversely affected. In other words, you should not simply assume that any contractual agreement by shareholders/directors about how they will act as directors, will be enforceable. Indeed, some courts may refuse to enforce even an agreement that actually injures no one, if the court concludes that the agreement effectively "sterilizes" the board of directors.

B. **The New York case law:** The leading line of cases limiting the enforceability of agreements that restrict the board's discretion has arisen in New York. We will consider two well-known New York cases, and then attempt to synthesize present New York law:

1. ***McQuade:*** In *McQuade v. Stoneham and McGraw*, 189 N.E. 234 (N.Y. 1934), the majority shareholder (Stoneham) and two minority shareholders (McQuade and McGraw) agreed that all would use their best efforts to keep one another in office as directors and officers at specified salaries. Subsequently, Stoneham and McGraw refused to try to keep McQuade in office as director and treasurer; after he was dropped from these posts he sued for breach.

   a. **Holding:** The New York Court of Appeals found that the shareholder agreement was ***invalid***, and thus held for the defendants. The court reasoned that stockholders may not, by agreeing among themselves, place "limitations . . . on the power of directors to manage the business of the corporation by the selection of agents at defined salaries." In other words, the board must be ***left free*** to exercise its own business judgment. The agreement here prevented the board from doing that, by purporting to restrict the board from firing McQuade from his treasurer's post. (Separately, the court also concluded that since McQuade was a New York City magistrate at the time of the contract, his employment was invalid under a local statute.)

2. ***Clark v. Dodge:*** But just two years later, the New York Court of Appeals seemed to soften its prohibition of contracts that restrict the board's discretion, in *Clark v. Dodge*,

199 N.E. 641 (N.Y. 1936). In *Clark*, P owned 25%, and D 75%, of two corporations. They signed an agreement whereby D was to vote for P as director and general manager, and to pay him one-fourth of the business' income, so long as he remained "faithful, efficient and competent." D argued that this agreement violated the *McQuade* rule, since it purported to restrict the discretion of the board of directors.

a. **Holding:** But the Court of Appeals ***upheld*** this business arrangement, despite *McQuade*. The court seemed to rely on two respects in which this agreement was different from the one struck down in *McQuade*: (1) ***all*** shareholders had signed the agreement, and there was no sign that anyone would be injured by the contract; and (2) the impairment of the board's powers was "negligible," apparently since P could always be discharged for cause, and his one-fourth of income could be calculated after the board determined in its discretion how much should be set aside for the company's operating needs.

3. **Synthesis:** Synthesizing *McQuade*, *Clark* and other New York cases, the law in New York seems to be that to be valid, the agreement: (1) must not harm creditors, the public or non-consenting shareholders; and (2) must involve only an ***"innocuous variance"*** from the rule that a corporation's business should be managed by the board. Also, it may be a requirement that ***all shareholders consent*** (or at the very least that the person now attacking the agreement have previously consented to it). See Nutshell, p. 174.

a. ***Zion:*** The New York courts today may in fact be more willing to uphold director-fettering arrangements than would be guessed from *McQuade* and *Clark*. For instance, in *Zion v. Kurtz*, 405 N.E.2d 681 (N.Y. 1980), all stockholders agreed that they would not cause the corporation to engage in any business transactions over Zion's objection. The corporation was incorporated in Delaware, and under Delaware law this arrangement would have been valid had the corporation elected to be treated as a statutory close corporation and placed in its articles of incorporation a special provision electing to have the corporation run by the shareholders rather than the directors. The corporation here had done neither.

i. **Arrangement upheld:** But the New York court viewed these omissions as technical ones that could be remedied by a court order; it therefore ***enforced*** the arrangement.

ii. **Significance:** It is hard to know what to make of this case, since it was a New York court interpreting Delaware law. However, the case probably indicates that the New York courts are now somewhat more willing to uphold director-fettering arrangements, at least those ***approved by all shareholders and injuring no one.***

C. **Other jurisdictions:** Other jurisdictions are probably also becoming more willing than they used to be to ***approve*** arrangements that interfere to some extent with the discretion of the board of directors, even if no statute expressly authorizes such an arrangement.

1. ***Galler* case:** Probably the leading non-New York case showing this modern liberal trend is ***Galler v. Galler***, 203 N.E.2d 577 (Ill. 1965).

a. **Facts:** The two principal owners of the corporation, Benjamin and Isadore, each owned 47.5% of the stock. They signed a shareholders' agreement in which they agreed to pay certain dividends each year and to pay, in the event either should die, a specified pension to his widow. Benjamin died, and Isadore refused to carry out the agreement.

b. **Holding:** The Illinois court upheld the agreement, even though it limited the discretion of the board of directors. The court required an agreement to satisfy three tests before it would be enforced: (1) there must be ***no minority interest*** who is ***injured*** by it; (2) there must be no injury to the public or to creditors; and (3) the agreement must not violate a clear statutory prohibition. This agreement satisfied these requirements.

c. **Importance to closely-held corporation:** Perhaps more importantly, the Illinois court in *Galler* stressed the importance of broad and enforceable stockholder agreements in the close corporation context. An investor in a close corporation "often has a large total of his entire capital invested in the business and has no ready market for his shares should he desire to sell. He feels, understandably, that he is more than a mere investor and that his voice should be heard concerning all corporate activity. Without a shareholder agreement, specifically enforceable by the courts, insuring him a modicum of control, a large minority shareholder might find himself at the mercy of an oppressive or unknowledgeable majority."

2. **Summary of modern view:** So the modern, increasingly prevalent view seems to be that a shareholder agreement that substantially curtails the discretion of the board of directors will nonetheless be ***upheld*** if it: (1) ***does not injure any minority shareholder***; (2) does not injure creditors or the public; and (3) does not violate any express statutory provision (the three requirements set forth in *Galler*).

IV. SUPER-MAJORITY VOTING AND QUORUM REQUIREMENTS

A. **Why super-majority techniques are used:** A common and effective technique for giving a minority shareholder effective veto power over the corporation's major decisions is the ***"super-majority"*** voting or quorum requirement. There are numerous variations on this technique, all of which require more than the usual "simple majority" (50%) vote or quorum. These requirements can be applied either to shareholder action (the percentage of votes needed to constitute shareholder approval, or the percentage of votes which must be present to constitute a quorum at the shareholders' meeting) or action by the board (again, the percentage of votes needed for a quorum, or the percentage of votes needed to pass the measure).

Example 1: A owns two-thirds and B owns one-third of the stock of Corporation. B is worried that A will cause Corporation to make unwise acquisitions. Therefore, A and B cause Corporation to amend its certificate of incorporation to require that 80% of shareholders approve any major acquisition. Now B has effective veto power over acquisitions.

Example 2: A, B and C each own one-third of the stock of Corporation. They hold the only three seats on the board of directors. Since A and B are brothers, and C is not related to either of them, C worries that A and B will vote together as a block on the board. Therefore, Corporation amends its charter to provide that board action must be by unanimous vote. Now, C can prevent A and B from "ganging up" on him at board meetings.

Example 3: A, B, C and D each own 25% of Corporation. If the usual "majority constitutes a quorum" rule applied for shareholder meetings, A, B and C could hold a meeting without D's presence, and two of the three could therefore deliver shareholder approval. To prevent this, they agree that a quorum for a shareholders' meeting will consist of at least 80% of all votes, and they amend the charter to so provide. Now, a meeting cannot be held unless all four shareholders are present, and (assuming that the usual majority vote rule is not changed), it will take three of the four of them to approve any measure.

B. Traditional restrictive view: Traditionally, courts have been ***reluctant*** to enforce such super-majority voting or quorum requirements, on the grounds that such requirements: (1) interfere with the democratic "majority rule" principle and (2) are likely to lead to deadlock. Courts have been most likely to strike down a super-majority provision if it requires ***unanimity***.

C. Modern statutes permit: But virtually all states today ***permit*** super-majority quorum and voting requirements, even ones setting unanimity as the required threshold. In most states, this has been accomplished by ***statutes*** that explicitly permit such techniques.

1. **MBCA:** For instance, the MBCA allows for super-majority requirements: Under § 7.27, a super-majority quorum or voting requirement for shareholders may be established if it is placed into the articles of incorporation. Under § 8.24(a), either the articles or the bylaws may set a super-majority quorum requirement for the board of directors, and under § 8.24(c) either the articles or bylaws may set a super-majority voting requirement for directors.

2. **Changing a requirement:** Observe that a minority shareholder who succeeds in having a super-majority voting or quorum requirement imposed through modification of the articles of incorporation or bylaws has really accomplished nothing, unless he has some way to prevent a simple majority from ***rescinding*** those provisions. For instance, if *A* owns two-thirds and *B* one-third of Corporation, a requirement in the articles of incorporation that acquisitions and mergers must be approved by a 75% vote of shareholders will be worthless if the articles of incorporation can themselves be amended by simple majority vote: *A* can simply vote to rescind the super-majority provision.

   a. **Protection:** Therefore, the stockholder who will benefit from the super-majority provision should make sure that ***the same super-majority vote is needed for an amendment of the provision***. Thus in the scenario set out just above, *B* should insist on a provision in the articles of incorporation stating that "any amendment to these articles shall be by a vote of 75% of the stockholders."

   b. **Automatic protection:** Some statutes give this kind of "anti-amendment" protection ***automatically***. Thus MBCA § 7.27(b) provides that "an amendment to the articles of incorporation that adds, changes, or deletes a greater quorum or voting requirement must meet the same quorum requirement and be adopted by the same vote . . . required to take action under the quorum and voting requirements then in effect or proposed to be adopted, whichever is greater."

V. SHARE TRANSFER RESTRICTIONS

A. Reasons for restrictions: The stockholders of a close corporation will usually agree to ***limit the transferability*** of shares in the corporation. For instance, they may agree that no holder may sell the shares to an outside party until the corporation has first been given the right to buy them at a pre-established price (***"first option"***), or the right to buy them by matching what the outside person is willing to pay (***"right of first refusal"***). Or, they may agree that the corporation has a firm obligation to buy the shares, and the stockholder has the obligation to sell them, at a pre-established price upon the happening of certain events (e.g., the stockholder's death, retirement or termination of employment with the corporation).

1. Rationale: There are three main reasons why most shareholders in close corporations believe that some sort of transfer restriction is a good idea:

a. Veto over new colleagues: First, in a close corporation stockholders are usually heavily involved in management, and must cooperate with each other. Each shareholder/manager is likely to want to have some say over whom he must work with. If *A* has the unfettered right to transfer his shares to whomever he wishes, this is tantamount to allowing him to thrust upon *B*, his fellow shareholder, an ***unwanted colleague***. Therefore, share transfer restrictions give the shareholders of a corporation a power analogous to the right of *delectus personae* in the partnership context, i.e., a right to ***veto the admission of a new partner***.

b. Balance of control: Second, the holders of a close corporation usually have worked out a fairly delicate ***balance of control***. This balance may be upset if shares can be freely transferred.

Example: A and B, the sole shareholders of X Corp., have worked together for years and have agreed on a balance of power whereby the Corporation will only take actions to which both shareholders agree. The Corporation has no share transfer restrictions, and B now sells half of his shares to C and half to D. Now the situation is unstable: C and A may combine to outvote D, D and A may combine to outvote C, or C and D may combine to create a stalemate. There is likely to be a lot of intrigue and uncertainty, which will probably be detrimental to the firm's ability to function.

c. Estate liquidity: Finally, if a stockholder ***dies***, a large portion of his estate may be represented by shares in a close corporation. Estate taxes will have to be paid on the actual market value of this stake, yet the lack of a ready market for a minority stake in a close corporation may prevent the estate from selling even enough shares to pay estate taxes. Therefore, a mandatory buy-sell agreement — whereby the corporation is obligated to buy, and the estate obligated to sell, some or all of the decedent's shares at a pre-established price — may be the best way of making sure that the estate can receive the necessary funds.

B. General rule: Courts are far more willing than they used to be to uphold share transfer restrictions.

1. Traditional rule: Traditionally, share transfer restrictions have been viewed as ***"restraints on alienation."*** Therefore, such restrictions have often been struck down on the grounds that they are ***unreasonable***.

2. **Modern view:** Today, courts still generally require that the restraint be ***"reasonable"*** before they will uphold it. However, courts generally find a broader range of restrictions to be reasonable than they used to. Furthermore, statutes have been enacted in many states that expressly validate certain types of restrictions. In general, courts today recognize more than they used to that share transfer restrictions often make sense for closely-held corporations, even if such arrangements would not be appropriate for a publicly held corporation. Clark, p. 764.

C. **Various techniques:** There are five principal techniques by which the transfer of shares in a closely-held corporation may be restricted:

1. **Right of first refusal:** Under a ***right of first refusal***, a shareholder may not sell his shares to an outsider without first offering the corporation or the other current shareholders (or both) a right to buy those shares at the ***same price and terms*** as those at which the outsider is proposing to buy. Usually the corporation has the first chance to exercise the right; if it does not do so, the other shareholders get the right in proportion to their holdings.

   a. **Advantage:** An advantage of the right of first refusal is that it gives the non-selling shareholders a way to keep the shares in the current "family", yet apparently does not cost the selling shareholder any funds — he is receiving the same price and terms as the outsider was willing to give.

   b. **Disadvantage:** However, the existence of a right of first refusal in fact probably makes it more difficult for the shareholder to ***find an outsider*** willing to buy his shares. The outsider faces the risk of going through the substantial effort of understanding a small business and negotiating a deal to buy an illiquid interest in it, only to have the deal "called away" at the last minute by exercise of the right of first refusal. S,S,B&W, p. 483. Also, the first refusal device works only when the shares are to be sold, not when they are to be transferred by ***gift*** or ***bequest***. *Id.*

2. **First option at fixed price:** A second device is the ***"first option."*** This is similar to the right of first refusal, except that the price is determined by the agreement creating the option. Usually this is done by inserting some kind of ***formula*** into the agreement (e.g., a provision that the option is at a price equal to "book value"). Valuation methods are discussed *infra*, p. 113.

   a. **Advantage:** An advantage of this method is that, unlike the right of first refusal, the option method can handle the situation where the shares are proposed to be transferred by ***gift*** or ***bequest***.

3. **Consent:** Third, a shareholder's transfer of stock may be made subject to the ***consent*** of the board of directors or the other stockholders.

   a. **Disadvantage:** Consent powers, since they might be used to unreasonably restrict alienation, are likely to be more closely scrutinized by the courts for "reasonableness" than the above two methods. See *infra*, p. 152.

4. **Buy-back rights:** The three above methods are triggered only if a shareholder makes a decision to transfer the shares. A ***buy-back right***, by contrast, is given to the corporation to enable it to buy back a holder's shares on the happening of certain events, ***whether the***

holder wants to sell or not. For instance, the corporation might be given the right to repurchase shares of a holder/employee upon that person's ***retirement*** or termination of employment. Clark, p. 765. The corporation is ***not*** obliged to exercise its buy-back right.

5. **Buy-sell agreement:** A ***buy-sell agreement*** is similar to a buy-back right, except that the corporation is ***obliged*** to go through with the purchase upon the happening of the specified event. Most often, the corporation and the shareholders will make a buy-sell agreement under which the corporation must re-purchase the shares upon the ***death*** of a shareholder/employee. This guarantees the holder's estate of a market for the shares and enough funds to pay estate taxes.

   For a good general overview of these five methods, see Clark, pp. 764-65.

D. **Who has right to buy:** Any of the above restrictions may run in favor of ***either*** the ***corporation*** or the ***remaining shareholders***.

1. **Purchase by corporation:** Typically, the ***corporation*** is given the first opportunity to purchase the shares, and only if it does not do so are the remaining shareholders given this right. An advantage of this approach is that it makes it easy to preserve the positions of the remaining shareholders relative to each other — the re-purchased shares are simply retired as treasury stock, and the remaining shareholders automatically maintain the same voting power vis-a-vis each other as they had before.

2. **Purchase by remaining shareholders:** If the corporation does not repurchase, or the restriction runs in favor of the remaining shareholders rather than the corporation, typically the shareholders have the right to repurchase in ***proportion*** to their existing holdings. If all exercise this right, their relative positions are preserved. If one or more do not repurchase, the unpurchased shares must generally be offered to the other shareholders *pro rata*. If there are more than a few shareholders, this process of offering and reoffering can get unwieldy, so it is usually better to have the offer run to the corporation, at least in the first instance. Nutshell, p. 211.

3. **Redemption vs. cross-purchase:** As a matter of nomenclature, if the corporation has the right to do the buying, the agreement is called a ***"redemption"*** agreement (the shares are "redeemed" by the corporation). If the other shareholders have the right, the agreement is called a ***"cross-purchase"*** agreement.

E. **Notice and consent to restrictions:** If a shareholder signs an agreement imposing a transfer restriction, he has clearly received notice of that restriction and consented to it, so the restriction will be applied to him as long as it is reasonable. But in a number of other situations, the holder will be able to argue either that he had no notice of the restriction at the time he purchased his shares, or that he did not consent to the restrictions. Special rules have evolved to determine whether the holder is bound in this situation. In general, the rule is that a holder who purchased without either ***actual or constructive notice*** of the restriction will ***not be bound*** by it. We must consider two different fact patterns:

1. **Subsequent purchaser without notice:** First, consider a person who purchases shares ***without actual knowledge*** of pre-existing restrictions at the time he makes the purchase. Such a purchaser will ***not be bound*** by the restrictions unless the restriction was ***conspicuously noted*** on the ***share certificates***. The reason is that UCC § 8-204(a) provides that "a

restriction on transfer of a security imposed by the issuer, even if otherwise lawful, is ineffective against any person without actual knowledge of it unless . . . the security is certificated and the restriction is noted conspicuously thereon. . . ."

a. **Meaning of "conspicuous":** UCC § 1-201(10) defines "conspicuous" as follows: "A term or clause is conspicuous when it is so written that a ***reasonable person*** against whom it is to operate ***ought to have noticed it***. A printed heading in capitals . . . is conspicuous. Language in the body of a form is 'conspicuous' if it is in larger or other contrasting type or color. . . ." Therefore, the certificate should have notice of the restrictions written in capital letters, larger type size, or color, in order to be certain to be conspicuous. Also, reference to the restriction should be on the ***front*** of the certificate. (But if the transferee has ***actual*** notice, then he is bound by the restrictions even if the certificate is silent.)

Example: A single line of small type on the front of the stock certificate refers to a 14-line small-type paragraph on the reverse. This paragraph in turn refers in very general terms to transfer restrictions in the articles of incorporation. *Held*, the transfer restrictions were not "conspicuous" as required by § 8-204(a), because "something must appear on the face of the certificate to attract the attention of a reasonable person when he looks at it." *Ling & Co. v. Sav. & Loan Ass'n*, 482 S.W.2d 841 (Tex. 1972).

2. **Non-consenting minority holder:** Now, consider a person who is ***already a shareholder*** at the time the restrictions are imposed. For instance, suppose the restrictions are imposed by an amendment to the articles of incorporation or the bylaws, and the shareholder does not vote in favor of these changes although he is aware that they are about to be implemented. Courts and statutes are ***split*** as to whether the non-consenting minority shareholder is bound.

a. **Modern trend:** The modern trend is probably ***not*** to bind the non-consenting shareholder. See, e.g., MBCA § 6.27(a), providing that "A restriction ***does not affect shares issued before the restriction was adopted*** unless the holders of the shares are parties to the restriction agreement or voted in favor of the restriction."

F. **Removal of restriction without consent:** Now consider the converse problem: If a restriction is in force, may it be ***removed*** without unanimous consent? If the restriction is embodied in a shareholders' agreement, this is of course a contract that may not be amended without unanimous consent. But if the restriction is imposed in the bylaws or the articles of incorporation, the issue is less clear, since the bylaws and the articles may normally be amended by majority vote. Probably most courts would hold that a ***unanimous vote is necessary***.

G. **Valuation:** All but one of the transfer restrictions described above require a ***valuation*** to be placed on the stock at some point. (The sole exception is the right of first refusal, in which the price is automatically set by what the outsider is willing to pay.) As you might expect, devising a method of setting the price at which the corporation or remaining shareholders are to acquire the disposing shareholder's shares is very tricky. Four methods are commonly used: (1) the "book value" method; (2) the "capitalized earnings" method; (3) the "mutual agreement" method; and (4) appraisal.

1. **The "book value" method:** Many companies use some variant of the ***"book value"*** method of valuation. "Book value" is an accounting concept, derived directly from the

corporation's ***balance sheet***. According to accepted accounting principles, book value is equal to the corporation's balance sheet ***assets*** minus its balance sheet ***liabilities***.

a. **Advantage:** One advantage of the book value method is that book value is a number that can be objectively determined by quick inspection of the balance sheet. Therefore, the parties are less likely to become embroiled in a dispute about this number than they are where other methods are used.

b. **Historical cost**: But a disadvantage is that book value will often be much less, or much more, than the company is really "worth" to an outside buyer. One reason for this is that under accounting conventions, assets are carried on the company's books at their ***historical cost*** rather than being adjusted to reflect market values. For instance, if the corporation acquired Blackacre, a parcel of land, in 1940 for $2000, the balance sheet will still show $2000 as the value of the asset, even if its market value is now $2 million. Therefore, the parties may be wise to agree in advance that book value shall be calculated only after marketable assets are adjusted to their current values.

   i. **Goodwill:** Conversely, balance sheets often include assets listed at historical prices that may never be realized. For instance, if Corporation acquires the stock of XYZ Corp, much of the purchase price may be allocated to the "***goodwill***" account. ("Goodwill" in an acquisition is roughly the amount by which the purchase price exceeds the book value of the acquired assets). This goodwill will probably remain on the books of Corporation indefinitely, even though it may have no practical value at all. Therefore, the parties may want to agree that book value should be computed without any value attributed to goodwill.

c. **Generally upheld:** Whatever method of computing the book value the parties agree upon, the court will usually ***enforce*** their decision, even if it turns out that the method chosen produces a figure that is shockingly low (or high) compared with the actual market value at the time of sale.

2. **The "capitalized earnings" method:** Alternatively, the shares may be valued by the ***"capitalized earnings"*** method. In theory, this method will produce the most accurate approximation of market value. Clark, p. 766. This method attempts to estimate the ***future earnings*** of the business, and then discounts these earnings to present value by using a discount rate that is appropriate for investments with similar characteristics. *Id.*

   a. **Refined method:** The main difficulty with this method is that reasonable people can disagree by a large factor as to the future earnings of the company and the appropriate discount rate. Therefore, most agreements using the "capitalized earnings" method refine it by: (1) taking recent ***past*** earnings as a predictor for future earnings and (2) agreeing on a discount rate (or a formula for calculating the discount rate) at the time the agreement is signed.

   Example: The parties might agree that future earnings will be calculated by taking the average earnings over the past three years prior to the sale, increasing this average by 15%, and then discounting by the then-current United States Treasury bill rate plus 3 percentage points. Suppose that the company has earned an average of $1 million per year over the last three years, and that the treasury bill rate at the time of sale is 8%. The value of the company would be computed as follows:

$$\frac{\$1{,}000{,}000 \times 1.15}{0.11} = \$10{,}454{,}545$$

See Clark, p. 766.

b. Salaries: Another difficulty in using the "capitalized earnings" method is that past or future earnings may be distorted by the fact that the principals have taken unusually large salaries. Therefore, the agreement will often compute earnings without subtracting any principals' salaries, or after subtracting only salaries that would be reasonable for the work actually performed.

3. The "mutual agreement" method: A third method, the "***mutual agreement***" method, typically has several stages. At the time the agreement is signed, the parties agree upon an initial fixed valuation (e.g., $2 million). But they also agree that at defined intervals (e.g., annually) or from time to time, they will ***mutually agree*** upon an adjusted number to reflect changes in actual market value.

a. Failure to agree: This method can produce dispute and inequity if the parties do not in fact attempt to revise the number as time goes by, or if the parties turn out to have sharply different interests so that they cannot agree on a fair revised number. For instance, if A is much older than B, and the parties agree to adjust from time to time the price at which the estate of the first to die will sell the shares back to the corporation, A will have the incentive to insist upon a much higher figure than B, and they may never be able to agree.

4. Appraisal: Finally, the parties can agree to have the price determined by an ***appraisal*** of the company at the time of transfer, to be performed by a neutral third party. If this method is chosen, it is important to agree upon a procedure for choosing the appraiser (e.g., by agreeing to have the appraisal performed by an arbitrator selected according to the rules of the American Arbitration Association). See S,S,B&W, p. 483.

H. Funding of buy-sell agreement: It may be a problem for the corporation or the remaining shareholders to ***fund*** their purchase of the transferror's shares. This problem is especially severe in the case of a ***buy-sell*** agreement, since here the corporation or remaining shareholders have a ***duty***, not merely an option, to purchase.

1. Life insurance: Since the main use of buy-sell agreements is to repurchase the shares of a stockholder who ***dies***, buy-sell agreements are often funded by having the corporation purchase ***life insurance*** on each shareholder. If the amount of the policy is enough to cover the estimated purchase price for that holder's shares, there will be no funds needed beyond those provided by the policy.

2. Installment payments: Alternatively, the parties can agree that the shares will be purchased by the ***installment*** method. Typically, there is a down payment, followed by quarterly or annual payments at a reasonable interest rate. Often this method is combined with the insurance method — the insurance policy furnishes the down payment, and the remaining payments are made out of the corporation's earnings over the following years. (Using the corporation's earnings to make the payments works best if the purchase is being made by the corporation rather than the surviving shareholders, since otherwise the survivors will have to pay taxes on the dividends they receive from the corporation before they turn around and pay out this money to the estate.)

I. Requirement of "reasonableness": Recall that at common law, share transfer restrictions are deemed "restraints on alienation." Even today, transfer restrictions are fairly strictly scrutinized, and will be upheld only if they are "***reasonable.***" Also, they will be ***narrowly*** construed. (For instance, a restriction on "transfer" may well be interpreted not to prevent a bequest or legacy. C&E, p. 501).

1. **Outright prohibitions and consent requirements:** Courts are especially likely to strike down an ***outright prohibition*** on the transfer of shares to third parties — the court is likely to hold that denying the shareholder the chance to sell to anyone except his fellow shareholders or the corporation is *per se* unreasonable. Nutshell, p. 207. Similarly, a provision that shares may not be sold to outsiders without the ***consent*** of the other shareholders and/or corporation is likely to be found unreasonable, if the provision is drafted in a way that permits the others to withhold their consent arbitrarily. *Id.*

2. **Options, first refusals, and buy-sell agreements:** The remaining types of restrictions — first option, right of first refusal, buy-backs and buy-sell agreements — are more likely to be found "reasonable." In general, if the mechanism chosen by the parties is reasonable ***at the time the method is agreed upon***, it will probably be found reasonable even though it turns out to produce a price that is much higher or much lower than the market price at the time of sale.

3. **Statutes:** A number of states have enacted ***statutes*** that expressly validate certain types of share transfer restrictions that might otherwise be held "unreasonable" at common law.

   a. **Delaware:** For instance, Delaware GCL § 202(c) specifically validates first refusals, first options, buy-sell agreements and consent requirements. § 202(c) even validates outright prohibitions on the transfer of shares to "designated persons or classes of persons" if such designation is "not manifestly unreasonable." (For instance, a corporation might flatly prohibit transfer of its shares to any ***competitor.***)

   b. **MBCA:** Similarly, MBCA § 6.27(d) expressly validates most types of restrictions. This section is very similar to the Delaware provision, except that consent requirements are upheld only if they are "not manifestly unreasonable." So a flat requirement that the corporation and all other shareholders consent to a prohibition (with no further provision that consent will not be unreasonably withheld) probably would be struck down by a court interpreting the MBCA, at least if the refusal to consent on the actual facts was unreasonable.

VI. RESOLUTION OF DISPUTES, INCLUDING DISSOLUTION

A. Dissension and deadlock: A close corporation is to some extent like a family. The shareholders are usually active in management, and if they do not get along well together the corporation's operations are likely to suffer. Advance planning — use of techniques like a shareholders' voting agreement, super-majority requirements and the other techniques described above — may reduce the likelihood that shareholders' disagreements will hurt the corporation, but they certainly do not eliminate this possibility. Furthermore, in many close corporations no advance planning is ever done, and the parties may find themselves at odds with nothing but the general corporation statute of the jurisdiction to guide them as to their rights. Therefore, the law must deal with two related inter-shareholder problems: ***dissension*** and ***deadlock***.

1. **Meaning of "dissension":** "Dissension" refers to squabbles or disagreements among the shareholders. For instance, the holders may disagree about whether to enter a new line of business, rent a particular piece of real estate, employ the son-in-law of one of them, or almost any other business-related matter.

2. **Meaning of "deadlock":** "Deadlock" refers to a scenario in which the corporation is ***paralyzed*** and prevented from acting. Usually deadlock arises from some aspect of the ***control structure*** that the shareholders have adopted.

    a. **Three types:** There are three common ways in which the corporation may become deadlocked:

        i. **Two 50% holders:** Two factions each own exactly 50% of the outstanding shares, and cannot agree;

        ii. **Even number of directors:** There is an even number of directors, each of the two factions has the voting power to elect exactly half of the directors, and the two sets of directors cannot agree; or

        iii. **Minority holder has veto:** A minority shareholder has, through a shareholder voting agreement, super-majority requirement or some other means, obtained a veto power over corporate action, and exercises that veto.

        See Nutshell, p. 258.

    b. **Deadlock at shareholder level vs. director level:** Observe that deadlock may occur at either the shareholder or director level, or both.

        i. **Shareholder level:** If deadlock occurs only at the ***shareholder*** level, the result is not usually immediately catastrophic: The holders may not be able to elect new directors, but in most states the directors elected before the deadlock arose will remain in office until successors are elected (see, e.g., MBCA § 8.05(e), to this effect), so there will still be a board that can take action.

        ii. **Director level:** Deadlock at the ***director*** level is more immediately dangerous. Here, the board's inability to take action may prevent the corporation from functioning (though a strong president may be able to run the company effectively, perhaps while ignoring the deadlocked board). See Nutshell, p. 259.

3. **Buyout of one faction:** Even if the disagreements are not resolvable, the shareholders will often be able to deal with the problem by a ***buy-out*** — one faction buys the other's shares at a mutually acceptable price.

    a. **Quandary of minority shareholder:** However, the factions will find it hard to come to a mutually acceptable buy-out arrangement if they have sharply different amounts of ***bargaining power***. For instance, consider the minority stockholder who has not been able to preserve any veto power by voting agreement, super-majority provision or otherwise. Such a minority holder may say to the majority holder, "Buy me out," but the majority holder has little incentive to do so at a fair price. Indeed, the majority holder has the ability to "soften up" the minority holder by refusing to have the corporation declare a dividend, refusing to employ the minority holder, or otherwise denying the minority holder economic benefits from his equity in the corporation; the majority holder can then make a "low ball" offer for the minority holder's shares, or can refuse to make any offer at all.

b. **No right to compulsory buy-out:** You might think that the law would deal with this situation by giving a minority holder the right to ***compel the majority*** to buy-out his shares at a fair price. But in fact, ***no state*** gives the minority holder an automatic right to compel a buy-out regardless of the circumstances. (A few states do allow the judge to order a buy-out at a fair price if specified statutory criteria are met, such as the existence of deadlock or oppression of the minority. See *infra*, p. 157.)

   i. **Rationale:** Probably the two main reasons for this absence of a general right to compel a buy-out are: (1) such a compulsory buy-out would give the minority holder a power to "***hold up***" the majority, i.e., the power to extract unfair concessions in return for not exercising this right; and (2) the existence of such a right might ***impede the corporation's operations***, by suddenly draining the cash needed for the buyout.

c. **Dissolution and other techniques:** Instead, the law attempts to deal with dissension and deadlock by giving courts a number of discretionary remedies. The most important of these is the ability to compel a ***dissolution*** of the corporation; judicially-ordered dissolution is discussed extensively below. Other techniques include: (1) the appointment of provisional directors, custodians and receivers; (2) the use of a judicially-ordered buy-out in lieu of dissolution; and (3) the modern trend of imposing on the majority a ***fiduciary obligation*** to the minority, for breach of which damages may be awarded. We consider each of these in turn following treatment of dissolution.

B. **Dissolution:** The most important judicial remedy for dissension and/or deadlock is for the court to order that the corporation be ***involuntarily dissolved***. Dissolution means that the corporation ***ceases to exist*** as a legal entity. The corporation's assets are sold off, its debts paid, and any surplus distributed to the shareholders.

1. **Powerful weapon:** A decree of dissolution thus offers a shareholder, especially a minority shareholder, a way to ***cash in*** on his investment in the corporation, without the consent of the other shareholders.

2. **No general right to dissolution:** However, ***no*** state gives a shareholder an ***automatic right*** to a judicially-ordered dissolution. Instead, each state has a statute setting forth the ***specific grounds*** for which dissolution may be granted. These statutes are usually ***strictly construed***, and only if the shareholder shows that one of the statutory grounds applies will the court order involuntary dissolution.

3. **Model Act:** The MBCA is fairly typical.

a. **Four showings:** Under MBCA § 14.30(a)(2), a shareholder may obtain dissolution only if he shows one of four things:

i. **Director deadlock:** that the ***directors*** are ***deadlocked*** in the management of the corporation's affairs, in a way that is causing injury to the corporation or its shareholders (§14.30(a)(2)(i)); or

ii. **Oppression:** that the directors or those controlling the corporation have acted in a manner that is ***"illegal, oppressive, or fraudulent"*** (§14.30(a)(2)(ii); or

iii. **Shareholder deadlock:** that the ***shareholders*** are ***deadlocked*** in voting power, and have failed to elect successor directors "for a period that includes at least ***two consecutive annual meeting dates***" (§14.30(a)(2)(iii)); or

iv. **Waste:** that the corporation's assets are being ***"misapplied or wasted"*** (§14.30(a)(2)(iv)).

b. **Harm usually required:** Observe that none of these four MBCA showings permits a shareholder to dissolve the corporation merely because he thinks he would be better off cashing out his investment. In fact, for three of the four, the shareholder must show actual and serious ***harm*** or abuse. Only in the "shareholder deadlock" situation is a finding of serious harm or abuse not needed, and there the shareholder will have to show that at least two annual meetings have occurred at which no successor directors could be elected. Nutshell, p. 260.

4. **Judge's discretion:** Most states have held that even if the statutory criteria are met, the decision whether to grant dissolution is left to the ***judge's discretion***. C&E, p. 523. Thus the court is usually free to deny dissolution if dissolution would be ***unfair*** to one or more shareholders. For instance, suppose that: (1) dissolution is requested by the dominant shareholder, (2) a forced sale will destroy any "going concern" value, and (3) the court believes that the shareholder requesting dissolution will be able to buy up the assets at a bargain price and continue in business without the other shareholder's receiving a fair portion of the business' going concern value. In this situation, the court is likely to ***deny dissolution*** even if the statutory criteria are met.

5. **Profitability:** If the corporation is ***profitable***, the court is less likely to use its discretion to dissolve, than where it is not profitable. However, "profitability is not an absolute bar to dissolution." C&E, p. 524.

6. **Dissolution as remedy for deadlock:** Nearly all states allow the court to order dissolution as a remedy for shareholder or director ***deadlock***. Again, however, remember that even where deadlock is shown, the court may decline to order dissolution because this would be unfair to shareholders.

7. **Dissolution as remedy for oppression:** More recently, many states have added ***"oppression"*** of a shareholder as a statutory ground for dissolution. If a minority shareholder can show that the majority has used its voting power to treat the minority holder unfairly, and to deprive him of the economic benefits of his ownership, the court is able to order dissolution in most states. The court may find such oppression even though the majority has not acted fraudulently or illegally.

Example: P1 works for Corporation for 42 years, and then resigns. P2 works for Corporation for 35 years, and is then fired. Each is a minority stockholder in Corporation. While the two were employed by Corporation, they received the benefits of corporate ownership in the form of either dividends or extra compensation, in proportion to their stockholdings. After the Ps leave Corporation's employ, the remaining shareholders change the method by which they pay out Corporation's earnings — instead of paying based on stock ownership, they pay based on services rendered to the corporation. The majority also alters a long-standing unofficial practice whereby Corporation buys back the shares of employee shareholders when they leave Corporation's employ. The Ps thus are left with no way to derive any economic value from their minority holdings in Corporation. They petition for dissolution.

Held, for the Ps. The New York statute permits judicial dissolution if the petitioners show that they hold at least 20% of a corporation's shares and have been "oppressed." The majority's conduct here constituted "oppression": "A shareholder who reasonably expected that ownership in the corporation would entitle him or her to a job, a share of corporate earnings, a place in corporate management, or some other form of security, would be oppressed in a very real sense when others in the corporation seek to defeat those expectations and there exists no effective means of salvaging the investment." Here, the Ps' expectation that they would receive distributions proportional to stockholdings, and that Corporation would buy back their shares if their employment ended, were objectively reasonable, so the change in corporate policy did oppress them. Therefore, the court will order dissolution of Corporation. (But the majority may avoid dissolution by buying back the Ps' shares for what the court determines to be a fair price). *Matter of Kemp & Beatley, Inc.*, 473 N.E.2d 1173 (N.Y. 1984).

a. **Definition of "oppression":** What kind of conduct by the majority constitutes "oppression" of the minority, so that the statutory right to dissolution is triggered? There seem to be two main classes of majority shareholder behavior that will constitute "oppression": (1) self-dealing; and (2) squeeze-out moves.

   i. **Self-dealing:** ***Self-dealing*** occurs when the majority holder engages in corporate transactions that ***benefit the holder at the corporation's expense.*** For instance, self-dealing might be found if the majority stockholder caused the corporation to ***purchase supplies*** at an inflated price from another company in which the majority holder had an interest. Clark, p. 792.

   ii. **Squeeze out moves:** ***Squeeze-out moves*** occur when the majority attempts to ***exclude the minority*** from either: (1) the ***economic benefits*** of corporate ownership; or (2) participation in the corporate ***decision-making process***. For instance, if the majority holder declines to pay dividends even though the corporation is profitable, declines to employ the minority holder, or declines to pay him anything more than an ordinary salary, this would cause the minority holder to lose the benefits of ownership. Or, if the majority holder used his control of the board to disregard all suggestions by the minority stockholder/director, or refused to let the minority holder be voted onto the board, this might be found to be such a denial of opportunity to participate in corporate decision-making that it would constitute "oppression". See generally Clark, p. 792.

b. **Relation to "fiduciary obligation" doctrine:** As we will see below, *infra*, p. 161, a number of courts have now begun to find a general ***fiduciary obligation*** on the part of the majority stockholder to the minority stockholder in a close corporation. In general, the kinds of acts by the majority that would violate this fiduciary obligation (e.g., refusal of employment, refusal to pay dividends, etc.) would also constitute "oppression." Clark, p. 792.

8. **Non-statutory grounds:** Some courts will occasionally grant dissolution based on ***non-statutory grounds***. For instance, if the applicable dissolution statute recognizes deadlock but not oppression as grounds for dissolution, in some states the court may use its ***equitable powers*** to compel dissolution for oppression even though this ground is not mentioned in the statute. However, it is generally not easy for the petitioner to convince the court to use its non-statutory dissolution powers. Clark, pp. 793-94.

9. **Buy-out in lieu of dissolution:** It will often make more economic sense for one shareholder to ***buy out*** the other rather than permit judicially-ordered dissolution to occur.

   a. **Rationale:** If the corporation is dissolved and its assets sold off piecemeal, any "going concern" value will be destroyed. Most businesses have at least some going concern value — that is, most businesses are worth more alive than dead. Therefore, in the usual case one party will buy out the other, or they will agree to sell the going business to a third party, instead of permitting the court to order a liquidation.

   b. **Judicial order:** Furthermore, a number of states have now enacted statutes that take account of the fact that a buy-out will often be more sensible than a dissolution. Some of these statutes give the party opposing dissolution the right to buy out the shares of the party seeking dissolution at a judicially-supervised fair price (even if the party seeking dissolution does not want this). Other statutes allow the court to ***order*** a buy-out in lieu of a dissolution. But under these statutes, the buy-out may only be ordered if the statutory criteria for dissolution are met; remember that no state gives a minority shareholder the automatic right, regardless of circumstances, to compel a buy-out of his interest (*supra*, p. 154).

C. **Dissolution of an LLC:** Most states allow for judicial dissolution of ***LLCs***, just as for corporations.

1. **Greater private-ordering:** But there is an important distinction between corporations and LLCs when it comes to dissolution. Shareholders of a corporation do not necessarily have (though they may have) a shareholder agreement detailing how the corporation is to be run, and dealing with such issues as dissolution and buyout. Members of an LLC, by contrast, *must* have an "operating agreement," detailing at least some aspects of how the LLC is to be run (see *supra*, p. 12). Therefore, it's more likely that the members of the LLC will have made their ***own private agreement*** dealing with issues like the break-up of the company than is the case for shareholders of a typical corporation. This ought to mean that use of judicial dissolution will be needed ***less often*** than in the corporation case — for instance, if the members of the LLC have signed an operating agreement giving any member the right to withdraw and receive the value of her membership interest, this "buyout" clause ought to reduce the need for judicial dissolution.

a. **Buyout as substitute for LLC's dissolution:** There is another reason why judicial dissolution is less likely in the LLC case than the corporate one. In the corporate setting, the "default" rule (i.e., the one that the court will follow if the parties have not reached their own agreement) is that ***no shareholder is entitled to compel the other(s) to buy him out*** if they have a disagreement — so dissolution is essentially the *only* statutory (as opposed to contract-based) remedy for impasse or oppression. But the default rule for LLCs, in most states, is exactly the ***opposite***: the default rule is that any member may resign, and thereupon ***withdraw the value of her membership interest.***

   i. **Delaware applies:** For instance, ***Delaware*** applies this default rule. See Del. LLC Act, §18-604: "[U]pon resignation, any resigning member is ... if not otherwise provided in [an operating] agreement, ... entitled to receive, within a reasonable time after resignation, the ***fair value of his [LLC] interest*** as of the date of resignation based upon his right to share in distributions from a limited liability company." So in Delaware, as in most states, if the agreement is ***silent*** on the issue of withdrawal and/or buyout, the dissident member is effectively ***entitled to a mandatory buyout*** under this default rule, making it less likely that dissolution will be needed.

2. **The "reasonably practicable" standard:** But suppose that the operating agreement ***specifies*** that a resigning member is ***not*** entitled to a mandatory buyout. Does the resigning member (or a member who would like to resign) have the ability to cash out the fair value of her interest by causing the LLC to be ***judicially dissolved*** over the objection of the other member(s)? The short answer is ***"no"*** — LLC statutes almost ***never*** give a member a ***unilateral right to dissolve the LLC*** if the operating agreement is silent on the issue of dissolution. Instead, state LLC statutes typically specify ***very limited grounds*** for which the court may decree dissolution. Most statutes allow dissolution only where it is ***not reasonably practical*** to carry out the business in the manner contemplated by the operating agreement.

   The ***Delaware*** LLC Act follows this approach. The Act lists ***only one ground*** for judicial dissolution: the court may decree dissolution of the LLC on application by any member "whenever it is ***not reasonably practicable*** to ***carry on the business*** in conformity with [the operating agreement]." §18-802.

   a. **Factors to be considered in Delaware:** The Delaware statute does not specify what factors the court should consider in determining whether it is "reasonably practicable" to carry on the business in accordance with the operating agreement. But the cases show that there are ***three circumstances*** that, when present, are likely to persuade the Delaware courts to approve dissolution. As the leading case on the subject puts it, these circumstances are that:

      [1] "[T]he members' vote is ***deadlocked at the Board level***";

      [2] "[T]he ***operating agreement*** gives ***no means of navigating*** around the deadlock"; and

      [3] "[D]ue to the ***financial condition of the company***, there is effectively ***no business to operate."***

Fisk Ventures, LLC v. Segal, 2009 WL 73957 (Del. Ch. 2009). The court in *Fisk Ventures* explained that the three factors ***need not all be present*** for the court to approve dissolution. But the cases suggest that typically, dissolution will be granted because either *both factors [1] and [2] exist* (i.e., a deadlock that cannot be navigated around) or *factor [3] exists* (bad financial condition prevents operation of a viable business), or all three.

b. Illustration (*Fisk Ventures v. Segal*): *Fisk Ventures*, *supra*, illustrates the kind of fact pattern in which the Delaware courts will decree a dissolution over the objection of some members of the LLC.

i. Parties: P (Segal) was a biochemist who formed Genitrix, LLC ("the LLC"). The business's main asset was a patent licensed from university research labs, which could not be assigned except pursuant to a sale of the entire business. D (Fisk Ventures) was a venture capital investor that invested nearly $1 MM in the LLC, in return for which it received various rights, including (1) certain anti-dilution protections if additional money was to be raised; and (2) a "Put Right," under which D had the right to require the LLC to buy back its stock after a certain date (which by the time of the litigation had long since arrived).

ii. LLC structure: The Board of the LLC had five members, with P and D each appointing two. The operating agreement said that no Board action could occur except by vote of 75% of the Board; this meant that either P or D could in effect ***veto any Board action***. The agreement also said that the LLC could be wound up or dissolved only by consent of 75% of the Board or by a decree of judicial dissolution.

iii. Conflict: The LLC ran out of money, and by the time of suit no longer had an office or any revenue. D brought suit to have the company dissolved and the patent license sold to the highest bidder. P objected to the dissolution on the grounds that it would be reasonably practicable to continue operating the business if only D would either (1) waive its anti-dilution rights so that additional money could be raised from third persons (which P was confident could be done), or (2) exercise its Put Rights so that the LLC could buy out D's interest and then raise new funds.

iv. Dissolution ordered: The Delaware Court of Chancery found for D, and ***granted a dissolution.*** The court concluded that all three of the circumstances (listed above) that should be looked to in deciding whether carrying on the business was no longer "reasonably practicable" were present.

[1] Deadlock: First, the Board was ***deadlocked***, since 75% of the Board members had to approve any action, and P and D could each prevent the 75% from being achieved by withholding their two votes. As the court put it, "This type of charter provision, unless a 'tie-breaking' clause exists, is almost always a recipe for disaster ... [and] unfortunately, the parties are behaving true to form."

[2] No way to navigate deadlock: There was no way to ***navigate this deadlock*** under the operating agreement. P argued that D should be required to exercise its Put Right, so as to avoid the deadlock. But the court held that the Put Right was an ***option belonging to D***, not to P or the LLC; "it would be inequitable for this court to force a party to exercise his option when that party deems it in its best interest not to do so."

[3] Lack of funds: The lack of funds made it ***impractical to carry on the business.*** Again, P argued that if the court simply ordered D to exercise its Put Right, P could then raise new funds to both carry out the buy-back of D's stock and exploit the value of the patent (perhaps by selling it to a third party). If the company were forced into dissolution, P argued, the value of the patent would be lost. But the court concluded that the value of the patent could likely be preserved just as well through a court-ordered dissolution and sale and through a continuation of the LLC's existence.

[4] "Unclean hands": P made one last-ditch argument: that D was trying to put the company into dissolution so that it could ***buy the assets at fire sale prices***, and was thus using its leverage under the operating agreement in an unfair way. Therefore, he argued, D had ***"unclean hands,"*** preventing it from being entitled to the equitable relief of court-ordered dissolution. But the court rejected this argument, too: D had expressly negotiated all of the rights it held under the operating agreement, and D was therefore "perfectly within its rights" to exercise its negotiated leverage to benefit solely itself. The court was "in no position to ***redraft*** the [operating agreement] for these ***sophisticated and well-represented parties***." Therefore, dissolution was the only available remedy.

D. Alternatives to dissolution: Dissolution is not the only way of dealing with deadlock and/or dissension in the close corporation. We consider briefly a number of other methods:

1. **Arbitration:** The shareholders may agree to have their disputes subjected to ***arbitration***. Most states now have a policy of encouraging arbitration; for instance, in most states arbitration agreements are irrevocable, and an arbitrator's award may then be entered as an enforceable judgment.

2. **Provisional directors:** A number of states allow the court to appoint a ***provisional director***. Most commonly, a provisional director can be appointed to ***break a deadlock*** on the board. See, e.g., Cal. Corp. Code § 308. Once the tie is broken, the provisional director is normally removed. The provisional director has no powers beyond those of an ordinary director. Clark, p. 797.

   a. **Impartiality:** Many state statutes explicitly require that the provisional director be ***impartial***.

      i. **Where statute is silent:** Where the statute does ***not explicitly say*** that the provisional director must be impartial, courts have tended to say that he need ***not*** be.

3. **Custodian:** Many states allow the court to appoint a ***custodian***. A custodian has the power to ***run the business***. See, e.g., Del. § 352, allowing the appointment of a custodian to run any deadlocked close corporation.

4. **Receiver:** Nearly all states allow the court to appoint a ***receiver***. Unlike a custodian, the job of the receiver is to ***liquidate*** the corporation rather than to continue it. Therefore, a receiver is usually only appointed for a dying corporation. Clark, p. 796.

5. **Statutory buy-out right:** As noted (*supra*, p. 157), some states allow the court to order a judicially supervised ***buy-out*** in lieu of dissolution, if the requirements for dissolution are met.

6. **Fiduciary obligation of majority to minority:** Last and probably most significant, a few states have formulated a theory of ***fiduciary obligation*** to resolve close corporation disputes. These courts, especially the Massachusetts courts, have held that ***a majority stockholder in a close corporation has a fiduciary obligation to a minority shareholder***, and must behave towards him in good faith. Violation of this obligation can be compensated by an award of ***damages***. This "fiduciary obligation" doctrine is important as a method of resolving disputes, because it gives the courts that apply it a method of rectifying the minority holder's grievances without the very strong medicine of dissolution.

   a. **Application to share repurchase:** For instance, an important Massachusetts case helps minority shareholders by holding that if a corporation ***repurchases*** shares from one stockholder, it must ***offer to repurchase from other holders on the same basis***. ***Donahue v. Rodd Electrotype Co.***, 328 N.E.2d 505 (Mass. 1975).

      i. **Facts:** The facts of *Donahue* illustrate how this "fiduciary obligation" doctrine can sometimes protect minority holders in circumstances where dissolution would formerly have been the only method of protecting them. P was a minority holder in a corporation who had inherited her shares from her husband, an employee of the corporation. The corporation had previously bought back shares from its majority stockholder at a high price. It refused to buy a similar portion of P's shares back from her at anything close to that price, thus leaving her with a largely unmarketable interest.

      ii. **Holding:** The court held that the corporation was ***required to repurchase shares from P in the same portion, and at the same price***, as it had purchased from the majority holder. The court phrased its rationale broadly: "Stockholders in the close corporation ***owe one another substantially the same fiduciary duty in the operation of the enterprise that partners owe to one another***. . . . [This is the duty of] ***utmost good faith and loyalty***. . . . [Stockholders] may not act out of avarice, expediency or self-interest. . . ." Where the controlling shareholder causes the corporation to buy back shares from him and not from minority holders, he is effectively using corporate funds for his personal benefit, in violation of this strict duty of good faith. (The court defined a "close corporation" to be one which has a small number of stockholders, no ready market for its shares, and substantial participation by the majority stockholder in the management of the company.)

   b. **"Squeeze-outs":** If the majority attempts a classic "squeeze-out" of a minority holder, the majority holder may be found to have violated this fiduciary obligation. For instance, if the majority ***refuses to pay dividends***, and refuses to employ the minority holder, so that the minority has no way to participate in the economic fruits of ownership, this may be a violation of the majority's fiduciary obligation.

i. ***Wilkes* case:** For instance, the highest court of Massachusetts extended the "fiduciary obligation" doctrine of *Donahue* to cover this kind of squeeze out in the later case of ***Wilkes v. Springside Nursing Home, Inc.***, 353 N.E.2d 657 (Mass. 1977). P and three other stockholders each owned 25% of the corporation. Each holder participated in management, and received an equal salary. Relations between P and one of the other stockholders deteriorated, and the other holders caused the corporation to ***terminate P's salary and to drop him from the board.*** The court found that the other holders had violated their fiduciary obligation to P by this squeeze-out, since it stripped P of his ability to obtain his expected return on his investment.

ii. **"Legitimate business purpose" test:** But the *Wilkes* court was careful to make it clear that not every act by the majority that is disadvantageous to a minority stockholder will be a breach of this fiduciary obligation. Instead, the majority's conduct will be upheld if there was a ***"legitimate business purpose"*** for it, and that purpose could not have been achieved by a different course of action less harmful to the minority holder. Here, the majority stockholders had not shown a legitimate business purpose in dropping P from the payroll and from the board, so they had violated their fiduciary obligation to him.

c. **Obligation of minority stockholder:** One lower Massachusetts court has even gone so far as to hold that a ***minority*** stockholder has a fiduciary obligation to his co-stockholders, if the minority holder has been given a veto power over corporate actions.

Example: Dr. Wolfson is one of four equal shareholders in a corporation that owns real estate. The corporation's charter gives each stockholder an effective veto power over any corporate decision. Over the objections of the other three stockholders, Wolfson refuses to allow the corporation to pay a dividend out of its surplus. Consequently, the corporation is assessed substantial penalties by the IRS for excess accumulations of earnings.

Held, Wolfson's refusal to allow a dividend was motivated more by his personal tax considerations and dislike for his fellow shareholders than for the corporation's benefit. Therefore, Wolfson must reimburse the corporation for the loss it suffered from his unreasonableness (the amount of the IRS penalties). The court will declare a dividend if Wolfson does not agree to one on his own. *Smith v. Atlantic Properties, Inc.*, 422 N.E.2d 798 (App. Ct. Mass. 1981).

d. **Non-Massachusetts cases:** So far, the doctrine that stockholders in a close corporation owe each other a fiduciary obligation of utmost good faith has principally been applied in Massachusetts. But a few non-Massachusetts cases have also applied the doctrine. See Clark, p. 800.

i. **Delaware rejects:** But other states, most notably Delaware, have ***rejected*** a special fiduciary-obligation approach to close corporations. The Delaware decision doing so is *Nixon v. Blackwell,* 626 A.2d 1366 (Del. 1993).

(1) ***Donahue* approach rejected:** The court rejected in *Nixon* the approach of Massachusetts in cases like *Donahue*. The court phrased the issue as "[w]hether there should be any special, judicially-created rules to 'protect' minority

stockholders of closely-held Delaware corporations," and concluded that "[i]t would do violence to normal corporate practice and our corporation law to fashion an *ad hoc* ruling which would result in a ***court-imposed stockholder buy-out*** for which the parties had not contracted."

Quiz Yourself on ***CLOSE CORPORATIONS*** *(ENTIRE CHAPTER)*

37. The Three Musketeers Toy Company, a close corporation, makes war toys — "My First Uzi," "Baby's Teething Grenade," "Battlin' Scuds 'N' Patriots," etc. Aramis owns 60% of Three Musketeers' voting stock; Athos and Porthos each own 20%. Three Musketeers's board of directors has three members, who are elected via cumulative voting. Athos and Porthos agree in writing that before voting for directors they will confer and agree upon a mutually-acceptable candidate, so that they will be sure that between them they elect at least one director to the board. The agreement is to last three years. Before the very next annual meeting, Athos changes his mind and votes his shares in favor of Aramis's nominees.

(a) Is the voting agreement valid? ____________

(b) Assume that the court finds the agreement valid. What relief will the court most likely award? ____________

38. March Hare and Mad Hatter are minority shareholders of Alice's Wonderland Travel Adventures, Inc., a close corporation. Hare and Hatter sign a document under which both agree that Hare will have the power to vote both his own and Hatter's shares on any issue put to a shareholder vote. At the same time, Hatter also transfers physical possession of his shares to Hare. The agreement has a duration of eight years. No one knows about the agreement except the two signatories, and Hatter's shares remain listed on the corporation's books as belonging to Hatter. At the next shareholder meeting, Hatter purports to vote his shares, but Hare says that he has the power to vote them (and shows the document to the corporate secretary). The secretary goes to court for a ruling as to who may vote the shares. Assume that the MBCA is in force.

(a) If you are representing Hatter, what argument will you make to the judge? ____________

(b) If you are representing Hare, what argument will you make to the judge? ____________

(c) What is the most likely result? ____________

39. The I-Say-Boy Dairy Company, a close corporation, has four shareholders, with Foghorn Leghorn and Miss Prissy between them owning 60% of the voting stock. The two minority shareholders are Dawg and Weasel. Foghorn and Prissy agree between themselves to elect themselves as two of the three members of the board of directors and to appoint themselves officers at a combined annual salary of $400,000, regardless of the company's level of sales and profits. Two years later (while the agreement is still in force), Foghorn and Miss Prissy stick to the agreement. The combined $400,000 in salaries is somewhat excessive in light of the company's modest sales and profits, but there's enough cash in the company till to pay the salaries for now. The agreement complies with applicable procedural statutes. Dawg sues to have the agreement declared invalid. Will he succeed? ____________

40. The Lady Macbeth Suicide Hotline, Inc., is a five-year-old close corporation. Macbeth owns 700 shares, and Banquo owns the remaining 300. At an annual meeting, Macbeth votes his shares to amend the bylaws to grant the company a right of first refusal on any subsequent stock transfer. Banquo votes against the amendment and, boy, does that make Macbeth mad. Thereafter, Banquo wants to transfer his shares to Fleance, who's willing to buy them for $10 a share. Under the prevailing modern approach, must Banquo first offer the shares to the company at $10 a share? ________________

41. The Jekyll & Hyde Cosmetics Company, a close corporation, has, and has always had, bylaws providing that, before a shareholder may sell his shares to a third party, the corporation has a 60-day option period during which the corporation can purchase the shares at the "book" (i.e. net asset) value as stated on the company's most recent balance sheet. This valuation method was agreed upon by the shareholders 20 years ago, at a time when book value was the most common method for valuing a business such as this one. Dr. Jekyll owns 10% of Jekyll & Hyde's shares. He wants to sell, and so notifies Jekyll & Hyde. Jekyll & Hyde's chairman, Shelley, writes back, offering the current book value, $25 a share. Jekyll balks, since the market value of the shares is now around $100 a share. (Cosmetics businesses now typically sell for a substantial multiple of book value, due to a change over the last 20 years in how the market values successful companies in this industry.) Jekyll tries to sell to Walton at $100 a share. The company refuses to issue a new certificate in Walton's name. The company seeks to rescind the sale and to compel Jekyll to accept the company's price. What result? ________________

42. Ricky Ricardo is founder, chairman of the board, and president of the Ricky Ricardo Babaloo Club, Inc., a close corporation. He owns 60% of Babaloo's voting stock. When he retires, Babaloo buys some of his shares for $1,000 a share. Lucy Ricardo, a minority shareholder, immediately thereafter offers her shares to the corporation at $1,000 each. Babaloo claims it can't afford to pay that much, offering instead $400 a share. (In reality, the corporation could easily afford to pay the $1,000.)

(a) If you represent Lucy, what argument will you make with respect to the company's obligation to Lucy? ________________

(b) Will you succeed with the argument you made in part (a)? ________________

Answers

37. (a) Yes. Virtually all courts today hold that voting agreements — including those which, like this one, are of the "agreement to agree" type — are valid and enforceable. [137]

(b) Specific performance, in that Athos's shares will be voted in favor of Porthos's nominee, so that that nominee is sure to be elected. With three directors, under cumulative voting it takes at least 26% of the shares to elect one director. (See the formula on p. 56). So if the court casts Athos's shares in favor of Porthos's nominee, putting 40% of the total voting power behind that nominee, the latter is certain to be elected.

Note that in earlier days, a court was more likely to cancel any votes cast by Athos in violation of the agreement than to order that Athos's vote be cast in a particular way. Such "relief" would be useless to Porthos, because Aramis would still elect the entire board, since Porthos's 20% would not be enough to elect a single director, even under cumulative voting. See *Ringling Bros. v. Ringling,* involving similar facts. [138] Porthos thus does much better under the modern approach.

38. (a) That this is an attempted voting trust, which is invalid because not previously disclosed to the corporation. Under MBCA § 7.30 (as under most modern statutes), "voting trusts" are legal, but only if several quite stringent requirements are met. In particular, "[T]he trustee shall prepare a list of the names and addresses of all owners of beneficial interests in the trust, together with the number and class of shares each transferred to the trust, and deliver copies of the list and agreement to the corporation's principal office." § 7.30(a). Such a trust does not become effective until "the date the first shares subject to the trust are registered in the trustee's name." § 7.30(b). Since the shares here were never registered to Hare as trustee, and the document was never filed with the corporation, if it's a voting trust it never became effective (you would argue on Hatter's behalf). [140]

(b) That the arrangement is a valid voting agreement, not an invalid voting trust, and that it's therefore specifically enforceable. MBCA § 7.31 says that "Two or more shareholders may provide for the manner in which they will vote their shares by signing an agreement for that purpose. A voting agreement created under this section is not subject to the provisions [on voting trusts]." If the court agrees that this is a "voting agreement" rather than an attempted "voting trust," it doesn't matter that the corporation wasn't aware of the arrangement, because there's no requirement of disclosure. If the court accepts this characterization, the agreement will be specifically enforceable. [139]

(c) Probably Hare's argument will prevail, and the arrangement will be specifically enforced. Other than the physical transfer of shares, there's nothing in this arrangement (so far as the facts tell us) that forces the conclusion that this was intended to be a true trust, as opposed to an agreement. So the court will probably conclude that the parties' intent will be better carried out by treating it as an agreement, and enforcing it, than by treating it as a nullity.

39. Yes, probably. Agreements restricting director discretion in a close corporation are generally valid if they comply with applicable statutes ***and*** they don't harm creditors or minority shareholders. [144] Here, the agreement between the majority shareholders that they will vote themselves excessive salaries harms the minority shareholders (Dawg and Weasel) by leaving less money for dividends and other corporate activities. (It may also harm creditors — the facts don't give us enough information to know.) Since the agreement harms the minority shareholders, a court will probably hold it invalid. At the very least, this will mean that if either Foghorn or Miss Prissy changes his/her mind about voting the high salaries, the other won't be able to sue. (It's less clear whether Dawg will be able to get a court to intervene if both Foghorn and Miss Prissy continue to vote for the high salaries once the agreement is struck down.)

40. No, because Banquo's shares aren't subject to the transfer restriction. The modern approach is to refuse to apply the restrictions to previously-issued shares. [149] For instance, MBCA § 6.27(a) provides that "A restriction does not affect shares issued before the restriction was adopted unless the holders of the shares are parties to the restriction agreement or voted in favor of the restriction." Here, since there is no "restriction agreement" (just a newly-enacted bylaw), and since Banquo didn't vote in favor of the bylaw, he's not bound as to any shares that he already owned at the moment the restriction came into effect. (But if he bought additional newly-issued shares, while on actual or constructive notice of the restriction, he *would* be bound as to these shares, even if he never agreed to the restriction.)

41. The company wins. The issue here is whether the bylaw, granting the corporation an option to repurchase shares from its shareholders at book value, is valid even where it produces a price that's much below market value. The general rule is that a restriction on stock transfer is valid if the person taking the shares has notice of the restraint and the restraint is "reasonable." The focus here is on the "reasonableness" element, since the shares are worth four times the option price. However, most courts say that if the mechanism chosen by the parties was reasonable *at the time the method was agreed upon*, the method will be deemed reasonable even though later trends make the price produced by the method very high or low viewed as of the moment of adjudication. [152] Since the facts tell us that the book-value method was reasonable at the time it was adopted, the fact that valuation methods have changed will not invalidate it. Thus even though the method produces a very below-market price now, the restriction is binding. At the very least, the court will allow the company to continue to refuse to recognize the transfer to Walton. If Jekyll is unlucky, the court will hold that Jekyll's notice of intent to sell gave the company a temporarily-irrevocable option to acquire the shares at the $25 price, and will order specific performance by Jekyll.

42. (a) That the company (and Ricky as controlling shareholder) owes a fiduciary duty to Lucy to treat her as favorably as it treated Ricky, and thus repurchase her shares at the same $1,000 price.

(b) Yes in Massachusetts; probably not in most other jurisdictions. A few states have in recent years held that a majority stockholder in a close corporation has a fiduciary obligation to each minority stockholder, such that the majority holder must behave in good faith towards the minority holder. If the state falls into this group, it would be likely to agree with this argument by Lucy that the company must repurchase Lucy's shares on the same terms as Ricky's, assuming that its financial condition still permits it to do so. The Massachusetts court in *Donahue v. Rodd Electrotype* so held, on almost exactly these facts. [161] However, *most* courts (including those in Delaware) would probably *not* agree that such a fiduciary obligation exists merely because of the close-corporation context, so Lucy would probably lose in most non-Massachusetts courts.

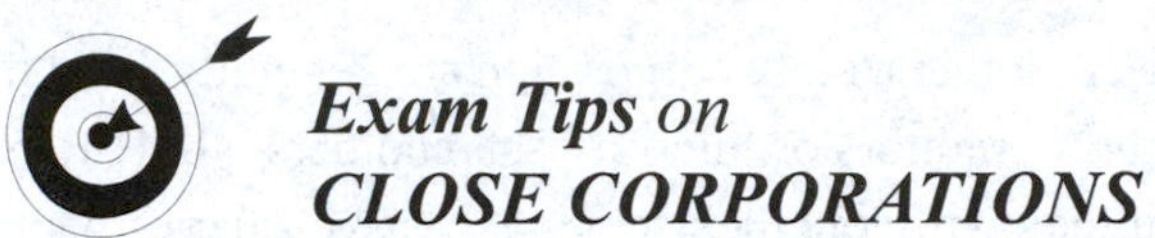

Exam Tips on CLOSE CORPORATIONS

The most frequently-tested issue regarding close corporations is the ***validity of s/h voting agreements.***

☛ Be on the lookout for agreements that ***limit the discretion of the board of directors***. Although s/h agreements are generally ***valid***, an agreement which substantially restricts the authority of the board will be ***struck down*** if it either: (i) violates a statutory provision; (ii) ***injures a minority s/h***; or (iii) injures the corp's creditors or the public.

- ☞ You're most likely to see a s/h agreement in which a majority of the holders agree to ***put and keep a particular person*** (perhaps one of the majority) into a ***key job***, and a minority-holder objects. Here, "injury to the minority-holder plaintiff" should be the focus of your answer.

  Example: A, B and C together control 75% of the stock of D Corp, and they are its sole directors. They sign a s/h agreement that says that unless all vote to cancel the agreement, all will cast their board votes so as to put and keep A in the President's position. P, a 10% holder, does not have a board seat, and now sues A, B and C (and the corp.) to have the voting agreement stuck down. If P can show that A is not doing an appropriate job running the business (or is otherwise injuring P by the way he's running it), the court may strike down the agreement. But if P doesn't show this, the court will probably uphold the agreement even though it substantially restricts the directors' freedom of action.

- ☞ Agreements under which each of the signers agrees to vote so as to ***elect all of the signers to the board*** are generally ***valid***.

  - ☞ A closer question is whether a person who then ***buys (or gets a gift of) stock from one of the original signers*** is bound by, or gets the benefit of, such an "all s/h's agree to elect all s/h's to the board" agreement. The answer is probably "yes," at least where the shares are conspicuously ***marked*** with the fact that there is a voting agreement that governs.

Example: A, B and C are the only s/h's in D Corp. All agree that all will vote so as to put all 3 on the board. C (who has too few shares to be able to vote herself to the board if no one else votes for her) dies, and bequeaths her shares to E. A and B refuse to vote E to the board. E sues to enforce the agreement. You should say that there's a good chance that a court will hold that the original signers intended that both the benefit and burden would "run" with the stock, in which case the court will require A and B to vote E onto the board (but E must vote for them as well). You should also point out that this result is more likely if the shares were marked with notice of the agreement than if they're not.

☞ Look for s/h agreements which contain ***share transfer restrictions.***

☞ Remember that a person who purchases shares ***without actual knowledge*** of pre-existing restrictions will ***not*** be bound unless the restrictions were ***conspicuously noted*** on the share certificates.

☞ If the fact pattern involves a right of ***first refusal*** (by the corporation or by the other shareholders), the restriction normally applies only if the shares are ***sold***, not if they are to be transferred by a ***gift*** or ***bequest***.

☛ Fact patterns on close corps sometimes pose the issue of whether one party can compel ***dissolution*** of the corp.

☞ Keep in mind that most statutes (e.g., the MBCA) allow the court to order dissolution at the request of one s/h, if certain conditions occur. Most states allow dissolution if:

❑ The ***s/h's*** or the ***directors*** are ***deadlocked*** in a way that prevents the corp. from operating; or

❑ The directors (or controlling s/h's) are ***oppressing*** or ***defrauding*** a minority holder; or

❑ The corp's ***assets*** are being ***wasted***.

☞ If the fact pattern involves an ***LLC*** rather than a corporation, remember that the jurisdiction probably allows judicial dissolution on factors similar to those for corporations. If it's a Delaware LLC, cite to the Del. LLC Act, allowing the court to decree dissolution of the LLC "whenever it is ***not reasonably practicable to carry on the business*** in conformity with the [LLC agreement.]"

☞ If the parties are ***deadlocked*** and the operating agreement doesn't supply a way to navigate around the deadlock, that's likely to be enough to make carrying on the business "not reasonably practical."

Example: LLC has two members, Al and Bill. The operating agreement says that an additional capital raising can only be done with the consent of both Al and Bill. The company runs out of money. Al is prepared to invest more for a bigger stake, but Bill doesn't like Al's terms and doesn't propose any terms of his own; instead Bill petitions for dissolution. The court (especially in Delaware) is likely to say that this deadlock is enough to making carrying on the business impractical, and therefore that Bill is entitled to judicial dissolution.

CHAPTER 6

THE DUTY OF CARE AND THE BUSINESS JUDGMENT RULE

ChapterScope

This Chapter discusses a director's and officer's fiduciary duty to exercise due care when making decisions. Key concepts:

- **Duty of due care:** A director or officer must behave with the level of care that a ***reasonable person*** in similar circumstances would use.
  - **Personal liability:** If the director or officer is found to have breached this duty of care, in a way that causes loss to the corporation, he may be held liable for ***money damages***, which are to be paid to the corporation.
- **Business judgment rule:** The court will not find an absence of due care merely because the officer/director's decision turns out to have been an unwise one. The "business judgment rule" says that there's ***no breach*** of the duty of care where 3 requirements are met:
  - the director or officer had ***no conflicting self-interest*** in the matter that he decided;
  - he made himself ***adequately informed*** about the facts relevant to the decision; and
  - his decision was ***"rational"*** as of the moment it was made.

I. INTRODUCTION

A. The duty of care generally: This chapter considers the duty of directors and officers to ***act carefully*** when they act on behalf of the corporation.

B. Broad statement of duty: Stated in its broadest form, a director's or officer's duty of care is as follows: He must, in handling the corporation's affairs, behave with the level of care that a ***reasonable person*** in ***similar circumstances*** would use. This sounds like the familiar negligence standard from tort law, and in many ways it is.

1. **Protection of "business judgment" rule:** However, a key rule called the ***"business judgment"*** rule in fact makes the duty of care much less burdensome than you might guess. Stated most briefly and generally, the business judgment rule says that courts will ***not second-guess*** the wisdom of directors' and officers' business judgments, and will not impose liability for even stupid business decisions so long as the director or officer (1) had ***no conflict of interest*** when he made the decision, (2) gathered a reasonable amount of ***information*** before deciding, and (3) did not act ***wholly irrationally***.

2. **Effect of combining the two rules:** When the duty of due care is combined with the business judgment rule, what we really have is a scheme that looks quite closely at the ***process*** by which the director or officer makes his decision, but then gives very little scrutiny to the substantive wisdom of the ***decision itself***. Thus a director who does not attend

board meetings, or who acts without a serious attempt to obtain the available facts, is likely to be found to have violated his duty of care. By contrast, a director who tries hard, gets most of the available facts, and then makes a decision which is clearly unwise (even when viewed *without* the benefit of hindsight) probably will ***not*** be found to have violated his duty of care — the business judgment rule will protect him as long as his decision was not totally irrational.

C. Liability for damages vs. injunction: If a director or officer violates his duty of care to the corporation, and this violation causes loss to the corporation, the director/officer will be ***personally liable*** to pay ***money damages*** to the corporation. Often, this will come about procedurally by means of a shareholder's derivative suit (see *infra*, p. 318), in which a shareholder sues "on behalf of" the corporation against the negligent director or officer; if the plaintiff is successful, the director/officer will have to pay damages to the corporation, and the shareholder/plaintiff will share *pro rata* with all other shareholders by virtue of the corporation's recoupment of its losses.

1. Injunction: However, there is a quite different context in which the duty of care and the business judgment rule may also be relevant. This is the situation in which the board of directors has approved (but not yet consummated) a transaction, and a shareholder or outsider sues for an ***injunction*** to block the proposed transaction. If the court concludes that the directors or officers have not acted with due care, and that shareholders as a whole would be injured, it may block the proposed transaction until it is approved with the required level of diligence.

a. Easier decision: In general, courts are probably willing to block a proposed transaction (especially in the takeover area) on less of a showing of a violation of due care than they would require before imposing personal liability on directors and officers. This is easy to understand: blocking a transaction that is unfair to shareholders probably will not directly (and certainly not unfairly) hurt the directors and officers who approved it, whereas making them personally liable for potentially huge damages as the result of their service to the corporation may severely hurt them, even bankrupt them.

D. Only rarely happens: In general, it is ***very rare*** for directors and officers to be found liable for breach of the duty of due care, as distinguished from breach of the duty of loyalty (discussed *infra*, p. 197). At least traditionally, most of the cases purporting to impose liability for lack of due care have probably really been cases in which the court believed that the directors were engaged in ***self-dealing*** (i.e., they violated their duty of loyalty), but because the proof of self-dealing was not strong enough, the court based its decision upon lack of due care.

1. Modern trend: However, beginning in the 1980s a few cases have found lack of due care even without indications of self-dealing. Therefore, the duty of care is becoming a duty that has some real practical impact upon how corporations are managed. See especially the dramatic and instantly-landmark case of *Smith v. Van Gorkom*, *infra*, p. 186, in which the Delaware Supreme Court found the directors of a corporation liable for damages because they did not obtain the highest possible price from a takeover bidder, even though the sale price was substantially higher than the stock had ever previously traded, and even though there was no apparent taint of self-dealing.

E. Directors vs. officers: The duty of care is imposed on both ***officers*** and ***directors***. Essentially the same duty is imposed upon each. However, the duty that is imposed is the duty to behave reasonably "under the circumstances," and the circumstances are obviously somewhat different for an officer than for a director. For instance, an officer will typically have deeper knowledge about the company's affairs than will an outside director, so facts which might not give an outside director cause to investigate might give the officer such cause, making his failure to investigate a violation of due care even though the director's failure would not be. In general, everything we say below applies to ***both directors and officers*** unless otherwise noted.

II. THE STANDARD OF CARE

A. The basic standard: Virtually all states impose, either by statute or case law, a duty of ***due care*** on all officers and directors. The director or officer "must exercise that degree of skill, diligence and care that a ***reasonably prudent person*** would exercise in ***similar circumstances***." Clark, p. 123.

1. **MBCA:** The MBCA spells out this duty in a way that is typical of the law of most states: "Each member of the board of directors, when discharging the duties of a director, shall act: (1) in good faith; and (2) in a manner the director ***reasonably believes*** to be in the ***best interests of the corporation***." § 8.30(a).

2. **No "accommodation" or "dummy" directors:** An important consequence of this duty of care is that there is ***no such thing*** as an ***"accommodation"*** or ***"dummy"*** director.

   Example: Suppose that X, who knows nothing about business, as a favor to his friend the President of ABC Corporation, accepts a director's post on ABC's board. President assures X that X will only be a "figurehead" who is not expected to have any significant function in ABC's affairs. Despite these assurances, a court will hold that X had a duty of care to ABC (and indirectly to its shareholders and creditors), and that he can be liable for damages if he does not act in accordance with this duty. "[A] person who accepts a directorship without assuming the responsibilities of a director is courting disaster." Nutshell, p. 310.

3. **Personal liability:** A director or officer who violates his duty of due care, and who thereby injures the corporation, may be held ***personally liable*** for the corporation's damages. This is true even if the director is paid little or nothing for his director's services, and otherwise had little or nothing to gain. In the case of a major corporation, the potential liability can be many times the director's net worth! (For this reason, most corporations now pay for directors' and officers' liability insurance. However, the existence of deductibles, co-insurance provisions and other limits means that even with insurance, a director is probably still significantly at risk if he violates his duty of due care.)

4. **Egregious cases:** However, this duty of due care is not as draconian as it might sound. First, under the "business judgment rule" (*supra*, p. 169), the actual business decisions made by a director or officer will not be second-guessed by the court as long as they are rational, made in good faith, and based on reasonable information. Therefore, liability for breach of the duty of due care generally arises only where the director or officer has failed

to comply with reasonable ***procedures*** for making decisions. Second, even where the director's procedures are inadequate, most courts hold that there is only liability for ***"gross negligence"*** or ***"recklessness."***

a. Total failure to act as director: Therefore, most successful claims against directors have come in cases where the director simply ***fails to do the basic things that directors generally do***. Thus a director might be found grossly negligent (and therefore liable) if he does some or all of the following:

[1] fails to ***attend meetings***;

[2] fails to ***learn anything*** of substance about the company's ***business***;

[3] fails to ***read reports***, financial statements, etc. given to him by the corporation;

[4] fails to ***obtain help*** (e.g., advice of counsel) when he sees or ought to see signals that things are going seriously wrong with the business; or

[5] otherwise "neglect[s] to go through the standard motions of ***diligent behavior***."

Clark, p. 125.

Example: Mrs. Pritchard is a director of Pritchard & Baird, a reinsurance broker. Pritchard & Baird goes bankrupt, and its trustees in bankruptcy sue Mrs. Pritchard for violating her duty of due care as a director. They show that two officers of Pritchard & Baird, Charles and William Pritchard (who are the other two directors, are Mrs. Pritchard's sons, and are the sole other stockholders apart from Mrs. Pritchard) have misappropriated $12 million from trust accounts held by the company on behalf of others. During the years the misappropriation took place, Mrs. Pritchard was elderly, alcoholic, and depressed over the death of her husband. She hardly ever attended board meetings (which were in fact rarely held), knew nothing of the corporation's affairs, never read or obtained any financial statements, and in general "did not pay any attention to her duties as a director or to the affairs of the corporation."

Held, Mrs. Pritchard (and after her death, her estate) ***breached her duty of due care to the corporation***, and is therefore liable for the losses caused by the misappropriations. Directors are not required to conduct a detailed inspection of day-to-day activities. But they must at least become familiar with the fundamentals of the business, and must keep informed in a general way about the corporation's activities. Here, had Mrs. Pritchard done even so little as to read the corporation's financial statements at any time, she would have noticed an item called "loans to shareholders" which dwarfed the company's assets, and which would have immediately put her on notice that her sons were effectively stealing trust funds. Had she noticed this, and asked her sons to stop, they probably would have done so (so that her negligence was a but-for cause of the losses). ***Francis v. United Jersey Bank***, 432 A.2d 814 (N.J. 1981).

b. Disguised "self-dealing" cases: Cases in which directors are held liable for failing to act with due care are often ***disguised "self-dealing" cases.*** That is, the court believes that the directors acted in pursuit of their own ends rather than for the good of the corporation, yet there is not enough evidence of this to make it the basis for the finding of liability; therefore, the court seizes upon lack of due care instead. Clark, pp. 126-28. For instance, in *Francis*, *supra*, the court was probably swayed by the fact that

D was the mother of the two miscreants, and her refusal to undertake any of the responsibilities of a director may have been motivated in part by her desire to let her sons enrich themselves at the corporation's expense. See Clark, p. 127-28.

B. Subjective vs. objective standard: The standard of care is basically an ***objective*** one. That is, the director will be held to the standard of care that would be exercised by a ***"reasonable person"*** in the director's position. Consequently, a director who is simply less smart, less able or less innately diligent than an "ordinary" reasonable director will nonetheless have to meet this higher ordinary standard.

Example: Consider Mrs. Pritchard in the *Francis* case, *supra*, p. 172. Even though she was elderly, alcoholic and depressed over the death of her husband, these factors were not taken into account by the court in determining what level of care was "reasonable" for her. Instead, she was required to conform to the level of directorial skill and diligence that an ordinary "reasonable" director would have shown under the circumstances.

1. Special skills of director: On the other hand, if the director has ***special skills*** that go beyond what an ordinary director would have, he ***must use*** those skills. For instance, if the director is by training an accountant, and he learns of facts which would make a trained accountant suspicious but would not raise the suspicions of an ordinary non-accountant director, he must behave as a reasonable accountant would behave under the circumstances. The rule would be similar for one with special ***legal***, ***banking*** or ***real estate*** training. Nutshell, p. 310.

C. Surrounding circumstances: The level of care required is that which is reasonable ***in the circumstances*** in which the director finds himself.

1. Nature and size of business: These "circumstances" include the ***nature*** and ***size*** of the particular business. For example, if the corporation is small and its operations relatively simple, the level of attention required of the director is probably somewhat less than if he sits on the board of, say, General Motors. Also, if the business serves as trustee or custodian for the ***funds of others***, probably a "reasonable" degree of care under the circumstances would include being on the lookout for misappropriation. Thus directors of banks are sometimes said to owe a "higher" standard of care; however, it would be more accurate to say that they owe the same "reasonable" duty of care as any other director, but that in a banking context this duty includes the obligation to be watchful for signs that depositors' accounts are being looted.

D. Reliance on experts and committees: Only rarely can a director, especially a director of a large corporation, directly ascertain the condition of the business. A director of IBM probably has no reasonable way to determine that the company's big supercomputer development program is way behind schedule, that its Singapore branch manager is fixing prices with his counterpart from Hitachi, or that the person overseeing the company pension plan is embezzling. Directors normally rely heavily on the ***expertise*** and ***assurances*** of others, including the company's officers, lawyers, accountants and other persons who are in a better position to know the facts. Generally speaking, the director is ***entitled to rely*** on these other people, and is not expected to go behind what they tell him.

1. **Model Act:** Thus MBCA § 8.30(b) provides that

   "(f) A director is ***entitled to rely*** ... on:

   > (1) one or more ***officers or employees*** of the corporation whom the director ***reasonably believes to be reliable and competent*** in the ***functions performed*** or the information, opinions, reports or statements provided;
   >
   > (2) ***legal counsel, public accountants***, or other persons ***retained*** by the corporation as to matters involving ***skills or expertise*** the director ***reasonably believes*** are matters (i) within the particular person's ***professional or expert competence*** or (ii) as to which the particular person ***merits confidence***; or
   >
   > (3) a ***committee*** of the board of directors of which the director is not a member if the director ***reasonably believes the committee merits confidence***."

2. **Reliance unreasonable:** On the other hand, it's vital to remember that the reliance must be ***reasonable***. Thus if the director knows facts which indicate that the officer, lawyer, or other third person is ***lying*** or is ***otherwise mistaken***, the director cannot bury his head in the sand and continue to rely on this third party's statements. As the MBCA puts it, the director may rely on the third party's statements, opinions, etc. (including financial statements) only so long as the director "does not have knowledge that makes reliance unwarranted[.]" § 8.30(e).

   Example: X is the director of Corporation, a large construction contractor. There have been persistent rumors that high-level officials of Corporation have bribed foreign officials to get foreign construction contracts, in violation of the federal Foreign Corrupt Practices Act. The board appoints a special board committee to investigate; the committee comes back and reports that there is no substance to these allegations. Ordinarily, X would be permitted to rely on the committee's report, since he "reasonably believes the committee merits confidence" (see MBCA § 8.30(b)(3)). But if X has actually been told by Y that Y and others have paid $10 million of Corporation's funds to Z to induce Z to give Corporation a contract, X's reliance on the committee is no longer reasonable, because of this actual knowledge. Therefore, X may not hide his head in the sand and say, in effect, "Everything's okay because the committee says so." He must instead explain what he knows, and at least attempt to prevent recurrences.

   a. **Tough standard for P to meet:** But it tends to be difficult for a plaintiff who is suing the directors to establish that the board's reliance on employees, experts, etc. was so unreasonable as to violate the duty of care. As we'll see in a little while (*infra*, p. 182), under the ***"business judgment rule,"*** if the board has no conflicts, is adequately informed, and merely makes a "rational" decision, that decision will not be deemed to violate the duty of care merely because it seems somewhat unwise or unreasonable after the fact. Therefore, the board's decision to rely on, say, an expert's recommendation will be protected under the business judgment rule ***so long as the board's procedures are reasonable***, even if the board does not make a very deep analysis of that recommendation before approving it.

      Example: The Board of Walt Disney Co. ("Disney") approves an employment contract for Michael Ovitz, under which Ovitz is appointed president (number two) at

Disney. The contract includes severance provisions under which if Ovitz is terminated without cause before the contract has run for seven years, Ovitz will receive a lucrative severance package. Ovitz in fact leaves by mutual agreement after 14 months, and ends up collecting the huge sum of $140 million in severance. In a derivative action, Disney shareholders sue the board, alleging that the board failed to use proper procedures in approving the contract, especially by failing to calculate how much severance Ovitz would receive in the event of an early no-fault termination. The complaint alleges that had the directors done such a calculation, they would have realized that the contract gave Ovitz a large incentive to exit the company by a no-fault termination as soon as possible. The complaint also says that the board was negligent in relying on the advice of its compensation expert, Graef Crystal, who himself did not seem to have calculated how much severance Ovitz would be entitled to if he left early. The Ds (the directors) move to dismiss for failure to state a claim.

Held, for the Ds. Even if the board did, as alleged, fail to calculate the potential cost to Disney of an early no-fault exit by Ovitz, the allegation fails to create a reasonable doubt that this constituted lack of due care. "It is the essence of the business judgment rule that a court will not apply 20/20 hindsight to second-guess a board's decision, except 'in rare cases [where] a transaction may be so egregious on its face that the board approval cannot meet the test of business judgment.' " Here, the board's reliance on Crystal, despite Crystal's failure to fully calculate the amount of potential severance, lacks egregiousness. "[T]he duty of care is still filled even if a Board does not know the exact amount of a severance payout but nonetheless is fully informed about the manner in which such a payout would be calculated. A board is not required to be informed of every fact, but rather is required to be reasonably informed." ***Brehm v. Eisner***, 746 A.2d 244 (Del. 2000).

E. **Passive negligence:** In some situations, the duty of due care arises in connection with a specific, affirmative, action by the board of directors. Thus the board may choose to write a certain loan, approve a certain acquisition, or otherwise make an explicit decision to take (or not take) certain action. In this situation, it's not too hard to determine whether the board members have acted with due care. Many if not most situations, however, involve what might be called ***"passive"*** negligence, or "nonfeasance." That is, circumstances exist which the board (arguably) ought to notice and do something about, but instead the board members do nothing. Most commonly, this kind of situation arises when the board fails to ***detect wrongdoing*** by officers or employees of the corporation.

1. **No duty to detect wrongdoing:** The directors certainly do not have any explicit duty to ***in fact detect wrongdoing***. That is, most courts would probably hold that the board members need not be suspicious sorts who go out of their way searching for evidence of embezzlement, bribery, self-dealing or other misconduct by operating-level managers or employees. As the Delaware Supreme Court has put it, "[A]bsent cause for suspicion there is no duty upon the directors to install and operate a ***corporate system of espionage*** to ***ferret out wrongdoing*** which they have no reason to suspect exists." *Graham v. Allis-Chalmers Mfg. Co.*, 188 A.2d 125 (Del. 1963).

2. **Actual grounds for suspicion:** On the other hand, of course, if the directors are ***on notice*** of ***facts that would make a reasonable person suspicious*** that wrongdoing is taking place, their duty of due care requires that they at least ***investigate further***.

3. **Duty to put controls into place:** Furthermore, many courts today hold that, while the board's duty of care may not require it to install a "system of espionage to ferret out wrongdoing" (*Graham*, *supra*, p. 175), that duty of care *does* require that reasonable ***control systems*** be put in place to ***detect wrongdoing***, even where the board has ***no prior reason to suspect*** that wrongdoing is occurring.

   a. **Limited burden:** But once the board does put in such a control system, the board won't be liable for failure to supervise merely because the control system (and or the persons using it) ***fails to detect wrongdoing.*** The case in the following example demonstrates this.

   Example: Caremark is a medical services firm, which provides various forms of therapy — including treatments for HIV/AIDS and hemophilia — to outpatients. The company participates in various Medicare and Medicaid programs. A federal law, the Anti-Referral Payments Law (ARPL), forbids firms such as Caremark from paying doctors to refer Medicaid and Medicare patients to it. Caremark pays physicians fees for monitoring certain patients, including Medicare and Medicaid patients, that are under the firm's care. Federal prosecutors indict the company on various felonies arising out of these monitoring fees, on the theory that the fees violate ARPL. The company settles these charges by pleading guilty to a single felony count, and then spends $250 million to settle various related civil claims against it. No senior officers or directors of the firm are charged with wrongdoing. Stockholders then bring a derivative suit on behalf of the company against all members of the Board of Directors, claiming that the board members failed to exercise their duty of due care, which (the suit asserts) required them to put in control mechanisms that would have prevented the violations of ARPL. The parties then propose to settle the suit, without the Ds paying any money, but with the company taking various steps to avoid future violations of law. The court is asked to approve the settlement.

   Held, the settlement is approved. In deciding whether a settlement involving no financial recovery is reasonable, the court must of course take into account the likelihood that the plaintiffs would have prevailed at trial. Notwithstanding *Graham*'s statement about "espionage," "A director's obligation includes a duty to attempt in good faith to assure that a corporate information and reporting system, which the board concludes is adequate, exists, and ... failure to do so under some circumstances may, in theory at least, render a director liable for losses caused by non-compliance with applicable legal standards."

   However, the burden on a plaintiff who wants to establish a breach of this obligation is a high one: "only a sustained or systematic failure of the board to exercise oversight — such as an utter failure to attempt to assure a reasonable information and reporting system exists — will establish the lack of good faith that is a necessary condition to liability." Here, there is no evidence that the director Ds were guilty of such a sustained failure of oversight. The mere fact that the corporation committed a criminal violation does not by itself establish such a failure of oversight by the board. Since the

Ps would be unlikely to prevail on the merits at trial, the settlement is reasonable despite its failure to call for any financial recovery. ***In Re Caremark Int'l. Inc. Derivative Litigation***, 698 A.2d 959 (Del. Ch. 1996).

b. Approved by Delaware Supreme Court (*Stone v. Ritter*): *Caremark, supra,* was a decision by the Delaware Court of Chancery, not the Delaware Supreme Court. But in a later decision, the Delaware Supreme Court affirmed the basic test articulated in *Caremark* for when directors could be liable for an omission. In ***Stone v. Ritter***, 911 A.2d 362 (Del. 2006), the court cited *Caremark* approvingly, and said that, assuming the corporation has an exculpation clause (see *infra*, p. 178), the ***directors will have liability for poor oversight only if:***

"(a) the directors utterly ***failed to implement any reporting or information system*** or controls; or

"(b) having implemented such a system or controls, ***consciously failed to monitor or oversee its operations[,]*** thus disabling themselves from being informed of risks or problems requiring their attention."

i. Knowledge of shortcoming required: The *Stone* court then continued: "In either case [i.e., failed-to-implement-a-system or failure-to-monitor/oversee-the-system], imposition of liability requires a showing that the directors ***knew that they were not discharging their fiduciary obligations***."

ii. Gross negligence not enough: So what might be called ***"oblivious gross negligence" won't be enough*** for director-liability in Delaware, at least where — as is usually the case — the corporation has elected to put into its charter an exculpation clause ***relieving directors of liability*** for violation of the ***duty of due care*** (see *infra*, p. 178). Unless the directors are ***conscious*** that they were not discharging their fiduciary obligations, ***no amount of inattention will be enough.*** As the Delaware Supreme court said in *Stone*, "a claim that directors are subject to personal liability for employee failures is 'possibly the most difficult theory in corporation law upon which a plaintiff might hope to win a judgment.' "

iii. Illustration: The facts of *Stone* itself, set forth in the following example, illustrate how hard it is for the plaintiffs to recover — or even get to trial — on a claim in Delaware that the directors should be held personally liable for failing to detect employee wrongdoing. In particular, Delaware courts will be careful not to use the ***benefit of hindsight*** to infer that directors' failure to spot wrongdoing establishes that the directors behaved with the required conscious knowledge that they were not discharging their fiduciary responsibilities.

Example: The plaintiff shareholders in a derivative action (see *infra*, p. 318) allege that the directors of AmSouth, a Delaware-chartered bank, should be held liable for money damages because they failed to detect that the bank's employees were not filing Suspicious Activity Reports (SARs), required by federal anti-money-laundering statutes. (The bank paid $50 million in fines and penalties to resolve the government's SAR claims.) Special procedural rules concerning derivative suits require that in order for the case to go to trial, the plaintiffs must show a substantial likelihood that the directors knew, at the time the derivative suit was begun, that they faced possible personal financial liability from the suit. Since AmSouth has a charter provision exculpating directors for non-bad-faith breaches of the duty of due care (see the discussion of exculpation clauses *infra*, p. 178), the directors face financial liability if and only if they acted in "bad faith." The directors move to dismiss on the grounds that there is no evidence of their bad faith.

Held, for the directors. Where the claim is that the directors failed to make a good-faith effort to supervise the corporation adequately, the plaintiffs must establish bad faith by showing either that the directors utterly failed to implement a reporting or control system, or consciously failed to monitor that system. In either case, liability requires a showing that the directors "knew that they were not discharging their fiduciary obligations." Here, there was unrebutted evidence that the board approved policies requiring the filing of SARs, and delegated to non-board employees the job of monitoring those filings and reporting back to the board about whether the policies were being followed. This is enough to rebut any claim that the directors knew they were not discharging their fiduciary obligations. "In the absence of red flags [which were not present here], good faith in the context of oversight must be measured by the directors' actions 'to assure a reasonable information and reporting system exists' and *not by second-guessing* after the occurrence of employee conduct that results in an unintended adverse outcome." *Stone v. Ritter, supra.*

iv. **Significance:** So in the usual case where a charter provision relieves the directors of money-damage liability for lack of due care, *Stone v. Ritter* establishes that directors of a Delaware corporation will have liability for failure of oversight only if they ***"knew that they were not discharging their fiduciary obligations."*** This is a ***nearly-impossible standard*** for the plaintiffs to meet — unless the plaintiffs can show that the board either (a) "utterly failed to implement *any* reporting or information systems or controls," or (b) "consciously failed" to monitor such a system once it was installed, the directors won't be liable, ***no matter how grossly negligent they were*** in failing to notice that wrongdoing was occurring.

c. **Federal statute on controls:** By the way, a federal statute now expressly requires that public companies institute a system of internal controls. § 13(b)(2) of the Securities Exchange Act of 1934 now requires every publicly-held corporation to "devise and maintain a system of ***internal accounting controls***" to guarantee accurate financial statements and to guard against misappropriation of assets. Most public companies have done this by creating an audit committee that works with the corporation's accountants to install such controls.

F. **The significance of "good faith," and director-exculpation provisions in charters:** The question of whether the directors satisfied their duty of due care is often intertwined with the question of whether the directors behaved in ***"good faith."*** For years, it was unclear whether the duty of good faith was an independent duty, or was instead an aspect of (1) the duty of care, which we've been discussing and/or (2) the duty of loyalty, which we will be discussing later (*infra*, p. 197).

1. **Director-exculpation clauses:** Why does it even matter whether the duty of good faith is an independent duty or part of some other duty (due care or loyalty)? At least in Delaware,

the most important reason it matters has to do with the right of a corporation to ***reduce or eliminate a director's liability for money damages*** for certain claims. Del. GCL § 102(b)(7) lets a corporation put into its certificate of corporation a provision "eliminating or limiting the personal liability of a director to the corporation or its stockholders for monetary damages for ***breach of fiduciary duty*** as a director[.]" However, (b)(7) does ***not*** permit the reduction of liability for any breach of the "duty of loyalty" or for any acts or omissions "***not in good faith*** or which involve intentional misconduct or knowing violation of the law."

a. **Claim of gross negligence as bad faith:** Until 2006, plaintiffs in shareholder derivative actions (*infra*, p. 197) often argued in Delaware that if the board behaved grossly negligently, this gross negligence amounted to bad faith, and thus automatically deprived the board of the protections of a GCL §102(b)(7) clause, which most public corporations have in their charters. (For instance, the plaintiffs in *Stone v. Ritter*, *supra*, p. 177, made such a claim.) But in a series of three decisions by the Delaware Supreme Court, beginning in 2006, the court has held that only a narrowly-defined ***conscious disregard of duty*** — and ***not mere gross negligence*** — can amount to bad faith and deprive the board of the protection of a § 102(b)(7) provision. We consider these three decisions in Paragraphs 2 through 4 immediately below.

2. **Claim rejected in *Disney*:** First, in ***In Re The Walt Disney Co. Derivative Litigation***, 906 A.2d 27 (Del. 2006) (also known as the final opinion in *Brehm v. Eisner*), the Delaware Supreme Court said that ***gross negligence without more*** — even including a failure to inform oneself of available material facts — ***cannot constitute "bad faith"*** of the sort that deprives the directors of the protection of a GCL § 102(b)(7) exculpatory clause.

   a. **Rationale:** The *Disney* court reasoned that the legislature, in enacting § 102(b)(7), desired to afford "***significant protections*** to directors of Delaware corporations." To read the statute in a way that "conflates the duty of care with the duty to act in good faith by making a violation of the former an automatic violation of the latter, would nullify those legislative protections[.]"

   b. **Consequence:** Therefore, according to *Disney*, to qualify as the sort of bad faith that will deprive a director of the protection of the § 102(b)(7) exculpation clause, a director's conduct must rise to the level of an "***intentional dereliction of duty***, a ***conscious disregard*** for one's responsibilities."[1]

3. **Failure of oversight:** Then, in ***Stone v. Ritter***, 911 A.2d 362 (Del. 2006), the court made it clear that this "gross negligence does not constitute bad faith" ruling covers claims that the directors ***failed to adequately supervise*** the corporation's operations. As we noted above (*supra*, p. 177), the directors will have liability for poor oversight only if they either:

   [1] "***utterly failed to implement any reporting or information system*** or controls"; or

   [2] "having implemented such a system or controls, ***consciously failed to monitor or oversee its operations[,]*** thus disabling themselves from being informed of risks

---

1. "Subjective bad faith" — where the director is "motivated by an actual intent to do harm" — will also qualify as conduct that deprives the director of the benefits of the exculpation provision, according to *Disney*.

or problems requiring their attention."

Furthermore, the court said in *Stone*, neither of the above two failures will be found to have occurred unless the plaintiff shows that the directors ***"knew that they were not discharging their fiduciary obligations***."

4. **The "offer to buy the company" scenario:** Then, in the last case of the trio, the Delaware Supreme Court held that this "gross negligence does not constitute bad faith" standard also applies to limit directors' liability for ***mishandling an offer to acquire the company.*** Only if the directors are shown to have "***utterly failed to attempt to obtain the best sale price"*** will they be liable for bad faith in the takeover context. ***Lyondell Chemical Co. v. Ryan***, 970 A.2d 235 (Del. 2009).

Example: The directors of Lyondell receive a $48/share buyout offer from Blavatnik at a substantial premium to the existing share price. Blavatnik says that this is his final offer, and must be accepted within one week or it will be off the table. During that week, the directors meet several time to consider the offer, solicit and follow the advice of their financial and legal advisors (which is to take the offer because it's higher than anyone else will likely pay), at least briefly attempt to negotiate a higher offer, and approve the agreement because they believe it's simply too good not to pass along to stockholders for their consideration. After the board accepts the offer and shareholders approve it, some investors bring a class action, alleging that the board showed bad faith in not doing more to get a higher price.

Held, summary judgment granted against the Ps. In the acquisition context, the directors will be liable for breach of the duty of loyalty only if they are shown to have "***utterly failed to attempt*** to obtain the best sale price." Here, the multiple board meetings, the soliciting and following of the advisors' advice to take the deal, and the members' belief that the offer was simply too good not to pass along to stockholders for their consideration, were more than enough to show that the directors did not fail to even attempt to obtain the best price. *Lyondell Chemical Co. v. Ryan*, *supra* (discussed further *infra*, p. 464).

5. **Summary of "gross negligence" vs "bad faith" in exculpation-clause cases:** Taken together, *Walt Disney*, *Stone v. Ritter* and *Lyondell Chemical* establish several propositions regarding director liability in the common situation in which the corporation has a § 102(b)(7) exculpation clause:

[1] Where there is an exculpation clause, the directors will ***not*** be liable for ***"gross negligence,"*** and will be liable ***only*** if they are shown to have acted in ***"bad faith."***

[2] "Bad faith" requires a showing that the directors ***"utterly failed to [even] attempt"*** to discharge their fiduciary duties.

[3] Consequently, where a Delaware corporation has an exculpation clause, it will take a ***very extreme fact pattern*** for the directors to be found liable for breach of the duty of loyalty, assuming the directors were not in a conflict position (see *infra*, p. 197). Essentially, the directors would have to have either (1) ***not even tried*** to discharge their responsibilities, or (2) been fully ***aware*** that the actions

they were taking conflicted with their duties.

G. **Failure to make disclosure:** Under some circumstances, directors' or officers' ***failure*** to ***make accurate disclosure of information*** to shareholders may constitute a breach of the duty of due care.

1. **Shareholder action sought:** The most straightforward example arises when directors seek ***shareholder approval*** of some corporate action — when they do so, their duty of due care (as well as their duty of loyalty, see *infra*, p. 197) requires that they ***communicate truthfully*** about the merits of the proposed action.

   Example: Suppose that the board of X Corp. wants to merge the corporation into Y Corp., in a transaction in which X Corp. shareholders will end up with shares in Y Corp. Assuming that state law requires the board of X Corp. to obtain informed shareholder approval of the proposed transaction (as most states would require — see *infra*, pp. 378, 390), the board's duty of due care and loyalty would require it to exercise reasonable care in disclosing to shareholders the facts needed for the holders to make an informed decision. For instance, suppose the board completely failed even to make reasonable efforts to ascertain, or to communicate to X's shareholders, the business prospects for a combined X Corp and Y Corp. A court might well hold that the board's failure to ascertain the facts and disclose them constituted a violation of the duty of due care, making the board liable in, say, a shareholder's derivative action (see *infra*, p. 318).

2. **Shareholder communication not required but given:** Now, however, suppose that the Board of Directors is ***not required*** to communicate with (or get approval of) shareholders on a particular matter, but chooses to do so anyway. If the board communicates incorrect information, can it be liable for a breach of the duty of due care? The Delaware Supreme Court answered "yes," in *Malone v. Brincat*, 722 A.2d 5 (Del. 1998).

   a. **Facts:** In *Malone*, the Ps were shareholders in Mercury Finance Co., and the Ds were directors of Mercury. The complaint alleged that the Ds intentionally and repeatedly overstated the financial condition of Mercury in reports to shareholders and the SEC, in breach of their state-law fiduciary duties. When the true facts were eventually disclosed, the share price collapsed.

   b. **Liability possible:** The court agreed with the Ps that liability was at least theoretically possible if the facts alleged in the complaint were proven. "When the directors disseminate information to stockholders when no stockholder action is sought, the fiduciary duties of care, loyalty and good faith apply. Dissemination of false information could violate one or more of those duties." (Because the complaint was poorly worded — the court couldn't even tell whether the claim purported to be a direct or a derivative one — the case was dismissed with leave to replead.)

   c. **Business judgment rule:** But it's unlikely that a mere error in reporting facts to shareholders would trigger a finding of breach of the duty of due care. The business judgment rule would normally give the board significant protection in the case of an "honest," even if negligent, mistake. However, if the board failed to put into place ***reasonable procedures*** for ***gathering accurate information***, a breach of the duty of care might be found.

H. Causation: Even if a director or officer has violated his duty of due care to the corporation, many cases say that he will not be personally liable unless this lack of due care is the ***legal cause*** of ***damage*** to the corporation. In other words, in many courts the traditional tort notions of ***cause in fact*** and ***proximate cause*** apply in this context.

1. **Cause would have happened anyway:** Thus if the loss ***would have happened anyway*** even had the directors all behaved with due care, many courts hold that there is no liability.

2. **Delaware rejects:** But some states, including ***Delaware***, ***reject*** the requirement of causation when directors are shown to have violated their duty of care. Thus in *Cede & Co. v. Technicolor, Inc.*, 634 A.2d 345 (Del. 1993) the Delaware Supreme Court held that once P shows that the directors breached their duty of care, that showing overcomes the protection that directors get from the "business judgment" rule (see *infra*, p. 182). At that point, P has established a *prima facie* case — ***even if he can't show that exercise of due care would have avoided the loss*** — and the ***burden of proof shifts to the defendants***: unless the defendants carry the burden of showing the "entire fairness" of the transaction, they will be liable.

3. **Joint and several liability:** When multiple directors are charged with breaching their duty of due care, each will (if she's smart) argue, "Even if I had behaved with due care, the rest of the board would probably not have listened to me, and the loss would have happened anyway." However, at least some courts hold that any board member who violates his duty of due care is ***jointly and severally liable*** with all other directors who have done so, as long as the board ***collectively*** was a proximate cause of the loss; each director is treated as a "concurrent cause" of the harm, and is liable even though his own due care probably would not have made a difference. See ALI *Prin. Corp. Gov.*, § 7.18, Comment d (taking "no position" on whether the liability should be joint-and-several or, instead, apportioned.)

III. THE BUSINESS JUDGMENT RULE

A. The rule generally: The "business judgment rule" may be thought of as a "judicial gloss" on what it means for a director to exercise due care. Even if the director's conduct might seem to lack due care when viewed from a general "reasonable person" benefit-versus-burden tort perspective, the more precise business judgment rule may save the director from liability.

B. Statement of the rule: There is no single universally-accepted statement of the business judgment rule. The basic idea behind the rule seems to be that "[business] decisions made upon ***reasonable information*** and with ***some rationality*** do not give rise to directorial liability ***even if they turn out badly*** or disastrously from the standpoint of the corporation. . . ." Nutshell, p. 310. In other words, the court will not find an absence of due care merely from the fact that the decision was ***unwise***.

> **Example:** The Ds are the directors of American Express Co. They have caused the corporation to distribute the shares it holds in a separate company, DLJ, to shareholders as a special dividend. P, an American Express shareholder, brings a derivative suit against the Ds; he alleges that they should have had American Express sell these DLJ

shares on the open market instead of distributing them as a dividend. He points out that this technique would have resulted in substantial tax savings to shareholders.

Held, for the Ds. P makes no claim that the Ds engaged in fraud or self-dealing. P is merely claiming that a different decision by the board would have been more advantageous. But a complaint alleging merely that some other decision would have been wiser does not state a cause of action, because of the business judgment rule. ***"More than imprudence or mistaken judgment must be shown."*** Here, the evidence shows that the directors considered the tax advantages of selling the stock rather than distributing it, but were worried that this path would hurt the corporation's reported earnings; their decision will not give rise to liability so long as it was reached in good faith. *Kamin v. American Express Co.*, 383 N.Y.S.2d 807 (N.Y.Sup.Ct. 1976).

1. **ALI definition:** The clearest definition of the business judgment rule is perhaps the one given in the ALI's *Principles of Corporate Governance*:

   §4.01(c) "A director or officer who makes a ***business judgment*** in ***good faith*** fulfills the duty [of care] if the director or officer

   (1) is ***not interested*** in the subject of the business judgment;

   (2) is ***informed*** with respect to the subject of the business judgment to the extent the director or officer reasonably believes to be appropriate under the circumstances; and

   (3) ***rationally believes*** that the business judgment is in the best interests of the corporation."

   a. **Interpretation:** Thus a director who asserts that he is protected by the business judgment rule has to prove three things under the ALI's approach:

      [1] that he was not "interested" (i.e., that he had no ***conflict of interest***, no personal stake in the outcome that was different from the corporation's stake);

      [2] that he gathered the reasonably needed ***information***; and

      [3] that he honestly, ***and rationally***, believed that his decision was in the company's best interest.

      So, assuming that the director has no conflicts and gathers adequate information, the essence of the business judgment rule is that ***mere rationality*** is ***all that is required*** — as long as the decision is not entirely crazy or outside the bounds of reason, the fact that (when judged by reference to the facts known to the director) it was ***very unwise***, will not be enough to make the director liable.

2. **Model Act:** The MBCA, by contrast, does not attempt to codify the business judgment rule at all. § 8.30(a) sets forth the general duty of due care (including the requirement that the director act in a manner that the director "reasonably believes to be in the best interests of the corporation"). The Official Comment to § 8.30 says that the elements of the business judgment rule, and its impact on the duty of due care, are left to the courts.

3. **Relation between general duty of care and the business judgment rule:** At first blush, the business judgment rule seems in conflict with the general duty of due care described above. Probably the best way to see how the pieces fit together is this: The duty of due care imposes a fairly stern set of ***procedural*** requirements for directors' actions —

the director must act in good faith (e.g., not be pursuing his own interests), and he must get all reasonably needed ***information*** before deciding. Once these procedural requirements are satisfied, however, the business judgment rule sets out a far more easily satisfied standard with respect to the ***substance*** of the business decision: that decision will be upheld so long as it is "rational" (a weaker requirement than that the decision be "reasonable").

4. **Rationale:** There seem to be three main reasons for limiting directors' liability by use of the business judgment rule:

   a. **Risk-taking directors:** First, a certain amount of ***innovation*** and ***risk-taking*** is essential if businesses are to grow and prosper. It is generally in the shareholders' interests to have their directors take at least rational risks on the corporation's behalf. Without the business judgment rule, directors would become much more conservative and anti-risk, and the overall economic performance of corporations generally would probably decline.

   b. **Courts are poor judges of business reality:** Second, directors — like executives — must constantly engage in a ***"risk/return calculus."*** Judges, especially acting from hindsight, are ***not very good*** at making this kind of calculus — they have no training in it — so they may reach inappropriate conclusions if we let them second guess business people. "A reasoned decision at the time made may seem a wild hunch viewed years later against a background of perfect knowledge." *Joy v. North*, 692 F.2d 880 (2nd Cir. 1982).

   c. **Directors as poor "cost avoiders":** Finally, imposing greater director liability would make directors a form of ***"cost spreaders."*** But any given director is a poor cost spreader, since he probably serves only a few companies, and cannot incorporate the cost of his mistakes into the price he charges for his services. (This is in contrast to the ability of, say, lawyers or accountants to buy malpractice insurance and therefore spread among many clients the cost of law or accounting mistakes.) Shareholders can spread the risk of business misjudgments far more easily by diversifying their portfolios than directors can spread this risk by serving on multiple boards.

   See generally *Joy v. North*, 692 F.2d 880 (2d Cir. 1982).

C. **Requirements for application of rule:** As we noted above, most courts appear to impose three requirements before the director or officer will gain the protection of the business judgment rule: (1) he must not have any private ***interest*** in the outcome different from the corporation's interests, i.e., there must be no taint of self-dealing; (2) he must have made the judgment only after gathering the reasonably needed ***information***; and (3) he must have ***"rationally believed"*** that his judgment was in the corporation's best interest. See ALI, Prin. Corp. Gov., § 4.01(c). We now consider each of these requirements in turn.

1. **No self-dealing:** First, the director or officer will lose the protection of the business judgment rule if he has an ***"interest"*** in the transaction. Thus if he is a ***party*** to the transaction, or is related to a party, or otherwise has some ***financial stake*** in the transaction's outcome that is adverse to the corporation's stake, the business judgment rule will not apply. So any taint of ***self-dealing*** by the director will be enough to deprive him of the business judgment rule's protection.

a. **Rationale:** The rationale behind the business judgment rule is that we want to protect honest (even if mistaken) cases of business misjudgment. But if the director has engaged in self-dealing, he has not really engaged in business judgment (in the sense of judgment on behalf of the corporation) at all — instead he has been engaged in pursuing his own objectives. This conduct is not the kind of action we want to protect with a special rule that makes recovery very difficult. Clark, p. 138.

Example: X is an officer and director of Printing Corp. He votes to have Printing Corp. purchase most of its paper from Paper Corp. Paper Corp. charges an average of 5% more for the same paper as is available, on substantially the same delivery and credit terms, from Discount Corp. Normally, X's decision to vote to have the purchases made from Paper Corp. would be protected by the business judgment rule (assuming that X acts with reasonable information, and his decision is not wholly irrational; see *infra*). However, it turns out that X is a secret substantial shareholder in Paper Corp., who will benefit financially by this large volume of business from Printing Corp. Therefore, X is "interested" in the transaction and he thus will not get the protection of the business judgment rule.

Note: The law governing self-dealing transactions is discussed extensively beginning *infra*, p. 197, and is an extremely important body of law. The point we are stressing here is that self-interested transactions, unlike other transactions, don't get any special benefit from the business judgment rule.

2. **Informed decision:** The requirement that has the greatest practical importance is that the decision must have been an ***"informed"*** one in order to be protected by the business judgment rule. That is, the director or officer must have gathered at least a ***reasonable amount of information*** about the decision before he made it. As one court has put it, the directors must inform themselves "prior to making a business decision, of ***all material information reasonably available to them***." *Aronson v. Lewis*, 473 A.2d 805 (Del. 1984).

   a. **Gross negligence standard:** However, even with respect to his duty to become "informed," the business judgment rule is not as tough as it might sound. Most courts would probably hold that a director loses the benefit of the rule only if he was ***grossly negligent*** in the amount of information he gathered. In other words, mere "ordinary" negligence in obtaining available information, like mere negligence on the substantive merits of the decision, will not be enough to cause liability.

   Example: Suppose that the directors of X Corp. are asked to approve X's acquisition of Y Corp. The President of X gives the directors ten years of financial information on Y, but director D only reads the last three years of this information. D (as well as his fellow directors) approves the acquisition, it goes forward, and it turns out disastrously because of embezzlements carried out by the founder of Y (who is kept on). Had D read the financial statement from seven years previously, he would have discovered in a footnote reason to doubt the honesty of the founder.

   On these facts, a court would probably hold that D gets the benefit of the business judgment rule (thus validating his decision to acquire as long as it was not completely irrational) so long as he was not "grossly negligent" in limiting his reading to the three most recent years. Probably a court would find that while this limited research may have been negligent, it was not "grossly" negligent. See, e.g., *Smith v. Van Gorkom* (discussed extensively *infra*, this page), in which the court said "we think the concept of gross negligence is . . . the proper standard for determining whether a business judgment reached by a board of directors was an informed one."

b. All circumstances considered: In determining whether the decision was an informed one, the court will generally consider ***all of the surrounding circumstances***. For example, if the board's decision had to be made in an extremely ***short time period***, a smaller amount of information will have to be gathered than if the court had months or years in which to make the decision.

c. The key case of *Smith v. Van Gorkom*: The requirement that the decision be an "informed" one is the key to the most important business judgment rule case to be decided in modern times, ***Smith v. Van Gorkom***, 488 A.2d 858 (Del. 1985). *Van Gorkom* represents a striking exception to the usual rule that if there is no taint of self-interest, and at least some attention paid to directorial responsibilities, the business judgment rule will shield the directors for liability for their decision.

i. Facts: The precise facts of *Van Gorkom* are of utmost importance, so we consider them in detail. The Ds were the directors of Trans Union Corp., including its chairman/CEO, Van Gorkom. Trans Union was publicly-held, and Van Gorkom held a sizeable, but minority, stake. Van Gorkom was near retirement age, and apparently wished to sell his shares prior to retirement. He had his chief financial officer compute the price at which a leveraged buyout could be done; the CFO reported that at $50 per share, the corporation's cash flow would easily support a buyout, but that at $60 a share the cash flow might not be sufficient. Van Gorkom then, without consulting with anyone else in senior management, proposed to his friend Pritzker (a well-known corporate acquirer) to sell him the company for $55 per share. The company's price on the New York Stock Exchange had recently fluctuated between $29 and $38, and in its history had never been higher than $39 1/2. Pritzker agreed to a $55 per share buyout price.

ii. Board approval: Van Gorkom did not attempt to get any other offers for the company. Nor did he ever commission a formal study of the company's value. Instead, he went to his board of directors and asked them to approve the sale to Pritzker at $55. He did not invite the company's investment bankers to the board meeting. He told the board that Pritzker was demanding an answer within three days. Most members of senior management opposed the deal on the grounds that the price was too low. The board was not shown the proposed merger agreement, or any documents concerning the value of the company; it relied solely on Van Gorkom's oral presentation, the chief financial officer's statement that the price offered was in the "low" range of appropriate valuation, and an outside lawyer's advice that the board might be sued if they failed to accept the offer. The board approved the buyout on this basis. The sale went through at $55 per share.

iii. Holding: The Delaware Supreme Court, by a three-two vote, held that the directors had been ***grossly negligent*** in failing to inform themselves adequately about the transaction that they were approving. The majority seemed especially influenced by the fact that: (1) it was Van Gorkom, not Pritzker, who promoted the deal and named the eventual sale price, and the board never ascertained this; (2) the board had made no real attempts to learn the "intrinsic value" of the company; (3) the board had no written documentation before it and relied completely on oral statements, mostly by Van Gorkom; and (4) the board made its entire decision in a two hour period, with no advance notice that a buyout would be the subject of the meeting, and in circumstances where there was no real crisis or emergency. (The board claimed that it had reserved the right to take any higher offer, but the court found that this reservation was illusory, because of tight limits that the Pritzker agreement placed upon the board's ability to accept higher offers from third parties. In any event, the two other bidders who came forward never made a serious offer, apparently in part because of limits placed on other offers by the board's deal with Pritzker.)

iv. Dissent: The two dissenters argued that the directors' decision to approve the merger should have been protected by the business judgment rule. One of them pointed out that the directors were highly sophisticated businessmen who were very well informed about the company's affairs.

v. Significance: The *Van Gorkom* decision is quite extraordinary. Here we have a buyout done at a price that was 40% above the highest price that the stock had ever traded for in its history. Yet the directors were held grossly negligent for approving the buyout! Perhaps the real key to the decision is that a majority of the court felt that the directors acceded to an autocratic leader (Van Gorkom), rather than making their decision in a collaborative manner. See Clark, p. 129.

vi. Large stakes: Observe that the stakes for the defendant directors in a case like *Van Gorkom* are enormous. Had the court finally decided that the buyout was $5 lower than a fully-informed transaction would have been done at, the 20 million shares outstanding would have produced a verdict of $100 million! In reality, the case was settled for $23 million (though this did not come out of the directors' pockets — about half came from directors' liability insurance and the rest from Pritzker, who apparently paid it voluntarily). S,S,B&W, pp. 714-15.

vii. Lesser guilt: Also striking is the fact that the other directors were held jointly and severally liable even though Van Gorkom was clearly the person primarily responsible for the transaction. The explanation is probably that the defendants pursued what turned out to be a poor litigation strategy: the court repeatedly asked them whether there were reasons to treat some directors differently from other directors, and they answered "no," preferring to pursue a "one for all and all for one" strategy. See Nutshell, p. 315; S,S,B&W, p. 714. Therefore, the court treated them as being jointly and severally liable.

viii. Significance: The *Van Gorkom* case seems most significant for the proposition that ***process*** is exceptionally important in obtaining the benefits of the business judgment rule. Had the board members reviewed the proposed merger agreement, and obtained an investment banker's opinion that $55 was a "fair" price, the court would probably have found that the decision was an "informed" one, and was therefore protected by the business judgment rule. Thus the actual merits of the decision — whether $55 was an appropriate price — wasn't what really made the difference in *Van Gorkom*.

d. Takeover context: As *Van Gorkom* illustrates, directors must do more than merely "go through the motions" in approving major business transactions. Especially in the ***takeover*** area, the directors must go out of their way to gather all relevant information, must take whatever time is reasonably available in the circumstances before deciding, and must interrogate management closely rather than merely "rubber stamping" management's recommendations.

3. The requirement of a "rational" belief: The final requirement for the business judgment rule, according to most courts, is that the director must have ***"rationally believed"*** that his business judgment was in the corporation's best interest. See, e.g., ALI Prin. Corp. Gov., § 4.01(c)(3). That is, the director must ***actually*** believe he is acting in the corporation's best interests, and this belief must be ***at least rational***.

a. Meaning of "rational": Observe that the requirement is merely that the belief in the soundness of the decision be "rational," not that it be "reasonable." In other words, so long as the belief is not ***totally beyond the bounds of reason***, it will be sustained even though most people might not have held that belief.

b. Refers to belief, not substance of decision: Also, keep in mind that what has to be rational is the director's *belief* that the decision is in the corporation's best interests, not the *decision* itself. Therefore, as long as the director (1) had a rational basis for believing that he had ***followed sensible decision-making procedures*** (e.g., he rationally believed that he had gathered the appropriate information before deciding), and (2) had a rational basis for believing that he was attempting to pursue the corporation's interests (rather than, say, his own interests), that will be the end of the matter.

i. No scrutiny of merits of decision: An important corollary of this emphasis on the rationality of the "belief," not the rationality of the underlying decision, is that the court ought to focus on the directors' decision-making ***process***, and ***ought rarely to consider the merits of the underlying decision***. As one court has put it, "it is obvious that a court must examine the ***circumstances surrounding the decisions*** in order to determine if the conditions warrant application of the business judgment rule. If they do, the court will ***never proceed to an examination of the merits*** of the challenged decisions, for that is precisely what the business judgment rule prohibits." *Cuker v. Mikalauskas*, 692 A.2d 1042 (Pa. 1997). So, for instance, if the case arises in the form of a shareholder's derivative suit (see p. 318, *infra*), and the decision in question is the board's decision to terminate the suit, the court will never consider whether the suit itself had substantive merit, but will merely consider such procedural issues as whether the board or its sub-committee was "independent" when it made the dismissal decision, whether it conducted a reasonable investigation into the merits of the derivative suit, etc.

(1) No 20/20 hindsight: The idea that a court deciding whether to apply the business judgment rule should not review the substantive merits of the underlying decision is often captured by saying that the court ***will not use "20/20 hindsight."*** See, e.g., *Brehm v. Eisner*, 746 A.2d 244 (Del. 2000) (discussed at length *supra*, p. 175): "It is the essence of the business judgment rule that a court will not apply 20/20 hindsight to second-guess a board's decision, except 'in rare cases [where] a transaction may be ***so egregious on its face*** that the board approval cannot meet the test of business judgment.' "

D. Exceptions to rule: Even where these three requirements for the business judgment rule are satisfied, there is at least one kind of situation (and possibly a second) where the court will find the rule ***inapplicable***.

1. **Illegality:** If the act taken or approved by the director is a ***violation of a criminal statute***, the director will ***lose the benefit*** of the business judgment rule. This is true even if the director was pursuing what he saw as the corporation's rather than his own interests, was acting based on full information, and rationally believed that his action would benefit the corporation (the three standard requirements for the rule). Even if there has been no criminal prosecution, if a civil plaintiff can show that the act was a criminal violation, the defendant will lose the benefit of the business judgment rule and his conduct will be evaluated solely based on the general duty of due care. (The director is then likely to lose, on the grounds that it is not due care to advocate or permit a violation of the criminal laws.)

   a. **Shareholders as protected class:** This "illegality" exception to the business judgment rule is especially likely to be invoked if the court concludes that shareholders are among the ***class meant to be protected*** by the criminal statute in question.

   Example: A statute forbids corporate charitable contributions. The purpose is to protect shareholders' financial interest. If a shareholder sues to recover illegal contributions, the court is likely to hold that the contributions violated the duty of due care if the board knew of them.Cf. *Miller v. American Telephone & Telegraph Co.*, 507 F.2d 759 (3d Cir. 1974).

2. **Pursuit of "social" goals:** Some courts recognize yet another exception to the business judgment rule: the pursuit by a director of broad ***social*** or ***political*** goals not related to the corporation's welfare. For instance, if the directors of a computer corporation (whose operations have very little to do with health care) were to donate, year after year, 50% of its net profits to a foundation for cancer research, a court might well hold that this extreme pursuit of social welfare goals at the expense of the corporation's profitability should not be protected by the business judgment rule. This might be the case even if the directors honestly, though mistakenly, believed that such donations were in the corporation's best overall interests (thus perhaps satisfying the "rationally believes" requirement for the business judgment rule).

   a. **Contrary view:** However, even in this kind of extreme situation, it is not clear that the court would refuse to apply the business judgment rule. Courts tend to give extremely ***wide latitude*** to directors' judgments that charitable or social (and perhaps even political) purposes mesh with the corporation's own financial interests. In any event, the corporation will usually be able to dress up its decision into one that is at least rationally related to the corporation's own financial interests.

   Example: P, a minority stockholder in the Chicago Cubs baseball team, brings a stockholders' derivative action against the directors of the team. P alleges that one of the Ds, Philip Wrigley (owner of 80% of the stock) has refused to allow lights to be placed in Wrigley Field, not because he thinks this will benefit the corporation but because he holds the personal social/political opinion that "baseball is a daytime sport" and that the installation of lights will have a bad effect upon the surrounding neighborhood.

Held, for Wrigley and the other defendant directors. It is not clear that these motives, even if proven, are contrary to the best interests of the corporation and its stockholders. For instance, if the neighborhood around the park were to deteriorate because of lights, the value of the corporation's property (the park) would deteriorate; also, patrons might be less willing to come to the park if it were now in a deteriorated, poorer, neighborhood. (The fact that all other teams have implemented night baseball is irrelevant, because "it cannot be said that directors, even those of corporations that are losing money, must follow the lead of the other corporations in the field.") *Shlensky v. Wrigley*, 237 N.E.2d 776 (Ill. App. Ct. 1968).

IV. MODERN STATUTORY MODIFICATIONS TO THE RULES OF DIRECTOR LIABILITY

A. **Reason for statutory modifications:** As the number of suits successfully holding directors liable for breach of the duty of due care has multiplied, many states have tried to ***counteract*** this trend by modifying their statutes. In general, these states appear to feel that increasing directors' and officers' risk of personal liability does not improve the economic efficiency of business as a whole, and certainly does not improve a state's ability to induce corporations to choose that state as their domicile.

B. **Some typical approaches:** There are at least four approaches that states have taken to reduce the practical burdens of director liability for money damages for breach of the duty of due care:

1. **Allow shareholders to amend charter:** Some states have allowed the shareholders to ***amend the corporate charter*** to eliminate or reduce directors' personal liability for violations of the duty of due care. For instance, Delaware GCL § 102(b)(7) allows the shareholders to modify the corporation's charter to eliminate money damages for breach of the duty of due care, so long as the director has acted in good faith without knowingly violating the law and without obtaining any improper personal benefit. (For more about this provision, see *supra*, p. 178.)

2. **Looser standard of care:** Some states have made the ***standard of care*** looser, so only more egregious conduct will give rise to personal liability. For instance, Indiana and Ohio now allow recovery only where the director has intentionally harmed the corporation or acted "recklessly." See Ind. Code § 23-1-35(1)(e)(2); Ohio Code § 1701.59.

3. **Limiting damages:** Some states have placed a ***limit*** on the amount of money damages that may be recovered against the director or officer. For instance, in Virginia personal liability is generally limited to $100,000 (or any lesser sum put in the company's charter by shareholder vote). Va. Code § 13.1-692.1.

4. **Greater right to indemnify:** Finally, many states now allow the corporation to completely ***indemnify*** directors and officers for any liability they may have for breach of the duty of due care. This topic is discussed extensively *infra*, p. 341.

See generally S,S,B&W, pp. 734-736.

Quiz Yourself on ***THE DUTY OF CARE & THE BUSINESS JUDGMENT RULE*** *(ENTIRE CHAPTER)*

43. Teddy Roosevelt is chairman of the board of a Delaware-chartered linen supply company, Bully Sheet, Inc. The board of directors is thinking of paying a dividend to the shareholders. (The directors are aware that the jurisdiction, like most, prohibits dividends when the effect would be to leave the corporation unable to pay its bill.) The directors therefore call in the company's chief financial officer, Ben Counter, who tells them that paying the dividend would not affect Bully Sheet's ability to meet its financial obligations. The directors are somewhat surprised by this, since they know that the company hasn't met its payroll recently. Nonetheless, relying on Counter's report, they go ahead and declare a dividend.

(a) A shareholder subsequently brings a derivative action against the directors, trying to hold them liable for improperly paying the dividend at a time when the corporation could not in fact afford to pay it. The directors defend by claiming that they satisfied their duty of care by relying on the opinion of an expert, Counter. Who's correct? ________________

(b) What could the board and shareholders of Bully Sheet do to make sure that future claims like the derivative claim in (a) could not possibly succeed? ________________

44. Carlo Bonaparte is majority shareholder of the Elba Real Estate Development Corporation. His two sons, Napoleon and Joseph, are minority shareholders, as well as officers and directors of the corporation. When Carlo dies, he leaves his interest in Elba to his widow, Letizia, who also becomes a director. Napoleon, as President, asks for board approval of the use of $1 million of corporate funds to attempt to acquire the island of Sardinia from an unaffiliated third party. In a 3-hour board meeting to consider the acquisition, Letizia and Joseph ask a number of questions, to which Napoleon gives answers that seem at least superficially reasonable. The board also reads a report on the proposed acquisition prepared by the company's accountants; the report concludes that the acquisition will probably be profitable, and that the price, though high, is within a reasonable range. At the conclusion of the meeting, Letizia says, "Well, I'd prefer that we stockpile our cash rather than going into this somewhat risky venture, but Nappy, if you really think it'll work out ok, I'll support you despite my doubts, because you've got a good feel for these real-estate purchase deals and I trust you to make money for the company."

Joseph votes against the acquisition, but between Letizia and Napoleon the proposal has enough votes to pass. A typical reasonably-able real estate investor would probably have voted against the transaction, because the price was about 25% above prevailing prices for such property, and the financial risks were clearly visible. The acquisition proves disastrously unprofitable, and causes the company to go broke. Joseph sues Letizia, alleging that she violated her duty of due care in voting for the acquisition.

(a) If you represent Letizia, what doctrine would you assert as a reason for holding Letizia not liable?

____

(b) If you make the argument referred to in part (a), what will be the likely result of the suit?

____

45. Lillian "Mama" Carlson is chairman of the board of Cincinnati Communications, Inc., (CCI) whose sole asset is radio station WKRP. Lillian rules WKRP with an iron fist, dominating the other seven board members — her son Arthur, Andy Travis, Jennifer Marlowe, Les Nessman, Venus Flytrap, Herb Tarlek, and Dr. Johnny Fever. Sosumi Inc., a giant Japanese communications company, offers to buy CCI for $50 a share. CCI is currently trading on the NYSE at $39 a share. Lillian wants to accept the offer, but realizes she needs board approval. At a special board meeting called on one day's notice, Lillian makes a 20-minute presentation about the offer. She doesn't supply — and the directors don't request — a valuation study or a written copy of the purchase terms. After her presentation, and with very little discussion, she calls for a vote. The directors unanimously approve the sale. They submit it to a shareholder vote shortly thereafter, with their recommendation. The shareholders approve it. Thereafter, a minority shareholder, Bailey Quarters, sues the directors for violating their duty of care to the corporation, asserting that the value was closer to $80 a share. (Assume that Quarters is correct, that another bidder could have been found who would have paid $80.) The directors claim that their decision is shielded by the business judgment rule. What's the likely result? ________________

46. Frank N. Stein wants to incorporate in Delaware his business, Frankie's Body Shop, which sells cadavers to be used in medical research. In order to lure qualified directors to his board, he agrees to put a clause in the articles of incorporation attempting to insulate the directors from breaches of the duty of care.

(a) Assume that the clause says, "No director shall be liable for money damages of any sort, arising from the violation of the duty of due care, regardless of the nature of the act or omission giving rise to the violation." Will the clause be enforceable as written? ________________

(b) Assume that the clause says, "No director shall be liable for money damages arising from the violation of the duty of due care, so long as the director acted in good faith, without knowingly violating any statute or other law, and without obtaining any improper personal benefit." Will clause be enforceable as written? ________________

Answers

43. (a) The shareholder. Directors can violate their duty of care through inactivity, as by failing to inform themselves of their corporation's business. They typically can fulfill their duty to keep themselves informed by relying on the advice of experts, such as lawyers and accountants. However, reliance on third parties shields the directors from liability for failure to exercise due care only when the reliance is ***reasonable***. Reliance is not reasonable where the director is on notice of facts or circumstances indicating that the expert is wrong. [174] Here, the directors know that Bully Sheet hasn't met its payroll recently; this flies in the face of Counter's statement that the company could pay a dividend and still meet its financial obligations. Once on notice of facts suggesting that Counter's statement was unreliable, the directors had at least a duty to inquire further, a duty that they did not discharge. Since the payment of the dividend in these circumstances seems to have brought harm to the corporation (by making it further insolvent), the directors are likely to be required to reimburse the corporation for the improperly-paid dividend.

(b) Placing an exculpation clause in the corporation's certificate of incorporation. Del. GCL § 102(b)(7) lets a corporation put into its certificate of incorporation "a provision eliminating or limiting the personal liability of a director to the corporation or its stockholders for monetary damages for breach of fiduciary duty as a director[.]" The provision can't cover a breach of the duty of loyalty or good faith, but it can cover a breach of the duty of care. Since only the duty of care is involved here, such a provision would make it virtually impossible for a shareholder derivative suit to succeed on these facts.

44. (a) You should assert that the "business judgment rule" bars liability. Under the business judgment rule, a director (or officer) who makes a business judgment in "good faith" fulfills the duty of care if the director (1) has no conflict of interest concerning the transaction; (2) is reasonably well-informed about the transaction; and (3) rationally believes that the business judgment is in the corporation's best interests. [183] You can make a pretty plausible case that Letizia's decision to vote in favor of the acquisition satisfied these requirements (see part (b) below).

(b) Letizia will probably win. As to requirement (1), there's nothing in the facts to indicate that Letizia had any conflict of interest regarding the transaction (for instance, the purchase was made from an unaffiliated third party.) As to requirement (2), the long board meeting, Letizia's detailed questions, and her reliance on the accountant's report, seem enough, taken collectively, to have made her "well-informed" about the acquisition. As to (3), Letizia's belief that Napoleon knew what he was doing seems to have been at least "rational," even if not fully "reasonable." Therefore, Letizia probably qualifies for the protection of the business judgment rule. If the court agrees, it won't hold Letizia liable even though an ordinary director of reasonable prudence would probably not have voted in favor of the transaction, based on the facts then known to the board.

45. The directors will probably lose. Directors have a duty of care toward the corporation, which they can violate either through inactivity or negligence. The directors will be protected from even a bad business decision under the business judgment rule, if they meet the three requirements described in the previous answer. The problem is that here, the directors have almost certainly not met requirement (2), that they be reasonably ***well-informed*** before taking the action. The fact that the directors didn't have a valuation study or see a copy of the acquisition agreement, the shortness of the advance notice to directors, the lack of discussion at the meeting — all of these things indicate a lack of reasonable information on the part of the board.

Since the board doesn't qualify for the protection of the business judgment rule, the question becomes whether the board's decision demonstrated "due care" or reasonable prudence. If another buyer really could have been found to pay $80, selling for $50 probably wasn't reasonably prudent. Therefore, the board will probably be held liable to reimburse the corporation for the money that was left on the table. See *Smith v. Van Gorkom*, so holding on roughly the same facts. [186]

Note that, had the directors not been procedurally careless — i.e., had they deliberated and done a valuation, but honestly, mistakenly valued the corporation too low — the business judgment rule probably *would* have protected their decision. (The prior question is an example of how this protection might have applied.)

46. (a) No, probably. Delaware, like most states, will not allow a corporation to nullify the duty of care as completely as this clause purports to do. In particular, this clause would absolve a director from liability even if he knew that the corporate action he was approving violated the law, or even if the director was engaging in self-dealing, and most state courts, including Delaware's, would not allow such a complete waiver of liability. See Del. GCL § 102(b)(7), listing a number of wrongs to which an exculpation clause may not apply, including an act or omission that violates the director's "duty of loyalty," that is "not in good faith," or that involves "intentional misconduct or a knowing violation of law."

(b) Yes. Because this clause requires good faith, and doesn't apply if the corporate action is known to be illegal or constitutes self-dealing, the clause meets the requirements of Delaware law (and probably that of most jurisdictions). See Del GCL § 102(b)(7), discussed in part (a) above. [190]

Exam Tips on THE DUTY OF CARE & THE BUSINESS JUDGMENT RULE

The duty of care — and its sibling, the business judgment rule — are two of the most frequently-tested subjects. Be alert to these issues whenever a fact pattern involves a decision by an officer or the board which could be characterized as ***unwise***.

☛ Never consider "duty of care" in the abstract — always discuss it in ***conjunction*** with the ***business judgment rule***. In other words, phrase the initial issue as "did the directors exercise due care?" but then say something like, "If the conditions for the business judgment rule are met, the court will find that the board satisfied its duty of care even though the transaction turned out badly or seems to the court to have been substantively unwise."

- ☞ Remember the ***three things*** a director must do to ***qualify*** for the business judgment rule:
  - ❑ she must ***not*** be ***"interested"*** (i.e., have a ***financial stake*** apart from the corp's own interest) in the subject matter of the action;
  - ❑ she must be ***reasonably informed*** about the decision she's making; and
  - ❑ she must ***rationally believe*** that the judgment she's making is in the ***best interests*** of the corp.
- ☞ Remember that ***absent directors*** are held to the same standard as directors who attended the meeting during which the board approved of a particular action. Thus if the board as a whole violated the duty of due care (i.e., didn't qualify for the business judgment rule), the absent directors will also be liable.
- ☞ Most frequently-tested aspect of the bus. judg. rule: the directors don't make an ***adequate investigation*** before they ***commit large sums of money*** to a project.

  Example: Pres., the head of Corp., wants to sell Corp. to Acquirer. Pres. is worried that the present demand for Corp.'s products will be transitory, and believes that the most favorable sale would be one that is accomplished rapidly. Therefore, Pres. urges the Corp. board to approve the sale without debate, and does not fully brief the board on the reasons why Acquirer's offer is the best one that can be gotten. Nor does Pres. or the board have an outsider review the price or other sale terms. The board probably does not qualify for the bus. judg. rule, because it was not adequately informed. If so, the board will be liable for failure to satisfy its duty of care, if its carelessness caused a disadvantageous sale to be made.

  - ☞ A variant is that a report describing the proposed transaction is prepared, but some directors ***don't read it*** — these directors don't get the protection of the bus. judg. rule, because they haven't taken the available steps to make themselves "reasonably informed."

- ☞ Questions sometimes involve board ***reliance*** on the ***opinions of others***. Here, the rule is that the board is entitled to rely on others where it is ***reasonable*** to do so. For instance, the board can typically rely on the opinion of the corp's CPAs, if the latter say that a proposed acquisition is a profitable business that is being sold for a standard multiple of earnings.

☞ Also, check whether the directors have acted in ***good faith.*** The requirement of good faith has two main components:

- ☞ First, the directors must have acted in a ***non-self-interested manner***. If they are acting so as to further their own business interests, at the expense of, say, a minority holder, the directors will not qualify for the bus. judg. rule.

  Example: The board refuses to pay out any of $5 million of accumulated earnings as dividends. P, a minority holder, sues to overturn this refusal, and the majority directors defend on the grounds that their dividend policies are protected by the bus. judg. rule. If P can show that the directors' purpose was to "freeze out" P — by depriving him of income so that he'd sell his shares back to the majority at a low price — the directors won't receive the protection of the bus. judg. rule.

- ☞ Second, the directors ***must not have been aware that they were not discharging their fiduciary obligations.*** (Cite to *Stone v. Ritter* on this point.) At least in Delaware, this means that the directors must have put in some sort of reporting or information system, and must have believed that they were doing some sort of monitoring of data from that system.

☞ A fact pattern will ***rarely fail*** to meet the ***"rational belief"*** requirement for the bus. judg. rule. Remember that so long as the directors' belief that the action was in the corp's interest is not ***wholly irrational***, this prong will be deemed satisfied. And this is true even if the action results in ***financial loss*** to the corp.

Example: To prevent a minority s/h from acquiring control, Corp. buys shares from 3 other s/h's at the asking price of $80/share, a price in excess of both book value and market value. As long as the decision was "plausible," the fact that the judge disagrees about the decision's wisdom — or the fact that later events showed that the shares were not worth the price paid — won't prevent the bus. judg. rule from applying.

CHAPTER 7

THE DUTY OF LOYALTY

ChapterScope

This Chapter covers the duty of "loyalty" owed to the corporation by its directors, officers and controlling shareholders (which we call "Key Players.") Key concepts:

- **Self-dealing transactions:** In a transaction where the Key Player and the corporation are on ***opposite sides*** (e.g., the Key Player sells property to the corporation), the transaction may be voided by the court, and the Key Player required to pay damages to the corporation, unless the conflict is disclosed in advance.
  - **Approval by disinterested holders or directors:** The best way for the Key Player to avoid self-dealing problems is for her to: (1) ***disclose*** the conflict and the nature of the transaction ***in advance***; and (2) have a majority of the ***disinterested directors*** or ***disinterested shareholders pre-approve*** the transaction after this disclosure.
  - **Fairness or ratification:** Alternatively, the Key Player will avoid self-dealing problems if either: (1) the transaction is basically ***"fair"*** to the corporation; or (2) disinterested directors or shareholders ***ratify*** the transaction after the fact, after receiving full disclosure about it.
- **Executive compensation:** Decisions about a senior executive's ***salary***, bonuses, stock options or pensions may be overturned if they are ***clearly "excessive,"*** taking into account the nature of the executive's services.
- **Corporate opportunity doctrine:** Before a director or senior executive may take for himself an ***opportunity*** that is likely to be of interest to the corporation (e.g., purchase of some property adjacent to the corporation's property), he must first ***offer that opportunity*** to the corporation. If he doesn't, he may be required to surrender the opportunity to the corporation after the fact, and/or pay damages.
- **Sale of control:** The owner of a controlling block of stock is generally allowed to sell his shares for an above-market ***"premium," without sharing*** that premium with other shareholders. However, there are several exceptions.

I. FIDUCIARY STATUS OF DIRECTORS, OFFICERS AND CONTROLLING SHAREHOLDERS

A. Key Players as trustees: It is sometimes said that directors, officers and controlling shareholders are in effect ***"trustees"*** of the corporation, and have a ***fiduciary obligation*** to it. As Justice Cardozo said (in a case involving a joint venture rather than a corporation, but a case which is often cited in connection with the duties of corporate directors and officers): "Joint adventurers . . . owe to one another . . . the ***duty of the finest loyalty***. Many forms of conduct permissible in a workaday world for those acting at arm's length, are forbidden to those bound by fiduciary ties. A trustee is held to something stricter than the morals of the market place." *Meinhard v. Salmon*, 164 N.E. 545 (N.Y. 1928).

1. **Partial truth:** However, the statement that officers, directors and controlling shareholders are in effect trustees of the corporation is only ***partly accurate***. It is true that these Key Players have varying duties to the corporation and its other shareholders that are somewhat similar to the fiduciary duties that a trustee incurs. But there are important differences. For example, a trustee must behave in a prudent manner, whereas the managers of a business enterprise are expected to take risks, sometimes big ones (and often ones that would be inappropriate for a trustee). Similarly, a controlling shareholder may have certain duties to the corporation and to the minority shareholders, but he nonetheless owns his shares, and within fairly broad limits is entitled to sell them when and how he wishes, without concern for the minority; again, this is quite different from the position of the trustee, who must put the interests of the beneficiary ahead of his own interests.

2. **Full-time employee:** There is one situation in which fiduciary responsibilities will be quite strictly enforced in corporate law: any full-time ***employee*** of the corporation (including an ***officer***) is an ***agent*** of the corporation, and is subject to all the fiduciary rules of agency, including a very strict ban on self-dealing.

   a. **Directors and controlling stockholders:** By contrast, an outside director, and a controlling shareholder who is not employed by the corporation, are usually held to at least a somewhat more lenient fiduciary standard. This difference is especially noticeable in the corporate opportunity context (*infra*, p. 219) — a business opportunity that a full-time employee learns about is much more likely to be found to "belong" to the corporation, than is a business opportunity that an outside director or non-employee major shareholder learns about.

II. SELF-DEALING TRANSACTIONS

A. **Kind of transactions we're concerned with:** The first context in which we need to consider the "duty of loyalty" is the context of the ***self-dealing transaction***. The key aspect of such transactions is that the Key Player (officer, director or controlling shareholder) and the corporation are on ***opposite sides*** of the transaction.

1. **Why we're concerned:** More precisely, we're especially concerned with transactions in which ***three conditions*** are met:

   ❑the Key Player and the corporation are on ***opposite sides***;

   ❑the Key Player has helped ***influence*** the corporation's decision to enter the transaction; and

   ❑the Key Player's ***personal financial interests*** are at least potentially ***in conflict*** with the financial interests of the corporation, to such a degree that there is reason to doubt whether the Key Player is necessarily motivated to act in the corporation's best interests.

   See Clark, p. 147. When we use the term "self-dealing transaction" in this book, we'll be referring to transactions that satisfy all three of these requirements.

   a. **Sale of property:** For instance, the paradigmatic illustration of the self-dealing transaction is the ***sale of property*** by a director to the corporation, or by the corporation to the director. If the director has influenced the corporation's decision to make the transaction, there is reason to fear that a sale by the corporation to the director will be at too low a price, and a sale by the director to the corporation will be at too high a price.

2. **If transaction with stockholder:** Observe that the fact that the Key Player happens to be a shareholder in the corporation does not remove this danger of unfairness to the corporation. For even though damage to the corporation will hurt the Key Player *qua* shareholder, the gain to him in his role as independent person will probably be greater than the loss to him as shareholder. This is true even if he is the majority shareholder.

   Example: Smith owns 70% of the stock of XYZ Corp. He is also president and one of the three directors. XYZ Corp is in the business of building hotels on property that it acquires. Smith happens to own Blackacre, a nice two acre parcel that he and his fellow directors agree is perfect for XYZ to build a hotel on. The board approves XYZ's purchase of the property from Smith at a price of $1 million.

   There is reason to worry that this price is too high and is therefore unfair to the corporation. True, if the price is $100,000 too high, Smith will bear $70,000 of this loss (because he owns 70% of the stock). But on the other hand, Smith ends up with $100,000 extra in his pocket, so he is ahead by a net amount of $30,000, and the minority shareholders are behind by $30,000. Since there is reason to think that Smith may have influenced the board's decision even if Smith himself didn't vote on the transaction (the other two directors know that they effectively serve at Smith's pleasure, and that he can decline to reelect them next time), we have all three ingredients for a self-dealing transaction that should be closely scrutinized: (1) a Key Player in a transaction with the corporation; (2) the Key Player possibly influencing the corporation's decision to enter the transaction; and (3) the Key Player's personal financial interests in conflict with those of the corporation (Smith wants to sell high, the corporation wants to buy low). Therefore, a court will probably scrutinize the transaction fairly closely, and will void it if it appears unfair to the corporation.

B. **Historical rule:** Courts have gradually become somewhat more tolerant of self-dealing transactions.

1. **Initial rule:** Until the late 1800s, courts were completely uncompromising: self-dealing transactions were ***completely prohibited***. For example, it didn't matter that the transaction was "fair" when viewed by an impartial observer, or that the transaction purported to have been approved by a majority of disinterested directors with full knowledge of the facts.

2. **Fair and ratified transactions:** By 1910, most courts had eased that prohibition somewhat: a self-dealing transaction would be allowed to stand if it was ***both*** approved by a majority of fully-informed disinterested directors, and was "fair" to the corporation (as determined by the court). But a contract in which a ***majority*** of the board was interested was voidable even if fair.

3. **Modern view:** By 1960, the still more liberal view that generally applies today was in place: a self-dealing transaction found by the court to be ***fair*** would be ***upheld***, whether approved by a disinterested board or not. (In most states, the rule is at least partly established by statute.)

   See generally Clark, pp. 160-61.

4. **Rationale:** The cases give no clear explanation for this dramatically increased tolerance for at least those self-dealing transactions that are found to be fair. Probably much of this tolerance comes from recognition that there will generally be an ***economic benefit*** to the corporation from allowing fair but self-dealing transactions — especially in the case of the close corporation (see *supra*, p. 133), transactions between a Key Person and the corporation may be the ***only way*** a corporation can obtain funds, goods or other things it needs.

   Example: Suppose that Close Corp. is formed by three shareholders, A, B and C. The corporation needs working capital to pursue its business (a service business which so far has no tangible assets). Banks are unwilling to lend to Close. A and B cause a corporation that they control to make an unsecured loan to Close at the prime rate. The transaction is never approved by the sole disinterested director, C, and it is never formally ratified by the stockholders acting as such.

   In the late 1800s or even 1910, a court would have voided the transaction at C's request, without considering its fairness to Close. But a modern court would probably determine that it was fair to the corporation (since it was not at an excessively high interest rate, and no better terms seemed to be available from other sources), despite the lack of direct approval by disinterested directors or shareholders. The reason is that the transaction has been beneficial to Close, since it enabled it to get funds that it could not otherwise easily obtain.

C. **Modern rule in detail:** Let us now consider in more detail the modern rule. You must keep in mind that there is substantial variation among states, and that we are merely trying to summarize the view of ***most*** courts.

1. **Statement of rule:** Most courts, acting by a combination of statutory interpretation and common-law principles where the statute is silent, seem to divide self-dealing transactions into three categories:

   a. **Fair transactions:** If the transaction is found to be ***fair*** to the corporation, considering all the circumstances, nearly all courts will ***uphold*** it. This is true ***whether or not the transaction was ever approved by disinterested directors or ratified by the shareholders***.

   b. **Waste/fraud:** If the transaction is so one-sided that it amounts to ***"waste"*** or ***"fraud"*** against the corporation, the court will usually ***void it*** if a stockholder complains. This is true even though the transaction has been approved by a majority of disinterested directors (acting with full knowledge of the transaction they were approving) or ratified by the shareholders.

   c. **Middle ground:** If the transaction does not fall into either of these categories — the court is not convinced it's perfectly fair, but the unfairness does not amount to waste or fraud — the court's response will probably depend on whether there has been ***director approval*** and/or ***shareholder ratification***. If a majority of disinterested and knowledgeable directors have approved the transaction, the court will probably uphold it; the court will similarly uphold it if it has been ratified by the shareholders. If neither disinterested director approval nor shareholder ratification has occurred, the court will probably invalidate the transaction. The ***burden of proof*** is on the ***Key Player***; he must show that the transaction was approved by either: (1) a disinterested and knowledgeable majority of the board ***without participation by the Key Player***; or (2) a majority of the shareholders ***after full disclosure*** of the relevant facts.

2. **Summary:** Thus the most important variable in the modern cases seems to be ***fairness***; clearly-fair transactions are always upheld, clearly-abusive ones (waste or fraud) are always struck down, and only if the transaction's fairness is ambiguous will the fact of disinterested director approval or shareholder ratification make a difference. See generally, Nutshell, p. 321.

3. **MBCA:** The corporation statutes of 38 states have explicit provisions dealing with transactions between the corporation and a Key Player. Most of these statutes deal solely with contracts between the corporation and a ***director***, not those between a corporation and a non-director officer or controlling shareholder. Probably the most important, and explicit, such statute is MBCA §§ 8.60-8.63. These sections were made part of the MBCA in 1988, replacing a much simpler single provision. Although these new sections have so far not been widely adopted by the states, they are likely to become increasingly influential.

   a. **Typical approach:** Also, the general pattern of these MBCA provisions — that a self-dealing transaction will be upheld if it is either approved by disinterested directors, ratified by shareholders or found by a court to have been fair — is typical of the approach of most states. Therefore, we consider the MBCA provisions in some detail. §§ 8.60-8.63 are usually collectively referred to as "Subchapter F" of the MBCA.

   b. **Key section:** The key section of the MBCA Subchapter F is § 8.61:

   §8.61 Judicial Action

   (a) A transaction effected or proposed to be effected by a corporation (or by an entity controlled by the corporation) may ***not*** be the subject of ***equitable relief*** or give rise to an ***award of damages*** or other sanctions against a director of the corporation, in a proceeding by a shareholder or by or in the right of the corporation, on the ground that the director has an ***interest*** in the transaction if it is ***not a director's conflicting interest transaction***.

   (b) A ***director's conflicting interest transaction*** may ***not be the subject of equitable relief,*** or give rise to an ***award of damages*** or other sanctions against a director, in a proceeding by a shareholder or by or in the right of the corporation, on the ground that the director has an ***interest respecting the transaction*** if:

   (1) ***directors' action*** respecting the transaction was taken in compliance with section 8.62 at any time; or

   (2) ***shareholders' action*** respecting the transaction was taken in compliance with section 8.63 at any time; or

   (3) the transaction, judged according to the circumstances at the relevant time, is established to have been ***fair to the corporation***.

   c. **Definitions:** Section 8.60 supplies a set of definitions for Subchapter F; these definitions are too long and convoluted to be reproduced here in full. However, we discuss a few of the definitions here.

   i. **"Director's conflicting interest transactions":** The core definition is that of "Director's conflicting interest transaction," defined in § 8.60(1) as follows:

   (1) ***"Director's conflicting interest transaction"*** means a transaction effected or proposed to be effected by the corporation (or by an entity controlled by the corporation)

   (i) to which, at the relevant time, ***the director is a party***; *or*

(ii) respecting which, at the relevant time, the ***director had knowledge and a material financial interest known to the director***; or

(iii) respecting which, at the relevant time, the director ***knew that a related person was a party or had a material financial interest***."

ii. "Related person": Another key definition is ***"related person."*** Under § 8.60(5), a "related person" encompasses principally the director's spouse, child, grandchild, sibling or parent (or any of these people's spouses), or any trust or estate as to which the director is a beneficiary or fiduciary. But the concept also includes any ***business or non-profit of which the director in question is a director or partner.***

iii. "Material financial interest": Next, there is a definition of ***"material financial interest"***: this means "a financial interest in a transaction that would reasonably be expected to impair the objectivity of the director's judgment when participating in action on the authorization of the transaction." § 8.60(4).

iv. "Required disclosure": Finally, there is a definition of ***"required disclosure,"*** which means "disclosure of (i) the ***existence and nature of the director's conflicting interest***; and (ii) all facts known to the director respecting the subject matter of the transaction that a director free of such conflicting interest would ***reasonably believe to be material in deciding whether or not to proceed with the transaction."*** § 8.60(6).

v. Explanation: Integrating these definitions: no matter whether the transaction involving the corporation is major or minor, it's automatically a "director's conflicting interest transaction" if *either* of the two following things is true:

[1] the director in question, or her ***close relative*** (or a business entity or non-profit that either the director or her close relative controls or ***serves as a director***) ***is a party*** to the transaction; or

[2] the director or her close relative (or a business entity or non-profit that either the director or her close relative controls or serves as a director) has (and knows she has) a ***"material financial interest"*** concerning the transaction.

Example of [1] (D is a party): A director (call him "D") of X Corp. uses his influence to cause the board of X Corp to authorize the purchase of $1,000 worth of office supplies from Z Corp., of which D is also a director. D is a multimillionaire, and does not benefit (or think he will benefit) in any way from the sale of supplies. Because D is a director of Z Corp., Z Corp. is a "related person" to D. D does not disclose to X's board that D is a director of Z Corp.

Since a related person to D is a direct party to the transaction with X Corp., the sale of supplies is a "director's conflicting interest transaction" as to D. Therefore (as we'll see in the next section entitled "three-part approach"), under the MBCA the court may enjoin it, or award damages against D in connection with it, if it's not approved by the Board or the shareholders of X Corp. after proper disclosure by D of his interest, and is "unfair" to X. So, for instance, if X is overcharged by $400, under the MBCA X can be required to pay the $400 back to X Corp. in damages, even though the small size and D's wealth meant that he did not have a "material financial interest" in the transaction. In other words, the fact that a "related person" to D (i.e., Z Corp.) was a party *automatically* made the transaction a "director's conflicting interest transaction" as to D.

Example of [2] (D has a "material financial interest" but is not a party): D (again a director of X Corp.) suggests to X Corp's board that X Corp. should purchase, for $1 million, a parcel of vacant land from Sell, an individual. Sell is not a "related person" to D. However, unbeknownst to any other board member or executive of X Corp., not only are D and Sell good friends, but prior to the transaction Sell has promised D that if Sell is able to sell the property for $1 MM to X Corp., then Sell will pay a $50,000 "commission" to D.

This quid pro quo has almost certainly given D a "material financial interest" concerning the purchase of the parcel from Sell (since the prospect of receiving a $50,000 fee "would reasonably be expected to impair the objectivity of the director's judgment when participating in action on the authorization of the transaction," the standard for whether the director has a "material financial interest.") If so, then under the MBCA a sale authorized by X Corp's board is a "director's conflicting interest transaction" as to D. Consequently, if D does not disclose the conflict and then get the transaction approved either by the Board or the shareholders of X Corp., then unless the transaction is "fair" to X Corp., a court acting under the MBCA could either enjoin it or award damages against D. And that's true even though D is not directly a party to the transaction — D's having a "material financial interest" is a substitute for D's being a party to the transaction. (The same would be true if, say, it was a *sibling or child* of D who would get the commission — if a "related party" to the director has a material financial interest in the transaction, it's the same as if the director himself had such an interest.)

d. **Three-part approach:** The guts of Subchapter F are set forth in § 8.61 (reproduced above). That section imposes two major rules:

i. **Non-conflict transactions:** Where a transaction is "***not*** a director's conflicting interest transaction" (under the definitions summarized in (c) above), the court may ***not*** enjoin it or set it aside on account of any interest which the director may have in the transaction.

ii. **Conflict transactions:** If the transaction ***is*** a "director's conflicting interest transaction," the corporation and the director receive a ***"safe harbor"*** for the transaction — and the court may thus not set it aside — if: (1) a ***majority of disinterested directors approved it*** after disclosure of the conflict to them (§8.62); or (2) a majority of the votes held by ***disinterested shareholders*** are cast in a vote ***ratifying*** the action, after disclosure of the conflict (§8.63); or (3) the transaction, "judged according to the circumstances at the time of commitment, is established to have been ***fair*** to the corporation."

e. **Commentary:** Here are several aspects of Subchapter F that may not be obvious:

i. **Exclusive definition of "conflicting interest":** First, the definition of "director's conflicting interest transaction" given in § 8.60 is ***exclusive***. That is, if the transaction does ***not*** fall within the definition given there, the transaction is automatically deemed ***non-conflicting***, and the court may not overturn it on grounds of director self-interest.

Example: D is a director of X Co. X Co. proposes to enter into a transaction with Smith, who is D's cousin. The transaction comes before the X Co. board for approval. D and Smith are not only cousins but extremely close friends, and D knows that Smith desperately needs the money which would come to him as the result of the proposed transaction. D does not disclose to the X Co. board the fact that Smith is his cousin, or that D wishes the transaction to go forward so as to aid Smith. D has no independent financial interest in the transaction. The board members listen to D's urging that the transaction be approved, and vote for approval. P, a shareholder, now sues the board and Smith, seeking to have the transaction set aside.

Under the MBCA approach, the court must conclude that there is *no conflict*, and may therefore not even consider overturning the transaction on conflict grounds. The reason is that a cousin is not "related person" under the definitions given in § 8.60(5), and D had no direct financial interest of his own in the transaction. Since the transaction is not a "director's conflicting interest transaction" as defined in § 8.60(1), § 8.61(a) requires that the court not enjoin it on account of any conflict arising out of the X-Smith relationship. (This example is suggested by an example given in Official Comment 1 to § 8.61.)

ii. **Directors only:** Second, Subchapter F covers only transactions between the corporation and one of its ***directors***. Transactions between the corporation and a non-director ***officer or shareholder*** are not covered by Subchapter F (and are in fact not covered by ***any*** provision of the MBCA having to do with self-dealing). Thus transactions with non-director officers or shareholders under the MBCA are left entirely to ***common-law principles*** (though the court is likely to approach these in almost the same way as a transaction between the corporation and a director).

iii. **Disclosure after controversy:** Third, the disclosure and approval can happen even ***after the transaction has been challenged*** by a dissident shareholder or third party. In other words, after-the-deal ***ratification*** by the board can suffice — pre-approval is not necessary. See Official Comment to MBCA § 8.62(a).

Example: A majority of disinterested directors approve Corp's purchase of land from Landco, a limited partnership. At the time of the approval vote, the directors don't know that Bob, one of the directors, is secretly a major partner in Landco. The purchase goes through. Steve, a minority holder in Corp., then learns of the conflict. He brings a derivative suit to have the transaction unwound. If nothing further happens (and if the court finds that the transaction was "unfair" to Corp.), the court will probably order the transaction unwound or at least order that Bob pay damages to Corp. But if, within a reasonable time after Steve brings suit, the board ratifies the transaction with full disclosure of the nature of the transaction and nature of Bob's ownership interest in the selling partnership, the court will not interfere.

4. **Three paths:** Under the MBCA and the statutes of most states, there are thus three different ways that proponents of a self-dealing transaction can avoid invalidation:

[1] by showing that it was ***approved by a majority of disinterested directors***, after full disclosure;

[2] by showing that it was ***ratified by shareholders***, after full disclosure; and

[3] by showing that it was ***fair when made***.

Let's now consider each of these branches in detail in Paragraphs D, E and F below.

D. Disclosure plus board approval: The general principle behind the "board approval" branch is simple to state: a ***transaction may not be avoided by the corporation if it was authorized by a majority of the disinterested directors, after full disclosure of the nature of the conflict and the transaction***. However, this formulation raises a number of questions:

1. What must be disclosed: ***What information*** is it that must be disclosed to the disinterested directors? Most courts (and the MBCA) require disclosure of ***two*** major kinds of information: (1) the material facts about the ***conflict***; and (2) the material facts about the ***transaction***.

a. Conflict: Often the fact that there is a conflict will be obvious to the disinterested directors (e.g., when the contract runs directly between the director and the corporation). But other conflicts will not be obvious, and must therefore be disclosed by the Key Person. This will be true, for instance, if the other party to the transaction is a ***corporation*** in which the Key Person has a significant pecuniary interest. (See the discussion of indirect conflicts, *infra*, p. 209.)

Example: XYZ Corp wants to buy an office building. D, a vice president of XYZ, owns all of the stock of Realty Corp, which owns an office building. D has a real estate broker offer the building to XYZ, and the board of XYZ votes to acquire it. The other directors are not aware that D has an interest in Realty Corp.

Even though all material economic facts about the underlying transaction (e.g., the condition and market value of the building) have been disclosed to the other board members, approval by the board of the contract will not insulate the transaction from attack, because D has not disclosed his financial interest in Realty Corp to the board. See MBCA § 8.62 (requiring disclosure to the board, before approval, of details regarding the director's conflict); § 8.60(6) (defining the required disclosure).

b. Disclosure of transaction: Apart from disclosure of the facts that cause a conflict, the Key Person must also disclose all facts about the ***underlying transaction*** that a reasonable observer would consider ***"material."*** This obligation goes far beyond the ordinary duty of one party to a contract to disclose essential facts to the other. For instance, if the Key Person knows of facts that are likely to make the proposed contract turn out to the disadvantage of the corporation, ***he must disclose those facts***, whereas a third party negotiating at arm's length with the corporation could remain silent.

c. When disclosure must be made: You might think that the requirement of disclosure means that the disclosure must take place ***before*** the transaction is entered into. But courts are in fact in disagreement about whether this is required.

i. Ratification allowed: Some courts will uphold the transaction based on board approval even if the disclosure does not come ***until*** after the transaction is entered into, so long as the directors then ***"ratify"*** it (by formally stating that they have no objection, or perhaps even by simply failing to raise an objection). Thus MBCA § 8.61(b)(1) insulates the transaction against judicial review if "directors' action respecting the transaction was ***at any time*** taken in compliance with § 8.62" (providing for approval by disinterested directors). The phrase "at any time" is intended to allow for post-transaction ratification.

ii. Contrary view: But other courts require the disclosure to occur before the transaction, or at least make it tougher for transactions to be ratified after the fact instead of approved beforehand.

2. Who is a "disinterested" director: The approval must be by a majority of the ***"disinterested"*** directors. Who is "disinterested" for this purpose? Most courts would probably agree with the MBCA, which says that a director is "qualified" (the MBCA's term for "disinterested") if (i) the transaction is not a "director's conflicting interest transaction" (see *supra*, p. 201 for what this means); *and* (ii) the director does not have a "material relationship" with another director as to whom the transaction is a "director's conflicting interest transaction." MBCA § 1.43(a)(3).

Example 1: The proposed transaction is between X Corp. and Z Corp., under which X Corp. will buy a piece of real estate from Z Corp. The issue is whether D, a director of X Corp., is "disinterested" (or under the MBCA, "qualified"), so that D's vote to approve the transaction can contribute to the required approval by a majority of disinterested directors. Assume that D is also a director of Z Corp. D is not qualified, because under the combination of MBCA §§ 8.60(1)(iii) and 8.60(5)(v), D's being a director of Z Corp. makes Z Corp. a related person to D, and the fact that D has a related person who has a "material financial interest" in a transaction makes the transaction a "director's conflicting interest transaction" as to D.

Example 2: Same basic facts as above example. Now, however, D has no direct relationship with Z Corp. However, D's boss, B, who also happens to be on X Corp's board, is a director of Z Corp. Since D has a material relationship with B (boss-subordinate would almost certainly be a material relationship), the fact that the transaction is a director's conflicting interest transaction as to B means that D, too (not just B) is not a disinterested or qualified director.

a. Outside professionals: Even outside directors who serve as ***professionals*** (e.g., outside counsel or outside accountant) to the corporation may be found to be "interested" in a transaction in which the CEO is a party. The theory for treating these professionals as "interested" is that they may be afraid they will no longer be engaged by the corporation if they annoy the CEO by voting against the transaction. Thus on the facts of Example 2 above, if D was not B's subordinate, but was instead a lawyer who relied on B for lots of business, D would likely not be disinterested.

3. Quorum: Often, especially in the case of a close corporation, a majority of the directors will be "interested" in the transaction. (For instance, the CEO may be a party to the transaction, and a majority of the directors may be full-time employees who owe their jobs to him.) In this situation, there will of course not be enough disinterested directors to constitute a quorum of the board. Therefore, a special rule exists in almost all states to facilitate approval by the disinterested directors: if a ***majority of the disinterested directors*** approve the transaction, this constitutes not only approval, but also a ***quorum***. (However, most statutes require ***at least two*** disinterested directors to approve the transaction.) See MBCA § 8.62(c), and Del. GCL 144(a)(1), both to this effect.

> **Example:** The board of XYZ Corp has five directors. Two of them propose to enter into a contract with XYZ, and are therefore interested directors. The other three are not interested. One of the three disinterested directors is absent from the board meeting. The other two disinterested directors are sufficient to constitute a quorum for approval purposes (since they represent a majority of the three disinterested directors). If these two approve the transaction, this will constitute the requisite disinterested-director approval.
>
> If, on the other hand, two of the three disinterested directors were absent, the third director's vote approving the transaction would not constitute either a quorum or approval, because there would not be approval by a majority of the total disinterested directors (those present and those absent).

4. **Presence or vote of interested director:** Ideally, the ***interested*** director should ***abstain*** from either voting or even lobbying the disinterested directors concerning the transaction. However, most statutes provide that participation by the interested director in the consideration or voting does ***not*** by itself nullify the approval by the disinterested directors — the interested director's presence and/or vote is simply ***disregarded***, and the sole question is whether a majority of the total disinterested directors has approved the transaction.

   a. **Different rule in MBCA:** But some statutes say that ***no interested director(s) may be either present or voting*** (presumably for fear that the interested director's mere presence may sway the others.) See, e.g., MBCA § 8.62(a)(1), which says that a vote by the disinterested directors authorizing the transaction will be effective only if the disinterested directors "have deliberated and ***voted outside the presence of and without the participation by*** any other [i.e., interested] director."

5. **Committee:** Under most statutes, approval by disinterested directors may be done at the level of a ***committee*** rather than the full board. Usually, this committee may be either one that already exists (e.g., the compensation committee), or one appointed specially to consider the particular transaction. In any event, all that is required for a quorum and for approval is the approval by a majority of the disinterested directors ***on the committee***, even if this is less than a majority of the total disinterested directors on the board.

6. **Immunization of unfairness:** Suppose a majority of disinterested directors (acting after full disclosure of all material facts) approves a transaction that, viewed later by a court, is clearly ***unfair*** to the corporation. Does the disinterested-director approval completely immunize the transaction against attack for self-dealing? Most statutes are written as if the answer were ***"yes."*** However, in practice courts often void such transactions if the unfairness is great, despite the disinterested-director approval; frequently, they accomplish this result by finding that the transaction constituted "waste." (The effect of unfairness is discussed more extensively, *infra*, p. 208.)

   a. **Shifting of burden of proof:** In most states, approval by the disinterested directors does seem to at least ***shift the burden of proof***: if the transaction has not been approved by disinterested directors (or shareholders), the burden is generally on the Key Player to prove that it was fair; once approved by disinterested directors, the burden shifts to the person attacking the transaction to show that it was unfair. See *infra*, p. 209.

E. Disclosure plus shareholder ratification: The second main branch for validating a self-dealing transaction is the ***ratification by shareholders***, following disclosure to them.

1. **Disclosure required:** As in the case of disinterested-director approval, the shareholder ratification will be effective only if it comes after there has been ***full disclosure*** to the shareholders of ***both the conflict*** and the ***material facts of the transaction itself***.

2. **Disinterested shareholders:** Recall that in the case of director authorization, a majority of the ***disinterested*** directors must approve. Does a comparable rule apply to shareholder ratification, or may interested shareholders vote and be counted towards a majority? The courts are hopelessly ***split*** and confused about this issue — some seem to say that shareholder ratification has no effect unless a majority of the disinterested shareholders approve, whereas others seem to hold that all shareholders may vote and be counted. A court is likely to give a more searching inquiry into the transaction's underlying ***fairness*** (*infra*, p. 208) in those situations where it is not clear that a majority of the disinterested shareholders has approved.

   a. **MBCA:** The MBCA takes a stringent view: under § 8.63(a), a majority of the ***disinterested*** shareholders must approve the transaction. (On the other hand, for purposes of determining whether the transaction is approved under general corporate action principles having nothing to do with the conflict, interested shareholder votes may be counted, and are part of the quorum.)

      Example: Assume that Parent Corp owns 60% of Subsidiary Corp. Parent Corp wants to merge Subsidiary Corp into itself. Because Parent Corp is a party to the transaction, the conflict will be deemed ratified by the shareholders only if at least half of the holders of the minority block approve it, under MBCA § 8.63(a) and (c). See Official Comment 3 to MBCA § 8.63. However, for purposes of determining whether the general requirement of shareholder approval for *any* merger under the MBCA has occurred, and for determining whether there has been a quorum for that approval, Parent Corp's votes may be counted.

F. Fairness as the key criterion: The final method of defending a self-dealing transaction against attack is by showing that it is, under all the circumstances, ***fair*** to the corporation.

1. **Fairness alone sufficient:** In nearly all states, ***fairness alone*** will cause the transaction to be ***upheld***, even if there has been ***no approval*** by disinterested directors and no ratification by shareholders.

   a. **Measured at time of transaction:** "Fairness" is generally determined by the facts as they were ***known at the time of the transaction***. See, e.g., MBCA § 8.61(b)(3) ("judged according to the circumstances at the relevant time[.]")

2. **No requirement of prior disclosure:** In most courts, the transaction will withstand attack if it is proven fair, even though ***no disclosure whatsoever*** is made by the Key Player to his fellow executives, directors or shareholders. Thus in the office building example on p. 205 *supra*, even if D never disclosed to anyone that he was a controlling shareholder in the firm that owned the building being sold to the corporation, most courts would hold that so long as the pricing terms were in line with what would have been produced by arm's length bargaining, the transaction may not be avoided by the corporation.

3. **Authorization/ratification does not immunize from unfairness:** In most states, fairness is really the ***key element***. As we've just seen, if the transaction is fair, lack of disinterested-director authorization or shareholder ratification will not make a difference. Conversely, if the transaction is found by the court to be grossly ***unfair***, under most statutes the fact that there *was* approval by disinterested directors, or ratification by shareholders, will ***not immunize*** the transaction.

   a. **Delaware allows immunization:** But some jurisdictions, probably a minority, do allow disinterested-director authorization or shareholder ratification to ***immunize*** even an unfair transaction from judicial review. Delaware, for instance, seems to allow such immunization. As the Delaware Supreme Court has stated: "Approval by fully-informed disinterested directors under § 144(a)(1), or disinterested stockholders under § 144(a)(2), permits invocation of the business judgment rule and limits judicial review to issues of gift or waste, with the burden of proof upon the party attacking the transaction." *Marciano v. Nakash*, 535 A.2d 400 (Del. 1987).

   b. **MBCA allows immunization:** Similarly, the MBCA forbids judicial review of the fairness of director-authorized or shareholder-ratified transactions. § 8.61(b) (as noted *supra*, p. 201) states that the court may not overturn a director-conflict transaction if the action was authorized by disinterested directors after disclosure, or ratified by disinterested shareholders after disclosure.

4. **Significance of director or shareholder approval:** If fairness is what really counts — that is, if fair transactions will be upheld even without director or shareholder approval, and unfair ones will be struck down even with shareholder or director approval — why bother to get approval by disinterested directors or by shareholders? The answer is that in most states, there is still some practical benefit to this kind of approval, a benefit which stems from ***standards of proof*** and the ***burden of proof***.

   a. **Standards of proof:** First, in most states, the ***degree of unfairness*** that must be shown to upset a transaction that has been approved by disinterested directors or shareholders is probably ***greater*** than where there has been no approval. Some courts accomplish this by saying that a director-approved or a shareholder-approved transaction will only be overturned if the unfairness is so great that it amounts to ***fraud*** or ***waste***. Others appear to look for "gross" unfairness, as opposed to the "ordinary" unfairness that will be enough for invalidation where there has been no approval.

   b. **Burden of proof:** Second, the ***burden of proof shifts*** in most states when there has been director or shareholder approval. Without such approval, the burden of proof is clearly on the ***Key Player*** to show why the transaction is fair. Once there has been disinterested-director approval or shareholder approval, the burden shifts to the person who is attacking the transaction, who must now come forward with evidence of the transaction's ***un***fairness. Most statutes do not expressly document this shift in the burden of proof, but courts seem to make the shift anyway.

G. **Indirect conflicts involving Key Player:** So far, we've generally assumed that the Key Player is himself directly a party to the transaction in question. But the rules against self-dealing also apply where the conflict of interest is ***"indirect."*** That is, self-dealing problems arise where the Key Player has an interest or association with ***some other entity***, and it is that entity that enters into the transaction with the corporation.

1. **Pecuniary interest:** In general, if a Key Player's ***financial interest*** in the other entity is such that this interest would reasonably be expected to ***affect his judgment*** concerning the transaction, the self-dealing rules apply. For instance, if the Key Player is a significant ***stockholder*** of the other corporation, or a partner in a partnership, the transaction involving that other corporation or partnership will be deemed self-dealing, and the rules described above will apply. The office building hypothetical on p. 205 is an example of this principle.

2. **Interlocking directors and other non-ownership problems:** Suppose the Key Player does not have a significant ownership interest in the other entity, but is a full time ***executive*** or a ***director*** of that other entity. Here, the self-dealing problem is usually thought to be less severe, so the full range of self-dealing rules does ***not*** apply. For instance, the fact that a person serves on the board of directors of both companies (the ***"interlocking directorate"*** problem) will not by itself usually cause a transaction between the two companies to constitute self-dealing by the director.

   a. **MBCA is different:** But again, in this interlocking-directorate scenario the MBCA is ***much stricter*** than the usual state statute. One of the ways a transaction will be a "director's conflicting interest transaction" is if the director "knew that a related person was a party or had a material financial interest" in the transaction. MBCA § 8.60(1)(iii). "Related person" is defined in § 8.60(5)(v) to include "a domestic or foreign ... business ... of which the director is a director." So a person who is a director of both corporations is not, under the MBCA, a disinterested (or "qualified," to use the MBCA's term) director as to any transaction between the two corporations.

      Example: D is a director of A Corp and B Corp. A Corp. proposes to buy a piece of real estate from B Corp. When A Corp's board votes on the transaction, D will not be a "qualified" (i.e., disinterested) director, because he is a director of a related person (related to him, that is) — B Corp — and that related person is a party to the proposed transaction. Therefore, D must be careful to make disclosure of his conflict, and then not participate (or be present at) the vote by A Corp's board.

H. Remedies for violation: Where there has been a violation of the rule against self-dealing, there are two possible ***remedies***: (1) ***rescission***; and (2) ***restitution*** in the form of money damages. The plaintiff will normally be the ***corporation itself***, or a shareholder who has brought a derivative suit (*infra*, p. 318) in the corporation's name.

1. **Rescission:** If it is possible to ***rescind*** the transaction, this is normally the appropriate remedy for self-dealing. For instance, in the office building sale hypothetical (*supra*, p. 205), if suit were brought by the corporation or a shareholder in a derivative suit, and the closing had not yet occurred, the court would simply order that the contract be cancelled. If there is to be rescission, the corporation must ***give back*** any consideration it has received in the transaction. For instance, if the corporation has sold corporate property to a Key Player in what turns out to be an unfair transaction, the corporation may obtain return of the property, but it must then return to the Key Player the price he paid.

2. **Restitutionary damages:** If because of the passage of time or the complexity of the transaction, it is not feasible to rescind it, the appropriate remedy is ***restitutionary damages***. That is, the Key Player will be required to pay back to the corporation any benefit he received beyond what was fair. For instance, in our office building sale hypothetical

(*supra*, p. 205), if Realty Corp received $1 million for the sale of the building, and the fair market price was only $800,000, D or Realty Corp would have to return to XYZ the $200,000 excess over fair value.

3. **Consequence:** Observe that neither rescission nor restitution is a very strong deterrent to self-dealing: In either case, the Key Player who has engaged in the wrongful self-dealing is merely ***returned to the same position*** he would have been in had he not done the transaction at all. See C&E, pp. 662-63. However, some courts have ordered the self-dealing Key Player to also return any ***salary*** he earned during the relevant period, have awarded ***punitive*** damages to the corporation, or have ordered the self-dealer to pay the corporation's ***counsel fees*** and other litigation expenses. C&E, pp. 663-64.

Quiz Yourself on
***THE DUTY OF LOYALTY** (SELF-DEALING TRANSACTIONS)*

47. Mr. Haney is one of six directors of the Green Acres Produce Company. Green Acres is interested in expanding its acreage. It wants to buy a 100-acre tract of land in Hooterville, which is owned by the Hooterville Limited Partnership. When the chairman of Green Acres Produce, Oliver Wendell Douglas, inquires as to a selling price, Hooterville's general partner, Mr. Ziffel, tells him it's $10,000 an acre. Mr. Haney doesn't go to the directors' meeting where the land purchase is discussed; the other five directors approve it unanimously. Unbeknownst to the other board members, Mr. Haney is one of the limited partners in the Hooterville Limited Partnership (he owns a 25% economic interest in the partnership). A minority shareholder of Green Acres finds out about the proposed purchase, and sues to prevent its consummation, on account of the fact that Mr. Haney is arguably on both sides of the transaction. Assume that the proposed price is 30% above market prices for the type of property in question, and that the Hooterville directors who voted in favor of the transaction knew this. Does the fact that the disinterested directors approved the transaction mean that the court should allow the transaction to go forward? ______________

48. The Addams Shroud Company provides funeral supplies. It has seven directors — Gomez, Morticia, Puggsley, Wednesday, Fester, Lurch, and Cousin Itt. Of the seven, four of them — Gomez, Morticia, Wednesday, and Puggsley — are also major shareholders of the Arsenic and Old Lace Fabric Company, which makes, among other things, black fabric. The Addams Shroud Company uses a lot of black fabric that it buys from various suppliers. Gomez negotiates a requirements contract on Addams Shroud's behalf with Arsenic and Old Lace. When it comes time for the Addams's board to approve the contract, the four "interested" directors abstain (after making sure that the others know the full details of the conflict and of the contract). The three remaining directors vote, 2-1, to approve the contract. The dissenter argues that the contract has not been properly approved, because a quorum of the board did not participate in the decision. Has the Addams's board properly approved the contract, in a manner that will immunize the contract from attack on conflict grounds? ______________

49. The Enterprise Tribble Company makes funny toys called, predictably enough, tribbles. James Kirk is one of the five directors of Enterprise. He is also majority shareholder of Romulan Card Stores, a chain of greeting card and novelty toy stores. Kirk believes that Romulan can sell Enterprise's entire tribble output. Romulan and Enterprise negotiate a contract, whereby Romulan agrees to pay $5 per tribble (a fair price based on what the parties know at the time), for two years, for 1,000,000 tribbles per year (which is likely to be most of Enterprise's output). Kirk fully discloses his conflict and the material elements of the contract to the other, disinterested members of the Enterprise board, who unanimously approve the contract. It comes as a surprise to everyone when tribbles feature prominently in a Star Trek episode shortly after the contract goes into effect, such that the demand for tribbles — and the price Romulan can charge for them — skyrockets. A minority shareholder of Enterprise, Scotty, can't take it any longer, and files a derivative lawsuit against Kirk, citing the unfairness of the deal and seeking to void it on grounds of conflict of interest. What result? ________________

Answers

47. No, because Mr. Haney didn't disclose his ownership interest in the land to the board. This was a director-conflict situation: Haney was a director of the buyer, and he also had a sufficiently large financial interest (25%, or $250,000) in the subject of the transaction that his impartiality can reasonably be questioned.

When a director has a conflict of interest involving a corporate transaction, there are three ways to avoid the transaction's voidability on conflict grounds: (1) full disclosure and disinterested director approval, (2) full disclosure and shareholder approval, or (3) overall fairness. (In practice, most courts require that the transaction be fair regardless of director or shareholder approval.) But the conflict won't be deemed to have been "disclosed" unless the disinterested directors (or shareholders) knew *both* the nature of the transaction *and* the *nature of the conflict*. See, e.g., MBCA § 8.62(a) (making board approval of a conflict transaction effective only if it comes after "required disclosure") and § 8.60(6) (defining "required disclosure" as disclosure of (i) "the existence and nature of the director's conflicting interest" and (ii) "all facts known to the director respecting the subject matter of the transaction that a director free of such conflicting interest would reasonably believe to be material in deciding whether or not to proceed with the transaction.")

Here, the disinterested directors didn't know that Haney was a significant partner of the selling entity, so they didn't know of the "nature of the director's conflicting interest." Therefore, there wasn't true disclosure, and the approval by the disinterested directors will be irrelevant. (It's also irrelevant that Haney didn't vote on the proposed transaction — as long as there was a conflict between Haney's role as director of Green Acres and his role as partner in Hooterville, the conflict rules apply, requiring disclosure.)

In fact, full disclosure would probably require not only that the Green Acres board be told that Haney was a partner in Hooterville, but also that the board be told the approximate size of his interest (e.g., that he owned about 1/4 of the economic interest.)

Observe that if the transaction were "fair" to the corporation, the court would probably approve it even without the prior disclosure; but the facts tell you that the price is quite high, thus making it probably unfair. Also, note that even *after the dissident shareholder filed suit*, under most conflict statutes it would not be too late for Haney to make full disclosure, and procure a truly informed approval by the disinterested directors. (See, e.g., Off. Comm. to MBCA § 8.62(a)). Such an after-the-fact vote would suffice to immunize the transaction from a court-issued injunction or an award of damages.

48. Yes. The contract will not be voidable on conflict grounds, because a majority of the disinterested directors have approved it after full disclosure.

A conflict arises when a director or officer has split loyalties. Here, the conflict is indirect — four Addams directors are shareholders of a corporation with which Addams Shroud is contracting. The prevailing rule is that such a contract is voidable at Addams's option unless either disinterested directors approve it on full disclosure, shareholders approve it on full disclosure, or it's fair. Most states hold that as long as a majority of the disinterested directors (with a 2-person minimum) approve the transaction, this counts not only as approval, but also as a quorum. See, e.g., MBCA § 8.62(c). Since a majority of the 3 disinterested directors have approved, this condition is satisfied. [206]

49. The deal isn't voidable, because it was approved by disinterested directors, and, besides, it's fair. The transaction here involves a conflict because Kirk is a director for one party to a contract and majority shareholder of the other. The general rule is that such a contract is voidable unless either: (1) the transaction and conflict are disclosed to directors, who approve it; (2) the transaction and conflict are disclosed to shareholders, who approve it; or (3) it's fair to the corporation. [200] Here, Kirk fully disclosed the material facts of the deal and the conflict to the disinterested directors of Enterprise, who approved it. This satisfies test (1), and is thus in and of itself enough to avoid voidability on grounds of conflict.

In any event, the transaction here was "fair" to Enterprise. A court will generally judge fairness as of the time the transaction was made. (See, e.g., MBCA § 8.61(b)(3)). [208] At the time this deal was made, everything suggested that the deal was fair to Enterprise. So the transaction satisfies (3), and would therefore not be voidable at Scotty's urging even if full disclosure and pre-approval by the board *hadn't* occurred.

III. EXECUTIVE COMPENSATION

A. Aspect of self-dealing: We turn now to what might be thought of as a "special case" or aspect of self-dealing, ***executive compensation***. When an executive is sufficiently senior that he can influence the corporation's decision on his compensation, we have a transaction that presents all the traditional dangers of self-dealing: since the executive is to some extent on both sides of the transaction, there is a risk that the corporation will not be treated fairly (because it will pay the executive more money than it ought to, and this will be money that belongs to the shareholders). As we will see below, the courts handle the question of executive compensation in much the same way they handle the more general self-dealing problems we reviewed above: they look essentially to the "fairness" of the transaction, and are influenced by the fact that there has been (or has not been) approval by disinterested directors and/or ratification by shareholders.

B. Forms of compensation: Before we get into the tests by which courts evaluate executive compensation, let us first review briefly the common forms that such compensation may take. Executive compensation arrangements may be grouped into three broad categories: (1) ***current*** payments (salary and annual bonus); (2) stock-based ***incentive*** arrangements (stock options, restricted stock, phantom stock and stock appreciation rights); and (3) pensions and other ***deferred cash*** compensation. We consider each of these groups briefly in turn.

1. **Salary and current bonus:** Executives almost always receive two types of ***"current"*** cash compensation: a salary that is paid throughout the year, and an annual cash bonus, typically paid at the end of the year. The bonus is usually geared in some way to the corporation's profits. Both the salary and bonus, if they are reasonable in amount, are ***deductible*** by the corporation when paid, in computing the corporation's taxable income.

2. **Stock-based incentive plans:** Especially in public companies, the corporation (and the outside directors who typically form the compensation committee) worry that senior executives who receive only a salary and an annual bonus will take a short-term view in managing the corporation. To get executives to think more like an "owner," i.e., a shareholder,

most publicly held corporations therefore give their executives one or more types of ***long-term incentive*** tied in some way to the performance of the company's ***stock***.

a. Stock options: The most common form of stock-based long-term incentive plan is the ***stock option***. A stock option is the right to buy shares of the company stock at some time in the future, for a price that is typically set today. If the stock price increases (presumably due in part to the executive's good performance) to where the stock is selling for more than the option price, the executive ***"exercises"*** the option by paying the now-bargain price, and then either immediately resells at a profit or holds onto the stock hoping for still more appreciation. If the stock price never rises above the exercise price, the executive never exercises the option, and has therefore not lost anything. There are two sub-types of options which differ sharply in their tax treatment.

i. Non-qualified stock options: A ***"non-qualified"*** stock option (i.e., any option that isn't an "incentive stock option" as described below) does not get any special tax treatment under the Internal Revenue Code. The executive does not receive income when the option is awarded to him; however, when he ***exercises*** the option, he receives immediate income equal to the difference between the exercise price and the present market value, of the stock. This can be burdensome if he wishes to hold onto the stock, since he has to pay taxes without having any cash with which to pay them. (On the other hand, the corporation gets a current deduction for the difference between the exercise price and the present market value, since this is in effect "compensation" and is therefore deductible as an ordinary and reasonable business expense.) See C&E, pp. 701; Clark, pp. 202-03, 210-11.

ii. Incentive stock options: The other kind of stock option is the so-called ***"incentive stock option."*** For an option to be an incentive stock option, it must meet several requirements set forth in the Internal Revenue Code (e.g., the option price cannot be less than the stock's per-share market value at the time the option is granted; the employee may not own more than 10% of the company's voting stock, etc.). Incentive options get special tax treatment: the executive is not taxed on any gain at the time he exercises the option, but only when he ***sells the underlying stock***. If the executive holds the stock bought under the option for a number of years, this deferral of gain has significant value. (On the other hand, the corporation never gets a tax deduction for creating the incentive option. Clark, pp. 210-11.)

b. Restricted stock: ***"Restricted stock"*** is a somewhat vague term that refers to stock that is awarded to an employee under a variety of limitations. For instance, an executive might be awarded 100,000 restricted shares, with 10,000 shares "vesting" in each of the next ten years, but only if the executive is still employed on that date. If the executive leaves, his unvested shares would be forfeited. Restricted shares are frequently issued free or at a dramatically reduced price. They are especially useful in a closely-held corporation that expects to go public in the future. C&E, pp. 704-05.

c. Stock Appreciation Rights: A ***Stock Appreciation Right*** (or "SAR") is the right to be paid a future cash bonus based on any ***increase*** in the price of the company's stock. For instance, suppose the company's stock sells for $10 a share on the date the SAR is granted; if the SAR is exercisable after two years, and the stock then sells for $15 a share, the executive would receive a cash payment of $5 ($15 minus $10) for each SAR. Clark, p. 208; C&E, p. 702-03.

d. Phantom stock: ***"Phantom stock"*** is quite similar to an SAR. However, the deferred cash bonus that the executive receives under a phantom stock plan is often equal to the ***total value*** of a share of the company's stock sometime in the future (whereas the SAR only pays him the ***increase*** in that value since the date of grant). Thus a phantom stock plan might entitle Executive to an amount of cash in three years equal to the then market value of 10,000 shares of the company's stock. Executive is not deemed to have received any compensation before the three-year-away settlement date, and he has no voting rights during the interim. He will not receive cash dividends during the interim, but might get some economic benefits from dividends (by having these treated as if he had reinvested them in more phantom stock). Clark, p. 208; C&E, p. 703-04.

3. Pensions and other long-term deferred compensation: Corporations also typically have long-term ***deferred*** compensation plans for senior executives. Most common is the ***pension plan*** or retirement plan, by which the executive will receive regular cash payments during retirement. If the retirement plan is qualified under the Internal Revenue Code, the company gets a current deduction for money it puts into the plan, the money inside the plan compounds tax-free, and the executive is not taxed until he actually starts receiving the cash payments following his retirement.

C. Corporate law problems: We're now ready to analyze the corporate-law issues which are raised by compensation schemes benefiting senior executives or directors. There are three main issues:

(1) How does one avoid the ***self-dealing*** problem, since the executive is influencing the corporation concerning his own compensation level?

(2) Must there be ***"consideration"*** for the compensation, and if so, what kind? and

(3) May a compensation plan be struck down because it is ***"excessive"***?

We consider each of these in turn.

D. The self-dealing problem: There is a self-dealing problem whenever the compensation is fixed for either: (1) a director; or (2) an executive who is sufficiently senior that he can influence the corporation's decision about how much he is to be paid.

1. General rule: In general, courts treat the self-dealing problems concerning compensation pretty much the same as they treat other kinds of self-dealing. Thus according to most courts, an executive or director compensation scheme is much more likely to be upheld if either: (1) a majority of the ***disinterested directors*** have approved it, following disclosure of all material facts about it; or (2) the ***shareholders*** have approved it, following such disclosure.

a. Fairness as key: As with other types of self-dealing transactions, the compensation scheme is much more likely to be upheld if in the court's judgment it is ***"fair"*** to the corporation. In the compensation context, the question, "Is the scheme 'fair' to the corporation?" becomes transformed into the question, "Is the compensation 'excessive'?" Excessive compensation is discussed *infra*, p. 216.

b. Shift of burden of proof: As with other types of self-dealing, if the disinterested directors or shareholders have approved the scheme, a much greater showing of unfairness will be needed to strike the plan, and the burden of persuasion shifts from the executive to the person attacking the plan. See, e.g., ALI Prin. Corp. Gov., 5.03(b).

c. **Presence of executive:** If the corporation wants to take advantage of the extra protection from "approval by disinterested directors," the executive should usually not only not take part in the directors' vote on his compensation, but he should not even ***be present*** at the meeting. Clark, p. 194.

2. **Business judgment rule:** The importance of approval by disinterested directors or shareholders is shown by the fact that in many courts, the disinterested directors' decision to approve a scheme will be awarded the protection of the ***business judgment rule***. Under the business judgment rule (see *supra*, p. 182), the directors' decision will be sustained by the court so long as it is rational, informed, and in good faith (despite the fact that the court might have reached a different conclusion about the desirability of the action).

E. **Consideration:** Courts insist that there be ***consideration*** for each element of a compensation plan. In the case of salary and current bonus, the consideration is clear: the executive is working for the company for a particular period, and is being paid for the period.

1. **Deferred compensation:** The requirement of consideration has real bite, however, when the compensation plan includes stock options, retirement benefits, or other consideration that is to be paid far in the future. In brief, the requirement of consideration means that it must be ***very likely*** that an executive will receive the deferred compensation ***only if he remains with the company***. For instance, a grant of stock options to all executives currently at the company, exercisable by them in the future regardless of whether they have remained with the company following the adoption of the option plan, would probably be struck down as lacking in consideration.

2. **Unbargained-for payments for past services:** Another situation in which the requirement of consideration may have some bite is where the corporation makes a large payment upon the ***death*** or ***retirement*** of a senior executive, without there having been a ***prior plan*** or ***contract*** to make such a payment. Although the corporation may defend such a payment on the grounds that the consideration was the "past services" of the executive, the challenger can make the following argument: Where there was no contract or plan to make the payment, the executive could not have been motivated by the prospect of receiving it while he was still working, so the payment amounts to a gift or a waste of corporate assets. Courts have sometimes accepted this argument, and have struck down large payments, made without a pre-existing plan or contract, to senior executives or their estates at retirement or death.

a. **Ways around:** Observe that there are a number of ways around this problem. Most obviously, the corporation can enact a formal plan of retirement or death payments while the executive is still active; his continued participation until death or retirement is therefore the consideration for the eventual payment. Second, even if there has not been advance planning, the executive can receive payments in retirement (though probably not after death) under a "consulting" contract or a non-competition agreement. Clark, p. 197.

F. **Ban on "excessive" or "unreasonable" compensation:** Even if a compensation scheme has been approved by a majority of the disinterested directors, or ratified by the shareholders, the court may still overturn it if the level of compensation is ***"excessive"*** or ***"unreasonable."*** As the idea is usually put, "the amount of compensation must bear a ***'reasonable relationship'*** to the ***value of the services*** performed for the corporation." Clark, p. 192.

1. **Easier to satisfy than "fairness" rule:** Recall that for most types of self-dealing transactions, the court will strike down transactions it believes to be ***"unfair"*** to the corporation. In the compensation area, the courts are more reluctant to strike down the transaction: it is harder to show that a compensation level is "excessive" than it is to show that a different sort of transaction is "unfair": "Executive compensation is scrutinized in a less exacting way than are other contracts with interested officers." *Id.*

   a. **Rationale:** The main reason for this judicial reluctance to strike down compensation as excessive is that courts feel they do not have the appropriate ***standards*** by which to judge the reasonableness of compensation. As one court put it, "[W]hat yardstick is to be employed? Who or what is to supply the measuring-rod? . . . If comparisons are to made, with whose compensation are they to be made — Executives? Those connected with the motion picture industry? Radio artists? Justices of the Supreme Court of the United States? The President of the United States? . . . [I]f a ceiling for these bonuses is to be erected, the stockholders who built and are responsible for the present structure must be the architects." *Heller v. Boylan*, 29 N.Y.S.2d 653 (1941).

2. **Few cases:** Consequently, there are relatively ***few*** cases in which courts have struck down executive compensation plans as being "excessive." At least where the compensation plan has been approved by disinterested directors or ratified by disinterested shareholders, courts will generally invalidate it only if it is so excessive as to constitute ***"waste."***

   a. **Standard for "waste":** The typical definition of "waste" is a very ***restricted*** one. Thus in Delaware, a transaction will not be invalidated as constituting waste unless it is "an exchange that is ***so one sided that no business person of ordinary, sound judgment could conclude that the corporation has received adequate consideration."*** *Brehm v. Eisner*, 746 A.2d 244 (Del. 2000). In the case of executive compensation, "If ... there is ***any substantial consideration received*** by the corporation, and if there is a ***good faith judgment*** [by the board] that in the circumstances the ***transaction is worth while***, there should be no finding of waste, even if the fact finder would conclude ex post that the transaction was ***unreasonably risky***." *Brehm, supra.*

      Example: Consider the facts of *Brehm*, *supra*, p. 175: the board of Disney gives Michael Ovitz a contract which, when terminated early by the company without any breach on the part of Ovitz, gives Ovitz a severance payment of $140 million. Notwithstanding the huge expense and the near-total lack of value actually received by Disney from having Ovitz as its president, the Delaware Supreme Court held as a matter of law that the Disney board did not commit waste in entering into the contract. The board had decided that an expensive compensation package would be required for Ovitz to take the job, and that he would be valuable to the company. Because "the size and structure of executive compensation are inherently matters of judgment," the board's decision could be labeled as waste only if the board acted irrationally or in good faith. And, here, the plaintiff had not "alleged with particularity" facts that would prove either irrationality or lack of good faith.

3. **Tax cases about compensation:** The strong reluctance of courts to strike down compensation as excessive under corporate law principles should be contrasted with the result in many ***tax*** cases. Under § 162 of the Internal Revenue Code, a corporation may deduct from its gross income its ordinary and necessary business expenses, including a "reasonable allowance for salaries or other compensation for personal services actually rendered." Quite frequently, the IRS attacks a particular manager's compensation as "excessive," and the courts have often agreed. In the tax context, the courts have focused on comparable compensation, i.e., how much executives who perform similar functions for similar companies earn. They do not seem troubled by the difficulty of making such comparisons (in contrast to the difficulties in making comparisons that the court in *Heller v. Boylan*, *supra*, p. 217, felt it faced). See generally, Clark, pp. 199-200.

Quiz Yourself on
***THE DUTY OF LOYALTY** (EXECUTIVE COMPENSATION)*

50. Mr. Bill is president of Sluggo Storage Systems, Inc. He earns $150,000 per year in that post. The company has no provision for a pension or death benefit for Mr. Bill (or for any other worker). Mr. Bill is killed in a freak accident when he is run over by a steamroller. At the next board meeting, the board unanimously votes to pay Mrs. Bill, Mr. Bill's widow, an annual pension of $75,000.

(a) You represent Spot, a minority shareholder of Sluggo. Spot is not too happy about the pension, but can't think of any grounds upon which to object. What grounds would you recommend?

____

(b) Will the grounds for objection that you recommended in part (a) be successful?

____

Answer

50. (a) Lack of consideration. The issue here is the validity of payments for past services. The general rule from contract law is that such payments are only valid when the basic specifics of the arrangement and the recipient's identity are established *before* the services are rendered (in the form of a contract, a formal bonus plan, or established company practice). Otherwise, such payments are without consideration, since "past consideration" is not consideration at all.

(b) Yes, probably. Mr. Bill was dead before the specifics of the pension were ever worked out, so the pension couldn't have been consideration for his performance of services while alive. Consequently, the court will probably order that the pension not be paid. (Alternatively, the court might say that paying a pension for which there is no consideration is a "waste" of corporate assets, since the corporation receives no benefit from the payment.)

IV. THE CORPORATE OPPORTUNITY DOCTRINE AND RELATED PROBLEMS

A. Introduction to problem: So far in our treatment of the duty of loyalty, we have focused on transactions between the Key Player and the corporation. We turn now to a different type of problem: the Key Player appropriates to himself some ***business opportunity*** or ***property*** that is found to "***belong" to the corporation***. Here, there is rarely an issue as to the "fair" price; instead, if the Key Player has taken something that belongs or ought to belong to the corporation, this is *per se* wrongful and the corporation may recover. There are three sub-problems:

[1] When may a Key Player ***compete*** with the corporation?

[2] When may a Key Player make ***personal use of corporate assets*** (e.g., by using the company plane to fly on a personal vacation)? and

[3] When does a Key Player, by taking advantage of a business opportunity, wrongfully usurp a ***"corporate opportunity"***?

Of these three areas, the third is the most difficult and important. We consider each in turn.

B. Competition with the corporation: A director or senior executive ***may not compete*** with the corporation, where this competition is likely to ***harm*** the corporation.

Example: Able and Baker are both senior vice presidents of Wannabe's, a large department store in downtown Cleveland. While they are on the Wannabe's payroll, they secretly form a new corporation, Newco, and cause Newco to sign a lease on a vacant building across the street from Wannabe's. They intend to set up a competing department store in this building. They then (still while on the payroll) tell some key suppliers that they'll be opening up a competing department store soon, and that they hope to buy from these suppliers. Able and Baker also tell their plans to two of Wannabe's key executives, Charlie and Devon, saying, "We hope you'll come with us in a month or so after we open the new store." This induces Charlie and Devon to work less hard for Wannabe's, since they figure that they, too, will soon be leaving to join the new store.

A court would probably hold that Able and Baker have violated their duty of loyalty to Wannabe's, by effectively competing with Wannabe's while still on the payroll. If so, the court will probably order them to pay money damages to Wannabe's (and might — though probably won't — enjoin them from soliciting any further employees from Wannabe's for some period of time.)

1. Seek approval or ratification: But as with other types of self-dealing, conduct that would otherwise be prohibited as disloyal competition may be validated by being ***approved*** by disinterested directors, or being ratified by the shareholders. With either of these methods, the Key Player must first make ***full disclosure*** about the conflict of interest and the competition that he proposes to engage in. See ALI, Prin. Corp. Gov., § 5.06(a)(2) and (a)(3). Thus had Able and Baker gone to the directors of Wannabe's in the above example, and announced that they wished to own a competing store, and had the disinterested directors approved of this by a majority vote, there would have been no violation of the duty of loyalty.

2. **Preparation to compete while still in corporation's employment:** Executives and directors seldom engage in active competition while still affiliated with the corporation. Much more commonly, they ***prepare***, while still on the company's payroll, to engage in later competition. For instance, they may acquire property that will be used in competing, hire employees, negotiate contracts, solicit customers for the soon-to-be-born firm, or otherwise pave the way. There are no hard and fixed rules for this situation, but in general courts tend to hold that these activities constitute disloyalty if they occur while the director or executive is still on the original corporation's payroll. A common remedy is for the court to order a ***return of all salary*** received during this preparation period.

3. **Competition after end of employment:** A quite different situation is presented where the executive or director first ***leaves the corporation*** and only then begins preparing to compete. Assuming that the executive has not signed any "non-compete" agreement, he is ***not barred*** from basic competition with his former employer.

   a. **Trade secrets:** However, he may not compete by the taking of the former employer's ***trade secrets***. Any of the following acts may be deemed to be a wrongful taking of trade secrets: (1) the systematic solicitation of a large number of the former employer's ***customers***; (2) the solicitation of the former employer's ***employees*** to become employees of the new company; and (3) the use of the former employer's secret ***processes*** or other methods of doing business.

   b. **Non-compete:** Additionally, the executive may be barred from competing if he has signed a valid ***non-competition agreement***. However, courts have become increasingly reluctant to enforce broad non-competition agreements, because they do not wish to unduly constrict the executive's ability to earn a living. Therefore, non-competition covenants will be enforced only if they are ***reasonable*** as to ***time***, ***area***, and ***scope***. H&A, p. 630.

      i. **Illustration:** For instance, suppose a dentist agrees with his employer not to compete by practicing dentistry at any place in New York City for a period of two years following the end of his employment; this would almost certainly be found to be too broad to be enforceable. But a promise not to practice oral surgery for six months in the same small town as the employer, by contrast, would probably be upheld.

C. **Use of corporate assets:** A Key Player may not ***use corporate assets*** if this use either harms the corporation, or gives the Key Player a ***financial benefit*** (including a financial benefit he receives as a stockholder that is not available to other similarly-situated stockholders). See ALI Prin. Corp. Gov., § 5.04(a) (reprinted *infra* p. 261). "Corporate assets," for this purpose, consist not only of tangible goods but also intangibles like ***information***.

   Example: D, the engineering director of a large aerospace company, learns that the company will be making huge purchases of platinum for a secret project. Only a few people inside the company (and no one outside of it) know that this will occur. D buys platinum futures, and when the news is announced, D sells at a substantial profit. A court might well hold that D has wrongfully used a corporate asset (information about the corporation's plans), in which case the corporation would be entitled to the profits rather than D.

1. **Approval or payment:** As with other types of self-dealing, ***approval*** by disinterested directors, or ***ratification*** by shareholders (in each case, only ***after full disclosure***) will help

immunize the transaction. Similarly, in the case of use of tangible corporate property, the transaction will not be wrongful if the Key Player pays the ***fair value*** for any benefit he has received. See ALI Prin. Corp. Gov., § 5.04(a)(1).

D. The "corporate opportunity" doctrine: Suppose that a senior executive or director of a corporation learns of an attractive business opportunity. Suppose further that this business opportunity is not in an area of commerce in which the corporation presently does business. May the executive or director pursue this opportunity on his own, rather than turning it over to the corporation? The brief, but unhelpful, answer is that the manager may not pursue the opportunity on his own, and must turn it over to the corporation, if the opportunity is one that can be said to ***"belong"*** to the corporation. The difficulty is that the rules for distinguishing between opportunities that "belong" to the corporation and those that do not are confusing, and vary substantially from court to court.

1. Effect of finding of "corporate opportunity": If the manager is found to have taken for himself an opportunity that "belongs" to the corporation (i.e., to have usurped a ***"corporate opportunity"***), the rules are very strict: this taking is ***per se wrongful*** to the corporation, and the corporation may recover damages equal to the loss it has suffered, or the profits it would have made had it been given the chance to pursue the opportunity. Often, the court will order any profits made by the manager from the venture to be held in ***constructive trust*** for the corporation, and may order the enterprise itself to be turned over to the corporation. See *infra*, p. 229.

Example: D is the president of Hotel Corp. D knows that Hotel Corp is looking for an appropriately zoned two-acre site in the village of Ames on which it can build a hotel. As D knows, the company's search for such a site so far has been notably unsuccessful. D learns through a friend of a good potential site at a fair price. Instead of allowing Hotel Corp to buy the site, he buys it himself, and resells it for a quick profit to a businessman who puts a car dealership on it. The court is likely to find that by buying the land, D has usurped a corporate opportunity, i.e., an opportunity that properly belonged to Hotel Corp. If the court does so conclude, it will order D's profit on the resale to be turned over to Hotel Corp. (And, in fact, if Hotel Corp is unable to get another site, D may even be liable to pay a larger sum equal to the profits that Hotel Corp could have made had it been offered the site and built a hotel there.)

a. No issue of fairness of price: Once the court decides that the manager has taken a corporate opportunity, most courts ***do not recognize any separate issue of "fairness."*** Thus suppose Manager buys Blackacre which, the court finds, he should have offered to the corporation that employs him. The fact that Manager has paid a fair market price for the property (and the fact that a subsequent increase in value is due to an unforeseen increase in values, or to Manager's own unusual efforts) is irrelevant — Manager will still have to account to the corporation for any profits he has made.

2. Delaware multi-factor test: Courts vary in the tests they use for whether an opportunity is a "corporate opportunity." The Delaware courts use a ***multi-factor test***, which has been influential in other courts. Therefore, we'll focus on the Delaware test here.

a. The multi-factor test: Under Delaware law, a business opportunity presented to a corporate officer or director will count as a "corporate opportunity" if it meets the following requirements:

- ❑ the corporation is "***financially able to exploit***" the opportunity;
- ❑ the opportunity is "within the corporation's ***line of business***";
- ❑ the corporation has an ***"interest or a reasonable expectancy"*** in the opportunity; and
- ❑ if the director or officer were to embrace the opportunity, he would thereby be placed in a ***conflict*** with his duties to the corporation.

See *Beam v. Stewart*, 833 A.2d 961 (Del. Ch. 2003), quoting the four-factor test originally set out in *Guth v. Loft*, 5 A.2d 503 (Del. 1939).

i. Either "line of business" or "interest or expectancy": The language quoted above from *Beam* sounds as though the opportunity must satisfy *both* the "line of business" and "interest or expectancy" standards. But in practice, the Delaware courts seem to hold that the opportunity must merely satisfy *either* the "line of business" or "interest or expectancy" test, not both. Clark, p. 228.

ii. Meaning of "line of business": Delaware cases often turn on the ***"line of business"*** element. The Delaware courts (and the courts of other states following the general Delaware approach) seem to take a fairly ***broad definition*** of line of business. Even if the activity is not a business that the corporation already engages in, the court is likely to find that the line-of-business test is satisfied if the court feels that the company has some ***special expertise*** that equips it to compete in the new area. Thus a ***"functional relationship"*** between the type of activity the corporation already engages in and the prospective activity may be enough, even though they are in different industries.

Example: Clark (p. 228) suggests that if a company already makes cold medicines, a business that makes contact lens wetting solution would be within its "line of business," because "the methods of marketing and distributing the products — through drug stores, for example — overlap ... enough to permit ***significant economies of scale*** if the businesses were to be combined."

3. Other factors (especially for determining "fairness"): Apart from the four factors applied under the Delaware test (*supra*, p. 221), there are a number of additional factors which courts consider in deciding whether an opportunity is a corporate one. These factors are especially likely to be considered by a court that uses "fairness" as a partial or sole standard:

a. Capacity in which offer received: whether the opportunity was offered to the officer or director as an ***individual***, or rather as a corporate manager who would convey the offer to the corporation. The case for regarding the opportunity as corporate is obviously stronger in the latter situation than in the former.

b. How insider learned of opportunity: whether or not the officer or director ***learned*** of the opportunity while ***acting in his role as the corporation's agent***. Thus if President learns of the opportunity while attending a meeting that relates solely to his company's business, the case for finding a corporate opportunity is stronger than where President learns of it while having drinks with a social friend.

c. Use of corporate resources: whether the officer or director ***used corporate resources*** to take advantage of the opportunity. An illustration of the use of corporate resources would be where President takes the company jet to scout out the opportunity.

i. **D's use of his own "company time":** Some corporate plaintiffs have claimed that when the defendant (an employee of the corporation) developed the opportunity while on ***"company time"*** (i.e., during working hours), this constituted the "use of corporate resources." However, this by itself is ***unlikely*** to be a very important factor, especially if the time used is not very substantial.

d. **Essential to corporation:** whether the opportunity is ***essential*** to the corporation's well-being. The more important the opportunity is to the corporation's well-being — i.e., the worse financial injury the corporation will suffer if it does not have the opportunity — the more likely the opportunity is to be regarded as corporate.

Example: Suppose Realty Corp, a real estate developer, is trying to complete an assemblage on which to build a single skyscraper. If an executive of Realty snatches away the last lot in the parcel, thus preventing Realty Corp from completing its assemblage, the critical importance to Realty of this last lot makes it very likely that a court will view the lot as an opportunity belonging to Realty.

e. **Distinction between outside director and full-time executive:** whether the person taking the opportunity is an ***outside director*** or a ***full-time executive***. A full-time ***executive*** is commonly understood to owe his ***entire efforts and loyalties*** to the corporation that employs him. An ***outside director***, by contrast, often has numerous other business interests, some of which will be (and may properly be) more financially important to him than the corporation that he serves only as a director. Therefore, the outside director should be ***more free*** to take an opportunity for himself.

i. **ALI approach:** The ALI's *Principles of Corporate Governance* recognize this distinction:

(1) **Employee:** Under § 5.05(b), an opportunity is a corporate one if it comes to a ***full-time employee*** who knows that the opportunity is ***"closely related*** to a business in which the corporation is engaged or expects to engage."

(2) **Outside director:** If the opportunity comes to an ***outside director***, by contrast, the fact that he knows or should know that the opportunity is closely related to the corporation's present or reasonably anticipated activities is ***irrelevant***; the opportunity is not deemed "corporate" unless the director either: (1) learned of the opportunity ***in connection*** with performing his duties for the corporation; (2) learned of it under circumstances where he should reasonably have believed that it was ***really being offered to the corporation*** and not to him personally; or (3) learned of it through the use of ***information or property belonging to the corporation*** (in which situation a full-time employee will also have to treat the opportunity as "corporate.")

See *infra*, p. 227, for a more complete description of the ALI approach to corporate opportunity.

4. **Delaware's "no need for pre-approval by corporation" rule:** Suppose that the Key Player (officer or director) who has the opportunity believes that under the relevant test (e.g., the multi-factor Delaware test described above, *supra*, p. 221), the opportunity is not

a corporate one. Must the Key Player ***disclose*** the opportunity to the board of the corporation ***in advance***, and give the latter the chance to argue that this is indeed a corporate opportunity that the corporation wishes to pursue? At least in Delaware, the answer is a clear ***"no"*** — the Key Player is always *free* to disclose the opportunity and try to get the corporation to say that it's not interested, but the Key Player is ***not required*** to make advance disclosure.

a. Significance: Of course, if the Key Player *doesn't* make advance disclosure, and takes the opportunity for herself, she faces the risk that if the opportunity proves lucrative, the corporation will sue the Key Player and try to unwind the transaction or collect the profits from it. If that happens, then a court will then second-guess the Key Player's judgment that the requirements of the opportunity doctrine were not satisfied. But the Key Player is entitled to take this risk — there is no formal requirement of advance disclosure, at least in Delaware.

Example: Broz is a director of CIS, a publicly-held corporation that offers cellular service in various parts of the country. Broz also owns his own smaller cellular provider, RFBC. Broz learns of the availability of an FCC license called "Michigan-4," entitling the holder to provide cell service in a rural part of Michigan. Broz speaks informally to a couple of CIS directors, and learns that they do not believe CIS would have an interest in the Michigan-4 license. However, Broz does not present the opportunity formally to the entire board of CIS. Instead, Broz causes his own company, FRBC, to buy the license. In so doing, he beats out a competing offer from PriCellular, another cellular provider that is at the time in early discussions about merging with CIS. Shortly after Broz causes FRBC to buy the license, PriCellular and CIS in fact merge. The management of the combined CIS/PriCellular then asserts that the Michigan-4 opportunity was a corporate opportunity of CIS, and that Broz was required to present the opportunity formally to the board of CIS before buying it for himself.

Held, for Broz. First, at the time Broz purchased, CIS was divesting most of its cellular operations, so the company did not have any "expectancy" regarding any new license. Second, it is irrelevant that Broz did not formally offer the opportunity to CIS' board: "It is not the law of Delaware that presentation to the board is a necessary prerequisite to a finding that a corporate opportunity has not been usurped." And the fact that there was some chance that CIS might complete a merger with PriCellular (which as Broz knew wanted the opportunity for itself) is irrelevant, since it was unclear that the merger would ever go through, or that PriCellular might want the opportunity post-merger. *Broz v. Cellular Information Systems, Inc.*, 673 A.2d 148 (Del. 1996).

5. Who is bound: Generally, courts seem to apply the corporate opportunity doctrine only to ***directors***, ***full-time employees***, and ***controlling shareholders***. Thus a shareholder who has only a ***non-controlling interest*** (and who is not a director or employee) will generally ***not*** be subjected to the doctrine.

a. Lower-level employee: There are not many corporate-opportunity cases involving ***lower-level employees***. However, such an employee probably has a ***similar duty*** to refrain from usurping a corporate opportunity, under the law of agency (which makes an employee a fiduciary for the employer). See *ALI Principles*, Introductory Note to Part V, sub-par. (b).

i. **Less likely to be "unfair":** However, when a low-level employee takes a given opportunity for himself, the taking is probably somewhat ***less likely*** to be found to be ***"unfair"*** to the corporation than where the taking is by, say, an officer. So to the extent that the jurisdiction considers "fairness" in deciding whether something is a corporate opportunity, the low-level employee is likely to have an easier time.

6. **Rejection by corporation:** Even if an opportunity is a "corporate opportunity," the Key Player is not necessarily barred from pursuing it himself. If he ***offers the corporation*** the chance to pursue the opportunity, and the corporation ***rejects the opportunity*** by a majority vote of ***disinterested directors*** or ***disinterested shareholders***, the Key Player may pursue the opportunity himself. S,S,B&W, pp. 809-10. See also ALI Prin. Corp. Gov., § 5.05(a)(3)(B) and (C).

   a. **Disclosure:** In order for the Key Player to be allowed to raise the defense that the disinterested directors or shareholders have rejected the opportunity on behalf of the corporation, most courts require that the Key Player have made ***full disclosure*** of the nature of the opportunity. Thus if President purports to offer the corporation the chance to pursue the opportunity but ***understates*** the potential benefits, or overstates the cost to the corporation, rejection by the disinterested directors or disinterested shareholders will probably not be a defense. See ALI Prin. Corp. Gov., § 5.05(a)(1).

   b. **Contemporaneous vs. subsequent rejection:** The safest path is for the Key Player to offer the opportunity to the corporation ***before*** he accepts it himself, and to wait until the disinterested directors or shareholders have rejected it before he acts. But if the Key Player accepts the opportunity himself, and then persuades the disinterested directors or shareholders to ***ratify*** his acceptance (and the corporation's rejection) of the opportunity after the fact, this post-facto ratification may ***still be enough*** to allow the Key Player to escape liability.

      i. **Close scrutiny:** However, courts probably would scrutinize such an after-the-fact ratification ***more closely*** on the theory that it is far less likely to manifest a truly voluntary consent than where the opportunity is offered to the corporation in advance, at a time when the corporation may truly benefit from it.

      ii. **ALI:** In fact, the ALI's Principles are stricter than most courts on this issue; under the ALI approach, there is a flat rule against a director's or senior executive's taking a corporate opportunity unless the opportunity has first been disclosed and offered to the corporation and rejected by it. In other words, under the ALI text, the director or senior executive may not take a corporate opportunity with no disclosure to the corporation, then receive after-the-fact ratification by disinterested directors or shareholders.

7. **Corporation's inability to take advantage of opportunity:** A Key Player who takes a corporate opportunity for himself often tries to defend the subsequent lawsuit by contending that the corporation would have been ***unable*** to take advantage of the opportunity itself, and has therefore suffered no damage. This is a troublesome defense, since if the court allows it, the Key Player will have absolutely no incentive to help the corporation overcome its difficulties — he will simply take the opportunity for himself, and count on

being able to make a later showing of corporate inability, a showing which is likely to be quite difficult for outsiders to disprove. Clark, p. 243.

a. Types of inability: There are a number of different types of corporate inability that Key Players have raised when sued for usurping a corporate opportunity: (1) the corporation's ***legal*** inability (e.g., because of antitrust or other regulatory restraints); (2) the ***refusal*** by the person offering the transaction to deal with the corporation; and (3) the corporation's ***financial*** inability to take advantage of the opportunity. Courts are especially reluctant to accept justifications of type (3), since if the opportunity is a good one, there should be a way to overcome financial constraints (e.g., by convincing a bank or other investor to lend money, by taking on a partner, by forming a joint venture, etc.) Clark, p. 243.

b. Strict rule: Courts are in disagreement about whether and when the defense of corporate inability should be accepted. A number of courts take a quite strict view, under which if the Key Player does not make full disclosure to the corporation and offer it the opportunity, he is ***simply not permitted to argue*** that the corporation could not have taken advantage of the opportunity. This "bright line" rule has the advantage of encouraging full disclosure (and honest efforts by the Key Player to help the corporation take advantage of attractive opportunities).

i. ALI: As noted, this is the approach followed by the ALI's *Principles of Corporate Governance*: If the Key Player does not offer the opportunity to the corporation, and make full disclosure about it, his taking of that opportunity for himself is flat-out wrongful, even if the corporation would have been totally unable to take advantage itself.

Example: D is the president of P, a corporate "club" that owns a golf course. On several occasions, D buys parcels of real estate that immediately adjoin the course. After each purchase, D informs the board of P that she has made the purchases; the board takes no action (it neither affirmatively votes to ratify D's purchases nor does anything to oppose or undo them.) More than 10 years after the earliest of these purchases, the board finally sues D to have the parcels held in trust for the club, on the theory that D usurped a corporate opportunity. D defends, in part, on the theory that the club never had the funds to have purchased the parcels when they became available.

Held (on appeal), for P: the case is remanded for a rehearing by the trial court, with the ALI principles to be applied. If the trial court concludes (as P alleges) that one or more of the parcels was offered to D in her capacity as club president, the opportunity must be found to be a corporate one. Assuming that D did not make disclosure to the board of the opportunity until after she bought the parcels, and that the board did not thereafter affirmatively ratify her conduct, then D will not be permitted to defend on the grounds that her failure to offer the opportunity was "fair" (e.g., fair because the club was not financially able to exercise the opportunity itself). "The central feature of the ALI test is the strict requirement of full disclosure prior to taking advantage of any corporate opportunity." (On remand, the trial court concludes that D did indeed usurp a corporate opportunity, but that no recovery is allowable, because of statute-of-limitations and laches problems.) *Northeast Harbor Golf Club, Inc. v. Harris*, 661 A.2d 1146 (Me. 1995).

(1) **Where Key Player *does* make offer to corporation:** On the other hand, if the Key Player *does* offer the opportunity to the corporation and the disinterested directors or shareholders reject it, the corporation's financial, legal or other inability to take advantage of the opportunity *are* to be considered as factors in determining whether they acted "rationally" in rejecting, an additional requirement for the "rejection" defense. See Comment to § 5.05(a).

c. **Lenient view:** Other courts, such as those of Delaware, take a more lenient view toward the defense of corporate inability than does the ALI test. For instance, in *Guth v. Loft, Inc.*, 5 A.2d 503 (Del. 1939), the court treated an opportunity as being a "corporate opportunity" only if the opportunity was one "which the corporation is financially able to undertake." Delaware courts have continued to apply this standard, and to hold that there is no requirement of advance disclosure if the corporation is not in fact financially able to exploit the opportunity.

8. **ALI approach:** The ALI's *Principles of Corporate Governance* are by far the most comprehensive statutory or statute-like treatment of the problems of the corporate opportunity doctrine. (By contrast, the MBCA doesn't deal specifically with the corporate opportunity doctrine at all, and leaves this area to case law.) Because of the specificity of the ALI treatment, and its growing acceptance by courts, we reproduce the relevant sections:

§ 5.05 Taking of Corporate Opportunities by Directors or Senior Executives

(a) *General Rule.* A ***director*** or ***senior executive*** may not take advantage of a ***corporate opportunity*** unless:

(1) [He or she] first ***offers*** the corporate opportunity to the corporation and makes ***disclosure*** concerning the conflict of interest and the corporate opportunity;

(2) The corporate opportunity is ***rejected*** by the corporation; and

(3) Either:

(A) The rejection of the opportunity is ***fair*** to the corporation;

(B) The opportunity is rejected in ***advance***, following such disclosure, by ***disinterested directors*** . . . in a manner that satisfies the standards of the ***business judgment*** rule; or

(C) The rejection is ***authorized*** in advance or ratified, following such disclosure, by ***disinterested shareholders***, and the rejection is not equivalent to a ***waste*** of corporate assets.

(b) *Definition of a Corporate Opportunity.* For purposes of this Section, a corporate opportunity means:

(1) Any opportunity to engage in a business activity of which a ***director*** or ***senior executive*** becomes aware, either:

(A) ***In connection with the performance*** of functions as a director or senior executive, or under circumstances that should reasonably lead the director or senior executive to believe that the person offering the opportunity ***expects it to be offered to the corporation***; or

(B) Through the use of ***corporate information or property***, if the resulting opportunity is one that the director or senior executive should reasonably be expected to believe ***would be of interest*** to the corporation; or

(2) Any opportunity to engage in a business activity of which a ***senior executive*** becomes aware and knows is ***closely related*** to a business in which the corporation is engaged or

expects to engage.

. . .

§ 5.12 Taking of Corporate Opportunities by a Controlling Shareholder

(a) *General Rule.* A ***controlling shareholder*** may not take advantage of a corporate opportunity unless:

(1) The taking of the opportunity is ***fair*** to the corporation; or

(2) The taking of the opportunity is ***authorized in advance or ratified*** by disinterested shareholders, following ***disclosure*** concerning the conflict of interest and the corporate opportunity, and the taking of the opportunity is not equivalent to a ***waste*** of corporate assets.

(b) *Definition of a Corporate Opportunity.* For purposes of this section, a corporate opportunity means any opportunity to engage in a business activity that:

(1) Is ***developed or received by the corporation***, or comes to the controlling shareholder primarily by virtue of its relationship to the corporation; or

(2) Is ***held out*** to shareholders of the corporation by the controlling shareholder, or by the corporation with the consent of the controlling shareholder, as being a type of business activity that will be ***within the scope of the business*** in which the corporation is engaged or expects to engage and will not be within the scope of the controlling shareholder's business.

(c) *Burden of Proof.* A party who ***challenges*** the taking of a corporate opportunity has the ***burden of proof***, except that the ***controlling shareholder*** has the burden of proving that the taking of the opportunity is ***fair*** to the corporation if the taking of the opportunity was ***not authorized in advance or ratified by disinterested directors or disinterested shareholders***, following the disclosure required by Subsection (a)(2).

a. **Special features:** Following are a few of the especially noteworthy features of the ALI's treatment of corporate opportunity. (We've touched on some of these above, but for convenience, we discuss the whole ALI approach here in a single place.)

b. **Requirement of advance disclosure:** If the opportunity is a "corporate opportunity," the insider (director, senior executive or "controlling shareholder") ***must offer it to the corporation***, with full disclosure of its nature before he may take it for himself. If he does not make this offer, he will not be permitted to defend a later suit on the grounds that the corporation was unable (for financial or other reasons) to take advantage of the opportunity. As one court has said in adopting the ALI approach, "the central feature of the ALI test is the strict requirement of ***full disclosure*** prior to taking advantage of any corporate opportunity." *Northeast Harbor Golf Club, Inc. v. Harris, supra*, p. 226.

c. **Disinterested directors or shareholders:** The mere fact that the corporation rejects the opportunity does not by itself get the Key Player off the hook. Unless the corporation's rejection is ***authorized*** by a majority of ***disinterested directors***, or a majority of ***disinterested shareholders*** (in either case, following full disclosure), the Key Player will have to show that the corporate rejection and the overall transaction were ***fair to the corporation.***

   i. **Effect of director authorization:** On the other hand, if a majority of disinterested directors ***does*** authorize the rejection, then the transaction is pretty much ***immunized*** against later attack. Only if the disinterested directors have violated the business judgment rule (i.e., they have behaved irrationally; see *supra*, p. 188) may the transaction be attacked.

ii. Effect of shareholder authorization: Similarly, if a majority of disinterested ***shareholders*** approves the corporation's rejection of the opportunity after full disclosure, the transaction may be attacked only if their action amounts to "waste."

d. Senior executive has stricter duty: As noted, *supra*, p. 226, a ***"senior executive"*** (i.e., a ***full-time*** high-level employee) is held to a somewhat ***stricter standard*** than an outside director. Any opportunity of which the senior executive becomes aware (even if this happens outside of the corporation's business, as at a purely social cocktail party) is "corporate" if the executive "knows [that the activity] is closely related to the business in which the corporation is engaged or expects to engage." § 5.05(b)(2). By contrast, if the outside director learns of the opportunity, and does so while not acting either on behalf of the corporation or by use of corporate information, the opportunity is not a "corporate" one. § 5.05(b)(1).

e. Controlling shareholder: A ***controlling shareholder*** is treated more like a senior executive than like an outside director. The opportunity is a "corporate" one as to the controlling shareholder if either: (1) she learns of it while ***acting on the corporation's behalf***; or (2) or the opportunity is one that is ***"held out to the [other] shareholders*** of the corporation" as being "a ***type of business activity*** that will be within the scope of the business in which the corporation is engaged or expects to engage and will not be within the scope of the controlling shareholder's business." (§5.12(b)(2).)

Example: Major is the controlling shareholder of newly-formed Corp, which is to invest in Connecticut real estate. Major also has a separate business that invests in real estate. Major tells his fellow investors, "I'll use my contacts to find good Connecticut real estate investments for Corp." No matter how Major learns of a particular Connecticut real estate investment, it will be a "corporate" opportunity, because Major has indicated to his fellow shareholders that such opportunities will be for Corp rather than for any other businesses in which Major is involved.

9. Parent-subsidiary problems: Suppose one corporation owns a controlling (but not 100%) interest in another corporation. In this ***parent-subsidiary*** context, suppose that the parent decides to take a business opportunity for itself rather than for the subsidiary. Does the corporate opportunity doctrine apply? In brief, the answer is probably "yes" — if the opportunity relates much more closely to the subsidiary's present or contemplated business than to the parent's, the parent probably violates its fiduciary obligation to the subsidiary and the subsidiary's minority shareholders by usurping it for itself. This problem is discussed more fully in the treatment of general parent-subsidiary fiduciary questions *infra*, p. 243.

10. Remedies: Once the court has determined that a Key Player has usurped what is properly viewed as a corporate opportunity, what ***remedies*** are available to the corporation or its shareholders? The usual remedy is quite draconian: the court may order the imposition of a ***constructive trust***, and may order the Key Player to account for ***all profits*** earned from the opportunity.

a. Constructive trust: If the court imposes a ***constructive trust***, this means that the property is treated ***as if it belonged to the corporation*** that owned the opportunity. The court probably may, but need not, require the corporation to pay the Key Player for the Key Player's direct investment made in creating the opportunity.

b. Accounting for profits: Also, the court will usually order the Key Player to ***account for the profits*** already made from usurpation of the corporate opportunity.

Quiz Yourself on

***THE DUTY OF LOYALTY** (THE CORPORATE OPPORTUNITY DOCTRINE)*

51. Mona Lisa Burgers, Inc. — "the burgers with the mysterious sauce" — is an enormous (and rapidly expanding) fast-food chain. Mike Angelo owns 5% of Mona Lisa's outstanding shares, which are publicly traded. Mike is not an officer or director of Mona Lisa, however. Mike knows (as anyone who reads the local business press would know) that Mona Lisa is considering putting a restaurant into the fast-growing suburb of David. Through friends on the David Township planning and zoning board, Mike learns the location of a new freeway that is about to be built through David. He snaps up nearby real estate, knowing that traffic will skyrocket, as will the value of the property. Mike never offers the property to Mona Lisa. Instead, he opens a fast-food restaurant of his own, Sistine Chicken & Ribs.

(a) Mona Lisa sues Mike for usurpation of a corporate opportunity, claiming (quite accurately) that the land would be ideal for a Mona Lisa burger joint. Is Mike likely to be liable? ________________

(b) Would Mike be liable if, in addition to the above facts, Mike were an outside (i.e., non-employee) director of Mona Lisa? ________________

(c) Would Mike be liable if he was not a director or stockholder at all, but was Mona Lisa's Senior Vice President in charge of sales and marketing? ________________

52. Alexis Colby is a director (but not an employee) of the Prime-Time Suds Oil Company. Because Alexis is proud of being exceptionally knowledgeable about the company's affairs, she annually (and at her own expense) takes a tour of some of Prime-Time's properties. While on one such trip to South America, she learns of mineral rights available in Antarctica that seem to have promise for oil. Alexis buys the mineral rights for herself, drills, and finds oil. Has Alexis usurped a corporate opportunity belonging to Prime-Time? ________________

53. Peter Pan is a senior employee, and one of seven board members, of the huge, public Darling Pharmaceuticals Company. Darling's area of focus is cancer treatment and prevention. Peter Pan learns about research at Hook University concerning "fairy dust," whose main value is that it makes people fly, but whose secondary value is that people who take it and fly are less likely to get cancer. Peter thinks that fairy dust represents a great commercial opportunity. He calls the chairman and 5% owner of Darling Pharmaceuticals, Wendy Darling, and discusses the opportunity with her at length (making full disclosure of what he thinks the benefits will be). Peter finally says, "So, whaddya think? Shouldn't Darling Pharmaceuticals be in on a deal like this?" Wendy pauses and says, "Naaaah. You take it." Peter buys the rights to fairy dust for himself, and it quickly becomes wildly successful. The corporation sues Peter on grounds of usurping a corporate opportunity.

(a) If you represent Peter, what defense will you raise? ________________

(b) Will this defense be successful? ________________

(c) Suppose fairy dust merely helps people fly, but doesn't prevent cancer. Assuming that the defense you raised in part (a) is unavailable, has Peter usurped a corporate opportunity? ________________

54. Peter Minuit is vice president of the New England Potato Company, which owns vast tracts of land in New York on which it grows potatoes. He learns through friends that Chief Firewater is willing to sell Manhattan Island, prime potato-growing land in New York, for $24. Peter knows that New England Potato is hard-pressed financially, doesn't have $24 on hand, and probably couldn't borrow it from a bank. He therefore doesn't mention the opportunity to New England Potato's board or president, and instead buys Manhattan with his own funds, with an eye toward putting a big apple orchard there. New England Potato sues Peter for usurpation of a corporate opportunity.

(a) If you represent Peter, what's the main defense that you should raise. ________________

(b) Is this defense likely to be successful? ________________

Answers

51. (a) No, because Mike doesn't owe Mona Lisa a fiduciary duty on these facts. The rule as to corporate opportunities is essentially that "insiders" may not exploit an opportunity that rightly belongs to the corporation. Only directors, employees and controlling shareholders will generally be deemed to be bound by the corporate-opportunity doctrine. [224] The mere fact that Mike owns 5% of the shares won't be enough to make him a controlling shareholder (and there's nothing else to indicate he controls the corporation); since he's also not a director or employee, he's free to buy the land without regard to whether it might be a valuable opportunity for the corporation.

(b) No, probably. If Mike were a director, he'd be barred from taking anything that was a true corporate opportunity. But the land here probably wouldn't be deemed to be a corporate opportunity. Where the Key Player is a director (but not an employee), fewer things are deemed to be corporate opportunities. Thus the ALI's *Principles* say that, vis-a-vis a director, something is a corporate opportunity only if the director either (1) learned of the opportunity in connection with performing his duties for the company; (2) learned of it under circumstances where he should reasonably have believed it was being offered to the corporation, not to him personally; or (3) learned of it through the use of information or property belonging to the corporation. [223] Since the facts suggest that Mike learned of the land (and of the routing of the highway) through means that had nothing to do with Mona Lisa or his director-work for Mona Lisa, the land did not represent a corporate opportunity. Consequently, the fact that the land might have been very useful to the company is irrelevant.

(c) Yes, probably. More things are held to be corporate opportunities when exploited by a full-time employee of the corporation than when exploited by an outside director. Thus the ALI *Principles* say that an opportunity is a corporate one if exploited by an employee who knows that the opportunity is "closely related to a business in which the corporation is engaged or expects to engage." [223] Since Mona Lisa is currently engaged in the business of putting up fast-food restaurants on vacant land near highways in fast-growing towns (and has already expressed interest in putting a store in David), this was a corporate opportunity vis a vis a full-time employee. Consequently, Mike was required to offer the property to Mona Lisa first, before buying it himself. (The fact that Mike's area of expertise was sales instead of, say, real-estate acquisitions, won't make a difference.) The court will probably impose a "constructive trust," under which Mike will be treated as holding the property for Mona Lisa's benefit. [229] (Mona Lisa would have to reimburse Mike for his costs before taking control of the property, however.)

52. Yes, probably. As explored in the previous answer, an opportunity is less likely to be found to "belong" to the corporation when exploited by a non-employee director than when exploited by a full-time employee. But even in the director situation, if the director found the opportunity ***in connection with company business***, the opportunity will generally be held to be a corporate one. [223] Since at the time Alexis learned of the Antarctic opportunity she was visiting company properties in connection with her role as director, that opportunity was a corporate one (which she improperly usurped). (If she had been traveling on a vacation that had nothing to do with Prime-Time affairs, she probably would *not* be deemed to have usurped any opportunity, even though the lease would have been of value to Prime-Time — see the answer to question 48(b).)

53. (a) That the corporation, through Wendy its President, rejected the opportunity.

(b) Probably not. Most courts do indeed hold that if the corporation rejects the opportunity after full disclosure, the Key Player may exploit the opportunity himself. The real issue here is whether "the corporation" has in fact rejected the opportunity. It's true that the President has rejected the opportunity. But most courts would probably hold that rejection does not occur unless either a majority of the disinterested directors, or a majority of the shareholders, have rejected it. [225] Since no disinterested directors other than Wendy have rejected it, true rejection did not occur here.

(c) Probably not. Although the opportunity is drug-related, Darling's focus — cancer — has nothing to do with a drug that merely helps people fly; Darling's marketing channels might not even be useful in selling the product. Thus, this probably wouldn't constitute an opportunity under the line-of-business test, even though "line of business" is typically interpreted very broadly. [222] Under the interest-or-expectancy test, Darling didn't have any interest or expectancy related to "flying" drugs, nor was such a drug essential to Darling's business. As a result, Peter would probably win with the argument that the opportunity wasn't a "corporate" opportunity at all.

54. (a) That the company was financially unable to take advantage of the opportunity, and thus hasn't been harmed.

(b) Unclear. Courts are split about whether and when the corporation's financial inability to take advantage of the opportunity constitutes a defense to a usurpation-of-opportunity claim. Many courts say that unless the defendant made full disclosure of the opportunity to the corporation in advance, he may not later rely on its probable financial inability as a defense. [226] Courts following this view reason that: (1) if the opportunity is attractive enough, the corporation might be able to raise the funds even if it doesn't already have them on hand; and (2) allowing financial inability to be a defense furnishes a bad incentive to corporate insiders, because the defense's availability discourages the insider from seeking a way to help the corporation raise the funds. Since Peter didn't notify anyone associated with New England Potato about the opportunity before taking it for himself, he won't be able to raise the "financial inability" defense later, under this view.

But other courts, including Delaware, don't require advance disclosure as a pre-requisite to a "financial inability" defense. So in those states, Peter's failure to notify anyone at the company before taking the opportunity for himself won't bar his use of the financial-inability defense.

V. THE SALE OF CONTROL

A. Nature of problem: A "controlling block" of shares in a corporation will often be worth more, per share, than a non-controlling block. This fact raises the key question that we discuss in this section: May the controlling shareholder sell his block for a significantly ***higher price*** than that available to non-controlling shareholders who also wish to sell, and keep the excess for himself? In general, the answer is ***"yes,"*** but with some important exceptions.

1. **What is a "controlling block":** First, let's consider what is meant by a "controlling shareholder" or a "controlling block" of stock. A person has effective "control" (and his block is a "controlling block") if he has the ***"power to use the assets of a corporation as [he] chooses."*** S,S,B&W, p. 1138.

   a. **Not necessarily majority:** A person who holds a ***majority*** of the shares of the corporation necessarily has control. But even a ***minority*** interest may be controlling. For instance, the holder of a substantial minority interest (e.g., 30% or more) will usually have effective control if he holds the largest single interest, and the remaining interests are quite fragmented. The existence of a controlling interest is a factual question — a 20% interest might be controlling in one corporation (e.g., a large corporation where no one else owns more than 2%) but not controlling in another (e.g., where someone else holds a majority or a larger minority position).

2. **Why control might be worth a premium:** Why should a control block sell for a ***"premium"***? ("Premium" is the term used to describe the excess that an acquirer pays for the control shares over what he would pay for non-controlling shares.) The answer is that a person with control has the ***"keys to the corporate treasury"*** (S,S,B&W, p. 1139), and may for a variety of reasons attach economic value to those keys. Depending on how this power over the corporate treasury is used, the controlling shareholder may be acting properly or improperly; even a "proper" use of control, however, may have real economic value for an acquirer.

   a. **Change of strategy:** For example, consider Investor, a skilled business person who has been successful at buying troubled corporations and "turning them around" by changing their strategy. If Investor buys a non-controlling interest in Target, he will not be able to influence Target's strategy, and will therefore have to depend for return on his investment on Target's operations and management as these now exist. If, however, he can acquire a controlling interest in Target, he can change the management, sell off assets, pursue new lines of business, or otherwise directly influence Target's future prospects. It would not be foolish for him to pay more, on a per-share basis, for a controlling interest than for a non-controlling interest in Target. (Observe that having Investor acquire a controlling interest in Target might well be advantageous to the non-controlling holders of Target; if Investor makes divestitures, starts new lines of business, etc., and thereby increases the value of the company, these minority holders benefit along with Investor.)

   b. **Use for personal gain at expense of others:** On the other hand, one who acquires control may use the corporation for less laudable purposes, and in fact for purposes which leave the non-controlling shareholders ***worse off*** than they were before the acquisition. For instance, Investor may pay a premium to get a controlling interest in Target, then convert some of Target's assets to his ***own personal use***. He might do this in a direct bald-faced manner (e.g., by selling corporate property to himself at a very below-market price) or he might do it in a way that would be harder to attack (e.g., by paying lower dividends on all stock, and using the savings to pay himself an above-market salary as self-appointed president of the company).

c. **Summary:** In any event, whether the acquirer plans to use his control for proper or improper purposes, he would rationally pay more per share for control than for a non-controlling interest.

d. **Seller demands control premium:** Conversely, the existing holder of control will often be unwilling to ***sell*** his stock without getting a control premium, i.e., without getting some compensation that is not given pro rata to other shareholders. After all, he already has control, and is presumably drawing some of the advantages of control (e.g., a cushy salary as president, which he probably will lose if he sells) that the non-controlling shareholders don't have.

3. **Ways of arranging control premium:** Therefore, we have an existing controlling shareholder and a would-be acquirer, each of whom has an incentive to arrange a transaction in which the controlling shareholder will receive a control premium. Buyers and sellers of control have shown almost limitless ingenuity in arranging ways to pay/receive extra for the control block.

Example 1: Buyer is willing to pay $1 million for the assets of Target, 60% of the shares of which are owned by Dominant. Instead of buying all shares for a total of $1 million (so that Dominant would get $600,000), Buyer buys just Dominant's shares, and pays $700,000 for them. Buyer now controls 60% of the stock. Buyer now causes Target to sell all of the assets to himself for $750,000. Buyer now liquidates the corporation, and receives back $450,000 (60% of $750,000). Buyer has paid the same $1 million net that he was always willing to pay for the assets ($700,000 to Dominant, $750,000 to Target, less $450,000 received back on liquidation of Target). Yet Dominant has received $100,000 more than he would have gotten by a pro rata sale, and the minority shareholders have gotten $100,000 less. See S,S,B&W, p. 998.

Example 2: Same facts as Example 1. However, Buyer merely buys Dominant's shares for $700,000, then continues to operate the business. The minority shareholders have no opportunity to sell, whereas Dominant has cashed out at an attractive price. Buyer may or may not operate the business in a way that benefits the minority shareholders, but clearly Dominant got an opportunity (to sell at a price valuing the whole company at $1 million) that the other holders have not gotten.

4. **General rule allows:** The general rule is that the controlling shareholder ***may sell his control block for a premium, and may keep the premium himself***. Clark, p. 478.

Example: The Ds and their families collectively own 44% of the stock of Gable Industries, Inc. The Ds sell their interests to Flintkote Co. for $15 per share at a time when Gable stock is selling on the open market for a little more than $7 per share. P, a small shareholder, contends that the minority shareholders should be entitled to share in this control premium (apparently by having the Ds not sell all of their shares, and allowing the minority holders to sell part of theirs to Flintkote).

Held, for the Ds. "[A]bsent looting of corporate assets, conversion of a corporate opportunity, fraud or other acts of bad faith, a controlling stockholder is free to sell, and a purchaser is free to buy, that controlling interest at a premium price." The relief sought by P would require that a controlling interest could be transferred only by means of an offer to all stockholders, i.e., a tender offer. Such a radical change should only be done by the legislature, not the courts. *Zetlin v. Hanson Holdings, Inc.*, 397 N.E.2d 387 (N.Y. 1979).

5. **ALI approach:** The ALI's *Prin. of Corp. Gov.* similarly recognize the general rule that a controlling shareholder may sell his control block for a premium (subject to various exceptions). See § 5.16.

6. **Exceptions:** But as *Zetlin, supra,* hints, there are ***exceptions*** to the controlling shareholder's general right to sell his control block for a premium. The three main such exceptions are:

   (1) the ***"looting"*** exception;

   (2) the ***"sale of vote"*** exception; and

   (3) the ***"diversion of collective opportunity"*** exception (which itself has two or three sub-branches).

   The remainder of our treatment of "sale of control" problems is devoted to these exceptions, which collectively have considerable importance.

B. **The "looting" exception:** Probably the most important exception to the general rule that a controlling shareholder may sell for (and keep) a premium, is the ***"looting"*** exception: "[A] holder of controlling shares may not knowingly, recklessly, or perhaps negligently, sell his shares to one who intends to loot the corporation by unlawful activity." Clark, p. 479.

1. **Investment companies:** The clearest "looting" cases are those in which the corporation's principal or sole assets are stocks, bonds and other ***liquid*** assets. (Such companies are usually called ***"investment companies."***) The "true," i.e., net asset, value of shares in an investment company is usually readily calculated. Therefore, a controlling shareholder who sells his shares to a buyer who is willing to pay more than this net asset value has reason to be suspicious — the high price is almost impossible to understand if the buyer plans to run the company honestly, but very easy to understand if he plans to steal the corporate assets. Clark, p. 479.

2. **Close corporation:** Apart from cases involving investment companies, plaintiffs have only very rarely been able to show that the seller knew or should have known that the buyer intended to loot the company; therefore, there are very few non-investment-company cases in which the plaintiff has prevailed.

3. **Factors considered:** Here are some of the factors that courts have treated as ones that would arouse the suspicions of a reasonably prudent seller and thus trigger a duty to conduct further investigation: (1) the buyer's willingness to pay an ***excessive price*** for the shares; (2) the buyer's excessive interest in the ***liquid*** and ***readily saleable assets*** owned by the corporation; (3) the buyer's insistence on ***immediate possession*** of the liquid assets following the closing, and on immediate transfer of control by resignations of incumbent directors; and (4) the buyer's lack of interest in the details of how the corporation operates. Nutshell, pp. 363-64.

4. **Negligence theory:** Most courts seem to base liability on a theory of ***negligence***: the selling shareholder owes a duty of care to the corporation, and is liable if he breaches that duty by acting negligently (or, worse, recklessly or with malicious intent). Because of this negligence foundation, the courts often award ***damages*** equal to the ***harm*** suffered by the corporation. This harm will often be greater than the "control premium" (the excess of

price paid over a fair market value of the shares), and might conceivably even be greater than the entire purchase price — the seller could find himself not only paying back every dime he received, but then some!

C. The "sale of vote" exception: A second major exception to the general rule allowing the controlling stockholder to sell for a premium, is the so-called ***"sale of vote"*** exception.

1. General ban on sale of office: To begin with, understand that as a matter of public policy, courts prohibit the bald sale of a corporate office.

Example: Smith is a director of Corporation, and sits on its nominating committee (which nominates candidates to fill vacancies on the board). Without Smith's vote, the board is equally divided on many important matters of policy. Smith decides to resign, and goes to one of the competing factions. He says that in return for $10,000, he will not only resign, but use his influence with his co-directors on the nominating committee to cause a candidate favored by that faction to be nominated and elected to fill the vacancy.

Virtually every court would strike down this agreement (and the ensuing nomination and election of a director stemming from it) as violating the public policy against sale of a corporate office. Smith, as a director, owes Corporation a fiduciary obligation, which includes the obligation to nominate the candidate he thinks is best for Corporation, not the one whose election will most benefit Smith personally. Clark, p. 480.

2. Application to sale of control context: This rule against the "sale of office" has occasionally been applied to the sale-of-control context, so that the person selling control has to return his control premium to the corporation or the minority shareholders. An illegal sale of office is most likely to be found in two situations: (1) where the control block is much less than a majority of the shares, but the seller happens to have unusual influence over the composition of the board; or (2) where the sale contract expressly provides for a separate, additional, payment if the seller delivers prompt control of the board.

3. Small minority: It may occasionally happen that a shareholder, even though he holds only a ***small minority*** of the shares, happens to have a large influence over a majority of the board of directors. If as part of this shareholder's sale of his shares, he causes this majority to resign and be replaced by directors controlled by the buyer, the court may find that the control premium amounts to a disguised sale of office, and will therefore force the seller to disgorge this control premium.

a. Sale of majority of stock: On the other hand, where what is being sold is a ***majority*** block, courts never strike down a control premium on the "sale of vote" theory — they recognize that the buyer will eventually be able to control the board through the regular stockholder election process, so they see no reason to require him to wait to achieve control.

b. "Working control" block: The sale-of-vote issue is hardest to resolve when what is being sold is something that is, at least arguably, ***"working control."*** Remember that this phrase refers to a block that is less than a majority but still large enough that, as a ***practical matter***, the possessor will ultimately be able to get his nominees elected to a majority of board seats (perhaps because there are no larger minority blocks and the remaining interests are very fragmented). For instance, a 20-40% block will often represent working control of a widely-held publicly traded company. One problem with analyzing such a situation is that there is no way to know in advance whether a substantial minority block will indeed turn out to be controlling in the buyer's hands — the buyer may expect that, say, a 25% block will give him control, yet discover to his chagrin that because of some unforeseen organized opposition, a competing tender offer, or some other reason, he does not get control. In this ambiguous situation, courts are split about whether the seller may legally charge and pocket a premium that depends in part on his delivery of immediate resignations of some or a majority of the directors.

i. ***Essex Universal* case:** In the principal case on this subject, *Essex Universal Corp. v. Yates*, 305 F.2d 572 (2d Cir. 1962), the two judges who discussed the issue (sitting together on the same panel) disagreed with each other. The block represented 28.3% of the stock, and the seller contracted to deliver to the buyer resignations of a majority of the directors and to cause the buyer's nominees to replace them. One judge believed that the court should presume that the 28.3% block would eventually confer control on the buyer, so that unless the plaintiff could show otherwise, the transaction should be allowed to stand. The other judge believed that (at least as a matter of policy though not as a matter of interpreting New York State law) the seller's agreement to deliver immediate control should be struck down unless it was "entirely plain that a new election would be a mere formality," which he thought was only true for cases involving the sale of a virtual majority, which 28% was obviously not.

4. **Separate payment for sale of control:** A second situation in which the sale of the control block may be found to be an "illegal sale of control" is if the sale contract provides for a ***separate payment*** to be paid only for, and upon, the delivery of directors' resignations and election of the buyers' nominees to the board. However, this is a pitfall that can be easily gotten around by careful drafting: the seller's lawyer must be careful that the contract states a single purchase price for stock and the resignations, rather than separate prices for each.

5. **Subsequent re-election as ratification:** Even where the court might otherwise order the seller to disgorge the control premium because he has in effect "sold his vote," the court may reach a contrary decision if the seller's nominees have been ***re-elected*** at a ***subsequent shareholders' meeting***. In this situation, the fact that the buyer's nominees have been re-elected by shareholder vote shows either that the buyer did have working control, or that the minority shareholders have not been damaged (since they have ratified the buyer's choices for the board); in either event, there is no reason to confiscate the seller's control premium.

D. **Diversion of collective opportunity:** The final major category of exceptions to the general rule allowing a control premium has been called the ***"diversion of collective opportunity"*** (Clark, p. 482), a phrase which we use here. This phrase refers to situations in which for one reason or another the control premium should really be found to belong either to the corporation or to all shareholders pro rata. The two main situations in which courts have found such a diversion of collective opportunity are:

[1] where the court decides that the control premium really represents a ***business opportunity*** that the corporation could and should have pursued ***as a corporation***; and

[2] where a buyer ***initially tries*** to buy most or all of the corporation's ***assets*** (or to buy ***stock***

pro rata from all shareholders), and the controlling shareholder instead talks him into buying the controlling shareholder's block at a premium instead.

1. **Displaced corporate-level business opportunity:** The first of these sub-types of "diverted collective opportunity" is somewhat amorphous: the idea is that the corporation as such has a ***business opportunity*** that it would normally pursue on its own, but for some extraneous reason the value of this opportunity is instead "sold" to the buyer of a control block in return for a control premium. The best-known (and perhaps the only) case clearly illustrating this "displaced company-level opportunity" theory (see Clark, p. 482) is the landmark case of ***Perlman v. Feldmann***, 219 F.2d 173 (2d Cir. 1955). Because of this case's importance, we consider it in some detail:

   a. **Facts:** Feldmann was the president and dominant shareholder of Newport Steel Corp. During the Korean War, the steel industry voluntarily refrained from increasing its prices, even though the war caused demand to skyrocket and shortages to develop. Wilport Co. was a syndicate of steel end-users who wanted to obtain more steel than they had been able to get. Wilport bought Feldmann's controlling interest in Newport for a price of $20 per share (at a time when the publicly-traded shares of Newport were selling for $12 a share, and its book value per share was $17). Once Wilport gained control, it apparently caused Newport to sell substantial amounts of steel to Wilport's members, though such sales were always made at the same prices Newport charged its other customers. Non-controlling shareholders of Newport sued Feldmann, arguing that the control premium Feldmann had received for his shares was directly due to the premium buyers were willing to pay for steel in a time of shortage, and that this premium was therefore essentially a corporate asset that should belong to all shareholders pro rata.

      i. **The Feldmann Plan:** The plaintiffs supported this assertion by pointing out that before the stock sale, Newport had been obtaining some extra benefit from the steel shortage by use of what was known as the "Feldmann Plan." Under the Plan, would-be customers would make interest-free advances in return for firm commitments to them of Newport's future steel production. Newport could then use these interest-free loans to build new plants, improve its existing plants, etc. In other words, use of the Feldmann Plan allowed Newport to in effect raise its prices (by obtaining interest-free loans in addition to the purchase price) without violating the industry's voluntary price guidelines. The plaintiffs apparently claimed (though this is not completely clear from the opinion) that after Wilport took control, it caused Newport to reduce or eliminate Feldmann Plan transactions, at least as to purchases made by Wilport's syndicate members.

   b. **Holding:** The Court of Appeals agreed with the plaintiffs that by selling his control block for a premium, Feldmann had ***violated his fiduciary duty to the other shareholders.*** The court made it clear that it was not imposing any general rule that sale of a control block for a premium was a violation of fiduciary obligations. But when there was an opportunity for ***corporate-level gain***, and instead the controlling shareholder appropriated that gain for himself, there was a breach of such obligations — Newport could have continued to realize its extra profits by maintaining and even expanding the Feldmann Plan; instead, this corporate opportunity was (apparently) transformed into abolition of the Feldmann Plan and dollars into Feldmann's own pocket.

c. **Remedy:** The court took the further unusual step of ordering that any recovery (the amount of the premium) be paid ***solely to the minority stockholders***, not to the corporation. That way, Wilport (now the owner of Feldmann's shares) would not get any benefit from the recovery.

d. **Dissent:** Judge Swan wrote a well-known dissent. He contended that the usual rule (that a controlling shareholder may sell for a premium and keep it) should be applied so long as there was no evidence that the sale of control, or the buyer's subsequent actions, injured the corporation or the minority holders. Here, he found no such evidence — he stressed that Wilport syndicate members paid the same price for Newport steel as any other customer did. (He conveniently ignored the apparent fact that Wilport caused Newport to eliminate the Feldmann Plan, thus effectively lowering prices charged to *all* buyers of Newport steel.)

e. **Significance:** The significance of *Perlman v. Feldmann* is fairly ***narrow***: if the corporation has an ***unusual business opportunity*** that it is ***not completely taking advantage of*** (e.g., the ability to raise prices, to obtain interest-free loans, or otherwise to prosper in a time of great demand for its products), this opportunity ***may not be appropriated by the controlling shareholder*** in the form of a ***premium for the sale of control.***

2. **Seller switches type of deal:** If the buyer proposes to buy the entire company, but the seller instead ***switches*** the nature of the deal by talking the buyer into buying just the seller's control block (at a premium), a court may take away the seller's right to keep the premium, on the grounds that all shareholders deserve the right to participate.

E. **ALI approach:** The ALI's Prin. of Corp. Gov. don't recognize the above three exceptions as such. Instead, the ALI approach sets out two more general exceptions to the general rule that the control block may be sold for a premium:

❑ The controlling shareholder may not fail to ***make disclosure*** to the other shareholders with whom he deals in connection with the transaction.

> **Example:** *A*, the 52% shareholder of Corp., agrees to sell his block to Acquirer at an above-market price. Simultaneously, as part of his arrangement with Acquirer, *A* recommends to the minority holders that they sell to Acquirer at the market price. *A* doesn't tell the minority holders that he's selling at a higher price. The *ALI Prin. of Corp. Gov.* say that *A* has violated his "duty of fair dealing" to the minority holders. See Illustr. 4 to § 5.16.

❑ The controlling shareholder may not sell his control block if "it is apparent from the circumstances that the ***purchaser is likely to violate the duty of fair dealing*** . . . in such a way as to obtain a significant financial benefit for the purchaser or an associate."

> **Example:** This covers the "looting" situation: if it should be apparent to the controlling holder that the purchaser will sell corporate assets to himself at a below-market price, or sell property to the corporation at an above-market price, the controlling shareholder can't carry out the transaction (even at a market price).

F. **Remedies:** As we've said above, in a normal situation the controlling shareholder may sell for, and keep, the control premium. But in those special situations where the general rule does not apply (sale to looter, sale of office, diversion of collective opportunity), what exactly is the

remedy that the plaintiff who succeeds on the merits will receive? The two basic possibilities are: (1) return of the premium to the corporation; and (2) payment of some portion of the premium directly to the non-controlling shareholders.

1. **Recovery by corporation:** For these three theories of recovery — sale to looter, sale of office and diversion of collective opportunity — the most logical form of recovery is ***by the corporation***. At least arguably, it is the corporation's assets that have been sold to produce the control premium, so it is the corporation that should get the premium back. This is indeed how some cases have been decided.

2. **Benefits purchaser:** But there is a big problem with having the control premium returned to the corporation: this remedy gives the ***purchaser*** — the very person who agreed to pay the control premium — an unanticipated and probably undeserved windfall. For instance, if Dominant owns 50% of Target, and sells that stake to Buyer for a $10 per share premium, if the premium is ordered returned to Target then half of it will effectively end up in Buyer's pocket (since he now owns 50% of Target's shares). Therefore, the court may decide to order the seller to repay ***directly to the minority shareholders*** their pro rata part of the control premium.

   a. ***Perlman v. Feldmann:*** This is exactly what happened on remand in *Perlman v. Feldmann, supra*, p. 238. The district court concluded that the premium had been $5.33 a share, or $2,126,280. The non-controlling minority shareholders owned 63% of the stock. Therefore, the court ordered that the selling controlling holder pay them $1,339,769 (63% of $2,126,280). See *Perlman v. Feldmann*, 154 F.Supp. 436 (D. Conn. 1957). This method allowed Feldmann to keep his pro rata share of the control premium, and prevented the buyers from getting back any of the benefit from the control premium they had paid.

Quiz Yourself on
THE DUTY OF LOYALTY *(THE SALE OF CONTROL)*

55. Abner Doubleday is a 55% shareholder of the NASDAQ-listed Splendid Splinter Baseball Bat Company, Inc. The fair market value of Splendid Splinter's stock on NASDAQ is $20. Doubleday decides he wants to give up the bat business and go into something really lucrative — forging sports memorabilia. Scuff Spitballer, a reputable businessman, offers to buy Doubleday's shares for $30 each, if he's willing to sell all of them. Doubleday accepts the offer. Splendid Splinter's minority shareholders sue Doubleday on behalf of Splendid Splinter, seeking the $10 premium he received for his shares over fair market value. Who wins? ________________

56. Ali Baba Art Galleries, Inc., buys and sells fabulously expensive works of art. Ali Baba, controlling shareholder of the galleries, sells his shares to Scheherezade, at a price $20 a share above market value. Scheherezade immediately begins to sell to herself the Galleries's inventory of art works at grossly understated prices. By the time minority shareholders wake up and sue Scheherezade, she has secreted the works (apparently in the vaults of an unidentified Swiss bank), and is thus effectively judgment-proof.

(a) You represent one of the minority holders. On what theory might you sue Ali Baba for the difference between the true value of the artworks sold by Scheherezade to herself and the price she paid?

____

(b) State the factors (not necessarily ones presented explicitly in the above statement of facts) that, if proved at trial, would support your theory of recovery. ________________

57. The Sleeping Beauty Sewing Machine Company has seven directors. Its shares are publicly traded, with a price hovering around $10 a share. Evil Stepmother decides she wants to acquire control of the company. Evil Stepmother approaches five of the directors — Grumpy, Dopey, Sleepy, Bashful, and Doc — and asks them to sign a document in which they agree that they will (1) immediately resign and (2) as a final act on the board, vote for Evil's nominees as their successors as directors. The document also states that Evil will pay each director $20 a share for his shares. The five directors together own about 7% of the company's stock. (The President owns about 25% of the stock, and the rest is held by the public at large.) The directors sign the agreement, then resign and vote as they've agreed to do.

(a) What is the best theory under which a minority holder in the company could sue the 5 resigning directors? ________________

(b) Will that theory succeed? ________________

Answers

55. Doubleday. The issue here is whether a controlling shareholder can sell his control at a premium — that is, a price above the fair market value of the shares. The *general* rule is that he may, in fact, sell his shares for whatever price he wants. [234] There are exceptions to this doctrine, but none of the exceptions applies here. (For instance, Doubleday has no reason to believe that the buyer will loot or otherwise harm the corporation, Doubleday hasn't explicitly agreed to transfer control of the board as a condition of the deal, and there's no reason to believe that the premium is a diversion of a "collective opportunity.") So Doubleday is within his rights in collecting something extra for his controlling stake, even though he's getting a benefit not available to other shareholders.

56. (a) That Ali Baba knew or should have known that Scheherezade was likely to "loot" the company. Part of a controlling shareholder's fiduciary duty to his corporation is that he cannot sell control to anyone whom he knows or should know will harm the company (e.g., by looting the company's treasury, committing fraud on the corporation after acquiring control, or implementing business policies that would harm the corporation or its shareholders). [235]

(b) Any facts that ought to have put Ali on notice of Scheherezade's intent-to-loot would be helpful. Look for pre-transaction facts known to Ali, such as Scheherezade's exaggerated interest in the corporation's liquid assets; any demand by her that control be transferred to her immediately following the closing; any sign that she had only a negligible interest in the corporation's operations; or evidence that as Ali knew, Scheherezade had engaged in similar self-dealing with corporations she'd bought in the past. [235] (Her mere payment of a substantial premium for control, by contrast, would be only a *weak* indication that she might intend to loot the corporation.)

57. (a) That the document constituted an illegal "sale of office." A director or group of directors, like any other shareholder, can normally sell for a "control premium." However, a director cannot baldly sell "his office," i.e., his directorship. [236]

(b) Yes, probably. Since the 7% stake bought by Evil would not normally have given her control of the board, and since the purchase agreement here was expressly contingent on the sellers' resignations and votes for Evil's board nominees, it's hard to imagine a more blatant sale of a directorship. So the court will probably order the selling directors to disgorge the control premium either to the corporation or (preferably) directly to the shareholders other than Evil. (If the 5 selling directors owned, and were selling, a *majority* of the shares, then probably no sale-of-office would be found; that's because Evil would have been able to get control of the board eventually, even without the resignations and succession votes by the sellers. The same would probably be true if the selling directors were selling Evil a "working majority." [236])

VI. OTHER DUTIES OF CONTROLLING SHAREHOLDERS

A. **Introduction:** So far in this chapter, we have looked at various contexts in which controlling shareholders, like directors and executives, have a duty of loyalty to the corporation. We now focus on a collection of miscellaneous contexts in which controlling shareholders, in particular, may have a special duty of loyalty to their fellow non-controlling shareholders. Of these special contexts, the most important is that involving a parent-subsidiary relationship — a parent that does not own all the stock of the subsidiary is generally held to have a fiduciary obligation to the subsidiary's minority shareholders. This topic is discussed beginning *infra*, p. 243.

B. **Possible general fiduciary duty:** Does a controlling shareholder have any kind of ***general fiduciary duty*** to his fellow non-controlling shareholders?

   1. **Not covered by statute:** Few if any states impose such a general fiduciary duty on the controlling shareholder by ***statute***. For instance, the MBCA is completely silent about the general fiduciary obligations (if any) owed by controlling shareholders. (Of course, if the controlling shareholder is also a director or executive, there are likely to be statutory duty-of-loyalty obligations explicitly imposed on him, such as MBCA § 8.31's rules on self-dealing transactions involving directors. But the point I am making here is that few if any statutes impose fiduciary obligations on a shareholder *qua* shareholder.) Therefore, any fiduciary obligations must be imposed as a matter of ***case law***.

   2. **Close corporation situation:** In the case of a ***close corporation***, some courts have expressly concluded that the controlling shareholder has a significant fiduciary obligation to his fellow shareholders. See, e.g., the landmark case of *Donahue v. Rodd Electrotype Co*, *supra*, p. 161. Thus Massachusetts (the state where *Donahue* was decided) as a matter of case law prevents a controlling shareholder in a close corporation from putting his own interests ahead of those of his fellow shareholders. For instance, the controlling shareholder may not cause the corporation to redeem some of his own shares at an attractive price, without also causing the corporation to offer a similar redemption arrangement to the minority shareholders. *Donahue, supra.*

   3. **Public corporations:** Where the corporation is ***publicly held***, the courts have been less quick to impose on the controlling shareholder a fiduciary obligation with any real bite. The fact that a controlling shareholder is generally allowed to sell his controlling interest at a premium (*supra*, p. 234) is one illustration of this lack of any generally-recognized fiduciary obligation to one's non-controlling co-shareholders.

a. **Possible duty of complete disclosure:** However, even in the public-company context, when a controlling shareholder or group deals with the non-controlling shareholders some courts say the controller owes the non-controllers a ***duty of disclosure*** (not a duty to behave with substantive fairness) with respect to the transaction, as a matter of state common law.

Example: Controlling shareholders in ABC give notice of the proposed buyback of a minority block of stock, without telling the minority holders that due to secret developments the minority holders would benefit by exercising certain conversion rights. A court might well hold that this failure to give complete disclosure violated the majority's common-law obligation to the minority. See, e.g., *Zahn v. Tansamerica Corp.*, 162 F.2d 36 (3d Cir. 1947), so holding.

C. **Parent/subsidiary relations:** Most cases involving the duties of a controlling shareholder to the non-controlling holders arise in the context of the relationship between a parent and its ***not-wholly-owned subsidiary***. In general, these parent/subsidiary cases are analyzed the same way as any other case involving the duties of a controlling shareholder to the non-controlling holders. Thus some courts say that the parent has a fiduciary obligation to the other shareholders in the subsidiary, but it is not clear how much bite this obligation has. We must look at different contexts (e.g., merger, dividends, parent-subsidiary contracts, etc.) to get a meaningful view of what the parent's obligations are, since these vary depending on the context.

1. **Merger:** It will often be the case that the parent wants to turn the subsidiary into a ***wholly-owned*** subsidiary, by ***buying out*** the minority shareholders and then merging the subsidiary into the parent. In these transactions, the general rule is that the merger must be at a ***fair price***. The main legal issues are: What price is fair? and How should the determination of fairness be made? This topic is discussed extensively beginning *infra*, p. 411; see especially the treatment of *Weinberger v. UOP*, *infra*, p. 425.

2. **Dividends:** The parent, by virtue of its controlling interest in the subsidiary, will be able to control or at least influence the subsidiary's ***dividend policy***. The minority holders may not like this dividend policy: they may feel that the dividend is too high (and the cash should instead be reinvested in the subsidiary's business rather than being paid out pro rata to the parent and to the minority holders); or, they may feel that the dividend is too low (and should be paid out rather than re-invested in the subsidiary's business). The minority holders can plausibly argue that when the parent sets the subsidiary's dividend policy, the parent is engaged in a self-dealing transaction (defined *supra*, p. 198), and that the policy should therefore be closely scrutinized by the court.

a. **Unsuccessful argument:** However, the minority holders in this parent/subsidiary situation have generally been ***unsuccessful*** at getting the courts to apply the self-dealing rules to dividend transactions. Courts generally are swayed by the fact that the dividends are paid ***pro rata*** to all shareholders, so the parent isn't getting any more money ***per share*** than are the minority holders. Courts that take this view ignore the fact that different shareholders have different preferences, and the fact that a given dividend policy that is good for the parent may be bad for other shareholders. In any event, the general rule seems to be: even though the parent may be controlling the subsidiary's dividend policy, so long as that policy satisfies the ***business judgment rule*** (i.e., it isset in good faith after reasonable investigation, and is not completely irrational;[1] see *supra*, p. 182), it will be ***upheld*** by the court.

Example: Sinclair Oil ("Sinclair") owns 97% of the stock of Sinclair Venezuelan Co. ("Sinven"). Sinclair controls the board of directors of Sinven. Sinclair causes Sinven to pay out extremely high dividends (in fact, dividends in excess of Sinven's earnings) during a 7-year period. The Ps (who are among the 3% minority stockholders in Sinven) sue Sinclair, arguing that this dividend policy violates Sinclair's fiduciary duty to Sinven.

Held, for D (at least on this point). The dividends were paid in proportion to stockholdings, so that Ps got their aliquot share (3%) of all dividends paid. Therefore, the setting of the dividend policy was not self-dealing by Sinclair. Instead, the policy must be judged by the business judgment rule. Since the Ps cannot show that the dividends resulted from "improper motives and amounted to waste," the business judgment rule is satisfied and the dividend policy must be upheld. (Other aspects of the case are discussed *infra*, p. 244). *Sinclair Oil Corp. v. Levien*, 280 A.2d 717 (Del. 1971).

3. **Self-dealing between parent and subsidiary:** As *Sinclair* indicates, the fact that Parent has set Subsidiary's dividend policy does not constitute self-dealing. But other types of transactions between Parent and Subsidiary may well be found to be self-dealing. If so, these transactions are judged by the same rules applied to self-dealing transactions outside of the parent/subsidiary context. (See *supra*, p. 200, for an explanation of these rules.) In general, the minority holders in Subsidiary can therefore get a self-dealing transaction struck down if they can show that it was ***not fair*** to Subsidiary and that it was not approved by either ***disinterested*** directors or disinterested shareholders.

   a. **Dominated board:** In the common situation where Parent dominates the entire board of Subsidiary, this means that unless the ***minority shareholders*** have been given a chance to ***ratify*** the self-dealing transaction, they can have the court strike down the transaction if it is not fair to them. In fact, once the minority holders of Subsidiary show that there has been self-dealing by Parent with respect to Subsidiary, the ***burden of proof shifts*** to Parent: Parent must now ***show affirmatively*** that the transaction was ***fair*** to Subsidiary.

   Example: Go back to the facts of *Sinclair*, *supra*. Sinclair and Sinven make a contract in which Sinven agrees to sell all of its crude oil and refined products to Sinclair at specified prices, payment to be made on receipt. The contract includes minimum and maximum quantities. Sinclair breaches the contract in several respects (e.g., it does not pay on receipt, and it does not order the contractually-specified minimums). The Ps (minority shareholders in Sinven) claim that the contract constituted self-dealing, and that it should be struck down unless Sinclair shows that the contract was fair.

---

1. Courts seem to ignore the third requirement for the business judgment rule, that the decision-maker not be ***"interested"*** in the decision. Thus even though it's the parent or its employees and directors, not independent directors of the subsidiary, who set the dividend policy, the policy will get the benefit of the business judgment rule if it's set in good faith, after reasonable investigation, and in a not-completely-irrational way.

Held, for the Ps. "Self-dealing occurs when the parent, by virtue of its domination of the subsidiary, causes the subsidiary to act in such a way that the parent receives something from the subsidiary to the exclusion of, and detriment to, the minority stockholders of the subsidiary." Here, the contract meant that Sinclair was taking Sinven's oil for itself, rather than allowing the oil to be sold on the open market. Therefore, the contract was self-dealing. Such a self-dealing contract will only be upheld if the parent satisfies the "intrinsic fairness" standard. Here, Sinclair did not bear the burden of showing why Sinven's failure to enforce the contract against Sinclair was "intrinsically fair" to the minority shareholders of Sinven. Therefore, Sinclair is liable to the minority holders for their share of the damages that Sinven could have obtained for breach. *Sinclair Oil Corp. v. Levien*, *supra*, p. 244.

b. **Other kinds of contracts:** *Sinclair* was a very clear example of self-dealing (even though the level of unfairness to the minority holders was apparently not great): Parent was buying all of Subsidiary's output. But courts have also found self-dealing — and struck it down on grounds of unfairness — where the presence of Parent on both sides of the transaction with Subsidiary was much more subtle. For instance, the court may hold that Parent's provision of legal, accounting, financial or other general ***corporate services*** to Subsidiary amounts to self-dealing, and must be struck down if unfair.

4. **Acquisitions and other corporate opportunities:** Recall that the doctrine of ***"corporate opportunity"*** prevents a Key Player from usurping for himself an opportunity that is found properly to "belong" to the corporation. This corporate opportunity doctrine may apply in the parent/subsidiary context: If Parent takes for itself an opportunity (e.g., an ***acquisition***) that the court finds really belongs to Subsidiary, the minority holders of Subsidiary will be able to reclaim that opportunity for Subsidiary, or at least recover damages.

   a. **Standard:** In general, courts have applied the same corporate opportunity doctrine in the parent/subsidiary context as they do in the ordinary non-subsidiary situation. See Clark, p. 256. For instance, if the court would apply a multi-factor test like Delaware's (p. 221) to a transaction in which President takes for himself a business opportunity that might have been taken by Corporation, the court would presumably also apply this multi-factor test to determine whether an opportunity taken by Parent belongs to Subsidiary.

5. **Disinterested directors:** Both for self-dealing transactions and for corporate opportunities, Parent may avoid claims of unfairness by Subsidiary's minority shareholders if Parent somehow (perhaps temporarily) "undoes" its domination of Subsidiary. For instance, if Subsidiary has some truly ***disinterested directors*** (e.g., directors elected by the minority shareholders), Parent could let these disinterested directors ***negotiate on behalf of Subsidiary.*** This would help immunize any contract between Parent and Subsidiary against a claim of self-dealing, and would permit Subsidiary to pursue any business opportunity on its own that was also being pursued by Parent.

   a. **Mergers:** In the case of a proposed ***merger*** of Subsidiary into Parent (and consequent forced buyout of the minority shareholders of Subsidiary), having Subsidiary represented by such an independent committee of directors is now the normal way of proceeding. See *infra*, p. 426.

Exam Tips on ***THE DUTY OF LOYALTY***

The duty of loyalty is the single most frequently-tested subject on exams. Duty of loyalty issues often appear in the same fact patterns as duty of care issues. Watch particularly for ***self-dealing transactions*** (transactions in which a director has a ***financial interest***) and situations in which a director or senior exec. takes personal advantage of an ***opportunity*** which might ***belong to the corporation.***

☛ ***Self-dealing transactions*** are usually easy to spot. Look for situations in which the corp. has ***conducted business*** with a director or senior exec. ("Key Player"), or with a member of a Key Player's family.

Once you spot a self-dealing transaction, remember that you have to do a ***multi-step analysis*** to determine whether it's a breach of the duty of loyalty:

Step 1: Did the Key Player ***disclose*** the conflict and the nature of the transaction ***in advance*** to either senior management or the entire board (whichever would normally be expected to make the decision for the corp. on whether to do the transaction)? If "yes," go to Step 2. If "no," got to Step 3.

Step 2: [For advance disclosure situations]: Did a majority of the ***"disinterested directors"*** (or a ***"disinterested superior"*** if the Key Player is not a director) ***approve*** the transaction? If "yes," there was ***no breach*** of the duty of loyalty. If "no," go to Step 3.

Step 3: [For situations where there was no advance-disclosure-plus-approval]: Did the Key Player ***disclose*** the conflict and nature of the transaction ***after*** it was entered into (either before suit or within a reasonable time after suit was filed), to either senior management or the board (as appropriate — see Step 1)? If "yes," go to Step 4. If "no," go to Step 5.

Step 4: [For after-the-fact disclosure situations]: Did a majority of the ***"disinterested directors"*** (or a "disinterested superior" if the Key Player is not a director) ***ratify*** the transaction? If "yes," there was no breach of the duty of loyalty. If "no," go to Step 5.

Step 5: [For situations where the board never gave proper approval or ratification]: Did a majority of ***disinterested shareholders***, following disclosure of the conflict and the transaction, either ***approve it*** in advance or ***ratify it*** afterwards? If "yes," go to Step 6. If "no," go to Step 7.

Step 6: [For situations where the disinterested s/h's approved]: Was the transaction a ***"waste"*** of corporate assets, viewed as of the time of s/h approval or ratification? If "no," there was ***no breach*** of duty of loyalty. If "yes," it ***is a breach*** of the duty of loyalty.

Step 7: [For sits. where there is neither board nor s/h approval or ratif.]: Was the transaction ***"fair"*** to the corp. when entered into? If "yes," there is no breach of duty of loyalty.

If "no," there is a ***breach*** of loyalty.

Example: Pres, the president of A Corp., negotiates an agreement for A Corp. to buy all of Y Corp's outstanding shares. Only one of A's 6 other directors is told by Pres. that Pres's immediate family holds all of Y Corp's shares. The board approves the transaction. Y Corp. proves to have little value. A minority s/h brings a derivative action against Pres. for damages from the purchase. You should say that since there was never disclosure of the conflict to all the independent directors [Steps 1 and 3 above], and since there was no shareholder approval [Step 5], the court will strike down the transaction unless it believes that the transaction was "fair" to the corporation [Step 7].

Other examples of self-dealing: (1) Pres. negotiates to have all of Corp's properties cleaned by X Co., and doesn't disclose that he has a large ownership interest in X Co. (2) B, a director of Corp., conveys equipment worth $50K to Corp. in return for $100K of stock, without disclosing that the equipment is only worth $50K (and while knowing that most directors think it's worth $100K).

☞ Always remember that ***pre-approval*** (after disclosure) by a majority of the ***disinterested directors*** or a majority of ***disinterested shareholders*** will ***immunize*** the transaction, and a court will not even consider whether the transaction is "fair." (See Steps 2 and 5.)

☞ Also, post-transaction ***disinterested-shareholder ratification*** of the transaction, made after disclosure and before suit, will always ***immunize*** the transaction (Step 5), and post-transaction disinterested-***director*** ratification will usually immunize it (Steps 3-4).

☞ Remember that if the facts suggest to you that the transaction was ***"fair"*** (i.e., not disadvantageous) to the corp., ***viewed as of the time it was made***, it won't be set aside or serve as the basis for damages, even if there was no disclosure, no independent-director approval and no shareholder approval. That is, fairness puts a ***complete end*** to the inquiry.

☛ Whenever a fact pattern indicates that a Key Player has taken personal advantage of an opportunity, consider whether the doctrine of ***corporate opportunity*** applies. Remember that this doctrine prohibits a Key Player from taking advantage of an opportunity which belongs to the corp., unless he first ***discloses*** the offer to the other directors or to senior management.

☞ Here are some factors which strengthen the inference that an opportunity is a corporate one:

- ❑ The Key Player ***learned*** of the opportunity while acting in his role as the ***corp's agent*** rather than as an individual;
- ❑ The opportunity is ***closely related*** to the corp's ***existing or prospective activities***;
- ❑ The opportunity is ***essential*** to the corp's ***well-being***; or
- ❑ The corp. had (and the Key Player knew that the corp. had) a ***reasonable expectation*** that the opportunity would be regarded as a corporate one.

Example: At a board meeting of A Corp., B, a director of the corp., learns that the corp. is planning on expanding, and that it's examining 3 parcels adjacent to one of its existing plants. B pays $3,000 for an option to buy one of those parcels for $120,000, and does not tell his fellow directors before doing this. B has probably usurped a corp. opportunity, since he learned of the parcel's availability from his work for the corp., the parcel is closely related to the corp's prospective activities (expansion), and the corp. reasonably expected that any parcels considered during the board meeting would be viewed as corporate opportunities. Therefore, B can probably be required to turn over the option to the corp.

☞ It generally takes less of a conflict for the corp. opportunity doctr. to apply when the Key Player is a ***full-time employee*** than where she is an ***outside director***.

☞ If the corp. opport. doctr. otherwise seems to apply, check whether the fact pattern contains signs that the corp. ***wouldn't have been able to take advantage*** of the opportunity even had it known of the opportunity. Say that courts are ***split*** about whether corporate inability (e.g., ***lack of financial resources***) can be a defense.

☛ Be alert for duty-of-loyalty issues where the fact pattern involves ***executive compensation***. Make sure that the corp. is receiving some benefit as a result of the compensation scheme — if it's not, it's likely to be invalid as a ***"waste"*** of corporate assets.

☞ If a compensation arrangement is ***approved in advance*** by ***disinterested directors or disinterested s/h's***, this pretty much ***immunizes*** it from s/h attack, even if a court might otherwise believe the compensation is ***"excessive."*** (Courts are split as to whether this is true even where the person receiving the compensation is a ***senior executive*** who has ***participated in the process*** by which the compensation was set.)

☞ ***Stock options*** are ordinarily acceptable, provided they do not result in clearly excessive compensation.

☞ ***Retirement benefits*** may pose a problem, especially if they are awarded at the ***moment of retirement,*** without being part of a general or pre-existing plan. Here, a s/h could claim that this is waste (or without consideration), because the corp. isn't getting anything in return. (*Example:* At the moment when Bill, a senior manager at A Corp., says he's retiring, Prexy [pres. of A Corp.] makes a written promise to pay Bill a $4,000/mo. pension for life. A Corp. does not have any general pension plan. A s/h might successfully attack this promise as being waste and without consideration, in which case the court may order the promise not to be enforced.)

☛ Sometimes you'll have a problem of ***interlocking directors*** (X is a director of two corps who do business with each other). Here, say that the duty-of-loyalty problems are typically ***not as severe*** as where a director deals for himself: unless the director's ***own financial interest is substantially at stake***, the fact that he sits on both boards won't create a conflict when the two corps do a transaction together (as long as there's disclosure of the fact that the director sits on both boards).

Example: X is a director of both A Corp. and B Corp., and each corp. knows this. At a B Corp. meeting, X votes to have B Corp. buy certain property from A Corp. Unless X's financial stake in A Corp. (and the size of the transaction) are enough to give X a significant financial incentive to have B Corp buy the property, X's voting for the transaction is ***not*** a breach of his duty of loyalty to B.

☛ Keep in mind that a ***controlling s/h*** may (it's not clear) have an obligation to behave in a ***fiduciary manner*** towards minority holders. This principle is most likely to be applied if the majority tries to ***"freeze out"*** the minority. Be especially alert to freeze-out and other mis-treatment-of-minority problems if the corp. is a ***closely-held*** one.

Example: A, B, C, and D each own 25% of Corp. Corp. has always paid generous dividends to each s/h, since Corp's own operations don't need much capital. A, B, and C learn that D is desperately in need of cash, and is counting on continuation of the dividend stream. The 3 vote to suspend dividends for the sole reason of pressuring D, so that they can induce him to sell his stock back to Corp. cheaply. This is probably a violation of the duty of loyalty, since A, B and C have served their own interests rather than the interests of all holders.

☛ Even if you conclude that there's been a breach of the duty of loyalty, be sure to check that the corp. has suffered an ***actual loss*** — if there's no actual loss, then there can't be any recovery.

CHAPTER 8

INSIDER TRADING (AND RELATED TOPICS)

ChapterScope

This Chapter mainly discusses the rules that prohibit corporate insiders from trading in their corporation's publicly-held stock while in the possession of non-public information. Key concepts:

- **Definition:** Most commonly, insider trading occurs when a corporate "insider" (generally an employee or director of the corporation whose shares are being traded) buys or sells the corporation's stock, at a time when he knows material non-public information about the company's prospects.
- **State laws:** State law provides very little protection against insider trading.
- **10b-5:** Federal law prohibits insider trading. The main federal prohibition comes from SEC Rule ***10b-5***.
  - **Private right of action:** A person who has been harmed by an insider's trading (e.g., a non-insider who sold stock while the insider was buying) has the right to bring a ***private civil suit*** against the insider for damages.
  - **"Insider," "tippee" or "misappropriator":** A person isn't liable for insider trading unless he is either an ***"insider,"*** a ***"tippee,"*** or a ***"misappropriator."*** An "insider" is one who learned the information either as an employee or director of the corporation whose stock is being traded (true insider) or as one who was performing services for the corporation, such as a lawyer or accountant (constructive insider). A "tippee" is one who learned the information from an insider. A "misappropriator" is one who learned the information from one other than the issuing corporation, and breached a confidence by trading on the information.
- **Short-swing trading profits:** Entirely apart from true "insider trading," § 16(b) of the Securities Exchange Act says that the profit from any purchase-and-sale or sale-and-purchase of a public company's stock within 6 months by an officer, director or 10%-shareholder must be repaid to the corporation. This is the ban on "short-swing trading profits." This rule applies even if the insider does not in fact have any non-public information at the time he trades.

I. INTRODUCTION TO INSIDER TRADING

A. Definition of insider trading: As the term is used in everyday discourse, a person engages in "insider trading" if he ***buys or sells stock in a publicly-traded company based on material non-public information about that company***. Clark, p. 264. This very broad definition is the one we will have in mind when we use the phrase "insider trading" in this book.

1. Not all kinds illegal: You might think that all kinds of insider trading (as we've just defined it) are illegal under federal or state law principles. But interestingly, this is not so.

a. **Illustration:** For instance, suppose that Jones is sitting by himself in a restaurant and happens to overhear Smith tell his dining companion at the next table, "I just heard that we brought in a huge new well off the coast of Saudi Arabia." Jones happens to know that Smith and his companion both work for Oilco, a major oil company. Jones can buy stock in Oilco with impunity, even though he is acting on material non-public information. (See the discussion of *Chiarella v. U.S.*, *infra*, p. 274, and our discussion of the limits of SEC Rule 10b-5 *infra*, p. 267.) In general, the federal securities laws (which are the most important laws in this area) bar only that insider trading that occurs as the result of someone's willful breach of a ***fiduciary duty***, and no one in our Jones-Smith example has committed such a breach.

b. **Broad meaning:** In any event, when we use the phrase "insider trading," we'll be using this broad "not-necessarily-illegal trading based on non-public information" sense of the term, and much of our discussion will be devoted to exactly when such trading is and is not illegal.

2. **Buying before disclosure of good news:** The paradigmatic example of insider trading (and in fact, insider trading of the clearly illegal variety) occurs when a high company official learns of some ***favorable development*** concerning his company, and buys stock in the company before this good news is disclosed to the public.

   Example: Prexy is the president of Oil Co., whose business is exploring for and then drilling for oil. Oil Co.'s stock is publicly traded, and investors interested in the company know that for some time, Oil Co. has been exploring a tract of remote Canada thought by most geologists to be unpromising. On July 1, Prexy learns that his exploration team has just struck what seems to be a substantial gusher at North Fork, Canada. He orders the team to keep silent about what they have found, and immediately purchases 10,000 shares of Oil Co. stock on the New York Stock Exchange at $20 a share. On July 2, he authorizes the company's public relations department to issue a press release stating "Major Gusher found by Oil Co. at North Fork." The stock immediately jumps to $30 a share. Prexy sells out the 10,000 shares, and pockets a profit of $100,000. (These facts are loosely adapted from *SEC v. Texas Gulf Sulphur Co.*, *infra*, p. 265.) Not only has Prexy traded on material non-public information, but his trading is of the clearly illegal variety, and he will face both criminal and civil liability under the federal securities laws.

3. **Selling on bad news:** Insider trading may also take the form of selling before the disclosure of ***bad news*** about the company's prospects.

   Example: Same facts as the prior example, except assume that on July 2, Prexy decides to hold onto his shares instead of selling them following the disclosure of the gusher. Then, on July 5, the gusher suddenly peters out, indicating that there was vastly less oil than the company (and the public) had thought. Before this news is disclosed to the public, Prexy now sells his 10,000 shares (plus another 5,000 he had bought long before) at $30 a share. The bad news is then disclosed to the public, and the stock sinks all the way back to $20 a share. Prexy has made a "profit" by this insider selling (in the sense that he has avoided a loss) of $150,000. His insider selling here is just as illegal as his purchases in the prior example, and he will be both civilly and criminally liable under the federal securities laws.

B. The Efficient Capital Markets Hypothesis: Before we delve into the harms (and possible benefits) from insider trading, we must understand an economic doctrine that has become very central to the way courts and commentators analyze insider trading problems. This is the so-called Efficient Capital Markets Hypothesis (ECMH). Essentially, the ECMH says that ***security prices at all times fully reflect available information***. See S,S,B&W, p. 899. In other words, the ECMH says that if on a particular day a share of IBM stock is selling for $126, then the $126 figure reflects everything that is now known about IBM's business prospects, and is therefore the true "value" of that share.

1. Three forms: Actually, there are three forms of the ECMH, which make progressively more broad-sweeping claims about the extent to which prices reflect available information:

a. Weak form: The ***"weak form"*** of the ECMH states that "prices fully reflect all information contained in the ***historical pattern*** of market prices." Cox, quoted in S,S,&B, p. 901. In other words, this form says that an investor cannot, merely by looking at the pattern of past prices of a particular stock (or, for that matter, past prices of the stock market as a whole), predict the course of future prices. To put it another way, according to the weak form of the ECMH ***stock price movements are random***. For instance, the mere fact that IBM stock has gone up three days in a row does not increase, at all, the likelihood that it will go up on the fourth day. This weak form of the ECMH is ***very well accepted*** by economists, but it is not so deeply relevant to the insider trading problem.

b. Semi-strong form: The ***"semi-strong form"*** of the ECMH says that "prices reflect all public information, including that in financial statements." Cox, *op. cit.* Thus if IBM is trading on a particular day at $126 per share, everything that is known to the public about IBM's business prospects is already reflected in that $126 price. If the "pure" form of the semi-strong hypothesis is accepted (that the "value" of IBM stock is always exactly reflected in the stock's price, insofar as that value can be determined from publicly available information), then two important corollaries emerge: (1) an investor without inside information ***can never systematically beat*** the market, and in fact the profession of "securities analyst" is worthless; and (2) an investor can always buy any share at any time at the prevailing market price without worrying whether the price is too high or too low, ***because the price will always be "fair"*** in the sense that the price will always reflect all publicly known information.

i. Significance: This corollary (2) is especially important for insider trading law, because it furnishes a way for an investor who has bought without the benefit of inside information to show that he has been harmed. For instance, in our example on p. 252, an investor who bought shares in Oil Co. on July 3 at $30 per share can say, "I relied on $30 per share being a fair price for Oil Co. stock, because I know that the market always reflects all available information about a company's prospects. Had Prexy made prompt disclosure that Oil Co. did not find as much oil as had previously been announced, the price would have dropped, I would have paid

$20 a share instead of $30 a share, and I would have avoided an ultimate loss of $10 a share." See the discussion of the "fraud on the market" theory, *infra*, p. 280.

ii. Widely accepted: The semi-strong form of the ECMH is fairly ***well accepted*** by economists. See S,S,&B, pp. 900-01. Actually, for purposes of analyzing insider trading, it doesn't even matter whether the true "value" of a company is always reflected in its stock. All that is required is that particular ***new pieces of public information*** become ***rapidly reflected*** in the company's share price. Virtually all economists would agree that the semi-strong version of the ECMH is correct in this "information arbitrage" sense. See S,S,B&W, p. 904. In other words, it is well accepted that when a material fact is disclosed, this information is immediately reflected in the stock's price, and the price of a stock is therefore always "fair" in this sense of reflecting all recent publicly known events.

c. Strong hypothesis: The ***"strong"*** version of the ECMH says that "prices fully reflect ***all*** information including ***non-public*** or ***'inside'*** information." Cox, *op. cit.* But here, there is a substantial body of evidence that the strong ECMH is ***wrong***, i.e., that stock prices do not always reflect information known to insiders but not known to the public. Cox, quoted at S,S,B&W, p. 903. This means that ***insider trading probably pays off in the long run*** — a person trading on insider information about his company will probably "beat the market." If this is true, it is important, because it means that: (1) insiders do indeed have a strong economic incentive to trade based on inside information; and (2) insiders who trade on their inside information will end up — arguably unfairly — richer than outsiders who play the same securities-trading game.

C. Harms from insider trading: What's wrong with insider trading? Why should there be a huge federal effort to stop it? The possible harms from insider trading can be divided into four main types:

1. Harm to corporation: Some people have argued that insider trading hurts the ***corporation*** whose stock is being traded. For example, if a corporation's top managers are seen to be routinely engaging in insider trading in the company's stock, the public may come to view the corporation itself as being sloppily and inefficiently run, and its management as dishonest. This might make it harder for the company to raise money by selling new stock, to find customers for its products, etc.

a. Weak effect: However, if this damage-to-the-corporation effect exists at all, it is probably very weak, and is certainly not sufficient to support the very strong public policy against insider trading. Clark, p. 266.

2. Harm to investors: Second, insider trading may cause harm to certain ***investors*** who trade during the period of non-disclosure. If investors are injured, the injured ones may be (but will not necessarily be) the ones who actually take the opposite side of the trade with the insider. The injured investors will, however, be the ones who trade ***opposite from the way*** the insider trades (i.e., those who buy when the insider is selling, or who sell when the insider is buying). How are these "opposite traders" harmed?

a. How harm might occur: First, realize that the question that should be asked is not "How has the outsider done less well than the insider?" Instead, the question should be "How has the outsider done less well than he would have done in the absence of insider trading?" In other words, an outsider should be viewed as having being harmed only if he somehow ***does something different*** than he would have done had there been no insider trading.

b. Traders who behave differently: If one believes the semi-strong form of the Efficient Capital Markets Hypothesis, once disclosure of the formerly inside information finally takes place the stock will trade at its "true" value. Therefore, the only investor who can be hurt by insider trading is one who trades ***during the period of non-disclosure***. Furthermore, even an investor who trades during this non-disclosure period is harmed only if his conduct is ***different than it would have been had there not been any insider trading***. For many if not most outsiders who trade during the period of non-disclosure, their conduct (and the financial results to them) are no different than they would have been had there been no insider trading at all — the outsider would have made the trade anyway, and at the same price.

i. "Induced" trader: On the other hand, some outsiders may indeed take a different action because of the insider's trading.

Example: Assume the same basic facts involving the oil well as in our example on p. 252. But this time, assume that Prexy's purchase of shares on July 1 was large enough relative to the other trading in the stock that it *raised the price* of Oil Co. shares from $20 to, say, $23 per share. Now, assume that Outsider would never have sold out at the pre-July-1 price of $20, but that the rise to $23 *induced* him to sell.

Here, we can at least make a plausible case that Outsider has been directly harmed by the insider trading: he has been "suckered" into selling for a small gain ($3 per share over the earlier price) whereas, had Prexy not caused the price to rise $3 by his insider trading, Outsider could instead have benefited from a sudden rise to $30 when the company eventually made its announcement about the gusher. So such an "induced" seller (and, conversely, an outsider who is induced to buy by a small drop that results from insider's selling before the disclosure of bad news) are the only kinds of investors who can really be said to have been directly harmed by the insider trading. See Wang, 54 S.Cal.L.Rev. (cited in S,S,B&W, pp. 910-11).

(1) Large traders: Observe that this harm to "induced" sellers and buyers will only occur where the insider trading is ***large enough*** relative to the non-insider trading in the stock that the insider trading ***affects the market price***. S,S,B&W, p. 911.

3. Delayed disclosure: Perhaps the most concrete harm from insider trading is that it interferes with the ***prompt disclosure*** of important corporate information that should (and would) otherwise be immediately released to the public. For instance, in our oil well example, Prexy might have caused Oil Co. to ***immediately announce*** the gusher as soon as it was discovered on July 1; his desire to trade on the inside information caused him to delay the disclosure at least long enough to carry off his insider trading.

a. Nature of harm: Why is such delayed disclosure bad? Three plausible reasons can be given:

i. **Inefficiencies:** First, it distorts the ***efficiency*** of the capital markets — stock prices are less often "correct" because the information they are responding to is more often out-of-date. Consequently, our economy will not be ***allocating its resources*** as well.

ii. **Equal access:** Secondly, most of us have a basic psychological and moral sense that the markets should function on the basis of ***equal access to information***. A market in which insiders have information that (because of delayed disclosure) outsiders do not have, is like playing in a card game where the other guy has a marked deck. Indeed, this generalized notion that fairness requires equal access to information is probably the single most important factor behind the rules against insider trading.

iii. **Harm to market:** A third, related, harm from delayed disclosure is that if investors in general believe that insiders have the advantage (that the game is "unfair"), they are likely to ***boycott the stock market***. If there are fewer investors than there otherwise would be (or if investors demand a higher return on their investment for putting up with the perceived unfairness of insider trading), firms' ***cost of capital will rise***. This will in turn disadvantage the corporate sector of the economy vis-a-vis other investments (e.g., treasury bills), and will make it harder for the corporate sector to grow.

4. **Harm to efficiency from secret profits:** Finally, the pursuit of insider trading may cause managers to run their companies in an ***inefficient manner***. If we completely legalize insider trading, insiders would probably be able to make trading profits that are much larger than the salaries they now receive. This might lead them to be less diligent in increasing shareholder value. (For instance, they might concentrate their energies on spotting opportunities to sell the company's shares short in anticipation of soon-to-be-released bad news, rather than on running the company well.) Also, they might be inclined to take ***riskier actions*** than the outsiders would want. (Their main incentive, as managers primarily interested in trading profits, would be to cause large changes in the company's prospects, to be followed by large moves in the stock; because of their ability to engage in either purchases or short-sales, they wouldn't care so much whether the results increased the company's share price.) See Clark, pp. 274-75.

D. **Arguments in support of insider trading:** A small group of commentators has argued that insider trading has ***beneficial*** effects, and should be tolerated if not encouraged. Here are the two principal arguments made in behalf of insider trading:

1. **Market price quickly reflects new information:** First, insider trading arguably causes the company's stock price to ***better reflect new (unannounced) developments***. There are two asserted sub-benefits: (1) stock prices ***move more smoothly***; and (2) a company's stock price is ***closer to its "true" value*** at most times, than where there is no insider trading and the previously secret information is suddenly announced, causing a sharp rise or drop in the stock price. (This, in turn, is asserted to be economically desirable because "correct" stock pricing helps allocate capital efficiently. See *supra*, p. 256.)

2. **Compensation for entrepreneurs:** Second, the advocates of insider trading argue that it often furnishes reasonable ***compensation*** for managers, and gives otherwise risk-averse

managers an additional incentive to take riskier, but nonetheless economically sensible, corporate action. Under this argument, "a manager will be more willing to take risks if he knows that he can profit by selling short prior to public disclosure of the failure." S,S,B&W, p. 914.

a. **Criticism:** But this argument is even more strongly criticized by the anti-insider-trading forces. The critics point out that if this argument is correct, the manager won't care whether the company does well or badly, since he can profit in either case. Therefore, his incentive to run the firm in a way that enhances its value for outside shareholders will be compromised. Also, it is doubtful whether the bulk of insider traders are corporate "entrepreneurs" who will if properly motivated create true value for the corporation; they are just as likely to be lower-level functionaries who will have no real impact on the firm's fortunes either way, and who therefore do not need any of this special insider trading "incentive compensation." See Clark, p. 279.

E. **Summary:** In summary, most observers believe that insider trading is, on balance, ***harmful***. Certainly federal law (and, increasingly, the laws of many states) reflect uniformly the belief that insider trading is unfair to public investors and economically inefficient.

F. **Summary of law:** There are three principal bodies of law that proscribe and punish insider trading (or, at least, certain types of insider trading). We will be considering each of these in some detail below. For now, let us just mention each:

1. **State common law:** A few states bar certain kinds of insider trading by the application of ***state common-law*** principles. The states are especially likely to bar trading by an insider that is accompanied by ***face-to-face fraud*** (e.g., the insider simply lies about the company's prospects while making a face-to-face trade with an outsider). In the more common situation of an insider buying or selling on the impersonal ***stock market***, while simply remaining silent about the existence of material non-public information, apparently ***only one state court*** has found the insider liable under common-law principles; see *Diamond v. Oreamuno*, *infra*, p. 261.

2. **Federal SEC Rule 10b-5:** Most importantly, the federal SEC Rule 10b-5 prohibits any fraudulent or manipulative device in connection with the purchase or sale of a security. This has been interpreted to bar ***most kinds of insider trading***. A violation of 10b-5 can give rise to criminal liability, to SEC injunctive proceedings, and to a private right of action on the part of outside investors who have been injured. Our extensive discussion of 10b-5 begins on p. 262.

3. **Short swing profits:** Finally, § 16(b) of the federal Securities Exchange Act makes insiders liable to repay to the corporation all profits they make from so-called ***"short swing trading profits."*** Briefly, if the insider buys and then sells within a six month period, or sells and then buys within a six month period, he must ***repay to the corporation*** all of the profits. This is true whether the insider is actually relying on material non-public information or not — it is a categorical rule designed to remove much of the incentive from at least short-swing insider trading. See *infra*, p. 305.

G. **Who can recover:** Even where it is clear that the insider is civilly liable for insider trading, an important issue remains: ***who*** can recover? Usually, the choice is between allowing recovery by the ***corporation itself***, or allowing the recovery to go to certain ***outside investors*** who have in some way been harmed by the insider's trading. In the Rule 10b-5 context, it is usually the private investors who recover. In the § 16(b) cases, by contrast, it is always the corporation that recovers.

II. STATE COMMON-LAW APPROACHES

A. **Common-law rules generally:** State common law has placed only very minor limits on insider trading. Therefore, most barriers to insider trading today come from federal rather than state regulation. However, because federal private suits against insider traders have become somewhat harder to bring since 1976, state law remedies may become more important. Therefore, it is worth spending some time on the state common law that pertains to insider trading.

B. **Suits by shareholders:** First, let's consider an action by a ***shareholder*** against the insider trader.

1. **Action for deceit:** A shareholder plaintiff who wants to sue an insider trader under state law will generally have to use the common-law action of ***deceit***. Traditionally, the plaintiff in a deceit action has been required to show five things: (1) that P justifiably ***relied***; (2) to his ***detriment***; (3) on a ***misrepresentation*** of a material fact; (4) made by the defendant with ***knowledge*** of its falsity (or at least with reckless disregard for its truth); and (5) with ***intent*** that the plaintiff rely. See S,S,B&W, p. 919-20.

   a. **Misrepresentation:** Where the insider makes an actual ***misrepresentation*** in a ***face-to-face*** transaction with the plaintiff, the plaintiff has a reasonable chance of winning in a deceit action. So if Insider says to Outsider, "Our profits are going to be down next quarter," and this knowing falsehood induces Outsider to sell to Insider cheaply, Outsider has a *prima facie* case for deceit at common law.

   b. **Half-truth:** In fact, the insider will be liable under general common-law deceit principles if he knowingly tells a ***half-truth***, i.e., he discloses part of the truth, but his failure to disclose the rest of the truth has the effect of misleading the other party. For instance, if Insider truthfully tells Outsider, "Profits will be down this quarter," but neglects to mention that a third party has offered to buy the company at an above-market price, Insider's statement is a half-truth that will probably give rise to liability for deceit if Outsider is induced to sell cheaply to Insider. C&E, p. 815.

   c. **Silence:** But where the Insider simply ***remains silent*** and buys or sells based on material non-public information, the common-law remedy of deceit is of little use. The problem is that, as noted above, one of the requirements for an action in deceit is a ***misrepresentation***, and the insider who silently buys has simply made no misrepresentation. The "silent insider" problem is discussed more fully immediately below.

2. **Silent trading:** In general, the common law does ***not*** impose upon a party to a transaction any ***duty to disclose*** facts known to him. There *is* a duty to disclose where the defendant has some ***fiduciary responsibility*** to the plaintiff, growing out of some special relationship between them. But the majority common-law rule is that an insider (officer, director or controlling shareholder) has a fiduciary obligation only to the corporation, not to other present or prospective shareholders. Therefore, there is simply ***no way*** for an

investor to bring a successful deceit action against the insider who buys or sells ***silently*** based on ***inside information***.

Example: D1 (president and director of Cliff Mining Co.) and D2 (a director of Cliff) are aware that an experienced geologist believes that copper deposits will be found under the company's land. At a time when the public (including P) does not know of this geological prediction, P sells his Cliff shares on the Boston Stock Exchange, and those shares happen to be bought by the Ds. P brings a common-law deceit action, arguing that had he known of the geologist's report, he would not have sold his shares.

Held, for the Ds. Directors and officers of a company may owe a fiduciary responsibility to the company, but they do not owe any fiduciary responsibility to individual shareholders. Therefore, the Ds had no obligation to P to make any kind of disclosure prior to the purchase. "An honest director would be in a difficult situation if he could neither buy nor sell on the stock exchange shares of stock in his corporation without first seeking out the other actual ultimate party to the transaction and disclosing to him everything which a court or jury might later find that he then knew. . . ." *Goodwin v. Agassiz*, 186 N.E. 659 (Mass. 1933).

a. **Impersonal transactions:** In the case of ***impersonal transactions*** on the stock exchange, *Goodwin* represents not only the majority but essentially the sole rule: the insider who ***buys silently on the exchange*** simply has ***no common-law liability to the other party*** to the trade.

b. **Face-to-face transactions:** Where the insider buys from the outsider in a ***face-to-face*** transaction, the majority rule still seems to be that the insider has ***no affirmative duty of disclosure***, and is therefore ***not liable if he simply remains silent.*** C&E, p. 814-15. But in this face-to-face situation, there are some well-accepted ***exceptions***, as well as a minority rule:

   i. **Fraud:** First, if the insider knowingly ***lies*** or tells a ***half-truth***, he will be liable under ordinary deceit principles, as discussed above.

   ii. **"Special facts" exception:** Second, many states recognize a ***"special facts"*** exception to the majority rule that silence cannot constitute deceit. Under this loose exception, if there are special facts that make the insider's conduct ***especially unfair***, he will be liable even though he remains silent. For example, if he ***seeks out*** the other party to the transaction, or if he makes affirmative efforts to ***conceal*** either his own identity or material facts about the company's fortunes, the court is likely to find the requisite "special facts" and impose liability.

   Example: D is a director and three-fourths owner of Philippine Sugar Co. The company is in bad financial shape, and the public knows that the only way the shares will go up is if the company is able to sell its properties to the U.S. government. The negotiations have dragged on for a long time, and the public believes they will fall through. D (who as three-fourths owner and director controls the price at which the company will sell) secretly resolves to consummate the sale to the government. D learns that P has some shares for sale. D has an intermediary use a broker to buy P's shares, in such a way that P never learns that D is the purchaser or that D is about to consummate the sale to the government. The price D pays for P's shares is one-tenth what the shares become worth three months later after the sale to the government is carried out.

Held, P can recover against D for fraud. The special facts here, including D's total control over whether and when a sale would be made to the government and his concealment of his identity from P, would make it unjust to deny P a recovery against him. *Strong v. Rapide*, 213 U.S. 419 (1909).

iii. Minority rule: Furthermore, a minority of states have imposed the more general rule that in face-to-face negotiations, an insider has an affirmative ***obligation to disclose*** material facts known to him. This minority rule is sometimes called the "Kansas Rule."

3. Summary: So at common law, if Insider buys from Outsider in a face-to-face transaction, Outsider can recover if any of the following is true:

(1) Insider ***affirmatively lies*** to Outsider about the company's prospects;

(2) Insider tells a ***misleading half-truth***;

(3) there are ***"special facts"*** making Insider's conduct unfair (e.g., he has ***concealed his identity*** from Outsider); or

(4) the jurisdiction follows the ***minority*** or "Kansas" rule, and Insider has failed to make full disclosure.

a. Not covered: But in cases where the transaction is not face-to-face, and is instead carried out through the impersonal stock exchanges, and in cases where the insider remains completely silent in a jurisdiction that follows the majority rule (as in *Goodwin*), the common-law approach leaves the outsider with no remedy for insider trading.

b. No recovery against seller: Also, apparently no case has ever awarded a recovery against an insider who ***sold*** on the basis of inside information. This may be because everyone has assumed that an insider couldn't possibly owe any kind of duty of disclosure to one who was ***not yet*** a stockholder. Clark, p. 311.

c. Weak remedies: So in general, the common-law remedies for insider trading have been very ***weak*** at best.

C. Recovery by corporation: Given the difficulties that individual shareholders find at common law in recovering for insider trading, may the ***corporation itself*** recover for insider trading in its shares by one of its officers or directors?

1. Harm to corporation: First, consider the situation in which the corporation is ***actually harmed*** by the insider's trading in its shares. There are practically no cases on the subject, but general duty-of-loyalty and duty-of-care principles (*supra*, pp. 197 and 169) suggest that the corporation could recover at common law for the damage to it. A court could quite plausibly hold that the insider information used by the officer or director was really a ***corporate asset***, and that the insider may not put his own interests ahead of the interests of the corporation in the use of that asset.

Example: Suppose that Insider, a director of Corporation, knows that Corporation will soon be buying back a large portion of its shares from public shareholders. Insider expects that the announcement of this buy-back will cause the shares to rise. Before the announcement, he buys an additional 5% of Corporation's shares himself, thereby driving up the price. When Corporation carries out its buyback, it is forced to pay a higher price because of the rise due to Insider's purchases. A court would probably allow Corporation to recover from Insider for the extra amount it had to pay, on the theory that Insider breached his duty of loyalty to Corporation by appropriating the information (knowledge of the impending buyback).

2. **No corporate harm:** But in the usual insider trading situation, the corporation will ***not*** suffer direct financial or other quantifiable harm. If the corporation suffers no direct loss, may it nonetheless recover against the insider on the theory that he has been unjustly enriched by his use of a corporate asset (the inside information)? Only ***one major case*** has ever answered ***"yes."*** This is the New York Court of Appeals' decision in *Diamond v. Oreamuno*, 248 N.E.2d 910 (N.Y. 1969).

   a. **Importance of *Diamond:*** In *Diamond*, the New York Court of Appeals essentially held that inside ***information is a corporate asset***, and that an insider who profits by trading upon that information has ***violated his fiduciary duty to the corporation*** and must ***turn over to the corporation any profits he has made*** (or losses he has avoided) from the trading, even though the corporation did not suffer direct financial loss.

   b. **Rejected by other courts:** ***No other state court*** has accepted the rationale of *Diamond*, and thus no court has allowed recovery on behalf of the corporation where the corporation cannot show direct injury from the insider trading. Nutshell, p. 340.

   c. **ALI follows *Diamond*:** But the ALI's Principles of Corporate Governance ***follow Diamond***. ALI § 5.04(a) provides that:

      §5.04 Use by a Director or Senior Executive of Corporate Property, Material Non-Public Corporate Information, or Corporate Position

      (a) *General Rule.* A director or senior executive ***may not use*** corporate property, ***material non-public corporate information***, or corporate position to ***secure a pecuniary benefit***, unless either: . . .

      (3) The use is solely of ***corporate information***, and is ***not in connection with trading of the corporation's securities***, is not a use of proprietary information of the corporation, and does not harm the corporation; . . .

      i. **Extensive liability:** The ALI says that even if the corporation does not suffer any actual harm, it may recover for ***"unjust enrichment"*** by the insider, under § 5.04(a)(5). In fact, the ALI section goes even further than any reported case has, to contemplate the possibility that a ***tippee*** (one who receives the non-public information from an insider, and uses it for his own benefit) may also be liable under this provision, perhaps on the theory that the tippee has knowingly participated in a breach of the duty of loyalty owed by the insider to the corporation. § 5.04, Comment d(2)(a).

III. SEC RULE 10b-5 AND INSIDER TRADING

A. Securities Exchange Act § 10(b): Section 10 of the Securities Exchange Act of 1934 (the "'34 Act") provides:

> **Regulation of the use of manipulative and deceptive devices.**
>
> It shall be ***unlawful*** for any person, ***directly or indirectly***, by the use of any means or instrumentality of ***interstate commerce*** or of the mails, or of any ***facility of any national securities exchange*** . . .
>
> (b) to use or employ, ***in connection with the purchase or sale of any security*** registered on a national securities exchange or any security not so registered, any ***manipulative or deceptive device*** or contrivance in ***contravention of such rules and regulations*** as the [SEC] may prescribe as necessary or appropriate in the public interest or for the protection of investors.

1. **Analysis:** Notice that nothing is directly made illegal by this § 10(b) — only to the extent that the SEC enacts a ***rule*** prohibiting certain conduct pursuant to this section can there be any criminal liability. Furthermore, observe that nothing in § 10(b) gives any hint that investors injured by fraudulent conduct of the sort that § 10(b) seems to be directed at would have a ***private right of action***.

B. SEC's enactment of Rule 10b-5: It was not until 1942 that the SEC finally enacted a rule that would put some meat into the general anti-fraud prohibition of § 10(b). The Commission did this by enacting ***Rule 10b-5*** (i.e., its fifth rule pertaining to section 10(b) of the '34 Act). That rule reads today as follows:

> It shall be unlawful for any person, directly or indirectly, by the use of any means or instrumentality of interstate commerce, or of the mails, or of any facility of any national securities exchange,
>
> (a) to employ any device, scheme, or artifice to ***defraud***,
>
> (b) to make any ***untrue statement of a material fact*** or to ***omit to state*** a material fact necessary in order to make the statements made, in the light of the circumstances under which they were made, not misleading, or
>
> (c) to engage in any act, practice, or course of business which operates or would operate as a ***fraud*** or ***deceit*** upon any person
>
> ***in connection with the purchase or sale of any security.***

1. **Purpose:** The rule was initially enacted to prevent insiders from making explicit fraudulent statements to investors about how ***badly*** the company was doing, so that the insiders could buy up the shares cheaply. At the time of its enactment, the Commission staff did not focus on the typical insider-trading paradigm (purchases or sales by insiders who remain completely ***silent*** about the company's condition). And the Commission certainly did not foresee that the rule might give rise to a private right of action by investors; it was intended solely to let the SEC stop fraudulent activity. *Id.*

2. **Broad application:** But the actual application of Rule 10b-5 has grown far beyond what the Commission intended at the time of drafting. Perhaps the three most important extensions are:

   (1) The rule applies to ***any form*** of deceit or fraud, including the garden-variety case in which the insider ***silently*** buys or sells on material non-public information (and thus never makes any affirmative misrepresentation);

(2) The rule applies to one who makes a ***misrepresentation*** that induces others to buy or sell, even if the ***maker*** of the misrepresentation ***never buys or sells*** himself; and

(3) Perhaps most dramatically, an investor who meets several procedural requirements may bring a ***private suit*** alleging a violation of 10b-5, and may recover damages for that violation.

Our detailed treatment of Rule 10b-5 will consider in detail each of these extensions, among other issues.

3. **What constitutes insider trading:** Before we get into the details of 10b-5, let's summarize, in a semi-accurate way, the elements that must be present before a defendant will be found to have insider-traded in violation of 10b-5. In this discussion, we're not considering who may sue.[1]

D will be found to have insider-traded in violation of 10b-5 if (and only if) all these elements are present:

❑ D ***bought or sold stock*** in a company (the "issuer"). The issuer will usually be, but need not be, a publicly-traded company.

❑ At the time D bought or sold, he was in possession of ***information*** that was ***"material,"*** i.e., would be considered ***important to a reasonable investor*** in the issuer's stock.

❑ The material information (referred to in the prior step) was ***non-public*** at the moment D bought or sold.

❑ D had a ***special relationship*** with the ***source*** of the information (either the issuer or someone else who possessed the inside information[2]). D meets this requirement if he was a true ***insider*** of the issuer (e.g., an employee), or was a ***"constructive insider"*** (i.e., in possession of confidential information that the issuer temporarily entrusted him with, such as a lawyer working as outside counsel for the issuer). He also meets it if he was a ***"tippee,"*** who was given the information by an insider (a "tipper") in violation of the insider's fiduciary duty. Lastly, he meets the requirement if he was a ***"misappropriator,"*** i.e., an "outsider" vis a vis the issuer who gets the information from ***one other than the issuer*** (e.g., from a potential acquirer of the issuer), in breach of a promise of confidentiality.

❑ D meets the ***jurisdictional requirements***. That is, he traded "by the use of any means or instrumentality of interstate commerce or of the mails, or of any facility of any national securities exchange." In the case of a publicly-traded stock, this requirement is always met.

C. **Development of 10b-5's application to insider trading:** It took two developments to make Rule 10b-5 a really useful weapon against insider trading: (1) the judicial conclusion that there

---

1. The plaintiff may be either a private person or the SEC. For the elements that must be satisfied by a private plaintiff in a damages action, see *infra*, p. 283.

2. Under the "misappropriation theory" recognized by the Supreme Court, it's enough if D is in a fiduciary relationship with *someone other than the issuer* (e.g., a company planning a tender offer for the issuer). See the discussion of the misappropriation theory and *U.S. v. O'Hagan, infra*, p. 291.

should be an ***implied private right of action*** for violations of 10b-5; and (2) the conclusion that 10b-5 covers insider trading that takes place ***without any affirmative misrepresentation*** by the insider.

1. **Implied private right of action:** Almost from the beginning, the courts have held that when a person violates 10b-5, an investor injured by this violation may bring a ***civil suit for damages***, based on the violation. The text of 10b-5 itself (or, for that matter, the text of § 10(b) of the '34 Act, under which 10b-5 was promulgated) nowhere mentions any private civil action — the Rule consists merely of the SEC's statement that fraudulent or manipulative devices will be "unlawful." But the courts have consistently held that since investors in a company's securities are members of the class that the Rule was designed to protect, they should be able to recover in damages for violations of the Rule. (This is really nothing more than a federal application of the well-known state common-law principle allowing tort claims to be based upon statutory violations, as in the negligence *per se* doctrine. See Clark, p. 313.)

   a. **Explicit statutory right of action:** At least some private actions based on 10b-5 are now ***expressly*** authorized by statute. In 1988, Congress enacted the Insider Trading and Securities Fraud Enforcement Act of 1988 (ITSFEA). Section 20A of the '34 Act (added by ITSFEA) allows P to sue D if D bought or sold on inside information, and P bought or sold on the opposite side of the trade ***"contemporaneously"*** with D's trades. Section 20A is discussed more extensively *infra*, p. 283.

2. **Application to insider trading:** Rule 10b-5 certainly does not expressly state that an insider who buys or sells based on material non-public information, without making any affirmative misstatements, has engaged in "fraud or deceit." So it is not obvious from the text of 10b-5 that it applies to garden variety "silent" insider trading at all. But the SEC concluded that such garden variety insider trading does violate 10b-5, in its landmark opinion in *In re Cady, Roberts & Co.*, 40 S.E.C. 907 (1961).

3. **"Disclose or abstain" rule:** *Cady, Roberts* is also noteworthy as the first case in which the SEC articulated its ***"disclose or abstain"*** rule. Proponents of insider trading (and defendants in insider trading cases brought under state and federal principles) often argue that if the insider is required to disclose the inside information, the disclosure will happen ***prematurely*** and the corporation may suffer. But the SEC's answer to this argument is that the insider has a ***choice***: he must ***either*** disclose the inside information or abstain from trading. In other words, the insider is ***never required by 10b-5 to make disclosure of any facts***, no matter how material; all that 10b-5 requires is that the insider ***not trade while in possession*** of such undisclosed information.

   a. **Affirmative obligations:** This "disclose or abstain from trading" rule remains the law. It also remains the case (at least as a matter of federal securities law) that ***companies*** and insiders ***never have an affirmative duty to disclose a material fact*** that, in their rational business judgment, they think would better serve the company's interests by remaining nondisclosed. Of course, in the case of a public company, eventually documents will have to be filed with the SEC (e.g., the 10-Q quarterly report and 10-K annual report) that must disclose material developments; also, the rules of the various stock exchanges typically require immediate disclosure of "ripe" material company information. And, of course, the company itself is an "insider," so if it has not released material news, it may not ***buy back*** its own shares or sell new ones to the public. But there is no federal provision that makes it a crime to fail to disclose material information, so long as no stock trading takes place during the period of nondisclosure.

4. **Private companies:** Perhaps surprisingly, Rule 10b-5 applies to fraud in the purchase or sale of securities in ***privately held*** companies as well as publicly held ones. 10b-5 itself refers merely to fraud, deceit, etc. in connection with the purchase or sale of "any security." "Security" is defined in § 3(10) of the '34 Act in a very general way, with no limitation to publicly held stock. Therefore, if D sells P all of the stock of Dry Cleaning Corp., a corporation solely owned and operated by D which runs a drycleaning business, P actually has a federal securities-law claim if he can show that D made intentional misrepresentations about the company (assuming the other procedural requirements for 10b-5 actions are met).

5. ***Texas Gulf Sulphur* case:** Before we begin looking at the individual issues raised by Rule 10b-5's application to insider trading, it's worth looking in detail at a seminal case: ***SEC v. Texas Gulf Sulphur Co.***, 401 F.2d 833 (2d Cir. 1968). This case is important for several reasons: (1) Because it involves complex, evolving facts (indeed, it reads a lot like a law school exam question!), it will give you a good sense of the various insider trading problems that can come up in ordinary corporate life; (2) It was the first major case in which a court (rather than just the SEC) asserted that silent trading in the impersonal securities markets on the basis of material non-public information violated 10b-5; (3) It was the first major case in which the SEC successfully compelled insiders to disgorge their trading profits, thus encouraging a raft of private actions for damages; and (4) It was decided by a very smart and well-respected court, the Second Circuit (sitting *en banc*).

   a. **Facts:** Texas Gulf Sulphur (TGS) had been looking for minerals in eastern Canada for a number of years. In early November, 1963, it drilled a test hole at K-55-1 near Timmins, Ontario. This test core showed a higher percentage of minerals (copper, zinc and silver) than TGS's geologists had ever seen before. From November until February, 1964, TGS stopped drilling to keep its find confidential (and so that it could obtain leases on additional nearby acreage).

      i. **Shares bought:** During this non-drilling period, various employees of TGS, including four members of the geological team, the president, the executive vice president, the general counsel and a director bought lots of TGS stock and "calls" (options to buy) on TGS stock.

      ii. **Options issued:** Also during this non-drilling time, TGS issued stock options to a number of high-level employees, including five who knew about the Timmins find. (The board of directors and the Stock Options Committee, at the time they awarded these options, did not know of the Timmins find.)

      iii. **Misleading press release:** Drilling resumed in late March, 1964, and immediately produced very favorable results. Rumors about a major ore strike began to circulate. To diffuse speculation the company released on April 12 a ***press release*** that said that the rumors "exaggerate the scale of operations" at Timmins, and that the work done to date "has not been sufficient to reach definite conclusions and any statement as to size and grade of ore would be premature and possibly misleading." But in fact, at the moment of the news release TGS had already discovered at least $150 million worth of minerals.

iv. **Final announcement:** TGS finally made the press release announcing a sizable strike on April 16. Some of the employees of TGS who knew of the strike continued to buy stock between the April 12 press release and the final April 16 announcement.

v. **Stock price:** The stock price had increased gradually during the entire time following the original November 8 test core: When drilling began, the stock traded at around $17. The day TGS finally announced the strike, the stock closed at $36.

vi. **SEC's suit:** The SEC sued the employees who had traded with knowledge of the probable strike between November 8 and April 16; it sought to make them disgorge their trading profits. It also sued TGS itself, on the theory that although TGS did not buy or sell its own shares during this period, by issuing the misleading April 12 press release it induced outsiders to sell at prices lower than they would have gotten had the misleading release not been issued.

b. **Holding:** The court found ***in favor of the SEC*** on virtually all points. A number of aspects of the court's holding are worthy of special notice:

c. **Court adopts "disclose or abstain" rule:** The court adopted the ***"disclose or abstain"*** rule urged by the SEC, under which an insider with material non-public information must choose between disclosing it to the public or abstaining from trading in the stock.

d. **"Material" inside information:** The court defined ***"material"*** inside information to be information "[to which] a reasonable man would ***attach importance*** . . . in determining his choice of action in the transaction in question." This definition was later adopted by the Supreme Court in *Basic Inc. v. Levinson*, *infra*, p. 272. The insiders were not required to give outsiders the benefit of their "financial or other expert analysis" or to disclose their "educated guesses or predictions." But the basic objective fact — that drilling had produced test cores with a high mineral content — was clearly the kind of fact that an investor would regard as important in deciding whether to buy, sell or hold, and was therefore "material."

i. **Importance attached by those who knew:** An interesting aspect of the court's treatment of "materiality" was that it attached great significance to the importance that a fact holds to ***those who know about it*** inside the company. Here, the frenetic pattern of trading activity by those who knew of the drilling results was strong circumstantial evidence that these insiders thought the fact was important, and thus strong evidence that the drilling results were "material."

e. **Time to disseminate information:** The court held that it is not enough that the insiders have waited until the company has made a public announcement of the inside information. Rather, they must wait until this information has been ***widely disseminated*** to the marketplace. For instance, the insiders were required to wait until the news had appeared over the most widely-circulated medium, the Dow Jones "broad tape," not merely until the news had been read to members of the press.

f. Receipt of stock options: The court held that it was a form of insider trading for a high-level executive to ***receive stock options***, where the executive knew the inside information and the committee awarding the stock options did not. In other words, receipt of stock options by, say, the corporation's general counsel occurred "in connection with the purchase or sale of any security" (Rule 10b-5's language) even though the options were in a sense "given" to him. (But option recipients below high-level management were found not have any duty to disclose or refuse the options).

g. Press Release: Finally, the court held that ***TGS itself***, even though it did not buy or sell its own securities, could be found to have ***violated*** 10b-5 if it failed to use due diligence in preparing its news release. The release's great generality (at a time when much more interesting and specific information was available) was itself enough to make the report "misleading." (Today, it remains the case that a corporation can have 10b-5 liability for misleading statements even where it does not buy or sell its own stock; however, the corporation must be shown to have known of the falsity or recklessly disregarded the danger of falsity, so that a mere lack of due diligence as in *Texas Gulf Sulphur* would not suffice. See *infra*, p. 268.)

h. Remand: On remand, the district court ordered all TGS insiders who had bought stock or call options before the April 16 press release to ***disgorge their profits***. That is, they were required to pay the difference between the average price for TGS stock the day after the final disclosure, and the amount they had previously paid for the stock. The insiders were also required to pay damages equal to any profits made by their ***tippees*** (i.e., outsiders who learned of the drilling from the insiders). All of these damages were to be held for five years in a fund, which would be used to pay damages to outside investors who were injured by the insider trading (e.g., those who sold during the non-disclosure period for less than they would have gotten had disclosure been made). Any sums not paid over to private claimants at the end of five years were to become the property of the ***corporation*** itself. (In other words, to the extent that there were no successful private claimants, the action would be treated as if it had been a shareholder's derivative action.) *SEC v. Texas Gulf Sulphur Co.*, 312 F.Supp. 77 (S.D.N.Y. 1970), *aff'd* 446 F.2d 1301 (2d Cir. 1971).

D. Requirements for 10b-5 private action: As we noted previously, an outsider injured by insider trading may bring a private damage action under Rule 10b-5. However, the Supreme Court has set up a number of hurdles that the plaintiff must jump over in order to recover in this manner. Several of these requirements were imposed after 1975, when the Supreme Court apparently decided to make such actions tougher to bring. These requirements apply to all 10b-5 actions, whether based on an affirmative misrepresentation, a half-truth, or an omission to state material facts. (The usual insider trading case — involving an insider's "silent" trading while in possession of material non-public information — falls into the "omissions" sub-category; this sometimes introduces a special twist to the rules, and I comment on these twists separately.)

In any event, today the requirements for a successful 10b-5 damages suit seem to be as follows:

1. Purchaser or seller: The plaintiff must be a ***purchaser*** or ***seller*** of the company's stock during the time of non-disclosure. For instance, it is not enough that the plaintiff ***declined***

to buy because of false statements made by the company or an insider. See *Blue Chip Stamps v. Manor Drug Stores, infra*, p. 269.

2. **Traded on material non-public info:** The defendant must have misstated or omitted a ***material*** fact. If the claim is that the insider has traded "silently" (rather than by making a misrepresentation), then the silence is an omission that is "material" only if the undisclosed fact would have been ***important to a reasonable investor.*** (Remember that the insider has no affirmative duty to disclose, merely a duty to ***either*** disclose or abstain from trading.)

3. **Special relation:** If the claim is based on insider trading, the defendant must be shown to have had a ***special relationship*** with the issuer (or with someone other than the issuer who possessed the inside information), based on some kind of ***fiduciary duty***. For instance, if D happens to overhear a conversation in a restaurant that relates to XYZ Corp., a company that he has no other contact with, D has no duty to disclose or abstain, and he can thus trade freely on this inside information. See *Chiarella v. U.S., infra*, p. 274. (Generally, this requirement of a special relationship means that D must be shown to be either an ***insider***, or one who learned the information from the insider with knowledge that the insider had a fiduciary responsibility to protect the information, or a "misappropriator" who steals the information from someone. See *Dirks v. SEC, infra*, p. 276; *U.S. v. O'Hagan, infra*, p. 291.)

4. **Scienter:** The defendant must be shown to have acted with ***scienter***. In other words, the defendant must be shown to have had a mental state "embracing intent to ***deceive, manipulate, or defraud***." In the usual "silent" insider trading situation, this requirement is of little practical importance. But in the case of a defendant who is accused of having made an affirmative misrepresentation or half-truth, the requirement is important, because it forecloses liability for mere negligence. See *Ernst & Ernst v. Hochfelder, infra*, p. 277.

5. **Reliance:** The plaintiff must show that he ***relied*** on the defendant's misstatement or omission. In the case of an omission (as in the usual "silent" insider trading situation), this requirement is of little importance, because it is generally satisfied by giving the plaintiff the benefit of a presumption that he relied on the market price's being "fair." See *Basic Inc. v. Levinson, infra*, p. 280. (In fact, § 20A of the '34 Act, added in 1988, expressly gives any person who has bought or sold stock the right to sue any person who insider-traded in the opposite direction at the same time; no showing of reliance on the defendant's omission is required. See *infra*, p. 282.)

6. **Proximate cause:** The defendant's conduct must be shown to have been the ***proximate cause*** of the plaintiff's loss. In the usual silent insider trading situation, this requirement, like the requirement of reliance, is of little importance. For instance, P need not show that he traded directly with D; the mere fact that P bought at the market price, and this market price would have been different had D discharged his duty to disclose before trading, will be enough to show proximate cause. See *infra*, p. 281.

7. **Jurisdiction:** Don't forget that there's a ***federal-jurisdictional requirement*** for a 10b-5 action: the defendant must be shown to have done the fraud or manipulation "by the use of any means or instrumentality of ***interstate commerce*** or of the ***mails***, or of any ***facility of any national securities exchange."*** ('34 Act, § 10(b).)

a. **Normally met:** In the case of any ***publicly-traded security***, this requirement will readily be ***met***, even if the defendant ***didn't himself or itself buy or sell.*** Thus an issuer or executive who issues, say, a misleading press release (as in *Texas Gulf Sulphur*) can be liable even though it/she never bought or sold stock, as long as the release is reasonably connected to someone else's purchase or sale (e.g., a member of the public).

b. **Private face-to-face transactions:** But where the fraud consists of deceit in a ***face-to-face sale of shares***, especially shares in a ***private company***, then the jurisdictional requisites may well be ***lacking***.

Example: Prexy, owner of a majority position in privately-held Corp., tells Dupe, in a face-to-face meeting, "Our financial position is extremely strong." In that same meeting, Prexy sells shares in Corp. to Dupe. Unless there's some other interstate aspect to the transaction (e.g., use of the mails in connection with it), Prexy will have no 10b-5 liability because the transaction does not meet the jurisdictional requirements of § 10(b) of the '34 Act. That is, the transaction didn't use "any means or instrumentality of interstate commerce or of the mails," and it didn't use any "facility of any national securities exchange."

8. **Detailed treatment:** We consider the first six of the above requirements in more detail beginning immediately below.

E. **Plaintiff must be purchaser or seller:** The plaintiff in a private 10b-5 action must be either a ***purchaser*** or ***seller*** of stock in the company to which the misrepresentation or insider trading relates. The Supreme Court so held in ***Blue Chip Stamps v. Manor Drug Stores***, 421 U.S. 723 (1975), a case which marked the beginning of the Court's efforts to make it much harder to bring a private 10b-5 action.

1. **Facts:** The Blue Chip Stamp Company agreed to settle an antitrust claim by offering shares in itself to certain retailers who had previously used the company's stamp service. This stock offer was on terms quite favorable to the retailers, and presumably Blue Chip knew that any shares not bought under this compulsory offering could later be sold to the public at higher prices; this is what in fact happened. Some of the retailers who did not buy in the compulsory offering then brought a class action suit claiming that Blue Chip had made its prospectus misleadingly ***pessimistic***, for the purpose of inducing them not to buy so that the shares could be sold to the public at higher prices.

2. **Holding:** The Court held that this class of disappointed retailers could not bring a 10b-5 action. Rule 10b-5 by its express terms prohibits only deceit that occurs "in connection with the purchase or sale of any security." (Last phrase of 10b-5.) The Court interpreted this phrase to mean that the plaintiff must have been an ***actual purchaser or seller*** of shares. Here, the retailers' claim was that because of the defendant's misrepresentations, they did ***not*** purchase shares, so the claim was simply not within the scope of 10b-5. The Court thus approved the "purchaser or seller" requirement previously imposed by nearly all lower courts, a rule that had become known as the "*Birnbaum*" doctrine.

3. **Practical consequence:** The practical consequences of the "purchaser or seller" requirement of *Blue Chip Stamps* are actually quite ***small***. Most cases involving misrepresentations in prospectuses are brought by those who actually buy in reliance on a misleadingly ***optimistic*** prospectus, and these plaintiffs of course satisfy the "purchaser or seller"

requirement. In the usual garden-variety insider trading case, the plaintiff will be one who sold without knowledge of the favorable news, or bought without knowledge of the unfavorable news; these plaintiffs, too, satisfy the requirement. As the Court in *Blue Chip Stamps* noted, there are really only three types of plaintiffs who are likely to be affected by the rule, and these will either be able to circumvent the rule or will rarely have a plausible claim even apart from the rule:

a. Potential purchasers who don't buy: The first class affected by the "purchaser or seller" requirement consists of potential purchasers of shares who claim that they decided not to purchase because of an ***unduly pessimistic statement*** (or omission of favorable material) by the issuer. The Ps in *Blue Chip Stamps* itself fell into this class. But such plaintiffs are quite rare.

b. Non-sellers: The second class consists of people who ***already owned*** shares in the issuer, who claim that they ***decided not to sell*** their shares because the corporation or its insiders made an ***unduly optimistic representation*** or ***failed to disclose negative material.*** These shareholders are affected by the "purchaser or seller" rule, because although they previously bought the shares, they did not do so "in connection with" the misrepresentation or omission.

c. Loss of value of investment: Finally, there are shareholders and creditors who have suffered loss in the value of their shares or claims, due to insider trading by the corporation's officials. The "purchaser or seller" rule has some real bite in this situation.

Example: P has been a long-time shareholder of XYZ Corp. Prexy, the president of XYZ, learns that XYZ's vice president has been embezzling for a long time, and has brought the company to the brink of insolvency. Instead of making a public announcement of this fact, Prexy secretly sells his entire holdings in XYZ at \$20 per share. XYZ then announces the embezzlement, and the stock sinks to \$5. P will not have standing to directly recover damages in a private 10b-5 action, because of the "purchaser or seller" rule. This is true even though he can say, plausibly, that Prexy has unfairly pocketed profits (or at least avoided losses) that should have been available to all shareholders equally.

i. Derivative action: But here, P may be able to bring a ***derivative*** action against Prexy. For instance, if Prexy sold some of his shares back to XYZ during the period of non-disclosure (making XYZ a "purchaser"), the derivative action can be brought. Similarly, if XYZ happened to sell some shares to the public or to some other insider (perhaps by means of issuance of stock options to employees) during the period of non-disclosure, it will be a "seller" and a derivative action may be brought in its behalf against Prexy. But if XYZ has neither bought nor sold during the period of Prexy's non-disclosure of the embezzlement, a derivative action will not be available under 10b-5, and thus neither disappointed stockholders nor the corporation will be able to recover from Prexy.

d. Options: Suppose that P is a person who neither bought nor sold stock in connection with D's misrepresentation or insider trading, but that P did buy or sell an ***option*** on the company's stock. Does P's purchase or sale of this option make him a "purchaser or seller" for 10b-5 purposes? The courts are ***split*** on this question.

4. **Defendant doesn't have to buy or sell:** Keep in mind that the "purchaser or seller" requirement for 10b-5 private actions applies ***only to the plaintiff***: it has never been required that the ***defendant*** be a buyer or a seller. Thus if an issuing company, or an insider at that company, makes an ***affirmative misrepresentation*** to the marketplace (e.g., an intentionally misleading press release), the company or the insider can be liable under 10b-5 even though it/he never bought or sold a share of stock. See *infra*, p. 300.

   a. **D buys or sells options:** Also, a defendant who insider trades by purchasing an ***option*** on a security is expressly covered by federal insider-trading provisions. See § 20(d) to the '34 Act, added in 1984, expressly bringing options traders within the scope of federal insider-trading prohibitions.

F. **Trading "while in possession" of info, vs. trading "on the basis of" info:** Until 2000, it was not clear just what the causal relationship had to be between D's *knowledge* of the inside information and his *decision* to trade the stock. Was it enough for liability that D was merely ***"in possession"*** of the inside information at the time of the trade, or did the government (or P in a private suit) also have to prove that D in some sense ***"used"*** the information in making his decision to trade? For example, suppose that D knew the inside information, but could conclusively prove that his decision was based entirely on other (public) factors — could D still be liable? The question was given a mostly ***"yes"*** answer in 2000 by the SEC's adoption of an important new rule, Rule 10b-5-1.

1. **"Awareness" test:** 10b-5-1 for the most part makes life tougher for possessors of inside information. The Rule starts by stating an apparently pro-defendant principle that Rule 10b-5 prohibits trading "on the basis of" material nonpublic information. But the Rule then defines "on the basis of" to *mean* ***"was aware of"*** the information at the time of the purchase or sale. In other words (except for a "safe harbor" which we'll discuss below), the government or private plaintiff merely has to show that D was ***"aware"*** of the inside information at the time he traded, *not* that the inside information in any sense ***caused or even affected*** D's decision to trade.

   a. **Safe harbor for preplanned trading:** But Rule 10b-5-1 also gives the insider an important ***"safe harbor"***: if before becoming aware of the inside information, the insider adopts a ***"written plan for trading securities"*** that ***locks the insider into making particular types of purchases or sales at particular times*** or under particular circumstances, sales that are made according to this preplanned trading arrangement won't be deemed to be "on the basis of" the inside information, even if the insider knows the information at the time the trade actually occurs. Cf. Hamilton (8th), p. 1053, n. 6.

   Example: Prexy, the head of XYZ Corp., owns $100 million of XYZ stock, and would like to gradually diminish the proportion that XYZ stock constitutes of his net worth. In late 2011, therefore, Prexy enters into an irrevocable written contract with Broker, under which Prexy instructs Broker to sell $5 million of Prexy's XYZ stock during the first week of each calendar quarter for the next three years. On June 25, 2012, Prexy learns that XYZ will soon need to announce poor quarterly earnings, which will likely lead to a decline in the stock. On July 2, before the poor earnings are reported, Broker sells $5 million of stock for Prexy.

Even though the sale took place at a time when Prexy was in possession of material nonpublic information, Prexy has not committed insider trading, because he has successfully used the preplanned-trading-arrangement safe harbor of Rule 10b-5-1. That is, Prexy has (in the language of the safe harbor provision) "entered into a binding contract to purchase or sell the security," has "provided a written formula or algorithm ... for determining amounts, prices and dates," and has shown that the sale was "pursuant to the prior contract." The idea is that because in late 2011 Prexy irrevocably made the decision to sell shares in the first week of July, 2012 — a decision that would bind him no matter what happened to the market price or status of XYZ — he won't be deemed to have sold "on the basis of" information that he didn't acquire until after making that irrevocable decision.

G. **Requirement of misstatement or omission (including trading on material non-public information):** The defendant must be shown to have made a ***misstatement*** or ***omission*** of a ***material fact***, in ***violation of some duty***.

1. **Affirmative misrepresentation:** If the plaintiff's claim is that the defendant has made an affirmative ***misrepresentation*** or told a ***half-truth***, the main impact of this requirement is that the plaintiff must show that the misstatement was ***"material."*** We discuss the meaning of "material" below.

2. **"Silent" insider trading:** In the case of garden-variety "silent" insider trading, the "misrepresentation or omission of a material fact" requirement means that the plaintiff must show not only that the defendant insider failed to disclose a material fact, but that he had a ***duty*** to make that disclosure. In general, this means that the plaintiff must show that the defendant ***bought*** or ***sold*** while in possession of the material non-public information, or that he knowingly gave a ***tip*** to someone else in order to allow the "tippee" to buy or sell.

   a. **"Disclose or abstain" rule:** In other words, the fact that the defendant was an insider who had material non-public information and failed to disclose it is never, ***by itself***, enough to expose him to a 10b-5 action. The rule is one of ***"disclose or abstain"***; the defendant must either: (1) disclose the information or (2) abstain from trading and from tipping others to allow them to trade. See the discussion of the *Texas Gulf Sulphur* litigation *supra*, p. 265.

3. **Meaning of "material":** The misrepresentation or omission must be as to a ***"material"*** fact. In a 10b-5 suit, a fact is material "if there is a ***substantial likelihood*** that a ***reasonable shareholder*** would consider it ***important***" in deciding whether to buy, hold, or sell the stock. ***Basic, Inc. v. Levinson***, 485 U.S. 224 (1988). Or, to put it a slightly different way, an omitted fact is "material" if there is a "substantial likelihood that the disclosure . . . would have been viewed by the reasonable investor as having significantly altered the ***'total mix'*** of information made available." *Id.* (This definition of "material" is the same as, and derived from, the definition of "material" for purposes of proxy materials, adopted in *TSC Industries, Inc.*, *supra*, p. 105.)

   a. **Application to mergers:** One situation in which the precise definition of "material" is likely to be important, is where an insider buys the company's stock at a time when secret ***merger negotiations*** are under way. If the company and its suitor have ***not yet agreed on price or important terms*** (and, indeed, if the company has not yet even agreed in the abstract that it is for sale), is the mere fact that a suitor is attempting to buy the company automatically "material"? In *Basic, Inc. v. Levinson*, the Court held that the answer is ***"not necessarily."***

i. Balancing: Where an event may (but will not necessarily) occur, materiality "will depend . . . upon a ***balancing*** of both the indicated ***probability*** that the event will occur and the anticipated ***magnitude*** of the event in light of the totality of the company activity." (Opinion in *Basic*, quoting from *SEC v. Texas Gulf Sulphur Co.*)

ii. Mergers: In the case of merger and acquisition discussions, the buy-out of the target company is the most significant event in that company's existence. Therefore, the possibility of that event becomes "material" at an ***earlier stage*** than where the event is a less important one (e.g., a rise in quarterly profits).

iii. Fact-based: In any event, the Court indicated in *Basic*, whether a particular set of merger negotiations has firmed up to the point of being "material" will be highly dependent upon the ***particular facts***, including such facts as whether the board has passed a resolution authorizing the company to conduct the discussions, whether investment bankers have been brought in, whether the principals have directly held negotiations, etc. (The issue is so fact-based that in *Basic* itself, the Court declined to decide whether the merger discussions there were "material," and instead remanded to the trial court on this issue.)

b. Fact need not be outcome-determinative: A fact does ***not*** have to be one that (if known to the investor) would have ***changed the investor's decision,*** in order to be "material." As one lower court has explained the significance of the Supreme Court's *Basic* "total mix" standard, "a material fact is one that would ***affect*** a reasonable investor's ***deliberations*** without necessarily ***changing*** her ultimate investment decision." *Folger Adam Co. v. PMI Industries, Inc.*, 938 F.2d 1529 (2d Cir. 1991).

4. Non-public fact: Where the wrong by the defendant is an ***omission*** rather than a misrepresentation, the omission must be of a fact that is ***non-public***. The main significance of this requirement is that an insider may not trade until the previously-undisclosed fact has been ***disseminated to the market at large***.

a. Press release: For instance, an insider may not buy a large block of XYZ stock one minute after XYZ's press release has been sent to the media, because the public at large has not yet had a chance to learn the news and act upon it; instead, the insider must wait until the media have disseminated the information. Thus in the *Texas Gulf Sulphur* litigation (*supra*, p. 265), the appeals court treated the news of the mineral strike as not becoming "public" until the story had been carried on the Dow Jones "broad tape," where a majority of investors could be expected to have learned of it; a trader who bought after Dow Jones and other news sources had been told of the strike, but before they had run the story, was held to have acted illegally.

H. Defendant must be insider, knowing tippee or misappropriator: In the case of silent insider trading, the defendant will not be liable in a private 10b-5 action unless he was either an ***insider,*** a ***"tippee"*** or a ***"misappropriator."*** In other words, merely trading while in possession of material non-public information is ***not by itself enough*** to make D civilly liable for insider trading under 10b-5.

1. **Violation of duty:** The key rule is that the duty to "disclose or abstain" only applies to ***"insiders," "tippees,"*** or ***"misappropriators."*** A person who is none of these simply has no duty to disclose-or-abstain.

2. ***Chiarella*** **case:** This main parts of this rule — that a person who trades on material non-public information is not liable unless he is an insider or tippee — were established most dramatically in ***Chiarella v. U.S.***, 445 U.S. 222 (1980).

   a. **Facts:** In *Chiarella*, D was a printer at Pandick Press, a financial printing company. Pandick received financial documents in connection with takeovers. The documents disclosed all the terms of the soon-to-be-launched takeovers, but the names of the suitor and target were left blank or replaced by phony names until the night of the final printing. D was able to deduce the identity of some of the targets by other information in the documents, and secretly used this information to buy shares in the targets. He was charged with violating Rule 10b-5.

   b. **Holding:** The Supreme Court held that D had not violated 10b-5, because he had not been under any duty to "disclose or abstain [from trading]". The duty to disclose or abstain only applied where there was a "***relationship of trust and confidence*** between parties to a transaction." Here, D had no direct fiduciary relationship with the target companies whose shares he traded in. Therefore, the mere fact that he traded while in possession of material non-public information was not enough to make him a violator of 10b-5.

      i. **Misappropriation:** The prosecution argued that D had violated a duty ***to his employer*** (Pandick Press), by "stealing" the partially identifying information contained in the takeover document. The Supreme Court did not reject this "misappropriation" theory on the merits, but the Court ignored the theory because it had not been presented to the jury at D's trial.

   c. **Dissent:** Chief Justice Burger, in a dissent, argued that the Court should accept the prosecution's "misappropriation" theory: "A person who has misappropriated non-public information has an absolute duty to disclose that information or to refrain from trading." Since D used information entrusted to him in confidence (the identifying clues in the tender offer documents), he was guilty of misappropriation, and should be found to have violated 10b-5, Burger argued.[3]

   d. **Significance of *Chiarella:*** *Chiarella* establishes the principle, which remains in force, that the mere trading on non-public information does not by itself violate 10b-5, and that there can be a 10b-5 violation only when the person has violated, or knowingly benefited from another's violation of, a fiduciary duty. But *Chiarella* itself would almost certainly be decided differently today.

---

3. For more about this theory — which the entire Supreme Court finally accepted in 1997 — that "misappropriation" of the information from even a non-issuer is enough to trigger 10b-5 liability, see *infra*, p. 289.

i. **Mail or wire fraud:** First, D could almost certainly be convicted of ***wire fraud*** or ***mail fraud*** for having misappropriated the information entrusted by the acquirers to Pandick and thence to him. See the discussion of *U.S. v. Carpenter*, *infra*, p. 290.

ii. **10b-5:** Second, the Supreme Court has finally accepted the misappropriation theory urged by Chief Justice Burger in *Chiarella.* See *U.S. v. O'Hagan*, *infra*, p. 291. Thus today, a person who improperly uses confidential information from one other than the issuer (e.g., from a company that is planning a tender offeror for the issuer), can be liable under 10b-5. Therefore, it is highly likely that if the Supreme Court were hearing the case today, it would hold that *Chiarella did* violate 10b-5, by ***misappropriating information entrusted to him by his employer.***

iii. **Consequence:** Therefore, the only situation in which the non-liability rule of *Chiarella* clearly applies is where the trader has learned the information ***without any breach of fiduciary responsibility by anyone.*** For instance, if *Chiarella* had learned the information by ***overhearing*** a chance remark in a restaurant or finding a slip of paper on the sidewalk, he would not be liable under 10b-5 even under the most expansive reading of later cases. See the discussion of this "inadvertent discovery" situation *infra*, p. 288.

3. **Meaning of "insider":** An "insider" will be liable under 10b-5 if he trades while in possession of material non-public information. What, then, is an ***"insider"***? The Supreme Court has never given a precise definition, but the concept seems to be that an insider is one who obtains information ***by virtue of his employment with the company*** whose stock he trades in.

   a. **High-level employees:** Thus ***officers, directors and high-level employees*** of a company are clearly "insiders," and are liable under 10b-5 if they trade in the company's stock while in possession of material non-public information about the company.

   b. **Lower-level employees:** Furthermore, even a low-level employee who ***learns information by virtue of his employment*** with the company is an "insider."

   Example: David is a secretary for Prexy, the president of XYZ Corp. One day, while David is straightening up Prexy's desk, David notices a letter from Suitor to Prexy, saying "We propose to acquire XYZ for $20 per share." David goes out and buys XYZ stock at $10 a share. David is almost certainly an "insider," and has thus violated 10b-5 even though he is a low-level employee. He has gotten the inside information by virtue of his employment by XYZ, and has a fiduciary responsibility to keep that information confidential and to not use it for his own purposes. (For instance, he is probably liable for misappropriation of company property under state law; see, e.g., *Diamond v. Oreamuno*, *supra*, p. 261; Clark, p. 323.)

   c. **"Constructive" insider:** People who do not work for the issuing company, but who are ***entrusted*** by it with confidential information, probably also become ***"constructive"*** insiders. For instance, if XYZ gives one of its outside ***professionals*** (e.g., its lawyer, accountant or investment banker) information about XYZ so that the professional can perform a service for XYZ, the professional is almost certainly a constructive insider, and may not trade on the information without violating 10b-5. This topic is discussed further *infra*, p. 288.

4. **Liability of "tippee":** The main other type of person who violates 10b-5 if he trades on inside information is the ***"tippee."*** A tippee is a person who is not himself an insider, but to whom an insider consciously gives inside information. Clark, p. 324. The most important thing to remember about tippee liability under 10b-5 is that this liability is ***derivative*** from the liability of the tipper — unless the insider/tipper has ***consciously violated his fiduciary responsibility*** to the company for personal gain, the ***tippee has no liability*** even if he trades on the information for his own gain. This is the core holding of the landmark case of ***Dirks v. Securities & Exchange Commission***, 463 U.S. 646 (1983).

   a. **Nomenclature:** Before we get into the facts of *Dirks*, let's review some nomenclature. A "tipper" is one who gives inside information to another. A "tippee" is one who receives insider information from an insider. A "secondary tippee" is one who receives inside information from a tippee. In the case of secondary tipping, a person can be both a tipper and a tippee.

   Example: Able, the president of XYZ Corp., is of course an insider with respect to the news that XYZ has just made a major new mineral discovery. If Able tells Baker, a friend not employed by XYZ, about this news, Able is a tipper and Baker is a tippee. If Baker now tells his cousin Carr about this news, Baker is both a tipper and a tippee, and Carr is a secondary tippee.

   b. **Facts of *Dirks:*** Ray Dirks was a securities analyst who specialized in insurance stocks. He received a call from Ronald Secrist, a former officer of Equity Funding Corp., a company that sold life insurance and mutual funds. Secrist claimed that Equity Funding's assets had been vastly overstated through various fraudulent practices (e.g., phony life insurance policies). Dirks then investigated by interviewing various officers and employees of Equity; senior officials refused to corroborate the charges but lower employees did so. Dirks tried to get the *Wall Street Journal* to publish a story on the fraud, but it declined to do so. Although Dirks and his firm did not trade in Equity Funding stock during his investigation, Dirks told some of his investor customers about his findings, and they sold Equity Funding stock. Eventually, due mostly to spreading rumors about Secrist's charges, the stock price collapsed, trading was halted, and the fraud was exposed. The SEC charged Dirks with a violation of 10b-5, on the theory that the fraud allegations were inside information that Dirks gave to his clients for the purpose of permitting them to trade in Equity Funding stock.

   c. **Holding:** The Supreme Court held that Dirks ***did not violate*** 10b-5. Dirks was clearly a tippee, not an insider. As such, any liability he might have for misusing the inside information must ***derive*** from the liability of his tipper (in this case, Secrist). "[A] tippee assumes a fiduciary duty to the shareholders of a corporation not to trade on material nonpublic information only when the ***insider has breached his fiduciary duty*** to the shareholders by disclosing the information to the tippee and the tippee ***knows or should know*** that there has been a breach."

      i. **Secrist's non-liability:** So the question became whether *Secrist*, by passing on to Dirks information about the fraud, had himself violated his fiduciary obligation to

Equity. Here, the Court held, there was no breach merely by virtue of the fact that Secrist passed on insider information; instead, an insider breaches his fiduciary duty to the corporation only if he ***"personally will benefit, directly or indirectly from his disclosure."*** Such a benefit might occur if the insider received some direct ***monetary*** or other ***personal benefit***, or if the insider was intending to ***make a gift*** of the confidential information (e.g., a gift to a relative or friend).

ii. Application to facts: But here, neither Secrist nor the other low-level employees who corroborated his charges received any monetary or personal benefit from Dirks, nor did they intend to make him a gift. Therefore, these insiders did not breach any fiduciary obligation. Therefore, Dirks had ***no derivative liability*** as tippee, and thus did not violate Rule 10b-5.

d. Dissent: Three dissenters in Dirks conceded that the tippee's liability should derive from the tipper's liability. But they believed that the tipper breaches a fiduciary responsibility to his company and its shareholders whenever he ***knowingly harms*** the shareholders, regardless of whether he is attempting to get a personal benefit. Here, Secrist knew that he would be harming Equity Funding shareholders (by disclosing damaging information which would drive down the stock's price); therefore, the fact that he received no personal gain should be irrelevant. Since Secrist violated his obligation of confidentiality to the shareholders, Dirks should have derivative 10b-5 liability, the dissenters contended.

e. Consequence: So *Dirks*' main importance is that it establishes that: (1) a tippee is liable under 10b-5 ***only if his tipper*** (the insider) has ***violated some fiduciary duty to the company*** or its shareholders; and (2) the insider/tipper violates a fiduciary duty only where he receives a direct ***"benefit"*** from disclosing the information, or intends to give something of pecuniary value to the tippee. Where the insider acts for some "altruistic" purpose (e.g., exposing fraud), his tippee cannot be liable under 10b-5 even if the tippee uses the information for his own direct personal benefit. (For instance, even if Dirks had bought Equity Funding stock himself, and reaped huge profits, under the majority's analysis he would not have been liable.)

f. Additional discussion: We discuss additional aspects of tippee liability — including when the insider/tipper receives a "benefit" — *infra*, p. 286.

I. Requirement of scienter: A defendant will be liable under 10b-5 only if he acted with ***scienter***, that is, with an intent to ***deceive, manipulate or defraud***. *Ernst & Ernst v. Hochfelder*, 425 U.S. 185 (1976).

1. Significance: This requirement of scienter has historically been important where the defendant was a ***professional firm*** (e.g., an accounting or law firm) charged with ***aiding and abetting*** a 10b-5 violation. Unless the plaintiff could show that the professional firm's conduct amounted to something worse than negligence, the firm would not be liable under 10b-5 despite its sloppiness.

2. Facts: Thus in *Ernst & Ernst* itself, defendants were a Big Eight accounting firm that had audited the books of First Securities Co., a small brokerage firm. First Securities' president had been carrying on a massive fraud for years, converting customers' accounts to his own use. The accounting firm missed a number of clues to the fraud (e.g., the fact that the president insisted on being the only one to open certain kinds of mail), yet there was no suggestion that the accounting firm ever intended to defraud or mislead those who relied on its audit.

3. **Holding:** A majority of the Court held that a showing of scienter was necessary in any 10b-5 action (at least any private action for damages).[4] The court relied heavily on the use of the word "manipulative," "device," and "contrivance" in § 10(b) of the '34 Act (under the authority of which the SEC has enacted 10b-5). These terms, the court held, connote "intentional or wilful conduct designed to deceive or defraud. . . ."

4. **What scienter means:** What exactly does "scienter" mean? As the Court says in *Ernst & Ernst*, the essential concept is an intent to "deceive, manipulate, or defraud." But even this phrase is somewhat vague.

   a. **Knowing falsehood:** Clearly if D misstates a material fact ***knowing*** that the statement is false, and with the intent that the listener rely on the misstatement, scienter is present.

   b. **Absence of belief:** Additionally, if the representation is made ***without any belief as to whether it is true or not***, this almost certainly constitutes scienter as well. See C&E, p. 930.

   c. **False statement of knowledge:** Similarly, if D states that he knows a fact to be true, when in fact D knows that he does not really know whether the fact is true or not, this is almost certainly scienter: D has intentionally defrauded his listener "not so much as to the fact itself, but rather as to the extent of [the speaker's] information." Prosser & Keeton on Torts, p. 742.

   d. **Recklessness:** Virtually all courts post-*Ernst* have concluded that if the defendant makes a misstatement ***recklessly***, he has scienter. C&E, p. 931.

      i. **Affirmative misstatement:** In the case of an affirmative misstatement, a person who makes the misstatement with total disregard whether it is true or false has acted recklessly.

      ii. **Omission:** Where the claim is that the defendant has failed to act or speak, rather than that the defendant has made a misstatement, the definition of "recklessness" for 10b-5 purposes is less clear. Most courts would probably agree that where the defendant has ***ignored a danger*** that is so obvious that any reasonable man would have known of it, he has acted recklessly (even if the defendant in fact did not know of the danger). Thus on the facts of *Ernst & Ernst*, if the clues to fraud were so blatant that any reasonable accounting firm would have picked up on the fraud,

---

4. In a post-*Ernst* decision, the Supreme Court ruled that there is *no private action for aiding and abetting* a violation of 10b-5. So the requirement of scienter is no longer of practical importance in private aiding-and-abetting suits against professionals, like *Ernst*, since these can't be brought at all. See *Central Bank of Denver v. First Interstate Bank of Denver, infra*, p. 282. (But scienter would still matter in an *enforcement* action brought by the SEC [see *infra*, p. 282] for aiding-and-abetting under 10b-5. Scienter would also still matter in a private direct [rather than aiding-and-abetting] insider-trading case, where the accusation was that the defendant traded while in possession of inside information [e.g., he thought the information was already public]. See *infra*, p. 282.)

the Ds' silence would constitute recklessness and thus scienter even if there is no explicit proof that the Ds had actual knowledge of the fraud.

5. **Insider trading:** Is there any practical impact of the scienter requirement on 10b-5 violations involving garden variety "silent" insider trading? The main impact of the scienter requirement here is that "the defendant must have ***known*** that the information to which he had access while trading was ***material*** and ***nonpublic***." Clark, p. 328. For instance, if D honestly (even if somewhat unreasonably) believes that the news of his company's mineral strike has ***already been released*** to the public, his purchase of shares in the company would not be a violation of 10b-5.

   a. **Failure to control another person's insider trading:** But there is one situation in which a defendant who is ***without scienter*** may nonetheless be liable for insider trading. Under the Insider Trading and Securities Fraud Enforcement Act of 1988 (ITSFEA), the SEC may obtain large civil penalties against D if D ***"controlled"*** X, an insider trader, and D "knew or recklessly disregarded the fact that [X] was likely to engage in the act or acts constituting the violation and ***failed to take proper steps to prevent such act or acts*** before they occurred." § 21A(b)(1)(A) of the '34 Act. So an issuer, law firm, accounting firm, investment banking firm, etc. can be liable even without scienter if it ***knew of or recklessly disregarded the chance that its employees might insider-trade,*** and ***failed to institute safeguards*** (e.g., warnings, and the walling-off of information from those without the need to know it) to prevent insider trading. See the further discussion of ITSFEA *infra*, p. 283.

6. **Pleading of scienter:** In the case of private class-action suits for 10b-5 violations, the plaintiff(s) must ***plead*** the facts relating to scienter ***"with particularity."*** See *infra*, p. 304.

J. **Actual causation, reliance:** The plaintiff in a 10b-5 private damage action must show that his harm was ***caused in fact*** by the defendant's wrongdoing. In other words, P must show that ***but for D's wrongdoing***, P would not have been injured. Sometimes, courts say that to prove causation, P must show that he ***relied*** on D in some way. (But as we'll see, this reliance need not always be shown.)

1. **Common law requires reliance:** In common-law deceit actions, "causation in fact" must be proven by showing that P ***relied*** on D's misrepresentation. Thus suppose D says to P, "This house I'm offering to sell you does not have termites," and P knows through an independent inspection that the house does have termites. If P buys the house anyway, he will not be able to sue D for deceit: he did not rely on D's misstatement, so even if the house falls apart due to termite damage P's loss has not been caused in fact by D's misstatement.

2. **Reliance under 10b-5:** In 10b-5 cases, most courts similarly assert that P must show that he relied on D's wrongdoing. But in 10b-5 cases, unlike the typical common-law face-to-face deceit situation, P can be hurt by D's misrepresentations or insider trading without having directly relied on D's conduct. (We'll see how in a moment.) Therefore, the frequently-asserted requirement of reliance in 10b-5 cases can be better understood as a more general requirement that P show that his losses were ***caused in fact*** by D's misconduct (i.e., would not have occurred without that misconduct).

3. **"Fraud on the market" theory:** The most important way in which P can show that he was harmed by D's misconduct even though he did not rely on anything D did or said, is by use of the ***"fraud on the market" theory***. P makes an argument that goes something like this: "The Efficient Capital Markets Theory (*supra*, p. 253) says that at any time, the price of any stock reflects all publicly-available information. When I purchased (or sold) stock in XYZ Corp., I relied on the current market price being a 'fair' one that reflected all known information. When D made a misstatement to the public about XYZ's prospects (or when D bought/sold XYZ stock secretly without complying with his duty to disclose material non-public information), his wrongdoing made the price different from what it would have been had he fulfilled his obligations. Therefore, when I bought/sold based on the market price, I paid more/received less because of D's wrongdoing, and my economic loss was caused in fact by that wrongdoing."

   a. **Accepted in *Basic* case:** The Supreme Court essentially accepted this "fraud on the market" theory, and consequently gave the plaintiff the benefit of a ***presumption of reliance*** on the defendant's misleading statements, in ***Basic, Inc. v. Levinson***, 485 U.S. 224 (1988).

      i. **Facts:** *Basic, Inc* was a case involving an alleged ***affirmative misrepresentation***. D (Basic, Inc.) was involved in merger discussions with another company, Combustion Engineering. Yet it publicly denied that any merger discussions were under way, and denied knowing of any other reason why the company's stock was trading heavily and setting new highs. A buyout of D was finally announced, and shareholders who had sold prior to the buyout announcement at less than the final buyout price brought a class action. The Ps claimed that they were injured by having sold shares in D at "artificially depressed prices" in a market that had been affected by D's misleading statements.

      ii. **"Fraud on market" theory accepted:** The Court first reiterated that reliance is an element of a 10b-5 claim. However, the Court gave Ps the benefit of a ***rebuttable presumption of reliance***: instead of requiring each P to prove that he personally knew of D's misstatements and relied on them in making his decision to sell the stock, the Court would presume that: (1) the price of D's stock at any time reflected everything that was publicly known about D's prospects; and (2) therefore, the price each P received was affected by any material misrepresentations made to the public by D (i.e., by any "fraud on the market" perpetrated by D).

      iii. **Rebuttable:** But the Court also stressed that this presumption is ***rebuttable***. In other words, if the defendants could show that the misrepresentation did not affect the market price, or that the particular plaintiff in fact did not rely on the "integrity" of the market price, the presumption would be rebutted (and presumably plaintiff would lose). For instance, if the defendants could show that the market was ***aware*** that the defendants were ***lying*** (so that the market price was not affected by their lies), the presumption would be rebutted; similarly, if the defendant can show that a particular plaintiff disbelieved the defendant's lies but sold anyway, the presumption would also be rebutted.

      iv. **Dissent:** Two justices ***dissented*** from the majority's use of a presumption of reliance based on the "fraud on the market" theory. Most fundamentally, they objected on empirical grounds to the proposition that an investor typically relies on the "integrity" of the market price. The very point of investing in stocks, they argued, is to buy when the price is less than the stock is really worth and sell when it is more than the stock is really worth, a technique that is at odds with reliance on the integrity (in the sense of accuracy) of the market price.

b. **Insider trading cases:** The "fraud on the market" theory, and the consequent presumption of reliance, are clearly important in those 10b-5 cases that involve *affirmative misrepresentations*. (The defendant's false denials of merger discussions in *Basic, Inc.* are one example.) But in the usual insider trading case, there is no representation (false or otherwise) being made by the defendant. Instead, he is simply ***silently trading***. Here, the whole requirement of reliance is really ***meaningless***: it doesn't make any sense to say that P relied on a fact that D was obligated to disclose but did not disclose. C&E, p. 868. Therefore, the "fraud on the market" theory is probably irrelevant in this typical "silent" insider trading context.

   i. **Causation:** Instead, the real question in these "silent" cases is ***causation***, not reliance: "[O]nce the plaintiff has shown that defendant omitted to disclose a material fact he was obliged to disclose, the burden is on the defendant to prove that the plaintiff would have made the same investment decision even if disclosure had been made." C&E, p. 869. (Remember that even in affirmative misrepresentation cases, reliance is really just one way of showing that the defendant's misstatement was the "cause in fact" of the plaintiff's damages.)

K. Proximate cause: In theory, there should also be a ***proximate cause*** requirement in 10b-5 cases. That is, under normal tort principles P should have to prove that his loss was the ***reasonably foreseeable consequence*** of D's misconduct. Clark, p. 337. But this requirement of proximate cause seems to have little practical impact in 10b-5 cases.

1. **Need not be in privity:** For instance, courts could have, but clearly have not, used the proximate cause requirement to impose a requirement of ***privity*** on the plaintiff. In other words, if D engages in insider trading or tells lies about the company, P can win ***without showing that he traded directly with D***.

2. **Misrepresentation:** In the case of a misrepresentation or half-truth told by D, the proximate cause requirement seems displaced by notions of the efficient market and the "fraud on the market" theory. Since D's lies (at least when they are on a material matter and are believed by some traders) affect the price of the stock, those lies not only are the cause in fact of the damage to any plaintiff who buys at a higher price (or sells at a lower price) than he otherwise would have gotten, but these lies are also the proximate cause (i.e., reasonably foreseeable cause) of P's damages.

3. **Insider trading:** In the garden-variety "silent" insider trading context, proximate cause similarly seems not to be required by courts. If the insider buys while concealing good news (or sells while concealing bad news), courts seem to say, implicitly, "It is reasonably foreseeable that had D made disclosure instead of concealing his inside information, anyone who traded in the market thereafter, including P, would have gotten a better price."

   a. **ITSFEA:** The irrelevance of proximate cause in ordinary insider trading cases also seems to be embodied in a federal statute. As part of the Insider Trading and Securities

Fraud Enforcement Act of 1988 (ITSFEA), Congress added § 20A to the '34 Act, which gives those who buy or sell during the time of insider trading a private right of action against the insider trader. § 20A does not say anything about causation, and seems to assume (as courts have done) that where P and D are trading on opposite sides at the same time, D's insider trading has proximately caused P's losses. See the further discussion of ITSFEA *infra*, p. 283.

L. Aiding and abetting: Suppose that a violation of 10b-5 is principally engineered by A, but that a second person, B, helps him commit the violation. Can B be civilly liable for ***"aiding and abetting"*** this 10b-5 violation? As the result of a 1994 Supreme Court case, the clear answer is now "***no.***"

1. ***Central Bank of Denver* case:** That 1994 decision was ***Central Bank of Denver v. First Interstate Bank of Denver***, 511 U.S. 164 (1994).

   a. **Facts:** In *Central Bank*, D was a bank that served as trustee for certain public housing bonds. The Ps (bond holders who lost money when the issuer defaulted) claimed that D had had suspicions that the issuer of the bonds was misrepresenting its financial situation, but that D delayed an independent review of that financial situation until after the issuer's default. Thus, the Ps claimed, D was liable under 10b-5 for aiding and abetting a misrepresentation, even though D itself never made any misrepresentation.

   b. **Holding:** But the Supreme Court, by a 5-4 vote, held that ***there can be no "aiding and abetting" liability*** under 10b-5. The majority reasoned that the plain text of the statute prohibits only the making of a material statement or omission or the commission of a manipulative act, and that this language simply does not extend to cover a person who merely helps another person commit such a statement or act. Nor did the majority believe that Congress would have created a private right of action against aiders and abetters had it thought about the subject.

2. **Suits against professionals:** *Central Bank of Denver* means that 10b-5 suits against ***professionals*** (the group against whom aider-and-abetter suits were most often brought) are now ***harder to bring***. But they are not impossible — professionals can still be sued when they make a misrepresentation (or, more likely, an omission). In other words, they can still be ***"primarily"*** liable even though not "secondarily" liable.

   Example: Suppose that ABC Partners, an accounting firm, certifies a company's financial statement while knowing that (or recklessly disregarding the risk that) the numbers are wrong. In this situation, ABC can probably be held liable, not as an aider-and-abetter, but as the actual "maker" of an material omission. (In this situation, the requirement of "scienter," see *supra*, p. 268, will be important.)

3. **SEC enforcement authority:** Although *Central Bank* establishes that private plaintiffs can't recover on an aider-and-abetter theory, the ***SEC*** now has authority to sue for an ***injunction*** against the aiding and abetting of securities fraud. Congress expressly gave the SEC this power, in a 1995 statute enacted in response to *Central Bank*.

4. **Tipper's liability:** Before *Central Bank*, plaintiffs often used an aider-and-abetter theory to sue the ***tipper*** in insider-trading cases, even where the tipper did not benefit directly

from the insider-trading, and did not himself buy or sell securities. *Central Bank* makes this no longer possible.

a. **Explicit private action against tipper:** But an aider-and-abetter theory is not really necessary to reach such a tipper. That's because § 20A(c), added to the '34 Act in 1988, gives a buyer or seller an ***express private right of action*** against the tipper: "Any person who violates any provision of this Title or the rules or regulations thereunder by ***communicating*** material, nonpublic information shall be jointly and severally liable . . . with, and to the same extent as, any person or persons liable under subsection (a) [giving a private right of action against the person who actually trades based on the inside information] to whom the communication was directed."

M. The Insider Trading and Securities Fraud Enforcement Act of 1988: Congress broadened and intensified the fight against insider trading with the Insider Trading and Securities Fraud Enforcement Act of 1988 (ITSFEA). Here are some highlights of ITSFEA:

1. **Express private right of action:** Recall (see *supra*, p. 264) that neither § 10(b) of the '34 Act, nor the SEC's rule 10b-5, expressly allows a private person who has bought or sold stock to bring a civil damages action against an insider-trader. But ITSFEA for the first time added into the '34 Act an ***express private right of action.*** Under § 20A:

> "***[A]ny person who violates*** any provision of this Title or of the rules or regulations thereunder by ***purchasing or selling a security while in possession of material, nonpublic information*** shall be ***liable in an action*** in any court of competent jurisdiction ***to any person*** who, ***contemporaneously*** with the purchase or sale of securities that is the subject of such violation, has ***purchased*** (where such violation is based on a sale of securities) or ***sold*** (where such violation is based on a purchase of securities) securities of the same class."

So if P is, say, buying shares in XYZ Corp at the same time D, an insider, is dumping them based on his own knowledge that XYZ's prospects are less good than the market believes, P now has an express statutory right to recover civil damages from D.

a. **Does not define "insider trading":** Neither § 20A nor any other part of ITSFEA attempts to ***define*** "insider trading," or to determine who is an "insider," or to determine what is "material nonpublic information." It is left to the courts to decide these questions, just as it has always been. All § 20A does is to make it clear that once P has convinced the court that D has insider-traded, P is permitted to recover damages. (Section 20A also places some limits on damages, and makes the tipper liable, as discussed below.)

b. **"Contemporaneous trader" requirement:** Section 20A(a) gives a right of action only to one who is a ***"contemporaneous trader."*** That is, P must show that at about the ***same time*** D was doing his insider trades, P was trading in the ***opposite direction***, though not necessarily directly with D. Thus P must have been buying at about the time D was selling, or vice versa.

c. **Person who is not "contemporaneous trader":** But even people who are ***not*** "contemporaneous traders" may be injured by insider trading. As to these people, § 20A does not affect their remedies, and they may still be able to persuade a court to allow an implied private right of action.

i. **Would-be acquirer:** For instance, a would-be ***acquirer*** may be able to obtain civil damages against an insider trader, even though the acquirer had not yet begun to buy up the target stock (but later had to do so at a higher price, because of an increased price triggered by the insider's purchases). See the fuller discussion of recovery by an acquirer *infra*, p. 292.

2. **Liability of tipper:** ITSFEA makes it clear that the ***tipper*** will be liable to the same extent as the tippee, even if the tipper did not benefit financially from the tip. See § 20A(c), discussed further *supra*, p. 282.

3. **Controlling person:** ITSFEA lets the SEC obtain substantial ***civil damages*** against a ***"controlling person"*** when the "***controlled*** person" commits insider trading. Under § 21A(a)(1)(B), the SEC may obtain a "civil penalty to be paid by a person who, at the time of the violation, directly or indirectly controlled the person who committed such violation." However, the SEC must show that the controlling person "***knew*** or ***recklessly disregarded*** the fact that such controlled person was likely to engage in the act or acts constituting the violation and failed to take appropriate steps to prevent such act or acts before the occurred. . . ." § 21A(b)(1)(A).

   a. **Extensive liability:** Under this provision, a ***law firm***, accounting firm, issuer, financial printer, newspaper, etc., could be liable for ***failing to take steps to guard against*** insider trading. The civil penalty can be "the greater of $1,000,000 or three times the amount of the profit gained or loss avoided as a result of such controlled person's violation."

   Example: X is an associate at Law Firm, in Law Firm's real estate department. X learns from Y, an associate in the firm's mergers and acquisitions department, that Raider, a client of Law Firm, will soon be launching a tender offer for the shares of Target Corp. Law Firm has never instructed Y or its other mergers-and-acquisitions lawyers not to discuss pending tender offers; nor has Law Firm enacted any written policy on insider trading. X insider trades, buying Target Corp stock at $20, which he is able to sell for $40 once Raider's $42-per-share tender offer is announced. A court might well find that Law Firm, as the "controlling person" of X, knew of or recklessly disregarded the chance that X or some other lawyer at the firm would insider trade, and neglected to take "appropriate steps" to prevent such insider trading. If the court so found, the SEC could recover from Law Firm penalties equal to the ***greater*** of $1 million or three times the profit gained by X.

4. **Bounty:** ITSFEA allows a person to receive a ***bounty*** for turning in an insider-trader. Under § 21A(e), the informant may receive a bounty of up to 10% of the civil penalties received by the SEC stemming from the tip.

N. **Damages:** Suppose that the plaintiff in a civil 10b-5 suit does jump through all of the hoops required for a successful action. What then is the ***measure of damages*** for P's recovery? The answer depends on a number of factors, most importantly whether D has made misrepresentations or has merely silently traded based on insider information.

1. **Misrepresentation by D:** Where the defendant has made a ***misrepresentation*** either to the public at large or directly to P, most courts seem to award P a measure of damages based upon what would be needed to ***put him in the position he would have been in had***

his trade been delayed until after the misrepresentation was corrected. Thus in the case of a plaintiff who sells in response to the defendant's falsely pessimistic statement, P will usually get the difference between what he actually received and what he would have received had he sold when the misstatement was shown to be false. A converse rule would be followed for the plaintiff who bought upon a false optimistic statement by D.

2. **D is silent insider-trader:** Where D is a ***silent insider-trader*** rather than a misrepresenter, the damage issue is somewhat trickier. First, there is no clearly-applicable "moment of wrongdoing": whereas in the misrepresentation case, the moment of the wrong is the moment the misrepresentation takes place, in the insider trading context it is not clear whether the time of wrongdoing is the time of trading or the (possibly long) period of nondisclosure before or after the trading. Also, causation in fact is much more difficult to determine in the insider trading context (see *supra*, p. 279), leading courts to be leery of using an unduly broad measure of damages.

   a. **Limited liability under ITSFEA:** Recall (see *supra*, p. 283) that a ***"contemporaneous trader"*** may sue the insider trader or tipper in an express private right of action now granted by § 20A of the '34 Act (added by the Insider Trading and Securities Fraud Enforcement Act of 1988). Congress has defined the measure of damages in such private actions relatively ***narrowly***. Under § 20A(b)(1), the total damages that may be recovered from the defendant in a § 20A action "shall not exceed the ***profit gained or loss avoided*** in the transaction or transactions that are the subject of the violation." Furthermore, the damages are to be ***reduced*** by the amount of any ***disgorgement*** recovered from the defendant by the SEC. § 20A(b)(2).

   Example: Tipper, an insider at IBM, learns that IBM will shortly be announcing a sharp rise in quarterly profits. Tipper tells his friend, Tippee, about this news, with the intention of letting Tippee buy some shares cheaply. At a time when the market has no inkling that this improvement will occur, Tippee buys 100 shares of IBM at $120 per share. Two weeks later, the favorable earnings report is released, and the stock jumps to $140 per share. During the two week period between Tippee's trade and the final disclosure, Paul, a large investor, sells one million shares of IBM at an average price of $125; he would not have made this sale had he known of the rise in quarterly profits (the inside information).

   Paul may sue Tippee and Tipper under the explicit private right of action given in § 20A. But Paul's recovery is limited to $2,000 (the profits earned by Tippee). Furthermore, if the SEC obtained a disgorgement order against Tippee (as the SEC may do under § 21A(a)(1)), Paul's recovery against Tippee would be further reduced by the amount of that disgorgement.

      i. **Limit not applicable to other types of actions:** Section 20A(b)'s limitation-of-damages provision applies ***only*** to actions brought by "contemporaneous traders." Other categories of people hurt by insider trading may have an implied private right of action, and if they do, it is up to the court to decide on the appropriate measure of damages. For instance, a would-be ***corporate acquirer*** probably has an implied right to recover damages against one who insider-trades in the target's stock and thereby drives up the price; if so, the acquirer might be permitted to recover damages in excess of the defendant's illegal gain; see the discussion of such suits by acquirers *infra*, p. 292.

3. **Civil penalty by SEC:** In addition to damages recoverable by a private plaintiff for insider trading, the ***SEC*** may also recover ***civil penalties*** against the insider-trader. Section 21A of the '34 Act (added by ITSFEA in 1988) lets the SEC recover up to ***three times*** the profit gained or loss avoided by the insider trader. § 21A(a)(2). This civil penalty may also be recovered against the ***tipper*** (even if the tipper did not benefit financially), so that the tipper can be required to pay three times the profits made by the tippee. Finally, anyone who "controls" a tipper or tippee and fails to take appropriate steps to prevent insider trading may be subject to civil penalties.

   a. **In addition to disgorgement:** The insider trader may have to pay the civil penalty ***in addition*** to being required to "disgorge" his illegal gains.

IV. RULE 10b-5 — WHO IS AN "INSIDER," "TIPPEE" OR "MISAPPROPRIATOR"?

A. **Introduction:** Recall that not everyone who trades based on material non-public information violates 10b-5 — only those traders who are found to be "insiders," "tippees" or "misappropriators" are covered by 10b-5. In this section, we take a closer look at various classes of people to see whether they are "insiders," "tippees" or "misappropriators," or, instead, are ones who may trade with impunity despite their possession of material non-public information. As we go through the various categories, keep in mind the three central rules established in *Chiarella* (*supra*, p. 274), *Dirks* (*supra*, p. 276) and *O'Hagan* (*infra*, p. 291):

   [1] a person is an ***"insider"*** only if he has some kind of ***fiduciary relationship*** that requires him to keep the non-public information confidential;

   [2] a person is a ***"tippee"*** only if

      (a) he receives information that is given to him in ***breach of the insider's fiduciary responsibility***, *and*

      (b) he ***knows*** that (or, perhaps, ***should know*** that) the breach has occurred, *and*

      (c) the insider/tipper has received some ***benefit*** from the breach (or intended to make a pecuniary gift to the tippee); and

   [3] a person is a ***"misappropriator"*** if he is an ***"outsider"*** who gets the information from one other than the issuer, in violation of an express or implied ***promise of confidentiality***.

B. **Who is a "tippee":** Let's first look in a little more detail at the three requirements for a person to be a "tippee" for 10b-5 purposes.

   1. **Breach of insider's fiduciary responsibility:** First, the tippee must receive the information from an "insider," and the disclosure must be ***in breach of the insider's fiduciary responsibility.*** This is the requirement that effectively makes the tippee's liability "derivative" from the tipper's liability.

Example: Driller works for Oil Co. Through Driller's job, Driller hears that an industry rival, Gas Co., has made a major find. Driller tells his friend Fred about this information, which is non-public. Fred buys Gas Co. stock. Assume that Driller is not an "insider" of Gas Co. (the issuer), nor has Driller's disclosure breached any fiduciary responsibility to Gas Co.[5] Therefore, Driller can't be liable for a 10b-5 violation, and consequently Fred (whose liability would have to be derivative from Driller's liability) can't be liable either.

2. **Tippee's knowledge:** Second, the tippee isn't liable unless he ***knows*** (or, perhaps, ***should know***) that the info being given to him is in violation of the tipper's fiduciary responsibility.

   Example: Same facts as the prior example, except now assume that Driller learned about Gas Co.'s find as the result of a job interview at Gas Co., in which he was told (before he was given the info), "Don't tell this information to anyone outside the company — it's top secret." Also, assume that Driller merely divulged the info to Fred, without giving Fred any reason to believe that Driller had promised to keep the info secret. Even if *Driller* is liable for a 10b-5 violation (which he may well be, if he intended to confer a financial benefit on Fred), *Fred* won't be liable, because he didn't know or have reason to know that Driller was violating a fiduciary responsibility.

3. **Benefit to tipper:** Finally, the tipp*er* must have ***received some benefit*** from the breach, or at least have ***intended to make a pecuniary gift to the tippee***. This means that a mere "did you know . . ." comment by the tipper, made without thought as to the possibility that the tippee will trade on the info, probably doesn't trigger liability on the tippee's part.

   Example: Executive gets drunk in a bar, and says loudly to Bartender, "My Company, Gas Co., just struck oil in Malaysia, so I'll probably be going out there next week, and I won't see you for a while." It never occurs to Executive that Bartender might trade on the info, and Executive certainly doesn't intend to get any benefit for himself (or to confer any financial benefit on Bartender) by the remark. Bartender hears, buys, and profits. Bartender isn't liable under 10b-5, because Executive didn't intend to give him a benefit or obtain his own (direct or indirect) benefit from the disclosure. So even though Bartender's own conduct is completely venal (and, most people would say, should be barred by 10b-5), Bartender gets off the hook.[6]

   Note: But if the tipper *does* intend to help the tippee make money, it's no defense (either to the tipper or the tippee) that the tipper didn't intend to ***benefit himself***. Thus if Executive in the above Example said to Bartender, "Why don't you buy some options on Gas Co.," Executive and Bartender would both be liable under 10b-5, because Executive has intended to confer a financial benefit on Bartender. And that

---

5. Since the Supreme Court has now accepted the "misappropriation" theory, see *infra*, p. 289, it would be enough if Tipper breached a fiduciary responsibility to *Oil Co.* (his own employer) by making the disclosure, and it wouldn't matter that Oil Co. wasn't the issuer whose stock was being traded. But on our hypo here, Tipper is not violating any fiduciary obligation to Oil Co. (there's no indication that Oil Co. cares about whether Tipper keeps the info secret), so use of the misappropriation theory won't affect the outcome of the hypothetical.

6. But Bartender probably has criminal liability under some *non-10b-5* federal statute(s), such as the wire-fraud statute (if he uses the telephone to place the buy order.) See p. 290.

would be true even if it never occurred to Executive to benefit himself in any way (as by asking Bartender to kick back some of the profits to him).

C. Information acquired by chance: As a consequence of the first requirement above (breach of fiduciary responsibility by the tipper), if an outsider acquires information ***totally by chance***, without anyone's violating any fiduciary obligation of confidentiality, the outsider may trade with impunity. For instance, this will be the case if the outsider, without breach of any fiduciary responsibility, randomly ***overhears*** the inside information, randomly sees a ***document*** containing the information, etc.

D. Information acquired by diligence: Similarly, if an outsider acquires non-public information through his own ***diligence***, he may trade upon it despite its non-public nature, so long as no one breached his own fiduciary responsibilities in passing the information on to the outsider. *Dirks* is itself the best illustration of this principle: Dirks ferreted out clearly non-public information about the fraud at Equity Funding, but since the people who told him about it were not violating any fiduciary duty of their own (because they received no personal financial benefit), Dirks never became a "tippee" and had no liability under 10b-5.

E. Intent to make a gift: If an insider gives an outsider information with the ***intent to make a gift*** of ***pecuniary value*** to the outsider, the outsider *will* be a "tippee," and ***both insider and outsider*** will be liable.

1. **No intent to make pecuniary gift:** On the other hand, if the insider discloses the information to the outsider for some reason ***other*** than intent to confer a pecuniary benefit on himself or on the outsider, then probably the outsider will not be a tippee. For instance, if the insider is merely ***indiscreet***, or is trying to right some wrongdoing (as in *Dirks v. S.E.C.*, *supra*, p. 276), the outsider typically does ***not*** become a tippee.

    Example: Remember the Executive/Bartender Example on p. 287. Executive probably won't be found to have breached a fiduciary duty to Gas Co. (even though he's guilty of serious indiscretion). Therefore, even if Bartender trades on the info, he's probably not a tippee, and won't be liable under 10b-5.

F. Disclosure between family members: Suppose that a person (let's call him X) learns information not from the issuer, but from X's ***relative***, who in turn has some connection with the issuer. Under what circumstances will X be deemed to be an insider? The principal case on the issue has held that X is only an insider if X had a ***fiduciary responsibility*** concerning the information, and ***the mere fact that X learned the information from a relative does not without more give rise to a fiduciary responsibility. U.S. v. Chestman***, 947 F.2d 551 (2d Cir. 1991). *Chestman* is a case that is especially important in light of the Second Circuit's great expertise and reputation in securities-law matters.

1. **Facts:** Ira Waldbaum, president of the publicly-traded Waldbaum supermarket chain, agreed to sell the company to A&P. The sale was to take place at $50 per share, at a time when the stock was trading at about $25. Ira told his sister, Shirley, about the transaction, advising her to keep quiet about it. Shirley told her daughter, Susan, about the proposed sale; Shirley warned Susan not to tell anyone except Susan's husband, Keith Loeb, because disclosure might ruin the sale. Susan told Loeb about the sale, and then warned him not to tell anyone because it could ruin the sale. Loeb then told Chestman, Loeb's stockbroker, that Loeb had "some definite, some accurate information" that Waldbaum

was about to be sold at a premium. Loeb asked Chestman what he thought Loeb should do; Chestman responded that he could not advise Loeb, and that Loeb should make up his own mind. Chestman then made several purchases of Waldbaum stock in the open market (at prices around $25); the purchases were for Chestman's own account as well as for some accounts whose investment decisions he controlled, including a purchase for the Loeb account. Later that same day, Loeb explicitly told Chestman to buy some Waldbaum shares for Loeb. Chestman was criminally charged with violating both Rule 10b-5 and the SEC's special tender-offer insider-trading rule, 14e-3 (discussed *infra*, p. 290). Here, we focus on the 10b-5 action.

2. **Holding:** By a narrow vote, the Second Circuit held that Chestman could ***not*** be convicted of a 10b-5 violation. The majority began by noting that Chestman could not be convicted of the 10b-5 violation unless there was evidence to show that: (1) Keith Loeb ***breached a fiduciary duty*** to the source of the information (his wife or her family); *and* (2) Chestman ***knew*** that Loeb had breached such a duty. The court then concluded that Loeb had ***not breached any fiduciary duty***.

   a. **Rationale:** The court reasoned that a mere familial relationship between the source of information and the tipper was not enough to impose a fiduciary duty on the tipper. Thus the mere fact that Loeb heard the information from his wife (and that she in turn had heard it from another family member) did not make Loeb a fiduciary as to the information. If Loeb and his wife had had a ***pre-existing*** fiduciary relationship (e.g., they had frequently discussed Waldbaum business matters, and Susan continued these discussions based on her understanding that her husband knew to keep them confidential), then the requisite fiduciary relationship regarding the new information would exist. Similarly, if Susan had demanded that her husband promise confidentiality ***before*** she discussed the new information with him, this would have been enough. But an after-the-fact admonition by Susan to Loeb, "Don't tell," was not enough to make Loeb a fiduciary. Therefore, Chestman was not learning information that had been transmitted in violation of a fiduciary obligation, and he could have no 10b-5 liability, any more than Ray Dirks (see *Dirks v. SEC*, *supra*, p. 276) had liability when he received information that was not the result of an insider's breach of fiduciary duty.

3. **14e-3 conviction affirmed:** But the *Chestman* court *affirmed* Chestman's conviction for violating SEC's ***Rule 14e-3(a)***, governing insider trading during the course of tender offers. This aspect of the case is discussed further *infra*, p. 290.

4. **SEC Rule:** Where non-public information is disclosed by a person to that person's close relative — the situation in *Chestman* — there is now an SEC Rule, ***Rule 10b-5-2***, on point that creates a ***rebuttable presumption*** that the recipient has a fiduciary duty to maintain the confidence. Where this presumption applies and can't be rebutted, the Rule reverses the result in *Chestman*. See *infra*, p. 293.

G. **Confidential information, but not from issuer (the "misappropriation" problem):** So far, we have assumed that the non-public information ***comes from the issuer*** (i.e., from the company whose stock is being traded). But suppose that material non-public information about company *A* comes from a source that has nothing to do with company *A* at all. Can a person who buys or sells shares of company *A* nonetheless be found to have violated Rule

10b-5? The answer is ***"yes,"*** at least in those situations where the trader has learned of the information by ***"misappropriating"*** it.

1. **Criminal liability under other provisions:** Before we look at whether 10b-5 is violated in this situation, let's first consider possible liability under ***other statutory provisions***.

   a. **Wire and mail fraud:** Most importantly, if a person misappropriates information from another, and trades based on that information, he will be guilty of violating the general federal criminal ***mail*** and ***wire fraud*** statutes.

      i. ***Chiarella:*** For instance, recall Vincent Chiarella (see *Chiarella v. U.S.*, *supra*, p. 222), the financial printer who used information about takeover bids that he learned on his job. Although the Supreme Court found that Chiarella did not violate *10b-5* because he bore no fiduciary duty to the targets in whose stock he traded (the information came from acquirers, not targets), Chiarella could almost certainly now be convicted of mail or wire fraud — Chiarella clearly "misappropriated" information from his own employer that was given to him in confidence, and this information would be deemed to be "property" covered by the federal wire and mail fraud statute.

      ii. **Government official:** Similarly, the wire and mail fraud statutes may cover broad ***market-related*** information that is not specifically tied to any one stock. This may often be true of secret ***government*** information. For instance, suppose that D is a member of the Federal Reserve Board, and learns at a regular monthly Fed meeting that the Fed will be raising interest rates, a move that is certain to depress the stock market. If D sells all his stock before the public announcement of the Fed's action, D is almost certainly guilty of mail and/or wire fraud, since he has misappropriated secret government information (and has probably used a phone call or Internet communication to carry out the trade).

   b. **SEC Rule 14e-3:** Furthermore, in the special case of ***tender offers***, a separate SEC rule makes it illegal to trade on the basis of non-public information, even if this information does not derive from the company whose stock is being traded (i.e., the target). Under SEC Rule 14e-3 (added after *Chiarella*), it is forbidden to trade based on tender offer information derived directly or indirectly from ***either*** the offeror or the target. Apparently, Vincent Chiarella would, today, fall right within this provision: his information about takeovers was derived indirectly from the acquirers. See Clark, p. 354.

      i. ***Chestman*** **case:** A post-*Chiarella* case shows how SEC Rule 14e-3 can lead to an insider-trading conviction even where the trader is not guilty under Rule 10b-5. In *U.S. v. Chestman*, 947 F.2d 551 (2d Cir. 1991) (also discussed *supra*, p. 289), D was a stockbroker who bought shares in Waldbaum Corp. based upon information from a member of the controlling family that the company was about to be taken over at a higher price. Even though D's conviction under *10b-5* was overturned on the theory that the information was not obtained in violation of a fiduciary obligation, D's conviction under *Rule 14e-3* was affirmed — 14e-3 dispenses with the requirement (imposed in 10b-5 cases) that the information have been obtained as a result of breach of a fiduciary duty.

2. **10b-5:** Now, let's consider whether ***10b-5*** is violated when a person trades based on confidential information whose source is other than the company whose stock is being traded. The answer is that the defendant ***is liable under 10b-5*** if he has ***misappropriated*** the information, by ***breaching a fiduciary relationship with the source of the information.*** This is the result of a major Supreme Court decision, ***U.S. v. O'Hagan,*** 521 U.S. 642 (1997).

   a. **Facts of *O'Hagan*:** The facts of *O'Hagan* make for a classic illustration of misappropriation from one-other-than-the-issuer, in this case from a company planning a ***tender offer*** for the issuer. Grand Met was planning a secret tender offer for Pillsbury. Grand Met hired the law firm of Dorsey & Whitney to represent it. D was a partner in Dorsey & Whitney, and learned what Grand Met was planning. (D didn't actually do any work on the matter — he just learned about it from others in the firm.) While the plan was still secret, D went out and made open-market purchases of thousands of Pillsbury shares and call options. When Grand Met announced its tender offer, Pillsbury shares skyrocketed, and D pocketed a $4.3 million profit. The U.S. government brings criminal charges against D for, among other things, violating Rule 10b-5.

   b. **The defense:** D claimed that he shouldn't be liable under 10b-5, because he hadn't taken information belonging to the issuer (Pillsbury). He won with this theory in the Eighth Circuit Court of Appeals.

   c. **Supreme Court rejects:** But ***D lost*** when the case got to the U.S. Supreme Court. In a 6-3 decision, the Court held that 10b-5 liability could be based upon the ***misappropriation of confidential data from a person other than the issuer.***

      i. **Statutory construction:** The case was a matter of statutory construction: what did Congress mean in §10(b) of the Exchange Act by its reference to conduct involving a "***deceptive device*** or contrivance" used ***"in connection with"*** the purchase or sale of securities? The Court found that both the "deceptive device or contrivance" requirement and the "in connection with a purchase or sale" requirement of the statute were ***satisfied*** when a person misappropriates confidential information from a non-issuer and then buys or sells the issuer's stock.

      ii. **Public-policy rationale:** The majority concluded that this interpretation of the statute furthered the general policies behind the anti-insider-trading rules, especially the policy of ***encouraging wide participation in the securities markets:*** "Although informational disparity is inevitable in the securities markets, investors likely would ***hesitate to venture their capital*** in a market where trading based on misappropriated nonpublic information is unchecked by law. . . . It makes scant sense to hold a lawyer like O'Hagan a §10(b) violator if he works for a law firm representing the target of a tender offer, but not if he works for a law firm representing the bidder."

   d. **Significance:** *O'Hagan* clearly broadens the population of people who can be liable for violating 10b-5:

      i. **Who can be covered:** Anyone who "misappropriates" confidential information ***from anyone*** can be liable for trading on that information.

         ❑ Thus one who learns of the information as the result of a fiduciary relationship with a company ***planning a tender offer*** for X Corp. can be liable for trading in X Corp. stock. (That's what happened in *O'Hagan* itself.)

- ❑ Similarly, one who learns secret information about X Corp. as the result of working inside a ***publisher or broadcaster*** that's about to publish a story on X Corp. would probably also be covered.

- ❑ Even a person who learns the information as the result of ***securities research*** done at a ***money-management company*** would be liable, if the information "belonged" to the money-management company.

ii. Meaning of "misappropriates": It's not fully clear what situations constitute "misappropriation" of insider information. The key concept seems to be ***"deception."*** Thus the Court in *O'Hagan* said that "the misappropriation theory premises liability on a fiduciary-turned-trader's ***deception of those who entrusted him with access*** to confidential information." Apparently if (and only if) the supplier of the information could bring some sort of ***"theft of information" tort claim*** against D, D will be liable under the misappropriation theory.

e. Recovery by acquiring corporation: *O'Hagan* was a case brought by the SEC and federal prosecutors. Suppose, instead, that a private 10b-5 action is brought by a would-be ***corporate acquirer*** against one who misuses the acquirer's information to trade in the target's stock. For instance, suppose that on the *O'Hagan* facts, Grand Met (the acquirer) sued O'Hagan, alleging that he had stolen Grand Met's information and, by his trading, caused the price of Pillsbury to go up, causing Grand Met to have to pay more to complete the tender offer.

i. Recovery may be allowed: Assuming that Grand Met can prove that: (1) D *knew* the information was the confidential property of Grand Met (highly likely); and (2) the increased price was the proximate result of D's trading (more questionable), probably Grand Met *can* recover, at least the actual profits earned by D and perhaps the entire "damages" (i.e., higher acquisition price) suffered by Grand Met.

f. SEC Rule 10b-5-2: Since *O'Hagan* establishes the misappropriation theory, application of that theory will turn on whether the recipient of the information indeed had a fiduciary responsibility — a duty of trust or confidence — not to trade on the information. (If the recipient has no duty of trust or confidence regarding the information, he will not be deemed to have "misappropriated" it to trade on it.) Yet the post-*O'Hagan* case law is very sketchy about when the relationship of trust or confidence should be deemed to exist. The SEC has tried to remove the ambiguity by setting forth, in ***Rule 10b-5-2***, adopted in 2000, a non-exclusive list of three circumstances in which ***a duty of "trust or confidence" will be found to exist*** on the part of the recipient of information:

- ❑ First, a duty of trust or confidence exists if the recipient ***"agrees to maintain*** [the] information in confidence";

- ❑ Next, a duty of trust or confidence exists if the discloser and the recipient "have a ***history, pattern, or practice of sharing confidences***, such that the recipient ***knows***

or reasonably should know that the [discloser] expects that the recipient will maintain its confidentiality."

❑ Finally, under a bright-line rule, there is a *presumption* of a duty of trust or confidence if the recipient is a ***"spouse, parent, child, or sibling"*** of the discloser. However, the recipient can then ***rebut*** this presumption by showing that, in light of the relationship between the two family members, the recipient "neither knew nor reasonably should have known" that the discloser expected that the information would be kept confidential. (This right of rebuttal won't apply if the recipient promised keep the information secret.)

g. Tippee who gets information from misappropriator: Presumably the rules of ***tippee*** liability will also apply to the misappropriator situation, though the Supreme Court hasn't yet confirmed this as of this writing (April 2013). Thus if a misappropriator gives the information to a friend, with intent to make a pecuniary gift, and the friend knows or has reason to know that the information comes from a misappropriation of confidential information, presumably the friend and the misappropriator will both be liable if the friend trades on the information.

Example: On the facts of *O'Hagan*, suppose that O'Hagan (the lawyer for the acquirer) had told Fred, his best friend, "Buy stock in Pillsbury, it's going to be taken over by one of my clients." Fred does so. It's highly likely that Fred will have tippee liability under 10b-5, since he had reason to know that the information was being given to him in violation of O'Hagan's fiduciary responsibility to his client. O'Hagan would also be liable, as a misappropriator/tipper (even if O'Hagan didn't trade himself), since he intended to give Fred a pecuniary benefit.

H. Information about one's own trading plans: Can information about ***one's own trading plans*** ever make one an "insider" for 10b-5 purposes? The question arises most interestingly when X buys in the open market with the knowledge that he (or an entity controlled by him) will ***shortly be making a tender offer***. It could be argued that the very knowledge that one will shortly be making a public tender offer (at a price higher than the market price) is inside information of the sort that should prevent one from trading without disclosure.

1. Not applied: However, such trading-in-advance-of-one's-own-tender-offer is virtually ***never*** regarded as a violation of 10b-5. Indeed, those planning tender offers make it virtually standard operating procedure to amass as much stock in the open market as they can before they are required to disclose their stake. (Rule 13d-1 under the '34 Act requires anyone who acquires more than 5% of any class of stock of any public company to file a disclosure statement to that effect on Schedule 13D within 10 days of the acquisition. See *infra*, p. 438.)

2. Rationale: The inapplicability of 10b-5 to this situation makes sense, since the information about one's own future plans does not derive from the issuer itself — one therefore does not have any fiduciary responsibility to the company or its shareholders concerning that information (thus taking the case outside of 10b-5 under *Chiarella*'s requirement that a fiduciary responsibility to the issuer be breached for there to be a 10b-5 violation).

Quiz Yourself on
INSIDER TRADING *(SEC RULE 10b-5)*

58. Aquaman is president of a marine research company, Wet Dreams, Inc. On April 1, the research director of Wet Dreams tells Aquaman they've come up with "Oxygum," a means of breathing underwater by chewing a special kind of gum. Aquaman knows a great product when he hears it. He delays announcing the invention to the public, so he can buy up all the Wet Dreams stock he can get his hands on. Sure enough, when Aquaman makes the announcement, the price of Wet Dreams stock immediately rises from $1 to $50 a share.

(a) What SEC rule, if any, is Aquaman likely to have violated? _______________

(b) Has Aquaman in fact violated that rule? _______________

59. Choo Choo Charlie is president of Good, Inc., a manufacturer of black licorice candy, whose common stock is traded on the NYSE. He negotiates an acquisition of Plenty, Inc., a company that makes hard candy coatings. After the acquisition, the company will be known as Good & Plenty, Inc. Once the main terms of the acquisition are finalized, Choo Choo Charlie waits a week before announcing it in a press release, so that Plenty can notify one of its vacationing directors. During that week, a Good shareholder, Olive Oyl, sells 1,000 shares of her Good stock at the market price, $10 a share. When Choo Choo Charlie finally announces the acquisition, Good stock rockets to $15 a share. Olive brings a private action against Charlie for violating SEC Rule 10b-5. Will Olive recover? _______________

60. Richard Squishy, CEO of HealthNorth Corp., has just learned from his CFO that the company has earned lower-than-expected profits for the just-completed quarter. He sells 100,000 shares of stock for gross proceeds of $2 million before the lower profits are announced to the public. When sued by the SEC for insider trading, he argues, "I concede that I knew about the lower earnings. However, I made the sale not for that reason, but because I needed the $2 million for a new house that I was contractually obligated to pay $3 million for the next week." Assuming that the trier of fact believes that Squishy is telling the truth about his motivation, is he liable for insider trading? _______________

61. Santa Claus is president of publicly traded Hohoho, Inc., a company that makes wooden toys and delivers them to children all over the world on Christmas Eve, charging parents. Hohoho's marketing VP, Rudolph Reindeer, convinces Santa that there are big "bucks" to be made in buying toys from other manufacturers and passing them on to parents at a higher price. On July 1, Santa negotiates a huge contract with Skintendo Computer Games. Santa then waits until July 15 before he announces the contract in a press release. During the period from July 2 through July 14, Santa buys 10,000 shares of Hohoho at $10. After the announcement, the shares quickly rise in price to $15. Then, over the next 2 months, they rise to $25. Cindy Lou Hoo, who dabbles in stock as a hobby, files a private 10b-5 claim against Santa. Cindy Loo alleges that: (1) she already owned 2,000 shares of Hohoho as of July 1; and (2) she would have bought an additional 1,000 shares of Hohoho stock on July 3, had Santa disclosed the Skintendo contract promptly. She therefore claims that Santa's failing to promptly disclose the contract, while trading in the stock, has cost Cindy Lou profits she would have made. Assuming that the court believes Cindy Lou's factual assertions, will Cindy Lou recover (and if so, how much)? _______________

62. The Nat King Coal Mining Company is always drilling at new test sites. One such site, on Nomansan Island, is quite positive. Nat King's chief geologist tells company insiders that in his judgment, there's a 30% chance that the Nomansan site has commercial quantities of coal; he also tells them that if the site is in fact commercially viable at all, it's probably a huge find, which will at least double the company's proven reserves. Immediately (and before anything is said to the public), the corporation's vice president of operations, Cole Dust, buys up all the Nat King Coal stock he can afford. Sure enough, the find turns out to be commercially viable, the stock price skyrockets, and Cole's a rich man. The SEC sues him for insider-trading in violation of 10b-5.

(a) If you represent Cole, what defense would you offer? ________________

(b) Will the defense you raise in (a) succeed? ________________

63. James Bond is sitting at a bar drinking a vodka martini, shaken not stirred. He overhears a man nearby telling a friend about how his company has secretly been buying up gold bullion on the world market, to such an extent that it now controls the market. Bond looks up and recognizes the man as Auric Goldfinger, chairman of the publicly traded Twenty-Four Carat Corp. Bond checks out the financial papers and finds out that this information hasn't been made public. He buys up all the Twenty-Four Carat Corporation stock he can, and, sure enough, when the information becomes public, the stock price skyrockets. Has Bond insider-traded in violation of Rule 10b-5? ________________

64. D.B. Cooper is president of Cooper Printing, Inc., a publicly traded company. He goes out for drinks one night at the Parachute Inn. He meets a woman, Brenda Starr, and they share a few cocktails. D.B. doesn't hold his alcohol too well, and he blabs to Starr that the reason Cooper Printing is doing so well is that, when the presses aren't busy, they print counterfeit money. He adds that the FBI is hot on their tracks, and will probably discover the counterfeiting operation soon. It never occurs to D.B. that he's conveying commercially-valuable information. However, Brenda drinks in this hot tip and, the next day, sells short as much Cooper Printing stock as she can. (That is, she sells borrowed shares, hoping the price will fall and she can buy them back at a lower price, pocketing the difference.) The SEC discovers all of the above facts, and charges Brenda with insider trading in violation of Rule 10b-5. Is Brenda liable? ________________

65. "King" Lear is director of research at the Bard of Avon Company, which produces men's cosmetics. A researcher at Bard of Avon, Dorian Gray, comes up with a treatment that stops aging. Lear knows a gold mine when he sees one, and, before the breakthrough is announced, he buys all the Bard of Avon shares he can afford — 10,000 shares at $5 a share — on the NYSE. That same day, Lady Macbeth sells 50,000 Bard of Avon shares at $5 a share. The following day, Gray's treatment is announced by Bard of Avon's president, Shakespeare, and the stock price shoots up to $10 a share. Lady Macbeth brings a claim against Lear for insider trading, under the federal statute giving an express private right of action in these circumstances. Assuming that Lady M. proves all elements of her claim, how much will she recover? ________________

66. Jim Kirk is president of Tribble Trouble Inc. ("TTI"), a closely-held corporation with 5 shareholders. TTI owns a tribble ranch, on which it raises fuzzy little tribbles that are sold as exotic housepets. Kirk phones Mr. Spock, a neighbor who is also a TTI shareholder, and tells him the ranch is having breeding troubles, and the outlook isn't very good. Kirk encourages Spock to sell Kirk Spock's shares for $50 each. At a face-to-face meeting the next day, Spock sells Kirk the shares at the $50/share price. In reality, the tribbles are reproducing like rabbits, and Spock's shares would really have been valued at $200 each by an investor who knew the full facts. When Spock finds out about Kirk's lie, he gives Kirk a Vulcan neck pinch at the next block party, and then files a 10b-5 claim against him in federal court. Kirk challenges the claim on the grounds that: (1) Rule 10b-5 does not apply to transactions in the stock of non-publicly-traded companies; and (2) 10b-5 does not apply where no instrument of interstate commerce is used in connection with the transaction. Which, if either, of these defenses will be successful? ______________

67. Same facts as the previous question. Now, however, assume that Kirk, instead of phoning Spock, rang Spock's doorbell, told Spock face-to-face how business was bad, and bought Spock's shares in that same meeting. What, if any, defense could Kirk raise to a 10b-5 suit, that Kirk could not have raised in the prior question? ______________

Answers

58. (a) SEC Rule 10b-5. That rule (roughly) makes it unlawful to "employ any device, scheme, or artifice to defraud . . . in connection with the purchase or sale of any security." [262]

(b) Yes. A person commits insider trading in violation of Rule 10b-5 if he (1) has a special relationship with the issuer of stock (e.g., he is an "insider" of the issuer), and (2) buys or sells the issuer's stock, while in possession of information that is (3) material and (4) non-public. [263] Aquaman, as president, was an insider of the corporation whose shares were being bought (Wet Dreams), so Aquaman satisfies (1) and (2). Information is "material" if a reasonable investor would consider it important in deciding whether to buy or sell the shares. [272] Information that in fact increases a company's share price from $1 to $50 is clearly "material" (satisfying (3)). The Oxygum invention hadn't been known to investors generally when Aquaman made his purchases, so the information about the invention was "nonpublic" (satisfying (4)). As a result, Aquaman is liable for insider trading in violation of Rule 10b-5.

59. No, because Charlie didn't trade in Good shares before the acquisition was made public. The rule on insider trading is that insiders may not *trade* in the company's stock while in possession of material inside information. 10b-5 does not require the prompt disclosure of material non-public information: the company and its insiders may delay disclosure indefinitely so far as the Rule is concerned, so long as they don't buy or sell in the interim. This is the "disclose or abstain" rule. [264] Here, Charlie abstained. Thus, he can't be liable to Olive.

60. Yes. An SEC Rule enacted in 2000, Rule 10b-5-1, forecloses Squishy's defense. The Rule starts by saying that Rule 10b-5 prohibits trading "on the basis of" material nonpublic information. But 10b-5-1 then defines "on the basis of" to *mean* ***"was aware of"*** the information at the time of the purchase or sale. Since Squishy was "aware of" the info when he sold, he's liable, even if the "motivation" for his sale was his need for house-acquisition funds rather than the inside info. (10b-5-1 would have given Squishy a "safe harbor" if, before he got the lower-earnings news, he had irrevocably committed to sell the shares as part of a pre-planned trading program, such as a commitment to sell a certain number of shares at the beginning of every quarter regardless of market conditions. But there's no indication on our facts that Squishy qualified for this safe harbor.) [271-272]

61. No — Cindy Lou Hoo loses, because only purchasers or sellers of the affected securities can be plaintiffs under 10b-5. More precisely, a person can only be a plaintiff if she bought or sold the company's stock *during the period of non-disclosure. Blue Chip Stamps v. Manor Drug Stores.* [269] Since Cindy didn't buy or sell any Hohoho stock during the period when the insider-trading was occurring — July 2 through July 14 — she can't recover, no matter how clear it is that Santa in fact violated 10b-5 (and it's very clear here that he did).

62. (a) That the non-public information was not "material." Insider trading violates Rule 10b-5 only if the defendant bought or sold while in possession of "material" non-public information. Cole can make a plausible argument that because there was only a 30% chance that the site would be commercially viable, the news about it wasn't material.

(b) No, probably. Information is "material" if there is a "substantial likelihood" that disclosure of that information "would have been viewed by a reasonable investor as having significantly altered the ***'total mix'*** of information made available." [272] A 30% chance that a coal company's proven reserves will at least double would almost certainly be viewed as significantly altering the "total mix" of information about the company's prospects.

63. No, because Bond had no disclose-or-abstain duty. Bond did trade on the basis of material, nonpublic information. However, that by itself doesn't violate 10b-5. Instead, the only people subject to liability are pure insiders (directors, officers, controlling shareholders, employees), temporary insiders (accountants, lawyers, investment bankers, etc.), misappropriators, and tippees (those to whom an insider knowingly discloses inside information in breach of a fiduciary duty). [273] Bond fits none of these descriptions. Instead, what he did was, essentially, to obtain market information by chance. It's perfectly OK to trade on the basis of such information.

If Goldfinger had *known* that Bond was listening, and had intended to give Bond the information so that Bond could make money by trading the company's stock, then Goldfinger would be a tipper and Bond would probably be liable as a tippee. [288] But since Goldfinger didn't even know that Bond was listening, Goldfinger is not a tipper and Bond is not a tippee.

64. Probably not. Here, Brenda is not herself an insider in Cooper Printing, so if she's liable at all it would be as a tippee. A tippee's duty to disclose or abstain derives from the liability of his tipper (here, D.B.) [276] A tipper is only liable for the disclosure if the tipper is breaching his fiduciary duty to the issuer's shareholders by making the disclosure. Furthermore (and this is the not-so-obvious step), the tipper will be deemed to be breaching his fiduciary duty only if he "personally will benefit, directly or indirectly, from his disclosure." *Dirks v. SEC.* [276] If D.B. had expected Brenda to make money from trading on the tip and give him a portion — or even if D.B. had just intended to make a pecuniary gift to Brenda by giving her information on which he expected her to trade — D.B. would be in breach of his fiduciary duty, and Brenda would be derivatively liable if she realized that D.B. was violating his duty. But here — where the facts tells us that D.B. has no idea that Brenda will use the info for personal gain — D.B. hasn't violated any fiduciary duty, so Brenda can't be derivatively liable no matter how bald-faced her conduct may have been.

65. $50,000 — 10,000 shares x $5 profit per share. Congress has given certain types of claimants an express private right of action for insider trading, under the Insider Trading and Securities Fraud Enforcement Act of 1988 (ITSFEA). Under that Act, damages "shall not exceed the profit gained or loss avoided in the . . . transactions . . . that are the subject of the violation." [285] Therefore, Lady M. is limited to the *lesser* of her own lost profits (50,000 x $5, or $250,000) and the defendant's gains ($10,000 x $5, or $50,000).

RELATED ISSUE: Say the plaintiff had been the *SEC*, not a private plaintiff like Lady Macbeth. The SEC could seek, among other remedies, *treble damages* under ITSFEA — the SEC is not limited to recovering the defendant's actual gains made or losses avoided. [286] (These damages would go to the Treasury.)

66. Neither. As to (1), this is simply a misstatement — 10b-5 applies to transactions involving any "security," whether publicly-traded or not. [265] So the fact that TTI is privately-held is irrelevant. As to (2), the statement of law is (roughly) correct, but it doesn't apply to these facts. That's because Kirk used the telephone as part of his scheme, and the telephone is considered to be an instrument of interstate commerce.

67. Lack of jurisdiction. The statutory section that supplies authority for Rule 10b-5 requires that D's fraud have been "by the use of any means or instrumentality of interstate commerce or of the mails, or of any facility of any national securities exchange." [268] Since on these facts neither phone nor mail (nor any other instrument of interstate commerce) was used, and the stock was not traded on a stock exchange, the transaction was a purely intrastate one and there is nothing to satisfy the quoted jurisdictional requirements.

V. RULE 10b-5 — MISREPRESENTATIONS OR OMISSIONS NOT INVOLVING INSIDER TRADING

A. Beyond insider trading: We now focus on those acts that may violate 10b-5 even though they do ***not*** involve conventional ***"silent"*** insider trading. Recall that 10b-5 prohibits any "fraud or deceit" in connection with the purchase or sale of any security. Certain ***misrepresentations***, and perhaps even omissions, may constitute violations of 10b-5 even though the case does not fall within the conventional pattern of a person who buys or sells based on non-public information about the company whose shares are being traded.

B. Breach of fiduciary duty as a kind of fraud: Recall that Rule 10b-5 forbids any "fraud or deceit upon any person, in connection with the purchase or sale of any security." Suppose a director, officer or controlling shareholder violates his ***state-law fiduciary duties*** in connection with buying or selling stock in the company. Can this violation of fiduciary duties constitute a "fraud" covered by 10b-5, even if there is no lie? If the answer is "yes," a shareholder would often prefer to bring a federal 10b-5 damage action instead of a state-law action, for various procedural reasons (e.g., better choice of venue, nationwide service of process, etc.). However, as we shall see, in the absence of an actual misrepresentation or half-truth, breach of state-law fiduciary duties does ***not*** give rise to a 10b-5 claim.

1. Lie to directors: First, let us consider a comparatively easy case: an insider (director, officer or controlling shareholder) ***lies to the board of directors*** or the compensation committee and induces them to ***sell him stock*** on favorable terms. Here, there is clearly a 10b-5 violation, even though the trade takes place directly with the corporation.

Example: D, the chief scientist of XYZ Corp., is aware that his employees have just made a major discovery that is likely to be translated into significantly higher earnings for XYZ. At a time when the board of directors of XYZ is not yet aware of the discovery, the board asks D whether there have been any major developments in his department, and he falsely says "no." The board then issues D stock, or a stock option, perhaps as part of a general plan of incentive awards for top executives. If D accepts the stock or options, he has violated 10b-5, because his false denial of significant developments is a "fraud . . . in connection with the purchase or sale of [securities]." (The same would be true if the board did not ask D about the development, he failed to disclose it, and he accepted the option they awarded him. This was one of the express holdings of the court in *SEC v. Texas Gulf Sulphur*, *supra*, p. 265.)

2. **Breach of duty without misrepresentation:** Now, consider the more difficult case in which D ***violates his fiduciary duties*** to the corporation of which he is an insider, but this violation does not involve any misrepresentation or, for that matter, any non-disclosure of something that D is obligated to disclose. Can the breach of fiduciary duty by itself be a violation of 10b-5, on the theory that it is a kind of fraud, perhaps "constructive fraud"? The answer is ***"no,"*** as the result of ***Santa Fe Industries, Inc. v. Green***, 430 U.S. 462 (1977).

   a. **Facts:** In *Santa Fe*, D (Santa Fe Industries, a corporation) owned 95% of the stock of Kirby Lumber Corp. Under applicable Delaware "short-form" merger provisions, a parent corporation that owns more than 90% of the stock of a subsidiary corporation may "cash out" the minority by buying their shares whether the minority consents or not. (A minority holder may then petition the court for an appraisal to determine the fair price for the stock, if he does not agree with what the majority holder is offering. See *infra*, p. 394.) D complied with all the terms of this short form statute, and thereby put through a merger under which the minority holders in Kirby were offered $150 per share. The Ps were minority holders in Kirby who were unhappy with the $150 per share price, but did not want to use their state-law appraisal rights. Instead, they brought a federal suit under 10b-5, claiming that when D put through the merger at what was (the Ps asserted) an unfairly low price, D was engaging in a kind of "fraud or deceit" upon the minority.

   b. **Holding:** But the Supreme Court ***rejected the Ps' argument,*** and held that they did ***not*** state any 10b-5 claim. As long as there was no "omission" or "misstatement" in the information given by D to the Ps, there was no "fraud" and thus no 10b-5 violation. 10b-5 simply does not, the Court held, cover situations in which "the essence of the complaint is that shareholders were ***treated unfairly by a fiduciary.***"

   c. **Rationale:** Perhaps the main reason why the Court found 10b-5 inapplicable to this "substantive unfairness" situation was that the Court did not want to ***federalize the law of fiduciaries***. Traditionally, the rules governing fiduciaries, especially corporate insiders, have been the subject of state, not federal, regulation. If a 10b-5 action could be brought any time an insider violated a state fiduciary rule, the federal courts would end up interpreting and applying state law, with which they have no expertise.

   d. **Fiduciary breach includes deception:** But it is important to keep in mind that *Santa Fe* only bars a 10b-5 action where there is ***no deception*** by the insider. If, as part of the insider's violation of his fiduciary obligations to the corporation and its shareholders, he ***deceives*** the corporation, its board or the minority shareholders, then a 10b-5 action will still be available despite *Santa Fe*. This exception is especially likely to be invoked where a ***majority*** or ***controlling stockholder*** causes the corporation to sell stock to him or buy stock from him, and the controlling stockholder ***does not make full disclosure*** to the company or its other shareholders.

      i. **Disclosure to disinterested board:** More specifically, the minority shareholders of a corporation may have a 10b-5 claim against the majority that sells stock to, or buys stock from, the corporation, if the transaction falls into ***either*** of two factual settings:

(1) **Shareholder approval required:** If ***shareholder approval*** was ***required under state law*** for the particular transaction, the Ps probably have a 10b-5 claim if they can show that they were not given ***full disclosure*** of the transaction. (We assume, of course, that the transaction involves a purchase or sale of stock in the corporation of which the Ps are stockholders.) In this situation, the fact that full disclosure was made to the board of directors is irrelevant.

(2) **Shareholder approval not needed:** If, under state law, shareholder approval was ***not*** required, the Ps may still be able to win if they can show that: (1) the disinterested ***directors*** were not given full disclosure; ***and*** (2) had full disclosure been made, the disinterested directors might well have rejected the transaction, or the court might well have blocked it as unfair. See S,S,B&W, p. 867.

C. Misrepresentation without trading: Suppose the corporation itself or one of its executives makes a ***false statement*** but ***does not trade*** in the company's stock. Can the corporation or the officer still be liable for a 10b-5 violation? The answer is "yes" — only the plaintiff, not the defendant, needs to have bought or sold the corporation's stock.

1. Scienter required: Remember, however, that the plaintiff in a 10b-5 action must always show ***scienter***, i.e., intent to deceive, on the part of the defendants. Thus if the defendant makes a false statement, but was ***honestly (even if unreasonably) mistaken***, there will be no 10b-5 liability. (On the other hand, if D speaks with ***reckless disregard*** of whether the statement is true or false, this recklessness ***will*** constitute scienter; see *supra*, p. 277.)

2. Merger discussions: The problem of false statements by non-traders occurs most frequently in the case of a company that is undergoing secret ***merger negotiations***. The target company will often have a strong interest in not acknowledging publicly that merger discussions are under way. First, the suitor may insist on this, because it does not want to be drawn into a bidding war, and will negotiate secretly or not at all. Secondly, the target may feel, perhaps quite reasonably, that the discussions are very preliminary and speculative, and that disclosure would attribute more importance to the discussions than they in fact warrant. Finally, the target may worry that public acknowledgment of the discussions will put the company "in play," i.e., subject it to a public bidding contest where management has little choice but to sell to the highest bidder.

a. Issue: Therefore, the issue becomes: If rumors start to fly about a possible merger, can the target company ***falsely deny*** that discussions are underway? In brief, the answer is "no": if the company knows that it is having even preliminary merger negotiations, it cannot flatly make statements such as "There are no merger negotiations underway" or "We know of no reason why the price and trading volume of the stock are rising." But there are at least two ways in which the company may be able to avoid liability without confirming secret discussions:

b. Materiality: First, one only has 10b-5 liability for ***material*** misrepresentations. If merger discussions are so ***preliminary*** and ***speculative*** that a reasonable investor would not consider them important in deciding whether to buy, sell or hold the stock, the discussions are not "material," and a false denial that they are occurring is not a misstatement of a material fact. See *Basic, Inc. v. Levinson*, 485 U.S. 224 (1988), *supra*, p. 272.

c. **Statement of no comment:** Perhaps more importantly, the company can almost always avoid 10b-5 liability by saying ***"no comment"*** when it is asked about the discussions. As the court said in *Basic, Inc.* (fn. 17) "***Silence***, absent a duty to disclose, is ***not misleading*** under Rule 10b-5. 'No comment' statements are generally the functional equivalent of silence." A company's right to remain silent about corporate developments is discussed further *infra*, pp. 302-302.

   i. **Difficulty:** Of course, if the company always explicitly and truthfully denies merger discussions when none are pending, and then suddenly switches to a "no comment" response when discussions really are pending, the "no comment" response will be seen as silent confirmation of the truth of the merger rumors, the very fact that the company presumably wants to keep secret. Therefore, the wisest thing for the company to do is to adopt ***in advance*** a "no comment" policy concerning ***any*** merger discussions, true or false.

   ii. **Insider trading problem:** Also, if material merger discussions are under way and the company uses the "no comment" policy, the company and insiders aware of the discussions may not ***buy or sell*** the company's stock. A purchase or sale by them would fall squarely within 10b-5's ban on insider trading.

   iii. **Exchange policies:** Finally, even if no insider trades on the stock, use of the "no comment" policy when important discussions were in fact underway would probably violate the requirements of any ***stock exchange*** on which the stock was traded. See, e.g., New York Stock Exchange Company Manual §§ 202.03 and 202.05.

3. **Reliance:** Where P claims that D has made an affirmative misrepresentation, must P nonetheless show that he directly ***knew*** of and ***relied*** upon the misstatement? The answer is ***"no"*** — P gets the benefit of "fraud on the market" theory, whereby he will be ***presumed*** to have relied upon the misstatement in the sense that the misstatement affected the market price at which P's purchase or sale took place. Indeed, *Basic, Inc. v. Levinson*, the case in which the "fraud on the market" theory was finally accepted by the Supreme Court, was a case in which the defendant company falsely denied that it was engaged in merger negotiations. See *supra*, p. 272.

4. **Fraud by one not associated with issuer:** Even a person ***not associated with the issuer*** can commit fraud (and thus violate 10b-5) by knowingly or recklessly making a false statement about the issuer or the issuer's stock.

   Example: Broker tells Client that XYZ Corp. has just made a major new invention, and that XYZ's stock price will probably soar as a result. Broker has no connection with XYZ, and Broker knows that his information is false. Client buys XYZ stock, as Broker hopes he will do. By making a false statement in connection with the purchase or sale of a security, Broker has violated 10b-5; this is so even though Broker has no connection with the issuer (XYZ).

D. **Statements made while one's own stock position concealed:** Concealment of ***one's own stock holdings*** may constitute the sort of "misrepresentation or omission" that can give rise to 10b-5 liability, even in the absence of conventional insider trading.

Example: D is a financial columnist for MoneyWeek Magazine. D buys lots of stock in XYZ Corp., then publishes a column in which he accurately summarizes XYZ's favorable characteristics and urges his readers to buy the stock. (He intends to influence the market price so that he can sell out at a profit if the stock rises.) The stock rises, and D sells out at a profit. D's column fails to mention D's own substantial position. Even though D's column is accurate (in the sense it does not contain any affirmative misrepresentations), D has probably violated 10b-5 because he has deceived his readers by making a misleading omission (that is, he has failed to disclose that he has a strong ulterior motive for his recommendation). Also, this conduct might be a "manipulation" of XYZ stock, similarly forbidden by 10b-5. See Clark, p. 348.

E. Omission by non-trader: Suppose that the company or an insider simply ***remains silent***, i.e., ***fails to disclose*** material inside information that it possesses. So long as the company or insider is not affirmatively ***misleading***, and so long as it or he does not buy or sell the company stock during the period of non-disclosure, there is ***no violation*** of 10b-5. This is true even if market rumors (correct ones as it turns out) are flying fast and furious, and the company's stock price and trading volume are being heavily affected.

1. **Exceptions:** But there are two ***exceptions*** to this general rule that the company cannot be liable under 10b-5 for a mere failure to disclose:

   a. **Leaks by company or its agents:** First, if rumors are the result of ***leaks*** by the company or its agents, the company probably has an obligation to confirm correct rumors or correct false ones.

   b. **Involvement in outsider's statements:** Second, the company may so ***involve*** itself with outsiders' statements about the company that the company will be deemed to have assumed a duty to correct material errors in those outsiders' statements.

   Example: X, a securities analyst, submits his estimates of ABC Corp.'s next quarterly earnings to ABC's investor relations director, W. W knows that these estimates are much too optimistic, but says nothing. X releases them to the public, the public is misled into bidding up the price of ABC stock, and the stock plunges when the real earnings are eventually released. ABC and/or W might well be held liable for violating 10b-5, on the theory that W's silence in the face of X's estimate was an implied representation that the estimate was reasonable.

F. Private class actions: An important aspect of 10b-5 liability not involving insider trading is the potential for ***private class-actions.***[7] Investors who have lost money based upon misleading statements by corporate insiders can sue en masse for those losses. Such actions can create potential liability in the billions of dollars.

Example: Suppose that XYZ Corp. is a large corporation with a $50 billion market capitalization. Rumors have started to float that XYZ's earnings will be down; the stock price has dropped from $50 to $35. On June 1, Prez, the company's chief executive, issues a statement saying, "Our business is as strong as ever — earnings are

---

7. Private class actions may be brought in insider-trading cases, too, but their biggest impact has been in misrepresentation cases not involving insider trading.

expected to be $1 per share for the quarter that will end June 30, compared with $.75 for the same quarter last year, and for the whole current year they are expected to be $4.25 compared with last year's $3.20." At the time Prez makes this statement, he knows that it's very unlikely that XYZ will in fact achieve anywhere near the earnings he's just promised. The stock rallies back to $45 on Prez' announcement. 8 weeks later, on August 1, the actual quarterly results are announced: the company loses $1.50 instead of making $1 (a loss that Prez in fact foresaw at the time he made the earlier pre-announcement). The stock plummets to $20.

A federal-court 10b-5 class action could be brought against Prez on behalf of all investors who bought XYZ stock between June 1 and August 1, for the difference between the price paid by each holder and $20 (the price after the misrepresentation was corrected). Since Prez made an intentional misrepresentation about a material fact and the class members presumptively acted in reliance on that misrepresentation, recovery ought to be allowed. If a large portion of the XYZ's outstanding stock changed hands during this period, the damages could easily amount to billions of dollars.

1. **Abuses:** In the early 1990s, there was increasing evidence that plaintiffs' class action lawyers were abusing the system by bringing frivolous 10b-5 ***"strike suits,"*** especially against high-growth technology companies. That is, lawyers were bringing suits "not because plaintiffs or their class action lawyers had any persuasive evidence of fraudulent conduct on the part of the defendants but primarily as an *in terrorem* device for ***extracting settlements*** from the defendants irrespective of the merits. ... [U]nwarranted settlements could be extracted because plaintiffs and their counsel, at relatively little cost and risk to themselves, were able to impose enormous ***discovery costs*** and the risks of ***astronomical damage awards*** on defendants." 51 Bus. Law 1009 (1996) (quoted in Hamilton (7th)).

2. **Reform Act to curb abuses:** Congress tried to curb these abuses by passing the Private Securities Litigation Reform Act of 1995 (the ***"Reform Act"***). A few of the key provisions of the Reform Act (all applicable only to *federal* securities-fraud class actions) are:

   - ❑ **Incentives for lawyers:** The ***incentives*** for ***class-action lawyers*** who represent just a few small shareholders are ***reduced***. For instance, the lead attorney's fees are capped at a ***"reasonable percentage"*** of the amount of damages paid to the class, and there is a presumption that the plaintiff with the largest financial interest should be the lead plaintiff, who then gets to select lead counsel.

   - ❑ **Discovery delayed: *Discovery*** (together with the large costs associated with it, especially on the defense side) is ***delayed*** until after the defense has had a chance to bring a motion to dismiss. This prevents plaintiffs from using discovery as a ***"fishing expedition."***

   - ❑ **Proportionate liability in some cases:** In many situations, defendants will ***not be jointly and severally liable*** — instead, there is ***"fair share" proportionate liabilty***, thereby decreasing the risk that any individual defendant will be ruined by a large, unexpected judgment. (Congress believed that the small but non-zero risk of total ruination contributed to settlements that were unreasonably large relative to the likely outcome on the merits.)

- ❑ **Pleading of state of mind:** Perhaps most important, where (as is usually the case) the result is dependent on the defendant's having acted with a particular state of mind, the complaint must "state with ***particularity facts*** giving rise to a ***strong inference*** that the defendant acted with the required state of mind." '34 Act, § 21D(b)(2).

See generally Hamilton (8th), pp. 1117-1122.

3. **Reform Act not wholly successful:** The Reform Act seems not to have been very successful. The number of federal securities-fraud class actions has actually gone up, not down, since the Act was passed, and the average settlement amount has increase fourfold. Hamilton (8th), p. 1122.

   a. **State-court suits:** Furthermore, the Reform Act seemed to spawn a dramatic increase in the number of securities fraud class actions filed in the ***state courts*** — plaintiffs' lawyers seem to have decided that if federal class action suits are now more difficult to bring and win, they should simply select a different forum, and a different body of law.

   b. **SLUSA:** Congress responded once again, by passing the Securities Litigation Uniform Standards Act of 1998 (***"SLUSA"***). SLUSA "***preempts*** most securities fraud class actions brought in ***state court.***" (Hamilton (7th), p. 1040.)

      i. **Traditional state-law actions preserved:** However, SLUSA does ***not*** preclude suits that are based on traditional areas of ***state corporate law.*** This exception is known as the ***"Delaware carve-out."*** For instance, under the carve-out SLUSA doesn't preclude traditional ***derivative suits*** (see *infra*, p. 318), where the claim is brought on behalf of the entire corporation. Nor does it preclude state class-action suits based on insiders' breach of state-law fiduciary duties regarding certain transactions between the corporation and its stockholders.

      ii. **Effect of SLUSA:** Despite the Delaware carve-out, SLUSA seems to be having some real impact. In the garden-variety scenario in which the claim is that some ordinary-course communication by the corporation or its insiders was fraudulent, any class-action will have to be in federal court. Thus in our example on p. 302 (fraudulent statement about what the level of earnings would be), any class action would have to be brought in federal court.

Quiz Yourself on

INSIDER TRADING (AND RELATED TOPICS) *(RULE 10b-5 — MISREPRESENTATIONS OR OMISSIONS NOT INVOLVING INSIDER TRADING)*

68. McSpeedy Gonzales is a corporation that runs a chain of very fast food restaurants. Mary McCheese, a stockbroker for the firm of Merrily Lynchem, tells Sylvester Katt in a phone conversation that McSpeedy Gonzales has just reported profits of $2 a share for the most recent quarter, and that in McCheese's opinion the stock is an excellent buy. McCheese knows that in fact the company has made only a $1 per share profit (down from the prior year), and that the $2 figure is due to a computational error by Merrily's fast-food analyst. Sylvester relies on his conversation with McCheese, and buys 1,000 shares of McSpeedy. The truth about McSpeedy's earnings comes out a week later, and the stock tanks. Sylvester sues

McCheese for a 10b-5 violation. McCheese defends on two grounds: (1) that she neither bought nor sold McSpeedy stock at any time; and (2) that she was not a McSpeedy corporate insider, nor did she learn her information by means of a breach by anyone of a fiduciary duty to McSpeedy. Therefore, she says, she can't have violated 10b-5. If McCheese's two factual assertions are correct, which, if either, of McCheese's defenses is valid? ______________

Answer

68. Neither. Rule 10b-5 prohibits (among other things) misstatements and omissions of material fact "in connection with the purchase or sale of any security." When D knowingly makes an affirmative misstatement of material fact to P about a security, and this induces P to buy or sell that security, P can recover from D for a 10b-5 violation even though D never bought or sold the company's securities, and even though D was not a company insider and didn't learn any nonpublic fact by means of a breach of fiduciary duty on the part of a company insider. [301]

If you got this question wrong, it's probably because you confused suit based on affirmative misrepresentation (which is what we have here) with a suit based on *insider trading*. If P's claim is that D has insider traded, then P must show both: (1) that D bought or sold the issuer's stock while in possession of material nonpublic information; and (2) that D was either an insider of the issuer or learned the information by means of a breach by someone of a fiduciary duty. But neither of these requirements applies to suits based on affirmative misrepresentation. So here, since McCheese knew that she was making an incorrect statement about McSpeedy's earnings, she's violated 10b-5 and Sylvester can recover. Thus in the garden-variety "fraud by a broker" scenario, the broker has typically violated 10b-5.

VI. SHORT-SWING TRADING PROFITS AND § 16(b)

A. Introduction: Entirely apart from Rule 10b-5, the federal securities laws contain another major statutory provision that was originally designed to combat insider trading. This is § 16(b) of the Securities Exchange Act of 1934, whose principal provisions read as follows:

> "For the purpose of preventing the unfair use of information which may have been obtained by [any beneficial owner of ***more than 10%*** of a ***class of stock***], ***director***, or ***officer*** by reason of his relationship to the issuer, ***any profit*** realized by him from ***any purchase and sale***, or any sale and purchase, of ***any equity security*** of such issuer . . . within ***any period of less than six months*** . . . shall inure to and ***be recoverable by the issuer***, irrespective of any intention on the part of such beneficial owner, director, or officer in entering into such transaction of holding the security purchased or of not repurchasing the security sold for a period exceeding six months. . . . This subsection shall not be construed to cover any transaction where such beneficial owner was not such ***both*** at the time of the purchase and sale, or the sale and purchase, of the security involved, or any transaction or transactions which the Commission by rules and regulations may exempt. . . ."

1. **Summary:** So to summarize how § 16(b) operates: if an ***insider*** (director, officer or 10%-stockholder) ***buys-and-then-sells*** (or sells-and-then-buys) with ***less than six months elapsing*** between the purchase and the sale (or the sale and then purchase), the insider is automatically required to ***pay back to the corporation all profits*** from the transaction.

2. **Purpose:** In enacting § 16(b), Congress reasoned that a "bright line" rule would be an effective way to stamp out at least some types of insider trading. Therefore, the rule

applies ***automatically***: if one of the statutorily-defined insiders buys stock in his company on, say, Feb. 1 and sells it at a profit on June 1 (or sells on Feb. 1 and repurchases it for less on June 1), he is ***automatically*** required to return the profits to the corporation, ***even if he had absolutely no insider knowledge***.

B. Overview: Here are some of the highlights of § 16(b)'s operation:

1. **Who is covered:** Section 16(b) defines quite specifically the insiders who are covered by it: ***officers***, ***directors***, and anyone who is directly or indirectly the ***beneficial owner*** of ***more than 10%*** of any class of the company's stock. Thus someone who might be an actual or constructive insider for 10b-5 purposes will not necessarily be an insider for 16(b) purposes — for instance, an outside professional (e.g., lawyer or investment banker) who is given information about the company, or a low-level employee who happens to learn important non-public information while on the job, is not covered by 16(b)'s short-swing profits rule unless he happens to be an officer, director, or more-than-10% owner.

2. **Only public companies:** Only officers, directors, and 10% shareholders of companies which have a class of stock ***registered*** with the SEC under § 12 of the '34 Act are covered. That is, the insider will be covered only if the company either: (1) is listed on a national securities exchange; or (2) has assets greater than $10 million and a class of stock held of record by 500 or more people. See § 12(g) of the '34 Act, and SEC Rule 12g-1. So as a practical matter, all "publicly held" companies are covered, but privately held companies are not. (Recall, by contrast, that SEC Rule 10b-5 applies even to the securities of "privately held" companies. See *supra*, p. 265.)

3. **Who may sue:** Suit may be brought by the corporation or by ***any shareholder*** (even one who did not own any shares when the insider's transactions took place). However, even if the suit is brought by the shareholder, any recovery goes into the ***corporate treasury***, not to the successful plaintiff-shareholder.

   a. **Attorneys' fees:** Why then would any shareholder ever bring a 16(b) action? Because the court will award ***attorneys' fees*** to the plaintiff's lawyer if the action is successful. Therefore, as a practical matter 16(b) actions are almost always engineered by the lawyer, and the plaintiff is typically someone with almost no financial stake in the corporation (e.g., a person who is persuaded to buy one share just prior to the litigation, for the purpose of being a named plaintiff).

4. **Public filings:** Any purchase or sale which could be part of a short-swing transaction under § 16(b) must be ***reported to the SEC***, under § 16(a). In fact, any § 16(b)-style insider (i.e., officer, director, or 10%-owner) must file a statement showing his ownership in the company's stock within 10 days after any calendar month in which that ownership changes. The SEC releases this information to the public, and private securities lawyers scan it looking for § 16(b) short-swing trades.

5. **Federal suit:** A § 16(b) action must be brought in ***federal court***.

6. **Not complete solution to insider trading:** Observe that while § 16(b) may catch someone who is not in fact trading on inside information, the converse is also true: a careful insider may avoid § 16(b) even if he is blatantly trading based on inside information. For instance, if Prexy buys stock in XYZ Corp., of which he is president, on Jan. 2, based on

the knowledge that the company will soon release favorable news, he will avoid § 16(b) liability so long as he holds on to the stock until at least July 3.

C. Who is an insider: As noted, § 16(b) covers only directors, officers, and more-than-10%-owners.

1. **Who is an "officer":** Who is an ***"officer"*** for 16(b) purposes? Unlike the status of being a "director," there is no simple, universally-agreed-upon definition of "officer" for 16(b) purposes.

   a. **Rule 3b-2:** The SEC's Rule 3b-2 under the '34 Act (applicable to § 16(b) liability) defines "officer" as follows: "[A] president, vice president, secretary, treasurer or principal financial officer, comptroller or principal accounting officer, and any person routinely performing corresponding functions with respect to any organization whether incorporated or unincorporated."

   b. **Case law:** The case law on who is an "officer" for § 16(b) purposes seems to boil down to these principles:

      i. **3b-2 title:** Anyone who holds any of the titles listed in the first phrase of Rule 3b-2 (president, vice president, secretary, treasurer, comptroller) is ***automatically*** an "officer" for 16(b) purposes.

      ii. **Functional analysis:** In addition, even a person who does not hold one of the titles enumerated in Rule 3b-2 will still be deemed an "officer" if he ***in fact*** performs executive duties similar to those typically performed by a holder of one of the named titles. This is essentially the "functional" approach of the second phrase of Rule 3b-2. Thus even someone who holds the title of, say, "production manager" might be an "officer" under § 16(b), if it were demonstrated that he was essentially an executive-level worker who would be likely to obtain material confidential information about the company's affairs in performing his job.

2. **Who is a "beneficial owner":** Even tougher issues are involved in determining who is "directly or indirectly the ***beneficial owner*** of more than 10%" of some class of the company's stock. (§ 16(a), incorporated by reference in § 16(b).)

   a. **10% of any class:** First, it's important to remember that a person falls within § 16(b) if he owns 10% or more of ***any class*** of the company's stock — he need not own 10% of the total equity in the company. For instance, if the company's equity is divided into 1,000,000 shares of common stock and 1,000,000 shares of preferred stock, D will be covered by § 16(b) if he owns 100,001 shares of preferred.

   b. **Attribution:** Remember that a person is covered under the "owner" prong of § 16(b) if he is "directly or ***indirectly*** the beneficial owner. . . ." Therefore, the court will sometimes ***attribute*** stock listed in A's name as being "indirectly beneficially owned" by B. The consequence of this attribution will be that A and B are treated as one "person," so that: (1) a sale of stock listed in A's name might be matched against a purchase in B's name; or (2) a purchase and sale of stock in A's name may come within § 16(b) because B is a director or officer of the company even though A is not. Probably most courts would agree to the following general attribution principles:

i. **Spouse and minor children:** A person will generally be regarded as the beneficial owner of securities held in the name of his or her ***spouse*** and their ***minor children***. See SEC Exchange Act Release No. 7824 (1966) (applying to the disclosure requirements of § 16(a), but probably relevant to 16(b) as well). Attribution is especially likely where the spouses ***share the economic benefit***, and/or one spouse ***influences*** or controls the other's investment decisions.

ii. **Grown children:** But a parent is less likely to have attributed to him the stock ownership of his ***grown children***.

3. **Deputization as director:** A corporation may be treated as a "director" of another corporation if the former appoints one of its employees to serve on the latter's board.

Example: ABC Corp owns a significant minority interest in XYZ Corp. ABC appoints E, its employee, to serve on the board of XYZ. ABC will be deemed to have "deputized" E to serve as director, so ABC will be treated as a constructive director of XYZ, and any short-swing trading profits reaped by ABC in XYZ stock will have to be returned to XYZ.

D. **When must the buyer/seller be an insider:** To be covered by § 16(b), must one be an "insider" (i.e., a director, officer, or beneficial more-than-10% owner) at ***both*** the time of purchase and the time of sale? The answer varies depending on whether the trader's insider status comes from his being an officer or director, on the one hand, or an owner, on the other.

1. **Director or officer at only one end of swing:** If D is a ***director or officer*** at the time of ***either*** his sale or his purchase of stock, § 16(b) applies to him even though he does not have the status at the other end of the trade. C&E, p. 963-64.

2. **10% ownership:** But the rule for 10% owners is different. Notice that under the last sentence of § 16(b), the entire section does not apply to any transaction "where such beneficial owner was not such both at the time of the purchase and sale, or the sale and purchase, of the security involved. . . ." So it is clear that a person is caught by the "10% owner" prong of 16(b) only if he has that more-than-10% status at ***both*** ends of the swing. But the interesting questions are: (1) Do we count the purchase that puts the person over 10%? and (2) Do we count the sale that puts the person under 10%?

a. **Purchase that puts one over 10%:** It is clear that the ***purchase*** that puts a person ***over*** 10% does ***not*** count for 16(b) purposes. In other words, a particular purchase will not be the first part of a buy-sell short-swing unless the buyer ***already owned more than 10%*** before the purchase. To put it another way, the purchase that ***lifts the buyer over 10%*** cannot be matched against a subsequent sale within six months. The Supreme Court so held in *Foremost-McKesson, Inc. v. Provident Securities Co.*, 423 U.S. 232 (1976).

i. **Rationale:** This rule makes sense, because we are trying to prevent people from buying on inside information and then reselling soon after; a person who at the moment he decides to buy does not yet own 10% is not an insider at the moment of decision, and thus presumably has no special information on the company's affairs. Clark, pp. 297-98.

b. Sale that puts person below 10%: But now consider the converse problem: suppose D already owns more than 10%, makes an additional purchase on Feb. 1, and then sells such a big chunk on March 1 that that sale brings him below 10%. Can the March 1 sale be partially matched against the Feb. 1 purchase, or do we measure D's 10% ownership status after the sale? This question ***has not been definitively resolved.*** However, the anti-insider-trading rationale of § 16(b) suggests that we should do this measurement ***before*** the sale — at the moment D ***decides*** to make the sale, he is still a more-than-10%-owner, and presumably has access to inside information about the company. See Clark, p. 298.

i. Two sales: Suppose D owns, say, 13% of XYZ Corp., and within six months of acquiring it, cleverly makes not one but ***two sales*** to dispose of his interest: first a sale of 3.5%, and then a sale of the remaining 9.5%. D will of course argue that his only § 16(b) liability is as to the initial 3.5% sale, and that since he no longer owned 10% at the time of the second sale, it is exempt. The Supreme Court ***agreed*** with this argument, over P's objection that both sales should be covered if they were part of a common design or plan, in *Reliance Electric Co. v. Emerson Electric Co.*, 404 U.S. 418 (1972).

E. What is a "sale," in the case of a merger: If the corporation ***merges into another company*** (and thus disappears), the insiders will not necessarily be deemed to have made a "sale" for purposes of § 16(b). D will escape short-swing liability for a merger or other unorthodox transaction if he shows that: (1) the transaction was essentially ***involuntary***; *and* (2) the transaction was of a type such that D almost certainly did ***not have access*** to inside information.

Example: Raider launches a hostile tender offer for Target. On Feb. 1, Raider buys 15% of Target pursuant to the tender offer. Target then arranges a defensive merger into White Knight, whereby each share of Target will be exchanged for one share of White Knight. The merger closes on May 1, at which time Raider (like all other Target shareholder) receives White Knight shares in exchange for his Target stock. On June 1, Raider sells his White Knight stock on the open market for a total greater than he originally paid for the Target stock.

Raider does not have any § 16(b) problem, because the overall transaction was essentially involuntary, and was of a type in which Raider almost certainly did not have access to inside information about White Knight's affairs.

F. Computation of profits: If § 16(b) applies, the defendant insider must forfeit to the corporation his "profit" realized by the purchase-sale or sale-purchase transactions. In the case of multiple purchases or sales within a six month period, the concept of "profit" is ambiguous. But what courts have in fact done is to perform the calculation so as to produce the ***maximum possible profits***.

1. Lowest purchase price matched against highest sale: In other words, the court will take the shares having the ***lowest purchase price*** and match them against the shares having the ***highest sale price***, ***ignoring any losses*** produced by this method. In other words, the courts do ***not*** match stock certificate numbers to determine the profits produced by the sale of particular shares (as they would do in a tax case). Nor do they use, say, a first-in-first-out computation, as an accountant might.

2. **"Profit" under § 16(b) despite overall loss:** This means that, paradoxically, an insider may have to fork over "profits" in a § 16(b) suit ***even though he had an overall loss*** in his transactions during the six-month period.

   Example: D is a director of XYZ Corp. He engages in the following sales and purchases of XYZ stock:

Transaction	Price	Date
Buy 200	$10	Feb. 1
Sell 200	$5	March 1
Buy 100	$20	April 1
Sell 100	$15	May 1

   Assuming that D never owned any other XYZ shares, a tax or accounting computation would conclude that D lost $1,500 on these transactions in total: he lost $1,000 on the first 200 shares, and another $500 on the last 100 shares. But in a § 16(b) case, the court would match 100 of the 200 shares bought at $10 against the 100 shares sold for $15; this would produce a $500 "profit," which D would have to surrender to XYZ despite his real loss on the set of transactions! See Clark, p. 300, fn. 17.

3. **Consequence:** Therefore, as a practical matter, if an insider makes a sale within six months of a purchase, or a purchase within six months of a sale, he does so only at his ***great peril.***

Quiz Yourself on

INSIDER TRADING (AND RELATED TOPICS) *(SHORT-SWING TRADING PROFITS)*

69. Joker is the president of the Metropolis By-Products Company, whose shares are publicly traded. Joker buys 11,000 Metropolis shares at $10 each on March 15. The by-products business is booming, and the shares are trading at $15 by June 1. On that fateful day, Joker trips on a catwalk at the factory and falls into a vat of chemicals. His ensuing medical bills are enormous, compelling him to sell 1,000 of the shares for $15 each on June 15. At the moment he sells the shares, Joker doesn't know anything about the company's operations that the general public doesn't know.

(a) You represent Robin, who owns a small number of Metropolis shares. What federal securities claim might you make against Joker? ______________

(b) Will your claim succeed? ______________

(c) Assuming the claim succeeds, how much will you recover, and to whom will it go? ______________

70. Fairy Godmother decides she's a real bozo for making wishes come true for nothing. As a result, she incorporates under the name Magic Wand, Inc., and begins taking on Fairy Godmother trainees, whom she teaches to perform miracles. The company grows by leaps and bounds, until it has sales of $100 million annually and has shares traded on the NYSE. Fairy Godmother owns 15% of Magic Wand's common stock. On March 1, she buys another 5,000 shares of the common stock at $10, and sells 1,000 shares at

$15 on April 1. On May 1, Rex Judicata, a lawyer, reads about these transactions. On June 1, he buys 50 shares of Magic Wand stock, and immediately pursues a derivative claim on Magic Wand's behalf, seeking Fairy Godmother's profit under §16(b). Does Judicata have standing to pursue the claim? ________________

71. Ariel, believing that seaweed is likely to become a major food source, buys 5,000 shares of publicly traded Little Mermaid Sea Harvests, Inc., on March 1. The shares cost $5 each, and her 5,000 shares represent 5% ownership of Little Mermaid. Ariel has no other connection with Little Mermaid. On April 1, Ariel buys another 10,000 shares at $5. On May 1, the U.S. government announces substantial government support for seaweed-based food products. Little Mermaid stock soars to $15 a share, prompting Ariel to sell her 15,000 shares on May 2. A §16(b) claim is filed against Ariel. How much, if anything, will Ariel owe? ________________

72. Calvin buys 1,000 shares of Hobbes Fantasy Vacations, Inc. stock at $10 a share on May 1. On June 1, Calvin is elected to Hobbes's board of directors. On July 1, he sells his 1,000 shares for $15 apiece. A 16(b) claim is filed against him. Will Calvin be liable under §16(b)? ________________

73. Albert Einstein is president of the Gone Fission Toy Company, which makes nuclear-powered toys. Gone Fission's stock is traded on the NYSE. On April 1, Einstein buys 500 shares of Gone Fission at $11 each. On May 1, he sells 500 shares at $8 each. On June 1, he buys 1,000 shares at $5 each. On July 1, he sells 1,000 shares at $6 each. If Einstein is sued under §16(b), how much, if anything, will he owe to Gone Fission? ________________

Answers

69. (a) A claim under § 16(b) of the '34 Act, to recover short-swing trading profits. Under this section, if an officer (or director or 10% owner) of a publicly-traded company buys and then sells (or sells and then buys) the company's stock within a 6-month period, all profits must be paid over to the company. [305]

(b) Yes. Joker, as president, is obviously an officer of Metropolis. Since he bought shares on March 15, and sold 1,000 of them on June 15 (less than 6 months after purchase), he's automatically liable under §16(b). The fact that he had no actual insider knowledge is irrelevant.

(c) $5,000, payable to Metropolis. The computation is simple, in this instance: on the 1,000 shares Joker sold, he made a profit of $5 per share, so he must disgorge the entire $5,000 profit to Metropolis. However, the plaintiff's lawyer will be entitled to reasonable attorney's fees out of this sum, with the corporation receiving only the balance. [306]

70. Yes; if the corporation itself doesn't pursue a § 16(b) claim against an insider, any shareholder can do so, regardless of when he became a shareholder. [306] Thus, the fact that Judicata wasn't a shareholder either at the time Fairy Godmother made her purchase or at the time she made her sale doesn't matter. Note that the lack of any "advance purchase" requirement gives attorneys an incentive to keep up with trades by insiders: such trades have to be reported to the SEC, and are then publicly disclosed. So an attorney can view the public record to spot a §16(b) violation, buy a few shares (or have a friend buy shares) in the corporation in question, press a § 16(b) suit derivatively, and collect attorney's fees.

71. $0. § 16(b) makes certain people engaging in purchases and sales of a corporation's securities within six months liable to pay any profits on those transactions to the corporation. The people covered are directors, officers, and 10+% shareholders. The issue here is whether Ariel fits the 10+% shareholder profile, since she was a 15% owner when she sold her shares. The answer is "no" — the Supreme Court has held that the purchase that *lifts* a person over the 10% threshold does not itself count under §16(b). [308] Since Ariel didn't make a later purchase (i.e., a purchase at a time when she already owned 10%+ of any class of stock), there's nothing against which the May 2 sale can be matched, so Ariel has no liability.

RELATED ISSUE: Say that, instead of selling shares on May 2, Ariel bought another 1,000 shares at $15. On May 15, suppose she sold all her 16,000 shares at $20. 1,000 shares of the 16,000-share sale could be matched against her May 2 purchase, since she was a 10+% owner immediately before that purchase. As a result, she could be required to surrender $5,000 of her profit (1,000 x [$20-$15]) to the corporation under § 16(b).

72. Yes. § 16(b) prohibits in-and-out purchases and sales of corporate securities by insiders, who can be directors, owners, or 10+% shareholders of the issuer. As the previous question shows, 10%-owners won't be covered unless they occupy that status both at the time of purchase and the time of sale. But the rule is different for directors or officers: these are covered by §16(b) if they hold that director or officer status at *either* the time of sale *or* the time of purchase. [308] Since Calvin was a director at the time he sold the 1,000 shares, he's liable under §16(b) (and will have to pay his $5,000 profit over to Hobbes).

73. $2,000. This is true even though Einstein lost $500 overall on his trades during the 6 months! § 16(b) makes insiders (and a President, as an officer, is clearly an insider) liable to the corporation for short-swing profits from trading in the corporation's stock. The court will match purchases and sales according to a *lowest-in, highest-out* formula, and will consider only those matches that produce profits. [309] Here, Einstein's "lowest in" is the 1,000-share lot he bought June 1 at $5. His "highest out" is May 1, when he sold 500 shares at $8. Matching 500 of the June 1 purchase against the May 1 sale results in a $1,500 profit (500 x $3). His next "highest out" is the 500-share sale at $6 on July 1; matching this sale against the remaining 500 shares from the June 1 purchase (at $5) results in a $500 profit (500 x $1). Any matching that produces a loss is ignored. Thus, Einstein's "profits" within a six month period are deemed to be $2,000, which he owes to the corporation.

Exam Tips on *INSIDER TRADING (AND RELATED TOPICS)*

Be alert to insider trading whenever a fact pattern involves the purchase or sale of stock based on ***information which was not available to the general public.***

☛ First, check for the core insider-trading scenario: a corporate insider has learned something non-public that will affect the price of the stock, and he then ***either buys or sells before the info becomes public.*** The insider has violated ***SEC Rule 10b-5.*** First, he can be sued civilly by the SEC. Second, ***any private person*** who has traded in the stock at a less favorable price during the time the insider was trading has an ***"implied private right of action"*** under federal law, and can therefore recover civil damages from the insider.

Example: D is a director of J Corp, a public company. He learns that J has developed a major new invention which it's about to patent, that will make the corp. more valuable. At a time when the public doesn't know about the invention, D buys J Corp. stock on the stock exchange, at $25/share. When J announces the deal, the stock goes to $50/share, and D sells. Both the SEC, and anyone who sold stock during the approximate time when D was buying, can bring a civil action against D. (Also, D has committed a crime.)

☞ Check to make sure that the private plaintiff ***bought or sold*** after the insider had the inside info. If not, P can't recover.

Example: Prexy says that Corp.'s earnings will be down next quarter. Prexy knows that in fact the earnings will be sharply up, and Prexy is in fact buying secretly for his own account. Joe shows that he would have bought had Prexy remained silent, but he declined to buy because of Prexy's false statement. Joe can't recover against Prexy under 10b-5, because only those who sell or buy while the insider is trading can recover.

☞ Remember that this "buy or sell" requirement means that the ***corporation itself cannot recover*** for insider trading under 10b-5, unless it was itself a purchaser or seller of shares at the same time as the insider trading was going on. (*Example:* On the facts of the above example, Corp. can't recover under 10b-5 against Prexy, if Corp. didn't issue any of its own shares while Prexy was buying.)

☛ Remember that the inside info must be ***"material."***

☞ You're most likely to have a materiality issue when the inside info is that ***merger negotiations have begun,*** but are very ***preliminary***. If all that's happened is that another company has approached, say, the target's CEO but the CEO has told them he's probably not interested, that may not yet be "material" inside info. (But once the CEO has decided to try to make a deal, and certainly once the CEO has gotten the board of directors involved in whether to sell, the info *is* now material.)

☛ Also, remember that the info must be truly ***"non-public."*** It's not enough that the other party to the transaction doesn't know of it — if a substantial number of members of the public do know of it, there can't be 10b-5 liability.

Example: Corp., a privately-held company, has just announced its new quarterly earnings, which are good. Prexy, Corp's president, buys stock from Pete in a face-to-face transaction. Pete hasn't heard the earnings report yet, but Corp. has already sent a press release to several local newspapers containing the info. The info isn't "non-public," so Prexy hasn't violated 10b-5.

☛ Keep in mind that 10b-5 also applies to ***private sales*** of ***non-publicly-traded stock*** based on insider info.

☞ But a ***facility of interstate commerce*** (phone, mail or a national securities exchange) must be used for any 10b-5 violation. This jurisdictional requirement is sometimes missing in private-sale fact patterns. (*Example:* Prexy buys stock directly from Dupe in a face-to-face transaction. Even if Prexy had insider info, there's no 10b-5 violation.)

☛ A large portion of 10b-5 questions turn on whether and when there's ***tipper liability*** and ***tippee liability.***

- ☞ The tipp*er* can be liable, ***even if he doesn't personally benefit,*** if he ***intends to make a pecuniary gift to the tippee.*** (*Example:* Prexy, head of Oilco, tells Fred, his friend, "We just struck a large well, so you might want to buy some stock quickly." Fred buys lots of stock, which rises after Oilco releases the news. Prexy is liable even though he did not buy or sell, and didn't get — or desire — any personal financial gain from tipping Fred; it's enough that he desired to confer a financial benefit on Fred.)

- ☞ Most importantly of all, the tipper is generally ***not liable unless he is an "insider"*** of the ***issuer.*** Normally, an insider is one who ***works for, or is a director of,*** the issuer (the company whose shares are bought or sold).

  - ☞ But ***non-employees*** can be ***constructive insiders.*** Thus ***lawyers***, investment bankers, accountants, etc., can be insiders if they've been given the info by issuer, to enable them to perform tasks on the issuer's behalf.

  - ☞ Someone who ***stumbles upon*** the inside info ***without having a fiduciary duty regarding that info*** is ***not*** an insider, and can't be liable as a tipper (or as a tippee). (*Example:* While sitting on a commuter train, D overhears Prexy, who he knows to be head of Oilco, tell Friend, "We just brought in a huge gusher today." If D tells E to buy Oilco stock, and E does so, neither D nor E is liable under 10b-5, because D didn't have any fiduciary duty regarding the info and thus isn't an "insider.")

  - ☞ When the inside info is news of an impending takeover, a person who works for or controls the ***bidder*** is ***not an "insider" of the target.*** (*Example:* Prexy, head of Bigco, is planning to have Bigco make a tender offer for Smallco. If Prexy personally buys shares in Smallco before announcing the tender offer, there's no 10b-5 violation, because Prexy is not an insider of Smallco, the issuer. Same result if Prexy tips Friend and Friend buys. But make sure Prexy is not a "misappropriator," as explained in the next paragraph.)

    - ☞ But remember that under the ***"misappropriation"*** theory, one who is an ***"outsider"*** (vis a vis the issuer) can still be a tipper, if he steals the information and trades on it or passes it on. (*Example:* Veep is a Vice President at Bigco, which is planning to make a tender offer for Smallco. Veep knows or should know that this information is secret and proprietary to Bigco. If Veep buys Smallco shares, he's liable under 10b-5 as a "misappropriator." If Veep passes on the info to his friend Leonard, who buys, Veep and Leonard are probably both liable, as tipper and tippee respectively.)

- ☞ The tipp*ee*'s liability is ***derivative from the liability of the tipper*** — if the conditions for tipper liability aren't satisfied, the tippee can't be liable no matter what the state of his knowledge or intent. (*Example:* On the earlier Prexy-Friend example, this principle is why Friend isn't liable under 10b-5 if Friend buys after being tipped by Prexy.)

- ☞ Even if the tipper is liable, the ***tippee won't*** be liable unless he ***knew or should have known*** that the tipper was ***breaching a fiduciary obligation*** to the corp. whose shares were traded.

  Example: Joe is a carpet installer. While installing carpet at the house of Prexy, head of Oilco, he sees an Oilco memo on Prexy's desk saying, "We just struck a huge gusher." Joe tells Fred, his friend, "You should buy Oilco stock right away, because I heard they just struck oil," but doesn't tell Fred how he learned the info. *Joe* is liable as a tipper [he knew he was breaching a fiduciary duty to Oilco and Prexy by stealing the info, and he intended to confer a benefit on Fred]. But *Fred won't* be liable as a tippee, since he didn't know, and had no reason to know, that Joe got his info as a result of a fiduciary breach.

☛ Next, consider the possibility that there may be a ***state-law*** cause of action for the insider trading.

- ☞ If all the insider did was to silently, and impersonally, buy or sell ***on a stock exchange*** while in possession of the information, there's probably no state-law (just federal law) liability.
- ☞ But if the insider buys ***face to face*** with someone (call him X), X may be able to recover against the insider under state common-law principles if either:
  - ☞ The insider made an ***affirmative misrepresentation.*** (*Example:* Insider says to P, "I'll sell you my stock at $15/share; the company will be reporting a good quarter soon and the stock will go up." In fact Insider knows that the quarter will be bad, and the stock goes down. P will probably be able to have the transaction rescinded and/or get damages.) ***or***
  - ☞ The insider remains silent, but ***uses unfair methods*** to seek out a buyer or to ***conceal his own identity.*** This is the ***"special facts"*** doctrine. (*Example:* Pres. has inside info that Corp's earnings will go up. Pres. has a broker locate X, a stockholder in Corp., and has the broker buy shares from X without disclosing that he's acting for Pres. A state recognizing the "special facts" doctrine will probably let X rescind the transaction or get damages.)
- ☞ Consider the possibility that the ***corp. itself*** may be able to bring its own state-law action against the insider-trader, to recover on behalf of all s/h's the profits the trader made. Say that the NY case of *Diamond v. Oreamuno* would allow corp. recovery here, but that most states do not. (*Example:* On above example, Corp. could recover from Pres the profits Pres made on the trade with X, under *Diamond.* This is true even though Corp. itself didn't suffer any direct loss — only X had direct losses, from selling his shares at a low price.)

☛ Finally, be on the lookout for situations in which an insider may be liable for ***short-swing profits.*** Remember that under § 16(b) of the Exchange Act, a corp. which is traded on a ***national stock exchange*** can recover ***profits made by a director, officer or more-than-10% s/h*** from the ***purchase-and-sale***, or the ***sale-and-purchase***, of that corp's securities ***within any 6-month period.***

- ☞ Remember that there's no § 16(b) cause of action unless there's been ***both a purchase and sale within the same 6-month period.***

  Example: On Feb. 1, Prexy, head of Corp., sells 1,000 shares of Corp. stock at $25. On March 1, Corp. discloses poor earnings, and the stock immediately falls to $10. If Prexy doesn't buy any stock back until Dec. 1, there's no 16(b) violation. But if he buys back 500 shares on July 1 at $10, he's automatically liable to Corp. for $15 x 500, regardless of whether he had any insider knowledge on either Feb. 1 or July 1.

☞ If D is a ***s/h*** (but *not* an officer or director), be sure that she was a ***more-than-10%*** s/h when she acquired the stock. § 16(b) won't apply to a s/h unless she owned more than 10% of the corp's stock at both the time of purchase and the time of sale. ***The purchase that lifts the buyer over 10% does not count*** for § 16(b) purposes.

Example: Prior to Dec. 1, Acquirer Corp. owned 50,000 shares (5%) of Target Corp. On Dec. 1, Acquirer buys an additional 140,000 shares (14%) of Target for $10/share, thereby becoming a 19% s/h in Target. On Feb. 1, Acquirer sells all its shares in Target for $20/share. Acquirer has no §16(b) liability, because there never was a time when it made a purchase while already — before the purchase — a 10% holder. (As to the sale, it's not clear whether we evaluate the 10% status before or after the sale, but there's a good chance that we measure that status *before* the sale.)

☞ However, where D is a ***director***, § 16(b) applies as long as he occupied that position on ***either*** the purchase date ***or*** sale date. Therefore, be alert for situations where the director ***resigned or was removed*** from the board before selling the stock, since these are ***covered***.

Example: D is a director of X Corp, a publicly-traded corp. with 100,000 shares outstanding. On March 1, D (who owns no X stock) buys 1,000 shares at $10. On July 1, D is removed from his seat for cause, on account of unauthorized expenses he charges to the company. On July 15, D sells his 1,000 shares at $15. X can recover $5,000 from D under §16(b), because D was a director at the time of the purchase, and it doesn't matter that D was no longer a director at the time of sale.

☞ When you calculate profits for §16(b), remember that the ***lowest purchase price is matched against the highest sale price,*** so as to ***maximize*** the corp's recovery. (Stock certificate numbers are not matched up, in other words.)

Example: D, a director of X Corp., buys 4,000 shares of X at $25 on Feb. 1. On March 1, D exercises an option to buy 1,000 shares at $15. On June 1, D sells 1,000 shares (whose certificates show that they were part of the 4,000-share lot), for $20 per share. X can recover $5,000 from D ($5 x 1,000), because we ignore the actual share certificates and match the lowest purchase price against the highest sale price.

CHAPTER 9

SHAREHOLDERS' SUITS, ESPECIALLY DERIVATIVE SUITS

ChapterScope

This Chapter covers suits brought by shareholders, especially the "shareholder's derivative suit." Key concepts:

- **"Derivative suit" defined:** A shareholder's derivative suit is a suit in which the shareholder sues "on behalf" of the corporation, on the theory that the corporation has been injured by the wrongdoing of a third person, typically an insider. (*Example:* A suit brought against an officer for engaging in self-dealing transactions with the corporation.)

- **Differences:** It's important to distinguish between when a suit should be brought as a derivative suit, and when it should be brought as an ordinary ***"direct"*** suit. Suits for breach of the ***duty of care*** and of the ***duty of loyalty*** are normally ***derivative***. Suits by a ***minority holder*** contending that the majority holder has behaved unjustly towards P (e.g., by refusing to pay dividends) are typically direct suits.

    - **Why distinguish:** The distinction between the two kinds of suits is important, because much more stringent ***procedural rules*** apply to derivative suits. (For instance, it's relatively easy for the board of directors to have the derivative suit discontinued if they don't think it has merit.)

- **Demand on board:** Most states require that before a derivative suit can be maintained, the plaintiff must make a ***"demand"*** on the board, in which he asks the corporation to take over the suit. If (as usually happens) the board declines, the court will often dismiss the suit.

    - **Demand excused:** But many states ***excuse*** the demand on the board in certain circumstances, such as where demand is likely to be "futile" (e.g., it's the entire board that's accused of wrongdoing, or of being under the wrongdoer's thumb).

- **Settlements:** Because there's a big risk that the plaintiff and the corporation will collude, any ***settlement*** of a derivative action has to be ***approved by the court***.

- **Indemnification:** The corporation may sometimes ***reimburse*** (***indemnify***) the director or officer for losses incurred relating to her actions on the corporation's behalf. In some situations, the corporation is ***required*** to indemnify, whether it wants to or not (***"mandatory"*** indemnification) and in others, the corporation ***may*** indemnify if it wishes to, but need not (***"permissive"*** indemnification).

I. INTRODUCTION

A. Remedy for fiduciary breaches: What happens when a person who owes the corporation a fiduciary duty breaches that duty? For instance, if X breaches his duty of loyalty to the corporation, or his duty of care to it, how can the corporation be made whole? In theory, the corporation itself, by vote of its board of directors, could decide to bring suit against the wrongdoer. But the wrongdoer will normally be an insider — a director, officer, or controlling shareholder — and the wrongdoer's fellow insiders will normally be reluctant to turn on one of their own.

1. **The derivative suit:** Therefore, courts in the United States (as well as in other common-law countries) have long allowed a peculiar form of action in order to deal with this problem: the ***shareholder's derivative suit***. In a shareholder's derivative suit, an individual shareholder (typically an ***outsider***) brings suit ***in the name of the corporation***, against the individual wrongdoer.

2. **Suit against insider:** The derivative suit may in theory be against anyone who has wronged the corporation, whether that person is an insider or outsider. Thus the defendant might be an officer who has breached the duty of due care or the duty of loyalty, or it might be an outsider who has injured the corporation in some other way (e.g., by breaching a contract with it, by committing a tort against it, etc.) But because the corporation itself, by vote of its board of directors, will usually not have any special reluctance to pursue claims against outsiders, the particular utility of the derivative suit is to pursue claims on the corporation's behalf against ***insiders.***

   a. **Breach of loyalty:** Most significantly, claims can be brought against an insider who has caused the corporation to enter into a ***self-dealing transaction*** with him (e.g., a sale of corporate property at below fair market value) or against an insider who has usurped a ***corporate opportunity*** (see *supra*, p. 219).

   b. **Breach of due care:** Derivative suits are also brought, though typically with less success, based on the insider's alleged violation of his duty of ***due care***. For instance, if Corporation's board of directors vote to acquire all of the stock of Small Corp., and the acquisition turns out to be disastrous, a shareholder might bring a derivative action against the individual directors who approved the transaction, alleging that they failed to use due care in making the acquisition.

B. **Pros and cons of derivative actions:** The entire area of derivative actions is a highly controversial one — strong arguments can be made both in favor of and against such suits.

1. **Favoring suits:** Those who find a lot of value in derivative suits, and who therefore argue for court rules that make it relatively easy to file and pursue such suits, make the following arguments:

   a. **Remedy for insider wrongdoing:** Such suits are practically the ***only effective remedy*** when ***insider wrongdoing*** occurs. The corporation itself (as represented by its incumbent board of directors) will rarely take action against an insider. The discipline of the marketplace (e.g., a decline in the market price of the company's stock when insiders are wronging the corporation) does little to deter wrongdoing, especially among insiders who own very little of the company's stock. Only an action brought by a shareholder whose investment has been made less valuable because of the wrongdoing will directly redress the injury to the corporation.

   b. **Deterrent effect:** A successful, or even threatened, derivative suit will have a useful ***deterrent*** effect — not only will the particular wrongdoer and the particular corporation in whose name the suit is brought be chastened, but potential wrongdoers in ***other*** corporations will think twice, lest they face the same kind of action.

c. **Legal fees:** The enforcement action is generally ***without direct cost*** (including attorneys' fees) to the corporation, since the plaintiff's attorney will only receive fees if he is successful, and he will then receive these fees only out of the recovery that is made on behalf of the corporation. (See *infra*, p. 339.)

2. **Against derivative suits:** But opponents of derivative suits make equally cogent arguments:

   a. **Waste of corporation's time:** The mere prosecution of a derivative suit often ***wastes a lot of the time*** and energy of the corporation's senior executives, and any resulting benefit to the corporation is less than the value of this time and energy.

   b. **Risk-averse managements:** Corporate managements will so fear derivative suits that they may become needlessly ***risk-averse***, and may thereby fail to maximize shareholder wealth.

   c. **Strike suits:** Because of the large waste of senior management time when a suit continues through trial, management will often be tempted to ***settle*** even suits that have little merit, in order to be rid of them. This incentive to settle in turn gives the plaintiff's lawyers an incentive to bring ***"strike"*** or ***"nuisance"*** suits, i.e., suits that have little probability of succeeding on the merits but are troublesome enough to induce the corporation to make a settlement. In the end, only the plaintiff's lawyers, not the corporation, are enriched.

3. **Early termination:** Most states recognize merit on each side of the controversy. Therefore, most states attempt to allow meritorious suits to be filed and to proceed to trial, while at the same time attempting to screen out suits without merit. The principal way this screening now occurs in most states is by allowing the corporation to appoint a special ***independent committee*** to assess the merits of the plaintiff's suit, and to recommend whether the suit should be continued or dismissed; if the committee is truly independent, conducts its investigation carefully, and recommends that the suit be discontinued, most courts accord that recommendation significant weight. The early termination of meritless derivative suits is the single most important issue in connection with derivative suits, and is discussed extensively beginning *infra*, p. 325.

II. DISTINGUISHING DERIVATIVE FROM DIRECT SUITS

A. **General distinction:** Not all suits by shareholders are derivative — in some situations, a shareholder (or a class of shareholders) may sue the corporation, or insiders, ***directly***. The procedural and substantive rules that govern direct actions are quite different from those that govern derivative actions. How, then, can we distinguish between an action that should be characterized as a derivative action and one that should be characterized as a direct action?

1. **General rule:** In the most general sense, the distinction is based on ***who has been directly injured***: if the injury is an injury ***to the corporation***, the suit to redress it is a derivative action; if the injury is to some or all shareholders, the suit is a direct one. See

the discussion of *Tooley v. Donaldson, Lufkin, & Jenrette, Inc.*, the Delaware case on the distinction, *infra*, p. 320.

2. **Illustrations of derivative action:** Thus most cases brought against insiders for breach of the fiduciary duty of ***care*** or ***loyalty*** are ***derivative***. Here are some examples:

   a. **Due care:** A suit against the board members for failing to use ***due care*** in overseeing the company's operations (e.g., by grossly negligently approving a disastrous acquisition);

   b. **Self-dealing:** A suit against an officer for ***self-dealing*** (e.g., by inducing the corporation to buy the property from him at an above-market price);

   c. **Excessive compensation:** A suit to recover ***excessive compensation*** paid by the corporation to its officers;

   d. **Corporate opportunity:** A suit against an officer alleging that he has usurped a ***corporate opportunity*** for himself (e.g., by acquiring a piece of property that the corporation would have been interested in).

   See Clark, p. 663.

   Note: Observe that in each of these above situations, it can be said that the shareholders have been injured, since their investment in the corporation is worth less than it would have been had there been no breach of duty. But the action is still a derivative, not direct, one because ***in the first instance*** it is the ***corporation*** that has been injured, and the shareholders have only been harmed secondarily.

3. **Illustration of direct actions:** Here, by contrast, are some of the types of suits that are generally held to be ***direct***:

   a. **Voting:** An action to enforce the holder's ***voting rights***, or to prevent some other shareholder from improperly voting his shares;

   b. **Dividends:** An action to compel the payment of ***dividends***;

   c. **Anti-takeover defenses:** An action to prevent management from improperly using the corporate machinery to ***entrench itself*** (e.g., a suit to enjoin the corporation from enacting a "poison pill" which would prevent a takeover);

   d. **Inspection:** An action to compel the ***inspection*** of the corporation's books and records.

   e. **Protection of minority shareholders:** A suit to prevent oppression of, or fraud on, ***minority shareholders, especially where the corporation is closely-held.***

   See ALI Prin. Corp. Gov., Comment c to § 7.01.

4. **Delaware law on the distinction (*Tooley*):** A 2004 Delaware case establishes a simple ***two-part test*** for distinguishing between direct and derivative actions. In *Tooley v. Donaldson, Lufkin, & Jenrette, Inc.*, 845 A.2d 1031 (Del. 2004), the Delaware Supreme Court said that the issue must turn "solely" on the two following questions:

   [1] "who ***suffered the alleged harm*** (the corporation or the suing stockholders, individually)?" and

[2] "who would ***receive the benefit*** of any recovery or other remedy (the corporation or the stockholders, individually)?"

a. **Probably must meet both parts to be direct:** The *Tooley* decision does not focus on what happens if the two answers point in different directions. The most likely reading is that to be "direct," the suing stockholders must ***both*** have ***suffered the alleged harm*** *and* be in line to ***receive the benefit of any recovery***. In any event, a split-answer should rarely happen — if the plaintiff shareholders have suffered a harm that is not dependent on an injury to the corporation, it is presumably those shareholders, not the corporation as a whole, who will also get the benefit of any recovery.

b. **Application to facts of *Tooley*:** The facts of *Tooley* illustrate how the two-part Delaware test will work. The Ps were former minority shareholders of brokerage firm DLJ. Prior to the events in question, this minority group owned 30% of the company, and AXA owned 70%. AXA as controlling shareholder put through a merger agreement in which all shares in DLJ — whether owned by AXA or the minority holders — would be exchanged for a mix of stock and cash in Credit Suisse, the acquirer. After the merger agreement was signed, the DLJ board agreed to give Credit Suisse extra time to cash out the minority shareholders. The minority shareholders sued the DLJ board (apparently consisting mostly of AXA-nominated directors), alleging that the grant of extra time violated the directors' fiduciary duty to the minority holders.

i. **Held to be direct:** Applying the new two-question test, the Delaware Supreme Court quickly concluded that the action was ***not a derivative suit.*** There was no claim that the corporation (DLJ) had been injured by the delay — only the minority stockholders claimed to have been injured (by having to wait longer for their money). And if there was a recovery, it was clear that that recovery would go just to the minority holders.[1]

5. **Direct action preferred:** Because the procedural rules imposed in derivative suits (see *infra*, p. 322) are generally tougher for the plaintiff than in a direct suit, the plaintiff will usually ***prefer to have his suit characterized as direct*** rather than derivative.

B. **Consequences of distinction:** As noted, the plaintiff will usually want his action to proceed as a direct rather than derivative one. Here are some consequences that flow from a court's decision to treat an action as direct or as derivative:

1. **Procedural requirements:** If the action is ***derivative***, the plaintiff must jump through a number of ***procedural hoops*** merely to be able to proceed at all. For instance, he must satisfy the "contemporaneous ownership" rule (*infra*, p. 322), by which he must have been a shareholder at the time the wrong complained of occurred; similarly, he may have to comply with a ***security-for-expenses*** statute.

a. **No jury trial:** Plaintiff in a derivative action also will typically face ***trial rules*** that are less favorable to him than he would in a direct action. For instance, most states hold

---

1. On the other hand, the court concluded, this was not yet a valid *direct* claim either, because the merger as extended had not yet closed, so the plaintiffs' claim had not yet "ripened." Once the merger closed, then plaintiffs could bring their direct claim.

that a derivative action is ***equitable***, and that there is therefore no right to a ***jury trial*** on it.

2. **Demand on board; termination:** Second, the plaintiff in a derivative suit is much more likely ***to lose control*** of his action than where the action is direct. For instance, the plaintiff must generally make a ***demand*** on the board of directors that it bring suit; the board of directors (or, increasingly, a special committee appointed by the board) may in most states investigate and recommend ***termination*** of the suit. The court will often respect this termination recommendation (see *infra*, p. 330), so that the plaintiff will simply not be allowed to proceed. In a direct action, by contrast, the plaintiff (or the plaintiff class) will get to proceed unless the defendant obtains a summary judgment, a much more difficult thing to get.

3. **Who gets recovery:** Finally, the distribution of the ***recovery*** is likely to be more attractive to the plaintiff in a direct than in a derivative suit. In a derivative suit, the recovery is always ***by the corporation***, and the plaintiff benefits only to the extent that his shares in the corporation (as well as the shares of everyone else) become more valuable due to the corporation's recovery. In a direct action, by contrast, the plaintiff may be able to put money directly into his own pocket. For instance, if P sues to compel the payment of a dividend, this money will be paid directly to him if he succeeds.

III. REQUIREMENTS FOR MAINTAINING A DERIVATIVE SUIT

A. **Rules, generally:** There are three main procedural requirements that, in most states, a plaintiff must meet in order to maintain a derivative suit: (1) P must have been a shareholder ***at the time of the acts complained of*** (the ***"contemporaneous ownership"*** rule); (2) P must ***still*** be a shareholder at the time of the suit; and (3) P must make a ***demand*** (unless excused) upon the board of the corporation, requesting that the board attempt to obtain redress for the injury the corporation has suffered.

B. **Requirement of a shareholder:** All states require that the plaintiff be a ***stockholder*** in the corporation on whose behalf the suit is brought. Before we look at the ***time*** at which the stock must be owned, let us first consider what is meant by "stockholder." The word means, essentially, "holder of an ***equity*** security" in the company.

1. **Bondholders not covered:** In other words, a ***bondholder*** or other creditor may ***not*** bring a shareholder's suit. C&E, p. 1002.

C. **"Contemporaneous ownership" rule:** A key requirement is that P have owned his shares at the ***time of the transaction*** of which he complains. See ALI Prin. Corp. Gov., Reporter's Note 6 to § 7.02. This is the ***"contemporaneous ownership"*** rule.

1. **Federal rules:** For instance, in derivative suits brought in federal court, Fed. R. Civ. Pro. 23.1 requires that the complaint allege "that the plaintiff was a shareholder . . . at the time of the transaction of which the plaintiff complains or that the plaintiff's share or membership thereafter devolved on the plaintiff by operation of law. . . ."

2. **Nearly universal requirement:** Nearly all states similarly impose this "contemporaneous ownership" requirement, most by statute but some by case law. See, e.g., MBCA

§ 7.41 (the shareholder may not commence or maintain a derivative proceeding unless she "was a shareholder of the corporation at the time of the act or omission complained of. . . .").

3. **Rationale:** Two reasons are usually given for the contemporaneous ownership rule: (1) it discourages litigious people from bringing frivolous suits, since they can't look around for wrongdoing and then buy shares that will support standing; and (2) a person who buys after the wrong with knowledge of it may ***pay a lesser price***, and would thus receive a windfall if he obtains a corporate recovery. ALI Prin. Corp. Gov., Comment c to § 7.02.

4. **Criticism:** But the rule is also frequently criticized, on the grounds that it screens out meritorious suits as well as frivolous ones, and screens out suits where there would be no unjust enrichment.

   a. **Illustration:** For instance, the contemporaneous ownership rule (in its traditional phrasing) would bar suit by P if he purchased the shares after the wrongdoing, ***even if neither P nor anybody else knew of the wrongdoing at the time of purchase.*** In this situation, P clearly did not buy in order to stir up litigation (since he did not know of the wrongdoing), and P would not be unjustly enriched by a successful suit (since he did not pay a lesser price to reflect the unknown wrongdoing).

      i. **ALI allows:** For this reason, the ALI's *Principles of Corporate Governance* merely require that the shares be bought before the material facts of the wrongdoing were "publicly disclosed or were known by [the plaintiff]." See ALI Prin. Corp. Gov., § 7.02(a)(1).

5. **"Continuing wrong" exception:** Partly because of these criticisms, courts sometimes use a number of techniques to avoid throwing the plaintiff out of court even though he did not buy until after the alleged wrongdoing took place. One such technique is by recognizing an exception for ***"continuing wrongs."*** Under this exception, P can sue to challenge a wrong that began before he bought his shares, but that ***continued after the purchase.*** C&E, p. 1029-30.

D. **The "continuing ownership" rule:** The plaintiff must ***continue*** to own the shares in the corporation not only at the time of suit, but right up until the moment of ***judgment***. In other words, P must continue to have an actual (even if tiny) economic stake in the outcome of the suit right until its conclusion.

   1. **Involuntary merger:** Normally, this requirement does not have much bite — since even a one-share holding by the plaintiff will suffice, compliance with the requirement is rarely difficult for the plaintiff. But there is one situation in which the continuing-ownership rule does have real bite: the situation in which all shares in the corporation are involuntarily ***exchanged*** into cash or shares in a different corporation, as part of a ***merger*** transaction. Here, many courts ease the unfairness that would result from mechanical application of the continuing ownership rule — they allow the shareholders in the no-longer-existing corporation to bring a non-derivative suit against the wrongdoers, or they allow the surviving corporation (or its shareholders) to bring suit. See ALI Prin. Corp. Gov., Reporter's Note 4 to § 7.02.

E. Demand on the board: Virtually all states require that, as a general rule, the plaintiff must make a ***written demand*** on the board of directors before commencing a derivative suit; the demand asks the board of directors to bring a suit or take other corrective action to redress the wrongdoing. Only if the board refuses to act may the plaintiff then commence suit.

1. **Excuse:** However, many jurisdictions also ***"excuse"*** the demand requirement where such a demand would clearly be ***futile.*** For example, if the essence of P's claim of wrongdoing is that the entire board of directors personally benefited in a pecuniary way from the transaction which they approved, most courts would excuse the would-be plaintiff from demanding that the board in effect sue itself.

   a. **MBCA:** The MBCA requires a demand on the board in ***all*** cases. See MBCA § 7.42(1). The shareholder must then normally wait 90 days after the demand, before suing (unless the board rejects the demand earlier). § 7.42(2).

2. **Later treatment:** The requirement of a demand on the board, and the accompanying doctrine that demand is sometimes excused, have extraordinary importance in the law of derivative actions. The reason for this is that in most states, the distinction between cases in which demand is required and those in which it is excused determines the ***scope of judicial review*** of the action: if demand is required and the board rejects the demand, the court will only very rarely allow the action to proceed; but if demand is excused, although the court may still terminate the action on the corporation's motion it is less likely to do so. Therefore, our treatment of the demand requirement is deferred until our treatment of the broad issue of early termination, *infra*, p. 325.

F. Demand on shareholders: Many states purport to require that the plaintiff also make a demand on the ***shareholders*** before he institutes the derivative suit. In theory, the shareholders would then vote on whether to maintain the derivative action, and if a majority voted against the action, the plaintiff would not be permitted to proceed.

1. **Some courts eliminate requirement:** But a number of important jurisdictions do ***not*** require a demand on shareholders in ***any*** situation. This is true, for example, in California (Cal. Corp. Code § 800) and New York (N.Y. B.C.L. § 626). The trend is ***away*** from requiring shareholder demand; for instance, the ALI's Prin. Corp. Gov. § 7.03(c), and Subchapter D of the MBCA both eliminate the demand on shareholders.

2. **Demand excused:** Even in those states that purport to require a demand on shareholders, the demand may be ***excused*** in a variety of situations. Usually, these demand-excused situations are so common that they virtually swallow up the requirement of a shareholder demand, so that the requirement has little practical bite. Here are some of the common grounds for excusing shareholder demand:

   a. **Large number of holders:** The number of shareholders is large enough that a demand would be very expensive or would result in substantial delay. This exception exists in almost every state with a shareholder-demand requirement, and as a practical matter ***eliminates*** shareholder demand in the case of ***any publicly-held corporation***.

   b. **Defendant controls:** The defendants have a ***majority or controlling block*** of the stock, so their disapproval of bringing the suit would not be disinterested; and

c. **Non-ratifiable:** The wrong is said (by the court) to be ***"non-ratifiable."*** Typically, this will be the case where the wrong is an ***illegal act***, or amounts to a ***fraud*** on the shareholders. Cases alleging ***self-dealing*** are often held to fall into this "non-ratifiable" category. The theory behind this exception is that fraud or illegality injures the objecting shareholders so deeply that it is simply not in the majority's power to approve (by rejecting the suit) the imposition of such an injury on the minority. See the discussion of non-ratifiable self-dealing *supra*, p. 207.

IV. DEMAND ON THE BOARD; EARLY TERMINATION BASED ON BOARD OR COMMITTEE RECOMMENDATION

A. **Problem generally:** Recall that a derivative action is brought "on behalf of" the corporation. Yet decisions about how the corporation's affairs should be run are ordinarily reserved to the board of directors (see *supra*, p. 50). If a plaintiff may litigate a derivative suit on the corporation's behalf even though the board opposes the action, the board's customary power to make major business decisions concerning the corporation's operations is effectively curtailed. Furthermore, the plaintiff or the plaintiff's lawyer will often have an incentive to bring frivolous claims for their "nuisance" or settlement value, and the corporation itself may suffer if the time of the board and senior executives is used up in dealing with a protracted meritless suit. These considerations support giving the board, or perhaps a special committee of the board, at least some power to review the action, to determine whether it is in the corporation's best interest, and if not, to have it dismissed.

1. **Insiders as defendants:** On the other hand, many serious derivative suits allege wrongdoing by corporate insiders, including (1) board members and/or (2) the senior executives who were responsible for the board members' getting their board seats in the first place. If left to its own devices, the board will rarely institute action against a corporate insider. Thus in precisely the situations where derivative actions serve their most worthy purpose, giving the board a substantial say in whether the action should proceed will undermine the very purpose of allowing derivative actions in the first place.

2. **Dilemma:** Courts have, therefore, struggled to find rules that will on the one hand maintain the board's ability to control the corporation's affairs and to terminate frivolous actions at an early stage, yet will on the other hand prevent the board from covering up for wrongdoing by its own members or other insiders.

   a. **Protect board's autonomy:** In general, courts and statutes have tried to protect the board's autonomy by (1) requiring a demand to be made on the board in most instances; (2) giving substantial weight to the board's decision not to pursue the action; and (3) increasingly, by giving significant weight to the recommendation of a specially-appointed board committee, made after investigation, that the suit be dismissed.

   b. **Block coverups:** At the same time, courts and statutes have tried to block coverups by: (1) excusing demand on the corporation in many instances, in which case the suit is typically allowed to go forward even though the board would or does oppose the suit; and (2) ignoring the board or special committee's opposition to the suit where the essence of the complaint is that the board, or persons who dominate the board, have received an improper personal financial benefit by the act complained of.

c. **Three topics:** Therefore, we can break down the topic of "early termination based on board or committee action" into three separate topics:

(1) When is demand on the board ***excused***, and what are the consequences of such an excuse?

(2) If demand is ***not*** excused, and the board ***rejects*** the demand, when should the court nonetheless ***allow the action to go forward***? and

(3) If demand is made, the board appoints a special ***independent committee*** to review the merits of the action, and the committee recommends dismissal, how much weight should the court give that recommendation?

We consider each of these questions in turn.

B. **Demand excused:** First, when is a demand on the board ***excused***, and what are the consequences of excuse? Let's consider these questions in reverse order:

1. **Consequences of excuse:** If demand on the board is excused, the action normally may ***proceed*** without any early judicial overview of its merits (except, perhaps, for a motion for summary judgment by the corporation or the defendants). However, even in cases where demand is excused, the board may appoint an independent committee to review the suit; if that committee investigates and recommends dismissal, the court usually may consider whether to accept that recommendation and dismiss the suit, just as if demand had been made and the committee appointed. (The whole issue of an independent committee's recommendation is discussed *infra*, p. 329.) But in general, the plaintiff will have a much ***easier time having his action go forward*** without close judicial scrutiny of the merits if the case falls in the "demand excused" category than if it falls within the "demand required" category. For this reason, the issue of whether the case is a "demand excused" or "demand required" one is typically subjected to bitter and protracted litigation.

2. **When is demand excused:** In the broadest sense, demand on the board is excused where it would be ***"futile."*** Typically, demand will be deemed excused if the board is accused of having participated in the wrongdoing — in this situation, the board is unlikely to, in effect, recommend suit against its own members collectively. On the other hand, courts vary with respect to what kind of board conduct the plaintiff must allege in order to escape the demand requirement.

   a. **Board wrongdoing alleged:** Most cases in which P argues that demand should be excused are ones in which the ***board itself*** is charged with some sort of ***wrongdoing*** (either breach of the duty of due care or breach of the duty of loyalty), and the issue is what kind of board wrongdoing will be sufficiently grave that a subsequent demand by P to the board should be deemed "futile" and thus excused.

3. **Delaware view:** In Delaware, a plaintiff who attacks a board decision as wrongful must nonetheless make a demand on the board, unless he carries the burden of showing a ***reasonable doubt*** about whether the board either: (1) was ***disinterested*** and ***independent***; or (2) was entitled to the protections of the ***business judgment*** rule (see *supra*, p. 132).

Example of category (1): P might bring the case into category (1) — board not disinterested and independent — by showing, for instance, that each member of the board was ***hand-picked*** by D (the president and controlling shareholder), and that when the board members approved, say, a very generous salary for D, they were motivated principally by a desire to ***ensure their continued re-election*** to the board.

Example of category (2): P might bring the case within category (2) — that the decision was not entitled to protection of the business judgment rule — by showing either that the board members did not follow ***adequate procedures*** in reaching their decision (e.g., they did not conduct a reasonable inquiry; see *Smith v. Van Gorkom*, *supra*, p. 186) or that the board's decision was, substantively, so ***irrational*** as to be outside the bounds of reasonable business judgment. *Aronson v. Lewis*, 473 A.2d 805 (Del. 1984).

a. **Difficult to do:** But Delaware makes it very ***difficult*** for the plaintiff to succeed in bringing the case within either category (1) or (2), and thus difficult to get demand excused. Here are some of the ways that Delaware courts do this:

   i. **Specificity:** Although P must merely ***plead*** (not submit evidence of) facts sufficient to get the case within (1) or (2), the facts must be plead with great ***specificity***. For instance, in *Aronson*, *supra*, P alleged that D, a 47% shareholder in the corporation, had personally hand-picked each of the directors, who had then approved a very generous retirement/consulting package for D. The court held that these allegations were not specific enough to show the board's lack of independence; instead, P had to come up with an even more particularized showing of how the board was under D's dominance at the time it approved his contract.

   ii. **Liability of board:** Similarly, the fact that the board itself is being charged with a violation of the duty of due care for having approved the transaction is ***not enough*** to render demand futile and thus excused.

   iii. **Discovery:** The plaintiff will not normally be able to obtain ***discovery*** in order to be able to make the particularized allegations that are required. S,S,&B, p. 1078.

   iv. **Self-dealing transaction:** Finally, even though the suit alleges gross self-dealing, usurpation of corporate opportunity or other breach of loyalty by an insider, and even though this self-dealing was ***approved*** in advance or after-the-fact by the board of directors, demand will still not be excused unless there is a particularized showing that the board was not independent or acted irrationally. *Id.*

   v. **Summary:** In summary, it will be a relatively rare Delaware case in which the plaintiff is able to allege board misconduct with enough specificity to get the demand excused.

4. **New York law:** New York seems to follow roughly the same approach as Delaware in distinguishing between situations in which demand is excused on account of futility and those in which demand is required. In *Marx v. Akers*, 666 N.E.2d 1034 (N.Y. 1996), New York's highest court gave a succinct summary of when demand will be excused. Demand will be ***excused*** if (and only if) the complaint alleges "with particularity" any of the following:

   [1] "that a ***majority of the board*** is ***interested*** in the challenged transaction." (A director

can be "interested" either because she has a direct self-interest in the transaction, or because, although she has no direct self-interest in the transaction, she has lost her independence by being "controlled" by a self-interested director.)

[2] that the board "***did not fully inform themselves*** about the challenged transaction to the extent reasonably appropriate under the circumstances." In other words, a director who merely "passively ***rubber-stamp[s]*** the decisions of the active managers" does ***not*** thereby exempt herself from liability.

[3] that "the challenged transaction was so ***egregious on its face*** that it ***could not have been the product of sound business judgment*** of the directors."

C. Demand refused: Suppose now that the case falls within the ***"demand required"*** rather than "demand excused" category. If the plaintiff makes his demand on the board, and the board ***rejects*** the demand and refuses to sue (as it almost always does), may the plaintiff continue with his suit?

1. Suit against unaffiliated third party: Where the suit is against a ***third party*** who is not a corporate insider, the plaintiff will almost never be permitted to continue his suit. In this situation, the board's rejection of demand constitutes a decision about how the corporation should ***conduct its ordinary business affairs.*** Therefore, the court will almost always give the directors' decision not to pursue the suit the protection of the ***business judgment rule***. (Remember that under this rule, *supra*, p. 182, the board's decision on a business matter will be respected by the court so long as it is made in good faith, with reasonable procedural safeguards, and is not totally irrational, even though the court may believe that the decision was substantively unwise.)

2. Suit against insider: Where (as is usually the case) the suit is against a corporate ***insider***, the situation is more complex. But here, too, the court will give the board's decision not to sue the protection of the business judgment rule, unless P alleges that the board: (1) somehow ***participated*** in the alleged wrong (e.g., they got some ***personal benefit*** from it); or (2) the directors who voted to reject the suit were ***dominated or controlled*** by the primary wrongdoer. Clark, p. 644. If P can show either of these two things, then the court will generally remove the cloak of the "business judgment rule" from the board's decision not to sue, and will allow P's suit to go forward.

a. Similarity to demand-excused rules: You will notice that these two situations (self-dealing and domination) that will allow P to sue notwithstanding the refusal of his demand are very similar to the factors that will cause the demand to be ***excused*** in the first place (see *supra*, p. 326). If this is so, the court's decision to put the case into the "demand excused" rather than "demand required" category doesn't make as much difference as is usually thought — the same factors of self-interest or domination will allow the plaintiff to proceed regardless of which category the case is placed in. But it is probably the case that, in most jurisdictions, it is somewhat easier to convince the court that demand would be futile (and thus should be excused) than to convince the court that the board's rejection of a required demand was so wrongful that it should not be protected by the business judgment rule.

i. Require demand in all cases: Because of the similarity between the factors required for excusing demand and those required for letting the plaintiff proceed despite the board's rejection of the demand, some commentators have argued that demand should be required in ***all*** cases, and that the board's self-interest or domination by wrongdoers should ***only*** be litigated after the board has rejected the demand.

(1) MBCA: The MBCA agrees: demand on the board is ***required in all cases***. See MBCA § 7.42(1).

(2) ALI: Similarly, the ALI's *Principles of Corporate Governance* require demand in all instances. See *infra*, p. 336.

ii. Contrary view: But others argue that requiring a demand in all cases, even where it would clearly be futile, creates delay and expense — "[w]hen directors receive a demand they inevitably embark on a flurry of defensive maneuvers at corporate expense, and the plaintiff's law suit is at least delayed until a reasonable time for their response has passed." Clark, p. 645. This delay and expense is a reason, though not a terribly powerful one, for not requiring a demand that is clearly futile.

D. Use of independent committee: The most important development in derivative litigation over the last few decades has been the wide-spread use by corporations of ***independent committees*** to defeat derivative litigation.

1. How the committee works: Here is how this process works: As soon as P files his derivative suit or makes a demand on the board, the board appoints a supposedly "independent committee" of directors to investigate P's allegations.

a. No financial stake: To ensure that the committee is "independent," only those directors who have ***no financial stake*** in the transaction that P is complaining about are put on the committee. If all directors are being sued, the board may even vote to enlarge itself by the appointment of one or more additional new directors, who are then immediately appointed as the committee.

b. Investigation and report: The committee typically procures independent counsel, and then goes on to make an extensive investigation, usually including extensive interviewing of witnesses, and culminating in an extensive written report.

c. Dismissal recommended: In virtually all instances, the committee recommends that P's suit be ***dismissed***. Sometimes, this recommendation is based on a finding that P's allegations simply have no substantive merit. Often, however, the committee reasons that although the allegations have merit, the burden to the corporation of pursuing the suit would outweigh any possible recovery.

2. Business judgment rule: Why does the corporation go through all this? Principally because of the hope that when the committee recommends dismissal of the action, and the board then seeks judicial dismissal based on the recommendation, the court will afford the recommendation and board decision the protection of the ***business judgment rule***. The court will not in fact always do so; indeed, when the court should and should not give the committee report business-judgment-rule protection is the main issue in connection with independent committees. But courts grant this protection often enough that corporations and their boards typically find it well worthwhile to undergo the considerable expense of setting up such a committee.

3. **Judicial review:** Courts do not simply rubber stamp an independent committee's decision not to pursue the suit. For instance, if P can show that the committee was not really independent, or did not conduct even a reasonably careful investigation, the court is unlikely to dismiss P's suit based on the committee recommendation. But the much more interesting question is whether, if the court is convinced that the committee was independent and used appropriate procedures, the court may nonetheless use its ***independent judgment*** about whether P's suit has merit. On this issue, courts vary widely. There seem to be two main positions, the New York position and the Delaware position.

   a. **New York:** The New York approach makes it very difficult for the plaintiff to overcome the independent committee's recommendation that the suit be terminated. The plaintiff is entitled to show that the members of the committee were not in fact independent (e.g., that they were dominated by the controlling shareholder who was accused of wrongdoing), or that the committee did not use reasonable procedures in reaching its conclusion (e.g., its investigation was very shallow). But once the court is satisfied with the committee's independence and procedures, the New York courts will ***not review the merits of the substantive recommendation that the suit be dismissed***.

      i. **Business judgment rule:** In other words, the court will not attempt to make an independent determination of whether the committee was correct in its conclusion that the probability of recovery was low, the costs of proceeding with the suit would be high, etc. Instead, the committee's substantive recommendation that the suit be dismissed, and the board's approval of that recommendation, ***receive the protection of the business judgment doctrine.*** See *Auerbach v. Bennett*, 393 N.E.2d 994 (N.Y. 1979).

   b. **Delaware view:** Delaware, by contrast, will in some situations let its courts ***review the substantive merits*** of the committee's recommendation that the suit be dismissed. The Delaware approach was articulated in the landmark case of ***Zapata Corp. v. Maldonado***, 430 A.2d 779 (Del. 1981), a case in which the Delaware Supreme Court tried hard to reconcile the need for early termination of meritless actions with the need to make sure that the independent committee does not simply rubber-stamp wrongdoing by insiders.

      i. **Two-step test:** Under *Zapata*, the Delaware courts will use a ***two-step*** test to determine whether the committee's recommendation of dismissal should be followed:

         (1) **Step 1:** The court will determine whether the committee acted ***independently*** and in ***good faith***, and whether the committee used ***reasonable procedures*** in conducting its investigation. If the answer to any of these questions is "no," then the court will ***automatically disregard the committee's dismissal recommendation***, and will ***allow the suit to proceed***. For instance, if the committee members are shown to have been dominated by a controlling shareholder, or to have been motivated by their own self-interest (e.g., they are themselves

accused of wrongdoing by the plaintiff), or if they conducted a shallow investigation, the committee recommendation will be disregarded.

(2) Step 2: Even if the committee passes all the procedural hurdles of step one, a court may go onto a second step: here, the court may determine, by ***"applying its own independent business judgment,"*** whether the suit should be dismissed. It is in this second step that the Delaware approach varies sharply from the New York approach: whereas the New York courts would never enter this second step at all (and would always dismiss the suit if the committee passed muster under Step 1), the Delaware courts retain the freedom to allow the suit to continue even though the committee acted with procedural correctness. In other words, in Delaware the committee's recommendation that the suit be dismissed will ***not be given the protection of the business judgment doctrine***. For instance, if the court feels that the suit has merit, and would probably result in a substantial recovery for the corporation, the court may allow the suit to go forward even though the committee (acting with procedural correctness, independence, and good faith) has recommended against continuation of the action.

ii. Only in "demand excused" cases: Apparently, it is only in cases falling into the "demand excused" rather than "demand required" variety that the court will use the two-step test of *Zapata*. If demand is ***required***, and the corporation responds by appointing an independent committee that then recommends not continuing the suit, the court will apparently treat the case just as it would treat a case in which the main board rejects the plaintiff's demand. In that situation, only the independence, procedural correctness, and good faith of the committee, ***not the substantive merit of its decision,*** will be reviewed by the court. See *supra*, p. 326.

4. The "structural bias" problem: The principal criticism that is usually lodged against the use of a committee of "independent" directors is that such directors are ***not really "independent,"*** in a ***psychological*** sense.

a. Rationale: There are two main reasons for this critique of independent-director committees:

(1) The "independent" directors are nonetheless directors. They sit on the same board with the non-independent directors (i.e., directors who have a clear interest in the outcome, and who are often themselves defendants in the action). The independent directors know that they may continue to sit on the board after the committee's investigation is completed, and that they will therefore have to ***get along with the interested directors.*** To the extent that the independent disinterested directors value the compensation, prestige or other aspects of directorship, they are likely to have at least an unconscious bias in favor of the defendants.

(2) The committee is typically appointed by a vote of the entire board, including the interested directors. Unless the interested directors are stupid, or lacking in insight, they will not appoint committee members who are known for their independent way of thinking or for sympathy to derivative plaintiffs.

See S,S,B&W, pp. 1105-07.

b. MBCA: Concerns about "structural bias" led the drafters of the 1989 revision to the MBCA to require that the independent committee be elected by majority vote of the independent directors. See MBCA § 7.44(b)(2).

c. Tough standard for independence in Delaware (*Oracle* case): Concern about whether the members of independent committees are really psychologically independent has led the Delaware courts to impose a ***heavy burden*** on the committee to demonstrate its members' independence. As the Delaware Supreme Court has put it, the committee "has the burden of establishing its own independence by a yardstick that must be 'like Caesar's wife' — ***'above reproach.'"*** *Beam ex rel. Martha Stewart Living Omnimedia, Inc. v. Stewart*, 845 A.2d 1040 (Del. 2004).

Furthermore, as the result of ***In Re Oracle Corp. Derivative Litigation***, 824 A.2d 917 (Del. Ch. 2003), the Delaware courts ***consider social ties*** — not just direct financial ties — in deciding whether the directors are really independent of the persons whose conduct they are investigating. And those courts will be relatively quick to conclude that the directors' social ties make them *not* sufficiently independent, in which case the committee's decision not to pursue the suit will not be accorded judicial deference.

i. Facts: In *Oracle*, plaintiff shareholders brought a derivative suit alleging insider trading by four Oracle directors, including CEO (and multibillionaire) Larry Ellison and non-executive directors Lucas and Boskin (we'll call all three the "Trading Defendants"). In response, Oracle formed a special litigation committee (SLC) of board members to evaluate the merits of the suit. The SLC consisted solely of two Stanford professors, Garcia-Molina and Grundfest, each of whom had also gotten graduate degrees from Stanford.

(1) SLC Report: The SLC investigated the insider-trading allegations extensively, and issued a report of that investigation. The report concluded that there was not credible evidence of insider trading, and that the suit should not be pursued. The report also concluded that the two SLC members, although they had minors ties to the trading defendants, were sufficiently independent of those defendants and of Oracle.

(2) Dismissal sought: Oracle then tried to have the suit dismissed, over the plaintiffs' objection. Oracle claimed (as is standard in cases where the SLC finds the suit without merit) that the committee's decision to discontinue the suit should be binding on the court.

ii. Ps claim the SLC was not disinterested: But the plaintiffs claimed that the two members of the SLC had not in fact been disinterested, because of their extensive social and business ties to the three Trading Defendants. Therefore, the plaintiffs said, the SLC report's conclusion that the suit should be dismissed as meritless was not entitled to judicial deference.

iii. Court agrees: The Delaware Chancery Court agreed with the plaintiffs, concluding that ***the SLC had not carried its burden of demonstrating that the two SLC members were sufficiently independent*** of Oracle and of the Trading Defendants. The court's decision focused on ***social*** rather than economic ties between the SLC members and the Trading Defendants. The ties that the court relied on arose out of the fact that the SLC members and the trading defendants all had extensive connections to Stanford University. And, while the SLC report itself disclosed some of these ties, the court gave great weight to additional Stanford-related ties that the report had not disclosed.

(1) Boskin: For example, Boskin (one of the Trading Defendants) had taught Grundfest (one of the two SLC members) at Stanford in the 1970s when Grundfest was a PhD candidate. Furthermore, the two were, at the relevant times, both members of the steering committee at a Stanford entity, the Stanford Institute for Economic Policy Research.

(2) Lucas: Similarly, there were Stanford ties between both SLC members (remember, they were both sitting Stanford professors) and another trading defendant, Lucas. Not only was Lucas a Stanford alumnus, but a Lucas family foundation, of which Lucas was chairman, had given almost $12 million to Stanford. And Lucas himself had given $4 million to the school.

(3) Ellison: Finally, Ellison, the Oracle CEO, was an ongoing benefactor to Stanford. A medical foundation he started had given or pledged nearly $10 million to Stanford. And at the time the SLC committee was formed, Ellison was discussing with Stanford funding a $170 million Ellison Scholars Program modeled on the Rhodes scholarship.

iv. "Domination and control" argument: Oracle argued that none of these Stanford-related ties should make any difference on the issue of independence. Oracle contended that the test for independence of the SLC members should be whether they were under the ***"domination and control"*** of the interested parties (i.e., the three Trading Defendants). Since the Trading Defendants did not have the practical ability to deprive either SLC member of his tenured Stanford position (and Stanford itself did not have any practical way to punish either of them if the university was displeased with any action the SLC member took against the Trading Defendants), Oracle argued, the SLC members were not under the Trading Defendants' domination and control, and were thus automatically independent.

(1) Argument rejected: But the court flatly ***rejected*** this argument by Oracle: "[A]n emphasis on 'domination and control' would serve only to fetishize much-parroted language, at the cost of denuding the independent inquiry of its intellectual integrity." The independent inquiry ***should not "ignore the social nature of humans[.]"*** Corporate directors are "generally the sort of people deeply enmeshed in social institutions," and such directors ***should not be assumed to be "persons of unusual social bravery***, who operate heedless to the inhibitions that social norms generate for ordinary folk." The social ties among the SLC members, the Trading Defendants and Stanford were "so substantial that they ***cause reasonable doubt about the SLC's ability to impartially consider*** whether the trading defendants should face suit."

(2) Boskin: For instance, as to the insider-trading claim against Boskin that the SLC was evaluating, the SLC members could not be counted on to be impartial for several reasons. First, Boskin was the committee members' fellow Oracle board member. Second, Boskin was a fellow member of the faculty at the university (Stanford) where both SLC members taught, and "To accuse a fellow professor — whom one might see at the faculty club ... — of insider trading cannot be a small thing — even for the most callous of academics." Finally, Boskin had taught one of the SLC members (Grundfest), and the two had maintained contact over the years, making it even harder for Grundfest to be objective about whether to recommend suit against Boskin. (There were similar ties between the SLC members and the two other Trading Defendants.)

(3) Conclusion: In summary, the various connections between the SLC members and the trading defendants were sufficiently extensive that these connections would ***"weigh on the mind*** of a reasonable [SLC] member in deciding whether to level the serious charge of insider trading against the Trading Defendants." (It didn't matter whether this "weighing on the mind" would make the SLC member *more* favorable or *less* favorable to the defendant — a risk that the SLC member would "lean over backward" not to favor the defendant would be just as bad from an independence standpoint.) Therefore, the court said, the SLC was not independent, and its conclusion should be disregarded by the court; the suit should proceed rather than being terminated as the SLC recommended.

v. Significance of *Oracle*: The significance of the *Oracle* case is that when a Delaware court is deciding whether a supposedly independent committee was sufficiently independent to entitle the committee's dismissal recommendation to judicial deference, independence should be evaluated by a ***broad, holistic method.*** The issue is ***not*** merely whether the committee members are under the ***domination and control*** of the interested parties, or whether the interested parties, if unhappy with the committee's decision, could inflict economic damage on the committee members. Instead, the whole range of "soft" non-economic ***social ties*** between the committee members and the interested parties must be considered. So, for example, the fact that a committee member and a defendant sit on the company's board together, or are graduates of the same schools, or work for the same large institution, or are even social acquaintances — any of these would be a factor (though not necessarily a dispositive one) pushing the court towards a conclusion that the committee is not truly independent.

(1) Non-Delaware courts: *Oracle* has been very influential — a number of courts outside Delaware have followed *Oracle's* approach of considering social, not just economic, ties between the committee members and the interested parties in determining independence. See Hamilton (10th Ed.), p. 740.

d. Court-appointed committee: Perhaps the best solution to the whole problem of finding a way to gain early dismissal of meritless derivative suits is to have the ***court***, not the directors, appoint an independent committee. Where the committee is appointed by the court, it need not consist of directors; the odds are therefore much better that such a panel will be truly independent of the defendants. Thus MBCA § 7.44(f) allows the court to appoint an independent panel, whose results will be in practice (though not as a strict matter of law) binding on the court.

E. The MBCA approach: The ***MBCA's*** procedures on derivative suits are covered in Subchapter D of Chapter 7, in §§ 7.40-7.47. The heart of Subchapter D is § 7.44, which spells out in unusually great detail when the court may dismiss the derivative proceeding at the corporation's request. The essence of § 7.44 is that the court ***must dismiss*** so long as the board vote to dismiss is made ***after reasonable inquiry*** and ***in good faith*** — the court may not insist that the action be continued merely because the court thinks that, objectively, the action has merit and would benefit the corporation.

1. **No distinction between demand required and demand excused:** Because the MBCA requires a written demand on the corporation in ***all*** situations (see § 7.42, discussed *supra*, p. 324), there is no distinction between the "demand excused" and the "demand required" situations, as there is in Delaware.

2. **Vote of independent directors:** When the directors vote to recommend discontinuance of the derivative action, the only votes that count are the votes of ***"independent directors."*** If independent directors constitute a quorum of the board, then all that is required is that a ***majority of these independent directors*** must vote to discontinue the action. (In other words, the entire board can vote, as long as a quorum of independent directors are present, and as long as a majority of the independent directors vote to recommend discontinuance.)

   a. **Committee:** Alternatively, a ***committee*** consisting of two or more independent directors may vote on discontinuance. This "committee" method is available in all circumstances, and is the required method where a majority of the full board is not independent. The committee must be selected by majority vote of the ***independent directors***. § 7.44(b)(2). This method of allowing only independent directors to select the independent committee members is designed to counter the problem of "structural bias," discussed *supra*, p. 331.

3. **Standard by which board or committee is to act:** What are the standards by which the board or the committee is to reach its decision? Under § 7.44(a), the majority of independent directors (or the majority of a committee of independent directors) must "determine[] . . . in ***good faith*** after conducting a ***reasonable inquiry*** upon which its ***conclusions are based*** that the maintenance of the derivative proceeding is not in the ***best interests*** of the corporation."

4. **Meaning of "independent" directors:** Subchapter D does not define an ***"independent"*** director. However, § 7.44(c) specifies several things that will ***not*** prevent a director from being deemed independent, including: (1) that she was ***nominated*** or ***elected*** to the post of director by ***vote of a defendant*** in the derivative proceedings; (2) that she is ***herself a defendant*** in the derivative proceeding; or (3) that she ***voted to approve the act*** being challenged (so long as the act resulted in no personal benefit to herself.) On the other hand, any showing that the director ***benefited*** from the challenged action, or that the director is ***beholden*** for her livelihood to a person who is charged with receiving a personal benefit from the challenged transaction, probably would be enough to lead a court to find that the director was not "independent."

5. **Significance:** The MBCA seems to make it relatively ***easy*** for the corporation to ***obtain a dismissal*** of the derivative action. If the board has a majority of "independent" directors

(as the boards of most publicly-held corporations probably do today), the plaintiff will bear the burden of showing that the independent directors did not act in good faith, or did not conduct a reasonable inquiry. Even where a majority of the board is not independent, the fact that the corporation merely has to show good faith and reasonable inquiry, rather than the objective reasonableness of its action, will mean that the court will have no choice but to dismiss the action most of the time.

V. SECURITY-FOR-EXPENSES STATUTES

A. Generally: About 14 states have so-called ***"security-for-expenses"*** statutes. These statutes require certain plaintiffs to post a ***bond*** to guarantee that if the corporation incurs expenses in connection with the derivative suit, the court can order those expenses reimbursed to the corporation by means of the bond.

1. **Rationale:** These security-for-expenses statutes reflect a basic hostility toward shareholder derivative actions, especially towards the possibility that a plaintiff's attorney might bring a frivolous action for the sole purpose of extracting a "nuisance value" settlement. The idea is that if the plaintiff is required to post a bond to cover the corporation's out-of-pocket expenses, P and his attorney will be less likely to bring such "strike suits."

2. **Criticisms:** On the other hand, critics of security-for-expenses statutes point out that such statutes are ***overinclusive***: they are almost as likely to screen out meritorious suits as meritless ones, since the bond required may be much greater than the amount by which a plaintiff would benefit even if the suit were found to have merit. Also, since most such statutes apply only in the case of small shareholders (see *infra*), they are criticized on the grounds that they discriminate against small holders and in favor of large ones.

3. **Small shareholders:** Most security-for-expenses statutes apply only to suits brought by ***"small"*** shareholders (i.e., those whose stake in the corporation is less than a certain size). For instance, New York's statute (B.C.L. § 627) requires the bond to be posted unless the plaintiff holds either: (1) 5% or more of some class of the corporation's shares; or (2) shares having a market value of more than $50,000.

4. **What are "expenses":** For most of these statutes, "expenses" covers much more than court costs. Typically, the court may order security posted to cover the corporation's anticipated ***legal fees*** in connection with the action. S,S,B&W, p. 1113-14. Even more important, "expenses" usually includes ***indemnification*** payments made by the corporation to the defendants (e.g., directors), which may be made by the corporation under a variety of circumstances (see *infra*, p. 341). The net result is that the court may order the plaintiff to post a bond in a sum that is likely to be out of all proportion to what the plaintiff or the plaintiff's lawyer can expect to recover if victorious.

B. Not substantial impediment: Therefore, you would expect that such statutes would be a serious impediment to the bringing of derivative suits. But the reality is that such statutes do ***not*** seem to have had that effect.

C. Many states do without: In any event, many jurisdictions have no security-for-expenses statute, and yet do not seem besieged by meritless derivative actions. For instance, neither Delaware nor the MBCA has such a provision.

1. **Limited:** A few other jurisdictions have security-for-expenses statutes that operate not on the basis of size of plaintiff's stake, but rather only where a court determines that the action is probably ***frivolous.*** For instance, under the California statute (Cal. Corp. Code § 800(c)-(f)), the corporation may only obtain a bond if it convinces the court that there is ***"no reasonable possibility"*** that the action will benefit the corporation or its shareholders.

D. Recovery against bond: Suppose that the plaintiff does post the bond, tries the suit, and loses. Generally, the corporation is ***not*** entitled to ***automatically*** recoup its expenses against the bond. Instead, it is usually up to the court to decide how much the corporation should get from the bond. For instance, under New York's B.C.L. § 627, the corporation may have recourse to the bond "in such amount as the court having jurisdiction of such action shall determine upon the termination of such action."

1. **No personal liability:** Also, the plaintiff is generally ***not personally liable*** for the corporation's expenses. In other words, he is not liable beyond the amount of the bond. C&E, pp. 1091-92.

VI. SETTLEMENT OF DERIVATIVE SUITS

A. Danger of collusion: Derivative litigation is essentially a three-party game. The three parties are: (1) the plaintiff shareholder (and his lawyer); (2) the corporation; and (3) the individual defendants charged with wrongdoing. Typically, parties (1) and (3) will be the most actively interested in the litigation, since they are the real protagonists; the corporation usually does little more than stand by and watch (with the board, assuming it is not charged with wrongdoing, not helping either party but probably rooting for the defendants for the reasons described *supra*, p. 278). If the plaintiff and the defendants could settle the litigation on their own, they would have a strong incentive to benefit themselves at the expense of the corporation and its non-party shareholders. For instance, they might agree to a token recovery on behalf of the corporation, accompanied by a substantial payment to the plaintiff's attorney as his "fee."

1. **Plaintiff doesn't object:** The plaintiff probably won't object to such a settlement, since the plaintiff is usually a nominal figure who has very little direct interest in the outcome (he benefits only to the extent that the value of his stockholdings increases).

2. **Corporation doesn't object:** Nor will the corporation typically object, since it (or at least its board of directors) is typically hostile to the action in the first place.

3. **Danger:** Yet the net result of such a settlement may be that a serious wrong to the corporation and its shareholders goes uncorrected, whereas a full trial of the action might have produced a substantial recovery for the corporation. In summary, there is a major risk of ***collusive settlements*** in derivative actions.

B. Judicial approval: Because of this danger of collusion, most states require that any settlement be ***approved by the court***. Clark, p. 657. Only if the proponents of the settlement (generally the plaintiff's attorney and the defendants) convince the court that the settlement is in the best interests of the ***corporation*** and its shareholders, will the court approve the settlement.

C. Notice to shareholders and opportunity to intervene: In the federal courts, and in many state courts, shareholders must be given ***notice*** of the proposed settlement, and the opportunity to intervene in the action to oppose the settlement. Statutes vary widely as to when notice is required, and what type of notice.

1. **Federal suits:** In ***federal*** suits, Fed. R. Civ. Proc. 23.1 is somewhat vague: "[N]otice of the proposed dismissal or compromise shall be given to shareholders . . . ***in such manner as the court directs.***" Usually, federal courts will order notice by ***mail*** to each shareholder of record. However, where such notice would be very costly, the court will sometimes use its discretion to allow for notice by ***publication***, or by a mailing to just a ***random sample*** of shareholders. *Id.* It is probably up to the discretion of the court which party shall bear the cost of notice.

2. **Intervention:** The main purpose of notice to other shareholders is that any shareholder may then ***intervene***, and argue at the court's hearing on the proposed settlement that the settlement should not be approved. The intervening shareholder might argue, for example, that the proposed settlement is a collusive one in which plaintiff's lawyer is maximizing his fees, defendants are paying relatively little to the corporation, and the corporation, after payment of the attorney's fees, will be left with far less than the true "value" of its cause of action. However, the intervenor will generally be a complete outsider who will have little ability to make such a showing.

3. **Res judicata effect:** If notice of the proposed settlement is given to all shareholders, the settlement will generally be ***binding*** on them. For this reason, the corporation and the defendants will often want notice to be given to all shareholders even if it is not required by the statute.

D. **Factors to be considered by court:** In deciding whether to approve the settlement, the court typically considers a number of factors, including: (1) the best possible recovery that might occur at trial; (2) the likely (as opposed to highest possible) recovery at trial; (3) the probable expense to the corporation of litigating through trial; and (4) the defendants' ability to pay a judgment higher than the proposed settlement amount.

1. **Key factor:** Of these, the most important factor is usually the relation between the size of the ***net financial benefit to the corporation*** under the settlement versus the probable net financial benefit to the corporation if the case were to be tried.

   a. **Subtract counsel fees and indemnification:** The court will often subtract anticipated ***counsel fees*** and ***indemnification payments*** that will be made by the corporation to the defendants (see *infra*, p. 341) in calculating the net benefit to the corporation, both under the settlement and as would be likely to occur at trial. Thus even where the defendants are paying the corporation a substantial sum, the court might not approve the settlement if it concludes that once the corporation pays the plaintiff's attorney's fees (and these fees are always paid by the corporation out of its recovery, see *infra*, p. 340), too little money will remain in the corporation's coffers.

2. **Non-pecuniary benefits:** Often, a proposed settlement will include ***non-pecuniary benefits*** to the corporation. For instance, the corporation may agree to add ***outside directors*** to its board, to beef up its internal financial controls so as to prevent similar wrongdoing in the future, to cancel stock options granted to the wrongdoers, or to take other action that does not put immediate dollars in the corporation's coffers. A court approving a proposed settlement will sometimes attribute some value to such non-pecuniary benefits. But in

general, courts are somewhat ***skeptical*** of such benefits, because they can "sometimes represent a means by which the parties can ***increase the apparent value*** of the settlement and thereby justify higher attorney's fees for plaintiff's counsel, who is often the real party in interest." ALI Prin. Corp. Gov., § 7.14, Comment e.

3. **Strength of case:** Obviously, in reviewing the settlement the court will consider the probable ***strength of the plaintiff's case*** — the stronger the claim, the more favorable to the plaintiffs the settlement will have to be.

E. All relief must go to corporation: An additional way in which courts discourage collusive settlements is that all payments made in connection with a derivative action must be ***received by the corporation***, not by the plaintiff.

F. Other terminations: As noted, a settlement must, in most jurisdictions, be approved by the court. Jurisdictions following this rule usually extend it to apply to a ***voluntary dismissal*** or ***discontinuance*** as well. Thus once P brings a derivative action against D, he cannot simply abandon the action without judicial approval in most states — there is too much risk that P (or more probably his lawyer) is being in effect "paid off" to drop the action. See ALI Prin. Corp. Gov., § 7.14(a). Similarly, if notice to shareholders would be required for a settlement, it is generally required for a voluntary dismissal. *Id.*

1. **Involuntary dismissal:** But where the court issues an ***involuntary dismissal*** of the action (e.g., it grants a summary judgment against P because of the legal inadequacy of the claim), no formal "judicial approval" or notice to shareholders is called for — there is little danger of collusion between plaintiff and defendant in this situation. ALI Prin. Corp. Gov., Comment c to § 7.14.

G. Settlement between corporation and insider: So far, we have been assuming that the settlement is between the plaintiff shareholder and the defendants. Suppose, however, that the ***corporation itself***, without the plaintiff shareholder's consent, tries to settle with the defendant on the underlying corporate claim against that defendant. May the corporation do this without judicial approval, and if it may, will this be binding on the plaintiff?

1. **Other jurisdictions:** Most states that require judicial approval of ordinary settlements in derivative actions seem to require such approval of settlements between the corporation and the defendants as well. See, e.g., ALI Prin. Corp. Gov., § 7.15. In any event, because a settlement between the corporation and the defendant that did not include judicial approval or shareholder notice probably wouldn't be binding on shareholders anyway, the corporation and defendants are quite unlikely (and unwise) to settle without such approval even if they could.

VII. PLAINTIFF'S ATTORNEY'S FEES

A. The problem: Normally, U.S. courts follow the so-called "American" rule about attorney's fees: each side pays its own attorney's fees. But adherence to this general rule in derivative actions would make such actions nearly impossible: the individual shareholder plaintiff almost never receives a sufficiently large financial benefit even from a successful suit to pay a reasonable attorney's fee out of the proceeds.

Example: Assume that P owns 10% of the shares of XYZ Corp. P brings a derivative action against D, an XYZ director, which results in XYZ's recovering $1 million from D. Assume (as is usually the case) that a reasonable attorney's fee for such an action would be around 20% of the recovery. Before payment of the fee, P has only benefited by $100,000 (since the value of his shares has been enhanced by his 10% holding times the $1 million received by the corporation). If P has to pay a $200,000 attorney's fee, he will have a net loss of $100,000 on the transaction.

1. **Benefit to non-plaintiffs:** At the same time, the shareholders who did ***not*** join in the action would benefit from a "windfall" — their shares would increase in value because of the recovery just as P's have, yet they would not have to pay any part of the attorney's fee. This problem is an aspect of the ***"free rider"*** problem, in which one party pays to bring about an event that benefits others who do not have to pay for it.

B. **The "common fund" theory:** To deal with this free rider problem, courts have adopted the so-called ***"common fund"*** theory. Under this theory, when a person's efforts result in the establishment of a fund that benefits others as well as himself, that person's attorney's fees and expenses may be taken out of the fund. In the derivative context, the common fund doctrine allows plaintiff's counsel to be ***paid out of the fund***, i.e., out of the recovery received by the corporation. All jurisdictions award the successful plaintiff attorney's fees on this basis.

C. **Amount of the fee:** On the other hand, courts are in disagreement about how the amount of the fee should be ***calculated***. There seem to be two main approaches:

1. **The "lodestar" method:** Under the ***"lodestar"*** method, the key component is the ***reasonable value of the time*** expended by plaintiff's attorney. This is computed by taking the actual number of hours expended by the attorney on the case, and multiplying it by a ***reasonable hourly fee*** for the type of work in question. After this number (the lodestar) is computed, the court can then ***adjust it up or down*** to reflect other factors. For instance, the court will often adjust it upwards to reflect the fact that there was a substantial ***contingency*** aspect to the case (i.e., P was by no means certain to prevail, so when he does prevail, the lawyer should get more per hour than where the lawyer was certain to be paid for each hour, as in the usual hourly fee arrangement).

2. **The "salvage value" approach:** The other common approach to fee calculation is the ***"salvage value"*** approach. Under this approach, the court calculates counsel fees by awarding a percentage of the total recovery. Typically, if the recovery is below $1 million, the award is in the 20-30% range, and if the recovery is more than $1 million, the award is between 15 and 20%. See ALI Prin. Corp. Gov., § 7.17, Comment c.

VIII. WHO GETS TO RECOVER

A. **Pro rata recovery by individuals:** The recovery in a derivative action must normally go ***to the corporation***, as we have seen (see *supra*, p. 339). Although individual shareholders are plaintiffs, the action they are asserting is one that is really "owned" by the corporation, and it is appropriate that the corporation, not the individual plaintiffs, should receive the recovery. But occasionally, it may be unjust or counterproductive to allow the corporation to recover. If so, the court may order that all or part of the recovery be distributed to ***individual shareholders*** on a ***pro rata basis*** (i.e., proportionally to their shareholdings).

1. **Situations where pro rata treatment appropriate:** Here are two common situations in which the court may well decide to award a pro rata rather than corporate recovery:

   a. **Wrongdoers in control:** If the alleged wrongdoers remain in substantial ***control*** of the corporation, the court might decide to award pro rata recovery to the non-controlling, innocent, shareholders. The court is especially likely to do this where there is a danger that any recovery paid to the corporation will simply be diverted again by these same wrongdoers.

      i. **Mere fact of continuing ownership:** By contrast, the mere fact that the wrongdoers continue as shareholders will ***not*** by itself lead the court to declare a pro rata recovery. Indeed, it is the ***defendant*** who will often urge a pro rata recovery in this situation, as a way of limiting the damages he must pay, but the court will usually ***reject*** this request.

   b. **Aiders and abettors:** The court may also award pro rata recovery when most of the shares are in the hands of people who in some sense ***aided and abetted*** the wrongdoing, even though they are not deeply culpable themselves.

      Example: Recall the facts of *Perlman v. Feldmann*, *supra*, p. 238, in which Wilport Co. (a group of steel end-users) bought D's control block in Newport Steel Corp. at a premium in order to get steel supplies at a time of shortages. After the court decided that D could not keep this control premium, it decided that this premium should be paid by D to the plaintiffs (the minority shareholders), not to Newport. The court reasoned that a payment to Newport would unjustly enrich Wilport, who had aided and abetted D's original wrongdoing by agreeing to pay the control premium to D.

IX. INDEMNIFICATION AND D&O INSURANCE

A. **Introduction:** A director or officer who is charged with breach of the duty of due care, the duty of loyalty, or other wrongdoing, can face very substantial damages. For instance, the defendant directors in *Smith v. Van Gorkom*, *supra*, p. 186, ended up settling the case for $23 million, even though they were guilty of at most gross negligence, not intentional wrongdoing. Because of this possibility of liability out of all proportion to compensation, directors and officers (and the corporations that will need their services) have struggled to find protection. The two principal methods for reducing the burden on individuals are: (1) ***indemnification***, in which the corporation reimburses the director or officer for expenses and/or judgments he incurs relating to his actions on behalf of the corporation; and (2) so-called ***"D&O"*** (directors' and officers') ***liability insurance***, which can be paid either to the corporation (to make it whole for any indemnification payments it makes to the individual) or directly to the director/officer.

   1. **Third-party vs. derivative actions:** In considering whether the corporation may indemnify or insure the director/officer against liability, it is important to distinguish between: (1) third-party actions brought directly against the individual; and (2) derivative actions brought in the name of the corporation. Statutes and case law are less likely to permit

indemnification of judgments or settlements in derivative actions, since that would in effect lead to ***circular recovery*** (the corporation recovers against the defendant, then pays the money right back out to him as indemnification).

2. **Self-dealing:** Also, be careful to distinguish between claims that allege self-dealing or other ***disloyalty***, and those that do not: statutes and case law are much more likely to permit indemnification and insurance where the defendant is guilty of breach of the duty of due care (even if his breach amounts to recklessness or gross negligence) than where his wrong consists of improperly receiving a financial benefit at the corporation's expense.

3. **Mandatory vs. permissive:** Lastly, you should distinguish between ***mandatory*** and ***permissive*** indemnification: In most states there are a few situations in which a corporation ***must*** indemnify a director or officer, but a large range of circumstances in which the corporation ***may*** indemnify him.

B. **Indemnification generally:** All states have statutes dealing with when the corporation may (or must) ***indemnify*** a director or officer against losses he incurs by virtue of his corporate duties.

1. **Who is covered:** In general, these statutes apply to both directors and officers (i.e., high-level executives). Even where the statute does not cover ***lower-level employees***, a court would probably hold that the corporation may offer the same indemnification to such an employee.

C. **Mandatory indemnification:** In most states, there are just two situations in which the corporation may be ***required*** to indemnify an officer or director: (1) when the director/officer is completely ***successful*** in defending himself against the charges; and (2) when the corporation has previously ***bound itself*** by charter, by law or ***contract*** to indemnify.

1. **Requirement of "success":** If the director or officer has been completely ***successful*** in defending himself against the charges of wrongdoing, he is ***entitled*** to indemnification in nearly all states. In other words, if the corporation refuses to reimburse him voluntarily, the director/officer may get a court order requiring the corporation to pay. However, the statutes vary somewhat as to what constitutes "success."

a. **Success not on the merits:** Most states provide mandatory indemnification so long as the defendant is successful, whether the success is "on the merits" ***or not***. See, e.g., Del. GCL § 145(c), N.Y. BCL § 722(a). Thus in most states, the director or officer who successfully raises a ***technical defense*** like the statute of limitations is entitled to indemnification — these states reason that the defendant should not have to go through an entire trial on the merits when he has a technical defense available, merely in order to assure himself reimbursement.

i. **Settlement by corporation but not by officer:** Suppose the suit ends with the officer paying nothing, but with the ***co-defendant corporation paying a significant amount.*** Here, the officer is likely to be found to have "succeeded" (and thus to be entitled to mandatory indemnification) despite the corporation's payment, as long as the officer did not intentionally *cause* the corporation to make the payment.

Example: P is a silver trader for Conticommodity ("Conti"), a corporation. He spends over $2 million in legal fees defending himself against civil lawsuits and an enforcement proceeding by the Commodity Futures Trading Commission (CFTC). The civil suits include Conti as a co-defendant. P eventually settles the CFTC suit by paying a $100,000 fine. The civil suits end when Conti, but not P, pays $35 million to the plaintiffs in those suits (which are then dismissed as to P as well as to Conti). P attempts to have Conti reimburse him for his $1 million in legal fees spent on defending the private suits. Conti argues that P has not "succeeded" in defending the private suits, but has merely been "bailed out" by Conti's payment of enough money to end the suits against both defendants.

Held, for P. The suit against P was dismissed "without his having paid a settlement," and "it is not [the court's] business to ask why this result was reached." The result might be different if P had sought, or acceded to, Conti's payment of the settlement; but he didn't. "Delaware law cannot allow an indemnifying corporation to escape the mandatory indemnification [provision] by paying a sum in settlement on behalf of an unwilling indemnitee." *Waltuch v. Conticommodity Svcs., Inc.*, 88 F.3d 87 (2d Cir. 1996) (construing Delaware law in a diversity case.)

b. Finding of non-liability: Generally, the director or officer will qualify for mandatory indemnification only if he is ***completely exonerated*** of wrongdoing. If the court finds that he has committed wrongdoing, but doesn't impose financial penalties, most states probably would regard D as ***not*** having been "successful," and would therefore not grant him mandatory indemnification.

2. Provision in charter, by law or contract: If the corporation ***obligates itself***, by a provision in its articles of incorporation, bylaws, or in a special contract with the director, to provide indemnification in certain circumstances, the court will ***enforce*** such a provision. In a sense, this can be viewed as "mandatory" indemnification — even if the corporation changes its mind and refuses to pay, the court will force it to do so.

a. Rationale: Why would the corporation lock itself in with a charter, bylaw or contractual provision; why not simply wait until the particular occasion arises, and then make a voluntary payment to the director or officer? The answer is that the director or officer may not be willing to take the post on this kind of wait-and-see basis. For instance, the director or officer may reasonably fear that after he takes a particular action, corporate control may change to one who is unfriendly to him, who would then cause the corporation to refuse indemnification. (In fact, since even the articles of incorporation or bylaws could be changed after an act by D but before a suit was brought, D's best protection is to have a ***contract*** with the corporation explicitly guaranteeing him indemnification under certain circumstances.)

b. Must not run afoul of specific statutory prohibition: A charter, bylaw or contractual provision will only be enforced if it does not run afoul of some explicit ***statutory prohibition***. As we will see in our discussion of permissive indemnification below, most states flatly prohibit indemnification in certain circumstances (e.g., where D acts in bad faith to obtain a wrongful personal financial benefit from the corporation, or D acts with knowing illegality). In such a "statutory prohibition" situation, the court will not enforce even a very explicit mandatory indemnification provision in a charter or contract.

D. Permissive indemnification: Virtually all states, in addition to their mandatory-indemnification provisions, allow for ***"permissive"*** indemnification. That is, there is a large zone of circumstances in which the corporation ***may***, if it wishes, indemnify the director or officer, but is not required to do so.

1. Limits: However, to prevent corporations from underwriting blatant wrongdoing by those in control, nearly all states place certain ***limits*** on permissive indemnification. That is, each state ***prohibits*** indemnification in certain circumstances. Typically, states prohibit indemnification where:

(1) D is found to have acted in ***knowing violation*** of a serious law;

(2) D is found to have received an ***improper financial benefit***;

(3) D pays a ***fine or penalty*** where the policy behind the law precludes indemnification; or

(4) the amount in question is a payment made by D to the corporation in a ***derivative action***.

We will consider various contexts in which even permissive indemnification may be prohibited by the state.

2. Model Act: The MBCA's permissive-indemnification provisions are reasonably typical of modern statutes. Therefore, to give you some idea of how the pieces fit together in a typical permissive-indemnification scheme, here is the text of MBCA § 8.51:

"§ 8.51 **Permissible Indemnification**

(a) Except as otherwise provided in this section, a corporation ***may indemnify*** an individual who is a party to a proceeding ***because he is a director*** against liability incurred in the proceeding if:

(1) (i) he conducted himself in ***good faith; and***

(ii) he ***reasonably believed***:

(A) in the case of conduct in his ***official capacity***, that his conduct was in the ***best interests*** of the corporation; and

(B) in all other cases, that his conduct was at least ***not opposed to the best interests of the corporation***; and

(iii) in the case of any criminal proceeding, he had ***no reasonable cause to believe his conduct was unlawful; or***

(2) he engaged in conduct for which ***broader indemnification*** has been made permissible or obligatory under a provision of the ***articles of incorporation***. . . .

(c) The termination of a proceeding by ***judgment***, order, ***settlement***, or conviction, or upon a plea of nolo contendere or its equivalent, is ***not***, of itself, ***determinative*** that the director did not meet the relevant standard of conduct described in this section.

(d) Unless ordered by a court under §8.54(a)(3), a corporation may ***not indemnify*** a director:

(1) in connection with a proceeding ***by or in the right of the corporation*** [e.g., a derivative action], except for reasonable expenses incurred in connection with the proceeding if it is determined that the director has ***met the relevant standard of conduct*** under subsection

(a); or

(2) in connection with any proceeding with respect to conduct for which he was adjudged liable on the basis that he ***received a financial benefit to which he was not entitled***, whether or not involving action in his official capacity."

a. **Delaware:** Delaware's permissive indemnification provision contains essentially the same language as MBCA § 8.51(a) and (c). Also, it forbids indemnification in suits by or on behalf of the corporation (including shareholders' derivative suits) in which D is found liable to the corporation, unless the court so orders. See Del. GCL, § 145(a) and (b).

3. **Third-party action:** First, let's consider suits brought directly against the director or officer by a ***third party***. In other words, we are not considering actions brought by the corporation against the defendant or officer; nor are we considering ***derivative actions*** (i.e., suits brought "in the name of" the corporation by a shareholder).

   a. **General rule:** As a general rule, most states allow permissive indemnification so long as the director or officer: (1) acted in ***good faith***; (2) was pursuing what he reasonably believed to be the ***best interests*** of the corporation; and (3) had no reason to believe that his conduct was ***unlawful***. See MBCA § 8.51(a)(1).

   b. **Breach of duty of due care:** Most importantly, this means that if a director or officer, while acting on behalf of the corporation, acts ***negligently*** (or even grossly negligently, but not dishonestly) the corporation will be able to indemnify him for his ***expenses*** in defending a third-party suit, and for any ***judgment*** or ***settlement*** he might have to pay.

   Example: D is the president and director of Auto Corp. He approves production of a new car, the Nino, without reading a design-and-safety analysis prepared by the company's engineering department. Had D read this report, he would have known that the design was extremely dangerous, in that the car was likely to explode if hit from the rear. P, a passenger in a Nino, is badly burned when just such a collision occurs. P sues D (as well as Auto Corp.) for gross negligence.

   Although D has acted with negligence or even with gross negligence, Auto Corp. will probably be allowed to indemnify D for: (1) his expenses (including legal fees) in defending the suit; (2) any judgment he may be required by the court to pay after the trial; and (3) any settlement he might decide to pay instead of going to trial. This is true because D appears to have acted in good faith, in the reasonable belief that he was acting in the best interests of Auto Corp., and with no reason to believe that his conduct was unlawful.

   c. **Bad faith:** But if the director or officer acts in ***bad faith***, then in most states he may ***not*** be indemnified. For instance, suppose that D in the above example reasoned, "I know that this design is unsafe, and that some people will be fried as a result. However, it would cost us more money to make a safe design than we'll have to pay in civil suits for this unsafe design, so let's go with the unsafe one." On these facts, D has clearly not behaved in good faith, so the corporation will be forbidden to indemnify him, even if it wished to do so (and even if in a narrow financial sense D's decision was indeed in the corporation's best interests.)

i. **Delaware agrees:** Delaware agrees with this general approach, that a director or officer ***may not be indemnified if she acts in bad faith***. See Del. G.C.L. § 145(a), which says that a corporation may indemnify an officer or director ***only*** if he "acted ***in good faith*** and in a manner he ***reasonably believed*** to be in or not opposed to the ***best interests*** of the corporation." The indemnitee must also have had "no reasonable cause to believe his conduct was ***unlawful***."

(1) **Provision cannot be overridden:** This "no indemnification for bad faith actions" provision is not just a default rule — it is a rule that ***cannot be overridden*** no matter what the corporation does.

d. **Illegality:** Similarly, if the case is a ***criminal*** proceeding, the corporation may not indemnify D if D had reasonable cause to believe that his conduct was ***unlawful.***

Example: D, a director of XYZ Corp., knowingly authorizes a company executive to pay bribes to an official of a foreign government, in violation of the federal Foreign Corrupt Practices Act. D is then charged with violating the act. If D is convicted, XYZ will not be permitted to indemnify D either for his legal expenses or any fine that he is required to pay.

e. **Improper personal benefit:** Most states do not allow a corporation to indemnify a director or officer who has received an ***improper personal benefit*** from his actions. See, e.g., MBCA § 8.51(d)(2).

i. **Insider trading:** For instance, a director or officer who is found liable for ***insider trading*** probably may not be indemnified by the corporation either for litigation expenses, fines, settlements or judgments paid. This is true even if the corporation itself has not been injured by the trading. See Official Comment 4 to MBCA § 8.51. (Also, in the insider trading situation D might have an additional problem because he was not acting ***in his official capacity***, something that many of the statutes require for indemnification.)

4. **Derivative litigation:** Now, let us turn to suits brought ***by or on behalf of the corporation***. Here, we are principally interested in ***derivative suits*** (since a corporation that brings a direct action against a director or officer is unlikely to be willing to make permissive indemnification payments). Since a derivative suit involves a charge that the corporation has itself been injured by the defendant's actions, states are less likely to allow the corporation to indemnify than in the case of third-party actions discussed above.

a. **Settlements or judgments:** Thus the vast majority of states do ***not*** permit the corporation to indemnify a director or officer for a ***judgment*** on behalf of the corporation, or for a ***settlement*** payment made by the defendant to the corporation. See, e.g., MBCA § 8.51(d)(1); Del. GCL § 145(b). This rule is easy to understand: if indemnification were allowed in the case of judgment or settlement on behalf of the corporation, there would be a ***circular recovery*** — the corporation would be receiving the judgment or settlement with one hand and paying it out again with the other hand in the form of indemnification.

b. **Expenses:** On the other hand, the defendant may have a somewhat easier time getting indemnified for his ***litigation expenses*** (including attorney's fees). Here, most statutes seem to permit these expenses to be indemnified if D has ***settled*** the case with the corporation, but do not permit them if D has been ***found liable*** by the court. In a state making this distinction between settlement and judicial finding of liability, the director or officer will thus have a powerful ***incentive*** to ***settle*** if his legal bills have been extensive.

5. **Fines and penalties:** Suppose the director or officer is ***fined*** or required to pay a ***penalty*** or ***punitive damages***. May he be indemnified for these? In general, the answer is "yes," so long as the defendant meets the other requirements for permissive indemnification (e.g., that he behaved in good faith, and that he did not have reason to believe that his conduct was illegal).

E. Who decides: Observe that the corporation's right to indemnify a defendant depends on one or more ***questions of fact***, such as: (1) whether D acted in good faith; (2) whether D reasonably believed that he was acting in the best interests of the corporation; and (3) whether D had reason to believe that his conduct was illegal. Therefore, the question becomes, ***who decides*** these issues of fact?

1. **Court proceeding:** Sometimes, these factual issues will be answered ***by the court*** as part of the basic action for which indemnification is later sought. Thus if the trial judge makes specific findings of fact in deciding against the defendant (e.g., "I conclude that D approved the automobile design plans with knowledge that they posed grave safety risks"), this finding will be binding. But the mere fact that D ***lost*** the case will ***not necessarily*** dispose of these factual issues.

   Example: Consider the facts of the basic automobile example *supra*, p. 345. Suppose further that the case goes to the jury, and the jury finds D liable on a negligence theory. This verdict does not dispose of the issue whether D acted in good faith or the issue whether he acted in what he reasonably perceived to be the best interests of the corporation. Therefore, someone else will have to decide whether D qualifies for permissive indemnification.

2. **Statutes vary:** When the basic suit does not dispose of these entitlement issues, statutes vary as to who may decide them. Typically, ***independent members*** of the ***board of directors*** (i.e., those who were not themselves involved in the action) may make these decisions, assuming that they make up a quorum of the total board. See, e.g., MBCA § 8.55(b)(1). Also, in most states the ***stockholders*** may decide them.

   a. **Independent legal counsel:** Additionally, some but not all statutes permit this decision to be made by ***"independent" legal counsel***. See, e.g., Del. GCL § 145(d)(3); MBCA § 8.55(b)(2).

      i. **Regular law firm:** Probably the corporation's regular outside law firm is not "independent" for this purpose, so a firm that has not recently done work for the corporation or for its insiders must be called in specially for this task.

F. Advancing of expenses: Not only is litigation expensive, but the legal bills must normally be paid as they are incurred. A director or officer who does not have the money to pay attorney's fees as the action proceeds would therefore find little comfort in the knowledge that at the end of the action he could obtain indemnification. Therefore, most statutes allow the corporation to ***advance*** to the director or officer money for counsel fees and other expenses as the action proceeds.

1. **Promise to repay:** Typically, the statutes require that the director or officer ***promise*** in writing to repay these advances if he is ultimately found not entitled to indemnification. See, e.g., Del. GCL § 145(e).

2. **Financial ability:** As long as the director or officer makes this promise, the corporation may generally make the advance even if there is reason to believe that the defendant would not be ***financially able*** to make the repayment. A few states require the defendant to post ***collateral*** to guarantee repayment, but most do not, on the theory that this would unfairly discriminate between poor and rich directors or officers. See, e.g., MBCA § 8.53(b), which says that "[t]he undertaking [to make repayment] . . . must be an unlimited general obligation of the director but ***need not be secured*** and may be accepted ***without reference*** to the ***financial ability*** of the director to make repayment."

G. **Insurance:** Nearly all large companies, and many small ones, today carry Directors' and Officers' ("D&O") ***liability insurance***. D&O policies are becoming as important as indemnification for directors and officers who are sued in connection with their duties.

1. **Typical policy:** The typical D&O policy has two parts:

   a. **Corporate reimbursement:** First, the ***"corporate reimbursement"*** part reimburses the ***corporation*** for indemnification payments it makes to a director or officer. Thus the corporation is made whole (at least up to the policy limits) when it indemnifies the director or officer, a fact which is likely to make the corporation much more liberal in granting indemnification in a particular instance than if the corporation were paying out of its own pocket.

   b. **Personal coverage:** Second, the ***"personal coverage"*** reimburses the director or officer directly for his losses (litigation expenses, settlements or judgments) to the extent that he is not indemnified by the corporation. This part of the policy comes into play if the corporation is unable to indemnify the individual (e.g., because the corporation is insolvent, or because indemnification on the particular claim would be prohibited by statute), or if the corporation is unwilling to indemnify in a circumstance where it could do so.

2. **Deductibles:** The D&O policy usually has a ***deductible*** (typically less than $10,000) for each officer or director as to the "personal coverage" part. Also, there is usually a much larger deductible for the "corporate reimbursement" part.

3. **Premium:** Usually the corporation, not the individual, pays the entire premium.

4. **Exclusions:** Nearly all D&O policies contain some important ***exclusions.*** Most policies contain at least the following major exclusions:

   a. **Personal profit or advantage:** A claim based on the individual's gaining a ***personal profit or advantage*** to which he was not legally entitled. (For instance, a claim that D usurped a corporate opportunity, or engaged in self-dealing by selling property to the corporation at an inflated price, or a claim that D improperly spent corporate funds to entrench himself in office, would all presumably be excluded under this clause.)

b. Active and deliberate dishonesty: A claim which results in a judgment that the insured acted with ***"active and deliberate dishonesty."*** (Thus knowing and willful ***violations of law***, such as the payment of bribes or of illegal campaign contributions, would be excluded.)

c. Illegal remuneration: A claim for return of ***illegal remuneration***, if a court agrees that remuneration was illegal. (For instance, compensation that is ruled by a court to have been ***excessive*** won't be covered.)

d. Libel and slander: A claim for ***libel*** or ***slander***.

e. Securities laws: A claim for return of ***short-swing profits*** under § 16(b) of the Securities Exchange Act of 1934 (*supra*, p. 305).

f. Fines penalties and punitive damages: ***Fines*** and ***penalties*** in ***criminal cases***. In a ***civil*** case, fines, penalties and punitive damages will also be uninsurable if insurance on them would be a violation of ***public policy***. (This will often be the case, since a fine, penalty or punitive damage award has as its main purpose ***deterrence*** rather than compensation, and the ability to insure against loss will remove much of the deterrent effect of that loss. See Clark, p. 670.)

5. Generally allowed: Most states explicitly ***allow*** the corporation to purchase D&O insurance.

a. May cover non-indemnifiable costs: Most importantly, a corporation may buy D&O insurance to cover a director's or officer's expenses ***even where those expenses could not be indemnified***. For instance, MBCA § 8.57 allows use of insurance to cover an individual "whether or not the corporation would have power to indemnify or advance expenses to him against the same liability under this subchapter."

6. Practical effect: Of course, many of the kinds of expenses that the corporation is forbidden to give indemnity for under most statutes, are also ***excluded*** from the typical D&O policy. For instance, just as the corporation may not generally indemnify for self-dealing (see *supra*, p. 344), so the typical D&O policy will not cover self-dealing. Similarly, knowing and culpable ***violations of law*** typically cannot be indemnified or insured against. Why, then, is it worthwhile to have insurance?

a. Individual's perspective: From the individual's perspective, there are some important instances in which insurance would cover an expense that could not be indemnified.

i. Derivative actions: Most significantly, money paid ***to the corporation*** as a ***judgment*** or ***settlement*** in a ***derivative action*** will usually be coverable by insurance (assuming the case did not involve blatant self-dealing or knowing illegality), even though such derivative action settlements and judgments are almost never indemnifiable (see *supra*, p. 346).

ii. Fact-finding: Second, whereas the corporation must generally make a ***formal written finding*** of indemnifiability before it may make final indemnification payments to the defendant (e.g., a report by an independent legal counsel, see *supra*, p. 347), no such formal fact-finding is required prior to insurance coverage — the insurer usually makes its decision about whether a particular claim is covered on a much less formal negotiated basis.

iii. **Legally able but practically unable or unwilling:** Finally, even if the corporation would be legally entitled to indemnify D for a particular loss, the corporation may be unable as a practical matter to do so (e.g., because it is insolvent), or may simply be ***unwilling*** to do so, in which case insurance is worthwhile. Clark, p. 674.

b. **Corporation's perspective:** From the corporation's perspective, the availability of insurance has two major virtues: (1) the corporation can avoid having to pay out more than a certain amount to cover directors' and officers' liability problems in any particular year (whereas if it has a broad indemnification policy, it may suddenly find itself with massive indemnification liability); and (2) the availability of insurance may allow the corporation to get ***better directors and officers*** than it would be able to get if it did not furnish them with insurance. See Clark, pp. 673-74.

Quiz Yourself on ***SHAREHOLDERS' SUITS*** *(ENTIRE CHAPTER)*

74. Chateau Marmoset, Inc., is a winery. Its board of directors wants to reduce the market price of Chateau Marmoset's shares (so insiders can buy the shares up more cheaply). Therefore, the board refuses to declare a dividend. This does, in fact, drive down the price of Chateau Marmoset stock. A Chateau Marmoset minority shareholder, Cher Donnay, brings suit against the directors to force them to pay a dividend.

(a) If you represent Cher, would you prefer that the court characterize your suit as a derivative suit, or a direct suit? ________________

(b) How will the court in fact characterize your suit? ________________

75. The Peter Minuit Real Estate Development Corp. has seven directors. One of them, Chief Floating Zone, owns an island he wants the company to buy from him for $24 and some subway tokens. (All directors are aware that Floating Zone owns the island.) There is some evidence before the board that the price is perhaps 20-30% above market rates. Five of the seven directors (one of whom is Floating Zone himself) vote to approve the transaction; the other two dissent. The transaction goes through. Manny Hattan, a Peter Minuit shareholder, bring a derivative claim against Floating Zone for self-dealing, and against the other four board members for breaching their duty of care in approving the high-priced transaction. (Hatten has not first made a demand on the board that they bring the suit instead of him.) The company files a motion to dismiss for failure to make a demand on directors. Assume that Delaware law is to be followed.

(a) What argument should Hatten make about why demand on the board should be excused? ________________

(b) Will this argument succeed? ________________

76. Snow White is a shareholder of Seven Dwarfs Microcomputers, Inc., which has seven directors. The Munchkinsoft Computer Co. makes a secret offer to the board of Seven Dwarfs to buy Seven Dwarfs at $25 a share. The directors instead collectively ask Munchkinsoft to give each director a consulting contract; in return, the directors promise to recommend to the shareholders that they accept *$20* a share for the Seven Dwarfs stock. The sale is approved at the $20 figure in part due to the directors' recommendation (which doesn't mention the $25 offer or the consulting contracts). The true facts about the recommendation later emerge. Snow White brings a derivative suit against the directors without first making a demand on them that they remedy the situation. The directors claim that the suit should be dismissed due to failure to make a demand on directors.

(a) Assume that Delaware law applies. What result? ________________

(b) Assume that the MBCA applies. What result? ________________

77. Peter Pan is a shareholder of the Fairy Dust Pharmaceuticals Corp. Three of Fairy Dust's seven directors, Wendy Darling, Captain Hook, and Tinkerbell, usurp a corporate opportunity of Fairy Dust's. Peter Pan, intending to file a derivative suit against them, makes a demand on the directors first. They appoint a special litigation committee, comprised of Wendy Darling, Tinkerbell, and a retired judge, Oliver Motor-Holmes. After a thorough investigation of the facts, the committee recommends that Fairy Dust not pursue a claim. Peter Pan files the derivative claim, and the directors respond by citing the committee's recommendation and filing a motion to dismiss. Will the court honor the committee's recommendation? ________________

78. Same basic facts as the prior question. Now, assume that only Wendy Darling is charged with usurping the corporate opportunity. All members of the board (with Wendy abstaining) vote to appoint a 3-member litigation committee, consisting of Captain Hook, Tinkerbell and Motor-Holmes. (There are no significant personal relationships between any of these three and Wendy.) The committee makes an extensive investigation into the facts. It concludes that Wendy has indeed acted on both sides of the transaction, did not make disclosure of the conflict to the board, and improperly benefited. However, the committee also formally concludes that "Although the suit might well be successful in recovering $100,000 from Wendy, the suit would cause considerable distraction to the company's officers and board, and the probable recovery would likely be outweighed by the negative impact of these distractions. Therefore, we recommend that the suit be dismissed."

(a) In most states, would the court accept the committee's recommendation? ________________

(b) In a state following the MBCA, would the court accept the committee's recommendation? ________________

79. Hannibal Lechter Foods, Inc., makes a popular meal extender for cannibals, "Manburger Helper" (". . . when you need a helping hand.").[2] The corporation is incorporated in (and based in) the mythical state of Atlantis. Robinson Crusoe, a 1% shareholder, believes that the directors are cooking the books; however, they refuse to allow him to see the corporation's books to find out if he's right. Nineteen other shareholders have the same problem. Among them, Crusoe and the other nineteen shareholders own 3% of the corporation's shares. When they sue the corporation in Atlantis state court to enforce their state-law right to inspect the books, the corporation asks that they be required to post bond for the corporation's litigation expenses. The Atlantis security-for-expenses statute is mandatory when the plaintiffs in a derivative suit own less than 10% of a corporation's outstanding shares. Will Crusoe and the other plaintiff/shareholders have to comply with the statute? ________________

---

2. Yes, we know you've seen this cheap pun (and this cheap basic fact pattern) before (p. 126). But we've varied the facts this time.

80. Catherine of Aragon is one of the directors of Henry VIII Dating Service, Inc. In her position as board member, she encourages Henry VIII to acquire another company, Marie Antoinette Cakes, Inc. Unbeknownst to the shareholders or directors of Henry VIII, Catherine is a large, secret shareholder in Marie Antoinette. Catherine honestly (and reasonably) believes that the acquisition, at the proposed price, will be beneficial to Henry VIII. After the acquisition goes through, a Henry VIII shareholder, Anne Boleyn, brings a derivative suit against Catherine, alleging that Catherine violated her duty of loyalty to Henry VIII by not disclosing the conflict. Catherine spends $20,000 litigating the suit; just before it goes to trial, she settles for a payment of $50,000 to the corporation. Henry VIII's charter authorizes indemnification of any director "for any liability which the director may have to the corporation for any breach of any obligation to the corporation, regardless of whether the director shall have acted in good faith." Catherine wishes to have Henry VIII indemnify her for both her $20,000 in litigation expenses and her $50,000 in settlement payments. The corporation wishes to pay these sums to Catherine, but wants to know whether it may properly do so.

(a) Under the prevailing approach, what result? ________________

(b) Under the MBCA, what result? ________________

(c) Assume now that the case went to trial. The court found that Henry VIII had paid a price that was $50,000 higher than a "fair" price for Marie Antoinette Cakes, and that this was due in part to Catherine's urging of the transaction, coupled with her failure to disclose her secret ownership interest in Marie Antoinette. The court therefore entered a judgment for $50,000 against Catherine in favor of Henry VIII. Catherine now seeks indemnification from Henry VIII for the $50,000 judgment, plus her litigation expenses (now $30,000). Henry VIII is willing to pay these sums. What, if anything, may Henry VIII properly pay her, under the MBCA? ________________

Answers

74. (a) You'd rather it be direct. A derivative suit has to jump many more procedural hurdles. For instance, demand has to be submitted to the board, and in most states if the board makes a reasonable inquiry and concludes that the claim has no merit, the court will probably terminate the action. Also, the plaintiff often has to post security for expenses, and the court has to approve any settlement. A direct action typically does not suffer from any of these shortcomings. [322]

(b) As direct. A case is a derivative suit only where the primary harm is to the corporation, not the individual plaintiff shareholder. Here, Donnay is complaining of an injury to her personally as a shareholder (failure to pay her dividends), not an injury to the corporation. The vast majority of derivative cases are against directors and/or officers for breaching their duties of care and loyalty to the corporation (e.g., wasting assets, self-dealing, excessive compensation, usurping a corporate opportunity). [320] That isn't what happened here. In general, a suit alleging that insiders have taken an action whose motive or principal effect was to injure a minority shareholder will be treated as direct.

75. (a) That demand would be futile, because the claim is that a majority of the board has breached its duty of care, and the board will almost certainly conclude that a claim of board-wrongdoing has no merit. It is indeed true that if the court becomes convinced that demand would be futile, the court will excuse the demand. [326] It's also true that in general, if the complaint charges a majority of the board with wrongdoing, the court is more likely to find demand to be futile than where only one board member, or a non-board-member, is charged with wrongdoing. [326] However (as discussed in part (b) to this answer), a Delaware court is likely to conclude that the wrongdoing charged here is not serious enough to excuse demand.

(b) No, probably. Delaware makes it very difficult to have a suit treated as demand-excused. The fact that a majority of the board approved the transaction doesn't, in and of itself, mean that demand on the board would be futile (says Delaware). [327] Demand will not be excused unless P shows in advance a reasonable likelihood that the board either: (1) was not disinterested or not independent; or (2) was not entitled to protection of the business judgment rule for its approval. [326]

There's no evidence of (1) (lack of disinterestedness or independence) on these facts. As to (2), the slightly-high price was not enough to make the board's approval "irrational," which is what would be required for an informed and distinterested board to lose protection of the business judgment rule. So the case will be dismissed until Manny makes a demand on the board. In other words, a charge that a majority of the board has violated its duty of care (as opposed to a charge that it has violated its duty of loyalty) will generally not be enough in Delaware to make the case demand-excused, unless there's substantial evidence of gross negligence or true irrationality. (A New York court, by contrast, would probably excuse demand here, merely from the fact that a majority of the board is charged with breach of the duty of care.)

76. (a) The demand will be excused, so the case won't be dismissed. As the prior question indicates, the main exception to the requirement of a demand on the board is where demand would be futile. Although Delaware makes it harder than most states to get a finding of futility, a claim (backed by some evidence) that a majority of the board has violated its duty of *loyalty* will suffice. Here, that's the case: all the directors have been offered lucrative consulting contracts with Munchkinsoft, in return for which they seem to have violated their duty to seek the best deal for the Seven Dwarfs' shareholders. As a result, Snow White needn't fulfill the demand-on-directors requirement.

(b) The demand must be made. The MBCA, in § 7.42(1), requires that a demand be made on the board in all cases, no matter how futile it would be. [335] (On the other hand, once the demand is made and the plaintiff waits the 90 days required by § 7.42(2), the court won't dismiss the action even if the board so recommends, unless the court believes that the independent directors have "determined in good faith after conducting a reasonable inquiry upon which [their] conclusions are based that the maintenance of the derivative proceeding is not in the best interests of the corporation." MBCA § 7.44(a). [335] So if the directors do a complete whitewash, the court will let the action proceed.)

77. No, because the members of the committee weren't "independent" or "disinterested." When the plaintiff in a derivative suit makes a demand on directors, the directors needn't make their own decision on whether to pursue the claim. They can, and sometimes do, leave the decision in the hands of a "special litigation committee." When they do so, and the committee recommends that the corporation not pursue the claim, the issue becomes whether the committee's recommendation is protected by the business judgment rule (in which case the motion to dismiss the claim will be granted). While states differ as to the deference courts should pay to committee recommendations, they all agree that each member of the committee must be "independent" from the defendants, and must not have any interest of their own in the transaction under attack ("disinterested"). [329] See, e.g., MBCA § 7.44(b)(2). Here, two of the three committee members were themselves defendants charged with serious wrongdoing (breach of the duty of loyalty), so they're not disinterested. As a result, their recommendation isn't subject to the business judgment rule, and the court will deny the motion to dismiss.

78. (a) Yes, probably. Most courts look principally at the committee's independence (see prior answer), disinterestedness (against see prior answer), good faith, and thoroughness in investigating. If the court is satisfied that the committee was independent, was disinterested, made a good-faith effort to reach a conclusion about what was best for the corporation, and investigated the available facts with reasonable thoroughness, the court will probably accept the committee's recommendation, without inquiring into the substantive validity of the suit. [330] Since the committee here seems to meet all these conditions, the court will likely accept its conclusions.

(b) Yes. MBCA § 7.44(a) says that a derivative proceeding "shall" be dismissed by the court if "one of the groups specified in [other sub-sections] has determined in good faith after conducting a reasonable inquiry upon which its conclusions are based that the maintenance of the derivative proceeding is not in the best interests of the corporation." [335] One of the groups that this section refers to is "a committee consisting of two or more independent directors appointed by majority vote of independent directors present at a meeting of the board of directors." The three committee members here are "independent," because they have no personal relationships with the person charged with wrongdoing (Wendy), and are not themselves charged with wrongdoing. See Official Comm. to § 7.44, "1. The Persons Making the Determination." Since all directors (and thus a majority of "independent" directors) voted to have the three elected to the committee, the committee qualifies. The facts don't indicate any reason to believe that the committee acted in other than good faith (for instance, there's no indication that they covered up their own misdeeds), and the facts tell us that the committee made a more-than-"reasonable" inquiry. So the court will not second-guess the committee's conclusion that the suit would not be in the corporation's best interests, and will dismiss the suit on the corporation's motion.

79. No, because the suit isn't derivative, it's direct. Security-for-expenses statutes generally require that "small shareholder" plaintiffs in derivative suits post a bond (or other security) for the corporation's litigation expenses, which the plaintiff will have to pay if he loses. Not all states have such statutes; however, even in the ones that do, only *derivative* suits are covered, not direct ones. [336] Here, Crusoe and the other shareholders are claiming that their *own* right to inspect the corporation's books has been violated; they aren't claiming that the corporation itself has been wronged. Therefore, the claim is direct, not derivative, so the security-for-expenses statute won't require the plaintiffs to post a bond (or other security) for the corporation's litigation expenses.

80. (a) The $20,000 in expenses, but nothing towards the $50,000 settlement amount. The vast majority of states do not permit a corporation to indemnify a director or officer for a settlement payment made by the defendant to the corporation at the conclusion of a derivative suit. [346] The reason is that if indemnification were allowed, there would be a circular recovery — the corporation would be receiving the settlement with one hand and paying it out again with the other hand as indemnification. However, most states *do* permit the defendant to be indemnified for his litigation expenses, if the derivative suit has been settled. [346]

(b) Same as in part (a) ($20,000 for expenses, only). Under MBCA § 8.51(d)(1), "a corporation may not indemnify a director: (1) in connection with a proceeding by or in the right of the corporation, except for ***reasonable expenses*** incurred in connection with the proceeding if it is determined that the director has met the relevant standard of conduct under subsection (a) . . . ." So no matter what Catherine's conduct was, she can't recover the settlement itself, since this is a "proceeding by or in the right of the corporation" (i.e., a derivative suit.) (The *court* still has discretion to *order* indemnification, under the "fair and reasonable" test of § 8.54(a)(3), but it's unlikely that the court will use this discretion, and the corporation may not make the indemnification payment without a court order.)

On the other hand, Catherine probably *can* recover the litigation expenses. These are clearly "reasonable expenses incurred in connection. . . ." The issue is whether Catherine's conduct met the requirements of § 8.51(a). That subsection requires that she have: (1) conducted herself in "good faith"; and (2) "reasonably believed . . . in the case of conduct in [her] official capacity, that [her] conduct was in the best interests of the corporation." The facts tell us that (1) is satisfied, and her belief that the acquisition would be a good one for Henry VIII probably means that (2) is satisfied as well. Therefore, Catherine can probably recover her litigation expenses.

(c) Nothing. MBCA § 8.51(d)(2) prohibits the company from indemnifying a director "in connection with any proceeding with respect to conduct for which [the director] was ***adjudged liable*** on the basis that he ***received a financial benefit to which he was not entitled***, whether or not involving action in his official capacity." This applies here: the court has found a breach of the duty of loyalty, leading to an unduly high price being paid, which price was shared in by Catherine. Therefore, without a court order the company may not even pay Catherine's litigation expenses, let alone indemnify her for the judgment. (The court might still order that Henry VIII reimburse the expenses, under § 8.54(a)(3), if this would be "fair and reasonable"; but the court does not have discretion to order indemnification for the judgment under any circumstances, under that same provision.)

Exam Tips on ***SHAREHOLDERS' SUITS, ESPECIALLY DERIVATIVE SUITS***

- Whenever the facts involve a shareholder suit, first determine whether the suit should be characterized as a ***direct action*** or a ***derivative action***.
  - Remember that if the injury is primarily to some or all s/h's "personally," the suit to redress it is a ***direct*** action. Here are kinds of suits that are usually "direct":
    - ❑ suits to enforce the s/h's ***voting rights***;
    - ❑ suits to ***compel payments of dividends***;
    - ❑ suits to ***prevent oppression of or fraud*** on minority s/h's;
    - ❑ suits to ***compel inspection*** of the corp's books and records.
  - Conversely, a ***derivative*** action is the exclusive remedy where the alleged harm is done primarily to the ***corporation***, rather than to an individual s/h. Examples of suits that are generally derivative:
    - ❑ suits claiming breach of the ***duty of care***;
    - ❑ suits claiming breach of the ***duty of loyalty*** (e.g., suits claiming self-dealing, usurpation of a corp. opportunity, or excessive compensation).
- If the action is derivative, confirm that the requirements for a derivative action have been met. In particular:
  - Verify that either the ***"contemporaneous ownership"*** rule is satisfied, or that some exception applies. Thus P must normally have ***already owned his shares at the time of the transaction of which he complains***. But there are two exceptions:
    - where the wrong began before P brought his shares, but ***continued after*** P bought

(the ***"continuing wrong"*** exception); or

- ☞ where P acquired his shares by ***"operation of law,"*** and his ***predecessor owned*** the shares before the wrongdoing (the "operation of law" exception). Shares which P acquired by ***inheritance*** are often part of the exam fact pattern, and fall within this exception.

☞ Check to see whether P has made a ***demand*** on the directors to redress the improper action. If not, determine whether demand is ***excused*** because it's ***likely to be futile*** (though not all states excuse demand even when futile).

- ☞ Keep in mind that in many states, demand is excused as futile where ***all or a majority*** of the ***board*** is ***charged*** with breach of the duty of ***due care*** or of the duty of ***loyalty***.

  Example: Trucking Corp. runs a trucking business. Its board has 15 members. Management has a consultant prepare a report that says that if the corp. doesn't buy $1 million worth of new trucks within the next year, the company will lose business and probably become insolvent. The report is given to every member of the board, but only 5 read it. The board unanimously votes not to buy new trucks, and to spend the $1 million available to buy another business. Trucking Corp. becomes insolvent shortly thereafter for lack of new trucks. S, a s/h throughout the relevant period, brings a derivative action against those board members who didn't read the report, for breach of the duty of care in not buying the trucks. In many states, demand on the board will be excused, because this demand would likely be futile since a majority of the board members are being accused of a breach of the duty of care.

☞ If P has made a demand on the board, and the board ***rejects*** the demand, the board's decision will generally receive the ***protection of the business judgment rule*** (so that as long as the decision not to bring the litigation is ***rational***, P will not be allowed to continue with his derivative action).

- ☞ But the court will allow P's suit to ***go forward*** despite the board's rejection of the demand, if either: (1) the ***board significantly participated*** in the alleged wrong; or (2) the directors who voted to reject the suit were ***dominated or controlled by the alleged wrongdoers***.

- ☞ Look for situations in which the board has appointed a special ***committee*** to evaluate the derivative action, and the committee has recommended dismissal. Confirm that the members of the committee are ***truly independent*** of the directors accused of wrongdoing — if they're not, the derivative action should be allowed to proceed despite the committee's recommendation.

  Example: The 5 directors of Corp. (most of whom are part of management) are fearful of a hostile takeover attempt. These 5 directors therefore vote to sell off valuable corporate assets at below-market prices, solely to make Corp. a less attractive target. The board then votes to expand to 9 members, and to stagger the terms so that only 3 directors can be replaced each year. The 4 new directors are all close friends of the existing directors. P brings a derivative action against Corp for damages from the asset sales. The board votes to create a litigation committee consisting of the 4 new directors. The committee votes to recommend dismissal of P's suit. You should say that the court should let the suit proceed, because the committee was not truly independent — its members were all close friends of the original directors accused of the wrongdoing.

☛ Look out for questions that require you to say whether a corp's ***indemnification*** of its officers or directors was proper.

☞ Recall that nearly all states ***permit*** the corp to indemnify any director or officer whose position is ***upheld*** in litigation, so questions on this fact pattern are easy. (In fact, most states ***require*** the corp. to indemnify in this "successful defendant" situation.)

☞ Conversely, remember that most states do ***not permit*** an agreement to indemnify a director or officer whose position is ***not upheld*** (e.g., a dir. or off. who's found liable to the corp. in a derivative action).

☞ Where the action is ***settled*** by means of a payment by the dir/off to the corp., usually state statutes say that the dir/off ***can*** be indemnified for his ***litigation expenses***, but ***can't*** be indemnified for the ***settlement payment***.

Example: Veep, a v.p. of Corp., is sued in a derivative action in which P says that Veep entered into an unfairly favorable contract to buy property from Corp. Veep spends $30,000 on legal fees, then settles by paying $20,000 to Corp. Corp. can probably indemnify Veep for the $30,000 legal fees, but not the $20,000 settlement.

☞ Make sure that the ***decision*** about whether to indemnify is made by a ***sufficiently independent party.*** Thus directors closely affiliated with the defendant(s) can't decide to allow the indemnification payment — a ***committee*** of independent directors (i.e., directors not charged with wrongdoing and independent of those who are so charged), should make this decision.

Example: P brings a derivative suit charging all members of Corp's board with selling Corp's assets at an unfairly low price to avoid a hostile takeover. The suit is settled with each board member paying $10,000. The entire board votes to pay the litigation expenses, including legal fees, of each board member. Probably this indemnification is invalid — since every board member was charged with wrongdoing, they couldn't make an arms' length decision to indemnify themselves.

CHAPTER 10

STRUCTURAL CHANGES, INCLUDING MERGERS AND ACQUISITIONS

ChapterScope

This Chapter discusses mergers, acquisitions and other structural changes in a corporation. Key concepts:

- **Different forms for acquiring:** There are various forms a business combination can take. A key distinction is between "merger-type" deals and "sale-type" deals.
  - **Merger-type deals:** In a ***merger-type*** transaction, shareholders in the "target" corporation (the one being in a sense "acquired") end up with ***stock*** in the acquiring corporation. The acquiring corporation, of course, now owns the acquired business as well as the acquirer's original business. So in a merger, the target's shareholders have a ***continuing stake*** in the newly-combined enterprise.
  - **Sale-type deals:** In a ***sale-type*** deal, the target's shareholders end up with cash (or, perhaps, some type of debt instrument issued by the acquirer, like notes.) Those holders thus ***no longer have any ongoing stake*** in either the target or the acquirer.
- **Appraisal rights:** In many types of business combinations, the target's shareholders have a "right of ***appraisal***" under state law. If a shareholder feels that he has not gotten a fair price for his shares (and he hasn't voted in favor of the sale or merger), that shareholder may have a court determine the fair value of the shares; if that fair value is greater than the amount actually paid, the acquirer is required to pay the shareholder the balance.
- **Freezeouts:** Courts try to protect minority holders from "freezeouts." In a freezeout, the controlling shareholders take exclusive ownership of the corporation by finding a legal way to eliminate the outsiders as shareholders.
- **Tender offers:** The principal way one publicly-held corporation takes over another publicly-held one is by means of a ***tender offer.*** In a tender offer, the acquirer (the offeror) offers to buy each public holder's stock directly. A tender offer can be carried out even over the objection of the target's board of directors and management (since it's up to each holder in the target whether to tender, i.e., sell, his shares to the offeror.) The tender offer is thus different from a sale of assets by the target to the acquirer, which requires the consent of the target's board.
- **Hostile takeovers:** Much of this chapter is concerned with ***"hostile takeovers."*** A hostile takeover is a process by which one corporation acquires another, over the objection of the target's board of directors. Takeovers are usually carried out by tender offers (see above).
- **Takeover defenses:** The management of a target that is the subject of a hostile takeover attempt has a number of tactics by which to repel the takeover. Much of this chapter is a review of these techniques, and of the ways in which courts have tried to restrict these tech-

niques so that the target's management cannot entrench itself at the expense of the target's shareholders' right to sell to the hostile bidder for a high price.

I. CORPORATE COMBINATIONS — GENERALLY

A. Types of transactions: Let us assume that Big Corp wants to acquire control of the business and assets of Little Corp. There are a number of ways that this can be brought about. We shall begin by summarizing some of the more important techniques for carrying out such a business combination.

1. **Merger-type deals vs. sale-type deals:** First, let's make a major distinction between what might be called ***"merger-type"*** deals and ***"sale-type"*** deals. A "merger-type" deal is one in which the shareholders of Little Corp will end up mainly with ***stock in Big Corp*** as their payment for surrendering control of Little Corp and its assets. A "sale-type" transaction is one in which Little Corp's stockholders end up with ***cash*** in compensation for their interest in Little Corp. Most types of transactions fall fairly clearly into either the merger-style camp or the sale-style camp (though there are some hybrid transactions, which we will be describing below, whose categorization is not so clear).

B. Merger-type transactions: There are four main techniques that fall into the ***merger***-style category:

1. **Traditional statutory merger:** First is the traditional ***"statutory merger."*** By following procedures set out in the state corporation statute, one corporation can merge into another, with the former (called the "disappearing" corporation) ceasing to have any legal identity and the latter (called the "surviving" corporation) continuing in existence. S,S,B&W, p. 399.

   Example: Suppose that Big Corp wants to acquire Little Corp through a statutory merger. The boards of directors of Big Corp and Little Corp will each approve a "plan of merger," which specifies that Little Corp will be merged into Big Corp, and which specifies that each share of Little Corp stock will be converted into, say, two shares of newly-issued Big Corp stock. The shareholders of Little Corp will have to approve the merger, and the shareholders of Big Corp may have to approve it also (depending in part on whether the number of outstanding Big Corp shares will increase materially by virtue of the merger; see *infra*, p. 379). After the requisite approvals, Big Corp will deliver articles of merger to the Secretary of State of its home state. Big Corp will issue new shares in Big Corp to Little Corp shareholders as prescribed in the merger agreement. Little Corp will cease to exist as a separate entity — it is "merged into" Big Corp. By automatic operation of law, Big Corp acquires all of Little Corp's assets and all of its liabilities. All contracts that Little Corp had with third parties now become contracts between that third party and Big Corp. Big Corp is referred to as the "surviving" corporation and Little Corp as the "disappearing" corporation. See MBCA §§ 11.01, 11.03, 11.05, and 11.06.

   a. **Diagram:** Thus after the completion of the statutory merger, we have the corporate structure shown in Figure 10-1 on p. 361.

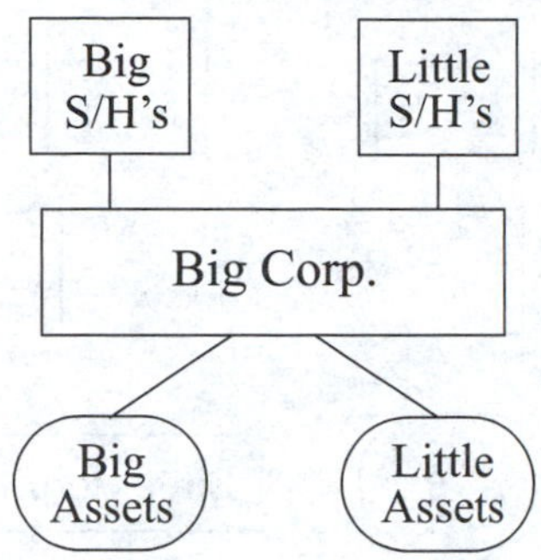

Figure 10-1
Statutory Merger

b. **Continuing ownership:** Probably the key feature of the statutory merger (at least when it is compared to the sale-type transactions we will be considering below) is that the shareholders of Little Corp, the "acquired" company, are ***not "cashed out"*** — instead, they continue to have an equity participation, though this participation is now in the combined Big Corp/Little Corp entity rather than being solely in Little Corp.

2. **Stock-for-stock exchange ("stock swap"):** There is a second method of producing almost exactly the same result as the statutory merger. This is the ***"stock-for-stock exchange"*** or, as it is sometimes called, the ***"stock swap."*** The essence of the stock swap is that the acquiring corporation, instead of entering into a plan of merger with the target corporation, makes a ***separate deal with each target shareholder***, giving that holder shares in the acquirer in exchange for the shares in the target.

   Example: Big Corp decides to acquire Little Corp by a stock-for-stock exchange ("stock swap") instead of by statutory merger. Big Corp will offer to acquire each Little Corp share in return for, say, two newly-issued Big Corp shares. Each Little Corp shareholder will independently decide whether to accept the offer to exchange. Big Corp might decide to make its offer contingent upon receiving some specified majority (e.g., 50%) of Little Corp's shares. In some states, if a majority of Little Corp shareholders approve the exchange offer, even those not approving will be forced to go along and exchange their shares.

   a. **Diagram:** At the end of the stock swap (at least assuming that all Little Corp shareholders accepted or were forced to accept the deal) the corporate form would look as shown in Figure 10-2 on p. 362.

   This corporate form is almost the same as that in the statutory merger situation (see Figure 10-1 above), except that Little Corp keeps its separate corporate identity (though it is now a subsidiary of Big Corp). Otherwise, the economic reality is the same as any statutory merger: Little Corp's shareholders now have a stake in the combined Big Corp/Little Corp, and Big Corp controls Little Corp's assets.

   i. **Subsequent liquidation and distribution:** In fact, if Big Corp wants to end up with ***exactly*** the same result as in the statutory merger situation, it merely has to take a simple second step: it can ***liquidate*** Little Corp, and distribute Little Corp's

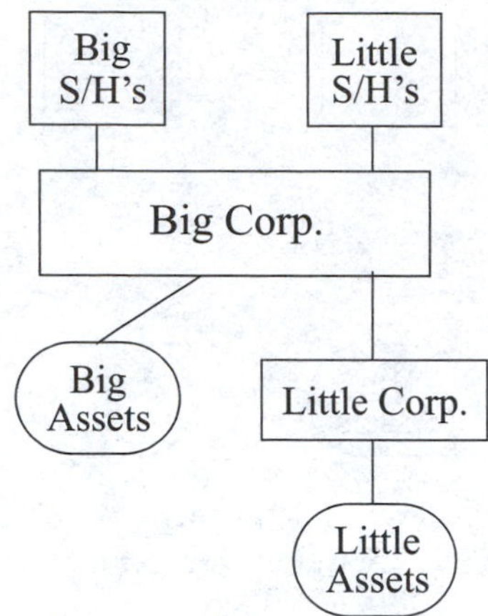

Figure 10-2
Stock-for-Stock Exchange
("Stock Swap")

assets to itself. The corporate form would then look exactly like Figure 10-1 on p. 361.

b. Rationale: Why would Big Corp want to use the stock-for-stock method rather than the statutory merger method? First, the statutory merger requires the ***consent*** of Little Corp's board, whereas the stock-for-stock exchange can be carried out over the board's opposition (Big Corp makes a tender offer for the Little Corp shares, and each shareholder is, at least in the first instance, free to accept or reject the exchange offer). Second, Big Corp might be able to avoid the need for a formal vote of approval by Little Corp shareholders (each Little Corp holder would effectively "vote" by tendering or not tendering his shares), whereas the Little Corp holders will certainly have to vote for a statutory merger. On the other hand, stubborn Little Corp minority shareholders who oppose the stock-for-stock deal may have the ability to maintain their Little Corp holdings (this depends on whether the state statute governing exchanges allows the majority to force the minority to go along with the exchange), whereas Little Corp shareholders who oppose the statutory merger would be out of luck, and would definitely be compelled, in all states, to accept Big Corp shares in substitution for their Little Corp shares.

c. Surviving minority interest: As the last sentence of the prior paragraph shows, a minority of shareholders in the target can seriously disrupt the share-for-share exchange, by simply refusing to tender their shares. The acquirer faced with this possibility may lose interest, since it is unlikely to want to be stuck permanently with a minority of shareholders in the target — this would subject it to fiduciary responsibilities of fairness to the minority holders, which may interfere with business flexibility. (See, e.g., *Weinberger v. UOP, infra*, p. 425.)

i. Plan of exchange: To deal with this possible "tyranny of the minority," a few states allow a share-for-share exchange to be made ***compulsory*** upon all of the target company's shareholders. The directors of the target corporation, in these states, can approve a ***"plan of exchange"***; if the plan is approved by a majority of the target's shareholders, then all target shareholders are required to exchange their shares for shares of the acquirer. See, e.g., MBCA §§ 11.03, 11.04 and 11.07(b), allowing for such a compulsory plan of share exchange. The net result of such a compulsory plan is that share exchanges very closely resemble mergers, in terms of the corporate action needed to bring them about. See S,S,B&W, p. 402.

3. **Stock-for-assets exchange:** Now, consider our third form of merger-type transaction: the ***stock-for-assets exchange***. In this kind of transaction, there are usually two steps: In Step 1, the acquiring company gives stock to the target company, and the target company gives all or substantially all of its assets to the acquiring company in exchange. In Step 2 (which usually, but not necessarily, follows), the target dissolves, and distributes the acquirer's stock to its own shareholders. If both steps are carried out, the net result is virtually identical to the result in the true merger scenario.

   Example: Big Corp wants to end up with all of the assets of Little Corp. It reaches a stock-for-assets exchange agreement with Little Corp, by which Big Corp issues to Little Corp a number of Big Corp shares having an aggregate market value equal to the market value of Little Corp's assets. In return, Little Corp conveys (by bill of sale for personal property, and deeds for real estate) all of its assets to Big Corp. Little Corp is now effectively a "shell" or "holding company," since its only assets are the Big Corp stock. Little Corp might continue to run as a holding company, receiving dividends and perhaps paying out those dividends to its own shareholders. More probably, however, Little Corp would dissolve, and make a liquidating distribution to Little Corp shareholders of the Big Corp stock. If this dissolution-and-distribution took place, the net result would be as if Little Corp had been merged into Big Corp.

   a. **Diagram:** Thus at the end of Step 1 (the initial exchange of Little Corp's assets for Big Corp stock), our corporate structure would look like this:

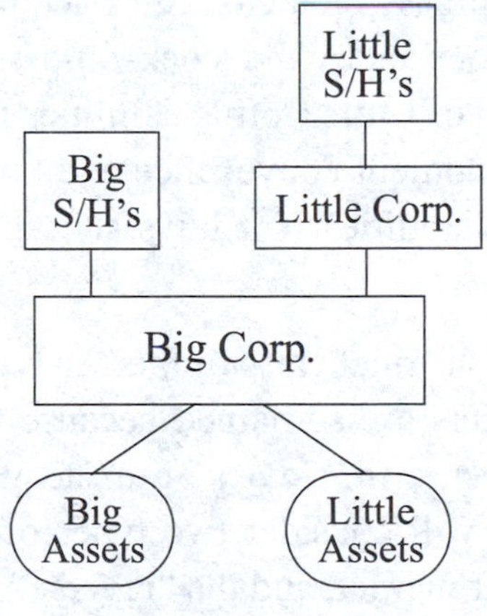

Figure 10-3a
Stock-for-Assets Exchange
(After Step 1)

      i. **Diagram after second step:** Then, if the second step occurs (Little Corp dissolves, and pays a liquidating distribution of the shares in Big Corp to Little Corp shareholders), we would have the corporate structure shown Fig. 10-3b on p. 364.

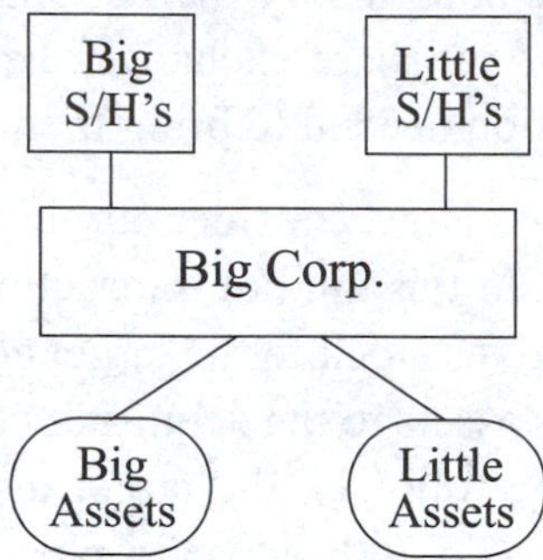

Figure 10-3b
Stock-for-Assets Exchange
(Little Corp. has dissolved)

Thus after the second step, we have a structure that is identical to Figure 1 (result of an ordinary statutory merger).

b. **Rationale:** Why would Big Corp proceed by a stock-for-assets exchange rather than by one of the other two forms we have considered? Big Corp's management might prefer the stock-for-assets arrangement to a statutory merger because Big Corp's shareholders might have to approve the statutory merger (see *infra*, p. 377), whereas they would not have to approve the stock-for-assets exchange (assuming that there were enough authorized but unissued Big Corp shares to fund the transaction, and assuming that the increase in the number of Big Corp issued shares that would result from the transaction would be reasonably small; see *infra*, p. 381). Big Corp might also prefer the stock-for-assets exchange over a stock-for-stock exchange for reasons of liability: Big Corp has some chance of acquiring just Little Corp's assets, without its liabilities, if it proceeds by the stock-for-assets form, whereas it will be automatically saddled with all of Little Corp's liabilities if it does a stock-for-stock deal. (However, the laws of fraudulent conveyance and bulk sales make it hard for Big Corp to avoid Little Corp's liabilities if it buys substantially all of Little Corp's assets; see *infra*, p. 373.)

4. **Triangular mergers:** Our final class of merger-type transaction is called a ***"triangular"*** merger. Triangular mergers are so named because they involve ***three*** parties rather than the usual two: the acquirer, a ***subsidiary*** of the acquirer created especially for the transaction, and the target. We will consider two types of triangular mergers: the "forward" or "conventional" triangular merger, and the "reverse" triangular merger.

   a. **"Conventional" or "forward" triangular merger:** In the ***"conventional"*** or ***"forward"*** triangular merger, the acquiring company ***creates a subsidiary*** for the purpose of the transaction. Usually, the subsidiary has no assets except shares of stock in the parent, which it receives in return for issuing all of its own stock to its parent. The ***target is then merged into the acquirer's subsidiary***. But unlike the usual merger, the target's shareholders do not receive stock in the surviving corporation (the subsidiary) but rather stock in the subsidiary's ***parent*** (the acquirer). The end result is very similar to what would have happened had the target simply merged into the acquirer, except that the target's business is now owned by the acquirer's subsidiary rather than directly by the acquirer.

Example: Big Corp wants to acquire the business of Little Corp. Big Corp sets up a subsidiary called Big-Sub. Big Corp transfers 1,000 of its own shares to Big-Sub, in return for all of the shares of Big-Sub. Big-Sub now enters into a merger agreement with Little Corp. (On the acquiring side, shareholder approval for the merger comes from a vote by Big Corp as the sole shareholder of Big-Sub, not from a vote by Big Corp's individual shareholders.) Little Corp now merges into Big-Sub.

In an ordinary merger, the shareholders of Little Corp (the disappearing corporation) would receive shares of the surviving corporation (Big-Sub). But in a special twist that is found in forward triangular mergers, Little Corp shareholders instead receive as a result of the merger shares in Big Corp rather than shares in Big-Sub. Little Corp loses its separate existence as a result of this merger. The end result is very similar to what would have happened had Big Corp directly done a stock-for-stock exchange with Little Corp (except that Little Corp's assets are now held by a Big Corp subsidiary called "Big-Sub" rather than by a Big Corp subsidiary called "Little Corp").

i. **Diagram:** Thus in terms of our diagrams, the situation following the forward triangular merger is as shown in Figure 10-4a:

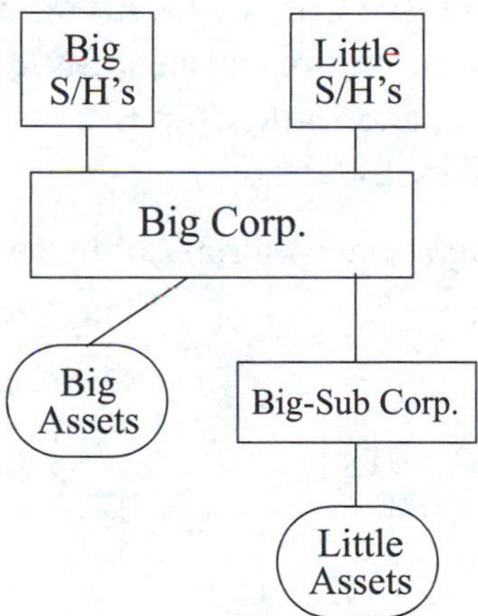

Figure 10-4a
Forward Triangular Merger

The configuration from Figure 10-4a is the same as Figure 10-2 (stock swap) except that Little Corp's assets end up being held by Big-Sub Corp (a subsidiary of Big Corp) rather than by Little Corp (a subsidiary of Big Corp).

ii. **Rationale:** One advantage of this technique, compared with the stock-for-stock exchange to which it is so similar in result, is that this forward merger technique is guaranteed to ***eliminate all minority interest*** in Little Corp's assets — ***every*** Little Corp shareholder is forced to become a Big Corp shareholder, whereas in the stock-for-stock exchange scenario a Little Corp shareholder could decline to participate (assuming that the "plan of share exchange" technique, *supra*, p. 362, is not used). Also, this technique has the advantage over the direct merger of Little Corp into Big Corp that the arrangement ***does not have to be approved by Big Corp's shareholders:*** approval on the Big side comes from Big-Sub's sole shareholder (Big Corp, probably in the form of a vote cast by Big's management rather than by vote of Big-Sub's ultimate owners, the shareholders of Big Corp). (But see Cal. Corp. Code § 1200(d), giving Big's shareholders the right to approve of the merger of Little into Big-Sub because Big's stock is being used in the merger.) See also C&E, p. 1175.

b. Reverse triangular merger: Now, let's examine the other kind of triangular merger, the exotically-named "***reverse*** triangular merger." This technique is the same as the forward triangular merger, except that the acquirer's subsidiary ***merges into the target***, rather than having the target merge into the subsidiary.

Example: Big Corp forms a wholly owned subsidiary Big-Sub, just as in the example, *supra*, p. 365. Again, all shares of Big-Sub are transferred to Big in return for a certain number of Big shares. Big-Sub and Little Corp are merged, just as in the prior example, except that this time, *Big-Sub disappears* and *Little* is the surviving corporation. In other words, under the merger agreement among the three parties, Big will have its shares in Big-Sub converted into shares of Little; also under that agreement, the former Little Corp shareholders will have their stock converted into Big Corp stock (namely, the shares of Big Corp stock that were previously owned by Big-Sub but that have become assets of Little Corp by means of the merger itself). See Clark, p. 431.

When all the transactions are finished, Little Corp's original shareholders are left with stock in Big Corp, and Little Corp is now a subsidiary of Big Corp (with Little Corp's assets still held by Little Corp).

i. Diagram: In diagrammatic terms, at the end of the transactions, here is what we have:

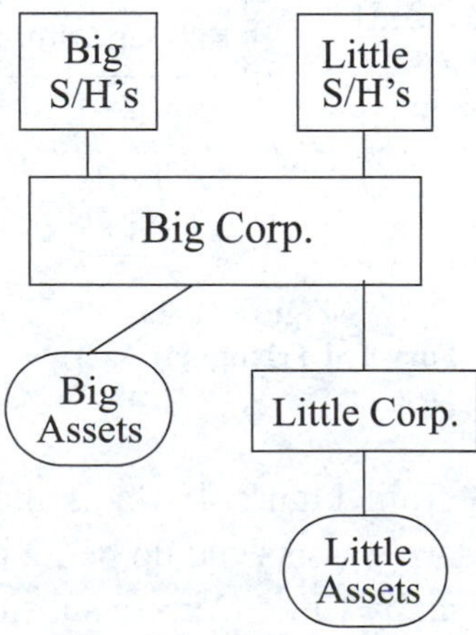

Figure 10-4b
Reverse Triangular Merger

(1) Comparable to share-for-share exchange: If you look closely at Figure 10-4b, you will see that the final result of a reverse triangular merger is ***exactly***

the same as that in a stock-for-stock exchange in which the acquirer succeeds in acquiring all of the target's shares (represented by Figure 10-2).

ii. Rationale: The reverse triangular merger form is quite popular, even though the notion of merging a piece of the acquirer into the target, instead of merging the target into the acquirer, seems bizarre. Merger lawyers often prefer the reverse triangular technique over each of the alternative forms because it has at least one significant advantage over each of these other forms:

iii. Advantage over stock-for-stock exchange: Since the net result of a reverse triangular merger looks to be exactly the same as the net result of a stock-for-stock exchange, let's begin by asking, "Why use the reverse triangular merger instead of a plain (and easily understood) stock-for-stock swap?" The principal answer is that in most states, a stock-for-stock exchange can be ***obstructed by minority shareholders of the target***, whereas the reverse triangular merger ***eliminates all shareholders in the target*** whether they wish to be eliminated or not.

Example: In the stock-for-stock exchange, *supra*, p. 361, some Little Corp shareholders might decide not to tender their shares in exchange for Big Corp shares. These minority Little Corp shareholders would thus persist in their partial ownership of Little Corp. Big Corp would be a majority, but not sole, owner of Little Corp. Any actions it took regarding Little Corp and its assets could be attacked for unfairness by the remaining minority Little Corp stockholders. (See, e.g., *Weinberger v. UOP*, *infra*, p. 425.)

By contrast, at the conclusion of the reverse triangular merger, all Little Corp shareholders have been forced to receive stock in Big Corp, whether they like it or not.

Observe that this advantage of the reverse triangular technique over a simple stock-for-stock exchange does not exist where state law authorizes a plan of exchange (*supra*, p. 362). Where a plan of exchange is allowed by statute, and is approved by both boards of directors and by the shareholders of the "disappearing" corporation (Little Corp in our example), the stockholders of the corporation being acquired are forced to accept the acquirer's shares in exchange for their own whether they want it or not, just as in the reverse triangular merger technique. Therefore, the reverse triangular merger technique is more popular in jurisdictions that do not allow a plan of exchange that is binding on all shareholders. See Clark, p. 432.

iv. Advantages over direct merger: The reverse triangular merger also has two potentially important advantages over simply merging the acquired corporation into the acquirer. To see these, let's compare the reverse triangular merger of BigSub into Little Corp with a straightforward merger of Little Corp into Big Corp (as on p. 364).

(1) Exposure to liabilities: First, if Little Corp is simply merged into Big Corp, Big Corp not only acquires all of the liabilities of Little Corp, but places ***its own assets*** at risk to satisfy those liabilities. (Remember that when a statutory merger occurs, the surviving corporation automatically, by operation of law, takes all of the liabilities of the disappearing corporation, whether it wants to or not.) Thus if Little Corp turns out to have some unsuspected major contingent liability that comes home to roost, the creditor(s) of Little Corp can collect not only against the assets that used to belong to Little Corp and now belong to Big Corp but also against Big Corp's pre-existing assets. If the reverse triangular technique is used, Big Corp has a good chance of limiting Little Corp's creditors to the assets of Little Corp (which still survives after having Big-Sub merged into it). See Clark, pp. 432-33.

(2) **Vote by acquirer's shareholders:** Second, as in the case of the forward triangular merger, the reverse triangular merger dispenses with the need for the acquirer's shareholders to approve the transaction. The plan of merger adopted as part of the reverse triangular technique will have to be approved only by Big-Sub's shareholder (Big Corp, probably acting by vote of its management), not by vote of Big Corp's individual shareholders. By contrast, a plan of merger of Little Corp into Big Corp might well have to be approved by Big Corp's individual shareholders (unless the transaction fell into the "whale/minnow" category, described *infra*, p. 379). See Clark, p. 433.

(3) **Advantage over forward triangular merger:** Finally, the reverse triangular technique has a potentially important advantage over the forward triangular technique: since the target ***survives as a separate legal entity***, certain rights and properties of the target are more likely to remain intact than if the target disappeared. For instance, Little Corp might have valuable contract rights, leases, licenses, etc., which might be lost if Little Corp were merged into Big-Sub; these will almost certainly not be lost if Big-Sub is merged into Little Corp which survives. Similarly, if Little Corp has had profits and paid taxes, any post-acquisition losses that the business might suffer have a better chance of being carried back against Little's pre-acquisition profits (resulting in a tax refund) if Little survives as an entity rather than being merged into Big-Sub. See Clark, p. 433.

c. **Non-merger types of triangular deals:** Often in a triangular merger the use of a subsidiary will be coupled with the use of a statutory merger. The triangular examples we've seen so far (Little Corp statutorily merges into Big-Sub, or Big-Sub statutorily merges into Little Corp) fall into this pattern. But there is no requirement that the statutory merger form be used merely because the triangular or subsidiary structure is used: ***the subsidiary and the target can combine using the other techniques just as well***.

i. **Stock swap:** For instance, Big-Sub could effectively acquire Little Corp by means of a ***stock-for-stock exchange***: Little Corp would trade all of its stock in return for the Big Corp stock held by Big-Sub.

ii. **Forward stock-for-assets exchange:** Or, the transaction could proceed as a ***stock-for-assets*** swap between the subsidiary and the target. Thus Big-Sub could buy all of Little Corp's assets in return for the Big Corp stock held by Big-Sub.

iii. **Reverse stock-for-assets swap:** Perhaps most ingeniously, a ***reverse*** triangular merger could similarly proceed as a stock-for-assets swap: Little Corp could "buy" all of Big-Sub's assets (namely, the Big Corp stock held by Big-Sub) in return for all of the stock of Little Corp. The key advantage of this somewhat bizarre structure is that this might avoid giving Little Corp's shareholders either the right to ***approve*** the transaction (since shareholder approval of a ***purchase*** of another company's assets is usually not required) or ***appraisal*** rights if they don't like the transaction (an appraisal right is the right of a stockholder who disapproves of a transaction to be "cashed out" at a fair value; see *infra*, p. 395).

(1) **De facto merger doctrine:** But if this reverse triangular stock-for-assets structure were seen by the court as being the substantial economic equivalent of a conventional merger, and were also seen by the court as being primarily motivated by the desire to deprive the target's shareholders of their appraisal rights, the court might apply the "de facto merger" doctrine to grant those appraisal rights anyway; see *Farris v. Glen Alden Corp.*, *infra*, p. 406, in which this is exactly what happened.

5. **Continuity-of-interest aspect:** All of these merger-type scenarios have one important factor in common: the shareholders in the acquired corporation have a ***continuity of interest*** once the transaction is completed. That is, rather than being "cashed out" of their equity investment in the target, they have in one form or another ***exchanged*** that equity investment for another equity investment, this time an investment in a pool of assets consisting of the target company's assets and the acquiring company's assets. In terms of our Big/Little hypothetical, after each of the merger-type scenarios Little Corp's shareholders own a piece of the combined Big/Little assets.

a. **Significance:** This "continuity of interest" is important for the ***tax*** treatment of these transactions. Little Corp shareholders would not pay any tax at the time of the exchange of Little Corp shares for Big Corp shares; instead, Little Corp shareholders would pay a tax when they eventually sold the Big Corp shares that they received in the exchange (but this tax would be computed by looking at the Little Corp shareholder's original cost for his Little Corp shares). See *infra*, p. 383.

C. **Sale-type transactions:** We now turn to the other side of the great divide, to what might be called ***"sale-type" transactions*** as opposed to merger-type ones. The key distinction between sale-type transactions and merger-type ones is that in the sale-type case the stockholder in the acquired company is effectively "cashed out." She gives up her equity interest in the target company for cash, or perhaps a combination of cash and debt (e.g., a debenture, see *infra*, or preferred stock, see *infra*, p. 415). The point is that the target company shareholder no longer has a common stock interest in the assets of either the target or the acquiring company.

1. **Two main types:** There are two main sale-type transactions: (1) a sale of the target's assets for cash, followed by a liquidation and distribution to shareholders ("asset-sale-and-liquidation"); and (2) a sale by each shareholder of his target company stock in return for cash, perhaps followed by a liquidation of the target ("stock sale"). We will consider each in turn.

2. **Asset-sale-and-liquidation:** The essence of the ***asset-sale-and-liquidation*** transaction is that it is carried out by ***corporate action*** on the target's part. The target's board of directors approves a sale of all or substantially all of the target's assets to the acquirer, and this proposed sale is approved by a majority of the target shareholders. The target conveys the assets to the acquirer, and the target receives the cash (or perhaps debt) payment from the acquirer. Typically, the target then ***dissolves***, and pays the cash or debt to the shareholders in proportion to their shareholdings, in the form of a ***liquidating distribution***.

   Example: Big Corp wants to end up with the assets of Little Corp, and does not want to have to dilute its own shareholders by paying for the purchase in the form of Big Corp shares (as would be the case with any of the merger-type transactions considered above). Therefore, Big Corp proposes to buy Little Corp's assets in return for a combination of cash and debentures. The transaction contemplates the payment of $1 million in cash and $1 million in five-year debentures, paying interest-only until maturity. Little Corp's board of directors approves the proposed asset sale. Little Corp's shareholders, by a majority vote, also approve the sale. Little Corp then conveys (by issuing bills of sale for personal property and deeds for real estate) all of its assets to Big Corp. Big Corp writes out a check for $1 million cash payable to Little Corp; Big Corp also issues $1 million in debentures to Little Corp.

   After this exchange is completed, Little Corp dissolves (pursuant to a plan of liquidation approved by the Little Corp shareholders at the same time they approved the asset sale to Big Corp). As part of the dissolution, Little Corp distributes to each shareholder his share (in proportion to his common stock holdings in Little Corp) of the cash and debentures.

   a. **Diagram:** Our diagram of the results of this transaction (assuming that Little Corp dissolved) would look like this:

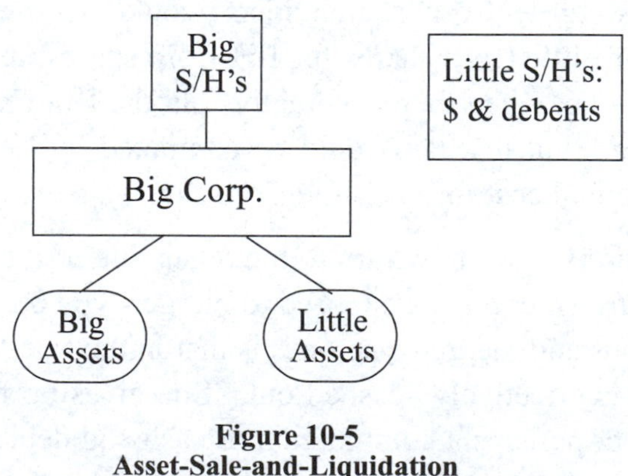

Figure 10-5
Asset-Sale-and-Liquidation
(Shown after liquidation of seller)

   Observe that in contrast to all of the merger-type transactions, Little Corp shareholders are not now shareholders of Big Corp, and in fact are not shareholders of anything; they are simply owners of cash and debentures.

3. **Stock sale:** Now, let's consider the other major sale-type transaction: the ***"stock sale."*** Here, no corporate level transaction takes place on the target's side. Instead, the acquirer ***buys stock from each target company shareholder.*** After the acquirer controls all or a

majority of the target company stock, it may take the second step of dissolving the target and distributing the assets to itself. (If there remain minority holders in the target, the acquirer would distribute assets both to itself and to those other minority holders, in proportion to their stockholdings.)

a. **Tender offer vs. individually-negotiated purchases:** There are two ways in which the acquirer might carry out this stock purchase plan: (1) by a classic ***tender offer***, in which the acquirer publicly announces that it will buy all (or, perhaps, a majority) of shares offered to it by the target company's shareholders; and (2) by ***privately negotiated purchases*** from some or all of the shareholders. The following example gives the flavor of what the tender-offer scenario might look like.

Example: Big Corp makes a tender offer for all of the common shares of Little Corp, at a price of $20 per share. The offer is publicized by Big Corp in newspaper advertisements, and in offering documents sent to each Little Corp shareholder. The offer is held open for 20 days. At the end of the 20-day period, 95% of Little Corp's shares have been tendered to Big Corp (since the $20 offer is $8 above the price prevailing at the time the offer was made). Little Corp's board may have approved the transaction and recommended that shareholders tender (a "friendly" takeover) or it may have opposed the tender offer and pursued defensive measures (a "hostile" takeover). In any event, immediately after the close of the offer on the 20th day, Big Corp writes out a check to each Little Corp shareholder for the shares tendered, and is now the 95% owner of Little Corp.

Probably, at a later date Big Corp will want to eliminate the 5% minority holders in Little Corp. It could do this in one of two ways: (1) it could liquidate Little Corp, distributing 5% of its assets to the minority holders and the balance to itself; (2) more probably, it will vote to merge Little Corp into itself, under a plan in which the 5% minority holders will receive either cash or Big Corp shares. "Back-end" mergers like this are discussed extensively *infra*, p. 448.

b. **Diagram:** Figure 10-6 on p. 372 shows two different stages of the corporate organization resulting from a stock sale: (1) after the stock sale but prior to any merger or liquidation of Little Corp (the drawing assumes that Big Corp buys 70% rather than all of Little Corp's shares); and (2) after Big Corp has carried out a "back end" merger of Little Corp into Big Corp (giving the minority Little Corp holders Big Corp shares instead).

4. **Differences between two techniques:** What are the differences between these two techniques, the "asset-sale-and-liquidation" technique and the "stock sale" technique?

a. **Corporate action by target company:** First, the asset sale requires ***corporate action*** by the target, and the stock sale does ***not***. Thus if the board of directors of Little Corp is opposed to the proposed transaction, it will be able to block an asset sale by simply refusing to approve the transaction or submit it to a stockholder vote, but it will not be able to block stock sales by the individual shareholders. For this reason, hostile takeover attempts (*infra*, p. 429) always proceed as tender offers for the target's stock, not as attempts at an asset sale.

Figure 10-6
Stock-Sale-and-Liquidation

10-6a. After Sale, but Before Liquidation
(Assumes Big Corp. buys 70% of Little's shares)

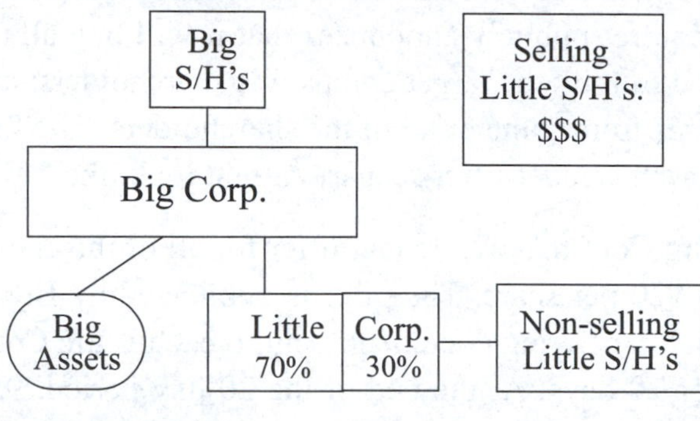

10-6b. After "Back-End" Merger of Little Corp. into Big Corp.
(Assumes minority shareholders of Little Corp. get shares in Big Corp.)

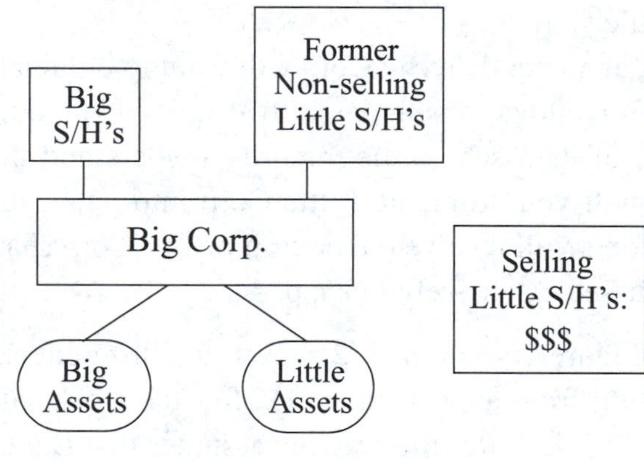

b. Shareholder vote: Similarly, the asset sale will have to be approved by at least a ***majority vote*** of the ***target company's shareholders,*** whereas the stock sale will normally not be subjected to a shareholder vote at all (each shareholder simply decides whether to tender his stock).

i. Plan of share exchange: However, a few states have amended their statutes to allow a target to cause all of its stock to be sold to an acquirer as a matter of corporate action. The target corporation's board approves a "plan of share exchange" under which the shares are to be exchanged for cash paid by the acquirer. If a majority of the shareholders approve the plan, then ***all*** shareholders are required to participate. See, e.g., MBCA § 11.03. (We saw this provision when we were discussing stock-for-stock exchanges *supra*, p. 361; this provision also applies where the target's holders vote to exchange their shares for cash or other non-stock consideration.)

c. **Elimination of minority stockholders:** As you should be able to see readily, the asset-sale technique gives the acquirer a much cleaner way to eliminate any minority interest in the acquired company than does the stock-sale approach. In an asset-sale deal, the acquirer pays the consideration directly to the corporation, and receives the assets free and clear of any minority interest. If the acquirer buys stock, by contrast, the acquirer may not succeed in getting ***all*** of the shares; the acquirer will thus be left with minority stockholders to whom it will owe a fiduciary responsibility. (These might be eliminated by a majority-stockholder-approved plan of share exchange, as discussed in the prior paragraph, or by an eventual "back-end" merger of the target into the acquirer, as discussed *infra*, p. 434, but these procedures will not always be available, and when they are they may be cumbersome.) Thus if the transaction is a "friendly" one (in the sense that it is welcomed by the target's board of directors), an asset sale is clearly superior to a stock sale from the standpoint of giving the acquirer complete control over the target's business.

d. **Liabilities:** Similarly, if the deal is done as an asset sale, the purchaser has a better chance of ***escaping the target's liabilities*** than if the purchaser buys stock. In an asset sale, the purchaser can normally specify which liabilities it is assuming, and will normally not be liable for any debts or contingent liabilities (e.g., lawsuits filed after the closing) that it does not specifically assume. (Of course, the law of fraudulent transfers, and the bulk sales provisions of the UCC, have to be complied with, or else the purchaser may be hit with these liabilities anyway. See *infra*, p. 408. Also, the de facto merger doctrine may be used to allow a creditor, especially a tort claimant, to go after the acquired assets even when the deal is cast as an asset sale. See *infra*, p. 405.) In a stock deal, by contrast, the purchaser in effect takes the target's liabilities along with its assets, whether it wants to or not.

e. **Tax treatment:** Asset sales and stock sales also differ significantly in their ***tax*** treatment. The tax treatment of an asset sale is generally less favorable for the seller — there would be both a corporate-level tax on the corporation's gain from the sale of the assets, and a shareholder-level tax when the corporation dissolves and distributes the cash sale proceeds to the shareholders; these two taxes can easily total nearly half of the total purchase price! Brode, Par. 2.2[2][c]. By contrast, when the stockholders sell their stock, there is only a single-level gain. These tax implications are discussed more extensively *infra*, p. 383.

D. **Comparing merger-type deals with sale-type deals:** What, then, are the big differences between the transactions on one side of our great divide and those on the other side: between merger-type transactions on the one hand and sale-type transactions on the other?

1. **Continuing interest:** The biggest difference is that the shareholders of the target in the sale-type scenarios are ***"disinvested"*** — they end up with cash (and/or debentures or other fixed obligations of the acquiring company), but they ***no longer have an equity stake*** either in the target's business or in the combined business of the acquirer/target. By contrast, in the merger-type transactions, the target shareholders do have an ongoing equity

interest — true, this interest has changed from an interest in just the target's business to an interest in the combined acquirer/target's business, but there is no "disinvestment."

a. **Illustration:** Putting it most concretely in terms of our ongoing Big/Little example, in all of the sale-type transactions the Little Corp shareholders are left with a pile of cash or bonds; in all of the merger-type transactions, by contrast, Little Corp shareholders are left with an ownership interest in the combined Big/Little business.

2. **The effect on acquirer:** Conversely, there is an important difference between the sale-type and merger-type scenarios as to the transaction's impact on the ***acquirer***.

   a. **Sale-type:** In the sale-type deals, Big Corp and its shareholders have not given up any claims to Big Corp's assets — Big Corp may have more debt or less cash (used to fund the acquisition), but Big Corp's shareholders still own the entire business (and, indeed, now also own Little Corp's business).

   b. **Merger-type:** In the merger-type scenarios, by contrast, Big Corp's shareholders now share ownership of Big Corp's business (and Little Corp's business) with a new group of people, the former Little Corp shareholders. "It is as if the [acquirer's] business operations were surrounded by a kind of legal cell membrane, and this membrane were then snipped open, stretched to engulf the former business operations of [the target] as well as the old ones of [the acquirer], and the membrane's ends reconnected." Clark, p. 404.

   c. **Voting power:** Apart from the fact that the ownership stake of Big Corp shareholders is diluted in the merger-type scenarios but not in the sale-type scenarios, the ***voting power*** of Big Corp's shareholders is also diluted in the merger-type cases but not the sale-type ones.

3. **Goodness or badness:** There is no way to say, in the abstract, that merger-type transactions are generally "better" or "worse" than sale-type ones, either from the perspective of the acquirer or the target. Mostly, this comes down to a matter of economics.

   a. **Illustration:** Assume that the purchase price is the "same" in the two scenarios, in the sense that Little Corp shareholders will receive $1 million of cash if the transaction is a sale-type one, and $1 million of Big Corp stock (valued at the current stock market price for Big Corp stock) if the transaction proceeds as a merger-type deal.

      i. **Little Corp's shareholders:** There is no way to say in advance which of these will be more advantageous for Little Corp's shareholders: this depends on whether the $1 million of Big Corp stock that they received in the merger-type deal performs better than the investment they make of the after-tax cash proceeds from a sale-type deal. Obviously, if the transaction takes place at a time when Big Corp's shares are selling for much more than their intrinsic value, Little Corp shareholders are more likely to rue a merger than if the merger takes place at a time when Big Corp's shares are undervalued. (Generally, acquirers tend to do merger-type transactions much more frequently when share prices are high than when they are low, so holders of purchased companies beware!)

      ii. **Big Corp's shareholders:** Conversely, Big Corp's pre-existing shareholders may do better by giving up $1 million of cash rather than $1 million of newly-issued Big Corp stock to fund the acquisition. But they may also do worse. If the Big shares given up in the merger become worth more than the $1 million cash savings becomes (when re-invested by Big), the merger will have been less good than a cash purchase from the standpoint of the Big Corp shareholders. If the shares turn out to be worth less than the amount to which the $1 million savings grows, the Big Corp holders will be lucky that there was a merger rather than a sale.

E. Sale-type transactions in detail: Let us now review some special issues that arise in the case of sale-type transactions. Recall that by "sale-type" transactions we mean principally: (1) a sale of the target's assets, followed by a liquidation of the target and the payment of the sale proceeds to the shareholders pro rata; and (2) a sale of stock by some or all target shareholders, possibly followed by a "back end" merger of the target corporation into the acquiring corporation. (These are the two transactions illustrated in Figures 10-5 (*supra*, p. 370) and 10-6 (*supra*, p. 372), respectively.)

1. "Substantially all" assets: If a corporation sells a small percentage of its assets in one transaction, this is a transaction that needs neither board nor shareholder approval. For instance, if Little Corp sells a machine that it has used to make some of its products, and the sale price of the machine is an amount equal to 10% of Little Corp's total assets, this sale could be consummated by management alone, without board or shareholder approval. On the other hand, state corporation statutes almost always have a special provision covering the sale of ***"all or substantially all"*** of the corporation's assets — such large-scale asset sales nearly always require ***both board approval and shareholder approval***. See, e.g., Del. GCL § 271(a); MBCA § 12.02(a).

a. Meaning of "substantially all": Because of these requirements of board and shareholder approval, it can be very important to determine whether a particular proposed sale is of "substantially all" of the corporation's assets. There is no hard-and-fast rule for determining what constitutes "substantially all."

i. Delaware law: The Delaware courts seem to take a very broad view of what constitutes "substantially all" of the corporation's assets. For instance, in *Katz v. Bregman*, 431 A.2d 1274 (Del.Ch. 1981), the court held that a sale of a corporation's Canadian operations, which constituted 51% of the corporation's total assets, 45% of its total sales, and 52% of its operating profit, was a sale of "substantially all" of the corporation's assets (and thus required shareholder approval).

b. MBCA's "significant continuing business" test: The MBCA no longer (since 1999) uses the "'substantially all" test for determining when shareholder approval is needed. Instead, that statute now requires shareholder approval "if the disposition would ***leave the corporation without a significant continuing business activity.***" MBCA § 12.02(a). The existence of a "significant" continuing business activity is, in turn, to be determined by comparing the remaining business activity to the corporation's business prior to the disposition — the bigger the company before the disposition, the bigger the remaining unsold piece must be in order to avoid the need for shareholder approval. Official Comment 1 to § 12.02.

i. **Safe harbor:** The MBCA also gives companies a ***"safe harbor"*** — if the retained activities constitute at least 25% of the company's pre-disposition "total assets", and also 25% of either the company's pre-disposition profits or its pre-disposition revenues, the company is conclusively deemed to have retained a significant continuing business activity. § 12.02(a), second sent. Such a safe harbor is useful when the company is planning an asset sale, because the firm does not have to run the risk that it will dispense with shareholder approval, yet later be found by a court to have failed to keep a significant business activity.

ii. **Contrast with Delaware law:** The MBCA subjects ***fewer transactions*** to the requirement of a shareholder vote than does Delaware law. For instance, the sale in *Katz*, *supra*, would have qualified for the MBCA safe harbor, and would therefore not have required shareholder approval.

2. **Shareholder vote:** Now, let's consider whether the ***shareholders*** of the ***selling*** corporation must ***approve*** the sale-type transaction. Whether a shareholder vote is required for a sale-type transaction depends on the structure of the transaction:

a. **Asset sale:** As we have just seen, if the sale takes place as a sale by the corporation of all or substantially all of its ***assets***, the target's shareholders must approve. In most states, this approval must be by a ***simple majority*** of all of the votes that ***could be cast*** (not merely a majority of the votes actually cast) on the transaction. Thus normally, more than half of the common stockholders must vote to approve a sale of all or substantially all the corporation's assets. See, e.g., Del G.C.L. § 271(a).

i. **Contrast with other shareholder votes:** Notice that the number of votes needed to approve a sale in most states is thus ***more*** than the number needed to constitute other shareholder action, such as approval of a shareholder resolution at the annual meeting. A shareholder resolution merely needs a majority of the votes actually cast (assuming a quorum is present and voting), so the resolution can pass with much less than a majority of shares outstanding. See *supra*, p. 81. (And a director can be elected just by beating other candidates, regardless of how few votes this takes, again assuming a quorum). So approval-by-a-majority-of-shares-outstanding represents a tough threshold.

ii. **MBCA has easier threshold:** But the MBCA now requires only a majority of the votes ***actually cast*** (assuming a quorum) for approval of an asset sale, as with other types of shareholder votes. § 11.04(e). Since a quorum is half of the eligible votes, the sale could thus be approved by as few as 25% + 1 of the eligible votes. (If there are multiple classes, then each class must approve the sale by this "majority of the majority" standard.)

b. **Stock sale:** A ***stock*** sale, by contrast, works quite differently: each individual shareholder would decide whether to sell his stock to the acquirer (and of course no board approval is necessary for some or all of the target shareholders to do this). On the other hand, once the acquirer controls the target corporation by means of having acquired a majority of its shares, the acquirer will not normally be able to eliminate the minority shareholders without some sort of vote of the target stockholders.

i. **Back-end merger:** Typically, the acquirer will want to do this by a "back-end merger" of the target into the acquirer or into a subsidiary of the acquirer. Normally, the acquirer can easily bring this about by casting its own (majority) of the target's shares in favor of this back-end merger.

ii. **Short form merger:** There may also be a second method: if the acquirer has acquired more than a certain percentage (90% in most states) of the target's shares, a "short form" merger statute (see *infra*, p. 380) is usually available, and entirely ***eliminates the need for a shareholder vote*** on the theory that this would be futile.

iii. **Majority of minority:** But some states, as an anti-takeover device, require the vote of a majority ***of the minority stockholders*** before such a back-end merger can take place under certain circumstances. These back-end merger statutes are described in detail *infra*, p. 447.

iv. **Plan of share exchange:** Also, remember that in some states, a stock sale may be carried out not by individual tenders by each shareholder of his stock, but rather, by corporate action in the form of board and shareholder approval of a "plan of share exchange." See *supra*, p. 362. Under such a scheme, if a majority of the shareholders approve the plan, ***all*** shareholders can be required to exchange their shares for cash, bonds, or other consideration.

3. **Approval by acquirer's holders:** What about the shareholders of the ***acquiring*** corporation; do they get to approve the transaction? The basic answer is ***"no,"*** in nearly all jurisdictions. Most corporation statutes are simply ***silent*** about whether the shareholders of a corporation that makes a cash acquisition of assets or stock have a right to approve the transaction. Therefore, by negative implication the shareholders do not have such a right. See Clark, pp. 415-16.

a. **Rationale:** Normally, in our various sale-type transactions (acquirer's cash for target's stock, or acquirer's cash for target's assets), the acquirer will be ***much larger*** than the target. Furthermore, the acquirer's shareholders will not be giving up any of their ownership of the acquirer's business, as they would be doing in a merger-type deal (though, of course, they would effectively be giving up their ownership of some of the acquirer's cash, or suffering a greater debt against the acquirer's assets). In general, then, the impact of a sale-type transaction on the shareholders of the acquirer is much less than the impact of such a deal on the target, so it's reasonable not to give the acquirer's shareholders the right to vote on the transaction.

i. **Exception:** But there are instances in which this is not true. For instance, Time, Inc., acquired Warner Communications in 1989 for $13 billion (mostly cash). Even though Time had to borrow hugely to fund the acquisition, and even though Warner's market value was nearly as great as (perhaps greater than) Time's, Time's shareholders did not get to vote on the transaction. This led some critics to argue that the acquirer's shareholders should get to vote on any acquisition that is very large relative to the acquirer's size or net worth.

4. **Appraisal rights:** Suppose a particular shareholder of the target does not approve of the target's proposed sale of all of its assets, or of a plan of share exchange (in a state allowing such a plan to be binding on the minority). By complying with various technical require-

ments, this dissenting shareholder may have the right to a judicial ***"appraisal"*** of his shares. Under the appraisal procedure, the shareholder will be entitled to be paid a fair price for his shares, which may be more than the price called for in the asset-sale or share-exchange agreement. Appraisal rights (which apply to mergers as well as sale-type transactions) are discussed more extensively *infra*, p. 394.

F. Mergers in detail, especially shareholder approval: Let's now focus on the corporate-law requirements for ***mergers*** in more detail. We are especially interested in when the ***shareholders*** of one or both corporations have the right to ***approve*** or disapprove the merger.

1. Statutory mergers generally: First, let's look at the classical ***statutory*** merger. As we saw (*supra*, p. 360), this is a device under which the surviving corporation and the disappearing corporation sign a plan of merger, and the disappearing corporation is "fused into" the surviving corporation, with shares in the surviving corporation being issued to the disappearing corporation's shareholders, and all assets and liabilities being taken over by the survivor by operation of law.

a. Board approval: In all states, the ***boards of directors*** of ***both*** corporations must approve the merger.

b. Approval by holders of target: In all states, approval by the ***shareholders*** of the ***disappearing corporation*** (i.e., the target) is also ***required***, unless some special exception applies to the particular merger at hand. See, e.g., Del. GCL § 251(c); MBCA § 11.04(b). This approval must normally be by ***majority vote*** of the shares permitted to vote (but many states allow the certificate of incorporation to set a higher threshold for approval, such as two-thirds; see, e.g., MBCA § 11.04(e)).

i. Majority of all shares, not just of shares voted: As with asset sales, in most states a majority of ***all shares outstanding*** — not just a majority of shares that are voted — must approve the merger. (But MBCA § 11.04(e) requires only that a majority of the shares actually voting approve, assuming a quorum is present.)

ii. Exception: There is an important exception in most states to the rule that the disappearing corporation's shareholders must approve the merger: this is the so-called "short form" merger, in which if one corporation owns the vast majority of stock in another, the latter may be merged into the former without shareholder approval. Short form mergers are discussed *infra*, p. 380.

c. Approval by holders of survivor: Similarly, the general rule is that the ***shareholders*** of the ***surviving corporation*** must also ordinarily approve the merger by a majority vote.

i. Rationale: At first, it may not seem obvious why the shareholders of the surviving corporation should have to approve the merger. The answer is that the survivor's shareholders are ***giving up some part of their claim*** on the business of the surviving corporation. For instance, suppose that Big Corp has 1 million shares outstanding, and that it proposes to have Little Corp merge into it for 500,000 newly-issued Big Corp shares. The pre-existing Big Corp shareholders will, after the merger, "own" only two-thirds of Big Corp's resulting business, rather than the 100% they had previously (though, of course, the "business" will be bigger, since it will now consist of both Big Corp's existing operations as well as the operations of Little Corp). Since Big Corp's shareholders are seeing their ownership materially "diluted," it is reasonable to give them a chance to veto the transaction. (But see the exception for "whale-minnow" mergers, *infra*, p. 379.)

d. Voting by classes: Under some statutes, if there are ***different classes*** of stock, each of the classes may ***vote separately*** on the merger, and each class must approve it. The purpose of such "class voting" provisions, which generally apply to the holders of ***both*** the disappearing as well as the surviving corporation, is to prevent the holders of one class of stock from forcing through a merger that would help that class but hurt a different class. See, e.g., MBCA § 11.04(f) and § 10.04.

Example: Little Corp has two shares of stock, Class A and Class B. These classes are the same except that the A shares have four times the voting power per share as the B shares. There are one million shares of each class outstanding, so the As will normally be able to outvote the Bs. Little Corp proposes to merge into Big Corp, under a scheme in which each A share is exchanged for two Big Corp shares, and each B share is exchanged for one Big Corp share.

Under MBCA § 11.04(f) and § 10.04(a)(1), the A shares and the B shares would vote separately on the proposed merger — even if the A holders overwhelmingly approved it, the merger could not go through if it did not receive the votes of a majority of the B holders. (Under MBCA § 10.04(a)(1), each group can vote separately on any change that would "effect an exchange or reclassification of all or part of the shares of the class into shares of another class," which would be the case here if the B shares were exchanged into Big Corp shares.) This would serve as a brake on the ability of the A holders to effectively "sell" their votes to Big Corp in return for a bigger piece of the merger pie.

e. Small-scale ("whale-minnow") mergers: There are two key exceptions to the general rule that the holders of both merging corporations must approve the transaction. The first of these is for ***"small-scale"*** mergers, or, as they have been picturesquely called, ***"whale-minnow"*** mergers. See Clark, p. 450. The basic idea here is that if a corporation will be merged into a ***much larger*** corporation, the shareholders of the surviving corporation ***need not approve*** the merger.

i. Typical provisions: Typically, corporate statutes today furnish an exception for approval by the surviving corporation's shareholders if the amount of surviving corporation stock outstanding after the merger does not increase by more than a ***certain percentage*** over what it was just before the merger. For instance, under Delaware law (GCL § 251(f)) and the MBCA (§ 11.04(g); § 6.21(f)), any merger that does not increase the outstanding shares of the acquiring company by ***more than 20%*** ordinarily need not be approved by the acquiring corporation's shareholders.

Example: The boards of Big Corp and Little Corp approve a plan of merger whereby Little Corp is to be merged into Big Corp, and Little Corp shareholders are to receive 100,000 shares of authorized but previously-unissued Big Corp stock. Before the merger takes place, there are one million Big Corp shares already outstanding. This merger will of course have to be approved by Little Corp shareholders, since their corporation will disappear. But because the merger will result in a less-than-20%-increase in the number of Big Corp shares outstanding (indeed, the increase will only be 10%, from 1 million to 1.1 million shares), the shareholders of Big Corp do not have to approve it and probably will not be asked to approve it. This is true under both Delaware law (§ 251(f)) and the MBCA (§11.04(g)(4), § 6.21(f)).

ii. **Rationale:** There is a sensible reason for this "whale-minnow" exception to the shareholder approval rules: the basic reason for requiring shareholder approval of mergers is that such events are very major structural changes to the corporation, and are likely to represent such a change to the shareholders' expectations about the nature of their investment that they should get some say in whether that change should be made. But where a "whale" swallows a "minnow," the nature of the whale's shareholders' investment has changed very little, so the rationale for shareholder approval does not apply. This is especially true in view of the not-inconsiderable expense involved in informing shareholders about the facts of the prospective merger, and obtaining their vote.

f. **Short-form mergers:** A second key exception to the usual requirements of shareholder approval is for so-called ***"short-form"*** mergers. The idea here is that if corporation P owns an overwhelming majority of the shares of corporation S, so that they are basically in a parent-subsidiary relationship, S may be merged into P without the approval of the shareholders of ***either*** P or S.

i. **Rationale:** A vote by S's shareholders would be futile, since P by definition holds more than enough stock to insure that a majority of total S shareholders will approve the transaction. (Indeed, in many states not even S's ***board of directors*** needs to approve the merger, on the theory that P will control the board as well, and the board would thus be a formality. But see *Weinberger v. UOP, Inc.*, *infra*, p. 425.) Approval by *P's* shareholders is also not required, probably on the theory that since the overwhelming majority of shares in S are already held by P, a final merger of S into P would not make much economic difference for P's shareholders.

ii. **Percentage required:** Both Delaware law and the MBCA allow a short-form merger where P holds ***90% or more*** of the stock in S. See Del. GCL § 253; MBCA § 11.05.

iii. **Minority holders of subsidiary:** Of course, there is a real possibility of unfairness to the ***minority shareholders*** of the subsidiary in a short-form merger. If the minority holders are being given stock in the parent in exchange for their stock in the subsidiary, they may be given too little parent company stock to make the exchange a fair one. If they are given cash or notes, here, too, the price may be unfairly low. Traditionally, the remedy of the minority shareholders has been restricted to ***appraisal rights***, i.e., the right to have a court determine the fair value of the minority shares, and the right to compel the parent company to pay the dissenting minority holder that fair amount. See *infra*, p. 395. But courts may occasionally give the minority shareholders the right to bring a class action for damages or an injunction if the terms of the short-form merger are dramatically unfair. See, e.g., *Weinberger v. UOP, Inc.*, *infra*, p. 425, a Delaware case in which this occurred.

2. **Hybrids:** Now, let's consider the ***"hybrid"*** transactions, ones that are "merger-type" but are not pure statutory mergers. Thus we'll look at the corporate-law requirements for: (1) stock-for-stock exchanges; (2) stock-for-assets exchanges; and (3) triangular mergers involving a subsidiary of the acquirer.

3. **Stock-for-stock exchanges:** The corporate law treatment of ***stock-for-stock*** exchanges is very simple. Indeed, one of the principal advantages of this form of acquisition is that the procedural requirements for it are relatively undemanding in most states.

   a. **Acquiring side:** On the acquiring company side, the exchange proposal will need the approval of the acquirer's board of directors. But the shareholders of the acquirer normally do ***not*** have to approve the transaction: so long as there are enough ***authorized but unissued*** shares to fund the transaction, board approval, and not shareholder approval, is all that is required on the acquirer side.

      i. **Not enough shares:** But if the number of authorized but unissued shares is ***not enough*** to fund the transaction, then the acquirer's shareholders will effectively have to approve the plan. The reason is that the number of authorized shares can only be increased by an amendment to the acquirer's ***articles of incorporation***, and such an amendment must be approved by the shareholders. See *supra*, p. 23. S,S,B&W, p. 402.

      ii. **Different rule:** Also, some statutes and stock exchange rules now require acquirer-side shareholder approval for those share exchanges that would increase the number of acquirer shares outstanding by more than a certain percentage.

         (1) **New York Stock Exchange Rules:** For instance, if the acquirer is listed on the ***New York Stock Exchange***, approval of the share exchange by its shareholders will be required if the new shares to be issued would increase the acquirer's total outstanding shares by 18.5% or more. See N.Y.S.E. Listed Company Manual, § 3.12.00(3)(b).

         (2) **MBCA requires approval:** Similarly, under the MBCA, approval by the acquirer's shareholders will be required if the new shares to be issued ***would increase the acquirer's total outstanding shares by 20% or more***. MBCA § 6.21(f)(1)(ii).

   b. **Target side:** On the target side, corporate law requirements for the stock-for-stock exchange are in a sense even simpler:

      i. **No board approval:** Approval by the target's board of directors is generally ***not*** required. The acquirer is simply arranging to buy shares from each target company shareholder in separate transactions, so no corporate action is taking place on the target side. For this reason, a hostile takeover attempt that is to be funded by the acquirer's shares will normally take the form of a stock-for-stock exchange proposal rather than a stock-for-assets proposal (which would require the approval of the target's board).

ii. **Shareholder approval:** Also, the stock-for-stock exchange proposal does ***not*** even have to be formally approved by vote of the target's ***shareholders***. Each target company shareholder "votes" only in the sense that he decides whether or not to exchange his shares or keep them. S,S,B&W, p. 402. (Of course, if the acquirer's exchange offer is made contingent on receipt of at least half the target's shares, as would usually be the case, then the target's shareholders are effectively voting on the transaction in the sense that if a majority don't tender, no transaction will take place.)

iii. **Minority can remain:** Observe that because there is no formal shareholder vote in the stock-for-stock exchange transaction, there is likely to be a minority who do not participate, and who thus remain as minority stockholders after the exchange is completed. (This minority might then be subsequently "cashed out" by a "back-end merger." See *infra*, p. 420.)

iv. **Plan of share exchange:** Also, remember that in some states (e.g., MBCA §§ 11.03, 11.07(b)) even unwilling shareholders may be ***forced*** to participate in the stock-for-stock exchange, if a "plan of share exchange" is: (1) approved by the target's board of directors; and (2) approved by a majority of the target's shareholders. See *supra*, p. 362.

4. **Stock-for-asset deals:** Now, let's look at ***stock-for-assets*** deals, in which shares of the acquirer are used to purchase all or substantially all of the target's assets. In brief, this type of transaction is treated on the acquirer's side the same as a stock-for-stock exchange, and on the target's side the same as a sale of assets for cash.

   a. **Acquirer's side:** Thus on the acquirer's side, board approval is necessary but shareholder approval is not, as long as there are enough authorized but unissued shares to fund the transaction. If the number of authorized shares must be increased, approval by the acquirer's shareholders is necessary since the articles of incorporation must be amended. Also, as in a stock-for-stock exchange context, if the acquirer is listed on the New York Stock Exchange, and the number of issued shares would increase more than 18.5% as a result of the transaction, the acquirer's shareholders must approve the transaction under New York Stock Exchange rules. See New York Stock Exchange Listed Company Manual, § 312.00(3)(b).

   b. **Target side:** On the target side, the stock-for-assets exchange is the equivalent of any other asset sale. Therefore, the target's board of directors must initiate and approve the transaction. It must then be approved by a majority of the stockholders. Clark, p. 426. Remember that for a sale of all or substantially all of the assets, the transaction must, in most states, be supported by the votes not just of a majority of the shares actually voting, but of a majority of the shares ***entitled*** to vote. (But the MBCA requires just a majority of those shares actually voting, assuming a quorum is present. § 11.04(e).)

   c. **Eventual liquidation of target:** Normally, the target will eventually ***liquidate***, and distribute its assets (which now consist of the shares of the acquirer received in the exchange) to the shareholders in proportion to their holdings.

5. **Subsidiary mergers:** Finally, let's look at the corporate law treatment of ***subsidiary*** or "triangular" mergers. These are the forward subsidiary merger (*supra*, p. 364) and the

reverse subsidiary merger (*supra*, p. 366). For simplicity, we'll assume that each uses the statutory merger provision (rather than the stock swap or assets-for-stock techniques).

a. **Forward merger:** First, consider the ***forward*** subsidiary merger. Recall that here, the acquirer (let's assume it's Big Corp) forms a subsidiary (let's call it Big-Sub), and the target (let's call it Little Corp) merges into Big-Sub in return for either cash or shares in Big Corp.

   i. **Acquirer's side:** On the acquirer's side, the transaction is easy. Big-Sub's and Big Corp's boards must both approve the transaction (but Big-Sub's board's approval is a formality since Big-Sub's directors either are the same as Big Corp's directors or are ones hand-picked by Big Corp). Shareholder approval is also easy, since only Big-Sub's shareholders have to approve the transaction, and Big-Sub's sole shareholder is Big Corp (which will vote in the manner determined by Big Corp's management). Thus approval from the acquirer's side is a mere formality.

   ii. **Target side:** On the target side, Little Corp's board and shareholders will have to approve the plan of merger, just as they would with any merger. Observe that once a majority of Little Corp shareholders approve the transaction, the dissenting Little Corp shareholders will be forced to go along anyway, since the form of the transaction is a merger.

b. **Reverse merger:** Now, let's look at the reverse subsidiary merger. Remember that the structure of this is the same as for the forward subsidiary merger, except that Big-Sub is merged into Little Corp instead of vice-versa.

   i. **Acquirer's side:** Here, the labels "acquirer" and "target" get a little confusing. Let's use the label "acquirer" to denote the ***real*** acquiring side, Big Corp (and Big-Sub, its subsidiary) in our example, and "target" to refer to Little Corp, even though Little Corp is in a sense acquiring Big-Sub. On the acquiring side, Big Corp's board and Big-Sub's board and shareholders (the sole shareholder being Big Corp) will have to approve the transaction, exactly as in the forward merger case.

   ii. **Target side:** On the target side, Little Corp's board and shareholders will have to approve, again just as in the forward subsidiary merger case. Thus in summary, exactly the same board and shareholder approvals are needed for the reverse subsidiary merger as for the forward subsidiary merger.

G. **Tax and securities-law treatment:** Let us now take a brief look at some of the ***tax*** and ***securities-law*** issues raised by corporate combinations.

H. **Taxation:** The ***federal income taxation*** of corporate combinations makes a very important distinction similar to our corporate-law distinction between "merger-type" deals and "sale-type" deals. Different jargon is used: in the tax world, what we have called "merger-type" transactions are generally referred to as ***"reorganizations"***; what we have called "sale-type" transactions would simply be "sales" under federal income tax principles.

1. **Tax deferral vs. immediate tax on gain:** Why does it make a difference for federal tax purposes whether a business combination is a "reorganization" or an ordinary sale? The brief answer is that in the case of a reorganization, there is ***no tax to the target's share-***

holders imposed at the time of the transaction. In an ordinary sale, by contrast, the target's shareholders must pay an immediate tax on their gain in the transaction.

Example: Suppose that Big Corp desires to acquire the business of Little Corp. Let's further assume that Option 1 for the transaction is a statutory merger, in which Little Corp will merge into Big Corp, and Little Corp's shareholders will receive Big Corp shares in return for their interest in Little Corp. Under this option, Little Corp's shareholders will not have to pay any federal income tax as part of the merger transaction. Only when the former Little Corp shareholders sell their Big Corp shares, which might not be for years or decades after the merger, will they pay any tax on the gain. However, when they do sell those Big Corp shares, they will pay a tax not on the difference between what they received at the time of sale and the value of those shares at the time of merger, but rather, the difference between what they received on sale of the Big Corp shares and their cost for the *original Little Corp shares*. Thus the merger structure gives the target's shareholders the opportunity for *deferral* of gain.

Now, contrast this with Option 2 for structuring the transaction: Here, Big Corp will pay cash for each Little Corp share, and will make that cash payment directly to each Little Corp shareholder. Under this option, each selling Little Corp shareholder will have to pay an immediate tax on the gain from sale. That is, he will pay a tax on the difference between what he originally paid for his Little Corp shares and what he is receiving in cash at the time of sale. That's the bad news. The good news is that that's all the tax the Little Corp shareholders will ever have to pay on the transaction (whereas under Option 1 the Little Corp shareholders will have a big tax hanging over their heads if they dispose of their Big Corp shares).

So the main consequence of the distinction between reorganizations and ordinary sales is that in the reorganization, the target shareholders defer any tax on their gain, whereas in the ordinary cash sale of stock, the target's shareholders have to pay an immediate tax on the gain.

2. **Various types of reorganizations:** Assuming, then, that the term "reorganization" refers to any acquisition in which the shareholders of the acquired corporation do not pay an immediate tax on the transaction, what types of transactions qualify as "reorganizations"? The Internal Revenue Code recognizes three distinct types of reorganizations:

(1) the ***"type A"*** reorganization, which is defined as a ***statutory*** merger;

(2) the ***"type B"*** reorganization, which is essentially a ***stock-for-stock*** exchange; and

(3) the ***"type C"*** reorganization, which is essentially a ***stock-for-assets*** exchange (the stock of the acquiring corporation is used to purchase substantially all of the assets of the target corporation).

In other words, each of the three "merger-type" transactions which we summarized previously — the statutory, stock-for-stock and stock-for-assets transaction — has a formally-defined counterpart under the Internal Revenue Code which will lead to tax-deferred status for the target company's shareholders. We consider each of these types of reorganizations in turn, mostly to examine in modest detail the criteria which a deal must meet in order to fall within that type of reorganization.

3. **"Type A" reorganization:** The basic requirement for a ***"type A"*** reorganization is that the transaction must be carried out according to state ***statutory merger*** provisions. A merger carried out according to some state's version of MBCA § 11.02, for example, would qualify. Thus the merger of Little Corp into Big Corp as described on p. 360 and represented in Figure 10-1 would qualify as a type A reorganization, and Little Corp's shareholders would not pay any tax at the time of the merger. See IRC 368(a)(1)(A). (By the way, the labels "type A", "type B" and "type C" reorganizations stem from the three subsections of IRC § 368(a)(1), each defining one type of reorganization.)

   a. **Continuity-of-interest doctrine:** Traditionally, state statutory merger statutes were used to facilitate transactions in which the target company's shareholders received ***common stock*** in the surviving corporation, and nothing else. However, most merger statutes have by now been amended to allow the merger device to be used even where what the target's shareholders receive at the end of the merger is something other than the acquirer's common stock, including ***cash***, ***bonds*** and ***preferred stock***. But recall that the principal reason for deferring the tax on shareholders in a reorganization is that the shareholders have a ***continuing investment*** that has merely changed form (e.g., changed from an investment in the target company's common shares to an investment in the acquirer's common shares). If all of the consideration in a statutory merger were to take forms other than common stock, the rationale for deferring the tax on the target's shareholders would no longer be applicable: they would have been "dis-invested", yet would not be paying a tax.

      i. **Consequence:** Therefore, the courts and the IRS impose a ***"continuity of interest"*** requirement which a type A reorganization must meet in order for the target's shareholders to avoid an immediate tax: the target's shareholders must preserve their continuity of interest in the business of the target, by receiving some ***stock in the surviving company.***

      ii. **Amount not clear:** It is not clear exactly ***how much*** of the total consideration received by the target shareholder in a type A reorganization must be in the form of the survivor's stock. But it is clear that so long as ***more than 50%*** of the total value that the target's shareholders receive consists of stock in the acquiring company, this "continuity of interest" requirement is satisfied. See Treas. Reg. § 1.368-1(b); Rev. Proc. 77-37 1977-to c.b. 568.

4. **"Type B" reorganization:** A ***"type B"*** reorganization — what we've called a "stock-for-stock exchange" when discussing mergers from a corporate-law point of view — occurs when one corporation acquires, in exchange for all or part of its voting stock (or the voting stock of its parent), a controlling stock interest in another corporation. IRC § 368(a)(1)(B).

   a. **Control:** For these purposes, the acquirer "controls" the target, if, following the exchange, the acquirer owns ***at least 80% of the voting power*** of the target, plus at least 80% of the total number of shares of all other (non-voting) classes of target company stock. Observe that this control requirement means that a target company shareholder deciding whether to tender into a stock-for-stock exchange can't know whether the exchange will be tax-deferred as to him, unless the acquirer explicitly makes the offer conditional upon receiving at least 80% of the target's shares.

b. **No "boot" allowable:** As we saw previously, a statutory merger can qualify as a type A reorganization even though up to 50% of the consideration paid by the acquirer is in the form of cash, debentures or other property that is not the voting stock of the acquirer. But the rules for type B reorganizations are not so generous: ***only*** the acquirer's voting stock (or voting stock of the acquirer's parent corporation) may be used. As a tax lawyer might say, there can be no ***"boot"*** in a type B reorganization. See Clark, p. 434, n. 10.

Example: Big Corp offers to exchange, for every share of Little Corp, one share of Big Corp plus $2 cash. Even if every Big Corp share is worth $50 (so that about 96% of the value of the purchase is paid in stock of the acquirer), this transaction will not qualify as a type B reorganization, because it is not funded solely by the stock of the acquirer or the acquirer's parent. Therefore, Little Corp shareholders would have to pay a tax on the difference between what they received for the Little Corp share they were giving up and what they paid for the share originally.

5. **"Type C" reorganization:** Finally, a ***"type C"*** reorganization — corresponding roughly to our "stock-for-assets exchange" category on the corporate-law side — is defined as the acquisition by one corporation, in exchange for all or part of its voting stock (or the voting stock of a parent corporation), of ***substantially all of the assets*** of another corporation. IRC § 368(a)(1)(c).

a. **Acquirer may use some non-cash consideration:** Recall that for a type B reorganization, the acquirer must pay ***only*** with its own shares. But the rules are not so strict for a type C reorganization: All that is required is that the acquirer's voting stock be used to pay for ***at least 80%*** of the value of the target's assets; the rest of those assets may be paid for by cash, bonds or other non-voting-stock.

Example: Big Corp wants to acquire all of Little Corp's assets. Using a transaction like the one illustrated in Figure 10-3a on p. 363, Big Corp agrees to pay $1 million for all of Little Corp's assets. It pays for these assets by issuing: (1) $850,000 (at present market value) of Big Corp common stock; and (2) $150,000 of Big Corp 10-year debentures (which are like bonds). Little Corp can now liquidate, and distribute to each of its shareholders its pro rata portion of both the Big Corp stock and the debentures. Because at least 80% of the payment by Big Corp was in the form of its voting shares, the transaction qualifies as a C reorganization. Therefore, neither Little Corp or its shareholders will have to pay an immediate tax on the Big Corp shares received in the acquisition (though they will have to pay a tax on the debentures, since these are "boot"; see *infra*, p. 387 for a discussion of "boot"). See generally Brode, Par. 7.1[1] and [2].

6. **Triangular subsidiary mergers:** ***Triangular*** mergers (i.e., mergers in which the acquirer is a subsidiary of the corporation whose stock is used to fund the transaction) can also qualify as tax-free reorganizations.

a. **Forward mergers:** First, consider the ***forward*** subsidiary merger (*supra*, p. 364). In terms of our diagram on p. 365 (Figure 10-4a), Little Corp will be merged into Big-Sub, and Little Corp shareholders will receive Big Corp stock. This merger of Little Corp into Big-Sub would qualify as a type A reorganization because a special IRC provision allows the subsidiary to use its ***parent's*** stock, instead of its own, to carry out the merger. See IRC § 368(a)(2)(D). (Similarly, Big-Sub could use its own stock in the merger. But it cannot use ***both*** its own and its parent's stock. Clark, p. 434, n.10.)

b. Reverse triangular merger: Similarly, the ***reverse triangular*** merger may qualify for tax-deferred reorganization status. Recall that in a reverse triangular merger, the acquirer's subsidiary merges into the target (as shown in Figure 10-4b, *supra*, p. 366). Here, too, the merger will generally be treated as a type A merger. Thus if Big Corp forms Big-Sub, of which it owns all the stock, and Big-Sub merges into Little Corp (with Little's shareholders receiving Big Corp stock at the end of the merger), Little's former shareholders will not pay any tax even though they are effectively trading their stock in Little Corp in exchange for stock in Big Corp. Brode, Par. 6.3[3].

7. Treatment of "boot": So far, we've generally been assuming that the shareholders of the target receive only stock in the acquirer, as the result of the reorganization. But a transaction might qualify as a reorganization even though some minority part of the consideration given to the target's shareholders is ***cash***, bonds, non-voting stock, or something other than common stock. The bad news for the target's shareholders is that, even though the transaction as a whole may still qualify for reorganization treatment, ***the non-common-stock*** proceeds are ***taxable*** to the target's shareholders. These non-common-stock proceeds are colloquially called ***"boot,"*** and the target shareholders' gain on the transaction is taxable up to the amount of this boot.

Example: Big Corp and Little Corp agree to a plan of merger, under which Little Corp will merge into Big Corp, and each Little Corp share will be exchanged for one share of Big Corp (worth $10) and one Big Corp 5-year debenture (worth $8). Able, a Little Corp shareholder, before the merger owns 100 Little Corp shares, for which he originally paid $5 each. The transaction will qualify as a type A reorganization, since it is done pursuant to a state merger statute and more than 50% of the total consideration paid to the target's shareholders is in the form of the acquirer's voting stock. (See *supra*, p. 385.) However, each shareholder is receiving $8 of "boot"; therefore, each Little Corp shareholder must pay an immediate tax on his gain up the amount of this boot. Thus Able has a gain of $1300 (he is receiving $18 of value for shares for which he paid $5, and he has 100 shares); he will have to pay taxes immediately on $300 of this gain ($8 per share of debenture, or "boot," less $5 per share of original cost). See Clark, p. 441.

8. Sale-type transactions: So far, our tax analysis has assumed that the transaction is a merger-type one. Now, let's take a brief look at the tax treatment of our two sale-type transactions, the sale by the target of its assets in return for cash, and the sale by the target's stockholders of their stock in return for cash. (See *supra*, p. 370, including Figures 10-5 and 10-6.)

a. Asset sale: First, let's consider the sale of assets by the target, in return for cash paid to the target. In terms of our example, *supra*, p. 370, Little Corp transfers all of its assets to Big Corp, and Big Corp pays cash to Little Corp.

i. **Corporate tax:** Little Corp will have to pay a ***corporate-level tax*** on the gain, to the extent that the cash received from Big Corp exceeds Little Corp's cost for the assets sold.

ii. **Individual-level tax:** Then, if Little Corp dissolves and pays out the cash received from Big Corp to its own shareholders in a ***liquidating distribution***, there will be a ***second tax***: Little Corp shareholders will each have to pay a tax on the amount by which the proceeds they are receiving exceed what they originally paid for their Little Corp shares.

iii. **Consequence:** These two levels of taxation, taken together, can mean that ***nearly half*** of the total proceeds from Big Corp can be eaten up in taxes by the time the proceeds get to the Little Corp shareholders! Thus the sale of assets followed by liquidation, while it is an attractive technique tax-wise for the acquirer, is disastrous for the target's shareholders. See Brode, Par. 2.2[2][c].

iv. **No liquidation:** One thing the target's shareholders can do to lessen this problem is to ***refrain from liquidating*** the target. Thus Little Corp might sell its assets to Big Corp and receive the cash, but then not liquidate or distribute the proceeds to Little Corp's shareholders. Of course, this alternative is not very satisfactory if Little Corp's shareholders are conducting the sale in order to get their hands on the cash.

b. **Sale of stock:** Now, consider the other kind of sale-transaction, that in which the target's shareholders ***sell their stock*** to the acquirer. Here, the tax implications for the target's shareholders are much better than in the sale-of-assets situation: there is only one level of taxation, in which the target shareholders each pay a tax on the difference between the cash they are receiving in the transaction and their original cost of the shares.

i. **Taxation for acquirer:** However, from the ***acquirer's*** perspective, the taxation of the stock-purchase approach is less attractive than the asset-purchase approach. In the asset-purchase scenario, the purchaser can ***depreciate*** or ***amortize*** much of the purchase price, both the price paid for the "hard" assets like plant and equipment. and the price paid for the "soft" assets (e.g., "goodwill," such as the acquired company's customer list.) These depreciation and amortization deductions let the buyer deduct from his income each year some part of the purchase price, over the useful life of the acquired assets.

(1) **Compared with stock purchase:** But where the acquirer buys ***stock***, these depreciation and amortization deductions are usually ***much lower,*** since they derive from the target's ***original*** cost for these assets rather than from the usually-higher price that the acquirer is effectively paying for these assets.

c. **Tradeoffs:** Therefore, the ***sellers will usually prefer a stock sale, and the buyers will usually prefer an asset sale.*** Because the bad consequences to the buyer from a stock sale are usually less terrible than the bad consequences to the sellers from an asset sale, most acquisitions of publicly-held targets nowadays are stock sales.

I. Federal securities law: Now, let's look at the federal ***securities law*** implications of the various types of combinations.

1. Sale-type transactions: First, let's consider the ***sale-type*** transactions.

a. Asset sales: If the transaction is a purchase by the acquirer of the target's ***assets*** for cash, the securities-law requirements are modest. Thus if Big Corp is acquiring Little Corp's assets for cash, and Little Corp is publicly held, the only aspect of the securities laws that comes into play are the ***proxy*** rules. That is, since under state law Little Corp's shareholders will have to approve of the transaction, Little Corp will need to send them a proxy statement describing in some detail the proposed transaction and the current status of Little Corp, so that shareholders may intelligently decide whether to vote in favor of the transaction. See Clark, p. 423. If Little Corp is expected to dissolve and pay a liquidating distribution after the asset sale, this fact, too, would have to be disclosed in the proxy statement, so that Little Corp's holders can decide whether to give their prospective approval to this dissolution step.

b. Stock sale: If the sale is to be a sale of ***stock*** by each target company shareholder to the acquirer, the securities-law aspects get trickier. If Big Corp wants to buy all or a large percentage of Little Corp's shares, (and Little is publicly held), Big Corp will normally need to proceed by a ***tender offer***. That is, Big Corp will make a public announcement and solicitation of Little's shareholders, to get them to sell their shares. (Tender offers are discussed more extensively *infra* p. 430).

i. Tender offer disclosures: If Big Corp does proceed by tender offer, it will have to send each Little Corp shareholder materials required by the Williams Act (an amendment to the Securities Exchange Act of 1934), giving substantial disclosure about the nature of Big Corp's offer, Big Corp's identity, the status of Little Corp's business, and other matters relevant to a Little Corp holder's decision about whether to tender. See *infra*, p. 440.

ii. Purchase by negotiation: On the other hand, if Big Corp merely tries to buy a controlling stock interest via ***individual negotiations*** with one or a few Little Corp major shareholders, this will not be a tender offer, and the securities laws will generally not come into play.

2. Merger-type transactions: Now, let's look at the securities-law implications of ***merger-type*** transactions. Remember that in these transactions, a major part of the consideration paid by the acquirer will be in the form of ***stock*** of the acquirer. As you might imagine, the securities laws take the position that the target's shareholders are entitled to know a considerable amount of information about the acquirer, in order to decide whether they should give up ownership of their shares in the target in return for shares in the acquirer. (By contrast, in the sale-type transactions discussed above, the target's shareholders receive little if any information about the acquirer and its finances, since in those transactions the target's shareholders are receiving cash rather than stock.)

a. Stock-for-stock exchange: Where the deal takes the form of a ***stock-for-stock exchange*** (see *supra*, p. 361), the securities laws have always treated this as the equivalent of a ***public issue*** of stock by the acquirer. Thus if Big proposes to acquire each share of Little in exchange for one share of Big, Big will have to file a ***registration statement*** and supply each Little Corp shareholder with a ***prospectus***. (See *infra*, p. 540.) Furthermore, this stock swap will normally be a tender offer, so the disclosure requirements applicable to tender offers will apply here if Little is publicly traded. See Clark, p. 435.

b. Statutory merger and stock-for-assets deal: The two other main merger-type structures, the ***statutory merger*** and the ***stock-for-assets*** exchange, are a little trickier.

i. Proxy materials: First, Little Corp's shareholders will clearly have to vote on either the statutory merger or the stock-for-assets swap, so Little Corp will have to send them a ***proxy statement*** containing information about the proposed deal in order that they may vote intelligently on whether to approve it. Since Little Corp's shareholders are being asked to take Big Corp stock as all or part of the consideration, the proxy materials must contain detailed information about Big Corp's business and finances.

ii. Registration statement: Second, the SEC takes the position that Big Corp's issuance of shares as part of the statutory merger or the stock-for-assets swap is sufficiently like a ***new sale of stock*** that Big Corp must file a ***registration statement*** and must supply a ***prospectus***. Under SEC Rule 145, however, the registration statement required in such merger or stock-for-assets deals is a simplified one, which consists of the proxy statement with a small amount of additional information. See Clark, pp. 740-41.

c. Triangular mergers: Triangular mergers will also normally require that a proxy statement be sent to the target's shareholders. For instance, suppose Big Corp establishes a subsidiary Big-Sub, and merges this subsidiary into Little Corp in return for all of Little Corp's shares (the transaction diagrammed in Figure 10-4b on p. 366 *supra*). Little Corp will have to send its shareholders a proxy statement when it requests their approval of the transactions, and that proxy statement will have to disclose full financial information about Big Corp. Rule 145 will probably also apply, so that Little Corp's holders will receive a combined registration/proxy statement. See Clark, p. 435.

J. Table: The following table summarizes the pros and cons of the various ***merger-type*** structures. Note that this table only covers the four main merger-type structures (statutory merger, stock-for-stock, stock-for-assets, and reverse triangular), and does not cover the sale-type deals (asset sales and stock sales).

Table 10-1
PROS & CONS OF VARIOUS MERGER-TYPE TRANSACTIONS

Objective	**Statutory Merger ("A" reorg.)**	**Stock-for-Stock Exch. ("B" reorg.)**	**Stock-for-Assets Exch. ("C" reorg.)**	**Reverse: (Triangular merger of A's Sub. into T)**
Corporate				
Reduce # of S/H votes required (1)	Poor	Good	Fair	Fair
Circumvent stubborn minority S/H's of T (2)	Good	Poor	Good	Good
Circumvent opposition by T's mgmt. (3)	Poor	Good	Poor	Poor
Taxes				
Flexibility on consideration rec'd by T's S/H's (4)	Good	Poor	Fair	Good
Other				
Insulate A from T's liabilities (5)	Poor	Fair	Good	Fair
Assign T's contract rights to A (6)	Fair	Good	Poor	Fair
Keep mechanics of transaction simple (7)	Good	Fair	Poor	Good

Symbols: **A** = Acquirer **T** = Target
Abbreviations: "A reorg." = Statutory merger
"B reorg." = A's stock exchanged for T's stock
"C reorg." = A's stock exchanged for T's assets
"reverse" = A forms subsidiary, and that subsidiary is statutorily merged into T

Notes:

(1) "A" reorg. is the worst — it will require votes by both T's and A's shareholders. "C" is better — A's shareholders usually won't have to vote, though T's will. "Reverse" is equally good — A's shareholders

won't get to vote, though T's will. "B" is best — neither side probably gets to vote formally (though T's effectively vote, by deciding whether to tender).

(2) In the "A," "C" and "Reverse" cases, all T shareholders are forced to go along, whether they want to or not. In the "B" case, T's minority shareholders can refuse to go along, and can continue to hold their stock after the acquisition (except in those few states allowing a "plan of share exchange" which is binding on minority, as in MBCA § 11.07(b)).

(3) If T's management opposes transaction, "A," "C" and "Reverse" transactions can be completely blocked. But T's management can't directly block "B" type (which is why hostile takeovers are generally "B" type or else cash purchases of T's stock).

(4) For "A," the only requirement is "continuity of interest," which will be satisfied if T's shareholders receive 1/2 or more of their consideration as A Corp stock. "C" is a little tougher — 80% of T's value must be paid for in the form of A Corp Stock. "B" is toughest — T's shareholders must receive ***only A Corp stock***; "Reverse" is basically like "A", though slightly tougher.

(5) "A" is the worst — by operation of law, in a statutory merger the surviving corporation (A) assumes all of the liabilities of the disappearing corporation (T), whether it wants to or not. "B" is somewhat better — A doesn't formally assume T's liabilities, but T's assets are burdened by these liabilities, so all the value of the acquired assets can be wiped out by unforeseen liabilities of T. "Reverse" is functionally identical to "B," since the acquired assets are burdened by the liabilities, but A's assets are not affected. "C" is the best, since A can take the assets without the liabilities — A assumes only those liabilities expressly mentioned in the asset sales agreement. (But remember that, especially in tort cases, a court may apply "de facto merger" theory to saddle A with T's liability even where the transaction was a "C" reorg.)

(6) "C" is the worse, because many contracts are not assignable without consent, and in a "C" reorg. every contract is being assigned. "A" is better, since the assignment happens by operation of law (but a personal-services contract might be held to terminate upon merger; see C&E, p. 1167-68.); "Reverse" is same as "A." "B" is the best — there is no change to the corporate entity (T) holding the contract, so no assignment happens at all.

(7) "C" is worst, because every piece of property must be conveyed by a formal document (deeds, bills of sale, etc.); also, each creditor of T must be notified under the bulk sales law. "A" and "Reverse" are easiest — there's just the plan of merger, and all transfers happen automatically once the plan is consummated. "B" is similar to "A" except that if T is publicly-held, there will have to be a complex (and expensive) tender offer that conforms to federal securities laws (see *infra*, p. 382). C&E, pp. 1167-70.

See generally C&E, pp. 1167-70; Clark, p. 437.

Quiz Yourself on
MERGERS AND ACQUISITIONS *(CORPORATE COMBINATIONS — GENERALLY)*

81. Guano Building Supplies Inc. has a thriving business recycling wild bird refuse into building bricks. Guano's board of directors votes to sell all of Guano's assets to the Rin Tin Tin House Construction Company.

(a) The directors of Guano call a shareholder meeting to vote on the sale. At the meeting, holders of 60% of the corporation's stock are present. 60% of the shares present are voted in favor of the sale. According to the majority rule, has the sale been approved by the shareholders? ________________

(b) Same facts as (a), but now assume that the case is governed by the MBCA rather than by the majority rule. Has the sale been approved by the shareholders? ________________

82. Same facts as in prior question. Now, the directors of Rin Tin Tin vote to make the acquisition of Guano. They do not call for a shareholder meeting to vote on the acquisition. Under the majority approach, is the acquisition duly authorized without a shareholders' vote? ________________

83. Sampson, Inc., manufactures beauty supplies. It has 100,000 shares of voting stock outstanding. Its board resolves that Sampson should purchase Delilah's Hairdressers, Inc., a chain of beauty parlors. To effectuate the merger, Sampson will issue 25,000 shares of authorized but previously-unissued stock to Delilah's shareholders. Whose shareholders must approve the transaction: Sampson's, Delilah's, both, or neither? ________________

84. Same facts as prior question. Now, however, assume that to effectuate the merger, Sampson will issue 10,000 shares of treasury stock to Delilah's shareholders. Whose shareholders (Sampson's, Delilah's, both or neither) must approve the transaction? ________________

85. The Paleolyric Music Publishing Co. owns 92% of the stock of the Tyrannosaurus Lex Publishing Co. Tyrannosaurus's and Paleolyric's boards of directors approve a merger, with Paleolyric to be the survivor. They file a plan of merger with the jurisdiction's Secretary of State, saying that the merger was duly approved. Terry Dactyl, a 2% owner of Tyrannosaurus, seeks to rescind the merger on grounds of lack of a shareholder vote. Assume that Delaware law applies, and that any special procedural requirements have been satisfied. What result? ________________

Answers

81. (a) No. In most states, a sale of substantially all of a corporation's assets must be approved by a majority of the corporation's *outstanding stock* — not just a majority of those present at a validly convened meeting. Here, only 60% of the shares were represented at the meeting, so a 60% approval represented only 36% of Guano's outstanding shares. As a result, the sale hasn't been approved by the shareholders and can't be carried out. [376]

(b) Yes. MCBA 11.04(e) requires only a majority of those shares actually voting, as long as a quorum (1/2 of eligible votes) votes. [376] Since 60% of those voting voted yes, and since more than half of all eligible shares voted, that's enough under the MCBA, even though fewer than half of all eligible shares voted yes.

82. Yes. In virtually all jurisdictions, the shareholders of a corporation that acquires another corporation's assets do not have to approve the transaction. [377]

83. Both. In virtually all states, if a company's shareholders will give up their existing shares in return for shares in some new entity, that company's shareholders must approve the transaction. (In other words, in a merger the "merged" company's shareholders must approve.) [378] Again in most states, the "default" rule is that the shareholders of the company which is "buying" assets in exchange for its shares must approve, as well. (In other words, the holders of the surviving party to the merger must approve.) See, e.g., MBCA § 11.04(a). [378] There are some exceptions, but none applies here.

84. Only Delilah's. As the prior question shows, ordinarily in a merger the shareholders of both the surviving and the disappearing company must approve. However, a different rule applies where the merger is what is sometimes called a "whale-minnow" merger, i.e., a merger in which the acquiring company is so much bigger than the to-be-acquired corporation that the former's shares outstanding won't materially increase. That's because the impact on the surviving corporation's shareholders isn't deemed great enough to give them a vote. In most jurisdictions, if the survivor's shares outstanding won't increase by more than 20%, the survivor's shareholders don't have to approve. MBCA §§ 11.04(g) and 6.21(f); Del. GCL § 251(f). [379] Here, Sampson had 100,000 voting shares before the merger and only 10%, or 10,000, more voting shares after the merger. As a result, Sampson's shareholders aren't entitled to a vote.

85. Dactyl will lose, because no shareholder vote is required in a short-form merger. Delaware, like many states, recognizes the "short-form merger" — that is, a scenario by which a corporation owning at least 90% of another corporation merges that corporation into itself. In such a merger, neither corporation's shareholders get a vote, on the theory that such a vote would be meaningless. Instead, only the boards of the two corporations need approve the merger. See Del. GCL § 253. [380] Since Paleolyric owns more than 90% of Tyrannosaurus, the short-form merger provision is available, and Paleolyric properly took advantage of it. (The protection that Dactyl gets is the right to an appraisal of his shares. See GCL § 253(d); § 262.)

II. CORPORATE COMBINATIONS — PROTECTING SHAREHOLDERS

A. Introduction: When a corporate combination takes place, there is a substantial risk that stockholders, especially stockholders of the acquired company, will be treated unfairly or at least differently from how they expected to be treated. In this section II, we cover three main ways in which courts and legislatures try to protect shareholders when a merger or acquisition occurs: (1) ***appraisal*** rights, by which the shareholder may demand payment of the value of his shares in cash, rather than being forced to accept other securities; (2) judicial scrutiny of the ***substantive fairness*** of the transaction; and (3) the ***"de facto merger"*** doctrine, by which courts occasionally will treat what is not formally a merger as in fact being one, usually for the purpose of conferring appraisal rights that would not otherwise exist.

B. Appraisal rights: As we have seen, a merger must normally be approved by majority vote of the stockholders of each of the corporations (and must *always* be approved by the stockholders of the disappearing corporation); similarly, a target's shareholders must approve its sale of its assets, and the same is true of the other types of corporate combinations we have looked at. But as long as the approval of the target's shareholders is not unanimous, there are likely to be unhappy shareholders.

1. Two problems: There are two main sources of possible unhappiness:

a. Unfairness: First, the majority-approval procedure gives no guarantee that the minority shareholders (i.e., those not approving the transaction) are being treated ***fairly***. This is especially true where there is a ***single shareholder*** or small tightly-knit group that controls a majority of the corporation's stock — this control group might engineer a sale or merger of the company on terms that are very generous to the control group but unfair to the outsider minority holders. (See the discussion of premiums for the sale of control *supra*, p. 234, for an illustration of some of the ways this may happen.)

b. Merger: Second, if the transaction is a ***merger*** of one corporation into another, even though the transaction may be "fair" in the strict economic sense each stockholder, including those opposing the transaction, is being forced to trade his investment for stock in a company that may be a stranger to him, and that may have most of its operations in a completely separate industry.

c. **Solution:** To deal with these twin problems arising out of corporate acquisitions — the possibility of outright unfairness to the minority holders, and the disappointed expectation interest of one who is forced to trade his shares for shares in a different company as part of a merger — nearly all states have created a legislative remedy called ***appraisal***.

2. **Nature of appraisal:** The basic idea behind appraisal is that this remedy permits a shareholder in certain circumstances to ***disinvest*** at a ***fair price***. Instead of being forced to trade his shares for shares in a different company (as would ordinarily happen in a merger or a plan of share exchange), and instead of being forced to receive cash consideration determined in a not-arm's-length manner (as might be the case in a short-form merger where the minority shareholders are redeemed for cash in an amount determined by the controlling parent corporation; see *supra*, p. 380), appraisal gives the dissatisfied shareholder a way to be ***"cashed out"*** of his investment at a price ***determined by a court*** to be fair. Appraisal is therefore a sort of ***safety valve*** that protects a minority shareholder against being forced to invest in an undesirable enterprise, and against other possible types of unfairness.

3. **MBCA's role:** Appraisal statutes vary widely from state to state. The MBCA's appraisal provisions are extensive, modern and well-thought-out. Therefore, it is on these MBCA provisions that most of our treatment of appraisal rights will center. These rights are spelled out in MBCA §§ 13.01-13.31.

4. **Mergers:** Nearly all appraisal statutes apply to a shareholder in a ***merger*** if the shareholder had a ***right to vote*** on the merger. In the garden-variety situation in which one corporation merges into another, and the disappearing corporation's shareholders receive shares in the survivor, nearly all states give appraisal rights to the disappearing shareholders. See MBCA § 13.02(a)(1).

Example: Little Corp merges into Big Corp. Each Little Corp shareholder, pursuant to the plan of merger, receives one share in Big Corp for each share he used to own in Little Corp. Able owns ten shares of common stock in Little Corp. Since Able had the right to vote on the merger (see *supra*, p. 378), Able also has appraisal rights, under MBCA § 13.02(a)(1). That is, instead of having to content himself with shares in Big Corp, he may require Big Corp to effectively "buy him out" at the fair market value of his Little Corp shares, computed as of just before the merger. That way, Able is not forced to exchange his investment in Little Corp (a corporation as to which he may have had special confidence, special knowledge, etc.) for shares in Big Corp (a corporation that he may know nothing about, in which he may completely lack confidence, etc.)

a. **Holders of surviving corporation:** Similarly, the ***surviving corporation's prior shareholders*** normally get a right of appraisal, too. See, e.g., Del GCL § 262(b) (giving appraisal rights to holders of stock in a corporation which is a "constituent corporation" in "any merger or consolidation"). (However, there's an important exception for the whale side of whale-minnow mergers, discussed in Par. (b) below.)

i. **Rationale:** The rationale for giving appraisal rights to the surviving corporation's pre-merger shareholders is that these holders are in effect being required to exchange their 100% interest in the survivor (as it existed prior to the merger) for a less-than-100% interest in a new, combined corporation. So these holders should be given a way to get cash instead of this new, mixed, security that they may not like.

ii. **Tied to right to vote on the merger:** Remember that the basic principle is that a shareholder whose shares are involved in a merger normally gets appraisal rights if she had the ***right to vote on the merger***. Giving appraisal rights to the prior shareholders of the surviving corporation fits into this scheme, since the survivor's holders normally get to vote on the merger. (See *supra*, p. 378).

b. **Whale side of whale-minnow mergers:** As we have just seen, the general rule is that any shareholder entitled to vote on a merger has appraisal rights as to that merger. The converse of this general rule is also true: a shareholder who does ***not*** have voting rights as to a merger will normally ***not*** have appraisal rights either. The main consequence of this converse rule is that in a ***"whale-minnow"*** merger — that is, a merger in which a corporation is merged into a much larger one, so that the increase in outstanding shares of the larger company is small — the ***surviving corporation's shareholders do not get appraisal rights.*** Thus under MBCA §§ 11.04(g)(4) and 6.21(f), the surviving corporation's shareholders do not get to vote on the merger if the increase in the survivor's outstanding shares will be less than 20%, so these shareholders do not get appraisal rights either. See MBCA § 13.02(a)(1)(i).

Example: Little Corp will be merging into Big Corp. Pre-merger, Big Corp has one million shares outstanding, and Little Corp has 150,000 shares outstanding. In the merger, each Little Corp share is exchanged for one newly-issued Big Corp share. Since the number of Big Corp shares outstanding will increase by only 15% (from 1,000,000 to 1,150,000) as a result of the merger, Big Corp shareholders do not get to vote on the merger, under MBCA §§ 11.04(g)(4) and 6.21(f). Therefore, Big Corp shareholders do not have appraisal rights as the result of this merger either. But the shareholders of Little Corp, which will be the disappearing corporation, do have such appraisal rights.

i. **Rationale:** The exclusion of appraisal rights for the surviving corporation's shareholders in whale-minnow mergers makes good sense. The merger is by hypothesis sufficiently small relative to the surviving corporation's business that the nature of the acquiring corporation's shareholders' investment has not really changed — this is much more like a sale-type acquisition by the surviving corporation than it is like a merger. Therefore, there is no need to protect the surviving corporation's shareholders (Big Corp shareholders in the above example) from the unfair results of being trapped in an investment very different from the one they anticipated, and there is thus no need for appraisal rights. See Clark, p. 450.

c. **Short-form mergers:** But in most states there is one very important ***exception*** to this general rule that if a shareholder could not vote on the merger, he will not have appraisal rights as to it. This exception is for the shareholders of the ***subsidiary*** in a ***short-form merger*** (i.e., a merger of a subsidiary into a controlling parent; see *supra*, p. 380). Because there is a significant risk that the outside, minority, shareholders of the subsidiary will be treated unfairly, it is reasonable to ***give them appraisal rights even though they would not have been able to vote on the merger.***

Example: Big Corp owns 92% of Big-Sub Corp. Under MBCA § 11.05(a), Big Corp may cause Big-Sub to be merged into itself without a vote of the shareholders of either corporation (since Big Corp owns more than 90% of the shares of Big-Sub). Remember that the rationale for dispensing with the vote of Big-Sub shareholders is that such a vote would be superfluous, since Big Corp would obviously vote all of its shares in Big-Sub in favor of the merger, so that the merger will go through even if all the outside Big-Sub shareholders voted against the merger. But under MBCA § 13.02(a)(1)(ii), the holders of the 8% of Big-Sub shares not held by Big Corp would have appraisal rights, since there is a substantial risk that the merger terms would be unfair to these minority Big-Sub holders (e.g., they might be given too few shares in Big Corp in exchange for their Big-Sub shares, or they might be given too little cash in the case of a "cash-out" merger).

i. **No appraisal rights for majority's shareholders:** On the other hand, the shareholders of the ***parent*** corporation in a parent-subsidiary or short-form merger do ***not*** get appraisal rights. Thus Big Corp's shareholders do not have appraisal rights on the facts of the above example. This, too, makes sense, since the economic impact of the merger on them is minimal (their corporation already owned, by hypothesis, at least 90% of the stock in the subsidiary).

5. **Sales of substantially all assets:** Appraisal rights also apply, in most states, to the corporation's ***sale of substantially all of its assets***. See MBCA § 13.02(a)(3).

a. **Sale for stock:** Thus if a corporation sells all of its assets in return for ***stock*** in the acquirer, the shareholders of the selling corporation usually ***have*** appraisal rights.

b. **Sale for cash, but without liquidation:** Similarly, if a corporation sells substantially all of its assets for ***cash***, but the corporation does ***not plan to liquidate***, its shareholders ***get*** appraisal rights in most states. *Id.* This makes sense, since the shareholders of the seller have been forced to trade their investment in an ongoing business for an investment in a pool of cash or in any assets purchased with the sale proceeds.

i. **Not all states give:** But not all states follow the MBCA in giving appraisal rights to the stockholders of a corporation selling all of its assets. For instance, Delaware does ***not*** give appraisal rights to the stockholders of a corporation that sells its assets; see Del. GCL § 262. This is true even though a corporation sells its assets in return for stock, the selling corporation then liquidates, and the acquirer's stock is distributed to the seller's stockholders (thus producing practically the same end result as if the seller had merged into the buyer). For this reason, if a Delaware target wants to sell itself in return for stock, and wants to avoid giving appraisal rights to its shareholders, a clever lawyer will structure the transaction as an asset-for-stock sale followed by liquidation; see, e.g., *Hariton v. Arco Electronics*, *infra*, p. 407, in which this technique was used successfully to deprive the seller's shareholders of appraisal rights.

c. **Sale for cash, followed by quick dissolution:** Suppose a corporation's assets are sold for ***cash***, and the corporation is quickly ***liquidated***, with the net cash proceeds being ***distributed*** to the shareholders. Here, in most states the seller's shareholders have ***no*** appraisal rights.

i. **Rationale:** This exception is easy to understand: The main purpose of the appraisal remedy is to give a shareholder who does not approve of a merger or sale a way out so that he is not trapped in a new investment of which he does not approve. But if all of a corporation's assets are sold for cash, and the cash is promptly distributed to the shareholders, then the shareholder is not trapped in an investment at all, and is instead already "cashed out." (True, the asset sale might be for an unfairly low price, but this problem is best addressed by having a court review the substantive fairness of the transaction, rather than by use of the appraisal remedy. See *infra*, p. 408, for a discussion of when and how a court will review the substantive fairness of a sale.)

6. **The "publicly traded" exception:** As we've noted, the main purpose of the appraisal remedy is to allow the shareholder to "cash out" at a fair price. If the corporation that is about to undergo a merger or asset sale is ***publicly traded***, why can't the shareholder who disapproves of the impending transaction simply ***sell his shares*** on the public market, and thus be "cashed out" in precisely the same way as he would be at the end of an appraisal? A number of states, using this reasoning, ***deny*** the appraisal remedy for ***publicly-traded*** stock. For instance, Delaware GCL § 262(b)(1) denies appraisal rights for any stock that is, at the time the stockholders are notified of the proposed merger, either: (1) listed on a national securities exchange; or (2) held of record by more than 2000 stockholders.

   a. **MBCA agrees:** The MBCA now agrees with this general approach — the code denies appraisal rights where the class of stock is either: (1) listed on either the New York Stock Exchange, American Stock Exchange, or NASDAQ national market; (2) not so listed, but has at least 2,000 shareholders plus a market value of at least $20 million. § 13.02(b)(1). In other words, transactions by companies whose shares are fairly ***"liquid"*** don't give rise to appraisal rights.

      i. **Exceptions:** However, there are also a couple of "exceptions to the exceptions" under the MBCA. Most importantly, there *are* appraisal rights even for publicly-traded companies, where there is a ***potential conflict of interest*** on the part of the company's board or senior executives (e.g., the company is being sold for all cash in a management-led buyout, a scenario in which management may not have been motivated to get the highest price for shareholders.) § 13.02(b)(4).

7. **Stock-for-stock exchanges:** Normally, a ***stock-for-stock exchange*** will not confer appraisal rights. This is because such an exchange is normally ***optional*** on the part of each shareholder — he may tender into the swap, or continue to keep his old shares. But recall that some states now have an alternative provision, the "plan of exchange," whereby each holder will be ***compelled*** to enter into the stock swap if the board and a majority of shareholders approve it. In this situation, it would make sense to give disapproving shareholders appraisal rights. The MBCA indeed gives appraisal rights in this "plan of share exchange" situation; see § 13.02(a)(2).

8. **Amendment of articles of incorporation:** Certain ***amendments to the articles of incorporation*** may so change and/or worsen a stockholder's position that state law may give

him appraisal rights. But most states' appraisal statutes do ***not*** give appraisal rights in this amendment-of-the-articles situation.

a. **Fractional share redemption under MBCA:** The MBCA gives appraisal rights in one important special situation involving an amendment of the articles of incorporation. As we will see later (*infra*, p. 422), one method of "squeezing out" minority shareholders is to conduct a ***reverse split***, coupled with a mandatory cash ***redemption*** by the company of any ***fractional share***. For instance, a company could amend the articles of incorporation to implement a 600:1 reverse split, and then require anyone with less than 1 new share (i.e., anyone with less than 600 pre-reverse-split shares) to sell the fractional share back to the company for cash. In this situation, the holder of the fractional share would ***have appraisal rights***. § 13.02(a)(4).

9. **Special provision:** Finally, some states allow the articles of incorporation, by-laws or board of directors to confer appraisal rights in certain situations where they would not otherwise be conferred by statute. See, e.g., MBCA § 13.02(a)(5).

10. **Triangular mergers:** What about ***triangular mergers***? Do shareholders on either side get appraisal rights? The answer depends in part on whether the transaction is a forward or a reverse merger, and also on whether the court applies the statute literally or instead uses the so-called "de facto" merger doctrine.

a. **Forward triangular merger:** First, consider the forward triangular merger (*supra*, p. 364). As you'll recall, in this transaction the parent (let's assume that it's Big Corp) forms a wholly-owned subsidiary (let's call it Big-Sub), and arranges for the target (let's call it Little Corp) to merge into Big-Sub in return for shares of Big Corp.

i. **Acquirer side:** In most states, Big Corp's shareholders will ***not*** get appraisal rights, because Big Corp shareholders don't get to vote on the transaction. (This, in turn, is because Big Corp isn't merging, Big-Sub is. See *supra*, p. 364.) Indeed, Big Corp's management's desire not to give its holders voting rights and appraisal rights is probably the main reason why management would use the forward triangular merger structure.

ii. **Target side:** On the target side, there generally ***will*** be appraisal rights: since Little Corp shareholders get to vote on whether to approve the merger (their corporation will disappear), they will also get appraisal rights under most statutes.

b. **Reverse triangular merger:** In the case of a ***reverse triangular merger***, the appraisal situation gets trickier. Using our same Big Corp/Big-Sub/Little Corp scenario (but remembering that this time, since it is a reverse merger, Big-Sub is going to merge into Little Corp instead of the other way around), here's what we would have:

i. **Big Corp shareholders:** Big Corp shareholders still probably do not have appraisal rights. Since Big Corp is not a party to the merger, its shareholders don't get to vote and consequently don't get appraisal rights. Big-Sub's shareholder (Big Corp) presumably does get to vote, and thus in theory has appraisal rights. But since Big Corp is the sole owner of Big-Sub, and wants the transaction to go forward, any appraisal rights that Big Corp may theoretically hold are irrelevant.

ii. **Little Corp side:** On the Little Corp side, observe that the appraisal story depends on the exact form by which Little Corp is combined with Big-Sub. If this is done by statutory merger (Big-Sub statutorily merging into Little Corp), Little Corp's shareholders probably have appraisal rights, since they have the right to approve the transaction. But if the combination proceeds by a stock-for-assets deal (Little Corp "buys" all of Big-Sub's assets — which happen to consist solely of Big Corp stock — and Little Corp funds this purchase by issuing more of its own stock), then a literal reading of most appraisal statutes would suggest that Little Corp's shareholders ***do not*** have an appraisal right. This is because most appraisal statutes do not give appraisal rights to the shareholders of a corporation that purchases the assets of another corporation (even if this purchase completely changes the nature of the acquirer's business). Indeed, depriving Little Corp's shareholders of appraisal rights (even though Little Corp was in essence being acquired rather than doing the acquiring) might well be a key motivating factor for structuring the transaction as a reverse triangular stock-for-assets deal. See, e.g., *Farris v. Glen Alden Corp.*, *infra*, p. 406.

iii. **"De facto merger" doctrine used:** But a court might use the ***"de facto merger"*** doctrine to give Little Corp's shareholders a right of appraisal in this reverse triangular stock-for-assets swap deal. The de facto merger doctrine (discussed further *infra*, p. 405) basically holds that where the purpose and economic reality of the transaction are equivalent to those of a merger, the court will treat the transaction as such even though its literal form is other than a merger. Thus in *Farris v. Glen Alden*, *infra*, p. 406, the court applied the de facto merger doctrine to give appraisal rights to the stockholders of the company that was in Little Corp's position, even though that corporation was literally buying assets in return for stock.

11. **Procedures for appraisal:** Let's look now at the ***procedures*** by which appraisal rights can be exercised. Again, let's assume that Little Corp is being acquired by Big Corp (in some way that triggers appraisal rights for Little Corp shareholders); let's also assume that Selwyn is a Little Corp shareholder who is unhappy about this acquisition. How can Selwyn go about exercising his appraisal rights? Again, we will concentrate on the MBCA's procedures, since these have been liberalized in important ways to make the appraisal remedy more adequate.

a. **Notice by Little Corp:** First, at the same time Little Corp gives Selwyn notice of the shareholders' meeting at which approval of the transaction will be sought, it must ***give him notice*** that if he opposes the transaction he has appraisal rights. MBCA § 13.20(a).

b. **Notice of payment demand by Selwyn:** Then, Selwyn must do two things in response: (1) he must give ***written notice*** to Little Corp, ***before the shareholder vote*** on the transaction, that he demands payment of the fair value of his shares (i.e., that he's asserting his appraisal rights); (2) he must ***not vote his shares in favor*** of the transaction. MBCA § 13.21(a).

c. **Deposit of shares:** Also, early in the process (in some states, before the vote is even held), Selwyn must ***deposit*** his shares with Little Corp. See, e.g., MBCA § 13.23(a).

i. **Rationale:** Why must Selwyn deposit his shares with Little Corp while awaiting payment? If this were not required, Selwyn might try to have his cake and eat it too: he might begin the appraisal process, observe the fortunes of Big Corp, and eventually decide to abandon the appraisal request (by selling his shares on the open market, and receiving a high price reflecting the fact that his Little Corp shares can now be converted into Big Corp shares by the buyer). If lots of shareholders did this, it would be very hard to consummate the merger and conduct the appraisal in an organized way. Clark, p. 451. Therefore, the MBCA (and virtually all other appraisal statutes) require one in Selwyn's position to effectively ***choose at the outset*** between using the appraisal remedy and selling his shares. Of course, for Selwyn, having his shares tied up during the entire appraisal proceeding makes the appraisal remedy less enticing then it would otherwise be.

d. **Little Corp's choice:** Once Little Corp receives Selwyn's payment demand and his shares, Little Corp ***must*** almost immediately pay to Selwyn "the amount the corporation estimates to be the fair value of [his] shares. . . ." MBCA § 13.24(a).

i. **Significance:** This requirement is probably the single most important modification the MBCA's appraisal procedures make to prior statutes. Under nearly all prior statutes, the corporation ***does not have to pay anything*** until a court finally determines what the fair value of the shares is. Under the MBCA, by contrast, the corporation must at least pay the amount that ***it*** concedes is the fair value of the shares, and any subsequent litigation will relate only to the amount by which the shareholder's demand exceeds what the corporation concedes to be the fair value of the shares. Since the shareholder knows he will get something, this provision should make appraisal more attractive to him.

e. **Shareholder's dissatisfaction:** If Selwyn is dissatisfied with the payment made by Little Corp (i.e., he thinks the fair value of the shares is more than Little Corp said they were worth), he may (and must) make a written demand to Little Corp within 30 days, stating what he believes the fair price to be. Little Corp must now either pay that amount, or else start a ***court proceeding*** to have the fair value of the shares determined. MBCA § 13.30. All shareholders seeking appraisal rights will be made parties to a single court proceeding. § 13.30(c). In this proceeding, the court will determine what it believes to be the fair value of the shares, and the corporation will have to pay this amount to each dissenter.

12. **Valuation method:** The central aspect of appraisal is that a court determines the ***"fair value"*** of the dissenter's shares, and the corporation is obliged to pay him this amount. How, then, do courts go about determining "fair value"? A brief answer might be, "not in a very realistic way."

a. **Exclude the influence of transaction:** One rule that most courts and statutes agree upon is that the fair value of the shares must be determined ***without reference*** to the transaction that triggers the appraisal right.

Example: On April 30, practically no one (including the management of Little Corp) suspects that Little Corp will soon be the recipient of an unsolicited merger proposal from Big Corp. On that date, Little Corp stock is trading at $20 per share. On May 1, newspapers publish unconfirmed reports that Big Corp will shortly be proposing a merger of Little Corp into Big Corp, whereby each Little Corp share will be exchanged for one Big Corp share (having, at the time of the published reports, a market value of $30 per share). The market price of Little Corp stock immediately jumps to $27. Big Corp indeed proposes the merger, it is approved by the shareholders, and Little Corp shareholders (at least those who do not demand appraisal rights) receive a share of Big Corp for each Little Corp stock, at a time when Big Corp stock is trading at $25 per share.

If Selwyn, a Little Corp shareholder, demands his appraisal rights with respect to this transaction, the court will determine the "fair value" of his Little Corp share ***without reference*** to the proposed merger into Big Corp. That is, the court will try to determine what the shares in Little Corp would be worth assuming that no merger would take place. Thus the value of the Big Corp shares that Little Corp shareholders in fact received in the merger would be totally irrelevant to this computation.

i. Rationale: This refusal to allow the proposed transaction to affect the "fair value" makes sense: since the dissenter is objecting to the transaction (and voting against it), he should not be able to gain the benefits of that proposed transaction if it makes his shares more valuable, yet at the same time he should not be burdened by that transaction if it makes the shares less valuable.

ii. Takeover talk: There is a trickier question, however: suppose that Little Corp has been ***persistently*** the subject of merger rumors, because it is perceived as having undervalued assets. Can Little Corp's value to some unspecified acquirer be considered in determining the value of the dissenter's Little Corp shares? Under most statutes, the answer is probably "yes." (In any event, to the extent that "fair value" includes a factor for "market value" as discussed below, the generalized possibilities for a takeover will normally be factored into fair value since they are almost always factored into the stock's market value.)

b. No discount for minority status or non-marketability: Should the court's appraisal of the value of the dissenter's shares take into account the fact that the dissenter is a minority shareholder, and that a minority block is normally worth less per-share than the corporation as a whole would be worth per-share? In other words, should the court apply a ***minority"*** or ***"non-marketability" discount***? Courts are split on this question, but the majority view seems to be that a minority/non-marketability discount should ***not*** be allowed. See, e.g., MBCA § 13.01(4)(iii) (saying that fair value is to be generally determined "without discounting for lack of marketability or minority status. . . .") Delaware follows this majority "no non-marketability discount" rule.

c. The "Delaware block" method: Now that we know what the court *cannot* count (i.e., any increase or decrease in value due to the proposed acquisition itself and, in most courts, any minority or non-marketability discount), what *can* the court consider in determining "fair value"? Most courts have, at least traditionally, applied the so-called ***"Delaware block"*** valuation method. Under the Delaware block method, the court normally considers ***three factors***: (1) the ***market price*** of the shares just before the transaction is announced, (2) the ***net asset value*** of the company, and (3) the ***earn-***

ings valuation of the company. Let's consider how these factors are pieced together, and then let's consider each of them in detail:

i. **Different weights:** Under the Delaware block method, the court is ***not*** required to give ***equal weight*** to each of these three factors. Instead, the court is generally free to choose what weight should be given to each factor, based on the court's estimate of the ***reliability*** of each factor on the particular facts of the case at hand. For instance, if the court believes that the market value of the stock just before the transaction is ***unrepresentative and unreliable*** (e.g., because the market for that stock is extremely thinly traded), the court can apply a lesser weight; similarly, if the court believes that past earnings are less representative of future earnings prospects (and thus of company value) than is usually the case, the court might underweigh the earnings factor. In any event, once the court assigns a percentage weight to each of the factors, the resulting "fair value" is simply a mathematical computation based on these weights.

ii. **Market value:** The court will often be disinclined to attach too much importance to the ***market value*** of the shares just before announcement of the acquisition. First, the shares in question may be ***thinly traded***, making it less likely that the market will be a fair estimate of the shares' true underlying value. Second, those in control of the corporation (the ones trying to put through the acquisition) may well wait until precisely the time when the market value most ***undervalues*** the shares to announce the transaction. This is especially likely in ***"going private"*** transactions. In general, the more broadly-traded the stock, the heavier weight the court is likely to give to the market value factor.

iii. **Net asset value:** The second factor is the so-called ***"net asset value."*** Usually, the court means by this the ***liquidating value*** of the company, i.e., what would be received if its various pieces were sold off one at a time. Occasionally, however, the court will instead use the "going concern" valuation (i.e., the amount that a willing buyer would pay for the corporation if he intended to continue its unified operations as these previously existed). (Generally, the "going concern" valuation will be higher than the "liquidation" valuation.)

iv. **Earnings valuation:** Probably the most subjective factor of all is the so-called "earnings valuation." Computation of the earnings valuation requires two steps: (1) the court computes the average earnings of the corporation for some prior period (usually the ***five years*** before the acquisition); (2) the court then selects a suitable ***"multiplier,"*** i.e., a factor by which these average earnings should be multiplied to produce the net present value of that future annual earnings stream. In step (1), the court usually excludes non-recurring or extraordinary items (e.g., earnings from the one-time sale of an asset, losses from a large one-time write-off from a plant closing, etc.).

v. **Criticism:** Courts often end up with an unrealistically low number for the earnings valuation factor. The main reason for this is the use of average earnings over the last five years rather than any attempt to ***estimate future*** earnings (which is what stock-market analysts and investors generally do). Since the economy is normally growing, and most corporations' earnings normally grow (if only due to inflation), taking a five-year average will produce a lower number than the most recent year's earnings, and even the most recent year's earnings will be lower than the probable future earnings. The result is that the earnings valuation chosen by most courts under the Delaware block approach is lower than either the market value number or the net asset value number; see Clark, p. 455, n. 30.

d. **Delaware abandons "Delaware block" approach:** Partly for the reason described in the prior paragraph, Delaware has ***abandoned*** the Delaware block approach, or at least no longer requires it. In *Weinberger v. UOP, Inc.*, 457 A.2d 701 (1983), the Delaware Supreme Court decided that the Delaware block approach was unduly rigid, and that Delaware courts must now allow proof of value "by any techniques or methods which are generally considered acceptable in the financial community and otherwise admissible in court. . . ." Thus while the Delaware courts may continue to look to market value, net asset values and earnings value, they must not ***restrict the proof*** to these items.

   i. **New types of evidence:** In particular, the Delaware courts will now usually have to allow two types of evidence of valuation that they would not have accepted under the Delaware block approach: (1) ***valuation studies*** prepared by the corporation for its own purposes, and (2) ***expert testimony*** about how much an acquirer would be likely to have paid in the present situation (including testimony about the ***"takeover premium,"*** i.e., the amount by which the price paid in a takeover generally exceeds the market value of the target just before announcement of the takeover). See Clark, p. 455, n. 31.

e. **Interest:** All states allow the dissenter to receive ***interest*** from the time of the merger. However, courts are split about whether the interest should be ***simple*** or ***compound***.

13. **Exclusivity of appraisal rights:** Suppose that Selwyn, the Little Corp stockholder, is unhappy with the proposed merger, yet for one reason or another is also not happy with the appraisal remedy. May he try to have the transaction ***enjoined*** in its entirety, or is appraisal his ***exclusive*** remedy? The answer depends on what grounds Selwyn is asserting in his suit for injunctive relief.

   a. **Illegality:** The appraisal remedy almost never prevents a shareholder from attacking the transaction on the grounds that it is ***illegal*** under the general corporation statute. For instance, if Selwyn could show that the transaction was explicitly ***prohibited*** by an enforceable clause in the corporation's ***articles of incorporation***, a court would probably enjoin it rather than saying to Selwyn, "You must content yourself with appraisal."

   b. **Procedural irregularity:** Similarly, if the parties to the transaction have not complied with ***procedural requirements***, Selwyn will be able to attack the transaction notwithstanding the availability of appraisal. For instance, if the transaction requires a shareholder ***vote***, and no such vote has been sought, the court will enjoin it (or, if the transaction has already occurred and is too difficult to set aside, the court might award damages to injured shareholders). The same would be true if the requisite board approvals were not obtained.

c. **Unfairness:** On the other hand, in most states appraisal *is* the exclusive remedy when the shareholder's contention is merely that the proposed transaction is a ***bad deal*** for the shareholders, or that it is in some sense ***"unfair"*** to them. At least, this is true where the transaction is an ***arm's-length*** one.

Example: Selwyn attacks the merger of Little Corp into Big Corp on the grounds that Little Corp shares have a true value of $30 per share (even though they have traded at $20 per share just before announcement of the merger), and that the shares of Big Corp that will be issued on a one-for-one exchange basis are really only worth $15 per share. Selwyn produces no evidence of self-dealing by Little Corp's insiders; his argument is merely that Little Corp's shareholders are getting much less than they are giving up, and that the merger is therefore a bad deal for them. In most states that supply an appraisal remedy (including the MBCA), that appraisal remedy will be the exclusive remedy on these facts, so Selwyn will not be able to get the transaction enjoined even though it may be "unfair" to him and others.

i. **Gross unfairness:** But even in this ostensibly "arm's length" situation, if Selwyn can show that the transaction is so ***grossly*** unfair as to constitute ***reckless indifference*** by Little Corp's insiders to the interests of Little Corp's shareholders, or ***intentional disregard*** by the insiders of the stockholders' interests, Selwyn might be able to get the transaction enjoined despite the availability of appraisal. A court might justify this conclusion by saying that Selwyn had established "constructive fraud." But it will be a rare arm's-length transaction that is shown to be so grossly unfair as to be enjoinable despite the availability of appraisal.

d. **Self-dealing:** Finally, suppose that Selwyn shows ***self-dealing*** by insiders to the transaction. Here, the court is much more likely than in the arm's-length situation to find that there has been a form of "'fraud' in the broad sense" upon shareholders, and that the transaction should be enjoined despite the availability of appraisal.

i. **Parent-subsidiary merger:** For instance, suppose that the transaction is a merger of a ***controlled subsidiary into the parent.*** If a minority outside shareholder of the subsidiary can show that the price set for the minority's shares was ***determined by the parent***, acting under a clear conflict of interest, the court is likely to enjoin the transaction rather than requiring the shareholder to use appraisal. In just such a case, *Weinberger v. UOP, Inc.* (discussed extensively *infra*, p. 425), the Delaware Supreme Court held that the appraisal remedy is not exclusive "where fraud, misrepresentation, ***self-dealing***, deliberate waste of corporate assets, or gross and palpable overreaching are involved."

C. **The "de facto merger" doctrine:** As we have seen, often there will be more than one way of structuring a business combination to produce a given result. For instance, if Acquirer wants to buy Target's business in return for Acquirer's stock, here are two ways of structuring the transaction that are substantially equivalent:

(1) Target merges into Acquirer, and Target's shareholders receive stock in Acquirer in lieu of their stock in Target; and

(2) Target sells all of its assets to Acquirer, in return for Acquirer stock; Target then liquidates, and distributes the Acquirer stock to its own shareholders.

Even though these two structures produce virtually the same end result (Target's shareholders now have stock in Acquirer in lieu of stock in Target, and Acquirer owns Target's business), these two structures may trigger very different rules regarding appraisal rights. For instance, if Target is incorporated in a state which does not give appraisal rights to the stockholders of a corporation that sells all of its assets (Delaware is one example of such a state), but that state does give appraisal rights to the stockholders of a disappearing corporation in a statutory merger, the result is that Target's stockholders will get appraisal rights under structure (1) above but not under structure (2). The question then becomes, can Target's shareholders demand appraisal rights under structure (2), on the theory that (2) is the "substantial equivalent" of a merger, and should therefore be treated as if it were one (including the award of appraisal rights)? The brief answer is that a few courts have ***accepted*** such a theory.

1. **Essence of the "de facto merger" theory:** The theory that a transaction which is not literally a merger, but which is the functional equivalent of a merger, should be treated as if it were one for purposes of appraisal rights and shareholder vote, is generally called the ***"de facto merger"*** theory. When the doctrine is accepted, the most common result is that selling stockholders get appraisal rights; however, there are other possible consequences, including: (1) that the selling stockholders get the right to ***vote*** on the transaction, which they might not otherwise have; and (2) that ***creditors*** of the seller may have a claim against the buyer, which they otherwise might not have.

2. **Only occasionally accepted:** Apparently, only a ***few*** courts have ever accepted the de facto merger theory, and they have done so only in specialized circumstances. There are no hard-and-fast rules to predict when a court will apply the de facto merger theory. In general, it is probably the case that the ***more like a merger*** the transaction is, the more likely the court is to apply the de facto merger theory.

3. ***Farris v. Glen Alden:*** Easily the best-known case applying the de facto merger doctrine is ***Farris v. Glen Alden Corp.***, 143 A.2d 25 (Pa. 1958). Because of the importance of this case (even though its result has rarely been followed elsewhere), its unfortunately-complicated facts must be understood in some detail.

   a. **Facts:** List was a large Delaware conglomerate. Glen Alden was a somewhat smaller Pennsylvania corporation. In economic terms, List agreed to acquire Glen Alden. However, the transaction took an unusual form, in which Glen Alden was to acquire List instead of the other way around. More precisely, the parties agreed to take the following steps: (1) Glen Alden would acquire all the assets of List; (2) Glen Alden would pay for these assets by issuing a large amount of its own stock to List (enough stock so that List would end up owning over three-quarters of Glen Alden); (3) Glen Alden would assume all of List's liabilities; (4) Glen Alden would change its name from Glen Alden Corp. to List Alden Corp.; (5) all directors of both companies would become directors of the new List Alden Corp.; and (6) List would be dissolved, and its assets (now solely stock representing a two-thirds interest in List Alden) would be distributed to the original List shareholders. Shareholders in both companies would thus end up in more or less the same position they would have been in had List simply bought Glen Alden in return for List shares.

   b. **Rationale for structure:** Why did the parties structure the transaction in this seemingly bizarre way? In particular, why did the parties use a stock-for-assets swap, instead of a statutory merger? The answer seems to be that under Delaware law, List's shareholders would not get appraisal rights (since shareholders of a corporation that sells substantially all of its assets don't get appraisal rights under Delaware law; see *supra*, p. 397), whereas List's shareholders would have had such rights had List statutorily merged with Glen Alden.

c. **Holding:** The Pennsylvania Supreme Court upset all of this fine plotting by the lawyers. The court held that ***this transaction was a de facto merger***, and therefore that Glen Alden's shareholders ***had appraisal rights***. The court said it would look at the "realities of the transaction" rather than its form. Here, the reality was that List was acquiring Glen Alden, not the other way around. Therefore, the Glen Alden shareholders had appraisal rights just as they would have had had Glen Alden been selling all of its assets in return for stock.

4. **Doctrine rejected:** But Pennsylvania is among the very ***small number*** of courts to have ever accepted the de facto merger doctrine under any set of facts. Most courts — including most notably ***Delaware — reject*** the doctrine.

a. ***Hariton* case:** For instance, in ***Hariton v. Arco Electronics, Inc.***, 188 A.2d 123 (Del. 1963), Arco and Loral took the following steps: (1) Arco agreed to sell all its assets to Loral in return for some shares of Loral (a stock-for-asset swap or "C reorganization," see *supra*, p. 386); (2) Arco's shareholders then approved the dissolution of the company; and (3) Arco then liquidated and distributed to its shareholders all the Loral shares it had received in return for its assets. The net economic result was exactly the same as had Arco merged into Loral. Yet Arco's shareholders did not get any appraisal rights, since under Delaware law the shareholders of a company that sells all of its assets do not get appraisal rights, and the shareholders of a company that dissolves and distributes its assets do not get appraisal rights either. P, an Arco shareholder, argued (as the plaintiff in *Farris* had successfully argued) that "substance should prevail over form" and that something that was in reality a merger should be treated that way.

i. **De facto doctrine rejected:** But the court decisively ***rejected*** the de facto merger doctrine. The Delaware legislature had created two distinct statutory procedures, one for mergers and the other for sale-of-assets. These two procedures were of "equal dignity," and a company could use either one. The fact that use of the sale-of-assets procedure, followed by a merger, might happen to produce the same results as the merger statute would have produced, was simply irrelevant to the issue of whether shareholders have appraisal rights in the sale-of-assets situation.

b. **Pennsylvania also now rejects:** Even Pennsylvania, the state whose Supreme Court applied the de facto doctrine in the landmark *Farris* case, seems to have subsequently rejected the de facto merger doctrine. See *Terry v. Penn Central Corp.*, 668 F.2d 188 (3d Cir. 1981), interpreting a post-*Farris* modification to the Pennsylvania corporation statutes as having abolished the de facto doctrine.

5. **Modern statutes lessen the problem:** In any event, many modern corporation statutes lessen or completely remove the need for the de facto merger doctrine. They do this by treating the various merger-type structures (statutory merger, stock-for-stock swaps and

stock-for-asset swaps) ***the same way***, in terms of shareholder approval and appraisal rights.

Example: Suppose that Big Corp is to acquire the business of Little Corp, and that Little Corp's shareholders are to be compensated in some fashion by receiving an interest in the combined Big/Little businesses. The transaction might proceed as: (1) a statutory merger of Little Corp into Big Corp; (2) a "plan of share exchange," whereby each Little Corp shareholder is required to exchange his Little Corp shares for Big Corp shares; or (3) a sale by Little Corp of its assets in return for Big Corp stock, to be followed by dissolution of Little Corp and a liquidating distribution by it to its shareholders of the Big Corp shares received in the stock-for-assets swap.

Under many modern statutes, in each of these scenarios Little Corp's shareholders would get the right to approve the transaction, and would get appraisal rights.

D. Judicial review of the substantive fairness of transactions: Suppose Corporation is about to be acquired or merged, and Shareholder thinks the deal is very unfair for Corporation's shareholders (or at least unfair for its non-insider shareholders). Can Shareholder get a court to review the ***substantive fairness*** of the arrangement, and to enjoin the transaction (or perhaps award damages) if the court agrees that the transaction is indeed unfair? The brief answer has three parts: (1) Most courts believe that they do indeed have the power to review the substantive fairness of a proposed acquisition or merger; (2) In an arm's-length arrangement, the court will set aside the deal only if the unfairness is very extreme; and (3) Where there is a strong ***self-dealing*** aspect to the transaction, the court will scrutinize it more closely, and is more likely to overturn it.

1. **Appraisal as exclusive remedy:** Before we begin looking at the court's review of substantive fairness, remember that the plaintiff shareholder's suit may be blocked right at the outset by the defendants' assertion that ***appraisal*** must be P's ***exclusive*** remedy. The exclusivity of appraisal is discussed *supra*, p. 404. Recall that in general, the availability of an appraisal remedy will prevent the stockholder from showing that the deal is in a general sense a bad one for him and his fellow shareholders, but will not prevent him from showing that the transaction is unlawful or fraudulent. Therefore, a clever shareholder will try to show that the proposed transaction has self-dealing aspects that rise to the level of "constructive fraud"; this will be much easier for him to do where the two parties to the proposed deal have a close pre-existing relationship, than where they do not (the "arm's-length" case).

2. **Arm's-length combinations:** First, let's consider judicial review of ***arm's-length*** combinations. By "arm's-length combination," we mean a deal between two entities which ***do not have a close pre-existing relationship*** at the time they negotiate the deal.

   a. **General rule:** Most of the case law in this area comes from Delaware. The Delaware courts will review the substantive fairness of even an arm's-length transaction. However, there are two important requirements that the plaintiff must meet in order to have the transaction set aside for substantive unfairness: (1) he must bear the ***burden of proof*** on the issue of fairness; and (2) he must show that the price is so ***grossly inadequate*** as to amount to ***"constructive fraud."*** Clark, p. 464.

i. **Result:** These two requirements are so tough that courts almost never strike down the transaction where it falls into this arm's-length category.

b. **The "side payments" problem:** Even in an ostensibly arm's-length combination, there will be the potential for a weak form of self-dealing on the part of the insiders of the selling corporation (or the disappearing corporation in a merger). This is the so-called ***"side payments"*** problem: the insiders of the seller may settle for a ***lower selling price*** in return for some form of payment to themselves. For instance, the insiders might negotiate unusually lucrative ***employment contracts***, consulting contracts, or a higher price for their own shares than is being received by the outside shareholders.

i. **Court rejects attack:** But in general, courts refuse to treat a sweet deal between the seller's insiders and the buyer as being sufficient to make the transaction "self interested"; these courts therefore refuse to apply the stricter scrutiny that they use in the self-dealing context (described below). The main reason for this refusal is that it is difficult or impossible for the plaintiff to show that the insiders of the seller have really intentionally traded off a higher purchase price in return for the above-market deal for the insiders.

Example: Big Corp would like to acquire Little Corp. Little Corp is publicly held, and its president, Peter, earns $200,000 a year (which is roughly average for heads of companies of Little's size and profitability). Big Corp would strongly prefer a friendly transaction. Big Corp therefore offers to pay $10 million for Little Corp, and to give Peter an employment contract to continue to run Little Corp (which will be a separately run subsidiary of Big Corp) for five years at $1 million per year. Peter agrees to the transaction, gets his board to rubber-stamp it, and recommends it to the shareholders; Little's shareholders approve, and the deal goes through.

Now, Gadfly, a Little Corp shareholder, brings a suit for damages, alleging that he and the other Little Corp shareholders have received less than the fair market value of their Little Corp shares. He argues that Little Corp really had a fair market value of $14 million, and that $4 million of this has been diverted from the shareholders to Peter in the form of an employment contract that will pay $800,000 more per year to Peter than the fair market value of his services (as measured by his prior compensation).

But Gadfly will almost certainly lose. The court will probably refuse to consider this transaction to be a self-dealing one, and will therefore use the easy-to-satisfy standard of review (by which the burden of proof is on the plaintiff to show that the consideration was so grossly inadequate as to constitute "constructive fraud"). The 28% or so alleged shortfall will almost certainly not meet this standard, so the transaction will be upheld. The reason the court is likely to take this position is that it will be almost impossible for Gadfly to show that Big Corp would really have paid $14 million or that Peter would have vetoed the transaction without the huge raise. (For instance, Big Corp and Peter can argue that Little Corp was worth far more to Big Corp with a well-compensated, highly motivated president running it than it would be worth if run by somebody who was merely receiving the same money as he could get from any other company.) See generally Clark, pp. 465-66.

3. **Self-dealing situations:** Now let's consider situations that, the court decides, involve ***self-dealing***. Recall that a self-dealing transaction is one in which a key decision maker ***stands on both sides of the transaction***. (See *supra*, p. 198.)

   a. **Higher standard:** Generally, courts subject self-dealing merger and acquisition transactions to a much ***stricter level of scrutiny***. For instance, in Delaware, the rule seems to be that the proponents of the transaction have "the burden of establishing its ***entire fairness***, sufficient to pass the test of ***careful scrutiny*** by the courts." *Weinberger v. UOP, Inc.*, 457 A.2d 701 (Del. 1983) (discussed more extensively *infra*, p. 425). This stricter scrutiny seems to be due mainly to the fact that there is a greater risk of unfairness to shareholders when an insider is on both sides of the transaction than where the two corporate parties are truly bargaining at arm's length.

   b. **Two-step acquisitions:** One situation that, at least arguably, involves self-dealing is the ***two-step acquisition***. This is a transaction in which an acquirer purchases some (usually a majority) of the target's shares in a cash tender offer, then in a subsequent second step eliminates the remaining shareholders by a cash or stock merger. Before we examine how courts have looked at the substantive fairness of such two-step transactions, let's see how such a transaction might work in practice:

   Example: Big Corp wants to acquire Little Corp, but Little Corp's management opposes. Big Corp therefore decides to proceed by a two-step hostile tender offer. At a time when Little Corp stock is trading at $20 per share, Big Corp offers to buy 51% of Little Corp's stock for $35 per share. Big Corp's tender offer documents also say that Big Corp will later merge Little Corp into Big Corp with the remaining Little Corp shareholders receiving $25 per share.

   Observe that this offer (which might be called a ***"two-tier front-loaded offer"***) has a somewhat coercive effect on a Little Corp shareholder trying to decide whether to tender his shares. If he tenders, he will get $35 for about half of his shares, and $25 for the remaining shares. But if he does not tender, he will be merged out anyway in the second stage, and will receive only $25 per share in that stage. Therefore, he has an enormous incentive to tender, even though he would really prefer to continue as a shareholder in an independent Little Corp. For this reason, two-tier front-loaded offers like this one are often criticized as unfair to the target's shareholders. (See the fuller discussion of such offers *infra*, p. 441.)

      i. **State court attacks:** A Little Corp shareholder might bring an attack on this transaction in state court. In particular, a Little Corp shareholder might wait until the second stage (the "back end" merger of Little Corp into Big Corp, in which the remaining 49% independently-owned Little Corp shares are cashed out) is about to be carried out; he could then argue that this second step is both substantively unfair and constitutes self-dealing (since Big Corp is effectively on both sides of the transaction, insofar as it already controls Little Corp).

      (1) P probably loses: However, the shareholder would probably ***lose***. A state court would be likely to reason that: (1) a majority of the stockholders effectively approved the transaction, by tendering 51% (or more) of their shares, while knowing what the terms of the back-end merger would be; and (2) there is no requirement that both steps in a two-step transaction provide an equal price to shareholders, as long as all shareholders have an equal opportunity to participate pro-rata at each step (which is certainly the case in our example, since any shareholder can have 51% of his shares bought in the first step for $35 and the other 49% bought for $25 in the back-end merger). See Clark, p. 471.

ii. **Federal law:** On the other hand, a Little Corp shareholder might have a slightly better chance of attacking the transaction in ***federal court*** on federal grounds. There is a small chance that a federal court might hold that the entire two-tier structure of the offer was "manipulative," and thus barred by SEC Rule 10b-5 (or by § 14(e) of the Securities Exchange Act of 1934, which forbids manipulation in connection with tender offers; see *infra*, p. 446). Also, if a Little Corp shareholder can show that Big Corp gave ***false information*** in its tender offer documents (e.g., by misrepresenting the terms of the eventual back-end merger), he would have a much better chance of successfully blocking the back-end merger or obtaining damages, under these federal anti-fraud provisions. Clark, p. 471.

c. **Parent-subsidiary merger:** A second, related, situation in which the transaction is likely to be considered self-dealing involves ***parent-subsidiary mergers***. Here, state courts are quite vigilant to protect the rights of minority shareholders of the subsidiary — the parent will have the burden of proving that the transaction is ***"entirely fair,"*** and the court will carefully scrutinize it. One way in which courts justify this stricter scrutiny is by saying that the parent corporation (as the majority stockholder in the subsidiary) has a ***fiduciary obligation*** toward the subsidiary's minority shareholders, and thus bears a heavier burden of behaving fairly than if the parent were negotiating at arm's length with the subsidiary.

i. **Hypothetical arm's-length deal:** Generally, in determining whether the merger terms are fair, the court will attempt to compare those terms with the terms that might be expected if the subsidiary were instead being merged into an acquirer with whom it had no pre-existing relationship, in a completely ***arm's-length*** transaction. Of course, the price at which such a hypothetical transaction would take place can be very hard to estimate. (Also, observe that the ***market value*** of the minority shares in the subsidiary may not be a good estimate of the subsidiary's fair price. Indeed, this market value may be ***higher*** than the subsidiary's fair price. This is because the market may anticipate that the majority will want to gain complete control and that the majority will "pay up" for that control.

ii. **Use of independent committee:** One way the parent can increase the chance that the court will find the transaction to be fair to the subsidiary's minority holders is by the use of an ***independent committee*** to approve the transaction. That is, the subsidiary's board should appoint some or all of those subsidiary directors who are ***not affiliated with the parent*** to form an independent committee to consider the merger proposal. If this independent committee approves the merger as being fair to the subsidiary, the court is likely to conclude that the merger was, in essence, an arm's-length transaction which should be overturned only for gross inadequacies of price.

4. **Freezeouts:** So far, we have looked principally at situations in which the public shareholders of the corporation that disappears in the merger are ***not*** "cashed out" — that is, these public holders receive stock in the surviving corporation, and the sole issue is whether the stock they have received is of value equal to the stock that they had in the disappearing corporation. The problem of substantive fairness can be even more acute when the public shareholders are "cashed out" or "disinvested," by a merger in which they receive cash or bonds rather than stock in the survivor. Here, the issue is not only whether the price was fair, but also whether the insiders had the right to ***eliminate*** the outside public shareholders from the venture. The special problems raised by cash-out mergers are discussed in our separate treatment of "freezeouts" *infra*, p. 419.

Quiz Yourself on

MERGERS AND ACQUISITIONS (PROTECTING SHAREHOLDERS)

86. Salome founds a successful privately-held company, Seven Veils Dancing Schools, Inc. Seven Veils's board of directors votes to merge the company into the Gypsy Moth Lee Costume Company, with Seven Veils holders getting one share of Gypsy Moth in exchange for each share they hold of Seven Veils. A Seven Veils's shareholder, John Baptist, opposes the merger, because he believes that a share of Gypsy Moth will prove to be worth much less than a pre-merger share of Seven Veils.

(a) If you represent John Baptist, what would you advise him to do? ________________

(b) What procedural steps will John have to take in order to implement your recommendation in part (a)? ________________

(c) Assuming that John takes your advice, and carries out all procedurally-required steps, what is the likely outcome? ________________

87. Same basic facts as prior question. Now, however, assume that Seven Veils is traded on the New York Stock Exchange, and has several hundred million dollars of annual revenues. Assume also that John makes a demand for appraisal, and takes all required procedural steps.

(a) If Seven Veils is a Delaware corporation, will John be entitled to appraisal? ________________

(b) If Seven Veils is incorporated in a state that follows the MBCA, will John be entitled to appraisal? ________________

88. Seinfeld, Inc., a privately-held producer of TV sitcoms about nothing, is controlled by Jerry Seinfeld and Cosmo Kramer. The board of Seinfeld votes to sell all the company's assets for cash, to Friends, Inc., a rival sitcom producer. The plan of sale calls for the company to reinvest the cash received into a coffee shop on the Upper West Side of Manhattan. A majority of Seinfeld shareholders approve the transaction. George Costanza, a minority shareholder of Seinfeld, votes against the transaction and gives prompt notice that he wishes to have the company buy his shares for fair market value. Seinfeld's certificate of incorporation is silent on all material issues.

(a) If Delaware law controls, must Seinfeld, Inc. buy George's shares for their fair market value? ________________

(b) If the MBCA controls, must Seinfeld, Inc. buy George's shares for their fair market value? ________________

89. Little Joe gets tired of working at the Ponderosa Ranch, and decides to start up a chain of hotels, Horsepitality Inns, Inc. About 20 other investors join him. A few years later, another chain, Mare-iott Hotels, Inc., a public company, proposes a plan of merger, whereby each Horsepitality holder will exchange his shares for an equal number of shares in Mare-iott. (Mare-iott has 1,000,000 shares issued and outstanding before the merger, and proposes to issue 100,000 new ones to Horsepitality holders in the exchange.) The boards of both companies approve the transactions, and the holders of each company approve the transaction by majority vote. (Mare-iott's holders don't have a formal right of approval under state law, but Mare-iott's board decides to solicit their consent anyway.) Answer the following two questions by reference to prevailing law (as opposed to the law of any particular jurisdiction).

(a) Hoss Cartwright, a Horsepitality holder, votes in favor of the merger. Shortly after the vote, and before the share exchange is consummated, Mare-iott releases very poor quarterly earnings, and Hoss no longer wishes to receive Mare-iott stock in exchange for his Horsepitality stock. Assuming that Hoss acts in a timely manner, can Hoss now assert appraisal rights? ________________

(b) Wyatt Earp is a holder of Mare-iott prior to the merger. He votes against the merger. Assuming that he acts in a timely manner, can Earp now assert appraisal rights? ________________

90. The Long Silver Company and the Dong Bell Company plan to merge, with Long Silver disappearing and its holders getting .5 shares of Dong Bell for each share of Long Silver they hold. The merger is approved by the boards and shareholders of both companies. Paul Revere, a Long Silver shareholder, votes against the merger (but does not demand appraisal). After the merger is approved, and before it is consummated, Revere sues in state court for an injunction against consummation. Revere's complaint asserts that the Long Silver stockholders are getting far less in assets and in "business value" than they are giving up. Revere's complaint does not make any other allegations of unfairness or wrongdoing on the part of either Long Silver, Dong Bell, or their directors or officers.

(a) If you represent the Long Silver board of directors, what procedural argument should you make in support of a motion to dismiss Revere's suit? ________________

(b) Will the argument you make in (a) be successful, under the prevailing view? ________________

Answers

86. (a) Demand appraisal of his shares. Nearly all states allow an unhappy shareholder in a merging company to demand appraisal of his shares, provided that he does not vote in favor of the merger. The basic idea is that the merging company will be required to buy the dissenter's shares at their fair market value, rather than forcing him to accept the surviving company's stock. [395]

(b) Submit a demand and deposit his shares. John will have to submit a written demand that the company purchase his shares for fair value. In many states (e.g., Delaware — see Del. GCL § 262(d)(1)), this demand must be made in writing *before the vote on the merger occurs*. [400] John will also probably have to deposit his shares with the company at the time he makes the demand (so he can't sell the surviving-company shares at a profit if the price runs up, thus playing "heads I win, tails you lose"). [400]

(c) The merged company will have to buy John's shares for their fair market value, judged as of the time of the merger. If the company and John can't agree on what that fair price is, a court will ultimately decide.

87. (a) No, because Seven Veils is publicly-traded. Delaware, like a number of states, denies appraisal rights as to public companies. Specifically, Del. GCL § 262(b)(1) denies the right of appraisal to holders of any company that is either traded on a national stock exchange, listed on NASDAQ, or held of record by more than 2,000 people. [398] In other words, in Delaware, holders of publicly-traded companies don't get appraisal rights (on the theory that such a holder can simply sell his shares in the open market for what the market views as their fair value, so he doesn't need the "escape hatch" of appraisal). Since Seven Veils is listed on the NYSE, that fact alone means that John doesn't have appraisal rights.

(b) No, because Seven Veils is publicly-traded. The MCBA was amended (in 1999) to furnish a "publicly-traded" exception similar to those existing in many states (see (a) above). Under MCBA § 13.02(b)(1), no appraisal rights exist if the class of stock in question is listed on a national stock exchange or NASDAQ (or meets certain other "liquidity" standards). There is an exception for certain transactions thought to pose conflict-of-interest problems, like management buyouts, but this exception does not apply here.

88. (a) No. Under Delaware law, the shareholders of a company that sells all of its assets (whether for cash or for some other property, such as shares of the acquirer) do *not* have appraisal rights. See Del GCL § 262 (giving appraisal rights only to holders of "a constituent corporation in a merger or consolidation" — an asset sale is not a "merger" or a "consolidation"). [397] (If the company's certificate of incorporation expressly provided for appraisal rights in the sale-of-assets scenario, Del GCL § 262(c) makes such rights enforceable. But the facts here tell us that the charter is silent on the issue, so the "default" rule that there are no appraisal rights for sale-of-assets transactions applies.) Therefore, even though George will effectively be forced into ownership of a business (coffee shop) that's quite different from the one he expected to be owning (sitcom producer), he's locked in.

(b) Yes. MBCA § 13.02(a)(3) gives stockholders of a company that's selling all or substantially all of its assets a right of appraisal. [397] There's an exception if the company is selling for cash and plans to distribute the cash to holders within one year after the sale, but this exception doesn't apply here. So (for the reasons suggested by the last sentence of the answer to part (a) above), the MBCA gives George the right to force Seinfeld, Inc. to buy out his shares for cash at their fair market value.

89. (a) No. In virtually all jurisdictions, the cardinal rule is that a holder who votes in favor of the merger cannot later assert appraisal rights. Indeed, in many jurisdictions the holder not only can't vote in favor, but has to announce his demand for appraisal *before* the vote is even held. See, e.g., MBCA § 13.21(a); Del. GCL § 262(d)(1). [400]

(b) No. The general principle is that only holders who were entitled by law to vote on the merger may assert appraisal rights. (There are exceptions, such as for a minority holder of a subsidiary in a short-form merger, but no exception applies on these facts.) Because this was a "whale-minnow" merger (i.e., Mare-iott's shares outstanding would increase by less than 20% as the result of the merger), Mare-iott shareholders didn't have a legal right to approve, even though Mare-iott's board decided to solicit their approval anyway. [396] Therefore, under the prevailing view Earp as a Mare-iott holder would not be permitted to demand appraisal.

90. (a) That appraisal is the exclusive remedy, thus foreclosing an injunction.

(b) Yes, probably. Most states make appraisal the exclusive remedy when the shareholder's contention is merely that the proposed transaction is a bad deal for him or for the company in which he is a holder. [405] So Revere's claim that Long Silver and its holders are not getting equivalent value would be foreclosed, under the prevailing view. It will make no difference that Revere did not in fact ask for appraisal:

he was entitled to ask for it, so this becomes the exclusive remedy even though he didn't avail himself of it.

III. RECAPITALIZATIONS — HURTING THE PREFERRED SHAREHOLDERS

A. The problem generally: A "recapitalization" is an adjustment of the capital structure of a corporation. For instance, the recapitalization may involve reducing or eliminating the par value of the common shares, creating new classes of securities, etc. One type of recapitalization poses special problems, and is therefore worth a special look: this is the ***elimination of accrued dividends owed to preferred stockholders***.

1. **Preferred stock generally:** "Preferred stock" is stock that has a ***preferential right***, vis-a-vis the common stock, with respect to the payment of ***dividends***, amounts distributable on ***liquidation***, or both. See Nutshell, p. 467. On the other hand, preferred shareholders generally do not have a right to dividends beyond a ***fixed annual amount*** specified in the preferred stock issue, and do not have a right to anything in liquidation beyond the amount specified in the issue. Preferred stockholders thus have rights that are actually more like those of bondholders than like those of stockholders: in return for the greater likelihood (compared with common stockholders) that they will receive some fixed dividend and some fixed amount in liquidation, they give up the right to share in the upside if the corporation does unexpectedly well.

2. **Why common wants to eliminate preferred:** Most preferred stock provides for ***"cumulative"*** dividends. That is, if the corporation is unable to make a particular dividend payment to the preferred stockholders, that dividend payment becomes an "accrued" obligation. This accrual means that all arrearages in preferred dividends must be paid before ***any*** dividend payment is made to the common stockholders. If the corporation has been in default on its preferred dividends for a long time, the result may be that the common stock is very far away indeed from receiving any dividends, a fact that of course makes the common shareholders unhappy. The arrearages may also hurt the corporation's ability to obtain new debt financing (since, even though the new debt financing would have a repayment priority ahead of the preferred, the lender may be worried that the corporation's cash flow will always be diminished by the need to slowly pay off the preferred arrearages).

3. **Eliminating preferred arrearages:** Therefore, if payment of preferred dividends is substantially in arrears, the common shareholders will often want to find some way to ***eliminate*** or at least dramatically restructure these accrued preferred dividends. Two questions arise: (1) How may the common shareholders accomplish this? and (2) To what extent may a court review the ***fairness*** of such an arrangement?

B. Methods of eliminating arrearages: There are basically two ways the common shareholders can go about eliminating the accrued preferred dividends: (1) by ***amending the articles of incorporation***; and (2) by indirect means, especially by the use of the ***merger*** statute.

1. **Amending the articles:** Under modern corporation statutes, the articles of incorporation may be ***amended*** at any time. The amendment will generally be valid so long as the provision that is added or deleted could have been present in, or omitted from, ***new*** articles of incorporation filed on the date of the amendment. See, e.g., MBCA § 10.01(a).

   a. **No vested rights:** In other words, even though a preferred shareholder has bought his preferred shares in reliance on a form of "contract" (i.e., in reliance on a provision in the articles of incorporation setting forth the preferential rights he will have as the owner of those shares), that contract can be amended at any time to change his rights. See MBCA § 10.01(b). As the concept is sometimes put, the preferred shareholder (or, for that matter, the common shareholder) does ***not*** have a ***"vested property right"*** arising from any particular articles of incorporation provision. *Id.*

   b. **Approval by preferred shareholders as group:** On the other hand, most corporation statutes do give the preferred shareholders ***as a group*** a key form of protection: the right to ***approve or veto*** the change. For example, the MBCA allows the articles to be amended to lessen or eliminate preferred dividends (either accrued or prospective) only if the preferred shareholders, voting as a group, approve this plan. See MBCA § 10.04(a)(3) and (8). The preferred shareholders get to vote as a group even if the articles of incorporation otherwise provide that the preferred shareholders do not get to vote. (Customarily, preferred stockholders do not get to vote.) MBCA § 10.04(d).

   Example: ABC Corp. has two classes of stock: common and preferred. There are one million common shares and 100,000 preferred shares. The articles of incorporation provide that the preferred shares do not get to vote. ABC falls upon hard times, and misses four years' worth of preferred stock dividends (which, under the articles of incorporation, cumulate). Then, the corporation's health improves somewhat. The common stockholders would like to be able to receive dividends themselves, but know that if the four years' worth of preferred payments have to be made up first, the common shareholders will have to wait a long time. Therefore, the common holders propose a recapitalization under which the arrearage in the preferred dividends is declared eliminated by an amendment to ABC's articles of incorporation.

   Under the MBCA, this change to the articles must be independently approved by a ***majority of the preferred stockholders***, voting as a separate group. See MBCA § 10.04(a)(8). Therefore, even if all one million common shares and 40,000 of the preferred shares are cast in favor of the amendment, it will fail. This requirement that a majority of any affected class approve any amendment hurting that class, prevents the common holders from taking unfair advantage of the preferred holders.

      i. **Why preferred might approve:** Why might the preferred ever approve the transaction by majority vote, if the sole purpose is to eliminate the preferred's rights? First, management controls the proxy machinery, and management will normally be in favor of the proposal (since management typically identifies more with common stockholders than preferred ones), so the proposal might go through simply because of inertia. Second, the common shareholders typically have the ability to make the lives of the preferred holders miserable, and will often be able to use this ability to extract unfair concessions. For instance, the common holders might effectively say to the preferred holders, "The company's financial condition does not permit us to pay any preferred dividend, and will not in the future. However, if the proposed recapitalization is approved, we will make a small payment to the preferred holders." In this situation, the preferred stockholders might rationally conclude that half a loaf is better than none, and therefore approve even a basically unfair recapitalization.

2. **Indirect techniques, including merger:** Alternatively, the accrued preferred dividends may be eliminated or reduced by ***indirect means***. Most commonly, this is done by ***merging*** the corporation into another corporation, and having the survivor's articles not provide for payment of any accrued preferred dividends.

   a. **Right to approve:** Again, modern corporation statutes will generally protect the preferred shareholders by giving them, as a class, a veto power over the proposed merger. For instance, the MBCA lets a particular class of stock vote as a "separate voting group" if a merger would "change the rights, ***preferences***, or limitations of all or part of the shares of the class" (§ 10.04(a)(3)); see also § 11.04(f). Therefore, even if the preferred shareholders would not otherwise be entitled to vote on the merger, a majority of them will have to approve the merger if a reduction or elimination of the accrued preferred dividends would result.

      i. **Delaware:** But under *Delaware* law, if the preferred is non-voting, it does ***not*** get to vote on a merger, even if the merger is being carried out solely for the purpose of eliminating the preferred dividends. See Del. GCL § 251(c).

   b. **Judicially allowed:** Of course, to an individual preferred shareholder who thinks the proposed merger is a bad deal, it is of little consolation to know that his contract has been changed without his consent merely because a majority of his fellow preferred shareholders have approved the transaction. This is even more dramatically the case where it is clear that the ***sole reason*** for the merger is to eliminate the preferred shareholders. Nonetheless, courts generally seem to ***allow*** the use of the merger technique for the purpose of eliminating the preferred shareholders, so long as all needed shareholder approvals are obtained.

C. **Judicial review of fairness:** In general, courts have been very reluctant to interfere with recapitalizations even where the recap seems to be objectively ***unfair*** to the preferred shareholders.

1. **Appraisal:** The risk of unfairness, however, is reduced by two factors. First, as we saw above, under modern statutes both of the main techniques for carrying out a recapitalization that removes the accrued preferred dividends (amending the articles of incorporation, and merging into a shell with a different capital structure) require the vote of a majority of the preferred shares. Secondly, these techniques will, in most states, trigger ***appraisal rights*** on the part of the preferred shareholders. For instance, the MBCA gives appraisal rights to a preferred shareholder whose dividend preference is reduced or abolished by merger (see MBCA § 13.02(a)(1)), though apparently not to such a shareholder whose preference is reduced by charter amendment.

Quiz Yourself on
MERGERS AND ACQUISITIONS *(RECAPITALIZATIONS — HURTING THE PREFERRED SHAREHOLDERS)*

91. Moby Dick Cruise Lines, Inc. — "Have a whale of a time with us" — has two classes of stock: preferred and common. It has 10,000 shares of nonvoting preferred outstanding and 40,000 shares of common. In order to raise funds, Moby Dick's board votes to authorize a new class of preferred shares with cumulative dividends of $5 a year. The existing preferred shares are noncumulative. At a valid shareholders' meeting, 30,000 of the common shares and 2,000 of the preferred shares are voted in favor of the amendment, and 5,000 of the common shares and 1,500 of the preferred shares voted against. (There were no abstentions.) The applicable statute and the corporation's charter, as a general principle, allow charter amendments based on a simple majority. The charter is silent about what constitutes a quorum.

(a) Assume that because the new class would have rights superior to the preferred shares, a state statute gives the preferred shareholders the right to vote separately on the issue. Under the majority approach, has the amendment been approved? ________________

(b) Under the MBCA, has the amendment been approved? ________________

Answer

91. (a) No, because it didn't receive a majority vote of the preferred shares. The issue here is the percentage by which nonvoting shares must approve an amendment to the articles when they are entitled to vote on such an amendment. The majority rule is that, if a class of nonvoting stock is entitled to vote on an amendment (as is the case here), a *majority of that class* must approve the amendment. [416] Here, although a majority of the *total* outstanding shares approved the amendment — 32,000 out of 50,000 — only 20% of the outstanding preferred shares approved it (2,000 out of 10,000). As a result, the preferred shares as a class didn't approve the amendment. Thus, the amendment has not been adopted.

(b) No, because although a majority of those preferred's voting voted "yes," no quorum of the preferreds was present. Under MBCA § 10.04(a)(5), holders of a class of stock have the right to vote as a separate voting group on a change to the articles of incorporation if the change would "create a new class of shares having rights or preferences with respect to distributions or to dissolution that are prior or superior to the shares of the class." [416] The proposed change here, by creating the new class of cumulative-preferred shares, would create a class that is superior to the non-cumulative preferred with respect to the payment of distributions (since dividends are a form of distributions). Therefore, § 10.04(a)(5) gives the existing preferreds the right to vote as a separate group. Now, MBCA § 7.25(c) says that when a separate voting group votes, the measure passes if a majority of those voting in the group vote for the measure. However, that is true *only if a quorum of that voting quorum* — that is, a majority of the votes in that voting group — *is present.* See MBCA § 7.25(a). Under § 7.25(a), second sent., a quorum of a voting group consists of a majority of the shares outstanding of that voting group, assuming that the charter does not provide otherwise (and the facts tell us that the charter here does not provide otherwise). Therefore, for the quorum requirement to be satisfied, 5,001 shares of preferred must have been "present" (i.e., voting for or against or abstaining). Since only 3,500 voted or abstained, no quorum was present. Consequently, the fact that a majority of those preferreds voting voted "yes" is irrelevant — the preferreds didn't validly give their approval, and without their separate approval the measure couldn't pass.

IV. FREEZEOUTS

A. Meaning of "freezeout": A ***"freezeout"*** is a transaction in which those in control of a corporation ***eliminate the equity ownership*** of the non-controlling stockholders. Clark, p. 499. In other words, the insiders somehow force the outsiders to ***sell their shares***, or the insiders find some other way of eliminating the outsiders as common shareholders. The net result of a freezeout is that the controlling shareholders go from mere control to ***exclusive ownership*** of the corporation.

1. Distinguished from "squeezeout": Generally, the term "freezeout" is used to describe only those techniques whereby the controlling shareholders ***legally compel*** the non-controlling holders to give up their common stock ownership. The related term ***"squeezeout,"*** by contrast, is usually used to describe methods that do not legally compel the outsiders to give up their shares, but in a practical sense coerce them into doing so. Squeezeouts are especially common in the close corporation context. For instance, the majority owners of a closely-held corporation might stop paying dividends in order to "soften up" a minority holder who needs the dividends to live on, thereby encouraging him to sell his stock back to the corporation. A minority holder's salary might be cut off for similar reasons. In general, we will be talking in this section about "freezeouts" rather than "squeezeouts"; but see the brief discussion of "squeezeouts" in our treatment of the close corporation context, *infra*, p. 428.

B. Various contexts: There are three common ***contexts*** in which a freezeout is likely to occur: (1) as the second step of a two-step acquisition transaction; (2) where two long-term affiliates merge; and (3) when a company "goes private." See generally Clark, pp. 516-17.

1. Two-step acquisition: First, recall the ***two-step acquisition***, in which one company acquires another previously-unrelated one in a two-stage transaction. (See *supra*, p. 410.) For instance, Big Corp acquires Little Corp in two steps: (1) Big Corp buys most of the shares of Little Corp in a tender offer from the individual Little Corp shareholders; and (2) in a second step, Big Corp causes Little Corp to merge into Big Corp.

a. Where "freezeout" comes in: We already considered the general danger of unfairness in two-step transactions *supra*, p. 410. There, however, we assumed that the target's minority stockholders were not disinvested as the result of the second-step merger, but were instead given shares in the acquirer, so that the only big questions were first, whether the minority received enough information about the acquirer's finances (relevant since they would be receiving acquirer stock) and second, whether they received a fair number of shares. The freezeout transaction, by contrast, is one in which the subsidiary's minority shareholders are ***entirely disinvested*** during the second step. Typically, the way this is brought about is that these minority holders are required to take ***cash*** rather than acquire stock in return for their interest in the target — this is usually done by the so-called "cash-out merger," described *infra*, p. 420.

2. **Merger of long-term affiliates:** The second context is the ***merger of long-term affiliates***. Here, one corporation has had a controlling but not sole interest in another corporation for a long time, and now decides to eliminate the minority interest in the latter. This transaction is one of a class that we called "parent-subsidiary mergers" and analyzed *supra*, p. 411. But again, we assumed there that the minority holders in the subsidiary would be given stock in the parent as part of the merger, and the only issues were proper disclosure and appropriate number of shares. The freezeout, by contrast, involves cashing out the minority stockholders: they are given cash rather than shares in the parent company, usually through a cash-out merger.

3. **"Going private":** Finally, we have the ***"going private"*** transaction. Here, the insiders (often but not always controlling shareholders) change a publicly held corporation into a closely held one. More specifically, the insiders cause the corporation (or at least its underlying business) to cease to be registered under the Securities Exchange Act of 1934, to no longer be listed on a stock exchange, and/or to no longer be actively traded over-the-counter. Clark, p. 500.

   a. **Relation to freeze-out:** Not all going-private transactions are "freezeouts," in the sense of a transaction in which the non-controlling shareholders are legally compelled to disinvest. However, going-private transactions often involve either a freezeout or a squeezeout. Furthermore, whereas two-step acquisition transactions and long-term-affiliate mergers often have a bona fide business purpose (the elimination of a parent-subsidiary relationship that may raise difficult problems of fiduciary responsibility between parent and subsidiary), the going-private transaction usually has ***no*** independent business purpose, and merely reflects a desire on the part of those controlling the transaction to eliminate public ownership. Therefore, courts will probably scrutinize a freezeout in the going-private context even more closely than in the two-step and long-term-affiliate-merger context.

4. **General rule:** The formal legal rules for evaluating freezeouts are pretty much the same for all three contexts listed above. Generally, the court will:

   (1) try to assure itself that the transaction is basically ***fair***, and

   (2) scrutinize the transaction somewhat more ***closely*** than where the minority stockholders are not being cashed out (as in a merger where the minority holders get stock in a new entity).

   These rules are discussed more extensively, *infra*, p. 424. However, as noted, courts give extra scrutiny to transactions that seem to have no purpose other than the elimination of minority public stockholders, and a going-private transaction is more likely to fall into this category than are the other two types of transactions.

C. **Various techniques:** How, then, can a freezeout be accomplished? Several techniques are used today.

1. **Cash-out mergers:** First is the simple ***"cash-out"*** merger. Here, the insider causes the corporation to merge into a well-funded shell, and the minority holders are simply paid cash in exchange for their shares, in an amount determined by the insiders.

Example: Public Corp is controlled by Shark, who owns 70% of its stock. Shark forms Private Corp, a corporation that has no assets, of which he is sole shareholder. Assume that the value of Public Corp is $1 million. Shark contributes $1 million to Private Corp's capital (perhaps raising this money in part by pledging his Public Corp shares in return for a $700,000 bank loan). Let's assume that Shark has the benefit of a modern statute allowing "cash out" mergers (e.g., MBCA § 11.02(c)(3), allowing a merger that will result in "converting the shares of [the disappearing] corporation into . . . cash [or] other property . . . ."). Shark causes both Public Corp and Private Corp to agree to a plan of merger whereby each of Public's one million shares will be exchanged in the merger for $1 in cash. The 30% minority holders will be completely eliminated by the $300,000 cash payment, and Shark will receive $700,000 that he can use to repay the bank debt that funded Private Corp in the first place.

a. **Common method:** This straightforward cash-out merger is probably the most common method of freezeout today. Of course, if the transaction is seen by a court as being unfair or for an improper purpose, the court may strike it down; but most courts do not have an objection to this cash-out merger structure *per se*.

2. **Short-form merger:** Insiders may also be able to use the ***short-form*** merger statute. Remember that where one corporation owns a large percentage (usually 90% or more) of another's stock, the "subsidiary" may be merged into the "parent" without vote of the minority stockholders. Since short-form merger statutes today allow the minority to be paid off in cash as well as in stock (see, e.g., MBCA § 11.05(c), which treats short-form mergers like any other merger for all purposes except board and shareholder approval, and § 11.02(c)(3), allowing payment to holders for any merger to be in cash.)

Example: Private Corp, solely owned by Shark, has owned 92% of Public Corp stock for some time. Shark decides that he would now like to get rid of the public minority stockholders in Public Corp. Using a short-form merger statute like MBCA § 11.04, he causes the board of directors of Private to agree to merge Public into Private. The plan calls for the 8% minority holders of Public to receive $1 in cash for each Public Corp share they own.

At the end of the transaction, Private Corp will have had to pay out 8% of Public's value to the Public minority shareholders, but Public's business will now be owned directly and solely by Private, and there will be no more minority shareholders to worry about.

a. **Advantage:** By use of the short-form merger statute rather than the long-form one, Shark avoids the necessity of having to go through the motions of getting approval by the Public Corp shareholders.

b. **Formation of new holding corporation:** Also, observe that even if Shark did not already hold his Public Corp shares in Private Corp, he could form a new corporation (let's call it Holding Corp), contribute his Public Corp shares to Holding Corp in return for all of Holding Corp's shares, and then use the short-form merger statute to merge Public into Holding. See Clark, p. 502. However, where Holding Corp is formed expressly for the purpose of carrying out a short-form merger (as opposed to the situation in our prior example, where Private Corp had held the shares for a substantial time, and was thus not formed solely to facilitate a short-form merger), a court is more likely to strike down the transaction. For instance, courts that follow the rule that a freezeout must have an "independent business purpose" (see *infra*, p. 427) might well conclude that forming Holding Corp solely to carry out the merger violates this rule.

3. **Reverse stock splits:** Finally, the insiders might eliminate the outsiders by use of a ***reverse stock split***. Such freezeouts take advantage of the fact that most corporation statutes allow a corporation to compel owners of ***fractional shares*** to exchange their shares for cash, so as to ease the corporation's administrative burdens.

   Example: Shark owns 80,000 of the 100,000 total shares outstanding of Public Corp. Of the 20,000 shares that Shark does not own, no single investor owns more than 500. Shark causes Public to enact a 600:1 reverse stock split (i.e., each 600 shares are exchanged for one new share). All shareholders except for Shark, since they own less than 600 shares, will receive a "fractional" share as the result of the reverse split. Then, using a statutory provision allowing for payment of cash in lieu of fractional shares (e.g., MBCA § 6.04(a)(1), which allows a corporation to "pay in money the value of fractions of a share"), Shark pays all the other stockholders cash at the rate of $10 per pre-split share for each of their old shares, rather than giving them fractional post-split shares. At the end of the day, Shark is the only person who continues to hold stock in Public Corp.

   a. **Sometimes attacked:** Courts have disagreed about whether reverse-split statutes may be used for the clear purpose of eliminating minority stockholders. See C&E, pp. 1208-09.

D. **What's wrong with freezeouts:** What's wrong with freezeouts anyway? Obviously, the frozen-out minority holders should be entitled to a ***fair price*** for their shares — but that entitlement is no different from their entitlement to a fair price when they are being given stock in the surviving corporation of a merger rather than being frozen out. So the question is, assuming that the minority holders are receiving a fair price, are they really harmed in a way that should lead the court to give stricter scrutiny to freezeout transactions than to other types of mergers where there is a risk of self-dealing? The minority holders seem to have especially little to complain about where the price they are paid is ***higher than the market price*** that obtained just before the freezeout was announced.

1. **Possible harms:** Nonetheless, the minority holders may suffer some significant harms even though they are paid a "fair" or even "premium" price (measured by reference to the previous market price).

   a. **Taxes:** For instance, the minority holders are forced to ***pay capital gains taxes***, which they would not have to pay if there were either no transaction or a conventional tax-free reorganization (see *supra*, p. 383).

   b. **Transaction costs:** Similarly, the outsiders will have to ***reinvest*** their proceeds, and will incur transaction costs (e.g., commissions) in doing so.

   c. **"Fairness" hard to measure:** Additionally, what appears to be a "fair" price (measured by reference to the earlier market price, or even by reference to recent earnings, net asset values, etc.) may in fact be an unfair price. After all, it is the insiders who are choosing *when* to launch the freezeout: they will be most likely to do this at a time when the market price and the recent earnings performance give an unfairly low indication of the company's true value. See also Clark, pp. 504-09.

2. **Possible benefits:** On the other hand, there may be some aggregate economic benefits to freezeouts as well.

   a. **Long-term affiliates merge:** For instance, when two long-term affiliates merge, eliminating the subsidiary's minority public shareholders, there may be significant gains in efficiency. For example, the subsidiary corporation no longer needs to comply with securities-law reporting requirements separately from the parent, and the parent no longer has to worry about instituting procedural safeguards to ensure that the public shareholders of the subsidiary are being treated fairly whenever the parent deals with the subsidiary. (See *supra*, p. 244.)

   b. **Going private:** Where the freeze-out has the result of taking the company private, there may be additional gains: for instance, the company may be able to be more generous in giving its stock to its key employees. Similarly, it may be better able to engage in long-term planning instead of having to manage its earnings quarter-by-quarter, as many publicly held companies feel they must do. See Clark, pp. 510-12.

E. **Rules of law on freezeouts:** In any event, most courts seem to ***scrutinize*** freezeout transactions fairly ***closely***, on the assumption that the minority outsider shareholders need to be aggressively protected against possible (maybe even likely) self-dealing by the insiders. Most of the important limits on freezeouts come from state rather than federal law, but we must first briefly examine the federal law in this area before getting to state law.

F. **Federal law:** A federal-law attack on a freezeout would be most likely to be based upon an alleged violation of SEC Rule 10b-5 (*supra*, p. 262). Alternatively, it might be based upon SEC Rule 13e-3, which deals specifically with going-private transactions.

1. **10b-5:** The probability of a successful Rule 10b-5 action by a shareholder who opposes a freezeout is likely to depend mostly on whether there has been ***full disclosure*** by the insiders.

   a. **Full disclosure:** If there *has* been full disclosure, then the plaintiff is unlikely to convince the court that 10b-5 has been violated, no matter how "unfair" the freezeout may seem to the court, and even no matter how great the insiders' deviation from ordinary fiduciary principles may have been. The reason for this is that 10b-5 bans only conduct that is "deceptive" or "manipulative," not conduct that is unfair or a violation of fiduciary duty.

   b. **Without full disclosure:** Now, however, suppose that the insiders, when they issued various disclosures required by federal law to carry out the freezeout (e.g., proxy statements, tender offer documents, etc.), ***concealed*** or ***misrepresented*** material facts about the transaction. If full disclosure would have given the plaintiff shareholders a good chance to attack the freezeout ***under state law***, a federal court may well hold that the failure to disclose was "material" and "deceptive," and thus violated Rule 10b-5. See, e.g., *Goldberg v. Meridor*, 567 F.2d 209 (2d Cir. 1977), also discussed *supra*, p. 299.

2. **SEC Rule 13e-3:** SEC Rule 10b-5 is a general anti-fraud provision, which itself imposes no affirmative disclosure obligations. Because the SEC felt that outside stockholders in going-private transactions were often not furnished adequate information, the commission adopted in 1979 a special rule, Rule 13e-3, which specifically requires ***extensive disclosure*** by the insiders when they ***propose a going-private transaction.***

   a. **Transactions covered by the rule:** Rule 13e-3 covers any transaction in which a corporation's stock will no longer be registered under the 1934 act (i.e., will no longer be held by 300 or more people, and thus will generally not have to comply with federal securities law disclosure requirements). It also applies to any transaction whereby the company will be ***delisted*** from a national securities exchange, or will be removed from the NASDAQ over-the-counter computer system. The rule applies not only to pure "going private" transactions (in which the entire business disappears from both direct and indirect public ownership) but also to many mergers of long-term affiliates (e.g., a subsidiary merges into its publicly held parent).

   b. **Disclosure required:** The insiders are required to disclose some things that they would often rather not disclose, including: (1) the ***purpose*** of the transaction; (2) the ***reason*** for the ***particular structure*** they have chosen for the transaction; (3) "a reasonably detailed discussion of the ***benefits*** and ***detriments*** of the . . . transaction to the . . . unaffiliated security holders" (see Sched. 13E-3, Item 7(d)(2)); and (4) "whether [they] reasonably believe . . . that the . . . transaction is ***fair*** or ***unfair*** to unaffiliated security holders" (see Sched. 13E-3, Item 8(a)).

      i. **Little effect:** Rule 13e-3 seems to have had little effect on either the structure of going-private transactions or on the case law in the going-private area. Clark, p. 524.

G. **State law:** The real guts of any successful attack on a freezeout transaction will probably derive from ***state*** rather than federal law. Nearly any freezeout transaction requires the insiders to be on ***both sides of the transaction*** (e.g., the insiders probably control the corporation's board of directors and are instrumental in having the board approve the transaction, but they also stand to benefit if the transaction occurs.) Therefore, the courts will give ***close scrutiny*** to the ***fairness*** of the transaction.

1. **General approach:** Most states require a freezeout transaction to meet at least the first, and possibly the second, of the following tests:

   (1) the transaction must be ***basically fair***, taken in its entirety, to the outsider/minority shareholders; and

   (2) the transaction must be undertaken for some ***valid business purpose***.

   Let's consider each of these tests in turn.

2. **Intrinsic fairness test:** Virtually all courts will carefully scrutinize the transaction to make sure that it is ***basically or intrinsically fair*** to the outsider/minority stockholders. There seem to be three aspects of "fairness" which must be established: (1) a fair ***price***; (2) fair ***procedures*** under which the corporation's board decided to approve the transaction; and (3) adequate ***disclosure*** to the outsider shareholders concerning the transaction. If any of these components is lacking, the court is likely to find the transaction unfair, and either

enjoin it or at least award damages to the minority plaintiffs in an amount sufficient to bring them up to the equivalent of a fair price.

3. ***Weinberger* case:** The leading case on what constitutes basic fairness in a freezeout transaction is a Delaware case, ***Weinberger v. UOP, Inc.***, 457 A.2d 701 (Del. 1983).

   a. **Deal proposed:** *Weinberger* fell into the "long-term merger of affiliates" category (see *supra*, p. 420). Signal Corp. owned 50.5% of UOP Corp., with the balance owned by public shareholders. Four key directors of UOP were also directors of Signal (and apparently owed their primary loyalty to Signal). Two of these directors prepared a feasibility study, which concluded that anything up to $24 per share would be a fair price for Signal to acquire the balance of the UOP shares. But Signal eventually offered to buy out the UOP minority holders for just $21 per share. This price was based upon a hurriedly-prepared fairness opinion by UOP's investment bankers. UOP's board approved the $21 price, but there was never any real negotiation between Signal and UOP on this price, and the non-Signal-affiliated UOP directors were never shown or told about the feasibility study indicating $24 as a fair price.

   b. **Deal goes through:** The acquisition by Signal of the non-Signal-owned shares at $21 (by means of a cash-out merger of UOP into Signal) was approved by a majority of UOP's stockholders, including a bare majority of the minority UOP stockholders. The merger was consummated, and some minority UOP stockholders who opposed the transaction (or at least the price paid by Signal for the shares) brought a class action for damages based on the transaction's alleged unfairness.

   c. **Not a fair transaction:** The Delaware Supreme Court concluded that the transaction did ***not*** meet the requirement of ***"entire fairness."***

      i. **Procedural fairness:** As to "procedural" fairness, the transaction failed miserably. Signal never really ***negotiated*** with UOP's board as to the price; it basically informed the UOP board that it would pay $21, and that was the end of the price discussions. Even more troublesome, Signal used confidential UOP data to prepare the feasibility study that showed $24 would be a fair price, yet never even disclosed to the non-Signal-affiliated UOP directors that this feasibility study existed or that the study had concluded that $24 would be a fair price. Finally, the only work done on behalf of UOP to ascertain the fairness of the $21 price — the investment banker's fairness letter — was hurriedly, and presumably not very carefully, prepared. In summary, the procedures used were not ones to assure that the UOP board's approval of the transaction would be made in a way that would protect the UOP minority shareholders.

      ii. **Fairness of price:** Similarly, the ***"fair price"*** aspect of fairness was not satisfied — the feasibility study itself demonstrated that a fair price would be closer to $24 than to $21 (even though UOP's market price at the time the merger was announced was only $14.50).

      iii. **Disclosure:** Finally, Signal and UOP did not make ***fair disclosure*** to UOP's minority public stockholders. For instance, the documents describing the merger, sent to the shareholders as part of the approval process, mentioned the investment banker's fairness opinion, but did not disclose the hurried manner in which this was prepared. Even worse, the minority stockholders were never told that Signal had prepared a feasibility study showing $24 to be a fair price.

d. Independent committee to negotiate: *Weinberger* makes it clear that one of the best steps insiders can take to insulate the transaction from subsequent attack is by making sure that a ***special committee*** of ***independent directors*** is appointed to negotiate the transaction. Thus the *Weinberger* court noted that had UOP appointed the non-Signal-affiliated directors to a special committee to negotiate with Signal at arm's length, "the result here could have been entirely different. . . ." *Weinberger*, n. 7. The court went on to say that "[p]articularly in a parent-subsidiary context, a showing that the action taken was as though each of the contending parties ***had in fact exerted its bargaining power*** against the other at ***arm's length*** is ***strong evidence*** that the transaction meets the test of fairness."

4. Actual economic power required: If the parent wants the "innoculation" benefits of having an independent committee review the transaction for fairness, the committee must have the ***practical economic power*** (not just the bare legal right) to ***say "no"*** to the proposed freeze-out. ***Kahn v. Lynch Communication Systems, Inc.***, 638 A.2d 1110 (Del. 1994).

Example: Alcatel owns 43% of Lynch Corp. Under a pre-existing supermajority provision in Lynch's charter, 80% of Lynch's shareholders must approve any business combination (giving Alcatel an effective veto). Lynch's management proposes to acquire Telco, but Alcatel vetoes this transaction, and instead proposes to buy the 57% of Lynch that it doesn't already own. A committee of independent Lynch directors is formed. Alcatel makes a final offer of $15.50 to the committee. The committee believes that this price is inadequate, but Alcatel says that it will proceed with an unfriendly tender offer at an even lower price if the committee does not approve the $15.50 transaction. The committee realizes that it has no real bargaining power, and therefore reluctantly approves the transaction, which occurs. A shareholder suit then seeks to set the transaction aside. Alcatel claims that because the independent committee (and a majority of the minority holders) approved the transaction, the burden of showing unfairness should be shifted to the plaintiffs.

Held, for the Ps. "[U]nless the controlling or dominating shareholder can demonstrate that it has not only formed an independent committee but also replicated a process 'as though each of the contending parties had ***in fact exerted its bargaining power at arm's length***,' the burden of proving entire fairness will not shift." Here, no such arms' length negotiation took place, because the independent committee's ability to "say no" was compromised by Alcatel's ability to veto any other transaction and its threat to launch a hostile tender at a lower price. Therefore, the burden of showing "entire fairness" remains on Alcatel. *Kahn v. Lynch Communication Systems, Inc.*, *supra.*

5. Summary of Delaware law on freezeouts: In light of *Weinberger* and later cases decided under it, here's a summary of Delaware law on some important aspects of freezeouts:

a. "Entire fairness" rule: A freezeout transaction, as well as any other transaction in which insiders are on both sides of the transaction, will be sustained only if it is

"entirely fair," as measured by fair procedures, fair price, and adequate disclosure. *Weinberger*.

b. Burden of proof: Under some circumstances, the ***burden of proof*** can ***shift*** to the plaintiff to show that the terms of the transaction were ***unfair***. For this burden-shifting to occur, however, all of the three following things must happen:

i. Approval by majority of minority: A ***majority*** of the ***minority*** shareholders must ***vote to approve*** the transaction. *Weinberger*.

ii. Disclosure: The defendants (the insiders trying to sustain the transaction) must carry the burden of showing that they made ***adequate disclosure*** of the transaction. *Weinberger*.

iii. Arms' length process: There must be a ***simulation*** of an ***arms'-length process***, in which ***representatives*** of the minority and the majority negotiate. Usually, this will be by a ***committee of independent directors***, who negotiate with the majority-holder. *Kahn*.

c. Damages: Plaintiff/shareholders attacking the fairness of a freezeout or other merger transaction, even if they win, will normally have to be content with a ***monetary recovery*** equal to what they would have gotten under ***appraisal***. *Weinberger*. This means that the plaintiffs will usually ***not*** be able to get an ***injunction***, and will not be able to recover in a class action for ***all*** the frozen out shareholders (including those who didn't request appraisal). Therefore, a plaintiff will normally have to comply with the appraisal statute (e.g., by giving notice, prior to the merger, that he dissents) before he will even be allowed to attack the transaction on grounds of unfairness.

i. Fraud or overreaching: On the other hand, an injunction and class-action damages *will* apparently still be available if the plaintiffs prove ***fraud***, ***misrepresentation***, or ***"gross and palpable overreaching***." See, e.g., *Rabkin v. Philip A. Hunt Chemical Corp.* 498 A.2d 1099 (Del. 1985) (injunction against freeze-out allowable if P can show "overreaching" by the majority).

6. The "business purpose" test: A number of courts impose an additional requirement (apart from the requirement that the transaction be "entirely fair") when evaluating a freezeout: this is the requirement that the transaction serve a ***"valid business purpose."*** The basic thrust of this requirement is that even if the insiders pay a fair price, ***they cannot put through a transaction whose sole purpose is to eliminate the minority (public) stockholders***. In other words, the transaction must serve some valid corporate purpose ***other than eliminating the minority stockholders***.

a. Delaware adopts, then abandons: For a brief period, from 1977 until 1983, Delaware adopted the "business purpose" requirement. But in *Weinberger*, decided in 1983, the Delaware Supreme Court decided that the business purpose requirement really gave little extra protection to minority shareholders, and should therefore be ***dropped***.

b. Other courts maintain: But other courts have maintained the "business purpose" requirement even after Delaware's abolition of it. New York and Massachusetts are among these states. See, e.g., *Coggins v. New England Patriots Football Club, Inc.*,

492 N.E.2d 1112 (Mass. 1986) ("Because the danger of abuse of fiduciary duty is especially great in a freeze-out merger, the court must be satisfied that the freeze-out was for the advancement of a legitimate corporate purpose.")

7. **Closely-held corporations:** So far, all of the freezeout cases we have considered involved publicly held corporations, in which the public shareholders are frozen out for the benefit of the insider/controlling shareholders. Often, however, freezeouts — and their close cousin, squeezeouts — take place in the ***close corporation*** context. Here, the majority shareholder or group of shareholders forces out the minority holders either (1) through legal compulsion (using techniques like cash-out mergers, just as in the public corporation context) or (2) by making the minority's stock ownership so unrewarding as a practical matter that the minority feels it has no choice but to sell to the controlling holders (e.g., by cutting dividends, by cutting the minority holder's salary if he is an employee of the corporation, or by otherwise taking away the economic rewards of stock ownership). This latter "practical rather than legal compulsion" method is the ***"squeezeout"***.

   a. **Greater damage:** Often, the burden on the frozen-out or squeezed-out holders is ***worse*** in the closely held corporation context. In the public corporation case, a minority holder who is frozen out typically suffers relatively small burdens, so long as he receives a fair price; after all, he can generally reinvest in some other publicly held corporation on at least roughly similar terms. But the damage to the frozen-out or squeezed-out minority holder of a closed corporation will often be much more severe and much harder to redress.

   Example: Private Corp is owned 80% by Shark and 20% by Pitiful, the company's long-time marketing director. The company has historically paid little or no dividends, but has given salaries to Shark and Pitiful that really constitute the distribution of profits not needed by the business (in the ratio of 80% to Shark and 20% to Pitiful, the ratio of stock ownership). Shark then attempts to squeeze out Pitiful by causing the board to approve a very sharp reduction in Pitiful's salary, so that he no longer receives enough in wages to live on. Shark then offers to buy back Pitiful's shares at an amount that would be fair considering the corporation's dividend and earnings history, but that would leave Pitiful in a far worse position than if he simply had his old salary and job back. The injury to Pitiful from this kind of squeezeout is far worse than would be likely to occur to a frozen-out minority stockholder in a public enterprise, since Pitiful is effectively losing his job and livelihood, not just his stock.

   b. **Consequence:** Therefore, some courts seem to ***scrutinize*** freezeouts and squeezeouts in the case of closely held corporations even ***more stringently*** than they do in the public corporation context. For instance, on the facts of the above example, a court might well hold that Shark as a majority stockholder had a fiduciary duty to Pitiful that he breached by the squeezeout; the court might issue an injunction against reduction of Pitiful's salary, or at least award him damages equal in some way to the value of his job. See generally, Clark, pp. 528-30. See also *supra*, p. 161, discussing the growing doctrine that those in control of a close corporation bear a general fiduciary duty to the minority holders (especially *Donahue v. Rodd Electrotype Co., supra*, p. 161).

Quiz Yourself on
MERGERS AND ACQUISITIONS *(FREEZEOUTS)*

92. Big Bad Wolf is the majority shareholder of the publicly-traded Red Riding Hood Grocery Delivery Service, Inc. Wolf doesn't want to share any of the business with the company's minority shareholders. As a result, at a properly-convened shareholders' meeting, he votes to sell all of Red Riding Hood's assets to another of his businesses, the Grandma Costume Company, at a fair price in an all-cash transaction. In documents sent to holders before this vote, Wolf makes full disclosure to the other holders about the value of the business and the nature of the proposed transaction. The founder of the company — Red R. Hood herself — who is now only a minority shareholder, opposes the transaction, because she thinks the delivery business will continue to grow and she doesn't want to be cashed out. In fact, nearly all of the holders apart from Wolf vote against the transaction, because they feel the same way as Red does. But because Wolf holds a majority and votes in favor of the transaction, it's approved. The sale of assets takes place, and Red is left with cash for her shares and no part of the business.

(a) If Red R. Hood sues in federal court to unwind the transaction or for damages, on the theory that Wolf unfairly eliminated all other holders from the ownership of the business, is Red likely to get relief?

____

(b) If Red sues in state court for an unwinding or for damages, on the same theory of unfairness, is she likely to get relief? ________________

Answer

92. (a) No. Federal laws governing takeovers and proxy solicitations essentially protect only against fraud and inadequate disclosure, not against substantive unfairness. [423] Thus If Wolf had engaged in deceptive conduct, Red could have challenged the freezeout under Rule 10b-5, or under the proxy solicitation anti-fraud rules. But since Red's claim is merely that she's been unfairly excluded from the business, federal law gives her no remedy.

(b) It depends on the state. Some states follow the Delaware approach, and require that a freezeout — that is, any transaction cutting out minority shareholders — need only meet the "entire fairness" test. [426] Here, the fact that Red got a fair price for her shares, after adequate disclosure, probably makes the transaction "entirely fair" to her. Other states (e.g., New York), however, require — in addition to fairness — a valid "business purpose" for a corporate freezeout. [427] Courts following this latter approach typically hold that a majority holder's mere desire to eliminate minority holders is not a valid "business purpose." In such a court, therefore, Red might well succeed either in getting the transaction unwound or at least in getting money damages from Wolf.

V. TENDER OFFERS — GENERALLY

A. Tender offers generally: For the rest of this chapter, we will be concentrating on ***tender offers***, especially a form of tender offer known as a "hostile takeover bid."

1. **What is a tender offer:** A tender offer is "an offer to stockholders of a ***publicly owned corporation*** to ***exchange their shares for cash or securities*** at a price above the quoted market price." S,S,B&W, p. 1174.

2. **Used in hostile takeovers:** Tender offers, especially ***cash*** tender offers, have become much more popular in recent decades. The principal reason is that the cash tender offer is the best way to successfully engineer a ***"hostile takeover."*** A "hostile takeover" is the acquisition of a publicly held company (the "target") over the opposition of the target's management.

   a. **Why tender offers work:** Virtually all of the other methods of acquiring control of a publicly held company require the ***consent*** of the ***board*** and ***management*** of the target. For instance, conventional mergers and asset sales (*supra*, p. 360 and p. 369), which can often be used in "friendly" acquisitions, will not work as hostile takeover devices because these methods require the approval of the target's board of directors. A cash tender offer, by contrast, need not be approved by the target's board to be successful. Instead, the bidder is making an offer to each of the individual stockholders, to buy their shares at the stated price — if a majority of the stockholders "tender" (i.e., sell to the bidder on the proposed terms), the bidder can effectively take control of the target even over the most devout opposition by the target's management and/or board.

3. **Analysis of hostile takeovers:** Therefore, our study of tender offers is really mostly the study of hostile takeover attempts. We will be focusing principally upon two areas: (1) procedures that the bidder must follow, and consequences if he doesn't do so; and (2) defensive maneuvers that the target's management may adopt, and judicial review of those defenses.

B. **How tender offers work:** Let's begin with a short overview of the entire tender offer process:

1. **Selecting target:** First, the bidder ***selects a target***. By definition, this target will always be publicly held. It may or may not be in the same industry as the bidder (assuming that the bidder is a corporation with a business at all, as opposed to an individual corporate "raider"). Generally, the bidder will select as the target a company that the bidder considers to be ***"undervalued,"*** i.e., a company whose "real" value is not currently reflected in the market price of the target's stock.

2. **Pre-offer transactions:** Once the bidder has selected a target, the bidder usually does not rush right out and announce the takeover. Instead, the bidder will often secretly ***purchase a small percentage*** of the target's shares before announcing the tender offer.

   a. **Advantage:** The bidder gets two advantages from this pre-announcement purchasing activity: (1) it will probably be able to buy these initial shares at a price that is lower than the eventual tender-offer price (since the shares have not yet run up in price due to any announcement); and (2) if the target defeats the takeover attempt or if a "white knight" (see *infra*, p. 434) comes along to buy the target at a higher price, the bidder will at least recoup some of its costs and perhaps make some money because it will make a profit on these initial purchases. S,S,B&W, p. 1177.

b. **Limits:** However, there are two important ***limits*** on the bidder's ability to load up on the target's shares before announcing the takeover. First, once the bidder acquires 5% of the target's shares, it will have to make a filing to that effect with the SEC under § 13(d) of the Securities Exchange Act of 1934 (discussed *infra*, p. 438). The bidder will normally have to declare its intention to acquire control in that filing, and the price will immediately run up. Second, the Hart-Scott-Rodino Antitrust Improvements Act will often apply, and will therefore prevent the bidder from immediately buying more than $15 million or 15% of the target's common stock. See *infra*, p. 442.

3. **Financing:** Still before it has made any announcement, the bidder will arrange its ***financing***. Occasionally, it will be able to handle the transaction out of its own assets. Much more often, however, it will need some kind of outside financing. Often, this will be a combination of bank loans and "junk bonds" (see *infra*, p. 434). Sometimes, the bidder's investment bankers will make a "bridge loan" allowing the bidder to complete the purchase, with the expectation that this bridge loan will be repaid from the proceeds of a subsequent junk bond offering.

   a. **Use of shell corporation:** Generally, the bidder will form a ***shell corporation*** to do the actual acquisition. This shell corporation will have no assets or ongoing business, except that at the last moment it will receive from the bidder the funds needed to carry out the share purchase. Once the shell company has acquired whatever shares it will acquire under the takeover (generally at least a majority of the target's outstanding shares), the shell company is ***merged into*** the target.

   Example: Raider, an individual, wants to take over Target Corp. He forms a shell corporation, Target Acquisition Corp ("TAC"), and has TAC make a tender offer for all of Target's outstanding shares, at a price of $20 per share (at a time when Target's shares sell for $12 on the open market). 95% of Target's shareholders tender their shares into the offer. TAC buys all of the shares, using a combination of bank loans and junk bonds (bought by insurance companies, high-yield bond fund managers, and other institutions). Once TAC owns 95% of Target's shares, it uses statutory merger provisions to merge itself into Target Corp. TAC therefore disappears, and Raider (owner of all of TAC's shares) becomes the owner of a 95% stock interest in Target. By virtue of the merger, Target Corp takes over (by operation of law) all of the obligations of TAC, including the bank loans and junk bonds. These bank loans and junk bonds are now therefore secured by a real business and real assets, namely the business and assets of Target Corp. See S,S,B&W, p. 1176.

   b. **Self-financing acquisition:** Observe that a clever bidder may sometimes be able to have the target company essentially ***pay for its own takeover***. That is, the bank debt and junk bonds needed to consummate the takeover will eventually be secured by the target's own assets (as in the above example), and the cash needed to pay off these loans and bonds will often be generated mostly or completely by the earnings of the target company itself. Thus in the above example, if Raider has been shrewd, Target will earn enough money to pay off the bank loans incurred and junk bonds issued to finance the takeover, and Raider will end up owning Target Corp without having used or placed at risk much if any of his own money.

i. **Heavy debt load:** Of course, using the target's assets to secure and pay off the acquisition debt means that the acquisition is ***heavily leveraged***, i.e., that it has debts that are very large relative to its assets and earning power. In terms of our above example, if Raider is to pay a 67% premium over market value ($20 tender offer price versus $12 market price), the price he is paying will probably be so high that virtually all of Target's earnings for some years to come will have to be used to pay off the $20 per share acquisition price. If the economy stumbles into a recession, or Target's own business does not continue to prosper, the risk of default is much higher post-acquisition than it would have been pre-acquisition. This heavy leveraging associated with many hostile takeovers is an important reason why such takeovers are often criticized.

4. **Public announcement:** Let's return to our chronological story. The bidder, once he has selected his target, perhaps made some initial share purchases in the open market, and lined up his financing, now ***publicly announces*** the tender offer.

   a. **Number of shares:** Often, the bidder will tender for (i.e., offer to buy) ***all*** of the target's outstanding shares. Sometimes, however, he will only tender for ***part*** of those shares. The tender offer will almost always be for at least a ***majority*** of the outstanding shares — after all, the bidder is unlikely to pay a premium over the market price in return for merely a minority of the outstanding shares, since the bidder wants to obtain ***control*** of the target in return for his premium price.

   b. **Stated minimum:** Usually, the tender offer will be made ***contingent*** upon the tendering of at least some stated ***minimum number*** of shares. For instance, if the bidder is seeking all of the target's outstanding shares, he may make the tender offer contingent upon receipt of at least 80% of the shares. If the requisite minimum is not tendered, then the bidder is free to return those shares that are tendered, without any obligation to purchase them.

5. **Pressure to tender:** The bidder generally wants to acquire as many shares as he can, at least up to the number being tendered for. Therefore, the bidder will want to ***pressure*** the shareholders as much as he can to induce them to tender to him.

   a. **Threat of back-end merger:** One way in which shareholders are effectively pressured to tender in virtually ***every*** tender offer is because of the implicit ***threat of a back-end merger***. Suppose that Raider has tendered for all of Target's shares. A knowledgeable stockholder in Target should reason as follows: "If I tender, I will receive $20 a share for a stock which the market recently valued at $12 a share. If I do not tender, I will be one of a small percentage (probably 10% or less) of non-tendering stockholders once the tender offer is completed. Under the short-form merger statute of Target's home state, Raider will be able to merge Target into his shell acquisition company (or the other way around), and I will receive whatever price per share Raider sets in the plan of merger. That price may well be less than $20, and if it is, my only remedy will be the costly and probably unsatisfactory one of appraisal proceedings (see *supra*, p. 345). Therefore, I'd better be safe, and tender into the offer, so that I'm sure to receive the $20." For this reason, unless some better offer comes along while Raider's tender offer is still in force, or Target's management makes some very dramatic move that puts cash in shareholders' hands (e.g., a restructuring that pays a large one-time dividend; see *infra*, p. 455), the vast majority of Target's shareholders are likely to tender into Raider's offer even if they disapprove of Raider or of hostile takeovers generally.

6. **Price:** In order to induce a large portion of the target's holders to tender, the bidder must generally offer a ***substantial premium*** over the target's market price.

7. **Function of "arbs":** Shortly after a takeover bid is announced, much of the target's stock ends up in the hands of ***"arbitrageurs"*** or ***"arbs."*** Arbs are professional risk-takers who buy up the target's shares from the public, with the expectation of eventually tendering it to the bidder (or to some as-yet-unannounced higher bidder waiting in the wings) at a profit. Arbs are often criticized as being greedy, evil, and/or operating on illegal inside information. But arbs serve the useful function of allowing an ordinary stockholder in a takeover battle to "lock in his profit" without waiting to see whether the takeover actually succeeds.

8. **End of the game:** Now, the publicly-visible part of the takeover battle begins. The target's management will generally oppose the takeover, by instituting various defensive measures. For instance, the target may seek a ***"white knight,"*** i.e., another bidder who will offer an even higher price, and who (the target's management hopes) will be friendlier to target management than would be the original bidder. Or, the target management may ***restructure*** the target, by taking it private in a management-led leveraged buy-out (*infra*, p. 434), or by borrowing lots of money and paying a large one-time dividend. Or, management may institute a "poison pill," among other defensive measures. (The various defensive tactics commonly used are discussed beginning *infra*, p. 450.)

9. **Final outcome:** There are a number of possible final outcomes to the battle:

   a. **Challenge beat back:** First, the target may (but rarely does) simply ***defeat*** the takeover attempt, i.e., persuade enough shareholders not to tender that the bidder does not receive the number of shares that he has stated to be his minimum for consummation of the offer. In recent years, at least in those situations where the bidder has the funds to consummate the transaction, this kind of outright victory by the target has almost never occurred.

   b. **Some other bidder wins:** Second, the initial bidder may be joined by ***other bidders***, and one of these other bidders may finally win the contest for control by offering the highest price on the best terms, or by waging the most skillful political/legal battle. Sometimes, this winner will be a "white knight" recruited by the target's management; often, it will simply be another unsolicited bidder who comes out of the woodwork.

   c. **Success by original bidder:** Finally, the ***initial bidder*** may ***win*** the contest. He might do so on the terms he originally has proposed. Alternatively, he might ***raise*** his offer one or more times during the battle, and end up with control, but only at a much higher price than he originally bid. The target's management will often consider itself "successful" if it can force or persuade the original bidder to raise its offer in this manner.

      i. **Eventually "friendly":** In fact, in those situations where the original bidder wins the contest, usually the target's management ends up ***approving*** the offer eventually, at the higher price. Thus in a sense, nearly all successful hostile takeovers eventually become ***"friendly"*** ones.

C. Glossary of takeover terms: Here is a brief glossary of takeover terms. (You don't necessarily need to absorb all these definitions at the outset. They're here mainly as a reference tool, and are referred to in the later materials.)

Arbitrageurs or arbs: In the takeover context, these are market professionals who buy up stock in the target after the tender offer has been announced but before it has been consummated. If the takeover goes through (or a higher bidder emerges), the arbs make a profit. If the deal falls apart and the target stock price retreats to its pre-tender offer level, the arbs take the loss.

Auction: A competition among two or more bidders for control of the target. Sometimes the auction occurs spontaneously; at other times, the target's management tries to promote the auction, in order to get the highest price for the target's shareholders (and, perhaps, to end up with a more palatable acquirer than the original bidder would be).

Back-End Merger: The second stage of a two-step acquisition program. In step one, the bidder makes a tender offer (usually a cash one) through a shell corporation, for most or all of the target's shares. If the tender offer is successful and the bidder owns a majority of the shares, it then institutes the Back-End Merger: the shell merges into the target, or the target merges into the shell. Those target shareholders who did not tender, or those shares that were tendered but not bought by the bidder because the tender was a partial one that was oversubscribed, are then eliminated in the merger, in return for either cash or debt securities in the target. Since the bidder's shell corporation has typically taken out bank loans or issued junk bonds to finance the takeover, it is only by this back-end merger that the target's assets and earnings can be used to secure and pay off the loans/bonds. Often, the value of the cash and/or securities paid in the Back-End Merger is less than that paid in the front-end tender offer portion. (This makes the transaction a *Two-Tier Front-Loaded* tender offer, see below.) Second-generation state takeover statutes (see *infra*, p. 448) usually work by placing restrictions on when and under what terms a bidder may carry out the Back-End Merger.

Bidder: The company seeking to acquire control of another company by tender offer. (The company the bidder is trying to acquire is the *Target.*)

Bust-Up Takeover: A takeover that is followed by the bidder's disposition of some or all pieces of the target. For instance, if the target is a conglomerate, the successful bidder might sell off some or all of the operating businesses, each one to the highest bidder, to raise cash to reduce acquisition-related debt.

Crown Jewel Option: The target's "crown jewels" are its most valuable businesses or properties. If the target is desperate to prevent the original bidder from acquiring the company, the target's management may grant a third party (perhaps a *White Knight*, see *infra*) an option to acquire those crown jewels at an attractive price, in order to induce the third party to enter the bidding. Not only does this increase the attractiveness to the third party of making a bid, but it also makes the target less attractive to the original, feared bidder — even if that bidder succeeds with his bid, he will be acquiring a target that no longer controls its most valuable asset. (The crown jewel option is one form of *Lock-Up,* see *infra.*)

Fair-Price Provision: A provision (either imposed by statute or placed in the target's articles of incorporation) requiring that a super majority (usually 80%) of the target's shareholders must approve any *Back-End Merger* (*supra*) with a bidder who at the time of the merger owns some specified percentage (usually 20%) of the target's shares. The shareholder-approval requirement typically does not apply if a majority of the target's board (as the board is constituted prior to the tender offer) approves the offer, or if the bidder pays the same cash price in the *Back-End Merger* as it did in the initial tender offer. The main effect of a fair price provision is to prevent discriminatory *Two-Tier Front-Loaded* tender offers (*infra*). See S,S,B&W, p. 1205. For an example of such a statutory provision, see Maryland Code §§ 3-601 through 603.

Golden Parachute: A contract between a company and its senior executives, providing for very generous payments to be made to the executives in the event the company is taken over and the executives are forced to leave the company. Golden parachutes are usually derided by the outside world as being a waste of shareholders' money, but they may have the benefit of persuading a target's management to stop opposing a hostile takeover and thus allow the target's stockholders to be bought out at a high price.

Greenmail: The payment by a target to a bidder of an above-market price for repurchase of shares in the target owned by the bidder. In return for a chance to sell his shares back to the target at a high price, the bidder usually agrees not to try to take the target over again for some specified period (e.g., 10 years). Arbs and other shareholders in the target hate bidders who take greenmail, because after the greenmail, the market price of the target's stock usually drops far below the greenmail price, since the immediate threat of a takeover (certainly the threat of a takeover by the greenmailing bidder) has disappeared.

In Play: When a company first is perceived to be a target. This may happen either when a takeover bid is publicly announced, or when a person who has been a hostile bidder in the past files a Schedule 13D (*infra*, p. 438) showing that he has acquired 5% or more of the company. When a company is "in play," the arbs assume that it will be acquired by someone, and the only question is by whom.

Junk Bond: A high-interest-bearing bond, usually of relatively low investment quality. In the takeover context, junk bonds are issued by the bidder to help pay for the takeover; the bonds are usually bought by insurance companies, managers of high-yield bond funds, and other institutions who are attracted by the high interest rates that the bonds offer. Interest and principal are repaid (if all goes well) by the earnings of the target, and the bond holders get to look to the target's assets for security.

Leveraged Buy-Out* or *LBO: A corporate acquisition funded by very little equity, and by a very large amount of debt. The debt is secured by the acquired company's assets. The transaction generally takes the company private. Often, the acquirer is the company's management (in which case it is a *Management Buy-Out*, see below). The debt is usually in the form of bank loans, junk bonds, or both. The acquired company's earnings are used to pay off this debt; therefore, if the acquired company does not do well, the company is more likely to become insolvent than if the transaction were not highly leveraged.

Lock-up: An advantage given by the target to one bidder over other present or potential bidders. The purpose is to make it more likely that the favored bidder will win in the auction that may arise, and to discourage other bidders. One form of lock-up is the granting of a *Crown Jewel Option* (see above). Another is the granting to the favored bidder of an option to buy some percentage of the target's stock at a favorable price (e.g., an option to buy 50%, so as to preclude a competing bidder.) Lock-ups are often overturned by courts; see, e.g., *Revlon v. MacAndrews & Forbes, infra,* p. 461.

Management Buy-Out: The acquisition of a company by its own senior management, or the acquisition of an operating subsidiary of a bigger company by that subsidiary's management. Most Management Buy-Outs are also *Leveraged Buy-Outs* (see above).

No-Shop Clause: A provision in a merger agreement between a target and a bidder in which the target (and its board) agree that the board will recommend the merger to shareholders, and will not "shop around" for a more attractive offer. The courts have split on the legality of such clauses, with some courts holding that they are unenforceable because they conflict with the board's duty to get the highest price for shareholders once the company is to be sold. See C&E, p. 1214.

Pac Man Defense: A defense in which the target makes a hostile tender offer for the bidder at the same time the bidder is tendering for the target. It takes its name from the popular video arcade game in which the players devour each other. It is theoretically possible (though it has apparently never happened) for each tender offer to go through, in which case each side controls the other, and both are therefore effectively paralyzed.

Poison Pill: This refers to a variety of provisions that will discourage a hostile takeover by making the target more expensive or less desirable to the bidder. The most common form of poison pill is a "call right." Typically, this right gives shareholders in the target the ability to buy shares in the target at ***half price*** whenever a bidder tenders for or buys more than a certain percentage of the target's stock (usually 20%). Poison pills are generally revocable by the target's board; therefore, they only block hostile, not friendly, takeovers, and their usual function is to pressure the bidder into making a deal with the target's board. Courts often scrutinize poison pills fairly closely, but sometimes sustain them; see, e.g., *Moran v. Household International, Inc.*, *infra*, p. 474, in which the Delaware Supreme Court upheld a poison pill defense. Poison pills are discussed in more detail *infra*, p. 452.

Raider: The pejorative term for *Bidder*.

Restructuring or Recapitalization: In the takeover context, a change of capital structure to defeat a hostile takeover attempt. Most commonly, the target raises money by issuing junk bonds or preferred stock, or by taking out massive bank loans, in order to pay a large one-time special "dividend" to stockholders. If the target is trading at $60 before the bidder emerges, for instance, and the bidder offers $90, the target might pay a one-time dividend of $60, and point out to the shareholders that they will still own a "stub" with a value of more than $30; this lets the target's management argue that the restructuring produces better shareholder value than the hostile bid does.

Shark Repellant: A provision in the target's articles of incorporation or bylaws designed to make hostile takeovers more difficult. *Poison Pills* (*supra*) fall into this class, as do charter amendments requiring a super-majority shareholder vote approving any merger between the target and a large pre-existing stockholder.

Standstill Agreement: A peace agreement between a bidder and a target, whereby the bidder agrees not to try to acquire control of the target or buy additional shares in the target for some specified number of years. Often, the target "buys" the standstill agreement by making *Greenmail* payments (see *supra*).

Stop, Look & Listen Letter: A letter written by the target's management to shareholders after a tender offer has been made, that takes no position about the offer and recommends that the shareholders wait for a later management recommendation before they decide whether to tender.

Target: The company that a bidder is attempting to gain control of by means of a tender offer.

Tender Offer: A public offer made by a bidder to a target's shareholders, in which the bidder offers a substantial premium above market price for most or all of the target's shares.

Two-Tier Front-Loaded Offer: A tender offer that contains two parts. In the first part, the bidder pays a high cash price for most (usually 51%) but not all of the target's stock. In the second, or "back end" step, the bidder acquires the remaining shares in the target by merging the target into itself (or itself into the target), in return for either a lower cash price or debt securities having a value lower than the price paid in the first step. Bidders like the device because it pressures the target's holders to tender into the offer: if they don't, all of their shares will be acquired at the lower back-end price. The device is used less frequently these days, probably because it is so unattractive to the bidder's holders that some better non-front-end-loaded offer is likely to come along.

White Knight: A suitor who is friendly to the target's management, and who at that management's request acquires the target so it won't be acquired by the original unwelcome bidder. Often, the white knight promises to keep the target's existing management in place after the acquisition (whereas the original bidder probably will not).

White Squire: A "friendly escort." At the request of the target's management, the squire buys up a less-than-majority interest in the target (usually 25% or less) so as to help shield the target from a hostile takeover. The use of a white squire is especially common now in Delaware, because any person who holds more than 15% or more of a target's stock can block an acquirer (even one who owns, say, 84% of the target stock) from executing a *Back-End Merger* (see *supra*) with the target. See the discussion of Del. GCL § 203 *infra*, p. 449.

VI. TENDER OFFERS — THE WILLIAMS ACT, AND OTHER FEDERAL REGULATION

A. The Williams Act generally: The federal "Williams Act," enacted in 1968, is a package of amendments to the Securities Exchange Act of 1934. The Act attempts to make takeovers fairer to the target's shareholders, by reducing the pressure upon them to make a quick decision and by ensuring that all shareholders will be treated equally. To understand the Act's provisions, we must first understand something about the evils the Act was designed to eliminate.

1. Pre-Williams-Act takeovers: Before the Williams Act was enacted, stockholders of a company that was the subject of a tender offer were (at least arguably) treated unfairly in two ways:

a. Lack of information: First, they were not given the ***information*** needed to make a rational decision about whether to tender. For instance, the bidder was not required to disclose anything about himself, his finances, or his plans for the company; therefore, the stockholder had no basis for comparing the tender offer price with the probable value of the shares if the holder declined to tender and thus remained invested in the target.

b. Pressure: Second, the bidder could ***unfairly pressure*** the target's stockholders. For instance, the bidder could tender for only ***part*** of the target's shares, and put the offer on a "first come, first served" basis. Holders would feel pressure to tender early, lest they be closed out of the offer, and left with minority shares that could be redeemed by the bidder at a low price in a *Back-End Merger* (see *supra*, p. 434), or otherwise left to the bidder's mercy. Therefore, holders did not have time to consider the offer rationally and deliberately, or to wait for a possible better bid to come along.

2. Brief summary of act: We will be looking at the Williams Act in detail below. For now, let's look at some of the highlights of the Act, which continues to constitute the general federal statutory law governing takeovers:

a. Disclosure for 5% owners: First, the Act requires anyone who purchases more than 5% of the stock of a publicly held company to ***disclose*** that fact promptly to the SEC. This disclosure is required even if the investor has no intention to make a tender offer or otherwise seek control of the company.

b. Tender offers: Second, the Act comprehensively regulates tender offers. In particular:

i. Disclosure rules: The Act requires comprehensive ***disclosure*** by any bidder of the bidder's ***identity, financing, plans*** for the company if the bid is successful, and other information. There are also extensive rules governing management's communications to shareholders about whether they should accept or reject the bid.

ii. Traffic rules: Perhaps the most important part of the Act is its tight limitations on the ***form*** tender offers may take. For instance, stockholders are given extensive rights to ***withdraw*** their shares even after they tender them into the offer; bidders are required to buy up stock from all shareholders equally on a ***"pro rata"*** basis, rather than on a "first come, first served" basis; all stockholders must be offered the ***same price***; and the offer must be left open for a ***minimum time***.

iii. Anti-fraud: Finally, the Act contains several ***anti-fraud*** rules, forbidding manipulation or deception in tender offers, just as SEC Rule 10b-5 (*supra*, p. 262) forbids similar deceptive conduct in connection with the ordinary purchase or sale of securities.

B. Disclosure by 5% owners: First, let's look at the mechanism by which the world can learn that a person has acquired more than 5% of the stock of a publicly held company. Under § 13(d)(1) of the '34 Act, any person who ***"directly or indirectly"*** acquires ***more than 5%*** of ***any class*** of stock in a publicly held corporation must ***file a statement*** on ***SEC Schedule 13D*** disclosing that acquisition.

1. Information disclosed: The filing on Schedule 13D must include more than the mere fact that the investor has acquired a more-than-5% stake. Some of the items that must be disclosed include: (1) the exact number of shares purchased by the person or group doing the filing; (2) the source and amount of the ***funds*** used to make the purchase (including details about who lent the money to the buyer, if part of the purchase price was borrowed); (3) the purchaser's ***purpose*** in buying the shares, including any plans he may have to ***seek control***, to cause a merger to take place, to sell a large part of the company's assets, etc.; and (4) any plans the filer has to take the company ***private.*** See the SEC's instructions for filing Schedule 13D.

2. "Beneficial owner": The ***"beneficial owner"*** of a more-than-5% stake must file. Thus if Ian has either the power to ***vote*** the shares, or to decide whether and when to ***sell*** them, he must file even though the record owner of the shares may be someone else (e.g., his broker). See SEC Rule 13d-3(a). Also, if Ian has an ***option*** to acquire the shares within 60 days, he will be a "beneficial owner" even though he doesn't really own the shares yet. Rule 13d-3(d)(1)(i).

3. When filing is due: The filing must be made ***within 10 days*** following the acquisition. Rule 13d-1(a).

a. 10-day window: Observe that this gives Ian, our hypothetical investor, an attractive ***"10 day window"*** in which to make further purchases of the company's stock before the filing has to be made. Ian theoretically purchases, say, an additional 20% of the company's stock before making the filing, and thus might be able to pay less for that

20% stake than he would have had to pay had the purchase come after his disclosure. The SEC would like to close this window by requiring Ian to file the very next day after crossing the 5% threshold (or at least requiring Ian to refrain from making any more purchases until he has filed), but Congress has not acted on the SEC's request, and the SEC so far has not attempted to make this change by rule-making alone. F,B&H, p. 62.

i. **Hart-Scott-Rodino:** However, a buyer may have to comply with the Hart-Scott-Rodino Antitrust Improvements Act of 1976, in which case the buyer would have to notify the government of his acquisition plans and wait at least 15 days before making purchases. Hart-Scott-Rodino is discussed further *infra*, p. 442.

4. **Additional acquisitions:** Suppose that Ian has owned 6% of Public Corp's stock for some time, and now buys another, say, 4%; must he file a new Schedule 13D? The answer is "yes." In general, anytime someone who is already a 5%-or-more owner acquires ***additional*** stock, he must refile on 13D.

   a. **Limited exception:** However, there is a limited exception to this general requirement that any additional purchase causes a duty to refile: if a person who is already a 5%-or-more owner makes a new purchase which, taken together with all other purchases by the same person during the prior twelve months, does not exceed ***2%***, there is no need to refile. For instance, suppose that Ian bought 12% of Public's common stock in 1995. During 1996, he buys (in the course of several transactions) an additional 2% of the common stock. Since he has not bought more than 2% of Public's stock during any 12-month period since his last filing, he does not have to refile.

5. **Groups:** The duty to file a Schedule 13D clearly applies to an ***individual*** who has bought more than 5% of a company's stock, to a ***corporation*** that has done so, to a ***partnership***, etc. But the duty to file also applies to ***"groups,"*** i.e., ***persons acting in concert.*** See '34 Act, § 13(d)(3). For instance, if Able and Baker agree that each will buy 4% of Public Corp, they are acting in concert and must therefore file a 13D even though neither of them separately owns more than 5% of Public's stock.

6. **Amendment based on change of plans:** Recall that a person who files a 13D must disclose his purpose and plans for the transaction, including, for instance, the fact that he does or does not intend to seek control. Section 13(d)(2) requires a person who has filed to ***amend*** his Schedule 13D if "any material change" occurs in the facts set forth on the initial filing. So if Ian reports in his original filing that he did not intend to seek control, but then decides that he does want to do so, he must re-file to make public his change of heart. (Also, as noted above, if Ian buys more stock, he will have to refile, unless he qualifies under the "2% or less during the past 12 months" exception described above.)

7. **Applies even where no tender offer intended:** Keep in mind that the requirement of filing under § 13(d) is a blanket requirement, that applies ***no matter what the purchaser's intent is.*** Thus even though Ian honestly intends to be a completely passive investor forever, and would never dream of commencing a tender offer, he must still file on Schedule 13D as soon as he buys 5% or more of Public.

   a. **Serious obligation:** Also, don't make the mistake of thinking of the § 13(d) filing requirements as mere technical or ministerial rules of little consequence. For instance, one of the counts on which financier Michael Milken went to jail in the 1980s was for having "parked" securities, by failing to disclose the fact that he was holding stock for third parties.

C. Rules on tender offers: Now, let's turn to the Williams Act's rules governing tender offers.

1. **Disclosure:** First, the '34 Act requires bidders to comply with ***disclosure*** rules that are somewhat similar to § 13(d)'s rules governing more-than-5% owners. Section 14(d)(1) imposes disclosure requirements on any tender offeror who, if his tender offer were successful, would own more than 5% of any class of stock of the target. The disclosure is made on SEC Schedule 14D-1.

   a. **Items disclosed:** As in a 13D Schedule (for more-than-5% owners), the tender offeror must disclose his identity, funding, and purpose. Thus if the offeror plans to sell off major pieces of the target, change the target's board of directors, change the target's dividend policy, take the company private, etc., all of these things must be disclosed on the 14D-1 form. Also, some information is required that is not required on the 13D Schedule, most notably information about the ***financial condition*** of the bidder. For instance, if the bidder proposes to pay part of the purchase price in the form of ***securities*** (e.g., preferred stock, common stock in the bidder, junk bonds, etc.), the bidder's financial condition will clearly be material to a stockholder's decision whether to tender, so the bidder must disclose his/its financial condition in some detail. See Item 9 to instructions for Schedule 14D-1.

   b. **Disseminate to stockholders:** Unlike a Schedule 13D more-than-5%-owner filing, the Schedule 14D-1 tender offer disclosure statement must not only be filed with the SEC, but must also be delivered to the target, to any other bidders, and to any stock exchange where the target's stock is listed. Furthermore, the bidder must make reasonable attempts to ***notify*** all of the target's stockholders about the existence of the tender offer; usually, this can be done in the form of ***newspaper advertisements*** listing the key facts about the tender offer (including price, minimum and maximum shares which will be purchased, the bidder's purpose, etc.). See Rules 14d-4 and 14d-6.

   c. **Solicitation to accept or reject bid:** The terms of the bidder's offer are not the only aspects of the tender offer process that are subject to extensive disclosure requirements. Any communications from either side advising stockholders to ***accept*** or ***reject*** the tender offer are similarly subject to disclosure rules. Thus anyone who solicits or recommends to the target's shareholders that they accept or reject the tender offer must file a separate disclosure statement with the SEC (on Schedule 14D-9), on which the recommender's identity, recommendation, and ***reasons*** for the recommendation are among the items listed. Copies of any written recommendations or solicitations (and even scripts of any oral solicitations) must accompany this filing, so that the SEC can see exactly what is going on.

      i. **Rationale:** These extensive disclosure requirements for the solicitation/recommendation process are consistent with the SEC's overall goal of neither aiding nor impeding tender offers, but rather making sure that full and accurate information is given to the target's shareholders by each side in a takeover battle.

2. **"Traffic" rules:** Entirely apart from the disclosure rules that govern tender offers, § 14(d) and the rules adopted under it actually govern in important ways the ***substance*** of tender offers. The rules do not govern anything so purely substantive as price, the number of shares which will be bought, or other basic aspects of the "deal" being proposed by the bidder. But these rules do govern in very important ways the terms of the deal that the bidder may propose. The main thrust of these rules is to guarantee ***equal treatment*** for all stockholders, and to prevent stockholders from being ***rushed*** or unfairly pressured. These procedural rules have been called ***"traffic rules"*** for tender offers. See Clark, p. 551.

   a. **Withdrawal rights:** The first of these protections is the ***right to change one's mind.*** A shareholder who tenders to a bidder has the right to ***withdraw*** his stock from the tender ***at any time while the offer remains open.*** See Rule 14d-7 (extending the more limited withdrawal rights given in § 14(d)(5) of the '34 Act). If the tender offer is ***extended*** for any reason (e.g., by voluntary act of the bidder, or because the bidder is compelled to extend it, on account of his having changed the price or number of shares he is seeking), the withdrawal rights are similarly extended until the new offer-expiration date.

      i. **Consequence:** One key consequence of this extended withdrawal right is that, from the bidder's perspective, nothing is certain until the offer has expired. For instance, suppose that Shark is tendering for 80% of Little Fish Corp, with the offer set to expire on June 1. Even if by May 27, 90% of the shareholders of Little Fish have tendered to Shark, a new bidder could emerge a day later, make a better bid, and all holders could withdraw their tendered shares from Shark and re-tender them to the new bidder. In tender offers, as in baseball, "It ain't over 'til it's over."

      ii. **Good for management:** As a corollary, the extended withdrawal rights are helpful to the target's management. Until the bidder's tender offer has expired, it's never too late for management to pull a rabbit out of a hat by coming up with a white knight who will make a higher bid, by restructuring, or by doing something else to induce the shareholders who have already tendered to the hostile bidder to withdraw their tendered shares.

   b. **Pro rata rule:** Second, if the bidder offers to buy only a ***portion*** of the outstanding shares of the target, and holders tender more than the number the bidder has offered to buy, the bidder must buy ***in the same proportion from each shareholder***. This is the so-called ***"pro rata rule."*** See '34 Act § 14(d)(6); Rule 14d-8.

      i. **Rationale:** The pro rata rule is perhaps the most important of the traffic rules added by the Williams Act. It prevents the bidder from making a tender offer on a "first come, first served" basis for less than all of the shares, a device that before the enactment of the Williams Act was used to coerce stockholders into tendering immediately and to prevent rival bids from shaping up.

   c. **"Best price" rule:** Often a bidder will set an initial price in a tender offer, and will then ***increase*** that price before the tender offer has expired. Section 14(d)(7) requires the bidder to pay this increased price to ***each*** stockholder whose shares are tendered and bought up, not merely to those who tender after the price increase. This is sometimes called the ***"best price"*** rule, since each tendering holder must be given the "best price" given to any other holder who tenders.

i. **Rationale:** The "best price" rule, like the other traffic rules, is designed to reduce coercion and ensure that all tendering shareholders are treated equally and fairly.

ii. **New tender offer at higher price:** But a clever bidder may be able to circumvent the "best price" rule by waiting until the original tender offer is completed, buying up the tendered shares at the originally-announced price, and only then announcing a ***new*** tender offer at a higher price.

d. **20-day minimum for offer:** The final traffic rule is that a tender offer ***must be kept open for at least 20 business days***. Rule 14e-1(a). Furthermore, if the bidder changes the price or the number of shares he is seeking, he must hold the offer open for ***another 10 days***, even if the original 20-day period was just about to expire. Rule 14e-1(b).

i. **Rationale:** Like the other traffic rules, this one ensures stockholders of enough time to carefully consider whether they want to tender.

3. **General anti-fraud provision:** Apart from the disclosure and "traffic" rules, the federal law governing tender offers includes a general ***anti-fraud*** provision, somewhat similar to Rule 10b-5 (see *supra*, p. 262). Section 14(e) of the '34 Act makes it unlawful, in connection with a tender offer, to: (1) "make any ***untrue statement of a material fact*** or ***omit to state any material fact*** necessary in order to make the statements made, in the light of the circumstances under which they are made, ***not misleading***"; or (2) to "engage in any ***fraudulent, deceptive, or manipulative*** acts or practices. . . ." The SEC is authorized to enact rules to prevent such fraudulent, deceptive, or manipulative acts. (In fact, it is a rule enacted under this section, Rule 14e-1, that requires tender offers to be open for a minimum of 20 business days, and for a minimum of 10 business days following any change in the terms of the offer, as described *supra*.) We will be discussing the § 14(e) anti-fraud provision in greater detail *infra*, p. 446, as part of our treatment of Williams Act litigation.

D. **Hart-Scott-Rodino Act:** So far, all of the federal regulation of tender offers that we have looked at has had as its source the Securities Exchange Act of 1934 and the Rules enacted pursuant to it. But there is another body of law that can have a considerable impact on tender offers: the ***Hart-Scott-Rodino Antitrust Improvements Act of 1976*** ("H-S-R"), 15 U.S.C. § 18a. H-S-R is designed to give federal ***antitrust*** regulators a chance to intervene to stop any corporate acquisition that would raise antitrust problems. H-S-R does not confer on the government any right that it does not otherwise have to stop acquisitions on antitrust grounds; but it does provide for ***notice*** to the government of certain proposed deals, and imposes a ***waiting period*** before the deal can be consummated (during which time the government can decide whether it wants to try to stop the deal on antitrust grounds).

1. **Notice and waiting period:** If a proposed acquisition is covered by H-S-R, the tender offeror (or other acquirer) must notify both the FTC and the Antitrust Division of the Justice Department about the proposed deal. The bidder must then ***wait for 15 days*** before buying any shares for cash under the offer, or for ***30 days*** before buying any shares for securities rather than cash. The notice to the government must include extensive details about the bidder and the target, to enable the government to evaluate the antitrust risk. If

the government needs more information, it can request it, which has the effect of extending the waiting period for another 10 days (for cash purchases) or 20 (for non-cash purchases). Such a request and additional waiting period "often is the kiss of death in a contested tender offer," since other bidders have more time to move in.

2. **Deals to which Act applies:** H-S-R applies, and thus requires notice to the government and the waiting period, only if one party to the transaction has sales or assets of more than $100 million and the other has sales or assets of more than $10 million. Also, it applies only where the bidder would end up with 15% or more of the target's stock, or stock worth more than $15 million. (Regulations under H-S-R narrow the class of transactions covered by H-S-R a little further. See 16 C.F.R. § 802.20.)

E. **Litigation under the Williams Act:** Let us now look in detail at a couple of areas in which the meaning of the federal takeover regulations has been actively litigated:

F. **The disclosure rules of § 13(d):** In connection with the disclosure rules of § 13(d) of the '34 Act, two main issues have been extensively litigated: (1) What is a "group"? and (2) What are the remedies for non-compliance?

1. **What is a "group":** Recall that if two or more persons act together as a ***"group"*** for the purpose of acquiring, holding, or disposing of stock, they must file a Schedule 13D disclosure statement so long as they collectively own more than 5% of a company, even if none of them separately own 5%. The issue is: ***What is a "group"*** for these purposes, and when is it deemed to have been formed?

   a. **No written agreement:** It is clear that a group can be formed ***without a written agreement***. So if Able and Baker orally agree that each will buy 4% of Target's stock, they are a "group" and must file a Schedule 13D. In fact, the existence of a "group" may be proved by ***circumstantial evidence***. For instance, if Able and Baker are brothers, and each of them buys 2% of Target's stock on May 1 and another 2% on May 14, a court might well find this to be adequate circumstantial evidence to establish that they acted as a group, even though there is no direct evidence of an agreement. See Clark, p. 556.

   b. **Sellers:** Also, ***sellers*** can constitute a "group" just as buyers can. For instance, suppose Able and Baker have long held, between them, 40% of Target's stock, and both sit on the board. (Let's assume that each filed an original Schedule 13D years ago, when he acquired his present stake.) Now, Able and Baker, while at a board meeting, get together and decide that they will try to sell their stake in Target (and thus control of Target) to a single purchaser. This agreement to pursue a joint sale makes Able and Baker a "group," and they must therefore file a Schedule 13D. See Clark, p. 557, n. 11. See also SEC Rule 13d-5(b)(1).

2. **Remedies for violation of § 13(d):** Suppose that a person does violate § 13(d), either by failing to file a Schedule 13D at all, or by filing but putting false information on the document. What remedies are available to: (1) the SEC; and (2) private parties?

   a. **SEC:** As to the SEC, the answer is that broad remedies are available. For instance, the SEC can get a judge to order the wrongdoer to comply (i.e., to file a 13D or to correct the previously-filed one). The Commission can also get an injunction against future violations. Clark, p. 558.

b. Private damage actions: But ***private*** actions alleging 13(d) violations are much less likely to succeed.

i. No implied right of action: Courts have decided that there is ***no implied private right of action for damages*** under Section 13(d). Clark, p. 558. This means that neither continuing shareholders nor issuers will have standing to sue for a 13(d) violation.

G. Meaning of "tender offer": A second major area of Williams Act litigation has concerned the meaning of the phrase ***"tender offer."*** § 14 of the '34 Act, and the many SEC regulations under it, impose all kinds of requirements that apply to "tender offers." Yet, perhaps surprisingly, neither federal statutes nor rules actually define "tender offer." Therefore, it has been up to the courts to determine, as best they can, whether particular facts do or do not constitute tender offers.

1. Much at stake: Observe that a lot will turn on whether an acquisition is a "tender offer."

a. If not tender offer: If an acquisition of stock is ***not*** a tender offer, the only federal securities-law requirement will be that the acquirer make a disclosure under § 13(d) after buying 5%. He can make the actual purchases (including ones made within ten days following his reaching of the 5% threshold) without any advance notice, and on any terms that he can get the other party(ies) to agree to.

b. If tender offer: But if the acquisition ***is*** a tender offer, then the acquirer is much more limited: (1) he must give ***advance notice*** of his plans, and more extensive disclosure than he would under § 13(d); (2) he will have to ***wait longer*** (since he will have to keep his offer open for at least 20 business days), during which time other bidders may materialize; (3) he will have to follow all of the ***"traffic rules"*** of § 14(d), including the withdrawal, pro-rata and best price rules, all of which are likely to make the acquisition more expensive; and (4) he takes the risk of a fraud action under § 14(e) (see *infra*, p. 446). See Clark, pp. 559-60.

c. Consequence: Therefore, it is not surprising that an acquirer will often try to structure a transaction so that it is not a tender offer. This is especially true where the acquirer only wants a relatively small percentage of the target's stock (small enough to be bought within a ten-day window following the buyer's reaching of the 5% § 13(d) disclosure threshold), or when a substantial percentage of the target's stock is in the hands of a few sophisticated holders with whom the buyer can negotiate privately.

2. SEC's eight-factor test: As you might expect, the SEC argues for a ***broad definition*** of "tender offer." In a number of litigations, the SEC has proposed an ***eight-factor test*** for determining whether a transaction is a tender offer. (The SEC apparently claims that even if most but not all of the factors are present, the acquisition should be considered a tender offer.) The eight factors are as follows:

a. Solicitation: An ***active and widespread solicitation*** is made of the target's public shareholders;

b. Percentage: The solicitation is for a ***substantial percentage*** of the target's stock;

c. **Premium:** The offer to purchase is made at a ***premium*** over the prevailing market price;

d. **Firm terms:** The terms of the offer are ***firm*** rather than negotiable;

e. **Contingent:** The offer is ***contingent*** on the tender of a ***fixed number of shares*** (and is perhaps, though not necessarily, subject to a ***fixed maximum number*** that will be purchased);

f. **Limited time:** The offer is open only for a ***limited period of time***;

g. **Pressure:** The offerees are subjected to ***pressure*** to sell their stock; and

h. **Public announcements:** The buyer ***publicly announces*** an acquisition program, preceding or accompanying his accumulation of stock.

3. **Courts sometimes accept:** Some, but by no means all, courts have accepted the SEC's eight-factor test.

4. **Vast quantities not sufficient:** One thing is clear: ***mere purchases of large quantities of stock***, without at least some of the eight factors listed above, do ***not*** constitute a tender offer. F,B&H, p. 25.

5. **Privately-negotiated purchases:** One kind of transaction that will generally not constitute a tender offer even though it involves large stock purchases, is the ***privately-negotiated purchase***. Even if the acquirer conducts simultaneous negotiations with a number of large stockholders, and buys from them at an above-market price, these purchases will not, without more, be a tender offer.

   a. **Widespread canvassing:** If, on the other hand, the acquirer makes personal contact with ***large numbers*** (e.g., hundreds) of holders of the target's stock, and tries to persuade each one to sell to him privately at some fixed price, this might well be found to amount to a tender offer.

6. **Open-market purchases:** Suppose that, instead of privately-negotiated purchases, an acquirer makes ***open-market purchases*** that amount to a large percentage of the target's stock. That is, the acquirer places orders on, say, the New York Stock Exchange, through a broker and without any knowledge of who the seller is. Can this be a tender offer? The answer is usually "no," though the precise outcome may turn on the degree of ***publicity*** concerning the acquirer's intent.

   a. **Secret intent:** First, let's suppose that the acquirer keeps completely ***secret*** its intent to acquire a significant stake in the target. (Obviously, the acquirer can do this only until at most ten days after it has crossed the 5% threshold, since at that time it has to file a 13D disclosure statement.) On these facts, nearly every court has concluded that there is ***no*** tender offer — the lack of publicity about the acquirer's intent means that sellers are not being subjected to pressure or put under any special time limit in deciding whether to sell in the open market, so there is no need to give them the protection that the tender offer rules confer. Clark, p. 563.

   b. **Publicly announced intent:** Now, let's consider the situation in which the acquirer buys his shares through open-market purchases, but does so after ***publicly announcing*** that he is considering a tender offer (or perhaps after a public disclosure that he is going to try to gain control by unspecified means). Here, a stronger case can be made for considering the resulting purchases to be a tender offer. After all, here individual stock holders presumably feel at least somewhat more pressure to sell while the acquirer is buying, than they do where the acquirer's intent is secret.

i. **Majority rule:** A few courts have, therefore, found a tender offer to exist on these facts. Clark, pp. 562-63. But most courts have held that even where the acquirer's intent to gain control is known, open market purchases will still ***not*** give rise to a tender offer.

H. Private actions under § 14(e): The last major area of Williams Act litigation concerns private suits for certain violations of the Act. § 14(e) of the '34 Act provides that:

> "It shall be unlawful for any person to make any ***untrue statement of a material fact*** or ***omit to state*** any material fact necessary in order to make the statements made, in the light of the circumstances under which they are made, not misleading, or to engage in any ***fraudulent, deceptive, or manipulative acts or practices***, in ***connection with any tender offer*** or request or invitation for tenders, or any ***solicitation*** of security holders in opposition to or in favor of any such offer, request, or invitation. The [SEC] shall, for the purposes of this subsection, by rules and regulations define, and prescribe means reasonably designed to prevent, such acts and practices as are fraudulent, deceptive, or manipulative."

We will be considering two main issues concerning this section: (1) Does it ban takeover conduct that is fully disclosed but ***substantively unfair***? and (2) What are the elements of a ***private cause of action*** for ***fraud or non-disclosure*** under this section?

1. **Does not cover substantive unfairness:** With respect to the first of these questions, the answer is quite clear: § 14(e) does ***not*** prohibit conduct by a bidder or, for that matter, by an issuer defending against a takeover bid, where there is no misrepresentation or failure of disclosure, and the only complaint is that the defendant's conduct is ***substantively unfair***. In other words, like SEC Rule 10b-5 (see *supra*, p. 262), § 14(e) only guards against ***misrepresentation*** or ***nondisclosure*** in connection with a tender offer, not against substantive unfairness. Therefore, any claim of substantive unfairness in connection with a tender offer, and any chance for the challenger to get either damages or an injunction on such grounds, must come from ***state law***.

2. **Remedy for misrepresentation or non-disclosure:** Now, let's consider whether and how § 14(e) offers a private remedy for misrepresentation or nondisclosure in connection with a tender offer.

3. **General review:** § 14(e) ***does*** give an ***implied private right of action*** for damages or injunctive relief to one who has been injured by a bidder's (or target's) misrepresentation or nondisclosure in connection with a tender offer. However, the plaintiff will have to show:

   (1) that the misrepresentation or nondisclosure was ***material***;

   (2) probably, that the defendant made it with ***scienter*** (i.e., with an intent to defraud or mislead); and

   (3) in most cases, that the plaintiff ***relied*** upon the misrepresentation.

4. **Standing:** Several types of people can bring a suit for a violation of § 14(e), including: (1) the target (which can seek an injunction against deceptive conduct by the bidder); (2) a ***bidder*** (which can get an injunction against the target's management or against another bidder, but which ***cannot*** get ***damages*** against anyone); (3) a ***non-tendering shareholder*** (who can get either damages or an injunction); and (4) a person who ***buys*** or ***sells*** shares in reliance on information disclosed or not disclosed in tender offer documents.

5. **Remedies:** A plaintiff suing under § 14(e) might seek either injunctive relief, damages, or both.

   a. **Injunction:** Any private party involved in or affected by a tender offer may obtain an ***injunction*** if he can show that the defendant has violated § 14(e). Most significantly: (1) the target's management can enjoin the bidder from ***consummating*** the tender offer if the bidder has not made the required disclosures; (2) the bidder can enjoin the target from making misrepresentations in connection with the target's opposition to the takeover attempt; and (3) one of two or more rival bidders can enjoin the other from proceeding without disclosure.

      i. **Temporary nature:** An injunction granted by a court under § 14(e) will rarely be permanent. For instance, when the injunction is issued against a bidder (at the behest either of the target or of a rival bidder), the court will simply prevent the bidder from acquiring the tendered shares until the bidder has complied with all disclosure requirements. F,B&H, p. 231. But a suit under § 14(e) can nonetheless buy a target extra time, during which it may be able to come up with a more permanent means of defeating the tender offer (e.g., a better bid by a white knight). *Id.*

   b. **Damages:** Most private plaintiffs will also be able to recover ***damages*** if they have been injured by a § 14(e) violation. For instance, the ***target***, tendering shareholders and even non-tendering shareholders (but not bidders) may all recover such damages.

VII. STATE ANTI-TAKEOVER STATUTES

A. **State regulation of hostile takeovers:** Federal regulation of takeover attempts, as we have just seen in considering the Williams Act, is basically even-handed: the federal laws are not designed to assist either a hostile bidder or the target's incumbent management, but are instead designed to make sure that shareholders receive all relevant information and can make a decision free of coercion. This even-handedness is most emphatically ***not*** true of ***state*** regulation of takeovers, especially hostile ones. States have a natural and strong incentive to ***protect incumbent management*** against hostile takeover attempts, especially attempts by out-of-state bidders.

   1. **Explanation:** There are several reasons why state legislatures tend to favor the managements of in-state companies: (1) If a hostile takeover by an out-of-stater is successful, there is a significant risk that the winning bidder will ***move operations out of state***, close in-state plants, and otherwise harm the local economy; (2) The incumbent management of an in-state company typically has a much stronger influence on the local legislature (e.g. through campaign contributions) than does an out-of-state bidder, or a widely-dispersed

stockholder population; and (3) The Secretary of State's office and the local corporate bar both have a strong interest in having local corporations incorporate in the state (rather than, say, in Delaware), and if management does not receive the anti-takeover protection it wants it may well reincorporate elsewhere.

2. **Anti-takeover statutes:** Therefore, it is not surprising that most states — at least 30 at last count — have enacted statutes whose purpose and effect is to make takeovers of in-state corporations more difficult and costly.

B. **Modern statutes:** Most modern anti-takeover statutes operate not by preventing the bidder from buying shares from the target's shareholders, but rather, by depriving the bidder of the ***benefit*** of his share acquisition. There are three main ways these statutes do this: (1) by preventing the bidder from ***voting*** the shares he has bought unless certain conditions are satisfied; (2) by preventing the bidder from conducting a ***back-end merger*** (see *supra*, p. 387) of the target corporation into the bidder's own shell, or vice versa; or (3) by requiring the bidder to pay a specified ***"fair price"*** in any back-end merger.

1. **The *CTS* case*:*** One fairly typical statute, that of Indiana, was upheld by the Supreme Court in *CTS Corp. v. Dynamics Corp. of America*, 481 U.S. 69 (1987).

   a. **Facts:** The Indiana Control Share Acquisitions Statute restricts hostile takeovers by preventing the bidder from ***voting*** the shares he has acquired. Whenever a person passes one of three thresholds of share ownership — one-fifth, one-third or one-half — of certain public corporations chartered in Indiana, he is not allowed to vote this controlling block unless he obtains approval by a majority of the target's pre-existing "disinterested" shareholders. The bidder can require management to hold a special shareholders' meeting within 50 days after the bidder so requests, at which the bidder can try to get this approval. If he fails to get the approval, the target may (but is not required to) redeem the control shares from the bidder by paying him their fair market value. The net result of the Indiana statute is to make hostile takeovers of an Indiana corporation more costly and risky in at least two respects: (1) the bidder must pay for the special shareholders' meeting if he wants to obtain prompt approval by the disinterested shareholders; and (2) if the bidder fails to get this approval, he may be stuck with shares that have no voting rights.

   b. **Statute upheld:** Even though the Indiana statute would probably make nationwide tender offers for Indiana companies more expensive and difficult, the Supreme Court ***upheld*** the statute. In so doing, the Supreme Court rejected two arguments by the bidder: (1) that the statute conflicted with the Williams Act, and was thus preempted by federal legislation; and (2) that the statute violated the Commerce Clause.

      i. **Williams Act:** On the first of these arguments, the majority in *CTS* found no conflict with the Williams Act. The majority conceded that it would usually take a bidder 50 days to get approval to vote the control shares, versus a mere 20-day waiting period under the Williams Act. But this small delay was not enough to constitute a real conflict with the Williams Act, especially since both the Williams Act and the Indiana statute were (at least the majority assumed) devoted to the identical purpose of giving shareholders a fully informed opportunity to decide their fate.

ii. **Commerce Clause:** The majority also concluded that the Act ***did not unreasonably burden interstate commerce.*** The majority pointed out that the statute dealt with the familiar subjects of state corporate regulation: voting rights, shareholders' meetings and shareholder approval. Furthermore, the statute applied *only* to corporations chartered in Indiana. Therefore, the state was merely using its long-accepted power to regulate the internal aspects of its domestic corporations, an activity that did not unduly interfere with interstate commerce. Even if the Indiana statute reduced the number of successful tender offers, this would not constitute an interference with commerce because "the very commodity that is traded in the 'market for corporate control' — the corporation — is one that owes its existence and attributes to state law. Indiana need not define these commodities as other States do; it need only provide that residents and nonresidents have equal access to them."

c. **Dissent:** There were three dissenters in *CTS*. They believed that the practical effect of the Indiana statute was to give the majority of a target's shareholders veto rights over a minority's practical ability to sell their shares to a bidder. Since this thwarted minority might (and usually would) be widely dispersed throughout the country, their inability to sell their shares to a bidder constituted, according to the dissent, an unconstitutional burden on interstate commerce.

d. **Significance:** *CTS* seems to give all states a very powerful weapon to discourage hostile takeovers of corporations chartered by the state. So long as (1) the statute applies only to corporations ***chartered by the state*** (rather than, say, corporations with a principal place of business in the state, large numbers of employees there, etc.), and (2) the statute operates by governing the familiar attributes of corporate law — voting rights, shareholder meetings, shareholder approval, etc. — rather than by blocking the actual transfer of "ownership," the statute will probably withstand constitutional attack. Therefore, in addition to statutes that deprive the bidder of voting rights over his shares (like the Indiana act upheld in *CTS*), statutes that flatly block back-end mergers between a bidder and the target, and statutes that block a back-end merger unless the bidder pays a "fair price," are probably also ***valid.***

C. **Delaware act:** Clearly the most important second-generation statute, and one that is almost certainly constitutional in light of *CTS*, is the ***Delaware*** anti-takeover statute. § 203 of the Delaware General Corporation Law, enacted in 1988, provides as follows:

1. **Combinations prohibited:** Any "business combination" between the corporation and an "interested stockholder" is ***prohibited*** for ***three years*** after the stockholder buys his shares. "Business combinations" are defined to include ***mergers***, significant ***asset sales***, and any other transaction between the corporation and the interested stockholder that confers a benefit on the latter. An "interested stockholder" is anyone who owns ***15%*** or more of the corporation's stock, and the "affiliates" and "associates" of such a person. (There are some exceptions which we won't go into.)

2. **Significance:** The Delaware statute therefore makes hostile takeovers less attractive by preventing the bidder from conducting a ***back-end cashout merger*** (see *supra*, p. 434) unless he either:

[1] gets ***board approval*** before he buys his stock;

[2] ***buys at least 85% of the stock***; or

[3] gets approval of the cashout from ***two-thirds of the stockholders*** who will be cashed out in the back-end step.

This impediment to back-end cashout mergers (and to the related technique of asset sales by the target to the bidder) is more significant than it might first appear: unless the bidder can arrange a merger or asset sale, he won't be able to ***use the target's assets as security for the loan*** that finances the share acquisition, and he won't be able to ***use the target's earnings and cash flow to pay off this debt.*** (See *supra*, p. 434.)

a. **85% purchases:** The practical effect, in turn, is usually to make hostile bidders for Delaware corporations seek at least ***85%*** of the target's shares. (Remember that if the "interested stockholder" owns 85% or more of the shares, he can conduct a merger or asset sale with himself, without worrying about the Act.) This fact in turn has spawned an entirely new defense: the target ***sells more than 15%*** of its stock to a friendly ***"white squire"*** (see *supra*, p. 434), who promises not to tender to any hostile bidder who may emerge, and who therefore prevents any hostile bidder from acquiring the requisite 85%.

VIII. HOSTILE TAKEOVERS — DEFENSIVE MANEUVERS, AND THE JUDICIAL RESPONSE

A. **Introduction:** When a corporation becomes the subject of a hostile bid, the management and board of the target corporation will usually try to repel the bid, either in the hopes of improving the offer, or in the hopes of somehow remaining independent. In this section, we look at methods that the target can use to repel the bidder or induce a sweetened price, as well as at the responses that courts make to these defensive maneuvers.

B. **Defensive maneuvers:** At the outset, let's look at the ***defensive maneuvers*** that may be employed by a target's management to defeat a hostile bidder. We will be focusing on the various techniques that incumbent management may use, and then on the ***limits*** that courts have placed on such defensive tactics.

1. **Catalog of tactics:** First, let's summarize the possible defensive techniques that a target's management might use to defeat a hostile bidder. We can divide these into techniques that are typically employed before an actual hostile bid surfaces, and those that are used after such a bid has arisen. (In general, measures put into place before an actual bid has surfaced have a better chance of being upheld by the courts.) For now, we will just be listing the techniques; later on (beginning p. 472 *infra*) we'll consider most of these in more detail, together with the judicial response to each.

2. **Pre-offer techniques:** ***Before*** a concrete takeover attempt has been announced, there are a number of things the target's management can do to make an attack somewhat less likely to occur, or somewhat less likely to succeed if it does occur. These are often collectively referred to as ***"shark repellants"*** (perhaps indicating management's hope that they will prevent any attack from happening at all, rather than the hope that if an attack does occur these devices will cause it to fail).

a. **Shareholder approval:** Most shark repellants are carried out by means of amendments to the corporation's articles of incorporation. Therefore, they almost always require ***approval by a majority of shareholders***. Since a shareholder who is asked to approve such measures knows that their very purpose is to make a hostile takeover bid (presumably at a much-above-market price) less likely to succeed, shareholders will not normally be enthusiastic about giving their approval. Nonetheless, due to inertia, management's control of the proxy machinery, and perhaps large stockholdings held by those friendly to management, shark repellants do often get approved by the requisite majority of shareholders.

b. **Super-majority provisions:** The target might amend its articles of incorporation to require that ***more than a simple majority*** of the company's common stockholders must approve any ***merger*** or any major ***sale of assets***. For instance, the target might require that ***80%*** of all stockholders approve any such merger or asset sale. Alternatively, the target might provide that a merger or asset sale must be approved by a ***"majority of the minority"*** — that way, if a bidder bought, say, 65% of the target's stock, the acquisition would still have to be approved by a majority of the remaining 35% holders. Such ***"super-majority"*** provisions are somewhat effective against partial tender offers and two-tier front-loaded offers (*supra*, p. 434), but are ***not*** very effective against bids for ***all*** of the target's shares. F,B&H, pp. 320-21.

   i. **Repeal:** Observe that for such a super-majority provision to have any chance of being effective, the provision itself must not be subject to amendment by a simple majority vote. Therefore, such provisions are generally set up in such a way that the same super-majority vote (e.g., 80%) must be cast to amend or remove the provision as must be cast in favor of the merger or asset-sale transaction under the provision. *Id.*

c. **Staggered board:** A target might put in place a ***staggered*** board of directors. (See *supra*, p. 51.) That is, only a minority of the board will stand for election in any given year. The theory behind the staggered board as an anti-takeover device is that even if the bidder acquires a majority (or, indeed, all) of the target's shares, he will not be able to gain control immediately, and will have to wait two or more years in order to elect his own hand-picked directors to the board.

Staggered boards are both a common anti-takeover device and a relatively effective one.

d. **Anti-greenmail amendments:** A target might amend its charter to prevent the paying of ***"greenmail,"*** i.e., the repurchase by the target of shares from a would-be takeover artist at a premium over market price. The theory is that a bidder will be less likely to attack a target where there is no possibility of greenmail as an outcome. But this technique seems not to be very effective, especially against a bidder who really wants control.

e. **New class of stock:** The company might create a ***second class*** of common stock, and require that any merger or asset sale be approved by each class (so that the new class has a veto power). Then, the new class of stock could be placed with persons friendly to management, e.g., the founding family. For example, many companies in the newspaper business have such two-class structures, with members of the original founding family holding enough of one class to block a hostile takeover even though the family does not have a majority of the overall shares. However, stock exchange restrictions, as well as the need for shareholder approval, make implementing such a plan difficult.

f. Poison pill plans: The best-known and probably most effective shark repellants tend to be so-called ***poison pill*** plans. There are numerous kinds of poison pill plans, and they grow more toxic all the time. What they have in common is that they try to ensure that bad things will happen to the bidder if it obtains control of the target, thereby making the target ***less attractive*** to the bidder. As of 2002, a majority of public companies had some kind of poison pill plan. Hamilton (8th), p. 1226, n. 1.

Most poison pill plans can be roughly divided into "call" and "put" plans.

i. "Call" plans: ***"Call"*** plans give stockholders the right to buy cheap stock in certain circumstances. They usually work by distributing to each target shareholder one "right" for each target share. The key feature of the right is usually a ***"flip over"*** provision, which is triggered when an outsider buys, say, 20% of the target's stock. Once the right has "flipped over" because of this outsider share acquisition, three things usually happen: (1) the rights become separately tradeable; (2) they are no longer redeemable by the target's management; and (3) most importantly, if the outsider gets control and causes the target to merge with the outsider, the right entitles its holder to ***acquire shares of the bidder at half price***. Effect (3) occurs because the right to buy cheap stock (the "call") is an obligation of the target, and by operation of law this becomes an obligation of the surviving corporation following a merger (see *supra*, p. 367).

Example: Suppose that Ford Motor Corp. issues a poison pill of the "call-right" variety. The right provides that if anyone acquires 25% of Ford, any Ford shareholder may buy one additional share of Ford at half the then market price. At a time when GM stock is trading at $50 a share, GM acquires 51% of Ford in a hostile tender offer. GM then merges Ford into itself. Upon completion of this merger, the poison pill will "flip over," thus giving each former Ford shareholder the right to buy a share of GM stock at $25 (half the current market price). The reason this "flip over" works is that when GM causes Ford to merge into itself, it takes over Ford's liabilities by operation of law, and the cheap call is one of those liabilities. In theory, the existence of the poison pill is supposed to make GM less interested in hostilely tendering for Ford.

ii. "Flip in" provision: The "flip over" provision described above will only work where the bidder merges with the target. A second type of poison pill call contains a ***"flip in"*** provision. A "flip in" provision works the same way as the "flip over" one, except that the right-holder's opportunity to buy cheap stock is triggered not only in the case of a merger but also in the case of other self-dealing transactions, including purchases by the bidder of assets from the target at below-market prices, loans by the target to the bidder, etc. As with the "flip over" provision, the "flip in" gives the right-holder the right to buy the cheap shares ***in the bidder***, not just in the target. Again, the theory is that the bidder will fear that the equity interest held by its own shareholders will be seriously diluted if the pill takes effect. See S,S,B&W,

p. 1205. But where a large well-capitalized company takes over a much smaller one, the dilution is less frightening, so both the "flip over" and "flip in" plans are usually less of a deterrent.

iii. "Put" plan: Finally, some poison pills are ***"put"*** plans. These calculate a price that the target's directors think is a "fair" price for the target's shares. If a bidder buys some but not all of the target's shares, the put gives each target shareholder the right to sell back his remaining shares in the target at the fair price. The fair price set in the plan may either be a fixed price (e.g., $60 per share) or a formula (typically, the highest price paid so far by the bidder for the target's shares). A put plan is effective against a two-tier front-loaded tender offer (see *supra*, p. 434), since it relieves the target's holders of the fear that if they do not tender, they will be cashed out on unfavorable terms in the back-end merger. But put plans are less effective against tenders for all of the target's shares: if the put price is not very high, the bidder may simply top it (making it moot), yet if it is too high, the court may invalidate it. See *infra*, p. 474.

iv. Other aspects: Here are a few other aspects of poison pills:

(1) Not always a pre-offer technique: A poison pill plan need not necessarily be put into place before a hostile bid has surfaced — targets sometimes implement a plan hurriedly after a bid has surfaced. One reason they are able to do this is that a plan typically does ***not*** require ***approval of shareholders***, since the company is simply distributing a call or put right to each shareholder pro rata.

(2) Usually not dispositive: A poison pill plan rarely keeps a hostile bidder completely at bay. But because the pill can make an acquisition much more expensive for a bidder, and because the plan generally allows the target's board to ***redeem (cancel)*** the put or call rights at its discretion, the pill makes it more likely that the bidder will ***reach an agreement*** with the target's board (probably at a higher price after negotiation) instead of going directly to the shareholders over the target management's unyielding opposition. S,S,B&W, p. 1206.

(3) "Dead-hand" and "no-hand" provisions: As just noted, most pills allow the target's board to redeem the rights, giving the board useful leverage in negotiating with the acquirer ("If you pay $x per share, we'll redeem the rights.") However, from the standpoint of the target's board, this ability to redeem the rights has a major downside: the acquirer may persuade a majority of the target's shareholders to ***elect new directors*** friendly to the acquirer, who will replace the old ones and then redeem the rights. Consequently, a number of plans in recent years have included ***"dead hand"*** or ***"no hand"*** provisions. A dead hand provision restricts the ability of the board — including any successor board — to redeem the rights. A no hand provision sets a minimum period of time that the board must wait before redeeming the rights. Dead hand and no hand provisions may, like any other aspect of a poison pill, be invalidated by a court if found to be unfair; see *infra*, p. 475.

3. **Post-offer techniques:** Here are some of the techniques commonly used by the target ***after*** a hostile bid has surfaced:

   a. **Defensive lawsuits:** The target's management can institute ***defensive lawsuits***. The target sues the bidder in either state or federal court, alleging that the offer violates state fiduciary principles, federal securities laws, etc. However, state law will rarely give the target's management much relief, unless the offer is unusually unfair (e.g., a clearly coercive two-tier front-loaded tender offer, see *supra*, p. 434). A federal suit based on the securities laws, as we have seen (see *supra*, p. 444), may slow the bidder down temporarily, and may require him to correct shortcomings in his disclosure documents, but it will almost never permanently block his offer. In general, litigation rarely does more than gain the target's management extra time to take other defensive measures. Clark, p. 572.

   b. **Finding a "white knight":** The target may find itself a ***"white knight"*** (*supra*, p. 434), who will acquire the target instead of letting the hostile bidder do so. For this technique to work, the white knight will generally have to offer a price at least as good as the one the hostile bidder is offering. Even when the target's management successfully uses this technique, its victory will be bitter-sweet: management loses its independence, but probably keeps its jobs.

      i. **Lock-ups:** To induce a third person to become a white knight, the target may give the third person some kind of ***"lock-up"*** (see *supra*, p. 434). The purpose is to make sure that the third person defeats the hostile bidder in any auction that may result. (That is, the special treatment enables the third person to "lock up" the acquisition.) For example, the target may give the would-be white knight a ***"crown jewels"*** option, i.e., an option to buy one of the target's most attractive businesses at a below-market price. This grant of an option does not require shareholder approval because it is not a sale of "substantially all" the target's assets; yet it will make the target much less attractive to any other bidder. Lock-ups are especially vulnerable to attack in state court; see, e.g., *Revlon, Inc. v. MacAndrews & Forbes Holdings, Inc.*, *infra*, p. 460.

      ii. **Stock option:** Alternatively, instead of giving the white knight a crown jewel option, the target may give the white knight an ***option*** on target's own ***common stock*** at a very favorable price or on favorable terms. For instance, when Paramount Communications was trying to keep from being acquired by Viacom, Paramount gave QVC, a white knight, a very favorable no-cash-required option to buy lots of Paramount stock in the event that Paramount's proposed sale to QVC didn't go forward. (This stock option was struck down by the court; see *infra*, p. 450.)

   c. **Defensive acquisition:** The target might make itself less attractive by arranging a ***defensive acquisition***. For instance, if the bidder owns daily newspapers in certain markets, the target may acquire radio or television stations in some of those markets, knowing that FCC rules would prevent the bidder from operating both newspapers and broadcast media in any given city.

i. **Large debt:** One form of defensive acquisition is the ***leveraged*** acquisition, in which the target borrows heavily to fund a large acquisition, and hopes that its new highly-leveraged status will make it unattractive.

d. **Corporate restructuring:** The target may ***restructure*** itself in a way that increases its short-term value to its stockholders. For instance, the target may borrow heavily from banks, and then give its shareholders a large one-time ***dividend*** of cash, bonds, and/or preferred stock. It is not unknown for a company whose shares are trading at $50 before a tender offer surfaces, to end up paying its holders $50 in cash plus preferred stock in order to defeat an $80 per share hostile tender offer — of course, the target's common stock then drops to very low levels, and its debt-equity ratio goes through the roof. Restructurings also often include the ***sale*** of ***whole divisions*** of the company. In fact, restructurings are similar to leveraged buyouts (see *supra*, p. 434), except that public equity participation is reduced rather than completely eliminated. S,S,B&W, p. 1208.

e. **Greenmail:** The target may simply decide to pay ***"greenmail"*** to the bidder. That is, the target buys back the partial stake that the bidder has already built, by paying him an above-market price. In return, the bidder enters into a "standstill" agreement (*supra*, p. 434), whereby he agrees not to attempt to re-acquire the target for some specified number of years. In an alternative version of greenmail, the target arranges for some ***third party*** to buy the bidder's stake at a premium; usually, the target will have to somehow make it worth the third party's while to pay the above-market price (e.g., by giving the third party an option to acquire on favorable terms some business owned by the target).

f. **Share manipulations:** The target's management may ***manipulate the shares*** of the target in a way that discourages a hostile takeover. Poison pill plans and greenmail are two devices that fall into this category. Others include the following:

i. **Sale to friendly party:** The target may sell a less-than-controlling block to a ***friendly party***, i.e., one that can be trusted not to tender to the hostile bidder. For instance, the target might sell newly-issued shares to its employees' ***pension plan***; this would be especially effective if the employees and their plan trustees perceive the bidder as one who would eliminate jobs, move the company, or otherwise harm the employees. This is sometimes called the ***"white squire"*** (as opposed to "white knight") technique. It is especially attractive to targets incorporated in Delaware, since a 16% stake in friendly hands means that a bidder will not easily be able to arrange a back-end merger. (See the discussion of Del. GCL § 203 *supra*, p. 449.)

ii. **Share repurchases:** If insiders hold a substantial but not controlling stake, they may cause the target to ***repurchase*** a significant portion of its shares from the public. This may be enough to give the insiders a controlling stake (i.e., a stake big enough to defeat the hostile bidder), or at least put them within a range where they can use their own resources to buy enough additional shares to get control. For instance, if insiders already own one-third of the stock, a repurchase by the target of one-third of its outstanding shares (assuming that the insiders do not tender any shares into this repurchase) would leave the insiders with 50% ownership. See Clark, p. 573.

g. Use of state anti-takeover measures: Lastly, don't forget the existence of ***state anti-takeover statutes***. Normally, these statutes will assist the target's management in repelling unwanted advances without much affirmative action by the target. See *supra*, p. 447. However, some statutes require the target to "opt in" by explicit corporate action in order to get the benefit of the statute. Where this is required, it can usually be done without shareholder approval (e.g., by amending the target's bylaws).

C. Judicial response: If targets and their managements were left free to use any and all of the above defensive measures, hostile takeovers would become almost impossible. But the courts have not stood idly by; instead, they (especially state courts) have tried to protect the interest of the target's shareholders, an interest which is often better served by encouraging hostile bids at premium prices. Generally, it is the hostile bidder, not the target's shareholders, who will try to get courts to prevent the target's management from using techniques like those summarized above. We first consider suits that seek to use federal-law principles to enjoin these defensive techniques, then we consider the much more extensive body of state law concerning when such defensive measures may be employed.

D. Federal securities laws: A bidder who wants to overturn the target's defensive measures will probably be ***unable*** to use the ***federal securities laws*** to do this.

1. Deception: Recall that § 14(e) of the '34 Act bars the use of "fraudulent, deceptive, or manipulative acts or practices" in connection with a tender offer. See *supra*, p. 446. This proscription applies as well to "any solicitation of security holders in opposition to . . . any such offer. . . ." Therefore, if a bidder can show that the target's management has actually ***deceived*** the target's shareholders as a part of management's defensive strategy, the bidder might be able to get a federal court to enjoin further violations (and to order the correction of past misrepresentations) under § 14(e).

Example: For instance, suppose the target's management writes to shareholders, "Don't tender your shares because the bidder is a convicted felon," and the bidder is not a convicted felon. This would be a § 14(e) violation that the court could correct by injunction.

2. Unfair tactics: But most of the time, the bidder will not be claiming that the target is actually lying. Instead, the bidder's claim will typically be that the defensive measures chosen by target's management are simply ***substantively unfair***. Here, neither § 14(e) nor the rest of the federal securities laws are likely to be much help to the bidder. Recall (see *supra*, p. 446) that some sort of ***deceit*** is a necessary element of a § 14(e) violation. A claim that the target's management is behaving in a way that is substantively unfair to the target's shareholders simply does not satisfy this requirement. Therefore, neither § 14(e) nor the rest of the federal securities laws (e.g., SEC Rule 10b-5) will be of much help to the bidder.

E. State case law, generally: A bidder's best shot at getting a court to invalidate the target's management's takeover defenses is through the use of ***state law***. The target's management and its board of directors have a fiduciary duty to the target's shareholders, of course. If the bidder can show that management, by implementing anti-takeover measures, was acting solely to

entrench itself, not to protect the shareholders, the court might hold that the defenses should be set aside like any other self-dealing transaction that was unfair to stockholders.

1. **Business judgment rule and rules on self-dealing:** What makes the problem especially difficult for courts is that the judicial response to defensive measures has to fit into the framework of two other doctrines: (1) the business judgment doctrine (*supra*, p. 182); and (2) the self-dealing rules (*supra*, p. 198), whereby a transaction in which management or the board have a direct personal economic interest can be set aside if it is not fair to the stockholders.

F. Delaware law, generally: Most of the important case law about when a court will overturn management's anti-takeover tactics comes from Delaware, since that is where most publicly held takeover targets are incorporated. Therefore, our focus will be on Delaware law, except where otherwise noted.

1. **General summary of Delaware law:** In general, the Delaware courts have followed a ***middle ground*** in reviewing attempts by the target's management to defeat hostile takeover attempts.

   a. **Business judgment doctrine:** The court does ***not*** automatically apply the ***business judgment doctrine.*** (Remember that under this doctrine, a business judgment made by the board will not be overturned by the court so long as the directors who made it had no direct financial interest in the other side of the transaction, and followed reasonable investigatory procedures. See *supra*, p. 182.)

   b. **Self-dealing rules:** At the same time, the court will ***not*** automatically apply the ***self-dealing rules*** that are used when a corporate insider stands on both sides of a transaction with the corporation. (Remember that under those self-dealing rules, the insiders have the burden of establishing the ***entire fairness*** of the transaction.)

   c. **Middle ground:** Instead, the Delaware courts apply what might be thought of as a ***"modified business judgment rule"*** — because of the higher-than-usual probability that the target's management and board will be acting for self-interested purposes rather than stockholder welfare when they institute anti-takeover defensive measures, management and board must make some ***special showings*** in order to qualify for the protection of the business judgment rule.

2. **Special rules:** There seem to be, in Delaware, four rules governing when the target's management and board will obtain the protection of the business judgment doctrine for the anti-takeover measures they have enacted:

   a. **Reasonable grounds for belief in corporate objective:** First, the board and management must show that they had ***reasonable grounds*** for believing that there was a ***danger to the corporation's welfare*** from the takeover attempt. To put it conversely, the insiders may not use anti-takeover measures ***merely to perpetuate themselves in power*** — they must have reasonable grounds for believing that they are protecting the ***stockholders'*** interests, not their own interests.

   b. **Reasonable response:** Second, the directors and management must show that the defensive measures they actually used were ***"reasonable in relation to the threat posed."*** For instance, if the threat is a particular takeover on what management reasonably believes to be terms unfair to the stockholders, management may not respond by instituting defensive measures that would foreclose ***all*** hostile takeovers, since this response would be out of proportion to the particular threat posed.

c. **Good faith and reasonable investigation:** Third, the board must make the two above showings by demonstrating that it acted not only in good faith but upon ***reasonable investigation***. Thus if the measures were hurriedly passed, without extensive discussion or analysis, and at the urging of management, the measures are less likely to be sustained than if they were carefully considered over a substantial period of time.

d. **Independent directors:** Finally, the court is much more likely to find that the first two requirements (threat to the corporation's welfare and a response that is reasonably proportional to the threat) are satisfied if the takeover measures were approved by a board a majority of whose members were ***disinterested*** (i.e., ***outside***) ***directors***. The court will presume that an independent director, who does not rely on the corporation for the bulk of his livelihood, will have less of a conflict of interest than a management that is trying to save its jobs, so approval by such an outside director is a more meaningful guarantee of fairness to shareholders.

e. **Business judgment doctrine:** Once the insiders have borne this initial burden of showing that they had reasonable grounds to perceive a threat to the corporate welfare, that the defensive measures they chose were in reasonable proportion to the threat, and that they acted after a reasonable investigation, the defensive measures will then get the ***protection of the business judgment doctrine***, and the court will not overturn the decision merely because the court thinks that the measures are "unwise."

See generally *Unocal Corp. v. Mesa Petroleum Co.*, 493 A.2d 946 (Del. 1985), and *Moran v. Household International, Inc.*, 500 A.2d 1346 (Del. 1985), the two main Delaware cases setting forth these requirements. (Each of these cases is discussed below.)

G. **How regulation works in Delaware:** Now that we've summarized these basic Delaware rules that the target's insiders must satisfy before their decision to implement takeover defenses will qualify for protection under the business judgment rule, let's look at each rule in more detail:

1. **Reasonable basis for fear:** The real meaning of the requirement that the insiders show a "reasonable basis for fearing danger to the corporate welfare" from the takeover attack is that the insiders must have acted from a good-faith desire to ***protect the corporation***, ***not merely to protect their own jobs***. If the court believes that the insiders acted mainly to entrench themselves, their takeover defenses will not get the protection of the business judgment rule, and will instead be reviewed like any other self-interested transaction (and will therefore be struck down unless shown to be "entirely fair" to the corporation's shareholders, a showing which the insiders will rarely be able to make).

a. **Dangers that may be considered:** What, then, are the kinds of dangers imposed by hostile takeovers that might be sufficient to meet this requirement? Here are some that would probably suffice:

i. **Change of business practices:** A reasonable belief that the bidder, if successful, will ***change the business practices*** of the corporation in a way that will be ***harmful*** to the corporation's ongoing business and existence. For instance, if the target's insiders have reasonable grounds to believe that the bidder will ***liquidate*** the corporation by selling off its parts to different buyers, or that the bidder will operate the business in an illegal or unethical manner, or that valuable corporate contracts might be lost (e.g., non-assignable government contracts or licenses), these will probably be sufficient to meet the "reasonable fears" requirement.

ii. **Coercive tactics:** Similarly, if the insiders reasonably believe that the particular takeover attempt is ***unfair*** or ***coercive*** to the target's stockholders, this will suffice to meet the "reasonable fears" requirement.

Example: For instance, if the bid comes at a time when the target's selling price is unusually depressed, the target's insiders might be able to plausibly argue that the price being bid is unfairly low and does not really reflect the company's intrinsic value. (On the other hand, if the bid is, say, 60% higher than the stock has ever traded for in its entire history, management's claim that the offering price is unfairly low probably will not pass muster.)

iii. **Excessive debt:** Finally, a reasonable fear that the tender offer will leave the target with ***unreasonably high levels of debt*** will probably suffice. For instance, if the bidder has indicated that he will finance the acquisition with high-yield "junk bonds" (see *supra*, p. 434) secured by the target's assets and paid off by its cash flow, a court may well conclude that such a highly-leveraged offer was one that the target's management could reasonably have viewed as posing a substantial danger to the corporation's welfare. This is especially true where the bidder has indicated that he will ***sell off major pieces*** of the company to reduce the debt. Clark, p. 587.

2. **"Proportionality" requirement:** The second requirement, that the anti-takeover defenses represent a response that is ***"reasonable in relation to the threat posed,"*** may be thought of as a ***"proportionality"*** requirement.

a. **Can't be "preclusive" or "coercive":** To meet the proportionality requirement, a defensive measure must ***not*** be either ***"preclusive"*** or ***"coercive."*** *Unitrin, Inc. v. American General Corp.*, 651 A.2d 1361 (Del. 1995).

i. **"Preclusive":** A ***"preclusive"*** measure is one which ***prevents the hostile bidder from succeeding*** in its tender offer no matter what the bidder does.

(1) **Foreclosing of all takeovers:** For instance, a ***poison pill*** "call" plan that gives each target shareholder the right to buy a share of the acquirer's stock at one-tenth of its market value, or a poison pill "put" plan that gives the target holder the right to sell back his shares at ten times their fair market value, might make all hostile takeovers so unpalatable to bidders as to foreclose all such attempts, in which case the pill would be found to be "preclusive" and thus violate the "proportionality" rule.

(2) **Absolute lock up:** If concessions given to a favored bidder amount to an ***"absolute lock up"*** — i.e., they create a structure that virtually guarantees that the favored bidder will end up acquiring the company — the concessions will be found to be "preclusive." See *Omnicare v. NCS Healthcare, infra*, p. 476.

ii. **Coercive:** A ***"coercive"*** measure is one which ***"crams down"*** on the target's shareholders a management-sponsored alternative.

(1) **Lower management bid:** For instance, a ***lower competing bid by management*** would probably be "coercive," if management had enough votes to veto the hostile bid and make it clear that it would use this power to block the hostile bid.

(2) **Waste of assets:** Similarly, a defensive measure that constitutes a ***waste*** of the target's corporate assets would probably be "coercive." For instance, suppose Target repurchases Raider's 25% stake for a price equal to three times the market value of Target's stock, as part of a "greenmail" transaction in which Raider signs a long-term standstill agreement. A Delaware court would probably view this as forcing management's alternative onto unwilling shareholders, and thus as being coercive. Similarly, if Target sells one of its most attractive core businesses at a ridiculously low price to a third party, in order to reduce its attractiveness to a particularly hostile bidder, this too might be coercive.

(3) **Absolute lock up:** Finally, an ***"absolute lock up"*** (see the discussion of this term above) given to a particular bidder will be considered "coercive." See *Omnicare, infra*, p. 476.

b. **Benefit to stockholders:** The rule of "proportionality" also means that the defensive measures must ***somehow benefit the stockholders***. The defensive measure may primarily benefit ***other constituencies*** (e.g., employees or creditors of the target), but there must be at least ***some benefit*** to the common stockholders, for it is to them that the target's board and management owe their primary duty of loyalty. For instance, the target's board cannot enact a takeover defense that better protects the company's creditors against the risk of default, but that clearly deprives the stockholders of the highest price for their shares; see *Revlon, Inc. v. MacAndrews & Forbes Holdings, Inc.*, discussed *infra*, p. 462.

3. **Investigation:** Third, remember that the target's board must conduct a ***reasonable investigation*** of the defensive measure before adopting it. For instance, if the target conclusorily and quickly brands the offer "inadequate" without doing a detailed financial analysis of it, this will probably not constitute adequate investigation. F,B&H, p. 291. Similarly, if the directors approve a proposed defensive measure (e.g., a poison pill) with very little discussion, and without advice from outside experts (e.g., investment bankers and lawyers), the requisite investigation will probably be found lacking. And if the outside directors are not given a chance to meet by themselves, and simply vote along with the inside directors, the required level of care in investigation is less likely to be found.

4. **Significance of independent directors:** Finally, consider the fourth aspect of the Delaware process for reviewing anti-takeover devices: the favorable judicial response to the fact that the device has been approved by a board a majority of whose members are ***inde-***

pendent. It is not really a requirement in Delaware that the device be approved by such a board — the fact of such approval merely makes the court ***more likely*** to find that the insiders have satisfied their burden of showing reasonable grounds for fear and a reasonably proportionate response to that fear.

a. Dissent: Apparently, the Delaware courts will attach this favorable presumption to the decisions of independent-majority boards even ***without*** detailed proof that a ***majority of the independent directors*** approved the transaction. For instance, suppose that a nine-member board has five outsiders and four insiders. Apparently, the Delaware courts will give the favorable presumption to the actions of this board, even though the board may have approved the action by, say, six-three, with three of the five outsiders being the dissenters. If this would indeed be the Delaware approach, it is illogical — a better rule would be that derived from the self-dealing context (*supra*, p. 205), whereby the directors' action serves to ratify the insiders' self-interested transaction only if the transaction is approved by a ***majority of the disinterested directors***, not merely approved by a board that has a disinterested majority.

b. Not dispositive: The fact that a board with an independent majority has approved the defensive measure does not ***insulate*** it — the independent directors may, for instance, have honestly but stupidly approved a measure that is wildly disproportional to the actual harm threatened.

c. Who is an "independent" director: The Delaware courts take a tough view of who is truly an "independent" director for these purposes. It is apparently not enough that a majority of the board consists of directors who are not full-time employees of the corporation. Instead, the court will treat the existence of other significant business or stockholding relationships with the corporation as making the director an "inside" rather than "independent" one. For instance, in *Revlon, Inc. v. MacAndrews & Forbes Holdings, Inc.*, discussed further *infra*, there were 14 directors on the target's board. Only six were employees. But because two others were significant stockholders, and four of the remaining six had had business relationships with the target, the court refused to treat the board as having a majority of "truly outside independent directors," and therefore refused to give the board's action the favorable presumption.

5. Consequences if requirements not met: What happens if one or more of these requirements are ***not*** satisfied? Will the Delaware court automatically strike down the defensive measure? The answer is probably ***"no."*** Instead, the court will treat the insiders' decision to adopt a takeover measure as it would treat any other instance of ***self-dealing***. In other words, the insiders will probably have the burden of showing that the transaction is ***entirely fair*** to the target's shareholders; if the insiders cannot satisfy this burden, then the court will strike down the measure.

H. Delaware law and the decision to sell the company: So far, we have implicitly assumed that a target's management and directors are staunchly opposed to ***any*** takeover, whether by the particular hostile bidder who has surfaced or by anyone else. Suppose, however, that the target's management and/or board have announced that they will consider ***selling*** the company. Once they make this announcement (or act in ways indicating a willingness to sell the company), the rules governing their actions ***shift dramatically***. At this point, the courts give ***"enhanced scrutiny"*** to the steps that the target's board and managers take.

1. **The "Level Playing Field" rule:** Most importantly, the Delaware courts impose on management and the board the duty to ***obtain the highest price for the shareholders***. This means, in turn, that the target's insiders must create a ***Level Playing Field: all would-be bidders must be treated equally***, and the insiders cannot favor one bidder (e.g., a would-be white knight) over another (e.g., the original hostile "raider").

2. **The *Revlon* case:** The key Delaware case illustrating the Level Playing Field rule is ***Revlon, Inc. v. MacAndrews & Forbes Holdings, Inc.***, 506 A.2d 173 (Del. 1986). This case dramatically illustrates how defensive measures that might be validly employed while the target is struggling to preserve its independence are likely to be ***invalid*** if used to ***favor one bidder over another*** once a ***decision to sell*** the company has been made.

   a. **Facts:** *Revlon* involved a long-fought battle in which Pantry Pride sought to acquire Revlon. In the early stages of the battle, Revlon's board rejected Pantry Pride's initial hostile tender offer of $45 per share as grossly inadequate, adopted a poison pill, and announced a share repurchase plan. Revlon also began looking for a white knight, and found one, Forstmann Little. Forstmann and Pantry Pride began topping each other's bids. The Revlon board finally approved Forstmann's bid of $57.25 a share, versus Pantry Pride's then-highest (but not yet final) bid of $56.25.

   b. **Lock-ups:** Revlon's board did not simply take Forstmann's bid because it was higher than Pantry Pride's when the auction ended. Instead, Revlon gave Forstmann several key concessions that effectively ended the auction: (1) it gave Forstmann a ***"crown jewels" option*** (*supra*, p. 434) to buy two key Revlon subsidiaries for between $100-175 million below market value if another acquirer (e.g., Pantry Pride) got more than 40% of Revlon's shares; (2) it agreed to a ***no-shop*** provision (i.e., it agreed not to deal with any other would-be acquirer, including Pantry Pride); and (3) it agreed to a $25 million cancellation fee. The Revlon board also gave Forstmann private financial information about Revlon that it did not make available to Pantry Pride. Among the reasons the Revlon board gave for approving the Forstmann offer rather than the Pantry Pride offer was that the Forstmann offer would better protect the holders of certain notes recently issued by Revlon, who had indicated that if they did not receive special protection they might sue Revlon and its directors.

   c. **Holding:** The Delaware Supreme Court ***enjoined Revlon*** from going ahead with the Forstmann deal.

   d. **Early defensive measures:** The court had no problem with the early defensive measures (the poison pill plan and the share repurchase plan). At that point, the Revlon directors apparently had a reasonable fear that the corporation's effectiveness would be impaired if the Pantry Pride offer succeeded, since Pantry Pride expected to use junk bonds and to sell off major pieces of the company to reduce the debt.

   e. **Auction:** But the nature of the board's duties ***changed*** dramatically, the court held, once the board recognized that some sort of sale of the company was inevitable. Thus on the day the Revlon board authorized management to negotiate a merger or buyout with a third party, the board was ***putting the company up for sale***. At that point, "The whole question of defensive measures became moot. The directors' role changed from defenders of the corporate bastion to ***auctioneers*** charged with ***getting the best price for the stockholders*** at a sale of the company."

f. Duty violated: The court found that the Revlon board ***violated*** this duty to "get the best price for the shareholders." True, the Forstmann offer that the board approved was $1 per share higher than the then-outstanding Revlon offer. But the auction was clearly not over, until the Revlon board brought it to a premature end by approving the Forstmann deal and granting the lock-up, no-shop and cancellation provisions. Where the board really made its key mistake, the court held, was in preferring the Forstmann bid because that bid gave ***better protection for the note holders***. Once a company is being sold, the court held, management's duty is to protect the ***stockholders***, not creditors (like the note holders), employees, or management itself. The note holders were protected by whatever contract governed their relationship with Revlon, and they were not entitled to extra protection at the expense of the stockholders. Since Revlon's acceptance of the Forstmann bid brought the auction to an end before Pantry Pride could top it (which it indicated it would do), the board had violated this principal duty to the stockholders.

g. Protection of directors: In fact, the Delaware court seemed heavily influenced by the fact that the Revlon directors were not really protecting the note holders out of fondness for the note holders — they were protecting the note holders because they feared that ***they themselves might be liable*** if they didn't do so. "[W]hen a board ends an intense bidding contest on an insubstantial basis, and where a significant by-product of that action is to protect the directors against a perceived threat of personal liability for consequences stemming from the adoption of previous defensive measures, the action cannot withstand the intense scrutiny which [prior cases] require . . . of director conduct."

h. Lock-ups: The court gave special treatment to the use of ***lock-ups***, such as the crown jewel option granted by Revlon to Forstmann. Lock-ups will not be per se illegal under Delaware law. But they must be used to ***expand the competition***, not to destroy it. For instance, if a lock-up were the only way to induce a second bidder to enter the competition, it might well be legal since it would be shareholder-value-maximizing. But here, Forstmann was already an active bidder, and the use of the lock-up merely ended the auction rather than enhancing it, so the lock-up violated the directors' duty to get the best price.

i. Consequence: So the *Revlon* case stands for several propositions:

(1) Once management decides to ***offer the company for sale***, or decides that a sale is ***inevitable***, it may ***no longer use defensive measures***, and must instead make every effort to achieve the ***best price*** for the stockholders;

(2) Getting the best price for stockholders means ***treating all bidders equally***, not preferring one bidder over another;

(3) The use of ***lock-ups,*** and the divulging of ***confidential financial information*** to one bidder rather than another, are the kinds of actions that probably constitute inappropriate favoritism;

(4) In choosing among offers, the board's sole duty is to the ***common stockholders*** (i.e., to get the highest price), and the board may not attempt to get extra protection for employees, creditors, management or itself at the expense of shareholders.

3. **Management interested:** Where the target's ***management*** is one of the competing bidders, the courts will be especially careful to ensure that the Level Playing Field rule is applied. This is even more the case when management has ***seats on the board*** — it will be almost essential that the ***independent directors*** make a full investigation of their own, and treat all bidders equally.

   a. **Use of special committee:** In this situation in which management is one of the bidders, the target should form a ***special committee of independent directors***, and this special committee: (1) should have truly independent legal and investment banking counsel; and (2) should itself conduct the negotiation and/or auction, rather than letting the inside directors serve on the target's side of the process.

4. **Taking an action that might "put the company in play":** Where the target's board takes an action which ***might*** have the effect of ***"putting the corporation in play,"*** i.e., attracting a hostile takeover bid, this action does ***not*** by itself trigger the Level Playing Field rule. Thus in *Paramount Communications, Inc. v. Time, Inc.*, discussed extensively *infra*, Time's board decided to merge with another company; the Delaware Supreme Court concluded that the fact that Time's directors knew that the merger might put Time "in play" (i.e., signal to Wall Street the company's vulnerability, and thus attract a hostile suitor) was not itself enough to trigger the Level Playing Field rule. Only when a corporation ***initiates an active bidding process*** for itself, or otherwise seeks some transaction involving a ***breakup of the company***, will the Level Playing Field rule apply. *Id.*

5. **Mere possibility that offer may soon be made:** If ***no formal offer*** to buy the company has ***so far occurred,*** the Level Playing Field rule is ***not triggered***, even if the board has specific reason to believe that a particular party may well ***soon make an offer.*** As the Delaware Court said in an important 2009 case, "*Revlon* duties do not arise simply because a company is 'in play.' The duty to seek the best available price applies only when a company ***embarks on a transaction*** — on its own initiative or in response to an unsolicited offer — that will result in a change of control." ***Lyondell Chemical Co. v. Ryan***, 970 A.2d 235 (Del. 2009).

   Therefore, even though the board may reasonably believe that an offer will soon be forthcoming, the board is ***free to "wait and see"*** whether the offer occurs, and need not take any concrete steps in anticipation, like ascertaining what other potential bidders might exist, trying to gauge the company's value to an acquirer, or plotting how to get the best price. Only when the board actually receives an offer ***and starts negotiating with the bidder*** need it take concrete steps to obtain the best price. *Lyondell, supra.*

   a. **Facts of *Lyondell*:** In May, 2007, Blavatnik, a European chemical tycoon, filed a Schedule 13D (see *supra*, p. 438) with the SEC, indicating that he controlled 8.3% of the stock of Lyondell, a U.S.-based chemical company, and might be interested in acquiring more. The board of Lyondell made no public response to this filing, deciding instead to "wait and see" what Blavatnik would do next. Then, on July 9 of that year, Blavatnik met with Lyondell's CEO, Smith, and offered to buy the entire company for $40 per share. Smith told Blavatnik that $40 was too low, and Blavatnik immediately raised his offer to $44-45. Smith responded that he believed the board would reject this offer, too, as being too low, since the company was not on the market.

i. **The final offer:** Later that afternoon, Blavatnik made what he described as a final offer to Smith of $48 per share, with no financing contingency. However, Blavatnik told Smith that to get that price, Lyondell would have to (a) sign a merger agreement by July 16, and (b) agree to a $400 million break-up fee if Lyondell later cancelled.

ii. **Negotiations:** Over the next week, the Lyondell board negotiated the terms of a merger agreement with Blavatnik, obtained several valuation models from its investment bank (which all concluded that $48 was a very attractive price), and finally signed the agreement on July 16, just before the offer was to lapse.

b. **The suit:** The deal was then approved by 99% of the voted shares, and was consummated at the $48 price. Shortly thereafter, some shareholders brought a class action against the board, claiming that the directors had breached their duty of loyalty in various ways. For instance, the plaintiffs asserted, the directors had shown bad faith by taking, during the two months between the 13D filing and the July 9 offer, no action to prepare for a possible acquisition bid, and by otherwise failing to discharge their *Revlon* duty to get the best price.

i. **High hurdle:** The suit, to survive, had to demonstrate a breach of the duty of *loyalty*, since Lyondell had enacted a § 102(b)(7) clause preventing liability for breaches of the duty of *care*.

ii. **Trial court allows suit to continue:** The trial court (the Delaware Chancery Court) denied the directors' motion for summary judgment. In reaching that conclusion, the court decided that the directors' *Revlon* duty to get the best price had begun as soon as Blavatnik filed the 13D, that there was some evidence that the directors failed in bad faith to discharge that duty (e.g., by not canvassing other potential buyers after the filing), and that this evidence precluded summary judgment on the bad faith issue.

c. **Supreme Court reverses:** But the Delaware Supreme Court ***reversed***, and ordered summary judgment for the directors. The court said that the directors' decision to take a "wait and see" approach "was an entirely ***appropriate*** exercise of the directors' business judgment." In contrast to the trial court's ruling, "the time for action under *Revlon* [to get the best price] did not begin until July 10, 2007, when the directors ***began negotiating the sale[.]"***

i. **"Utter failure to attempt" standard:** Furthermore, the court held, the lower court had incorrectly assumed that once the time for action began, the plaintiffs could carry their burden to show director bad faith merely by showing that the board did not do everything that it (arguably) should have or could have done to obtain the best sale price. Instead, the proper inquiry was "whether [the] directors ***utterly failed to [even] attempt*** to obtain the best sale price."

ii. **Several steps taken:** As to this point, the court pointed out, during the one week that the directors had between the start of negotations and the announced end of the offer, the directors had ***met several times*** to consider the offer, which was at a substantial premium to the prior stock price. During that week they had also ***solicited and followed the advice of their financial and legal advisors***. They had at least briefly ***attempted to negotiate a higher offer***, and had been rebuffed by Blavatnik's "take it or leave it" stance. They had then finally approved the agreement because they believed that it was simply too good not to pass along to stockholders for their consideration.

iii. **Plaintiffs lose:** These steps were more than enough to demonstrate that the plaintiffs ***had not come forward with evidence*** from which a reasonable jury could find an "utter fail[ure] to attempt to obtain the best sale price," which was the only basis on which a jury could have found the requisite bad faith breach of the duty of loyalty.

6. **Offer by controlling shareholder:** The "Level Playing Field" rule, when it applies, means that the target must try to get the "best price reasonably available." The rule does ***not*** mean that the target must ***treat all bidders precisely equally***, because the bidders themselves may not truly be equal. One example of this "not necessarily equal" fact is that where a ***controlling shareholder*** makes an offer for the rest of the company, the board doesn't necessarily have to take actions that would make the target attractive to outside bidders — the board may actually be able to take a relatively ***low offer*** from the controlling shareholder, in recognition of the reality that that shareholder can veto any outside offer.

I. **Sale of "control":** *Revlon* establishes that where the board decides to "sell the company," the court will give enhanced scrutiny both to the process that the directors followed and to the substantive fairness of the result. A similar enhanced scrutiny will be given to transactions in which the board ***"sells control"*** of the company to a single individual or group. This result stems from the Delaware Supreme Court's decision in ***Paramount Communications, Inc. v. QVC Network***, 637 A.2d 34 (Del. 1994).

1. **Deal with Viacom:** After Paramount unsuccessfully tried to merge with Time (see *infra*, pp. 469-471), Paramount's directors decided that if they didn't arrange a defensive merger, they might be the subject of a hostile takeover bid themselves. Therefore, the directors agreed to have Paramount merge into Viacom, another media company. Viacom was under the control of lawyer-turned-entrepreneur Sumner Redstone, who knew enough about takeovers to want to make very sure that the Viacom-Paramount merger deal didn't simply put Paramount "in play" in a way that would lead to someone else's getting the prize instead of Viacom.

2. **Lock-ups and other protective measures:** Therefore, Viacom insisted that the Paramount-Viacom merger agreement contain a number of unusual features that would make it very hard for Paramount to abandon the deal and merge or sell to someone else. The Paramount board complied. Thus the agreement provided these special protections for Viacom:

a. **No-shop provision:** First, a ***"No-shop"*** Provision severely limited the Paramount directors' right to offer to sell or merge the company with some third party. Not only couldn't Paramount do this on its own initiative, but it couldn't even respond to unsolicited offers from third parties, unless two conditions were satisfied: (i) the unsolicited third-party offer was not "subject to any material contingencies relating to financing"; and (ii) the Paramount board decided that discussions with the third-party were necessary for the Paramount board to comply with its fiduciary duties.

b. **Termination Fee provision:** Second, under a ***"Termination Fee"*** provision, Viacom would get a $100 million fee if any of several things happened to end the deal with Viacom: Paramount got sold to someone else, or the Paramount board declined to recommend the Viacom deal to shareholders, or Paramount holders decided on their own not to approve the transaction.

c. **Lock-up Stock Option:** Finally (and probably most importantly in economic terms), a ***"Stock Option Agreement"*** gave Viacom the right to purchase 19.9% of Paramount's outstanding stock at a fixed price of $69.14 a share (the price at which Viacom would be buying Paramount under the deal) if any of the events that would trigger the termination fee (see *supra*) occurred (i.e., if the deal fell apart.) Although such "lock-up" stock options were not unusual in friendly merger transactions, this one had two highly unusual features:

   i. **No cash:** First, Viacom did ***not have to put up any cash*** to exercise the option: it could pay by giving an essentially-unsecured "note" for the price (and the note would be of questionable marketability given Viacom's finances).

   ii. **"Put" right:** Second, Viacom could, instead of exercising the option, require Paramount to ***pay it cash*** representing the difference between the $69.14 option exercise price and the market price at the time of the exercise. This "put" option meant that Viacom wouldn't have to exercise the option and then sell the stock on the open market (which might have depressed the price it got); it could instead require Paramount to simply pay it cash equal to the "market value" of its option. And since there was no "cap," this was an open-ended liability to Paramount.

d. **QVC bid:** After the deal with Viacom was agreed on, another bidder, QVC, came on the scene. QVC's offer had a face value that exceeded the Viacom offer by over $1 billion. But Paramount's management portrayed the QVC offer to the board as having lots of contingencies (e.g., ones relating to financing), while ignoring comparable contingencies in the Viacom offer. (Paramount management appears to have favored the Viacom deal because Paramount's chairman would remain in power, whereas he would not with the QVC deal.) Paramount responded to the QVC offer by improving the deal with Viacom slightly, but only by getting a bit more compensation, not by bargaining for the removal of the No-Shop Provision, the Termination Fee or the Stock Option Agreement.

3. **Court strikes down:** The Delaware Supreme Court agreed with the Chancery Court that the revised Viacom-Paramount deal was ***unreasonable***, and ***enjoined the parties*** from going through with it. The Court reached this decision in two main parts:

a. **"Sale of control" triggers enhanced scrutiny:** First, the Court held that ***"enhanced scrutiny"*** — the kind of close review given, for instance, in Revlon — must be given whenever there is a ***"sale of control."*** So it's not just when the entire company is put up for a cash sale that there will be enhanced scrutiny; this will also occur whenever control of the corporation would pass from the public to a single individual or single entity.

   i. **Redstone:** In the present transaction, it was not the fact that Paramount shareholders would be exchanging their shares for shares in Viacom that made this a "sale of control." It was, rather, the fact that Paramount shareholders were getting most of their compensation in non-voting Viacom stock, coupled with the fact that Viacom had a controlling shareholder, Sumner Redstone. These two facts taken together meant that after the transaction, the control of Paramount that once rested in public hands would now be in the hands of one individual, Redstone.

   ii. **Rationale:** Why should the sale of control be the thing that triggers enhanced scrutiny? The Paramount court's answer was this: "The acquisition of majority status and the consequent privilege of exerting the powers of majority ownership come at a price. That price is usually a ***control premium*** which recognizes not only the value of a control block of shares, but also ***compensates*** the minority stockholders for their resulting ***loss of voting power***. . . . Once control has shifted, the current Paramount stockholders will have ***no leverage in the future*** to demand another control premium. As a result, [they] are entitled to receive, and should receive, a control premium and/or protective devices of significant value. There being no such protective provisions in the Viacom-Paramount transaction, the Paramount directors had an obligation to take the maximum advantage of the current opportunity to ***realize for stockholders the best value reasonably available***."

b. **Deal fails "enhanced scrutiny":** The second part of the opinion applied the enhanced-scrutiny test to the facts of the case. The Viacom deal failed this enhanced scrutiny, the Court found.

   i. **Procedural defects:** Procedurally, the Paramount board gave "insufficient attention" to the ways in which the various features of the Viacom deal impeded the board's ability to get the "best deal" for shareholders.

   ii. **Substantive defects:** Substantively, the ***result*** achieved for stockholders was also ***"not reasonable."*** Even after the Paramount board had made the original deal with Viacom, the board clearly had the clout (stemming from the QVC offer) to revise the deal and remove the unreasonable competition-thwarting provisions (e.g., the Stock Option). But, the court found, the board "remained paralyzed by their uninformed belief that the QVC offer was 'illusory,' " and thus "squandered" their final chance to "seek the best value reasonably available."

c. **Special features struck down:** Finally, the court ***struck down*** the ***No-Shop*** Provision, the ***Termination Fee*** and the ***Stock Option***. Since these were all unreasonable (because designed to limit a competitive offer), they were simply unenforceable.

4. **Significance:** The main significance of *Paramount v. QVC* is that enhanced scrutiny now occurs whenever the board proposes a transaction that would result in a ***"shift of control"*** from the public to a ***particular individual or small entity***.

   a. **Criticism:** This can produce a result that some think is anomalous: a merger transaction in some cases either will or will not trigger close judicial scrutiny, depending solely on ***whether the acquiring corporation has a controlling shareholder***.

      Example: Consider the directors of small publicly-held software company (let's call it Soft Co.) who have a choice of whether to merge into IBM or Microsoft. If they propose a stock merger into IBM — i.e., the stockholders will get IBM stock in exchange for their Soft Co. stock — there will be no enhanced judicial scrutiny of the merger, because IBM has no controlling shareholder (so that post-merger, control of the combined entity will remain vested in the "fluid aggregation of unaffiliated stockholders," to quote the *Paramount* court.) Instead, the transaction will be subject only to the "business judgment" rule, and will receive great deference from the courts.

      But if the Soft Co. directors propose a merger into *Microsoft*, it's a different story. Assume that one individual (Bill Gates) is a controlling shareholder of the acquiring company (with about 25% of the stock), so he'll be in control of the merged entity. Therefore, the Delaware courts will give enhanced scrutiny to the transaction as they did in *Paramount* (e.g., they'll check closely to see that the "best price reasonably available" was achieved). It is not clear that it is "sensible industrial policy" to make the friendly transaction with Microsoft harder to do than the friendly transaction with IBM.

J. **Board's right to "just say no":** Suppose that Raider makes an ***all-cash tender offer*** at a ***much-higher-than-market price***, for all of Target's shares. Does Target's board have the right to ***"just say no"***? That is, may Target's board refuse to redeem a previously-enacted poison pill defense scheme, refuse to let Target's shareholders vote on the transaction, or otherwise side-step the attractive offer? In Delaware, the general answer is ***"yes."*** This principle is illustrated by ***Paramount Communications, Inc. v. Time, Inc.***, 571 A.2d 1140 (Del. 1989).

1. **Facts:** *Paramount* involved the efforts of Paramount Communications to interfere with a pending merger between Time, Inc. and Warner Communications, and to acquire Time for itself in a cash tender offer. (This transaction came before the Paramount-Viacom transaction described *supra*, p. 466-469.)

   a. **Initial merger:** Time and Warner, both large media conglomerates, decided to merge in a stock-for-stock transaction. Warner's stockholders would have ended up owning 62% of the combined Time-Warner stock, but Time would in some senses (including board control) have been the "surviving" corporation. Under New York Stock Exchange rules, this proposed merger would have had to be approved by a vote of Time's stockholders (as well as Warner's). At the same time the Time board agreed to the merger plan, it adopted several defensive tactics (e.g., it purchased agreements from various banks that the banks would not finance any third-party attempt to acquire Time).

b. **All-cash offer from Paramount:** After the proposed merger was announced, and in fact after proxy statements were sent to stockholders so that they could vote on the transaction, Paramount, another large media conglomerate, made a surprise all-cash offer of $175 per share for all outstanding Time shares. (Just before the offer, Time's stock was trading at $126.) This offer was not subject to any financing contingencies, but was subject to certain legal contingencies (e.g., the need for Paramount to get regulatory approval of various cable franchise transfers from Time).

c. **Offer rejected:** The Time board met several times to consider this offer, but rejected it, principally on the grounds that it presented a threat to Time's "control of its own destiny and retention of the 'Time Culture.' " Instead, Time's board recast the Warner deal into an acquisition of Warner by Time for cash and securities (all cash for 51% of the stock, and a later mixture of cash and securities for the remaining 49%). This way of doing the deal had the disadvantage that Time would have to assume $7-10 billion worth of debt. But this structure would have the advantage of not requiring approval by Time shareholders.

d. **Offer raised:** In response to the new Time-acquires-Warner-for-cash deal, Paramount boosted its tender offer to $200 per share. Time's board rejected this offer as well. Paramount then (together with various Time, Inc. shareholders) sued Time in Delaware to enjoin the Time-Warner transaction.

2. **Injunction denied:** The Delaware Supreme Court rejected the request for injunction. In so doing, it denied both claims asserted by the various plaintiffs: (1) a *Revlon* claim (see *supra*, p. 462), i.e., that Time was effectively being sold and all bidders must be given a "level playing field"; and (2) a *Unocal* argument (see *supra*, p. 458), that the behavior here of the Time board — especially the decision to acquire Warner for cash — was a defensive response, which should be struck down because it was not a proportional response to a reasonable threat to Time's business.

3. **The *Revlon* argument:** The court first concluded that Time's decision to acquire Warner for cash did not trigger *Revlon* ***"level playing field"*** duties. *Revlon* duties will arise where either: (1) a corporation initiates an active bidding process seeking to sell itself; or (2) in response to a bidder's offer, the corporation "abandons its long-term strategy and seeks an alternative transaction also involving the breakup of the company."[1] However, the court decided, neither of these circumstances existed here.

4. **No violation of *Unocal* principles:** Similarly, the conduct of Time's board did not violate any duties under *Unocal*, which governs what defensive responses are proper.

a. **First prong:** *Unocal*'s first prong requires that the board have reasonable grounds for believing that a ***danger to "corporate policy and effectiveness"*** exists. Here, this prong was satisfied, because the board could reasonably have believed that Time's shareholders might elect to tender into Paramount's cash offer in ignorance or in a mistaken belief about the strategic benefits which a business combination with Warner might produce. The court rejected Paramount's argument that where an acquirer

1. The later case of *Paramount v. QVC* (*supra*, p. 466) added "sale of control" as a third situation in which level-playing-field duties would be triggered.

makes an all-cash, all-shares tender offer at an above-market price, there cannot *be* any threat to corporate policy or effectiveness. Instead, the court reasoned, the board may consider ***long-term values and strategies***, and may decide that the tender offer poses a threat to these long-term values, as the Time board did here.

b. Second prong: The second prong of the *Unocal* test — that the target's board's ***response*** to the perceived threat be ***"reasonable"*** and ***"proportional"*** to the threat — was also satisfied here. Time's decision to restructure its merger into an asset acquisition of Warner was a reasonable response to Paramount's threatening tender offer, because "the carrying forward of a pre-existing transaction in an altered form . . . was reasonably related to the threat." This was true even though the cost to Time and its shareholders of recasting the transaction into an asset purchase was that Time would be burdened by very heavy debt.

5. Significance of case: *Paramount v. Time* illustrates that the target's board may in general ***"just say no"*** — it may refuse to take affirmative steps so as to give the shareholders a chance to approve the transaction. Of course, normally shareholder approval for a tender offer is not necessary — the shareholders simply decide whether to tender their shares, and each shareholder acts individually. But where an acquirer makes a tender offer that is conditional upon acts by the board (e.g., conditional upon the board's decision to redeem a previously-issued poison pill, or the board's agreement to cancel some other pending transaction, as Paramount demanded that Time do concerning the Warner acquisition), the board may simply refuse to take that action, as long as this board response is a "reasonable response to a perceived threat" (the *Unocal* test). And it will apparently take very little to convince the Delaware courts that this "reasonable response to a perceived threat" standard is satisfied.

K. When "enhanced scrutiny" applies: As we've seen over the past pages (pp. 461-471), sometimes the Delaware courts ***apply "enhanced scrutiny"*** to the target's actions, and sometimes they don't. When they apply enhanced scrutiny, the courts are likely to: (i) enjoin or reverse the transaction unless they are convinced that the target's board and management have obtained the ***best price reasonably available*** for the shareholders; and (ii) ***strike down defensive measures*** that materially lessen the interest of other bidders. When the Delaware courts *don't* apply enhanced scrutiny, they typically find the target's directors' actions protected by the business judgment rule. Therefore, it's worth recapitulating in one place the situations in which Delaware does and does not apply enhanced scrutiny:

1. Scrunity used: There are three major situations in which Delaware ***applies*** enhanced scrutiny:

a. Active bidding process: When the corporation ***"initiates an active bidding process seeking to sell itself*** or to effect a business reorganization involving a clear break-up of the company." *Paramount v. Time* (*supra*, p. 469). In other words, enhanced scrutiny applies where the company ***"puts itself on the market."***

b. Abandonment of long-term strategy: When the corporation, in response to a bidder's offer, ***"abandons its long-term strategy*** and seeks an alternative transaction involving the ***break-up*** of the company." Id.

c. **Sale or change of control:** When approval of a transaction would result in a ***"sale or change of control,"*** i.e., control would pass to a ***single individual*** or ***small entity***. *Paramount v. QVC* (*supra*, p. 469).

See generally *Arnold v. Soc. for Savings Bancorp*, 650 A.2d 1290 (Del. 1994), listing these three situations.

2. **Scrutiny not used:** Delaware does ***not*** apply enhanced scrutiny (and instead uses the unadorned business judgment rule) in the following situations:

   a. **Board says "no":** When the target receives an ***unsolicited offer***, and the board essentially ***"says no"*** to the offer. *Paramount v. Time* (*supra*, p. 469). This scenario also applies where the board ***refuses to undo some previous defensive measure***, or takes new defensive measures.

      i. ***Unocal*** **duties:** However, if the target takes defensive measures (or refuses to undo prior measures), the measures must satisfy the *Unocal* danger-to-corporate-effectiveness/proportionality rules; see *supra*, p. 470.

   b. **Merger into uncontrolled public company:** When the target, without putting itself up for sale or break-up, proposes to ***merge*** into another public company that is ***not controlled by any one person or small group***. *Arnold v. Soc. for Savings Bancorp, supra*.

L. **Particular anti-takeover devices:** Now, let us look briefly at how courts, especially those of Delaware, have reacted to ***particular types*** of anti-takeover devices.

1. **Greenmail:** Courts have generally given a target's directors and management considerable leeway to ***pay greenmail***. For instance, Delaware applies its general analysis (see *supra*, p. 457) to greenmail payments:

   a. **Justifiable fears:** If the board shows that it is worried that a particular hostile takeover will ***damage the corporation's existence or business policies***, and buying back the raider's shares at a premium in return for a standstill agreement will prevent the hostile takeover, the Delaware courts will generally ***approve*** the transaction even though it enriches the bidder at the expense of the corporation's treasury. See *Cheff v. Mathes*, 199 A.2d 548 (Del. 1964), upholding a greenmail payment on the grounds that the board justifiably feared the hostile bidder's poor reputation.

   b. **Entrenchment:** But if the decision to pay greenmail is shown to have been motivated mostly by the board's or management's desire to ***retain their positions***, the greenmail payment will be ***struck down***.

   c. **Size of premium:** Interestingly, the ***size of the premium*** paid above market value seems not to be a key aspect of the Delaware decisions, except perhaps that a very large premium will increase the chance that the court will find the board to have been motivated primarily by self-interest.

2. **Exclusionary repurchases:** Recall that one technique by which the target may try to repulse a hostile bidder is by embarking on its own aggressive program of ***share repurchases*** — if the target offers a higher price for its own shares than the bidder is offering, the target's holders will be less likely to tender to the bidder. The interesting question is:

May the target ***exclude the bidder*** from participating in the share repurchase program? At least in Delaware, the answer will generally be "yes." The Delaware Supreme Court upheld such a selective share repurchase program in one of the main cases setting out Delaware's general approach to reviewing defensive measures, ***Unocal Corp. v. Mesa Petroleum Co.***, 493 A.2d 946 (Del. 1985).

a. **Facts:** Mesa, which already owned 13% of Unocal, instituted a two-tier front-loaded tender offer for another 37% of Unocal. The offer indicated that if it were successful (giving Mesa half of Unocal), Mesa would then bring about a back-end cash-out merger in which the remaining half of Unocal stock would be bought out for highly subordinated junk bonds. Unocal's board then offered to have Unocal repurchase up to 49% of its shares in exchange for debt that Unocal claimed to be worth $72 per share. But this repurchase program would backfire if Mesa was allowed to participate by reselling its shares to Unocal for the $72 debt package — Unocal would be subsidizing Mesa's takeover efforts, by paying $72 for shares that Mesa had just bought for $54. Therefore, Unocal's offer to repurchase its shares specifically excluded Mesa.

b. **Upheld:** The Delaware Supreme Court ***upheld*** the share repurchase program, including its exclusion of Mesa. The Unocal directors had the burden of showing reasonable grounds to believe: (1) that Mesa's takeover threat posed a danger to the corporation's welfare (not just to the directors and management); and (2) that the repurchase program undertaken as a defensive measure was proportional to the threat posed. (These are the two basic requirements consistently imposed by Delaware in reviewing defensive measures; see *supra*, p. 457.)

   i. **Danger of coercion:** Here, requirement (1) was satisfied because Mesa's bid was reasonably perceived to be an unfair coercive front-loaded tender offer (shareholders would tender because they would be scared of being left out and forced to take inferior junk bonds in the back-end merger).

   ii. **Proportionality:** Requirement (2) was satisfied because: (a) it might defeat the Mesa bid entirely; and (b) if it didn't defeat the bid, non-mesa shareholders would at least be better protected, because shares not bought by Mesa would be exchanged for senior debt securities rather than highly subordinated junk bonds.

c. **Independent directors:** The court in *Unocal* also attached importance to the fact that Unocal's board, which approved the plan, had a ***majority of outside independent directors***, and the board acted only after considerable investigation and thought (e.g., advice by investment bankers and lawyers).

d. **SEC's "all holders" rule:** Today, Unocal's discriminatory share repurchase program would probably ***violate federal securities law.*** Following the *Unocal* decision, and in response to criticism that companies like Unocal should not be allowed to discriminate among various stockholders, the SEC enacted its Rule 14d-10 under the '34 Act. That rule prohibits any tender offer "unless . . . [t]he tender offer is open to all security holders of the class of securities subject to the tender offer. . . ." This so-called ***"all holders"*** rule presumably applies to issuers' self-tender offers as well as to third-party tender offers, and would thus prevent Unocal from excluding Mesa from the share repurchase program today. See F,B&H, p. 80.

3. **Poison pill plans:** In general, courts have upheld the validity of ***poison pill*** plans (see *supra*, p. 452). But a few plans have been struck down. A key element to the fate of a poison pill plan is likely to be the ***degree*** to which it discourages hostile takeovers: if the plan so economically burdens bidders that practically no bidder is likely to come forward, the court is much more likely to strike down the plan than if it has merely a minor impact on the whole takeover process.

   a. ***Moran*** **case:** The leading case on the validity of poison pill plans is ***Moran v. Household International, Inc.***, 500 A.2d 1346 (Del. 1985), in which the Delaware Supreme Court sustained a plan of the "call" variety.

      i. **Facts of *Moran:*** In *Moran*, the target (Household International Inc.) gave each of its shareholders a call right with a ***"flip over"*** (see *supra*, p. 452) provision. Under the flip over, if anyone acquired 20% or tender offered for 30% of Household, and then merged with Household, each Household shareholder would get to buy stock in the surviving company at half price. The board could "redeem" the rights (i.e., cancel them) for a nominal payment at any time until an acquirer obtained 20% of Household's shares. The plan was put into effect before there was a specific hostile bid on the table (allowing the board to claim that it was worried about two-tier front-loaded offers, even though one never emerged).

      ii. **Plan upheld:** The Delaware Supreme Court ***upheld*** the rights plan, holding that it was a reasonably proportional response to a reasonable fear (the fear of two-tier front-loaded coercive offers), and that it was enacted by an adequately-informed board having a majority of independent directors. (These general requirements, as articulated in *Moran*, are discussed further *supra*, p. 457.)

      iii. **Does not stop all hostile takeovers:** The plaintiff's key contention in *Moran* was that the poison pill plan would effectively block any hostile tender offer (since the offeror would be worried about dilution of its own shares through the "flip over"). But the court rejected this contention on factual grounds: a hostile bidder could avoid the flip over by making its offer ***conditional*** upon redemption by the board of the rights, by tendering for the rights as well as the shares, or by other means. Furthermore, if an actual hostile bid materialized and the bidder requested that the board redeem the rights, the board could not arbitrarily refuse to do so, and any refusal would be treated as a new form of board action that could be set aside by the court if motivated by a desire for entrenchment. Finally, the court noted that a poison pill plan is generally less damaging to the corporation than many other defensive maneuvers that are sometimes sustained (e.g., a restructuring by means of a large increase in corporate debt, or the payment of greenmail).

   b. **Consequence:** Therefore, at least in Delaware, the adoption of a poison pill plan will probably ***rarely*** be ***invalidated***. As long as the plan does not substantially foreclose hostile tender offers, it will be sustained if it is enacted in response to the board's reasonable fears of damage to the corporation.

      i. **Redemption:** On the other hand, once the company does go up for sale, the board's handling of the rights will probably be judged by reference to the Level Playing Field rule (*supra*, p. 461). For instance, the board can't tell one bidder that it will redeem the rights for that bidder, but refuse to do so for another bidder offering approximately the same price.

ii. Dead hand and no hand provisions: Furthermore, there is one feature of some poison pill plans that is quite likely to be invalidated right after its enactment, without reference to the Level Playing Field rule. This is the ***dead hand*** (or a variant, the ***no hand***) feature. Recall (see *supra*, p. 453) that a dead hand provision prevents the board of the target from redeeming previously-granted poison pill rights, thus preventing a hostile bidder from persuading a majority of the target's shareholders to elect new directors who will redeem the pill. Similarly, a no hand provision forces any successor board to wait some designated period of time before redeeming a pill. In an important 1998 decision, the Delaware Supreme Court struck down a no hand provision on the grounds that it inappropriately ***limited a successor board's ability to carry out its fiduciary duties***. *Quickturn Design Syst. v. Shapiro*, 721 A.2d 1281 (Del. 1998).

(1) Significance: The decision in *Quickturn* seems to mean that in Delaware, when a board enacts a poison pill, ***the board cannot significantly restrict the ability of a successor board to cancel or redeem the pill.*** This in turn means that as long as the acquirer is able (perhaps in a proxy fight), to convince the target's shareholders to replace a majority of the board, the poison pill should offer little barrier to a merger between the acquirer and the target.

4. Lock-ups: Of all anti-takeover devices, the ***lock-up*** is the one most closely scrutinized by courts, and ***most likely to be invalidated.*** The most common form of lock-up is the ***"crown jewel option"*** (*supra*, p. 454). Usually the crown jewel option is given to a third party bidder favored by management, who in return for entering the bidding war as a white knight gets the option to buy one or more of the target's best businesses at a very low price if the third party's bid is eventually topped by the hostile bidder. The mere existence of the crown jewel option makes the white knight much more likely to prevail, because the target is (with its best businesses under option) less attractive to the hostile bidder than if the option were not in existence.

a. Usable to promote better offer: Lock-ups are ***not per se illegal*** in most jurisdictions. For instance, a lock-up might be used properly if its result is to ***produce an auction*** where none would otherwise exist.

Example: Raider makes a hostile bid for Target at $30 per share (at a time when Target is trading for $20 per share). No other potential acquirers of Target come on the scene of their own volition. Target's management finds a leveraged buyout firm, White Knight Inc, which is not inclined on its own to make a bid for Target higher than $30. But in return for an option to buy Target's Crown Jewel Division for $100 million (it has a fair market value of $150 million), White Knight is induced to make a bid of $32 per share for all of Target — the option will only be exercisable if Target accepts a higher bid for the whole company from some other bidder (including Raider).

A court would probably hold that this crown jewel option was valid, since its effect was to produce a higher bid for the entire company, and to create the possibility of an auction where none otherwise existed.

b. Used to end auction: But if a crown jewel option or other lock-up is given to ***end an auction*** rather than to create one, the court is much more likely to find that the grant of the option violated the Level Playing Field rule (see *supra*, p. 461). For instance, if two bidders, A and B, are ***already*** each trying to win control of Target, and management gives a crown jewel option to B because it would rather have B win the auction instead of A, the court is likely to find that this preference violated Target's board's duty to get the highest price obtainable once it was clear that the company would be sold anyway. This is what happened in *Revlon* (*supra*, p. 461), in which the Delaware Supreme Court struck down a crown jewel option.

c. "Force the vote" and other deal-protection measures (*Omnicare* case): A prospective buyer will often take steps to ***avoid being used as a "stalking horse" bidder***, i.e., one whose bid is used merely to extract a higher bid from someone else to whom the target ends up selling. As a result of an important 2003 Delaware decision, at least some combinations of ***deal-protection measures*** given to satisfy the first bidder's "I won't be a stalking horse" demand (and thus to lock up the deal for that bidder) will be found to ***violate*** the Level Playing Field rule.

That case was ***Omnicare, Inc. v. NCS Healthcare, Inc.***, 818 A.2d 914 (Del. 2003), where the Delaware Supreme Court struck down a combination of (1) an absolute agreement by the target's board to a "force the vote" provision (i.e., a requirement that the board submit the proposed merger to the target shareholders even if the board by then no longer supported the deal) and (2) an advance agreement by the target's controlling shareholders that they would vote their shares in favor of the merger. The case seems to stand for the proposition that ***an "absolute lock up"*** that makes approval of the merger a ***mathematical certainty*** will be ***invalid*** in Delaware, even if the bidder is the only or highest bidder in the picture and will walk away if not given the lock up.

i. Facts: NCS, the target, was on the verge of bankruptcy and had tried to sell itself without success. Finally, Genesis offered to buy it in a stock-for-stock merger. But Genesis made it clear that it wasn't willing to risk being a stalking horse bidder whose bid might be used to extract a better bid from someone else, particularly a bid by Omnicare (a competitor who had bested Genesis in a prior bidding war for a different company). Therefore, Genesis was only willing to sign the proposed merger agreement if it got three protections:

[1] a ***voting agreement*** by the two controlling shareholders of NCS,[2] ensuring that they would vote for the proposed merger no matter what else happened (e.g., a higher bid from someone else);

[2] a ***"force the vote" agreement*** by the NCS board, i.e., an agreement that the board would submit the proposed merger to stockholders for approval even if

---

2. These two holders together owned a majority of the common stock.

the board had subsequently determined that the merger was not in the shareholders' best interest; and

[3] the ***omission*** of any ***"fiduciary out"*** clause from the merger agreement, i.e., omission of any provision that the board would not be bound by the force-the-vote provision if the board's fiduciary responsibilities required it to oppose the transaction.

Because the board and the two controlling shareholders were afraid the company would go bankrupt if the Genesis deal fell through, the board and those two holders agreed to all of these conditions, and the agreement with Genesis was signed.

(1) Omnicare bids higher: Hours after the NCS-Genesis merger agreement was signed, Omnicare made a clearly superior tender offer for all NCS' shares. The NCS board withdrew its recommendation that shareholders approve the Genesis transaction, but the three Genesis-favorable conditions that NCS had already agreed to effectively ensured that the inferior Genesis transaction, not the later, better Omnicare offer, would be consummated. Omnicare sued for an injunction preventing the Genesis transaction from being completed.

ii. Omnicare wins: In a highly unusual 3-2 decision, the Delaware Supreme Court found for Omnicare, and ***invalidated the three deal-protection clauses*** in the NCS-Genesis transaction.

(1) Rationale: The majority reasoned that when the court gives "enhanced judicial scrutiny" to a company that has put itself up for sale, the company's board may agree to measures that protect the proposed merger transaction only if these measures are ***neither "coercive" nor "preclusive."*** The package of three clauses that NCS agreed to here was, the court said, *both* coercive and preclusive.

(2) Fait accompli: The heart of the majority's analysis was that the three merger-protective devices — the controlling shareholders' agreement to vote for the transaction, the board's "force the shareholder vote" agreement and the lack of any "fiduciary out" clause for the board — made it ***"mathematically impossible"*** and ***"realistically unattainable"*** for any later transaction to succeed no matter how superior it was. Thus although the minority shareholders were not forced to *vote* for the Genesis merger, they were "required to ***accept it*** because it was a fait accompli." Therefore, the combination of protective devices was unenforceable.

(3) "Fiduciary out" clause required: As a second rationale, the majority said that the merger-protection devices here were unenforceable because they ***"circumscribe[d] the directors' fiduciary duties."*** A target's board may give the other party to a proposed merger ***"reasonable structural and economic defenses [and] incentives"*** to make the merger agreement, but these incentives ***may not amount to an "absolute lock up."*** And the absence of a fiduciary-out clause here constituted an absolute, and thus illegal, lock up.

iii. Dissent: The two dissenters argued that the NCS board had behaved reasonably, and that the protections it agreed to should therefore have been enforced. The board had reasonably concluded that the Genesis deal was the "only game in town," and the board got the best deal it could from Genesis. Indeed, it was only the signing of the Genesis merger agreement that made the later, better, offer from Omnicare possible. And there was not really any "coercion" of the minority shareholders — they knew going in that the two controlling shareholders could force consummation of any transaction, so having those two controlling shareholders cast their votes in advance did not take away any right the minority would otherwise have had.

(1) Bad incentives: Conversely, the dissenters said, the majority's rule, unless narrowly interpreted, would ***worsen the position of stockholders in target companies.*** "By deterring bidders from engaging in negotiations like those present here and requiring that there must always be a fiduciary out, the ***universe of potential bidders*** who could reasonably be expected to benefit stockholders could ***shrink or disappear."***

iv. Decision narrowed: Post-*Omnicare* Delaware decisions suggest that the case will be ***limited*** more or less to its facts, and that other combinations of deal protections will be ***upheld*** even though they may significantly discourage other bidders.

(1) Significance: In other words, *Omnicare* merely stands for a narrow proposition: a set of lock-up arrangements that, in combination, make completion of a merger ***mathematically certain*** will be struck down in Delaware. But arrangements that, while they make a merger very *likely* to be completed, don't make completion a mathematical certainty, are likely to be *valid.* So, for instance, a provision that the deal will go through only if a majority of the outside shareholders approve it will probably be enough to ***immunize*** the agreement, even though controlling shareholders bind themselves to vote for the transaction, and even though the board agrees (without any "fiduciary out" clause) to put the merger to a shareholder vote. Cf. *Orman v. Cullman*, 2004 WL 2348395 (Del. Ch. 2004).

5. Stock option: A different type of lock-up, an ***option*** to the acquirer to ***buy stock in the target***, may be either upheld or struck down, depending on the circumstances.

a. Chilling effect on other bidders: Where the stock option is for so many shares, or for so low a price, or on such burdensome terms, that its mere existence has a materially *chilling effect on whether other bidders will emerge*, the option is likely to be struck down. For instance, the option in *Paramount v. QVC* (*supra*, p. 467) — which was for 20% of the company, could be exercised without the acquirer's paying any cash, had no cap in value, and which the acquirer could force the target to redeem for cash value — was struck down. (At the time the litigation in *QVC* began, this option was worth almost $500 million!)

(Main discussion continues on p. 494, after Table 10-1.)

	Table 10-2 ***RECAP:* Analyzing Takeovers of Public Companies** This table helps you analyze three common takeover scenarios: **Scenario 1:** a ***"friendly"*** takeover by an ***insider*** of the target; **Scenario 2:** a takeover attempt by an ***"outsider"*** that ***turns friendly***; and **Scenario 3:** a ***hostile*** takeover that the target's board opposes until the bitter end. The table will help you figure out how a court should rule on various claims raised in a class action brought by stockholders who oppose the takeover. The table assumes that ***Delaware law applies*** as to all state-law questions.
	Scenario 1 **Cash Tender Offer for Target's Shares by Bidder who is an *Insider*; Deal is Recommended by Target's Board and Results in Bidder's Receiving Tenders for More than 90% of Target's Stock.**
Scenario 1: Deal Assumptions	Here are the details of the assumed "deal" in Scenario 1: [1] ***"Target"*** is a public company (listed on a national securities exchange), and chartered in Delaware. [2] ***"Bidder"*** is the entity that is now trying to acquire at least 85%, and ideally all, of Target's outstanding stock. At the outset, Bidder (and anyone affiliated with Bidder) owns no more than 15% of Target's stock, all of which was acquired in the last year. [3] The person in charge of Bidder is an ***"insider"*** of Target, i.e., a person who already holds a meaningful minority stake in Target and/or influences Target's board, so that he might be said to be already in "control" of Target. (For ease of description, we'll refer to this person as being himself "Bidder," even though the actual Bidder is an entity.) [4] A majority of Target's board consists of ***"non-independent directors"*** (i.e., directors over whom Bidder has significant influence). [5] Bidder has made a ***cash tender offer*** contingent on Bidder's receiving tenders for at least 85% of Target's total shares outstanding. [6] Target did not have any board-initiated ***takeover defenses*** at the beginning of the process, and the ***board did not initiate any*** such defenses after Bidder indicated his desire to acquire control. [7] The board of Target has ***recommended***, by majority board vote, that shareholders of Target accept the offer by tendering their shares. [8] ***91% of Target's shareholders*** have just ***tendered*** to Bidder. [9] Immediately after getting the 91% of Target's stock, Bidder now proposes a statutory ***"cash-out" short-form merger*** (i.e., a merger of a subsidiary into a parent, with the subsidiary's shareholders receiving cash) of Target into Bidder (or into Bidder's special-purpose subsidiary shell set up for this purpose) under Del. GCL § 253. Under this § 253 merger, non-tendering Target shareholders will be cashed out for the same price per share as those who tendered, and Target's independent existence will end. Target's board has approved this merger. No vote of Target's non-tendering shareholders (the remaining 9%) has been scheduled, because such a vote is not required for a short-form merger under § 253. [10] The Ps are, at all relevant times, minority ***shareholders of Target*** who didn't tender, and who now ***bring a class action*** that seeks to (1) ***enjoin consummation of the cash-out merger*** on the grounds that it is unfair because of low price; (2) ***recover damages*** for themselves against the directors of Target who voted for the transaction, based on alleged breach of the duty of care and/or the duty of loyalty, with damages to be set in an amount by which the tender price is below what the Ps say is the minimal fair price. They also seek to

	Table 10-2, Scenario 1 (cont.)
	exercise whatever ***appraisal rights*** they may have.
Scenario 1, Q1	[Verify applicability of this Scenario] Is ***Bidder*** someone who has ***significant influence*** over a ***majority of Target's board members?*** **1(a).** If yes, this Scenario is the correct one. Go to Note 1 below. **1(b).** If no, this Scenario is ***not applicable***. Go to Scenario 2 (p. 485) or Scenario 3 (p. 488).
Note 1	Once the main board ***entered into negotiations with Bidder***, those negotiations triggered the board's *Revlon* ***"Level Playing Field"*** obligations (p. 462), i.e., the obligations: (1) ***not to favor Bidder*** over other potential bidders; and (2) to make all reasonable efforts to ***get the "best price"*** for the company. Continue to Q2.
Q2	Does Target have a GCL § 102(b)(7) ***exculpatory clause*** in its ***charter***? [Save answer for later, and go to Q3.]
Q3	Did Target's board do ***both*** of the following: (1) appoint a ***Special Committee of independent directors***, all members of which are financially and socially "independent" of Bidder and (2) authorize the Committee to ***negotiate*** with Bidder to get a ***higher price***? **3(a).** If yes, go to Q4. **3(b).** If no, go to Note 5.
Q4	[You should be here if a Special Committee was appointed and authorized to negotiate with Bidder over price.] Did the Special Committee ***approve*** the proposed takeover? **4(a).** If yes, go to Q6. **4(b).** If no, go to Q7.
Note 5	[You should be here if a Special Committee was ***not*** appointed with authority to negotiate with Bidder] **5(a).** If you answered "yes" to Q2 (does the charter have an exculpatory clause?), go to Q8. **5(b).** If you answered "no" to Q2, go to Q9.
Q6	[You should be here if a Special Committee was appointed, and it approved the deal.] Assume that all events recited through #9 in the "Deal Assumptions" have occurred. In other words, the board of Target has approved the deal, and recommended that Target's shareholders accept, and tender their shares; 91% of holders have tendered, and the cash-out merger is about to occur. **6(a). Injunction issue:** Assume that dissident shareholders have just sued to ***enjoin consummation of the cash-out short-form merger*** on the grounds that the price is unfairly low. Should the court deny the injunction and let the merger be consummated? **Answer to 6(a):** The answer to this question probably does not vary depending on whether Target's charter does or doesn't have an exculpatory clause. In either event, the court will evaluate the transaction under the ***"entire fairness" test,*** because that test is used in Delaware whenever a merger has aspects of ***self-dealing*** (and Bidder's status as an insider with control of Target's board constitutes self-dealing). The plaintiff shareholders won't win (i.e., won't get the transaction blocked or rescinded) unless they prove "specific acts of ***fraud, misrepresentation***, or other items of misconduct to demonstrate the unfairness of the merger terms to the minority." *Weinberger v. UOP, Inc.*, 457 A.2d 701 (Del. 1983). Furthermore, the fact that the Special Committee of independent directors ***approved*** the

	Table 10-2, Scenario 1 (cont.)
	merger will be "***strong evidence*** that the transaction ***meets the test of fairness.***" *Id.* So it's very ***unlikely*** that the court will ***block*** the transaction.
Scenario 1 Q6 (cont.)	**6(b). Breach-of-duty issue:** Can the plaintiffs recover against the board for ***breach of duty*** (either of the ***duty of care*** or the ***duty of loyalty***)? If you answered "yes" to Q2 (does the charter have an exculpatory clause?), go to 6(b)(1) below. If you answered "no" to Q2, go to 6(b)(2). **Answer to 6(b)(1):** [Be here if Target's charter ***has an exculpatory clause***.] It's ***very unlikely*** that the plaintiffs can recover for *either* the duty of care or the duty of loyalty. *Duty of care:* The exculpatory clause ***completely blocks*** liability for breach of the ***duty of care.*** *Duty of loyalty:* For the plaintiffs to recover for breach of the ***duty of loyalty***, they would have to prove ***"bad faith"*** by the board. Bad faith would require a finding that the board ***"utterly failed to even attempt"*** to get the best price. *Lyondell Chemical v. Ryan*, 970 A.2d 235 (Del. 2009) (p. 180). The fact that the board appointed a Special Committee, which then approved the transaction, is almost certainly enough by itself to avoid the necessary finding that the board "utterly failed to even attempt" to get the best price. So recovery is extremely unlikely. **Now, go to Q9 [Delaware anti-takeover statute]** **Answer to 6(b)(2):** [Be here if Target's charter ***doesn't have an exculpatory clause***.] It's ***unlikely*** that the plaintiffs can recover for *either* the duty of care or the duty of loyalty. *Duty of care:* The fact that the board appointed a Special Committee is probably enough to demonstrate that there was ***no breach of the duty of care.*** The approval of the transaction by the Special Committee would almost certainly be enough to trigger the application of the ***"business judgment" rule***. *See Benihana of Tokyo, Inc. v. Benihana, Inc.*, 906 A.2d 114 (Del. 2006): "After approval by disinterested directors, courts review the interested transaction under the business judgment rule[.]" Once the court applies the business judgment rule, the directors will not have liability for failing to use due care as long as their decision was ***rational***. The decision to defer an acquisition decision to the judgment of a Special Committee of independent directors would certainly be at least rational. *Duty of loyalty:* The ***duty-of-loyalty issue*** would be treated the same way whether Target does or doesn't have an exculpatory clause (since such a clause affects only the duty of care, not the duty of loyalty). For the reasons described in 6(b)(1) above, the plaintiffs would be extremely unlikely to succeed in proving a breach of the duty of loyalty. **Now, go to Q9 [Delaware anti-takeover statute]**
Q7	[You should be here if a Special Committee was appointed, and the Special Committee ***did not approve*** the deal.] We'll assume that the ***board approved the deal*** even though the Special Committee had advised against doing so (since otherwise there wouldn't likely be anything that a plaintiff wanted to litigate). We'll assume that all non-independent directors voted in favor, that all independent directors voted against, and that the approval occurred because the non-independents constituted a majority of the board. We'll also assume that the Special Committee was authorized to, and did, try to ***negotiate a higher price*** with the Bidder, but failed to get the price up, leading the Committee to recommend against the deal on the grounds that the price was unfairly low. **7(a). Injunction issue:** Will the court approve the cash-out merger? **Answer to 7(a):** The answer to this question probably does not vary depending on whether Target's charter has an exculpatory clause or not. In either event, the court will examine the transaction for ***"entire fairness"*** (since it's an interested transaction, due to the Target's

	Table 10-2, Scenario 1 (cont.)
Scenario 1 Q7(a) (cont.)	board's domination by Bidder). To pass this test, the transaction must be both ***substantively*** fair (i.e., have a ***fair price***) and ***procedurally*** fair (be arrived at by "fair dealing," which usually includes ***adequate disclosure*** to the side with less information and ***arms-length negotiating***). *Weinberger v. UOP, Inc.*, 457 A.2d 701 (Del. 1983). Here, the Special Committee reviewed the deal and refused to approve it. The court is likely to conclude that the transaction was ***not "entirely fair."*** The court will probably find ***"substantive fairness"*** lacking, given that the Special Committee thought the transaction involved a transaction price that was unfairly low. The court will also likely find ***procedural unfairness*** (since board approval occurred only by means of the participation of the non-independent directors, whose decision-making was tainted by their close relationship with Bidder, and who made up a majority of the board). If the court finds that the transaction was unfair under this "entire fairness" standard, it will likely ***block*** the transaction if it hasn't yet been consummated. If the transaction has already gone through in a way that cannot be easily rescinded (i.e., the merger has been completed, with minority holders having received cash for their shares in Target), the court can and likely will award ***"rescissionary damages."*** That is, the court will likely order the person controlling Bidder to pay an amount that would be enough to put the minority shareholders in the position that they would have been in had they received what the court believes to be the minimum fair price. **Go to Q7(b).**
Q7(b)	**7(b). Breach-of-duty issue:** Can the plaintiffs recover against the board for ***breach of duty*** (either of the ***duty of care*** or the ***duty of loyalty***)? If you answered "yes" to Q2 (does the charter have an exculpatory clause?), go to 7(b)(1) below. If you answered "no" to Q2, go to 7(b)(2). **Answer to 7(b)(1):** [You should be here if Target's charter ***has an exculpatory clause***.] It is fairly unlikely that the board will have liability for either duty of care or duty of loyalty. *Duty of care:* The exculpatory clause blocks liability for breach of the duty of care, no matter how careless the board was. So the fact that the board has ***overruled the Special Committee's recommendation*** that the transaction not be done will not be enough to overcome the exculpatory clause, and there will be no liability for any breach of the duty of care. *Duty of loyalty:* On the other hand, the plaintiffs have some chance (but not a good one) of showing that the board has violated the duty of ***loyalty***. The test is whether the board ***"utterly failed to even attempt"*** to obtain the best sale price. That's a tough test for the plaintiffs to meet: they must show either that (1) the board ***did not even try*** to discharge their responsibilities, or (2) the board was fully ***aware*** that the actions they were taking ***conflicted with their duties***. *Lyondell Chemical Co. v. Ryan*, 970 A.2d 235 (Del. 2009). As to (1) above, the appointment of the Special Committee authorized to try to get a higher price probably ***constitutes an "attempt" to obtain the best price.*** And given that the board appointed the Special Committee and authorized it to negotiate with Bidder, the fact that the board then overruled the Special Committee is probably ***not*** enough to demonstrate an "awareness" by the board that it was violating its duty of loyalty (even though interested directors were part of the final decision-making process). So it's quite likely that the plaintiffs will ***lose*** on the duty-of-loyalty claim. **Now, go to Q9 [Delaware anti-takeover statute]** **Answer to 7(b)(2):** [You should be here if Target's charter ***does not have*** an exculpatory clause.] *Duty of care:* The plaintiffs have a small but respectable chance of recovering for breach of the ***duty of care.*** When the board rejected the Special Committee's recommendation, the

	Table 10-2, Scenario 1 (cont.)
Scenario 1, Q7(b)(2) (cont.)	board was ***dominated by the interested directors***. (We know this because #4 in our list of Assumptions says that "A majority of Target's board consists of 'non-independent directors' [i.e., directors over whom Bidder has significant influence].") Since most directors were interested, this aspect of self-dealing will ***prevent*** the board's recommendation ***from being entitled to the protection of the business judgment rule.*** Instead, the court will use ordinary common-law concepts to decide whether the board behaved negligently. However, assuming that (1) the board ***adequately informed itself*** about the merits of the proposed transaction, and (2) the board authorized the Special Committee to ***try to negotiate a higher price*** (that's something that had to be the case for you to have answered "yes" to Q3, and you shouldn't be here unless you gave that "yes" answer to Q3), the fact that a majority of the directors who made the decision were not "independent" of Bidder probably ***won't*** be enough to constitute a breach of the duty of due care. *Duty of loyalty:* The ***duty-of-loyalty issue*** would be treated the same way whether Target does or doesn't have an exculpatory clause (since such a clause affects only the duty of care, not the duty of loyalty). For the reasons described in 7(b)(1) above, the plaintiffs would be quite ***unlikely*** to succeed in proving a breach of the duty of loyalty. **Now, go to Q9 [Delaware anti-takeover statute]**
Q8	[You should be here if a Special Committee was ***not*** appointed, and Target's charter ***has an exculpatory clause***]. As noted, once the main board ***entered into negotiations with Bidder***, those negotiations triggered the board's *Revlon* ***"Level Playing Field"*** obligations. See Note 5 for details. **8(a). Injunction issue:** Will the court approve the cash-out merger? **Answer to 8(a):** The answer to this question probably does not vary depending on whether Target's charter has an exculpatory clause or not. In either event, the court will examine the transaction for ***"entire fairness"*** (since it's an interested transaction, due to the Target's board's domination by Bidder, and the absence of any Special Committee of independent directors). So the court will likely enjoin the transaction if the court believes that the transaction was either ***substantively unfair*** (i.e., involved a transaction price that was unfairly low), or ***procedurally unfair***. The court will view the substantive and procedural aspects together (there's no concept of separate "passing grades" for each aspect standing alone). Since the approval came from a board a majority of whose members were non-independent, and whose decision-making was thus tainted by their close relationship with Bidder), if the court thinks the price was also somewhat on the low side, there's a respectable chance that the court will enjoin the merger. For more about the court's likely actions, see the discussion of 7(a) above. **8(b). Breach-of-duty issue:** Can the plaintiffs recover against the board for ***breach of duty*** (either of the ***duty of care*** or the ***duty of loyalty***)? If you answered "yes" to Q2 (does the charter have an exculpatory clause?), go to 8(b)(1) below. If you answered "no" to Q2, go to 8(b)(2). **Answer to 8(b)(1):** [Be here if Target's charter ***has an exculpatory clause***.] It is fairly unlikely that the board will have any liability. *Duty of care:* The exculpatory clause automatically ***blocks liability*** for breach of this duty, no matter how careless the board was. So even the board's failure to appoint a Special Committee (despite the board's knowledge that a majority of directors would be deemed to be "interested" in the transaction) won't result in liability for breach of duty care. And that will be so even if the board made absolutely no effort to inform itself about the proposed takeover.

	Table 10-2, Scenario 1 (cont.)
Scenario 1, Q8(b) (cont.)	*Duty of loyalty:* The court will ask whether the board ***"utterly failed to even attempt"*** to obtain the best sale price. That's the only way the board could have breached the duty of loyalty. (See answer to 6(b)(1) above.) In answering this question, consider that if the board so much as (1) hired an investment banker who unsuccessfully contacted other potential buyers to try to get a better offer, *or* (2) unsuccessfully asked Bidder to raise his offer, that's probably enough effort to avoid having "utterly failed to attempt" to get the best price. If your answer to the above "utterly failed" question is ***"yes"*** (unlikely), the board can be liable for breach of the duty of loyalty. So, as an extreme example, if the board spent just 10 minutes before approving the transaction, did absolutely no investigation into whether anyone else would pay more, did not hire an investment banker, and never asked Bidder whether he'd pay a higher price, this might be one of those very rare instances where there would be a breach of the duty of loyalty. If your answer to the "utterly failed" question is ***"no,"*** the board cannot be liable for breach of the duty of loyalty. So, for instance, if the board did *even a single one* of the things it didn't do in the above "yes" example, that would probably be enough to constitute an "attempt" to obtain the best price, and to foreclose duty-of-loyalty liability. **Now, go to Q9 [Delaware anti-takeover statute]** **Answer to 8(b)(2):** [Be here if Target's charter ***does not have*** an exculpatory clause.] Plaintiffs have a respectable chance at establishing breach of the ***duty of care***, but very little chance as to ***duty of loyalty***. *Duty of Care:* Plaintiffs have a respectable chance of holding the board liable for breach of the duty of ***care.*** Even though the board members presumably knew (and at least should have known) that they were majority-non-independent, and that they were making the decision to sell to an insider who dominated most of them, they did not even bother to take the easy step of appointing a Special Committee of independent directors. If the court also finds that the board did not adequately inform itself about the merits of the transaction (e.g., by hiring an investment bank to give an opinion about the reasonableness of the price, or by trying to find a bidder who would pay more), the court might let the lack-of-care claim go to a jury trial, in which case the plaintiffs might well win. *Duty of Loyalty:* Even without a Special Committee, the court is very ***unlikely*** to find a breach of the duty of ***loyalty***. As in cases where there is an exculpatory clause (which can only block liability for lack of care, not lack of loyalty), the test is whether the board ***"utterly failed to even attempt"*** to obtain the best sale price. As is described further in Q 7(b)(1), the plaintiffs can recover only if they show either that (1) the board ***did not even try*** to discharge their responsibilities, or (2) the board was fully ***aware*** that the actions they were taking conflicted with their duties. Even where the board is majority-interested, the Ps will very rarely succeed in making either of these showings. **Now, go to Q9 [Delaware anti-takeover statute]**
Q9	**9.** Does the Delaware ***anti-takeover statute*** (GCL § 203) prevent the cash-out merger? **Answer to Q9:** No. Ordinarily, § 203 prohibits any "business combination" between the corporation and an "interested stockholder" for ***three years*** after the interested stockholder buys his shares. The short-form cash-out merger between Bidder and Target is a "business combination" as § 203 defines that term. Therefore, if no exception to § 203 applies, the merger can't occur until three years from the time Bidder acquired (via the tender offer) its significant stake. And nowhere near three years have passed. However, there are three exceptions to § 203's operation. And two of them ***apply*** here:

	Table 10-2, Scenario 1 (cont.)
Scenario 1, Q9 (cont.)	[1]The acquirer (Bidder) got ***board approval*** of the proposed business combination from the target before the acquirer bought its stock (something we know happened from #7 in our set of Deal Assumptions); and [2] The acquirer now ***owns at least 85%*** of Target's total shares outstanding (and we know from our assumptions that Bidder owns 91%). Therefore, the three-year waiting period of § 203 ***doesn't apply***. (That's why Bidder was wise to ***condition*** its tender offer on Bidder's receiving tenders for at least 85% of Target's total shares outstanding — that way, Bidder knew that if the conditions were satisfied, § 203 couldn't possibly apply, even if Target's board refused to approve the eventual back-end merger.) **Now, go to Q10 [appraisal rights]**
Q10	**10(a).** Do the plaintiffs have ***appraisal rights*** for their shares? **10(b).** If so, what do those rights entitle them to? **Answer to 10(a):** Yes. Normally, you cannot answer a question about whether stockholders of a company being subjected to a merger have appraisal rights without looking at exactly what type of consideration the stockholders are receiving. But in the special case of a merger of a subsidiary into a parent corporation that owns 90% of the subsidiary's stock (i.e., the sort of § 253 merger we have here), any remaining minority shareholder is ***automatically*** entitled to appraisal rights. Del. GCL § 262(b)(3). **Answer to 10(b):** The minority holders are entitled to receive what the Del. Chancery Court determines to have been the ***"fair value"*** of the stock at the time of the merger. For this purpose, "fair value" does not include "any element of value ***arising from the accomplishment or expectation of the merger***." (So what counts is probably the fair value of Target stock right before Bidder announced its tender offer.) But fair value *does* include ***interest*** from the time of the merger, up until the time of the award. 262(h).

	Scenario 2 **Possibly-Friendly Cash Tender Offer for Target's Shares by Bidder, who is an *Outsider*; Board starts as Neutral towards the Offer, then *Recommends* the Offer to Shareholders, who Tender a Majority of Their Stock to Bidder**
Deal Assumptions	All details in this Scenario are assumed to be the ***same as those in Scenario 1*** (see p. 479 *supra*), except: [1] Bidder (and the person in charge of Bidder) is an ***"outsider"*** of Target, i.e., someone who ***has no prior relationship with Target***, and has no influence over any Target director. A typical instance of this scenario would be that Bidder is a "financial" buyer (e.g., a private equity fund) that has no prior operations in the industry that Target is part of. At the outset, assume Bidder doesn't know whether the Target's board will be hostile or friendly. Also, assume that Target has no significant takeover defenses at any time (except the one given automatically by Del. GCL § 203, which Target has not opted out of). [2] Target ***does not have a controlling shareholder***, and its board has a ***majority of "independent" directors*** (i.e., ones who are not under the significant influence of Target's management). [3] At a time when Target's stock is trading at \$30, Bidder offers \$36, a 20% premium. [4] Target's board begins by being ***neutral*** to the idea of being acquired by Bidder. The board

	Table 10-2, Scenario 2 (cont.)
Scenario 2: Deal Assumptions	then gathers a reasonable amount of data about the company's likely value to other potential bidders, and uses this data in deciding to recommend the transaction to shareholders. A board representative (Target's CEO) then asks Bidder if it will raise its offer; Bidder responds that it has already given its "last and best" offer. [5] Then, as in Scenario 1, Target's board eventually votes to recommend that shareholders of Target accept the offer by tendering their shares. 91% of Target's shareholders have just done so (the same percentage as in Scenario 1). [6] Bidder now seeks to consummate a ***parent-subsidiary merger*** under GCL § 253, by which a company that owns at least ***90%*** of the shares of another company can merge this "subsidiary" into itself without approval by the shareholders of the subsidiary. [7] As in Scenario 1, the Ps are minority ***shareholders of Target*** who didn't tender, and who now ***bring a class action*** to (1) ***enjoin consummation of the cash-out merger*** on the grounds that it is unfair because of low price; and/or (2) ***recover damages*** for themselves against the directors of Target who voted for the transaction, based on alleged breach of the duty of care and/or the duty of loyalty. They also seek to exercise whatever ***appraisal*** rights they have.
Q1	[Verify applicability of this Scenario] **1.** Is ***Bidder*** someone who has ***significant influence*** over a ***majority of Target's board members?*** If yes, this Scenario is ***not applicable***. (Consider whether Scenarios 1 or 3 applies.) If no, this is the correct Scenario. Go to Q2.
Q2	**2.** Does Target have a GCL § 102(b)(7) ***exculpatory clause*** in its charter? [Save answer for later, and go to Note 3.]
Note 3	Observe that in contrast to Q3 in Scenario 1 (p. 479), here it shouldn't matter whether Target's board ever appointed a Special Committee of independent directors. That's because a majority of the board itself is assumed to be independent of both Bidder and Target's management, so there is no initial reason to suspect that the board will engage in self-dealing. Go to Note 4.
Note 4	Once Target's board entered into negotiations with Bidder, the board triggered its *Revlon* ***"Level Playing Field"*** obligations. That's true even though Bidder was not an "insider," so the Board can't be reasonably suspected of favoring him. It's also true even though a majority of the board is independent of Target's management and thus not at great risk of merely doing what management wants regarding the offer. So despite the absence of reason to fear self-dealing by the board, the board was nonetheless obligated: (1) ***not to favor Bidder*** over other potential bidders; and (2) to make all reasonable efforts to ***get the "best price"*** for the company. If you answered "yes" to Q2 (does the charter have an exculpatory clause?), go to Q5. If you answered "no" to Q2, go to Q6.
Q5	[You should be here if Target's charter ***has an exculpatory clause.***] **5(a). Injunction issue:** Will the court approve the cash-out merger? **Answer to 5(a):** The transaction is ***presumptively entitled to the protection of the business judgment rule***. Unless the presumption is rebutted, the court won't even analyze the transaction to determine whether it is "entirely fair." (See paragraph beginning "Therefore" below for what application of the business judgment rule will mean.) In order for the plaintiffs to avoid the business judgment rule, they will have to prove ***one of three things,***

	Table 10-2, Scenario 2 (cont.)
Scenario 2, Q5(a) (cont.)	each of which is likely to be very hard-to-prove here: [1] that the Target board ***engaged in self-dealing***. (Since Bidder is an outsider with no influence over Target's board members, and since the board ultimately approved rather than fought the transaction to keep their seats, a finding of self-dealing is very unlikely). [2] that the board did not ***gather the reasonably needed information***. (But our assumptions state that they did, so the plaintiffs won't succeed on this prong.) and [3] that the board ***did not "rationally believe"*** the transaction was ***in the stockholders' interest.*** (That's a hard-to-meet standard, and one that is not supported by any evidence in our assumptions). Therefore, the Board's decision to recommend the takeover, and to approve the back-end merger, will almost certainly be ***entitled to the protection of the business judgment rule.*** And once the decision gets that protection, the court won't even analyze the transaction's fairness. Instead, the business judgment rule means that the court will enjoin the transaction only if the court believes that the board's decision to approve the transaction was completely ***"irrational,"*** which is very unlikely to be found to be the case here. See p.183. **5(b). Breach-of-duty issue:** Can the plaintiffs recover against the board for ***breach of duty*** (either the ***duty of care*** or the ***duty of loyalty***)? It is fairly unlikely that the board will have liability for *either* duty of care or duty of loyalty. *Duty of care:* The board ***can't*** be liable for lack of care; the exculpatory clause in the charter negates even the possibility of such liability. *Duty of loyalty:* The plaintiffs have a theoretical chance of showing that the board violated its duty of loyalty, but their practical chances of showing this are remote. The test is whether the board ***"utterly failed to even attempt"*** to obtain the best sale price. That's an extremely difficult test to meet: the plaintiffs must show either that (1) the board ***did not even try*** to discharge their responsibilities, or (2) the board was fully ***aware*** that the actions they were taking conflicted with their duties. *Lyondell Chemical Co. v. Ryan*, 970 A.2d 235 (Del. 2009). Here, the absence of evidence that the board was self-interested (since we know that they were not under Bidder's influence, and there's no indication they were trying to derive some benefit for themselves not available to other shareholders) makes it especially unlikely that the plaintiffs can make either of these showings. Furthermore, the fact that the board gathered some relevant data, and (unsuccessfully) asked Bidder to raise its price, will be enough to prevent the plaintiffs from demonstrating (1). So it's nearly certain that the plaintiffs will lose on the duty-of-loyalty claim. **Now, go to Q7 [Delaware anti-takeover statute]**
Q6	[You should be here if Target's charter ***does not have an exculpatory clause***.] **6(a). Injunction issue:** Will the court approve the cash-out merger? **Answer to 6(a):** Same analysis as in Q5(a). In brief, the Board's decision to recommend the takeover, and to approve the cash-out merger, will almost certainly be entitled to the ***protection of the business judgment rule***. And once the decision gets that protection, the court won't analyze its fairness, and will strike it down only if it's highly "irrational," which is very unlikely to be found to be the case here. **6(b). Breach-of-duty issue:** Can the plaintiffs recover against the board for ***breach of duty*** (either of the ***duty of care*** or the ***duty of loyalty***)? It is fairly unlikely that the board will have liability for *either* duty of care or duty of loyalty. *Duty of Care:* The absence of an exculpatory clause makes it at least theoretically possible

	Table 10-2, Scenario 2 (cont.)
Scenario 2 Q6(b) (cont.)	that the plaintiffs will succeed in showing a breach of this duty. But as with the court's decision whether to approve the cash-out merger (see 6(a) above), the court's evaluation of the board's handling of its duty of due care will be heavily influenced by whether the court applies the business judgment rule to the board's conduct. As in 6(a), the board's conduct will ***almost certainly be entitled to the protection of the business judgment rule.*** And once the decision gets that protection, the court won't even allow the due-care claim to go to trial unless the court finds that there is enough evidence to allow a reasonable jury to conclude that the board's behavior was highly "irrational," a very unlikely finding here. *Duty of Loyalty:* As in cases where there *is* an exculpatory clause (which can only block liability for lack of care, not lack of loyalty), the test is whether the board ***"utterly failed to even attempt"*** to obtain the best sale price. The analysis will be the same as in 5(b) above. Under that analysis, it's nearly certain that the plaintiffs will lose on the duty-of-loyalty claim. **Now, go to Q7 [Delaware anti-takeover statute]**
Q7	**7.** Does the Delaware anti-takeover statute (GCL § 203) prevent the cash-out merger? **Answer to Q7:** No. As noted in Q9 of Scenario 1, § 203 ordinarily prohibits any "business combination" (which would include the cash-out merger here) between the corporation and an "interested stockholder" for ***three years*** after the interested stockholder buys his shares. However, there are three exceptions to § 203's operation, and the same two that applied in Scenario 1 apply here. The most obvious one applies where the acquirer now ***owns*** at least 85% of Target's total shares outstanding. We know from our assumptions that Bidder owns 91%. Thus § 203 won't apply. **Now, go to Q8 [appraisal rights]**
Q8	**8(a).** Do the plaintiffs have ***appraisal rights*** for their shares? **8(b).** If so, what does that right entitle them to? **Answer to 8(a):** Yes. The analysis is the same as in Q10(a) of Scenario 1. In the special case of a merger of a subsidiary into a parent corporation that owns 90% of the subsidiary's stock (i.e., the sort of § 253 merger we have here), any remaining minority shareholder is ***automatically*** entitled to appraisal rights. Del. GCL § 262(b)(3). **Answer to 8(b):** As is described more fully in Q10(b) of Scenario 1, the minority holders are entitled to receive what the Del. Chancery Court determines to have been the ***"fair value"*** of the stock at the time of the merger.

	Scenario 3: ***Hostile* Stock-for-Stock Tender Offer for Target's Shares by Bidder who is an Outsider; Board Resists by *Enacting a Poison Bill*, and Opposes the Merger until the Bitter End** This Scenario illustrates a typical hostile takeover attempt that is strongly resisted by Target's board. Target then makes various attempts to fight off the takeover.
	As in Scenario 2 (see p. 485), Bidder (and the person in charge of Bidder) is an ***"outsider"*** of Target, i.e., someone who ***has no prior relationship with Target***, and has no influence over any Target director. All details in this Scenario are assumed to be the ***same as those in Scenario 2***, except as otherwise noted here. Here is a recap of the most important aspects of the set-up:

	Table 10-2, Scenario 3 (cont.)
Scenario 3: Deal Assumptions	[1] Bidder has made an informal overture to Target's CEO, offering to exchange all outstanding shares of Target for stock in Bidder having (at the time of the exchange) a market value of $40/share. At the time of the overture, Target's shares are trading at $30. (But 6 months ago, the shares were trading at $42, before some possibly-temporary bad news about Target's prospects became public.) [2] Target's board has ***rebuffed*** these initial overtures from Bidder. The board has publicly disclosed these overtures, and says that (1) the price being offered by Bidder is far lower than Target's true value; (2) Bidder's shares are overvalued, so that Target's holders will really be getting much less than $40 in value; and (3) in any event, the board believes Target should and will remain independent. [3] Target ***does not have a controlling shareholder***, and the Board has a majority of "independent" directors (i.e., ones who are not under the significant influence of Target's management). [4] Target has long had a shareholder-approved ***"poison pill" of the flip-over variety*** (see p. 452) under which: (a) If anyone tenders for more than 30% of Target's shares, and then merges with Target, each existing non-acquirer-related holder has the ***option to buy stock in the surviving company at a 70% discount*** from the then-market price in a large enough quantity to give these option-exercising holders collective control of the merged entity; but (b) Target's board can ***"redeem" (cancel)*** the plan at any time. [5] Target has no other specialized takeover defenses, and it has no staggered board terms (so its entire board is ***up for re-election each year***). [6] As soon as Target's board hears the first overture from Bidder, the board votes to ***amend the bylaw that incorporates the poison pill,*** by adding a ***"no hand" provision*** (see p. 453) to the pill. The effect of the amendment is that if an acquirer were to buy more than 30% of Target's stock, and then attempt a back-end merger, the board (including any successor board voted in after the acquirer's acquisition of shares) would have to ***wait two years*** before redeeming the pill. This means that the pill will remain in force even if Bidder buys 99% of the outstanding stock and replaces Target's entire board. That would make an acquisition while the pill is in place highly toxic to Bidder (since the pill will effectively stop a back-end merger for two years after Bidder gets control). This Scenario has ***three "stages,"*** each of which poses its own set of questions and decisions.
Scenario 3, Stage 1	<u>Stage 1:</u> <u>Suit to Undo Poison Pill Amendment</u> Bidder now sues Target's board in Delaware state court, seeking to have the amended poison pill ***judicially invalidated.***
Q1	In deciding whether to invalidate the poison pill amendment, the court will ask two questions. The amendment will be struck down unless the court answers "yes" to each of these questions: **1(a).** When Target's Board voted to amend the poison pill, did the board have ***reasonable grounds*** for believing that there was a ***danger to the Corporation's welfare*** from the takeover attempt? (See p. 457.) **Answer to 1(a):** Since Target's stockholders are being asked to surrender control in return for a bet on the value of the combined companies (note that Target's holders will merely get stock in the combined company), the court is likely to answer "yes." If the answer is "yes," go to 1(b). If the answer is "no," go 1(d) below.

	Table 10-2, Scenario 3, Stage 1 (cont.)
Scenario 3, Stage 1, Q1(b)	**1(b).** Was the decision by Target's Board to amend the poison pill a response that was ***"reasonable in relation to the threat posed"*** (i.e., ***"proportional"***)? (See p. 457.) **Answer to 1(b):** To meet the "proportionality" requirement, Delaware courts hold that the defensive measure cannot be *either* ***"preclusive"*** or ***"coercive."*** *Unitrin, Inc. v. Amer. General Corp.*, 651 A.2d 1361 (Del. 1995). Under cases such as *Quickturn Design Syst. v. Shapiro*, 721 A.2d 1281 (Del. 1998), a poison pill provision that ***significantly delays*** a successor board's ability to cancel the pill, where the delay would make a takeover much less attractive to the bidder, (a) is ***"preclusive"*** and (b) unlawfully interferes with the successor board's ability to ***discharge its fiduciary duties*** to shareholders. Therefore, the amendment here is probably illegal for both of these reasons. Furthermore, the ***offer*** here is at least on its face relatively ***attractive*** to Target's shareholders, since it is for an apparent premium of 33% over Target's immediately-prior stock price (though this value is contingent on Target's holders' ability to take the shares of Bidder they will acquire in the exchange and resell them at the $40 price; so Target's holders will take the risk of a last-minute downturn in Bidder's share price). Given the relative attractiveness of the premium, the court will probably answer ***"no"*** to this question. In that case, go to 1(d). But if the court instead surprisingly answers "yes," go 1(c).
Q1(c)	[You should be here only if the court answered "yes" to the questions in both 1(a) and 1(b).] **1(c).** Will the court give Target's board's decision to amend the poison pill the ***benefits of the business judgment rule***? **Answer to 1(c):** Yes. Therefore, except in the very unlikely event that the court concludes that the amendment, or the overall pill plan, was ***completely irrational***, the court will ***leave the amendment in place***. If that happens, we'll assume that Bidder ***abandons its intent to make a formal tender offer***, due to the likely horrible consequences to Bidder of having Target's shareholders be able for two years to buy lots of cheap stock in the merged company if Bidder takes control and wants to do a prompt back-end merger (which virtually any acquirer would want to do in these circumstances). ***This is the end of the analysis,*** because Bidder goes away (and Target's board has succeeded in keeping Target independent, at least for now).
Q1(d)	[You should be here if the court answered ***"no"*** to either Q1(a) or Q1(b). Since the answer to 1(b) was likely "no," (i.e., the plan was ***not proportional*** to the threat), there's a good probability you will be here.] **1(d).** Will the court leave the amended poison pill in place? **Answer to 1(d):** No. The court will likely strike the amendment, but ***leave the pre-amendment poison pill in place.*** Consequently, Bidder knows that if it can buy a majority of Target's stock in the tender offer, it will only have to wait for the next board election (which can't be more than one year away) to vote in new directors that it controls, and to have those directors approve a short-form merger of Target into Bidder. We'll assume that Bidder launches its tender offer, covered in Stage 2. **Go to the start of Stage 2.**
Scenario 3, Stage 2	Stage 2: Tender Offer is Made, and Target Considers Federal-Court Suit [You should be here if the judge struck down the "board can't repeal" amendment to the poison pill.] Now that the worst aspects of the poison pill plan have been judicially removed, assume that

	Table 10-2, Scenario 3, Stage 2 (cont.)
Scenario 3, Stage 2 (cont.)	Bidder ***makes a formal tender offer*** to all of Target's shareholders, under the following terms: [1] Bidder offers to exchange ***stock in Bidder*** for all of Target's shares. The amount of Bidder stock given in exchange will have a market value of $40 (measured as of ten days before the exchange occurs) for each Target share, regardless of the market value of Target's shares or Bidder's shares at the time. [2] Consummation by Bidder is subject to Bidder's being tendered ***at least 85%*** of Target's outstanding shares. In support of the tender offer, Bidder sends Target's shareholders a document (on SEC ***Schedule 14D-1***) that contains full and accurate financial data on both Bidder and Target. (Bidder has to do that, since Target's shareholders are being asked to take stock, the value of which depends on the soundness of Bidder's business.) [3] Target's board ***refuses to approve the tender offer***, stating that the package of stock being offered by Bidder will be worth significantly less than the board believes the true value of Target stock to be. The board therefore recommends that shareholders not tender their shares.
Q2	**2.** Assume that Target's board now sues Bidder in federal court for violations of the Williams Act (which gives some federal regulation over the takeover procedures; see p. 437). Assume further that the board persuades the federal judge that the offer probably substantively undervalues Target. Will the judge grant the board an injunction against the tender offer as presently constituted, or any other meaningful relief? **Answer to Q2:** No. Private litigation under the Williams Act is governed by § 14(e) of the '34 Act. § 14(e) gives a takeover target a federal-court private action against the bidder for any ***"fraudulent, deceptive, or manipulative acts or practices***, in connection with any tender offer[.]" But neither this section nor anything else in the Williams Act prohibits conduct by a bidder where there is ***no misrepresentation or failure of disclosure***, and the only complaint is that the defendant's conduct is ***substantively unfair*** (e.g., offers an unfairly low price). See p. 446. So unless Target's board can point to something in Bidder's Schedule 14D-1 that contains either a material misrepresentation or a material omission, the board has no viable Williams Act claim. Since our facts indicate that the 14D-1 contains "full and accurate financial data," we'll assume that the Target's board's federal-court suit is dismissed. **Go to Stage 3, immediately below.**
Scenario 3, Stage 3, Deal Assumptions	Stage 3: Tender Offer is Successful, and Target Tries to Block Back-End Merger Here are the events that take place at the beginning of Stage 3: [1] ***82%*** of Target's shareholders tender into the offer. [2] Bidder decides to ***waive the 85% minimum***, and acquires all tendered shares. Bidder finances the deal by means of a short-term ***"bridge loan"*** against Bidder's own assets. (Assume Bidder owns zero shares apart from the tendered ones. Also, assume that Target's officers, directors and employee stock plans own virtually no stock.) [3] The tendered shares are acquired by Bidder on Jan. 2, 2011. [4] After the closing of the tender offer, there are 1 million shares outstanding now, of which Bidder owns 820,000 (82%). [5] Next, Bidder proposes a ***statutory merger*** of Target into Bidder, under Del. GCL § 251. (Since Bidder has less than 90% of Target's shares, Bidder can't use the short-form parent-subsidiary merger provision of GCL § 253. Instead, it has to use § 251, which is a "regular" merger provision that requires approval by the acquired company's shareholders.)

	Table 10-2, Scenario 3, Stage 3 (cont.)
Scenario 3, Stage 3, Deal Assumptions (cont.)	[6] Bidder's object in seeking the merger is to enable Bidder to ***borrow***, post-merger, against Target's assets and ***upstream the loan proceeds*** to Bidder's bank account, and use them to ***repay the original bridge loan*** that funded the share acquisition. The merger plan provides that upon completion of the merger, any remaining non-Bidder holders of Target shares will receive $40 in cash. [7] Target's (existing) board ***refuses to approve the merger.*** Target's board is ***not staggered*** (i.e., all directors stand for annual re-election.) [8] At the next annual shareholder meeting of Target, on Feb. 1, 2012, Bidder casts all of its votes so that it can ***elect 9 of 13 directors*** of Target, i.e., approximately its 82% share. [9] On Feb. 3, 2012, the 9 Bidder-appointed directors of Target vote to ***approve the merger***; since they constitute a majority of Target's board, the approval vote passes. [10] The newly-constituted Target board then submits the merger plan to a ***vote of stockholders***, as required by GCL § 251(c), which requires that a "majority of the outstanding stock" of the non-surviving company vote to approve the transaction. Bidder votes all of its 820,000 shares in favor. Of the 180,000 shares held by persons other than Bidder, 91,000 are voted in favor, 35,000 are voted against, and the rest don't vote. [11]A ***class action*** brought in Delaware state court on behalf of the minority shareholders of Target (who hold 18% of Target's shares) is filed on March 1, 2012. The sole relief sought by the suit is an ***injunction against the merger***, on the grounds that the merger would violate Del. GCL § 203 (the statutory anti-takeover provision). As noted above (p. 484), § 203 prohibits any "business combination" between the corporation and an "interested stockholder" for ***three years*** after the interested stockholder buys his shares; § 203 will block this merger unless some exception to § 203's application applies. Assume that Target has never amended its charter to waive the application of § 203 (something that can only be done by affirmative vote of a majority of shares outstanding; see § 203(b)(3)).
	The Delaware judge hears the suit the day after it's filed (March 2, 2012). Following are the questions that the judge will have to ask, in order to decide whether there has been a violation of § 203, justifying an injunction against the merger.
Q3	**3. Approval by Target's Board:** *Before* Bidder became an "interested shareholder" in Target (which happened when Bidder closed on the tender offer for the 82% worth of shares), did Target's board ***give approval*** either to the merger or to completion of the tender offer? **Answer to Q3:** If the answer were "yes," § 203 wouldn't apply, and the merger could go forward. See Del. GCL § 203(a)(1) (target's board approval of the transaction causes § 203 not to apply). But we know from the deal assumptions that the answer is "no" (Target's board didn't approve until the replacement board was seated, long after Bidder became an interested shareholder). So the answer is "no." Therefore, the § 203(a)(1) exception doesn't apply. Go to Q4.
Q4	**4. Ownership of 85% of Target stock by Bidder:** Did Bidder own ***at least 85%*** of Target's stock after Bidder closed on the tender offer? **Answer to Q4:** Again, if the answer were "yes," § 203 wouldn't apply. See § 203(a)(2). But we know from the facts that after the closing of the tender offer, Bidder owned only ***82%*** of Target's outstanding shares. So the answer is "no." Therefore, the § 203(a)(2) exception doesn't apply. Go to Q5.
Q5	**5. Approval by Target's Minority Shareholders:** Is it the case that at least ***two-thirds*** of the shares that were owned by ***persons other than Bidder*** as of the date of the shareholder approval vote were voted ***in favor*** of the merger?

	Table 10-2, Scenario 3, Stage 3 (cont.)
Scenario 3, Stage 3, Q5 (cont.)	**Answer to Q5:** Once again, if the answer were "yes," § 203 wouldn't apply. See § 203(a)(3). But we know from the facts that there were 180,000 independently-held shares, so 120,000 of these would have had to be affirmatively voted in favor. Yet only 91,000 were actually voted in favor. So the required two-thirds of all independently-held shares (***not*** just two-thirds of the shares ***actually voted***) were ***not*** voted in favor. So the answer is "no." Therefore, the § 203(a)(3) exception doesn't apply. Go to Q6.
Q6	**6. Three Years since Acquisition:** Have ***3 years elapsed*** since Bidder acquired its 82% of the shares? **Answer to Q5:** If the answer were "yes," § 203 wouldn't block the merger. See § 203(a), first sentence (§ 203 only blocks the merger for 3 years after the controlling stockholder gains his interest). But we know that only a little more than ***one year*** (from Jan. 2, 2011 to March 2, 2012) has elapsed. Since the answer is "no," § 203 makes the merger unlawful until Jan. 2, 2014. Therefore, ***the judge must issue the injunction***. Bidder will have to wait another two years before it can merge Target into itself, and thereby borrow against Target's assets in a way that permits the loan proceeds to be used to pay off Bidder's bridge loan. (Since Bidder already controls Target's board, Bidder can cause the board to approve a loan to Target secured by Target's assets; but ***payment of the loan proceeds to Bidder*** would likely be a ***fraudulent conveyance***, void against Target's other creditors and probably void against the minority shareholders of Target who still own 18% of the company.) *Moral of the story:* Bidder made a bad mistake by waiving the "we must receive tenders for 85% of the shares" requirement in its tender offer. Had Bidder closed on the tender only after buying a total of 85% or more of Target's shares, § 203 wouldn't have applied at all. That's why most hostile bidders who bid for Delaware targets condition their tender offer on receiving tenders of 85% of all outstanding shares that the bidder doesn't yet own.

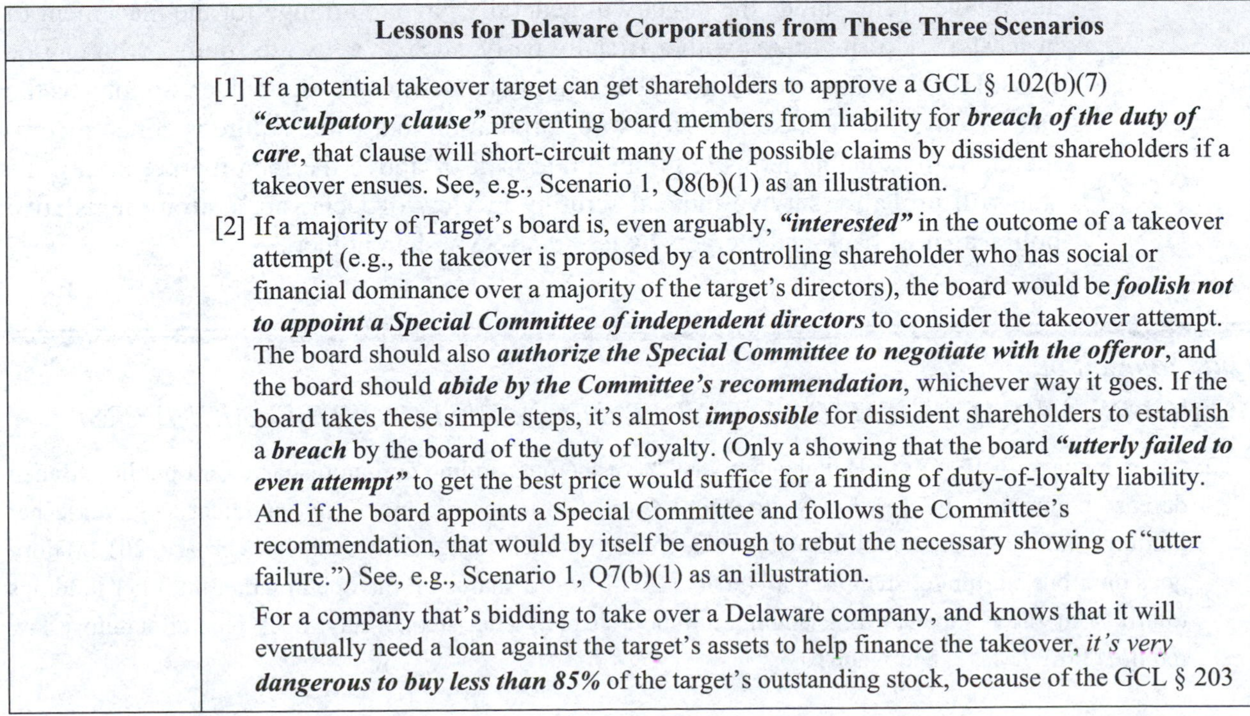

	Lessons for Delaware Corporations from These Three Scenarios
	[1] If a potential takeover target can get shareholders to approve a GCL § 102(b)(7) ***"exculpatory clause"*** preventing board members from liability for ***breach of the duty of care***, that clause will short-circuit many of the possible claims by dissident shareholders if a takeover ensues. See, e.g., Scenario 1, Q8(b)(1) as an illustration. [2] If a majority of Target's board is, even arguably, ***"interested"*** in the outcome of a takeover attempt (e.g., the takeover is proposed by a controlling shareholder who has social or financial dominance over a majority of the target's directors), the board would be ***foolish not to appoint a Special Committee of independent directors*** to consider the takeover attempt. The board should also ***authorize the Special Committee to negotiate with the offeror***, and the board should ***abide by the Committee's recommendation***, whichever way it goes. If the board takes these simple steps, it's almost ***impossible*** for dissident shareholders to establish a ***breach*** by the board of the duty of loyalty. (Only a showing that the board ***"utterly failed to even attempt"*** to get the best price would suffice for a finding of duty-of-loyalty liability. And if the board appoints a Special Committee and follows the Committee's recommendation, that would by itself be enough to rebut the necessary showing of "utter failure.") See, e.g., Scenario 1, Q7(b)(1) as an illustration. For a company that's bidding to take over a Delaware company, and knows that it will eventually need a loan against the target's assets to help finance the takeover, ***it's very dangerous to buy less than 85%*** of the target's outstanding stock, because of the GCL § 203

	Table 10-2, Lessons for Delaware Corporations (cont.)
	takeover statute, which will likely block any back-end merger of the target into the bidder for three years, if the takeover remains hostile. See Scenario 3, Stage 3, Q6 as an illustration.

   a. **No chilling effect:** But if a stock option's effect is merely to give the acquirer a ***fair return for having put a first deal on the table*** (thus perhaps inducing additional bidders to enter the fray), the option is likely to be upheld. For instance, an option giving the would-be acquirer the right to buy 10% of the target, for a cash price equal to the market price prevailing just before the time that acquirer's deal was announced, would probably be upheld.

6. **Termination fee:** Similarly, a ***"termination fee"*** (sometimes called a "breakup fee"), payable if the merger should be terminated by the target, may be upheld or struck down, again depending on the circumstances. The size of the fee will of course be significant, as will the other circumstances. Thus in *Paramount v. QVC*, a $100 million termination fee was struck down; but that fee was set in conjunction with other anti-competitive-bid devices (e.g., the stock option discussed above), so it might have passed muster had it stood alone.

7. **Use of state anti-takeover statutes:** Among the sometimes-successful anti-takeover devices are ones that take advantage of state anti-takeover ***statutes***. See *supra*, p. 447. Sometimes, these statutes impede takeovers even without affirmative action by the target. For instance, New York's stringent statute (BCL § 912) virtually prevents back-end mergers for five years after a person purchases control, whether the target's board does anything beforehand or not. But other statutes will typically require some sort of action by the target to be fully effective.

   a. **Delaware:** For instance, Delaware's anti-takeover law (*supra*, p. 449) is largely ineffective if a hostile bidder acquires 85% of the target's shares. Therefore, to take full advantage of the statute the target will generally have to arrange for the placement of at least 15% of its shares with a friendly party, such as a "white squire" who can be trusted (or who has agreed by contract) not to tender to a hostile bidder. So long as the sale of, say, a 16% stake in a Delaware corporation to a white squire is done on commercially reasonable terms (e.g., the price is at or above the then-market price), the sale will probably survive judicial scrutiny in view of Delaware's strong legislative policy against back-end mergers by less-than-85% shareholders.

Quiz Yourself on
MERGERS AND ACQUISITIONS *(TENDER OFFERS AND HOSTILE TAKEOVERS)*

93. As of January, 2012, Glory Hallelujah owns 2% of the outstanding common shares of a publicly traded defense contractor, the Terrible Swift Sword Corp. Glory doesn't announce her intent to increase her holdings, nor does she solicit any other shareholders to sell to her. However, in February, 2012, Glory goes on a buying binge, snapping up Terrible Swift Sword shares on the open market until her holdings total 8% of the company's outstanding common shares. What step, if any, does federal statutory law require Glory to take, and when? ________________

94. Alexis Colby wants to take over the Carrington Oil Company, a public company. She doesn't own any Carrington stock and intends to launch a tender offer for 51% of it. She's concerned, however, that, as soon as she announces her tender offer, her rival, Krystal Carrington, will make a rival bid. To minimize the possibility of this, Alexis would prefer to leave her offer open for only five days. If you represent Alexis, how would you advise her on the subject of how long she should or must leave open her offer?

____

95. Charlie owns 3% of the stock in the Willy Wonka Chocolate Factory, Inc., a public company. He wants to increase his holdings to 6%. On June 1, he makes a tender offer to the other shareholders, seeking 600,000 shares at $5 a share. The offer is to be open one month. After two weeks, only 200,000 shares have been deposited with Charlie. As a result, on June 15 Charlie raises the offer to $8 a share to induce additional shareholders to sell. Coco Nutt has already tendered her 5,000 shares on June 10, in response to the $5 offer. Assuming that Charlie buys some shares at the $8 figure, what price must he pay Coco Nutt for those of her shares that he wants to purchase? ______________

96. Mickey wants to take over the Mouse Von Trapp Company, a public company. On March 1, Mickey launches a tender offer of $10 a share for all of Mouse Von Trapp's common shares, the offer to remain open until April 15. On March 15, Minnie tenders her 100 shares to Mickey. On April 1, Pluto launches an offer to all Mouse Von Trapp shareholders at $12 a share. Can Minnie revoke her acceptance and accept Pluto's offer? ______________

97. Richie Rich intends to eventually make an offer to purchase a majority of the shares of the Getrich Qwik Food Company. For the time being, however, he contents himself with a spending spree, buying up 15% of Getrich Qwik's common stock on the open market. (He files all required disclosure documents in a timely manner.) Has Richie violated any law by failing to make a formal tender offer and by failing to follow the Williams Act's procedural rules for tender offers (e.g., the rule that offers must be open for at least 20 business days)? ______________

98. Queen Victoria is chairman of the board of a publishing conglomerate, Not Amused Publications, Inc., which is publicly held and which is incorporated in Delaware. Queen owns about 3% of Not Amused's common stock. Albert Prince owns Hanover Press, a rival publisher. After first trying (unsuccessfully) to convince Queen Victoria to merge Not Amused with one of his companies, on April 1, 2012 Albert launches a tender offer to Not Amused's common shareholders at $60 per share. (The market price before the tender offer was $40.) As of April 1, Albert holds only a trivial amount of Not Amused stock. In an effort to fend off the attack, the Not Amused board immediately votes to issue to every Not Amused stockholder of record on March 30 a "special call." This special call gives the holder the right to buy an additional share of Not Amused for $1. The special call will become exercisable only if there is a "change of control" in Not Amused, defined as the acquisition of 20% or more of Not Amused stock by a person who, as of March 30, 2012, owned less than 1% of the stock. The call also provides that it may not be exercised by any person who at the time of exercise owns more than 20% of Not Amused. Finally, the call provides that if Not Amused is merged into some other entity controlled by a person who has acquired a more-than-20% stake in Not Amused, the call may be exercised against the surviving entity.

(a) What is the popular name for the anti-takeover device which the Not Amused board has attempted to put into place? ______________

(b) Do the shareholders of Not Amused need to approve the device before it becomes effective? (Assume that Not Amused has a sufficient number of authorized-but-not-outstanding shares that even if all the calls were issued and exercised, the number of shares would not exceed the authorized number.) _______________

(c) In what court — Delaware state, or federal — does Albert have the best chance of getting the device invalidated? _______________

(d) What is the likely outcome of a suit brought in the court you identified in part (c)? _______________

99. James Bond makes a hostile tender offer for all shares of Her Majesty's Secret Laundry Service, Inc., a Delaware company, at $30 per share. Her Majesty's Secret has no controlling shareholder or group — it's held by the public at large. The directors of Her Majesty's Secret decide that the company is now "in play," and that control will almost inevitably change, one way or another. The board therefore grants a "crown jewels" option to SMERSH, Inc., another public company. Under this option, SMERSH has the right to buy, at a below-market price, Her Majesty's most valuable subsidiary, which owns all the company's washing machines and dryers. (The board of Her Majesty knows that another bidder is not very likely to acquire Her Majesty without this subsidiary.) The board has given SMERSH this option because the board thinks that SMERSH will keep Her Majesty's existing executives in their posts and will treat the existing board members fairly — the board fears that Bond will not do either. The board has also begun to negotiate a merger agreement with SMERSH for the whole company, at a price of $31 (but the negotiations have not yet been completed). Bond goes to Delaware state court to get an order invalidating the option. Will Bond succeed, and why? _______________

Answers

93. Glory must file a statement of ownership within 10 days of the time she became a more-than-5% owner of Terrible Swift's common stock. SEC Rule 13d-1(a) says that if a person becomes a more-than-5% owner of any class of stock in any publicly-traded company, the person must file a statement of ownership on Schedule 13 within 10 days of the time the person acquired that status. [438] So Glory must file a 13D, showing the number of shares she owns, the date of acquisition, and other information. The fact that Glory did not conduct a "tender offer" is irrelevant to the 13D filing obligation. (If Glory *had* conducted a tender offer, then she would have had to make disclosures even before acquiring the shares in connection with the tender offer; but these disclosures would have been on a different form, 14D-1, and pursuant to different rules, grouped under Regulation 14D under the '34 Act.)

94. Tell her she must leave it open for at least 20 business days. Under the Williams Act, tender offers must be left open for at least 20 business days. SEC Rule 14e-1(a) under the '34 Act. [442] Thus, regardless of Alexis's concerns about Krystal, she can't make a five-day offer. Note, by the way, that it's just this kind of competition that the 20-day rule is designed to encourage, so that shareholders will get the best possible deal.

95. $8 per share. Under the "best price rule," if the consideration offered in a tender offer for a target's shares is increased, the increased price must be paid to all the target's shareholders who accepted at the earlier, lower price. [441] As a result, Charlie will have to pay Coco an extra $3 a share. '34 Act, § 14(d)(7).

96. Yes. Under SEC Rules enacted pursuant to the Williams Act, a shareholder who tenders to a tender offeror may revoke the tender, and withdraw the shares, at any time so long as the offer remains open. See Rule 14d-7. [441] Since Mickey's offer remains open, Minnie may revoke and tender her shares to Pluto up until April 15.

97. No, because Richie has not made a tender offer. The Williams Act doesn't explicitly define tender offers. However, courts and the SEC cite eight elements (not all required in any given situation) in deciding whether a person has made a tender offer: active and widespread solicitation for a substantial percentage of the stock at a premium over market price, a firm price, an offer for a limited time and contingent on the tender of a fixed number of shares, an offer that is publicly announced before or during a buying spree, and the placing of pressure on shareholders to sell. [444] The most important elements are the fixed price of the offer and its limited time.

The only element present here was the buying spree. A court would almost certainly conclude that Richie's widespread open-market buying, in and of itself, wasn't enough to constitute a tender offer. Such a conclusion would be consistent with Congress's intent to protect shareholders from making hasty, ill-informed choices — on these facts, with private purchases and no actual offer to buy control at a particular price at a particular time, no real pressure on shareholders existed. This would be true even if Richie told the world that he expected to someday seek control. (Note that since Richie's purchases put him over 5%, he was required to file a Schedule 13D ownership statement, and on that statement was required to disclose that he intends some day to attempt to acquire control.)

98. (a) A "poison pill." [452]

(b) No. Generally, the issuance of shares is within the control of the board, as long as the shares are within the "authorized" number (which must normally be set in the charter, and which requires a shareholder vote to amend). Indeed, that's a big advantage (from the target's board's perspective) of a poison pill plan — since no shareholder approval is typically needed, the board can act quickly, and on its own. [453] (If holder approval were needed, the holders might well vote down the plan, since it reduces their chance of getting a premium price from a hostile bidder.)

(c) Delaware state court. Nothing in the federal securities laws generally bars a target company from using defensive measures, especially where the target's management has not solicited shareholder consent to the measure. [456] (If Not Amused had solicited shareholder approval of the call options, and had made misstatements or omissions in the materials accompanying the solicitation, then there *would* be a federal securities-law violation, which could be addressed in federal court.) Any relief that Albert is to obtain will have to come from Delaware state court, and will have to derive from Delaware law.

(d) That the call will be struck down as an unreasonable barrier to a hostile takeover. In evaluating anti-takeover measures taken by a target's management or board, the Delaware court considers four factors: (1) whether the target's board had reasonable grounds for believing that the raider posed a danger to the corporation's welfare; (2) whether the defensive measures were "reasonable in relation to the threat posed"; (3) whether the board acted in good faith and after reasonable investigation; and (4) whether the measure was approved by a board a majority of whose members were outside (as opposed to employee) directors. [457] If the court finds that the answer to all questions is "yes," the court generally gives the defensive measure the protection of the business judgment rule (and upholds it without second-guessing its substantive merits); but if the answer to one or more questions is "no," the court will make the target's management carry the burden of showing that the transaction is "entirely fair" to shareholders, something management usually can't do.

As to (1), there is no evidence on these facts for Not Amused's board to have any special fear about what Albert will do to operations. As to (2), Albert can make a very strong case that the call plan here was not "reasonable in relation to the threat posed" — the call seems to be a "preclusive" one (one which will make it very unlikely that Albert will go through with his tender offer, because of the horrible consequences to him if he does), and a preclusive measure will almost always be found to be unreasonable. As to (3), the fact that the board has acted "immediately" suggests that they didn't do much investigation about what Albert's offer really means for shareholders, and are acting mostly to protect their own posts. Therefore, even if the board satisfied (4) (the facts don't tell us whether it did), the court is very likely to conclude that the call plan should not receive the protection of the business judgment rule. In that event, the court will probably go on to find that the plan is not "fair" to Not Amused's shareholders, because it will probably prevent them from having the opportunity to be bought out at a premium. Consequently, the court is likely to invalidate the plan.

99. Yes, probably, because the board has not treated both bidders equally. Once the management of a Delaware company decide to sell control of the company, the board bears the obligation to get the highest price for shareholders. This obligation normally means that the board must treat all bidders substantially equally, rather than favoring one (because a bidding war normally offers the best chance to get top dollar for the company). This is the "level playing field" rule. [462] On these facts, it's quite clear that the board of Her Majesty is trying to steer the sale to SMERSH instead of to Bond, even though Bond might well be willing to offer more than the $31 price that SMERSH is talking about. So the Delaware court will probably invalidate the crown-jewel option, and order Her Majesty's board to negotiate equally with both Bond and SMERSH.

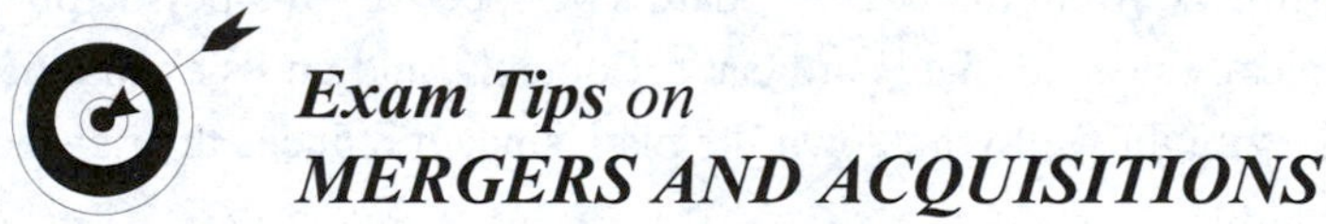

Exam Tips on MERGERS AND ACQUISITIONS

When you're analyzing an exam question on Mergers & Acquisitions, focus first on whether the transaction is "friendly" or "hostile." The issues that get tested are generally quite different depending on which category the transaction falls into.

Analyzing "friendly" acquisitions:

When you're analyzing a "friendly" acquisition (with no other, hostile, bidder in the picture), the main thing to check is whether the transaction violates the rules on ***self-dealing***.

☛ If the Target's board or management receives some "goodies" for themselves (not being given to other shareholders), and then recommend the acquisition, refer in your answer to the fact that the transaction is somewhat self-interested.

☞ However, indicate that as long as the court believes that the transaction was, overall, ***"fair"*** to the stockholders, the presence of some element of self-interest by Target's board or management won't cause the court to enjoin the transaction or award damages.

For instance, a large ***side-payment*** to Target's ***board or management*** won't usually result in the deal's being enjoined, if the price paid to shareholders is "fair."

Example: Target's stock is trading at $30/share. Acquirer offers to buy all shares at $60/share. Acquirer also promises to keep as officers the President and Treasurer of Target, at four times their current salaries, and to pay each other board member of Target a bonus equal to 4 times their annual directors' fees. All board members vote to recommend the acquisition to Target's shareholders. While the lucrative deals given to board members may make the transaction slightly self-interested, the court will let the transaction go through, and not award damages against the board, if the court thinks the transaction is "fair." Since the offering price is much higher than the prior market price, the court will probably conclude that the transaction is fair.

☞ Check to see if Target's board appoints an ***"independent committee"*** to approve the merger. The committee is probably "independent" so long as it's composed of board members who aren't on the Acquirer's side of the transaction — the fact that some committee members might get some benefit from the sale (as in the above example) won't be enough to make them non-independent.

☞ If an independent committee approves the deal, after ***reasonable investigation*** and ***deliberation***, the court usually ***won't even examine the "fairness"*** of the transaction. Instead, the court will probably hold that the transaction is ***protected by the business-judgment rule***, so long as the price and other terms aren't ***irrational***. (This assumes that the court believes the board has behaved in a way likely to get the highest available price. See the discussion of the "level playing field" rule, below.)

So where an independent committee has investigated and approved the deal, even a pretty low price won't be enough to cause the court to enjoin the transaction or award damages for the board's failure to exercise due care (but a price so low as to be completely irrational might be).

☛ Make sure that there was compliance with ***procedural formalities.*** In particular, if the friendly transaction is a merger or asset-sale (as opposed to a tender offer), make sure that ***stockholders have approved it***, by the requisite majority.

☞ Unless the charter says otherwise, only a ***simple majority*** of shares must approve. But this must be a majority of ***all shares outstanding***, not just a majority of shares voting. So abstentions hurt.

☞ The majority for approval can include ***insiders***, even insiders who will be on the other side of the transaction (e.g., management in a management-led buyout).

☞ Make sure that the shareholders received ***proper disclosure*** about the transaction before the vote. For instance, if it's a stock merger, and holders weren't given accurate info about the acquirer's finances or business prospects, the court may enjoin the transaction or award damages against the board.

☛ If shareholders have a right to vote on the transaction, keep in mind that an unsatisfied shareholder may have the right of ***appraisal***, i.e., the right to have the corporation ***buy his shares*** for a "fair price." In other words, in a stock merger, or in a sale of substantially all of the Target's assets for cash that won't be promptly re-distributed to the holders, the right of appraisal probably exists.

☞ But remember that a holder who ***votes for the transaction*** (or doesn't comply with other procedural requirements, like giving prompt notice of a demand for appraisal) ***forfeits*** her appraisal rights.

☞ Also, remember that where a holder has appraisal rights, these are usually her ***exclusive remedy***. So a holder who has appraisal rights usually can't sue to block the transaction as unfair, even if the circumstances are ones that would otherwise support an injunction (e.g., an excessively low price).

Analyzing Hostile Takeovers

Exams often focus on hostile takeovers and the defensive tactics used by the Target to repel the hostile bid. When you've got a question involving a hostile bid, here's what to look for:

☛ First, check whether all parties have complied with the ***Williams Act***.

☞ A party needs to comply with § 13(d)'s ***disclosure requirements*** if she directly or indirectly ***acquires more than 5% of any class*** of Target's publicly-held stock. A person needs to comply even if she has not made (and doesn't intend to make) a tender offer, and doesn't intend to purchase more stock.

☞ The disclosure requirement also applies when two or more people agree to ***act in concert*** in acquiring new stock, or even in voting stock they already own (as long as, together, they own at least 5% of a class of stock).

Example: Sam and Harold are officers of Target, and together own 47% of Target's stock. Raider makes a tender offer for all Target shares. Sam and Harold agree to try to block Raider's offer. In particular, they agree that they will vote together to oppose the offer, and will work together to persuade other holders to do the same.

Sam and Harold are required to file a Schedule 13D disclosure form (showing that they have agreed to work together) even though they are not intending to acquire any new shares. That's because their combination has increased their effective voting power, and is a transaction by a more-than-5% holder.

☞ If a person makes a ***"tender offer,"*** the person has to comply with ***additional disclosure*** rules under §14(e). But an offer to buy a large percentage of a corporation's stock doesn't automatically make the offer a "tender offer" — widespread solicitation, a firm price, and a time limit, will usually all have to be present for a tender offer. Open-market purchases usually won't suffice.

☞ But even if you spot a §13(d) or §14(e) disclosure-rule violation, don't assume that the court will ***block*** the transaction. Usually, the court will ***let the acquirer acquire and vote the shares***, even though he got them while failing to make disclosure. (A holder will have to be content with a civil-damages action).

☞ Any time you have a shareholder solicitation in connection with a takeover attempt, check whether the ***solicitation materials*** were ***accurate***. If they're not, any holder has an ***implied private right of action*** against the soliciter under §14(e) of the '34 Act. But P has to prove that:

- ❑ the misrepresentation or nondisclosure by D was ***material***;
- ❑ D acted with ***"scienter"*** (recklessness or intent to mislead); and
- ❑ P ***relied*** on the incorrect materials (if D's error was a misrepresentation, rather

than an omission).

Example: Acquirer makes a tender offer for all of Target's shares, at $65/share. Acquirer tells Prexy, the head of Target, that Acquirer will keep all product lines. Acquirer promises Prexy that Prexy will still have a job after the acquisition. Spoiler comes along and tells Prexy that he'll bid $70/share for a controlling interest in Target; Spoiler says he'll liquidate the company, and fire Prexy. Prexy tells these facts to Target's board. The board approves solicitation materials that recommend that each holder tender to Acquirer's offer. The materials don't mention the offer from Spoiler. Holder, a shareholder in Target, receives these materials, votes for the merger, then finds out the materials didn't mention the higher offer from Spoiler.

Holder can recover civil damages from Prexy and the rest of Target's board, because: (1) the omission about Spoiler's offer was "material" (existence of a higher offer would almost always be important to a holder who's deciding whether to tender); (2) the board knew about the other offer, so the omission was probably at least "reckless," and thus constituted "scienter"; and (3) Holder probably doesn't need to show he read the materials and relied, because you can't really rely on an omission (as opposed to an affirmative misrepresentation).

☛ Analyze any ***defensive measures*** employed by Target. Unless the facts tell you that some other body of law applies, you'll usually do well to apply the Delaware approach, which is well-developed and specific. (We'll apply Delaware rules here.) The court will probably invalidate the defensive measure unless four requirements are met:

❑ First, Target's board and management must have ***reasonable grounds*** for believing that there's a ***danger to Target's own welfare*** (as opposed to the welfare of management). Management and the board ***can't act merely to perpetuate themselves*** in power.

Example 1: Target is faced with a hostile takeover. Target's board adopts a plan stating that all employees of Target will receive a severance payment of one year's salary for every five years with the company. The payments are to be made only if the employee is fired after a change of control in Target. A court might well hold that this provision was intended mainly to perpetuate Target's management in power and defeat the takeover, not to benefit shareholders. In that case, the court will probably invalidate the measure.

Example 2: Target is faced with a hostile takeover from Raider. Target's stock is trading at $10/share, after having been $20 just six months previously. Raider is offering $13. Target's board reasonably believes that the 50% selloff is due to general stock-market conditions, not long-term problems with Target's business operations (which the board believes to be sound and improving). The board therefore recommends that holders not tender. The board also votes to have Target issue new shares representing a 15% stake, which Target sells at $11/share to White Knight, a buyer who has indicated that he will support incumbent management in any takeover battle.

Probably these measures satisfy the "reasonable grounds for fearing threat to corporate welfare" test (and will be upheld if they meet the other tests, which they probably do).

- ❑ Second, the anti-takeover defense must be ***reasonable in relation to the threat posed***. The response can't be ***"preclusive"*** (one that makes it almost impossible for the hostile bid to succeed) or ***"coercive"*** (one that forces holders to accept management's own alternative to the hostile bid).

  Example 1: Target is faced with a hostile bid from Raider. Target's board announces a contract to sell Target's most profitable subsidiary at a below-market price to Newcorp, a new company set up by Target's management; the contract will only take effect if Raider's bid is successful. If Raider (or a stockholder in Target) challenges this contract, it will probably be invalidated as being a waste of Target's assets and thus coercive.

  Example 2: Raider announces a hostile bid for Target at $200/share. Target has 152,000 shares outstanding. In response to Raider's offer, Target: (1) sells to White Knight 48,000 shares of Target at $150/share in return for White Knight's agreemen that he won't acquire any further shares without management's consent for 5 years; (2) buys back 100,000 shares from other holders. Simultaneously, Prexy, the head of Target, promises White Knight that Prexy won't sell Prexy's 3,000 shares in Target to anyone but White Knight, in return for White Knight's promise that if White Knight gets control of Target, it will employ Prexy.

  A court would almost certainly hold that this package of defensive measures is "preclusive," in that it prevents anyone but White Knight from getting control of Target no matter what they do. Therefore, the court will invalidate the measures.

- ❑ Third, the board must take the defensive measure not only in good faith, but only after ***reasonable investigation***.

- ❑ Finally, in a close case the court is more likely to approve the defensive measure if it was adopted by a board a ***majority*** of whose members were ***disinterested*** (i.e., ***outside***) members.

☛ If Target's board decides ***to sell the company*** (or control of the company), then remember that the board's main duty is to ***obtain the highest price*** for shareholders.

☞ This means that Target's board must create a ***"level playing field"*** — the board ***can't favor a white knight over a hostile bidder***.

Example: Target has just learned that Raider, a notorious hostile bidder who often liquidates his prey, has acquired 6% of Target and may be about to acquire more. With board approval, Target's management approaches Friendly Corp. about the possibility of Friendly's acquiring all of Target's assets. Target then gives Friendly nonpublic financial data about Target and declines to give the same data to Raider. Since Target's board (by approaching Friendly) has indicated that the company is for sale, Target had an obligation to obtain the highest price, and to treat all bidders more-or-less equally in order to obtain that highest price. By favoring Friendly in disclosure, Target violated these duties. The court will order Target to give the same data to Raider, and will probably enjoin any deal made with Friendly in the absence of the required "level playing field."

- ☞ But remember that the "level playing field" rule ***does not get triggered*** until the Target's board ***starts negotiating with a bidder*** (or starts ***actively looking*** for bidders). The mere fact that the board knows that a bid is ***likely to come soon*** is ***not*** enough to trigger the rule — so the board can just ***"wait and see"*** whether a bid arrives, without taking active steps to get the best price. [Cite to *Lyondell Chemical* on this point.]

- ☞ Also, keep in mind that the board ***won't be personally liable*** for breach of the duty of loyalty from its handling of a takeover bid unless the board ***"utterly fails to even attempt"*** to get the best price. So even a small effort by the board (e.g., an unsuccessful single attempt to get the Bidder to raise his initial offer) will likely be enough to avoid liability for breach of the duty of loyalty/good faith. [*Lyondell Chemical*.]

☞ The "level playing field" rule applies not only where Target's management is selling the entire company, but also where management or the board has decided to sell ***control*** to a single individual or entity.

Example: On the facts of the above Target/Raider example, suppose that Target offered to sell Friendly not Target's assets, but, instead, stock representing a 30% interest in Target. Assuming that 30% would be a controlling stake in Target (which would be the case if no one else had, say, more than a 15% stake), the offer to sell "control" to Friendly would be enough to trigger Target's "level playing field" obligations. So Friendly would have to give the same financial data to Raider (and would not be allowed to consummate the 30%-deal with Friendly if this would be less favorable for Target's shareholders than the bid from Raider).

☞ Finally, remember that Target's board always has the right to ***"just say no"*** when it receives an unsolicited offer. In other words, the board may refuse to approve the transaction or recommend it to shareholders, even if this has the effect of blocking the deal. (But if the board tries to make an alternative deal — like selling to a white knight — then the board isn't just "saying no," and it must comply with the "level playing field" rule.)

CHAPTER 11

DIVIDENDS AND SHARE REPURCHASES

ChapterScope

This Chapter covers two ways in which a corporation commonly distributes its earnings or assets to its shareholders: by paying dividends, and by repurchasing some of its own shares from shareholders. Key concepts:

- **State limits:** The main focus of this chapter is on how states limit dividends and share repurchases so as to ***protect creditors*** of the corporation. A secondary focus is on the extent to which courts will supervise a corporation's dividend or share-repurchase policies to protect ***minority shareholders***.
- **Dividends:** A dividend is a ***cash payment*** made by a corporation pro rata to each shareholder.
  - ❑ **State limits:** All states limit the payment of dividends in order to make sure that the corporation will remain able to ***pay its creditors***. States differ in how they do this; most states prohibit a dividend if this payment would leave the corporation with less ***"capital"*** than the amount originally contributed by stockholders. All states also prohibit dividend payments that would leave the corporation ***"insolvent."***
- **Stock repurchases:** A corporation may buy back a portion of its own stock, either on the open "public" market (if the corporation is publicly-traded) or from selected individual stockholders. Most states limit share repurchases so as to protect creditors.

I. DIVIDENDS — PROTECTION OF CREDITORS

A. Nature of a dividend: A "dividend," as the term is usually used, is a cash payment made by a corporation to its common shareholders pro rata. For instance, XYZ Corp might declare a quarterly dividend of fifty cents for each share of its common stock. Normally, the dividend is paid out of the ***current earnings*** of the corporation, and thus represents a partial distribution by the corporation to its stockholders of the corporation's profits.

1. How decided: The decision to pay a dividend must be made by the ***board of directors***. The decision to pay a dividend, and its size, are normally matters protected by the business judgment rule (*supra*, p. 182), so that a court will normally neither reverse the board's decision nor hold the directors liable, even if it thinks that they have made a bad decision. But there are two important exceptions:

[1] nearly all states place certain ***legal limits*** (mostly financial ones) on the board's right to pay dividends, and directors who disregard these limits may be liable (see *infra*, p. 514); and

[2] if the directors' choice of dividend policy is made not for the purpose of furthering the corporate welfare, but in ***bad faith*** or for the directors' own ***personal purposes***, the

court might overturn this policy (see *infra*, p. 516).

2. **Periodic vs. ad hoc dividends:** The nature of a corporation's dividend policy is likely to depend in large part on whether the corporation is publicly held or closely held.

   a. **Public corporations:** If the corporation is ***publicly*** held, it will typically try to have a ***regular***, predictable dividend policy. Usually, the corporation will do this by fixing upon a particular ***"payout ratio"***: the corporation will aim to distribute, say, 50% of its earnings as dividends. As earnings gradually increase over time, so the dividend will also be increased. Generally, public corporations try desperately hard to avoid ever having to ***cut*** their dividend. For instance, if the corporation's earnings decrease, the corporation will often temporarily increase the payout ratio in order to keep the dividend at its former level.

   b. **Close corporations:** Where the corporation is closely held, by contrast, the dividend policy is likely to be much more erratic. Typically, the stockholders/directors of a closed corporation will also be its managers, and they will take most of the entrepreneurial profits out of the corporation in the form of salaries, bonuses, fringe benefits, etc., rather than in the form of dividends.

      i. **Rationale:** The main reason for this is that dividends are ***taxed twice***: first, there is a tax at the corporate level (since the corporation does not receive any deduction from its income tax to reflect the fact that it pays out the dividend); second, the shareholder will be taxed on the dividend when he receives it. By contrast, salaries, bonuses and fringe benefits are taxed at most once (since they are deductible to the corporation), and sometimes not at all (in the case of many fringe benefits).

      ii. **Minority stockholders:** Therefore, in a close corporation, the pressure to pay dividends will usually arise only if there are minority stockholders who are not employed as executives by the corporation. Such stockholders are not getting generous salaries or other compensation, so they can participate in the corporation's profits only by either selling their stock (for which there may be no liquid market) or by receiving dividends. We will be treating the rights of minority shareholders to compel payment of dividends in closely-held corporations beginning *infra*, p. 518.

B. **Need to protect creditors:** A corporation's ***creditors*** reasonably expect that the corporation will maintain sufficient assets to pay the creditors' claims. True, a creditor should ordinarily recognize the possibility that a corporation may have so many debts that it is unable to pay them all. But a creditor is normally entitled at least to reasonable assurances that a corporation's ***common stockholders*** will not be paid "before" the creditor, in the sense that the stockholders receive money and the creditor is left with an unpaid claim against an insolvent corporation. Since the creditor has given up any chance to participate in the "upside" of the business in return for a fixed promise of payment, and since the stockholder has given up any right to a fixed payment in return for a chance to participate in this upside, payments to the shareholders at the expense of creditors would unfairly reverse the parties' basic understanding. Yet if corporations had unlimited rights to pay dividends to their shareholders, creditors might indeed be frequently left unpaid while the shareholders got back their original investment plus perhaps even a profit.

1. **Limits on dividends:** Therefore, ***all states*** have placed ***financial limits*** on the payment of corporate dividends. These statutes all attempt to protect creditors by assuring that dividends will not be paid if the payment will leave the corporation unable to pay off its creditors. However, as we shall shortly see, most of these statutes are a woefully ineffective way of accomplishing this goal — since a clever board of directors (and corporate counsel) can almost always find a way around these statutes to funnel dividends to the stockholders while leaving creditors holding the bag.

2. **Accounting principles and terminology:** Before we can examine these statutory limits on dividend payments, however, we unfortunately have to master some accounting principles and terminology, because these form the basis for most such statutes.

   a. **"Legal" or "stated" capital:** ***"Legal capital"*** — or as it is often called, ***"stated capital"*** — is the most important of the terms. (We'll use "stated capital" throughout our discussion.) The basic idea behind the concept of stated capital is that it represents the stockholders' ***permanent investment*** in the corporation. (We discuss the concept further *infra*, p. 530.)

      i. **Par stock:** If the stock has ***"par value,"*** stated capital is equal to the ***number of shares outstanding times the par value of each share***. (Originally, nearly all stock had a par value assigned to it; today, this is no longer the case. See *infra*, p. 533.)

      ii. **"No-par":** If the stock is ***"no-par"*** stock, as is now permitted in most states, stated capital is an arbitrary amount that directors decide to assign to the stated capital account. (This amount will be at most equal to what the shareholders paid for their stock at the time of its original issue, but is otherwise whatever the directors decide it should be at the time the stock is issued.) C&E, p. 1340.

   Example 1: XYZ issues 1,000 shares of stock having a $10 par value. The stock issued to the original investors has a selling price of $30 per share. The corporation's stated capital will be $10,000 (1,000 shares times the $10 per share par value). The remaining $20,000 paid in by the shareholders as part of their original investment will be called "capital surplus" (and, more narrowly, "paid-in surplus"; see *infra*, p. 510).

   Example 2: The directors of XYZ Corp, at the time it is formed, decide to issue no par stock instead of par stock. They issue the same 1,000 shares as in the prior example, at the same $30 per share initial issue price. But because the stock is "no par," the corporation's stated capital will be whatever the board decides it should be. Suppose that the board decides that $5,000 should represent the stated capital. Then, in addition to this $5,000 of stated capital, the corporation will have, initially, $25,000 of "capital surplus" or "paid-in surplus."

   b. **"Earned surplus":** The second key term is ***"earned surplus."*** "Earned surplus" is equal to the ***profits*** earned by the corporation during its existence, less any dividends it ever paid out. "Earned surplus" is the same as what is today usually called ***"retained earnings."***

   Example 3: In year 1 of its operations, XYZ Corp earns an after-tax profit of $1,000. In year 2, it earns $3,000 after taxes. In year 3, it has a $2,000 after-tax loss. At the end of year 3, XYZ's "earned surplus" will be $2,000, the sum of all of its annual profits and losses. On a modern-style balance sheet, this $2,000 figure would probably be labeled "retained earnings."

c. **"Capital surplus":** Finally, we have ***"capital surplus."*** This is defined (not very helpfully) as everything in the corporation's "capital" account that is not "stated" capital. A capital surplus can come from a number of sources, the most important of which is ***paid-in surplus***. Paid-in surplus is the difference between the amount paid by stockholders at the time of initial share issuance and the stated capital.

Example: Same facts as Example no. 1, above. The stockholders paid in a total of $30,000 for the 1,000 shares of stock. Of this, only $10,000 was stated capital (that is, $10,000 was the aggregate par value of the stock issued). The balance of $20,000 was paid-in surplus, a form of capital surplus. (Similarly, in Example 2 above, because $5,000 was arbitrarily assigned as the stated capital represented by the no par stock, the balance paid by the shareholders, $25,000, would be paid-in surplus.)

C. **Traditional statutes:** We are now ready to see how these concepts of stated capital, earned surplus and capital surplus are used in most states to limit the payment of dividends.

1. **Method of most statutes:** Most statutes allow a dividend to be paid only if ***both*** of the following general kinds of requirements are satisfied: (1) payment of the dividend will not impair the corporation's ***stated capital***; and (2) payment will not render the corporation ***insolvent***.

a. **Impairment of stated capital:** Most states use the concept of stated capital, and the companion notion of surplus, to limit the payment of dividends.

i. **"Earned surplus" statutes:** The strictest of these statutes allow dividends to be paid only out of "earned surplus." These are discussed *infra*, p. 509.

ii. **Impairment of capital:** Other statutes are somewhat more liberal: dividends may not be paid out of stated capital, but may be paid out of ***any kind*** of surplus, whether it is earned or unearned. For instance, these statutes allow dividends to be paid out of paid-in surplus. These statutes are generally referred to as "impairment of capital" statutes, and are discussed *infra*, p. 509.

b. **Insolvency:** Entirely apart from the above limits based on concepts of legal capital and surplus, nearly all states prohibit the payment of dividends if it is ***"insolvent,"*** or if it would be rendered insolvent by the payment. Some statutes use the "bankruptcy" sense of the word "insolvent" — a corporation is insolvent if its liabilities are greater than its assets. Others use the "equity" sense of "insolvent" — a corporation is insolvent if it is unable to pay its debts as they come due. Some statutes use both meanings, i.e., they prohibit dividends where the corporation would be insolvent under either test. See, e.g., MBCA § 6.40. The insolvency tests are discussed more extensively *infra*, p. 512.

c. **Payment out of current earnings:** Finally, some states relax their requirements somewhat by allowing the payment of dividends from ***"current earnings,"*** even where the dividend would not otherwise be allowed because the relevant capital test is not satisfied. Delaware falls into this category. These special current-earnings provisions are sometimes called ***"nimble dividend"*** rules, and are discussed *infra*, p. 511.

2. **"Earned surplus" statutes:** Most states still impose an ***earned surplus*** restriction: dividends ***may only be paid out of the profits which the corporation has accumulated*** since its inception. These statutes generally derive from the pre-1979 version of the MBCA, which generally allowed dividends to be paid "only out of unreserved and unrestricted earned surplus of the corporation. . . ." § 45(a), 1969 MBCA. (The 1969 Act also prohibited payment of dividends where the corporation is or would thereby become insolvent.)

   a. **Rationale:** The rationale of these "earned surplus" statutes is that "[d]ividends are supposed to be the fruit of the tree, and unless fruit has been borne, nothing can be picked." S,S,B&W, p. 258.

   Example: To see how the earned-surplus test would restrict the payment of dividends, assume that XYZ Corp has 1,000 shares of $1-par-value stock outstanding, that the shareholders paid $2 for each of these shares, and that XYZ's balance sheet looks as follows:

Assets		**Liabilities and Shareholders' Equity**	
Cash	$ 2,000	Total Liabilities	$ 500
Inventory	2,000	Shareholders' Equity	
		Stated Capital	1,000
		Capital Surplus	1,000
		Retained Earnings	1,500
	$ 4,000		$ 4,000

   In an earned-surplus jurisdiction, XYZ could pay a cash dividend of no more than $1,500. That is, its maximum dividend would be limited to its earned surplus (shown on our financial statement under the more modern term "Retained Earnings"). Even though the company has more than $2,000 of cash on hand, it may not make a dividend that would have the effect of reducing the balance sheet entry for either stated capital or capital surplus. (Also, of course, XYZ's board would have to comply with whatever version of an insolvency test the statute contains, as is discussed below.)

3. **"Impairment of capital" statutes:** A second group of states, smaller in number than those following the earned-surplus approach, follow the ***"impairment of capital"*** approach. These states are ***less strict*** about the payment of dividends. To be precise, they allow the payment of dividends from ***either*** earned surplus or ***unearned surplus***.

   a. **Delaware and New York:** Two very important statutes, those of Delaware and New York, fall into this "impairment of capital" category. Thus Delaware GCL § 170(a) allows a corporation to pay dividends "out of its surplus," and then defines "surplus" to be the corporation's net assets less the aggregate par value of its shares (i.e., net assets less stated capital). See Del. GCL § 154. Similarly, New York BCL § 510(b) says that dividends "may be made out of surplus only, so that the net assets of the corporation remaining after [payment] shall at least equal the amount of its stated capital. . . ."

   b. **Why they're called "impairment" statutes:** We call these statutes "impairment of capital" statutes because they impose only the relatively lenient requirement that the corporation's capital (by which they mean "stated" capital, usually the ***aggregate par value***) not be "impaired," that is, ***not be reduced below what it originally was.***

4. **Types of unearned surplus:** So the "impairment of capital" statutes are less strict than the "earned surplus" statutes to the extent that they allow dividends to be paid out of ***"unearned surplus"*** (or, as it is sometimes called, "capital surplus"). What is "unearned surplus"? There are three important varieties: (1) paid-in surplus; (2) revaluation surplus; and (3) reduction surplus.

   a. **Paid-in surplus:** ***"Paid-in"*** surplus is a concept we have already encountered. See *supra*, p. 436. This is the difference between what the shareholders pay for their shares at the time they are originally issued, and the stated capital represented by those shares (usually the aggregate par value). For instance, in our illustration on p. 509 the entire $1,000 item shown as "capital surplus" is paid-in surplus, since the stockholders paid $2 per share for each of the 1,000 issued shares, yet the par value of each share was only $1.

      i. **Can pay out paid-in surplus:** Thus under an "impairment of capital" statute (but not under an earned-surplus statute), the corporation may pay out this entire paid-in surplus as a dividend. On the facts of the above illustration, XYZ could therefore pay a dividend of $2,500 (its $1,500 of retained earning plus its $1,000 of paid-in capital surplus).

   b. **Revaluation surplus:** Second, many if not most "impairment of capital" states would allow a board of directors to create so-called ***"revaluation"*** surplus. Normally, a corporation's assets as shown on its balance sheet reflect the ***historical costs*** of each individual asset. For instance, if the corporation bought a piece of raw land in 1927 for $1,000, and that land is worth $3 million today, the corporation's balance sheet (if prepared according to generally accepted accounting principles) will show a value of $1,000, not $3 million. But for purposes of dividend statutes, most states would probably permit the corporation to "write up" its assets to their ***current market value***. The increase resulting from this write-up process would be shown on the left asset side of the balance sheet as an increase in the value of certain assets, and shown on the right (liability and net worth) side as "revaluation surplus."

      i. **Delaware allows:** Delaware follows this majority approach, allowing the board to create a revaluation surplus. See *Klang v. Smith's Food & Drug Centers, Inc.*, 702 A.2d 150 (Del. 1997).

   c. **Reduction surplus:** Finally, a corporation may have something called ***"reduction surplus."*** Reduction surplus is caused by ***reducing the corporation's stated capital***.

      i. **No par stock:** If the corporation stock is ***no par***, the stated capital can simply be reduced by a ***board resolution*** that is approved by a majority of the stockholders. See, e.g., 1969 MBCA § 69.

      ii. **Par value:** Where the corporation's shares have a par value, creating a reduction surplus by reducing the stated capital is a little trickier. Here, the par value has to be reduced, and this generally requires an amendment to the articles of incorporation (which in turn requires shareholder approval).

5. Nimble dividends: A number of states allow the payment of so-called ***"nimble dividends."*** These are dividends paid out of the ***current earnings*** of the corporation, despite the fact that the corporation otherwise would not be entitled to pay the dividend (e.g., the corporation has no earned surplus in an earned-surplus state, or the payment would impair the corporation's stated capital in an impairment-of-capital state). The phrase derives from the fact that the directors must be "nimble" in declaring and paying the dividend — under most such statutes, the dividend must be paid based on earnings from the ***prior*** or ***current*** fiscal year.

a. When used: Payment of nimble dividends is most useful when the corporation has had a number of years of ***losses***, and then one or two years of ***earnings***. These earnings are not enough to create an earned surplus or to repair the damage to stated capital; but the directors believe that the good times will continue, and they would like to give stockholders a dividend without having to wait, for, say, an earned surplus that would otherwise be required.

b. Delaware: The most famous nimble dividends provision is Delaware's, in Del. GCL § 170(a). That provision allows payment of dividends even if there is no "surplus," if the dividend is paid "out of [the corporation's] net profits for the fiscal year ***in which the dividend is declared*** and/or the ***preceding*** fiscal year."

Example: XYZ Corp, a Delaware corporation, issues 1,000 shares with a $10 par value, for $10 apiece. Therefore, XYZ initially has legal capital of $10,000, and no capital surplus. The corporation loses $1,000 during each of its first four years in business, leaving it with a negative earned surplus of $4,000. Then, in year 5, XYZ earns $3,000. At the end of year 5, its balance sheet appears as follows:

Assets		**Liabilities and Shareholders' Equity**	
Cash	$ 2,000	Debt	$ 1,000
Inventory	6,000	Shareholders' Equity	
		Stated Capital	10,000
		Earned Surplus (Deficit)	(1,000)
	$ 8,000		$8,000

Under the ordinary Delaware provisions, XYZ could not pay any dividend here, because a dividend may be paid only out of surplus, whether earned or unearned. (In other words, Delaware is an "impairment of capital" state; see *supra*, p. 509.) But the nimble dividends provision allows the directors of XYZ to pay in year 6 a dividend of up to $3,000 (the amount earned in the prior fiscal year); in fact, they could add to this dividend the amount they estimate the corporation will earn in the current fiscal year (year 6).

i. Protection of preference: But even under the Delaware nimble dividends provision, the capital of any class having a ***preference*** on the distribution of assets must be protected. For instance, suppose that XYZ, in the above example, also had 1,000 shares of $10 preferred stock (i.e., these preferred shares would be entitled to the first $10,000 of assets upon the liquidation of XYZ). Now, the nimble dividend described in the prior example could ***not*** be paid — only if the corporation's capital and capital surplus, less the amount of its earnings deficit, was at least equal to $10,000, could this dividend be paid. The purpose of this special provision, of course, is to make it reasonably likely that there will indeed be $10,000 of assets for the preferred shareholders if XYZ is liquidated.

6. **Insolvency tests:** Entirely apart from the earned-surplus or impairment-of-capital standards discussed above (at least one of which is on the books in most states), virtually every state prohibits the payment of dividends that would ***leave the corporation insolvent***. Sometimes, the prohibition on dividends that would lead to insolvency is contained in the corporation statute itself. See, e.g., NY BCL § 510(a). Often, however, the prohibition is instead in some non-corporation statute designed to ***protect creditors***, which prohibits any person or entity (including corporations) from making any payment without consideration that would lead to insolvency — since a dividend is made "without consideration," it will generally be "fraudulent" (and thus illegal) under these creditor-protection statutes if the corporation is insolvent either before or immediately after the payment. For instance, 25 states have enacted the ***Uniform Fraudulent Conveyance Act***, or UFCA, which would have the effect of prohibiting a dividend by an insolvent corporation. See H&A, p. 890, n. 5.

   a. **Two meanings of "insolvent":** There are two quite distinct definitions of "insolvent." The particular state statute prohibiting the payment of dividends by insolvent corporations may use one, the other, or both of these definitions.

   b. **"Equity" meaning:** First is the ***"equity"*** meaning of "insolvent": the corporation is insolvent if it would be ***unable to pay its debts as they become due***. This can be thought of as the ***"cash flow"*** sense of insolvency. For instance, suppose that XYZ Corp has a large bank loan coming due next month, and has no strong reason to believe that the loan can be rolled over. Assume also that XYZ has less cash on hand than the amount of this loan. If in the ordinary course of business XYZ would probably be unable to pay the loan back next month, it may not pay a dividend now, if the state prohibits dividends by insolvent corporations and uses the equity meaning of "insolvent." This would be true even though the corporation might have a capital surplus (i.e., its assets exceed its liabilities by more than the amount of its stated capital).

      i. **Most states apply:** This "equity" meaning definition of insolvency is the one that is in force in most states. Nutshell, p. 389.

   c. **"Bankruptcy" meaning:** The second definition of "insolvent" is often called the ***"bankruptcy"*** meaning: a corporation is insolvent if the ***market value of its assets is less than its liabilities***. Whereas the equity meaning concentrates on cash flow (ability to cope with the bills as they roll in each month), the bankruptcy emphasis is on ***liquidation***: in a forced sale, could all debts be paid off? A corporation with valuable but illiquid assets (e.g., real estate or a hard-to-sell machine) might well be insolvent in the equity sense but quite solvent in the bankruptcy sense. Conversely, a debtor with large, but very long-term, bank debt might be insolvent in the bankruptcy sense, but quite solvent in the equity sense since its day of reckoning is not near.

d. MBCA: The MBCA's dividend provisions (which we discuss more extensively *infra*, p. 514) include ***both*** meanings of insolvency. That is, a dividend is prohibited if the corporation is or would thereby become insolvent in ***either*** the equity or bankruptcy sense. See MBCA § 6.40(c).

7. Summary: You can probably see by now that the traditional corporate dividend statutes do not provide very much meaningful protection for creditors.

a. Stated capital: The concept of "stated capital" is especially unhelpful to creditors. First, the rise of no-par and low-par stock means that the board of directors as a practical matter can initially set stated capital so low that this "cushion" practically disappears. Furthermore, even if stated capital is set at a number high enough to be meaningful, the board's and shareholders' ability to reduce it (and transfer the amount of the reduction to "reduction surplus"; see *supra*, p. 510), and the board's ability to create "revaluation surplus" by revaluing the assets upward in an overly-optimistic way, means that the creditor cannot even count on a continuation of this cushion.

b. Earned surplus: The "earned surplus" requirement of most states seems stricter, but it, too, can usually be undermined both by the devices mentioned in the prior sentence as well as by other ones (e.g., payment of nimble dividends).

c. Consequence: Therefore, the only meaningful prediction creditors usually get comes from the ***insolvency rules***, though these are often ambiguous in their application to corporations, and may not provide a good remedy (e.g., it is not clear that the directors will be liable under such statutes; see *infra*, p. 514).

d. Contractual restrictions: Therefore, many creditors, especially lenders, now take matters into their own hands. That is, before they will issue credit to the corporation, they will insist upon ***contractual*** restrictions that protect them better than any statute ever could. Thus a bank lender will often require that the corporation agree to ***"negative covenants"*** restricting the corporation's right to pay dividends while the loan is still outstanding. For instance, the bank might require the corporation to agree that it will not pay any dividend which would leave the corporation with equity (assets minus liabilities) equal to an amount smaller than the amount of the debt. Such covenants are so common, and so much more effective than the dividend statutes, that the latter are now mainly important for the protection of ***trade creditors*** (i.e., suppliers), who extend credit without the knowledge or bargaining clout to impose the kinds of restrictive covenants that a bank lender can impose.

D. Modern statutes: Because of the poor creditor-protection given by traditional statutes built around the concept of capital, there is a slight modern trend toward abandoning that concept, and instead focusing on insolvency and on the kinds of measures on which sophisticated lenders rely.

1. Financial ratios: Thus at least one state, California, has enacted a statute that relies on ***financial ratios*** of the sort that bankers usually look to, rather than on any concept of capital. § 500 of the Cal. Corp. Code allows payment of dividends either out of retained earnings or if both of the following tests would be met after payment of the dividend: (1) the corporation's assets are at least 1 1/4 times its liabilities; and (2) its current assets are at least equal to its current liabilities (except that companies that have not recently earned an amount equal to their interest charges are required to meet a stricter ratio: their current assets must be equal to 1 1/4 times their current liabilities).

2. **MBCA:** The MBCA similarly abandons the concept of capital. But rather than looking to financial ratios as the California statute does, the MBCA focuses tightly on the notion of ***insolvency.***

   a. **Text of rule:** The gist of the MBCA's dividend rule is given in § 6.40(c), which provides that,

   "***No distribution may be made*** if, after giving it effect:

   (1) the corporation would ***not be able to pay its debts as they become due*** in the usual course of business; ***or***

   (2) the corporation's ***total assets*** would be ***less than the sum of its total liabilities plus*** (unless the articles of incorporation permit otherwise) the amount that would be needed, if the corporation were to be dissolved at the time of the distribution, to satisfy the ***preferential rights*** upon dissolution of shareholders whose preferential rights are superior to those receiving the distribution."

   b. **"Equity" and "bankruptcy" meanings:** Observe that under this MBCA provision, a dividend will be prohibited if the corporation would thereby become insolvent under ***either*** the "equity" ("unable to pay debts as they mature") or "bankruptcy" ("assets less than liabilities") meanings of "insolvent."

   c. **Protection of senior classes of stock:** Notice also that the MBCA gives special protection to ***senior classes*** of stock. Thus if a dividend is to be paid to the common stockholders by a corporation which also has preferred stock outstanding, it must be the case that after the dividend, the corporation will still have net worth (assets minus liabilities) in an amount equal to the aggregate liquidation preference of the preferred stock.

   d. **No cushion required:** The MBCA appears to protect creditors better than traditional statutes based on the concept of capital, since the MBCA at least focuses on a corporation's real-world ability to pay its debts. But the MBCA has been criticized for not requiring any ***cushion*** that would protect creditors. For instance, the "bankruptcy" part of the MBCA's insolvency test merely requires that after the dividend, there not be a negative net worth (so that a dividend that would result in the corporation's assets exactly matching its liabilities would be permitted). Observe that the California statute summarized *supra,* by contrast, does require a cushion of 25% if the dividend is not paid out of retained earnings.

   e. **Popular:** MCBA § 6.40(c)'s approach to when dividends may be paid has turned out to be quite ***popular***: about 37 states have adopted it either wholly or with minor variations. Hamilton (8th), p. 489. (But some large or commercially-important states have *not* jumped on the bandwagon and have kept their own traditional statutes, including Delaware, New Jersey, New York and Ohio. *Id.*)

E. **Liability of directors:** Suppose the board of directors does violate the applicable dividend statute, by authorizing and paying a dividend forbidden by the statute. Are the directors ***personally liable***? The answer is surprisingly complicated, and varies from state to state.

1. **Bad faith:** If the directors are shown to have ***known*** that the dividend was improper, they will probably be personally liable in nearly all states. Even if the dividend statute is silent about director liability, the payment of a forbidden dividend would presumably be a violation of the directors' more general duties of good faith and loyalty (see *supra*, p. 197). Therefore, a receiver or a trustee in bankruptcy for the corporation (after it becomes insolvent) could probably recover from the directors an amount equal to the improper dividend, or at least an amount equal to the claims of creditors who have not been paid but who would have been paid had the dividend not been issued. See generally C&E, pp. 1371-73.

2. **Innocent mistake:** If the directors have acted in ***good faith*** but have ***negligently*** failed to notice that the dividend is forbidden, they have a much better chance of escaping liability. Some states protect the director from liability if she acts in good faith (e.g., she relies on what appears to be reasonable financial statements).

3. **Non-negligent:** If the directors are not even negligent, they will probably be immune from liability in all states, even if they have approved a dividend which turns out to be forbidden (e.g., the corporation's capital was impaired, but this was not readily apparent to them because the corporation's financial statements were misleadingly prepared).

4. **Action by creditor:** Even if a director might be liable for approving an improper dividend, it is not clear that a ***creditor*** has standing to sue the director.

   a. **Some states allow:** Some states explicitly allow such a suit. For instance, N.Y. BCL §§ 719 and 720 allow the creditor to sue a director who negligently approves an improper dividend.

   b. **Others reject:** But in many other states, the right to recover against the director belongs only to the ***corporation***, and the creditor is left with no standing unless he can bring a shareholder's derivative suit. (But to bring a derivative suit, he will, as noted *supra*, p. 322, generally have to have owned stock at the time of the improper dividend, something that will usually not be the case). See C&E, p. 1372.

5. **MBCA:** MBCA § 8.33 explicitly allows the corporation to recover from a director the amount of any improper dividend (or other distribution) for which the director voted. However, under § 8.30 the director is protected from this liability if he acted in ***good faith*** and "in a manner the director reasonably believes to be in the best interests of the corporation." He is explicitly entitled to rely on financial statements and other financial data prepared by the corporation's accountants or executives, if he has reason to believe that they are competent to prepare such documents. § 8.30(f)(2). Thus only if the director behaves negligently in approving an improper dividend will he be liable under the MBCA.

F. **Liability of shareholders:** A ***shareholder*** who receives an improper dividend may also be liable. This liability may stem from common-law principles, from the corporation statute, or from other statutes (e.g., ones dealing with fraudulent conveyances).

   1. **Common law:** At common law, the shareholder will be ***liable*** and required to ***return the improper dividend***, if either: (1) the corporation was ***insolvent*** at the time of, or as the result of, the payment; or (2) the shareholder ***knew***, at the time he received the dividend, that it was ***improper***. But if the corporation is solvent, and the shareholder takes the divi-

dend in good faith (i.e., without notice that the dividend violates the state dividend statute), he will ***not*** have to return it, at common law. C&E, pp. 1376-79.

2. **Corporation statute:** The ***corporation statute*** may (but will not necessarily) make the shareholder liable to return the improper dividend. Occasionally, the statute imposes such liability on the shareholder directly. More often, this shareholder is made ***indirectly*** liable: directors who approve the payment are made primarily liable, but are then given a right to ***contribution*** from the shareholders who received the dividend with knowledge of facts indicating its illegality. See, e.g., MBCA § 8.33(b)(2).

3. **Other statutes:** Additionally, the shareholder may be liable under non-corporation statutes, especially ones dealing with ***fraudulent conveyances***. For instance, § 9 of the Uniform Fraudulent Conveyance Act allows a creditor to have a fraudulent conveyance set aside; a dividend paid either by an insolvent corporation (§ 4) or under circumstances that leave the corporation with "an unreasonably small capital" (§ 5) would be fraudulent, and could thus presumably be reclaimed by the creditor on behalf of the corporation. See Clark, p. 40, n. 1. Similarly, if the corporation becomes ***bankrupt***, the trustee in bankruptcy will probably be able to recover a dividend made while the corporation was insolvent or when it had unreasonably small capital; see 11 U.S.C. § 548. See generally C&E, pp. 1379-80.

G. **Stock dividends:** So far, we have been speaking only about cash dividends. What about the payment of a ***stock*** dividend?

1. **Meaning of "stock dividend":** A stock dividend is the distribution by a corporation of ***additional shares*** to the existing stockholders. For instance, the corporation might declare a 5% stock dividend, in which case it would distribute one new share of stock for each 20 existing shares (and would give either fractional shares or "scrip" representing fractional shares to those who held less than 20 shares).

2. **No limits:** Unlike a cash dividend, a stock dividend is not a distribution of the corporation's assets. The corporation has exactly the same total assets, and net worth, after the stock dividend as before it. Therefore, state corporation statutes generally ***do not apply to the payment of stock dividends***, and the corporation may declare one pretty much whenever it wishes. A stock dividend is quite similar to a stock split — it is merely a device for increasing the number of shares, and decreasing the percentage of ownership represented by each share. Nutshell, p. 384.

II. DIVIDENDS — PROTECTION OF SHAREHOLDERS; JUDICIAL REVIEW OF DIVIDEND POLICY

A. **Protection of shareholders generally:** It will often happen that a particular shareholder is unhappy with the corporation's dividend policy. Most commonly, the shareholder will want the corporation to pay ***more dividends*** than it is paying. For instance, the insiders (board members and executives) who control the dividend policy may want to reinvest all profits to expand the business, or to pay themselves huge salaries and bonuses that reduce the sums available for dividends, or to otherwise pursue personal or corporate objectives that result in low or no dividends being paid. The question therefore becomes, may the disgruntled shareholder persuade a court to intervene and to order the corporation to pay higher dividends? The answer is that the shareholder will only ***rarely be successful*** in getting a court to order a dividend increase.

1. **General rule:** There are virtually no statutes specifying when the corporation must (as opposed to when it may not) pay dividends. Therefore, the matter is left to common-law principles, especially the business judgment rule. Under the general approach of most courts (at least in cases involving ***publicly held*** corporations), the plaintiff must show both that: (1) the low-dividend policy is ***not justified by any reasonable business objective***; and (2) the policy results from ***improper motives***, and harms the corporation or some of its shareholders. Clark, p. 602.

2. **Difficult for plaintiff to win:** The plaintiff will only ***very rarely*** be able to satisfy both of these requirements. In particular, she will generally face the problem that the insiders can almost always point to some ostensibly valid business reason for paying low or no dividends (e.g., the need to accumulate cash in case of a downturn in the company's fortunes). It will be very difficult for the plaintiff to prove that this alleged justification is just a subterfuge, and that the insiders are really pursuing their own improper objectives. Furthermore, even if the plaintiff can make this showing of a subterfuge, the court may refuse to look behind the valid business objective, and may hold that the stated objective automatically justifies the dividend policy regardless of whether the objective was in fact the motivating force behind that policy.

   a. **Plaintiff occasionally successful:** But plaintiffs have, very occasionally, successfully persuaded the court to order a public corporation to institute or increase its dividend. Generally, this will only happen where the insiders are so unlucky (or incompetent) as not to be able to come up with ***any*** business justification for their no- or low-dividend policy, ***and*** the insiders are dumb enough to leave around evidence of their own improper motives.

   Example: Ford Motor Company, under the leadership of the original Henry Ford, reaps incredible financial success. For instance, by 1916 its working capital exceeds $48 million and its surplus is almost $112 million. From 1911 to 1915, it pays $41 million in dividends. Then, in 1916, Henry Ford announces that the company will no longer pay any dividends, and will reinvest all profits in the business. The Ps (the Dodge brothers, who are minority stockholders in Ford but who also are running their own car company) sue to have the court order Ford to resume payment of dividends. The Ps prove that Henry Ford has frequently stated that (1) the company is already making enough money, and (2) he wants to reduce the price of cars to benefit the working man instead of increasing corporate profits.

   Held, the company must pay a dividend of $19 million (half of its cash surplus as of the start of the suit). A corporation is organized for the benefit of stockholders, not for charitable purposes. Therefore, it was not up to Henry Ford to say that the company was already making enough money, and that no dividend was appropriate. (On the other hand, the court will not affirm the lower court's injunction of Ford from expanding its plants.) *Dodge v. Ford Motor Co.*, 170 N.W. 668 (Mich. 1919).

3. **Special rules for closely-held corporations:** Courts are probably more willing to order payment of some or higher dividends when the corporation is ***closely held***. Unlike the stockholder of a publicly traded corporation, a holder of closely held stock normally has no ready market if he wishes to sell his shares at their true "business" value. Therefore, he is much more dependent on dividends as a source of return on his investment. This is especially true where he is not employed by the corporation, and the controlling shareholders are not only employed but drain off most of the corporation's profits as salary or bonuses.

   a. **Emerging rule:** Therefore, courts have shown an increasing willingness to order close corporations to pay dividends even where there is some plausible corporate objective to be served by not paying them. Courts seem increasingly inclined to hold, in the close corporation context, that minority stockholders who are not employed by the corporation are entitled to a ***return on their investment*** in the form of a dividend, even in the face of an otherwise valid corporate objective such as expanding the business. Often, courts reach this conclusion by holding that the insiders have violated their ***fiduciary duty*** to behave fairly to the outside minority holders (see *supra*, p. 161).

III. STOCK REPURCHASES

A. **Repurchases generally:** Corporations often ***buy back*** their own stock. This may happen in a number of ways:

   1. **Self-tender:** A publicly traded company may make a ***self-tender***. For instance, XYZ Corp might offer to repurchase, at a stated price, 10% of its shares. It would be up to each stockholder to decide whether to sell some or all of his shares back to the company. Self-tenders are subject to essentially the same rules as third-party tender offers. See *supra*, p. 440.

   2. **Open market repurchases:** Second, a publicly traded company might make ***open market purchases*** of its own shares. Thus XYZ might from time to time buy its own shares on, say, the New York Stock Exchange, when it thinks the price is attractive. Usually the company will announce beforehand that it will be making such purchases, though it need not state when and at exactly what price it intends to do so.

   3. **Selective face-to-face purchases:** Finally, either public or closely held companies may make ***selective*** purchases directly from individual stockholders. Thus a public corporation might buy back a large stake held by an insider, or a stake held by a would-be hostile bidder (perhaps paying the bidder "greenmail," *supra*, p. 434, to get her to agree to sell). Even more commonly, a closely held corporation might buy back the stake of one of its stockholders, perhaps because the stockholder is leaving the company's employ, is retiring, or has died. Often, such repurchases are carefully planned in advance, and are indeed required by the terms of the "redemption" or "cross purchase" agreement among the company and the individual stockholders. (See *supra*, p. 148.)

B. **Problems similar to those posed by dividends:** A corporation's repurchase of its own shares poses many of the same problems posed by dividends. A repurchase is effectively a distribution of assets — the corporation pays cash (or, sometimes, gives a note or pays property), in return for getting the shares back. If the repurchase is completely ***pro rata***, it will have exactly the same economic consequences as a dividend (e.g., it can injure creditors if the corporation is left with insufficient assets). If the repurchase is not pro rata, it may injure not only creditors but also other shareholders — for instance, if the company repurchases shares from X at an above-market price, this may injure not only creditors but the shareholders who have not had a chance to sell at this attractive price, and who may now be left with a company that is worth less per outstanding share than before the repurchase from X.

1. **Statutory and judicial controls:** Therefore, most states have statutes that limit share repurchases (often but not always the same statute that limits the payment of dividends). Furthermore, courts will sometimes intervene to prevent share repurchases that would harm creditors or other shareholders.

2. **"Redemptions" distinguished:** When we use the term "repurchase" here, we will be referring to a corporation's purchase of its own shares in the absence of any previously-negotiated arrangement. Thus the self-tender, open-market-purchase, and greenmail scenarios described above are "repurchases." Similar to a "repurchase" but not identical is what we shall call a ***"redemption."*** A redemption, as we use the term here, occurs when a corporation buys (and generally cancels) some shares pursuant to a ***previously-negotiated arrangement***.

   a. **Preferred shares:** Often, a redemption will be of ***preferred*** shares (see *supra*, p. 415). Preferred shares are usually made redeemable at the corporation's option, on specified terms. For instance, preferred stock sold for $50 per share might be governed by the following provisions placed in the corporation's charter: (1) the shares are not redeemable by the corporation at all for the first five years after their issuance; (2) for the following five years, they are redeemable at $52 per share; and (3) thereafter, they are redeemable at par (i.e., at the original $50 issuance price).

   b. **Difference:** The economic effect of a redemption is similar to that of a repurchase. However, since the redemption occurs pursuant to a previously-negotiated "contract" with the shareholders, statutes and court rules that might prohibit a repurchase are less likely to prohibit a redemption (especially where the redemption is at the option of the stockholder rather than the corporation). See generally Clark, p. 625.

C. **Why corporations repurchase:** Why might a corporation repurchase its own stock?

1. **Redemption:** It is easy to see why a corporation might want to arrange to ***redeem*** its ***preferred*** stock. Preferred stockholders are more like bondholders than they are like common stockholders: they have lent the corporation money in return for a fixed dividend that is analogous to interest. Just as the corporation will want to have the freedom to prepay its bond debt or bank debt, so it will want to be able to redeem the preferred shareholders to avoid these fixed compulsory dividends. Therefore, if the time comes when the corporation no longer needs the money represented by the preferred stockholders, it will often exercise this redemption privilege. Clark, p. 626.

2. **Repurchase of common stock:** It is less obvious why a corporation might want to repurchase its common stock. Here are reasons that are sometimes given:

a. Excess cash: The corporation may have ***excess cash***, which it cannot productively reinvest in the corporation's business. Therefore, it may make sense to return this cash to the shareholders by repurchasing shares. Here, the repurchase is performing a function similar to that performed by the payment of dividends, with two differences: (1) each shareholder gets to decide whether to sell, so holders get to follow a policy that matches their own economic desires; and (2) the corporation can fine-tune its policy, buying at one time and not buying at another, whereas with the dividend policy it is usually more or less locked in to a particular, periodically-increasing, amount.

b. Raising earnings per share: A close corollary of this "repurchase rather than reinvest in the business" rationale is that a repurchase may ***raise earnings per share*** for the remaining shareholders. This will depend on how cheap the stock is relative to its earnings power. For instance, suppose that XYZ Corp is a mature business in a mature industry, and that additional capital invested in the company's main line of business will produce an after-tax return of, say, 7%. If XYZ buys back its shares for eight times earnings (so that $1 spent on share repurchase will make 12.5 cents of earnings available for the non-selling shareholders), the company's earnings per share will be higher than they would be if the earnings were reinvested in the business. Since earnings per share is probably the most important single determinant of share prices, the market value of the remaining shares is likely to rise.

c. Undervalued stock: Still another corollary is that a wise repurchase program lets non-selling shareholders get the benefit of the fact that the company's stock is temporarily ***undervalued***. Corporate managers often say that they are having the company repurchase its shares because those shares are temporarily "undervalued by the market." If they are correct in this, then the non-selling shareholders (presumably those who agree with management's assessment that the shares are undervalued) will be rewarded, since they will get a bigger piece of this undervalued pie at no additional cash outlay.

   i. Management must be correct: But there are two criticisms that can be lodged against this "repurchase because our shares are undervalued" strategy: (1) management may be kidding itself, and paying a fair price or more than a fair price because the company's shares are already being fairly valued by the market, in which case non-selling shareholders will be less well off rather than better off after the repurchase; and (2) even if the shares really are undervalued, management should be strenuously communicating to present and prospective shareholders why this is the case, rather than taking advantage of the market's ignorance to "sucker" some shareholders into selling for the benefit of other holders. See Clark, p. 629.

d. Greenmail: A publicly traded corporation that is under attack might want to ***buy back the hostile bidder's shares***, perhaps paying him ***greenmail*** (see *supra*, p. 434). Usually, such a move, though it may temporarily protect management's jobs, will be heartily detested by the other shareholders — not only has the corporation spent more of its assets for the share buy-back than the market currently thinks the shares are worth, but shareholders have been denied a chance to sell their shares into a takeover bid at a high price, something the vast majority of shareholders would love to have the chance to do (whatever they might think about hostile takeovers in the abstract).

e. **Close corporation:** Finally, there are special reasons why a ***closely held*** corporation might want to buy back its stock. Most importantly, if one of the manager/shareholders ***leaves the business*** or ***dies*** or ***retires***, the only way she or her estate can liquidate the investment may be to sell to the corporation. (The individual shareholders may simply not have the resources to purchase the shares.)

   i. **Maintains same proportions:** Furthermore, a repurchase by the corporation will preserve the remaining shareholders' interests in the ***exact same proportions***, thus avoiding the kind of control struggle that might be triggered if the remaining shareholders competed with each other to buy back the departing holder's shares.

   ii. **Redemption agreement:** For this reason, shareholders in a closely held corporation will often sign a ***redemption agreement*** in ***advance***, in which each agrees to sell his shares back to the corporation (and the corporation agrees to buy them) at some designated price or at a price produced by some designated formula. See *supra*, p. 147.

D. **Protection of shareholders:** A corporation's repurchase of its own shares has the potential to injure the non-selling shareholders. Most obviously, if the corporation pays too much for the shares it repurchases, the non-selling shareholders are less well off than they were before (since the corporation's loss of assets is not counterbalanced by the reduction in the number of outstanding shares). Perhaps even more troublesome are those situations where the corporation's offer to repurchase is not open to all shareholders — here, holders who would like to sell into the repurchase, but are not permitted to do so, are even more likely to be injured.

1. **No general rule:** There is no single rule summarizing how courts will respond to arguments by a plaintiff shareholder that he has been injured by the corporation's repurchase of shares from some other shareholder. At the broadest level, the court will use the familiar concepts of the duties of due care (*supra*, p. 169) and loyalty (*supra*, p. 197), and the business judgment rule (*supra*, p. 182). Therefore, so long as the board, in authorizing the repurchase, (1) behaves with reasonable care (i.e., makes reasonable inquiries into the corporation's financial health and the value of its shares before authorizing the repurchase) and (2) does not violate the duty of loyalty (e.g., the directors are not buying from themselves at an above-market price, without giving other shareholders the right to participate), the repurchase decision will almost certainly be upheld.

   a. **Business purpose:** In deciding whether the duty of loyalty was breached, courts are likely to use a ***"business purpose"*** test similar to the one they use in reviewing a corporation's dividend policy: if there appears to be a ***valid business purpose*** for the share repurchase, the court will generally not go out of its way to determine whether the repurchase was in fact motivated by improper purposes (e.g., a desire by the board to consolidate its control).

2. **Greenmail:** One context in which the courts are likely to scrutinize the repurchase transaction extra closely is ***greenmail***. Even here, however, if the corporate purpose is to avoid a hostile takeover (as it usually will be), courts will frequently, maybe even usually, uphold the transaction. *Cheff v. Mathes*, discussed *supra*, p. 472, is an example of how the

Delaware courts will approve the payment of greenmail as part of a repurchase scheme, if the directors reasonably believe that the hostile takeover would be damaging to the corporation's existence or to important aspects of its business.

3. **Self-dealing by insiders:** A court is similarly likely to look extra closely at a repurchase that appears to ***benefit the insiders*** unduly, and that appears to be clear self-dealing.

   Example: Suppose Isadore, who owns 40% of XYZ Corp (a publicly held company), dominates the board of directors. Isadore decides that he wants to retire from the company's affairs and to sell his stock, but does not want the entire company sold. He induces the board to have the corporation repurchase his holdings for $20 per share, at a time when the market price is $14 per share.

   A court would probably treat this as a case of potential self-dealing, and apply the special self-dealing rules described above (*supra*, p. 200). If there were no truly independent directors, or if a majority of the independent directors did not approve the transaction, Isadore will have the burden of showing that the transaction is "entirely fair" to the corporation and its remaining shareholders. Of course, he may succeed in making the showing (for instance, by showing that he could have sold his control block at the same $6 per share premium to an outsider, who would then use it as a wedge in taking the company private), but the point is that the court would not simply approve the transaction without analysis.

E. **Protection of creditors; financial limits:** A corporation's repurchase of its own shares may seriously injure the corporation's ***creditors***. A repurchase is a distribution of the company's assets, just like a dividend. While a non-pro-rata repurchase differs from a dividend in that the relative ownership of the various stockholders changes in the former but not in the latter, the effect on ***creditors*** is ***the same for a repurchase as for a dividend***: the corporation has fewer assets with which to pay creditors' claims.

   1. **Same rules:** Therefore, modern statutes generally treat share repurchases in much the same way as they treat dividends: a share repurchase that takes place when there is no earned surplus, that would impair capital, or that would leave the corporation insolvent, is likely to be forbidden if a dividend of the same amount would be forbidden.

   2. **Liability for improper repurchase:** Generally, the rules on ***who is liable*** for an improper share repurchase are the same as those on who is liable for an improper dividend. Thus depending on the statutory scheme, either the board of directors, the shareholder who has sold his stock back to the corporation, or both, may be liable for the payment if creditors or preferred shareholders are injured. C&E, p. 1389. (The rules on liability for improper dividends are discussed *supra*, pp. 514-516.)

Quiz Yourself on

DIVIDENDS AND SHARE REPURCHASES *(ENTIRE CHAPTER)*

100. In late 2010, Cleopatra founds a chain of pet stores, the "You Bet Your Asp" Stores, Inc. You Bet Your Asp sells 500 shares of its $5 par-value common stock for $10 a share. At the same time, it sells another 500 $5 par value common shares in return for retail space to be occupied by it in the future, worth $2,500 total.

(a) What is You Bet Your Asp's stated capital (and why might it matter)? _______________

(b) Assume that You Bet Your Asp makes a profit of exactly $0 in its first year of operations, 2011. Assume further that it hasn't yet used the rental space worth $2500. Ignore issues of insolvency. In a state allowing the payment of dividends out of any sort of surplus (whether earned or unearned), how much in dividends may You Bet pay, in early 2012? _______________

101. The balance sheet of the 100 Dalmatians Restaurant — don't ask what happened to the 101st dalmatian — looks like this:

Assets		Liabilities & Owners' Equity	
Cash	$300	Current Liabilities	$100
Inventory	$100	Long-term debt	$400
Other Assets	$400	Owners' Equity:	
		Stated Capital	$ 50
		Paid-In Surplus	$100
		Retained Earnings	$150

(a) Assume that the state of Disney, in which the restaurant is incorporated, follows the strict "earned surplus" test for determining sources of dividends. Assume further that the state also uses the balance-sheet test for insolvency. What's the most 100 Dalmatians could pay out in dividends? _______________

(b) Now, assume that the state follows the MBCA's rules on when dividend payments are allowed. What's the most 100 Dalmatians could pay out in dividends? _______________

102. Jed Clampett discovers oil on his property, and begins selling it under the auspices of his Clampett General Store, Inc. His balance sheet, prepared by his very conservative accountant, looks like this:

Assets		Liabilities & Owners' Equity	
Cash	$ 50	Current Liabilities	$100
Oil reserves, at cost	$ 400	Long-term debt	$200
		Owners' Equity:	
		Stated Capital	$ 50
		Paid-in Surplus	$ 50
		Retained Earnings	$ 50

Jed has just received an appraisal of his oil reserves, done by an expert. That appraisal shows that the fair market value of the reserves is now $1,000 (compared with the $400 Jed paid to acquire them). Jed would like to declare as big a dividend as possible. Assume that the state's dividend statute allows payments out of any source of capital surplus, whether earned or unearned. Assume also that the balance-sheet method is the state's only test for insolvency.

(a) What change should Jed make to his balance sheet, and how should he go about making that change? _______________

(b) Can Jed pay a $600 dividend after taking the step you recommend in (a)? _______________

103. The Jacques Cousteaudian Houseboat Cleaning Service, Inc., is formed. Each share's par value, $10, is the amount that the shareholders actually pay for the shares. For the first three years of the corporation's existence, it loses a total of $75,000. In its fourth and fifth years taken together, however, the service cleans up, to the tune of a $30,000 profit. Declaring a $1,000 dividend would leave the corporation solvent (regardless of the test used for solvency). Just before the end of Year 5, the directors declare a $1,000 dividend.

(a) Under the majority rule, was the $1,000 dividend properly declared? ______________

(b) Under Delaware law, was the $1,000 dividend properly declared? ______________

104. The directors of the Universal Solvent Soup Company declare a $5 a share dividend on the corporation's 1,000 shares of common stock, payable out of the company's cash on hand. Minnie Strone, who owns 50 common shares of Universal Solvent, receives her $250 dividend.

(a) Assume that the company was insolvent at the time of the dividend payment, and that the payment was therefore a violation of state law. Assume further that Minnie had no knowledge of the company's financial position, and thus neither knew nor had reason to know that the company was insolvent. Under the common-law rule, could Universal Solvent's creditors recover the $250 from Minnie (assuming that Universal Solvent refuses to sue her)? ______________

(b) Same facts. Now, however, assume that the company was not insolvent at the time of the payment, but that the company had no retained earnings at the moment of payment. The jurisdiction prohibits dividends except out of retained earnings. Again, assume that Minnie did not know, and had no reason to know, that the payment would violate the only-out-of-retained-earnings statute. Under the common-law approach, could Universal Solvent's creditors recover the $250 from Minnie? ______________

105. The Shortt Sirkit Electronics Company makes radios and TVs. Joe Electron is the President, and 35%-stockholder, of Shortt Sirkit. Joe decides he wants to lighten up on his holdings of Short Sirkit stock. He proposes to the board that the company repurchase his shares for $20 each, at a time when the public market price is $17. Joe indicates to each director that if that director votes against this proposal, he, Joe, will take this into consideration in deciding whether to renominate the director for re-election the next year. All directors (except for Joe, who abstains) vote in favor of the repurchase, and it goes through. Charles Capacitor, a minority shareholder, brings a derivative suit on the company's behalf against Joe, seeking recovery of the amount by which the corporation's payments to Joe exceeded the then market price. Will Charles succeed? ______________

Answers

100. (a) $5,000 — that is, 1,000 shares outstanding multiplied by $5 par value. Stated capital (a/k/a legal capital) is the par value per share multiplied by the number of outstanding shares. [507] Here, the par value is $5 and there are 1,000 shares outstanding, making $5,000 in stated capital. The remaining $2,500 paid for the shares (in cash or prepaid rent) would be "paid-in surplus." The "stated capital" figure might matter because in most states (regardless of their precise rules on when dividends may be paid), dividends may not be paid "out of" stated capital. [508] That is, a dividend cannot be paid if following the payment, the company's net worth (assets minus liabilities) would be less than its stated capital. So here, prior to operations, the company could not make a payment that would cause its net worth to go below $5,000.

(b) $2,500. The company has an "earned surplus" of $0 (i.e., it has a lifetime total of $0 in "retained earnings"). However, it has an "unearned surplus" of $2,500. This unearned surplus comes entirely from the "paid-in surplus," that is, the amount by which the company collected cash or property for share-issuance in excess of the $5,000 stated value. [508] This paid-in surplus is, of course, represented by the $2,500 in pre-paid rent that's shown as an asset on the company's books.

So in a state — like Delaware or New York — that allows dividends to be paid out of either earned or unearned surplus, a dividend of $2,500 could be paid. (On these facts the company probably doesn't have *cash* to pay out the $2,500 dividend. But it could borrow the $2,500 from a bank, and then pay that cash out as a dividend, because this would just "use up" the value of the prepaid rent. This might leave the company "insolvent" — in the sense of "unable to pay its debts as they come due" — which is why the question tells you to ignore any issue of insolvency. Note that in virtually all states, regardless of your surplus situation you can't pay a dividend if the payment would leave the company insolvent.)

101. (a) $150 — that is, the amount in the retained earnings account. Under the "earned surplus" test, a dividend can only be declared to the extent of the contents of the retained earnings account, which represents the accumulated but undistributed lifetime profits of the business. [509]

In addition, the facts tell us that the dividend is further restricted in that it can't leave the corporation insolvent, with insolvency to be measured by the balance-sheet test. Under this standard, the dividend won't be allowed if, after it's paid, the corporation's liabilities would exceed its assets. [512] Since paying a $150 dividend would leave the corporation with $650 in assets and $500 in liabilities, payment is not prohibited by the balance-sheet test. (After the dividend is paid, the cash account would be left with $150, and the retained earnings account would be empty.) Notice, by the way, that if the state allowed dividends to be paid from paid-in surplus as well as from retained earnings, this would leave another $100 for dividends, since after payment the company would still have $550 in assets and $500 in liabilities.

(b) $200, probably. Under the MBCA test, § 6.40(c), a corporation must essentially meet two tests of solvency (but no tests relating to surplus). First, a dividend can't reduce the company's assets below its liabilities (using any fair measure of assets, including fair market value). Second, the company must be able to pay its bills as they mature (the so-called "equity," as opposed to balance-sheet, test for insolvency.) [514] The pay-bills-as-they-mature standard more or less means that the company can't deplete its cash below its current liabilities. Under the MBCA, then, 100 Dalmatians could pay out $200 in dividends (since its cash is $200 more than its current liabilities, and its total assets exceed its total liabilities by $300). (Actually, if the company could show that it would soon collect additional cash — say from receivables — in time to pay already-accrued liabilities, the dividend might be ok even if it would leave cash on hand at less than current liabilities. Conversely, if the company knew that it would be receiving a huge bill soon that it couldn't pay when due, the fact that the company would, today, be left post-dividend with more cash than current liabilities, would not protect it. But "cash greater than current liabilities" is at least a good first *approximation* of whether the company is "able to pay its debts as they mature.")

102. (a) He should have his board declare a "revaluation surplus" of $600. For purposes of dividend statutes, most states probably permit a corporation to "write up" its assets from their "historical cost basis" to their "current market value." [510] This should typically be done by a resolution of the board of directors.

(b) Yes. After the revaluation surplus is declared, (and before the dividend is paid) the balance sheet will look like this:

Assets		Liabilities & Owners' Equity	
Cash	$ 50	Current Liabilities	$100
Oil reserves, at market	$1,000	Long-term debt	$200
		Owners' Equity:	
		Stated Capital	$ 50
		Paid-in Surplus	$ 50
		Retained Earnings	$ 50
		Revaluation Surplus	$600

The corporation can now pay dividends out of three types of surplus: paid-in surplus ($50), retained earnings ($50), and revaluation surplus (the difference between historical cost and market value, or $600), for a total of $700. If Jed wants to pay $600, the capital-surplus test doesn't block him. He'll have to borrow the money (since he doesn't have enough cash). If he borrowed the full $600 (as long-term debt), and used this to pay the dividend, his balance sheet would now look like this:

Assets		Liabilities & Owners' Equity	
Cash	$ 50	Current Liabilities	$100
Oil reserves, at market	$1,000	Long-term debt	$800
		Owners' Equity:	
		Stated Capital	$ 50
		Paid-in Surplus	$ 50
		Retained Earnings	$ 50

Since the company's assets ($1,050) still equal or exceed its liabilities ($900), payment of the dividend did not violate the balance-sheet insolvency test, so the dividend was legal in this jurisdiction. (In a state following the "able-to-pay-debts-as-they-mature" test for insolvency, the dividend probably wouldn't be legal, because the corporation now has $50 in current assets, and $100 in current liabilities.)

103. (a) No, because the company's retained earnings show a loss of $45,000 (the $75,000 loss less the $30,000 profit), and it has no paid-in surplus. Most states still impose an "earned surplus" restriction. That is, in most states dividends may only be paid out of "retained earnings" (a/k/a "earned surplus"), i.e., the profits which the corporation has accumulated since its inception. [509] Jacques Cousteaudian doesn't pass this test, because it has negative retained earnings (i.e., over its lifetime, it's lost a net of $45,000). Even in a more liberal state allowing payment out of "unearned surplus," the company still couldn't pay the dividend, because there is no paid-in surplus (since holders only paid par for their shares), and there is no other source of unearned surplus.

(b) Yes, because of Delaware's "nimble dividends" provision. Del. GCL § 170(a) allows payment of dividends — even if there is no surplus — if the dividend is paid "out of [the corporation's] net profits for the fiscal year in which the dividend is declared and/or the preceding fiscal year." [511] Since in Years 4 and 5 the company has earned a net of $30,000, the company could actually pay the entire $30,000 as a dividend in Year 5, at least as far as the surplus (as distinguished from insolvency) test goes. So the $1,000 payment is ok, even though there is no earned or unearned surplus. (But if the corporation just broke even in Years 6 and 7, it could no longer declare even the $1,000 dividend, because this would no longer be from the "current or preceding fiscal year" — the provision is called "nimble" dividends because the board has to act promptly after earning the money.)

104. (a) Yes, even though she wasn't on notice that the dividend was illegal. The issue here is whether an innocent shareholder can be required to repay a dividend that is paid by an insolvent corporation, even if the shareholder does not know, or have reason to know, of the insolvency. The majority approach at common law is that the company (or its creditors) may recover the payment despite the shareholder's lack of guilty knowledge or even lack of negligence. [515] As a result, Minnie can be required to repay the $250 she received, even though she had no reason to know anything was amiss at Universal Solvent.

(b) No. Where the problem is not the corporation's insolvency, but merely its surplus status, the majority common-law approach is that the stockholder can be required to disgorge only if she ***knew*** that the payment was improper. [515]

105. Yes, probably, because the repurchase was not for a proper purpose. In general, a corporation has the right to repurchase its shares. And there is no general rule that the corporation must treat all shareholders equally in making such a repurchase. (So, for instance, most courts say that a privately-held corporation can repurchase the controlling holder's shares for a fair price while refusing to do the same for the non-controlling holders.) But most courts say that the corporation must be acting for a valid "business purpose" when it makes a repurchase, and that the transaction must not violate the rules against self-interested transactions. [521] The purchase here seems to have no valid business purpose, merely the purpose (on Joe's part) of enriching him, and the purpose (on the board's part) of staying in power. Since the board was not "independent" and "disinterested" when they voted, the court will probably treat the purchase as being a self-interested transaction, and therefore probably won't give the directors' decision to repurchase the benefit of the business judgment rule. Consequently, the court will probably hold that the repurchase violated Joe's duty of loyalty to the corporation, and that the repurchase was not fair to the other stockholders. In that event, the court will order Joe to disgorge his profits (or will even rescind the entire transaction).

Exam Tips on *DIVIDENDS AND SHARE REPURCHASES*

Issues regarding dividends and share repurchases are easy to spot — just look for fact patterns in which a corp. has declared (or failed to declare) a cash dividend, or repurchased shares.

- Remember that a board's decision to pay (or not pay) dividends is generally protected by the ***business judgment rule***. So either way it goes, the decision won't be reversed so long as it's rational, unless there's fraud, illegality or self-dealing.
  - Therefore, first check to see whether the dividend policy is ***rational*** — if there's some ***plausible business purpose*** behind it, the court normally won't second-guess.

    Example: For the past 5 years, Corp. has racked up pre-tax earnings equal to 50% of its sales. Yet Corp. has not paid a dividend during this time. The board has done this so that Corp. will have substantial retained earnings, and will thus be more attractive to an acquirer. P, a minority s/h, sues to compel payment of a dividend. P's suit will probably fail, since the board's action is rational (and there's no allegation of fraud, illegality or self-dealing by the directors).

  - Second, check to make sure that the directors' decision on dividends wasn't ***fraudulent***, ***illegal***, or in ***bad faith***.
    - A common scenario is that the majority directors ***refuse to declare*** a dividend from available cash, because they want to ***squeeze out a minority s/h*** (e.g., by coercing her into selling out cheaply). If the court thinks that this is what happened, the court will order a dividend to be declared.
  - Conversely, check for situations where the directors ***declare a dividend*** that they ***shouldn't***.
    - Of course, a dividend isn't legal if its payment would result in the corp's becoming ***insolvent***.
    - Also, check the source out of which the dividend is being paid — in most states, dividends may be paid only out of ***earned surplus***, i.e., historical profits the corp.

has earned since its inception.

☞ But a few states let dividends be paid from ***revaluation surplus***, which is created when the corp's assets are revalued upward to reflect their current fair market value rather than their historical cost.

Example: Corp. is founded in 2004, and has a $50,000 total operating loss in 2004-2006. In 2006, it buys property from S for $60,000, but the board later in the year concludes that the property is now worth $120,000. Now, in late 2006, Corp. pays a $10,000 dividend to s/h's. If the state doesn't allow revaluation surplus as a source for dividends, then this dividend payment is illegal (since there's no operating surplus, only a $50,000 lifetime operating deficit). But if revaluation surplus *is* allowed as a dividend source, then the dividend is ok (since there's $60K worth of reval. surplus less $50K of operating deficit) — but anything more than a $10K dividend would still be illegal.

☞ Also, recall that some states allow payment of ***"nimble dividends"*** — dividends from the corp's ***current earnings*** (or its earnings from the last two years), even if the corp. does not have a "lifetime" surplus.

☛ If the facts describe a ***share repurchase***, remember that a corp's decision to repurchase outstanding shares is generally subject to the ***same conditions as the declaration of dividends*** (i.e., there must be adequate funds available). So check whether the same amount could be spent on dividends. Also, check whether the ***price paid*** by the corp. is ***reasonable***.

☞ Also, check to make sure there's no ***self-dealing*** in the repurchase.

☞ For instance, if a ***controlling s/h*** causes the corp to buy his shares, that s/h will probably have to show either that: (i) the price was ***"entirely fair"***; or (ii) a majority of ***disinterested directors*** or disinterested s/h's ***approved*** or ***ratified*** it. (But remember that there's ***no blanket rule*** that requires that the corp. buy back the minority holders' shares just because it's buying the controlling s/h's shares.)

CHAPTER 12

ISSUANCE OF SECURITIES

ChapterScope

This Chapter discusses both state and federal laws that regulate the issuance of securities. Key concepts:

- **Par value:** A corporation may choose to declare a ***"par value"*** for its shares before they are issued. If the corporation does so, then it may not issue the shares for ***less*** than this par value amount.
- **Payment in goods or services:** States put some — though not many — limits on a corporation's right to "sell" stock to insiders in return for ***goods and services*** rather than cash.
- **Preemptive rights:** Corporations sometimes opt to give shareholders ***"preemptive rights."*** A preemptive right permits an existing shareholder to ***maintain his existing percentage of ownership***, by guaranteeing him the right to buy a portion of any newly-issued shares.
  - **Exceptions:** There are some important exceptions to the coverage of preemptive rights, even when those rights exist. For instance, if the corporation issues shares in return for services or property, other shareholders' preemptive rights don't become triggered.
- **Public offerings:** The issuance of shares to "the public" (i.e., to large numbers of buyers simultaneously) is tightly regulated by federal law.
  - **Exemptions:** A large part of our treatment of public offerings consists of rules defining the borderline between offerings that are "public" (and thus tightly federally-regulated) and those that are "private" (subject to less regulation). Federal law has a number of ***"exemptions"*** that transform an offer that would otherwise be public into a private one. For instance, offerings to fewer than 35 affluent people, and offerings aggregating less than $1 million, are generally given an exemption.

I. STATE-LAW RULES ON SHARE ISSUANCE

A. Subscription agreements: Suppose that A, B, C, D, and E all want to form a new business that will operate as XYZ Corporation. Each is willing to put $10,000 into the venture, but each wants to be sure that he will not have to actually come up with the cash unless everybody else also comes up with the cash. One way the five would-be shareholders could do this is by having XYZ enter into a separate ***subscription agreement*** with each of the prospective investors. Each person's agreement might say that he promises to pay $10,000 for 100 shares in XYZ, but that this obligation is contingent upon the corporation's simultaneously selling at least 400 shares for $40,000 to one or more other investors. Once these agreements are signed, XYZ's promoter can begin arranging for workers, facilities, etc., confident that the $50,000 in capital will be available when needed.

1. **Installment plan:** Apart from this "reliance" objective, a second reason why promoters might want to use subscription agreements is that some or all of the stockholders may want to pay for their shares in ***installments***. The subscription agreement could then set out the size and timing of the installments, the remedies for default, etc.

2. **Less used today:** Subscription agreements are less frequently used today than formerly. If the corporation will be formed as part of a public offering, then the SEC's public offering procedures (*infra*, p. 539) will be used instead of the subscription-agreement procedure. If the corporation will begin its operations as a small privately held one, it will often be easier for the investors to simply form a shell and then simultaneously each purchase the shares, instead of having a pre-capitalization period in which the parties' expectations are protected by a subscription agreement.

3. **Law governing:** Nonetheless, subscription agreements are sometimes used, so it's worthwhile to understand the general principles governing them.

   a. **Revocation:** Suppose the subscription agreement is entered into ***before*** the formation of the corporation that will be issuing the shares. A key question is whether this agreement may be ***revoked*** by the signing shareholder if he attempts to do so before the corporation is formed.

      i. **No statute:** In a state where there is no statute on this subject, a court is likely to hold that the subscription agreement is only a ***continuing offer*** to a proposed corporation, and that the investor is ***entitled to revoke*** before the corporation is formed. In fact, some courts allow the investor to revoke even after the corporation is formed, so long as the corporation has not yet indicated that it intends to treat him as bound.

      ii. **Statute:** But many states have statutes making the subscription agreement ***irrevocable*** for some stated period. Usually, this period is ***six months***. See, e.g., MBCA § 6.20(a) (subscription agreement is irrevocable for six months unless it provides for a longer or shorter period; however, it may be revoked at any time if ***all*** the subscribers agree to revocation). See also Del. GCL § 165 (irrevocable for six months unless all other shareholders consent to revocation).

   b. **Liability:** Subscription agreements are generally ***enforceable*** by their terms. This means that a subscriber is ***liable*** for the unpaid portion of his subscription price. Clearly the corporation may recover against the recalcitrant subscriber; courts are split about whether the ***creditors*** of an insolvent corporation may recover from the subscriber.

B. **Par value:** You will remember from our discussion of dividends the historical importance of ***par value***. (See *supra*, p. 507.) To recapitulate briefly: traditionally in most states, stock was issued at a particular par value. This par value per share, when multiplied by the number of shares outstanding, constituted the corporation's "stated capital" or "legal capital." As we saw in the treatment of dividends, most states have statutes ostensibly prohibiting the payment of dividends where the payment would be greater than the corporation's "capital surplus" and would thus impair "stated capital." Now we focus on the other key aspect of the concept of par value: as a ***minimum price at which shares must be issued***.

1. **General rule:** The key rule about par value in connection with share issuance is this: ***the corporation may not sell the shares for less than their par value***. Nutshell, p. 105. If the corporation does sell shares for less than their par value, the shareholder who received them may be ***liable to the corporation*** or to the corporation's ***creditors***, a liability known as ***"watered stock"*** liability (discussed *infra*, p. 531).

   Example: XYZ Corp is authorized to issue 1,000 shares of $100 par value stock. XYZ issues 1,000 of these shares to Promoter for $10 per share. (Assume that Promoter has not given XYZ any past property or services, and that he has not promised to do so in the future as additional payment for the shares.) This issuance of shares to Promoter violates the fundamental rule that the price for shares must be at least equal to their par value. Therefore, Promoter will probably be liable to XYZ Corp (or to XYZ's creditors, if XYZ becomes insolvent) for $90,000 (the difference between the $100,000 aggregate par value of the shares he received, and the $10,000 he actually paid).

   a. **Rationale:** In theory, two different groups of people are protected by this insistence that shares not be issued for less than their par value.

      i. **Creditors:** First, a corporation's ***creditors*** are protected. Thus on the above example, if a creditor of XYZ knew that all 10,000 authorized shares had been issued, and knew (from reading XYZ's articles of incorporation, a public document) that the par value was $100 per share, he could rely on XYZ's shareholders' having contributed, as the corporation's "permanent capital," at least $1,000,000. In theory, this might lead the creditor to lend money to XYZ that he might otherwise not have lent.

      ii. **Other shareholders:** Second, the rule that shares be sold for at least par value might protect one ***shareholder*** against unfair favors being extended to another. Thus if Able and Baker both bought shares in XYZ, and Able bought at the $100 par value figure, he could know that XYZ could not legally sell shares for less to Baker — Able would therefore be reassured that he was being treated fairly as compared with prior or subsequent purchasers (but only assuming that Able paid par, not some amount greater than par).

   b. **Significance:** The rise of no-par and low-par stock has greatly impaired the ability of the par value scheme to protect either creditors or other shareholders. This is discussed *infra*, p. 533. For now, just understand that there remains on the books of virtually all states that recognize par value, a rule that shares must not be sold at a price less than par value.

2. **Amount of consideration (the "watered stock" problem):** What, then, happens if the corporation violates this rule against selling shares for less than their par value? The brief answer is that the purchasing stockholder may be liable to the corporation and/or its creditors, a liability known as ***"watered stock"*** liability.

   a. **Different types:** Observe that there are three different ways in which a corporation might sell stock for less than par value.

i. **Bonus shares:** First, shares having a par value might simply be issued for ***no consideration*** at all (either paid or promised). These are commonly called ***"bonus"*** shares.

ii. **Discount shares:** Much more commonly, a corporation might sell shares for cash, but a cash amount less than the par value per share. (Our example above in which Promoter buys $100 par value stock for $10 per share is an illustration of this.) These are commonly called ***"discount"*** shares.

iii. **Watered shares:** Finally, most statutes allow the corporation to issue shares in return for ***property or services***. If the corporation accepts the property or services as being equal to the par value of the shares given in exchange, but the property or services are in fact ***overvalued***, the shares are referred to as ***"watered"*** stock. (Sometimes, the term "watered" stock refers to discount and bonus shares as well as to the kind of watered stock we are specifically talking about here.) C&E, p. 1328.

b. **Recovery by creditors:** The main issue that arises in connection with watered stock ("watered" here will be used to refer to "bonus" and "discount" shares as well as shares issued for overstated property or services) is: May ***creditors*** of a corporation recover against the stockholder who received the watered stock? This issue usually arises only after the corporation has become ***insolvent***. There are several theories under which the receiving shareholder might be liable to the corporation's creditors.

i. **"Holding out" or "misrepresentation" theory:** A majority of the courts that have recognized any common-law liability to creditors have done so on a ***"holding out"*** or ***"misrepresentation"*** theory. The key concept behind this theory is ***reliance***: only to the extent that the creditor has relied on the corporation's (false) assertion that all shares were issued for at least par value, may the creditor recover. Under this theory, one who becomes a creditor ***before*** the wrongful issuance, and one who becomes a creditor after the wrongful issuance but with ***knowledge*** of it, may not recover, since by definition they have not "relied."

3. **Kind of consideration:** Most of the time, of course, stock is issued to the shareholders in return for cash. But it will often be desirable to award stock in return for something other than cash. This "something other than cash" might be ***property*** held by a would-be shareholder. Or, it might be ***services*** that have been performed by a promoter during the pre-incorporation. Finally, the consideration might be a shareholder's ***promise*** to pay cash, turn over property, perform services, etc., ***in the future***.

a. **Usual rule:** Statutes vary as to which of these forms of consideration are acceptable. One common scheme, however, is that existing property and past services are valid, but ***promises*** to perform services, donate property in the future, or pay cash in the future, are ***not***. See, e.g., N.Y. BCL § 504(a) ("Consideration for the issue of shares shall consist of money or other property, tangible or intangible, or labor or services ***actually received by*** or ***performed for*** the corporation or for its benefit or in its formation or reorganization. . . .") Similarly, Delaware apparently does not allow a promise to perform future services to be consideration (at least with respect to the par value or "stated capital" part of the payment). See Del. GCL § 152.

b. MBCA liberalizes: But the MBCA is much more liberal. Under § 6.21(b), virtually ***any kind of consideration*** will be valid, so long as the board of directors acts in good faith and with reasonable care in concluding that the consideration is adequate. Thus ***promissory notes*** and promises to ***perform future services*** would both be valid consideration under the MBCA, whereas they would not be under the New York scheme.

i. Rationale: Preserving the board's ability to give stock in return for promises of future payment or future services makes good economic sense. For instance, suppose that XYZ has just been formed, has no operating business yet, and could benefit enormously from the skills of Peter, an experienced executive who is willing to become president in return for stock. There is little reason why XYZ should not be permitted to give Peter stock in return for his promise to run the company for, say, three years — if XYZ cannot do this, it may be deprived of the ability to lure Peter away from his existing job.

(1) Risk to corporation: Of course, there is a risk that after receiving the stock, Peter will ***not in fact perform*** the services. But the MBCA makes the judgment that this problem can best be solved by requiring the board of directors to fulfill their duty of due care and loyalty (see *supra*, pp. 169 and 197) as they determine that this promise-for-stock exchange is a good idea, rather than by completely prohibiting all exchanges of stock for promises.

ii. Remedies: If the promised payment or services do not in fact come about, the corporation probably has a ***contract claim*** against the shareholder to pay/perform. Alternatively, MBCA § 6.21(e) lets the corporation ***escrow*** the shares until the future services or payments are fulfilled. What is significant about the MBCA's liberalization is that creditors or other shareholders cannot force the shareholder to pay with immediate cash instead of services or future installment payments.

4. Valuation of consideration: If the board of directors sells stock to a stockholder in return for past or future services or property, the board's good faith ***computation of the value*** that should be attributed to those services or property will usually ***not be overturned*** by a court. See, e.g., Delaware GCL § 152 ("in the absence of actual fraud in the transaction, the judgment of the directors as to the value of such consideration shall be conclusive").

5. Decline of par value's significance: Today, both the use of par value stock and the importance of "watered stock liability" are dramatically ***reduced***.

a. Par concept not recognized or not required: Most states today don't even require the par concept at all. As of 2002, only 22 states required the articles of incorporation to state the par value of shares. Hamilton (8th), pp. 392-93. The remaining states have all either eliminated the concept of par value entirely, or have left to the corporation the decision whether to use the concept. The MBCA follows this trend: § 2.02(1)(2)(iv) makes par value optional, and § 6.21 on "Issuance of Shares" does not even mention the concept.

b. No-par stock allowed: Furthermore, in the minority of states still imposing the concept of par stock, each state allows the corporation to choose ***no-par stock*** (and most also allow ***low-par stock***). As a consequence, only a very misguided lawyer will normally let his corporate client issue stock having any significant par value.

i. **Effect on watered stock liability:** This increased use of no-par and low-par stock makes the watered stock liability problem almost disappear. Generally, a stockholder is liable only for the difference between the par value of the shares issued to him and the value of what he has contributed. If the stock issued to him has no par value or nominal par value (as it will when low-par stock is used), then the shareholder will have almost always contributed an amount at least equal to this low or nonexistent number.

C. **Preemptive rights and related issues:** A ***"preemptive right"*** is a right sometimes given to a corporation's existing shareholders that permits them to ***maintain their percentage of ownership*** in the corporation, by enabling them to buy a portion of any newly-issued shares. To understand the dangers that preemptive rights theoretically protect against, consider the following example.

Example: Inventor has invented a marvelous new mousetrap, which is guaranteed to be a commercial success if only he can raise the funds to produce it. Capitalist agrees to put up the money needed to exploit the mousetrap. Together, they form Mousetrap Corporation, with Capitalist receiving 51% of the stock (in return for advancing all of the capital) and Inventor 49% (in return for assigning to the corporation all of his rights to the invention.) A nine-member board of directors is set up, with Capitalist controlling five seats and Inventor four seats. There are 1,000 shares outstanding, held 510 by Capitalist and 490 by Inventor. The business is an overnight success.

Capitalist wants to increase his percentage of ownership, and decrease not only Inventor's percentage of the economic pie but also Inventor's participation in decision making. He therefore causes his five directors to authorize the issuance of an additional 1,000 shares, at $500 per share (a fair price given Mousetrap's current economic prospects). He causes the board to offer these shares to (and only to) Capitalist's own personal holding corporation, PHC, Inc.; PHC immediately accepts the offer, and buys the shares for $500,000. Now, Capitalist controls three quarters of the company, and Investor has only one quarter. True, Investor now has an equity stake in a company that has $500,000 of extra cash, but Investor's share of any future increases in the company's value is reduced to half of what he thought it was at the time he made the arrangement.

1. **Rationale for preemptive rights:** If Mousetrap Corp, in our example, had preemptive rights, Inventor might have had some protection against the dilution of his interest. Under a typical preemptive rights scheme, Mousetrap would have been required to offer to Inventor 49% of any new issue of shares. Thus had there been preemptive rights, and had Inventor been able to get hold of about $250,000 on short notice, he could have maintained his 49% ownership position.

2. **Common-law rule:** Formerly, most states recognized preemptive rights as a common-law matter. Although the right was subject to many exceptions and varied a lot from state to state, the basic concept was that if the corporation offered newly-authorized stock to anyone, it had to offer to ***each*** existing stockholder the right to buy as many shares as

would keep his percentage ownership from decreasing. The shareholder exercising the preemptive right was obligated to pay the same price as was being paid by the other buyers. See, e.g., *Stokes v. Continental Trust Co.*, 78 N.E. 1090 (N.Y. 1906) (holding that the corporation "could not lawfully dispose of [the new] shares without giving [an existing shareholder] a chance to get his proportion at the same price that outsiders got theirs").

3. **Statutes:** Today, every state governs preemptive rights by ***statute***. All modern statutes allow the corporation to ***dispense*** entirely with preemptive rights if it so chooses. Nutshell, p. 148. This choice by the corporation is embodied in the articles of incorporation.

   a. **"Opt out" provision:** Some statutes give the corporation an ***"opt out"*** election — the corporation has preemptive rights unless it expressly specifies, in the articles of incorporation, that it does not want such rights. See, e.g., N.Y. BCL § 622(b) and (c).

   b. **"Opt in" election:** But the modern trend is toward an ***"opt in"*** scheme — that is, the corporation does ***not*** have preemptive rights unless it ***expressly elects***, in the ***articles of incorporation***, to have such rights.

      i. **MBCA:** The MBCA follows this "opt in" pattern; see § 6.30(a). Section 6.30 also simplifies the job of the drafter of a corporation's articles of incorporation: if the drafter wants preemptive rights, he simply puts in a clause that "the corporation elects to have preemptive rights," and this will cause the corporation to have the fairly detailed preemptive rights scheme set forth in § 6.30(b) (including terms of waiver, exceptions for such items as shares issued for property or to satisfy stock options, and other procedural aspects).

4. **Exceptions:** Both at common law and under the modern statutes, only certain kinds of share issuances are subject to preemptive rights. Thus the following kinds of share issuances are generally ***not*** covered even if the corporation has preemptive rights:

   a. **Initially authorized shares:** Most important, preemptive rights usually do not apply to shares that are part of the amount that is ***initially authorized*** at the time the corporation is first formed. Here, the theory is that a diligent shareholder should understand at the time he makes his initial purchase that the corporation may ultimately be selling to persons other than himself the entire rest of the initially-authorized amount.

      i. **Time limit:** On the other hand, if years go by without any sale of these remaining initially-authorized shares, the statutory scheme may cover the shares. Thus under MBCA § 6.30(b)(3)(iii), initially-authorized but unissued shares become covered by the preemptive rights scheme (if the corporation has elected to have one) once ***six months*** have elapsed from the date of incorporation. N.Y. BCL § 622(e)(5) applies a similar rule to initially-authorized shares that are sold more than ***two years*** after incorporation.

   b. **Treasury shares:** Under most statutes, ***treasury shares*** (that is, shares that were once outstanding, but that have been repurchased by the corporation) are not covered; see, e.g., N.Y. BCL § 622(e)(4). But the MBCA does not exclude such shares.

   c. **Property or services:** Shares that are issued in exchange for ***property*** or ***services*** are generally not covered. The theory is that the corporation has to be able to make special deals for hard-to-get property or services, and it would be a logistical nightmare to have to let existing shareholders participate proportionately (since usually the existing shareholders will not have comparable property or services to contribute, and it will be hard to equate their money with the outsider's property or services). Similarly, shares issued to allow the exercise of employee ***stock options*** generally are not covered.

5. **When to use:** As a matter of corporate planning (rather than law), when is it wise for a corporation to adopt preemptive rights? It is important to distinguish between publicly held and closely held corporations.

   a. **Publicly held:** It will very rarely be wise for a ***publicly held*** corporation to have preemptive rights. A preemptive rights scheme will cause substantial ***delays*** in financing — before the corporation offers shares to the public, it must make a "rights offering" to each existing shareholder, a complex procedure. Conversely, preemptive rights are rarely necessary to protect an existing shareholder in the public corporation — if he wants to maintain his proportional share of the corporation's equity, he can simply buy additional shares in the open market.

   b. **Closely held corporations:** But the reality is quite different in the context of the ***closely held*** corporation. Here, a stockholder (especially a minority one) is likely to find it very important to make sure that his equity percentage cannot be decreased without his consent. For instance, in our example on p. 534, a preemptive rights scheme would have offered Inventor the chance to maintain his 4/9's control of the board of directors, and thus the chance to preserve his voice in how the company should be managed.

      i. **Limited effectiveness:** But preemptive rights are only of limited effectiveness, even in a close corporation. Most significantly, they will only work if the existing shareholder has the ***financial resources*** to participate in the new stock issue. For instance, on the facts of our example on p. 534, even if Inventor got the benefit of preemptive rights, he would still have had to come up with $250,000 immediately to prevent dilution of his equity stake, a sum he might well not have had or been able to borrow. (In theory, Inventor could sell his preemptive rights to a third party, and at least receive some compensation if those rights entitled the holder to buy stock at less than its fair market value. But in the typical close corporation context, an outsider will usually not pay very much for the chance to be a minority stockholder in a company controlled by another — such as Capitalist — where the controlling shareholder does not welcome the new minority investor.)

6. **Emerging "fiduciary duty" theory towards dilution:** Because preemptive rights are often either waived by the corporation or not effective (for the reasons described just above), some modern courts are shifting to a new common-law theory for protecting minority stockholders against dilution. These courts have occasionally articulated a theory of ***"fiduciary obligation"***: the majority stockholder has a fiduciary duty not to cause the issuance of new shares where the purpose is to ***enhance his own control at the expense of the minority.*** Courts that have imposed such a duty do not, of course, block the controlling shareholder from ever causing the issuance of new shares over the objection of the minority; instead, these courts typically require that there be a valid ***"business purpose"*** for the new shares, so that the shares cannot be issued solely to enhance the majority's control.

a. **Unfair price:** The court is most likely to impose this fiduciary duty where the new shares are issued at a ***bargain price*** to those who are already in control.

b. **Bona fide business purpose required:** But ***even if the price is fair***, many courts will not sustain a sale of new stock by the corporation to its controlling shareholders if there is ***no valid business purpose*** behind the sale. For example, if the court becomes convinced that the controlling shareholder has caused the sale to take place solely for the purpose of ***enhancing his own control***, the court is likely to strike the transaction even though the price was fair.

c. **Preemptive rights as a defense:** As we've just seen, even where preemptive rights do not apply, the court will sometimes recognize a fiduciary obligation on the part of the board to offer all shareholders the opportunity to buy new shares on the same terms. But suppose that preemptive rights *do* apply, the plaintiff declines to participate (perhaps because he doesn't have enough money), and he then attacks the sale of new shares to other existing shareholders on the grounds that the price is ***unfairly low***. In this situation, courts are split:

   i. **Defense:** Some courts hold that the fact that P was offered the shares on the same terms under the preemptive rights plan constitutes a ***complete defense*** (and the court will therefore not inquire into whether the shares were sold at an unfairly low price.)

   ii. **Not a defense:** But other courts have held that the existence of preemptive rights is ***not*** a defense, and that the board must bear the burden of showing that the price was at least within the range of fairness. See, e.g., *Katzowitz v. Sidler*, 249 N.E.2d 359 (N.Y. 1969) (shares offered at one-eighteenth of present book value; P declined to exercise his preemptive rights; *held*, despite the availability of preemptive rights, board must show that the issuing price fell "within some range which can be justified on the basis of valid business reasons" — the corollary of preemptive rights is "the right not to purchase additional shares without being confronted with dilution of [one's] existing equity if no valid business justification exists for the dilution").

Quiz Yourself on ***ISSUANCE OF SECURITIES*** *(STATE-LAW RULES)*

106. Attila the Hun wants to buy 100 shares of newly-issued Pillage & Plunder Construction Equipment Company stock. The stock is worth $10,000. As payment, Attila gives Pillage & Plunder a document signed by him, which says, "In consideration of 100 shares of P&P stock to be issued immediately, I promise to perform for P&P pillaging and plundering services equal in value to at least $10,000. The services shall be performed, on the schedule requested by the company, over the next 2 years."

(a) May Pillage & Plunder properly issue the 100 shares? (Assume that the company is located in a state that follows the majority approach to issues raised by this question.) ________________

(b) Now, assume that the MBCA is in force. May Pillage & Plunder properly issue the 100 shares? ________________

107. On April 1, the Old King Coal Company incurs a $10,000 liability to the Keepon Trucking Co., for trucking that Keepon did for Old King Coal. On August 1, Old King Coal issues stock having par value of $25,000 to LaBrea Tarpit, in return for property that is worth (as LaBrea knows) only $10,000. On Sept. 1, Old King Coal becomes insolvent. Keepon Trucking sues LaBrea for $10,000, on the theory that Keepon may, as creditor of Old King, recover against LaBrea on account of LaBrea's having received $15,000 of "watered" stock. Assume that in the jurisdiction, the issuance of stock to LaBrea was in fact improper. Assume further that the jurisdiction follows the majority view on all relevant matters, and that there is no statute on point. May Keepon recover the $10,000 from LaBrea? ________________

108. Torquemada is a fabulously successful TV producer, his most popular program being "Wheel of Torture." His TV production company, a close corporation called Thumbscrew Productions, Inc., has 2,000 shares of common stock authorized and outstanding. Lucrezia Borgia owns 500 of those shares. Because the company needs more capital, Thumbscrew's board and shareholders vote to amend its articles to increase the company's authorized common stock from 2,000 to 3,000 shares. The board offers all 2,000 shares to Torquemada, at a fair price. Lucrezia would like to buy some of these shares for herself (so her percentage interest in the company won't be reduced). The company's charter is silent on all relevant issues.

(a) What doctrine or property concept is relevant to whether Lucrezia has the right to buy any of the newly-issued shares? ________________

(b) Assume that the MBCA is in force. Does Lucrezia have the right to buy any of the newly-issued shares? ________________

109. Same basic facts as prior question. Now, however, assume that the corporation's charter expressly awards preemptive rights.

(a) For this question, suppose that the events occur at a time when the corporation's authorized shares still total the originally-authorized 2,000 shares, of which only 1,000 were ever issued (750 to Torquemada and 250 to Lucrezia). Five months after the corporation is formed and the first 1,000 shares were issued, the board votes to sell an additional 500 shares (out of the initially-authorized batch) to Torquemada. Does Lucrezia have a right to buy enough shares to keep her ownership at 25%? ________________

(b) Suppose that after the company has raised its authorized shares to 3,000, the board enters into a employment contract with Torquemada, under which Torquemada gets 500 of the newly-authorized shares as compensation, in addition to salary. Does Lucrezia have the right to purchase as many new shares as will keep her percentage of ownership at its prior levels? ________________

Answers

106. (a) No. The issue, of course, is whether Attila has supplied adequate consideration for the shares. The majority approach — followed in New York and Delaware, among others — is that existing property and services are valid as consideration, but that promises to supply cash, property or services *in the future* are not valid. See, e.g., N.Y. BCL § 504(a) ("Consideration for the issue of shares shall consist of money or other property, tangible or intangible, or labor or services *actually received by or performed for* the corporation . . .") [532] Since Attila has supplied only his unsecured promise to perform the services, rather than the services themselves, under the prevailing view Attila has not supplied adequate consideration, and Pillage may not validly issue the shares.

(b) Yes. MBCA § 6.21(b), unlike the prevailing approach, allows a very broad range of things to suffice as consideration for share issuance. In particular, that section says that if the board so authorizes, consideration may consist of "contracts for services to be performed." [533] Since Attila has bound himself contractually to perform the services, his agreement constitutes valid consideration.

107. No. Not all courts recognize any common-law right on the part of a creditor of an insolvent corporation to recover against a recipient of "watered stock." Of those courts that do recognize such a right, most apply the "holding out" or "misrepresentation" theory. Under this theory, only a creditor who has ***relied*** on the corporation's (false) implied or express assertion that all shares were issued for at least par value may recover. [532] Here, Keepon extended credit to Old King Coal *before* Old King Coal even issued the stock to LaBrea. Therefore, Keepon could not possibly have relied on any express or implied assertion by Old King Coal that no watered stock had been issued. Since Keepon didn't rely on any assertion, it can't recover anything from LaBrea. (But there may be a statute, or case law, letting *Old King Coal* or its trustee in bankruptcy recover from LaBrea for the amount of "water.")

108. (a) The doctrine of preemptive rights. A preemptive right is a right, sometimes given to a corporation's existing shareholders, permitting them to maintain their percentage of ownership in the corporation by enabling them to buy a portion of any newly-issued shares. [534] If preemptive rights applied here, Lucrezia would be guaranteed the right to buy 25% of any newly-authorized batch of shares, at the same price as was offered to anyone else.

(b) No. The MBCA, like many modern statutes, follows an "opt in" approach to preemptive rights. That is, stockholders don't have preemptive rights unless the articles of incorporation specifically confer such rights (as opposed to an "opt out" approach, under which holders have such rights unless the charter says that they don't). See § 6.30(a). [535] Since the facts say that Thumbscrew's charter is silent on all relevant issues, Thumbscrew has not "opted in," and there are no preemptive rights. Therefore, the board can choose to offer all the new stock to Torquemada. (Where there are no preemptive rights, and the price is fair, courts generally say that the board can offer the stock to whomever it wishes.)

Notice that the facts say that the stock is being issued to raise needed capital. If this had not been true — if the stock was instead being issued solely to increase Torquemada's control — a court might hold that there was no "valid business purpose" for the issuance, and that Torquemada had used his control in violation of a fiduciary duty to the minority holders. In that event, even without preemptive rights the court might strike down the issuance to Torquemada, or order that Lucrezia be permitted to participate pro rata.

109. (a) No. Preemptive rights generally do not apply to shares that are part of the initially-authorized shares at the time the company is formed. [535] Some states provide that after a certain lapse of time, the initially-authorized-but-unissued shares do become subject to preemptive rights. But virtually no state would make this happen in as little as the five months specified in the facts. (MBCA § 6.30(b)(3)(iii) makes it happen 6 months from the date of incorporation; NY BCL § 622(e)(5) makes it happen after 2 years.)

(b) No. Shares that are issued in exchange for property or services generally are not deemed to trigger preemptive-rights schemes. [535]

II. PUBLIC OFFERINGS — INTRODUCTION

A. Regulation of public offerings generally: We turn now to a major new topic: federal regulation of the process by which securities are ***sold to the public***.

1. **The Securities Act of 1933:** Federal regulation of securities issuance is principally governed by the Securities Act of 1933 (which we will refer to as the " '33 Act").

   a. **Distinguished from '34 Act:** You must constantly distinguish between the '33 Act and the Securities Exchange Act of 1934 (the " '34 Act"). The '33 Act is virtually limited to the regulation of ***new issues*** of securities to the public. The '34 Act, by contrast, regulates nearly all securities-law aspects of publicly held companies apart from new issues. Thus the proxy regulations (*supra*, p. 97), the main insider trading and other anti-fraud rules promulgated by the SEC (such as Rule 10b-5, *supra*, p. 262), and the requirement of periodic financial disclosure (*supra*, p. 95), are all imposed by the '34 Act. So it may loosely be said that the '33 Act regulates "new issues," and the '34 Act regulates "companies."

2. **Section 5 of the '33 Act:** The key provision of the '33 Act is § 5. In brief, § 5 makes it unlawful (subject to some exemptions) to ***sell any security*** by use of the mails or other facilities of interstate commerce, ***unless a registration statement is in effect for that security***. This "registration statement" must contain a large amount of information about the security being offered and the company that is offering it (the "issuer"). Additionally, § 5 prohibits the sale of any security unless there is delivered to the buyer, before or at the same time as the security, a ***"statutory prospectus,"*** which contains the most important parts of the registration statement. (This way, the investor does not have to go to the SEC to read the registration statement.)

3. **Disclosure:** The '33 Act, like the other securities laws, reflects one key policy determination by Congress: that the best way to regulate securities markets, and to protect against fraud, is by requiring ***extensive disclosure***. The SEC has no power to decide that a particular stock issue should be prohibited on the grounds that it is too risky, overpriced, or otherwise inappropriate on the merits — so long as full disclosure is made in the registration statement and prospectus, there is no security too worthless to be offered to the public.

4. **What is covered:** The '33 Act does not apply only to "stocks," as you might expect. Instead, it applies to all ***"securities,"*** including ***bonds*** and other forms of debt. The meaning of "security" is discussed further *infra*, p. 541.

B. **The distribution process:** Before we can understand how the '33 Act regulates public offerings, we must first understand something about the system by which securities are distributed to the public. This entire distribution process is usually referred to as the ***"underwriting"*** process.

1. **"Firm commitment" underwriting:** Most securities offerings are handled through what is known as ***"firm commitment"*** underwriting. If the security is viewed as a "good," the firm commitment process can be viewed as a wholesale-retail distribution channel. The issuer (the company whose stock or bonds is to be sold) is in a sense the "manufacturer." There is a group of investment banking firms, known as the ***"underwriters"*** or the "underwriting syndicate," who function in effect as wholesalers — these underwriters contract in advance to ***purchase the entire issue*** at a stated price from the issuer. By means of this contract, the risk of a price decline, or of the unpopularity of the shares, is passed by the issuer onto the underwriters. The underwriters then "wholesale" the securities to a group

of retail securities ***dealers***, usually called the ***"selling group."*** These dealers then sell the securities "at retail" to institutional or individual investors. S,S,B&W, p. 283.

a. **Compensation:** The underwriters and dealers are compensated by receiving ***discounts*** on the securities. Generally, the total discount on stocks is somewhere between 6 and 15%. For instance, if the stock is being sold to the public for $10, the underwriters might pay the issuer $9, and the dealers might pay the underwriters $9.50. C&E, pp. 1415-16.

2. **"Best efforts" underwritings:** There is a second type of underwriting, known as ***"best efforts"*** underwriting. This method is used only by firms that are smaller and/or less well-established. Here, the underwriters do not give a hard contractual commitment to buy the stock issue and resell it to the public; instead, the underwriter merely commits to use its "best efforts" to sell the stock ***as agent for the issuer***. If the market turns out to be weak or the issue is overpriced, it is the issuer rather than the underwriter who takes the loss; the underwriter and the dealers under him are merely paid a commission for what they do sell. C&E, p. 1415.

C. **What is a "security":** Since the '33 Act applies only to sales of "securities," it becomes vital to know what constitutes a ***"security."*** Section 2(1) gives a definition of the term that is vastly broader than you might expect — the term is defined to include a list of items too long to reprint here, but one that includes any "note," "stock," "bond," "evidence of indebtedness," "certificate of interest or participation in any profit-sharing agreement," "investment contract," "certificate of deposit," or any put, call, or other option on any of the above. Here are some of the key rulings on what constitutes a "security," rulings that have emerged as a result of a substantial body of litigation[1]:

1. **Stock:** A share of ***stock*** will almost always be a security. Thus in the usual case of a for-profit corporation that issues shares of stock to represent an interest in the corporation's assets and future profits, these shares are clearly "securities."

a. **Sale of all stock in a closely held business:** Suppose that the owners of a ***closely held corporation*** sell ***all of the stock*** in the business to a purchaser who expects to manage the business himself. Does the fact that the ***entire business*** is being sold, rather than just a portion of it, prevent the stock sold from being a "security"? The answer seems to be ***"no" — even the sale of all the stock of a business will be the sale of a "security," and must therefore comply with the '33 Act***. See *Landreth Timber Co. v. Landreth*, 471 U.S. 681 (1985), in which the Supreme Court so held — the Court found that the federal securities laws were intended to apply not only to sales to "passive investors," but also to "privately negotiated transactions involving the transfer of control to 'entrepreneurs.' "

2. **Debt instruments:** A ***debt instrument*** may or may not be a "security." At one end of the scale, we have, say, a "note" given by a small-business owner to a bank, in return for a

---

1. By the way, the definition of "security" is essentially the same in the '34 Act as in the '33 Act. K,R&B (5th), p. 405. So if the buyer of, say, corporate stock wants to bring a civil suit against the seller for fraud or misstatement under SEC Rule 10b-5 (promulgated under the '34 Act — see *supra*, p. 262), the precedents we are exploring here concerning the meaning of "security" under the '33 Act will apply to that '34-Act-based claim.

loan; this is clearly not a "security." At the other end of the spectrum we have, say, a multi-million dollar set of bonds issued by a large corporation, and held by many institutions or even the general investing public; each of these bonds is almost certainly a "security." Other debt instruments will fall closer to the dividing line.

a. **Bank loans:** A note or other debt instrument that is issued to a single, or small number, of ***banks*** will normally ***not*** be a security. This is especially true where the loan is for some specific business purpose (e.g., to correct a seasonal cash flow shortage).

3. **"Investment contract":** The trickiest aspect of the definition of "security" involves whether a given money-raising scheme involves the sale of an ***"investment contract"*** (listed in § 2(1) as one of the types of "securities"). In general, the courts and the SEC have interpreted the phrase "investment contract" very ***broadly*** to reach agreements that a lay person would not think of as being "securities." The key concept seems to be that if A pays B money as an investment in a venture whose economic success will depend solely on the efforts of B or third persons (and not at all on A's own efforts), the deal will be held to have involved a security.

a. **Sale of LLC interest:** What about the sale of an ***interest in an LLC*** — can that be an "investment contract," so that the '33 Act applies? Again, the answer is likely to turn on whether the profitability of the LLC after the acquisition will depend in part on the buyer's efforts (in which case the buyer's interest is *not* an "investment contract") or will instead depend solely on the efforts of persons other than the buyer (in which case the buyer's interest probably *will* be an investment contract).

III. PUBLIC OFFERINGS — MECHANICS

A. **How filing works:** Recall that under § 5 of the '33 Act, no security may be sold in interstate commerce unless a registration statement has been filed for it. In fact, § 5 requires that, prior to the sale, the registration statement not only have been filed but also have become ***"effective."*** To understand the impact of this requirement of an effective registration statement prior to the sale of securities, you must understand something about the mechanics of the registration process.

1. **Filing the registration statement:** The process begins when a registration statement is ***filed*** with the SEC. The registration statement must contain considerable disclosure about the issue and the issuer. What goes into the registration statement is discussed more extensively *infra*, p. 545.

2. **20-day waiting period:** The issuer must now wait for the registration statement to become ***"effective,"*** because only when the statement is effective can the issuer actually sell the securities. Normally, the statement becomes effective ***20 days*** after it is filed. '33 Act, § 8(a).

a. **Letters of comment:** During this 20-day waiting period, the SEC staff reviews the registration statement to make sure that all required information is disclosed. If, as is usually the case, there are shortcomings, the staff notifies the issuer's lawyers of the problems in one or more ***"letters of comment,"*** also known as ***"deficiency letters."***

3. **Stop orders and refusal orders:** The registration statement automatically becomes "effective" on the 20th day after filing, regardless of whether the Commission finds it satisfactory. However, the SEC has the power to act affirmatively to delay or suspend the effectiveness of a registration statement. It can issue a "refusal order" (to prevent the statement from becoming effective) or a "stop order" (to suspend the effectiveness of an already-effective registration statement). In practice, however, it rarely has to use these devices, because issuers usually voluntarily comply with the wishes of the Commission's staff. See Ratner, pp. 39-40.

4. **Price amendment:** For a registration statement to be complete and therefore legal, it must include the ***price*** at which the securities will be offered to the public. But because markets are volatile, no underwriter is willing to commit himself to a fixed price 20 days before the public issue will take place. Therefore, what invariably happens is that the registration statement is initially filed ***without the price***, and the statement is then ***amended*** to include the price term.

5. **No investigation of underlying merits:** It is important to understand that in the registration process, the Commission does not conduct any ***independent investigation*** into the truth of the matters disclosed in the registration statement. True, the Commission staff inspects the documents carefully to see whether they appear to be complete and accurate ***on their face***; also, the staff generally compares the information in the registration statement against other information about the issuer in the Commission's files. But the Commission does not look into other sources of information (e.g., newspaper reports). Therefore, in the event of a later civil suit for a falsehood in the registration statement (see *infra*, p. 558), the issuer may not raise as a defense the fact that the Commission reviewed the statement and found it accurate. In fact, § 23 of the '33 Act makes it a crime to tell any prospective buyer that the fact that the Commission has allowed the statement to become effective means that the Commission has found the statement to be truthful.

B. Rules during the three periods: We can think of the offering process as having three distinct periods: (1) the ***pre-filing*** period, i.e., the period when the offering is being planned but the registration statement has not yet been filed with the Commission; (2) the period between filing and the effective date of the registration statement, usually called the ***"waiting period"***; and (3) the period ***after*** the registration statement has become effective. There are important rules about what activities by the issuer, underwriters and dealers are permitted during each of these periods.

1. **Pre-filing period:** During the ***pre-filing*** period, not only sales but also ***offers to sell*** are completely ***forbidden***. '33 Act, § 5(c).

   a. **Exception for preliminary negotiations:** There is one important exception: the issuer may conduct ***preliminary negotiations*** with the underwriter(s) and the underwriters may negotiate among themselves.

   b. **Definition of "offer":** But all other "offers" to sell are forbidden, and the term "offer" is defined quite broadly. For example, the term goes far beyond the usual contract-law meaning of soliciting an expression of willingness to purchase. For instance, any ***publicity*** by the issuer or the underwriter whose purpose or principal effect is to ***stir up interest*** in the planned offering is an "offer" and is thus forbidden.

i. **Oral offers:** Even an ***oral*** effort to stir up interest is forbidden during the pre-filing period. Thus it is unlawful for a broker at Merrill Lynch to telephone his clients and say, "We'll be underwriting a new issue of XYZ Corp stock next month, would you like me to put you down for 1,000 shares?" Similarly, it is unlawful for the president of XYZ to phone friends or relatives to ask them whether they would like to buy stock at the upcoming offering. Clark, p. 721.

ii. **Press release:** However, Rule 135 under the '33 Act does allow an issuer to put out a ***press release*** or other written notice of an offering during the pre-filing period, so long as the notice only lists the name of the issuer, and the purpose and basic terms of the offering (without listing the underwriters).

2. **Waiting period:** During the ***"waiting period"*** (after filing but before effective date of the registration statement), things loosen up a bit. Now, some types of offers to sell and offers to buy are allowed, but ***sales*** and ***contracts to sell*** are still not allowed.

a. **Oral offers:** Thus several types of offers are allowed during the waiting period. For instance, virtually any kind of ***oral offer*** is allowed during the waiting period, so long as it is truthful. Thus dealers may call all of their customers to ask whether they would like to enter a tentative order for the securities; similarly, the executives of the issuer may orally solicit their friends or customers to buy.

b. **Written offers:** On the other hand, ***written*** offers are still tightly regulated. Section 5(b) of the '33 Act has the effect of barring any type of written offer about the securities unless the offer is of a type that is specifically allowed.

i. **Preliminary prospectus or "red herring":** The main type of written "offer" that ***is*** allowed during the waiting period is the ***preliminary prospectus***, known in securities industry jargon as a ***"red herring."*** This is the prospectus as the issuer believes it will ultimately become effective, but minus the details about price and underwriters, details that will be supplied as an amendment just before the effective date (see *supra*, p. 543). (The "red herring" gets its name from the fact that there must be printed on the front of the document, in red ink, a statement explaining that the document is preliminary and that sales may not yet take place.)

(1) **Must be sent to customers:** Rule 15c2-8 under the '34 Act requires brokers and dealers to ***send*** the red herring to anyone who requests one in writing, and to anyone who is ***expected to receive a confirmation*** of sale.

ii. **Tombstone ad:** Another writing which the issuer or the underwriters may produce during the waiting period is the ***"tombstone ad,"*** that is, a newspaper ad which contains only certain tightly-specified information about the offer. (The name comes from the fact that the ad is usually enclosed in a black border.) See Rule 134 under the '33 Act.

iii. **"Free writings" prohibited:** But ***"free writings"*** are prohibited during the waiting period. Thus a brokerage firm that is offering the securities may not send its customers, say, a ***research report*** explaining why the firm's research department thinks that the issue will be a good investment. Clark, p. 722.

c. **No binding offers to buy:** Furthermore, no offer to buy or acceptance occurring during the waiting period will be deemed ***binding***. Thus suppose that Broker asks Customer, "Would you like to buy any shares of XYZ Corp? You won't have to take the shares or pay for them until after the offering becomes effective, which will be on July 1." Even if Customer says, "Yes, I'll take 1,000 shares," and even if Customer puts this acceptance in writing, Customer is ***not bound*** to take the securities or pay for them.

3. **The post-effective period:** Once the registration statement becomes effective, underwriters and dealers may make offers to sell, and actual sales, to anyone. However, the final ***prospectus*** (complete with the final price and underwriter information) must be sent to any purchaser ***before or at the same*** time he receives the securities. '33 Act, § 5(b)(2). (Thus the investor does not have to receive the prospectus until he is receiving the securities, a time when his investment decision has already been made. So the final prospectus is not likely to be very helpful in the investment decision-making process. That's why the SEC requires widespread dissemination of the preliminary prospectus, as described above, p. 544.)

C. **What must be in registration statement:** What must be in the registration statement? A great deal of information about the issuer and the particular security must be disclosed, including such items as "Risk Factors," "Use of Proceeds," "Selling Security Holders" (that is, which existing stockholders of the issuer are selling stock, if any), an extensive description of the issuer's business, detailed three-year financial information, etc. These requirements are laid down in the mammoth Regulation S-K, which coordinates all disclosure information under both the '33 and '34 Acts.

1. **Previously-public companies:** Companies that are already public, and that are therefore already making periodic reports to the SEC under the '34 Act (see *supra*, p. 96), can file a simpler registration statement than companies that are going public for the first time. Whereas companies going public must file on the very comprehensive Form S-1, already-public companies can file on the shorter Forms S-2 or S-3, which permit much of the required information to be incorporated by reference to other disclosure documents (e.g., the 10-K annual report) previously filed with the Commission.

IV. PUBLIC OFFERINGS — EXEMPTIONS

A. **Importance of exemptions:** The ordinary corporate lawyer, assuming that he is not practicing the specialty of securities law, does not need to know the intricacies of how to draft a registration statement or how to supervise a public offering. But because of the exceptional breadth of the securities laws, many more transactions will be held to be "public offerings" (and thus governed by the registration requirement) than a non-lawyer might expect. Therefore, it is exceptionally important that the corporate lawyer have a good sense of the complex scheme of ***exemptions*** from the securities laws — unless a particular issuance of stock falls within one of the exemptions, it is likely to be governed by the '33 Act; if so, the issuer, any financial intermediaries (and perhaps even the lawyer himself) could be found liable for distributing unregistered securities in violation of the '33 Act, something for which the potential penalties are staggering (see *infra*, p. 561). Therefore, we must examine this pattern of exemptions with great care.

B. Broad sweep of § 5: Section 5 of the '33 Act appears on its face to cover virtually ***any*** sale of a security. Section 5(a) provides that "unless a registration statement is in effect as to a security, it shall be unlawful for any person, directly or indirectly — (1) to make use of any means or instruments of transportation or communication in interstate commerce or of the mails to sell such security through the use or medium of any prospectus or otherwise. . . ." When this is combined with other parts of § 5, § 5 seems to say that ***virtually any "sale" of a "security" must be registered as if it were a public offering.***

1. **Exemptions:** However, other section of the Act grant important exemptions. Section 3 exempts certain securities, and § 4 exempts certain transactions. It is these exempted securities and transactions that we will be focusing on in this section. But the general point remains: ***if something constitutes a "sale" of a "security"*** (and the terms "sale" and "security" are very broadly defined; see, e.g., *supra*, p. 541), ***the registration requirement applies*** — and the sale must be treated as if it involves a public offering — ***unless some specific exemption applies***.

2. **Two key exemptions:** There are two types of exempted transactions that are so basic that we will consider them briefly here, though their intricacies will be explored below.

   a. **Persons other than issuers, underwriters and dealers:** The first of these is the exemption given in § 4(1) for ***"transactions by any person other than an issuer, underwriter, or dealer."*** So if a person can show that he is neither an issuer, underwriter or dealer, he doesn't have to worry about the registration requirements. Furthermore, nearly all sales by a "dealer" are exempted under § 4(3). Boiling it all down, therefore, registration will generally be required only where the transaction is being carried out by a person who is an ***"issuer"*** or ***"underwriter."*** But these two terms turn out to have broad, and sometimes unexpected, meanings, which are discussed below.

   b. **Non-public offerings:** The second key exemption is given in § 4(2): "transactions by an issuer ***not involving any public offering***." So if an issuer can show that its sale of securities was "non-public" rather than "public," it need not comply with the registration requirements.

3. **Organization of our discussion:** Our discussion of exemptions is organized into the following pieces: (1) non-public offerings; (2) "small" offerings, for which special SEC Rules have been enacted; (3) sales by persons other than the issuer (including sales by "underwriters," sales by controlling persons, and sales by non-controlling persons of shares bought at an earlier non-public offering); (4) mergers; and (5) some miscellaneous other exemptions (including the exemption for intrastate transactions).

4. **Illustration of issues:** Before we get enmeshed in the details of the various exemptions, it is useful to see how transactions that a lay person would never dream might be covered by the securities laws may in fact or at least arguably be covered. Let's consider the following hypothetical scenario:

   Example: Paul, a skilled lawyer and would-be journalist, is tired of practice and wants to go into the law school study aid publishing business. He therefore forms Outline

Corp. By telephone and mail, he solicits some prospective investors, including Vickie (a wealthy doctor who likes to back small ventures) and four of Vickie's friends. The various investors put up a total of $1 million of capital in return for 1 million total shares; Paul receives 75% of the shares for $500,000, Vickie receives 15% for $300,000, and Vickie's four friends collectively pay $200,000 for 10% (which they split evenly).

The first problem is that Outline Corp has "sold" "securities" to Paul, Vickie and the others, and this sale has involved interstate commerce (because the telephone and mail are instruments of interstate communication). Therefore, unless some exemption applies, Outline Corp (and probably Paul, as a promoter) have sold unregistered securities in violation of the '33 Act. (However, either the exemption for private offerings, or the exemption for small offerings, will probably apply, as we shall see later.)

Now, suppose that one year after the initial stock in Outline Corp is issued, Vickie wants to cash in her chips and go on to the next investment. She is unable to find a buyer for her shares among her circle of existing friends, so she asks her stockbroker to solicit a wider group of potential buyers. Her broker solicits 50 wealthy investors on his client list, and finally turns up Ned, who buys the shares. Assuming that this Vickie-to-Ned transaction does not qualify as a private or small offering (which it may not, in part because of the large number of buyers solicited), Vickie may have violated the '33 Act. While Vickie doesn't sound like an "issuer" or "underwriter," the broad definition of "underwriter" in the '33 Act will include Vickie if her purchase and subsequent resale is found to be part of the initial distribution. (This might be the case if a court finds that at the time she initially bought, she was already thinking about reselling within a year or two.) Vickie's problem is analyzed further *infra*, p. 557.

Finally, five years after the formation of Outline Corp, Paul grows tired of the grind of annual editorial revisions, and wants to sell his 75% interest. He hires Broker to find him a buyer for this controlling position. Broker locates Xavier, who buys Paul's interest. Because five years have passed since the formation of Outline Corp, the sale by Paul through Broker is unlikely to be found to be part of the original distribution, so the problem faced by Vickie won't apply here. But because Paul would be an "affiliate" of Outline Corp, he will be treated as an "issuer." Broker may therefore become an "underwriter," but will consequently lose the exemption given for ordinary sales by brokers on behalf of their customers. Thus both Paul and Broker may be guilty of selling unregistered securities in violation of the '33 Act when Broker arranges the sale by Paul to Xavier. See *infra*, p. 554.

C. **Private offerings:** Probably the most important exemption from the '33 Act's registration requirements is for ***non-public*** offerings (usually called "***private*** offerings"). Today, there are two paths by which an offering may qualify as "private" and thus exempt: (1) by means of the general exemption in § 4(2) of the '33 Act; or (2) by means of the special, and much more specific, exemption given in SEC Rule 506.

1. **Statutory exemption:** As noted, § 4(2) of the '33 Act gives an exemption for "transactions by an issuer ***not involving any public offering.***" The term "public offering" is not defined in the '33 Act, so defining it has been left to the courts and the SEC. These have recognized a number of basic categories of private-offering transactions:

a. **Sales to institutions:** Most important (at least in dollar volume) are sales to ***institutional investors***. If a corporation sells a large block of stock, bonds, or other securities to one or a few large and sophisticated institutions (e.g., insurance companies or pension funds), the transaction will be a private offering for which no registration statement is needed. This makes good sense: such institutions are powerful enough and sophisticated enough that they will insist on appropriate disclosure as a condition to committing their funds, and they therefore do not need the protection of the '33 Act's disclosure rules.

b. **Sales to key employees:** A second important category consists of ***stock sales to key employees***. Thus if a corporation offers stock (or stock options) to, say, its three most senior and important executives, this will almost certainly not constitute a public offering. As in the case of the institutional investor, these key executives presumably have such sophistication and knowledge about the company's affairs that they do not need the protection of the '33 Act's disclosure scheme.

c. **Acquisition of closely held corporation:** Similarly, suppose that Public Corp, a large company whose shares are publicly traded, wants to acquire Private Corp, a small closely-held outfit. The parties would like to do the transaction as an exchange of stock (see *supra*, p. 361), but Public Corp would like not to have to file a registration statement, since the transaction is small and all of the newly-issued Public Corp stock will go to Prez, the sole stockholder of Private Corp. Assuming that Private Corp's sole stockholder is reasonably sophisticated, Public's "sale" of its stock to Prez will probably qualify as a private offering under § 4(2).

d. **Money-raising offerings to small numbers of people:** Finally, the § 4(2) exemption may be used in the case of a ***money-raising offering*** to a ***small number*** of offerees. Here, the applicability of the exemption is more questionable than in the three prior categories, and more likely to depend on the precise facts of the case. In general, the two key factors seem to be:

   (1) how many offerees — not buyers — there are (with, obviously, the exemption becoming less applicable the more offerees there are); and

   (2) the degree of sophistication and knowledge about the company's affairs possessed by the offerees.

   Factor (2) means that even if there are very few offerees, if they do not have a reasonable level of sophistication and a substantial degree of ***knowledge*** about the company's affairs, the offering will not fall within the § 4(2) exemption.

   Example: Ralston Purina Co. allows any "key employee" to buy unregistered stock in the company. The company defines "key employee" very broadly to include any individual "who is eligible for promotion" or who "especially influences others." "Chow loading foreman," "clerical assistant," "production trainee," and "stenographer" are some of the people who are permitted to buy under the plan. The company claims that since its offering is limited to "key employees," the offering is private under § 4(1) (now § 4(2)).

   Held, this was not a private offering. The fact that an offering is only to a small number of people, or to a tightly-defined class, is not sufficient to make it "private."

The availability of the statutory exemption should turn on "whether the particular class of persons affected need the protection of the Act." The offerees here were not shown to have had ***access*** to the kind of information about the company that registration would have disclosed, so they could not fend for themselves and needed the protection of the Act. *SEC v. Ralston Purina Co.*, 346 U.S. 119 (1953).

i. **Later cases:** Cases after *Ralston Purina* seem to establish that an employee can "fend for himself" (so that an offering to him qualifies as private) if it is the case that ***either***: (1) the employee had ***access*** to the kind of data about the company that a registration statement would have disclosed (which will generally be the case for a ***senior executive***); or (2) the offeror makes actual ***disclosure*** of such information to him (so that if Ralston Purina had given each of the "key employees" a disclosure statement containing information similar to what would be provided in a registration statement, it would probably have won the case). See, e.g., *Doran v. Petroleum Management Corp.*, 545 F.2d 893 (5th Cir. 1977).

2. **Rule 506:** Relying on the § 4(2) statutory exemption to establish that an offering is "private" is a risky undertaking: there are no firm standards, and the offeror is at the mercy of how a particular court will construe prior case law. Therefore, the SEC has created a "safe harbor" — if a transaction satisfies the requirement of SEC ***Rule 506***, it will be deemed "private" regardless of whether it would meet the requirements of cases (like *Ralston Purina*) decided under the basic § 4(2) statutory exemption. Rule 506 is part of the broader SEC Regulation D, which sets forth a number of rules governing both "private" and "small" issues. (The other rules within Regulation D are discussed in our treatment of small offerings, *infra*, p. 550). Rule 506 imposes a somewhat mechanical test based on the number of purchasers.

   a. **Gist:** The gist of Rule 506 is that an issuer may sell an ***unlimited amount*** of securities to: (1) any number of ***"accredited"*** investors; and (2) up to ***35 non-accredited*** purchasers.

      i. **Meaning of "accredited":** The term ***"accredited investor"*** is defined in Rule 501(a). The full definition is too intricate to reproduce here. However, the key concept is that an investor is accredited if he is sufficiently ***rich***. In the case of an individual, he is accredited if either: (1) his ***net worth*** is more than $1 million (not counting his personal residence) (501(a)(5)); or (2) he has had an ***income*** of more than $200,000 in each of the two most recent years ($300,000 when his income is combined with that of his spouse), and has a "reasonable expectation" of reaching the same income level in the current year (501(a)(6)).

   b. **Accredited can be dumb:** If an investor is "accredited," he can be completely dumb about financial matters, and his purchase will not prevent the offering from qualifying under Rule 506. Thus if Promoter can find 100 very gullible millionaires, he can raise unlimited sums from each while still having the transaction be "private" under Rule 506.

   c. **Sophistication:** On the other hand, a ***non-accredited*** investor must be ***sophisticated***. More precisely, the issuer must ***"reasonably believe"*** that the non-accredited investor "either alone or with his purchaser representative(s) has ***such knowledge and experi-***

ence in financial and business matters that he is ***capable of evaluating the merits and risks*** of the prospective investment." (A "purchaser representative" is defined in Rule 501(h) to be a person of sophistication in financial and business matters who is helping the investor evaluate the merits of the investment.)

d. No dollar limit: There is ***no dollar limit*** on the securities that may be sold under Rule 506.

e. No advertising: The issuer may not make any general ***solicitation*** or ***advertising***, if the offering is to qualify under Rule 506 and the issuer wants the right to sell to up to 35 non-accredited investors. However, as the result of the 2012 "JOBS" Act, an issuer that is willing to sell ***only to accredited investors*** may now conduct general solicitations and advertising.[2]

f. Filing with the commission: The issuer must file a ***notice*** with the SEC that it will be making a Rule 506 offering. See Rule 503.

g. Disclosure: If the offering is ***solely*** to ***accredited*** investors, the SEC does not impose ***any disclosure requirements***. But if even one investor is ***non-accredited***, then ***all*** purchasers (whether accredited or not) must receive specific disclosures, as set forth in Rule 502(b)(2). The precise information that must be disclosed varies with the size of the offering and with whether the company is already filing SEC reports under the '34 Act. But even where disclosure is required, complying with Rule 502(b)(2) is much simpler and less expensive than filing a full-fledged registration statement. Clark, p. 731.

h. Not exclusive: Observe that Rule 506 is merely a ***"safe harbor,"*** not the exclusive method of demonstrating that the issue is a private offering. Therefore, if the issuer gets tripped up on one or two of the technical requirements of Rule 506, he still has the opportunity to prove that he qualifies as a private offering under the more general § 4(2) statutory exemption (discussed above).

Example of Rule 506's use: Rule 506 might have been quite useful in our Outline Corp example on p. 546. So long as Vickie and her four friends were each either "accredited" investors, or persons who (together with their "purchaser representative") had adequate sophistication to evaluate the offering, they would be appropriate investors under Rule 506. (Paul, as the promoter, would presumably have been either a director or officer of Outline Corp prior to the offering; if so, he would be an accredited investor by virtue of this insider status. See Rule 501(a)(4).) So long as Paul and Outline Corp did not conduct a general advertising or solicitation campaign, and gave an adequate disclosure document in the event that Vickie or one of her friends was not accredited, the other substantive requirements of Rule 506 would be met. But remember that if even one of the investors was non-accredited, all investors (accredited or not) would have to be given the appropriate disclosure document.

D. Small offerings: Rule 506, although often applicable, will not suffice for every case in which a small business wants to raise financing. The principal problem is that each investor

---

2. The amendment to Rule 506 that's needed to carry out this JOBS Act provision has been proposed by the SEC, but not yet finally enacted as of this writing (April, 2013).

must be either "accredited" or sophisticated (though sophistication can come from the purchaser representative). Suppose that Entrepreneur simply wants to raise a few hundred thousand dollars of seed money from his friends and relatives, who are neither rich nor sophisticated. Rule 506 will not do. Fortunately, the SEC has adopted two rules, Rules 504 and 505, that give a safe harbor for certain ***small size*** offerings, without reference to the degree of sophistication of the investors.

1. **Rule 504:** Rule ***504*** allows an issuer to sell up to a total of ***$1 million*** of securities. (For purposes of calculating the $1 million limit, all sales in any ***12 month period*** made under Rule 504 or the companion small-offering provision, Rule 505, must be added together.) For these very small offerings that fit under Rule 504, there are practically no significant restrictions:

   a. **Unlimited number:** There is no limit on the ***number*** of investors who may purchase. (Contrast this with Rule 506, where the number cannot be more than 35 non-accredited plus any number of accredited investors.)

   b. **Disclosure:** No particular ***disclosure*** is required. (However, the issuer must still comply with the general anti-fraud provisions of the federal securities laws, including Rule 10b-5.)

   c. **Advertising:** Generally, the offering may ***not*** be ***publicly advertised*** or accomplished by ***widespread solicitation***. But even here, an exception will sometimes be available: If the offering is made solely in states whose own laws require registration and the delivery of a disclosure document, an offering that is in compliance with the state requirements may be advertised and sold by solicitation.

   d. **No "development stage" companies:** "Development stage" companies — companies that ***don't yet have real business operations*** (including companies set up to ***acquire other not-yet-identified companies***) — ***cannot use*** Rule 504. See R. 504(a)(3).

   e. **Illustration:** The following example shows how Rule 504 might be used.

   Example: Return to our Outline Corp example from p. 546. Assume that the issuance of stock to Paul was lawful even without reliance on Rule 504 (or its companion small-offering rule, Rule 505, discussed below). If so, the amount of stock being sold to Vickie and her friends aggregates less than $1 million, so the Rule 504 exemption is available. This makes Paul's life much easier: he will not have to make any specific disclosure to Vickie or her friends, and will not have to worry about whether they are all sufficiently sophisticated to understand the nature of the investment. (But Outline Corp will have to file a Notice of Sale with the SEC within 15 days after it makes the first sale to Vickie or her friends. See Rule 503.)

2. **Rule 505:** Rule ***505*** "can be understood as a rule that straddles 504 and 506." Clark, p. 733. It allows a higher dollar amount than Rule 504, yet imposes less stringent requirements on who may invest than does Rule 506.

   a. **Gist:** Under 505, the issuer can sell up to ***$5 million*** of securities in any 12-month period (counting sales not only under 505 but also those under 504). As with Rule 506, the number of investors is limited to 35 non-accredited and any number of accredited investors.

b. **Disclosure and advertising:** If the issuer is selling to any non-accredited investors, it must make the same ***disclosure*** to all investors as would be required under 506. Similarly, the no-advertising and no-solicitation rules (*supra*, p. 550) that apply to Rule 506 offerings that are sold to non-accredited investors apply equally to Rule 505 offerings.

c. **Why used:** Given that the number-of-investor limits, disclosure rules, and anti-advertising rules that apply to 506 also apply to 505, and that 505 limits the offering to $5 million whereas 506 has no dollar limits, why would anyone ever use 505? The answer is that there are no requirements concerning the ***type of investor*** — unlike 506, the investor need not be either accredited or sophisticated. "Thus, the lawyer counselling her client about the availability of this exemption may be able to achieve ***greater certainty*** than if the [Rule 506] private offering exemption were invoked." Clark, p. 733.

Example: Return once again to our Outline Corp example from p. 546. Suppose, however, that Paul wants to have Outline Corp sell $2 million of stock to Vickie and her friends, rather than $500,000. Now, Rule 504 will not apply (because of its $1 million limit). Outline Corp will certainly want to get under 505 rather than 506 if it can, since under 505, Outline Corp and Paul will not have to form a belief about whether Vickie and her friends have "such knowledge and experience in financial and business matters that [they are] capable of evaluating the merits and risks of the prospective investment" (as Rule 506(b)(2)(ii) requires).

3. **Table 12-1:** Table 12-1 shows some of the more important aspects of the three main rules of Regulation D, Rules 504-506.

E. **Sales by persons other than the issuer:** We have now seen most exemptions that apply to sales by an "issuer." (Several others are briefly covered below, including mergers, intrastate offers, and Regulation A.) Let us now turn to the rules governing sales by persons ***other than the issuer***.

1. **We only worry about "underwriters":** Remember that § 4(1) of the '33 Act exempts from the registration requirements "transactions by any person other than an issuer, underwriter or dealer." Furthermore, virtually all sales by a "dealer" are exempted by § 4(3), except for those taking place during the first 40 days of a public offering. Therefore, our discussion of sales by persons who are not issuers is mostly a discussion of who is an "underwriter" — if a person is not an "underwriter" (and does not sell "through" an underwriter — see the problem of sales by controlling shareholders *infra*, p. 554), he probably does not need to worry about the registration requirements.

2. **Resales:** Another way to look at this topic of "sales by persons other than the issuer" is to think of it as a discussion of when ***resales*** are allowed. In terms of our Outline Corp example from p. 546, the kinds of problems we are interested in here are questions like: (1) May Vickie make her sale to Ned, one year after the original stock issuance, without registering her shares?; and (2) May Paul sell his shares to Xavier, five years after the initial stock issuance, without registration?

Table 12-1

COMPARISON: SEC REG. D EXEMPTIONS FOR "PRIVATE" AND "SMALL" OFFERINGS

	Rule 504	**Rule 505**	**Rule 506**
Maximum Amount (in any 12-month period)	$1 million	$5 million	Unlimited
Maximum Number of Investors	Unlimited	35 non-accredited; unlimited accredited	35 non-accredited; unlimited accredited
Investor Qualifications	None	None	Accredited, or sophisticated (alone or with Purchaser Representative)
Disclosure Requirements	None	If 1 or more investors are non-accredited, disclosure required by Rule 502(b)(2). If all investors are accredited, no specific disclosure required	Same as for Rule 505

Adapted from C&E (6th Ed.), p. 1509

3. **Ordinary brokerage transactions:** At the outset, let's consider ordinary ***secondary-market*** trading. If Investor buys registered shares at an initial public offering, and then wants to resell those shares on a stock exchange or in the over-the-counter market sometime later, why doesn't he have to file a registration statement to cover this sale? Assuming that investor has no special affiliation with the issuer, he is protected by the main exemption of § 4(1) (exempting any transaction that is not by an "issuer, underwriter, or dealer") as long as he is not an "underwriter." We will be discussing in detail who is an "underwriter." For now, you can simply assume that if Investor is an ordinary small investor with a small stake in the company, he is not an underwriter and can therefore resell on the open market without registration.

4. **Meaning of "underwriter":** The term ***"underwriter"*** is defined in § 2(11) of the '33 Act to mean "any person who has purchased from an issuer with a view to, or offers or sells for an issuer in connection with, the distribution of any security. . . ." This definition is a broad one. It doesn't just cover institutions that call themselves "underwriters," and that formally contract to buy a new issue from the issuer and resell it to the public by means of tombstone ads and the like. Instead, ***anyone***, even an individual, who "buys

from" or "sells for" the issuer with a "view to . . . distribution," is potentially an underwriter.

5. **Sales by or for controlling persons:** Because of the very broad definition of "underwriter," sales by or for a person who ***controls*** the issuer will often turn out to ***require separate registration*** (even if the issuer is already a "public" company with properly-registered shares in public hands).

   a. **Broad definition of "issuer":** To see how this can come about, first consider the last sentence of § 2(11) of the '33 Act: "As used in this paragraph [defining "underwriter"] the term 'issuer' shall include, in addition to an issuer, any person directly or indirectly ***controlling*** or controlled by the issuer. . . ." If we couple this broad definition of "issuer" with the definition of "underwriter" as meaning anyone who "sells for an issuer in connection with the distribution of any security," then it follows that ***a broker who sells shares for a controlling stockholder may be acting as an "underwriter"*** (in which case the key exemption given in § 4(1) for "transactions by any person other than an issuer, underwriter, or dealer" will not be available).

   b. **Liability of controlling shareholder:** As I just noted, a broker can be liable for selling unregistered securities if he makes sales for one who controls the issuer, and the sales are found to constitute a "distribution." But the ***controlling stockholder*** can ***also*** be similarly liable for unregistered sales: since the broker is acting as an "underwriter," the sales are not "transactions by any person other than an issuer, underwriter, or dealer," so the controlling shareholder loses his key § 4(1) exemption and is illegally selling unregistered securities unless he can find some other exemption.

   c. **Rule 144:** So the key concept is "distribution": if a broker sells for a controlling shareholder in what is found to be a "distribution," then both the controlling shareholder and the broker can be liable for selling unregistered securities. Fortunately for brokers and controlling shareholders, the SEC has adopted a special rule, ***Rule 144***, that provides a ***safe harbor***: if the terms of the rule are complied with, no "distribution" is deemed to occur, so the broker and the controlling shareholder get the § 4(1) exemption for "transactions by any person other than an issuer, underwriter, or dealer," and are not required to register the offering. In the case of a sale by or for a ***controlling shareholder*** of the issuer (what the rule defines in 144(a)(1) as an ***"affiliate"*** of the issuer), Rule 144 is available only if all of the following conditions are satisfied:

      i. **Limit on amount of sales:** The sales must be made ***gradually***. More precisely, in ***any three-month period*** the controlling shareholder may not sell more than the greater of: (1) ***1% of the total shares outstanding***; or (2) the ***average weekly trading volume*** for the four prior weeks. These volume limits mean that unless the stock is ***fairly actively*** traded (i.e., with more than 1% of its shares traded in an average week), a controlling shareholder will be likely to have to wait a ***very long time*** to sell a significant chunk of his holdings under Rule 144. For instance, it would take a ***30% holder*** more than ***seven years*** to sell off his holdings if less than 1% of the company's stock traded in an average week. Therefore, controlling shareholders who want to dispose of their entire holdings will generally find that as a practical matter, they must register their offering rather than rely on Rule 144. Clark, p. 740.

ii. Holding period: The controlling shareholder must normally have held the securities ***for at least two years*** before reselling them. (But the holding period does not apply if he bought the shares in a public offering.)

iii. Disclosure: The issuing corporation must be a "public" company, i.e., one which makes periodic reports to the SEC under the '34 Act (see *supra*, p. 95). Alternatively, there must be equivalent information about the company publicly available. So if the issuer is a typical closely-held corporation about which little financial information is publicly known, Rule 144 is not available to permit the controlling shareholder to sell shares.

iv. Ordinary brokerage transactions: The stock must be sold in ***ordinary brokerage transactions***, or sold directly to a "market maker." The main thrust of this requirement on the manner of sale is that the controlling shareholder's broker may not ***solicit*** orders to buy the stock — the broker must merely respond to unsolicited buy orders or sell on the open market, rather than, say, phoning his customer list to find out whether anybody is interested.

v. Notice: Finally, a ***notice*** of each sale must normally be filed with the SEC at the time the order to sell is placed with the broker. A notice must also be filed with any stock exchange on which the issuer's shares are traded.

Illustration of operation: Let's return to our Outline Corp hypothetical from p. 546 to see how Rule 144 might apply to a sale by a controlling shareholder. Recall that five years after the founding of the company, Paul wants to dispose of his interest, which consists of 750,000 of the 1,000,000 shares outstanding. If Broker simply calls up various customers and solicits orders for a large portion of Paul's stake, these sales are likely to be held to be a "distribution," and both Paul and Broker will be guilty of selling unregistered securities. Rule 144 might furnish Paul and Broker a way to sell off his stake without registration.

The biggest problem is the requirement that the shares be sold either to a market maker or in ordinary brokerage transactions. As a practical matter, this probably means that unless Outline Corp has not only "gone public" at some time in the past five years but is somewhat actively traded, Paul and Broker will simply not be able to use Rule 144 — without a reasonable "float," or number of shares in public hands, Broker could only move the shares by soliciting orders, and this is precisely what the "ordinary brokerage transaction" requirement prohibits.

Assuming that Outline Corp is already publicly traded, the "company disclosure" requirement will also be satisfied: Outline Corp will be making periodic reports to the SEC under the '34 Act.

The holding-period rule will not cause any problem: Paul is required to have held his shares (since they were not obtained in a public offering) for at least two years. But he has in fact held them for five.

But the volume limits will be a problem. Paul may not sell in any three month period more than the greater of: (1) 1% of the total outstanding shares of Outline

Corp common stock; or (2) the average weekly trading volume for the stock over the prior four weeks. Therefore, unless more than 1% of Outline Corp stock trades in an average week, Paul will be limited to 10,000 shares (1% of the company's total outstanding stock) in any three-month period; thus for him to sell his 750,000 shares, it will take him 75 three-month periods, or more than 18 years! So unless Paul is content to dribble out his shares over such a long schedule, he will have no choice but to file a registration statement for his shares.

If Paul does proceed by Rule 144, he will have to file with the SEC a notice of sale at the time each sale order is placed with Broker.

6. **Sales by non-controlling person:** ***Non-controlling persons*** will also sometimes have to worry about being classed as "underwriters" if they sell their unregistered shares. The principal situation in which a non-controlling shareholder needs to worry about being an "underwriter," and would like to be able to use Rule 144, is where the person has previously ***bought stock from the issuer in a private transaction*** and now wishes to resell that stock. Especially where the investor has not held the stock for very long, there is a chance the court will hold that he ***bought with an intent to resell*** rather than to hold for investment; if so, the resale is likely to be deemed part of the original "distribution," the investor will therefore be an "underwriter," and the resale will be an illegal sale of an unregistered security.

   a. **Rule 144 helps:** ***Rule 144*** may help in this situation of a resale by a non-controlling shareholder, just as it may help in the case of sales by controlling shareholders. In fact, the conditions which must be met before Rule 144 applies are actually ***easier*** in the non-controlling shareholder case, as we shall see shortly. Our discussion assumes that the non-controlling shareholder is holding ***"restricted securities,"*** that is, securities bought from the issuer in a non-public offering. (If the shares were bought in a public offering, he will generally not have to worry about his re-sales being considered "distributions," so he does not need the protection of Rule 144.)

      i. **Held less than three years:** If the non-controlling shareholder has held his restricted stock for ***less than three years***, then he may only use Rule 144 if ***all*** the requirements listed above for controlling-shareholder sales are met. That is, he is subject to the sale volume limits and the two-year minimum holding period, the issuer must make periodic SEC reports (or supply equivalent disclosure to the public), the sales must be made in ordinary brokerage transactions, and the SEC notice must be filed, all exactly as if the seller were a controlling shareholder.

      ii. **Held for more than three years:** But if the non-controlling shareholder has held his restricted stock for ***more than three years***, life gets dramatically easier under Rule 144. The volume limits, company-disclosure rules, "ordinary brokerage transaction" requirement, and SEC filing requirement are all ***removed***. So we have a simple general rule: ***a non-controlling shareholder who buys stock in a private offering and then holds that stock for three years may sell to whomever he wishes, in whatever amounts he wishes, by whatever type of transaction he wishes*** (so long as the resale does not itself involve a brand new public offering), without reference to whether the company ***files SEC reports***, and without any need to file any notice with the SEC.

Illustration: Returning once again to our Outline Corp example from p. 546, let's see how Rule 144 might have helped Vickie dispose of her 15% interest in Outline Corp. The Rule would not have helped Vickie at all with respect to her sale made one year after Outline Corp first distributed stock. Therefore, Vickie could be charged by the SEC with illegally selling unregistered shares — if a court found that she bought with an intent to resell rather than hold for investment, the court might well hold that her resale was a "distribution," thus making her broker an "underwriter" and depriving both Vickie and her broker of the key § 4(1) exemption for transactions not involving an underwriter, issuer or dealer.

But if Vickie held her Outline Corp stock for two years, she could then sell it under Rule 144, provided she met all of the stringent requirements of that Rule. For instance, assuming Outline Corp stock was lightly traded, she would be limited to selling 1% of all Outline Corp shares (i.e., 10,000 shares) in any three month period, so it would take her almost four years to dispose of her 15% position. Similarly, Outline Corp would have to be "public," in the sense that it either filed periodic reports under the '34 Act or made comparable information available to the public; the sales by broker would have to be "ordinary" ones in which the broker did not solicit for buyers and merely filled orders; and a notice with the SEC would have to be filed each time Vickie told her broker to sell some shares.

Assume, however, that Vickie is willing to wait until ***three years*** have passed since she first got her shares. Now, her life will be much easier: since she is not a controlling stockholder, she can sell all her shares whenever she wishes to whomever she wishes in any kind of transaction (as long as her sales activity doesn't independently constitute a new public offering), without reference to whether Outline Corp files SEC reports, and with no need on her part to file any notice with the SEC.

F. **Other exemptions:** Let us now review very briefly two other exemptions to the registration requirements: (1) the exemption for "intrastate" offerings; and (2) the Regulation A exemption.

1. **Intrastate offerings:** Section 3(a)(11) of the '33 Act exempts from the registration requirements "[a]ny security which is part of an issue offered and sold ***only to persons resident within a single State*** . . . where the issuer of such security is a . . . corporation, ***incorporated by and doing business within, such State***. . . ." This is the ***"intrastate offerings"*** exemption.

   a. **Stringent requirements:** Several stringent requirements make the intrastate exemption very hard to use. One writer says that these requirements render the exemption "virtually useless for making public offerings except in ***isolated areas far from any state border***." Ratner, pp. 62-63.

2. **Regulation A:** Regulation A is a set of SEC Rules that gives an exemption for certain issues of up to ***$5 million.***

   a. **Eligibility:** All offerings made under Regulation A during any 12-month period must be added together, and this total must be less than $5 million.

b. **Disclosure requirements:** Regulation A imposes substantial ***disclosure requirements*** on an issuer. The issuer must file an "offering statement" with the local SEC regional office before beginning the offering. This offering statement must include material that is fairly similar to what would have to be in a registration statement, although in less detail, and without audited financials.

c. **Employee benefit plans:** Regulation A is rarely used today, because it is not that much simpler to comply with than the true registration process (especially since the registration statement for smaller offerings can now be filed on a simple form that is hardly more burdensome than the Regulation A form). The main use of Regulation A is for offerings made under ***employee stock option*** and stock ***purchase*** plans. C&E, p. 1449.

V. PUBLIC OFFERINGS — CIVIL LIABILITIES

A. **Liabilities generally:** The '33 Act contains four ***liability*** provisions:

1. **Section 11:** Section 11 imposes liability for ***false statements in a registration statement***. It is probably the most important of the '33 Act liability provisions.

2. **Section 12(1):** Section 12(1) imposes liability on anyone who offers or sells a security in violation of § 5 of the '33 Act. Its main use is where stock should be registered but is not, i.e., an ***unregistered public offering***.

3. **Section 12(2):** Section 12(2) is a general ***anti-fraud*** provision. Unlike §§ 11 and 12(1), it is not keyed into registration. Thus even if the offering is exempt from registration, if the seller tells a lie orally or in writing in connection with the sale, he will be liable.

4. **Section 17(a):** Section 17(a) is an even more general anti-fraud provision. Like § 12(2), it applies without reference to whether registration is required, so it can apply to sales of securities that are exempt from registration. The fraudulent conduct it prohibits is phrased more broadly than the prohibition in § 12(2) (since 12(2) applies only to statements or omissions, whereas § 17(a) applies to "any device, scheme, or artifice to defraud"). However, unlike § 12(2), § 17(a) does not explicitly give a civil remedy to the buyer, and courts are in dispute about whether such a remedy should be implied.

B. **Liability under § 11:** Section 11 is the best reason for an issuer or underwriter to make sure that a registration statement is done carefully, for it comes fairly close to imposing ***strict liability*** for errors in registration statements.

1. **Basic provision:** Section 11 provides that if a registration statement, at the time it became effective, "contained an ***untrue statement of a material fact*** or ***omitted to state a material fact*** required to be stated therein or necessary to make the statements therein not misleading," anyone who buys the stock thereafter may sue not only the issuer but a number of other people. Remember that the registration statement includes the prospectus, so any prospectus error will trigger § 11.

2. **Who may sue:** A § 11 suit may be brought by ***anyone*** who buys the stock covered by the registration statement. Thus the plaintiff does not have to be someone who bought at the

initial public offering — he can be a ***secondary*** buyer (one who bought from one who bought at the initial offering).

3. **Reliance:** Even better still for the plaintiff, he does not have to show that he ***relied*** on the registration statement. Even if it is clear that he never read the prospectus, and that he would have bought the stock no matter what the prospectus said, he is still permitted to sue.

   a. **Actual knowledge:** However, the defendant is given an affirmative defense: he will avoid liability if he can bear the burden of showing that the plaintiff purchaser ***knew of the untruth*** or omission at the time he purchased.

   b. **Release of subsequent earnings report:** Also, if the plaintiff bought the stock after the issuer made public an earnings statement covering the first 12 months of operations following the effective date of the registration, then the plaintiff must prove that he in fact relied on the registration statement. § 11(a).

4. **Who may be sued:** A wide range of people may be sued under § 11. The categories include:

   (1) everyone who ***signed*** the registration statement (which always includes at least the issuer, the principal officers, and a majority of the directors);

   (2) everyone who was a ***director*** at the time the registration statement was filed (or who was named with his consent in the statement as being about to become a director);

   (3) every ***expert*** who consented to being named as having prepared or certified a part of the registration statement (including accountants, engineers, and appraisers); and

   (4) every ***underwriter***.

   So even if the issuer is bankrupt by the time suit is commenced, the plaintiff typically has a number of other deep-pocketed parties to sue.

5. **Standard of conduct:** The ***issuer's*** liability is ***absolute***; even if the misstatement or omission was inadvertent and in fact non-negligent, the issuer is strictly liable. But all other defendants are given the chance to raise the so-called ***"due diligence"*** defense. That is, a defendant who shows that he exercised due diligence in connection with the registration statement will escape liability. The due diligence test applies differently with respect to portions of the registration statement prepared by experts and those portions not prepared by experts, so we consider each of these situations separately:

   a. **Distinction between "expertised" and "non-expertised" parts:** A portion of the registration statement that makes extensive use of an ***expert***, and that lists the expert as having prepared that portion, is called the ***"expertised"*** portion. All other parts are referred to as "non-expertised" portions. In general, courts define the "expertised" parts narrowly. For instance, the fact that the entire registration statement is prepared by lawyers does not mean that the entire statement is "expertised" by the lawyers. See *Escott v. BarChris Construction Corp.*, 283 F.Supp. 643 (S.D.N.Y. 1968), discussed further *infra*. Typically, the expertised portions will be: (1) the ***financial statements***, expertised by the accountants who prepared them; (2) any ***engineering*** reports dealing with such items as structural soundness of properties; and (3) ***appraisals*** of property.

b. "Non-expertised" portions: With respect to the ***non-expertised*** parts of the registration statement, the due diligence defense is phrased affirmatively: the defendant must show that: (1) he made a ***reasonable investigation***; and (2) after that investigation, he was left with ***reasonable ground to believe***, and did ***in fact believe***, that there was no material misstatement or omission.

i. Can't be delegated: In general, this duty to make a reasonable investigation ***cannot be delegated***. For instance, suppose that an outside director says to the president of the issuer, or to the representative of the underwriter, "Have you checked out this registration statement completely?" and the insider or underwriter says, "Yes we have, and everything is alright." This will ***not*** constitute "reasonable investigation" on the director's part, so he will not succeed with his due diligence defense if this is all that he has done. *Escott v. BarChris Construction Corp.*, 283 F.Supp. 643 (S.D.N.Y. 1968) (where newly-appointed director relies on assurances of president and chief executive officer that all data in the registration statement is accurate, director has not made a "reasonable investigation" of the non-expertised portions).

c. "Expertised" portion: With respect to the ***"expertised"*** part of the registration statement, somewhat different rules apply:

i. The expert: The same standard that applies to all defendants concerning the non-expertised portion is applied to the ***expert*** in connection with the expertised part that he has prepared. In other words, the expert must make the affirmative showing that he conducted a reasonable investigation that left him with reasonable ground to believe (and the actual belief) that the part he prepared was accurate.

ii. Non-experts: But all other persons get the benefit of an easier standard for due diligence in connection with the expertised portion: they merely have to prove the ***negative*** proposition, that they ***"had no reasonable ground to believe and did not believe"*** that there was any material misstatement or omission. For instance, an ordinary director can leave to a financial expert (typically, the accounting firm) the preparation of the audited financial statements that are to appear in the registration statement; so long as the director does not have reason to believe, and does not in fact believe, that the financials are inaccurate, he will be protected even though he did not conduct any independent investigation of his own.

6. Measure of damages: The ***measure of damages*** in § 11 cases is the difference between: (1) the ***price*** the plaintiff ***paid*** for the stock (but not more than the public offering price); and (2) the ***value*** of the stock at the time of the suit (or the price the plaintiff got when he sold the stock). So the measure of damages essentially covers the plaintiff's ***out-of-pocket loss***.

a. Affirmative defense: But the defendant may get the damages reduced by showing that the decline in value was caused by ***factors other than the error*** in the registration statement. For instance, suppose that D shows that the entire stock market declined substantially between the offering and the suit; the court may well reduce the plaintiffs' damages by an amount that approximates the general percentage decline in the market.

C. **Section 12(1):** Section 12(1) is very brief: it imposes liability on "[a]ny person who . . . offers or sells a security in violation of Section 5. . . ." Section 12(1) therefore imposes liability on anyone who sells a security that ***should have been registered*** but was not.

1. **Strict liability:** Liability under § 12(1) is ***strict*** — even if the seller made an honest mistake, and indeed a non-negligent mistake, in concluding that the stock did not need to be registered, he is liable.

2. **Liable only to his purchaser:** ***Privity*** is required for a § 12(1) suit. In other words, a buyer of stock that should be registered and is not may sue only the person who sold to him, not someone further back in the distribution chain.

3. **Damages:** The plaintiff gets the equivalent of ***rescission***. In other words, he collects damages equal to the difference between what he paid and what the stock was worth at the time of suit (or the amount he received when he re-sold it).

D. **Section 12(2):** Section 12(2) is somewhat similar to § 11, in that it establishes liability for ***untrue statements of material fact*** and for ***omissions of material facts***. But there are some important differences, and some key situations in which suit will be possible only under § 12(2), not § 11:

1. **Not in registration statement:** Unlike § 11, § 12(2) is ***not limited to misstatements made in the registration statement***. Section 12(2) imposes liability for misstatements made ***orally***, or in a writing other than the registration statement. It also applies regardless of whether the security is registered or required to be registered. Thus if Promoter falsely tells Investor orally, "I've got a great private placement for you; management is honest and the company is profitable," § 12(2) may allow recovery even though § 11 does not (because there is no registration statement containing any error) and even though § 12(1) is unavailable (assuming that this is indeed a private placement that does not need to be registered).

2. **Negligence standard:** Section 12(2) effectively imposes a ***negligence*** standard. This is because it gives the seller a defense if he can show "that he did not know, and in the exercise of reasonable care could not have known, of such untruth or omission." (This is a bit different from the § 11 standard for non-expertised parts of the registration statement, where the defendant has the burden of showing that he conducted a reasonable investigation and did not learn of the error.)

3. **Broad class of defendants:** Under § 12(2), the buyer may sue anyone who was a ***substantial factor*** in the sale. Thus the class of possible defendants is not limited to the seller. For instance, a broker who merely handles the transaction as the seller's agent, or a public relations consultant who works for the seller, might each be liable if he makes an untrue statement or a material omission in connection with the sale. Loss, pp. 891, 1017-22. (By contrast, § 11 probably applies only to those defendants who fall within the precise classes specified in that section.)

E. **Section 17(a):** Finally, § 17(a) is a ***general anti-fraud provision***, which makes it unlawful, in the offer or sale of any security, to: (1) "employ any ***device, scheme, or artifice to defraud***"; (2) "obtain money or property by means of any untrue statement of a material fact or any omission to state a material fact . . ."; or (3) "engage in any transaction . . . which operates or would operate as a fraud or deceit upon the purchaser."

1. **Similarity to Rule 10b-5:** Observe that what is forbidden by § 17 is almost identical to what is forbidden by Rule 10b-5 (*supra*, p. 211). However, there is one main reason why a plaintiff might want to bring suit under § 17 rather than Rule 10b-5: subsections (a)(2) and (a)(3) (categories (1) and (2) listed above) probably do not require a showing of ***scienter***, i.e., of intentional falsehood, on the part of the defendant, whereas scienter is required under Rule 10b-5. See Loss, p. 979; see also *supra*, p. 277.

2. **Probably no private right of action:** On the other hand, whereas the other three liability provisions we have just discussed (§§ 11, 12(1), and 12(2)) all explicitly give an injured buyer the right to bring a private civil action, § 17(a) is silent about whether the buyer can sue. Courts are split about whether a private right of action should be implied; "The weight of recent opinions seems to be against a private right of action." Clark, p. 748.

F. **Rule 10b-5:** Apart from these provisions that deal expressly with public issuance of securities, a defrauded buyer may also be able to sue under the much more general Rule 10b-5 (*supra*, p. 262). In other words, even if a particular buyer would have an express right of action under, say, § 11 for an error in a registration statement, he may elect instead to proceed under 10b-5 (which he might want to do, for instance, because of 10b-5's longer statute of limitations). See Loss, p. 975.

VI. PUBLIC OFFERINGS — STATE REGULATION

A. **State "Blue Sky" laws generally:** So far, we have assumed that all regulation of securities issuance occurs at the federal level. But this is not true: ***every state*** regulates some aspects of securities transactions as well. Ratner, p. 295. These state securities regulations are collectively known as ***"blue sky"*** laws (perhaps because they were aimed at promoters who "would sell building lots in the blue sky in fee simple;" Loss, p. 8).

B. **'96 Act changes rules:** However, Congress ***took away*** a large portion of the states' Blue Sky powers, in the ***National Securities Market Improvement Act of 1996***. Except for a few small, regional or intrastate securities offerings, ***state regulation of securities issuance is now pre-empted by federal regulation.*** So an issue of securities that either satisfies the registration requirements of the '33 Act, or that falls within some exemption (e.g., Rules 504 or 505) need not comply with any state regulations.

1. **Fraud or deceit:** State regulators are still free to ***combat securities fraud or deceit*** that takes place in their state. But the '96 Act gets them out of the business of regulating the ***issuance*** of securities.

Quiz Yourself on

ISSUANCE OF SECURITIES (PUBLIC OFFERINGS AND EXEMPTIONS)

110. Rocky Raccoon is the sole shareholder of Roadkill Family Restaurants, Inc., a restaurant chain that obtains its ingredients mainly by harvesting them from the nation's highways and byways. Rocky would now like to raise about $2.5 million of additional capital for the company, to fund expansion. He tells you that he has two friends who are multi-millionaires that would like to invest around $1 million each. He says he also has an additional 20 or so friends who are "working stiffs," who each earn under $100,000 and don't have many assets; Rocky thinks that these friends might invest an average of about $20,000 each. A public offering (which would require a registration statement and subject the company to all sorts of SEC regulation) is out of the question at this time, so the money will have to be raised without one.

(a) If you are drafting and structuring the offering, what SEC exemption should you rely on? ________________

(b) Does the SEC regulate the types of financial and business disclosures you will have to make to the investors, when you rely upon the exemption you chose in (a)? ________________

(c) Suppose that Rocky tells you, instead, that he only wants to raise the money from his two very rich friends. You and Rocky both want to be sure that the transaction won't be a public offering, so that you won't have to prepare a registration statement. Do you need to find a particular SEC Rule that gives you an exemption from the public offering requirements (and if so, what Rule applies)? ________________

Answer

110. (a) Rule 505 under the '33 Act. SEC Rule 505 allows a company to raise up to $5 MM. [551] There can be any number of "accredited" investors (those having a net worth of more than $1 MM or income of more than $200,000 in each of the past two years), plus up to 35 non-accredited investors. The 20 "working stiff" friends thus qualify as non-accredited investors.

(b) Yes. You'll have to obey the pretty precise disclosure requirements laid out in SEC Rule 502. Some of the financial information (e.g., the balance sheet) will have to be audited.

(c) No. §4(2) of the '33 Act exempts from the registration requirements any transaction that does not involve a "public offering." Certain SEC Rules give a "safe harbor," by preventing certain transactions from being public offerings; Rule 505, discussed above, is one such. But a transaction can also avoid being a public offering just by complying with judicial decisions that define "public offering." [548] An offer to a very small number of very rich people would almost certainly be held by a court not to be a public offering. Therefore, Rocky can make his offer to his two rich friends, and take their money, without complying with any particular SEC Rule. The advantage of this non-Rule-based approach is that Rocky won't have to comply with any particular SEC-defined disclosure requirements (as he would if he went with SEC Rules 504, 505 or in some instances 506).

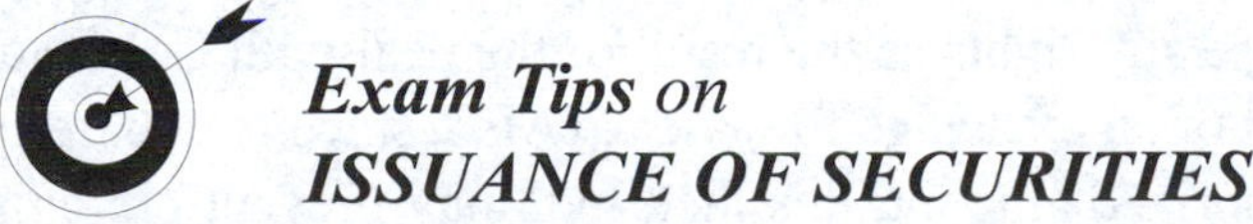

Exam Tips on *ISSUANCE OF SECURITIES*

The most common exam topics from this chapter are: (1) subscription agreements; (2) preemptive rights; and (3) watered stock.

☛ Concerning ***subscription agreements***, the most frequently-tested issue is whether a subscriber may ***revoke*** a pre-incorporation subscription. Here, recall that there are two principles applicable in most states:

☞ First, most states say that the subscription is ***irrevocable*** for some period, usually 6 months.

Example: G, and A and B agree to pay $3,000 each for all of the stock of Corp., a corp. to be formed by G. One week later, before anything further has happened, A and B write to G, stating "We hereby revoke any agreement to buy stock in Corp." In most states (incl. Del. & under the MBCA), G can form the corp. and have it sue A and B for the purchase price, because the subscription acts like an offer to the corp. that is irrevocable for some time, probably 6 mos.

☞ Second, even states making the subscription irrevocable for some time allow ***all s/h's, acting together, to rescind*** the agreement. (But if even one subscriber insists, the subscription remains in force.) (*Example:* On the facts of the above example, G, A and B could get together and all agree to rescind, but A and B by themselves can't.)

☛ Questions on ***preemptive rights*** are surprisingly common. A preemptive-rights issue can pop up even where the question does not use the phrase "preemptive rights" — you should look for such an issue whenever s/h *A* buys shares, then shares are offered to s/h *B* without *A*'s getting a chance to avoid dilution by buying additional shares.

☞ Don't forget that under most statutes, pre-emptive rights work on an ***"opt in"*** basis: unless the corp. in its charter specifically provides that there will be pre-emptive rights, such rights won't exist.

☞ Actually, most preemptive-rights issues involve the three main situations in which such rights ***don't apply***:

❑ ***Previously-authorized, but unissued, shares***. (However, under some statutes the unauthorized-but-unissued shares become covered by the pre-emptive rights scheme after passage of a certain amount of time, e.g. 6 mos., following formation.)

❑ ***Treasury stock*** (i.e., shares that were once outstanding, but that have been repurchased by the corp.).

❑ Most often-tested of all, shares ***exchanged for services or assets.***

Example: Corp. was incorporated 2 years ago with initial authorized capital of 10,000 shares of $100 par value stock. Corp. then issues 5,000 shares, 2,500 each to A and B. Later, Corp. issues 1,000 shares to C in return for C's transfer of title to Blueacre, which Corp. wants for a future plant site. Even if Corp. has pre-emptive rights, A can't exercise any rights as the result of the deal with C, because C got his shares as the result of an exchange for assets. (Also, since C's shares were part of the originally-authorized amount, this fact, too, may prevent pre-emptive rights from arising in A, though the passage of 2 years might be enough under the statute to cause pre-emptive rights to re-attach to the 5,000 authorized-but-originally-unissued shares.)

☛ Issues relating to the ***form*** and ***amount*** of ***consideration*** paid for stock are also common on exams.

☞ The principal issue relating to the ***"form"*** of consideration is the distinction between ***past*** services or property given in exchange for stock, and promises of ***future*** services or property:

☞ If the consideration is ***past services*** to the corp., or ***existing property*** already transferred to the corp., this is clearly ***valid*** consideration (at least if it's got a value that's ***no less than the par value*** of the stock).

☞ But if the consideration is a ***promise*** of ***future*** services, or a promise to ***transfer property in the future***, some statutes make this ***invalid*** consideration. (But most modern statutes, including the MBCA, allow such promises to be consideration.)

☞ As to the "amount" of consideration, you mainly have to worry about the problem of ***"watered stock."*** That is, if the shares are exchanged for money, property or services whose ***value is less than the stated par value of the shares***, in many states the transaction is an illegal issuance of watered stock.

Example 1: Corp. issues 100 shares, each with par value of $100, to A in exchange for A's promissory note for $7,500. This presents a watered-stock issue, because the value of the thing received by the corp. (the note) is less than the $10,000 aggregate par value of the stock.

Example 2: Corp. issues 100 shares, again each with par value of $100, to A in exchange for A's promise to work for Corp. for one year at a salary of $100,000. If the market value (and value to Corp.) of A's services for a year is less than $110,000, the issue may be invalid as watered stock.

But again, it's the ***exceptions*** that are usually tested. Most important:

❑ There's a ***"good faith"*** (or ***"business judgment"***) exception to the "no watered stock" rule: as long as the board in its good faith business judgment ***believes*** that the funds, property or services to be received in exchange are worth at least the par value, the court won't second-guess. Thus in Example 2 above, if the board honestly and plausibly believes that A's services for a year are worth $110K, the court won't find the stock to have been watered, even though the court might not agree with the board's assessment of A's value.

❑ Also, when stock is exchanged for property, don't be tricked into thinking that the stock is watered just because the recipient ***obtained*** the property for less than the par value of the stock. What's relevant is the value of the property at ***the time the stock is issued***, not how much the recipient originally paid for the property.

Example: Corp. issues 100 shares of $100 par value stock to A in return for office equipment currently appraised at $11,000. A had bought the equipment 6 months earlier at an auction, for $8,000. The stock isn't watered, because the present value (measured by the appraisal) is greater than the par value of the stock; it doesn't matter how much A originally paid for the equipment.

- ❑ Finally, remember that if the corp. has placed the legend ***"fully paid"*** on shares that were sold at a discount, in some states the corp. is ***"estopped"*** from later claiming otherwise — so the corp. or another s/h cannot later have the transaction rescinded, or recover the discounted amount from the issuee.

☞ Sometimes you'll see a question in which the person complaining about watered stock is not another s/h (as in the above examples), but a ***creditor***. This will generally happen only if the corp. is now ***insolvent***.

- ☞ The most common theory for letting the creditor recover against the s/h who received the watered stock is the ***"holding out"*** or ***"misrepresentation"*** theory. Under this theory, the creditor can recover from a s/h the amount of the "water" (the difference between par value and value of what the s/h paid) if the creditor shows that he extended credit in ***reliance*** on the corp's assertion that all stock previously issued was for par value. (Because of the reliance requirement, creditors usually can't use the holding-out theory where they lent ***before*** the watered-stock issue, or lent after but with ***knowledge*** of the watering.)

ESSAY EXAM QUESTIONS AND ANSWERS

The following Essay Questions are taken from the Corporations volume of *Siegel's Essay & Multiple Choice Questions & Answers*, a series written by Brian Siegel and published by Aspen Publishers. The full volume contains approximately 25 essays (with model answers), as well as approximately 100 multiple choice questions. (The essay questions were originally asked on the California Bar Exam, and are copyrighted by the California Board of Bar Examiners, reprinted by permission.) The book is available from your bookstore.

QUESTION 1: Starco, stockbrokers, in attempting to market 1,000,000 common shares to be issued by Durmac, offered 500,000 shares to the Ennis Corp. at $50 per share. Already the owner of a substantial interest in Durmac, Ennis's financial condition was such as to make a large, immediate acquisition of additional shares of Durmac desirable.

Ennis's by-laws provided that a quorum consisted of five out of its seven directors. After due notice to the four resident directors, but without notice to the three non-resident directors, a special emergency board of directors' meeting was held. Resident directors Almon, Barnes, and Chester with a proxy executed by Grabe, the fourth resident director, attended the meeting. Also present was Webster, a non-resident director. The directors present unanimously voted to purchase 400,000 additional Durmac shares. Upon conclusion of the meeting, Webster signed a waiver of notice.

Immediately following the meeting, Ennis purchased and paid for 400,000 shares of Durmac stock at $50 per share.

At their next regular meeting, attended by all directors, the board voted unanimously to ratify the action taken at the special emergency meeting.

Before the actual offering of Durmac shares to Ennis, Starco had offered, for one day only, a few thousand shares of the new Durmac shares at $42 each, cash, to a few select persons. Among the offerees was Almon, who purchased a total of 2,000 shares for his own account. Almon subsequently disposed of these shares at a substantial profit. However, by the time Ennis shareholders became aware of the foregoing facts, the market price of Durmac shares had declined sharply.

1. Was the acquisition of Durmac shares by Ennis a proper corporate action? Discuss.

2. Are any of the Ennis directors liable to their corporation for the decline in value of Durmac shares? Discuss.

3. What, if any, is Almon's liability to Ennis for profits he made on his purchase and sale of Durmac shares? Discuss.

Do not discuss federal statutory securities issues.

QUESTION 2: Art has been president of Exco, a publicly held corporation with net assets of approximately $50 million, for the past six years. Exco manufactures computers. Two years ago, Art negotiated an agreement for the purchase by Exco of all of the outstanding shares of Yang, Inc., a privately held maker of computer components, for $5 million cash. The purchase was made about one and one-half years ago. At the time, other members of Art's immediate family were holders of the outstanding shares of Yang. This information was not known except to Art, Yang's management, and Bob, an Exco director.

Art negotiated Exco's purchase of Yang stock and executed the purchase agreement on behalf of Exco, relying on his authority as its president. Before the purchase documents were signed, Art discussed the proposed acquisition individually with Bob, Curt, and Don. Curt and Don are Exco directors who, with Art and

Bob, comprise a majority of Exco's seven-person board of directors. Bob, Curt, and Don each told Art that he approved of the transaction.

After the purchase of Yang stock by Exco, at the next regular meeting of the Exco board one month later, Art informed all of the directors of the acquisition. While some questions were asked, there was no vote on the acquisition at the meeting. Except for Bob, no Exco director was informed of the previous ownership of Yang stock by Art's family members. Since Bob believed the acquisition was beneficial to Exco, he never mentioned to any of the other Exco directors his knowledge of the prior ownership of Yang stock by members of Art's family. The existence of such prior ownership could, however, have been discovered by a review of Yang's corporate records.

Since the stock purchase by Exco, Yang has been consistently and increasingly unprofitable. At the annual Exco shareholders meeting two months ago, Art, Bob, Curt, and Don were not re-elected as directors. Last month, Exco's new board replaced Art as president.

1. Can Exco rescind the purchase of Yang stock? Discuss.

2. Can Exco recover damages for Yang's unprofitability from any or all of the following:

a. Art? Discuss.

b. Bob? Discuss.

c. Curt and Don? Discuss.

QUESTION 3: Gasco is a State X Corporation involved in the petroleum industry. Its stock is traded on the New York Stock Exchange. Its board of directors hired Media, a public relations firm, to campaign against the passage of a State X ballot proposition to use gasoline tax receipts for the development of a statewide public transit system. The contract provided that Gasco's financing of the campaign should not be made public by Gasco or Media.

A group of Gasco shareholders, calling themselves Citizens Against Pollution (CAP) learned of the contract. They submitted to Gasco management, for inclusion in the next proxy statement and for presentation to the Gasco shareholders at the next shareholder meeting, proposals to:

(1) remove from the Gasco board those directors "who voted to authorize the Media contract or otherwise sought to prevent passage of the gasoline tax proposition";

(2) hire an auditor to go over Gasco's books; and

(3) consider the use of non-polluting cleansing products in all company-owned gas stations.

CAP has complied with all SEC procedural requirements.

A State X statute requires public disclosure of all corporate expenditures "designed to influence the outcome of issues to be decided by public ballot."

Pursuant to a valid Gasco by-law, only three of the nine Gasco directors are to be elected at the next shareholder meeting. The Gasco charter provides that the board of directors may, by majority vote, remove a director for "sufficient cause."

Discuss and decide the following:

1. Is management required to present the CAP proposals to the shareholders and include them in the proxy statement?

2. If adopted at the shareholder meeting, would the proposals be binding on the board of directors?

3. If a new Gasco board repudiates the Media contract, may Media nevertheless have it enforced?

ANSWER TO QUESTION 1:

1. Acquisition of Durmac ("D") shares by Ennis:

It could be contended that the vote on the acquisition of D stock was improper because (1) not all of the directors were noticed (only four of the seven were sent notice), and (2) there was not a quorum (only 4, rather than the required 5, directors were present).

As to the latter contention, it could be argued that (i) Almon should not be counted, since he was interested (i.e., owned shares of D stock), and (ii) directors usually cannot give their proxies to other directors to vote at a board meeting (and so Grabe's vote should not be counted). Thus, only three directors were present for purposes of a quorum. (Additionally, a special rule exists in almost all states providing that, if a majority of the disinterested directors approve the transaction, this number will constitute a quorum. In that case, four disinterested votes in favor out of a total of six disinterested directors would have been sufficient. However, since there were only three legally-cast disinterested votes if Almon's vote is excluded, even under the special rule there would have been no quorum.)

Notwithstanding the foregoing, since the decision to purchase D's stock was unanimously ratified at the next regular board meeting, the corporate action was properly taken. While Almon should have disclosed his interest and refrained from voting on the D stock purchase, his failure to do so is probably not be an adequate basis to avoid the purchase. The resolution would still have passed 6-0, even if he had abstained.

2. Liability of Ennis directors for the decline in D's shares:

Under the business judgment rule, a corporate director is required to exercise the due care with respect to corporate matters as he would with respect to his own assets. The facts are silent as to whether Almon or the other members of the Ennis board should have realized that the market price of D shares could decline sharply. It is also unclear as to whether Almon had any special basis to perceive the subsequent decline in D stock. If Almon was aware of the possibility of an imminent decline in D's shares, he probably had a fiduciary obligation to disclose such information to the board of directors of Ennis. If he failed to do so, and such data could have dissuaded the board from making the acquisition, Almon would be liable to Ennis for the losses resulting from the decrease of D stock.

Assuming the decline in D stock was the result of market conditions which could not reasonably have been perceived by the board of Ennis, the latter group has no liability to its shareholders. On the other hand, since Ennis was expending $2,500,000, the board of directors may have violated the business judgment rule by making such a major expenditure without a thorough investigation of D.

Assuming the board of Ennis violated the business judgment rule, the two non-resident directors and Grabe could probably not successfully defend against liability. Non-resident directors are ordinarily held to the same standard as local directors, and Grabe waived notice of the meeting. Also, all of the directors later ratified the action taken at the emergency meeting.

3. Liability of Almon to Ennis for the purchase and sale of D's shares:

Ennis could attempt to recover from Almon under the "corporate opportunity" doctrine.

Under this theory, a director is obligated to refrain from gaining any personal advantage to the detriment of his company as a consequence of information derived through his corporate position. Thus, the board of Ennis could contend that Almon should have (1) advised it of the possibility of purchasing D stock at $42 per share, and (2) permitted Ennis to purchase the shares at that rate.

However, the facts are silent as to whether (1) the offer to Almon was made as a consequence of the latter's position at Ennis, (e.g., Almon may have simply been on a mailing list of wealthy individuals), and (2) Almon had reason to believe that D stock would subsequently be offered to Ennis at a higher rate. Assuming either inquiry is answered in the negative, Almon has no liability under the corporate opportunity doctrine.

In summary, Almon probably has no liability to Ennis.

ANSWER TO QUESTION 2:

1. Can Exco ("E") rescind the transaction?

There are three independent theories pursuant to which E could attempt to rescind the transaction with Art's family (the "Sellers").

Breach of fiduciary duty

Where a director has a personal interest in a transaction which his corporation is considering, he is ordinarily obliged to (1) disclose that interest to the entire board of directors, (2) refrain from voting upon it, and (3) disclose any information indicating that the transaction may not be in the corporation's best interests. A transaction involving a director's immediate family would probably constitute a "personal" interest. While it is unclear from the facts whether or not Art believed the transaction was not in E's best interests, he clearly failed to meet the initial two requirements.

It will be difficult for Art to successfully claim that the transaction was subsequently impliedly ratified by a majority of the board (e.g., when Bob, Curt and Don advised him that they approved of the transaction), since (1) there was never a formal vote upon it, (2) he and Bob never disclosed to the other members of the board that the Sellers were members of Art's immediate family, and (3) there is no clear majority in favor of the purchase if Art's vote is discounted. Of these problems, (2) is the most important, since ratification requires a full disclosure of the underlying facts, including the facts that demonstrate the conflict.

Lack of authority

The President ordinarily oversees the day-to-day operations of a corporation. While this officer usually has the power to bind the corporation in routine transactions, a five million dollar acquisition (constituting 10% of E's assets) would probably not be within this implied authority.

SEC Rule 10b-5

Under SEC Rule 10b-5, it is unlawful to employ any scheme to defraud another in connection with the purchase or sale of a security. If it could be shown that (1) Art had reason to know that the Yang stock was overvalued, or (2) Sellers knew (or should have known) that Art was effectuating the sale for the purpose of paying them an excessive amount for their Yang shares, the transaction is probably violative of SEC Rule 10b-5; *Superintendent of Insurance v. Bankers Life & Casualty Co.*, 404 U.S. 6 (1971).

Under rescission (1) E would tender the Yang stock back to the Sellers, and (2) the Sellers would return the purchase price of the shares to E.

Sellers could contend that rescission (an equitable remedy which is discretionary with the court) is not appropriate, since (1) laches is applicable (i.e., E's board was informed of the transaction one and one-half years ago, and yet no action has been taken), and (2) Yang's decreased profitability may be due to actions undertaken by E or subsequent market conditions.

Unless E can show that (1) the decline in value of Yang stock was not due to market conditions, or (2) the Sellers knew that Art was deliberately paying them an excessive purchase price, rescission will probably not be granted.

2.

a. Can E recover for Yang's unprofitability from Art?

In addition to the theories described above, a derivative action against Art might also be sustained under the business judgment rule (i.e., a director must exercise the due care with respect to corporate matters as he would with regard to his own assets).

It is unclear from the facts as to whether Art investigated the transaction with the thoroughness which a five million dollar acquisition deserves. Assuming (1) he did not, and (2) the price paid by E was excessive, E could probably recover (under the business judgment rule and the other theories described above) from Art the diminishment in the value of Yang stock between the (1) time of purchase, and (2) trial. This amount would be reduced to the extent, if any, that Art could show that Yang's decreased profitability was due to mismanagement by E.

b. Can E recover for Yang's unprofitability from Bob?

The discussions above with respect to the business judgment rule and (for the most part) a director's fiduciary duties would be applicable to Bob. Although Bob did not conduct the transaction, he was probably under a fiduciary obligation to disclose Art's conflict of interest to the entire board (even though Bob, in good faith, believed the transaction to be beneficial to E). No action would lie under SEC Rule 10b-5 against Bob, since the scienter (desire or intent to deceive the corporation) element is lacking.

c. Can E recover for Yang's unprofitability from Curt and Don?

The discussion above with respect to the business judgment rule would be equally applicable to Curt and Don. Since the transaction had not been consummated at the time they were originally informed of the prospective acquisition, they (presumably) could have prevented its consummation.

ANSWER TO QUESTION 3:

1. Management's obligation to present the CAP proposals to shareholders and include them in the proxy statement.

Since Gasco's stock is traded on a national exchange (e.g., the NYSE), it is subject to the proxy rules promulgated under Section 14 of the Securities Exchange Act of 1934. Under Rules 14a-8(a), a shareholder is ordinarily entitled to submit, for inclusion in management's proxy solicitation, proposals which he intends to present at the upcoming shareholder's meeting. However, there are several exceptions to management's obligation to include such materials.

a. *Proposal to remove directors who authorized Media contract and sought to impede the gas tax proposition.*

Management may omit a proposal if, under the laws of the corporation's domicile, it is not a proper subject for shareholder action. It is unclear from the facts as to whether stockholders can remove a director in this state. We are advised only that Gasco's charter provides that the board may remove a director for sufficient cause.

Nevertheless, in most jurisdictions there is a common-law right of shareholders to remove directors for cause. However, "cause" typically exists only if a director has committed fraud, waste, or otherwise overtly misused his position. This standard is arguably satisfied by the directors' deliberate effort to circumvent the State X statute requiring disclosure of corporate expenditures made for the purpose of influencing public ballot measures.

However, the directors could contend in rebuttal that, unless this law provides for significant criminal penalties in the event it is violated, removal is not proper. They were only attempting to promote corporate objectives by preventing action which would presumably make Gasco's business less profitable.

While a close question, unless the directors' actions were criminal in nature, their removal is probably not a proper subject for shareholder action.

b. *Proposal to hire an auditor to review Gasco's books.*

The directors could assert that retaining auditors to review the corporation's books is a matter which relates to the "conduct of the ordinary business operations" of the company, and therefore should be excluded.

However, given the board's deliberate effort to avoid the State X statute, the request for an independent party to determine if there was other misconduct by Gasco seems appropriate.

Thus, the directors can probably be compelled to include this proposal in their proxy materials.

c. *Proposal to require non-polluting products only in company-owned gas stations.*

Directors may omit a proposal if it relates to a "personal claim or grievance." It can be argued that this proposal is nothing more than a general environmental grievance which reflects the personal views of the complaining shareholders.

The stockholders could respond that, even if the proposal emanates from the desire to have an environment free of pollutants, it nevertheless relates to an aspect of Gasco's general business policy. The courts and the SEC have shown a tendency to require inclusion of proposals that relate to major ethical, social and political issues that have a tangible link to the corporation's affairs. The use of non-pollutants in company-owned gas stations would place Gasco on the cutting edge of environmentally-conscious energy companies, which would arguably constitute a unique advertising appeal to its consumers.

Therefore, the most likely result is that the directors must include the proposal because it relates to major social/political issues with a tangible link to the company's affairs.

2. Binding effect of proposals.

As already discussed, unless there has been a serious criminal violation, dismissing the directors for involvement in the Media contract is probably not sufficient "cause." Thus, it is not includible nor is it binding upon the directors. Additionally, if it were includible, it would still not be binding, because a director must ordinarily have an opportunity to defend his actions and obtain judicial review of an unfavorable decision.

It might also be argued that, since only three of the nine directors are to be elected at the shareholder meeting, removing all of the directors (assuming the decision to enter into the contract with Media was approved unanimously) would result in there being no management of Gasco. However, Articles of Incorporation ordinarily provide for interim appointments or elections if a director is removed. Thus, the six vacancies could be filled by the three newly elected directors soon after the meeting.

The proposal to have an auditor review Gasco's books relates to verifying past conduct of the directors, and should be binding upon the board.

The third proposal, if found to have some tangible link to the corporation's affairs, would be includible but not binding upon the board. Management decisions are the exclusive province of the directors.

3. The contract with Media.

Two arguments can be made that this agreement is unenforceable.

First, it might be asserted that the contract is *ultra vires*, since it requires Gasco to do something which is contrary to law (e.g., refrain from disclosing corporate spending which is designed to influence public ballot issues).

However, a court could simply strike the illegal provision and permit the balance of the contract to stand. This remedy seems appropriate since the provision, having become known, has ceased to have any effectiveness.

Second, Gasco might argue that it and Media are in *pari delicto* with regard to an illegal provision, and therefore the contract is unenforceable. However, since the provision was presumably inserted at Gasco's insistence, a court would probably not permit Gasco to evade its contractual responsibilities under these circumstances.

Thus, Media can enforce the contract.

TABLE OF CASES

REFERENCES TO THE MODEL BUSINESS CORPORATIONS ACT

1969 Version of MBCA

REFERENCES TO DELAWARE GENERAL CORPORATION LAW

REFERENCES TO THE NEW YORK BUSINESS CORPORATION LAW

REFERENCES TO THE CALIFORNIA CORPORATIONS CODE

REFERENCES TO THE '33 AND '34 FEDERAL SECURITIES ACTS

REFERENCES TO SECURITY EXCHANGE COMMISSION (SEC) RULES

SUBJECT-MATTER INDEX